CompTIA Server+ Certification
2005 Objectives

Student Manual

THOMSON ™
COURSE TECHNOLOGY

Australia • Canada • Mexico • Singapore
Spain • United Kingdom • United States

CompTIA Server+ Certification
2005 Objectives

VP and GM, Training Group:	Michael Springer
Series Product Managers:	Charles G. Blum and Adam A. Wilcox
Developmental Editor:	Don Tremblay
Copyeditors:	Robb Tillett and Ken Maher
Series Designer:	Adam A. Wilcox
Cover Designer:	Abby Scholz

For more information contact:

Course Technology
25 Thomson Place
Boston, MA 02210

Or find us on the Web at: www.course.com

For permission to use material from this text or product, submit a request online at: www.thomsonrights.com

Any additional questions about permissions can be submitted by e-mail to: thomsonrights@thomson.com

Trademarks

Course ILT is a trademark of Course Technology.

Some of the product names and company names used in this book have been used for identification purposes only and may be trademarks or registered trademarks of their respective manufacturers and sellers.

Disclaimers

Course Technology reserves the right to revise this publication and make changes from time to time in its content without notice.

The logo of the CompTIA Authorized Quality Curriculum (CAQC) program and the status of this or other training material as "Authorized" under the CompTIA Authorized Quality Curriculum program signifies that, in CompTIA's opinion, such training material covers the content of CompTIA's related certification exam.

The contents of this training material were created for the CompTIA Server+ exam covering CompTIA certification objectives that were current as of December 2005.

CompTIA has not reviewed or approved the accuracy of the contents of this training material and specifically disclaims any warranties of merchantability or fitness for a particular purpose. CompTIA makes no guarantee concerning the success of persons using any such "Authorized" or other training material in order to prepare for any CompTIA certification exam.

ISBNs:

    1-4239-1455-4 = Student Manual + MeasureUp
    1-4239-1457-0 = Student Manual + MeasureUp and CBT

Printed in the United States of America

1 2 3 4 5 6 7 8 9 PM 08 07 06 05

Contents

Introduction

After reading this introduction, you will know how to:

A Use Course Technology ILT manuals in general.

B Use prerequisites, a target student description, course objectives, and a skills inventory to properly set your expectations for the course.

Topic A: About the manual

Course Technology ILT philosophy

Course Technology ILT manuals facilitate your learning by providing structured interaction with the software itself. While we provide text to explain difficult concepts, the hands-on activities are the focus of our courses. By paying close attention as your instructor leads you through these activities, you will learn the skills and concepts effectively.

We believe strongly in the instructor-led classroom. During class, focus on your instructor. Our manuals are designed and written to facilitate your interaction with your instructor, and not to call attention to the manuals themselves.

We believe in the basic approach of setting expectations, delivering instruction, and providing summary and review afterwards. For this reason, lessons begin with objectives and end with summaries. We also provide overall course objectives and a course summary to provide both an introduction to and closure on the entire course.

Manual components

The manuals contain these major components:

- Table of contents
- Introduction
- Units
- Appendix
- Course summary
- Glossary
- Index

Each element is described below.

Table of contents

The table of contents acts as a learning roadmap.

Introduction

The introduction contains information about our training philosophy and our manual components, features, and conventions. It contains target student, prerequisite, objective, and setup information for the specific course.

Units

Units are the largest structural component of the course content. A unit begins with a title page that lists objectives for each major subdivision, or topic, within the unit. Within each topic, conceptual and explanatory information alternates with hands-on activities. Units conclude with a summary comprising one paragraph for each topic, and an independent practice activity that gives you an opportunity to practice the skills you've learned.

The conceptual information takes the form of text paragraphs, exhibits, lists, and tables. The activities are structured in two columns, one telling you what to do, the other providing explanations, descriptions, and graphics.

Appendix

The appendix lists all CompTIA Server+ 2005 exam objectives along with references to corresponding coverage in this manual.

Course summary

This section provides a text summary of the entire course. It is useful for providing closure at the end of the course. The course summary also indicates the next course in this series, if there is one, and lists additional resources you might find useful as you continue to learn about the software.

Glossary

The glossary provides definitions for all of the key terms used in this course.

Index

The index at the end of this manual makes it easy for you to find information about a particular software component, feature, or concept.

Manual conventions

We've tried to keep the number of elements and the types of formatting to a minimum in the manuals. This aids in clarity and makes the manuals more classically elegant looking. But there are some conventions and icons you should know about.

Convention/Icon	Description
Italic text	In conceptual text, indicates a new term or feature.
Bold text	In unit summaries, indicates a key term or concept. In an independent practice activity, indicates an explicit item that you select, choose, or type.
`Code font`	Indicates code or syntax.
`Longer strings of ▶` `code will look ▶` `like this.`	In the hands-on activities, any code that's too long to fit on a single line is divided into segments by one or more continuation characters (▶). This code should be entered as a continuous string of text.
Select **bold item**	In the left column of hands-on activities, bold sans-serif text indicates an explicit item that you select, choose, or type.
Keycaps like ⏎ ENTER	Indicate a key on the keyboard you must press.

Hands-on activities

The hands-on activities are the most important parts of our manuals. They are divided into two primary columns. The "Here's how" column gives short instructions to you about what to do. The "Here's why" column provides explanations, graphics, and clarifications. Here's a sample:

Do it!

A-1:   Creating a commission formula

Here's how	Here's why
1 Open Sales	This is an oversimplified sales compensation worksheet. It shows sales totals, commissions, and incentives for five sales reps.
2 Observe the contents of cell F4	[F4 ▼] [= =E4*C_Rate]
	The commission rate formulas use the name "C_Rate" instead of a value for the commission rate.

For these activities, we have provided a collection of data files designed to help you learn each skill in a real-world business context. As you work through the activities, you will modify and update these files. Of course, you might make a mistake and, therefore, want to re-key the activity starting from scratch. To make it easy to start over, you will rename each data file at the end of the first activity in which the file is modified. Our convention for renaming files is to add the word "My" to the beginning of the file name. In the above activity, for example, a file called "Sales" is being used for the first time. At the end of this activity, you would save the file as "My sales," thus leaving the "Sales" file unchanged. If you make a mistake, you can start over using the original "Sales" file.

In some activities, however, it may not be practical to rename the data file. If you want to retry one of these activities, ask your instructor for a fresh copy of the original data file.

Topic B: Setting your expectations

Properly setting your expectations is essential to your success. This topic will help you do that by providing:

- Prerequisites for this course
- A description of the target student at whom the course is aimed
- A list of the objectives for the course
- A skills assessment for the course

Course prerequisites

Before taking this course, you should be familiar with personal computers and the use of a keyboard and a mouse. Some experience with servers and network basics would also be beneficial. While this course does not require CompTIA A+ certification as prerequisite, either this certification or similar is recommended.

Target student

This course will prepare you for the CompTIA Server+ exam (2005 Objectives). The CompTIA Server+ certification credential validates advanced-level technical competency of server issues and technology, including installation, configuration, upgrading, maintenance, environment, troubleshooting and disaster recovery. You should consider this certification is you want to certify your advanced technical knowledge in areas such as RAID, SCSI, multiple CPUs, and the like.

CompTIA certification

CompTIA is a non-profit information technology (IT) trade association. CompTIA's certifications are designed by subject matter experts from across the IT industry. Each CompTIA certification is vendor-neutral, covers multiple technologies, and requires demonstration of skills and knowledge widely sought after by the IT industry.

In order to become CompTIA certified, you must:

1   Select a certification exam provider. For more information, visit www.comptia.org/certification/general_information/exam_locations.aspx.

2   Register for and schedule a time to take the CompTIA certification exam at a convenient location.

3   Read and sign the Candidate Agreement, which will be presented at the time of the exam. The text of the Candidate Agreement can be found at www.comptia.org/certification/general_information/candidate_agreement.aspx.

4   Take and pass the CompTIA certification exam(s).

For additional information about CompTIA's certifications, such as their industry acceptance, benefits, or program news, visit www.comptia.org/certification.

To contact CompTIA with any questions or comments, please call (630) 678-8300 or e-mail questions@comptia.org.

Course objectives

These overall course objectives will give you an idea about what to expect from the course. It is also possible that they will help you see that this course is not the right one for you. If you think you either lack the prerequisite knowledge or already know most of the subject matter to be covered, you should let your instructor know that you think you are misplaced in the class.

Note: In addition to the general objectives listed below, specific CompTIA Server+ exam objectives are listed at the beginning of each topic. For a complete mapping of exam objectives to course content, see Appendix A.

After completing this course, you will know how to:

- Explain various motherboard buses and describe how clock frequency affects performance; identify common server processors and various types of memory; and configure the BIOS and identify common server configuration items.

- Identify basic physical hard disk components, compare physical and logical drives and describe their functionality, and identify major file systems; identify characteristics of the IDE interface and configure IDE cabling and connectors; identify characteristics of the SCSI interface; configure SCSI cabling and connectors; and become familiar with Fibre Channel technology and storage area networking, and identify and configure various types of RAID.

- Optimize server placement and diagram server plans; plan the server environment and physical site readiness; and implement sound physical server security practices.

- Identify features of server power supply and correctly implement an uninterruptible power supply (UPS); and plan optimum placement of equipment in a server rack, configure a keyboard, video, mouse (KVM) console, and list tips for installing equipment in racks. Identify thinnet, shielded twisted-pair, unshielded twisted-pair (UTP), and fiber optic cable characteristics, and make straight-through and crossover cables.

- Prepare for a server upgrade, verify availability of system resources, and adequately test and pilot the server upgrade; upgrade the processor and memory; and upgrade the BIOS, power supply, UPS, and adapters.

- Discuss general network operating system (NOS) characteristics and versions, list NOS hardware requirements, and perform NOS installations and upgrades; and identify the major NOS characteristics and versions, list hardware requirements, perform an installation and a proper shutdown of each NOS.

- Identify and understand major network operating system services; discuss other NOS services such as e-mail, Web, FTP, and fax; and discuss the different ways that servers run network applications and specify the functions of the server as a network device, router, and firewall.

- Describe the primary types of hardware used to back up critical data; discuss the primary types of software used to back up critical data, and the strategies to their use; describe the need for high server availability/redundancy, and identify key areas for SNMP monitoring; and determine key server management and disaster recovery strategies for preserving system uptime.

- Effectively use performance monitoring tools; establish a baseline; and recognize acceptable and unacceptable performance thresholds, and provide solutions to performance bottlenecks.

- Utilize sound troubleshooting logic to determine and solve problems, document problems and solutions, and check for common causes of server failure; utilize network, connectivity, NOS, and hardware diagnostic tools; troubleshoot from a remote location; recognize and solve boot, virus, and hardware problems; and locate help from vendors and peers.

Skills inventory

Use the following form to gauge your skill level entering the class. For each skill listed, rate your familiarity from 1 to 5, with five being the most familiar. *This is not a test.* Rather, it is intended to provide you with an idea of where you're starting from at the beginning of class. If you're wholly unfamiliar with all the skills, you might not be ready for the class. If you think you already understand all of the skills, you might need to move on to the next course in the series. In either case, you should let your instructor know as soon as possible.

Skill	1	2	3	4	5
Identifying computer components					
Identifying system board components and their functions					
Explaining various motherboard buses					
Describing how clock frequency affects performance					
Identifying common server processors and types of memory					
Configuring the BIOS					
Correctly implementing an uninterruptible power supply					
Planning optimum placement of equipment in a server rack					
Comparing physical and logical drives					
Identifying major file systems					
Configuring IDE cabling and connectors					
Configuring SCSI cabling and connectors					
Upgrading the processor and memory					
Identifying bus, ring, and star network topologies					
Discussing NetBEUI, IPX/SPX, and TCP/IP protocols					
Specifying the purpose of bridges, switches, hubs, and routers					
Listing various cable characteristics					
Making straight-through and crossover cables					

Skill	1	2	3	4	5
Discussing general network operating system (NOS) characteristics and versions					
Discussing NOS services such as e-mail, Web, FTP, and fax					
Describing the types of hardware used to back up critical data					
Identifying key areas for SNMP monitoring					
Using performance monitoring tools					
Establishing a baseline					

Topic C: Re-keying the course

If you have the proper hardware and software, you can re-key this course after class. This section explains what you'll need in order to do so, and how to do it.

Computer requirements

To re-key this course, your personal computer must have:

- A keyboard and a mouse
- A Pentium 3, 500 MHz (or higher) processor
- At least 256 MB RAM
- 2 GB of available hard drive space
- A CD-ROM drive
- An SVGA or higher resolution monitor set to 800×600 resolution
- Internet access for downloading the latest updates from www.windowsupdate.com and for Web activities

Setup instructions to re-key the course

Before you re-key the course, you will need to perform the following steps.

1 Install Microsoft Windows Server 2003 on an NTFS partition according to the software manufacturer's instructions. Set up each machine as a stand-alone server. Then, install the latest critical updates and service packs from www.windowsupdate.com.

2 Adjust the computer's display properties as follows:

a Open the Control Panel and double-click Display to open the Display Properties dialog box.

b On the Settings tab, change the Colors setting to True Color (24 bit) and the Screen area to 800 by 600 pixels or higher.

c On the Appearance tab, set the Scheme to Windows Classic, if necessary.

d Click OK. If you are prompted to accept the new settings, click OK and click Yes. Then, if necessary, close the Display Properties dialog box.

3 In order to make Web browsing easier, you might want to remove the Internet Explorer Enhanced Security Configuration, if it's active after you load the OS. Here's how:

a Choose Start, Control Panel, Add or remove programs.

b On the left pane, click Add/Remove Windows Components.

c Clear the check box for Internet Explorer Enhanced Security Configuration.

d Chick Next.

e Click finished.

4   To complete the independent practice activity in the unit on server planning, you will need the trial version of ConceptDraw V Professional, a network and systems diagramming program. The free download and installation instructions are at www.conceptdraw.com. You can use a different version, or even a different program (such as Visio), but you'll need to adjust the activity instructions accordingly.

Note on Web activities: Many of the activities in this book have you research topics on the Web. Given how often Web sites change, you should be prepared to adjust Web activities as necessary.

Unit 1

Motherboard architecture, processors, memory, and BIOS

Unit time: 120 minutes

Complete this unit, and you'll know how to:

A Explain various motherboard buses and describe how clock frequency affects performance.

B Identify common server processors.

C Identify various types of memory.

D Configure the BIOS and identify common server configuration items.

Topic A: Motherboard architecture

This topic covers the following CompTIA Server+ exam objectives:

#	Objective
1.1	Know characteristics, purpose, function, limitations, and performance of the following system bus architectures: • PCI bus mastering • PCI hot swap • PCI-Express • PCI-X • Hierarchical PCI bus • Peer PCI bus • I2O—intelligent input/output • Hot plug PCI • PCI expansion slots • PCI interrupts • EISA
1.11	Know the characteristics of hot swap drives and hot plug boards.
2.2	Install hardware using best practices. Hardware includes: • Boards • Processors and power modules • Memory

3.4	Configure external peripherals. Supporting knowledge includes:
	• Know available cable types for peripheral devices:
	  • Firewire
	  • USB
	  • Serial ATA (SATA)

4.6	Upgrade adapters (e.g. NIC's, SCSI cards, RAID, etc). Supporting knowledge includes:
	• Available bus types:
	  • PCI-X
	  • PCI-Express
	  • Hot swap PCI
	  • PCI (bus architecture, bus speed)
	  • EISA
	• Implementation of hot swappable PCI in servers

#	Objective
4.7	Upgrade peripheral devices, internal and external. Verify appropriate system resources (e.g. expansion slots, IRQ, DMA, etc.). Resources include: • Expansion slots • Expansion cards

The motherboard

Explanation

The motherboard provides the system "bus," the transportation medium for data to and from processors, memory, peripherals, and input/output (I/O) devices. Knowing about these server components helps you to make educated decisions in the server equipment you procure. The motherboard—sometimes referred to as the system board or backplane—is the "mother of all circuit boards." The processor(s), memory, buses, adapter cards, I/O ports, mass storage—just about every component in the system—are connected directly or indirectly to the motherboard. The various hardware components attached to the motherboard require basic management using a *BIOS* (*basic input/output system*), which identifies and confirms correct hardware installation and configuration.

Exhibit 1-1: Newer systems require plenty of cooling; this one has two case fans and a fan and heat sink on both the Pentium 4 processor and the graphics card processor

The bus

The bus is to the server what a highway is to a transportation system. The *bus* provides the data path to and from server components such as the processor and memory on the motherboard, the foundation of the computer. The motherboard attaches to the chassis and includes slots, sockets, and other connections for server components. A foundational architectural factor of the motherboard and its components is the bus width, in bits. Motherboard bus width corresponds to individual data wires that transmit data. The more wires a component such as the motherboard has, the more data it can transmit in a given period of time. Current motherboard data bus architecture is either 32 bits wide or 64 bits wide, which you could equate with a 32- or 64-lane data "highway." Of course, the 64-bit data highway will be able to deliver twice the data in the same amount of time as a 32-bit data highway. The current common expansion busses are PCI (Peripheral Components Interconnect), PCI-Express, and AGP (Accelerated Graphics Port) for graphics cards. You might still find machines with ISA or EISA expansion slots, but these are obsolete. The speed of each bus is dependent upon the motherboard clock frequency.

Clock frequency

Each bus and every device that connects to the motherboard bus depends on the clock frequency of the motherboard. *Clock frequency* (sometimes called the clock speed, cycle, or clock cycle) is the number of times in one second that an electrically charged quartz crystal located on the motherboard vibrates (oscillates). Clock frequency is measured in megahertz, a hertz equaling one cycle per second and "mega" meaning million. If a motherboard has a clock frequency of 66 MHz, then it cycles 66 million times per second. (Most new motherboards have a bus clock speed of 100 or 133 MHz.) The importance of the clock speed is that the processor requires at least one cycle (and usually more cycles) for each instruction that it executes. Therefore, the more times the motherboard clock cycles, the more instructions the processor can perform per second. A 3 GHz (Gigahertz) Pentium processor has about 3 billion opportunities per second to perform an action, subtracting wait states in which the processor uses empty clock cycles to wait for another instruction or hardware function to complete. Other system components, such as buses attached to expansion slots, also depend upon the clock cycle to determine the speed with which they operate.

This unit makes no attempt to explain every type of bus, peripheral, and port, because many simply do not apply to current technology or to servers. (Examples include VESA and MCA buses and game ports.) However, several buses do apply to PC servers, in particular PCI buses, which are explained in this unit.

Chipset function

In early personal computers, the entire system and its components operated on one bus and ran at 4.77 MHz. This fact seems unimportant until you consider the dramatic changes in bus speeds in the computing industry. Various hardware components require differing bus speeds in order to perform well. Faster components can run without waiting for slower devices to complete their tasks, because the devices operate in an independent bus context. If all components continued to run on a single bus as in early PCs, the resulting bottlenecks would significantly defeat computing efficiency.

Using different buses in the system requires a way to divide the motherboard into separate parts. The chipset (see Exhibit 1-2) is a group of motherboard chips that operate at the same speed as the motherboard clock and provide the boundary that divides one bus from another and controls the flow of bus data. Choosing a motherboard is mostly choosing a chipset.

Exhibit 1-2: The chipset is identified directly on the chip

Intel's Web site at http://support.intel.com/support/motherboards/server displays a current listing of server motherboards/chipsets. Intel is the primary manufacturer of PC-based server boards, and regardless of the name on the server case, most PC server vendors use Intel chipsets. Other vendors also make chipsets that are compatible with Intel processors, but again, they tend to be low-cost alternatives and often focus on the desktop computer market. For our purposes throughout the remainder of this course, only systems supporting two or more processors shall be considered servers unless stated otherwise. Also, this course does not address other chipsets such as those designed for AMD processors because AMD tends to focus on desktop computers with the exception of the AMD Sledgehammer (see the section on processors in this unit), which is developing a following in the Linux community. Nevertheless, AMD provides excellent low-cost, high-speed processors and is making significant headway into the desktop PC market. For more about AMD products, visit www.amd.com.

Hierarchical bus

PC-based bus systems use what is known as a *hierarchical bus*, because several buses actually comprise the (collective) "bus," each running at different speeds and with the slower buses hierarchically structured beneath the faster buses. Dividing the bus into the front side bus, PCI bus, and ISA buses allows slower components to operate without negatively impacting the faster components. (There is also a back side bus, which we will discuss later.) Intel architecture utilizes a North Bridge, South Bridge, and Super I/O chipset (see Exhibit 1-3) to divide the PCI bus from fastest to slowest and facilitate communication between buses in the order listed:

- *Front side bus*—A 64-bit data pathway that the processor uses to communicate with main memory and the graphics card through the North Bridge chipset. The *North Bridge* chipset divides the processor bus from the PCI bus, and manages data traffic between the South Bridge and between components on the front side bus and PCI bus. This core bus runs at motherboard clock speed. The front side bus is also known by several other names, including processor bus, memory bus, and system bus.

- *PCI bus*—A 32-bit data pathway for high-speed I/O for expansion adapter cards, USB, and IDE ports. The CMOS (defined later in this unit) and system clock also connect to the PCI bus. The PCI bus connects to both the North Bridge and the South Bridge. The *South Bridge* separates the PCI bus from the ISA bus.

It might be helpful for you to know the throughput capabilities of the following types of ports and buses, because many times you will need to transfer data through these ports, even as a temporary solution. For example, you might need to transfer diagnostic data from one server to another or to a laptop through a special serial cable known as a *null modem cable*. This type of cable uses special crossed wires to simulate a modem presence, allowing data to travel between the two hosts. In addition, many devices such as UPS systems are now connecting to the server via a USB port instead of a serial port, and new external hard disk storage devices can connect through a FireWire (IEEE 1394) port. The following table shows the various interfaces and their maximum throughput from the slowest to the fastest.

Port or bus	Maximum throughput
Serial	230 or 460 Kbps with a 16650 UART*
Parallel	500 KBps to 2MBps with ECP**
USB 1.1	12 Mbps
USB 2.0	480 Mbps
IEEE 1394 (FireWire)	400 or 800 Mbps
SCSI-3 (Ultra320)	320 MBps

* UART is Universal Asynchronous Receiver/Transmitter, a special serial port chip that increases throughput.

** ECP is Enhanced Capabilities Port, a high-speed, bidirectional parallel port.

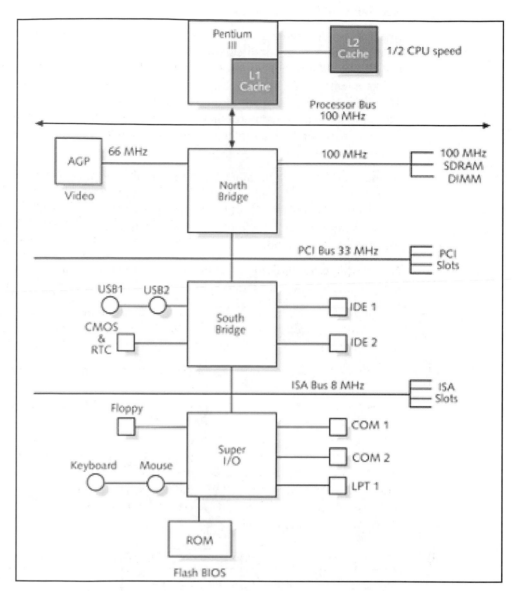

Exhibit 1-3: Typical North Bridge/South Bridge motherboard architecture

Accelerated hub architecture

Intel has implemented a new hub architecture to replace the tried-and-true North Bridge/South Bridge architecture, which connects the various buses described above through the PCI bus. The *accelerated hub architecture* connects buses to the system bus independently through a dedicated interface to the PCI bus, yielding throughput of up to 266 MBps—twice as much throughput as 33 MHz PCI. The independent buses do not share the PCI bus, thus increasing PCI bus bandwidth available to PCI-connected devices. Also, the hub architecture improves traffic throughput between slower I/O buses and the system bus.

In an accelerated hub architecture (see Exhibit 1-4), the North Bridge is called the *Graphics Memory Controller Hub* (*GMCH*), and the South Bridge is called the *I/O Controller Hub* (*ICH*). This architecture allows devices directly connected to the ICH (such as high-speed ATA-66 and ATA-100 disk controllers and USB 2.0 interfaces) much greater throughput.

North Bridge/South Bridge architecture is common on Intel 44*X* series chipsets, such as the 440LX, and the accelerated hub architecture is the current architecture in Intel 8*XX* series chipsets, such as the 840NX.

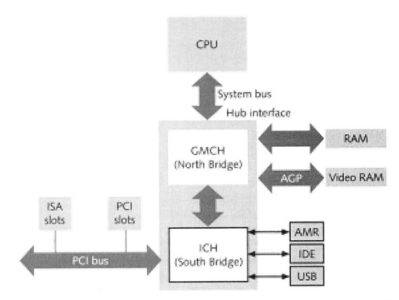

Exhibit 1-4:The accelerated hub architecture improves I/O traffic between slower I/O buses and the faster system bus

Bus interfaces

The front side bus, ISA bus, and PCI bus are only useful if there is a way to connect devices to each respective bus. The front side bus uses a slot or socket on the motherboard to connect the processors and memory. The ISA and PCI buses use expansion slots. Although PCI is quickly becoming the only slot available on new motherboards, you might still see the older ISA/EISA slots on some motherboards, so we briefly discuss them as well.

EISA

The 32-bit *Extended ISA* (*EISA*) bus provides backward compatibility with older ISA devices and a maximum bandwidth of about 33 MBps. Even though EISA performance is better than ISA, most motherboards do not include EISA buses any more because most manufacturers engineer devices that are compatible with the better-performing PCI bus interface.

PCI

The purpose of the *Peripheral Components Interface* (*PCI*) *bus* is to interface high-speed devices with the system bus so that slower devices do not create a bottleneck. For example, an older computer with a 16-bit ISA, 8 MHz video card would create a significant bottleneck for the rest of the system (mostly the processor) because it can only transfer a maximum of 8 MBps, and would use clock cycles that could otherwise be used by other devices. The processor would have to wait for the ISA video card to complete its task before being able to use the system bus. Using the bridge or hub architecture, faster PCI devices can use the PCI bus, reducing or removing the bottleneck. Continuing the video card example, a PCI video card uses a 32-bit 33 MHz card for much faster performance and better throughput at 132 MBps. Other devices such as network cards and hard disk controllers can also take advantage of this improved performance.

As for usability, one of the most significant benefits of PCI is that a Plug and Play operating system such as Windows 95 or later can automatically detect and assign system resources to new devices. Other buses such as ISA required BIOS configuration and/or manual configuration of jumpers and switches on devices. PCI 2.2 is the current specification of PCI, and PCI-X is soon to supercede it.

The PCI standard is compatible not only with PC platforms, but also with Macintosh, Sun, and Alpha platforms using platform-specific chipsets.

PCI-X

PCI-X (PCI-eXtended) is actually Addendum 1.0 to the PCI 2.2 specification. The basic advantage to PCI-X is simple: much higher bandwidth and correspondingly higher performance. PCI-X utilizes 64 bits and up to 133 MHz, yielding a maximum bandwidth of 1064 MBps. Devices that are designed according to the PCI-X standard will be able to utilize the full maximum available bandwidth, provided no other processes or devices contend for the same bandwidth. Also, relaxed ordering arranges real-time audio and video instructions in an efficient order instead of the first in/first out (FIFO) method of previous PCI versions.

Other efficiency enhancements to the PCI-X bus help to free up bandwidth and reduce wait states, with the net result of a nearly tenfold performance increase over 32 bit, 33 MHz PCI. Motherboard designers divide the PCI-X bandwidth in one of several slot combinations for each PCI-X bus segment: one 133 MHz slot, two 100 MHz slots, or four 66 MHz slots. The following table shows PCI and PCI-X performance statistics.

Data path width (bits)	Bus speed (MHz)	Max bandwidth (MBps)
32	33	133.33
32	66	266.66
64	33	266.66
64	66	533.33
64	133 (PCI=X)	1066.66 (PCI=X)

Bus mastering

Most devices utilize the processor to control the flow of information through the bus. As a result, a processor laden with the task of controlling requests from various devices is not as available to process more important productivity functions, slowing down overall performance. In PCI architecture, hardware designers can use *bus mastering* to bypass the processor and directly access memory, resulting in an overall increase in processor performance. Bus mastering is actually a form of direct memory access (DMA) known as first-party DMA. "First party" refers to the device directly controlling memory access, and compares to a third-party DMA transfer using a motherboard DMA controller. Also, bus mastering devices can communicate among themselves over the bus without CPU intervention. Video adapters and disk controllers commonly utilize bus mastering.

PCI Interrupts

Devices issue requests for system resources using an ISA-based interrupt request. An *interrupt request (IRQ)* is an electrical signal that obtains the CPU's attention in order to handle an event immediately, although the processor might queue the request behind other requests. Most devices utilize one of several IRQs on the motherboard. However, there are a limited number of available interrupts, and the number of devices is often greater than the available IRQs.

The BIOS utilizes the PCI bus to assign special *PCI interrupts* to PCI devices using the designation INTA#, INTB#, INTC#, and INTD# (sometimes known simply as #1-#4). Single-function PCI cards always receive INTA# according to PCI specifications. Chips or cards with multiple functions can receive assignments for INTB# through INTD# as needed. The PCI interrupts map to one of four corresponding ISA IRQs, usually IRQ 9-12. For example, if you have three single-function PCI cards, they all receive INTA#; however, each device still requires a unique ISA IRQ mapping. Functionally, the result is not that much different than if each device was a standard ISA device in the first place, because each device still receives unique, non-shareable IRQs. The benefit of the PCI interrupt appears when no more ISA IRQ addresses are available. With no more available IRQs, the PCI interrupt utilizes another PCI function known as *PCI steering*, in which the PCI interrupt assigns two or more PCI devices the same ISA IRQ.

PCI hot swap

PCI hot swap, otherwise known as *PCI hot plug*, means that you can add, remove, or replace PCI devices without first powering down the server. Note that even though it sounds like you can just take off the cover and rip out a card, many devices and PCI slots require you to follow specific steps. For example, most servers require you to turn off the power to the slot using management software (as with many Dell and HP systems) or using a switch or button (as with Compaq systems) before removing the device (see Exhibit 1-5). The power switch is often a button located near the actual slot. After you turn off the power to the slot, then remove and replace a card, you can turn the power back on. If the NOS is Plug and Play compatible (such as Windows 2000), it should be able to detect the new device and load (or request) the appropriate drivers. Hot swapping is truly a lifesaver in servers that require 24/7 operation.

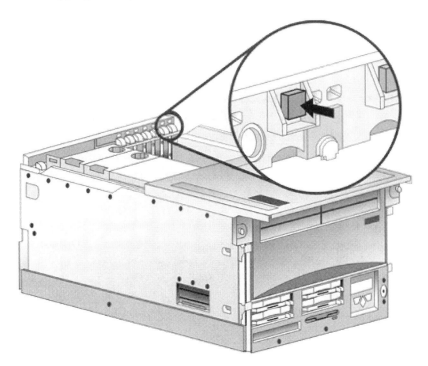

Exhibit 1-5: To turn off power to a PCI slot, use a button (as shown) or management software

Peer PCI bus

The *peer PCI bus* is usually a server-specific function that both increases available PCI bandwidth and expands the number of PCI expansion cards from the usual limit of four with a minimal impact on overall system bus bandwidth. This architecture usually involves dual peer PCI buses and two North Bridges, which connect to a primary PCI bus and a secondary PCI bus. PCI expansion slots connect to each respective PCI bus and are either integrated into the motherboard or installed as add-on daughtercards. Many motherboards use this expanded functionality not only to increase the number of expansion slots, but also to offer flexible PCI bus width and speed. For example, Bus #1 could offer four standard 32-bit 33 MHz PCI slots, while Bus #2 offers two additional 64-bit 66 MHz PCI slots, and devices in both buses can simultaneously access their respective buses. Peer PCI slots allow the administrator to load balance the system. For example, if you have two high-speed network cards for which you expect a great deal of traffic, you could place each one on a separate PCI bus to balance the load.

That way, they can each handle I/O without waiting for the other to complete a task on the PCI bus. You can extend the same load-balancing benefits to other devices such as high-throughput SCSI controllers. High-end servers such as the HP Netserver running Windows 2000 Datacenter Server offer up to 32 processors and 96 PCI slots!

Compare peer PCI slots with the bridged PCI bus, in which an additional PCI-to-PCI bridge is inserted below the North Bridge. This only increases the number of available slots, but does not offer better PCI load balancing because all expansion slots actually use a common data path to the system bus. In the peer PCI architecture, separate buses independently communicate with the system bus for more efficient load balancing.

I2O

Intelligent Input/Output (I2O) is an initiative to improve I/O performance via an I2O processor and driver model. The I2O driver communicates with the I2O processor, which is located on the device itself, as a separate add-in card, or integrated into the motherboard. Even on the PCI bus, which is designed to relieve traffic from the system bus, frequent PCI interrupts to the processor slow overall performance. With I2O, devices intelligently perform much of the processing function on their own. Also, I2O devices can communicate among themselves when necessary instead of using the processor to manage their communication. The I2O driver utilizes a "split driver" model in which the Operating System Module (OSM) handles I/O interaction between the device and the operating system, and the Hardware Device Module (HDM) manages interaction between hardware controllers and I2O-compatible devices. The I2O specification goes a long way toward developing a common standard that hardware and software vendors can use to simplify and reduce the costly, time-consuming process of driver development. Most I2O-enabled devices are network cards or storage devices because they typically require the highest I/O levels in the system. The I2O specification can work with OS/2, but don't expect to see great strides in I2O technology on the OS/2 platform. Windows NT 4.0 initially offered no participation with I2O; however, Windows 2000 and NetWare 5.x fully support the I2O specification.

The latest I2O specification (2.0) includes several new features, the most significant of which are:

- 64-bit addressing accommodates increased memory capabilities for newer CPUs.
- Hot-plug capability lets you change the adapter without shutting down the entire system.
- Direct memory access (DMA) allows direct access to memory instead of first utilizing the processor. High-speed I2O RAID disk controllers in particular benefit from DMA.

Accelerated Graphics Port (AGP)

The Accelerated Graphics Port (AGP) is designed to relieve the system bus and CPU of traffic and processing. Producing graphics is a very complex function, requiring memory usage and significant processing power. In the past, graphics functions used portions of main memory and depended on the main CPU to process much of the graphics load. Later, as video adapters matured, they performed much of their own graphics processing by adding memory chips and onboard processors specially designed for graphics functions. Nevertheless, the graphics card would frequently request attention from the system bus and the processor.

The AGP specification introduced in 1996 utilizes a single AGP slot on standard motherboards, and further relieves the processor and system bus of video burdens. The slot is brown in color and fits only AGP cards—so you can't accidentally insert any other type of card into the slot.

The initial specification offered both a 1X and 2X mode, representing a performance multiplier of 2, doubling the effective clock speed of a 1X card. Later, a 4X mode appeared; however, most cards are still produced at the 2X speed. There is also an AGP Pro spec, which uses a longer slot and more pins for higher voltage. In November 2000 the AGP 8X was introduced, but at this writing there are no cards available for it. The following table lists AGP performance statistics.

AGP mode	Effective clock speed (AGP mode × 66 MHz)	Throughput
1X	66 MHz	266 MBps
2X	133 MHz	533 MBps
4X	266 MHz	1066 MBps
8X	533 MHz	2133 MBps

AGP has an immediate and obvious benefit to overall system performance; however, AGP provides the greatest benefit to graphics-intensive computing, such as PC gaming, computer-aided drafting (CAD), graphic design, and other high-end graphics applications. Some servers come with AGP, particularly dual-processor machines that could just as easily serve as high-end graphics workstations. High-end servers normally do not include AGP because it is not necessary and adds a potential point of failure. Manufacturers try to ensure highest availability for servers by not including complex graphics features. You are not likely to be playing PC games on the server, so there is really no need for AGP graphics. High-end servers usually include a motherboard-integrated video adapter at 1024×768 screen resolution and only 256 colors. By graphics standards, this is video from the late 1980s. However, its simplicity avoids potential graphics problems on the server. Also, it does not matter from the administrator's perspective that the graphics are unimpressive, because most day-to-day server administration is actually done remotely on a desktop PC workstation.

PCI-Express

PCI-Express, formerly called 3GIO (third generation I/O), is designed to replace PCI, PCI-X, and AGP. PCI-Express is not just an upgraded PCI; it's based on a different model. Rather than using a 32- or 64- bit shared bus, PCI-Express uses a point-to-point serial connection with each device or slot. Packets of data are sent over transmit/receive pairs, much like an Ethernet connection. The theoretical maximum speed of one PCI-Express serial pair, or "lane," is 2.5 GB/s each way, or 5GB/s total. The actual performance is slower, but a device, such as a network card, using a single lane is still at least twice as fast as a regular PCI device. Furthermore, devices in need of more bandwidth can have several of the individually-clocked lanes. For instance, the PCI-Express replacement for AGP is a 16-lane, or x16, slot.

Because the link is serial and not parallel, PCI-Express requires smaller connectors. An x1 device has 36 pins, compared to the 120 required in a regular PCI slot. A system board can have a mixture of PCI-Express slots, including x1, x4, x8, and x16 slots. A device can fit into a slot that is larger than it needs – the extra contacts will be ignored.

Although older PCI devices won't fit in PCI-Express slots, compatibility with PCI addressing, and thus drivers and software, has been maintained. Other features that will be available to operating systems and applications include advanced power management, hot swap/hot plug ability, and data integrity and error handling.

Do it!

A-1: Discussing motherboards

Questions and answers
1 How does the bus bit width affect data throughput?
2 How does clock frequency affect server performance?
3 What is the function of a chipset?
4 What is a hierarchical bus?
5 How does PCI-Express differ from previous PCI versions?

Topic B: Processors

This topic covers the following CompTIA Server+ exam objectives:

#	Objective
1.5	Know the characteristics of the following types of memory and server memory requirements: • Hardware compatibility list • Memory caching
1.12	Know the features, advantages, and disadvantages of multiprocessing

1.14	Understand the processor subsystem of a server
	• Multiprocessing systems
	  • What they are
	  • How they differ from dual-processor systems
	• 64-bit server environments
	  • What they are
	  • Why and when they are important
	  • What are the different architectures

Hardware compatibility

Explanation

Before you buy or put together a server, you should ensure that all the components will work with the operating system to plan to use. Most OS makers publish a hardware compatibility list, or HCL, that lists in detail the motherboards, hard drives, expansions cards, etc. that have been tested with the OS. Untested components might work, but there's no guarantee.

Processor clock speed

Three primary factors—clock speed, data bus, and cache—contribute to the effective speed of the processor (CPU).

Clock speed, or processor speed, is the number of cycles the processor can execute in a single second, measured in millions of cycles per second, or megahertz (MHz). Instructions executed by the processor require a certain number of cycles, so the more cycles the processor can handle per second, the faster it operates, or "thinks." Current processors are also *superscalar*—that is, they can execute more than one instruction in a single clock cycle. The processor architecture design uses a multiplier methodology to provide the processor's speed. For example, a Pentium III 600 MHz processor installed on a motherboard with a system bus speed of 100 MHz uses a multiplier of 6 (100 MHz system bus speed × multiplier factor of 6 = 600).

Data bus

Data bus refers to the number of data bits that can pass into or out of the processor in a single cycle. Data bus width is typically 32 bits. Think of a 32-lane highway over which data travels. Some new processors offer 64-bit bandwidth, equivalent to a 64-lane data highway. Because of other internal engineering modifications, a 64-bit processor utilizes its resources more efficiently than a 32-bit processor and is, therefore, more than twice as fast. Data bus width and RAM have a direct relationship such that a 64-bit processor can also utilize 4,294,967,296 times more memory than a 32-bit processor (assuming that the 64-bit architecture extends throughout the entire system).

Cache memory

Cache memory is a small amount of memory that stores recently or frequently used program code or data, reducing the latency involved in retrieving data from RAM or disk. Cache memory appears in a number of places on the server, including the hard disk, CD-ROM, and processor. Processors use two types of cache memory: L1 (level 1) and L2 (level 2).

L1 cache

L1 cache is a small amount of memory (usually 32–64 KB) that provides extremely fast access to its data because of its proximity to the processor and because it runs at the same speed as the processor itself—not at the speed of the motherboard. For example, a Pentium III 850 running on a 100 MHz motherboard utilizes an L1 cache that also runs at 850 MHz, not 100 MHz. L1 cache provides an advantage to system performance, because the processor can access data directly from the L1 cache instead of having to fetch the data from memory, which is slower, or from the hard disk, which is painfully slower. Also, if the data in the L1 cache is the result of a processing action such as a complex calculation, retrieval from the L1 cache conserves valuable processor utilization because a recalculation is not necessary. While the size of the cache seems too small to be of any use, it is a great benefit because frequently used chunks of code or data are constantly served from extremely fast L1 cache.

L2 cache

L2 cache provides the same basic benefits as L1 cache, but it is larger, ranging from 256 KB to 2 MB. In the past, L2 cache was not stored on the processor die, but was instead stored on a separate chip inside the processor housing. This orientation is known as *discrete L2 cache*. The data path used to access the L2 cache was called the *back side bus*, and it ran at half the processor speed. For example, a Pentium III 450 MHz processor utilizes a 512 KB L2 cache running at 225 MHz. Some Pentium III 500s run a 512 KB L2 cache at half the processor speed and some run a 256 KB L2 cache at full processor speed. Most processors after the Pentium III 500 locate the L2 cache directly on the processor die (similar to the L1 cache) and run it at full processor speed. This *Advanced Transfer Cache (ATC)* is 256 bits wide and eliminates the need for a back side bus.

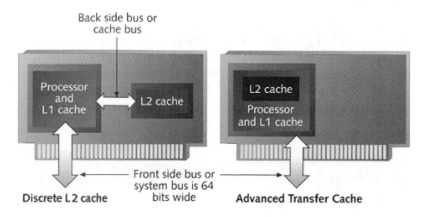

Exhibit 1-6: L1 cache, L2 cache, and Advanced Transfer Cache

SMP

Although clock speed, data bus, and cache are components of both servers and workstations, servers are typically more powerful in each respect. Also, servers often utilize *symmetric multiprocessing (SMP)*, which is the simultaneous use of multiple processors on the same server. SMP results in a corresponding increase in performance such that two processors are about twice as fast as one, four processors are about twice as fast as two, and so forth.

Many 32-bit applications can benefit from SMP if the code allows *multithreading*, which is the ability to run two or more program threads at once. For example, if a program runs two threads on an SMP system with two processors, each processor can handle a thread simultaneously. With a single processor, the program can still run multiple threads but the processor can only execute a single thread at one time. There is some overhead coordinating of multiple processors, so the performance isn't quite doubled when the processors are. Also, SMP is most useful on a server fielding many requests from different users. An individual using a standalone computer would not see appreciable improvement from using SMP.

Server processors

In existing servers, you are likely to find processors no slower than Pentium II 233 MHz or Pentium Pro 200 MHz. Servers also utilize an additional processor model not typically found in home or standard desktop PCs—the Pentium Xeon (pronounced "zeon"; see Exhibit 1-7). Xeon processors differ from standard Pentium models in the following respects:

- Type of enclosure
- Cache size
- Cache speed
- Amount of addressable memory
- SMP (symmetric multiprocessing)

Exhibit 1-7: The Intel Pentium III Xeon

The Xeon uses a Slot 2 single-edge contact (SEC) enclosure and is larger than a Pentium III in order to accommodate the internal board with more L2 ATC memory—up to 2 MB of error checking and correction memory. The Xeon uses a 256-bit data path to the L2 cache—a fourfold improvement over the standard Pentium II/III 64-bit data path. On the Xeon, both the L1 and L2 cache can run in parallel, offering simultaneous access and further reducing latency. The Xeon increases the number of fill buffers, the interface between the CPU and main memory, from four to eight, and increases bus queue entries, which hold outstanding bus and memory operations, from four to eight.

The amount of memory that the processor can use is a factor of the processor bit width and motherboard chipset. Typically, the processor can address more memory than the motherboard allows. A 32-bit processor can address 4 GB of memory (2^{32} = 4,294,967,296 bytes, or 4 GB). In the home desktop and corporate workstation, you are unlikely to find a motherboard with physical space and chipset design to allow for this much memory. Server processor design, however, is changing to allow substantial amounts of addressable memory by modifying the motherboard and/or chipset. Intel Pentium II Xeon and later processors let the processor utilize 36 bits to address memory using Intel's *Physical Address Extension (PAE)* feature, allowing up to 64 GB of addressable memory (2^{36} = 68,719,476,736, or 64 GB). While even 4 GB sounds like an immense amount of memory (and it is), large, real-time server applications such as online transaction processing (OLTP) and e-commerce require large amounts of data to reside in RAM for fast access. A Pentium III motherboard configuration accepts either single or dual processors.

A Xeon SMP configuration can use up to four processors, though by adding another processor bus (often called a *mezzanine bus*), eight processors are possible, and some manufacturers engineer buses that can use up to 132 processors (though four or eight is more common). A dual-processor system is known as "2-way," four processors as "4-way," eight processors as "8-way," and so on.

Newer processors are coming out all the time. Visit http://www.intel.com for the latest information. Characteristics of some Intel Pentium server processors appear in the following table:

Processor	Processor speed (MHz)	L1 cache (KB)	L2 cache (KB)	System bus speed (MHz)
Pentium Pro	200	16	256, 512, 1MB	60, 66
Pentium II	233, 266, 333, 350, 366, 400, 450	32	256, 512	66, 100
Pentium II Xeon	400, 450	32	512, 1MB, 2MB	100
Pentium III	400, 450, 500, 533, 550, 600, 650, 667, 700, 733, 750, 800, 850, 866, 933, 1 GHz, 1.3 GHz	32	256, 512	100, 133
Pentium III Xeon	550, 600, 667, 733, 800, 866, 933, 1 GHz	32	256, 1MB, 2MB	100, 133
Pentium 4 Xeon	1.4 – 3.2 GHz	8	512, 1MB, 2MB	533
Pentium 4	1.3 – 3.4 GHz	16	256, 512, 1MB	400, 533, 800
Pentium 4 Extreme Edition	3.2 or 3.4 GHz	8	512 L2 (2MB L3)	800

Notably absent from the general discussion to follow is the Celeron processor, because it is designed for the low-cost home PC market. Intel reduces the cost by utilizing a smaller cache and cheaper packaging, although the core Celeron II/III is the same core as the basic Pentium II/III. Also absent are the Classic (original) Pentium and the Pentium MMX because it is unlikely that you will find these in servers—although MMX video technology is still present in server processors. The Pentium 4 processor offers significant performance benefits over the Pentium III; however, it is not capable of SMP and is geared toward the high-end workstation or demanding home user.

64-bit processors

As with motherboard buses and adapter cards, the bit width on a processor correlates to the amount of data that it can transmit. Each bit corresponds to a wire connector through the socket or slot for data transmission between the processor and the motherboard. Most Pentium processors function internally at 64 bits, and then the data results are passed on to the 32-bit external bus interface.

Most server processors use 32-bit bus interfaces, but new processors from Intel and AMD are 64-bit processors both internally and externally. Although these processors are not in final form at this writing, they are likely to affect the future of PC server computing very soon.

Intel Itanium

The 64-bit Intel Itanium and Itanium2, using Intel's IA-64 technology, represents a departure from the 32-bit x86 Intel architecture, and performs optimally with 64-bit operating systems and applications (all editions of Windows Server 2003 have 64-bit versions). Co-developed with HP, the Itanium depends upon new compiler technology. (A *compiler* translates a high-level programming language into the lowest language the computer can understand, machine language.) In addition, 32-bit applications running on the Itanium processor utilize the Itanium's hardware emulation to adapt the 32-bit instructions for the 64-bit architecture. Because of the translation process, 32-bit applications will usually run more slowly on the IA-64 than on fast 32-bit Pentium III Xeon processors. The Itanium processor runs on Intel's upcoming 460GX chipset.

One of the reasons many large organizations migrate to the Itanium 64-bit platform (IA-64) is not so much the core processor speed as the 64-bit memory addressability. With 64 bits, the processor can address up to 18 billion GB:

```
2^64 = 18,446,744,073,709,551,616 bytes
```

This seems like an absurd amount of memory, but at least it doesn't appear as if there will ever be a memory ceiling again, and memory-hungry applications such as databases will make good use of any available memory. In addition to a large L2 cache, the Itanium also supports a 2 or 4 MB Level 3 motherboard cache (much like L2 cache before ATC).

The IA-64 architecture uses Explicitly Parallel Instruction set Computing (EPIC), allowing the processor to simultaneously process as many as 20 operations. New motherboard designs will take advantage of IA-64 architecture to also allow handling of up to 64 bits of data at a time. This type of functionality will be an especially powerful feature when applying 64-bit processing to encryption schemes such as RSA encryption/decryption. Intel estimates that an IA-64 processor will outperform the fastest RISC-based processors by a factor of eight or more.

AMD Sledgehammer

The AMD Sledgehammer (built on the AMD Athlon core) is also a 64-bit processor, but there is otherwise little similarity between the Itanium and the Sledgehammer (or "Hammer"). The latest versions of these are the Opteron and Athelon 64. AMD decided to extend Intel's original x86 architecture in the Hammer design with AMD's x86-64 architecture. In fact, 32-bit operating systems and applications can run on the Hammer without complicated hardware emulation, resulting in minimal performance overhead. This strategy could prove to be a wise marketing move for AMD, because few enterprises will be able to switch all operating systems and applications to 64-bit overnight. The Hammer allows organizations to gradually merge 64-bit functionality into their existing framework. Unfortunately, Microsoft has committed to creating 64-bit operating systems and applications only for the Intel IA-64 platform, not the AMD x86-64 platform. The Linux community, however, has a 64-bit version of Linux, and Sun Microsystems also ported Solaris UNIX to the x86-64 platform.

Do it!

B-1: Discussing processors

Questions and answers

1 What is the purpose of L1 and L2 cache?

2 Which characteristics differentiate the Intel Pentium III Xeon from the Pentium III?

3 What is an advantage of the Intel Itanium?

4 How will you know if hardware you're considering buying will work with your operating system?

Topic C: Memory

This topic covers the following CompTIA Server+ exam objectives:

#	Objective

1.5	Know the characteristics of the following types of memory and server memory requirements.
	• Memory types:
	  • EDO
	  • SDRAM
	  • DDR
	  • DDR-2
	  • RAMBUS
	• Memory interleaving
	• EDD vs. non-ECC vs. extended ECC
	• Unbuffered vs. buffered vs. registered

4.4	Increase memory
	• Activities include:
	  • Verify memory compatibility
	    • EDO
	    • DDR
	    • RAMBUS
	    • ECC/non-ECC
	    • SDRAM/RDRAM
	  • Verify that server and OS recognize the added memory
	  • Perform server optimization to make use of the additional RAM (BIOS and OS level)
	• Supporting knowledge includes:
	  • Number of pins on each type of memory
	  • How servers deal with memory pairings

RAM Overview

Explanation

Many types of memory have been available in PCs and servers over the past few decades, but this section describes only the types of memory most likely to be found in servers today. Desktop PCs and servers share many of the same memory characteristics, but servers often have additional memory features, such as registered memory and ECC memory. Several *dynamic RAM (DRAM)* memory chips are installed on a printed circuit board (PCB), which is collectively referred to as a module. DRAM is dynamic random access memory—referred to as dynamic because the information requires continuous electrical refresh, or else the data can become corrupt or lost.

In general, you might still find servers with 168-pin SDRAM, as this was used with Pentium 2 and Pentium 3 computers, which still work fine for many services. Newer computers come with DDR or DDR-2 memory.

DIMM modules

DIMMs (dual inline memory modules) dramatically improved memory performance over earlier SIMMs by expanding the module to 64 bits (nonparity) or 72 bits (parity or ECC) using 168 pins (see Exhibit 1-8). The contacts on both sides of the module are separate (hence the *dual* in DIMM). Recall that the more bits available for the data, the more data that can be processed in a given period of time. Because a DIMM uses 64 bits (instead of 32, like a SIMM), it yields a performance increase.

Exhibit 1-8: A 168-pin DIMM

EDO

Early DIMMs are known for the Extended Data Out (EDO) RAM technology (sometimes called "hyper page mode"), which relates to locations in memory known as memory addresses. A memory address references rows and columns. Instead of providing only the exact location requested, EDO can send the entire row address so that subsequent references to the same row require only a column lookup, saving time. This functionality is the same as an older technology known as Fast Page Mode (FPM) RAM, and also adds the ability to eliminate a 10 ns delay prior to issuing the next requested memory address.

SDRAM

Closely associated with a DIMM is *SDRAM* (*synchronous dynamic RAM*), because a DIMM is the physical platform of SDRAM. SDRAM removes the FPM and EDO DRAM signal-controlled bottleneck that emerged as buses faster than 66 MHz appeared. At 60–80 ns, the processor would request information faster than memory could serve it over the bus. SDRAM operates at clock speed; if the system bus is 100 MHz, then SDRAM matches that frequency, which functionally operates at about 10 ns. SDRAM memory is referred to with a PCXXX, where XXX is the bus speed for which the memory is designed. For example, PC100 refers to memory designed with a rated speed for use in 100 MHz motherboards. However, manufacturers actually make SDRAM run at 125 MHz on a 100 MHz bus for added margin because of extremely tight nanosecond timing. SDRAM is also available at 133 MHz at about 7.5 ns. Expect even faster SDRAM to match increasing speeds of newer buses. To identify the speed in nanoseconds upon visual inspection of the memory chip, look at the digits at the end of the product number. You should see 10 for 10 ns, 8 for 8 ns, and so on. The following table shows common SDRAM speeds.

Speed (ns)	Manufactured speed (MHz)	Rated speed (MHz)
15	66	PC66
10	100	PC66
8	125	PC100
7.5	133	PC133

RDRAM

RDRAM (*Rambus DRAM*) is an invention of Rambus Technology. Rambus does not actually manufacture memory, but it developed the technology and charges royalties against memory manufacturers. RDRAM memory chips fit on a narrow, 16-bit-wide RIMM memory module. (RIMM is not an acronym; it's a Rambus-patented name.) RDRAM provides extremely fast 800 MHz internal clock speed on a 400 MHz bus, because data is transferred on both the leading and trailing edge of each clock cycle. This adds up to 1.6 GB throughput (16 bits × 800 MHz / 8 = 1.6 GB). Intel has expressed the most interest in RDRAM, making it the memory of choice in the 820 chipset for PC desktop platforms, the 850 series for Pentium 4 platforms, and the 840 chipset for high-end workstation and server platforms. However, because of the licensing royalty and tight production tolerances, other chipsets (such as AMD-based chipsets) avoid RDRAM, preferring DDR SDRAM instead. The RDRAM data path must travel through each RIMM from beginning to end, adding a delay when data exits the modules. Compare this to DIMMs, with parallel connections to the motherboard, which allow independent data throughput for each DIMM. Because of the unique data circuit of RDRAM, empty RIMM sockets must be filled with a C-RIMM, a device that has no memory but provides continuity to complete the memory data path. The RIMM is uniquely identifiable because you can't see the actual memory chips as with other memory types. Instead, an aluminum sheath called a "heat spreader" covers the RDRAM to help diffuse the high heat levels brought on by the fast access and transfer speeds.

DDR SDRAM

Double data rate SDRAM (*DDR SDRAM*) is the current generation of SDRAM, and also uses a 184-pin, 64-bit DIMM with future plans for a 128-bit DIMM. DDR SDRAM (or SDRAM II), like SDRAM, is synchronous with the system clock. However, DDR SDRAM transfers data twice per clock cycle, similar to RDRAM, but at a lower cost because DDR SDRAM is an open standard charging no royalties. If the bus is 133 MHz, DDR SDRAM transfers data at 266 MHz. In addition, it retains the data pathway of DIMMs, offering faster data transfer from the actual DIMM to the bus with parallel construction, as opposed to the continuity requirement of RDRAM.

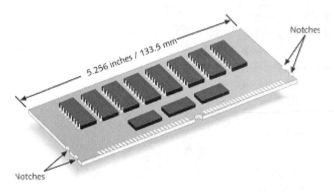

Exhibit 1-9: A 184-pin DDR SDRAM DIMM

The following table summarizes the memory technology of the various types of RAM:

Technology	Calculation of throughput	Data throughput
RDRAM	(16 bits × 400 MHz) ÷ 8	800 MBps
RDRAM	(16 bits × 800 MHz) ÷ 8	1.6 GBps
SDRAM on 100 MHz bus	(64 × 100 MHz) ÷ 8	400 MBps
SDRAM on 133 MHz bus	(64 × 133 MHz) ÷ 8	532 MBps
DDR SDRAM on 133 MHz bus	64 bits × 266 MHz	1064 MBps
DDR SDRAM on 166 MHz bus	128 bits × 332 MHz	2656 MBps

DDR-2

DDR-2 picks up where DDR leaves off, with speeds ranging from 400 MHz to 667 MHz. It is similar to DDR, with some improved features, such as 4-bit prefetch (up from 2), enhanced registers, and on-die termination. DDR-2 requires 240 pins, as opposed to DDR's 184. Both use a 64-bit interface. DDR-2 operates at 1.8 volts, about half that of DDR. Currently, DDR-2 memory does not significantly outperform DDR memory, but the technology should allow for improvement in the future.

Interleaving

Interleaving allows memory access between two or more memory banks and/or boards to occur alternately, minimizing wait states. For interleaving among banks on the same board, you must completely fill the first bank, and then completely fill the second bank with memory that is identical in size and speed.

For example, if you have two banks of memory with four slots each, Bank A and Bank B, and Bank A has 256 MB RAM in each slot totaling 1 GB, then Bank B must have exactly the same memory configuration (see Exhibit 1-10).

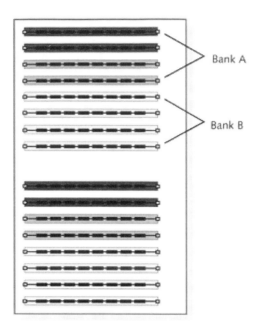

Exhibit 1-10: Interleaving between banks of memory—Bank A and Bank B must be filled identically

If you use larger memory configurations, such as with servers that have separate dedicated memory boards, you can interleave not only among banks on a board, but also among the boards. This configuration also requires you to configure RAM pairs identically. To interleave boards, each pair on one board must exactly match the corresponding pair on the other board (see Exhibit 1-11). See more about your vendor's specific interleaving requirements. For example, HP has several other considerations for their Netserver Lxr8000 servers (*www.netserver.hp.com*—search for board-to-board interleaving).

Interleaving configurations are described in an X-way format, where X is the number of interleaved banks in use. For example, if you have two memory boards with two memory banks, you have four-way interleaving (2 boards × 2 banks = 4-way).

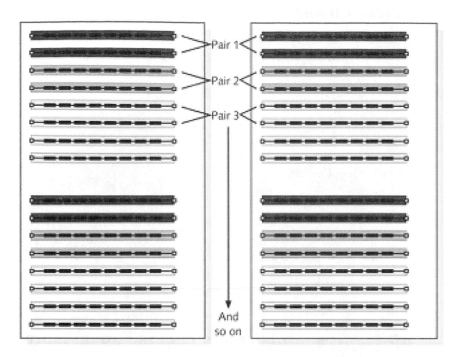

Exhibit 1-11: Interleaving between banks of memory—corresponding pairs between boards must be filled identically

Buffered and registered memory

Buffered memory is a function of FPM or EDO memory, and is an older memory technology. The purpose of both buffered and *registered memory* (which is more common in current computers) is to re-drive (amplify) the signal entering the module. Buffered or registered modules, which have a synonymous function, also assist the chipset in handling the larger electrical load when the system has a lot of installed memory, allowing the module to include more memory chips, which is one reason that servers often use registered modules. (With desktop PCs, SIMMs are likely to be unbuffered, because the chipset manages the buffering function.) You find registered memory on servers or high-end workstations, but rarely on a desktop PC. Registered memory also enacts a deliberate pause of one clock cycle in the module to ensure that all communication from the chipset arrives properly. Registered memory is useful on heavily loaded server memory, and was designed for SIMMs containing 32 or more chips.

Error Correcting Code (ECC)

Servers commonly use *error correcting code* (*ECC*) SDRAM. Although error correction is more expensive and involves a slight performance penalty, it is well worth it on a server, where data integrity is critical and other high-performing system components help make up for memory latency. ECC calculates check bits and appends them to the data during memory writes. For memory reads, ECC decodes the appended check bits and compares the write and read check bits. If there is a discrepancy in the check bits, then an error has occurred, and the NOS can be notified. If only a single bit error occurs, ECC can correct the error, but ECC cannot correct the more rare 2-, 3-, or 4-bit errors (multiple bit errors).

To find out more about specific memory modules, or to order memory for your servers, check the following Web sites:

- www.crucial.com
- www.micron.com
- www.kingston.com
- www.pny.com

Do it!

C-1: Researching processors and memory

Exercise
1 Using your Internet browser, access http://developer.intel.com and click the link for server components and products, then click the link for server boards. Choose a model to research.
2 How many processors does this board support?
3 What kinds of processors are supported?
4 What kind of memory is used?
5 What is the maximum amount of memory supported?
6 What are some ideal applications for this board?

Topic D: CMOS, BIOS, and POST

This topic covers the following CompTIA Server+ exam objectives:

#	Objective
2.2	Install hardware using best practices
	• Installation activities include:
	• Verify power-on via power-on sequence

CMOS

Explanation

The *CMOS* is a complimentary metal oxide semiconductor that includes a small amount of memory, the purpose of which is to store the BIOS settings such as the boot order (floppy, CD-ROM, hard disk, and so forth), hard disk configuration, power management settings, and more. The CMOS can store data for as long as power is available. The power supply provides power when the system is on; and a small, nonrechargeable, metal oxide battery (similar to a watch battery) supplies power when the server is off. Unlike desktop PCs, servers are usually powered on continuously except for regular maintenance, hardware upgrades, and troubleshooting when you must necessarily power off. Typical batteries can last for more than five years on desktop PCs, and somewhat longer on servers since the battery charge naturally dissipates as a matter of time instead of actual use. Server replacement might precede battery replacement, so sometimes battery life is not an issue. However, you should stock a few of the most common batteries in use on your servers just in case. You identify the specific battery in use by reading the identification stamped into the battery surface. Batteries near the end of their life usually lose time on the real time clock, so you should replace batteries on systems with slowing time.

BIOS

The *Basic Input/Output System* (*BIOS*) is a series of software programs that is the lowest-level interface between the hardware and the operating system. The BIOS programming is stored on a *flash BIOS* memory chip, also known as *EEPROM* (*electrically erasable programmable read-only memory*). The administrator can configure the BIOS programming to suit his or her needs and preferences, and the configuration is stored in the CMOS, which is powered by a small battery that retains the settings even when the power fails or is turned off. As its name implies, the BIOS is a series of input and output configuration settings for peripherals, adapters, and on-board components. Phoenix Software, Award Software, and American Megatrends Inc. (AMI) create most base BIOS programming, though individual server manufacturers often add modifications to provide functionality with their specific hardware. Phoenix Technologies acquired Award Software in late 1998, so a newer system will usually use either a Phoenix or an AMI BIOS. The BIOS controls all of the hardware on the system board and acts as a bridge for various NOS hardware drivers.

Accessing CMOS settings

Most of the time, when you turn on the power, the display tells you a specific key or keyboard combination to press in order to access the BIOS settings in CMOS. Typically, this is F1, F2, Esc, Del, or some combination of Ctrl+Alt (such as Ctrl+Alt+Shift, Enter, Esc, or S). Compaq computers usually use F10. A simple instruction such as "Press F2 to enter settings" often appears on the screen. Several manufacturers display a manufacturer-promoting splash screen that would prevent you from seeing such instruction, although pressing the Esc key often removes it. (In the unusual instance that the display does not indicate a method for accessing the BIOS, you can trick the system into allowing you to access the BIOS by pressing and holding virtually any key immediately after you power on the computer. The BIOS will often interpret your action as a keyboard problem and provide an opportunity for you to access the BIOS.)

When the system powers on, a procedure known as the *POST* (*power-on self-test*) verifies functionality of motherboard hardware. If the settings do not match, one or more beeps occur. Check system documentation to interpret the meaning of beep codes, which usually also accompany an on-screen error notification code. During the POST, if a device has its own BIOS such as a video card or SCSI card, the POST allows the device to perform its own diagnostics and then resumes when the diagnostics are finished. The POST checks the following:

- Video card and monitor
- CPU stepping (specific incremental version of the CPU)
- CPU model and speed
- BIOS version
- RAM
- Keyboard (which it enables)
- Various ports such as USB, serial, and parallel
- Floppy and hard disk drives
- Disk controllers using separate BIOS
- CD-ROM or DVD-ROM
- Sound cards
- Operating system (which it finds and loads)

Protecting the CMOS

Protecting the CMOS for both the server and workstation is an important security precaution. For example, anyone with physical access to the server could access the BIOS settings in CMOS to ensure that the system can boot from a floppy disk. Then, after booting from an MS-DOS or Windows 98 boot floppy, he or she could gain access to local hard disks and steal, alter, destroy, or otherwise damage data or the operating system. Protecting the CMOS first involves physical security, and then applying a password to the CMOS. The BIOS menu system is usually easily navigable, and you should be able to locate where to designate a password for the BIOS settings in CMOS. The CMOS usually includes two levels of password protection: a password to access and change the BIOS configuration, intended to prevent the curious from viewing the CMOS settings, and a password to boot the system. After setting the password(s), be sure to record and store them in a secure location.

In the event that you cannot find a server's CMOS password, you have no choice but to reset the CMOS, which clears password settings in addition to any configuration settings. Reset the CMOS in one of two ways. First, use jumper pins to short the battery circuit to the CMOS. To find the exact jumper pins, refer to the motherboard manufacturer's manual. In absence of a manual, you can also search for labeling on the circuit board. Usually the label is something like CPW (clear password), RPW (reset password), or the unmistakable "Short here to clear CMOS." Without battery power, BIOS settings drain from the CMOS, and the password resets to the original null (none) password setting. Second, you can simply remove the battery for a few seconds to clear the BIOS configurations, and then replace it. Either way, when you reboot, there will be no password required to boot or access BIOS settings.If you clear the BIOS settings, the operating system, hardware devices, or system preferences such as power conservation settings might not function as expected. Although a BIOS maker provides the basic BIOS, the server manufacturer has likely shipped the computer with default settings. Without these default settings, items such as the hard disk might not be accessible, making a boot impossible. After resetting the CMOS (or after you replace a dead battery), navigate the menu system to locate a setting that restores default settings to get back to a workable starting point. (Fortunately, the BIOS interacts with several hardware components to automatically configure settings, as in the hard disk configuration and memory detection.)

Common BIOS settings

It would be impractical to list all common BIOS settings from all manufacturers. A general list of configuration categories usually revolves around the system time/date, hard and floppy disks, disk controller (IDE), keyboard, processor(s), memory, ISA/EISA/PCI expansion buses, system resources (IRQ, DMA, etc.), serial/parallel ports, and boot configuration. However, you should know some common features that you are more likely to find on a server than a workstation. After you access the BIOS settings in CMOS, use the menu system to navigate to various settings (see the following table). The BIOS menu system varies from one manufacturer to the other, and a BIOS from a particular BIOS maker might be different from one machine to the next because server manufacturers often modify the menu system for uses specific to their computers.

Feature	Description
Ultra DMA settings	Configures the high-throughput UDMA disk controller.
Processor	On a server, displays information about processor stepping (version) and L2 cache size. You can view the settings for each of the installed processors and test each one.
PCI bus mastering	Enables/disables devices as PCI bus masters and sets the number of clock cycles that a device can master on a PCI bus during a single transaction.
RAM testing	Selects the degree to which the system tests the installed memory (e.g., each 1 MB, 1 KB, or each byte boundary).
Memory scrubbing	Allows capable chipsets to automatically detect and correct single-bit memory errors.
Security	Allows the system to boot as usual, but prevents use of keyboard or mouse until the correct password is entered. Included on many servers, this secure boot mode also requires the password to boot from a floppy or CD-ROM. Some vendors secure the power and reset switches, which also require a password to use. You can usually configure a hot-key combination or countdown timer that places the server back in secure mode.
Management port	Specifies a serial port to which you can connect another device (a laptop, for example) to externally diagnose the server—even with the server turned off. You can configure management port settings such as whether a password is required to use the port, the connection type (port or modem), and so forth.
Logging	Logs system events in a small segment of nonvolatile memory.
Management interrupt	Allows system management to issue a non-maskable interrupt (NMI), which takes priority over standard interrupt requests. An NMI is useful to stop the system or issue a message in the event of critical events such as failing memory.
General hardware	Displays hardware information such as part and serial numbers for information about the board, chassis, and system.
I2O drives	Allows you to specify the maximum number of I2O drives that will be assigned a DOS drive letter, usually one or four.

Most servers also include an additional management utility that provides similar management to that seen in the BIOS, except using a manufacturer-specific interface and settings. The settings are usually saved in BIOS, but settings can go beyond basic BIOS settings. For example, Intel's System Setup Utility also allows you to save *field replaceable unit* (*FRU*) information. (An FRU is a system with replaceable CPU, CMOS, CMOS battery, RAM, and RAM cache.) Typically, the management utility is a DOS-based utility run from floppy disk(s) or a CD-ROM. In some server types, however, these devices are not replaceable without sending the server to the manufacturer.

Do it!

D-1: Accessing the BIOS

Here's how

1 Boot your computer and access the BIOS configurations.

2 How much memory is installed in the computer?

3 How large is the hard disk?

4 In what order does the BIOS search for bootable media?

5 Attempt to exit the BIOS configuration. You are prompted to save your settings. Choose to discard the changes.

Unit summary: Motherboard architecture, processors, memory, and BIOS

Topic A

In this topic, you learned that a motherboard includes a **front side bus**, sometimes a **back side bus**, and three primary **I/O expansion buses**: Industry Standard Architecture (**ISA**), Extended ISA (**EISA**), and Peripheral Components Interconnect (**PCI**). Newer motherboards include only the PCI expansion bus. You learned that the speed of each bus is dependent upon the motherboard clock frequency, and that PC-based bus systems use what is known as a **hierarchical bus**, because several buses actually comprise the (collective) "bus," each running at different speeds and with the slower buses hierarchically structured beneath the faster buses.

Topic B

In this topic, you learned that **processor speed** is a measure in MHz of the number of opportunities per second that the processor can execute an instruction. You learned that the processor architecture design uses a multiplier methodology to provide the processor's speed, and that **Cache memory** is a small amount of memory that stores recently or frequently used program code or data, reducing latency. You also learned that cache memory appears in a number of places on the server including the hard disk, CD-ROM, and the processor, and that processors use two types of cache memory: **L1** (level 1) and **L2** (level 2).

Topic C

In this topic, you learned that **DIMMs** (dual inline memory module) dramatically improve memory performance over the SIMM predecessor by expanding the module to 64 bits (nonparity) or 72 bits (parity or ECC), and the contacts on both sides of the module are separate (hence the *dual* in DIMM). You also learned that **SDRAM** operates at clock speed; if the system bus is 100 MHz, then SDRAM matches that frequency, which functionally operates at about 10 ns. **RDRAM** provides extremely fast 800 MHz internal clock speed on a 400 MHz bus, because data is transferred twice during each clock cycle. This adds up to 1.6 GB throughput (16 bits × 800 MHz / 8 = 1.6 GB). You learned that Double data rate SDRAM (**DDR** SDRAM) is most commonly used in new machines, and uses a 184-pin, 64-bit DIMM, while the newer **DDR2** uses a 240-pin DIMM and less voltage than DDR.

Topic D

In this topic, you learned that the **CMOS** is a complimentary metal oxide semiconductor that includes a small amount of memory in order to store the **BIOS** settings such as the boot order, hard disk configuration and power management settings. You learned how to access the CMOS settings and learned about some common BIOS settings. You also learned what happens during the power-on self-test, or **POST**

Independent practice activity

1 Access the Intel Web site at http://developer.intel.com/products/chipsets/index.htm.

2 Under Server, click the link to the Intel 7501 Chipset.

3 How many processors can the chipset use?

4 What kind of processors does it use?

5 What type of memory does this chipset use?

6 What are some new technologies used on in this chipset?

Review questions

1 What is the main data transportation medium in the server?

A The PCI bus

B The motherboard

C The ISA bus

D ECC memory

2 How does the bus bit width affect data throughput?

A A wider bus results in less data throughput.

B Bus width does not affect data throughput.

C A wider bus results in more data throughput.

D A wider bus accepts higher voltage, allowing for overclocking.

3 If a server offers uptime of five nines, how many minutes a year might it be down?

A 5 minutes

B Five increments of nine minutes each

C Nine increments of five minutes each

D 59 minutes

4 How does clock frequency affect server performance?

A Each clock cycle represents a period of latency during which components cannot perform actions.

B Each clock cycle represents an opportunity for a component to perform an action.

C Only the processor, not clock frequency, affects performance.

D Slowing clock frequency means you should replace the CMOS battery soon.

5 What is the function of a chipset?

A Manage data traffic and separate buses

B Perform mathematical functions on behalf of the processor

C Cache data to accelerate performance

D Provide electrical continuity between the CPU and memory

6 What is a hierarchical bus?

A A bus that is the latest in a series of buses based on the same technology

B Multiple motherboards in the same server

C A motherboard that uses a mezzanine bus to expand memory and/or processors

D The structuring of slower buses beneath faster buses

7 Which of the following motherboard buses is the fastest?

   A commuter bus

   B front side bus

   C PCI bus

   D Universal Serial Bus

8 What is bus mastering?

   A The ability of a device to bypass the processor and directly access memory

   B A description of the system bus

   C A description of the North Bridge's control over the system bus

   D The ability of the MCH to direct traffic between the processor and memory

9 How is a PCI interrupt beneficial?

   A It allows PCI devices to have a priority when directing interrupt requests to the processor.

   B It arbitrates between two PCI devices contending for processor time.

   C It allows PCI IRQ steering to assign two or more devices the same IRQ.

   D Divides a single PCI bus into two separate, faster PCI buses

10 What do most servers require you to do before performing a PCI hot swap?

   A Shut down the server power

   B Shut down power on the PCI slot

   C Reboot the server

   D Place the server in sleep mode

11 What do most servers require you to do before performing a PCI hot swap?

   A Shut down the server power

   B Shut down power on the PCI slot

   C Reboot the server

   D Place the server in sleep mode

12 What is the purpose of I2O? (Choose all that apply.).

   A improve I/O performance

   B Simplify driver development

   C Provide a wider I/O bus

   D Provide a faster I/O bus

13 Why is AGP not included on some servers?.

    A AGP is incompatible with the Intel Xeon processor.

    B Servers include a separate, independent bus to handle video.

    C Servers do not require high performance graphics functionality.

    D AGP places too many demands on the processor.

14 What is the purpose of L1 and L2 cache?

    A These two caches do not have the same purpose.

    B To store recently or frequently accessed data to reduce latency

    C Short-term storage in case of data corruption

    D To cache data streams from the PCI bus

15 Which of the following characteristics does not differentiate the Intel Pentium III Xeon from the Pentium III?

    A Enclosure type

    B Cache size

    C Cache speed

    D Core clock speed

16 Which of the following is an advantage of the Intel Itanium?

    A Direct compatibility with 32-bit operating systems and applications

    B Windows 2000 will be ported to 64-bits, taking advantage of the wider data path

    C Support for up to eight processors

    D Cost effective alternative to the Pentium III

17 What makes SDRAM faster than standard DRAM?

    A SDRAM operates at PCI speed.

    B DRAM operates at bus speed.

    C SDRAM operates at bus speed.

    D They are the same speed.

18 Why is DDR SDRAM faster than standard SDRAM?.

    A DDR SDRAM transfers data twice per clock cycle.

    B DDR SDRAM is not faster, it only has a wider data path.

    C SDRAM can only run at half bus speed.

    D SDRAM is only 32-bits wide.

19 Why do servers use ECC memory?.

   A Increase performance

   B Increase latency

   C Increase data reliability

   D Purge memory in case of data errors

20 How does the BIOS relate to the CMOS?.

   A CMOS is the configuration programming that is stored in BIOS.

   B CMOS stores BIOS configuration settings.

   C BIOS and CMOS both provide I/O configuration settings for hardware.

   D BIOS is an error-correcting utility for the CMOS .

21 What two benefits do BIOS passwords offer?.

   A Ability to disable the power switch

   B Ability to prevent access to operating system

   C Ability to prevent access to BIOS settings

   D Ability to prevent booting

Unit 2

Storage

Unit time: 120 minutes

Complete this unit, and you'll know how to:

A Identify basic physical hard disk components, compare physical and logical drives and describe their functionality, and identify major file systems.

B Identify characteristics of the IDE interface and configure IDE cabling and connectors.

C Identify characteristics of the SCSI interface.

D Configure SCSI cabling and connectors.

E Become familiar with iSCSI, Fibre Channel, and FCIP technology and storage area networking.

F Identify and configure various types of RAID.

Topic A: Hard disks

This topic covers the following CompTIA Server+ exam objectives:

#	Objective
4.3	Add hard drives
	• Activities include:
	• Verify that the drives are the appropriate type
	• Supporting knowledge includes:
	• Difference between a RAID partition and an OS partition
4.7	Upgrade peripheral devices, internal and external. Verify appropriate system resources (e.g. expansion slots, IRQ, DMA, etc.)
	• Peripheral devices include:
	• Disk drives
7.2	Use diagnostic hardware and software tools and utilities
	• Supporting knowledge includes:
	• Know common diagnostic tools
	• FDISK
	• Basic hard disk tools

Hard disk overview

Explanation

The physical hard disk is the focal point of the enterprise. The operating system, applications, and data are stored on the hard disk, and without hard disk storage, there is nothing for anyone to "do" on the network. Therefore, it makes sense that server storage be protected against failure and that administrators configure storage so that it is as fast as reasonably possible. This unit opens with a brief inventory of hard disk physical components, differentiates physical and logical drives, and describes the major file systems commonly in use on servers. To operate the hard disk, an IDE or SCSI controller and attachment interface are necessary. Also, you will need to be aware of rules that govern appropriate connections and compatibilities for a given hard disk configuration, especially for SCSI.

Although desktop users commonly use only a single physical hard disk, server administrators often manage dozens of hard disks—most of which require high performance, redundancy, or both using various RAID implementations. When administrators add or replace a drive, it is vital to do so with minimal disruption (if any) to users, and this unit shows you various ways to do this. Part of administering server storage is proper maintenance, and you will learn about several such utilities. Finally, you will learn about network storage, including a new technology known as Fibre Channel that provides outstanding performance.

Hard disk components

Although we use the term "hard drive" or "hard disk," a hard disk is really multiple physical platters inside a sealed, dust-free housing. The manufacturing process is extremely controlled—there is no tolerance for contaminants (such as dust particles)—and manufacturing specifications are extremely tight. Most hard disks include the following major physical components (use Exhibit 2-1 for reference as you read the rest of this section):

- Disk platters
- Drive heads

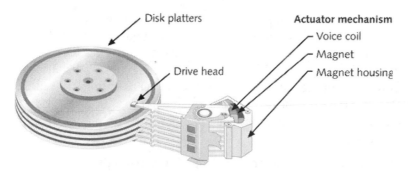

Exhibit 2-1: Hard disk components

The hard disk also consists of the following components not visible in Exhibit 2-1:

- Spindle motor
- Logic board
- Connectors
- Jumpers

Though it would be impractical to exhaustively describe each hard disk component, you should be aware of their basic functionality.

Disk platters

The *disk platter* is a rigid disk inside the sealed hard disk enclosure. In the past, disk platters have been composed of a metallic aluminum/magnesium alloy, a lightweight and rigid material. On the surface, a syrup containing iron-oxide particles was evenly spread across the disk using centrifugal force. It is this material that stores the magnetic data on the platter. With the cover off the sealed enclosure, you can see that the platter is a brownish or amber color. While you might still have disks in use that were manufactured using this process, it is not implemented in current manufacturing because the oxide medium is soft, making it susceptible to damage if the drive head touches the surface during operation, usually due to a jolt or vibration. (This is known as a *head crash*.) A head crash often (but not always) corrupts the data or compromises the integrity of the recording media.

Current manufacturing procedures have abandoned the metal platter in favor of a glass platter (actually a glass-ceramic composite) because it does not flex as metal can, allowing the platter to be about one-half the thickness of a metallic platter. Thinner platters allow room for more platters in the same drive housing, hence higher-capacity drives. Most current hard disks utilize four platters, but high-capacity drives can use upward of 11. Also, the glass platter is more thermally stable than metal, minimizing the expansion or contraction that occurs with temperature changes.

One way to apply the medium to the platter is to process the platter through a series of chemical baths that leave several layers of metallic film in an electroplating method similar to that used to affix chrome to car bumpers. A better, newer method is to apply a thin-film magnetic medium over the glass platter, providing greater density. The thin-film medium is more expensive than electroplating, and it is applied through a process known as "sputtering" in which the material is applied in a continuous, nearly perfect vacuum. Thin-film media are much harder than oxide media. The result is that it is more difficult (nearly impossible) to crash the media. Thin-film media are like a silvery mirror in appearance.

Drive heads

The *drive head* reads and writes data to the magnetic media on the disk platter. Each platter has two drive heads: one that reads media from the top and another that reads media from the bottom. When stationary, the drive heads are actually parked on the media surface. When the drive is in use and spinning, the air pressure from the movement of the platter separates the drive heads from the surface of the media. Because the drive heads are ganged together in a head rack to a single actuator mechanism, each head moves across its respective platter in unison with the other heads of the drive.

Older hard disks required a program to manually park the heads when powered off to avoid having the heads skitter across the surface, causing damage. Today, drives automatically park their heads using a spring and magnetic force. When the drive powers off, the magnetic force of the voice coil actuator dissipates, and a spring drags the head rack to a park-and-lock position.

The *actuator mechanism* is the mechanical component that physically positions the drive heads at the appropriate location on the disk platter to read or write data. Most actuator mechanisms today use the *voice coil* construction, which derives its name from audio speaker technology using an electrically charged coil. Fluctuations in the electrical charge move the coil to various positions over the platter similar to the way a speaker coil moves to create audible vibrations in a speaker cone. The actuator mechanism has no intelligence of its own in determining the appropriate location; it depends upon the *servo mechanism*, which detects precise cylinder locations on the platter using *gray code*, a special binary code written to the drive by the drive manufacturer that identifies physical locations on the drive. You cannot alter or erase this code, even with the FDISK utility or FORMAT command.

The physical components described above are relatively durable considering their precise nature. For example, specifications for many drives indicate the MTBF is approximately 1,200,000 hours (that's almost 137 years) and can sustain shock up to 300 Gs (the force of gravity times 300).

The environment is still extremely important for hard drives, particularly the temperature. We have already discussed adequate ventilation and cooling, but if your office is in a colder environment, also consider condensation. When a drive comes delivered to you from a cold truck in the middle of winter, allow plenty of time for the drive to warm up (acclimate) to room temperature before using the drive to prevent condensation on internal components. If the drive has been in an environment colder than about 50 degrees F (10 degrees C), allow it to sit at room temperature for several hours before opening the package.

Partitions and logical drives

Nearly all operating systems use a storage system that begins with basic Microsoft MS-DOS hard disk partitions. During OS installation, many operating systems (NetWare, for example) might modify the partition or create another partition. To further subdivide and organize storage on partitions, you create logical drives. This section briefly discusses partitions and logical drives.

Creating a partition

The operating system—whether it is as simple as MS-DOS or as sophisticated as NetWare—requires a defined boundary on the hard disk on which to place its files. The purpose of the partition is to provide this boundary. A partition can be a primary partition or an extended partition (see the section on logical drives). A *primary partition* is a bootable partition on which you can install operating system files. The MS-DOS *FDISK* utility is usually used to create the partition. You can create up to four primary partitions using Windows NT/2000/2003 disk management, but this will be unusual unless you intend to install multiple operating systems on the same server (as in a classroom or lab environment). Typically, you create one primary partition and an extended partition, which can, in turn, contain logical drives.

After creating the partition(s), you must reboot before using the *FORMAT* command to create the file system. If you try to format without rebooting, you will get an error message.

Even if you don't use Windows 98 in your environment, obtain a Windows 98 startup disk because it has several useful utilities, including FDISK and FORMAT. Booting from the Windows 98 startup disk automatically loads drivers that work with most CD-ROMs, avoiding the need for you to create a customized disk with your specific CD-ROM drivers. Also add the SMARTDRV.EXE utility and load it prior to installing the NOS because its ability to cache file reads in advance significantly decreases installation time.

Run the FDISK utility by typing FDISK at the MS-DOS command prompt. With more recent versions of FDISK (as in Windows 95B or later), notification that the hard disk is larger than 512 MB appears, and a lengthy prompt asks if large disk support is desired over 2 GB. Nearly always, you want to respond Yes to this option. The series of FDISK menu options is easy to navigate; however, the following table lists the common options.

Option	Notes
Create DOS partition or Logical DOS Drive	DOS partition can be a primary or extended partition. Logical DOS drive first requires an extended partition.
Create Extended DOS Partition	Contains logical drives.
Set active partition	The BIOS searches for a bootable, active partition, so you must set this to start the operating system. Some operating systems automatically set the partition active at installation.
Delete partition or Logical DOS Drive	Deletes the partition—be careful, you cannot recover data on a deleted partition!
Display partition information	Shows partitions on the drive. Note that any non-FAT file system (described later in this unit) might appear as a non-DOS partition.

There are third-party alternatives to FDISK and FORMAT. One alternative is GDISK from Symantec, a command line utility that works much faster and offers more flexibility than FDISK and FORMAT. GDISK accompanies Symantec Ghost, a disk duplication software product. Another alternative is PartitionMagic from PowerQuest, which has a more intuitive graphical interface and is a favorite among administrators for quickly resizing and moving partitions as well as converting them from one file system to another.

Logical drives

A *logical drive* is a section on the hard disk that appears to the operating system as if it were a separate, distinct hard disk and has its own drive letter. A logical drive requires an extended partition, which can take the place of one of the four primary partitions. You can have a maximum of either four primary partitions or three primary partitions and one extended partition.

The sole purpose of the *extended partition* is to store logical drive(s). Logical drives can be lettered up to Z. Within available disk space limitations, you can create as many logical drives in the extended partition as you want. You can use FDISK to create the logical drives, but operating systems like Windows 2000/2003 provide disk utilities to manage drives and volumes, as shown in Exhibit 2-2.

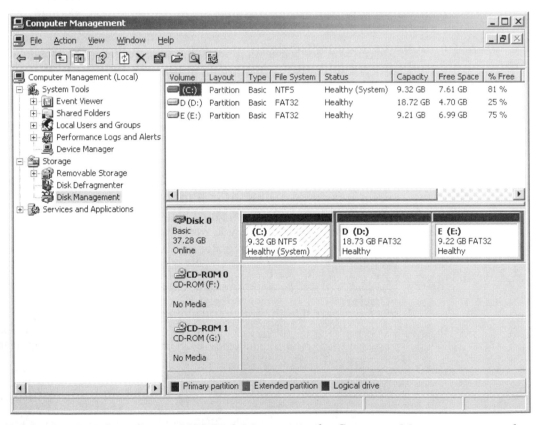

Exhibit 2-2: Windows Server 2003 Disk Manager in the Computer Management console

Once the partitions and/or logical drives are created, you must reboot the system and then format the drives. If you do not reboot the system prior to formatting, you are likely to receive an error message. Because the partition is only a storage boundary, you also need to format the partition or logical drive before you can store files on it.

Many operating systems include utilities that allow you to create and manage additional logical or primary partitions. For example, Windows 2000 Server and 2003 include the Disk Management console with which you can create additional partitions and software RAID configurations.

While a typical IDE hard drive will plug and play, most utilities for configuring and monitoring the health and performance of SCSI drives, RAID arrays, and external storage devices are vendor-specific. At least vendors of these devices will provide utilities, tough you may choose a third-party offering instead.

Do it!

A-1: Viewing drive details

Here's how

1 Turn on the power to the computer. Access the BIOS (look for a message telling you how or ask the instructor).

2 Navigate the menu system and locate information about the drive. Who is the manufacturer? How many megabytes are on the drive? (Not all BIOS will allow you to view this information. If so, proceed to Step 3.)

3 Navigate to where you can adjust the boot order. If necessary, adjust the boot order to boot from the floppy disk first, then the hard disk.

4 Exit the BIOS, saving changes. Boot back into Windows.

5 Choose **Start**, **Administrative Tools**, **Computer Management**. This will start the management console.

6 In the left pane, select **Disk Management**. Observe the drives on your machine.

7 In the right pane, right-click on **Disk 0** and choose **Properties**, as shown

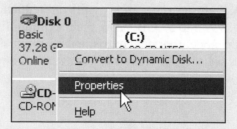

8 Note the properties of the physical drive. Click the Volumes tab and note the properties of individual volumes.

9 Close the properties windows and the computer management console.

File systems

Explanation

A file system is a structure that an operating system uses to name, store, and organize files on a disk. As you administer various operating systems, it is important to understand the basics of each file system. (The following are general descriptions, and are not intended to be exhaustive.)

FAT/FAT32

The Microsoft-based *File Allocation Table* (*FAT*) file system is compatible with nearly any operating system and uses an invisible table near the top of the partition that points to the physical location of data on the disk. It is the simplest file system, and the network operating systems discussed in this text can all be installed with a FAT file system, though you will often choose to convert to another file system during or after the installation, primarily because of the following FAT limitations:

- *Small volume size*: FAT only supports volumes up to 2 GB in size—tiny even by current home user standards.

- *Large cluster size*: The file system stores data on the drive in 32 KB "chunks" known as clusters or allocation units. If you save a file that is only 2 KB in size, it must use all 32 KB of the cluster, wasting the remaining 30 KB. The space of wasted kilobytes is known as *slack*. Even with hard disk storage at a relatively inexpensive level in recent years, the excessive slack of the FAT file system is undesirable and quickly adds up to several megabytes of wasted space.

- *Limited file size*: The maximum file size is 2 GB. While this seems large, it is woefully insufficient for most corporate databases.

- *Security*: FAT offers no local security. Therefore, any passerby with a boot floppy can fully access the files on the local hard disk. Of course, physical security measures should prevent local access; nevertheless, administrators usually prohibit a strictly FAT file system on the server.

FAT32 is the next (and last) generation of the FAT file system. It overcomes the first two weaknesses of the FAT file system by offering large disk support up to a theoretical 2 TB and using only 4 KB cluster sizes for a significant reduction of slack. However, Windows 2000 only allows up to 32 GB. Also, the maximum file size is 4 GB, but that's still too small for many corporate requirements. Administrators also avoid FAT32 because it does not offer security. Microsoft offers a secure file system with the NTFS file system.

NTFS

The *NT File System* (*NTFS*) is the Microsoft Windows NT file system. NTFS is compatible only with Windows NT 3.1 or later, including Windows 2000/2003 and XP, and is not directly compatible with other operating systems. An NT/2000/2003/XP machine can have both FAT and NTFS volumes at the same time. NTFS volumes offer the following benefits:

- *Large volume size*: NTFS can support extremely large volumes, though the practical limit according to Microsoft is 2 TB.

- *Small cluster size*: NTFS formats clusters at 4 KB each by default on partitions larger than 2 GB, though you can select a cluster size from 512 bytes to 64 KB.

- *Large file size*: File size is limited only by the available drive space.

- *Security*: Unless using hacker's tools, passersby cannot boot and access files on a local NTFS volume unless they also have a user account that is authorized to access those files. Also, administrators can apply very specific levels of file and folder security that are unavailable on a FAT file system. For example, you could allow a user to save a file or folder but not delete files or folders.

- *Compression*: Though FAT offers compression through Microsoft utilities, these utilities are not considered reliable enough to be practical for server use. NTFS allows you to compress files and folders using a highly reliable compression scheme, conserving disk space.

- *Data integrity*: NTFS includes mechanisms designed to ensure that data is properly and completely written to the drive.

- *Windows 2000/2003 NTFS features*: Under Windows 2000/2003/XP, a variety of new features appear in NTFS 5. You can encrypt files and folders with a nearly unbreakable encryption scheme, and set quotas so that users do not abuse file storage privileges. Besides the file system itself, the operating system offers many useful capabilities for managing partitions and files, including the *Distributed File System* (*Dfs*) to deploy what appears to be a single directory structure over multiple physical file servers. Windows 2000 also has offline storage to migrate seldom used files to a slower and less expensive storage medium such as tape.

Linux/UNIX file systems

There are dozens of different "flavors" (versions) of UNIX in use. For the most part, this text and the CompTIA Server+ exam gravitate toward Linux as the specific implementation of UNIX. UNIX implementations generally use the *UNIX File System* (*UFS*), the *Network File System* (*NFS*), or *AFS*, which stems from Carnegie-Mellon's *Andrew File System*. Linux often uses the *Filesystem Hierarchy Standard* (*FHS*), which is more a directory structure than a file system (see www.pathname.com/fhs for the complete standard). Finally, you can also create Linux-specific partitions—Linux swap, Linux native, and Linux RAID.

UNIX file systems have a higher administrative learning curve—you must use an arcane command line interface. However, several interfaces (such as X Windows) now allow you to perform many UNIX administrative functions using a GUI. Also, various flavors of Linux characteristically include a GUI.

NetWare

The traditional *NetWare file system* competes directly with Microsoft's NTFS, and therefore offers similar features: You can use very large volumes and files, and the cluster size is efficient. Using the traditional NetWare file system, you can create a NetWare *volume*, which is a collection of files, directories, subdirectories, and even partitions. You can combine separate partitions that together comprise a volume. File storage is also efficient because NetWare volumes can use suballocation. A NetWare volume can subdivide a block (a Microsoft cluster is a NetWare "block") to minimize slack space. Unfilled blocks are subdivided into 512-byte suballocation blocks, which can then be used to store data from one or more other files.

Like NTFS, NetWare offers file compression. You can manually activate compression by flagging files and directories with the IC (immediate compress) command or by using the SET command at the server console to configure a file inactivity delay, after which compression occurs automatically. NetWare offers a distributed file system and offline file storage similar to Windows 2000 Dfs and offline file storage, respectively.

NetWare 5.x also includes additional features in its optional *Novell Storage Service* (*NSS*) file system. The purpose of NSS is to increase performance and total storage capacity. NSS offers several improvements over the traditional NetWare file system:

- *Large files*: Instead of the traditional 2 GB limitation, files can now be up to 8 TB each! Also, you can store *trillions* of files in a single directory, compared to the 16 million entries per volume under traditional limitations.

- *Performance*: Large files typically take a long time to open, but NSS provides rapid access regardless of size. Also, mounting a volume (preparing it for use) is much faster.

- *Flexible storage management*: You can create up to eight NetWare partitions on a single disk and create unlimited volumes per partition.

Note: you can't just install an NSS file system; you have to first have the traditional NetWare file system and then add NSS.

Do it!   **A-2:   Discussing file systems**

Questions and answers

1   Why can larger cluster sizes waste disk space?

2   In what ways does FAT32 improve over FAT?

3   What limits the file size in NTFS?

4   What file systems are used by UNIX and Linux?

Topic B: The IDE interface

This topic covers the following CompTIA Server+ exam objectives:

#	Objective
1.7	Know the differences between different ATA (IDE) solutions, their advantages, limitations, and specifications
	• ATA 33
	• ATA 66
	• ATA 100
	• ATA 133
	• SATA (Serial ATA)
	• SATA II (SATA II v1.2)
	• Ultra DMA
	• Cabling and connectors
	• Master/slave/cable select (CSEL)
	• Jumper settings
2.2	Install hardware using best practices
	• Hardware includes:
	• Drives
4.3	Add hard drives
	• Activities include:
	• For ATA/IDE drives, confirm cabling, master/slave and potential cross-brand compatibility

IDE basics

Explanation

Integrated Drive Electronics (*IDE*) can refer to any hard disk with an integrated controller. However, it is more technically accurate to apply the term *ATA* (*AT Attachment*) to what we usually call an IDE drive, because the drive plugs into the 16-bit ISA bus known as the AT bus. In spite of this technicality, this text and most references use the terms IDE and ATA synonymously. Recall that an IDE drive includes the controller in the circuitry attached to the drive. When people colloquially say that they are installing an "IDE controller," what they really mean is that they are installing a *host adapter*, the more accurate term for what is usually referred to as an IDE or SCSI hard disk controller. The host adapter is the physical interface between the hard disk and the computer bus. As you can see, disk interface terminologies are replete with inaccuracies (and we have only gotten started). As we delve into the IDE interface and its variations, you'll learn synonyms for various interfaces.

Other devices besides hard disks can plug into the ATA interface, usually CD-ROM drives and tape drives. These devices require a variation on the ATA specification known as the *ATAPI* (*ATA Packet Interface*) specification. The SCSI interface, discussed later in this unit, can also accept other devices. For this unit's purposes, however, we are only concerned with hard disks for both interfaces.

ATA-1

The following major features characterize the *ATA-1* standard:

- Signal timing for DMA and Programmed I/O (PIO), which utilizes the processor to handle disk transfers but is superceded by DMA and Ultra-DMA
- 40/44-pin cable connections (44-pin connections use four more pins to supply power to notebook hard drives)
- Determination of master, slave, or cable select using jumpers
- Transfer rate of 3.3 MBps to 8.3 MBps depending on the PIO or DMA mode

ATA-2

The following major features characterize the *ATA-2* standard:

- Large drive support for up to 137.4 GB (previously 8.4 GB)
- Faster PIO and DMA transfer specifications
- Power management support
- Removable device support
- PCMCIA (PC card) support
- Reports drive characteristics to software (useful for Plug and Play)
- Transfer rate of 8.3 MBps to 16.6 MBps depending upon the PIO or DMA mode

Before proceeding, let's sort out some more terms. ATA-2 is synonymous with the unofficial marketing terms Fast-ATA, Fast-ATA-2, and Enhanced IDE (EIDE). EIDE has become one of the most accepted terms, and it applies in a general way to ATA-2 or better. The true published specification is AT Attachment Interface with Extensions, but people seldom use that title.

ATA-3

The following major features characterize the *ATA-3* standard:

- Includes Self Monitoring and Reporting Technology (S.M.A.R.T.), a predictive technology that enables the operating system to warn of a device's degradation. S.M.A.R.T. has its basis in preceding technologies known as Predictive Failure Analysis (IBM) and IntelliSafe (Compaq). Drives might use one of the three technologies, or a combination. For example, some Compaq systems use both IntelliSafe and S.M.A.R.T. If the hard disk begins to show signs of failure, you will see messages in the server's system log, RAID log, or in a vendor-supplied monitoring and reporting utility.
- Optional security mode that protects access to the drive with a password.
- Transfer rate of 11.1 MBps to 16.6 MBps depending on the PIO or DMA mode.

S.M.A.R.T. has made its way into the SCSI world of hard disks as well. This significantly adds to the administrator's ability to monitor the health of internal and external SCSI disks and RAID configurations.

ATA-4

The following major features characterize the *ATA-4* standard:

- Addition of the ATAPI standard to attach other types of devices
- Advanced power management
- Specification of an optional 80-conductor, 40-pin cable-select cable to reduce noise
- Improved BIOS support for a theoretical capability of 9.4 trillion gigabytes, though the actual ATA standard is still limited to 137.4 GB
- Ultra-DMA (UDMA) support, increasing the transfer rate to 33 MBps

ATA-4 is probably the most groundbreaking standard in terms of current IDE performance. It introduced a level of performance (which was increased even further with ATA-5 and ATA-6) that had been formerly available only on the SCSI interface. Other terms for ATA-4 include Ultra-DMA and Ultra-ATA. In reference to the transfer rate, you might also see UDMA/33 or Ultra-ATA/33. In previous ATA implementations, data is transferred once each clock cycle. Ultra-ATA differs in that data transfers twice for each clock cycle, once at the rising edge and once at the trailing edge. Ultra-DMA also adds a cyclical redundancy check (CRC) to ensure the integrity of data.

To support Ultra-ATA/33 and later, a compatible drive, BIOS, operating system, and host adapter interface must be in use. In the BIOS, most manufacturers now include an artificial "32-bit" transfer. Recall that IDE operates at 16 bits on the ISA interface, even though the host adapter is usually a PCI card. The BIOS now includes functionality that allows for two 16-bit transfers to occur at once, hence the "32-bit" transfer.

Under ATA-4 and higher, a single drive on the IDE cable must be at the end of the cable (no "stub" allowed). Otherwise, signaling problems can occur. Under earlier ATA versions, a stub was OK but inadvisable.

If you have any older ATA-1 through ATA-3 drives, don't throw them away just because current standards are ATA-4 or better. The ATA specification requires successive ATA iterations to be backward compatible. For example, you could still attach an ATA-1 drive to an ATA-4 or higher host adapter for cheap (but slower) storage. Note that as a general rule, if you mix ATA standards on the same cable, both devices operate at the performance level of the slower standard.

ATA-5

The following major features characterize the *ATA-5* standard:

- 80-conductor cable required (as opposed to optional) in order to achieve the maximum transfer rate. You can use a standard 40-pin cable but only at a maximum transfer rate of 33 MBps.
- Added to the ATA-5 specification is an IEEE-1394 (FireWire) link that allows use of an ATA drive on the FireWire interface. (FireWire is an extremely fast bus allowing up to 63 connected devices and up to 3200 Mbps throughput in the latest version.)
- Transfer rate of 66 MBps, achieved by reducing setup times and increasing the clock rate. Later implementations of ATA-5 achieve 100 MBps under the marketing title of Ultra-DMA/100. This came about as a result of manufacturers that could match the 100 MBps transfer rate of the ATA-6 standard but did not want to wait for the completed standard.

Starting with ATA-5 and ATA-6, you are most likely to have to add an adapter to achieve the maximum throughput because it takes several months and sometimes over a year for motherboard IDE interfaces to catch up to the latest ATA standard.

ATA-6

This standard includes all features of previous ATA standards plus a formalized 100 and 133 MBps specification.

SATA

The next step in IDE/ATA technology is *Serial ATA*, or *SATA*. Rather than using the usual parallel communication with a 40-pin IDE ribbon cable, SATA uses point-to-point serial communication. This requires much smaller cables and connectors with seven pins – one pair for transmit, one pair for receive, and 3 pins for ground. The connector has a key at on end to ensure proper insertion. First examples of SATA drives have transfer rates of 150 MBps. SATA II doubles the transfer rate and adds other enhancements.

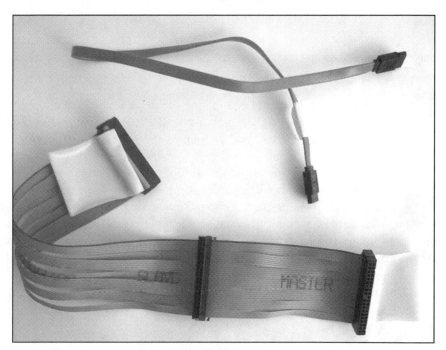

Exhibit 2-3: A 7-pin SATA cable (top) compared to a standard 40-pin IDE cable

Like a USB port, a SATA interface may be made available to external ports for peripherals such as external drives.

The following table summarizes the IDE standards covered in the previous sections:

IDE standard	Also known as	Performance
ATA-1		3.3–8.3 MBps
ATA-2	AT Attachment Interface with Extensions, Fast-ATA, Fast-ATA-2, and Enhanced IDE (EIDE)	8.3–16.6 MBps
ATA-3	EIDE	11.1–16.6 Mbps
ATA-4 (ATA-33)	Ultra-DMA, Ultra-ATA, UDMA/33, or Ultra-ATA/33	33 MBps
ATA-5 (ATA-66)	Ultra-DMA/100 for 100 MBps implementations	66–100 MBps
ATA-6 (ATA-100 and ATA-133)		100-133 MBps
SATA/SATA II (Serial ATA)		150/300 MBps

ATA cable

The standard ATA cable connecting the drive to the host adapter is a 40-pin ribbon cable (see Exhibit 2-4). To prevent incorrect connections, a cable key (protruding notch) on the cable matches a corresponding gap in the IDE connection on the hard drive. The cable should have one striped wire (usually red, sometimes blue) that indicates Pin 1. Pin 20 is not used and is usually absent from the drive, and a corresponding block in position 20 appears on the cable, also preventing backward insertion (see Exhibit 2-4 and Exhibit 2-5). Orient the connection so that Pin 1 on the cable is adjacent to the power cable connection. Because the cable is not shielded, you are limited to a length of 18 inches (457.2 mm). A longer cable could be more sensitive to timing and electrical noise issues, resulting in data corruption. The host adapter connected to the other end should also have a cable key, stripe, and absent Pin 20, and most manufacturers include a marking on the PCB (printed circuit board) that indicates Pin 1.

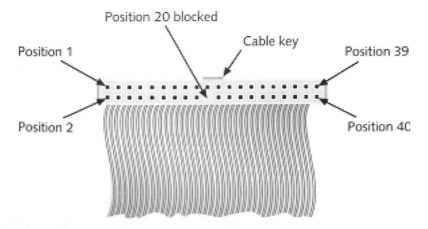

Exhibit 2-4: Standard 40-pin IDE connector

The cable length of 18 inches (457.2 mm) is usually plenty for a desktop workstation, but in full-size server tower cases in which the controller is farther away from the drive bays, this might cause a problem. If the ATA host adapter is a card (as opposed to integrated on the motherboard), move it as close as possible to the drive locations. Otherwise, if you need longer lengths, you can obtain a longer, custom-made IDE cable, but at the risk of performance degradation and data loss.

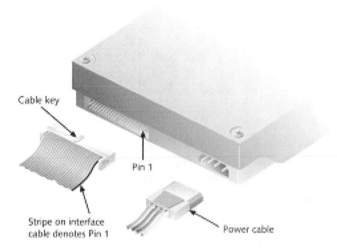

Exhibit 2-5: Correct orientation of the IDE cable on the drive

You can connect a maximum of two devices to a single ATA connector. The cable and its dimensions appear in Exhibit 2-6. Also, 80-conductor cables are identical except for an additional 40 grounded conductors. At one end of the cable, an IDE port connector is blue. Two more connectors appear on the cable—the first one is at the opposite end and is black and the middle one is gray. Connect the first hard disk to the black end connector. If you only have one hard drive, also make sure you connect it to this one and not the middle connector. Otherwise, the dangling connector on the end (the "stub") is not well terminated. Although it is not against ATA specifications, attaching a single drive to the middle connector is not recommended. Connect a second hard drive to the middle gray connector.

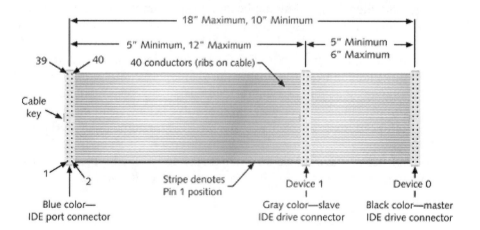

Exhibit 2-6: ATA 40-pin color-coded cable

As an option, you can use the 80-conductor 40-pin cable with ATA-4, but it is required with ATA-5 and ATA-6 (see Exhibit 2-7). An 80-conductor 40-pin cable begs the question: If there are 80 conductors, why isn't it an 80-pin cable? The additional 40 conductors are connected to ground only, and do not have a corresponding pin on the drive. Remember that an IDE cable is not shielded in any way, and is susceptible to electrical noise, usually crosstalk from adjacent conductors (hence the ground wires between signal wires). The extra grounded conductors absorb much of the electrical noise that would otherwise defeat the added performance of ATA-4 and better drives.

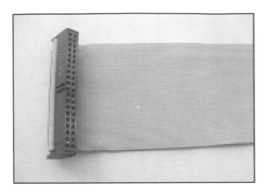

Exhibit 2-7: An 80-conductor, 40-pin cable

If you connect a faster device such as a hard disk and a slower device such as a CD-ROM to the same IDE cable, the hard disk performance will suffer while waiting for the CD-ROM to finish its tasks. Because IDE is not capable of simultaneous I/O, one device must wait for the other before performing tasks. In this case, it would be better to obtain another ATA host adapter and keep slower devices (such as CD-ROMs and tape drives) on one IDE connector and hard drives on the other.

Master, slave, and cable select

Because you can place two drives on an IDE host adapter, there must be a determination as to which one is the *master* and which one is the *slave*, especially because the master receives a drive letter assignment from the operating system first, and is also the device on which a boot record must be found. Otherwise, the master and slave drives are equivalent despite the implication of the names. You can use two methods to specify which drive is master and which is slave: First, you can set the jumper on the drive to indicate a master or slave setting. The drive manufacturer specifies these jumper settings in the drive manual or online documents. For example, Exhibit 2-8 shows the settings downloaded from Maxtor for the Diamondmax 80 Ultra-DMA/100. Most manufacturers also include an indication on the PCB or somewhere on the drive case as to which jumpers to set for master, slave, or cable select. Although you might need to change the jumper setting to specify master or slave for some older IDE drives, newer drives allow *cable select*, which means that the drive's position on the cable indicates whether it is a master or slave. Place the drive on the end of the 80-conductor cable to make it a master, and on the middle connector to make it a slave.

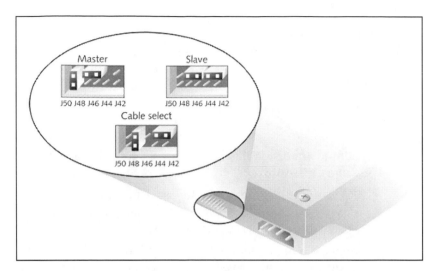

Exhibit 2-8: Jumper settings for master, slave, or cable select

It's not as much an issue as it used to be, but sometimes if you mix two drives from different vendors on the same IDE channel, you may experience problems. For example, the system might be unable to detect one of the drives, or if the drives are different sizes, report both drives at the smaller size. If you experience problems of this kind and are certain jumpers and locations on the IDE cable are correct, consider placing drives of the same manufacturer (and perhaps the exact same model) on the same cable.

The pros and cons of IDE/ATA

Current ATA implementations have some compelling advantages for use in the server world, but also have several disadvantages. If the disadvantages outweigh the advantages, and budgeting is sufficient, you will probably choose the more expensive SCSI interface.

Pros

- *Inexpensive*—Both the drives and host adapters are very inexpensive; even administrators on the tightest of budgets can probably afford a few new IDE drives.
- *Reasonable performance*—In less demanding situations where the server is not a heavily utilized file server, the reasonably good performance might be acceptable considering the low cost.
- *Simple configuration*—Plug it in and format the drive. That's pretty much it, and you don't usually have configuration complications, which you might experience with SCSI, for example.

Cons

- *Only two drives*—Two drives might seem like a lot for a workstation, but a server often connects to many more drives for purposes of performance, redundancy, and total available storage.
- *Slower device throttling*—Mixing slower devices with faster ones can drag the performance of the faster one.
- *Cable length*—18 inches (457.2 mm) is very limiting in a full-size server.
- *No simultaneous I/O*—Only one IDE device can operate at a time on a single IDE channel. SCSI, which does permit simultaneous I/O, might be much more attractive in terms of performance.
- Despite advertised transfer rates, most of the time you only get that rate from cached data. Data retrieved fresh from an Ultra-ATA/100 hard disk can usually only be sustained at about 40 MBps.

Although simultaneous I/O is not supported on a single IDE channel, you can place two drives on separate IDE channels. In this configuration, each drive can operate simultaneously. (More information about ATA/IDE can be found at www.ata-atapi.com and especially www.pcguide.com.)

Do it!

B-1: Discussing the IDE interface

Questions and answers

1 What is an advantage of IDE/ATA?

2 Which two ATA implementations can use 100 MBps?

3 What are the transfer rates for SATA?

4 What is a synonym for an IDE or SCSI controller?

Topic C: The SCSI interface

This topic covers the following CompTIA Server+ exam objectives:

#	Objective
1.6	Know the differences between different SCSI solutions, their advantages, and their specifications. • SCSI-1, 2, & 3 • SCSI bus speed (Fast and Ultra, Ultra Wide, Ultra 2, Ultra 160, Ultra 320, iSCSI, SAS)
2.2	Install hardware using best practices • Hardware includes: • Drives
4.9	Upgrade service tools (e.g. diagnostic tools, EISA configuration, diagnostic partition, SSU, etc.) • Service tools include: • SCSI utility

SCSI basics

Explanation

SCSI (Small Computer System Interface) technology, like ATA, has seen multiple generations of specifications, and includes an abundance of technical details beyond the scope of this book. However, as a server administrator, you must be aware of the major SCSI standards in order to provide the best available compatibility solution with the best possible performance. Properly configuring your SCSI hard drives also avoids complex troubleshooting.

As with IDE, SCSI drives include the controller circuitry directly on the hard disk assembly (HDA). In fact, some sources claim that hard disk manufacturers nearly mirror their drives in all physical respects and only change the circuitry to distinguish IDE and SCSI, often differentiated by only a single chip. What most people call the SCSI "controller" is actually the SCSI host adapter—similar to the inaccurate reference to an IDE "controller." However, although an IDE device communicates directly on the system bus, a SCSI device first communicates with the CPU through the SCSI host adapter.

Each succeeding version of the SCSI standard is backward compatible with all preceding versions. In theory, you could put a SCSI-1 hard disk on a SCSI-3 host adapter. However, such drastic implementations are not recommended because of complicated cabling adapters, termination incompatibilities, and performance limitations.

SCSI-1

SCSI-1 is obsolete, and it is unlikely that you'll find it on any current server. *SCSI-1* started off as just "SCSI" but was later renamed SCSI-1 to avoid confusion with successive SCSI standards. The following major features characterize the SCSI-1 standard:

- 8-bit *parallel bus*, meaning that multiple wires on the cable can transmit data at the same time. This is what allows SCSI to use simultaneous I/O.
- 50-pin Centronics-style external connector and low-density pin header internal connector
- Single-ended (SE) transmission
- Passive termination (the simplest type of termination, but also the least reliable; see later section on SCSI termination)
- Optional bus parity checking
- 5 MHz operation
- Transfer rate of 4 MBps (asynchronous) or 5 MBps (synchronous)

SCSI-1 is now considered obsolete and has been retired by ANSI and replaced with SCSI-2.

SCSI-2

SCSI-2 is essentially SCSI-1, plus the following optional features:

- *Fast SCSI* operating at 10 MHz instead of 5 MHz
- *Wide SCSI* utilizing 16-bit transfer instead of 8-bit (which is "narrow")
- 50-pin high-density connectors
- Active termination (see later section on SCSI termination)
- High Voltage Differential (HVD) is used to extend bus length. HVD is now considered obsolete in favor of Low Voltage Differential (LVD). (HVD and LVD are covered later in the unit.)
- *Command queuing* allows the host adapter to send as many as 256 commands to the drive. The drive stores and sorts the commands for optimum efficiency and performance internally before responding to the host adapter. Multitasking operating systems such as OS/2, Windows NT, and Windows 2000/2003 can take advantage of command queuing.
- Transfer rate of 10 MBps at 16 bits and 5 MHz (Wide SCSI), 10 MBps at 8 bits and 10 MHz (Fast SCSI), or 20 MBps at both 10 MHz and 16 bits (Fast and Wide).

SCSI-3

SCSI-3 is the most confusing of the SCSI standards, because manufacturers have used misleading marketing language. In addition, the SCSI-3 standard is not a complete standard of its own. Instead, it is more a collection of documents covering new commands, electrical interfaces, and protocols. A manufacturer could comply with only one of the major SCSI-3 additions and still label the product "SCSI-3." Nonetheless, subdividing SCSI-3 into several smaller standards helps SCSI-3 implementations to develop more quickly than waiting for the entire standard to be published and approved.

SPI SCSI-3 parallel interface

SPI is the SCSI-3 Parallel Interface, better known by the marketing terms Ultra SCSI or Wide Ultra SCSI. Along with this standard is the separate *SCSI Interlock Protocol* (*SIP*) defining the parallel command set. This standard was published as three documents offering the following features:

- 10 MHz bus speed, which is really no faster than SCSI-2. This is an example of how a manufacturer could use the 10 MHz bus speed (Fast SCSI) and call it SCSI-3 even though it offered no performance advantage.
- Fast-20 offers transfer rates up to 40 MBps using 20 MHz signaling.
- 68-pin P-cable and connectors for Wide SCSI

SPI-2

Also known as Ultra2 SCSI and Wide Ultra2 SCSI, *SPI-2* is characterized as follows:

- Single Connector Attachment (SCA-2) connectors. A successor to the problematic original SCA connector, this is the connection type that is mostly used in a chassis that contains several hot-swappable SCSI drives.
- Fast-40 40 MBps transfer rate on a narrow (8-bit) channel or 80 MBps on a wide (16-bit) channel. LVD is required for these data rates.
- LVD signaling to replace the previous SE signaling is required to achieve the faster throughput of Ultra2 or Ultra2/Wide speeds (40/80 MBps). You can use an SE device on the LVD SCSI chain, but doing so switches the chain to SE mode, which throttles the performance of the chain to SE-level performance at a maximum of 40 MBps and shortens the total cable length to as little as 5 feet (1.5 meters) in Fast-20 mode.
- 68-pin Very High Density Connector (VHDC) makes the connectors and ribbon cables smaller. This is important in SCSI because the older connectors and ribbon cables could be quite large and cumbersome.

SPI-3

SPI-3 was still in the draft stage at the time of this writing, although SCSI manufacturers have already implemented many of its features, including:

- Improving the earlier parity check, the *cyclical redundancy check* (*CRC*) is a calculation used by the sending device based on the data in the packet. The data arrives at the destination target and another calculation is performed using the same "formula." If the calculation in the packet matches the calculation performed by the destination device, the data is complete and considered error free.

- Domain validation improves the robustness of data transfer. In the past, the host adapter would send an inquiry to the SCSI device to determine its supported transfer rate. If the interconnection between host and device did not support the full transfer rate, then the device became inaccessible. With *domain validation*, the determined transfer rate is tested, and if errors occur, the rate is incrementally reduced and again tested until no errors occur.

- *Double transition* (*DT*) *clocking* transmits data on both the rising and falling edges of the clock. On a 16-bit, 40 MHz bus, this yields a transfer rate of 160 MBps.

- *Packetization* reduces the overall communication method to transfer data. Previously, data was transferred over the SCSI bus using a series of phases to set up and transfer data. Packetization streamlines this process by combining the process into a packet, reducing overhead.

- *Quick Arbitration and Selection* (*QAS*) eliminates the previously required *arbitration* method in which devices contend for control of the bus. Much of the prioritization is based on the device's priority level based on its *SCSI ID*, a unique number for each SCSI device. Because no data transfer can occur during the time that arbitration takes place, it adds overhead to the bus. QAS reduces overhead by reducing the number of times that arbitration must occur and by allowing a device waiting for bus access to do so more quickly.

SPI-3 is also known as Ultra3 SCSI.

Ultra160 and Ultra160+

The five features listed for SPI-3 sometimes cause a problem in the way a SCSI product is marketed. A manufacturer might include only one of the five items and call its product SCSI-3. Most manufacturers prefer to have more stringent requirements, so for the Ultra160 and Ultra160+ standards, the product must include:

- DT clocking at 160 MBps
- Domain validation
- CRC

QAS and packetization are optional for Ultra160, but required for Ultra160+.

Ultra320

Ultra 320 or *SPI-4* doubles the transfer rate to a burst rate of 320 mb/s. This data rate is accomplished by doubling the bus speed from 40 MHz to 80 MHz and using DT clocking. Like previous versions, it uses LVD, packetization, and QAS.

The following table summarizes SCSI standards and performance:

Standard	Also known as	Performance
SCSI-1 Async	Asynchronous	5 Mhz/8-bit/4 MBps
SCSI-1 Fast-5	Synchronous	5 MHz/8-bit/5 MBps
SCSI-2 Fast-5/Wide	Wide	5 MHz/16-bit/10 MBps
SCSI-2 Fast-10	Fast	10 MHz/8-bit/10 MBps
SCSI-2 Fast-10/Wide	Fast/Wide	10 MHz/16-bit/20 MBps
SPI (SCSI-3) Fast-20	Ultra	20 MHz/8-bit/20 MBps
SPI (SCSI-3) Fast-20/Wide	Ultra/Wide	20 MHz/16-bit/40 MBps
SPI-2 (SCSI-3) Fast-40	Ultra2	40 MHz/8-bit/40 MBps
SPI-2 (SCSI-3) Fast-40/Wide	Ultra2/Wide	40 MHz/16-bit/80 MBps
SPI-3 (SCSI-3) Fast-80DT	Ultra3 (Ultra160)	40 MHz/16-bit/160 MBps
SPI-4 (SCSI-3) Fast-160DT	Ultra320	80 MHz/16-bit/320 MBps

SAS

The next step in SCSI evolution is *Serial Attached SCSI*, or *SAS*. Like PCI-Express and SATA, SAS abandons shared parallel connections for serial, point-to-point technology. More like an Ethernet connection than previous versions of SCSI, SAS requires just two pairs of wires to connect to each drive – one pair to transmit and one to receive – providing full duplex communication at a steady rate of 300 MBps, with higher speeds on the way. Fewer wires also means much smaller cables and connectors compared to SCSI. The cables and connectors are the same for SAS and SATA, and a machine with SAS technology can support SATA drives also, though the reverse is not true.

Do it!

C-1:   Discussing SCSI

Questions and answers
1 What does a SCSI parallel bus allow?
2 Which version of SCSI introduced both Fast and Wide implementations?
3 A Wide SCSI implementation would use how many pins?
4 What does an SCA-2 connector allow you to do?
5 How does double transition (DT) clocking improve SCSI performance?
6 Why is an SAS cable smaller than a SCSI cable?

Topic D: SCSI configuration

This topic covers the following CompTIA Server+ exam objectives:

#	Objective
1.6	Know the differences between different SCSI solutions, their advantages, and their specifications.
	• SCSI bus width (narrow and wide)
	• SCSI connectors, cables, termination (passive, active, multi-mode)
	• SCSI ID's and LUN's
	• Single-ended devices
	• Low voltage differential (LVD)
	• High voltage differential (HVD)
	• BUS lengths
	• Multi-tasking
	• Multi-threading
	• Disconnect and reconnect
2.2	Install hardware using best practices
	• Installation activities include:
	• Verify the SCSI ID configuration and termination
	• Supporting knowledge includes:
	• SCSI cabling, termination, and hot plug configuration
3.4	Configure external peripherals
	• Supporting knowledge includes:
	• SCSI cabling and termination
4.3	Add hard drives
	• Activities include:
	• Confirm SCSI termination and cabling
4.6	Upgrade adapters (e.g. NIC's, SCSI cards, RAID, etc)
	• Supporting knowledge includes:
	• Characteristics of SCSI
	• Levels
	• Cabling
	• Termination
	• Signaling
4.7	Upgrade peripheral devices, internal and external. Verify appropriate system resources (e.g. expansion slots, IRQ, DMA, etc.)
	• Resources include:
	• SCSI ID's

SCSI cables and connectors

Explanation

Although you won't see every possible combination of cables and connectors listed here, you should be aware of those that are most commonly used. A narrow bus width (8 bits) is physically and logically smaller than the wider 16-bit bus. The 8-bit, 50-conductor cable is also known as *"A" cable* and the 16-bit, 68-conductor cable as *"P" cable*. (Other cables have been proposed, but have not come to fruition because the standards never caught on with manufacturers.)

The "A" cable is a low-density cable with a Centronics-style connector (see Exhibit 2-9) and 50 conductors. The "A" cable is used only in 8-bit (narrow) implementations. If you have both narrow and wide cables, you can continue to use both standards with special adapters such as the one in Exhibit 2-10, which reduces a 68-conductor cable to a 50-pin connector.

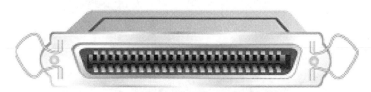

Exhibit 2-9: 50-pin, low-density "A" cable connector

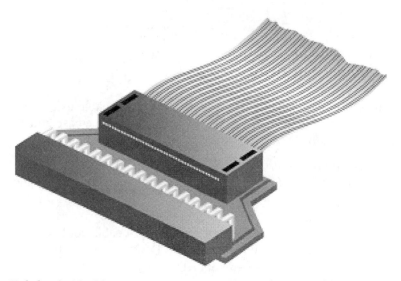

Exhibit 2-10: 50-pin connector on a 68-conductor cable

Thankfully, in the SCSI-2 standard, a high-density 50-pin SCSI connector was introduced to save space, because large SCSI connectors such as the Centronics type are cumbersome and can quickly take up space in a cabinet. Also, instead of using the wire latches on either side of the connector to attach and remove the connector, you use squeeze-to-release clip locks.

On the SCA-2 connector, the chassis has the female connector and the drive has the male connector. (Recall that this is the connector that allows hot-pluggable hard drives.) On the outside edges of both connectors are advanced grounding contacts that allow you to pull out or plug in a SCSI drive without negative electrical consequence (see Exhibit 2-11). Because you can't see the actual connection take place inside the chassis, this is known as *blind connector mating*. The connector provides both signal and power, and is an 80-pin connector offering only wide (not narrow) SCSI.

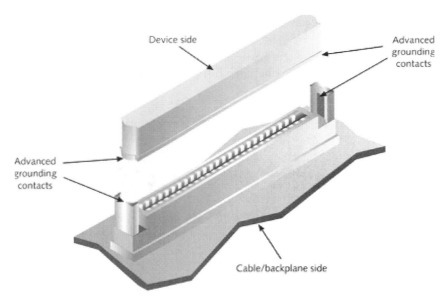

Exhibit 2-11: SCA-2 SCSI attachment

With SCSI-3, you most often find the wide SCSI cable using a 68-pin connector both internally (inside the case) and externally (outside the case and connected to the server's SCSI host adapter).

Some SCSI connectors, though rare, are 25-pin connectors created for economy of both design and dollars. This connector is streamlined compared to the 50-pin cable, and accomplishes this design mostly by removing grounding—an inadvisable practice. Recall that grounding is a contributor to signal integrity. Because the signal quality is not as good as standard 50-pin or greater SCSI cable, and because the connector is visually identical to the commonly used DB25 parallel cable connector, this style of cable/connector is not recommended.

Connectors are designed for either internal or external use. External cables are usually round with thumbscrews or clip-lock connections on the connector. The round cable is highly shielded and well engineered against signal degradation and interference. As a result, it is also relatively expensive. Internally, you will see ribbon cable in any of several types.

Signaling

In order to obtain the correct accessories for your SCSI chain, you must first know what kind of signaling is in use on the bus. *Signaling* generally describes transmission of data using electrical impulses or variations. These electrical transmissions represent data that the sender originates and the receiver translates based upon a mutually agreed-upon method. There are three types of signaling on the SCSI bus, detailed in the following sections. You must be careful about mixing devices intended for one type of signaling with devices intended for another type of signaling, because one or more devices might stop functioning or become damaged. Also, you must know the signaling before you can properly terminate a SCSI bus.

Disconnect-reconnect

Disconnect-reconnect refers to the SCSI ability to be multi-tasking and multi-threaded. Either the initiating or the target device can disconnect from the SCSI bus if it experiences a delay in processing a request, then reconnect when it is ready to proceed. This keeps the bus free for other devices in the event of one device's delay.

SE

Single-ended (SE) signaling, the original signaling method used on the SCSI-1 bus, uses a common signaling method in which a positive voltage represents a one and a zero voltage (ground) represents a zero, resulting in binary communication. SE signaling is available for any SCSI-1 or SCSI-2 implementation as well as SCSI-3 SPI-1. With most electronic signaling methods, you have a built-in opposition: the faster the transmission speed, the shorter the maximum cable length. Of the three signal types, SE is most susceptible to this limitation. On a Fast-20 bus, for example, an SE cable can only be 5 feet (1.5 meters) long.

HVD

High Voltage Differential (HVD) signaling is also available for any SCSI implementation up to SCSI-3 SPI-1. If you can use SE for the same SCSI implementations, then why use HVD? HVD, as the name implies, uses comparatively more electrical power than the other two types of signaling, resulting in greater allowable bus lengths. Whereas the SE cable is limited to 5 feet (1.5 meters) over Fast-20, an HVD cable can reach 82 feet (25 meters). The "differential" in HVD represents a kind of signaling in which the signal is comprised of the difference in a pair. A one is represented when one wire in the pair transmits a positive voltage, and the other wire transmits zero voltage. The receiving device detects the "difference" between the voltages, and translates it as a one. To transmit a zero, both wires carry a zero voltage. This signaling method is much less susceptible to interference, signal degradation, signal bounce, and crosstalk, allowing HVD to transmit over such a great distance.

Do not mix HVD and SE devices on the same bus. Because of the significantly higher voltage of HVD, SE devices could get smoked—literally.

It is rare to find HVD in PC servers. It is more often found in older minicomputers and never gained the popularity of SE, primarily because of a higher cost factor.

LVD

Low Voltage Differential (LVD) signaling is the signaling method you are most likely to find today, and it is similar to HVD except, as the name implies, it uses a lower voltage. Advantages of LVD are that you can use both LVD and SE devices on the same bus without electrical hazard, and it allows a longer maximum cable length—up to 39 feet (12 meters). Many SCSI devices are multimode devices; that is, they can operate as either LVD or SE depending on the signaling method of the other devices on the chain.

Multimode devices can be indicated in several ways, usually depending on the preference of the company marketing the product. However, it is usually abbreviated as LVD/MSE (where M is multimode) or LVD/SE.

Note the following about using LVD:

- A single SE device among LVD devices on the same chain will drop all devices to SE compatibility. This could have a significant impact if the cable is over 5 ft. (1.5 m) when you add the SE device, because the cable would now be too long.

- Some multimode devices have a jumper setting that forces SE operation. If you want to use LVD, be sure that no devices have enabled this setting.

- Use either LVD or multimode LVD/SE terminators.

- You cannot operate both HVD and LVD on the same bus for reasons of electrical incompatibility, which could damage LVD devices.

- LVD is the only available signaling method for Ultra3, Ultra160, Ultra160+, Ultra320, and probably any other standards that emerge in the near future.

Because the connectors are identical regardless of the signaling method, look for a special symbol on the connector. This will help ensure that you do not mix signaling standards, especially by adding HVD among SE or LVD devices. The signaling symbols appear in Exhibit 2-12.

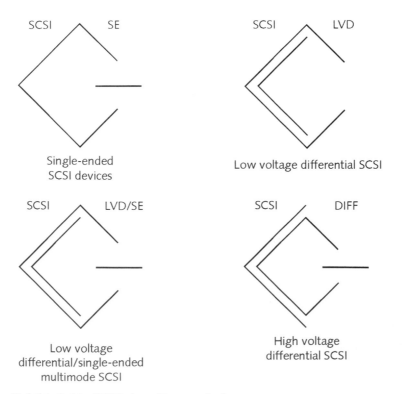

Exhibit 2-12: SCSI signaling symbols

SCSI termination

Termination (using terminators at the ends of a SCSI chain) is critical to assure error-free operation on the SCSI chain. A *terminator* absorbs the transmission signal to avoid signal bounce, making it appear to the devices that the cable is of infinite length. Terminators also regulate the electrical load, and are therefore critical in establishing a reliable communications medium. Proper termination requires a terminator at both ends of the SCSI cable. Some devices (and most high-performance host adapters) either automatically terminate or have a setting that allows you to specify termination. Otherwise, obtain a terminator to place over the last connector on the chain. If the last position is in use by a device that does not terminate itself, you can place a terminator over the connection, which allows signal transfer to and from the device while also providing the necessary termination. This is known as *pass-through termination* (see Exhibit 2-13).

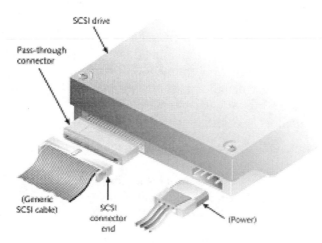

Exhibit 2-13: Pass-through termination connects the chain on the side of the terminator and the device on the other side

The terminators must also have terminator power supplied, or they cannot properly terminate. If the host adapter does not supply power to the terminator, you can configure a setting on one of the SCSI devices (usually via a jumper) to supply power to a terminator. (Some administrators configure all SCSI devices to supply power to terminators; that way it never slips through the cracks.)

The following list describes the various types of SCSI terminators:

- *Passive termination*—This is the simplest type of termination, but is also the least reliable. Passive terminators use resistors to terminate the SCSI chain, similar to terminators on coaxial Ethernet networks. Passive terminators usually work best on short, SE SCSI-1 buses. It is unlikely you will find many passive terminators in servers.

- *Active termination*—A requirement for faster, single-ended SCSI, active termination adds voltage regulators to provide a more reliable and consistent termination. Another type of active termination is active negation termination, which uses a more complex circuit to stabilize the voltage supply level, further eliminating electrical noise from the signal. Negation terminators are usually only a little more expensive than plain active terminators ($5–10).

- *Forced perfect termination (FPT)*—In this technology, the termination is forced to a more exact voltage by means of diode clamps added to the terminator circuitry. This advanced form of active termination is very clean and is the best termination available for an SE bus.
- *HVD termination*—A high voltage bus requires a high voltage terminator.
- *LVD termination*—A low voltage terminator for the LVD bus. Many LVD terminators are LVD/SE terminators to accommodate buses with multimode devices. When operating in SE mode, the terminator functions as an active terminator.

Be careful if your server environment mixes narrow SCSI technologies with newer, wider SCSI technologies. First, to place both narrow and wide devices on the bus, you will have to provide an adapter to convert from one width to the other. Converting wide devices to a narrow bus wastes 8 bits of transmission and severely limits the potential of the wide device. On the other hand, converting from 8 bits to 16 bits does nothing to improve the performance of attached 8-bit devices because 8 bits is the highest level of operation anyway. Along with the conversion, you must also consider how termination will affect the two widths. Do you terminate for the 8-bit devices? If so, what about the 16-bit devices? Terminating only for the 8-bits would leave the 16-bit devices with 8 unterminated bits. These dangling bits are called the *high byte* (also known as high 9), and when you have a mix of wide and narrow devices, you can obtain special multimode terminators.

Multimode terminators flash colors indicating which signaling method is in use. For example, if it's running SE, it might blink yellow, and if it's running LVD, it might blink green. This can be useful in troubleshooting the SCSI chain if you wonder why it seems to be running slow or unreliably over 3-meter lengths—it could be running SE, (just check the light to verify) when you want LVD so that you can benefit from faster speed and longer cable.

Drive configuration (SCSI ID and LUN)

Knowing the various SCSI technologies, cables, connectors, and termination is fine, but of course you have to also plug it all in. The problem is that with SCSI, misconfiguration can cause many hours of baffling troubleshooting. This section shows you how to correctly configure the devices on the SCSI bus.

Topology

Topology, the physical and/or logical layout of equipment, is simple for SCSI: Use a bus topology because that's all that's available (logically similar to a network bus topology). *Daisy chain* your SCSI devices so that they appear one after the other along the cable. In complicated configurations, you might accidentally connect the bus to itself somewhere along the line, creating a loop. Don't do that or the bus won't work. When configuring a chain from scratch, one end usually connects to the terminated host adapter (unless it's between an internal and external chain) and the other end is terminated as well. The order of the drives (and other SCSI devices, if any) doesn't matter in terms of performance or priority. That's one of the advantages of SCSI—a slower device on the bus doesn't bottleneck all the other devices. In a simple configuration using two SCSI hard disks and a SCSI scanner (see Exhibit 2-14), the layout is a bus and both ends are terminated.

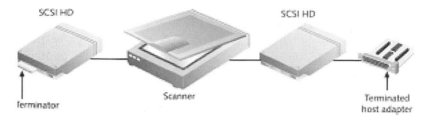

Exhibit 2-14: A simple SCSI bus topology with terminators at both ends

Realize that although termination takes place at the end of the SCSI bus, the SCSI host adapter is not always at one end of the chain. Because most host adapters have connections for both internal and external devices, a host adapter so connected would appear in the middle of the SCSI chain. In this case, you will have to be sure not to terminate the host adapter (see Exhibit 2-15).

You are likely to find a SCSI host adapter with multiple channels in many implementations. The primary benefits to multiple channels are twofold: First, having two separate channels allows for twice as many devices. Second, you can configure the two channels to support different signaling technologies. For example, if you have a few SE devices and a few LVD devices, you don't want to mix them or else you'll suffer the performance and length limitations of SE for all the devices. Instead, make one channel SE and the other LVD. That way, the LVD devices can operate at full capacity.

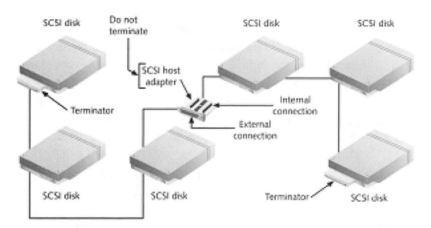

Exhibit 2-15: Do not terminate a host adapter appearing in the middle of the SCSI chain

SCSI ID Assignment

Each device on the SCSI chain must have a unique SCSI ID number. You configure the device SCSI ID using jumpers, a wheel, or a button on the device, and the adapter is usually preset at ID 7, though you can change it (possibly with a jumper but usually through a software utility). Although you can change the host adapter's SCSI ID, it is highly inadvisable. ID 7 is the highest priority of all the SCSI numbers. The range of available IDs depends on whether you are running narrow (8 IDs) or wide (16 IDs). SCSI ID assignment is important not only to uniquely identify each device, but also to establish which devices have priority when arbitrating over the bus. Arbitration occurs when it must be determined which of two or more devices have control over the bus. Usually, you want to assign a higher priority to slower devices such as scanners or tape drives to make sure that faster devices do not dominate the bus.

The priority of SCSI IDs range from the highest to lowest as follows: 7, 6, 5, 4, 3, 2, 1, 0. On a wide bus, the range is 7, 6, 5, 4, 3, 2, 1, 0, 15, 14, 13, 12, 11, 10, 9, 8. When you install an internal hard disk—simply a matter of screwing it into an available drive bay and plugging in the power and SCSI cables—you also need to configure a SCSI ID using jumper settings. External SCA devices, however, usually configure their own SCSI IDs automatically as soon as you swap the drive into its bay. This is needed to reduce the configuration time, as time is usually of the essence in swapping these drives.

Along with the unique SCSI ID number is the *logical unit number* (*LUN*). The LUN is a subunit of the device, and is used to identify items within the device. For example, a multi-disc CD-ROM changer probably assigns a unique LUN to each disk. If the CD-ROM drive is SCSI ID 5, the first LUN is probably LUN 0, the second is LUN 1, and so forth. Some host adapters do not support LUNs—the absence of LUN support makes the bus scan process during startup faster; so if you need LUN support, make sure the SCSI host adapter supports it. Administrators are not normally concerned with changing LUNs because the device manufacturer defines them.

SCSI pros and cons

SCSI has many pros and cons, but as mentioned earlier, the pros far outweigh the cons in most enterprises, and particularly for servers.

Pros

The benefits of SCSI are as follows:

- *Performance*—Aggregating the performance of multiple disks as in a RAID array (covered later in this unit) generates an appreciable performance gain. The more disks you add, the better the performance (up to the available throughput of the SCSI channel).
- *Expandability*—Several meters of cable length is enough for most SCSI implementations. Most use LVD, which allows for 12 meters. Also, compared to ATA standards that limit you to two disks, the expandability of using up to 15 devices on a SCSI chain is impressive.
- *Redundancy*—Several RAID implementations including RAID-1 and RAID-5 protect your data even if a hard disk fails.

Cons

The drawbacks of SCSI are as follows:

- *Difficult to configure and troubleshoot*—SCSI has so many varying standards, and there are so many opportunities for incompatibility and wrong termination, that it might take a while to get SCSI rolling, especially if you are trying to piece together a SCSI implementation out of existing equipment. If you build from scratch using consistent standards, it's much easier.
- *Expensive*—Smaller organizations or those that have a tight budget might not be able to afford SCSI.
- *Performance*—The performance improvement is not that noticeable if you're only using a single SCSI disk. SCSI shines when using multiple disks for performance and fault tolerance. Otherwise, you're better off saving the money and using ATA-4 or better.

Server administrators usually prefer SCSI because of its advantages in an enterprise environment.

SCSI summary

Remember the following about SCSI:

- 8-bit SCSI can connect up to seven devices (actually it's eight devices, but the host adapter counts as one).

- 16-bit SCSI can connect up to 15 devices (actually 16, but the host adapter counts as one).

- Exception to the number of devices: SPI (SCSI-3) Fast-20/Wide can use 15 devices on an HVD cable and seven devices on an SE cable.

- "A" cable is always used for 8-bit SCSI.

- "P" cable is always used for 16-bit SCSI.

- SPI-1 SCSI can use SE at 10 feet (3 meter) lengths, but only 5 feet (1.5 meters) if four or more devices are on the chain.

- Maximum length for all HVD signal cable is 82 feet (25 meters).

- Maximum length for all LVD signal cable is 39 feet (12 meters), but if the chain consists of the host adapter and only one device, you can extend length to 82 feet (25 meters).

Do it!

D-1: Discussing SCSI configuration

Questions and answers

1 Why shouldn't you mix HVD devices with LVD devices?

2 What is the best form of termination for an SE bus?

3 What is the SCSI ID of most host adapters?

4 What is one major drawback to SCSI?

Topic E: Network storage

This topic covers the following CompTIA Server+ exam objectives:

#	Objective
1.8	Know the features and benefits of fibre channel hardware • Storage arrays • Disk drives • Adapters • Cables, connectors, GBIC's, SFP GBIC's • Single- and Multi-mode • 1 Gbit, 2 Gbit, 10 Gbit • Bus lengths • Point-to-point vs. switched vs. LOOP
1.9	Know the features and benefits of iSCSI and FCIP • Storage arrays • Adapters • Cables, connectors • 1 Gbit, 2 Gbit, 10 Gbit • Bus lengths
1.15	Know the basic specifications of and differences between SAN and NAS • Block and file
3.4	Configure external peripherals • Supporting knowledge includes: • Fibre channel cabling

iSCSI

Explanation

Internet SCSI, or *iSCSI*, is not an internal SCSI standard; rather, it is a protocol that enables a computer to communicate directly with remote SCSI storage over IP networks. SCSI commands from the computer are encapsulated in IP packets, given a packet header, and sent out over Ethernet. At the other end, the commands are decoded and sent to the SCSI controller. The process is repeated in the other direction as the data is sent back to the requesting machine.

Fibre Channel

Fibre Channel (FC) is a storage technology that can use gigabit Ethernet networks but is primarily intended for fiber optic cable, as the name implies. (FC has roots in Europe, hence "Fibre" instead of "Fiber.") FC is a form of storage categorized under the *storage area network (SAN)* umbrella. SAN is a general term that refers to any network-based storage solution that is not server-based. SAN is becoming huge in the server world. Comprehensive coverage of SAN is beyond the scope of this text because it encompasses more than just server issues. In this section, you learn the basics of FC.

First, let's separate out from the discussion another growing storage solution that is sometimes confused with FC—*network attached storage (NAS)*. NAS is one or more storage devices attached to a network, most commonly Ethernet. A NAS device is easy to configure and use, because you just attach it to the rack, plug it into the network, flip its power switch, and it's ready to use. NAS devices are as accessible as any other device on the network. For smaller organizations, you can use a freestanding NAS device, or for the enterprise, rack models are available. Regardless, when you attach and power up the device, it receives an IP address and identifies the type of network in use. If you want to configure a static IP address, configure security settings or access privileges, or configure RAID, you can launch a management utility (usually browser-based so you can launch it from anywhere in the enterprise) and make changes. NAS devices are very inexpensive compared to FC. NAS devices as well as SAN storage have a significant benefit over traditional file servers in that you don't have a file server. This removes an expensive piece of hardware and greatly reduces administration.

In a SCSI FC implementation, a special SCSI host adapter designed for FC connects to the FC bus, which can be up to 10 kilometers (more than 6 miles) in length with single-mode fiber optic cable (multi-mode cable allows for 500 meters between devices). That's the benefit of using fiber instead of copper. Network adapters can connect to fiber with the use of a Gigabit Interface Converter, or *GBIC*. Small Form-factor pluggable GBICs (SPF GBIC) are used in network switches.

FC is run in its own storage "network" of either *Fibre Channel Arbitrated Loop* (*FC-AL*) or switched fabric. In FC-AL, you can connect 126 storage devices to a special fiber hub in a physical star, logical loop topology. However, all devices on the FC-AL share the available bandwidth, which is okay in many implementations if it meets the needs of the enterprise (see Exhibit 2-16).

In high-level implementations, you can use a switched fabric to connect to up to 15.5 million storage devices, and the full bandwidth of the channel is available to each device. As you might guess, this implementation is extremely expensive. The term *switched fabric* is somewhat vague in terms of its physical configuration. Simply put, it means that servers storing information on an FC device can reach the device using any number of physical paths. This is analogous to a phone call to a friend in another state. Call her today, and the phone company will route your call using the best path it deems practical. Call her tomorrow, and the phone company might or might not use the same path. However, it doesn't matter to you or to her, so long as the call connects.

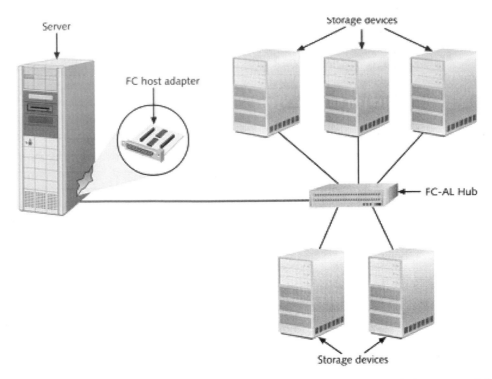

Exhibit 2-16: An FC-AL configuration connects to a fiber hub and shares available bandwidth

Some people have prematurely dismissed FC as too slow at its rated throughput of 100 MBps (200 MBps full duplex), especially compared to Ultra160, which can reach up to 160 MBps. In reality, FC is much faster because SCSI cannot sustain speeds of 160 MBps; that's just its burst speed when feeding data from cache. Instead, it will usually dish data out at a sustained rate of around 50 MBps. FC, on the other hand, can sustain data transfer at about 97.5 MBps. The storage media can be whatever file format suits you, and you can use RAID if you like. Developments in fibre channel now allow for transfer speeds of 1, 2, and 10 Gbps.

Typically administrators do not purchase the FC equipment and configure it themselves. Instead, you contract with a SAN storage company specializing in FC to supply the equipment and connect it all together. Maintenance is not usually an issue either, as the storage company also provides maintenance. Larger enterprises often have full-time employees from the storage company on site at all times to maintain and administer the storage and tapes.

The expense of FC is very high, and thus is usually seen in enterprises that need to store terabytes of data, such as in a large data center. The storage devices for a single terabyte of data alone can cost up to $750,000 before installation and costs of other associated equipment, with many implementations totaling millions of dollars.

FCIP

Like iSCSI, Fibre Channel over IP (FCIP or FC/IP) enables fibre channel storage to operate of IP networks, allowing for geographically distributed storage facilities.

Do it!   **E-1:   Discussing Fibre Channel**

Questions and answers

1   What's the difference between SAN and NAS?

2   What's the maximum fibre channel bus length with single-mode fiber-optic cable? with multi-mode?

3   What's FCIP?

4   How does iSCSI differ from other SCSI standards?

Topic F: RAID

This topic covers the following CompTIA Server+ exam objectives:

#	Objective
1.10	Know the features and capabilities of the following RAID levels, when they apply, and how each relates to fault tolerance and high availability (non-proprietary).
	• RAID 0
	• RAID 1
	• RAID 3
	• RAID 5
	• RAID 5+1
	• RAID 0+1
	• RAID 0+5
	• RAID 1+0
	• RAID 5+0
	• RADIOS
	• Zero Channel RAID
	• Differences between hardware RADI and software RAID and the advantages of one over the other.
1.13	Know the attributes, purpose, function, and advantages of clustering, scalability, high availability, and fault tolerance.
3.1	Check/upgrade BIOS/firmware levels (system board, RAID controller, hard drive, etc.)
3.2	Configure RAID
	• Activities include:
	• Use manufacturer's tool to configure the array
	• Testing (simulate failure)
	• Supporting knowledge includes:
	• Familiarity with OCE
	• Characteristics, purpose, and function of RAID cache including when to turn off write caching
	• How to calculate storage capacity
	• Functionality of RAID controller battery

#	Objective
4.3	Add hard drives

- Activities include:
    - Make sure RAID controller can support additions
    - Add drives to array
    - Replace existing drives
    - Integrate into storage solution and make it available to the operating system
- Supporting knowledge includes:
    - Available types of hard drive array additions and when they are appropriate
    - What "hot swappable" means
    - Difference between a RAID partition and an OS partition

4.6	Upgrade adapters (e.g. NIC's, SCSI cards, RAID, etc)

- Supporting knowledge includes
    - Implications on the array of changing RAID controller types

4.9	Upgrade service tools (e.g. diagnostic tools, EISA configuration, diagnostic partition, SSU, etc.)

- Service tools include:
    - RAID utility

RAID basics

Explanation

RAID stands for either Redundant Array of Inexpensive Disks or Redundant Array of Independent Disks. It doesn't really matter—it's just that the history of RAID has changed over the years and the acronym has changed with it. What matters is how you use RAID in the enterprise, and that you understand the characteristics of several levels of RAID, particularly RAID-0, RAID-1, RAID-5, and RAID-0+1.

The main purpose of RAID is to use multiple disks to improve performance, provide redundancy, or both. You configure a RAID array via host adapter hardware or software, though in most cases hardware RAID is preferred for reasons we will discuss at the end of this section. To the operating system and applications, the drives are logically a single drive.

With a controller that supports it, you can obtain a significant performance benefit using a *RAID cache*. Regardless of the version of RAID you use, the host adapter can have a certain amount of memory, usually a minimum of 32 MB, though better adapters have at least 128 MB. The memory is often supported by a battery backup for data integrity, similar to CMOS. The RAID cache fills with data sequentially beyond the actual requested data in anticipation that the next data will soon be requested. If the data is indeed required, the RAID cache serves data more quickly than if data must be retrieved directly from disk.

RAID-0

RAID-0, also known as *disk striping*, lays down data across two or more physical drives. RAID-0 provides no redundancy—if one of the drives fails, all the data is lost, so you must provide another solution for redundancy such as tape backup or RAID-0+1 (see later section). RAID-0 yields a performance advantage because you can aggregate the performance of multiple drives. The SCSI bus can deliver data in a matter of microseconds, but the data transfer of a single disk takes milliseconds, hence a bottleneck at even the fastest drives. RAID-0 helps to mitigate this bottleneck because multiple disks can simultaneously deliver data at once. For example, a RAID-0 array consisting of four drives provides roughly four times the performance of a single drive serving the same data because all four drives on a SCSI chain can operate at once. In Exhibit 2-17, the letters on each of the drives represent a portion of data, illustrating how the data appears on the drives. In any of the RAID levels, you can further improve performance by dedicating a single drive to each host adapter. (Using two host adapters and one drive on each is known as *duplexing*.) It is possible to use RAID-0 in an IDE implementation, but because IDE can operate only one drive at a time, there is no performance advantage.

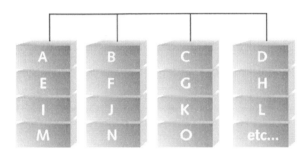

Exhibit 2-17: This RAID-0 array uses four drives to quadruple hard disk performance

Part of the POST process involves searching for a configurable BIOS from other hardware, particularly SCSI host adapters. To configure a RAID-0 drive once the proper SCSI connections have been made, enter the SCSI adapter's BIOS. Typically, a message appears instructing you to press a keyboard combination to access the BIOS. Then, use the menu system to specify the type of RAID you want to use and save changes.

RAID-1

RAID-1, also known as disk mirroring, requires at least two disks to provide redundancy. It can also provide improved performance, but only if using duplexing. In a RAID-1 array, the controller writes the same exact data to two disks at the same time. You can configure multiple adapters, each having two channels with a disk on each channel and capable of simultaneous I/O, to further increase performance (see Exhibit 2-18).

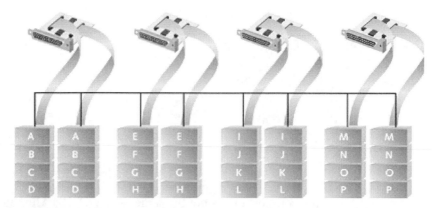

Exhibit 2-18: RAID-1 using multiple controllers provides both mirroring and high performance

RAID-1 has a higher cost factor or "overhead." If you have two mirrored 40 GB drives, the total raw storage available is 80 GB, but you can only use 40 GB because 40 GB must be available for the mirror. The overhead is 50% because you only use half of the actual disk space. Also, if the drives are not the same size, the mirror is the size of the smaller drive. You can configure RAID-1 through software (using Windows NT/2000/2003, for example), but it requires processor utilization; so in performance terms you're better off using hardware RAID through the controller.

In the event of a failed drive in a RAID-1 array, simply pull out the failed drive and insert a new one. Depending on the method used to configure RAID, you must manually regenerate data from the remaining drive to the new drive through software or BIOS, or the mirror regenerates automatically. With automatic regeneration, the user experience is not disrupted, although performance may suffer temporarily until all data is regenerated to the new drive.

RAID-0+1

As the name implies, *RAID-0+1* offers the best of both worlds: the performance of RAID-0 and the redundancy of RAID-1. In this implementation, two channels and at least four drives are required. Data is striped across two or more disks in the first channel (RAID-0), and the data from the first channel is mirrored to disks in the second channel (RAID-1) in the same striped layout as shown in Exhibit 2-19. This implementation has a 50% overhead.

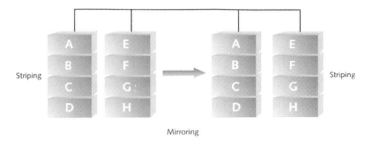

Exhibit 2-19: A RAID-0+1 array

Contrary to some sources, this is not the same as RAID-10. Although RAID-10 also uses both mirroring and striping, one channel mirrors the data and the other channel stripes the same data. In RAID-10, overhead is higher, although two disks could fail and you would still have enough fault tolerance to rebuild the data.

RAID-3

RAID-3 uses striping like RAID-1 but also adds redundancy by use of parity. In the case of RAID, *parity* is an encoding scheme that represents data appearing on other drives. RAID-3 saves the all the parity information to a single parity drive. The more commonly used RAID-5 spreads the parity and data across all the drives in the set.

RAID-5

RAID-5, sometimes called striping with parity, requires at least three hard disks to implement. The host adapter writes data to drives 1 and 2, and on disk 3 writes parity data. At the next write, data writes to drives 2 and 3, and on disk 1 writes parity data, and so on in round-robin fashion (see Exhibit 2-20). If the first disk fails, replace it. Then, the system regenerates the data that was supposed to be on the first drive using the parity on disk 2 and disk 3. SCSI is the best choice for this RAID implementation because it offers simultaneous I/O; that is, data reads occur from multiple drives at the same time.

RAID-5 has a lighter overhead in terms of disk space than RAID-1. Overhead is $1/X$ where X is the number of disks in the array. For example, a five-disk RAID-5 array would have an overhead of 1/5, or 20%. The overhead space is utilized by the parity data.

RAID-5 arrays can take quite a while to rebuild data to a new replacement drive. Also, parity calculation requires CPU cycles, and can significantly affect server performance, especially while rebuilding data to a replacement drive.

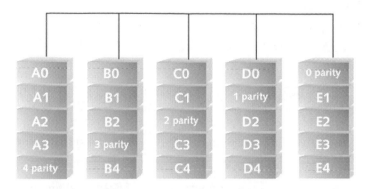

Exhibit 2-20: RAID-5 writes parity bits across members of the array, and uses the bits to reconstruct data if a drive must be replaced

RAID-1 and RAID-5 reconstruct data with the least amount of disruption if the hard disks are hot-swappable and data is reconstructed on the fly as opposed to rebooting and accessing the BIOS to reconstruct the data. (Although manufacturers such as Promise Technology offer EIDE host adapters providing RAID-0, 1, 5, and 0+1, performance benefits are best with SCSI because EIDE cannot perform simultaneous I/O.)

Many RAID systems support *hot plugging* or *hot swapping* of drives, meaning a failed drive can be pulled from its slot and replaced, and the new drive rebuilt, without ever turning off the machine or interrupting network service.

Regardless of the RAID configuration you choose (if any), be sure to optimize the hard disk so that it performs at its best. One of the most useful utilities for this purpose is defragmentation software, which arranges the data on your hard disk in a sequential fashion so that reads require less back-and-forth action to locate all the data.

Other RAID combinations

Like RAID 0+1 and RAID 10 described above, other RAID levels can be combined to achieve greater levels of capacity, speed, or redundancy. For instance, in RAID 5+1, entire RAID-5 striped sets are mirrored, while RAID 0+5 is a RAID 5 array made up of RAID-0 sets.

Software RAID vs. hardware RAID

Network operating systems such as Windows 2000/2003 and Novell NetWare offer software RAID. Software RAID has advantages and disadvantages, as described in the following table:

Advantage of software RAID	Disadvantage of software RAID
Software RAID is built into the NOS and is less expensive than hardware RAID.	Less robust than hardware RAID. If the operating system becomes corrupt, the array is at risk.
Generally an easy-to-use graphical interface. You can create a RAID array in a matter of minutes, perhaps without rebooting the system.	Limited configuration capabilities. You are usually limited in the types of RAID configurations you can use. In Windows 2003, for example, you can create a RAID-0, RAID-1, or RAID-5 array but not other RAID configurations such as 10 or 0+1.

Uses the CPU to perform parity calculations. |

Hardware RAID also has advantages and disadvantages, as described in the following table:

Advantage of hardware RAID	Disadvantage of hardware RAID
More reliable and robust	More expensive.
Faster performance because it is dedicated to RAID functions. Also, parity calculations are handled by hardware RAID (not the main CPU), which is faster than software RAID.	If you need to access the SCSI BIOS, a reboot is required.
The array remains regardless of corruption to the operating system.	

In Windows 2000/2003, software RAID is set up in the disk manager. For instance, two volumes of the same size can be configured as a mirrored set. By contrast, drives mirrored via hardware RAID-1 would be invisible to the operating system, appearing in disk manager as one drive.

All things considered, experienced administrators usually recommend hardware RAID as a better solution because of its dependability and performance.

RAIDIOS, MROMB, and ZCR

An open standard developed by Intel, RAIDIOS, or RAID I/O Steering, is a specification for an I/O controller embedded on the motherboard. This controller is tied to a PCI or PCI-X expansion slot, called a RAIDIOS-enabled PCI slot, and can act as a standard I/O controller or a RAID hardware controller. This setup is referred to as Modular RAID On Motherboard, or MROMB. A Zero Channel RAID card, or ZCR card, provides the rest of the picture. The ZCR card doesn't have all the chips necessary to support RAID on its own, but it makes use of the MROMB system. This modular implementation of on-board controllers and expansions cards makes each component simpler, more flexible, and less expensive.

Do it!

F-1:   Discussing RAID

Questions and answers

1 Why use RAID?

2 What are the advantages of software RAID?

3 What are the advantages of hardware RAID?

Unit summary: Storage

Topic A

In this topic, you learned that the **File Allocation Table (FAT)** file system is a Microsoft-based file system compatible with nearly any operating system and that it has a limit of 2 GB partition size and offers no security, while **FAT32** offers a 2 TB partition size. You learned that **NTFS**, the native file system for Windows NT and Windows 2000/2003, can support extremely large volumes, but it reaches a practical limit at 2 TB. You also learned that NTFS supports other features such as encryption, compression, and disk quotas. You learned that Linux and UNIX can use **UFS**, **NFS**, or **AFS** file systems, and that NetWare uses a NetWare volume in its file system, and a NetWare volume is created during installation, and you can add more as necessary. Recent versions of NetWare also offer the **NSS** file system, which increases performance and storage capacity.

Topic B

In this topic, you found that **IDE** and **ATA** are interchangeable terms, though IDE (and **EIDE**) is actually a marketing term and not a true standard. You learned that ATA/IDE operates at a current maximum of 100 MBps and uses no more than two drives per channel, and that ATA does not support simultaneous I/O.

Topic C

In this topic, you learned that **SCSI** has several versions, each with different benefits and capabilities. You learned that SCSI-3 Ultra320 is the fastest available standard, and that SCSI uses 8- or 16-bit implementations, A or P cables, and lengths from 5 feet (1.5 meters) to 82 feet (25 meters).

Topic D

In this topic, you learned that the **SCSI chain** is a bus **topology** and must be properly terminated at both ends using passive, active, forced perfect, **HVD**, or **LVD** terminators.

Topic E

In this topic, you learned that **Fibre Channel (FC)** is intended for very large storage needs, often in the terabyte range, and that FC is very expensive but has extremely fast sustained throughput and room for lots of devices.

Topic F

In this topic, you learned about the different levels of **RAID**. You learned that **Hardware RAID** is usually better than **software RAID** because it is faster and more reliable.

Independent practice activity

In this activity, you will explore some features of NTFS.

1 Choose Start, Programs, Administrative Tools, Computer Management. In the left pane, select Disk Management. Take note of the number of disks and partitions your computer has, and the file systems of each. Close the Computer Management window.

2 Create a new folder on the desktop and name it anything you want. Create a new text document in the new folder (you don't need to add any text to it.)

3 Right-click on the new text document and choose Properties.

4 Click the Security tab. What permissions can you set on the file?

5 Click the General tab, then click the Advanced button. Note the available options. Check Encrypt contents to secure data, then click OK. Click OK to close the Properties window. Read the Encryption warning, then click OK to accept the default.

6 Delete the new folder and file.

Review questions

1 Which of the following are physical hard disk components? (Choose all that apply.)

   A disk platters

   B spindle motor

   C compact disc

   D head actuator mechanism

2 A head crash is:

   A the drive head colliding with the sprocket

   B the drive head colliding with the disk platter

   C the drive head in contact with a stationary platter

   D the inevitable conclusion to a wild party

3 A primary partition:

   A is contained in an extended partition

   B contains logical drives

   C always represents the entire hard disk

   D can contain a bootable operating system

4 Which of the following is not a hard disk utility?

   A GDISK

   B FDISK

   C FORMAT

   D TETRIS

5 What is "slack" on a hard disk?

   A corrupt data on the physical media

   B cluster space that is only partially occupied

   C excessive free space

   D unterminated SCSI signals

6 The better technical term for IDE is:.

   A EIDE

   B ATA

   C SCSI

   D FC-AL

7 Which two ATA implementations can use 100 MBps?

   A ATA-3

   B ATA-4

   C ATA-5

   D ATA-6

8 What is an advantage of IDE/ATA?

   A up to 15 devices on a single channel

   B connects to a very fast switched fabric

   C inexpensive

   D up to 82 ft/25 meter cable length

9 What is a synonym for an IDE or SCSI controller?.

   A host adapter

   B array control unit

   C domain controller

   D SCA connector

10 What does a SCSI parallel bus allow?.

   A arbitrated I/O

   B simultaneous I/O

   C LVD

   D multiple channels on a single controller

11 Which version of SCSI introduced both Fast and Wide implementations?.

   A SCSI-1

   B SCSI-2

   C SCSI-3

   D SCSI Fast and Wide have been formally introduced as a standard

12 What is command queuing?

   A a method that allows the host adapter to send up to 256 commands to the drive

   B ordering of I/O operations on the IDE host adapter

   C a memory queue that caches sequentially read hard disk data

   D a management system that reorders unprocessed commands to the host adapter

13 A Wide SCSI implementation would use which of the following items?

    A 8-bit cable

    B 50-pin connector

    C 68-pin connector

    D 16-bit cable

14 What does an SCA-2 connector allow you to do?

    A replace disk platters on the fly

    B hot swap hard disks

    C hot swap terminators

    D convert from a 50-pin device to a 68-pin cable connector

15 How does double transition (DT) clocking improve SCSI performance?

    A transmits data twice per second

    B transmits data on the rising and falling edges of the clock cycle

    C fills the RAID cache during idle periods

    D relieves the main CPU of parity processing burdens

16 Why shouldn't you mix HVD devices with LVD devices?

    A The LVD devices can be damaged by the higher voltage.

    B The HVD devices will block communication on the bus.

    C The HVD devices will shorten the overall cable length.

    D The LVD devices can damage the HVD devices.

17 What is the best form of termination for an SE bus?

    A LVD termination

    B HVD termination

    C passive termination

    D FPT

18 What is the SCSI ID of most host adapters?

    A 0

    B 1

    C 7

    D 15

19 Which of the following is not a benefit of Fibre Channel?

    A simple installation

    B extremely high performance

    C extremely high storage quantity

    D extremely high number of connected devices

20 If you want both high performance and redundancy, which two RAID implementations would be suitable?.

    A RAID-0

    B RAID-1

    C RAID-5

    D RAID 0+1

Unit 3

Server planning

Unit time: 120 minutes

Complete this unit, and you'll know how to:

A Plan the server environment and physical site readiness.

B Implement sound physical server security practices.

Topic A: Planning physical site readiness

This topic covers the following CompTIA Server+ exam objectives:

#	Objective
2.1	Conduct pre-installation planning activities • Activities include: • Verify power sources, space, UPS and network availability • Supporting knowledge includes: • UPS sizes and types • Server power requirements • Power issues (stability, spikes, etc.)
6.2	Recognize and report on server room environment issues • Issues include: • Temperature • Humidity • ESD • Power surges • Back-up generator

Site preparation

Explanation

The physical server environment is one of the most critical aspects in determining where to place servers. In fact, you might have to significantly modify a particular room to ensure that the conditions are optimal for server reliability and uptime. Variances in the physical environment can also affect the lifetime of the server and its components. The two most significant factors affecting the health of a server are temperature and humidity. Other elements about the site's physical readiness include floor space, power availability, and the possibility of a fire or flood.

The physical site plan for your server room is vital to the success of your network. However, you cannot plan a new server room yourself, regardless of how much you know about servers and networking. Several key planning considerations require the involvement of an architect, electrical and mechanical engineers, and a general contractor. For example, you probably do not want to design a fire suppression system on your own. For that, you would use a mechanical engineer to ensure the best possible solution for your environment and to avoid liability on your part and that of your organization. Also, these professionals can ensure that the server room installation complies with federal OSHA requirements and local building codes.

Temperature

Servers run hot. When you consider individual factors that contribute to server heating and put them all into a single box, temperature problems quickly compound. The hottest element is and will probably always be the processor(s). The processor consists of around 40 million tiny transistors, each charged with electricity, albeit a small amount at about 1.7–3.5 volts. (A transistor is an electronic device that opens or closes, or turns on or off to provide a logic gate or switch, and provides the "thinking" capability of the processor.) Maximum temperature tolerance for the processor is about 185° Fahrenheit (85° Celsius); however, you should never allow the temperature to get this high. Fans and other cooling measures dedicated to the processor help to keep the temperature at 90–110° F (32–44° C). If you have an SMP system with multiple processors, potential temperature problems multiply accordingly.

Other hot components in the system are the hard drives, which on a server often have cooling fans of their own, and the motherboard. Internal components in the server collectively contribute to the overall heat of the server room. The increased heat in the air results in warmer air entering the server and aggravates the heat issue, which is why the server room should have dedicated air conditioning.

Generally, a series of fans inside the case help keep the system cool and achieve maximum effectiveness if the ambient (surrounding) room temperature is also cool. To provide cool ambient temperature, keep the air conditioning in the room as cool as possible. To compromise between human comfort and cooling server equipment, you can usually keep the server room temperature between 68° and 72° F (20–22° C). However, be sure to keep the temperature at a constant setting, because fluctuations cause expansion and contraction of server components, shortening the server's life span.

Because equipment in the server room generates heat disproportionate to the heat level in the rest of the office, setting a thermostat in general areas cannot adequately cool the server room. A thermostat set at 70° F (21° C) for general areas will allow significantly higher temperatures in the server room. Therefore, it's important to provide a separate air-conditioning system and thermostat in the server room. If the budget allows, also consider installing two air-conditioning units and thermostats in the same server space for redundancy (Exhibit 3-1). If one unit fails, the other should be able to cool the room.

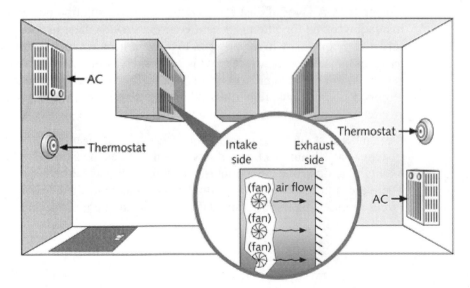

Exhibit 3-1: Use separate thermostats and air conditioners in addition to internal equipment fans to cool equipment

Regardless of the ambient room temperature and adequacy of server cooling fans, the server cannot adequately cool itself unless you provide good airflow to the server. This is an often overlooked factor for a number of reasons. For example, server rooms often lack adequate space. As administrators cram more equipment into the server room, they are often forced to shove equipment closer to the wall to create more usable floor space. Or, someone receives a new carton of equipment and, for lack of a better place, simply places it in front of the server rack—unaware that he or she has just blocked the ventilation slots to the server. Space in front of and behind the server or server rack is critical. According to most specifications, about three feet of clearance is required both in front of and behind the rack (Exhibit 3-2).

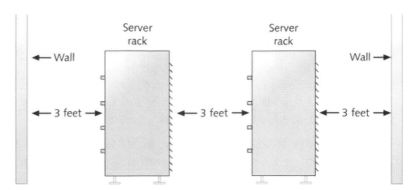

Exhibit 3-2: Allow three feet in front of and behind server equipment

Air quality

While air quality sounds like a health-related issue for people, it is also an important issue for server equipment. Air quality in a server context means that the air must be clean and as free as possible from dust particles. Rooms designed to house server equipment often have added filtration beyond the usual air filters installed in the general-purpose HVAC (heating, ventilation, and air conditioning) system.

Excessive dust in the air directly relates to the previously discussed issue of temperature. A layer of dust effectively becomes insulation on server components. Insulation is fine for a home, where you want to keep heat inside, but it's *not* fine on server components, where you want to prevent heat as much as possible. Also, dust particles can adversely affect moving parts such as floppy and hard disks. Dust accumulation can also present a fire hazard. Take regular measures to clean dust off of all server components, regardless of air cleanliness. Add supplemental air filtration to any server room that does not already have it.

Remember that dust begets more dust. Passersby or air movement from the HVAC system easily disturbs a layer of dust. While you as the administrator are responsible for maintaining dust-free components, a cleaning service can remove dust in general areas. There are contractors who specialize in cleaning controlled environments, such as your server room, using highly trained crews. An example is Data Clean Corporation.

Several server components—such as the power supply fans, supplemental cooling fans, server racks and cabinets, and hard disks—might also include supplemental filters. For example, a force-filtered server uses one or more filtered fans to supply main internal airflow throughout the server. Other cooling fans inside the server only draw upon this filtered air, creating a *positive pressure* environment (Exhibit 3-3). In server rooms that are extremely sensitive to dust, you can also install an adhesive pad in front of the server room door that collects dust particles from the bottom of shoes as people enter the room.

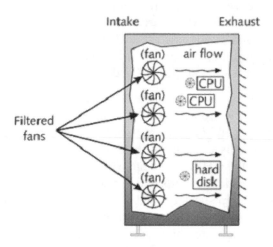

Exhibit 3-3: A positive pressure environment helps ensure clean air inside the server

Do it!

A-1:   Researching cleaning services

Questions

1 Data Clean Corporation provides cleaning services for controlled environments such as server rooms. Using your Web browser, access www.dataclean.com. Click the **services** link, read the Web page, and then answer the following questions:

2 Why is it important to have the floor plenum cleaned?

3 What is important about cleaning the floor surfaces?

Humidity

Explanation

Humidity factors vary widely depending upon the physical location of the site. For example, the desert climate of Phoenix is not as likely to present the same humidity issues as the rain-soaked climate of Seattle. Humidity affects the health of electronic server components because a drier environment presents a greater occurrence of electrostatic discharge.

Electrostatic discharge (ESD) is static electricity that can damage, destroy, or shorten the life of the server's electrical components. Many servers specify operating allowances between 20 percent and 80 percent *noncondensing relative humidity* (noncondensing means there is no moisture accumulation, such as on the outside of a cold glass). However, you should strive to humidify or dehumidify the air as needed to keep the humidity range between 40 percent and 60 percent.

High humidity presents the possible problem of condensation on equipment, which could obviously drip onto electronic components and generate significant damage—not to mention an electrocution and fire hazard to personnel. Even high-humidity environments do not normally cause condensation unless the temperature changes drastically—perhaps due to an HVAC outage. Higher humidity can create corrosion on metal components such as adapter cards and memory chips, and accelerate deterioration of magnetic media such as tape backups and floppy disks. Few environments contend with high humidity because both heating and air conditioning automatically remove humidity. However, you might find higher levels of humidity in basements or other subterranean locations, or environments that do not have a quality HVAC system in place.

If humidity is too high or too low, HVAC companies can offer a variety of solutions to add or remove humidity. Typically, HVAC modifications add humidity to the air that flows from the heating or air-conditioning unit. Utilize a dehumidification solution from the HVAC company as well. For economic reasons, you might be tempted to utilize a household dehumidifier in smaller server rooms. However, these units cannot be recommended for at least two reasons. First, these units are designed to cycle on and start dehumidifying based on a humidity threshold setting. When the unit powers on, it might cause a brief dip in power level if it is on the same circuit as server equipment. Second, these units usually remove the humidity from the air by condensing it into water in a pan. The pan must be emptied regularly—an overflowing pan threatens safety (slick floors) in addition to electrical hazards.

Do it!

A-2: Researching an HVAC company

Here's how

1 Using your Web browser, access www.liebert.com

2 Click the **Precision Air Conditioning** link

3 Scroll down to the High Capacity section, and click the **Deluxe System3–60Hz** link

4 Under Sales Literature, click **Brochure (4pg) - Upflow Applications (R 11/98) - 23KB** and read the document (click **Next** at the bottom to access all the pages)

5 On the second page, which of the airflow methods is specifically designed for a raised floor?

6 Exit the Web site and your browser

Flooring

Explanation

In a server room, flooring is much more than a location on which to place equipment. Flooring can have a direct effect on the health of your servers, particularly in respect to the risk of ESD and the efficiency of cooling. In practical terms, flooring also affects where you put cable and smoke alarms. Choose from either a flat floor or a raised floor—each has its own characteristics and advantages.

A flat floor usually involves commercial-grade floor tiles on top of concrete. Check with your architect for floor tiles that can withstand the pressure of heavy server equipment and are static-resistant. Inevitably, some equipment will scar or crack tiles, which is not a functional issue if the damage is only cosmetic. To plan for future equipment additions and rearrangements in the server room, be sure to request extra replacement tile. Also consider no-wax flooring to avoid the time-consuming and messy job of stripping and applying wax, in addition to the regular maintenance of machine buffing, which can generate a flurry of dust. Avoid carpet because it can retain dust and presents a static risk despite manufacturers' best efforts to make static-resistant carpet.

A flat floor requires you to place cable, power lines, and HVAC ducts inside walls and above ceiling tiles between the actual ceiling and the dropped ceiling—a space known as the *plenum* (Exhibit 3-4). Running cable in the plenum might not always be possible (for example, in an older building that does not have a plenum area).

A raised floor attaches to supports that provide a subfloor between the concrete floor and the floor panels (see Exhibit 3-5). This space (also called a plenum or under-floor cavity) serves the same purpose as the plenum in the ceiling—you can run cables, power lines, and HVAC vents in this space.

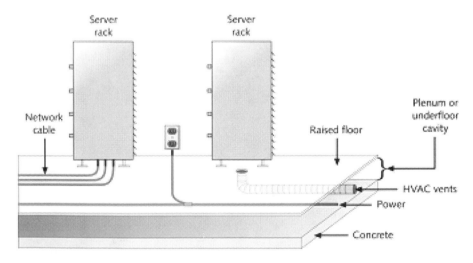

Exhibit 3-4: The plenum is useful for cable runs, HVAC vents, and power lines

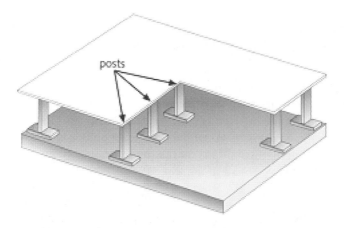

Exhibit 3-5: A raised floor rests on posts and provides plenum space

The depth of the subfloor varies from one design to another, but it usually involves 2-foot-by-2-foot panels 11 inches above the concrete. (You can adjust the height using different sized supports.) Raised floor installations were quite common in the era of large mainframes, and then became less common as more compact PC-based servers played a larger role. Server rooms became smaller as organizations decentralized from a very large room containing all servers to multiple smaller server rooms. Now, many organizations use a datacenter to house space-consuming equipment or consolidate contents of departmental server closets into a single, centralized, larger server room. (*Datacenter* is a term with two meanings, depending upon the context. It can refer to a consolidation of the majority of computer systems and data into a main location, or it can refer to one or more very powerful servers optimized as database servers—sometimes configured with as many as 32 processors. This context references the former.)

Heavy-duty floor panels are designed to withstand an enormous amount of weight (over 1000 lbs each) and are often steel filled. Some floors use an I-beam construction for added stability at the edges of the panel. These panels can be very heavy, weighing up to 45 lbs each, and require a floor puller with suction cups to lift them off the supports (Exhibit 3-6). The floor surface is specially coated to reduce ESD.

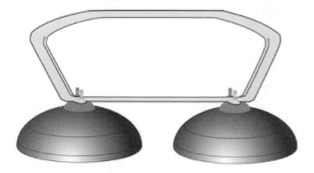

Exhibit 3-6: A floor puller uses suction cups to remove floor panels

When running cable in either the ceiling or floor plenum, consider using cable trays or other cable organizers to prevent a tangled mess and minimize future troubleshooting efforts. Also consider pulling the cable through a conduit to minimize interference with other mechanical equipment and to make replacing cable more feasible should the need arise.

Raised floors (Exhibit 3-7) offer excellent grounding to avoid ESD. Many designs ground each supporting post and offer grounding points for server racks, cabinets, or other equipment. You can place HVAC vents beneath cabinets or racks to force cooled air up through the equipment. A cabinet usually includes at least one 10-inch (25.5-cm) fan (and several supplemental fans) at the top to draw cool air through the opening at the bottom and expel warm air at the top.

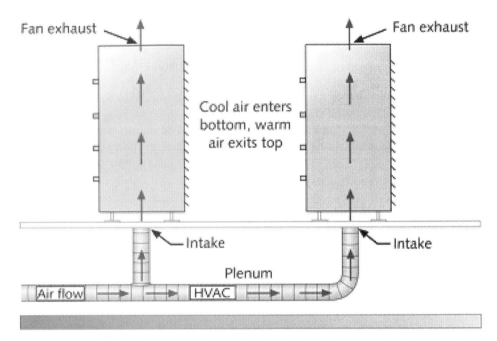

Exhibit 3-7: Raised floors can assist in the cooling of server cabinets and racks

Coordinate raised floor installations with your architects, engineers, and general contractors. Raised floor materials are available from many vendors. For a good start on the physical installation of raised floors and server rooms in general, visit the following Web sites:

- www.beanfield.com
- www.accessfloorsystems.com
- www.compucraftconstruction.com

Power

Designing an appropriate power solution for the server room is one of the trickiest considerations and should fall almost completely to the electrical engineers. Just tell the engineers what you want and the level of redundancy you require, and depend upon them to provide the solution. When providing planning objectives to the engineers, be sure to consider the factors of availability, quality, and susceptibility to electromagnetic interference.

Availability

Three power sources provide power to the server room: the main power supply, the uninterruptible power supply (UPS) for temporary power, and backup generator power for extended, system-wide outages. Make sure to request dedicated circuits to the server room that are separate from the building's main power supply. Calculate the total power the current equipment requires, including servers, monitors, routers, hubs, and switches. Add to this calculation anticipated amperage requirements for future expansion, and ask the electrical engineers to oversupply the power requirements just to be sure. (Also make sure to install plenty of easy-to-reach electrical outlets.)

Although you should rely on an electrical engineer to design server room power, you might also want to keep on hand the IEEE (Institute of Electrical and Electronic Engineers) publication *IEEE Recommended Practice for Powering and Grounding Sensitive Electronic Equipment* (ISBN 0-7381-1660-2). This book is also known as the "emerald book" in reference to its cover color, and provides complex electrical information such as reducing electrical noise and ensuring proper grounding. You might find it hard to locate in retail stores, but you can obtain it from www.ieee.org.

Administrators can probably determine what kind of UPS to use; however, the engineer should plan main power and backup generator power. The purpose of the UPS and backup generator is to provide redundancy, ensuring that power is available at all times. The UPS supplies power temporarily while administrators perform a graceful shutdown of server equipment. Otherwise, the sudden loss of power to the server can be extremely damaging to the operating system, applications, and open data files. Exhibit 3-8 shows a typical power configuration for a server room.

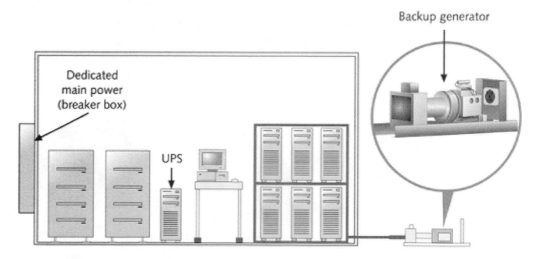

Exhibit 3-8: Main power, UPS systems, and backup generator provide power to the server room

Backup generators can be extremely expensive depending upon the amount of power they provide. Some generators cost about $250,000 and require a facility of their own, separate from the main building. Backup generators operate for as long as diesel fuel or natural gas is available. You will still need UPS systems because it usually takes about 15 seconds for the generator to start up and supply power. Of course, only organizations that absolutely require 24/7 operation would opt for such an expensive generator, which might also provide main power to the rest of the organization.

Quality

Clean power extends the life of the server and its components. "Clean power" means the absence of surges, spikes, dips, or poor grounding, which can lead to short circuits, tripped electrical breakers, and possibly damage to equipment or people. Use a receptacle tester (also known as a polarity tester) to test receptacles for power and grounding, especially in older buildings that might have questionable electrical wiring.

Request that the electrical engineer provide a connection to the earth ground in the server room. The earth ground of a home typically connects to the plumbing outside that provides water into the home. In a commercial building, electrical engineers usually design the earth ground to utilize a rod that is driven deep into the ground.

The electrical engineer takes measures to ensure clean power, but the administrator also ensures clean power to the server by using good surge protectors, UPS systems, and possibly line conditioners, which supplement power in the event of a brownout and/or minimize electromagnetic interference (EMI).

Electromagnetic interference

EMI is a byproduct of electricity and can disrupt or corrupt data traveling along network cable as well as disrupt other electrical equipment. Design data cable routes to and from the server room so that they avoid electrical equipment such as fluorescent lights, heavy electrical equipment, motors, and so forth. Make sure your electrical engineer is aware of the types of other equipment (such as heavy manufacturing equipment) in your organization so that he or she can design around potential EMI pitfalls.

Shielded twisted-pair (STP) network cable includes a foil inner jacket, adding a level of protection against EMI (Exhibit 3-9); however, you should avoid EMI sources when possible.

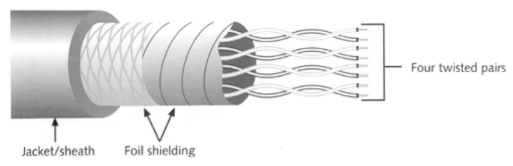

Four twisted pairs

Jacket/sheath   Foil shielding

Exhibit 3-9: STP cable includes a foil inner jacket to protect against EMI

Because servers and associated equipment are electrical devices, they also produce a level of EMI. While most equipment manufacturers take precautions to minimize the production of EMI, a certain level is unavoidable. If you find that certain server equipment exhibits strange, intermittent problems that do not seem to be associated with a specific component or the NOS, try moving the equipment to a different location where there might be less EMI from surrounding equipment. Also be sure to cover any open drive bays and expansion slots, and leave covers attached to servers when you are not servicing them. Otherwise, these exposures can radiate EMI.

If a situation arises in which you need to shut off a breaker, the description next to the breakers might be blank, incomplete, vague, or just plain wrong. Verify that you are about to switch off the correct breaker so that you do not inadvertently shut down other systems. You can use a circuit breaker finder, which is actually two pieces. The first piece (the transmitter) plugs into an electrical outlet on the circuit you wish to shut off. The second piece (the receiver) emits a tone when you physically pass it over the correct breaker.

Do it!

A-3:   Discussing site readiness

Questions and answers
1 What is a plenum?   Why is it useful?   2 What three power sources provide power to the server room?   3 What is clean power?   Why is it important?   4 What is electromagnetic interference (EMI)?

Topic B: Disaster planning

This topic covers the following CompTIA Server+ exam objectives:

#	Objective
6.1	Recognize and report of physical security issues • Activities include: • Limit access to the server room and backup tapes • Ensure physical locks exist on doors • Establish anti-theft devices for hardware (lock server racks) • Supporting knowledge includes: • Fundamentals of server security (importance of physically securing a server)
6.2	Recognize and report on server room environment issues • Issues include: • Fire suppression • Flood consideration

Fire detection and suppression

Explanation

A fire presents an obvious threat to people and equipment. Most buildings are built (or remodeled) according to relatively stringent OSHA regulations and local building codes. As a result, people sometimes dismiss the threat of a fire. However, alert administrators must remain keenly aware of the possibility of a fire (particularly an electrical fire) in both planning and daily operations. If there is a single location at which a fire is most likely, it is probably a single room filled with complex electrical equipment—the server room.

First, in the event of a developing fire, you must ensure that people in the server room are notified of the danger. Smoke alarms serve this purpose, and commercially available alarms can alert emergency services and people within the organization in addition to setting off an audible alarm. While most smoke detectors are in the ceiling, they can also be in the subfloor in a raised floor design. If they are in the subfloor, you should mark the surface of the floor panel above the smoke detector with adhesive signs, so that if it goes off you can more easily find it when it's time to reset or maintain it.

In years past, halon was the primary fire suppressant in server rooms because water has an obvious negative impact on electronics. Essentially, a fire is a chemical chain reaction. Halon breaks the chain reaction by substituting hydrogen atoms with halogen atoms. Halon leaves little or no residue and does not cause electrical short circuits. However, some suspect that halon can cause corrosion on computer components. Because halon is harmful to the earth's ozone layer, the Environmental Protection Agency (EPA) has banned the production of new halon, although you can purchase recycled halon. Because halon is being phased out, you might want to choose a different chemical fire suppressant. Consult EPA's list of halon substitutes at:

www.epa.gov/ozone/title6/snap/halonreps.html

Unfortunately, converting to another fire-protection chemical involves more than replacing the gas canisters—you must replace the entire system. Whatever product you use to extinguish fire, consider that you might also need an emergency ventilation system to expel gasses from the suppressing chemicals or burnt objects.

If you choose to supplement the chemical extinguisher, consider using a dry system instead of a water sprinkling system. A dry system uses water but only fills the pipes when there is a fire, ensuring that a damaged or leaking sprinkler head does not harm equipment. When a fire alarm trips, the pipes fill with water. Then, heat sensors release water from only areas of the room that indicate heat caused by fire. This prevents the unnecessary release of water in areas where there is no fire threat. Also, when the fire is extinguished, the sprinkler head can automatically close to prevent excess water release. Consider including floor drains for quick removal of water. Make sure the drains include a backflow prevention system so that sewer water backups do not flood the server room.

Flood considerations

In a flood, there is good news and bad news. The bad news is that there is not much you can do to prevent a flood. The good news is, at least you have less planning to do. Depending upon the cause, you might be able to prevent some types of flooding. For example, you could avoid placing the server room in locations where plumbing runs above or below the floor. A burst pipe could cause immense damage to server equipment. Also, remember to request floor drains with a backflow prevention system to prevent sewer backups into the server room while allowing fire sprinklers or other sources of water to evacuate.

If the flood is caused by a natural disaster, placing the server room as centrally as possible and away from exterior walls might allow other rooms to absorb the brunt of the initial water flow, although it may eventually reach the server room. General plumbing principles dictate that your floor drains seldom work when a large-scale flood is in progress. Your flood disaster plan will primarily determine the best way to minimize damage and move equipment quickly, instead of trying to avoid the flood. In an evacuation plan, move anything storing data first—file servers and backup tapes in particular. A well-planned system design calls for redundant copies of data, so you probably have off-site copies of your data. However, off-site copies are usually not as recent as local copies. Even though the servers are expensive, they are replaccable—whereas the organization's data is probably not replaceable. Remember that much server equipment is extremely heavy and cannot be lifted by a single individual. Also, some server NOSs feature built-in redundancy. For example, the Windows 2000/2003 Active Directory automatically replicates its database between domain controllers.

Using space effectively

In addition to technical issues relating to servers and networking, other factors can affect your server planning. Some factors might be specific to your organization, and others might be common to most situations, as in the following list:

- *Choose a central location:* If you have a choice (as in new construction), try to locate the server room centrally (Exhibit 3-10). A central location makes it easier to provide good connectivity to the rest of the network and saves cabling costs. Try to design Internet and WAN traffic to and from your organization so that it flows freely and with as few intermediary devices as possible (switches or routers, for example).

- *Consolidate space:* The best way to get the most bang for the buck out of server floor space is to use racks and cabinets. (A cabinet is similar to a rack, except that it has a locked enclosure and cooling fans.) That way, you can store several pieces of equipment in a single horizontal floor space.

- *Restrict foot traffic:* Place the server room in a low-traffic area to minimize the risk of unauthorized access.

- *Avoid exterior windows and walls:* Place the server room away from exterior building windows and walls for environmental and security purposes. In event of inclement weather, exterior windows might leak wind or rain, and sunlight contributes unwelcome warmth to the server room. A window that displays your server equipment to the outside world presents a security risk because someone can surmise much about your network design by viewing the equipment. Also consider that an evildoer could break the window and access the server room.

- *Be prepared to budget extra financing for server room design:* A server room is expensive. It requires expensive equipment and special design considerations. If you are responsible for budgeting the server room, bear this in mind and warn management in advance. As a general rule, you can multiply the cost per square foot of the building's general office space times four to arrive at the cost of server room space.

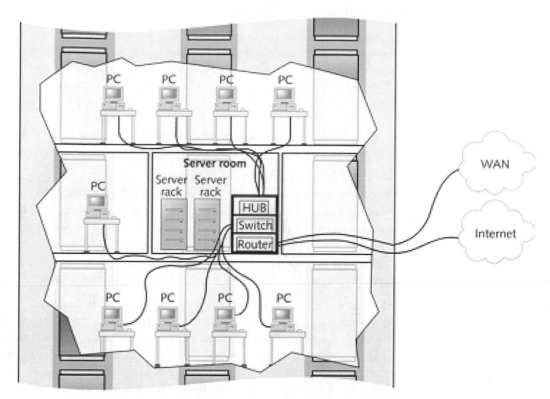

Exhibit 3-10: Centralize the server room for accessibility and reduced cable costs

Planning a secure location

Administrators of larger corporations are responsible for hundreds of millions and even billions of dollars worth of vital company data, such as customer databases, company secrets, accounting records, confidential employee records, and scores of other types of information—not to mention the value of the server equipment. Even if the organization is small, protecting company assets is still the administrator's vital concern. Securing the server room protects both the physical assets and the information stored on the servers. Although electronic security is designed to protect against hackers, viruses, malicious Internet users, and the like, physical security protects the actual server facility and equipment.

Physical security can be sophisticated, but it is not complicated. It is as simple as physical security has always been for everything from precious documents to currency—place the valuables in a safe and lock it. The server room is really a very large safe, and you as an administrator are responsible for ensuring that it is not accessed by unauthorized people. In fact, some corporate contractors to the United States government run servers and a few highly secure workstations in steel vaults.

All other security measures are only as effective as the level of physical security. You might have extremely restrictive permissions and detailed auditing records on who can access company payroll records. While hackers are always a threat over the Internet or internal network, anyone with physical access to the server can utilize special utilities that allow access to the data stored on the hard disk even though they are not authorized for such access. For example, a utility known as NTFSDOS allows the user to boot the server from an MS-DOS floppy and gain complete control of the NT file system on an otherwise secure hard disk. Monitoring security starts with your own IT staff.

Cutting your losses

A common source of company loss is employees, especially in the server room where there are a great many valuables. Sometimes, a security breach could be an innocent oversight—perhaps a new administrator provided a tour of the new server room to unauthorized outside persons. Or the security breach could be a deliberate, mean-spirited attack. Perhaps a disgruntled IT employee might want to seek revenge against the company before leaving for another job and, using his or her administrative privileges, destroys company data. It is wise to assume that anybody can steal or damage company assets—so implement sound security measures to remove or reduce such opportunities.

Always log off before leaving your computer. Otherwise, any passerby can access the local computer and network with the same authority you have, and any trace of improper activity will be logged to your account. Operating systems such as Windows allow you to lock your computer, requiring a password to unlock. Also consider logging on under only a general user account with no specific administrative privileges, and log on with administrative rights only when you need to perform administrative actions.

Restricting access to the server room

As discussed earlier, you should place the server room in an area that has minimal traffic. This minimizes the opportunity to access the server room and makes unwelcome visitors more obvious. Also, be very discriminating when determining who should see the server room. It is not a good practice to provide tours of the server room, even to employees of the organization. Next, make sure that the door you place on the server room is a solid, heavy, secure door made of solid wood, steel, or steel clad with a heavy-duty lock. The type of lock you choose depends upon the level of security you want or can afford. A simple keyed lock might be sufficient; however, most organizations probably want more controlled access, such as the following:

- *Keypad:* Enter a number into an electronic keypad to unlock the door. This number might be a shared number that all IT staff knows, or it might be unique for each user. You should reset the number on a regular basis to ensure the secrecy of the number. A keypad provides minimal security because a passerby might be able to see a number as the user enters it.

- *Card scanners:* Issue authorized persons a card that is read by a scanner at the entrance to the server room. The cards are available in a number of formats. Some have embedded magnetic data that uniquely identifies the user. Others are smart cards that have digital certificates with metal contacts read by the scanner. These are nearly impossible to duplicate. Administrators can set conditions on the cards so that they grant access to the room only at certain times—to prevent employees from sneaking into the server room and performing malicious deeds when no one else is around, for example. When the scanner reads the card, an electronic lock unlocks the door for a few seconds. One of the only drawbacks to this system is that people tend to lose, misplace, borrow, or steal the access cards. Provide a written policy to your staff that specifies penalties for missing access cards. Also make sure that employees always wear the access card. Most cards include a photograph of the person, helping to ensure that only the person to whom the card was issued uses it.

- *Bio-recognition:* This is an emerging technology that verifies a person's identity based upon physical identifiers such as fingerprints, retinal scans, voice imprints, or some combination thereof.

For maximum security, require some combination of access methods. For example, employees might insert a smart card into a reader and also type a password. This method would ensure that the card was not stolen.

Monitoring access to the server room

Despite your best security efforts, unauthorized persons might still find a way to access the server room, or authorized users might damage the server room. If such unfortunate occurrences take place, utilize a method of record keeping that allows you to know which persons were present at the time of the deed. Some of the following methods monitor access to your server room:

- Sign-in: Clearly the least secure method, a sign-in sheet depends upon the honor system, and persons who are a security risk are unlikely to be "honorable." A sign-in system should implement one or both of the next two methods that follow.

- *Security guard:* Because of the high cost associated with staffing a facility with a 24/7 security guard, this option might not be practical for all environments. However, a security guard adds an observer to unauthorized security breaches and is useful for quick apprehension and prevention as well as adding a visible level of deterrence. A security guard might also check contents of all bags going into the server room.

- *Video surveillance:* Video surveillance captures activity in the server room or at the server room door 24/7. Some facilities keep video tapes indefinitely, but most rotate tapes on at least a seven-day schedule. Be sure to replace tapes periodically, because older, worn tapes do not provide a clear image. Video surveillance is only as good as the area it covers. If you cover the server room, be sure to also cover wiring closets, areas where you store backup tapes, and so forth.

- *Logs:* Most controlled access methods such as scanners or electronic keypads keep logs that show who entered the server room and when. In addition, you can configure the NOS to track certain resources so that if someone attempts to access a resource (whether successfully or unsuccessfully), a log records the name of the logged-on user and time and date of access.

In securing the server room, do not forget to also secure other sensitive, physically accessible areas. You should, for example, secure patch panels and wiring closets, which provide a point of convergence for network cabling, making it easier to manage. In seconds, someone could access an exposed patch panel and start ripping out cable, causing considerable damage to network operations. Also, place backup media in secured data storage areas to prevent stolen tapes. In the IT context, your organization is not the server room; it is the data. Stolen tapes are a severe security risk. Secure the telco room, which is the access point for telephone communications and often shares its connections with a WAN or Internet connection.

Further secure the contents of the server room by placing locks on server equipment. For example, most server cabinets require a lock, and you can optionally lock individual components of the server rack. One reason for rack-mounted equipment is easy portability from one rack to another. However, you do not want someone easily porting the equipment into a backpack or briefcase. Do not leave spare parts lying around—secure them in a locked cabinet as well, and record parts with serial numbers.

Do it!

B-1:   Researching disaster planning

Here's how

1 Open http://www.dupont.com/fire/products/index.html.

2 From the FE Family list, select **FE-13** and click **Go**.

3 What are a few reasons that FE-13 would be good for use in server rooms?

Unit summary: Server planning

Topic A In this topic, you learned that **physical site readiness** is one of the most critical aspects in determining where to place servers, and that such readiness involves controlling temperature, humidity, and dust. You also found that there are three sources of power to the server room: the main power, the **uninterruptible power supply (UPS)** for temporary situations, and the backup generator power for extended, system-wide outages. You learned that **Clean power** extends the life of the server and its components, and that **Electromagnetic interference (EMI)** is a byproduct of electricity, can disrupt or corrupt data traveling along network cable, and can disrupt other electrical equipment.

Topic B In this topic, you learned that **disaster planning** is essential to site readiness: threats from fire or water damage are real, and chemical extinguishers and backflow preventers are often necessary.

Independent practice activity

For this activity, you will need the trial or full version of ConceptDraw Professional, a network and system diagramming program.

1 Choose Start, Programs, ConceptDraw V Professional Trial, ConceptDraw V Professional Trial.

2 In the Template Gallery, under Categories, select Computers and Network. In the right pane, select Logical Network Diagram, and then click OK.

3 Take some time to look at the icons in the left pane under Basic Network and Additional Network.

4 Under Basic Network, drag the Server icon to left side of the workspace.

5 Drag the Ethernet icon to the right of the Server icon in the workspace.

6 Drag the icon for Tower PC with flat screen monitor to the right of the Ethernet icon, and then drag another under the first.

7 Select the Ethernet symbol in the workspace. Drag a green line end to the side of the server, and drag line ends to the sides of the PC symbols in the workspace. Your diagram should now look something like Exhibit 3-11. Notice that a line end turns red when it is connected to a device – this indicates that you can now drag the symbols and the lines will stay connected.

8 You now have a basic network diagram. Choose File, Template Gallery. On the right side, select Logical Network Diagram and click OK. Browse through the icons in Internet Symbols, Network Devices, and PC and Peripherals.

9 Experiment, as time allows, with creating more detailed diagrams. Perhaps you can diagram your own organization's network.

10 When you are done, close ConceptDraw.

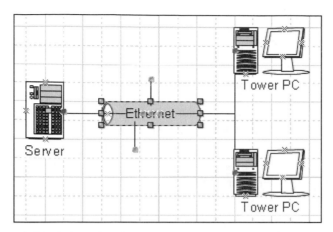

Exhibit 3-11: The ConceptDraw workspace after step 7

Review questions

1 Why is a server room hotter than other rooms in the building?.

   A Electrical components generate heat

   B It is hotter by design to reduce humidity

   C Optimum placement by exterior windows allows heat from sunlight

   D It is by design to make people uncomfortable in the server room

2 Besides fans in server equipment and cabinets, what can you do to keep the server room cool?

   A Prop the server room door open at all times

   B Add one or more dedicated air conditioners to the server room

   C Add oscillating fans wherever possible

   D Open a window

3 Why is a lack of adequate humidity detrimental to the server room?

   A Increases EMI

   B Might cause electronic circuitry to crack

   C Causes expansion and contraction of server components

   D Increases chances of ESD

4 Why is dust in the server room a problem?

   A Dust accumulation creates an unprofessional appearance

   B Dust acts as an insulator, increasing heat problems

   C Dust particulates can adversely affect moving parts

   D Dust is no more a problem in the server room than it is in other rooms

5 A positive pressure environment:

A Provides filtered air to internal server cooling fans

B Encourages people to do good deeds

C Forces filtered air into the server room at a greater rate than it escapes

D Is a server room condition that occurs when temperature, humidity, and dust control are all within acceptable parameters

6 High humidity can cause:

A Mold spores on server components

B Increased occurrences of ESD

C Increased occurrences of EMI

D Corrosion on metal components

7 Which of the following are advantages of a raised floor? Choose all that apply.

A Makes the ceiling closer, thereby easier to service the ceiling plenum

B Excellent grounding to avoid ESD

C Provides plenum space for cables, power, and HVAC

D Handy plenum space for storing spare parts

8 Why should you use a UPS even if you already have a reliable backup generator?

A The backup generator can only run for a few minutes

B The backup generator might not provide clean power, and the UPS can condition the power as necessary

C Backup generators normally serve the general building, not the server room

D The backup generator requires about 15 minutes to start – the UPS provides power in the mean time.

9 Why might you choose to install a dry system for fire suppression?

A To avoid water in event of a broken or leaking sprinkler head

B To avoid rust

C To reduce the weight of pipes in the plenum

D To avoid use of harmful chemical-based fire suppression systems

10 In case of a flood, what should you first attempt to move to a safe location?

A The mainframe

B Spare parts

C Anything storing company data

D The Chia pet

Unit 4

Server power and rack installation

Unit time: 90 minutes

Complete this unit, and you'll know how to:

A Identify features of server power supply and correctly implement an uninterruptible power supply (UPS)

B Plan optimum placement of equipment in a server rack, configure a keyboard, video, mouse (KVM) console, and list tips for installing equipment in racks

C Describe thinnet, shielded twisted-pair, unshielded twisted-pair, and fiber optic cable characteristics; and make straight-through and crossover cables

Topic A: Server power

This topic covers the following CompTIA Server+ exam objectives:

#	Objective
2.1	Conduct pre-installation planning activities
	• Activities include:
	• Plan the installation
	• Verify the installation plan
	• Verify hardware compatibility with the operating system
	• Verify power sources, space, UPS and network availability
	• Verify network protocols, naming conventions, domain names
	• Verify that all correct components and cables have been delivered
	• Supporting knowledge includes:
	• Cables and connectors required
	• UPS sizes and types
	• Server power requirements
	• Power issues (stability, spikes, etc.)
	• BTU's for the UPS and associated equipment
2.2	Install hardware using best practices
	• Installation activities include:
	• Install UPS (depending on environment)
3.4	Configure external peripherals
	• Peripherals include:
	• UPS
	• Supporting knowledge includes:
	• Proper layout of equipment
	• Requirements of the server installation environment (UPS, network, availability, space, power)

Before you start installation

Explanation

Before you begin installing your servers, you should take the time to be sure you're ready.

- Plan the installation carefully, and verify the plan with others who will help or will be affected.
- Verify that your hardware is compatible with your OS.
- Verify that you have enough space, enough power and power backup, and sufficient network connections.
- Verify your network protocols, naming conventions, IP addresses, and any other connectivity issues.
- Check that you have all the power cords, cables, and connectors you'll need.

Hardware compatibility

Most OS makers publish a hardware compatibility list, or HCL, that lists in detail the motherboards, hard drives, expansions cards, etc. that have been tested with the OS. Untested components might work, but there's no guarantee.

Supplying power to the server

Obviously, without power you don't have a working server. Selecting a server with the type of power supply you need and ensuring its continued operation through the use of an uninterruptible power supply (UPS) is the first step in ensuring solid uptime percentages.

Power supply

On the most basic level, an entry-level server probably has one power supply of at least 330 watts (W), whereas most workstations are probably as low as 145 W. A high-end, 8-way server probably provides between two and four power supplies rated between 375 W and 750 W each. The power supply, also known as the *power supply unit (PSU)*, attaches to the server chassis. Low-end servers and high-end workstations might not have hot-swappable and/or redundant power supplies. This means that in order to replace the power supply, you must remove the server case cover and disconnect power supply connectors to the motherboard, hard disks, floppy disks, and CD-ROMs before removing the screws attaching the PSU to the chassis and lifting out the power supply. This type of power supply installation is no different from the procedure on a typical desktop workstation because the chassis includes space for only a single, non-hot-swappable PSU. Well-configured servers, on the other hand, offer at least two hot-swappable power supplies. You can replace one of the power supplies without turning off the server.

Typically the server can operate acceptably with only a single PSU. The second power supply provides load balancing to reduce demands placed on a single PSU, as well as failover in case one of the power supplies fails. Often, a server includes three power supplies—two to provide continuous power and a third on standby in case one of the first two fails. Server management software and warning lights on the server should alert you to failed or unstable power supplies, usually indicated by a fan that does not spin at appropriate levels (see Exhibit 4-1).

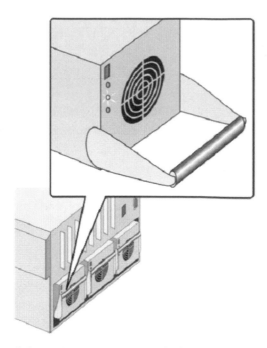

Exhibit 4-1: Most PSUs include a warning light that notifies you of problems

If one PSU fails, a standby comes online automatically and without interruption in service. (Some server configurations such as the Intel AD450NX server platform include support for an optional fourth PSU.) Because most networks require server availability 24/7, PSU failover is critical to a true server-level configuration. Also, the hot-swappable power supply does not require separate connectors for hard disks, CD-ROMs, the motherboard, and so forth. A hot-swappable PSU has sockets that plug directly into the power system of the server, which supplies power cables to server components. The power cord does not attach directly to the PSU (which would require a separate power cord for each PSU). Instead, a single power inlet serves all power supplies.

Many servers offer N+1 expandability for critical components, particularly the processor and the PSU. "N" is a variable that refers to the quantity of a given component installed in a system, such as two power supplies. The "+1" refers to a spare component. For example, a server with three power supplies might be referred to as 2+1, in which two power supplies provide ongoing power while an additional power supply provides redundancy. N+1 can also refer to a chassis designed with space to accommodate additional components.

Calculating server power requirements

Before calculating power requirements, make sure that the power from the building to the server room is sufficient to service your equipment. Although most building outlets are 110 volts (V), like household power outlets, server rooms usually also have 208/220 V outlets to accommodate the high power demands of larger servers with multiple power supplies and racks full of equipment. As part of your server room design, make sure the electrical engineers provide plenty of 208 V outlets for present and future needs. In a rack configuration, a *power distribution unit (PDU)*, similar in function to a household "power strip" but with much higher capacity, often plugs into the 208 V outlet and supplies power to internal rack components. Server power supplies automatically detect the voltage of the power source and adjust as needed.

Calculating the power supply needs for a server requires you to know how much power the motherboard, processor, internal adapters, and peripherals require. The power supply in the server can probably handle additional components without any problems; however, if you fill all expansion slots and drive bays, you might exceed power supply ratings. Though some components might list power requirements on the device or with its documentation, power requirements for other components might be difficult to locate. In that case, you should err on the safe side and calculate based on the maximum wattage allowed for a given type of device. The following table is a starting point.

Component	Wattage requirement
ATX motherboard (without CPU or RAM)*	30 W
RAM (approx. 10 W per 128 MB)	40 W for 512 MB
Pentium III 750 MHz	25 W
Floppy drive	5 W
IDE 50X CD or 10X DVD	25 W
4X AGP	30 W
PCI Card (5 W each)	30 W for six cards
IDE 5400 RPM drive**	10 W
IDE 7200 RPM drive	15 W
SCSI 7200 RPM drive	25 W
SCSI 10000 RPM drive	40 W

* 30 W represents a single, basic motherboard. Motherboard power requirements vary greatly depending on whether the server uses riser or mezzanine boards, which in turn require additional power.
** Hard drives require much more power during the spinup phase: 7200 RPM IDE drives require up to 30 W, and 10,000 RPM drives up to 40 W. Power requirements listed include *drive logic*, which is the circuitry included in the floppy or hard drive that interfaces with the disk controller. Many current hard drives are much more efficient in power requirements than the drives listed here.

When a high-powered server or rack power is turned on, a sudden, temporary surge of power to the system takes place (known as *inrush power*). To account for this, be sure that the electrical engineer not only knows the amperage requirements for equipment that is up and running, but also accounts for inrush power, usually at least 20 amps (A) per PDU. Otherwise, you won't be able to power up a rack of equipment all at once without tripping the breaker.

Some devices might list volts, watts, amps, or combinations thereof. Use the information you gather to calculate power according to the following formula:

```
watts = volts X amps
```

This formula involves slight rounding, but should suffice for calculating general power requirements. For example, a PCI slot requiring 5 V of 5 A current would require 25 W.

Computer components require positive power voltages in +3.3, +5, and +12 V. For example, a hard disk requires +12 V, and the processor usually requires +3.3 V. You might also find a negative power voltage of –5 V for backward compatibility with the ISA bus. The motherboard can be designed to supply negative voltages if the power supply does not. Assume all voltages in this text to be positive unless stated otherwise.

Add the total power requirements for all server components, and subtract the total number from the power rating for the power supply. You should have plenty of power to spare, preferably about 6%, if you want the system to be as reliable as possible. If available power is marginal, you might consider moving certain components to other servers if possible, or upgrading the power supply.

Older computers use a paddle switch located on the power supply to turn on the computer. More recent servers and workstations use a remote power switch, which runs cables from the power source connecting leads to connectors on the switch. Be sure that if you are working inside the case with these wires, you disconnect the power cable first because the wires carry 110 V AC at all times. Accidentally touching the ends of the leads together might result in an unpleasant shock.

Do it!

A-1: Calculating server power requirements

Questions and answers

1 Server rooms usually require what voltage outlets?

2 In a rack configuration, a PDU functions as what common household item?

3 What is the formula for calculating server power requirements?

Uninterruptible power supply

Explanation

An uninterruptible power supply (UPS) temporarily supplies power using batteries to the *load equipment* (anything connected to the UPS that draws power, usually servers and possibly other network equipment) in the event of a power outage. The UPS also supplements power in case of a brownout, where utility power continues but is below acceptable operating voltages.

A UPS typically provides backup power in that the load equipment constantly receives power from one or more backup batteries. The batteries receive a constant charge from utility power. If the utility power fails, the batteries continue to provide power just as they always have, minus the battery-charging function from utility power. The primary purpose of a UPS is not to continue normal operations for the entire duration of a brownout or power failure. Instead, the UPS provides a few minutes of power to give administrators enough time to send network messages to users (giving them time to save and close files) and gracefully shut down the server using normal procedures in the NOS. Otherwise, users can lose data from open files and the NOS can become corrupt or unstable.

Power protection systems fall under three major architectures:

- *Standby/Offline:* A transistor momentarily switches a large transformer, which stores a small amount of power, before transferring power to the UPS battery. These UPS systems are better suited for home PCs, workstations, and so forth.

- *Line Interactive:* Similar to Standby/Offline, but adds automatic voltage regulation to stabilize power levels during brownouts and overvoltages without using battery power. Used in PC desktops as well as smaller servers, and usually provides up to 3 kilovolt/amps (kVA).

- *Online/Double Conversion:* AC utility power enters UPS where the rectifier converts to DC and then back to AC out to the load equipment. This conversion process cleans the power stream to near perfection. Used for higher-end, mission-critical servers, and is commonly used where more than 3 kVA is required. (Extremely large power requirements over 3000 VA often require a huge amount of space, and might be centrally located with specially wired UPS-supported building circuits or power distribution strips.)

Several sources recommend that you do not purchase *standby power supply* (*SPS*) equipment, which detects an interruption in line power and switches to a transformer to bridge the period of time it takes to switch to battery power. This is no longer an issue, as it was in the 1980s and 1990s, because the quality of UPS equipment and server power supplies can easily survive the momentary transition without ill effects. The switch might take 2–4 ms, while power supplies can usually handle a 100–200 ms pause.

Understanding UPS operation

The following description and Exhibit 4-2 describe what takes place during normal operation of an online UPS when utility power is at normal, uninterrupted levels:

1   The UPS receives AC power.
2   The UPS uses a rectifier to convert AC power to DC power.
3   Some DC power is siphoned off to charge the battery.
4   An inverter converts DC power back to clean, nearly perfect AC power.
5   Power passes through the transformer to the load equipment.

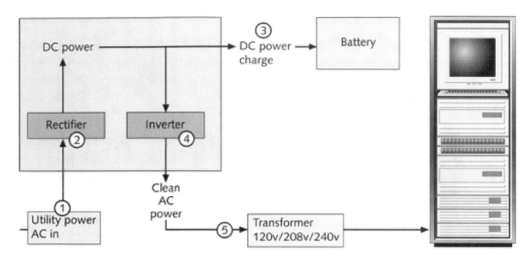

Exhibit 4-2: Normal online operation

The following steps and Exhibit 4-3 describe what takes place during a power failure:

1   Because there is no AC in, the battery discharges DC power to the inverter.
2   The inverter converts DC power to clean, nearly perfect AC power.
3   Power passes through the transformer to the load equipment.

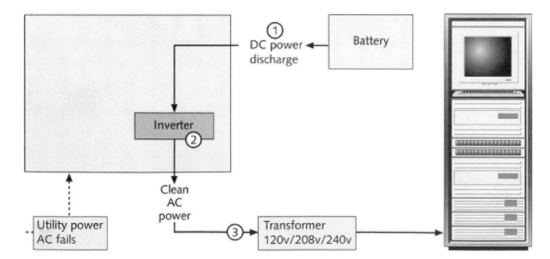

Exhibit 4-3: Battery operation

UPS software

UPS software such as American Power Conversion (APC) PowerChute can also assist the administrator by automatically shutting down the server and safely storing data that might otherwise be lost. The UPS connects to a port on the server (usually a serial or USB port) and sends a message to the server when backup functionality activates. The message serves as a trigger to the software, which begins to perform administratively predetermined functions such as data backup and system shutdown. Many UPS manufacturers are including increasingly sophisticated administrative software that goes beyond these basic functions. For example, Tripp-Lite offers software that allows you to remotely manage UPS systems of most major manufacturers from an Internet connection.

Failover for the UPS

Backup batteries eventually fail or lose their ability to retain a charge. Server-level UPS systems usually also offer N+1 functionality that allows you to replace a battery while another battery (or batteries) continues to power the unit, ensuring that the UPS is not temporarily unavailable. Also, you can use multiple UPS units so that you can service one UPS while the remaining units continue to supply power (see Exhibit 4-4).

Generally, administrators seek about 15 minutes of backup power for servers. Depending upon the business need, administrators might seek up to eight hours of backup power, such as for PBX telecom systems and Internet connections. However, UPS equipment providing eight hours of backup is large and expensive. If you want backup power for an extended period of time, consider a backup generator with a UPS. The primary power service in the event of an outage comes from the generator, not the UPS. However, the generator usually takes several seconds to come fully online (known as *generator kick*, *kick*, or *kickstart*). The UPS in this context provides power during the seconds required for the generator to come online.

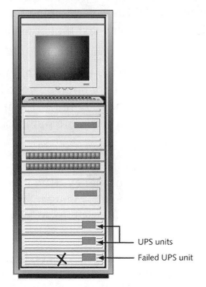

Exhibit 4-4: N+1 redundancy—if one UPS is unavailable, the remaining units continue to supply power

Determining UPS requirements

Determining your exact UPS requirements involves several variables, including power requirements of individual servers and networking equipment and/or rack power, one or more monitors, and so forth. The best way to calculate these needs is to add the total power requirements of the rack or server. Some sources recommend looking at the UL (Underwriters' Laboratory) sticker (if present) on the back of the unit to determine its total power requirement; however, the UL sticker is a measure only of what the manufacturer submitted as the default configuration for this server, and servers often include additional equipment. Instead, measure the wattage required by your load equipment. Let's say that on a particular server, you need 600 W (which includes 50% overhead, as recommended earlier). When you visit the Web site of a UPS manufacturer, you only see UPS systems rated in volt-amps (VA), and notice that a volt-amp is calculated using the same formula as watts: volts X amps. Since the formula is the same, does that mean watts and VA are the same thing? No, they are not. The difference is "where" the power occurs.

Power coming "in" from the utility company is measured in watts. That's what you pay for on your electric bill, and it is also sometimes called *actual power* or *true power*. However, as the electricity passes through the server's power supply, capacitors, inductors, and other equipment, we must account for a difference between the power that comes "in" to the power supply and power that goes "out" of the power supply. Power going "out" is known as *apparent power*. The difference between actual power and apparent power is known as the *power factor*, which is usually a difference of about 60%.

To boil it all down, it comes to a simple factor in determining UPS power requirements. Take the VA rating of the UPS and multiply that number by .60 to determine the number of watts that this UPS will support. For example, if the UPS is 1000 VA, then the watt rating for the same UPS is 600 W (1000 X .60 = 600 W). In the example stated at the beginning of this discussion, a 1000 VA UPS would exactly meet the 600 W power requirements of the server equipment. However, to plan for future expansion and add a margin of safety, you should increase to the next higher available VA rating from the UPS manufacturer.

It is important to realize that adding batteries to the UPS does not increase its volt-amp rating. For example, adding an extra battery will not upgrade your 1000 VA UPS to 1500 VA. Instead, it only extends run time. If the run time is 15 minutes, adding an extra battery will power the 1000 VA UPS for a few more minutes. The only way to increase VA is to use a more powerful UPS.

Next, determine the amount of time (known as the *run time*) you require to power the server. Realize that VA X high run time = lots of money. Run time is not a calculation you make on your own; you have to contact the UPS manufacturer to make that determination. This is best accomplished by visiting a UPS Web site and using online tools to arrive at the best product for your needs.

Avoid including printers in the total UPS power requirements, because documents can usually be printed any time; risk of data loss is a more immediate concern. Also, printers can be electrically "noisy," drawing varying levels of power; when performing a print operation, they are extremely demanding, electrically speaking. (Inkjet printers require much less power than laser printers and are better to include on a UPS if you absolutely must have a printer during a power outage.)

Site preparation

In addition to calculating the total power requirements for your servers, you must also consider the physical space that a UPS requires. Batteries can be quite large, and several models allow you to daisy chain multiple external battery packs together to extend UPS run time. This can require a great deal of space. One solution is a rack-mounted UPS. All vendors are moving to rack-mounted models in various formats. You can connect UPS units either in the same rack or in adjacent or back-to-back racks to increase run time or provide UPS fault tolerance. Also, you can use a rack-mounted UPS with an external battery pack (see Exhibit 4-5). These solutions are not something administrators arbitrarily piece together. Instead, always consult the UPS manufacturer, which will advise you on permissible physical connections, safety, power capacity, and run time.

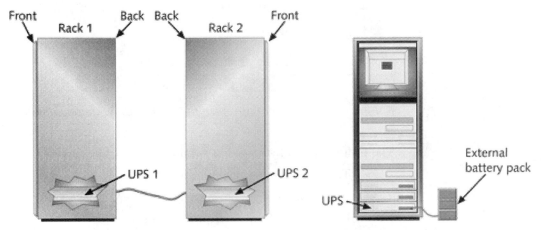

Exhibit 4-5: To provide extra power, connect two UPS systems back to back or use an external battery pack

Rack-mounted UPS systems, especially larger ones, are extremely heavy and usually require assistance to install and service. Because of the weight, you should place them at or near the bottom of the rack.

The largest UPS systems can be huge. For example, the APC Silicon DP3500E is 70 inches high, 94 inches wide, 31 inches deep, and weighs a staggering 5500 pounds. Regardless of the size, the following checklist will help you to plan site requirements, particularly for larger systems:

- For larger UPS systems, notify building engineers, electricians, and electrical engineers; for extremely heavy systems, also notify structural engineers. Verify that all aspects of the site are safe.

- Do not place monitors or other devices that are highly sensitive to electromagnetic fields (EMF) near the UPS. A larger UPS might emit an EMF that affects computer monitors, but probably not other equipment.

- UPS systems generate heat. Make sure the HVAC system can accommodate the heat output.

- Plan for any rewiring so that load equipment can reach the UPS. To prevent overloading the circuit, place larger UPS systems on a single, dedicated circuit.

- Verify sufficient clearance for adequate airflow, probably around 12 inches (0.31 m) behind a freestanding UPS array and 48 inches (1.22 m) in front (see Exhibit 4-6). Ensure adequate space to reach all switches, jacks, outlets, and so forth.

- Many UPS units have an optional earth ground to which you can ground the unit (in addition to existing AC grounding). Locate a suitable ground location reachable from the UPS.

- Get help—even in smaller units, the batteries are surprisingly heavy.

- Some larger freestanding units are on rolling casters to make movement easier. Make sure you lock the wheels when not moving the unit.

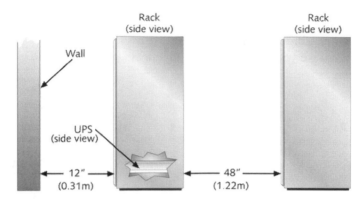

Exhibit 4-6: Allow enough space for airflow and equipment access

The following is a list of major vendors of UPS equipment:

- Tripp-Lite—www.tripplite.com
- American Power Conversion (APC)—www.apc.com
- Best Power—www.bestpower.com
- Liebert—www.liebert.com
- MGE—www.mgeups.com
- Oneac—www.oneac.com
- Sutton Designs—www.suttondesigns.com

Do it!

A-2: Discussing the UPS

Questions and answers

1 What is considered load equipment?

2 What is the purpose of a UPS?

3 What good is N+1 redundancy with a UPS?

4 What is the simplest way in determining UPS power requirements?

Topic B: The rack

This topic covers the following CompTIA Server+ exam objectives:

#	Objective
1.3	Know the basic purpose and function of the following types of servers.
	• Description of the following hardware types, including module types, basic spec, limitations and requirements (especially power and cooling)
	• Blade servers
	• Tower servers
	• Rack-mount servers
2.1	Conduct pre-installation planning activities
	• Activities include:
	• Plan the installation
	• Verify the installation plan
	• Supporting knowledge includes:
	• Server power requirements
	• Power issues (stability, spikes, etc.)
	• Server storage issues (rack requirements, rack sizes)
	• Uses of common server types (desk server, rack mount server, blade server) and the pros and cons of each
2.2	Install hardware using best practices
	• Installation activities include:
	• Mount the rack installation (if appropriate)
	• Install external devices (e.g. keyboards, monitors, subsystems, modem rack, etc.)
	• Supporting knowledge includes:
	• Physical infrastructure requirements (e.g. proper layout of equipment in the rack, adequate airflow, etc.)
	• Cable management
	• KVM management
	• Rack Mount security
4.3	Add hard drives
	• Activities include:
	• Upgrade mass storage
	• Supporting knowledge includes:
	• Available types of hard drive array additions and when they are appropriate
	• Expansions
	• Extensions

#	Objective
4.7	Upgrade peripheral devices, internal and external. Verify appropriate system resources (e.g. expansion slots, IRQ, DMA, etc.)
	• Peripheral devices include:
	• KVM devices
5.4	Perform physical housekeeping
	• Activities include:
	• Cable management

The advantage of racks

Explanation

In addition to configuring the system itself, you must determine the best physical orientation for the server—freestanding or rack mounted, and except for the smallest networks, you should plan to install servers in racks.

Racks provide an advantage in server rooms where the need for server and network equipment grows but floor space does not. By stacking equipment in a rack, you increase computing assets vertically in the same floor space that would have otherwise consumed precious floor space. This space savings is known as *density*. For example, in Exhibit 4-7, six servers on a table require about six feet of floor space. Using racks in the same six feet, you can install 18 8-way servers.

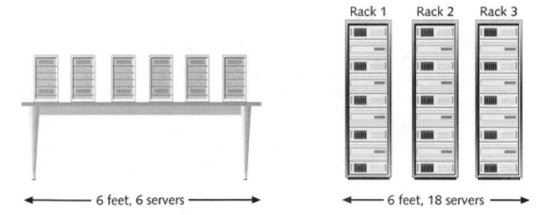

Exhibit 4-7: Density allows for more equipment in the same horizontal floor space

If you have existing servers in the tower configuration and want to place them in a rack, you can either place them on a vented shelf that mounts inside the rack or obtain a vendor kit that adapts the server to lay on its side and install it in the rack along telescoping rails. Nearly all network equipment (except, perhaps, for small workgroup hubs or switches) is rack-mountable. When you decide to use a rack, you must carefully consider several factors, including heat, ventilation, power, weight, grouping, and accessibility.

Physical characteristics

Physical rack characteristics vary from one vendor to the next. However, general characteristics are listed here. All aspects of equipment installation revolve around the physical dimensions of the rack as follows (see Exhibit 4-8):

- *Units*: Rack equipment is measured in *EIA* (*Electronic Industries Alliance*) units, or *U*. One EIA unit (1U) is equal to 1.75 vertical inches (4.45 cm). For example, Tripp-Lite makes a rack-mounted UPS that is only 1U in size. Server appliances are usually between 1U for network appliances dedicated to a single purpose and up to 7U (12.25 inches, or 31.12 cm) for 8-way servers. Datacenter servers larger than 8-way (such as a 32-way) are usually in their own dedicated enclosure.

- *Height*: Including frame, bezels, and feet or rolling casters, a full-height rack (42U) is about 6 feet (1.8 m). Various manufacturers make smaller racks as well, with common sizes at 22U, 24U, and 36U. Some manufacturers offer rack extensions, which add about 8U to the height. See the following table as a reference (casters or feet not included).

Units	Inches	Centimeters
22U	38.5	97.8
24U	42.0	106.7
36U	63.0	160.0
42U	73.5	186.7

- *Depth*: Racks are about 36 inches (.98 m) deep, with usable depth around 28 or 29 inches (between .71 and .73 m). Try not to use space beyond the usable depth, because you will still need room at the back to work, and for PDUs, cables, and other specialized devices that you do not need to see from the front.

- *Width*: Rack-mountable equipment requires a RETMA (Radio Electronics Television Manufacturers Association) industry standard opening of 19 inches (48.26 cm). Exterior width is usually about 23–24 inches (58.5 cm).

- *Weight*: Weight varies depending upon whether the rack includes ballast or doors, which weigh about 30 pounds each. 42U racks can weigh around 160–250 pounds empty, and can accommodate about 2000 pounds of equipment. (IBM has a heavy-duty rack that weighs 575 pounds empty!) 24U racks are about 210 pounds empty, and can accommodate about 1000 pounds of equipment.

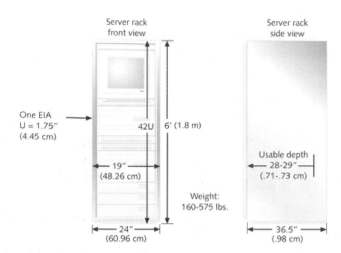

Exhibit 4-8: 42U rack dimensions

Racks can also include several other items:

- *Stabilizing feet*: Moving rack equipment in and out while servicing it presents a physical danger of the rack falling over. Stabilizing feet extend beyond the rack and help prevent it from tipping over when you work on equipment. The HP Rack System/E includes both a front and rear retractable anti-tip foot for added safety.

- *Leveling screws*: Similar to the leveling screws under a washing machine (but capable of much greater weight loads), you turn the screws until the rack is level.

- *Wheels*: Usually made of polyurethane to reduce the effect of bumps, jolts, and uneven floors when moving the rack. The wheels can support a great deal of weight, usually 1000 pounds *each*.

- *Filler panels*: Purely cosmetic, these panels cover up empty slots for a more professional, finished look.

- *Side panels*: Also cosmetic, side panels cover up the exposed sides of the rack. These are unnecessary where you join two racks together.

- *KVM/concentrator/switchbox*: A *keyboard, video, mouse* (*KVM*), also called a concentrator or switchbox, enables you to control multiple servers from a single keyboard, video monitor, and mouse.

- *Cable management arm*: It is important that when you service equipment and pull it out of the rack, all the cables do not come loose. Instead of bunching up the cable slack in a tangled mess at the back, you can Velcro cables to a *cable management arm* (*CMA*) that keeps cables neat while allowing them to extend when you pull out equipment. Cable management brackets also can be used to guide cables vertically within the rack.

- *Ballast*: Dead weight placed vertically, at the sides of the rack or at the bottom of the rack, to add stability when heavy equipment is required higher in the rack. A single ballast usually weighs about 30 pounds.

- *Short rear door*: The rear door has a gap of a few inches at the bottom to facilitate cabling out of the rack while maintaining security.

Cooling

Many racks include an option for front and rear lockable doors. Most doors are perforated safety glass or steel, providing about 60% opening for adequate ventilation, which in most racks is through convection (see Exhibit 4-9). Some manufacturers (such as Compaq) offer a multi-angled door design that enhances convection cooling. Warm air rises to the top of the rack, which may also be perforated.

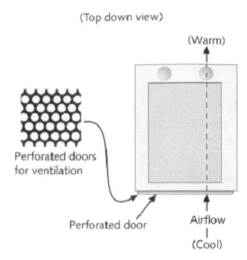

Exhibit 4-9: Perforated doors assist cooling through convection and fan-propelled airflow through equipment

To ensure adequate cooling in the rack, you can install fans in the top panel to increase availability of cool air inside the rack and draw warm air out (see Exhibit 4-10). Other temperature-control solutions cool from the front to the back, which is a function of the equipment in the rack. For example, a server might have a fan at the back of the unit that draws air into louvers at the front, and expels warm air out the back. Even in this case, you might still install fans at the top, which will help to more quickly expel naturally rising warm air while also drawing cooler air from the bottom of the rack. (Recall that some floors have air-conditioning vents beneath the racks.) This is also a more significant concern when the rack includes items that run hot, such as UPS systems and disk arrays.

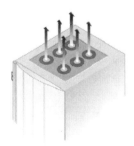

Exhibit 4-10: Fans in the top of the rack draw warm air out while cool air enters from the bottom

Be careful not to place anything on the top surface of the rack, which would inhibit dissipation of warm air. Be careful not to place racks so that the back of a rack faces the front of another to avoid the intake of warm air. Instead, you should place racks back to back and allow adequate space between rows of racks (see Exhibit 4-11).

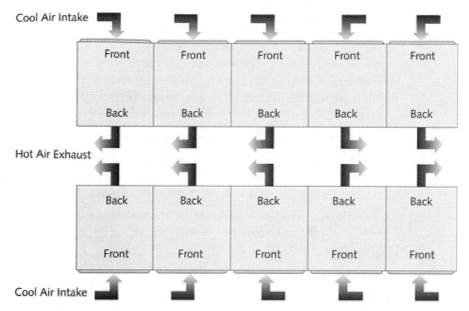

Exhibit 4-11: Arrange rows of racks in a back-to-back configuration

Configuration

Configuring the rack well directly affects the level of practical usability and prevents the need to rearrange equipment in the future. Major vendor Web sites offer rack configuration utilities as either downloadable programs or Web-based applets. These utilities are the most effective way to configure a rack, especially if all rack equipment is from the same vendor. If you make an unwise choice, the utility might alert you and ask if you want to select an alternative. Even if you do not stay with the same vendor for all equipment in your rack, you can use a rack configuration utility to approximate similar equipment. For example, the HP Netserver LXR8500 is very similar in power requirements and dimensions to the Dell PowerEdge 8450. The following is a short list of vendors offering rack configuration utilities:

- Dell—www.dell.com (download). A good, basic rack configuration utility.

- Compaq—www.compaq.com (Web-based). Offers the advantage of not having to install yet another program on your computer. Offers two modes, one for novices and one for those more experienced in rack configuration.

- Hewlett-Packard—www.hp.com (download). This one is excellent in terms of usability and has a low learning curve.

- IBM—www.ibm.com (download). The most detailed tool, but it will take a little longer to learn its usage and options (see Exhibit 4-12).

While very useful and educational, these utilities cannot account for every contingency, and you'll have to monitor the results for accuracy and practicality in your own real-world environment. Also, most of these utilities do not fully consider the implications of joining two racks together, especially in terms of sharing cabling between the racks. Therefore, you should be able to wisely configure a rack for weight distribution, device grouping, and cable management as described in the following sections.

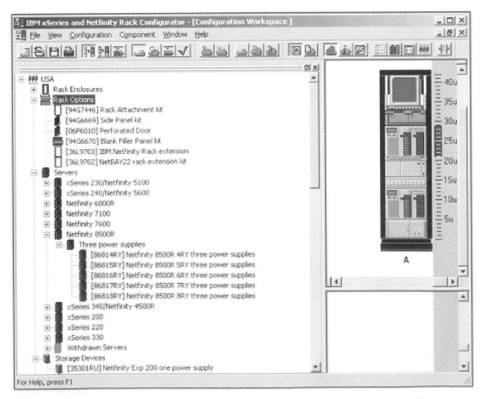

Exhibit 4-12: The IBM Netfinity Rack Configurator is an excellent tool

Weight distribution

Larger 8-way rack servers can weigh upward of 175 pounds, and UPS systems like the APC Smart-UPS 5000 RM is 5U and weighs 320 pounds! The general rule of thumb is to place the heaviest items at the bottom of the rack, which minimizes the chances of the rack tipping over. Therefore, unless the UPS is small (1U or 2U), you should almost invariably place it at the bottom. If other planning factors such as device grouping prevent you from placing all the heavier items at the bottom, try to avoid placing heavier items any higher than 36 inches (.91 m) up the rack, and consider adding one or more ballasts. Each ballast is 1U and weighs 30 pounds. Other heavy items include mass storage items such as a DLT (Digital Linear Tape, a backup device) and a disk array. (HP recommends placing the DLT just above the UPS.) It should not adversely affect weight distribution if you need to insert a keyboard/mouse between heavy devices. (See Exhibit 4-13.)

It is very important that you pull out only one piece of rack equipment at a time to avoid tipping. Even equipment that is only moderately heavy has a greater impact on server balance when it is pulled "out of center." A rack can easily exceed 1000 pounds, and could seriously injure or kill someone if it fell over. When working on a rack, don't forget to extend stabilizing feet if they are available.

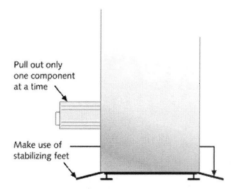

Pull out only
one component
at a time

Make use of
stabilizing feet

Exhibit 4-13: Pull out only one device at a time, and use stabilizing feet to prevent tipping

Device grouping

Grouping devices involves a delicate balance between weight distribution and logically placing components where cables from one component can reach other components. Also, for purposes of usability, some types of equipment should be placed where they are most usable. For example, although the keyboard is lightweight, placing it at the top of the rack would make it inaccessible to administrators. If administrators work on the server in a standing position, you should place the keyboard in the middle of the rack (or a little lower if administrators will be seated). The logic of some devices is also important. For example, certain devices might need to be closer to one another for cables to reach.

Another reason to group equipment in a different way than you would if only considering weight might be clustering. Recall that clustering involves two or more servers serving data from the same physical media (hard drives). In the rack, you might have (starting from the bottom) at least one UPS, Cluster Server 1, a disk array that contains data, and then Cluster Server 2 (see Exhibit 4-14).

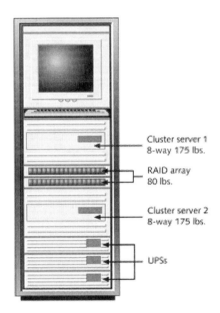

Cluster server 1
8-way 175 lbs.

RAID array
80 lbs.

Cluster server 2
8-way 175 lbs.

UPSs

Exhibit 4-14: A cluster might change the usual weight distribution order

Cable management

One of the primary goals in cable management is neatness. While this might sound compulsive, organization is critical in the server room. When equipment fails, administrators must have minimal distraction in finding the proper equipment. When trying to access equipment at the back of the rack (to replace a power supply, for example), you do not want to fight your way through a mess of cable. With cables neatly aligned along a CMA and placed out of the way with cable management brackets, guides, and so forth, you should be able to quickly access the equipment you need.

Another factor that affects where you place equipment is cable length. The effective cable reach of pieces using a CMA will be shorter because several inches (perhaps 28 or more) will be used by the arm. However, the shorter cable reach is well worth the improved organization and secure connections that a CMA provides (see Exhibit 4-15).

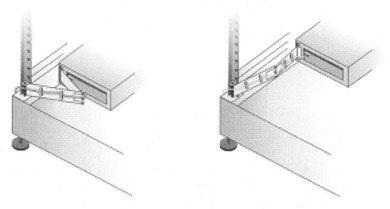

Exhibit 4-15: The CMA expands and contracts when you move the server

If cable lengths are too short, you might have to place dependent equipment closer to one another. For example, a light, 1U Web server near the top of the rack must back up its content to a DLT located at the bottom of the rack. If the cable lengths are not sufficient, you might have to move the heavy DLT higher in the rack, lower the 1U Web server, or move the 1U Web server to an adjacent rack in a lower position closer to the DLT. Many devices cannot use an extension to make up the shortfall in cable lengths. For example, there is no such thing as a SCSI cable extension.

Cable lengths become a more visible restriction when you consider a monitor, which is usually placed higher in the rack than the server. Typically, the monitor cable can reach the server over a maximum of 29U. If necessary, you can purchase an inexpensive VGA extension cable. Use as short a length as necessary (hopefully 6 feet or less), because longer lengths are not good for video signal integrity.

In the absence of a CMA, you might consider using a straight point-to-point cabling method with no intermediate cable management. However, this is the least desired method because the rack becomes more difficult to manage when you have cables hanging in the way. Also, unless there is a method to secure the cable ends (such as thumb screws), they are more likely to fall off. Some rack equipment has a cable tray option extending from the back of the equipment. The point of the cable tray is to lessen the pull of gravity on the cable connection and reduce the likelihood of the cable falling out (see Exhibit 4-16).

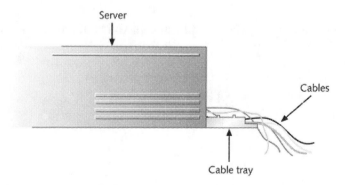

Exhibit 4-16: A cable tray helps cables to stay plugged in

Sometimes you need to use multiple devices from several racks that connect to a physical and logical center. For example, Exhibit 4-17 shows a centrally located server that connects to several devices such as DLT backup equipment, a SCSI disk array, and a Fibre Channel disk array. If other planning factors prevent you from placing all the equipment in the same rack, then centrally locate the server between racks containing the equipment.

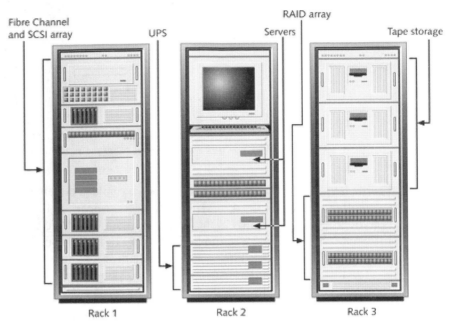

Exhibit 4-17: Place the server central to the other equipment to which it connects

Do it!

B-1: Discussing rack configuration

Questions and answers

1 What is a primary advantage of a rack?

2 How big is 1U?

3 Where should you generally place the heaviest items in the rack?

4 What helps to manage cables in the rack?

Power

A UPS is only as good as its availability, so each piece of rack equipment must be able to connect to the UPS. The UPS has a limited number of outlets (perhaps six), and in a fully loaded rack, that's probably not enough. However, by using a rack-mounted PDU, you can create more outlets (see Exhibit 4-18). Make sure that the devices you attach to it do not exceed 80% of the PDU's power rating. You can install the PDU in the rack in any of several configurations. Usually, you try to locate the PDU at the rear of the rack and as close to the bottom as possible.

Vertically installed PDUs attach to either the left or right rack post (see Exhibit 4-19). However, most PDUs use 11U vertically, so you can probably only install three on one rail, left or right. Another factor that limits PDU installation is the type of server. Some servers slide out of the rack at the rear instead of the front (the HP NetServer LXr Pro8, for example). In this case, a horizontal PDU in the same space as the server would interfere with server removal. In a vertical PDU configuration, also be careful not to install the PDU at the location of the locking latch, and face the PDU inward so that rack covers do not block outlets.

Exhibit 4-18: The PDU provides the functionality of a power strip at much higher power capacity

Exhibit 4-19: A vertical PDU installation

A horizontal installation usually allows for cleaner routing of power cables, and can be mounted behind most rack equipment in the same EIA unit except for very deep, large rack components such as some large servers. If installation behind a unit is not acceptable, you can also mount PDUs in the bottom of most racks (see Exhibit 4-20).

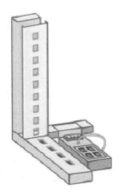

Exhibit 4-20: Mounting in the bottom of the rack does not interfere with other equipment

Many PDUs, especially those with higher voltage, have locking plugs that plug into a locking receptacle to prevent accidental disconnection. The rack utility software from several vendors calculates the VAs required to service the equipment you propose, and also suggests the quantity and type of PDUs you will need. For an added level of power redundancy, you can use a PDU designed for utility power from two independent circuits. If one of the circuits fails, the other transparently continues to provide service (see Exhibit 4-21).

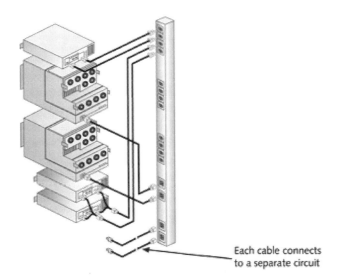

Each cable connects
to a separate circuit

Exhibit 4-21: For added redundancy, use a PDU that connects to two independent circuits

The KVM

It is impractical to have a separate keyboard, video display, and mouse for each server in the rack. A 42U rack can have 42 separate 1U servers! Instead, it makes more sense to install a single keyboard, video display, and mouse (KVM) that can service all of the connected servers, collectively referred to as a *console* (see Exhibit 4-22). A KVM console also reduces air-conditioning costs by eliminating multiple heat-generating monitors. You can obtain a basic, inexpensive KVM console for any configuration of workstations or servers, most of which operate between four and eight systems. Some can also be set to continually cycle between servers every few seconds so that you can observe activity on each server.

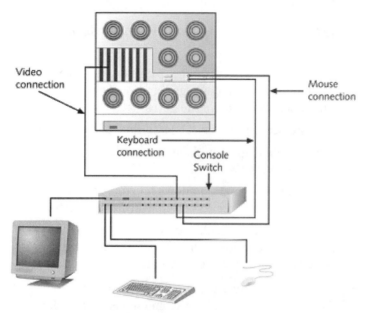

Exhibit 4-22: Use one keyboard, video, and mouse to control servers through a KVM console

For the rack, you can use several KVM components to arrive at the configuration you want:

- 1U fixed keyboard/mouse tray
- 2U retractable keyboard and mouse tray
- Full-size (about 11U) video display
- 1U or 2U integrated keyboard, trackball, and video display (see Exhibit 4-23)

Whichever configuration you decide on, the clear advantage is that you conserve space by using a single KVM console to manage multiple servers. Also, since each KVM console often manages up to eight servers, vendors usually offer the option to cascade the consoles, which allows you to manage dozens of servers. Some consoles are wireless, and with signal amplification they can allow you to control more than 60 servers.

The keyboard, mouse, and video monitor each connect to the KVM console. Then you need one extension cord (male to female) each for the keyboard, video monitor, and mouse for each server. If you have four servers, then you need four sets of extension cords. You can usually purchase the set as a bundled pack from any computer supply source.

Exhibit 4-23: An integrated keyboard, trackball, and pop-up video display

KVM switches are available from nearly all major server vendors and most computer stores. APC manufactures an outstanding KVM console that, in addition to standard functions, includes the following features:

- Password security to the KVM console adds an extra level of security.
- An on-screen display with customizable menus allows you to graphically switch between servers.
- Hot-pluggable operation allows you to add servers without having to first power off the KVM or other servers attached to the KVM.
- Mouse reset circumvents a frustration with KVM systems in which the mouse ceases to respond to actions. This feature also allows you to regain control of the mouse without powering down the KVM or the server.

Alternatively, you can usually administer servers from the comfort of your own desktop with a full-screen monitor, keyboard, and mouse, depending on the operating system. Windows 2000/2003 offers administrative tools that you can run from any Windows computer on the network. NetWare offers similar management control.

Blade servers

Blade servers are large cards containing the essential elements of a server – processors, memory, and hard disks—that slide into a chassis alongside like servers, like books on a shelf.

The blade server chassis, which can typically hold six to twelve or more blades, provides redundant power supplies, fans, network connections, KVM switches, and connections for external storage. The chassis mounts in a regular rack and reduces the number of needed cables. In addition to easy deployment and replacement of servers, management software allows for centralized management of individual servers or whole groups of servers.

Rack installation tips

The following tips can help you to properly configure the rack:

- Begin building the rack from the bottom up, with heaviest devices at the bottom (as previously discussed).
- If using multiple racks, be consistent in the server numbering scheme in relation to port numbers on the KVM, which helps you to quickly access the right server from one rack to the next instead of using a hit-or-miss method.
- Place servers attached to the same KVM console in close proximity to it so that you can easily view server activity while at the keyboard.
- Group servers that serve a particular purpose in the same physical area. For example, put Web servers in one location, file servers in another, application servers in another, and so forth. This helps to minimize trips across the server room when configuring or troubleshooting.
- Remember that at times you must access the rear of the server. Make sure there is adequate space behind the server to open the rear door.
- Place servers that require frequent access (such as those with backup devices) in more easily accessible locations.
- Place servers according to security need. Position high-security servers in highly visible locations where it is more obvious if someone is accessing them.
- For added security, lock the rack doors and install an alarm that trips when the door has been breached.
- Fully loaded racks are extremely heavy, so limit the number of racks that you tie together if you plan to move them, even for routine cleaning. It can be very difficult to roll three attached racks, even with assistance.
- When sliding equipment in and out of a rack, watch your fingers! The slide rails are pinch points.

Hundreds of pages about rack planning and installation can be found at the following sites:

- http://netserver.hp.com/netserver/docs/download.asp?file=g_rack_cabling.pdf
- http://support.dell.com/docs/systems/smarcon/en/index.htm
- ftp://ftp.compaq.com/pub/products/storageworks/techdoc/racksandoptions/14255e2.pdf
- www.ibm.com (search for the Netfinity Rack Configurator)

Do it!   ## B-2:   Discussing power and the KVM

Questions and answers

1 Where should you usually mount a PDU in the rack?

2 What is a KVM console?

3 What is the advantage of using a KVM console?

Topic C: Network cabling

This topic covers the following CompTIA Server+ exam objective:

#	Objective
2.2	Install hardware using best practices
	• Installation activities include:
	• Cut and crimp the network cabling
	• Supporting knowledge includes:
	• Basic understanding of network cabling and connector types

Cabling

Explanation   An important part of designing and deploying a network is selecting the appropriate cable medium. The cable provides the conduit for all network communications. The network media access method standard of the NIC and the physical topology affect the cable choice and implementation. The most common types of LAN cabling in use today are coaxial (thinnet and thicknet), shielded twisted pair, unshielded twisted pair, and fiber optic.

(Although this unit primarily addresses physical cable media, there are wireless options that comply with the new Ethernet 802.11b standard to allow transmission at rates up to 11 Mbps using radio frequency within a specific radius.)

Thicknet

Thicknet is based the 10Base5 standard, which transmits data at 10 Mbps over a maximum distance of 500 meters (1640.4 feet). Thicknet is about 1 cm thick and has been used for network backbones because of its durability and maximum length. Many current thicknet implementations are being replaced by fiber optic media.

Thinnet

Thinnet is based on on the 10Base2 standard (10 Mbps/Baseband transmission) that utilizes RG-58 A/U or RG-58 C/U 50 ohm coaxial cable with maximum segment lengths of 185 meters (606.9 feet). The RG-58 cable is less expensive and easier to install than the thicknet cable used for the 10Base5 standard, mostly because it is thinner (approximately 0.5 cm or .2 inch) and more flexible. While thinnet is gradually fading into networking history, you will still find it in several existing (but not new) network implementations. Cables in both the 10Base5 and 10Base2 systems interconnect with BNCs (British Naval Connectors) (see Exhibit 4-24). The network interface card in a computer requires a T-connector to attach two cables to a NIC. A BNC barrel connector connects two cables. Any unused connection must have a 50 ohm terminator to prevent signal bounce.

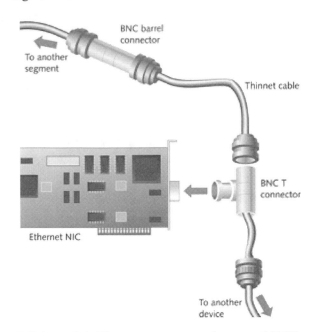

Exhibit 4-24: Thinnet uses several types of BNCs

Shielded twisted pair (STP)

Shielded twisted-pair (*STP*) cable includes screened twisted-pair cable and foil twisted-pair cable and provides reliable connectivity. STP involves two copper wires, each encased in its own color-coded insulation, and then twisted together to form a "twisted pair." Multiple twisted-pairs are then packaged in an outer sheath to form the twisted pair cable (see Exhibit 4-25). The cable minimizes the possibility of *crosstalk* (intruding signals from an adjacent twisted pair or cable) by increasing the number of twists per inch. Early telephone signals were actually sent over a form of twisted-pair cable, and almost every building today still uses twisted-pair cable to carry telephone and other signals. Although coaxial and fiber optic cable were developed to handle higher-bandwidth applications and support emerging technologies, twisted-pair cable has evolved so that it can now carry high-data-rate signals.

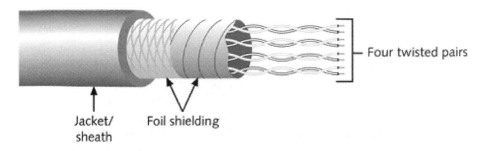

Exhibit 4-25: STP cable

STP cable encases the wires in a conducting metal shield to reduce the potential for EMI. Recall that electric motors, power lines, fluorescent lighting, and a variety of other devices cause EMI and, as a result, disruptions in network communications. STP cable effectively prevents radiation and blocks interference as long as the entire end-to-end link is shielded and properly grounded. The maximum length of STP is 100 meters (328.08 feet) with a speed of up to 500 Mbps. Although length becomes a problem with STP, it is inexpensive and easy to install.

STP cable can use several types of connectors, but only RJ-45 connectors are used in current networking contexts. *RJ-45* (*registered jack-45*) is an eight-wire connector that connects Ethernet network devices. RJ-45 connectors look similar to the RJ-11 connectors that are used for connecting telephone equipment, but they are wider because they connect eight wires instead of four (see Exhibit 4-26).

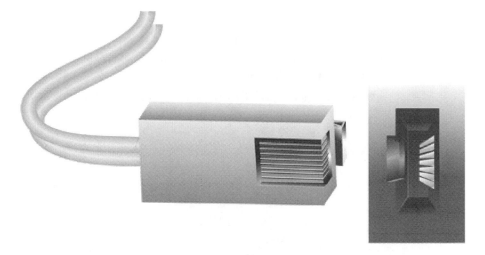

Exhibit 4-26: RJ-45 male and female connectors

Unshielded twisted pair (UTP)

Unshielded twisted-pair (*UTP*) cable, on the other hand, does not rely on physical shielding to block interference, but uses balancing and filtering techniques to reduce signal interference. Noise is induced equally on two conductors, which cancel out at the receiver. With correctly designed and manufactured UTP cable, this technique is easier to maintain than the shielding permanence and grounding of an STP cable. UTP cabling does not offer the high bandwidth or the protection from interference that coaxial or fiber optic cables do; however, millions of nodes are wired with UTP cable due to its lightweight, thin, and flexible nature. UTP cabling is a low-cost, manageable solution that is widely used for LANs and telephone connections. It is also quite adaptable and dependable, even for higher-data-rate applications. Like STP, UTP uses RJ-45 connectors. UTP has a maximum length of 100 meters (328.08 feet) and can support speeds of up to 100 Mbps.

The following table summarizes the various network cable types discussed so far:

Cable types	Maximum length	Maximum speed
Thicknet (10Base5)	500 meters (1640.4 feet)	10 Mbps
Thinnet (10Base2)	185 meters (606.9 feet)	10 Mbps
Shielded twisted pair (STP)	100 meters (328.08 feet)	10, 100, 1000 Mbps depending on the category of cabling
Unshielded twisted pair (UTP)	100 meters (328.08 feet)	10, 100, 1000 Mbps depending on the category of cabling

UTP cable has evolved over the years, and different varieties are available for different needs. Improvements such as variations in the twists, individual wire sheaths, or overall cable jackets have led to the development of several standards for STP/UTP cabling. Here are some of the most popular specifications, each using four wire pairs:

- *Category 3 (Cat 3)*—Provides signal throughput up to 10 Mbps. Cat 3 is permissible for 10 Mbps Ethernet; however, the slightly more expensive Cat 5 is more common and reliable. You can also find Cat 3 cable in older 4 Mbps Token Ring network implementations.

- *Category 4 (Cat 4)*—Provides signal throughput up to 16 Mbps. Cat 4 is common in 16 Mbps Token Ring network implementations. Cat 5 is preferred over Cat 4 in most cases.

- *Category 5 (Cat 5)*—Provides signal throughput up to 100 Mbps. Cat 5 is the most common network cable in use today, and is used for Ethernet as well as other fast networking technologies. Cat 5 can be used for 10BaseT, 100BaseT, 1000BaseT, and Token Ring networking. Note that Enhanced Cat 5 (Cat 5e) is available for optimum reliability and performance. Cat 5e is only marginally more expensive yet reduces crosstalk by using a twisted string or plastic rib to separates the pairs and keeps the wires in proper position along the whole length of the cable. Cat 5e also uses better insulation and a thicker jacket.

- *Category 6 (Cat 6)*—A heavily shielded implementation of twisted-pair cabling. Each of four pairs is wrapped in foil insulation, and even more foil wraps around the bundle of pairs. A fire-resistant sheath covers the outer foil layer. Cat 6 cabling provides excellent resistance to crosstalk and can support up to six times the throughput of Cat 5.

RJ-45 pin assignments

Cables normally connect to RJ-45 connectors in what is known as a "straight-through" configuration. This means that whatever color insulated wire is on the first pin on one end is the same color insulated wire on the first pin of the connector on the other end, and so on through all eight wires. Straight-through cabling is the most commonly used configuration and connects servers and workstations to wall connectors, hubs, and other network equipment.

While there are a few standards for determining the wiring order within the jack, it really doesn't matter as long as the wires on one end correspond exactly to the wires on the other end and the scheme is consistent throughout your organization. For reference sake, Exhibit 4-27 shows the Electronic Industries Association/Telecommunications Industry Association (EIA/TIA) 568A and 568B cable end standards. Generally speaking, 568B is more common in business and industry, and 568A is required in certain government installations. For straight-through cable, just make sure that both ends use the same configuration.

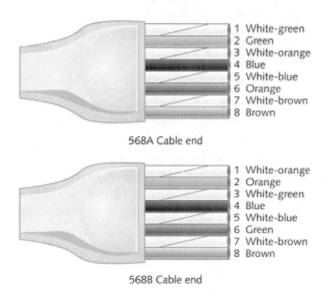

Exhibit 4-27: The EIA/TIA RJ-45 wiring standard

Crossover cables

Crossover cables are useful in connecting two computers directly to one another. This is handy for quick connectivity without intermediate hubs or other network equipment as well as diagnostic contexts in which you want to isolate a host from the network and connect to it directly. Crossover cables are also required to daisy chain network devices. For example, crossover cables would interconnect a series of stackable hubs or switches (see Exhibit 4-28).

Exhibit 4-28: Crossover cables daisy chain network devices such as hubs

In a crossover configuration, you simply reverse the green and orange pairs. A simpler way to view this is to look at Exhibit 4-27 again. Recall that a straight-through cable uses the exact same pin configuration on both sides of the cable. For a crossover cable, simply use the 568A configuration on one end and the 568B configuration on the other.

How to cut and crimp RJ-45 connectors

Although you can buy premade cables up to 25 feet (7.62 m) in length with guaranteed connectivity from manufacturers such as Belkin (*www.belkin.com*), you might find it worth your while to make your own cable under the following circumstances:

- You require lengths of cable longer than 25 feet (7.62 m).
- It is more economically feasible to purchase cable-making materials in bulk than premade cables.
- You want to create both standard and crossover cables.
- You want to choose your own color cable, useful for identifying cable runs to various parts of the building.

(Many organizations choose orange cable to uniquely identify crossover cables.)

To make your own cable, you will need the following materials:

- *Modular plug crimp tool*—These pliers allow you to crimp the connector onto the cable (see Exhibit 4-29) and often include sharp blades for stripping the jacket and insulation from cable.

Exhibit 4-29: Most crimp tools include strippers and can crimp four to eight wires

- *Universal UTP stripping tool*—This optional tool is useful if you strip a lot of cable; it strips both round and flat cable (see Exhibit 4-30).

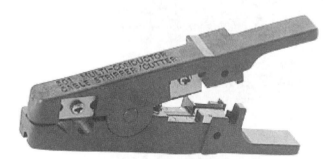

Exhibit 4-30: A universal UTP stripping tool

- *Diagonal cutters*—Use "diags" to cut cable off of the reel and to evenly trim pair ends during cable assembly (see Exhibit 4-31).

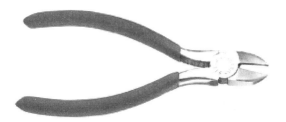

Exhibit 4-31: Diagonal cutters neatly cut and trim cable

- *Spooled cable*—UTP bulk cable is wound onto a spool inside a box (see Exhibit 4-32), and many manufacturers include an outlet from which to pull cable. There may also be a metering device so that you can measure the amount of cable pulled.

Exhibit 4-32: Spooled cable feeds through an outlet

- *Snagless boots*—Optionally, add a snagless boot to prevent the clip on RJ-45 cable from overextending and snapping off, which is a common problem when handling Cat 5 cable.

Cut and crimp your network cable as follows:

1   Pull the amount of cable you require. Cable is relatively inexpensive, so consider overestimating—too little cable requires you to start over, but seldom do you have too much.

2   Use the diags to cleanly cut the cable.

3   If you want to use snagless boots, thread two (one for each end) onto the cable. Make sure they are a few inches away from where you will crimp the ends to keep them out of the way.

4   Using the stripper or crimper, strip about an inch of the outer jacket off the end of the cable. Be careful not to cut into the insulation of the pairs inside. Although you can use the diags or some other tool to do the same task, you'll like the neatness of a stripper/crimper. Insert the end under the blade, lightly squeeze the crimper, and twist. This action cuts the outer jacket, which should then easily pull off.

5   Separate each of the four wire pairs and straighten them into the wiring order you choose (refer to Exhibit 4-27).

6   Evenly snip the end of the wires using the diags to expose a half inch of the wire pairs. (Originally, we cut one inch off of the jacket, but that was just to make handling the small wire pairs easier.) This should allow you to insert the wire pairs all the way into the end of the RJ-45 connector without leaving too much untwisted wire, which would cause crosstalk signaling problems. Also, half-inch exposure positions the jacketed portion of the cable under a plastic plug or wedge that clamps down onto the jacket. (Some sources recommend stripping the end of each individual wire, which is completely unnecessary and extremely time-consuming, as the crimper forces connection pins to pierce the insulation, making a solid connection.)

7   Insert the wire ends all the way into the RJ-45 jack—be careful not to get the wires crossed or bent. Once you get the wires into their respective grooves in the jack, the rest is easy.

8   Confirm that the wiring order is correct.

9   Hold the cable (not the plug) and insert the plug into the crimper tool. If the crimper tool has plugs for multiple connectors, look for the one marked "8P."

10 Squeeze the crimper around the connector. Most crimpers are ratcheted so that the crimpers hold their place if you lose or need to readjust your grip partway through. The crimper includes two plungers that attach the connector (see Exhibit 4-33). The leftmost plunger depresses a plug or wedge onto the jacket to prevent strain from dislodging the connector. The second plunger depresses a two-pronged metal pin into each wire, creating the actual connection.

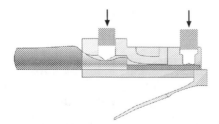

Exhibit 4-33: Two plungers attach the connector to the cable

11 Inspect the cable with the RJ-45 clip facing away from you. You should be able to see the wiring order through the clear plastic, as seen in Exhibit 4-34. If it's wrong, just use the diags to snip off the connector and start over again. (And don't feel bad—everybody goofs a plug sooner or later.) Also, give it a gentle tug; the connector shouldn't budge.

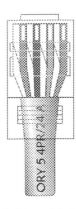

Exhibit 4-34: Inspect the wiring order

12 Repeat all steps for the other end of the cable.

13 Finally, if you included snagless boots, push them over the connectors.

10BaseT

The 10BaseT standard (also called twisted-pair Ethernet) uses a twisted-pair cable (such as Cat 5) with maximum lengths of 100 meters (328.08 feet). The cable is thinner and more flexible than the coaxial cable used for the 10Base5 or 10Base2 standards. If you were cabling for a 10BaseT network, the use of two pairs of Cat 3 wires would be sufficient; however, Cat 5 is a better choice in new implementations for purposes of signal quality and future upgrades.

100BaseT

The committee responsible for 100BaseT kept the 100 Mbps Ethernet standard as close to the original Ethernet definition as possible. Therefore, 100BaseT utilizes the Carrier Sense Multiple Access with Collision Detection (CSMA/CD) shared-media access method supported in earlier versions of Ethernet. The simplicity of this media access method might make it attractive to companies using traditional Ethernet. Because it is 10 times faster than Ethernet, it is often referred to as Fast Ethernet. Officially, the 100BaseT standard is called IEEE 802.3u. There are several different cabling schemes that can be used with 100BaseT, including the following:

- *100BaseT4* uses an extra two wires (four pairs) of normal-quality twisted-pair wires for use with Cat 3 UTP cable.

- *100BaseTX* Fast Ethernet uses two pairs of high-quality twisted-pair wires for use with Cat 5 UTP cable. The 100BaseTX standard has become the most popular due to its close compatibility with the 10BaseT Ethernet standard.

- *100BaseFX* is used with fiber optic cable that, for the most part, connects hubs and switches either between wiring closets or between buildings. 100BaseFX uses multimode fiber optic cable to transport Fast Ethernet traffic.

Fiber optic cabling

Fiber optic cable employs a technology that uses glass (or plastic) threads (fibers) to transmit data using light pulses from one end of the cable to the other. A fiber optic cable consists of a core of glass threads, each of which is capable of transmitting light pulses. A cladding surrounds the fibers, mirroring light back into the core. Plastic and braided Kevlar form the protective jacket (see Exhibit 4-35). The receiving end of the message converts the light signal to binary values. The maximum length is 25 km (15.5 miles) with speeds up to 2 Gbps. Fiber optics is not a particularly popular technology for workstations because it is so expensive. However, it is often used for a network backbone. Fiber cabling has been deployed as the primary media for campus and building backbones, offering high-speed connections between diverse LAN segments. Today, with progressively more complicated applications such as high-speed ISPs and e-commerce, optical fiber may soon become the primary media providing data to the desktop. Fiber has the largest bandwidth of any media available. It can transmit signals over the longest distance at the lowest cost, with the fewest repeaters and the least amount of repairs.

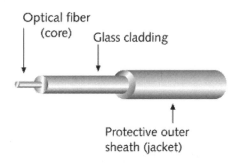

Exhibit 4-35: Fiber optic cable

Following are advantages of fiber optics:

- Fiber optic cables have a much greater bandwidth than metal cables to carry more data.
- Fiber optic cables are less susceptible to interference than metal cables.
- Fiber optic cables are much thinner and lighter than metal wires.
- Data can be transmitted digitally rather than in analog format.
- Fiber is immune to EMI and radio frequency interference (RFI). Because it does not conduct electricity, fiber optic cable can also be useful in areas where large amounts of EMI are present, such as on a factory floor.
- There are no crosstalk issues.
- Fiber is impervious to lightning strikes and does not conduct electricity or support ground loops.
- Fiber-based network segments can be extended 20 times farther than copper segments.
- Fiber cable cannot be tapped, so it's very secure.
- Fiber transmission systems are highly reliable.

Despite the numerous advantages of fiber, the cables are expensive to install, are more fragile than wire, and are difficult to split.

Do it!

C-1: Discussing network cabling

Questions and answers

1 How is a crossover cable different from a straight-through cable?

2 What is the most common type of network cable in use today?

3 With all of its advantages, why isn't fiber optic cable used more frequently?

Unit summary: Server power and rack installation

Topic A

In this topic, you learned that a **power supply unit** is a necessary piece of hardware in any server room, and a server can usually operate acceptably with only a single PSU; however, a second PSU provides load balancing to reduce demands placed on a single PSU and also provides **failover**, in case one of the power supplies fails.

Topic B

In this topic you discovered that racks provide an advantage in server rooms where the need for server and network equipment grows but floor space does not. You learned that by stacking equipment in a rack, you increase computing assets vertically in the same floor space that would have otherwise consumed precious floor space, and this space savings is known as **density**.

Topic C

In this topic, you learned that there are many different types and categories for cabling solutions. **Thinnet** is based on the 10Base2 standard (10 Mbps/Baseband transmission) that utilizes RG-58 A/U or RG-58 C/U 50 ohm coaxial cable with maximum segment lengths of 185 meters (606.9 feet). **Shielded twisted-pair** (**STP**) cable involves two copper wires, each encased in its own color-coded insulation, which are twisted together to form a "twisted pair." **Unshielded twisted-pair** (**UTP**) cable uses RJ-45 connectors. UTP has a maximum length of 100 meters (328.08 feet) and can support speeds up to 100Mps. **Fiber optic cable** employs a technology that uses glass (or plastic) threads (fibers) to transmit data using light pulses from one end of the cable to the other.

Independent practice activity

In this activity, you will research blade servers.

1 Open your Web Browser.

2 Look up "blade server" in a major search engine such as Google. Alternately, you can go directly to web sites of manufacturers like IBM, Intel, and Sun.

3 Read about and compare two or three blade server chassis.

4 Answer the following questions:

What models did you research?

Is the system designed for a specific use?

How many blades can the chassis hold?

What types of blades does it take (number of processors, platform, etc.)?

What hardware components does the chassis provide?

What software is provided to manage the servers and chassis, and what are some of its features?

5 Write down any other notable features of the hardware and software.

Review questions

1 Which of the following power supply wattages is likely to be found in a server?

   A 145W

   B 200W

   C 250W

   D 375W

2 How is the physical connection of a non-hot-swappable power supply different from a hot swappable power supply? Choose two answers.

   A You must remove individual power connectors

   B You must remove the server case cover

   C The PSU plugs directly into the chassis without individual cable connections.

   D The wattage is much higher.

3 What is N+1 redundancy?

   A It is a measure of the number of functioning hard disks + 1 hot spare hard disk

   B N refers to the quantity of a given component and +1 refers to a spare.

   C It is a modem command that dials without waiting for a dial tone.

   D It refers to the number of processors +1 redundant processor.

4 What might prevent you from turning on an entire rack of equipment at once?

   A Nothing, as long as a UPS is attached

   B A UPS with too low a capacity

   C Inrush power

   D A UPS with too low a runtime

5 How many amps might a PCI slot use (in amps)?

   A 2

   B 3

   C 4

   D 5

6 What is the load equipment?

   A Anything connected to the UPS that draws power.

   B Relatively heavy rack equipment

   C Any device requiring more than 1 amp

   D UPS batteries

7 What is the purpose of a UPS?

    A To provide extended runtime in event of a power failure

    B To allow the server to go into a low power, energy saving state

    C To conserve electricity

    D To provide enough power for a graceful shutdown

8 What is the advantage of the on-line/double conversion UPS?

    A No switchover time

    B Reduced energy efficiency

    C Low cost

    D Only converts DC current to AC during a blackout or brownout

9 How does the UPS trigger the UPS software to perform actions when power fails?

    A Using a USB or serial port to communicate with the software

    B Nothing. The software detects dips in power or blackouts by itself.

    C Infrared signals

    D A directed send through the network

10 What good is N+1 redundancy with a UPS?

    A Provides additional runtime in event of a power failure

    B If a UPS fails, the other continues to provide power redundancy

    C Provides additional power capacity

    D N+1 is not a UPS function

11 Where in the rack should you usually place UPS equipment?

    A At the top

    B In the middle

    C It doesn't matter

    D At the bottom

12 Where are you likely to install additional fans in the rack?

    A In one of the side panels

    B In the bottom panel above the floor

    C In the top panel

    D In the back of the server

13 What is a primary advantage of a rack?

   A Increased density

   B Less heat buildup

   C Quieter operation because of the doors

   D Better organization of equipment

14 How big is 1U?

   A It varies depending on the rack manufacturer

   B 1.75 inches (4.45 cm)

   C 2.4 inches (6.07 cm)

   D 1.57 inches (3.99 cm)

15 How much total approximate weight can a full height rack accommodate?

   A 2000 lbs

   B 1000 lbs

   C Limited only by floor support

   D Virtually unlimited

16 Where should you generally place the heaviest items in the rack?

   A Top

   B Middle

   C Bottom

   D It doesn't matter as long as overall balance is good

17 What helps to manage cables in the rack?

   A Cable management arms

   B Zip ties

   C Duct tape

   D The PDU

18 What is the purpose of a KVM?

   A To use a single console to control multiple computers

   B To use multiple consoles to control a single computer

   C To shorten the cable length of I/O devices

   D To use multi-monitor capabilities of Windows 2000

19 How does a PDU differ from a standard power strip

    A The number of outlets

    B The power capacity is higher

    C The power capacity is lower

    D No difference

20 What is the purpose of ballast?

    A To add weight near the top of the rack

    B To add weight to the side of a rack

    C To fill empty spaces in the front of the rack

    D To add weight near to bottom of the rack

21 A crossover cable:

    A Uses the same wiring order on both ends

    B Uses exactly the opposite wiring order on both ends

    C Connects a computer to a hub

    D Reverses orange and green pairs

22 What is the most common type of network cable in use today?

    A Thinnet

    B Cat 3

    C Cat 4

    D Cat 5

Unit 5

Server upgrades

Unit time: 90 minutes

Complete this unit, and you'll know how to:

A Prepare for a server upgrade, verify availability of system resources, and adequately test and pilot the server upgrade.

B Upgrade the processor and memory.

C Upgrade the BIOS, power supply, UPS, and adapters.

Topic A: Preparing for a server upgrade

This topic covers the following CompTIA Server+ exam objectives:

#	Objective
4.2	Add processors

- Activities include:
    - Perform OS upgrade to support multiprocessors
    - Perform upgrade checklist, including:
        - Review FAQs, instruction, facts and issues
        - Test and pilot
        - Schedule downtime
        - Confirm that upgrade has been recognized
        - Review and baseline

4.3 Add hard drives

- Activities include:
    - Perform upgrade checklist, including:
        - Review FAQs, instruction, facts and issues
        - Test and pilot
        - Schedule downtime
        - Confirm that the upgrade has been recognized
        - Review and baseline

4.4 Increase memory

- Activities include:
    - Verify hardware and OS support for capacity increase
    - Perform upgrade checklist including:
        - Review FAQs, instruction, facts and issues
        - Test and pilot
        - Schedule downtime
        - Confirm that the upgrade has been recognized
        - Review and baseline

4.5 Upgrade BIOS/firmware

- Activities include:
    - Perform upgrade checklist including:
        - Review FAQs, instruction, facts and issues
        - Test and pilot
        - Schedule downtime
        - Confirm that the upgrade has been recognized
        - Review and baseline

#	Objective

4.6   Upgrade adapters (e.g. NICs, SCSI cards, RAID, etc). Activities include:

- Perform upgrade checklist including:
  - Review FAQs, instruction, facts and issues
  - Test and pilot
  - Schedule downtime
  - Confirm that the upgrade has been recognized
  - Review and baseline

4.7   Upgrade peripheral devices, internal and external. Verify appropriate system resources (e.g. expansion slots, IRQ, DMA, etc.)

- Resources include:
  - IRQ
  - DMA
- Activities include:
  - Perform upgrade checklist including:
    - Review FAQs, instruction, facts and issues
    - Test and pilot
    - Schedule downtime
    - Confirm that the upgrade has been recognized
    - Review and baseline

4.8   Upgrade system monitoring agents. Activities include:

- Perform upgrade checklist including:
  - Review FAQs, instruction, facts and issues
  - Test and pilot
  - Schedule downtime
  - Confirm that the upgrade has been recognized
  - Review and baseline

4.9   Upgrade service tools (e.g. diagnostic tools, EISA configuration, diagnostic partition, SSU, etc.) Activities include:

- Perform upgrade checklist including:
  - Review FAQs, instruction, facts and issues
  - Test and pilot
  - Schedule downtime
  - Confirm that the upgrade has been recognized
  - Review and baseline

4.10   Upgrade UPS. Activities include:

- Perform upgrade checklist including:
  - Review FAQs, instruction, facts and issues
  - Test and pilot
  - Schedule downtime
  - Confirm that the upgrade has been recognized
  - Review and baseline

When to upgrade the server

On a simple level, an administrator might perform an upgrade in just minutes without notifying anyone. For example, perhaps a server just needs more memory costing less than $200. In many organizations, administrators have discretionary spending for smaller amounts, and it should only take a few minutes to shut down, install the memory, and restart the server. However, upgrading a server can require a significant investment in time, planning, and money—especially for larger upgrades that noticeably impact the operations of the IT department, users, or your business audience.

For example, if an organization primarily employs eight NetWare 3.12 servers and would like to upgrade the servers to Windows Server 2003, it is likely that the new system will need significantly more powerful hardware, as the minimum system requirements for NetWare 3.12 are much lower than for Windows 2003. (Granted, this is a drastic upgrade, but it makes very clear the effect that an upgrade can have on a network.) The organization will likely have to upgrade all major components, including the processors, memory, hard disks, and possibly even the motherboards. A mass migration and upgrade like this would probably be more cost-effective if the servers were replaced with new ones.

Moreover, this upgrade affects more than just how the IT department administers the servers—network resources for users might be located differently. Logon scripts mapping to NetWare printers won't work anymore, and users that have manually created shortcuts to network resources will no longer be able to access those resources. The impact of an upgrade this drastic would require significant planning, proper timing, a smoothly executed upgrade process, adequate personnel, and plenty of communications with the users notifying them of the upgrade and its impact on their day-to-day functions.

Many times, upgrading the server is a necessary step in response to poor server performance. To fully justify expenditures in time and money, you should create a performance *baseline* so that you can define an acceptable level of performance. If you see that the server begins to perform poorly on a regular basis when compared to the baseline, consider upgrading components that might be a bottleneck. For example, a heavily utilized database server will have higher demands placed on the processor than a simple file server. Upgrading or adding another processor might help the system to perform better.

Before upgrading a server component, pause to verify identification of the actual bottleneck. For example, a server that shows heavy hard disk utilization might not need a larger or faster hard disk. Instead, first check memory utilization. Most NOSs utilize a swap file mechanism that substitutes hard disk space for memory in a low memory situation. Therefore, heavy hard disk utilization could actually be a memory issue that would be minimized with a memory upgrade.

You might take that same database server and consider upgrading it not only to an acceptable level of performance, but beyond current needs in a proactive approach to extend the server investment. This might prevent the repeated expense of upgrading again in a few months as demand on the server grows. For example, if the database server has one 700 MHz Pentium Xeon processor now, you might consider installing two 1 GHz processors, if the motherboard supports it. A proactive upgrade like this is sometimes also in anticipation of financial timing. For example, if the department does not use its entire budget in a given time, the next budget allocation might shrink because of a perception that the department does not need as large a budget since it didn't spend the entire budget last time. Although this kind of budgeting model has obvious weaknesses in logic and wisdom, it is nevertheless a reality in many organizations.

Other reasons for a proactive approach might include the anticipation of an upcoming merger with a new parent company. Perhaps your current intranet is for general information only and does not have a high hit rate. However, the new parent company requires you to post a great deal of company information on the intranet, such as details on employee benefits, company announcements, Web-based collaboration software, and so forth. In this case, you might consider several upgrades, including adding another NIC to the server, to increase network throughput in anticipation of a higher hit rate.

Timing the upgrade

Generally, the IT professional tries to keep as low a profile as possible within his or her organization. Why? Because when the administrator has a high profile, it's usually because something is wrong with a server or the network, and users tend to immediately think of administrators as having caused the problem. When users don't notice your presence in the organization, it usually means you are doing your job well. An ill-timed server upgrade (or scheduled maintenance) can give the administrator a very high profile; therefore, you should make sure that days or weeks before the upgrade, you monitor server utilization to determine periods of peak usage and periods of lowest usage. Of course, you want to perform any upgrades that make the server unavailable only during periods of low usage. If your organization is most active during business hours, you can stay late or arrive early to perform your upgrades while nobody else wants to access server resources. However, many organizations, especially larger ones, operate continuously. In addition, if the organization is global, users on one side of the globe might access resources while users on the other side of the globe are sleeping. This type of continuous access means that some types of upgrades will definitely take place while some users are attempting to gain access to resources. If the server must be taken offline, you can either temporarily transfer the role of server to another server or you can notify users in advance so they don't expect access during the time of the upgrade. Some upgrades (such as adding a disk to an array) might not require any downtime, and users will never notice the difference. On the other hand, upgrades such as adding processors or memory require the server to be turned off, and you should schedule an appropriate time and notify users in advance.

Notifying users

Notifying users of a server upgrade helps to reduce the administrator's visibility and avoid unnecessary calls to the IT department. Even if you try to upgrade the server during the lowest usage periods, someone will still wonder why the server is unavailable, so the notification should help. Also, a public advance notice such as an e-mail broadcast shows that you made a reasonable effort to notify users.

Broadcast company e-mail is a common notification method, as are notices on the company Internet or intranet. Start notification as far in advance as is practical, which will vary from one organization to the next. (Some well-organized organizations have a written administrative policy for planned downtime notification.) An initial notification far in advance is recommended; and then as the upgrade approaches, notify a few more times with increasing frequency up until the actual upgrade event.

Notify the users when the server will be unavailable and for how long. If possible, also state how the planned downtime benefits the user. This helps to psychologically cushion the inconvenience for users when they understand it is ultimately for their benefit. For example, most users would be grateful if you were to add more storage to the e-mail server so they could store more messages.

When a server goes offline unexpectedly and not as a result of upgrades or maintenance, you should attempt to send out a message to all users to stem the certain flood of calls about the inaccessible server.

Try to maximize the upgrade process so that other tasks can be completed in the same approximate time without increasing the impact on user access. For example, any time you want to work inside the server case, you might as well get a vacuum or a can of compressed air and eliminate the dust. Since that's probably also a regularly scheduled maintenance item, doing it now saves the separate task of doing it later.

Confirm that you have necessary upgrade components

Avoid unproductive downtime during an upgrade by confirming that all the necessary components for a successful upgrade are accounted for. For example, some hardware might not respond appropriately to the operating system without the proper BIOS upgrade, so you need both the BIOS upgrade and the hardware itself. When you perform an upgrade, be careful about the drivers that come with the hardware. (A *driver* is a software interface that allows the hardware to function with the operating system.)

You do not know how long the device has been on the shelf, and the drivers might be outdated. Save yourself the task of time-consuming troubleshooting after the upgrade that might occur due to an outdated or incompatible driver. After checking to see if the device is compatible with the other hardware and network operating system (NOS), download the most recent driver from the vendor's Web site. While you're there, check the FAQ section to address and prepare for any issues you might encounter during the upgrade.

Download and expand the drivers into a permanent network directory from which you install the drivers. You might need to reinstall the drivers from time to time, and many NOSs default to installing drivers from the original installation path. Also, the drivers are immediately available to other servers on which you perform the same upgrade. Make sure you dedicate each directory to only a specific vendor and a specific device, because driver files might have the same name (especially from the same vendor) and you might accidentally overwrite files.

Similarly, check with the NOS vendor to see if there are known problems with the particular device and/or driver you want to install. A Readme.txt file often accompanies drivers and updates. Although this file is usually a statement of obvious information ("this driver upgrades your network card"), it might also contain important information ("this update only applies to Windows 2000"). Many administrators ignore this little file, but at the very least, you should scan it for any red flags or installation tips. The NOS Web site often informs you of incompatible devices and provides solutions. Often, the solution is to avoid specific conflicting hardware devices or to install a NOS upgrade, patch, or hot fix. If the NOS vendor's support team does not list any known problems, check with other sources, such as newsgroups focused on the specific hardware and/or NOS vendors.

The level of precaution recommended in these pre-upgrade tasks might seem overly cautious. If you were performing a simple upgrade on a home PC, it might be. However, because of the impact the server has on an organization, every precaution is necessary.

Planning for a failure

Anybody who has administered computers for more than a few weeks knows that even the most meticulous and professional upgrade attempt sometimes encounters unanticipated problems, conflicts, or incompatibilities. In preparing for this possible contingency, administrators should prepare adequate failsafe measures to quickly recover from the problem or continue service to users through redundancy while troubleshooting the failed upgrade.

Always back up the server before performing any hardware or software upgrades. Do not depend upon the normally scheduled backup rotation, because if a problem occurs, the backup can be slightly outdated. For example, most backups take place in the middle of the night, but if you perform the upgrade after everyone leaves work but before the backup, then one day's working data is in jeopardy if a problem occurs. Instead, take the server off the network so that new data cannot be written to it. Next, perform a full backup of at least the data, and possibly also the operating system. Now you have a snapshot of the system before the upgrade, and if necessary, a restore should replace the data intact.

Consider using imaging software such as PowerQuest DriveImage or Norton Ghost. This exactly duplicates the hard disk to a single image file for restore should a problem occur. You can store the image on a network share or one or more CD-ROMs, and protect it with a password in case the CD-ROM falls into unauthorized hands. Alternatively, many network cards are now bootable, allowing you to access the network and restore the image to the server from the network share. If you have to restore the image, it is much faster than reinstalling the operating system, reinstalling all of the server applications, and then restoring the data from a conventional backup.

In addition to creating a backup, other failsafe methods can also ensure server availability. For example, recall that clustering is utilization of two or more servers hosting the same application. If one of the servers is unavailable (as might occur during an upgrade), the remaining servers in the cluster continue to provide service. With a mission-critical server or application, you probably already have clustering enabled.

Absent a cluster, administrators might have a *hot spare*, which is a specific component (usually a hard drive) or a complete server that can immediately be available on the network and transparently perform the exact same functions as the original.

Verifying system resources

You never seem to have enough PCI slots for the devices you want to install in a server. While you might have a free ISA slot, you probably don't care because fewer devices are ISA compatible. However, PCI slots represent valuable slot real estate that quickly fills up. In a typical server, you probably have five PCI slots. Account for two network cards for better throughput and availability, a SCSI card for tape devices, and another for hard disks, and you're almost out of expansion slots already. If so equipped, you can add a mezzanine or riser board to the motherboard to expand the number of available slots. Whatever the case, in larger environments the administrator probably does not know offhand exactly how many expansion slots remain in each server. Before making plans to add a device, verify that sufficient slots are available.

Even if a slot is available, you might encounter issues with available IRQs, DMAs, or I/O ports. These are each limited resources that most devices require to communicate with the operating system and other devices, and they are defined as follows:

- An *interrupt request* (*IRQ*) is a request that the device uses to "interrupt" the processor to ask for processor resources. There are 16 IRQs, numbered 0–15. Several IRQs are preassigned. For example, the COM1 serial port usually has IRQ 4. PCI IRQ steering can allow multiple devices to use the same IRQ if no more unique IRQs are available. However, ISA devices cannot take advantage of this benefit.

- A *Direct Memory Address* (*DMA*) is a resource that ISA devices use to directly access memory without first having to access the processor, both increasing device performance and reducing processor load. There are eight DMA channels, numbered 0–7.

- An *I/O port* is a location in memory that the processor uses to communicate with a device.

- A *memory address* is a dedicated region in system memory that some devices reserve and that is unavailable for use by any other device, application, or the operating system. This can help device stability by ensuring that nothing else trespasses the memory, which causes system errors.

If you are out of IRQs and IRQ steering is not available, or if you are out of available DMAs, then you must remove (or disable) an existing device that requires those same resources, or you cannot upgrade the server. I/O ports are usually plentiful, and if two devices request the same I/O port, you can usually reassign one of them to an alternate port.

Depending upon the chassis and power supply, you might not have sufficient expansion space to add more hard disks, tape drives, or removable storage such as Zip drives, CD-ROMs, or DVD devices, all of which require a drive bay, either internal or external. Drives installed in an internal drive bay are neither accessible nor visible when the case is attached. Most commonly, you install hard disks internally. It would be impractical to install removable storage or CD-ROM/DVD drives internally, so you want to use an external drive opening, which means that you can access and see the drive. Besides drive bay availability, you need a power supply that can handle the additional power requirements of the devices and has sufficient power connectors for each drive. You can use a Y-cable split that converts a single power connector to two, but if you're using several of these, you might be overloading the power supply. Generally, the more powerful the power supply, the more power connectors it includes.

A standard desktop or entry-level server tower case has space for perhaps four internal drives and two or three external drives. A server has significantly more storage space. For example, the Compaq ProLiant 8000 has internal drive cages for 21 hot-plug hard disks. Regardless, verify available drive bays as necessary.

If you plan to install a large quantity of internal hard disks, consider adding one or more additional cooling fans to compensate for the additional heat.

Making an inventory

One of the most frustrating things about installing hardware is finding it. Even relatively small organizations quickly accumulate quite a few loose components, chips, hard disks, and so forth. When a server fails, you must know exactly where to find replacement parts, so you should carefully inventory (and lock up) all parts that have any value. Organize smaller loose parts in appropriately sized storage bins, trays, and cabinets. Having an inventory also helps you to control and be aware of possible theft.

In addition, you should know what equipment is in each server for proper asset tracking, budgetary projections, and warranty service. Especially in large environments, manual inventory of installed hardware is an arduous and seemingly endless task, further complicated when there are multiple sites. You might want to procure software that can automatically scan your entire network to inventory not only installed hardware in your servers and clients, but also installed software. Some programs can also identify network devices such as hubs, routers, switches, and so forth. One of the most popular programs is Microsoft Systems Management Server, for which you can find detailed inventory instructions at www.microsoft.com/technet/SMS/c0318341.asp or perform a search for the title "Administering Inventory Collection." Also check into the following other vendors:

- Hewlett Packard's OpenView at www.openview.com
- IBM Tivoli at www.tivoli.com
- Computer Associates Unicenter TNG at www.cai.com

Note that all these products require hardware that is capable of responding to queries from the software. You can still manually inventory hardware that does not automatically respond to the software, but this is becoming less of an issue as more hardware is designed to be compatible with inventory software.

When receiving new equipment or equipment transferred from another office, always request that an inventory list be included with the shipment. This helps to ensure that equipment arrives as promised and that the server from the home office that has 512 MB RAM doesn't suddenly appear in your office with only 128 MB. Another reason for the inventory list is that it helps you in assembling the equipment. Many servers and their associated equipment involve dozens of parts, including zip ties, cable management systems, fans, screws, keys, books, warranty cards, power cords, and so forth. It is extremely frustrating to unpack and assemble an entire server and rack, only to find that you are missing a vital component that you would have known about had you compared the physical parts to an inventory list.

Test and pilot

The potential impact of some upgrades (both if they succeed and if they fail) might require an isolated *pilot program* in which you thoroughly test the upgrade for reliability and performance prior to deployment throughout the organization. A pilot program isolates a server upgrade in a portion of the network that makes performance easier to determine and lessens negative impact should some part of a major upgrade fail. Some organizations require a pilot program for nearly any hardware, operating system, or software change. However, pilot programs are not usually intended for common upgrade items such as installing a hard disk, network card, or memory. Most implementations might involve something like an upgraded NOS, an entirely new NOS (migrating from UNIX to NetWare 5.x, for example), or a change in hardware architecture (such as a change from UNIX-based Alpha architecture to Windows-based Intel architecture). If the upgrade works well in its initial pilot, you can extend the pilot programs to other segments of the network to see if the results are also successful under different circumstances. Finally, when the upgrade is fully tested and has satisfactorily passed the pilot phase, you can deploy the upgrade throughout the remainder of the organization as necessary. As an example for the current context, which focuses mostly on hardware, consider a pilot program for upgrades of the BIOS, motherboard, processor (especially if changing platforms from, say, AMD to Intel), and anything else you think might significantly impact the network if it fails or requires isolated analysis.

Once you successfully implement the upgrade changes, make sure that the improvement is more than just a perception. Start recording the performance of the server and/or network as it applies, and compare it to the previous baseline and performance prior to the upgrade. You should be able to find an improvement in the targeted upgrade area. For example, if you added another processor, you should see overall processor utilization drop to a lower percentage (where lower percentages equal better performance). After recording performance statistics, you should be able to change the baseline's level of acceptable performance. In most organizations, the baseline is a moving target that you periodically reset as server demands increase. If responsible parties (you and management) determine that network or server responsiveness no longer meets an acceptable range of performance, then a decision must be made: Either reset the baseline at the new level of performance or modify network or server equipment to return to the original (or better) level of baseline performance.

When confirming a successful upgrade, you can check for the obvious items such as proper functionality of the hardware. Don't forget, however, that most NOSs have logs that might also record errors in a problematic upgrade.

Be sure that after performing the upgrade, you record it to an easily accessible source for troubleshooting and asset-tracking purposes. Some organizations might have a log book next to the rack where changes are hand-written; others might have a computer-based log, such as a database or a spreadsheet, saved to an administrative network share. For many administrators, the latter is preferable because the log is accessible from any administrator's desktop. For example, in troubleshooting a server in Denver, an administrator in Phoenix can open the server log on a network share and see if any recent hardware upgrades might have caused a problem.

Do it!

A-1:   Discussing preparing for an upgrade

Questions and answers

1 When should you upgrade the server?

2 Why should you notify users of a planned upgrade?

3 What is an IRQ?

4 Why is a pilot program useful?

5 Before an upgrade, why would you perform a full backup instead of depending upon the normal tape rotation?

Topic B: Upgrading the processor and memory

This topic covers the following CompTIA Server+ exam objectives:

#	Objective

2.2	Install hardware using best practices
	
	• Hardware includes:
	   • Processors and power modules
	   • Memory
	   • Internal cable
	   • Internal fans

4.2	Add processors
	
	• Activities include:
	   • On single processor upgrade, verify compatibility
	   • Verify N+1 stepping
	   • Verify speed and cache matching
	   • Perform BIOS upgrade
	   • Perform OS upgrade to support multiprocessors
	   • Ensure proper ventilation
	   • Perform upgrade checklist, including:
	      • Implement ESD best practices
	• Supporting knowledge includes
	   • What it means to verify stepping

4.3	Add hard drives
	
	• Activities include:
	   • For ATA/IDE drives, confirm cabling, master/slave and potential cross-brand compatibility
	   • Perform upgrade checklist, including:
	      • Implement ESD best practices

4.4	Increase memory
	
	• Activities include:
	   • Verify memory is on hardware/vendor compatibility list
	   • Verify memory compatibility
	      • Speed
	      • Brand
	      • Capacity
	   • Perform upgrade checklist including:
	      • Implement ESD best practices

#	Objective
4.5	Upgrade BIOS/firmware
	• Activities include:
	• Perform upgrade checklist including:
	• Implement ESD best practices
4.6	Upgrade adapters (e.g. NICs, SCSI cards, RAID, etc)
	• Activities include:
	• Perform upgrade checklist including:
	• Implement ESD best practices
4.7	Upgrade peripheral devices, internal and external. Verify appropriate system resources (e.g. expansion slots, IRQ, DMA, etc.)
	• Activities include:
	• Perform upgrade checklist including:
	• Implement ESD best practices
4.8	Upgrade system monitoring agents
	• Activities include:
	• Perform upgrade checklist including:
	• Implement ESD best practices
4.9	Upgrade service tools (e.g. diagnostic tools, EISA configuration, diagnostic partition, SSU, etc.)
	• Service tools include:
	• System configuration utility
	• Activities include:
	• Perform upgrade checklist including:
	• Implement ESD best practices
4.10	Upgrade UPS
	• Activities include:
	• Perform upgrade checklist including:
	• Implement ESD best practices
6.2	Recognize and report on server room environment issues
	• Issues include:
	• ESD

Avoiding electrostatic discharge

Explanation

Before touching anything inside the server, it is critical to exercise precautions against *electrostatic discharge* (*ESD*). You have probably experienced ESD at no significant harm to yourself many times, particularly if you live in an area where winters are cold and the wind blows (Chicago, for example). Once you are in from the cold and touch a door handle (or pet the cat), an ESD occurs. ESD occurs when two objects with differing electrical potential come into contact with one another because the electrical charges seek to equalize. While you are outside in the cold wind, the energy from the wind can build up electrical potential in you. When you touch an object in the house with less electrical potential, static electricity discharges from you to that object. Although people are hearty enough to sustain a static shock, servers and their components are not. Before you touch a server for any reason, including component installation or inspection, you must be certain that you present no ESD threat.

Although it doesn't seem like much, if you can feel the static discharge, then you probably discharged around 3500 volts. If you also hear the discharge, then you probably discharged around 5000 volts, and if you see the discharge in a lighted room, then you probably discharged around 8000 volts. It is easy to build up this voltage—walking across the floor can generate 15,000 volts; removing bubble pack from a carton can generate as much as 26,000 volts. It only takes 100–1000 volts to negatively impact server components, and at lower levels you might not feel, hear, or see the discharge.

You might unknowingly damage a component with ESD in two ways. First, an upset failure affects only the reliability and/or performance of a component. This is perhaps the worst of the two types of damage because it is difficult to detect and consistently reproduce. (For example, it takes 200–3000 volts to damage a server's CMOS.) The second way ESD affects a component is a catastrophic failure, which immediately damages the component so that it ceases to function properly.

To prevent static discharge, implement ESD best practices as follows:

- *Touch the chassis*—This grounds you and equalizes the voltage levels between you and the server. This is not a sufficient precaution, however, because as you work, voltage can build up again, particularly if you are wearing leather soles on carpet. Touching the chassis is only a temporary, initial precaution. If you can't use a better method, like an ESD protection kit, touch the chassis periodically.

- *Unplug the power*—Many people assume that because the power cord is plugged into a grounded outlet, the case is protected against ESD. While it is true that the plug does lead to earth ground, that is not what is important in preventing ESD. What you are seeking is equalization in electrical potential. Plugged or unplugged, touching the chassis temporarily equalizes electrical potential. Moreover, it is safer to unplug the server. By leaving the server plugged in, you risk accidentally bumping the power switch. Installing or removing a device with the power on is catastrophic to most components (unless they are hot-swappable) and introduces the risk of system-wide electrical damage, not to mention the unpleasant surprise of receiving an electric shock. Also, many power supplies continue to supply low-voltage power to the motherboard, even when switched off. By implementing proper grounding measures and unplugging the server, you can avoid a potential mishap.

- *Use a grounding kit*—These come in several forms. At the lowest end, a portable grounding kit uses a wrist strap with an alligator clip that attaches to the server chassis as in Exhibit 5-1. (Be sure to attach it to an unpainted surface for best contact.) This has the same effect as touching the chassis to equalize electrical potential, except it is not temporary because the connection is constant.

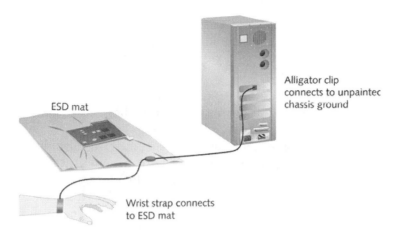

Alligator clip
connects to unpainted
chassis ground

ESD mat

Wrist strap connects
to ESD mat

Exhibit 5-1: A portable grounding kit and mat

A hardware repair bench normally includes a grounded floor mat (also called a map) that connects to earth ground at a nearby electrical outlet (this does not affect the operation of other devices plugged into that outlet). Another mat on the benchtop is also grounded—either to the floor mat or independently to another electrical outlet. The user wrist strap connects to either mat or the server chassis (see Exhibit 5-2). Because both mats, the wrist strap, and the chassis are all grounded, they possess the same electrical potential, eliminating the risk of ESD. The wrist strap usually includes a resistor designed to negate a high-voltage electrical charge, in case the technician accidentally touches a high-voltage item such as internal components in the power supply or the monitor. Both items retain high amounts of voltage even when unplugged. Full-time repair facilities normally ground the entire workbench.

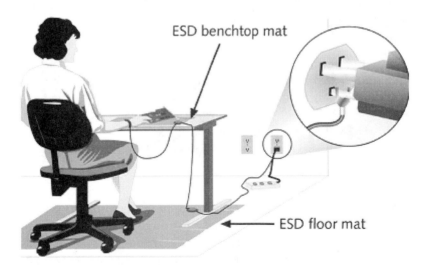

ESD benchtop mat

ESD floor mat

Exhibit 5-2: A workstation grounding kit

For more information on specific grounding kits, refer to the following Web sites (also see www.3m.com/ehpd/esd_training for more about ESD in general):

- Specialized Products Company at www.specialized.net
- 3M Corporation at www.3m.com/ehpd/workstation
- Jensen Tools at www.jensentools.com

Other tips for avoiding ESD include:

- *Take it to the mat*—As you install and remove components, be sure to place them on the mat. You might be tempted to place the computer itself on the mat, but that is unnecessary, provided you grounded it properly. Leave it off the mat so that you have some workspace.

- *Handle with care*—If you find yourself without ESD protection, be sure you handle loose adapter cards by the metal bracket that attaches to the chassis. The internal ground circuitry of the card is connected to the bracket, so touching the bracket prevents ESD from damaging the card components. If the device does not have a bracket (a motherboard, for example), handle it by the edges and try to avoid touching any of the items on the surface of the card. Do not touch the metal edge of the adapter that goes inside the expansion slot, because even minor soiling from oils in your hand can contribute to corrosion. Do not stack components.

- *Bag it*—Place loose components into ESD-resistant bags. Remove any other type of packing material, such as Styrofoam, bubble wrap, or cellophane, because they tend to build and hold a static charge.

- *Take off the jewelry*—Metal jewelry can conduct electricity. It is a good idea to remove any jewelry from your hands and wrists (watch, rings, bracelets) before working on the server. Also, jewelry can catch onto components and wiring and hinder your dexterity.

Now that you've made all the preparations for a server upgrade and have ensured that you are protected against ESD, you can proceed to upgrade server components.

Upgrading the processor

Before upgrading the processor, perform a few tasks to prevent serious problems or damage. Primarily, you want to verify that the BIOS and motherboard support the processor and, if using SMP, that the new processor is compatible with the existing processor.

Generally, it's a good idea to keep your BIOS version as up-to-date as possible—this unit addresses this issue later. Because the BIOS directly affects the communication between the processor and the rest of the system, the importance of BIOS compatibility is obvious. Besides keeping up-to-date, also access the BIOS settings and verify that it supports SMP. A PC server usually allows 4-way SMP unless a mezzanine board or other motherboard modification allows you to expand to 8-way or greater SMP.

Next, check the motherboard to see if the proposed processor is compatible. The form factor of a given processor might physically fit in several different motherboards, but that does not mean it is compatible. Recall that a processor operates at multiples of the bus speed. This is one of the factors that limits the available upgrade path in your server. For example, you cannot replace a 700 MHz Pentium III with a 900 MHz Pentium III. The 700 MHz Pentium III is designed to operate on a 100 MHz bus. However, the 900 MHz processor is designed to operate on a 133 MHz bus, which will not allow the processor to function properly on a 100 MHz bus. Also, a given chipset might not be compatible with the proposed processor. To determine the compatible processor upgrade path for the server, you could research the motherboard manufacturer's Web site. However, it is better to verify the upgrade path with the actual server vendor because they might have integrated something else into the system that affects upgrade compatibility.

Adding another processor to an existing processor involves more than simply making sure that both processors are the same speed. The processors should be identical in every way, including cache size, form factor, and stepping. For example, there are at least eight different 700 MHz Pentium III Xeon processors. While they all operate at 100 MHz, they vary in L2 cache size—either 1024 KB or 2048 KB—and the new processor cache must match the existing processor cache size. When adding another processor, verify that the new processor's *stepping* (the processor version) matches that of the existing processor. As Intel manufactures processors, minor problems, incompatibilities, or inaccuracies might be discovered from time to time. While the chances that these flaws will negatively affect server operation or compatibility are minimal, Intel usually corrects them when practical, so two processors of the same speed and cache still might not be exactly the same. You can also look on the processor to find its specification number (or *S-spec*)—an alphanumeric code that uniquely identifies each processor version and is more specific than the processor stepping. Exhibit 5-3 shows an S-spec (the last item on line 3, SL4MF). Notice also that the first line indicates 1000 MHz, 256 KB L2 cache, 133 MHz bus speed, and 1.7 V power.

Exhibit 5-3: The S-spec on this processor is SL4MF

Processor slots and sockets

The processor and its respective slot or socket appear in two primary formats. Sockets accommodate a processor format known as the *Pin Grid Array* (*PGA*) processor, which can be a flat, thin ceramic device with hundreds of gold pins on the bottom. These types of processors fit inside a motherboard socket receptacle that accepts each of the pins on the processor.

The most recent implementation is the *Staggered Pin Grid Array* (*SPGA*), which staggers the pin arrangement to squeeze more pins into the same space (see Exhibit 5-4). The PGA has two formats: standard PGA and the flipped chip PGA (FCPGA), referring to the fact that the processor die is "flipped" upside down on the die. The PGA format makes no difference in the actual installation except that FCPGA includes a fan in addition to the heat sink (described later in this section).

Exhibit 5-4: An SPGA processor

The slot format processor can be a larger device that stands upright inside a motherboard slot, similar to adapter or memory slots (see Exhibit 5-5). This format is called the *Single Edge Contact Cartridge* (*SECC*). The *Single Edge Contact Cartridge2* (*SECC2*) format is similar, except that it exposes the contacts at the bottom. The slot format processor includes a specially constructed plastic and metal housing that often includes an on-board cooling fan. Processor manufacturers have flip-flopped over the years regarding which format they use. Most processors use the socket format; however, Intel seems to favor the SECC slot format for the Xeon at this point. Whichever format is used, we'll consider the housing and CPU collectively to be the processor.

Exhibit 5-5: A Pentium III Xeon processor in the SECC format

The following table lists the types of sockets and slots in current use:

Socket or slot	Processor
Socket 370 (or PGA370)	Socket versions of the Intel Pentium III and Celeron
Socket 7 (or Super 7 when faster than 66 MHz)	Intel Pentium, Pentium MMX, AMD K5, K6, K6-2, K6-3
Socket 8	Pentium Pro
Socket A	AMD Duron and PGA format Athlon
Slot 1 (or SC-242)	Slot versions of the Intel Pentium III, Celeron, and Pentium II
Slot 2 (or SC-330)	Intel Pentium II and III Xeon
Slot A	AMD Athlon

Inserting the processor, either AMD or Intel, into a socket is an easy matter. Look carefully at the pins on the processor and match them to the socket on the motherboard. You will usually see a bevel that prevents you from accidentally inserting the processor in the wrong orientation. Simply match the bevel on the processor to the bevel on the socket. Before you insert the processor, lift up a lever next to the socket. The lever is the lock that holds the processor in place, and the feature is known as *zero insertion force* (*ZIF*) because when you insert the processor, gravity alone should be enough to seat the processor into the socket (see Exhibit 5-6). Sometimes you might have to help gravity a little bit, but very little pressure is required. If the processor does not seem to drop easily into the socket, do not force it. If you do, you may be buying another new processor.

Slots are keyed so that, again, you can only insert the processor in one orientation. However, be aware that it requires significantly more force to insert the processor into a slot, and the retention mechanism has guiding slots that facilitate this (see Exhibit 5-7). Use the retention mechanisms on either end of the processor to release it from the slot if you need to remove it later, but sometimes that can be a challenge as well. Most current processors require a slot.

Removing the slotted processor properly is a matter of experience and getting a feel for removing the processor, which is usually seated very firmly in the slot. You have to balance the objective of removing the processor with a prudent degree of restraint, and this might require some experience. A safer method is to procure a processor extraction tool. Flotron (www.flotron.com) makes such a tool (see Exhibit 5-8).

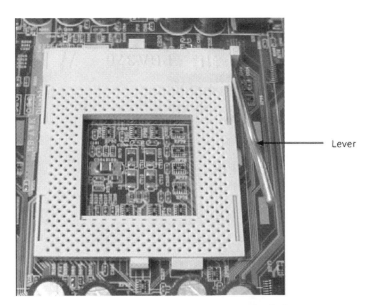

Lever

Exhibit 5-6: A ZIF socket uses a lever to lock the processor in place

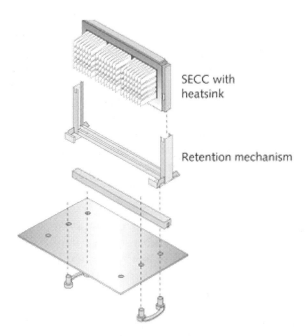

Exhibit 5-7: The slot and its retention mechanism

Exhibit 5-8: A processor extraction tool

Processor cooling

Processors can get very hot, and you must exercise care in cooling them properly using a heat sink—an attachment to the processor that either dissipates heat passively, through aluminum cooling fins, or actively, using a small cooling fan, usually in addition to cooling fins. When you purchase a "boxed" processor, it includes a cooling solution from the manufacturer. If it is "bare," then it has no cooling solution and you must determine a way to cool it yourself. Processors with only passive cooling depend upon airflow from the power supply and/or other cooling fans in the system. Use active cooling even when only passive is required and even if the boxed processor only includes passive cooling. (Other server components, particularly ribbon cables for hard drives, can block airflow. Be sure to route cables so as not to impede airflow.)

Socket processors usually have a fan mounted on top of the cooling fins. The short fan power cable is usually sufficient to reach the motherboard power connection for the CPU, and is often marked on the motherboard as "CPU FAN." Attaching this type of heat sink to the CPU (see Exhibit 5-9) typically uses a clip that you hook to a notch on one side of the socket. On the other side, you press down on the clip until it hooks onto the notch on the other side of the socket. Exhibit 5-9 shows the aluminum cooling fins, clip, fan, and thermal tape.

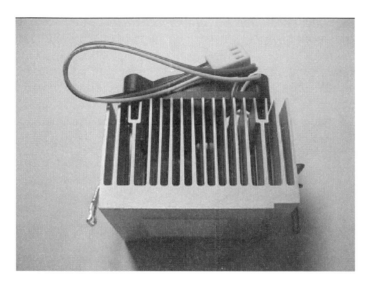

Exhibit 5-9: A heat sink

Exhibit 5-10 shows the installed heat sink, fan, and fan power connection to the motherboard. Inserting the heat sink might take considerable force; take care that the heat sink is oriented and aligned properly.

Exhibit 5-10: The installed heat sink, fan, and fan power connection

If you want to provide maximum cooling, you can buy third-party heat sinks and fans that are usually much larger than those that come from the manufacturer and provide even better cooling. Normally, these are no more than $50.

Processors that go into slots, such as the SECC for the Pentium II/III or the SECC2 for the Pentium III Xeon processor, use a similar cooling method to the socketed processors, except that the form factor is rectangular and larger to accommodate the larger slotted processors.

Most heat sinks include a small amount of thermal tape located at the contact point between the bottom of the heat sink and the surface of the processor. The purpose of the thermal tape is to act as a conductor through which heat is transferred from the processor to the heat sink. Otherwise, there would be a narrow gap of air between the processor and heat sink, and air by itself is not a good conductor. Many technicians prefer to apply inexpensive thermal grease instead. A small amount of grease fills the gap and draws away heat better than thermal tape.

Notifying the operating system

In Windows NT and Windows 2000/2003, you must notify the operating system of a change from one processor to multiple processors; otherwise, the operating system does not recognize or use the additional processor(s). The steps to make this change in Windows 2003 are as follows:

1   Click Start, then right-click My Computer and choose Manage.

2   Select Device Manager in the left tree pane.

3   Expand the Computer node in the right tree pane. The type of computer appears under Computer, such as ACPI multiprocessor PC.

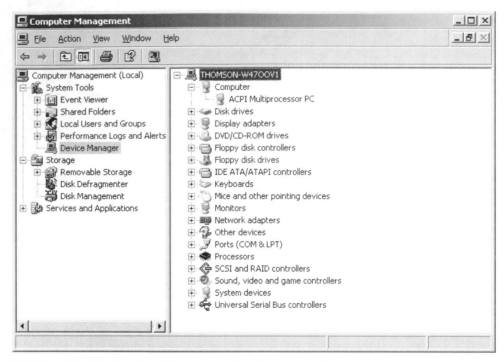

Exhibit 5-11: The Device Manager in the Computer Management console

4   Whichever type of computer appears, right-click it and choose Properties.

5   Click the Driver tab of the Properties sheet.

6   Click the Update Driver button.

7   Select Install from a list of specific location (Advanced). Click Next.

8   Select Don't search. I will choose the driver to install, and then click Next.

9   Check Show compatible hardware, if necessary.

10 Select the multiprocessor option that matches your computer, and proceed to the end of the wizard.

In current servers, it is uncommon to have to set a jumper to the correct voltage, CPU multiplier, and bus speed, but check documentation first, especially for Socket 7 or Super 7. If the voltage is set improperly, the processor might not function correctly or excessive voltage might damage the processor. Socket 370, Slot 1, Slot 2, and Slot A each adjust the voltage automatically. However, BIOS settings might be available to overclock the performance (not recommended for servers).

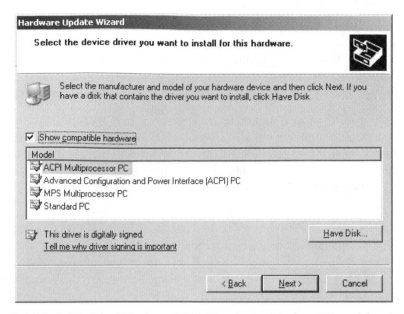

Exhibit 5-12: The Windows 2003 Hardware Update Wizard for the processor driver

Do it!

B-1:   Discussing ESD and processor upgrades

Questions and answers

1 Absent any grounding equipment, what can you do to protect against ESD?

2 Why should you keep your BIOS version updated?

3 What is a SECC?

4 Why are thermal tape or grease sometimes used during cooling fan installations?

Upgrading memory

Explanation

Memory module upgrades will usually be DIMMs. Fortunately, you cannot accidentally install the incorrect memory technology because the memory units have different installation notches, pin count, or length. For example, you cannot install a DIMM in an RDRAM slot. However, you will still need to verify that the memory you are upgrading is of the proper speed and matches other memory already installed in the system.

Technically, you can mix different speeds of memory, although it is not a good practice. For example, you can install 133 MHz SDRAM modules on a 100 MHz bus with existing 100 MHz modules. However, performance of all modules will be limited to 100 MHz. You cannot mix memory speed within a single SIMM memory bank.

Identifying memory

Identifying existing memory and the memory the motherboard supports is more time-consuming than actually placing the memory modules. Absent the documentation that came with the server, you can identify memory modules by reading the actual chips on the module, counting the chips, and measuring the length. You can read the numbers on the module's memory chips to determine the speed in nanoseconds (ns), which correlates to a manufactured speed. For example, if the number ends in –10, then you have 10 ns speed designed for a 66 MHz bus.

SDRAM speed in ns	SDRAM speed in MHz
15	PC66
10	PC66
8	PC100
7.5	PC133

Determine if an error correcting function such as parity or ECC is present in the module. There are several ways to verify this, but the simplest and most foolproof method is to count the number of chips on the module. If the number is evenly divisible by three, then you have either ECC or parity memory. For example, nine chips on the module is evenly divisible by three (9/3 = 3), identifying the module as ECC or parity. If the part number on each chip is the same, then you have ECC, which includes the error correcting function in each chip. If one of the chips has a different part number, then you have parity memory, because the chip that is different is solely responsible for the parity function on behalf of all the memory chips on the module.

Identify a 168-pin DIMM with two notches at the bottom, measuring 5.26 inches, or 133.8 mm (see Exhibit 5-13). The notches in the bottom are spaced slightly differently. The left notch spacing defines the module as registered, buffered, or unbuffered, and the right notch spacing defines the module voltage at 5.0 V or 3.3 V. Again, the notching makes it impossible to make a mistake with buffering or voltages when installing the modules.

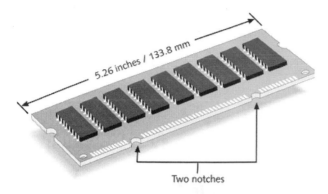

Exhibit 5-13: A 168-pin DIMM

The next generation of SDRAM, the 184-pin DDR DIMM, is an important memory module with which you should be familiar. High-end workstations and servers are increasingly requiring DDR SDRAM because of its extremely high throughput (up to 2656 MBps). You physically insert this module into the slot in the same way as the 168-pin DIMM; however, you can identify it with a single key notch at the bottom indicating its voltage (2.5 V) and with two notches on either end. The module is the same length as a standard SDRAM DIMM, measuring 5.256 inches, or 133.5 mm (see Exhibit 5-14).

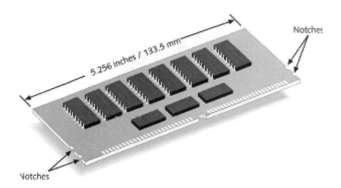

Exhibit 5-14: A 184-pin DDR SDRAM DIMM

Also look at the physical characteristics of the module. Recall that RDRAM RIMMs have identifiable metal heat spreaders covering the memory chips (see Exhibit 5-15). Another verification of RDRAM is if empty memory slots on the motherboard have a C-RIMM that completes the continuity, allowing memory data to pass through each slot.

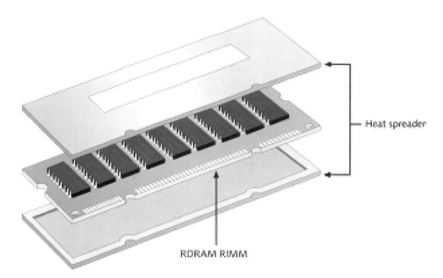

Exhibit 5-15: An RDRAM RIMM with heat spreaders pulled away

Installing memory

Installing memory is a straightforward matter. DIMMs have notching that prevents you from installing them in the wrong slots. The trick is to make sure that you have fully seated the memory into the slot. (Memory modules are particularly sensitive to ESD, so be sure to exercise appropriate precautions.)

DIMMs require 90-degree, straight downward insertion into the DIMM slot. Locking ejector tabs automatically clamp onto the module when the DIMM is fully seated, though you might also press them into place to verify proper locking (see Exhibit 5-16). To remove the DIMM, press down on top of both ejector tabs simultaneously, and the module should come out.

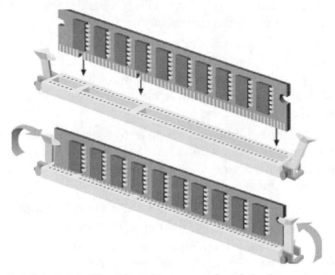

Exhibit 5-16: The DIMM is inserted with locking ejector tabs

Remember the following guidelines when installing memory:

- Match the manufacturer of existing memory when possible. Production variances are probably slight, but might produce an unacceptable risk in mission-critical servers. On desktop PCs, mixing manufacturers is a more acceptable risk.

- Try to plan server purchases with as few modules as possible to maximize future upgrade possibilities. For example, instead of two 64 MB DIMMs, install a single 128 MB DIMM.

- If the memory modules vary in size, install the largest modules (in megabytes) in the lowest numbered slot for best performance.

- Verify that the operating system is capable of recognizing the memory you install. For example, Windows NT 4.0 can utilize only 4 GB of memory regardless of motherboard capacity.

- Installing large quantities of memory (2–4 GB or more) might require special configuration of the NOS. Check with the vendor to verify. For example, Windows 2000 Advanced Server allows you to access large amounts of memory by adding the "/PAE" switch (enabling Physical Address Extension) to the Boot.ini bootup file.

- Large quantities of memory might also require specific hardware compatibility. For example, Windows 2000 Advanced Server can utilize PAE only with a Pentium Pro processor or later, 4 GB or more of RAM, and an Intel 450 NX or compatible chipset or later.

- Although the current motherboard and BIOS will automatically detect new memory, verify this in the BIOS to confirm proper seating of the memory.

- Most NOSs include a virtual memory feature that corresponds to the amount of physical memory installed in the system. When you increase the amount of physical memory, also increase the amount of virtual memory, which might be referred to as a swap file. However, in large memory implementations, it might be impractical to create a 4 GB swap file that matches 4 GB of physical memory. In this case, about 2 GB is usually acceptable.

Memory modules and sockets designed for low-cost appeal might use tin contacts. Many sources tell you to avoid mixing gold modules with tin sockets (and vice versa) because contact between the two creates an oxidization known as "fretting corrosion," affecting good electrical contact and possibly creating all kinds of instability and memory error problems. However, this issue is less of a problem than it used to be because tin contacts are rarely produced, especially for server platforms. All industry-standard DIMMs use gold contacts.

Do it!   **B-2:   Reseating memory**

Here's how

1 Open your computer's case and look at the memory module(s) installed on the motherboard. Using the information presented in this unit, identify what kind of memory it is; include information on parity, ECC, and speed where relevant.

2 Remove the memory module and reinstall it.

3 Start the PC. If the system does not POST, the module is not fully seated in the socket. Turn off the power and try again.

Topic C: Updating the BIOS, upgrading power supplies and adapters

This topic covers the following CompTIA Server+ exam objectives:

#	Objective
2.1	Conduct pre-installation planning activities. Supporting knowledge includes: • How to get drivers and BIOS updates
3.1	Check/upgrade BIOS/firmware levels (system board, RAID controller, hard drive, etc.)
4.2	Add processors. Activities include: • Perform BIOS upgrade
4.5	Upgrade BIOS/firmware. Supporting knowledge includes: • When the BIOS/firmware upgrades should be performed • How to obtain the latest firmware • Be aware the most hardware companies include self-installing installation applications for their components • Implications of a failed firmware upgrade • Multi-BIOS systems • Firmware recover options available • Backup flashing (when applicable) • Failed flash implies inoperable device • Issues surrounding multi-BIOS systems (how to properly upgrade, etc.) • Need to follow manufacturers flash instructions
4.10	Upgrade UPS • Activities include: • Firmware updates • Battery replacement • Battery disposal • Determine physical requirements • Determine load requirements • Verify whether UPS supports hot swap replacement • Supporting knowledge includes: • Some UPSs support shot swap battery replacement • Some UPSs support smart cabling • What can be upgraded • UPS MIBs • Management card • Management software

Obtaining and applying BIOS updates

Explanation

In years past, it was impossible to update the BIOS without first removing the BIOS, which might involve soldering tools. Current PCs and servers offer *flash BIOS*, which means you can download the most recent update from the vendor's Web site and apply it to the server without replacing the chip.

To keep on top of the most recent updates, consider checking with the server vendor to see if they offer a notification service that sends you an e-mail when a BIOS update (or other updates such as a driver) is available. Dell, for example, offers such a service.

Before updating the BIOS, read all available documentation about the update (a Readme.txt file usually accompanies the BIOS update). This is important to determine the purpose of the update and if it solves any problems you might be experiencing.

Update the BIOS as follows:

1   Download the BIOS update from the system vendor. Although major BIOS manufacturers such as Phoenix Software, Award Software, and American Megatrends Inc. (AMI) make most BIOS found in servers, you should not seek or use updates from the BIOS manufacturer. Server vendors work extensively to tailor a specific BIOS exactly for the server vendor's motherboard.

2   Execute the downloaded file. Typically, this will copy all necessary flash BIOS files to a blank floppy disk. Note: the boot disk should be as clean as possible. It should be a system disk containing only basic boot files (IOS.SYS, MSDOS.SYS, COMMAND.COM) but no memory management drivers such as HIMEM.SYS.

3   Record current CMOS settings. Most BIOS updates either automatically reset the CMOS for you or recommend that you manually reset the CMOS to default settings. You can use the recorded CMOS settings to reconfigure the CMOS to your preferences after the update is complete. (Instead of writing down each setting, consider using the Shift+PrtScn—Print Screen—keys to send the CMOS configuration screen to a locally attached printer. You will have to perform a manual form feed on laser printers to print the page.)

4   Boot from the flash BIOS disk. If the extracted files do not create a bootable system disk, use any DOS or Windows 9x system to first format the disk as a system disk.

5   The flash BIOS usually presents a list of options for what you want to do. Select the option to update the BIOS.

6   After the BIOS update is finished, manually reboot the computer if the updated BIOS does not do so automatically.

7   Upon reboot, access the CMOS settings and reset the values back to default. Otherwise, the system might not function correctly.

8   Reboot the server and again access the CMOS settings, entering in your preferred settings recorded in Step 3.

Recovering the BIOS

If the BIOS is corrupt, you cannot boot the system at all—not even with a valid flash BIOS disk. In fact, the display adapter is probably unavailable, further complicating matters. A corrupt BIOS can be caused by a number of things, including ESD to the BIOS EPROM, an interrupted flash BIOS update, or a virus. Regardless of what causes the corruption, the system cannot function until you repair the BIOS. While some systems might vary (specific instructions are probably in the documentation), the following are the usual steps to take in recovering the BIOS:

1 Turn off the system power.

2 Having removed the server cover, look for a motherboard jumper that allows you to enter recovery mode. Check motherboard documentation to find the jumper if it is not printed obviously on the motherboard.

3 Insert the latest flash BIOS update into the floppy drive.

4 Turn on the system power. A corrupt BIOS usually means that even the video display is not functioning, so you will have to listen to beep(s) to track what is taking place in the BIOS recovery:

   • The BIOS sounds a single beep when it passes control to DOS on the bootable flash BIOS floppy. DOS executes the Autoexec.bat file on the floppy, which in turn runs the flash BIOS update executable.

   • A single beep indicates commencement of the flash operation.

   • Two beeps indicate a recovered system BIOS.

   • Two more beeps indicate successful completion of the recovery.

   • A constant series of beeps indicates a failed recovery attempt.

   The recovery process usually takes between three to five minutes.

5 Remove the recovery diskette, and turn off server power.

6 Restore the motherboard jumper to its original position. (The server might have a read-only jumper position that prevents viruses from writing to the BIOS.)

7 Turn on the system power, and access the BIOS settings to enter your preferences.

After rebooting, a CMOS checksum error or some other problem might appear. Try to reboot again (by powering off and on) to see if that resolves the problem. If not, enter the CMOS setup utility to check and save settings. You can often resolve CMOS checksum errors by accessing CMOS settings, saving the settings, and then rebooting.

Upgrading a power supply

If you suspect a power supply is not performing reliably or to specifications, you can first verify this using a *digital multimeter (DMM)*. The DMM measures AC voltage, DC voltage, continuity, or electrical resistance (see Exhibit 5-17). In this section, we are mostly concerned with the DC voltage readings.

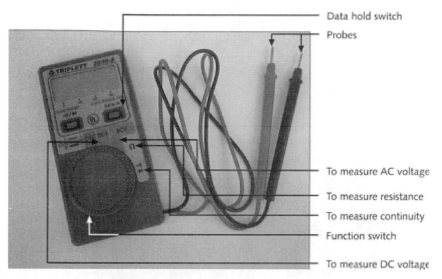

Exhibit 5-17: A digital multimeter

Memory parity check error messages are often an indicator of a problematic power supply. Recall that memory must be continually charged to retain its data. If the power to memory fluctuates, you are likely to lose data. If parity check messages consistently identify the same location in memory, then the problem is probably with a bad memory module. If the parity check messages are in different locations, then the problem is probably power-related.

Using a multimeter

A multimeter should help you clarify whether a power supply is operating within specifications. Although a multimeter can be analog (using a needle to show measurements), you should use a digital multimeter for best accuracy.

To check the operating voltage of a power supply using a DMM, use the following procedure:

1   Take the server cover off and power up the system.

2   The DMM has two probes: red and black. Find the power supply connector that connects to the motherboard, and locate the Power_Good pin (pin 8; third pin from the left on the unnotched side). Insert the red probe into the connector at pin 8 (see Exhibit 5-18). Inserting the probe alongside a live connection like this is known as *backprobing*.

Backprobe inserted in pin 8

Exhibit 5-18: Backprobing the ATX power supply connector

3   Touch the black probe to a ground, such as the chassis.

4   The DMM should read between +3 V and +6 V. If not, then the system cannot see the Power_Good signal and does not start or run correctly.

5   Repeat this process for other connectors (use the following tables as a reference). Connectors are in the +/-3.3 V, +/-5.0 V, and +/-12.0 V range. You should not see more than 10% variance from this range, and only 5% variance is acceptable for high-quality power supplies.

If the voltage readings are outside an acceptable range, replace the power supply.

If the DMM requires you to specify a maximum voltage range before testing equipment, set it at 20 V, because servers use +5 V or +12 V. Setting it too low might "peg the meter," overloading the DMM and possibly damaging it. Many higher-quality DMMs have autoranging capability to automatically determine the best setting.

Pin assignments for the ATX power connection		
Pin number*	**Color**	**Voltage**
1	Orange	+3.3 V
2	Orange	+3.3 V
3	Black	Ground
4	Red	+5 V
5	Black	Ground
6	Red	+5 V
7	Black	Ground
8	Gray	Power_Good
9	Purple	+5 VSB (Standby)
10	Yellow	+12 V
11	Orange (or Brown)	+3.3 V
12	Blue	-12 V
13	Black	Ground
14	Green	PS_On (power supply on)
15	Black	Ground
16	Black	Ground
17	Black	Ground
18	White	-5 V
19	Red	+5 V
20	Red	+5 V

*Pins 1-10 appear on the non-keyed side, and 11-20 on the keyed side.

Drive connections		
Pin number	**Color**	**Voltage**
1	Yellow	+12 V
2	Black	Ground
3	Black	Ground
4	Red	+5 V

Replacing the power supply

Wise server choices include redundant power supplies, so hopefully replacing a power supply, while urgent, does not involve downing the server. Many redundant power supplies include lights, beeps, or both to alert you of an impending failure as well as total failure. Naturally, you want to replace the power supply when warning of impending failure occurs, instead of waiting for total failure. Check with the vendor documentation for specific instructions on replacing the power supply (PSU). Generally, replacing a hot-swappable redundant power supply is quick and easy:

1   Verify that the replacement PSU is compatible. For hot-swappable server PSUs, use the server vendor PSU instead of a third-party PSU for best reliability.

2   If necessary, unscrew the power supply from the chassis. Normally, redundant power supplies use a lever or handle instead of screws to attach to the chassis. Flip the lever/handle or unscrew, and then pull the PSU out of the server (see Exhibit 5-19). You will probably perform this action from the back of the server in most cases, so make sure you have enough space to either slide the server out of the rack far enough to reach behind the server from the front of the rack or that sufficient space exists behind the server to both open a door (if present) and remove the power supply from the back of the rack. Be sure to use both hands when removing the PSU; it might be heavy.

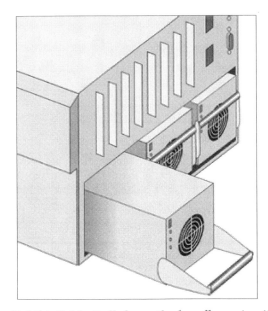

Exhibit 5-19: Pull down the handle and pull out the hot-swappable PSU

3   Replace the power supply by reversing the steps above. Hot-swappable PSUs plug directly into connections on the server without requiring you to remove the cover and attach power cables individually.

If the replacement power supply is an upgrade, not a matter of replacing a failed PSU, then you can perform the above steps one PSU at a time until all are up to the new level. Be sure to verify vendor documentation to see if the server supports the new power level.

For power supplies that are not hot-swappable, continued operation of the server is not possible when the power supply fails, and replacing the PSU is an immediate concern. Do *not* attempt to repair the PSU; even unplugged it retains a high level of dangerous electricity. It is more prudent to spend the money on a new PSU. Also, if it suits you, there is more flexibility in choosing a different vendor with non-hot-swappable power supplies. Make sure that the new power supply will fit the chassis. Some server vendors use specially designed PSU form factors that prevent you from choosing a generic replacement.

Replace the non-hot-swappable PSU as follows:

1 Power down the system if it is running.

2 Unplug the power cable.

3 Remove the server cover. (At your discretion, consider not grounding yourself in this rare case. If there is a chance that the PSU might ground to you, extremely high voltage could be discharged, resulting in serious injury. Just keep touching the chassis and be extra careful about not touching other ESD-sensitive components.)

4 Unplug all PSU cable connections to the motherboard, fans, drives, and so on.

5 Unscrew the PSU from the chassis. Non-hot-swappable PSUs do not have handles or levers to release them from the chassis. Some servers might require that you first remove other components such as adapters or hard disks in order to reach the PSU.

6 Remove the PSU. (If you have time, this is a good time to blow out or vacuum out dust.)

7 Replace with a new PSU by reversing the steps above. (Older AT power supply connections use two connectors to connect to the power supply. If you see this, make note of the connector orientation, because mixing them up can burn up the motherboard or components. Also, it's easy to accidentally make the "off by one" connection where you skew the connector to the board by one pin. Remember that the two black ground wires in each connector should be adjacent to avoid a mix-up (see Exhibit 5-20). ATX-style motherboards, on the other hand, use a single connector that is keyed to prevent backward installation.)

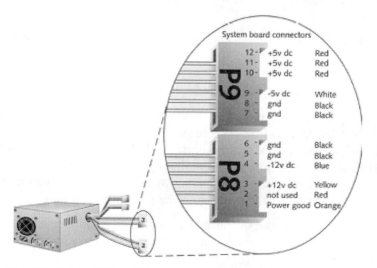

Exhibit 5-20: Older AT power supply connections

Upgrading adapters

Upgrading adapters is a fairly straightforward process. Actually, you cannot normally upgrade the adapter itself—to install new features, you simply replace the adapter. When installing the adapter into a slot, the following guidelines define what you can do:

- A 32-bit PCI card can fit into a 32-bit or 64-bit PCI slot.
- A 64-bit PCI card only fits into a 64-bit PCI slot.
- An AGP video card fits only into an AGP slot
- Currently, PCI 2.2 devices will work in PCI Express slots

When installing the adapter, apply firm, even pressure when guiding the adapter into the slot. Be sure to orient the server so that you apply downward pressure (toward the tabletop) instead of sideways to avoid tipping the server over. Try to visually line up the card with the slot to ensure success. Often, you will have to remove adjacent cards first for better visibility and more working room. As you press down on the adapter, you should feel the card "sink" into the slot (see Exhibit 5-21). If the retaining bracket is not flush against the chassis, then the card is probably not fully seated. Once the card is seated, screw in the retaining screw. Be sure to cover empty slot openings on the back of the chassis to help provide good airflow.

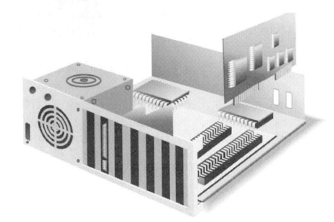

Exhibit 5-21: Inserting an adapter into its slot

Though unusual with quality components, some cards can not be fully seated because the retaining bracket is flush against the chassis, preventing further downward motion. If this is the case, you should choose a different adapter. Otherwise, you might have to use a pair of needle-nose pliers and carefully bend the adapter to make it fit.

The AGP graphics slot is further away from the fastening point on the chassis than other bus interfaces, such as PCI. As a result, AGP cards are a little more susceptible to "walking" out of the slot during shipment. When you receive a new server, press down on all removable components, including the AGP adapter, to ensure proper seating of cards. New motherboards often include an AGP card retention mechanism that snaps over the slot and locks the card into place via a retention notch.

Upgrading adapter drivers is normally a matter of connecting to the vendor Web site, downloading the drivers, extracting them to a temporary location on the hard drive, and installing them.

Upgrading the UPS

When upgrading the UPS, realize that the upgrade requires you to power down all systems connected to the UPS, because an "upgrade" is really a replacement. For example, if a rack has three 8-way servers in it and a large UPS for redundant power, and the administrator knows that the UPS will not supply adequate power after adding another 8-way server, he or she might proceed as follows:

1. Power off all load equipment attached to the UPS.
2. Replace the UPS with a model having sufficient power capacity and runtime.
3. Plug in all equipment and again power up the systems on the new UPS.

Of course, because the servers must be offline while the UPS is being replaced, redundant servers must perform the same services. If this redundancy is not available, notify the users of the planned downtime and perform the upgrade during low usage periods. Also, perform a backup prior to the upgrade. The batteries on a new UPS probably do not hold enough charge to provide adequate runtime if utility power were to fail soon after the upgrade, and a recent backup will assist the recovery.

Alternatively, if the rack has N+1 UPS redundancy, then the administrator can upgrade one UPS while another continues to provide redundancy. If utility power is interrupted during the upgrade, the redundant UPS will continue to supply power.

Server upgrade checklist

The following checklist should help you to perform carefully planned upgrades:

- Set a baseline of acceptable performance.
- Confirm NOS compatibility.
- Notify users if the upgrade affects them.
- Record settings if applicable (e.g., CMOS settings prior to BIOS upgrade).
- Verify available resources for the device (IRQ, DMA, I/O).
- Download the most recent driver(s) and BIOS upgrade.
- Read instructions, FAQs, and newsgroups.
- Inventory delivered parts.
- Perform a tape backup.
- Upgrade to the latest BIOS version.
- Perform the physical installation using sound ESD practices.
- Test and pilot the implementation.
- Reset the baseline.

Do it!

C-1: Discussing BIOS and hardware upgrades

Questions and answers

1 What should you do prior to a flash BIOS upgrade?

2 What does a digital multimeter (DMM) measure?

3 Hot-swappable PSUs are typically identified by what feature?

Unit summary: Server upgrades

Topic A   In this topic, you learned that before performing the upgrade, you should apply the latest flash BIOS upgrade and the most recently available drivers, and you should be sure to read all documentation and available FAQs or newsgroups relevant to the upgrade and NOS installation. You learned to perform **baseline performance tests** before and after the upgrade to measure any changes in performance, and to log upgrades to an easily accessible location to assist in troubleshooting and asset tracking. You also learned that you should always **back up the server** before performing any hardware or software upgrades.

Topic B   In this topic, you found that when **upgrading a processor**, you should verify that the motherboard and BIOS can accept the new processor, and if you're adding a processor for SMP, match the new processor's stepping, cache, form factor, and speed exactly to the existing processor. Also, you should be sure to match the **memory module manufacturer** when possible. You also learned to plan server purchases with as few modules as possible to maximize future upgrade possibilities. You also learned that if the memory modules vary in size, you should install the largest modules (in megabytes) in the lowest numbered slot for best performance.

Topic C   In this topic, you learned that current PCs and servers offer **flash BIOS**, which means that you can download the most recent update from the vendor's Web site and apply it to the server without replacing the BIOS. You learned that before you perform a flash BIOS upgrade, you should record existing CMOS settings because you might need to reenter them after the upgrade. You learned that you could recover a corrupt BIOS using a flash BIOS floppy, but only by using beeping sounds to track progress, because the display is not available. You also learned that if you suspect a power supply is not performing reliably or to specifications, verify PSU performance by using a **digital multimeter (DMM)**.

Independent practice activity

In this activity, you explore a possible BIOS upgrade for your computer.

1 Choose Start, All Programs, Accessories, System Tools, System Information. You should see something like Exhibit 5-22. Write down the BIOS makcr and version for your computer. Also note the make and model of your computer.

2 Write down the BIOS maker and version for your computer. Also note the make and model of your computer.

3 Use a search engine, if necessary, to locate the BIOS manufacturer's home page. Find the information for BIOS upgrades. Answer the following questions:

   Is your BIOS the newest version?

   If not, what is the latest version?

   What are the instructions for obtaining and applying the new BIOS?

   What other interesting BIOS-related information did you find?

4 Close the browser and the System Information window.

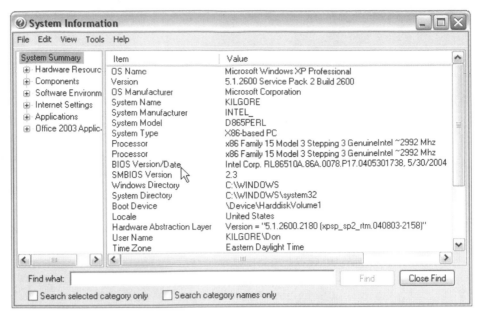

Exhibit 5-22: Determining the BIOS version in Windows System Information

Review questions

1 Which of the following might be cause to upgrade the server? Choose all that apply.

    A You want the latest technology

    B Server performance is insufficient

    C Timing in relation to the budget

    D Planning for future events

2 When should you upgrade the server?

    A During peak utilization

    B During lowest utilization

    C Between 12:00AM and 3:00 AM

    D During the weekend

3 Why should you notify users of a planned upgrade? Choose two.

    A To inform users as to how the upgrade benefits them

    B To increase visibility of the administrator so that people know you're actually working

    C To reduce support calls during server downtime

    D So users know who to call if the upgrade seems to be taking too long

4 Which of the following is an important factor in ensuring that the hardware operates correctly with the operating system?

A BIOS

B Parity memory

C Error Correcting Code (ECC)

D Bus speed

5 If the cover is off the server during the upgrade, you might as well:

A Leave it off for optimum cooling

B Clean the dust from the inside

C Test each electrical lead

D Upgrade the memory

6 Where can you check to see if an upgrade might cause a problem? Choose all that apply.

A Vendor's web site

B FAQs

C Newsgroup

D All of the above

7 A pilot program: (choose two).

A Ensures safety for passengers

B Ensures that the upgrade is reliable

C Ensures that an upgrade failure affects a smaller scope

D Ensures that the upgrade is successfully deployed across the organization simultaneously

8 In a real production enterprise, you should use a pilot program for: (choose two).

A Any hardware change, no matter how small

B Upgrading to a different NOS

C Changing the processor platform

D Upgrading the monitor to a larger size

9 The purpose of the log book is to:

A Blame someone else if a problem occurs

B Assist in troubleshooting upgrades

C Record system errors

D Record when tape backups are performed

10 Before an upgrade, why would you perform a full backup instead of depending upon the normal tape rotation?

   A The normal tape rotation might not be as current

   B Because the tape in the rotation might not have sufficient remaining space

   C The normal tape rotation might not backup all the data

   D You want the backup to reflect the most recent changes to the data

11 Which of the following is a resource you should verify is available prior to a hardware upgrade?

   A IRQ

   B Serial port

   C Parallel port

   D Electrical load

12 If you touch a server component and discharge static, it is only a problem if:

   A You can see the spark

   B You can feel the electrical discharge

   C You can always damage components with static discharge

   D You can hear the electrical discharge

13 Absent any grounding equipment, what can you do to protect against ESD?

   A Touch the server power cable

   B Touch the server chassis

   C Discharge ESD against something else first

   D Leave the server plugged in

14 What is the purpose of taking inventory? (Choose two)

   A To fairly distribute server equipment amongst all sites in the enterprise

   B To assist in budgetary projections

   C To avoid having to halt the upgrade because of missing parts

   D None of the above

15 Which of the following is not important in upgrading the processor?

   A Verifying stepping, cache size, and speed

   B Verifying that the new processor is compatible with the motherboard

   C Verifying that the new processor is compatible with the BIOS

   D Verifying that the processor is at least 400 MHz

16 Into which of the following socket or slot can you install a Pentium III Xeon 700 MHz processor?

A Socket 370

B Socket 490

C Slot 2

D Socket A

17 What can you identify about a memory module with nine chips, one having a different numbering on it than the others?

A The memory is a RIMM

B The memory is EDO memory

C The memory is ECC

D There is insufficient data to make a determination

18 What should you do prior to a flash BIOS upgrade?

A Record all BIOS settings

B Reset BIOS to default settings

C Remove the CMOS from the motherboard

D Remove the CMOS battery

19 Which of the following does a multimeter not test?

A Resistance

B Voltage

C Continuity

D MHz

20 A hot swappable power supply: (select all that apply).

A Is removable with a handle or lever

B Screws onto the chassis

C Is not technically hot-swappable: you must first plug/unplug all power cables

D Does not supply redundancy unless you have an N+1 configuration

Unit 6

Configuring a network operating system

Unit time: 120 minutes

Complete this unit, and you'll know how to:

A Discuss general network operating system (NOS) characteristics and versions, list NOS hardware requirements, and perform NOS installations and upgrades.

B Identify Novell NetWare characteristics and versions, list hardware requirements, and perform an installation and a proper shut down.

C Identify UNIX/Linux characteristics and versions, list hardware requirements, and perform an installation and a proper shut down.

D Identify Windows NT Server characteristics and versions, list hardware requirements, and perform an installation and a proper shut down.

E Identify Windows 2000 and 2003 characteristics and versions, list hardware requirements, perform an installation and proper shut down, and update the NOS.

Topic A: General NOS configuration concepts

This topic covers the following CompTIA Server+ exam objectives:

#	Objective
2.1	Conduct pre-installation planning activities • Activities include: • Verify network protocols, naming conventions, domain names

2.2	Install hardware using best practices
	• Characteristics of common network interface protocols
	   • Ethernet
	   • Fast Ethernet
	   • Gigabit Ethernet

3.3	Install NOS

3.5	Install NOS and driver updates to design specifications
	• Activities include:
	   • Lab testing
	   • Installation
	   • Testing

7.2	Use diagnostic hardware and software tools and utilities • Activities include: • Perform shutdown across the following OS's: Microsoft Windows NT/2000/2003, Novell Netware, UNIX, Linux

Hardware requirements

Explanation

This unit is organized by network operating system, and each respective section lists the minimum system hardware requirements for that NOS, including requirements for processor, RAM, and hard disk space. Each NOS also requires a keyboard, mouse, CD-ROM, network card, and VGA or better video display, but for this unit, we assume that these items are always present.

Vendors list the minimum requirements as a standard practice and also to qualify for various types of contracts for which a bid is required (government contracts, for example). However, these requirements are usually sufficient to install only the operating system. How well it runs is another matter. A production server languishes in attempting to provide service to the network with only the vendor's recommended minimum requirements.

Preparing server hardware for NOS installation involves the right perspective. Instead of trying to get away with as little as possible, the administrator's perspective should be nearly the opposite: obtain hardware that's powerful enough for current and future requirements. Administrators must remember to anticipate what kinds of demands will be placed on the server. Is it a file server? Better have a lot more hard disk space than the manufacturer recommends. Is it going to run applications, such as a database? Better also add a lot of memory and much more processing power. Will the server provide intranet or Internet Web content? Add another network card or two for load balancing or adaptive fault tolerance.

NOS installation

A common task in server administration is installation of the NOS. Before you start the installation, be certain that the installed hardware meets at least the minimum system requirements recommended by the vendor, and also be certain that installed devices are compatible.

Before you begin any NOS installation, write down the following information for which the installation may prompt you: an IP address for the server, an IP address of a DNS server, the name of your domain, the name of your computer, and so forth.

Virtual memory/swap files

In addition to giving hardware requirements for various NOSs, this unit also explains how each NOS deals with virtual memory, an important area of configuration for a network operating system. *Virtual memory* uses a portion of hard disk space to extend RAM. It's a logical (as opposed to physical) memory area that's supported in conjunction with physical RAM. Think of virtual memory as an alternate set of memory addresses. Programs use these virtual addresses rather than real addresses to store instructions and data. These virtual addresses are then converted into real memory addresses when the program or data is actually required. The main goal of virtual memory is to enlarge the address space that a program can use. To facilitate the copying of virtual memory into real memory, the operating system divides virtual memory into pages, each of which contains a fixed number of addresses. Each page is stored on a disk until it's needed. When the page is needed, the operating system copies it from disk to main memory and translates the virtual addresses into real addresses.

The process of translating virtual addresses into real addresses is called *mapping*. Copying virtual pages from disk to main memory is known as *paging* or *swapping*. Swapping is a useful technique that enables a computer to execute programs and manipulate data files larger than main memory. The operating system copies as much data as possible into main memory and leaves the rest on the disk. When the operating system needs data from the disk, it exchanges a portion of data in main memory with a portion of data on the disk. Each time a page is needed that isn't currently in memory, a *page fault* occurs. An invalid page fault occurs when the address of the page being requested is invalid. In this case, the application is usually aborted. All major NOSs require virtual memory. This unit explains how to create swap-file space for each respective NOS.

Performing upgrades

Sometimes it isn't necessary to "flatten" the system (use FDISK to repartition and format the disk). Although a clean install has advantages, sometimes it can be disruptive, time-consuming, and unnecessary. When upgrading a system from one released version to the next (Windows NT 4.0 to Windows 2000, for example), it might be best to take 15 minutes or half an hour to perform an upgrade, which retains all the existing applications and many configuration settings. Compare this to perhaps a day for a clean install, depending on the number of applications and configurations that you need to make. When Microsoft initially began the daunting task of upgrading its data center of more than 350 servers, administrators flattened NT 4.0 systems and performed clean installs of Windows 2000. Microsoft decided to perform upgrades instead on some servers and noticed that there was no appreciable difference in stability or function. Thereafter, Microsoft upgraded the rest of its systems.

While upgrades don't work smoothly for everyone under all circumstances, you should consider the time saving involved. Although NOS upgrades aren't specifically a CompTIA Server+ exam item, they are an important part of administration. Administrators considering a mass upgrade will want to test and pilot first, and if successful, perform the remaining upgrades.

Proper shutdown

Although servers ideally run indefinitely without need for maintenance, whether planned or unplanned, you'll eventually have to shut down or reboot a server. Often, this is necessary to return a server to healthy status when its performance is poor or it seems unstable. Most network operating systems also require a reboot any time you make a significant change, such as adding hardware, a service, or an application. A shutdown might also be required for the mundane but regular task of blowing dust out of the case. For whatever reason, you should know how to shut down various operating systems properly, because an improper shutdown can corrupt data files, applications, and the operating system itself.

When performing a planned server shutdown, it's critical for system administrators to have a good grasp of how the servers and clients are being used and actively involve users in scheduling downtime. The concepts behind performing a proper shutdown are fundamental to all network operating systems. For example, on most systems, a server shutdown causes all user processes to be killed. If users on a system are running tasks that take a long time to complete, then shutting the system down and killing all of the processes will severely impact the productivity of users, possibly resulting in data loss. Also, user workstations might lock up or hang while waiting for some kind of response from the server. Therefore, whenever possible, administrators should give users as much lead time as possible when scheduling a shutdown. Server operating systems discussed in this text are generally stable enough to need a shutdown seldom, if ever, except for regular maintenance.

Do it!

A-1:   Discussing NOS configuration concepts

Questions and answers

1 What should you check before an NOS installation?

2 What network information is important for an NOS installation?

3 What's virtual memory?

4 Why is a proper server shutdown important?

Ethernet

Explanation

Network communication requires a *media access method*, a way to place the data packets transmitted from the NOS to the physical network device (such as a NIC) and then to the wire.

Ethernet is by far the most widely used media access method today, because it offers a nice balance between cost, speed, and ease of installation. Since Ethernet utilizes shared media between nodes, there are rules for sending packets of data to avoid collisions and protect the data. Though Ethernet collisions are unavoidable, you want to minimize their occurrence as much as possible to optimize available bandwidth and not waste it with excessive collisions. A large number of collisions can occur, because there are too many users on the network contending for bandwidth. Segmenting (subnetting) the network into separate, smaller networks joined together with a switch or router is one way of reducing traffic on an overcrowded network. The Institute for Electrical and Electronic Engineers (IEEE) has defined standards for Ethernet, collectively known as the *802.3 Standard*, which define how to configure an Ethernet network as well as how elements in an Ethernet network interact with one another. By following the 802.3 standard, network equipment and network protocols can communicate properly.

Carrier Sense Multiple Access with Collision Detection (CSMA/CD) describes the method Ethernet devices used to negotiate access to the wire and retransmit in case of collisions. The sending host monitors the voltage level of the wire, and if no transmission is occurring, the host sends data. If two or more hosts determine that the network is clear and begin sending data at the same time, Collision Detection (CD) handles timely attempts to retransmit data for each host.

Although electrical signals on Ethernet travel at speeds nearing the speed of light, it still takes a finite amount of time for the signal to travel from one end of a large Ethernet network to another. In larger network designs, the signal quality begins to depreciate as segments exceed their maximum length. Ethernet hubs repeat the signal, extending the maximum length, and connect two or more Ethernet segments of any media type. A *hub* provides a universal link for devices in a network and sends all incoming data out to all ports (hence, to each node). There are several types of hubs, including:

- A *passive hub*, which provides a channel for the data, enabling it to go from one device (or segment) to another.

- An *intelligent hub* (or *managed hub*), which includes additional components that enable administrators to monitor the traffic passing through the hub and to configure each port in the hub.

- A *switching hub*, which reads the destination address of each packet and then forwards the packet to the correct port.

If the hub is attached to a backbone, then all computers can communicate with all the hosts on the backbone. A very important fact to note about hubs is that they allow users to share only Ethernet bandwidth. A network of hubs/repeaters is called a "shared Ethernet," meaning that all member hubs contend for data transmission on a single network (collision domain). The number of hubs in any one collision domain is restricted by the 802.3 rules. This means that individual members of a shared network get only a percentage of the available network bandwidth.

Ethernet is governed by the "5-4-3 rule" of repeater placement. This rule means that the network can have only five segments connected; it can use only four repeaters; and of the five segments, only three can have users attached to them—the other two must be inter-repeater links. If the design of the network breaks these rules, then the timing guidelines won't be met and the sending node will resend that packet, resulting in lost packets and excessive resent packets. This can adversely affect network performance by slowing down the network and creating problems for applications.

Fast Ethernet

Fast Ethernet (IEEE 802.3u) offers higher transmission speeds than 802.3 Ethernet. (Fast Ethernet is also known as 100BaseT.) Fast Ethernet allows for fewer repeaters, because the data travels so quickly that host NICs can't always compensate for collision detection and consequent retransmissions in a timely manner. In Fast Ethernet networks, there are two classes of repeaters. Class I repeaters have a latency of 0.7 microseconds or less and are limited to one repeater per network. Class II repeaters have a latency of 0.46 microseconds or less and are limited to two repeaters per network. Fast Ethernet can be deployed to desktops and servers by installing Fast Ethernet NICs and using Fast Ethernet switches and repeaters. This standard raises the Ethernet speed limit from 10 Mbps to 100 Mbps with no changes to the existing cable structure or connectors. Most of today's networks have a mixture of standard Ethernet networks (10 Mbps) and Fast Ethernet (100 Mbps).

Full-duplex Ethernet

There is another variation of Ethernet called *full-duplex Ethernet*. By simply adding another pair of wires (for a total of six wires) and removing collision detection, you can double the connection speed. Hosts can simultaneously send and receive data similar to a telephone conversation in which both parties can speak at once. (Half-duplex would be more like a CB radio conversation.) In terms of Fast Ethernet, 200 Mbps of throughput is the theoretical maximum for a full-duplex Fast Ethernet connection. This type of connection is limited to a node-to-node connection and often links two Ethernet switches. Full duplex is just another method used to increase bandwidth to dedicated workstations or servers by doubling the bandwidth on a link, providing 20 Mbps for Ethernet and 200 Mbps for Fast Ethernet. To use full duplex, special NICs are installed in the computers and a switch is programmed to support full-duplex operation.

You can't use full-duplex with a hub, because the nature of full-duplex requires a dedicated connection. Therefore, you'd have to use a switch, which provides full bandwidth to each port, instead of a hub, which shares bandwidth with other ports.

Gigabit Ethernet

Gigabit Ethernet is a newer version of Ethernet that supports data-transfer rates of 1 Gigabit (1000 megabits) per second. The first Gigabit Ethernet standard (802.3z) was ratified by the IEEE 802.3 Committee in 1998 and is defined by the frame format, the use of CSMA/CD, the use of full-duplex, the use of flow control, and the management objects defined by the committee. Gigabit Ethernet is basically Ethernet, only faster. Most organizations use Gigabit Ethernet as a backbone technology and for server connections. Gigabit Ethernet is a future technology that promises a migration path beyond Fast Ethernet. The next generation of networks will support even higher data-transfer speeds. The first installations require fiber optic media, for long connections between buildings, and short copper links, for connections between servers and hubs. Over time, as the market for workgroup and desktop Gigabit Ethernet services develops, customers will demand Gigabit links that are compliant with the installed base of Category 5 UTP wiring that's used for standard Ethernet. (Wiring specifics appear later in this chapter.)

Do it!

A-2: Discussing Ethernet

Questions and answers
1 What are three basic types of hubs?
2 What's the 5-4-3 rule?
3 What are the respective data speeds of standard and Fast Ethernet connections?

Protocols

Explanation

Recall that a protocol is a set of governing standards that determines how network devices communicate with one another. Also, a protocol defines how computers identify each other on a network, the form that the data should take in transition, and how this information is processed once it reaches its final destination. Protocols also define procedures for handling a lost or damaged packet, the electronic package that contains the network data. A protocol determines the type of error checking to implement, the data compression method (if any), how the sending device indicates that it's finished sending, and how the receiving device indicates that it's finished receiving.

There are several standardized protocols from which administrators can choose, each having its own particular advantages and disadvantages. Common protocols include NetBEUI, IPX/SPX, and TCP/IP. This unit addresses TCP/IP more thoroughly than the other protocols, because TCP/IP is more common and includes several utilities that you'll certainly use to troubleshoot network connectivity and configuration.

Ultimately, all protocols are only a means to transport the network message to the node's physical address, known as the MAC (Media Access Control) address, which globally and uniquely identifies a network device. To find the MAC address of a network interface card (NIC), look at the MAC address printed on the NIC, or you can type IPCONFIG /all from a command prompt, which shows the MAC address as shown in the following example: Physical Address. . . . . : 00-03-47-12-39-FF. (See more about IPCONFIG later in this unit.)

NetBEUI

NetBEUI is the *NetBIOS Enhanced User Interface*. Recall that NetBEUI is a fast protocol designed for small networks and requires no configuration. However, it isn't a routable protocol and isn't efficient in larger networks, because it frequently rebroadcasts to locate other nodes on the network. It doesn't cache previously located nodes, and it doesn't use name resolution services such as DNS or WINS.

IPX/SPX

IPX/SPX (*Internetwork Packet Exchange/Sequence Packet Exchange*) is the default Novell protocol implementation for all versions of NetWare until 5.0, which can also use TCP/IP. IPX/SPX might require some configuration to identify the network on which the node exists, and like NetBEUI, it doesn't have name resolution services. However, IPX/SPX includes a caching mechanism so that it isn't necessary to rebroadcast to locate recently accessed nodes. IPX/SPX was most popular when Novell NetWare networks required it, but current versions of NetWare can use TCP/IP instead, and many organizations are phasing out IPX/SPX.

TCP/IP

TCP/IP (*Transmission Control Protocol/Internet Protocol*) is actually a suite of protocols commonly in use on most networks and the Internet. However, administrators consider TCP/IP to be a single protocol. TCP/IP is scaleable and routable, which is why it's the protocol of the Internet and most enterprise networks.

Covering all aspects of the TCP/IP protocol—including theory, configuration, and planning—is beyond the scope of this text. However, if you want to know more about TCP/IP, read any of dozens of comprehensive TCP/IP books.

The Internet (IP) address

All protocols require a way to identify nodes uniquely. TCP/IP uses a unique IP address, similar to the way the U.S. Postal Service uses a combination of ZIP Code, state, city, and street name to find its "nodes." An IP address appears as four sets of digits, each separated by a dot, for example , 215.161.122.231. A host with this IP address must be unique on the LAN to avoid conflicts with other hosts, and it must be globally unique if the host IP address is exposed to the Internet. Each IP address also requires a *subnet mask*, another series of numbers which, when compared against the IP address, identifies the specific network to which the host belongs. As an example, Exhibit 6-1 shows a screen shot of an IP address and subnet mask for a Windows 2000 server.

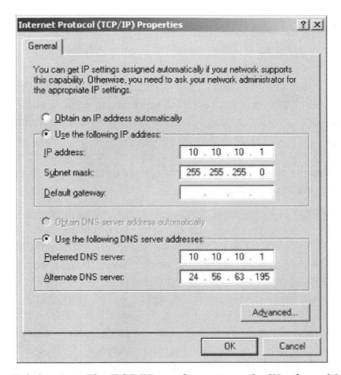

Exhibit 6-1: The TCP/IP configuration of a Windows 2000 server

Subnetting the network

Administrators also use a subnet mask to divide a range of IP addresses into multiple smaller networks. The reason for doing this is twofold. First, you might not need all the IP addresses available on a single network. Instead, you can split the IP address range among several separate networks. Second, administrators subnet their networks to split up a collision domain, characteristic of Ethernet networks. (A *collision domain* refers to a network boundary in which multiple nodes could potentially attempt to access the network at the same time.) This unit addresses Ethernet in more detail later, but for current purposes, understand that hosts on Ethernet networks have no arbiter to negotiate when network access is available (unlike the token of a ring network). As a result, network traffic grows exponentially as the number of nodes on a single network increases. Subnetting a larger network into smaller networks reduces the number of data collisions (and subsequent retransmissions) that take place when two hosts attempt to communicate at the same time. (A *collision* results when two devices or hosts transmit packets to the network at the same time.)

You can increase effective throughput to and from servers by installing network adapters with multiple ports, or multiple NICs in a single server. Such an installation makes the server multihomed. Similarly, you can use port aggregation software to combine multiple ports from the server into what's perceived as a single connection to the network but with bandwidth that's multiplied times the number of ports. Note that both multihoming and port aggregation increase throughput only of available bandwidth. The effectiveness of both methods diminishes with overutilized bandwidth.

Verifying TCP/IP configuration and connectivity

Connectivity or configuration problems with TCP/IP networks can involve lengthy and baffling troubleshooting. Fortunately, most network operating systems include a suite of TCP/IP configuration and troubleshooting tools to help diagnose problems.

Ping

Ping (*packet internet groper*) is an all-purpose utility for verifying that a remote host is accessible by sending small packets of data to which an accessible host responds. Ping tests connectivity at different stages between the host and destination to determine the point of failure at which a packet is dropped and also tests basic networking connectivity. For example, an unplugged network cable would prevent Ping from reaching its destination, alerting you to a physical network problem (provided all the TCP/IP configuration is correct).

In an IP network, Ping sends a single short data burst packet and then listens for a single packet in reply. Ping places a unique sequence number on each packet it transmits, and reports on the sequence numbers that come back to it. This is how Ping determines if packets have been dropped, duplicated, or reordered. Ping checksums (checks for errors) in each packet it exchanges. Ping places a time stamp in each packet, which echoes back and computes the length of time for packet exchange. This is called the *round-trip time* (*RTT*). Some routers silently discard undeliverable packets. Others mistake that a packet transmits successfully when it hasn't. Therefore, Ping may not always provide reasons why packets go unanswered. Ping doesn't perform analysis and can't tell you why a packet was damaged, delayed, or duplicated.

There are common situations, typically involving crowded wide area networks (WANs), in which even modern TCP implementations can't operate without dropping packets. Since TCP retransmits missing data, there's no reason for alarm unless a large number of retransmissions noticeably affects network performance.

IPCONFIG

IPCONFIG is a Microsoft utility that displays a wide variety of IP configuration data for a Windows system, including the IP address, subnet mask, default gateway, and other information (see Exhibit 6-2).

```
C:\Documents and Settings\Administrator>ipconfig /all

Windows IP Configuration

        Host Name . . . . . . . . . . . . : thomson-w47oov1
        Primary Dns Suffix  . . . . . . . :
        Node Type . . . . . . . . . . . . : Unknown
        IP Routing Enabled. . . . . . . . : No
        WINS Proxy Enabled. . . . . . . . : No
        DNS Suffix Search List. . . . . . : rochester.rr.com

Ethernet adapter Local Area Connection:

        Connection-specific DNS Suffix  . : rochester.rr.com
        Description . . . . . . . . . . . : 3Com 3C900B-TPC Ethernet
        Physical Address. . . . . . . . . : 00-50-DA-C5-7E-C1
        DHCP Enabled. . . . . . . . . . . : Yes
        Autoconfiguration Enabled . . . . : Yes
        IP Address. . . . . . . . . . . . : 192.168.1.101
        Subnet Mask . . . . . . . . . . . : 255.255.255.0
        Default Gateway . . . . . . . . . : 192.168.1.1
        DHCP Server . . . . . . . . . . . : 192.168.1.1
        DNS Servers . . . . . . . . . . . : 24.92.226.9
        Lease Obtained. . . . . . . . . . : Monday, August 08, 2005
        Lease Expires . . . . . . . . . . : Tuesday, August 09, 2005

C:\Documents and Settings\Administrator>
```

Exhibit 6-2: IPCONFIG /all displays complete IP configuration information

The most commonly used IPCONFIG switches are:
- /all—displays all available IP configuration information
- /release—releases IP configuration for DHCP clients
- /renew—renews the DHCP-assigned client IP address; useful when the DHCP configuration changes and you want to apply the changes to the DHCP client

ARP

ARP (*Address Resolution Protocol*) displays the resolution between the IP address and the physical (MAC) address on the NIC by building a table as IP addresses resolve to MAC addresses. You can also modify the ARP cache and table entries. For example, you can use the –s switch to add a static host-to-MAC address entry to the ARP table. The advantage of this would be to improve IP-address-to-MAC-address resolution time. To view the ARP table, type ARP –a, and to add an ARP entry, type ARP –s <IPAddress> <MAC address>.

TRACERT

TRACERT is the trace routing utility that works like Ping but shows the actual router hops taken to reach the remote host. This is handy if you want to find at which point a packet is being dropped or where a bottleneck may exist on the network (see Exhibit 6-3).

```
C:\Documents and Settings\Administrator>tracert www.course.com

Tracing route to www.course.com [198.80.146.30]
over a maximum of 30 hops:

  1    <1 ms    <1 ms    <1 ms  cpe-24-93-10-1.rochester.res.rr.com [24.93.10.1]
  2    <1 ms    <1 ms    <1 ms  fas0-1-0.rochnybpt-rtr01.nyroc.rr.com [24.93.0.225]
  3    <1 ms    <1 ms    <1 ms  srp7-0.rochnymth-rtr04.nyroc.rr.com [24.93.3.118]
  4    <1 ms    <1 ms    <1 ms  srp3-0.rochnymth-rtr02.nyroc.rr.com [24.93.3.178]
  5    <1 ms    <1 ms    <1 ms  son0-0-3.albynywav-rtr03.nyroc.rr.com [24.92.224.17?
  6     7 ms    <1 ms    <1 ms  pop1-alb-P2-0.atdn.net [66.185.133.233]
  7    <1 ms    <1 ms    <1 ms  bb1-alb-P0-0.atdn.net [66.185.148.96]
  8    <1 ms    <1 ms    <1 ms  bb2-nye-P3-0.atdn.net [66.185.152.71]
  9    <1 ms     2 ms    <1 ms  pop1-nye-P1-0.atdn.net [66.185.151.51]
 10    <1 ms    <1 ms    <1 ms  204.255.173.33
 11    <1 ms    <1 ms    <1 ms  0.so-6-0-0.XL2.NYC4.ALTER.NET [152.63.21.82]
 12     3 ms    <1 ms    <1 ms  0.so-4-0-0.CL2.CMH2.ALTER.NET [152.63.68.86]
 13    <1 ms    <1 ms    <1 ms  188.ATM4-0.GW2.CMH2.ALTER.NET [152.63.66.141]
 14    <1 ms    <1 ms    <1 ms  65.206.182.82
 15     *        *        *     Request timed out.
 16    <1 ms    <1 ms    <1 ms  www.mycourse.com [198.80.146.30]

Trace complete.

C:\Documents and Settings\Administrator>
```

Exhibit 6-3: Windows TRACERT identifies each router hop

NETSTAT

NETSTAT shows TCP/IP protocol statistics using any of several options. One of the most useful options is –r, which shows the routing table (see Exhibit 6-4). This feature is useful in verifying the efficiency of the routing tables.

```
C:\Documents and Settings\Administrator>netstat -r
d:\srv03rtm\net\tcpip\commands\netstat\netstat.c built Mar 24 2003 22:37:36

IPv4 Route Table
===========================================================================
Interface List
0x1 ........................... MS TCP Loopback interface
0x10003 ...00 50 da c5 7e c1 ...... 3Com 3C900B-TPC Ethernet Adapter (Generic)
===========================================================================
===========================================================================
Active Routes:
Network Destination        Netmask          Gateway       Interface  Metric
        0.0.0.0          0.0.0.0      192.168.1.1   192.168.1.101     30
      127.0.0.0        255.0.0.0        127.0.0.1       127.0.0.1      1
    192.168.1.0    255.255.255.0    192.168.1.101   192.168.1.101     30
  192.168.1.101  255.255.255.255        127.0.0.1       127.0.0.1     30
  192.168.1.255  255.255.255.255    192.168.1.101   192.168.1.101     30
      224.0.0.0        240.0.0.0    192.168.1.101   192.168.1.101     30
255.255.255.255  255.255.255.255    192.168.1.101   192.168.1.101      1
Default Gateway:       192.168.1.1
===========================================================================
Persistent Routes:
  None

C:\Documents and Settings\Administrator>_
```

Exhibit 6-4: NETSTAT –r shows the routing table

Do it!   **A-3:   Discussing protocols**

Questions and answers

1 What do you call a node on a TCP/IP network?

2 IPX/SPX is the default protocol of which NOS?

3 What's the purpose of a subnet mask?

4 Which protocol should you use for IP-address-to-MAC-address issues?

Topic B: Novell NetWare

This topic covers the following CompTIA Server+ exam objectives:

#	Objective

7.2	Use diagnostic hardware and software tools and utilities
	
	• Activities include:
	
	    • Perform shutdown across the following OS's: Microsoft Windows NT/2000/2003, Novell Netware, UNIX, Linux
	
	    • NOS shutdown procedures
	
	        • Novell Netware

NetWare basics

Explanation

Novell NetWare is a local area network (LAN) operating system that was developed by Novell Corporation. NetWare runs on a variety of LANs, including Ethernet and IBM Token Ring networks, and was arguably the NOS market leader until the mid 1990s, when Windows NT 4.0 came on the scene. NetWare offers users and programmers a reliable interface that's independent of the underlying hardware that transmits data. Depending on the version, NetWare uses either a bindery or directory service design to manage the majority of the resources.

A *directory service* is a network service that identifies all the resources on a network and makes them available to applications and users. These resources can include e-mail addresses; user, group, and computer accounts; and devices such as printers. A main goal of a directory service is to make the physical network topology and protocols invisible, so that a network user can access any resource without knowing where it is or how it's physically linked. One of the most important directory services is *Lightweight Directory Access Protocol* (*LDAP*), a standard that defines a method of creating searchable network resources and is used primarily for accessing information directories such as Windows 2000 Active Directory and NetWare Directory Service (NDS), which is used on Novell NetWare networks. Virtually all directory services are based on the *X.500 ITU* standard, originally a standard for searching e-mail directories. However, the standard is so large and complex that no vendor complies with it completely.

The NetWare operating system has the following characteristics:

- NetWare 3.x uses a bindery to provide network clients with the information that's stored on the NetWare server's local directory partitions. A bindery is restricted to the server on which it resides, and users can use only resources managed in the same bindery to which they log on. If users want to access resources located in another part of the network, they must log on to another server's bindery.

- NetWare 4.x and 5.x use the more advanced *Novell Directory Services* (*NDS*). NDS uses a scalable tree structure that extends throughout the enterprise. The administrator can plan and configure the NDS tree so that users from anywhere in the organization can access resources throughout the organization with a single logon.

- NetWare 5.1 incorporates new Web and application server technologies that extend an organization's contact to the realm of e-business and Web-based network management. NetWare 5.1 includes tools to make the once-complicated process of Web application development, deployment, and management much simpler. Novell NetWare works well with most client operating systems, ranging from MS-DOS to OS/2 and any version of Microsoft Windows.

- NetWare 5.1 offers a GUI interface known as *ConsoleOne*, which is a central management point for performing NetWare administration. This console remedied complaints about the text-only administration of previous versions of NetWare (see Exhibit 6-5).

- *Zero Effort Networks* (*Z.E.N.* or *ZENworks*) is a NetWare suite of software management tools that administrators use to manage the user or server operating system environment by automatically distributing applications and controlling the user desktop using ZENworks for Servers and ZENworks for Desktops.

- Using NetWare 5.1, your network can run in a pure IP environment without retaining older IPX-based functionality. (Older versions of NetWare used IPX/SPX as the default network protocol.)

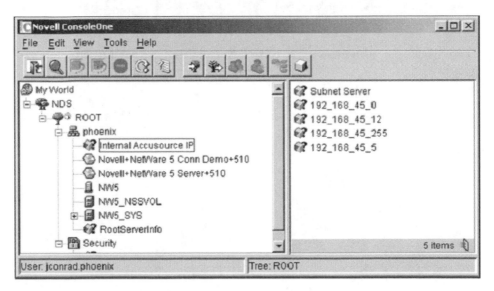

Exhibit 6-5: The NetWare 5.1 GUI interface, ConsoleOne

Prior to the Internet's rapid growth, using IPX/SPX wasn't a significant administrative concern. However, administrators trying to merge existing IPX/SPX networks with other IP-based servers and the Internet will appreciate the simplification of using a single protocol. By using only IP traffic, your organization can:

- *Reduce the routing burdens associated with forwarding multiple protocols.* This benefit is twofold: First, the administrator doesn't have to program and maintain routers with both IPX and IP forwarding information. Second, reducing the routing load to a single protocol extends the effectiveness of the router. For example, you might have to replace a saturated router in the IPX/SPX and TCP/IP environment. However, scaling down to only TCP/IP might reduce router traffic to the point that you can save a great deal of money by keeping the existing router.

- *Conserve valuable network bandwidth.* Instead of transmitting two protocols over the wire, each host transmits only one.

- *Eliminate the need to support other client protocols* on desktop computers.

- *Optimize remote connectivity.* Transmitting multiple protocols makes an already slow dial-up modem connection even slower.

Versions

There are several versions of NetWare in use today. The most recent version, and the subject of the rest of this section, is NetWare 5.1. Here are the various versions of NetWare:

- NetWare 2.12
- NetWare 386 (became NetWare 3.11)
- NetWare 3.12
- NetWare 4.0 – 4.1
- IntraNetware 4.11
- NetWare 5.0
- NetWare 5.1

You're most likely to find NetWare 3.12 or later in production environments.

NetWare 5.1 minimum requirements

The minimum hardware requirements for a NetWare 5.1 server are as follows:

- A server-class PC with any Pentium II or higher processor.
- A DOS partition that starts the server and loads the NetWare operating system. While the partition can be as small as 30-35 MB, Novell recommends 100 MB, which is very little, considering the size of modern hard disks.
- At least 1.3 GB of disk space on the SYS volume beyond the DOS partition is needed for the standard NetWare components and WebSphere Application Server for NetWare. (*WebSphere* is an IBM application for building and managing Web-based applications.)
- 128 MB of RAM is required for the standard NetWare components. Installing the WebSphere Application Server for NetWare requires 256 MB. Novell recommends 512 MB for higher-end servers.

The base software requirement to start the installation is DOS 3.3 or later. You can use a non-Microsoft version of DOS. Caldera DR-DOS 7 is included on the NetWare 5.1 License/Cryptography disk. The other software components that you need are the NetWare 5.1 Operating System CD, the NetWare 5.1 License disk, and the Novell Client for DOS and Windows 3.1x. This client is useful for installing NetWare from an IPX NetWare server over the network. You need the proper DOS CD-ROM drivers for your CD-ROM as well, unless the CD-ROM is bootable.

(If this is the first NetWare 5.1 server on your network, you must make sure that this server is a reliable, accessible, and continuous part of the network, because it lays the groundwork for the remainder of the enterprise installation and must be available.)

You must have Supervisor rights, which allow you to perform administrative tasks,) at the root of the NDS tree. If this isn't the first NetWare 5.1 server on the network, you must have Supervisor rights to the container where the server will be installed. (A *container* is a general term for an Organization or Organizational Unit, which consists of hierarchical components of the NDS tree. All network objects must reside in a container in the tree.) You need to have read rights to the Security container object for the NDS tree as well.

You may also need some optional client connection utilities for installing from a network, such as the Novell Client for DOS and Windows 3.1x. This allows you to boot a computer from DOS or Windows 3.x, connect to an IPX network share on a NetWare server running IPX, and install NetWare. If connecting to an IP server, use the IP Server Connection Utility instead.

Creating a floppy that both loads the appropriate network card drivers and connects to an IP host over the network can be quite time-consuming, frustrating, and filled with trial and error. Fortunately, Novell includes specific instructions for creating such a floppy in the file named Products\serverinst\ipconn.txt on the Novell client CD. Although these instructions don't work for every network card and every IP network connection, at least they provide a good groundwork for creating your own IP network boot floppy.

This text makes no attempt to detail each individual step in performing an operating system installation. Instead, the purpose of each respective operating system's installation section is to provide an overview of the installation process.

Installing NetWare 5.1

To install NetWare 5.1 on a server:

1 Create an MS-DOS primary partition and set it to active, using FDISK. This will be your boot partition that boots to DOS and loads NetWare, as well as any drivers for your CD-ROM, SCSI drives, and so forth. The installation will suggest a partition size for you. If you want to record *memory core dump* data (a representation of the contents of memory in the event of a problem, also known as simply a "memory dump"), size the partition to the recommended size plus the amount of RAM in system. For example, if the installation recommends 100 MB and you have 512 MB of RAM, the optimum partition size would be 612 MB. Most server operating systems offer some facility to store memory dump data, but it's extremely complex and usually meaningful only to programmers adept at its interpretation.

2 If you boot from the CD-ROM, the installation automatically seeks a suitable boot partition and, if none is found, offers to create one for you. This partition will contain the necessary files to start NetWare. (Creating a bootable partition during installation deletes all data on the hard disk, even data on other partitions.)

3 Booting from the NetWare 5.1 installation CD starts the installation for you. If using a boot floppy to access the CD-ROM, insert the NetWare 5.1 CD. At the CD drive or network drive prompt, enter Install. The initial screens of the installation program display in text-based mode. You can accept the detected and default settings, or you can modify the settings to meet the needs of your networking environment. You can also start the installation by booting with the network floppy mentioned earlier to access the installation files from a server. Booting from a floppy requires you to create a bootable MS-DOS system disk with drivers for your CD-ROM drive. Also, you must create an Autoexec.bat and Config.sys file and make sure that the logical file name of your CD drive (specified in the Config.sys and Autoexec.bat files) isn't CDROM or CDINST. The Config.sys file must contain a FILES=40 and BUFFERS=30 statement.

4 As you go through the installation, you see prompts to confirm or select various hardware in the system. For example, Exhibit 6-6 shows that NetWare detected several drivers that would work for the installed NIC, so the administrator had to choose the correct one. Use a NIC that's known to be detected automatically by the installation. Otherwise, you must specify the make and model of the network card from a list or provide the drivers from a floppy. Unfortunately, some NIC manufacturers no longer make a NetWare driver, so this might be limiting. After specifying the NIC, specify its resources, such as IRQ, I/O port, and so forth. This process can involve a great deal of trial and error as you determine which resources are available and which resources work with that particular network card. Automatically detected cards usually don't require you to specify resources manually.

5 Choose how you want to partition the hard disk space (see Exhibit 6-7). The first volume NetWare creates is called the SYS volume, and Novell recommends that you make it at least 200 MB (a complete install with all documentation requires about 600 MB). This volume should be used only for NetWare system files and *NetWare Loadable Modules* (*NLMs*) (NetWare programs and applications), not for user data. This setup makes recovering a problematic system easier and faster, especially for backup and restore. And if you need to reinstall the SYS volume, doing so doesn't destroy user data.

6   Continue with the installation and into the GUI mode, answering the questions based on your organizational requirements. During the text-based installation, much of your hardware is automatically detected, but don't expect this detection to be as thorough as Windows Plug and Play. Be familiar with the exact hardware in the server, because you might have to inform the installation of several items, such as storage adapters (IDE or SCSI), PCI hot plug capability, or network boards. For example, if installation doesn't properly detect your network card, you have to select it manually from a list of network boards or have the NetWare drivers for the card available on disk. And you might also have to enter the hardware resources that the board requires (IRQ, I/O address, and so forth).

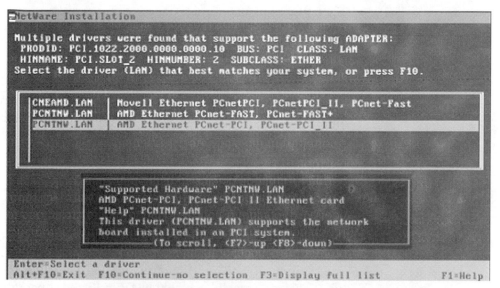

Exhibit 6-6: Verify or select the correct hardware during NetWare installation

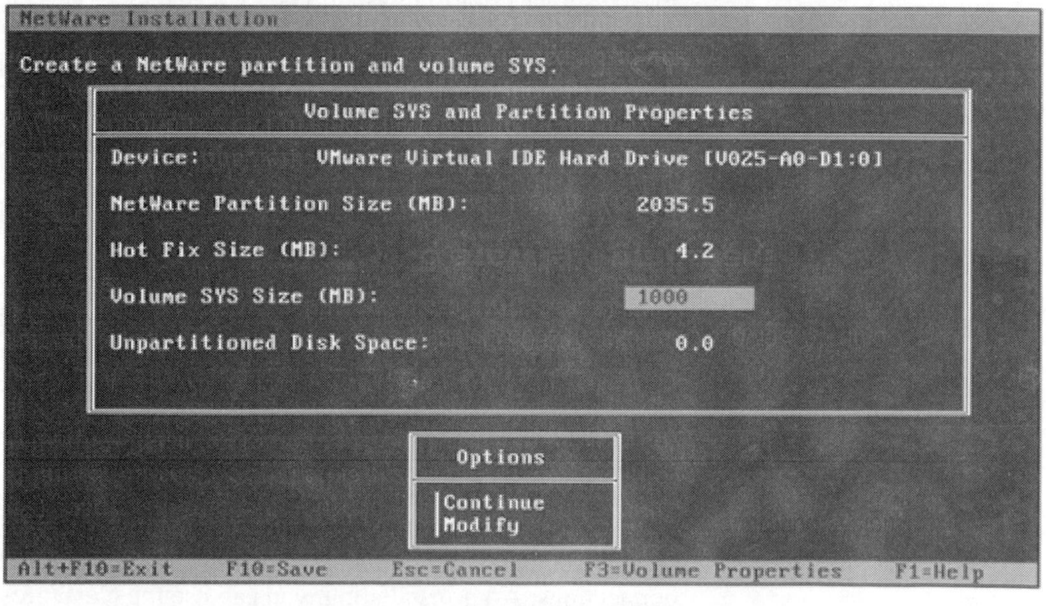

Exhibit 6-7: Choose how you want to partition the hard disk space

Most of the NetWare 5.1 installation steps are self-explanatory. However, there are some key issues that you need to address during the installation process, as follows:

- Decide which version of NDS you'll use. NetWare 5.1 allows you to use either NDS 8 (default) or NDS 7. NDS 8 provides the enhanced NDS functionality needed by many new Web networking products, such as WebSphere. If your NDS tree hasn't already been updated for NDS 8, you must have Supervisor rights at the root of the NDS tree to install NDS.

- You can create two types of volumes during the installation process: traditional NetWare volumes or Novell Storage Services (NSS) volumes. If you want an NSS volume, you must leave unallocated space on the hard disk and create the NSS volume after you've installed NetWare and booted the server.

- Specify the amount of space for a *hot fix* redirection area on the hard disk. NetWare verifies the integrity of all disk writes, and if a write fails this verification, the data is redirected to the hot fix area, and the original destination is marked as unusable. The default size of the hot fix area is a small percentage of a partition's total size.

- As mentioned earlier, NetWare 5.1 can process IP network packets and traditional IPX packets. You can install networking protocols to support IP, IPX, or both. In the GUI installation stages, you can specify protocols. Novell's IPX allows you to continue using IPX-based applications. If IPX is the only protocol installed on your server, it actively processes IPX packets and ignores packets using other protocols, such as IP. If you have network clients or applications that require IPX and IP, you can install both protocols at the expense of more network traffic from clients, as both protocols broadcast and communicate. (You can also install IP with IPX Compatibility. This binds both protocols to a network card, with preference for communicating over IP. IPX is in passive mode, dormant until an IPX request arrives. Then, NetWare communicates using IPX. This is a graceful way to transfer to IP and support both protocols at a low cost to network bandwidth.)

- Don't forget to enter a *host name record* (otherwise known as an *"A" record*) for the server prior to installation on your DNS server. During installation, you enter one or more DNS name servers, and the NetWare server must be able to locate the name server and verify the host record. This data is required in order to allow clients to find the server using its host name.

- You either join the server to an existing tree or create a new one. A NetWare tree defines the structure of the organization, its subdivisions, and the objects contained therein. Objects (resources such as servers, printers, users, and groups) reside in a context within the tree. Think of a context as a subdivided portion of the tree. For example, you install a file server for the graphics department of a company named KidHelp in Phoenix. The tree might be named KidHelp, and within that tree is the context. The context of the file server might appear something like O=Phoenix,OU=Graphics. (The root name is implied. You don't need to specify it when naming objects.)

- Finally, NetWare 5.1 must have a valid license in order to function as a server. You can install the license from the NetWare 5.1 License/Cryptography disk or browse to a directory that contains NetWare 5.1 licenses. Although the server can be installed without a license, the unlicensed server allows only two user connections. After installation, you can use the NetWare Administrator utility to install additional licenses.

NetWare servers by default start from the MS-DOS partition when you turn on the server. If you like, you can start the server manually, as follows:

1   Turn on the power, and the system boots to an MS-DOS prompt on the boot partition (usually C:\).

2   Start the server by accessing the nwserver directory—type *CD \nwserver* and press Enter.

3   Type *server* and press Enter. The server starts and launches into the GUI. Many experienced NetWare administrators prefer to do a lot of the administration at the command line. You can close the GUI, if you like, and perform administration from the command console.

You can also place these actions in Autoexec.bat to start the server automatically.

Creating NetWare swap-file space

Except for the SYS volume, NetWare volumes don't have default swap-file space. It isn't advisable to use only the SYS volume for swap files, because this volume is typically already very busy. Instead, you should place one or more swap files on other high-performance volumes with plenty of free space. To add a swap file to a volume, execute the SWAP ADD command from a server console prompt. It doesn't matter if the volume is *mounted* (that is, ready for use). If not mounted, the swap file is created once you mount the volume. Swap files are deleted when the volume is dismounted, requiring you to recreate the swap file when it's mounted again. To avoid this inconvenience, you can add the SWAP ADD command to the startup file, Autoexec.ncf. NetWare swap files are dynamic, becoming larger or smaller as necessary. You can learn more about the SWAP command by typing *swap add* at a server console prompt.

Performing an upgrade to NetWare 5.1

If you're upgrading an existing server from a previous version of NetWare, the installation detects the previous version and prompts you either to upgrade or start a new installation. Upgrading retains all your server data, such as files, directory structures, partitions, and volumes. During an upgrade, the upgrade program may skip entire sections otherwise seen in a new installation, as the upgrade program automatically detects and configures several of the setup tasks. You can upgrade an existing server running NetWare 3.x, NetWare 4.x, or NetWare 5 to NetWare 5.1.

Before introducing a NetWare 5.1 server into an existing network that contains NetWare 4.x servers, run the NetWare Deployment Manager to prepare the NetWare 4.x version of NDS for an upgrade to NetWare 5.1 NDS.

To update an existing NetWare 4.x network to NetWare 5.1, you must log on from a Windows 95/98 or NT workstation as a Supervisor. Next, run NetWare Deployment Manager (Nwdeploy.exe) from the NetWare 5.1 Operating System CD and complete the network preparation tasks.

After you've completed the Network Preparation section of NetWare Deployment Manager, you should prepare the computer to be a NetWare server. NetWare 5.1 simplifies the NDS upgrade process by verifying that your NDS tree is ready for the version that you choose to implement.

Performing a proper NetWare shutdown

To shut down a NetWare server properly:

1 Close the GUI by clicking the red Novell item in the lower-left corner of the screen.

2 Select the Close GUI item, and answer "Yes" to the confirmation prompt. When the GUI closes, you're left at the Servername: prompt, where servername is the name of the NetWare server.

3 Type *down* and press Enter to close all services and files. A handy feature of NetWare is that, in this process, a notification of the downed server is delivered to all attached workstations. If you'd rather just reboot the server, type *restart server* and press Enter. (For NetWare 4.11, you must also type *exit* and press Enter.)

4 At the C:\NWSERVER prompt, turn off the power.

Do it!

B-1:   Discussing Novell NetWare

Questions and answers

1 What's a directory service?

2 How's the use of Novell Directory Services (NDS) more beneficial than a bindery?

3 What's the base software requirement to start an installation of NetWare 5.1?

4 What GUI interface makes managing NetWare more intuitive for the administrator?

Topic C: UNIX/Linux

This topic covers the following CompTIA Server+ exam objectives:

#	Objective
7.2	Use diagnostic hardware and software tools and utilities
	• Activities include:
	• Perform shutdown across the following OSs: Microsoft Windows NT/2000/2003, Novell Netware, UNIX, Linux
	• NOS shutdown procedures
	• UNIX/Linux

Unix basics

Explanation

UNIX is an interactive time-sharing operating system invented in 1969 by Ken Thompson. Brian Kernighan and Dennis Ritchie, the inventors of C, are also considered coauthors of the operating system. *UNIX* is a popular multiuser, multitasking operating system designed to be small and flexible and used mostly by programmers. Although it's developed significantly over the years, UNIX still uses its original cryptic command names along with its general lack of user friendliness. This is changing, however, with graphical user interfaces such as *X Windows* and *GNOME*.

UNIX has been a popular choice among universities and corporations because of its low cost and the fact that programmers familiar with the C high-level programming language can modify the code to specific requirements. UNIX has split into two main dialects: AT&T's System V and the University of California, Berkeley, version known as BSD 4.1, 4.2, or 4.3. Within the two main versions, there are dozens of other modified versions, or "flavors".

Most UNIX flavors are designed for CISC-based computing. For our purposes, we focus on *Linux*, because it's a PC-compatible flavor of UNIX, the CompTIA exam is PC-centric, and most anything that would be true of Linux for our purposes also applies sufficiently to UNIX.

Linux is a version of UNIX that, like other flavors, is open source code. Linus Torvalds authored early versions of Linux with the objective of creating a relatively small UNIX source code that would run on Intel-compatible computers (as opposed to the CISC-based processors of other UNIX versions). Boxed versions of Linux available from the vendors listed in the next section of this unit are preferable in many cases, because although you have to pay for the boxed version, the coding has already been tested, associated tools are included, and technical support is available. Linux has become one of the hottest operating systems in the past few years and has unexpectedly begun to compete strongly against Microsoft Windows.

One potential challenge to the new Linux user is the plethora of new commands, features, applications, and other components. As you familiarize yourself with Linux, realize that much of its administration, especially with early versions of Linux, involves the command line. If you're accustomed to MS-DOS commands, you have to make a point of *not* using MS-DOS commands in Linux: They don't work. You can tap into more about Linux commands by looking on the hard disk at the /usr/doc files after installation is complete. On all Linux distributions, there's a huge amount of miscellaneous documentation stored in this /usr/doc/ directory. Each version of Linux makes its own directories under /usr/doc, where it places files like FAQs and installation guides. There are many sources of information on Linux on the Internet as well. One central clearinghouse is the Linux documentation project located at www.linuxdoc.org.

Linux offers all the services and features you'd expect to see on a server, including:

- IP services like DHCP, DNS, Web hosting, and firewall support
- Application support for a wide range of applications, such as IBM's mainstream database product, DB2, Sun Microsystem's office suite, StarOffice 5.2, and Computer Associates' ArcServIT backup software
- Mail server services
- File and printer services
- SMP support
- E-commerce support
- Clustering and load balancing

Versions

There are several versions of Linux because of its open source code, and there are many vendors from whom you can obtain boxed sets of Linux. The major Linux vendors are listed here:

- *SuSE Linux*. You can find an installation guide in several different formats for SuSE on an FTP server at ftp://ftp.suse.com/pub/suse/i386/current/docu/.
- *Caldera Linux*. This company also offers Caldera Volution, which is a Linux management solution designed for network management. You can get more information on this flavor at www.caldera.com.
- *Mandrake Linux*. The install guide for this Pentium-optimized Linux version can be found at www.linux-mandrake.com.
- *Debian Linux*. You'll find the "Guide to Installing the Free Software Foundation's Debian Linux on Intel-Based Machines" at www.debian.org.
- *Red Hat Linux*. This is probably the most popular build of Linux. The Red Hat "Getting Started Guide," installation FAQs, and other important documentation can be downloaded from www.redhat.com/support/. The FAQs list minimum system requirements in addition to more technical issues. Unless stated otherwise, Linux references in this book are to the Red Hat version.

Linux minimum hardware requirements

Unlike some other versions of UNIX for the PC, Linux is very small. You could actually download one of the smaller, free releases and run an entire system from a single high-density 5.25-inch floppy. To run a complete Linux system on today's computers, there are obviously other hardware requirements. Linux, because of its open source nature, is continuously expanding, with more features being added every day. Hardware compatibility is very broad, especially compared to the earliest releases of Linux. Check with the Linux vendor, but most commonly available video cards, SCSI drivers, NICs, and so forth should be supported.

Linux hardware requirements are humble but particular. You don't need to have the most advanced or most recent server to run Linux. As with all operating systems discussed in this unit, there are two primary options for obtaining a computer to run Linux. The first option is to buy a computer with Linux preinstalled. In our view, this is the best alternative if you need a business server or high-performance workstation, and it applies to all NOSs. You can choose from brand-name machines such as Dell, Compaq, HP, and many other top PC manufacturers. Red Hat posts a list of certified systems by manufacturer on its Web site (www.redhat.com). Also look for upcoming systems that will use the 64-bit processing power of the AMD Sledgehammer.

A second viable option is to use an existing PC or assemble one and then perform a custom Linux installation. This is somewhat more common in the Linux community because of a do-it-yourself attitude prevalent among Linux fans. A disadvantage to rolling out your own Linux implementation is that there's no support except for what's freely available through newsgroups and Web sites. If a critical Linux server experiences a failure, you're unlikely to have the patience required to post a newsgroup message and then wait a couple of days for an answer, if any. With major server vendors, you usually have 24/7 emergency software and operating system support, as well as overnight delivery for failed hardware.

Hardware compatibility is most important if you're installing on an older system or building a new system from scratch. Red Hat Linux 7.x should be compatible with most hardware in systems that were factory-built within the last couple of years. With hardware specifications changing almost daily, however, there's never any guarantee that your hardware is 100% compatible. Therefore, you should collect all of the system hardware information that you can. *The Official Red Hat Linux Reference Guide* on the Documentation CD has instructions in the Installation-Related Reference area (including instructions for Windows users) that can assist you. You can also use Red Hat's online resources to make sure that your hardware is compatible. The easily navigable hardware compatibility list is located at hardware.redhat.com.

Linux hardware requirements are somewhat inexact, since multiple vendors have various requirements. However, for a basic installation, most any server should suffice, because Linux code is exceptionally trim compared to larger operating systems, such as Windows 2000 Server with its 40 million lines of code. However, as with other NOSs, remember that more is better when it comes to running a production server. General minimum hardware requirements for Linux are as follows:

- *Intel 80386 processor or higher.* Intel-compatible processors such as AMD and Cyrix also work with Linux.
- *32 MB of RAM.* Although you can locate and download very thin Linux versions requiring as little as 2 MB, feature-complete Linux versions such as Red Hat Linux usually recommend 64 MB.
- *500 MB of hard disk space.* Although if you install absolutely all features in a Red Hat installation, you need nearly 2 GB. (So much for the trim Linux OS.)

Installing Linux

Linux is very flexible about coexisting with other operating systems, and the *Linux Loader* (*LILO*) allows you to select which operating system you want to boot when you start the server. As a general rule, configuring the system to boot to more than one operating system is usually a smoother process if you install the other operating system(s) first and Linux last.

When you read Red Hat Linux documentation, you might see mention of a partitionless installation. Don't mistake this to mean that the installation doesn't use a partition at all. A *partitionless* installation is a reference to using an existing DOS or Windows partition instead of creating a partition manually during installation with FDISK or Red Hat's *Disk Druid* partitioning tool.

Although you can choose from several methods to install Red Hat Linux, this unit assumes installation from the CD-ROM. Absent the CD-ROM, you can make an installation floppy disk to initiate an installation, for example, because you downloaded Red Hat Linux rather than purchasing an official boxed set. You need to use the Linux boot floppy to launch the installation as opposed to booting an MS-DOS floppy and running Setup.exe. To begin the process, you need a blank, formatted, high-density (1.44 MB) 3.5-inch floppy disk. The images directory in the Red Hat Linux source files contains the boot images for various contexts, such as a standard boot to the Linux installation program, activating a PCMCIA socket, or booting to a Linux network share location. Extract the image file to a floppy using the *rawrite* utility found in the dosutils directory.

If your system doesn't support a CD-ROM (*El Torito*) boot, Red Hat Linux offers another choice that still allows you to start the installation directly from a CD-ROM. Use a boot floppy that loads your CD-ROM drivers, such as the Windows 98 boot floppy, and run the Autoboot.bat file from the \dosutils directory on the Linux CD-ROM to start the installation. You can't just boot to the floppy and then run a Setup.exe or Install.exe file from the CD-ROM.

Although you can use a text-based Linux installation, we assume use of a GUI installation. You can select the same options during both installations, except that the GUI version also offers explanations of your options to the left of the screen, and it's more intuitive. At the opening installation screen, press Enter or wait 60 seconds for the GUI installation to begin automatically. (If you insist, you can type *text* and press Enter at the Welcome screen to enter text-based setup.)

As with the other NOS installations addressed in this unit, not every installation step and option is listed. However, the basic Red Hat Linux 7.0 steps are as follows:

1   Select the installation type: Workstation, Server System, or Custom System. One of the primary differences in these installations is how the partitions are handled (see Exhibit 6-8).

   *   *Workstation*: Removes all existing Linux partitions on all disks and then uses all available unpartitioned space for the installation. Non-Linux partitions are left alone, and you can still boot to them after the Linux installation.

   *   *Server System*: Removes all partitions on all drives!

   *   *Custom System*: Provides an opportunity for you to manipulate free space and existing partitions to your liking.

We proceed here under the assumption that you're installing a Custom System.

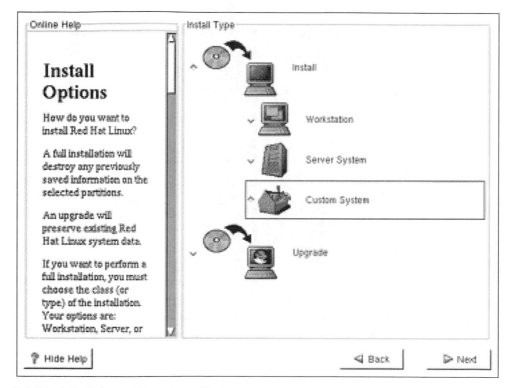

Exhibit 6-8: Select a Linux installation type

2 Configure partitions using either the Red Hat Linux Disk Druid utility or FDISK. As a minimum, you need:

- Root partition ("/"), which is the main repository for files except boot files.

- Swap partition equal to the amount of RAM in the system or 16 MB, whichever is larger.

- Boot partition ("/boot"), which contains the OS kernel, and as the name implies, boots to Linux. This partition doesn't need to be large, being usually no larger than 16 MB.

- Using the Disk Druid utility, you can also create a RAID 0, 1, or 5 array, and other partitions as suits your needs. Exhibit 6-9 shows the Disk Druid utility being used to create partitions.

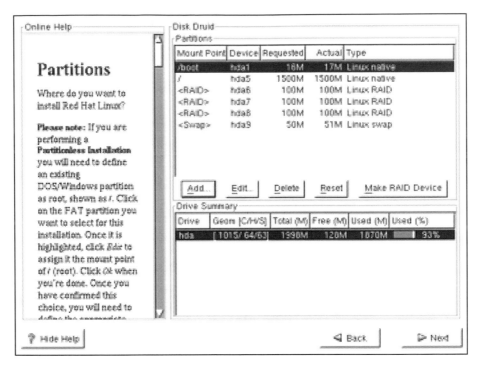

Exhibit 6-9: Creating partitions with Disk Druid

3   Enter the server's network configuration, including IP configuration, host name, gateway, and DNS server(s) (see Exhibit 6-10).

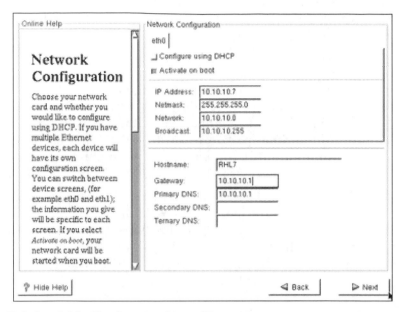

Exhibit 6-10: Configuring Linux IP settings

4   Select a root password, which allows you to administer the server completely. Also add one or more user accounts.

5   If you want to use security mechanisms, such as MD5 passwords or Kerberos, configure the appropriate information.

6   Select the various features you want to install and proceed through the installation. Setup creates partitions as specified and copies installation files to the hard drive.

As addressed in Step 2 in the Installing Linux section, you create Linux swap-file space during installation using the Disk Druid utility.

Performing a proper Linux shutdown

There are three possible states you can end up in when you shut down a Linux server. You can place the server in one of these states either from a GUI interface or an *X Term* session, which is a text-based terminal interface within your GUI.

- The first state, while not technically a shutdown, is *single-user mode*. System administrators often bring a UNIX system down to single-user mode, which closes user connections, to perform full backups of the file system, ensuring that there are no locks on open files. This isn't a complete shutdown, because the operating system is still running, and the processor is still active. From a network user perspective, however, it is. To enter single-user mode, access a boot prompt and enter *Linux single*. When finished, you can restart the computer by pressing Ctrl+Alt+Del or entering the shutdown –r command (see below).

- A second state is to shut down the system completely so that it's ready to be powered off. A complete shutdown is often performed when hardware maintenance is planned for the machine or at any other time the machine is to be powered off. A shutdown of this type uses the shutdown –h command (-h meaning "halt") to specify that the system should be completely shut down and the processor halted. When you halt the system, all processes are killed, and the sync command is called to write the memory-resident disk buffers to disk, after which the CPU is halted. If you truly want the power to be turned off with the shutdown command, press the power switch on the server. The shutdown –h command only kills processes and halts the CPU, but the power remains on.

- The third state is when the system is being rebooted. The shutdown –r command (-r meaning "reboot") accomplishes a reboot. If you're in text mode instead of a GUI (not a virtual console), press Ctrl+Alt+Del. On an MS-DOS computer, this reboots with any running applications still active and files still open, possibly damaging the system or data. A Linux computer closes files and kills services and applications before rebooting.

You can log out, reboot, or halt from any of the GUI interfaces such as GNOME using the Start style button in the lower left of the screen. Select Logout and make your choice (see Exhibit 6-11).

Exhibit 6-11: Choose to logout, halt, or reboot the Linux server

Once a system is brought up to *multi-user mode*, meaning that the server and its resources are available to network clients, it's common for the system to run for many days, possibly even months, without being shut down or rebooted.

Do it!

C-1: Discussing UNIX/Linux

Questions and answers

1 What's the Linux Loader (LILO)?

2 Which utility do you use in Red Hat Linux 7 to make a boot diskette under MS-DOS?

3 Linux is free over the Internet, and PCs are inexpensive. Why not build your own Linux server?

4 You want to create a partition for swap-file space during the Linux installation. Which partitioning utility should you use?

5 Why would you proceed with caution before installing a Linux server system?

Topic D: Windows NT Server

This topic covers the following CompTIA exam objectives:

#	Objective
3.9	Implement the server management plan (OS-dependent and OS-independent components)
	• Plans typically include:
	• Security plan
7.2	Use diagnostic hardware and software tools and utilities
	• Activities include:
	• Perform shutdown across the following OSs: Microsoft Windows NT/2000/2003, Novell Netware, UNIX, Linux
	• NOS shutdown procedures
	• Microsoft Windows NT/2000/2003

NT basics

Explanation

Corporations aren't quick to change server operating systems when they have servers that do the job reliably and securely. Thus, you'll find that Windows NT 4.0 is still used in many environments.

Windows NT 4.0 offers the following operating system characteristics:

- A Windows 95-based interface makes it easy to locate administrative tools and applications and makes it easier to operate compared to command-line-based operating systems, such as the earlier versions of NetWare and Linux.

- The interface and architecture make Windows NT capable of running local user applications: word processors, spreadsheets, and even a game of Solitaire if nobody's looking. Other network operating systems, such as earlier versions of NetWare, aren't designed for local application support. Even though you can install user applications on a server, it's better to avoid this option. Fewer applications mean lower overhead in terms of memory, processor, and hard disk utilization, freeing those resources for true server functions. Also, using an application on a local server requires you to log on, and this isn't prudent for most production servers because of the security risk involved if a passerby accesses your logged-on server while you're away from the server.

- Windows NT supports all the major TCP/IP services necessary for an IP network, including DNS, DHCP, and even a basic routing facility, though software routing can't usually compare to a true hardware router.

- The architecture of Windows is such that it allows a simple user interface while simultaneously limiting what the user can do. Even Windows NT 4.0 Workstation doesn't allow users to make major changes to the system, such as installing applications. This limitation significantly reduces the administrator's support burden, because user-installed applications often adversely affect the stability of the operating system.

- Windows NT introduces domains to the network. A Windows NT *domain* is different from an Internet domain, which is the hierarchical naming facility of the Internet, and is mostly implemented as a security boundary. For example, users in Domain A can access resources in Domain A. If the organization also has a Domain B, users in Domain A can't cross domains to access resources unless administrators specifically create a trust relationship between the two domains.

- The NTFS file system is Microsoft's first effort at securing hard disk resources, and especially for a first effort, they did a great job. Only persons to whom permission is granted can access a given file or folder.

- Windows NT supports multiple protocols, including NetBEUI, IPX/SPX, and TCP/IP.

Windows NT Server 4.0 minimum hardware requirements

Windows NT Server 4.0 has fairly high hardware requirements compared to NetWare 3.x and 4.x, which was Windows NT 4.0's primary competition at its introduction in 1996. However, at current levels of commonly available hardware, the requirements shouldn't be difficult to match or exceed. The minimum system hardware requirements are as follows:

- Intel-compatible 486/25 MHz processor
- 16 MB of RAM
- 124 MB of hard disk space

Each NOS lists minimum hardware requirements that are well below what you'd actually want in a production environment, but the NT minimums are probably the least realistic. Access the Hardware Compatibility List (HCL) from the Microsoft Web site at www.microsoft.com/hcl.

Installing Windows NT 4.0 Server

Installing Windows NT 4.0 Server is a fairly straightforward process. First, you must find a way to access the CD-ROM. The easiest way is to configure the BIOS settings in an El Torito-compatible system that can automatically access and boot from the CD-ROM. If your system is not El Torito-compatible, you can use the three floppy disks in the Windows NT boxed set. Boot from the first floppy and change disks when prompted. These disks also load CD-ROM drivers so that you can access the source files on CD-ROM. Finally, and as a last resort, use any MS-DOS system boot floppy, such as a Windows 98 startup disk, that also loads your CD-ROM drivers.

Though you can launch setup after booting from a Windows 98 startup disk, it has several drawbacks. Windows NT doesn't recognize FAT32 partitions. So, if you use a Windows 98 startup disk to create partitions, be sure to answer "N" (no) at the FDISK prompt to enable large disk support, which causes partitions to be formatted for FAT32. Otherwise, Windows NT won't be able to locate a suitable partition in which to copy installation files. Also, booting from a Windows 98 startup disk locks the hard drive, which means that the Windows NT installation won't be able to copy files to it. If you use a Windows 98 startup disk, type "lock c:" at a command prompt to remedy this situation. Also, there must be an existing FAT partition of at least 123 MB to store setup files. These drawbacks make booting from the Windows 98 floppy the least attractive choice, but it will do if necessary.

1   After booting from the CD-ROM or NT boot floppies, setup begins automatically, and you can skip to Step 4. If booting from a boot floppy with CD-ROM drivers, change to the CD-ROM drive (let's assume it's drive D). Installation proceeds much faster with both Windows NT and Windows 2000/2003 if you first copy the Smart Drive executable to the boot floppy. Smart Drive caches read from the CD-ROM. At the MS-DOS prompt, simply type SMARTDRV to load Smart Drive. This applies only to installations that use a manually configured MS-DOS or Windows 98 boot floppy, because the Windows NT boot floppy and bootable CD-ROM automatically load caching.

2   Go to the \i386 directory. This is the directory used for installing NT to an Intel-based PC server. However, you can also install Windows NT on a PowerPC, MIPS, or Alpha-processor-based server.

3   Type winnt /b and press Enter. This initiates the text mode portion of setup, which starts by copying setup files to the local hard disk (see Exhibit 6-12).

4   Proceed through the setup process, following the prompts. You're prompted to specify any additional storage devices, such as SCSI cards, that might not have been detected by setup (see Exhibit 6-13). If you have devices that weren't detected and for which you have the drivers on a floppy, supply the drivers from the floppy disk. (If you booted from a generic floppy, a reboot occurs between Steps 3 and 4).

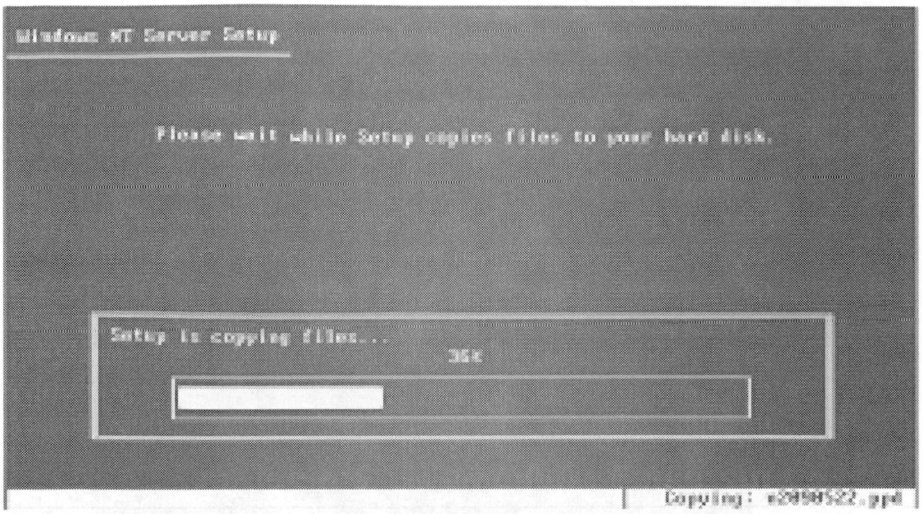

Exhibit 6-12: The Windows NT 4.0 file copy stage of text mode setup

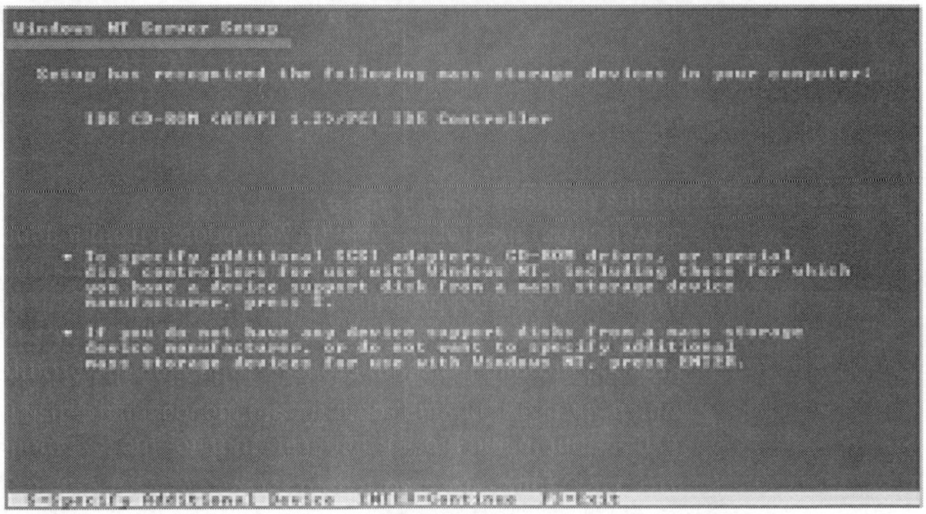

Exhibit 6-13: Add additional drivers for devices not detected by setup

5 Basic hardware detection finds hardware, such as keyboard, mouse, and display adapters. This level of device detection is very basic; a more in-depth and accurate detection occurs closer to the end of the setup process (see Exhibit 6-14).

6 Select a partition in which to install the operating system. If none of the existing partitions suits you, you can delete or create other partitions. Assuming that you started with a FAT partition, setup offers you the chance to convert to an NTFS partition. For the sake of performance and security, it's normally better to choose the NTFS conversion at this point (see Exhibit 6-15).

7 Setup copies more files to the hard disk. When prompted, press Enter to reboot the system. If you opted to convert from FAT to NTFS, the conversion takes place. This concludes the text portion of the setup process. The graphical portion begins after the reboot.

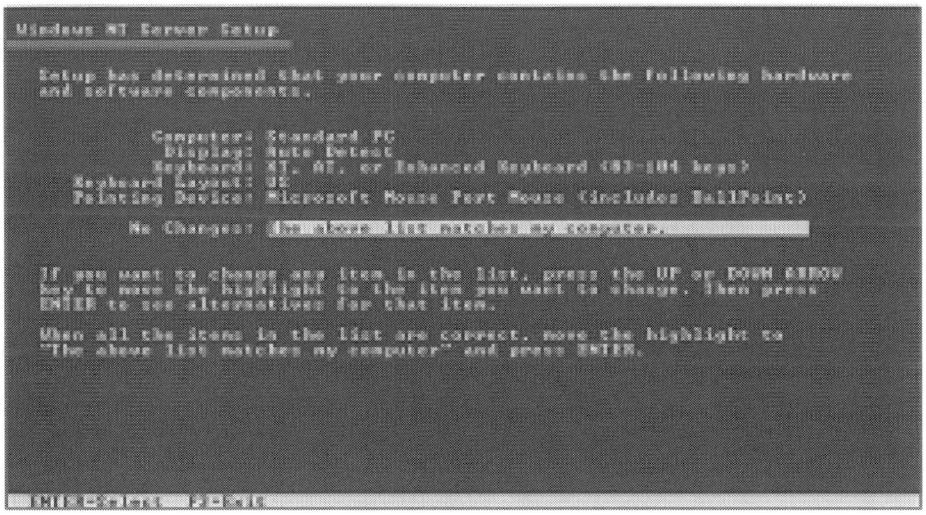

Exhibit 6-14: Basic device detection as determined by Windows NT 4.0

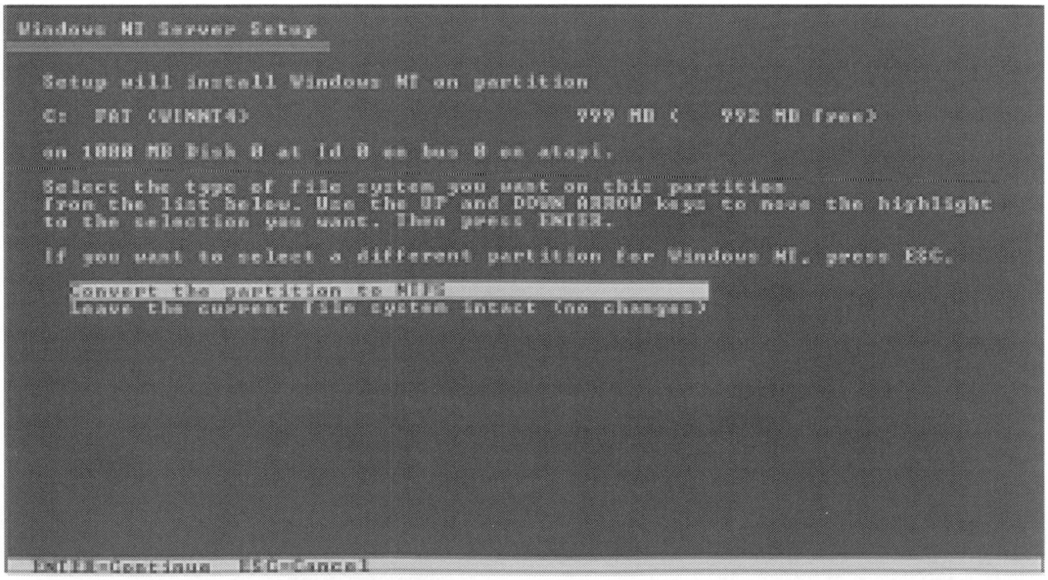

Exhibit 6-15: Convert partitions to NTFS

8   Enter your name and organization. (The name you enter here is the name of the person legally liable for properly licensing the product. So if at all possible, enter your boss's name.)

9   Enter the CD Key that accompanied the product.

10   Select a licensing mode (see Exhibit 6-16):

 • *Per server*: Enter the number of concurrent connections allowed under the licensing scheme you purchased. Choose this method if clients will usually connect to only one server. If you have 100 users connecting to four servers, then each server would require 100 licenses—a total of 400. This wouldn't be cost-effective.

 • *Per seat*: Each client that connects to this server must be properly licensed. This is much more cost-effective than the per-server licensing scheme if clients connect to multiple servers. Continuing the earlier example, a per-seatlicensing solution would require only 100 client licenses, one for each user workstation regardless of the number of servers to which the client connects. You can convert from per server to per seat, and money spent on per-server licensing can be directly applied to the new per-seat licensing scheme. Conversion is a one-time, one-way event. You can't convert from per seat back to per server.

11   Enter a computer name. This name is how the server is identified and must be unique within the network.

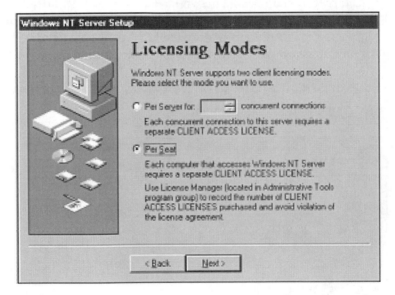

Exhibit 6-16: Select the per-server or per-seat licensing mode

12 Choose the role of this NT server (see Exhibit 6-17):

- *Primary Domain Controller (PDC)*: Stores the only read/write copy of the directory database. This database is a record of user and computer accounts and is used for logging on users.

- *Backup Domain Controller (BDC)*: Stores a read-only copy of the directory database and is useful as an extension to the PDC for logging on users and computers. You must have a PDC before you can have a BDC.

- *Stand-alone Server*: Doesn't store the directory database and isn't a member of the domain. This type of server doesn't share users or groups from the domain controller but is useful for other resources and services for which users don't require direct access (for example, a Web server allowing anonymous access or a DNS server).

- *Member Server*: Is a member of the domain but doesn't contain a copy of the directory database. Because it's a member of the domain, administrators can configure access permissions to its resources using domain user and group accounts. To configure a member server, you install it as a standalone server and later join it to the domain. A member server can be useful as a file, print, or application server, or it can provide one or more services.

13 Continue through the installation, answering prompts and choosing installation options. You'll enter a password for the local Administrator account (don't forget it) and install a network adapter, if one isn't detected automatically. If you experience difficulty installing the network card at this point but want to proceed with the installation, choose the MS Loopback Adapter, which is a software trick allowing you to install networking components without an actual physical network adapter.

14 When finished with all the setup prompts, the system boots to the standard Windows NT 4.0 desktop.

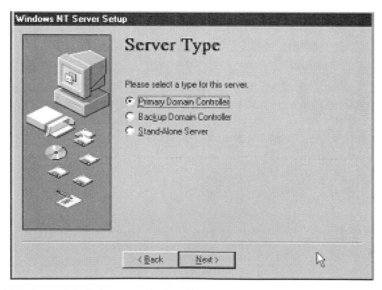

Exhibit 6-17: Select a role for the server

Upgrading to Windows NT 4.0 Server

To initiate the upgrade, just insert the Windows NT 4.0 Server CD into the CD-ROM drive. A prompt appears to begin installation automatically or you can run Winnt32.exe from the \i386 directory. Despite Microsoft's own success in upgrades, a clean install is recommended whenever possible, because an upgraded system can inherit remnant bugs or files that aren't used in Windows NT 4.0.

Winnt.exe executes the Windows NT/2000/2003 setup process from MS-DOS. From within existing Windows operating systems that you want to upgrade, use Winnt32.exe.

Creating Windows NT 4.0 swap-file space

Windows automatically creates its own swap file as part of installation. Typically, the swap-file defaults are of acceptable size, though you might want to change the drive on which the paging file appears for performance reasons.

To modify *paging file* configuration, as it's called in NT 4.0/2000/2003:

1 Right-click My Computer on the desktop (or double-click the System icon in Control Panel).

2 Select Properties from the menu.

3 Click the Performance tab, and then click the Change button in the middle of the dialog box (see Exhibit 6-18).

4 Specify the drive, initial size, and maximum size. Remember to click the Set button after configuring the paging file.

5 Click OK twice.

6 Reboot the system.

Exhibit 6-18: Adjusting the virtual memory paging file

Performing a proper Windows NT 4.0 shutdown

Shutting down any Windows operating system is very easy. Simply click Start, click Shut Down, and select from a list of options to shut down the computer, restart the computer, or close all programs and log on as a different user (see Exhibit 6-19). When the computer is "shut down," you must still turn off the power if the machine doesn't shut down automatically. You can click a Restart button if you want to reboot the operating system.

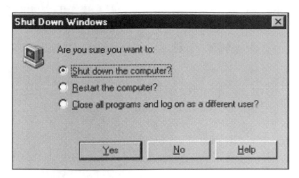

Exhibit 6-19: Choose to shut down, restart, or log off

Do it!

D-1: Discussing Windows NT

Questions and answers

1 What's the difference between a standalone server and a member server in an NT 4.0 domain?

2 On the installation CD, what command do you run from the i386 directory to upgrade to NT within a previous version of Windows? Which command starts a clean installation from DOS?

3 Which shutdown option restarts the computer and reloads the OS?

Topic E: Windows 2000 and Server 2003

This topic covers the following CompTIA exam objectives:

#	Objective
2.3	Develop the server management plan (in-band and out-of-band management).
3.5	Install NOS and driver updates to design specifications • Activities include: • Obtain update • Ensure there is a backup and recovery plan • Make sure that the old drivers are available for reinstallation • Supporting knowledge includes: • Know how to obtain OS updates • Why updates might be needed • How updates can be used • How to decide whether an update is necessary
3.9	Implement the server management plan (OS-dependent and OS-independent components) • Plans typically include: • Server management software installation • Availability • Server change management requirements • Supporting knowledge includes: • Purpose and function of server management tools
4.2	Add processors. Activities include: • Perform upgrade checklist, including: • Locate/obtain latest drivers, OS updates, software, etc. • Review FAQ's, instruction, facts and issues
4.3	Add hard drives. Activities include: • Perform upgrade checklist, including: • Locate/obtain latest drivers, OS updates, software, etc. • Review FAQ's, instruction, facts and issues
4.4	Increase memory. Activities include: • Perform upgrade checklist including: • Locate/obtain latest drivers, OS updates, software, etc. • Review FAQ's, instruction, facts and issues

#	Objective
4.5	Upgrade BIOS/firmware. Activities include:
	• Perform upgrade checklist including:
	• Locate/obtain latest drivers, OS updates, software, etc.
	• Review FAQ's, instruction, facts and issues
4.6	Upgrade adapters (e.g. NIC's, SCSI cards, RAID, etc). Activities include:
	• Perform backup
	• Perform upgrade checklist including:
	• Locate/obtain latest drivers, OS updates, software, etc.
	• Review FAQ's, instruction, facts and issues
4.7	Upgrade peripheral devices, internal and external. Verify appropriate system resources (e.g. expansion slots, IRQ, DMA, etc.)
	• Activities include:
	• Perform upgrade checklist including:
	• Locate/obtain latest drivers, OS updates, software, etc.
	• Review FAQ's, instruction, facts and issues
	• Supporting knowledge includes:
	• Validation via hardware compatibility list, tips, documentation, and FAQ's
4.8	Upgrade system monitoring agents. Activities include:
	• Perform upgrade checklist including:
	• Locate/obtain latest drivers, OS updates, software, etc.
	• Review FAQ's, instruction, facts and issues
4.9	Upgrade service tools (e.g. diagnostic tools, EISA configuration, diagnostic partition, SSU, etc.). Activities include:
	• Perform upgrade checklist including:
	• Locate/obtain latest drivers, OS updates, software, etc.
	• Review FAQ's, instruction, facts and issues
4.10	Upgrade UPS. Activities include:
	• Perform upgrade checklist including:
	• Locate/obtain latest drivers, OS updates, software, etc.
	• Review FAQ's, instruction, facts and issues
7.2	Use diagnostic hardware and software tools and utilities. Activities include:
	• Perform shutdown across the following OS's: Microsoft Windows NT/2000/2003, Novell Netware, UNIX, Linux
	• NOS shutdown procedures
	• Microsoft Windows NT/2000/2003

Windows 2000

Explanation

The Windows 2000 operating system family provides a significant advancement in features, stability, and increased runtime over its NT predecessor. While we'll continue to see Windows NT 4.0 on servers for a few more years, Windows 2000 has already eclipsed NT 4.0 in many organizations. The characteristics of Windows 2000 are:

- The primary characteristic of Windows 2000 is arguably its new directory service, known as Active Directory. *Active Directory* is a comprehensive database capable of storing millions of objects, such as users, groups, computers, and more. In terms of functionality, Active Directory users can log on and access resources anywhere in the enterprise regardless of geographic location or where the user account was originally created.

- Active Directory domains evolved from the original Windows NT 4.0 domains. Whereas, under Windows NT, an organization might have multiple domains in a flat namespace such as Domain A, Domain B, and Domain C, Active Directory uses a DNS hierarchy, such as DomainA.DomainB.DomainC. Also, Active Directory provides a structure allowing administrators to consolidate all NT 4.0 domains into a single domain. (NetWare administrators will notice some similarities between the tree structure of NetWare 4.x and later and Windows 2000 Active Directory. These similarities result from both operating systems using the LDAP standard.)

- In the past, Microsoft environments have relied heavily on WINS as the name resolution service for Microsoft network NetBIOS hosts. Windows 2000 allows the administrator to shed the need for WINS because DHCP clients can automatically register themselves in the DNS database using Dynamic DNS. In the past, someone would have to enter DNS registrations manually. However, Windows 2000 still offers the WINS service to support NetBIOS clients.

- Windows 2000 offers strong *scalability* (the ability to grow in terms of the number of processors) in that you can use 4, 8, or even 32 or more processors in a single SMP system. To be fair, we should emphasize that all NOSs in this unit support SMP. Microsoft claims to have an extremely efficient architecture that allows SMP systems to obtain a high level of performance.

- Up to 8 GB of memory support allows Windows 2000 Advanced Server to handle large and demanding files and applications.

- No other operating system offers as much broad hardware compatibility support, thanks to true Plug and Play capabilities.

- Built-in clustering support in Windows 2000 Advanced Server and Windows 2000 Datacenter Server allows a server in a cluster to fail or be removed for routine maintenance, while remaining members of the cluster continue to provide service.

- Windows file protection prevents new software installations from replacing critical Windows 2000 system files. This makes Windows 2000 more stable than past Windows versions. Also, Microsoft has instituted a thorough testing process for hardware manufacturers, in which their drivers must be proven safe and stable under Windows 2000. If a driver passes Microsoft's tests, a validating certificate is attached to the drivers.

- Administrators were frequently aggravated when a seemingly minor change to Windows NT 4.0 required a reboot before the change could take effect. Microsoft greatly reduced the number of events for which you have to reboot the system in Windows 2000. For example, you can change the IP address on a running system, and the change takes place after a few seconds without a reboot.

Versions

Windows 2000 comes in the following versions:

- *Windows 2000 Professional*. Though not a server operating system, this is the ideal client for Windows 2000 servers, especially for purposes of centralized administration and automated software distribution. Windows 2000 Professional supports up to 4 GB of RAM and 2-way SMP.
- *Windows 2000 Server*. The core server product capable of 4 GB of RAM and 4-way SMP.
- *Windows 2000 Advanced Server*. Windows 2000 Server plus support for clustering, up to 8 GB of RAM and 8-way SMP.
- *Windows 2000 Datacenter Server*. Windows 2000 Advanced Server plus support for up to 64 GB of RAM and 32-way SMP.

Windows XP is the desktop successor to Windows 2000 Professional but has mostly the same platform and architecture and is designed finally to replace the Windows 9.x architecture. Windows Server 2003 is the upgrade to Windows 2000 Server.

Windows 2000 minimum hardware requirements

Windows 2000 Server lists somewhat more realistic minimum hardware requirements than Windows NT 4.0 Server. However, you should still obtain server equipment that's as capable as possible. Minimum system hardware requirements are as follows for Windows 2000 Server and Windows 2000 Advanced Server:

- Intel-compatible 133 MHz processor or higher. (Windows 2000 Datacenter Server requires the same minimum hardware, except that the processors must be Pentium III Xeon or higher)
- 128 MB of RAM, though Microsoft strongly recommends at least 256 MB
- 2 GB hard disk with 1 GB of free space

You can verify the compatibility of specific hardware by checking the hardware compatibility list on the Microsoft Web site at www.microsoft.com/hcl.

You can't purchase Windows 2000 Datacenter Server off the shelf and install it wherever you like. Instead, only system integrators can purchase the product and sell it preinstalled with the server.

Installing Windows 2000 Server

The general steps for installing Windows 2000 are very similar to those for Windows NT 4.0:

1   If booting from the CD-ROM, setup begins automatically, and you can skip to Step 4. If booting from a boot floppy with CD-ROM drivers, change to the CD-ROM drive (we'll assume it's drive D).

2   Go to the \i386 directory. This is the directory used for installing NT to an Intel-based PC server. Windows 2000 installs only on Intel-based processors.

3   Type winnt and press Enter. This initiates the text mode portion of setup. Windows 2000 doesn't create the boot floppies by default, so the /b option isn't necessary, as it was for NT 4.0.

4   Proceed through the setup process, following the prompts such as license agreement, partitioning, and additional storage devices that might not have been detected by setup, such as SCSI adapters. If so, supply the drivers from a floppy disk. If you booted from a generic DOS floppy, a reboot occurs between Steps 3 and 4.

5   Basic hardware detection finds hardware such as keyboard, mouse, and display adapters. This level of device detection is very basic; a more in-depth and accurate detection occurs closer to the end of the setup process.

6   Select a partition in which to install the operating system. If none of the existing partitions suits you, you can delete or create other partitions. Assuming that you started with a FAT partition, setup offers you the chance to convert to an NTFS partition. For the sake of performance and security, it's normally best to choose the NTFS conversion at this point. You can also convert from FAT to NTFS after installation. A Windows 2000 server automatically applies security permissions appropriately when converted to NTFS.

7   Setup copies more files to the hard disk. When prompted, press Enter to reboot the system. If you opted to convert from FAT to NTFS, the conversion takes place at this point. This concludes the text portion of the setup process. The graphical portion begins after the reboot.

8   Confirm the locale and keyboard settings and then enter your name and organization.

9   Select a licensing mode under the same guidelines discussed in the Windows NT 4.0 section.

10 Enter a computer name. This name is how the server is identified and must be unique within the network. Then enter the password for the Administrator account.

11 Continue through the installation, answering prompts and choosing installation options.

12 Select Typical or Custom networking settings. Choosing Typical settings really means that the computer is configured as a DHCP client. Choosing Custom settings exposes the network property sheet, so that you can manually configure IP settings (see Exhibit 6-20).

13 Choose to make the computer a member of a workgroup or a domain. In Windows NT 4.0, you'd choose the server role during installation. But Windows 2000 servers always install as member servers (member of a domain but not a domain controller) or a standalone server (not a member of a domain). After installation, you can make the Windows 2000 server a peer domain controller by running DCPROMO from a command line, which launches a domain controller installation utility. All Windows 2000 domain controllers are peer domain controllers. This means that each domain controller has both a read and write copy of the directory database.

14 When finished with all the setup prompts, more files copy to the hard disk, and a prompt requests that you reboot.

15 After the reboot and logon, you see the standard Windows 2000 desktop.

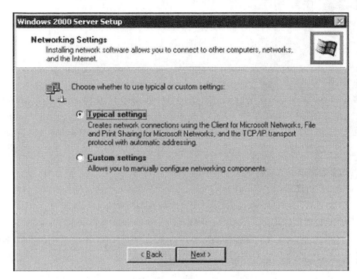

Exhibit 6-20: Choose Typical for DHCP clients, or Custom for manual IP configuration

Upgrading to Windows 2000 Server

You can upgrade a Windows NT 3.51 server or Windows NT 4.0 server to Windows 2000 Server. You can't upgrade any desktop client operating system to Windows 2000 Server. The easiest way to upgrade to Windows 2000 is simply to insert the CD and allow Autoplay to start setup. If Autoplay is disabled, you can run Winnt32.exe from the \i386 directory. A prompt asks whether you want to perform an upgrade or clean install (see Exhibit 6-21).

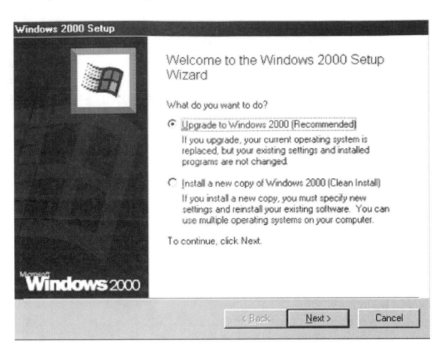

Exhibit 6-21: Select an upgrade or clean install

Creating Windows 2000 swap-file space

As with most Windows installations, Windows 2000 automatically configures a swap file for virtual memory use. You can adjust the size, move, or split the paging file among available drives using the System Properties as follows:

1 Right-click My Computer and click Properties or select System from the Control Panel. The System Properties dialog box opens.

2 Click the Advanced tab and select the Performance Options button.

3 In the Performance Options dialog box, click the Change button.

4 The dialog box that appears next is nearly identical to the Windows NT 4.0 Virtual Memory dialog box (refer to Exhibit 6-18). Enter the size of the swap file, click Set, and then click OK. Adjusting the swap file is one of the few reboot events in Windows 2000.

Performing a proper Windows 2000 shutdown

Shut down a Windows 2000 server in a way similar to shutting down a Windows NT 4.0 server. Click Start, click Shut Down, and select your shutdown option (see Exhibit 6-22). Windows 2000 has better power management than Windows NT 4.0, and it's more likely to turn off the power through the operating system. On some systems, you still press the power button to turn off power to the server. Just wait for the message that says it's safe to turn off the server. On the other hand, on many newer systems, pressing the computer's power button initiates a graceful shutdown in the OS.

Windows 2000 also allows you to place the system in a low-power standby state, or *hibernation*, which saves the complete contents of RAM to disk. When you turn on the power again, the contents on disk are reloaded into RAM. This is faster than a standard startup of the operating system.

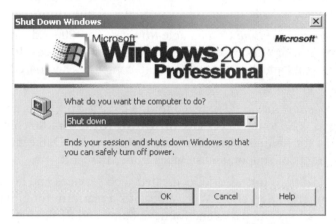

Exhibit 6-22: Windows 2000 allows log off, shut down, restart, stand by, and hibernate

Do it!

E-1:   Discussing Windows 2000

Questions and answers

1 What program can you run that helps Windows NT 4.0 or Windows 2000 installations to proceed much faster?

2 Windows 2000 offers what new directory service?

3 Why aren't there PDCs and BDCs in a Windows 2000 domain?

Windows Server 2003

Explanation

Windows Server 2003 is an improved and updated version of Windows 2000. There aren't major changes between 2000 and 2003 as there were between NT and 2000, so an administrator of Windows 2000 will be quite comfortable using 2003. Installation is virtually identical.

Editions

Windows Server 2003 has no client/workstation version. Desktop clients stick with Windows NT Workstation, Windows 2000 Professional, or Windows XP Professional. Windows Server 2003 comes in the following editions:

- *Standard Edition*: Like Windows 2000 Server, this edition is designed for departmental and standard workloads for file and printer sharing and desktop application deployment. It supports up to 4 processors and 4 GB RAM.

- *Enterprise Edition*: Comparable to Windows 2000 Advanced Server, it's designed for mission-critical applications and services. It supports up to 8 processors and 32 GB RAM for x86 computers and 64 GB RAM for Itanium-based computers.

- *Datacenter Edition*: Designed for the largest workloads and highest reliability, it supports up to 64 processors and 64 GB RAM for x86 computers and 512 GB RAM for Itanium-based computers. It offers the Datacenter High Availability Programs of support and services from Microsoft.

- *Web Edition*: Intended for dedicated Web services and hosting with Internet Information Server 6.0 Web server, it's a platform for building and hosting Web applications and pages and for developing and deploying XML services. It supports up to 2 processors and 2 GB RAM. There's no analogous version of Windows 2000.

- *Small Business Server*: This isn't actually an edition but a suite aimed at providing a complete package for small businesses. It includes Windows Server 2003 Standard Edition and other server software, such as Exchange Server 2003 and Shared Fax Service.

Hardware requirements

Requirements vary depending on edition. Standard and Web Editions require 550 MHz processor speed, while Enterprise and Datacenter Editions call for at least a 733 MHz processor speed. Minimum RAM is 128 MB for all editions except Datacenter, which is 512 MB. Recommended RAM is twice the minimum for each edition. All editions require 1.5 GB of disk space for setup, with final use depending on the edition and installed options.

Manage Your Server

As soon as you install Windows 2003, and every time you start it, the Manage Your Server window opens by default. This is a centralized management tool that provides links to other administrative tools, Windows Update, and help and support resources. It also allows you to add roles to your server, such as print and file sharing, application server, mail server, DNS server, DHCP server, and more. The tools and options available through Manage Your Server will be familiar to Windows 2000 administrators.

Exhibit 6-23: The Manage Your Server management tool

You can return to the Manage Your Server console at any time by choosing Start, Administrative Tools, Manage Your Server.

Performing a Proper Windows Server 2003 Shutdown

To shut down Windows Server 2003, click Start, Shut Down, and select your shutdown option. In addition to the options found in other Windows operating systems – Log off, Shut Down, Stand By, Hibernate – Windows Server 2003 adds the Shutdown Event Tracker tool (see Exhibit 6-24). When activated, this tool helps an administrator keep track of shutdown/restart reasons across the network by requiring a reason to be picked from a list before shutdown is completed. There's also a check box to indicate weather the shutdown was planned (such as a scheduled upgrade) or not. This tool doesn't require or track reasons for logging off or hibernating.

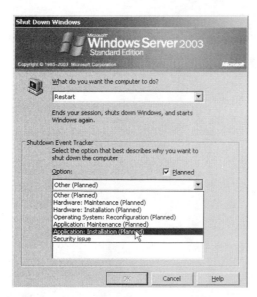

Exhibit 6-24: Windows Server 2003 Shut Down dialog box with Shutdown Event Tracker

Do it!

E-2: Discussing Windows Server 2003

Questions and answers

1 What's the Workstation version of Windows Server 2003?

2 Which edition of 2003 can handle the biggest workload?

3 What tool in Windows Server 2003 helps administrators track reasons for server shutdowns on their network?

Updating a network operating system

Explanation

Although there arc slight differences among patches, fixes, and updates, the differences don't matter for our purposes. We'll collectively call them all updates. All operating systems require periodic updates. There are many possible reasons for this, including:

- *Security vulnerability.* These updates usually come out as quickly as possible from the vendor. Unless thcre exists a compelling reason to avoid them, you should nearly always apply security updates for obvious reasons.

- *Incompatibility.* Even after rigorous testing, an operating system is likely to encounter compatibility problems with some number of applications. How quickly an update is relcased depends on the severity of the problem.

- *Poor functionality.* An operating system simply doesn't function as promised and requires an update to fix the problem.

- *Added features.* Prior to the release of the next major version of an operating system, a vendor might release additional features for free. For example, Microsoft released the Option Pack for Windows NT 4.0, which improved NT 4.0's Internet server features.

Regardless of the reason for an update, you should regularly check with the software vendor to see if there are any updates available that might be useful to you. In the server context, we discourage applying an update just because one exists. While an update might be designed to fix one problem, it might accidentally create another problem or incompatibility. So you should thoroughly test updates before placing them into production. Study relevant FAQ's, instructions, and issues before applying any updates.

Be sure to have backups of working drivers. You should also have a backup and recovery plan in case the update causes total failure. If possible, test the update on a lab machine. If the test goes well, install it on the production machine and test it there, including comparing before and after baselines.

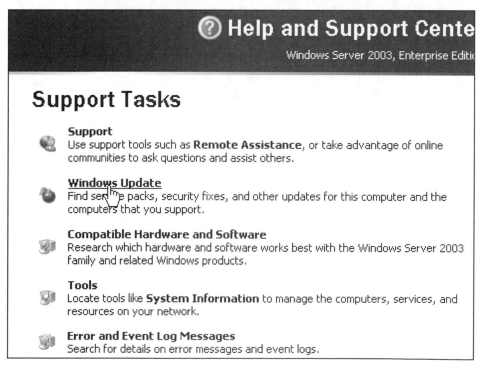

Exhibit 6-25: The Help and Support Center provides a direct link to available updates

To help you keep abreast of important updates, some vendors send you e-mail when one is released. With Windows 2000/2003/XP, Windows Critical Update Notification periodically checks the Microsoft Web site to see if a new update is available and notifies you of the update with a visual indicator. The Windows Update site scans your system and offers updates available for your system. You check off the upgrade items you want and apply the updates over the Internet (see Exhibit 6-26). This process simplifies the more cumbersome one in Windows NT 4.0 in which you have to download an update, extract the files to a temporary location, and run the update.

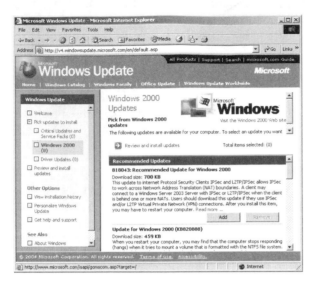

Exhibit 6-26: The Windows Update site automatically scans your system and notifies you of updates available for your system

Not all updates install with the same procedures.The best practice is to read the Web site documentation that describes the update to find out how to apply it. For example, Red Hat site updates have an encrypted authentication that you decrypt to verify that the update is truly a Red Hat update and not from a malicious source.

Do it!   **E-3:   Discussing Windows Updates**

Questions and answers

1   What reasons are there for manufacturers to provide OS updates?

Unit summary: Configuring a network operating system

Topic A   In this topic, you learned that the vendor's recommended minimum hardware is rarely adequate and that preparing server hardware for NOS installation involves the right perspective. Instead of trying to get away with as little as possible, the administrator's perspective should be nearly the opposite, that is, to obtain hardware that's reasonably powerful enough for current and future requirements. You learned that **Ethernet** is the most widely used access method, because it offers a nice balance between cost, speed, and ease of installation. And because Ethernet utilizes a shared medium between nodes, there are rules for sending packets of data to avoid conflicts and protect the data. You learned the four types of Ethernet: standard, **Fast**, **full-duplex**, and **Gigabit**.

Topic B   In this topic, you learned that Novell **NetWare** is a widely accepted LAN operating system developed by Novell Corporation. You learned that NetWare runs on a variety of LANs, including Ethernet and IBM Token Ring, and that it offers users and programmers a reliable interface that's independent of the underlying hardware that transmits data. You learned that, depending on the version, NetWare uses either a bindery or directory service design to manage the majority of network resources: NetWare 3.x uses a bindery, but NetWare 4.11 and later versions use NDS.

Topic C   In this topic, you learned that **UNIX** has been a popular choice among universities and corporations because of its low cost and the fact that programmers can modify the code to specific requirements. You learned that UNIX has split into two main dialects: AT&T's **System V** and the University of California, Berkeley version, known as **BSD 4.1**, **4.2**, or **4.3**. Within the two main versions, there are dozens of other modified versions or "flavors." You learned that **Linux** is a version of UNIX that, like other flavors, is open source code. Linus Torvalds authored early versions of Linux with the objective of creating a relatively small UNIX source code that would run on Intel-compatible computers (as opposed to the CISC-based processors of other UNIX versions). Several vendors offer Linux in boxed sets.

Topic D   In this topic, you learned that the **Windows NT** operating system has a Windows 95-based interface and allows you to run local user applications. It introduces a security boundary known as an **NT domain**, which isn't the same as a **DNS domain**.

Topic E   In this topic, you learned that **Windows 2000** introduces its LDAP directory service, **Active Directory**, which can store several types of objects and uses the DNS hierarchical namespace. You learned that **Dynamic DNS** services allow clients to self-register their host names. You also learned about **Windows Server 2003**, which has only server versions and improves upon Windows 2000.

Independent practice activity

In this project, you'll explore other possible updates for your operating system.

1 Choose Start, Help and Support.

2 Click the link for Windows Update. Your system is scanned for necessary and suggested updates.

3 Are there any critical updates to be applied?

4 In the left pane, click Windows 2003 to see the non-critical, Windows 2003-specific updates available. List the name and size of five of these and briefly describe each.

5 Click view installation history and note previous updates run on this computer.

6 Close the browser.

Review questions

1 What is the purpose of a swap file?

A To boost the effectiveness of the processor

B To allow processes to alternate between processors in an SMP server

C To transfer data from slower pages in RAM to faster pages in RAM

D To extend the range of physical RAM to virtual memory on the hard disk

2 Which of the following is a widely accepted local-area network (LAN) operating system that was developed by Novell Corporation that runs on a variety of different types of LANs, including Ethernet and IBM token-ring networks?

A NetWorks

B GateWare

C Warp

D NetWare

3 What GUI interface makes managing NetWare more intuitive for the administrator?

A Crayon Manager

B Program Manager

C InterfaceOne

D ConsoleOne

4 How can you simultaneously support both IPX/SPX and TCP/IP on a NetWare network with minimal additional network traffic?

A Segment the network into a separate IPX/SPX and TCP/IP network

B Install IP with IPX compatibility

C Use switches instead of routers

D Remove all IPX/SPX applications

5 How can you automatically create swap file space on one or more NetWare volumes when the operating system boots?

  A Create a visual basic script

  B Add the SWAP ADD command to the AUTOEXEC.NCF file

  C Access the System properties in Control Panel and select the Advanced tab

  D You cannot; NetWare does not support swap files

6 How can you simultaneously support both IPX/SPX and TCP/IP on a NetWare network with minimal additional network traffic?.

  A Segment the network into a separate IPX/SPX and TCP/IP network

  B Install IP with IPX compatibility

  C Use switches instead of routers

  D Remove all IPX/SPX applications

7 How can you automatically create swap file space on one or more NetWare volumes when the operating system boots?

  A Create a visual basic scrip

  B Add the SWAP ADD command to the AUTOEXEC.NCF file

  C Access the System properties in Control Panel and select the Advanced tab

  D You cannot; NetWare does not support swap files

8 How should you prepare NetWare version 4 for an upgrade to version 5.1?

  A No actions are necessary, just insert the 5.1 CD and setup automatically begins.

  B Run the NetWare Deployment Manager.

  C Uninstall NetWare 4 first, then install NetWare 5.1.

  D First upgrade to NetWare 5.0, then upgrade from 5.0 to 5.1.

9 Which of the following is a network component that identifies resources like e-mail addresses, computers, and peripheral devices on a network and makes them available to applications and users?.

  A network operating system

  B local area network

  C redirector

  D directory service

10 Which one of the following is an interactive time-sharing operating system invented in 1969 by Brian Kernighan and Dennis Ritchie, the inventors of C?

A Linux

B NetWare

C OS/2

D UNIX

11 Which utility do you use in Red Hat Linux 7 to make a boot diskette under MS-DOS?

A Rawrite

B Dosutils

C Dd

D Makedisk

12 Linux is free over the Internet and PCs are inexpensive. Why not build your own Linux server?

A A server from a major vendor with Linux preinstalled offers better support and reliability.

B You cannot obtain Linux off the shelf, it must come preinstalled on a server.

C There is no way to do it without violating the Linux licensing agreement.

D Linux does not work with PC servers, only CISC based processors such as Alpha.

13 Which of the following offers you the chance to boot from multiple operating systems?

A NWLoader.nlm

B LELA

C MultiBoot

D LILO

14 You want to create a partition for swap file space during the Linux installation. Which partitioning utility should you use?

A FDISK

B Partitions-R-Us

C Disk Druid

D LVM

15 Why would you proceed with caution before installing a Linux server system?

   A It requires significantly more system resources than the workstation installation.

   B It removes all partitions on all drives.

   C It flushes the cache, possibly discarding important data.

   D It automatically creates a root volume but no boot volume.

16 To properly shut down Linux:

   A Hit the power button, and all services and files automatically close.

   B Enter shutdown –r and then turn off the power.

   C Enter shutdown –h and then turn off the power.

   D Enter die, die, die, and turn off the power.

17 What program can you run that will help Windows NT 4.0 or Windows 2000 installations to proceed much faster?

   A SMARTDRV

   B QUICKTIME

   C POGOSTCK

   D SPEEDISK

18 Windows 2000 offers what new directory service?

   A NDS

   B DDNS

   C WINS

   D Active Directory

19 Why aren't there PDCs and BDCs in a Windows 2000 domain?

   A Those initials are way too confusing.

   B All domain controllers in Windows 2000 are peer domain controllers.

   C All Windows 2000 servers are member servers only.

   D All Windows 2000 servers are stand-alone servers only.

Unit 7

Services and applications

Unit time: 90 minutes

Complete this unit, and you'll know how to:

A Identify and understand major network operating system services.

B Discuss other NOS services, such as e-mail, Web, FTP, and fax.

C Discuss the various ways that servers run network applications and specify the functions of the server as a network device, router, and firewall.

Topic A: DHCP, DNS, and WINS

This topic covers the following CompTIA Server+ exam objectives:

#	Objective
1.3	Know the basic purpose and function of the following types of servers. • Server types include: • Client/server • DNS server • WINS server • DHCP server
2.1	Conduct pre-installation planning activities • Activities include: • Verify network protocols, naming conventions, domain names

Client-server

Explanation

Client-server can refer specifically to a network topology where one or more client computers access a local server for data, applications, or network services. It's also a general term that refers to any time a client computer obtains a service from one specialized computer, even if that server isn't part of its LAN or WAN. These services include such things as storing files, running applications, providing IP addresses, handling e-mail or chat communications, and hosting multi-player games.

DHCP

Each host on a TCP/IP network must have a unique IP address. If two hosts on the network have the same IP address, communication problems occur. In Windows NT, the first host that enters the network with a given IP address retains it when a second Windows NT host with the same IP address enters the network. The second host, however, cannot communicate. Both hosts enter a record of the duplicate IP address problem in the System log. Duplicate IP addresses are one of the most common problems in IP networks with *static IP addresses*, that is, where someone manually enters a permanent IP address for a host, which includes IP configuration such as the subnet mask, name servers, and routers. Human error and a lack of good records can lead either to wrongly configured IP addresses that don't communicate properly on the network or to duplicate records. Furthermore, it requires a significant investment in time for technicians to enter static IP addresses manually on hundreds or thousands of individual clients.

This kind of problem can be avoided by the use of a *Dynamic Host Configuration Protocol* (*DHCP*) server. A *DHCP server* automatically allocates IP addresses to hosts on the network. Recipients of DHCP-allocated IP addresses are known as DHCP clients, and in order to receive the IP address, you must specify this in the client's network properties. For example, Exhibit 7-1 shows the TCP/IP properties for a Windows network connection. Obtaining an IP address and a DNS server address automatically means to search for a DHCP server.

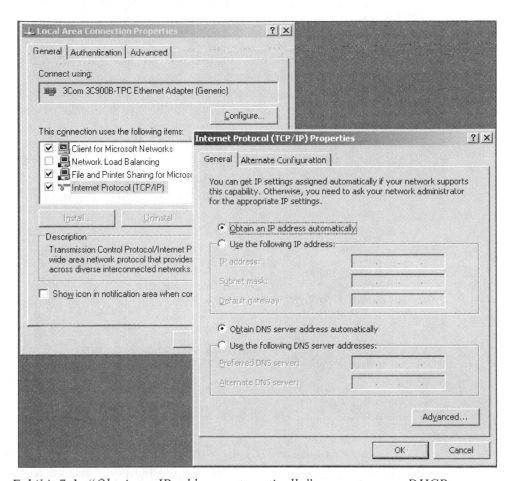

Exhibit 7-1: "Obtain an IP address automatically" means to use a DHCP server

The lease process

When a client receives an IP address from the server, it's obtained a *lease*. Similar to the lease of real estate or a car, this lease is for a limited duration. Administrators can adjust the length of the lease from a few hours to several days, depending on the nature of client access. For example, in a typical office building where the network hosts are mostly desktop computers and very few changes occur on the network, you might configure leases that last for days. However, if you run an ISP, the lease duration is probably an hour or less, because you don't want users who have disconnected to retain the address lease while it would otherwise be available to the next user.

The client initiates the lease process with a *discovery broadcast* seeking a DHCP server. A broadcast to all hosts is necessary, because the host doesn't yet have an IP address with which to communicate, nor does it know the IP address of the DHCP server. All available DHCP servers respond to the client with an *offer* of a specific IP address and configuration. The client responds with a *request*, which is an acceptance of the offer from one of the randomly selected DHCP servers, while rejecting offers from the rest. Finally, the server issues the IP configuration, which it confirms with an *acknowledgment*. Using the first letter of each of the four steps, you can easily remember the process with the mnemonic "DORA." Figure Exhibit 7-2 illustrates this process.

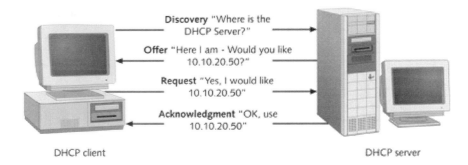

Exhibit 7-2: The DORA lease process

Although using DHCP for client IP address configuration helps ensure accurate IP addressing and reduces the administrative burden of manual configuration, it's best not to use DHCP for servers, printers, and network equipment, so that those addresses are always consistent. You don't want a printer, for example, to lease a changing IP address, because it becomes unavailable to clients attempting to access the printer's original address.

A DHCP server usually distributes not only the IP address and subnet mask to the client, but also many other configuration items, such as the IP address of the gateway (router) and DNS (Domain Name System) and WINS (Windows Internet Naming Service) name servers. In Windows 2000 or 2003, you can configure DHCP by opening the DHCP item (Start, Programs, Administrative Tools, DHCP). NetWare also has a GUI console that you can use to configure both DHCP and DNS. Exhibit 7-3 shows the Windows DHCP management console interface.

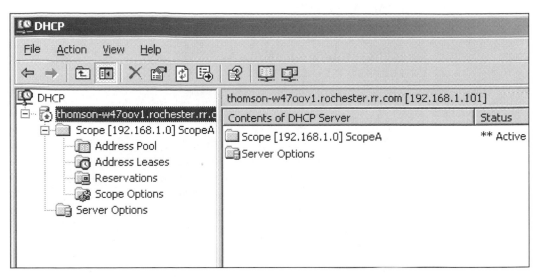

Exhibit 7-3: The Windows 2003 DHCP management console

When configuring DHCP, you must know the range of IP addresses you want to use on the network. This range is known as a *scope*. You can use private IP addresses, which are practically limitless and for which there's no direct access from Internet hosts, or you can use public IP addresses. As a security precaution, most administrators prefer private IP addresses for their network hosts. Once you determine the scope you want to use, you enter a starting IP address and an ending IP address on the DHCP server. Hosts then lease the IP addresses one at a time in sequential order. The administrator ensures that enough IP addresses are available in the scope to service all hosts on the network, and usually add a margin for growth.

Be careful about testing IP scopes on the network. If someone introduces a DHCP server with incompatible or duplicate addresses on the network and the organization is large, then the new DHCP server starts to answer DHCP client requests. Those clients are then incorrectly configured in the network, and it could be very difficult to find out exactly where the rogue DHCP server is and shut it down. Windows 2000 requires administrators to perform an additional step of authorizing a DHCP server before it functions on the network. This requirement helps to ensure that a rogue DHCP server doesn't enter the network.

For the sake of network availability and redundancy, implement more than one DHCP server. If one server fails, another DHCP server can continue to provide service. The redundant DHCP server(s) have a compatible range of IP addresses usable on the network, but none of the IP addresses overlaps from one DHCP server to the next. If it isn't practical to use two DHCP servers in the same network segment, you can program routers to forward BOOTP or DHCP broadcasts to another DHCP server on a different segment. Also, the operating system might include a mechanism by which a host listens to DHCP discovery broadcasts and forwards the discovery inside a packet that's sent directly to the IP address of a DHCP server. For example, in Windows NT and Windows 2000, the DHCP relay agent performs this function.

Some organizations consider the use of a DHCP server as a security threat. The concern is that a stranger could enter the building as a visitor and locate an available network jack. Then, by turning on a laptop and leasing an address, the stranger's laptop becomes part of the network and can begin to explore the network to provide information that would allow unauthorized access to resources.

DNS

People tend to remember names better than numbers. However, network hosts are identified using numbers. Though administrators are likely to have memorized the IP addresses of several key network resources, such as printers, routers, Web servers, mail servers, and logon servers, nobody memorizes the IP addresses of an entire enterprise. When users want to access a network resource or Web site, they don't type in an IP address such as www.199.227.124.246.net. Instead, users type the name, www.accusource.net.

It's the DNS server that transparently allows users to operate this way, because the *Domain Name System* (*DNS*) server stores a record of both the IP address and host name and uses these records to service name resolution requests. DNS is actually a replacement for the HOSTS plain text file used in all major NOSs. The *HOSTS file* contains static, manual entries of host-to-IP address mappings, much like this entry for a computer named Websrv6:

```
109.54.94.197 Websrv6.accusource.net
```

With the growth of the Internet, using a HOSTS file to resolve Web sites became impractical years ago. DNS also requires manual configuration but is much more flexible in its administration. However, many organizations still use the HOSTS file, because at boot time, the file is loaded into memory for quick resolution of a network host without a DNS server.

DNS name resolution

Although the length of time you wait for most host name resolution requests to resolve is perceptibly short, the resolution process might actually take place through several DNS servers across a wide geographic area. For example, when you type www.accusource.net into a Web browser, the computer issues a query to its configured DNS server, which then resolves the name to an IP address. As the Internet is large and even the most capable DNS server doesn't have all DNS records, the DNS server often references other DNS servers to answer a request. Forwarding the request like this is known as a *recursive query*. While waiting for another DNS server to resolve the request, the original DNS server becomes the resolver, while the client simply waits for an answer. In a recursive query, the resolution burden rests with the DNS server either to resolve the name itself or to do so using other DNS servers. Compare this to an iterative query, explained in the following section. This process is illustrated in Exhibit 7-4.

Internic is the governing body responsible for naming and managing the DNS domain namespace. The domain space is a hierarchical tree of names created to manage DNS requests using separate authoritative DNS servers to manage each domain space, such as .com, .gov, .edu, .net, .org, and so on. See more about Internic at www.internic.org.

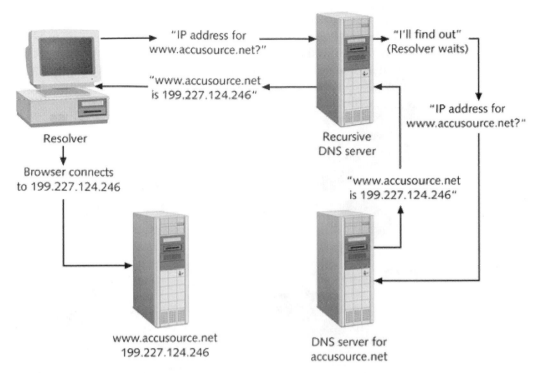

Exhibit 7-4: A recursive query

The DNS server can also be configured to work in an *iterative query* mode. When the DNS server receives a request for which it doesn't have an answer, it refers the resolver to more authoritative DNS servers further up the hierarchical DNS namespace tree, as illustrated in Exhibit 7-5. The iterative DNS server is then relieved of the resolution burden, because it's the client resolver that references other DNS servers. In turn, the next DNS server to which the resolver passes the request might forward the request to yet another DNS server.

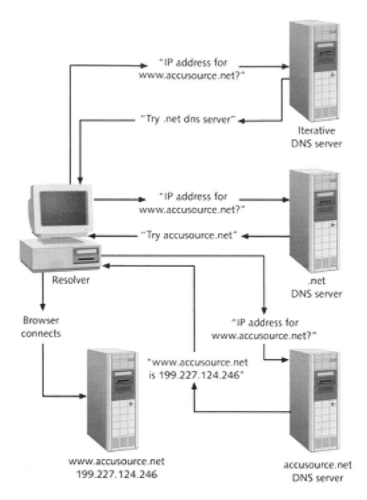

Exhibit 7-5: An iterative query

For infrequently accessed Internet sites or sites that have only recently become registered, a client Web browser might time-out on the first attempt while waiting for various DNS servers to resolve the request. Often, if you try a couple more times, DNS servers through which the request passed the first time will have cached some results, helping to speed up the resolution.

DNS zones

Many large organizations have one or more full-time employees whose main function is to create and maintain DNS database records. Except for Dynamic DNS records, which this unit discusses later, most DNS records require someone to make a manual entry on the DNS server. Each NOS has a different interface for creating such records, but if you know DNS, then you can create the DNS records on almost any GUI, once you get used to its interface. For example, the DNS/DHCP Management Console for NetWare 5.1 has a handy toolbar for configuring DNS (see Exhibit 7-6).

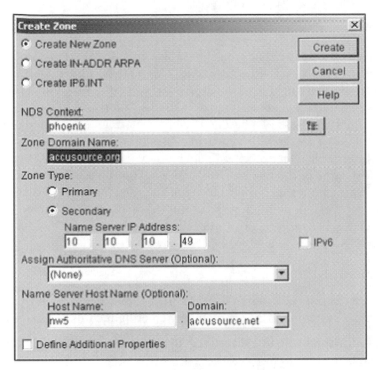

Exhibit 7-6: Use the DNS/DHCP Management Console to create DNS servers and zones

This section provides some basics and helps you learn some of the most commonly used types of records. The rest is a matter of learning the interface.

Before you go about creating DNS records, you need a DNS zone. The *DNS zone* is a naming boundary that you probably see every day when using the Internet. For example, in www.course.com, "course.com" is a zone and "www" is the name of the Web server in that zone. The zone contains the records. When you create a zone, you also add a record for the DNS server that's the *Start of Authority* (*SOA*) *server*. The SOA server is the authoritative source for information about the domain, and the domain can't function without it. In the configuration screen for a new zone, the NOS might include fields for you to provide the name SOA record, as shown in Exhibit 7-6, where the NetWare console labels it "Assign Authoritative DNS Server." Windows 2000 automatically assumes that the SOA server is the DNS server on which you create the zone and creates it for you. If this isn't correct, you can manually change this. An SOA record is also required for the reverse lookup zone.

If you use UNIX/Linux, then you need to learn the text-based format in which you add zones to the named.conf file, and then create separate database files (*.db) that store the individual records for each zone. One of the major flavors of UNIX is BIND (Berkeley Internet Name Domain), and it has a very reliable, time-tested facility for DNS. In fact, Internet DNS servers are typically UNIX servers. You can use BIND DNS on a Linux server. Although the service is very reliable, however, the interface is text-based and not as intuitive as other NOSs. For example, here's an excerpt from a named.conf file for accusource.net:

```
zone "accusource.net" {
type master;
file "accusource.db";
```

After you create the zone, you should also create the *reverse lookup zone*, otherwise known as the IN-ADDR.ARPA zone. This zone performs the reverse of a normal query: Instead of resolving a name to an IP address, you're resolving an IP address to a name. A reverse lookup is not as frequently used as a forward lookup, but it's useful if you know the IP address of a host and want to determine its name. For example, if you suspect that a server with a particular IP address is returning errors but can't remember which server has that specific IP address, by using the *PING* -a command, which returns the host name of the associated IP address, you can see the host name of the server. The host name implies its physical location and role, making it easier to find the specific server. Reverse lookups are also useful for verifying the claimed identity of a connecting host as a security precaution. Another reverse lookup tool is the NSLOOKUP tool available with Windows NT/2000.

DNS records

Creating records is a straightforward process that, again, is mostly a matter of using the operating system interface or manually entering records in UNIX/Linux.

The following list isn't exhaustive, but it itemizes the main DNS records of which you should be aware:

- *SOA record.* As discussed earlier, an SOA record identifies the authoritative name server for a given domain.
- *Name Server (NS) record.* This specifies what DNS servers are delegated servers for the domain, meaning that the server specified in the record can resolve queries authoritatively.
- *PTR (pointer) record.* This is the actual record used in reverse lookups.
- *Address (A) record.* Also known as a host record, this is the actual record that resolves the host name to the IP address.
- *Mail Exchanger (MX) record.* This routes mail to the appropriate server(s) for members of the domain. If you have multiple MX records for the same domain, you can prioritize the mail servers with numbers between 0 and 65,535, with lower numbers having the highest priority.

- *CNAME record.* This stands for canonical name record and is an alias that points to another host. You use CNAME records every time you browse the Internet. When you type www.xyz.com into a Web browser, "www" represents a server located in the xyz.com domain. However, very few companies actually name their Web servers "www." Let's say that the xyz.com domain's Web server is actually named Websrv13. That would make its true Internet address Wcbsrv13.xyz.com. However, for security reasons, most organizations prefer not to expose the true names of their Web servers on the Internet. The xyz.com DNS administrator would then create a CNAME record that directs inbound requests for www.xyz.com to Websrv13.xyz.com in a completely transparent way to the users. CNAME records are also useful in directing inbound requests to any of multiple servers. For example, if xyz.com has 13 Web servers, a CNAME for each server can be used to direct inbound requests to any one of the 13 Web servers.

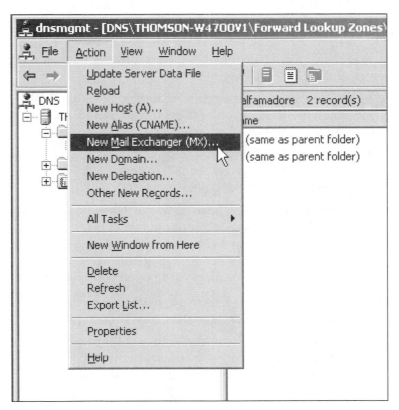

Exhibit 7-7: Creating a new record in the Windows 2003 DNS management console

A common way of directing inbound requests to any of multiple Web servers is to use the round-robin method, which you configure using the DNS server properties. DNS directs the inbound request to a host and then sends the host to the bottom of the list. DNS directs the next request to the next host and, in turn, sends that host to the bottom of the list and so on, until the original host returns to the top of the list.

Be meticulous about DNS administration. DNS is a critical service, because it points to other services. For example, it might direct network clients to mail servers, logon servers, Web/intranet servers, and so on. DNS problems can bring down an entire network. In fact, some major Web sites have become unavailable for hours or days because of an incorrect DNS record.

A relatively new technology, *Dynamic DNS (DDNS)*, greatly reduces the burden of manually creating DNS records. In network environments where Microsoft operating systems exist, NetBIOS names, instead of host names, identify network nodes. Introducing the mechanisms necessary to use and resolve NetBIOS names adds overhead and administration to the network. Beginning with NetWare 5.1 and Windows 2000, you can now rid the network of reliance on NetBIOS, because you can use DDNS instead. With traditional DNS, this would have required the administrative nightmare of manually creating, updating, and deleting DNS records, which usually makes registering hundreds or thousands of desktop clients completely impractical. Now, because of an interaction with the DHCP service, DDNS can accept automatic registrations from clients when they receive their IP configuration from the DHCP server. This capability isn't limited to NetWare 5.1 and Windows 2000. Any environment, including UNIX, that implements RFC 2136 can use DDNS. (RFC is "request for comments" and is the titling method used by the Internet Engineering Task Force to identify documents.)

Types of DNS servers

There are three main types of DNS servers: primary domain servers, secondary domain servers, and caching-only servers.

- *Primary domain servers* are the starting point of all DNS records, containing a read/write-capable zone database: you can add, remove, or modify DNS records from a primary domain server.
- *Secondary domain servers* receive a read-only copy of the zone database from a primary domain server. Secondary domain servers are useful for providing redundancy and load balancing.
- *Caching-only servers* have no zone database, either of their own or copied through a zone transfer from a primary domain server. Caching-only servers mostly function only to improve performance by reducing the number of forwarded queries. When a caching-only server retrieves a resolved query, it stores the result in memory for a period of time known as the *time to live* (*TTL*).

When a DNS zone is created, there's a master-slave relationship between the primary master server, master servers, and slave servers as follows:

- *Primary master servers* are the first and final authority for all hosts in their domains. There's only one primary master server per zone, and it's the source for records that are copied to master or slave DNS servers.
- *Master servers* are authoritative DNS servers that transfer zone data to one or more slave servers. ("Authoritative" means that the server is configured to host the zone and return query results.)
- *Slave servers* are authoritative servers that receive the *zone transfer* (a copy of the zone DNS database) from the master server and are named in the zone by NS records.

Windows 2003 Server roles

Windows Server 2003 refers to the many services a server can provide as *roles*. These roles, such as file serving and DNS and DHCP services, can be added, removed, and managed centrally from the Mange Your Server Console. This console opens by default every time you start the server, and you can also open it by choosing Start, Administrative Tools, Manage Your Server.

Do it!

A-1: Exploring service roles on Windows Server 2003

Here's how
1 Choose **Start**, **All Programs**, **Administrative Tools**, **Manage Your Server**.
2 Click **Add or Remove a role**.
3 Observe the preliminary steps, then click **Next**.
4 Observe the list of server roles. Select **DHCP server**.
5 Click the **Read about DHCP servers** link. The help system opens with the topic of configuring your server as a DHCP server.
6 Close the help window.
7 Select and read about other server roles.
8 Close the help window and the Manage Your Server console.

WINS

The *Windows Internet Naming Service* (*WINS*), as the name implies, is a Microsoft invention. In a Microsoft network, there are two types of names, and a client might possess one or both of them: a host name, as discussed in the previous section on DNS, and a NetBIOS name. WINS is a service that performs a function similar to that of DNS, except that it resolves NetBIOS names instead of host names. (Recall that *NetBIOS* is a broadcast-based name resolution scheme where a client simply broadcasts the NetBIOS name of the computer it wishes to reach to all of the computers on a subnet.) The broadcast message identifies a computer that acknowledges the broadcast and establishes a communication link. The limitations of this are clear from the fact that it's a broadcast message and therefore can't be routed to another subnet. This resolution method also creates more traffic on the subnet due to the nature of broadcast messages. WINS mitigates both of these problems by registering the NetBIOS names and resolving them to IP addresses that are routable and destination-specific. WINS is only a necessary evil to overcome the inherent limitations of NetBIOS names. Some network applications use WINS to locate network hosts. Also, mapping drives using the *NET USE* command use WINS.

Windows 2000 changes this reliance on WINS for name resolution by registering Windows 2000 computers, servers, and domain controllers via DDNS (as discussed earlier in this unit). In a strictly Windows 2000 networking environment, DNS is the only name resolution service that's necessary. However, if you have pre-Windows 2000 Microsoft clients, or if you have network applications that require a NetBIOS interface to resolve host names, you likely need to run the Windows NT or Windows 2000 WINS service.

WINS is a method by which user-friendly NetBIOS computer names can be resolved to IP addresses for the purpose of allowing such communication between hosts on different subnets. In order for this resolution to occur, network hosts must have a way to add, remove, or update their names dynamically in the WINS database. The WINS database is only as good as the accuracy of the records that are contained in it. The database must reflect any changes made to a client's configuration with as little delay as possible. The administrative overhead required to make these changes manually would be prohibitive, so the need for a dynamically updated database is clear.

Name registration occurs when a WINS client requests the use of a NetBIOS name from the WINS server. The WINS server can either accept or reject the request for a NetBIOS name made by the WINS client. The response that's given depends on several factors. If the requested name doesn't already exist in the WINS database, the WINS server accepts the request and creates a record containing the name of the NetBIOS client and its IP address, among other things. The WINS server also sends an acceptance message containing the TTL parameter to the requesting client.

Resolving NetBIOS names

Windows 2000 client name resolution follows a very specific order. WINS is one step in that order and is used only after exhausting the first two options. When a Windows 2000 client attempts to reach another host by name, the client determines whether or not to use DNS. DNS resolves the name for the client if there are more than 15 characters or if there are periods in the name. NetBIOS names must be 15 characters or fewer and can't contain periods, making DNS the only service that could properly resolve the name.

If the name is 15 characters or fewer and doesn't contain periods, the second step is for the client to check its remote name cache stored in RAM for resolution to the IP address. (This is the first step for non-Windows 2000 clients.) The remote name cache is a location in memory that stores recent NetBIOS names to IP address resolutions. This is the most efficient method of name resolution, because all the client reads is its own memory.

If the name isn't in the cache, the client contacts the configured (either statically or through DHCP) WINS servers to see if there's a record in the database for the requested computer name. If there's a record for the NetBIOS name, the WINS server returns the IP address to the requesting client. The client then uses the address to connect to the desired server.

If the name isn't in the WINS database, the client broadcasts the name to the subnet in the hope that the desired server responds. The main limitation of broadcasts is that routers can't forward broadcast messages to another subnet, so a client that's on another subnet can't respond.

If the broadcast fails, the client checks its LMHOSTS file to see if there's a static entry for the NetBIOS name. The *LMHOSTS file* is a static text file that lists NetBIOS-name-to-IP-address mapping and is the NetBIOS equivalent of the HOSTS file. You can configure entries in the LMHOSTS file to load individual records into the remote name cache at system startup. Therefore, Windows 2000 queries those LMHOSTS records at the very beginning of this process.

If the LMHOSTS file fails to provide resolution, the client queries the DNS resources. First, it queries for HOSTS files. For example, if you know that a client needs to access a specific logon server, adding the name of the host separated by the host's IP address automatically loads the name mapping into memory. If this fails, the client queries the configured (static or DHCP) DNS servers. Exhibit 7-8 illustrates the process of NetBIOS name resolution.

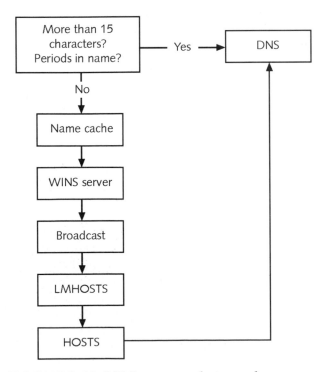

Exhibit 7-8: NetBIOS name resolution order

WINS replication

As a network becomes larger than just one subnet, and for the sake of redundancy, you should use more than one WINS server. No matter how many WINS servers you have in your network, you still have only a single WINS database. With multiple servers and one database, *replication* (copying the database from one server to another) is extremely important to ensure that all the WINS servers have a consistent copy of the database.

You configure each WINS server with one or more replication partners in such a way that all the WINS servers eventually receive each change that occurs on a single WINS server. When a WINS client registers its name and IP address with a WINS server, that server is the owner of the record and the record propagates to all the other WINS servers through a series of replication partners. WINS replication is incremental, meaning that only the changes in the database replicate, not the entire database. The entire database replicates only when you install a new WINS server on the network.

Every WINS server maintains an owner-version mapping table that it builds dynamically and stores in memory. WINS servers use these tables in the replication process to identify the server's replication partners and the version of the information that's contained on that server. The field in the table that's important for replication is the Highest ID field, which stores the highest known version ID that's contained on the replication partner. Remember that all records have a Version ID field, which records the highest value contained in all the version IDs received from a particular replication partner.

Pull replication partners

A *pull replication partner* is a WINS replication partner that requests and then accepts changes from its push replication partners. At specified intervals and when a WINS server starts, the pull replication partner requests all records from the push partner that have a higher version number than the last entry received from that particular pull partner. The amount of time between pull requests is called the *replication interval*, which can be set globally for all WINS servers or can be set at each WINS server that's configured as a pull partner.

The pull replication partner initiates the replication by sending a *replication trigger* message to a push replication partner. When the push replication partner receives the trigger, it scans for the highest version ID contained in the database for all WINS servers on the network. This highest ID for each owner is compared to the highest ID records that the pull replication partner currently has. All the records that have version ID numbers that fall between the two replicate to the pull partner initiating the replication.

Push replication partners

A *push replication partner* is a WINS replication partner that responds to requests for changes from its pull replication partners. Push replication occurs when the WINS server starts or when a set number of name-to-address changes have occurred in the replica contained in the push partner. You can set this value in the properties of the push replication partner WINS server. By default, the number of changes that are required to initiate a push replication is 20. If you enable persistent connections, which isn't the default, the number of changes required to initiate a push replication is set to zero, and any changes are replicated as soon as they're made. You can configure a push replication partner in this situation to initiate changes less frequently. The push/pull replication process is illustrated in Exhibit 7-9.

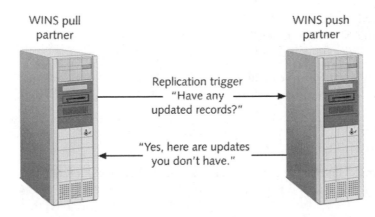

Exhibit 7-9: The WINS replication process

Push/pull replication partner

A push/pull replication partner acts as both a push and a pull replication partner. This is the default replication functionality for Windows 2000 WINS servers. In general, setting up WINS servers to be push/pull replication partners is the simplest and most effective way to ensure full replication between replication partners.

Avoid the use of unidirectional replication partners. There are some cases in large networks where the use of unidirectional partners can limit the amount of traffic created over slow WAN links. When configuring unidirectional partners, you should be careful that each server has at least one replication partner. Also, balance unidirectional partners configured over a WAN link with another link in the opposite direction to some other location in the network. Finally, configure primary and secondary WINS servers as direct replication partners of each other.

WINS proxy agent

Non-WINS clients use broadcast messages to locate other nodes on the network by default. Broadcast messages aren't routed, so that if the client attempts to contact another computer located on another subnet, the non-WINS client must use a statically configured LMHOSTS file to resolve the IP address so that the client can be contacted.

A *WINS proxy agent* is a WINS-enabled computer that you configure to listen on the subnet for WINS broadcast messages, such as query, refresh, release, and register. The WINS proxy then communicates with the WINS server to resolve or register NetBIOS names.

When a non-WINS client sends a broadcast query for a node on the network using a NetBIOS name, the node with that name responds if it's on the same subnet as the broadcasting node. The WINS proxy agent doesn't respond to a query message if the non-WINS client is on the same subnet. The WINS proxy agent determines that it's on the same subnet as the requesting client by comparing its address with the address of the requesting client using the subnet mask.

If the node isn't on the same subnet, the WINS proxy agent intercepts the broadcast and checks its own cache to see if it has a record of the NetBIOS name and its associated IP address. If it's in the cache, the WINS proxy agent sends the IP address to the non-WINS client so that it may now send routable, directed packets to the desired node.

If the name isn't in the cache, the WINS proxy agent queries the WINS server using directed packets. The WINS server then responds with the IP address that's associated with the NetBIOS name. The WINS proxy agent then forwards the information to the non-WINS client and stores the information in its cache for future use.

To configure a WINS-enabled Windows 2000 computer, you must edit its Registry by adding the value EnableProxy to the HKEY_LOCAL_MACHINE Registry subkey as follows:

```
HKEY_LOCAL_MACHINE\SYSTEM\CurrentControlSet\Services\
Netbt\Parameters
```

You must set the value to 1 to enable the WINS proxy agent. The type of data is REG_DWORD and is shown in Exhibit 7-10.

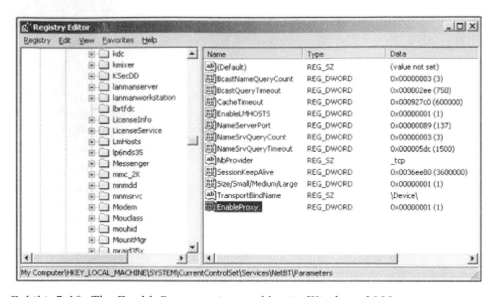

Exhibit 7-10: The EnableProxy registry subkey in Windows 2000

Do it!   ## A-2:   Discussing NOS services

Questions and answers
1   Which service automatically distributes IP configuration to clients?
2   What's the correct order in the lease process?
3   DNS is an alternative to which text file?
4   What's a resolver?
5   What's a DNS zone?

Topic B: Other services

This topic covers the following CompTIA Server+ exam objectives:

#	Objective
1.3	Know the basic purpose and function of the following types of servers.
	• Server types include:
	• Mail server
	• FTP server
	• SNA server
	• RAS server
	• Fax server
	• Web server
3.9	Implement the server management plan (OS-dependent and OS-independent components)
	• Plans typically include:
	• Security plan

E-mail protocols

Explanation

E-mail used to be available only for internal communications within the office. However, with the ever-expanding Internet, e-mail has become a global medium for both internal and external communications. E-mail is now possibly the most heavily utilized service in most organizations and is also the most visible to users. If the Web site goes down, users might not notice for a while and can probably continue most of their job functions. If e-mail services fail, users start calling immediately. Running e-mail services involves knowing the main components, adequately preparing the hardware, and planning for disaster.

E-mail requires a transport protocol to get it from one place to another. Each e-mail protocol has its own unique purpose, as listed below:

- *Simple Mail Transport Protocol* (*SMTP*). As the name implies, this protocol is very simple. In fact, by itself it transports only basic text. You couldn't use SMTP alone to send a binary e-mail attachment such as a multimedia file. MIME (see next) adds this functionality. SMTP is the protocol that transfers or forwards mail to an e-mail server. However, when clients retrieve e-mail, they typically use IMAP or POP3.

- *Multipurpose Internet Mail Extensions* (*MIME*). This protocol adds the mail capability of attaching and transferring multimedia files. To use MIME, you must also have an e-mail client capable of decoding the MIME format.

- *Post Office Protocol 3* (*POP3*). Both POP3 and IMAP (see next) use the SMTP protocol for the actual transfer of information, and both allow messages to be stored on the mail server for incoming e-mail. Then, when you log on, you download all the e-mail using POP3 with no selectivity.

- *Internet Message Access Protocol* (*IMAP*). In its current version (IMAP4), IMAP allows the e-mail client to leave messages on the mail server even after logging on, instead of downloading each one. This is useful for keeping e-mail in a central location, where it can be organized, archived, and made available to remote locations. You can also search through mail for certain keywords, while it's still on the mail server, and selectively download messages that match the search. IMAP integrates with MIME, so that users can read the mail header information and then decide whether to download the attached files separately. Compare this to having to download the files with the e-mail before you can read the header, which can take considerably longer with large files.

Notice that some of the e-mail protocols depend upon or interact with others. The protocols aren't mutually exclusive, and one e-mail transaction might require several protocols. For example, a friend might send you an e-mail with an attached JPEG picture from his vacation. The message is sent to the server using SMTP, and MIME allows the JPEG picture as an attachment. You dial up to an ISP with IMAP capability and see the header that reads, "A great picture from my vacation." Because you're on a very slow dialup line and expect the JPEG to be large, you decide not to download it. However, you are expecting an important JPEG file from a co-worker that you want to use in a presentation the next day, so you search for it, again because of IMAP capability. IMAP allows you to find the message, which can then be downloaded.

E-mail server applications and requirements

E-mail has in many ways reduced paper communications, such as the formerly ubiquitous interoffice memo. Software products such as Novell GroupWise and Microsoft Exchange extend the basic communication features of e-mail, offering a host of features, such as online collaboration, calendars, newsgroups, contact information, chat functions, and more. Mail servers must also be able to store the messages until the client requests and downloads them. These functions significantly contribute to the hardware requirements of a mail server, which vary broadly, depending on the product and utilization. For example, Linux can use the BIND Sendmail program, which requires light hardware resources, because it offers primarily plain e-mail functionality and doesn't include many of the shiny new features found in some other e-mail server products. Nevertheless, Sendmail is a longstanding favorite among e-mail administrators, as it's highly reliable. Find out more about Sendmail at www.sendmail.org.

Because a mail server is highly visible, it must be protected with regular backups and additional servers for purposes of redundancy and failover. Also make sure that additional DNS servers are available. Outgoing mail from your organization could go to any of countless other domains, and if you're suddenly without a DNS server to instruct the mail server as to the location of these other servers, the mail won't go.

Consider creating an alliance with another organization so that you can act as fault-tolerant partners. If one organization's site goes down and is unavailable to receive mail, the other organization receives and temporarily stores mail until the other site is back up. Otherwise, the e-mail is likely to bounce back to the sender.

Prepare other servers and network functions in the organization to send and receive mail. The following list represents a minimum starting point:

- Most organizations have firewalls to protect the network from the Internet. Be sure to open the firewall to the protocols mentioned in the previous section so that messages can pass into and out of your organization.

- Add the appropriate MX records to identify and prioritize the e-mail servers. If you also have a backup remote site with mail servers, be sure to configure the MX priority number to be higher than the local mail servers.

- Provide plenty of hardware. If there's any server that you can't underestimate, it's the mail server. Mail taxes every main hardware component, including memory, processors, and hard disk storage. For example, Microsoft Exchange 2000 Server requires 128 MB of RAM (256 MB recommended), 500 MB on the hard disk where you install Exchange 2000, and 200 MB of additional space on the system drive. Note that this is on top of the Windows 2000 operating system, which has minimum requirements of its own, and that a server configured with these minimums can handle only very light mail traffic. A production mail server is likely to have in excess of 1 GB of RAM and several gigabytes of disk space to store all the messages.

- Mail programs allow the administrator to set quotas on the user mailbox size. Mail quotas conserve disk space and improve backup and restore time. A large credit card company once made the mistake of not implementing quotas, and many users had mailboxes over 1 GB in size. The strain was so heavy on the mail system that, about every week, a hard disk failed.

- Mail server hard disk performance quickly degrades because of the constant write activity. Be sure to defragment the hard disk regularly.

- Mail is also very taxing to network bandwidth. Make sure that you have plenty of available bandwidth and also consider using a multihomed NIC configuration, such as adapter teaming.

- Because mail service is so active and demanding, mail servers should generally be dedicated to mail instead of serving multiple purposes. If necessary, you might include a relatively light additional service such as DHCP, but also using the mail server as a heavily utilized database application server would be out of the question.

- E-mail is often the primary vehicle by which viruses invade a network. It would be foolish not to implement a comprehensive and reliable antivirus solution to check e-mail.

- Choose your mail server product very carefully. If you later decide to change to another product, it can be very disruptive, even though most products include a means by which a competitor's mail service can be converted. Also, the mail product can alter the operating system. For example, Exchange 2000 adds modifications to the Windows 2000 Active Directory schema that are permanent. Even if you uninstall Exchange 2000, the schema changes remain. On the plus side, the mail product can greatly simplify administration. For example, you might be able to create a user account and simultaneously create a mail account instead of creating them separately. Likewise, carefully select the e-mail client to reduce licensing expenses and support burdens.

- Prepare for legal issues. Most companies consider employee e-mail to be company property when delivered to a company address using company equipment. Many employees disagree. When users are hired, be sure to notify them in writing that e-mail is neither the property of the employee nor private, if that's the company position.

Web and FTP servers

Even small and medium-sized organizations usually have a Web presence. A Web site seems to be more necessary than company stationery. A few years ago, some segments of the IT talent pool knew how to set up a Web site, usually on a UNIX server. Now, it's a given that administrators know at least the basics of Web site configuration and administration. This section addresses the server's role as a Web and FTP server.

Web server requirements

As with mail servers, Web and FTP servers (which we collectively refer to here only as Web servers) are normally dedicated solely to those respective functions. The specific type of Web server you run depends largely on the needs of the organization, the number of hits (visits) on the site, and the type of access. For light-duty Web service, virtually any server might be able to run the site. An administrator might configure Internet Information Server (IIS) on a Windows NT server, create some basic content, and probably have the site running and available in less than an hour. However, a Web site of this scale won't suit most active business concerns.

A medium-sized or large organization usually requires Web service with:

- Dedicated bandwidth to Internet traffic that's separate from the LAN connection to the Internet. Although you could share the bandwidth, LAN traffic might adversely affect the responsiveness of the Web site and vice versa.

- A large, fast, and redundant disk storage solution, such as Fibre Channel RAID, for multimedia or file downloads. Consider placing download files on an FTP server, because it's a more efficient file transfer protocol than HTTP. You can configure the link on the Web page to point to an FTP site to initiate the download. The user doesn't have to type in an FTP address. Plain Web page content by itself doesn't usually require a great deal of hard disk space.

- Adequate processing power. Processing power requirements vary greatly. For example, a Web server can answer thousands of hits per day yet have relatively little processor utilization if the Web content is simple. However, more complex functions, such as online transaction processing (OLTP), as required for Internet credit card purchases, can require significantly more processing power. The transaction itself takes place in a backend database on another server. However, the encryption required to validate the server and clients requires processing power. That's why, if you visit your bank's Web site, the home page probably loads quickly (little processing involved). But logging in using 128-bit Secure Sockets Layer (SSL) encryption to access your bank account requires a lot more processing power, and it may take several seconds to access your information.

- A digital certificate that validates the organization to the public. The digital certificate is an authentication mechanism using a form of digital identification, which enables SSL encryption between clients and hosts. For example, VeriSign (www.verisign.com) is a leading source of digital certificates. When visitors access a site, they want to know that the site is reputable and trustworthy, especially for online SSL transactions. A certificate is like a recommendation from the Better Business Bureau, only better.

- Adequate memory. As much of the entire Web page content as possible (except for download files and streaming media) should fit into main memory. As visitors access the site, the pages load into cache, where they're available at a much faster rate than by using disk retrieval.

- Redundant servers. If the Web site is simply "Here's some info about our company," then it might not be worthwhile to invest in one or more redundant servers. However, if the site contributes directly to your business's revenues, redundancy is critical so that, if a Web server fails, another can continue to provide service, usually through clustering. In a large Web site with frequent traffic, a Web server farm probably has several clusters, each comprised of several servers.

- A secure firewall if the site is connected to your LAN. However, it's a better practice to protect normal traffic to and from the LAN and to place Web content on a physically separate and independent Internet connection. This is a security precaution ensuring that, even if a malicious Internet user breaches your Web security, the LAN is still unreachable.

- One or more Webmasters to create and manage the content. In a smaller organization, the network administrator might fulfill this function, but larger organizations have full-time employees or contractors.

Most Webmasters are experts at creating Web content only. They aren't Web server administrators and shouldn't be given access to Web administration tools.

In the past few years, all major server manufacturers have brought 1U or 2U servers to market. These are dedicated network appliances that serve only one purpose and aren't intended for multiple services or applications. High-density, low-cost Web servers are increasingly popular for serving Web content. The local hard disk stores only the NOS and Web server software, while the Web content is usually on a separate array, so only a single local hard disk is required. You can also consider using caching-only servers that cache only Web content for increased responsiveness. These servers can cache inbound Internet traffic (known as *forward proxy*) to improve performance for your users or for your Web site. *Reverse proxy* caches your site's content for Internet clients accessing your Web servers. This offloads incoming requests for static content, increasing the number of concurrent users or connections the Web server is able to maintain, while at the same time improving the browsing experience for those users pointing their browsers to the Web server.

After configuring the Web servers with adequate hardware, you have another issue to consider: Where do you put the server? You can place the server in your local organization, except that if the site is large and busy, the physical plant might not be sufficient, and building another server room might not be practical. Many organizations co-locate their Web servers at a company whose primary business is to provide a highly available physical site for your Web. This arrangement provides many advantages:

- Co-locators provide the physical plant, including power and environmental controls. Using co-location is generally very cost effective compared to building from scratch.

- Site traffic has no impact on your local network utilization, and because the site is physically disconnected from your LAN, a breach in Web security doesn't directly affect local operations.

- Bandwidth availability is excellent, as most co-locators are directly tapped into the Internet backbone and usually offer extremely high throughput and redundancy through a *SONET* ring, which is a fiber optic transmission medium that's self-healing. If a line is cut, traffic redirects to another ring.

- Co-locators offer guaranteed uptime. While policies vary from one co-locator to the next, redundant power (including UPS systems and backup generators), redundant Internet connections, fire detection and extinguishing, and a high level of security help make sure your site stays available. In addition, co-locators provide on-site personnel 24/7.

- Stringent security requires administrators visiting their servers to have a passkey of some kind to open the door and access the site. Security cameras are everywhere.

- Administrators can still remotely monitor and manage the site over the Internet.

Colloquially speaking, administrators refer to a co-location arrangement as "ping power pipe." You can "ping" the server from anywhere on the Internet to see if it responds, "power" is always available, and the "pipe" is the line to the Internet.

Configuring a Web server

Each major NOS offers its own product for Web management, as listed below:

- UNIX/Linux—Apache: a text-based tool that, as usual for UNIX products, is open source code, highly reliable, and not at all intuitive. However, a newer version of Apache for Windows NT is in development and should be more intuitive. (Perhaps the reliability of UNIX and Apache is best attested to by Microsoft itself. For years, Microsoft ran a version of UNIX known as FreeBSD and Apache Web services for the Microsoft Hotmail Web site. In 2000, Microsoft finally switched to its own products: Windows 2000 and IIS 5.0.)

- Windows NT/2000—Internet Information Server (IIS): the best testament to IIS is that Microsoft's own Web site, one of the largest and busiest in the world, runs IIS 5.0. The GUI is simple to operate, yet rich in features.

Do it!

B-1: Researching a co-location facility

Questions

1 Using your Web browser, access the www.inflow.com Web site.

2 What kind of physical security does Inflow have?

3 When can you expect Inflow personnel to be available to monitor your applications and equipment?

4 What facility controls does the staff monitor?

5 How does Inflow ensure uninterrupted power?

Remote access service

Explanation

Remote access service (*RAS*) is the ability of a server to accept a connection from a client even when physically disconnected from the LAN. Users establish the connection on their end through dialup modem connections or existing Internet connections using a *virtual private network* (*VPN*). Once the connection is established, the user experience is the same as if directly connected to the local LAN, except that over a dialup connection, network responsiveness is much slower. A VPN connection can be much better because, although it usually takes place over the public, unsecured Internet, the session is protected inside an encrypted virtual tunnel that's extremely difficult for intruders to breach. The VPN can be just as slow, or slower because of the encryption overhead, if the Internet connection is dialup, but with the availability of high-speed Internet access, a user might experience significantly better performance.

Regardless of the method, RAS represents another arena of responsibility for the administrator. You provision the server to accept RAS connections, and you also ensure that the connections are secure.

You can also create VPNs inside your LAN to guard further against intruders. For example, if you wanted to protect a server that contained sensitive information, you could open it up only to users permitted to connect through a VPN, in addition to setting appropriate file and logon permissions as usual. Anyone intercepting the VPN session between user and server is very unlikely to retrieve any useful information.

Although a persistent hacker could obtain the phone numbers for dialup connections, you should make it as difficult as possible. Instruct users not to share the phone numbers with persons outside your organization. If you suspect a compromised number, change it as soon as possible.

Protocol support

You're already aware of basic protocols like TCP/IP, IPX/SPX, and NetBEUI. You can usually use each of these protocols to communicate with a RAS server. However, there are additional protocols that are used to establish and secure the connection.

The first type of protocol is a line protocol. Network protocols are designed for network media, such as 10BaseT Ethernet over CAT5 cable. When RAS clients dial in to the server over a phone line, TCP/IP alone won't work, because it's incompatible with conventional phone lines. Instead, when clients dial up the modem and establish a connection, a line protocol encapsulates the network protocol. Encapsulated packets are then sent across the connection where the server unwraps the line protocol packet. The packet then transmits over the network like an ordinary network packet. This process is illustrated in Exhibit 7-11, in which the PPP packet encapsulates a TCP/IP packet.

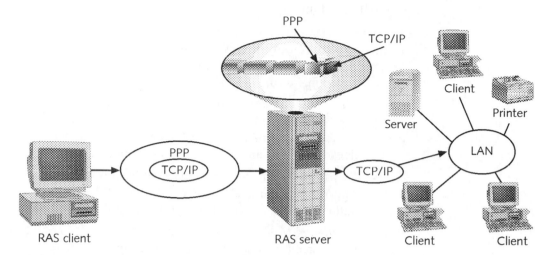

Exhibit 7-11: Line protocol encapsulation

The following are the two most common line protocols:

- *Point-to-Point Protocol* (*PPP*). A very flexible line protocol, PPP interoperates with a variety of RAS software packages. PPP supports the NetBEUI, IPX/SPX, and TCP/IP protocols, data compression and encryption, and authentication protocols (addressed later in this unit). The NetWare implementation of PPP is PPPRNS (Point-to-Point Protocol Remote Node Service) and is very similar, though it doesn't support NetBEUI.

- *Serial Line Internet Protocol* (*SLIP*). A more common line protocol in the past than it is today, SLIP uses only the TCP/IP protocol and is useful for UNIX connections. In Windows, when you connect with SLIP, a Windows Terminal dialog box opens allowing you to perform an interactive logon with the UNIX server. SLIP is very basic and doesn't support authentication protocols, encryption, or compression.

In addition to a line protocol, you need a tunneling protocol in order to establish a VPN connection. There are two primary tunneling protocols:

- *Point-to-Point Tunneling Protocol* (*PPTP*). A popular and easy-to-configure tunneling protocol. Configure both the server and the client to establish the VPN connection using PPTP and make the connection.

- *Level 2 Tunneling Protocol* (*L2TP*). A newer VPN protocol that requires an established certificate authority. Clients establishing a connection must download a certificate from the certificate authority. The certificate then validates the connection attempt over the VPN connection attempt.

Security protocols

Logging on remotely exposes the connection to eavesdroppers who could tap the connection and retrieve user name/password combinations. To avoid this vulnerability, you need to select an encryption method. The most common ones are listed below and are supported in varying degrees by all the major NOSs.

- *Password Authentication Protocol* (*PAP*). PAP sends logon information in clear text. Using a packet sniffer, an eavesdropper can analyze the packet and retrieve the logon data. PAP is the last resort: Use it only when the server you dial into doesn't support any of the other authentication protocols.

- *Shiva Password Authentication Protocol* (*SPAP*). Shiva products (acquired by Intel) are a popular alternative to Microsoft RAS solutions. Shiva encrypts authentication credentials for Shiva LAN Rover software.

- *Challenge Handshake Authentication Protocol* (*CHAP*). CHAP is a flexible and common authentication protocol that supports encryption for a variety of operating systems. Microsoft has two specific implementations: MS-CHAP for all Windows clients and MS-CHAP v2 for Windows 2000 clients.

Configuring RAS on a server

Explanation

Each network operating system has unique methods for configuring a RAS server. The important thing is to know about all the protocols discussed so far in this unit, because a critical matter in configuring client/server RAS communication is ensuring that settings on both sides match. Mismatched settings don't cause a poor connection; they usually prevent connection altogether. You must then determine what caused the problem. Most of the time, connection problems relate to mismatched security protocols. For example, if you're trying to connect using PAP but the RAS server accepts only MS-CHAP v2, the client logon attempt is denied.

Exhibit 7-12 shows a Windows 2000 dialup client with authentication settings for PAP, SPAP, and CHAP. As a rule, connection attempts first try the most secure available method and, failing that, move to the next most secure method, until all available authentication methods are exhausted. Exhibit 7-13 shows the default Windows 2000 Server dial-in settings. The client shown in Exhibit 7-12 won't succeed in the connection attempt to this server, because only MS-CHAP and MS-CHAP v2 are permitted.

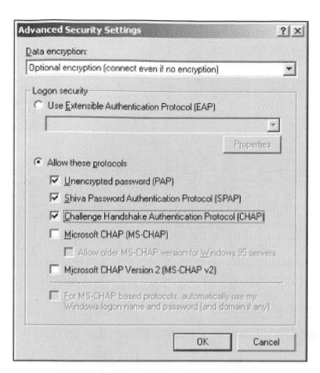

Exhibit 7-12: Windows 2000 dialup client authentication

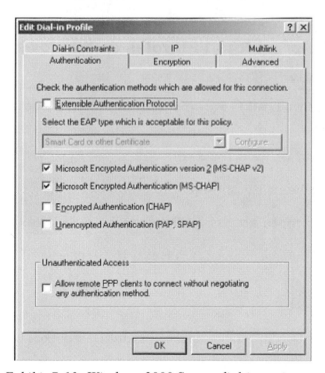

Exhibit 7-13: Windows 2000 Server dial-in settings

In Windows Server 2003, RAS and VPN can be set up by adding the appropriate roles in the Manage My Server console. This initiates the Routing and Remote Access Server Setup Wizard, as shown in Exhibit 7-14.

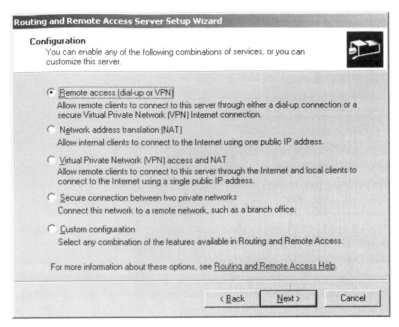

Exhibit 7-14: The 2003 Routing and Remote Access Server Setup Wizard

Do it!

B-2:   Exploring RAS/VPN roles on Windows Server 2003

Here's how
1 Choose **Start**, **All Programs**, **Administrative Tools**, **Manage Your Server**
2 Click **Add or Remove a role**
3 Observe the preliminary steps, then click **Next**
4 Select **Remote access / VPN server** and click **Next**
5 Observe the summary and click **Next**. The Routing and Remote Access Server Setup Wizard opens
6 Click **Next**
7 Observe the configuration options. Discuss what options would be appropriate for various situations
8 Cancel the wizard and close the Manage Your Server console

Fax services

Explanation

A fax server comes in two basic hardware formats: turnkey and computer-based. *Turnkey fax servers* are self-contained, freestanding devices in which fax software and hardware are already installed, and except for some company-specific configurations, they're ready to use right out of the box. Our attention focuses on the alternative, computer-based fax servers, which require separate hardware and software.

Fax hardware can consist of a simple fax modem that's shared from a single PC. While this might be acceptable for a small workgroup requiring only light-duty fax service, our focus is on higher-volume solutions for which you need one or more fax boards. Besides the fact that a single fax board can send or receive many times more faxes than a conventional fax machine, a fax board offers several other characteristics and advantages:

- Fax boards are specially tuned for fast *handshakes* (that soothing squawking noise that faxes and modems make when establishing a connection) and fax compression. This feature saves only a few seconds, but when multiplied by the number of users and the long distance rate of faxes, especially overseas, it makes a big difference. In addition, fax boards have a higher throughput than conventional faxes, so even at 14.4 Kbps, they can send a page in about 15 seconds instead of 60 seconds. (The most common fax speed remains 14.4 Kbps, even though there's also a 28.8 Kbps standard available.)

- Resolution is usually better on a fax server than most conventional fax machines. Also, the fax software often includes the ability to clean up unclear faxes.

- Security-sensitive documents are vulnerable to the curious on a conventional fax machine. On a fax server, you fax from the desktop, and nobody else sees it.

- A fax server saves users the frustration of clearing jams, replacing toner and paper, and waiting in line.

- Most fax machines collect data on inbound and outbound faxes, but you print it out and that's that. A fax server allows you to organize the data and use software products specially designed for reporting, such as Crystal Reports. Reports are useful for determining which users or departments send and receive the most faxes, finding out when fax traffic is heaviest, and so on. Reports are also as permanent a record as you like, whereas fax machine logs must be periodically cleared.

- Inbound faxes can go to a departmental printer or remain electronic and go to fax software or, better yet, to an e-mail inbox on the user's computer.

- The fax software automatically fills in cover sheet information, such as who's sending the document and the number of pages. Broadcast fax cover sheets can name individuals instead of all parties.

- Mobile users might be unavailable to receive a physical fax at the office. Using client fax software, they can have the fax forwarded to their e-mail inbox or to a printer at their current location.

Fax boards are PCI, and therefore can be installed in most computers, PC or otherwise. However, fax server software is usually a UNIX, NetWare, or NT/2000 product. Many vendors also include software that integrates with Lotus Notes, Microsoft Exchange, Novell GroupWise, SMTP/POP3, and more.

You can combine other services or functions with a fax server, but be aware of the kinds of resources it requires. First, faxing requires processing power for compression, error correction, data packet creation, and other fax-related processes. So you shouldn't share any processor-intensive functions with the fax server. An exception for this can be made if the fax board itself offloads these duties from the processor. Second, if faxes are stored on the server, plan for plenty of hard disk space. Calculate for the average size of inbound faxes and the length of time they're likely to be stored. In many cases though, you offload the faxes to another server, such as a Novell GroupWise or Microsoft Exchange Server. Memory requirements aren't high. You usually need only enough to run the fax software, probably 32 MB.

For more about fax servers, consult:

- www.faxserverfaq.com
- www.dialogic.com
- www.facsys.com

SNA Server

Systems Network Architecture (*SNA*) *Server* harkens back to 1974 and IBM's networking standards for mainframes. In those days, users sat at dumb terminals that accessed a mainframe server through a text-based terminal session. The reason why this history is important is that the basic mainframe architecture still exists today, and access to many midrange systems is similar, for example, IBM's AS/400 and AS/390 servers. Users must connect to these servers but usually don't sit at dumb terminals anymore. Now, users usually sit at Microsoft Windows clients and connect to the mainframe using a terminal emulator that appears to the server as if it were a dumb terminal. However, making a straight connection like this from Windows and maintaining all the features of Windows and the mainframe at the same time isn't always practical or possible. SNA Server is a Microsoft product that acts as a gateway between the client and the mainframe.

Microsoft has a successor to SNA Server: Host Integration Server, which is compatible with Windows NT 4.0 and integrates with Windows 2000. For the sake of our discussion, we collectively refer to these products as SNA Server.

The following list briefly describes several main features of SNA Server:

- Windows users connect to the mainframe (known in this context as a host, not to be confused with simply a TCP/IP host) through client software. From a Web browser, a user can click on a link that automatically downloads the necessary client software to the local computer. The client software allows users to be clients to the host and run whichever terminal emulation software or application suits their needs.

- Users have difficulty remembering passwords and experience even more difficulty if they must log on more than once, first to a Windows 2000 server and then to a host. Often, the accounts aren't synchronized (the username and/or password is different), further complicating matters. Using SNA Server, administrators can synchronize user accounts so that they're consistent between the host and the Windows NT or Windows 2000 domain, and changing the password on one system automatically synchronizes with the other.

- Database availability is improved, because SNA allows users to access mainframe-based databases such as DB2 (an IBM database).

- Uniform performance monitoring allows the administrator to use Windows NT/2000 Performance Monitor to analyze server performance on hosts.

- Administrators streamline the burden of file resource access. SNA applies Windows NT/2000 file security on shared folders as if the resource was on a local Windows NT/2000 server. This allows you to apply the same security permissions and access rights as with any other file.

- Print compatibility is improved, because users can send mainframe print jobs to LAN printers without changing host applications.

- SNA server failure has less impact on user productivity, because multiple SNA servers and be used for failover and load-balancing purposes.

- By itself, a logon using a 3270 terminal, for example, is sent in clear text, making it easy for someone intercepting the sign-on to read the username and password. SNA Server encrypts the data streams between the server and client.

Do it!

B-3: Discussing other services

Questions and answers

1 How might RAM improve Web server performance?

2 What's the difference between PPP and SLIP?

3 How are fax servers better than fax machines?

Topic C: Application servers

This topic covers the following CompTIA Server+ exam objectives:

#	Objective
1.3	Know the basic purpose and function of the following types of servers. • Server types include: • Server as a gateway • Server as a router • Server as a bridge • Firewall server • Proxy server • Database server • Application server • File and print server
1.4	Know the function of the following application server models. • Dedicated application • Distributed application • Peer to peer application
3.6	Install service tools • Service tools include: • SNMP • Supporting knowledge includes: • Identity, purpose, and function of service tools • How to set up SNMP
4.8	Upgrade system-monitoring agents • Supporting knowledge includes • Purpose and function of the following management protocols: • SNMP • DMI • IPMI 1.5 and 2.0 • Function and monitoring agents • Dependencies between SNMP and MIBs
5.5	Monitor, maintain and follow the server management and service plan • Activities include: • Follow the changes management protocol

Types of Application servers

- *Dedicated application.* As discussed with some of the services earlier in this unit (e-mail services, for example), servers sometimes run only a single application or service and nothing else. This helps to assure that application performance is unhindered by interference from other applications and services and also contributes to the stability of the server. The application software doesn't run on the workstation, though a client piece might, such as using Outlook Express to retrieve e-mail from a UNIX Sendmail dedicated server.

- *Distributed application.* The application runs on the server. The client can send requests to the server but doesn't run the application or perform processing. Probably the most common example of this type of application is a database. Typically, the client machines run the user interface, or "front end," of the application, while the server runs the "back end." It stores the data, runs data queries, and returns results to the client.

- *Peer-to-peer (P2P) application.* A P2P application server primarily exists to run software that allows peer computers to communicate with one another. An important issue with P2P servers is that they provide appropriate security measures so that users can search for and download files from other users without being able to access unauthorized materials.

Sharing resources

The simplest type of service isn't even an application; it's the sharing of resources, such as files and printers. For instance, a small office can have one machine with lots of storage and a good printer attached. This saves money on equipment, provides a central place for important files, and makes backing up important data easier, because only one machine needs to be backed up.

Monitoring protocols

Most networks are much larger than the administrator can practically administer if he or she had to visit each server and network device physically. Therefore, a means by which administrators can access remote servers is necessary. Each network operating system allows general administration from afar using various administrative tools. For example, you can manage a NetWare 5.1 server using the NWAdmn32.exe program from any Windows client, regardless of geographic distance. However, administrators also require a way proactively to monitor servers and network equipment, such as routers, hubs, and switches. How does the administrator know when a router becomes saturated beyond its ability to function? Is there a way that administrators can see an increasing trend in network traffic and prepare a proactive solution? The answer to both questions is found in the monitoring protocol.

There are two primary monitoring protocols: Simple Network Management Protocol (SNMP) and Desktop Management Interface (DMI), with SNMP being the most prevalent.

SNMP

Simple Network Management Protocol (*SNMP*) is really of no use by itself. Its usefulness is comprised of several elements that work together with the ultimate purpose of informing the administrator of a changing trend in the use of an object or alerting the administrator of an error, failure, or other condition. For example, an administrator might want to know well in advance when the 100 GB disk array is down to 10 GB so that he or she can make sure that more storage is available. This knowledge prevents the reactive response in which users complain about out-of-disk-space errors and the administrator must scramble at the last minute to find additional storage. With third-party SNMP software, the administrator can be notified in a number of ways about the low-storage problem. The administrator can configure a response in any of several forms, such as an e-mail message, pager alert, or network message to a workstation at which the administrator is logged on.

A useful SNMP solution consists of several individual components:

- *SNMP management system*. Also known as a management console, this is the computer that runs SNMP management software. The software can run on any compatible computer. It doesn't have to be a server, though it often is. The SNMP management system sends requests for information from the monitored system, known as the SNMP agent. Except for an alarm-triggering event, the SNMP agent doesn't normally initiate messages.

- *SNMP agent*. A service that runs on the actual object you want to manage or monitor. For example, if you have a Web server and want to receive an alert when the number of concurrent connections exceeds a certain threshold, you configure the Web server as an SNMP agent.

- *Management Information Base* (*MIB*). A database of definitions for the specific device being monitored. For example, one of the MIB values associated with a particular device could be sysUpTime, which specifies the elapsed time since the managed device was booted. Similar to hostname-to-IP-address mapping, a MIB value has an official name and a dot notation. For example, the dot notation for sysUpTime is 1.3.6.1.2.1.1.3.0, though it's obviously easier to use the official name.

- *Communities*. A group of hosts that use the same community name. You can name the community whatever makes sense for your organization. The community name isn't so much a grouping as it is a small measure of security. When SNMP queries are issued to a community, only members of that community respond, and the community name functions as a rudimentary password.

SNMP has no security of its own, and a malicious user with a packet sniffer could retrieve SNMP traffic, and then through impersonation, return false information to the SNMP management system. Newer implementations of SNMP are introducing public key/private key verification techniques to prevent this situation.

- *Traps*—When the SNMP agent issues a message to the SNMP management system, it's known as a trap.

As an example of configuring an SNMP agent, look at the Windows 2000 SNMP Service Properties dialog box in Exhibit 7-15. The check boxes in the Service frame specify what type of device is involved. For example, if the device is a router, you select the Internet item. For explanations of the other devices, use the online Help function.

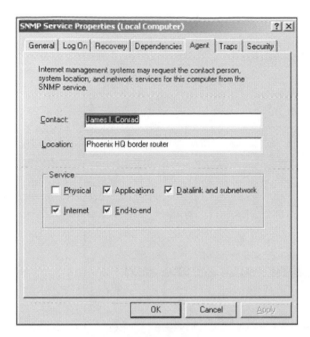

Exhibit 7-15: The SNMP Agent tab

Continuing the Windows 2000 example, notice the Traps tab shown in Exhibit 7-16. Here, you specify the community name and the trap destination. The agent can send messages only to hosts that know the community name.

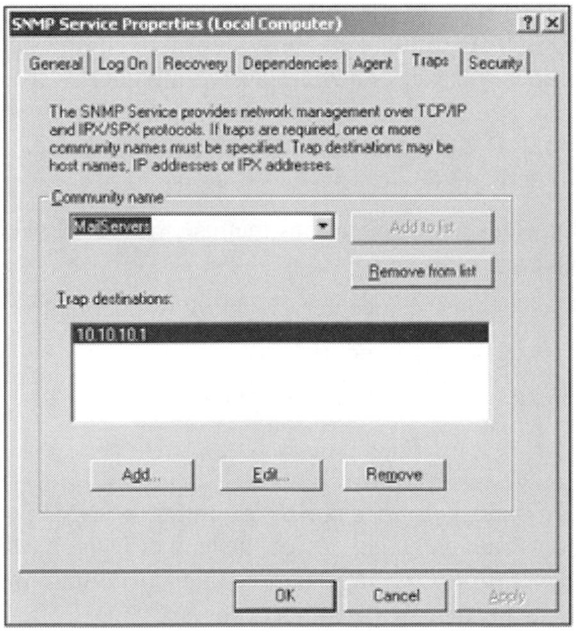

Exhibit 7-16: The SNMP Traps tab

Finally, specify rudimentary security on the Security tab, where you select accepted management systems with which the agent is allowed to communicate (Exhibit 7-17).

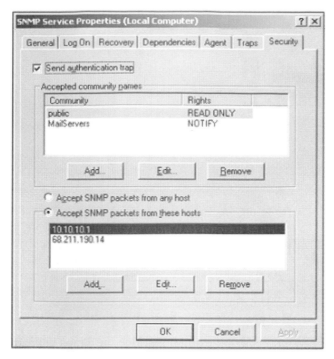

Exhibit 7-17: The SNMP Security tab

You might also find RMON on certain network devices. *Remote monitoring (RMON)* is an extension of the SNMP protocol and provides more comprehensive network monitoring capabilities. Instead of devices answering queries from the SNMP management system, RMON proactively sets off alarms for a variety of traffic conditions. As the full RMON protocol is quite comprehensive, only portions of it are usually placed into network devices such as routers.

There are several utilities and applications that use SNMP. However, the three most significant vendors are:

- Computer Associates' Unicenter TNG (www.ca.com)
- IBM's Tivoli (www.tivoli.com)
- Hewlett-Packard's OpenView (www.hp.com)

DMI

The *Desktop Management Interface (DMI)* is similar to SNMP, except that it contains specific information about an actual device. Instead of using a MIB, DMI uses a *Management Information File (MIF)* database that can contain information such as model ID, serial number, memory, and port addresses. DMI often runs in conjunction with SNMP. For example, when an SNMP query arrives at the agent, DMI can enter MIF information in the SNMP MIB.

The server as a network device

Network operating systems can enable a server to fulfill roles traditionally reserved only for hardware network devices, such as routers, bridges, and firewalls. Try to stick with the faster and more reliable hardware solutions for the most part, because servers must simultaneously cope with countless other activities and variables. For example, how often does a router crash because of a software bug? Never. But a server functioning as a router must not only perform routing functions but also simultaneously load millions of lines of operating system code into memory, run a few services just to stay alive (if not perform additional functions), share processor utilization with other functions, depend upon many other physical devices in the server (each one representing another possible point of failure), and so on.

Nevertheless, for the smaller, value-conscious organization or smaller department in an organization, a server network device might suit your needs. For example, even if you work for a gigantic organization, if it has a small satellite office in Nome, Alaska, with only five workstations and one server, it's probably not cost effective to install a Cisco router costing thousands of dollars to connect the office to a WAN. Instead, you'd use the existing server. Because there's likely to be very little network traffic going through the server anyway, the risk is reduced to the point of being acceptable.

The server as a router

Configuring the server as a network device, such as a router (also known as a gateway for our purposes) requires at least two network cards. In the case of a server configured as a router, one NIC connects to one network or subnet, and the other NIC connects to another network or subnet. The static IP address you assign to each respective NIC is in the same network range as the subnet to which it connects, as illustrated in the NetWare 5.1 example in Exhibit 7-18. You also configure the NICs the same way if the server functions as a firewall or bridge.

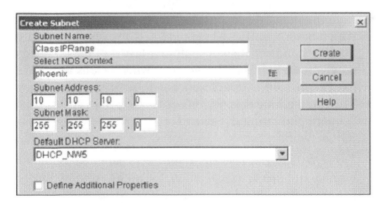

Exhibit 7-18: The NIC for each respective network matches the network address of the subnet to which it connects

After configuring the NICs, it's only a matter of configuring the respective operating system to perform the function you want. For example, to configure Windows 2000 as a router, you'd use the Routing and Remote Access (RRAS) tool (Start, Programs, Administrative Tools, Routing and Remote Access). If this is the first RRAS function you've configured, a wizard guides you through the process. Otherwise, you have to add a routing protocol, such as RIP or OSPF, manually and then specify the NICs participating in the routing function. A brief explanation of these routing protocols follows.

RIP

Router Information Protocol (*RIP*) is a distance vector-based protocol, which identifies the best route for a destination based on the number of hops (number of routers that the message passes through). RIP has the following advantages:

- *Configuration.* You enable RIP on the router interface, and no further configuration is necessary.

- *Simplicity.* Routing table advertisements are very simple (compared to OSPF) and easier to read.

- *Compatibility.* Most routers are compatible with RIP.

RIP is a fine protocol for simple purposes, but it can run into problems in more complex routing scenarios. Its disadvantages include:

- *Delayed convergence. Convergence* is the state in which all routers connected to a network have the same updated information. RIP exchanges routing tables in an unsynchronized and unacknowledged manner. Consequently, internetwork convergence might take several minutes, a costly lapse in a production network.

- *Larger routing table size.* Multiple routes to a network destination can appear as multiple entries in the routing table. Though this might not affect smaller networks, large networks with multiple paths can generate hundreds or thousands of entries in the RIP routing table.

- *Greater network traffic overhead.* Because of the larger routing tables generated by RIP, route advertising requires more network overhead. Route advertising continues to update routing information every 30 to 90 seconds, even after convergence. This means that the router's entire routing table is passed to all other known routers.

- *Poor scalability.* RIP broadcasts its entire routing table, making them much larger than OSPF tables. This generates an unreasonable degree of network traffic on larger networks. Also, RIP accepts up to only 15 hops.

- *Routing loops.* When a router learns of a downed link, it notifies a neighbor, which in turn notifies its neighbors. However, if an upstream neighbor issues its 30-90 second update table before it learns of the downed link, then all its downstream neighbors view the downed link as available again. This routing loop is difficult to troubleshoot and usually requires manual intervention to fix. The routing loop description here is only one type of routing loop, known as "counting to infinity." Several other types of routing loops could occur within a RIP network.

- *Less efficient.* Because RIP builds best path determination based only upon the number of hops to a destination, the path can sometimes be less efficient. For example, it might take only three hops to get from Network A to Network F. However, one of the hops must take place over a 56 Kbps demand-dial link. A faster route might exist over a four-hop T1 link, but a RIP-based router won't use it.

OSPF

The *Open Shortest Path First* (*OSPF*) routing protocol builds its routing tables using a link-state algorithm, which calculates the shortest path to each host based on the network topology, not just the fewest number of hops (as with RIP). The algorithm uses not only hop count, but also other factors, such as available bandwidth and network congestion, to determine the best path to a destination. Routing tables are smaller and update more often, but they're more efficient and converge more quickly than RIP. OSPF is quickly replacing RIP in most implementations. OSPF has the following advantages:

- *More rapid convergence*. OSPF routers converge much more quickly than RIP routers and aren't susceptible to routing loops.
- *Smaller routing table size*. Instead of storing every possible path to a destination, the SPF algorithm calculates the best path and stores only that path in the routing table.
- *Less network traffic overhead*. Because of smaller routing tables, and because routing tables aren't broadcast redundantly, OSPF requires less network traffic.
- *Hop count*. There's virtually no limit on hop count.
- *Scalability*. All of the above features make OSPF more scalable and suitable for large networks.
- *Compatibility*. Most current network devices can accept and use the OSPF protocol.

The OSPF routing protocol also has some disadvantages, but they're largely outweighed by the advantages:

- *Greater use of resources*. The database of link-state advertisements and the SPF calculations required for path determination require more memory and processor use than RIP.
- *More complex configuration and use*. Link-state protocol implementation requires careful planning, and the configuration options are more extensive than for RIP. Link-state protocols are also more complex and difficult to understand than RIP. However, this might not be a direct concern, unless you need to perform detailed network analysis.

As a rule, most network administrators prefer the scalability, flexibility, and accuracy of the OSPF protocol over RIP.

The server as a firewall

Recall from earlier discussions that a firewall protects your LAN from other networks, usually the Internet. A *proxy server* serves the same function by impersonating the internal client and is a term we use interchangeably with firewall. The proxy accepts Internet requests from the LAN client, represents the client on the Internet, and issues the request to the Internet destination host. When the Internet host returns an answer, usually a Web page, the proxy forwards the content to the original LAN client. The proxy server performs this function for all its internal clients and, to the Internet at large, appears to be a single, very busy Internet client. The proxy also prevents LAN users from accessing sites forbidden by the organization.

A firewall server can be a hardware or software solution and, in itself, is a form of routing. However, server firewalls can offer very sophisticated and advanced features, making potential weaknesses in operating stability a more acceptable risk, especially when there are redundant proxy servers.

Besides protecting the LAN, a proxy server improves Internet performance for the clients by using caching. When the proxy server delivers a Web page to a client, it also caches the page in memory and on a hard disk cache. The proxy server delivers the same content to the next client that wants to view the same page. This saves Internet network bandwidth and greatly improves responsiveness for frequently accessed pages.

Although you can configure the basic NOS to perform some firewall functions, such as allowing access only to certain IP addresses, you configure a proxy server using additional server software in most cases. For example, Novell NetWare uses an add-on product called BorderManager, and Windows NT/2000 uses Microsoft Proxy Server 2.0 or Internet Security and Acceleration (ISA) Server.

Do it!

C-1: Discussing application servers

Questions and answers

1 You receive a message on your pager that a particular router is flooded. Which service made this notification possible?

2 What's an SNMP agent?

3 What's RIP?

4 Why is Open Shortest Path First (OSPF) superior to RIP?

Unit summary: Services and applications

Topic A

In this topic you learned that **DHCP** automatically distributes IP addresses to DHCP clients, avoiding the error-prone and time-consuming process of manually entering IP configuration on hosts. The DHCP lease process uses a **discovery**, **offer**, **request**, and **acknowledgment** process. **DNS** resolves IP addresses to names and vice versa, replacing the need for a **HOSTS file**. The **resolver** is the client waiting for a name resolution answer. If a DNS server doesn't have the answer to a request, it can use other DNS servers in a **recursive query** or use an **iterative query**, which simply refers the original resolver to another DNS server. **WINS** is a method by which user-friendly NetBIOS computer names can be resolved to IP addresses for the purpose of allowing such communication between hosts on different subnets.

Topic B

In this topic you discovered that mail services are a critical part of most organizations. E-mail requires one or more of several protocols, including **SMTP**, **MIME**, **POP3**, and **IMAP**. Your Web servers should have plenty of Internet bandwidth, which is best accomplished by separating it from LAN bandwidth using a dedicated Internet connection. Plan for plenty of fast hard disk space for file downloads and streaming multimedia. **Remote access service (RAS)** is the ability of a server to accept a connection from a client even when physically disconnected from the LAN. Users establish the connection on their end through dial-up modem connections or existing Internet connections using a **virtual private network (VPN)**. **Fax servers** offer advantages over fax machines, such as greater speed, improved resolution, better security, better reporting, routing, and forwarding to another fax machine or e-mail inbox. Fax servers consist of a fax board and fax software.

Topic C

SNMP is a management protocol. Its usefulness is comprised of several elements that work together with the ultimate purpose of informing the administrator of a changing trend in the use of an object or alerting the administrator of an error, failure, or condition. **Desktop Management Interface (DMI)** is similar to SNMP, except that it contains specific information about an actual device. Instead of using a **Management Information Base (MIB)**, DMI uses a **Management Information File (MIF)** database that can contain information such as model ID, serial number, memory, and port addresses. A server can also function as a network device such as a **router** (using **RIP** or **OSPF**) or a firewall/proxy. Routing functions are best performed by hardware routers unless it isn't necessary or cost effective.

Independent practice activity

In this activity, you'll add the role of File Server to a 2003 server.

1 Choose Start, Administrative Tools, Manage Your Server. This opens the Mange Your Server console.

2 Click Add or remove a role.

3 Note the preliminary steps and click Next.

4 Select File server from the Server Role list, as shown in Exhibit 7-19.

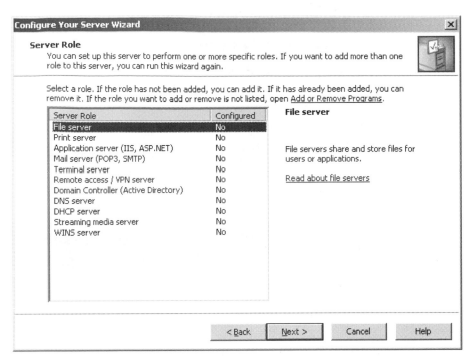

Exhibit 7-19: Adding the role of File Server

5 Leave the disk quotas as they are and click Next.

6 Leave the Indexing Service off and click Next.

7 Read the summary and click Next. The Share a Folder Wizard starts, as shown in Exhibit 7-20. Click Next.

Exhibit 7-20: The Share a Folder Wizard runs as part of adding the file server role

8 Select a folder to share, for instance, C:\Documents and Settings\All Users\Shared Documents. Click OK.

9 Accept the default share name and click Next.

10 Leave access as read-only and click Finish. The wizard shows a summary. Click Close. You're returned to a Manage Your Server screen that tells you that the server is now a file server.

11 Click Finish to close the message and return to the main console screen.

12 Observe that the role has been added to the console along with management options, as shown in Exhibit 7-21.

13 Close the Manage Your Server console.

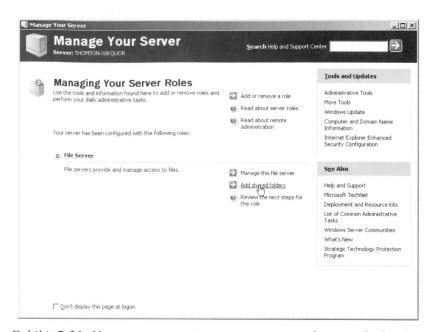

Exhibit 7-21: New management options appear in the console for the new role

14 Type a name for the zone. This should be the name of the zone only, not the name of existing or planned hosts. If you had a server named Mail1 and a domain named accusource.net, you'd enter only accusource.net here, not Mail1.accusource.net.

15 A file stores the DNS database. Leave the default value and finish the wizard.

Review questions

1 Which service automatically distributes IP configuration to clients?

   A DHCP

   B DNS

   C SNA

   D DISTIP

2 Which of the following is the correct order in the lease process?

   A Offer, discovery, acknowledgement, request

   B Discovery, acknowledgement, offer, request

   C Discovery, acknowledgement, request, offer

   D Discovery, offer, request, acknowledgement

3 DNS is an alternative to which text file?

   A LMHOSTS

   B HOSTS

   C Readme.txt

   D HOST

4 A resolver is:

   A An authoritative server that solves conflicting IP address issues

   B A service that removes outdated WINS records

   C A server that returns iterative queries

   D A client that requests DNS name resolution

5 A DNS zone is:

   A A physical boundary where a host must reside in order to become a resolver

   B A naming boundary

   C Another term for a Windows NT/2000 security domain

   D The authoritative server for all name resolution within a domain

6 Which of the following DNS records resolves the host name to an IP address?

   A PTR records

   B SOA records

   C MX records

   D A records

7 Which of the following DNS servers does not have any permanent DNS records?

   A caching only

   B slave

   C secondary

   D primary

8 Which operating system primarily uses NetBIOS names?

   A Linux

   B Bob's OS

   C Windows

   D NetWare

9 What does DDNS do?

   A Automatically registers NetBIOS names

   B Automatically registers DNS names

   C Recognizes when DNS server records are out of date and automatically replicates a more up-to-date zone

   D Dynamically configures a host's IP configuration

10 What does a push partner do?

   A Responds to pull partner replication trigger and sends WINS updates

   B Responds to other push partners replication trigger and sends WINS updates

   C Automatically replicates WINS data to DNS servers

   D Forces an update on pull partners

11 Which of the following mail protocols allows you to search for specific mail on the server and download only select items?

   A POP3

   B SMTP

   C MIME

   D IMAP

12 What special hardware factors might you consider for an email server?

   A Additional hard disk space

   B Powerful processing capability

   C Additional RAM

   D All of the above

13 Why might you want to have a dedicated, separate Internet connection to the web server? Choose two.

A So that LAN traffic does not affect web server responsiveness

B So that Web traffic does not affect LAN responsiveness

C This is a requirement for an effective firewall

D A separate connection offers no practical benefit

14 How might RAM improve web server performance?

A Web server software is particularly memory hungry

B RAM is not particularly an issue with web content

C More web content can be cached into RAM and served faster than from the hard disk

D FTP and streaming media can be stored wholly in memory

15 What is one of the disadvantages of most UNIX services?

A The GUI based interface is not consistent from one version of UNIX to another.

B The text-based administration is not intuitive

C UNIX services are historically less stable than other operating systems' services

D The UNIX services are completely incompatible with any other operating system

16 How are fax servers better than fax machines? Choose all that apply.

A Fax boards transmit faxes much faster

B Fax servers can better protect sensitive documents from prying eyes

C Fax servers automatically fill in some information

D Fax servers do not jam

17 What is the purpose of an SNA server?

A To connect Macintosh clients to the same network as Windows clients

B To connect clients to mini and mainframe hosts over a terminal session

C To separate the public Internet from the private LAN

D To allow dial up clients to access the LAN as if connected locally

18 You receive a message on your pager that a particular router is flooded. Which service made this notification possible?

A PAGER

B SNMP

C RAS

D PPTP

Unit 8

Disaster planning

Unit time: 90 minutes

Complete this unit, and you'll know how to:

A Describe the primary types of hardware used to back up critical data.

B Discuss the primary types of software used to back up critical data and the strategies for their use.

C Describe the need for high server availability/redundancy and identify key areas for SNMP monitoring.

D Determine key server management and disaster recovery strategies for preserving system uptime.

Topic A: Backup hardware

This topic covers the following CompTIA Server+ exam objectives:

#	Objective

3.4	Configure external peripherals
	• Peripherals include:
	  • Backup device
	  • Data storage subsystems

4.6	Upgrade adapters (e.g. NIC's, SCSI cards, RAID, etc) • Activities include: • Perform backup

4.7	Upgrade peripheral devices, internal and external. Verify appropriate system resources (e.g. expansion slots, IRQ, DMA, etc.)
	• Peripheral devices include:
	  • Backup devices
	  • Optical devices

8.1	Read and follow the disaster recover plan
	• Supporting knowledge includes:
	  • Types of backup hardware and media
	    • DAT
	    • SDAT
	    • DLT
	    • Super DLT
	    • Optical backup device
	    • AIT
	    • LTO
	    • Disk to disk
	    • Libraries vs. stand-alones

Importance of backups

Explanation   Although fault-tolerant hardware and devices can reduce total system downtime, the greatest potential loss in the event of a system failure of any kind is the loss of data. Even during normal day-to-day operations, data can become corrupt or lost. For example, users sometimes accidentally overwrite their own files with blank data, or perhaps an application crashes while a file is open, resulting in a corrupt file. Having that data available for restoration is the highest-priority item in the preparation for disaster recovery.

The basic theory behind backing up data is simple: Never put yourself in a position where critical data for the survival of your network or business is permanently unavailable.

There are many backup devices from which to choose and several backup methods that can be employed, but the goal is never to be without your mission-critical data. You also have to decide who's going to be responsible for accomplishing the backups and to what level these backups need to be secured. Which devices and methods you choose aren't as important as the choice to develop and deploy a backup strategy.

Hewlett-Packard cites industry experts who estimate that the quantity of data increases 50% annually. If these figures hold true for your organization, then the need for accurate backup and restore operations is obvious, as is the need to select appropriate backup hardware and strategies.

Types of backup hardware

Factors to consider when you purchase a backup unit include:

- The amount of data you need to back up
- Whether your backup software supports the unit
- The amount of money you want to spend
- The amount of time it takes to back up and restore data

You also need to consider the value of your data: Put a price tag on your data and on the time you'd need to rebuild the data if you lost it. Be willing to spend as much money on a device as some ratio of what you calculate your data to be worth.

There are many types of backup media and devices, from removable media cartridges to CD-ROMs and magnetic tape. You need to determine the best balance between speed of data backup, speed of restoration, the quality and function of supported backup programs, and storage media requirements. Then, choose a unit that provides the technology you need to back up and restore data efficiently and effectively within the parameters of your situation.

For example, some products use optical disks, which are a great solution for *Hierarchical Storage Management* (*HSM*), in which infrequently used data is moved from fast, expensive hardware (hard disks) to slower, less expensive media, such as optical disks or magnetic tape. (An *optical disk* is any disk written and read by laser, including CD-R, CD-RW, DVD, and so forth.) However, optical disks are a poor solution if you want to back up large amounts of data quickly. In that case, you usually turn to the ubiquitous and cost-effective tape drive. Tape drives offer the lowest cost per megabyte of storage, the greatest degree of flexibility compared to comparable-capacity devices, and are very portable.

The choices available in backup devices have greatly expanded over the last few years due to advances in technology. The following table introduces the most common backup solutions in the server realm: tape and CD laser devices.

Device (category)	Media type	Pros	Cons
Tape drives (magnetic)	DAT, DDS, DLT	Inexpensive media, faster transfer rate	Expensive drives
CD (laser)	CD-ROM, CD-R, CD-RW	Inexpensive media	Limited software support for drive interface, not as flexible in terms of recording data as other solutions, slower than tape

Tape devices are generally the most popular server backup devices. Some devices support multiple tape formats, and others support only one. Some are very expensive, and some aren't. The faster units are more expensive, as are units that have larger media capacities and/or automated handling of multiple media. One factor that often forces you to choose the large, more expensive drives is the backup window. The *backup window* is the optimal period of time in which you can perform a backup and is usually when most files are closed. If your organization has a very small backup window, you need a very fast and expensive tape backup solution.

Tape devices are known for their long-lasting performance between hardware failures, which is partly attributable to the reliable tape drive mechanics and robotics that some systems include. Despite this reliability, you should research a vendor's service contract to ensure that the contract includes same-day on-site or overnight cross-shipping service if the unit fails.

Competition in the tape backup arena has created an abundance of dubious performance claims. You need to determine the type of files the vendor used to test the drive and the type of test the vendor ran, because many claims are a result of using totally compressible files. These tests don't take into account that many file types can't be compressed, so the tests don't simulate real-world scenarios.

Whichever type of tape drive you install, consider the importance of the tape drive driver. Plug and Play operating systems, such as Windows 2000 and Linux, might automatically detect hardware and install drivers of their own for the tape device. However, there might be features of the device that don't become available until you install the driver directly from the manufacturer. For example, many tape drives include hardware compression in which tape drive electronics compress data as it writes to tape, relieving the compression burden from the processor. However, unless you use the vendor drivers, the feature might not be available, and you would then have to fall back to software compression utilizing the processor.

Be sure to upgrade tape drivers when upgrading from one drive to another. For example, upgrading from a standalone tape device to an autoloader without also upgrading the driver will likely result in a unit that won't back up at all or might only back up to a single tape.

No matter what type of drive you choose, versions of most backup products are available with a choice of SCSI, EIDE, or parallel port interfaces, except for the very high-end products, which all have SCSI interfaces. Additionally, some older, low-end products, particularly tape drives, also come in versions that connect to the floppy disk controller. Parallel port and floppy disk interfaces aren't considered further in this discussion of server backup solutions.

Departmental servers that might not require extremely high-capacity backup solutions might require only a single standalone EIDE tape device. These devices provide reasonably good performance at up to about 20 GB of compressed data. For the best backup performance, especially for use on higher-end workstations and certainly for all servers, the interface option of choice is SCSI. When assessing the cost of your backup solution, you need to add the price of a good-quality SCSI interface card for your server, if you don't have one already, though most high-end workstation PCs and servers are already based on SCSI disk subsystems and therefore won't require an additional interface. In either case, check the type of physical SCSI connector fitted to a drive before buying to make sure you won't need additional cables or adapters. An additional benefit of SCSI is system responsiveness. With EIDE tape drives, some tape operations, such as cataloging the contents of the tape or re-tensioning, temporarily dominate the system and affect responsiveness. Because of the nature of SCSI, you can perform nearly any tape function with minimal impact on overall system responsiveness.

If it isn't cost prohibitive, take performance a step further and choose a tape solution that's Fibre Channel compatible.

Automated tape solutions

For a large-scale enterprise, none of the backup solutions outlined so far are sufficient. Instead, you should probably investigate a backup technology that can automatically change tapes in a largely unattended fashion.

Often large and extremely expensive, these automated tape devices are typically tape libraries that use autoloaders (see Exhibit 8-1). A *tape library* is a self-contained tape backup solution that's preloaded with several tapes. Most tape libraries include *autoloaders* to load and swap tapes automatically. In addition to automatic tape rotation, these devices can automatically clean tape heads.

Exhibit 8-1: A tape library using an autoloader

Automated backup solutions also mitigate potential human error. What if someone backed up Server_A and accidentally marked the tape Server_B? Restoring Server_A data might never occur unless someone manually goes through all the tapes searching for the data. Automated backup solutions won't write a label for you, but once you place the first set of tapes in the drives and properly configure the software, you can remove the human error factor from the tape backup. In addition, backups can be a tedious chore fraught with misplaced tapes, unmarked or mismarked tapes, incompatible tapes, and so on. (Many of the problems listed here relate to multiple persons performing backups. Make sure that only designated individuals perform the regular backups and that a written, logical procedure is defined.)

Also, a properly configured tape library takes only a fraction of the time otherwise required for a manual backup. This becomes more of an issue as more data centers operate around the clock instead of during business hours, because the available backup window grows smaller.

Another big advantage of automated backup libraries is the extensive *online retention period* (*OLRP*), the period for which data can be restored from tape without manual intervention. Because a library can store several generations of backups at once, if you want to restore a file from, say, five weeks ago, you don't have to rummage through the storage cabinet to find the right tape. Instead, you can use the tape library software to locate and restore from the correct tape for you.

You might not have an automated backup device available, but at the very least, use a single tape drive to schedule nightly backups. Once you configure the scheduling software, all you have to do is replace tapes as necessary.

At the highest level, you'll see tape libraries that can support dozens of drives and hold several hundred cartridges (see Exhibit 8-2). At that level, you probably won't configure the tape solution yourself; you'll tell vendor representatives what your objectives are, and they'll configure the library for you or provide guidance.

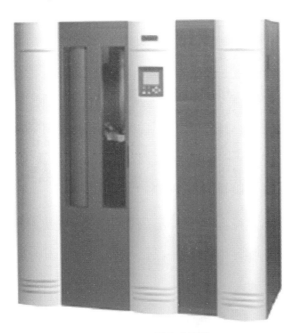

Exhibit 8-2: The StorageTek L700 can store up to 678 tapes and has up to 20 drives

Types of backup tape media

Tape media fall under a number of standards. The most common for smaller tape devices is probably the *Quarter Inch Cartridge* (*QIC*), which, as the name implies, is a quarter inch wide. QIC cartridges have evolved over the years, starting at about 20 MB and progressing to 80 MB. The QIC Wide (8 mm) tape was developed to squeeze more data into tape cartridges, but you probably won't see QIC or QIC Wide in use on servers anymore. However, you should keep some drives on hand that can at least read this format, as there are about 200 million QIC cartridges worldwide, and it might be necessary to restore an older archive. In 1994, a 3M spinoff (Imation) created a new QIC standard known as *Travan*. A Travan drive can reach compressed capacity of about 20 GB and is useful for home, small office/home office (SOHO), or small departmental backups. Because Travan drives accept the QIC format, they're usually backward read compatible with preceding QIC standards.

Travan NS (network series), as shown in Exhibit 8-3, is the most recent implementation of the Travan standard and addresses two main issues: compression and verification.

Exhibit 8-3: The Travan NS tape cartridge

Before Travan NS, data compression was always software based, taxing the processor and severely limiting other server functions. Travan NS tapes and drives offer hardware compression instead, relieving the compression burden from the CPU.

Any tape backup job still affects system responsiveness regardless of the tape format and drive technology. Whenever possible, perform backups during off-peak times. This helps to assure that fewer files are open, which might prevent them from being backed up and cause inconsistency when comparing them against a backup verification. Also consider performing backups remotely from servers or workstations that don't carry a significant role on the network. The following table provides a summary of Travan cartridge information:

Cartridge name (alias)	Native capacity / Compressed capacity	Read/write capability	Read capability
Travan-1 (TR-1)	400 MB 800 MB	QIC-80, QW-5122	QIC-40
Travan-2 (TR-2)**	800 MB 1.6 GB		
Travan-3 (TR-3)	1.6 GB 3.2 GB	TR-2, QIC-3020, QIC-3010, QW-3020XLW, QW-3020XLW	QIC-80, QW-5122, TR-1
Travan-8 GB (Travan 4, TR-4)	4 GB 8 GB	QIC-3095	QIC-3020, QIC-3010, QIC-80, QW-5122, TR-3, TR-1
Travan NS-8	4 GB 8 GB		QIC-3020, QIC-3010, QIC-80
Travan NS-20 (TR-5)	10 GB 20 GB	QIC-3220	Travan-8 GB, QIC-3095, TR-4

* Not every Travan standard is described in this text, but this chart is useful when you need to determine backward compatibilities. Compatibilities may vary from one drive manufacturer to another.
** Travan-2 never really got off the ground.

Another type of tape drive found on backup systems is a *digital audio tape* (*DAT*) drive. DAT was originally designed as a high-fidelity digital replacement for standard analog audiocassettes and, as happened with CD audio disks, the format was quickly picked up by the computer industry. While the mechanics of reading and writing to Travan, QIC, and similar format tapes are analogous to the way audio signals are written to a standard audiocassette, writing data to a DAT is similar to the way video signals are written to a videocassette. Rather than the tape being moved linearly across a static head, it's moved across an angled, rotating head, as illustrated in Exhibit 8-4. The result of this *helical scanning* is that a DAT can hold a higher density of data in a given area than other tape technologies. However, it's mechanically much more complex and potentially more expensive to repair should something go wrong. Such devices are usually significantly faster than more conventional linear drives, both in the time taken to read or write data and in how quickly an individual file can be located.

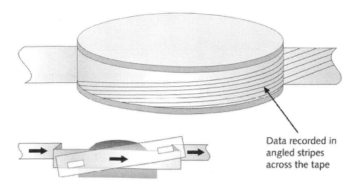

Data recorded in angled stripes across the tape

Exhibit 8-4: An angled DAT drive head stores more data on the tape

Only QIC tapes and drives read or write to QIC tapes and drives. In other words, you can't use a digital tape in a QIC drive or a QIC tape in a digital drive. In the digital arena, larger tape drives of each category are backward-compatible with smaller drives of the same type.

When Sony released its 8 mm videocassette technology, which is mechanically and conceptually similar to 4 mm DAT technology but with an 8 mm rather than a 4 mm tape width, its potential as a backup medium was once again seized upon by the computer industry. But unlike the case for 4 mm data drives, where a large number of makes and models are available, only a very few manufacturers took up the 8 mm helical scan challenge.

A variation of the 8 mm helical scan technology called *Advanced Intelligent Tape* (*AIT*) has recently become available. AIT is a Sony invention that makes backup and restore operations faster because of an optional Memory in Cassette (MIC) chip that's able to locate quickly which of the 256 tape partitions contain the data. Compare this to traditional methods in which you must scan the tape to locate data. Larger amounts of compressed data can fit onto one tape, making it the highest-capacity helical scan format available and allowing it to compare more favorably in terms of capacity with another commonly found tape format, *digital linear tape* (*DLT*), which is illustrated in Exhibit 8-5.

Exhibit 8-5: A DLT cartridge

Depending on the drive and media used, the DLT format allows up to 70 GB of compressed data to be stored on one rather large tape, which, unlike 8 mm or 4 mm helical scan technology, passes linearly over a fixed head.

Like Travan NS technology, DLT drives can simultaneously read and write, allowing them to perform extremely well and, in some cases, even better than an 8 mm helical scan tape. Because they're significantly faster and more capacious, in general, than any other technologies, AIT, conventional 8 mm helical scan, and DLT drives are also more expensive.

One of the latest tape formats is the ultra-high-capacity *Ultrium* format. The Ultrium format is actually a subset of the *Linear Tape Open* (*LTO*) technology—a collaborative effort headed up by HP, IBM, and Seagate. Ultrium features include:

- *Single reel.* Internal cartridge mechanics maintain the tape, and because it's pre-threaded inside the cartridge, as opposed to threading tape through the tape drive, Ultrium-compatible drives will potentially be less complicated. Exhibit 8-6 shows a cutaway of the Ultrium tape cartridge.

- *High storage capacity.* Ultrium tapes offer a native capacity of up to 200 GB and data transfer of 20-40 MBps. The Ultrium LTO format is expected to be available in four different generations as the technology advances, culminating in up to 1.6 TB per cartridge and up to 320 MBps (see table on facing page).

- *Cartridge memory.* Ultrium cartridges can contain *LTO-CM* (*Linear Tape Open - Cartridge Memory*) right on the cartridge that stores a redundant file log and user-defined information. If you want to know what's on a given tape, you can use an external reader to access the memory. The LTO-CM uses an RF (radio frequency) interface. Compare this to the lengthy process required of other tape types for which you insert the tape into the drive and then use the backup software to build a catalog. This process can take several minutes, whereas Ultrium memory allows immediate access.

- *Error correction.* LTO technology provides two levels of error correction that can recover data even when longitudinal scratches appear on the media. Simultaneous read/write capability allows for real-time verification of data.

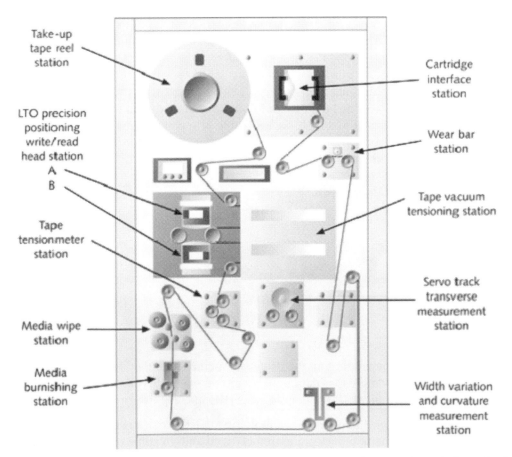

Exhibit 8-6: The Ultrium tape cartridge uses single spool and is pre-threaded inside the cartridge

Feature	Generation 1	Generation 2	Generation 3	Generation 4
Capacity:				
Native	100 GB	200 GB	400 GB	800 GB
Compressed	200 GB	400 GB	800 GB	1.6 TB
Transfer rate:				
Native	10-20 MBps	20-40 MBps	40-80 MBps	80-160 MBps
Compressed	20-40 MBps	40-80 MBps	80-160 MBps	160-320 MBps

Another LTO format known as Accelis proposes extremely fast data retrieval from anywhere on the tape in between 6.3 and 9.6 seconds. At this writing, Accelis is only a paper standard, and many speculate that Accelis drives and tapes may never actually be produced.

Tape and tape drive maintenance

Tape media are relatively delicate, and you should exercise care when handling them. The magnetic metal oxide that coats the film on the tape is susceptible to wearing off slightly over time. For the most part, this won't have an effect on the ability of the tape to store data. However, it does affect the drive itself, as literally miles of tape stream over the heads, capstans, and roller components. Just like a VCR, a tape drive requires regular cleaning of the components that come into contact with the media. Without proper cleaning, tape backups can lose integrity when the heads have difficulty reading or writing through the "gunk" that forms over the heads. Some newer media, such as AIT, include a built-in head cleaner. However, even in the cleanest environments, tape drives eventually accumulate contaminants. Dirty capstans and rollers can cause media to stick to the components and create a horrible mess when you have to untangle yards of loose tape from inside the drive. Some devices include automatic cleaning capability. Otherwise, you have to either procure cleaning tapes or use the old cotton swab and cleaning solution method.

Be careful about how you repurpose a previously recorded tape. In the past, when administrators had an old tape that they wanted to recycle to store new data, they'd bulk-erase the tape using a big magnet. Obviously, since tape is a magnetic medium, bulk erasing wipes out the existing data. With current tape technology, don't erase tapes in this way. Tapes now come preformatted, and bulk erasure removes important markings from the tape. Once erasure occurs, there's no way for the tape drive to orient the tape to a known starting position or locate boundaries to store the data logically. If you want to erase a tape, use tape backup software, which can usually perform a quick erasure by removing the table of contents, or a secure erasure, which overwrites the tape with zeros and ones.

A tape written under one software vendor's program usually can't be read by another vendor's program. This makes a corporate-wide policy that uses the same backup software critically important.

If you've performed even a single tape backup, then you know by listening that the drive fast-forwards and rewinds the tape quite a lot. This is okay and is the nature of the backup. However, over time and especially if only part of the tape is used, the level of tension varies at different places on the spool, and this inconsistency can affect read/write reliability. Temperature changes, which cause the tape to expand and contract, and dropping a tape can also affect its tension level. Tape software offers utilities to *re-tension* the tape, as illustrated in Exhibit 8-7, which fast-forwards to the end without reading or writing data, and then rewinds all the way to the beginning again. This process makes tension even throughout the tape.

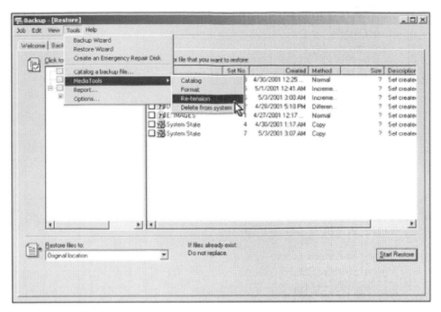

Exhibit 8-7: For even tension throughout the tape, the Windows Backup utility re-tensions the tape

Do it!

A-1:   Discussing backup hardware

Questions and answers
1   What's Hierarchical Storage Management (HSM)?
2   What's online retention period (OLRP)?
3   What's a QIC?
4   What's an optical disk?

Topic B: Backup software and strategies

This topic covers the following CompTIA Server+ exam objectives:

#	Objective
3.5	Install NOS and driver updates to design specifications. Activities include: • Ensure that there is a backup and recovery plan
3.6	Install service tools. Service tools include: • Backup software
4.1	Perform backup • Activities include: • Update the ERD/recover disk (if applicable) • Verify backup • Supporting knowledge includes: • When full backups might be necessary • How to select the appropriate type of backup • Differential • Appended • Copy • Full
5.1	Perform regular backup • Activities include: • Update the ERD/recovery disk (if applicable) • Verify backup • Supporting knowledge includes: • When full backups might be necessary • How to select the appropriate type of backup • Differential • Appended • Copy • Full
8.1	Read and follow the disaster recover plan • Activities include: • Confirm and use off site storage for backup • Supporting knowledge includes: • Identify types of backup and restoration schemes • Grandfather schemes • Differential and incremental backups

Software

Explanation
On the whole, lower-cost tape drives and some disk-based devices intended for use with stand-alone PCs come bundled with backup software. For example, Windows 2003 comes with backup software, as illustrated in Exhibit 8-8. The software tends to be quite basic, but it usually does the job it's intended for. Such software isn't capable of servicing more sophisticated backup solutions, such as automatic tape changers, remote backup, or backing up open files. On the other hand, most high-end tape drives and most disk-based products don't come bundled with software. This should be taken into consideration when comparing costs, because the software is an additional several hundred dollars per server. Software for high-end tape drives includes many more features and at a reduced cost per remote station.

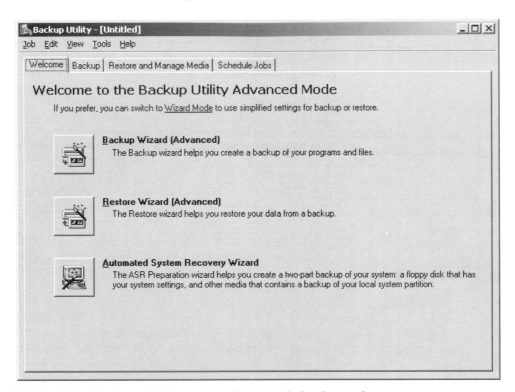

Exhibit 8-8: Windows 2003 comes with versatile backup software

If you need software as part of your backup setup, there are a number of packages available, ranging from replacements for bundled software to high-end products capable of backing up a whole room full of servers onto several tape drives, in some cases simultaneously. Depending on your needs, features to look for in backup software include the following:

- The ability to restore your hard disk in its entirety without requiring you to reinstall the operating system manually. This software feature creates an image of the disk and stores it on tape. This is not unlike Symantec Ghost or PowerQuest DriveImage, which store the image on a hard drive.

- The ability to treat a backup tape as a virtual hard disk, albeit a very slow one. This capability sometimes uses the right-click menu from Windows Explorer, allowing you to perform the backup in a way similar to using the Send To item when copying a file to a floppy disk.

- A built-in data compression capability should your drive not include its own hardware data compression facilities.

- The ability to scan for viruses during backup or restore operations.

- Built-in tape management facilities that can tell you when to replace or swap tapes. Robotic or automated media-switching devices often require proprietary drivers and administrative software to be installed.

- The ability to create an account for you that has access rights to back up all data regardless of ownership. In a Windows environment, this account would belong to the Backup Operators group. The account is usually able to log on as a service and, therefore, perform backup without an administrator performing an actual logon.

- The ability to perform unattended backups. The software often creates a special account that can log on by itself at scheduled times to start the backup.

- The ability to run commands before and after the backup. This is useful for stopping services or applications that would interfere with the backup utility and restarting them afterward.

Storing and securing backups

There are several steps that you can take to enhance the security and operation of your backup and restore operations. You should also take steps to secure your backup cartridges.

When you develop a backup plan, consider the following recommendations:

- Secure both the storage device and the backup cartridges. Data can be retrieved from stolen cartridges and restored to another computer.

- If the software supports it, add security measures to the tape. You might be able to protect the media with a password or allow restore operations only by the Administrator or Owner accounts, as in the Windows 2000 backup.

- Back up an entire volume by using the normal backup procedure. In case of a disk failure, it's more efficient to restore the entire volume in one operation than to include differential or incremental backups also.

- Keep at least three current copies of backup cartridges. Store one copy at an off-site location in an environmentally controlled, secure environment. Check for a service bureau in your area that can provide this storage. Most service bureaus also have tape drives that can read and restore the tapes for you if necessary. In preparation for disaster recovery, know how long it takes to retrieve the tapes physically from off-site locations. Store another copy near a server that can restore from the tape in a secure, locked, fireproof cabinet. The last tape can be stored wherever it suits you. Its main purpose is redundancy in case one of the other tapes becomes damaged or defective. Some organizations with a WAN infrastructure send a copy of the normal backup to another office across the WAN. That way, if the local off-site location and the local office become unavailable (as in a natural disaster), you still have the copy that was sent to the other office.

Backup types

A *normal,* or *full, backup* copies all selected files and clears the archive bit on each one. This identifies the file as having been backed up. The next time the file is modified, the archive bit is automatically set (added). Files or directories that have been moved to new locations aren't marked for backup. Most backup software allows you to back up only files with this marker set and to choose whether or not to mark files when they're backed up. The archive bit is significant in relation to the incremental and differential backups. Normal backups are the easiest to use for restoring files, because you need only the most recent backup file or tape to restore all of the backed-up files. Normal backups take the most time, because every file that's selected is backed up, regardless of whether it's changed since the last backup.

An *incremental backup* backs up only those files that have been created or changed since the last normal or incremental backup, which can reduce the amount of time that's required to complete the backup process. It marks files as having been backed up by clearing the archive bit. You should create a complete normal backup of your system before you run incremental backups. If you use a combination of normal and incremental backups, you must have the last normal backup set as well as every incremental backup set that's been made since the last normal backup, in chronological order, to restore your data. (The archive bit is easily observable by viewing the properties of a file. For example, in Windows Explorer, you'd right-click a file and view its properties.)

The advantage of an incremental backup is that the backup process is typically faster than both a normal or differential backup. The disadvantage is that it takes longer to restore the backup because you might have to supply multiple incremental tapes created since the last normal backup.

A *differential backup* copies files that have been created or changed since the last normal or incremental backup, which can reduce the amount of time that's required to complete the backup process. It doesn't mark files as having been backed up. You should create a complete normal backup of your system before you run differential backups. If you're doing normal and differential backups, you must have the last normal backup set and the last differential backup sets to restore your data.

The advantage of the differential backup is that it's faster than the normal backup and requires only two backup sets to restore data: the original normal backup and the corresponding differential backup. The disadvantage is that differential backups take longer to back up data.

A *copy backup* copies all selected files, but it doesn't mark each file as having been backed up. Copying is useful to back up files between normal and incremental backups, because it doesn't affect other backup operations. A *daily backup* copies all selected files that have been modified on the day that the daily backup is performed. The backed-up files aren't marked as having been backed up.

Backups protect against data loss caused by a virus. Because some viruses take weeks to appear, keep normal backup tapes for at least a month to make sure that you can restore a system to its uninfected status.

Using incremental backups

Let's say that you implement a normal backup, and that you don't want to do a normal backup every day. Performing an incremental backup makes the most sense in order to keep track of what files are backed up (unlike a differential backup). For example, suppose you're doing an incremental backup of 850 MB of data. If you did the normal backup on Monday, all 850 MB are placed on the tape on that day. On Tuesday, the incremental backup day, only the files that you've created or changed since Monday are backed up, so you may back up only a few megabytes at that time. On Wednesday, you back up only the files that you've created or changed since Tuesday, and so on. Because each incremental backup backs up data only since the last normal or incremental backup, the backup is relatively fast.

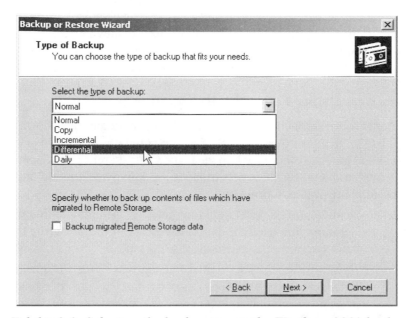

Exhibit 8-9: Selecting the backup type in the Windows 2003 backup software

Unfortunately, incremental backups have their disadvantages. Although they're quicker than normal backups, it takes longer to restore a file when incremental backups are involved in the process. For example, suppose you needed to restore a file you backed up on Monday. This file would be included in the first backup of the set, since you performed a normal backup on Monday. However, to ensure that you were restoring the most recent version of the file, you'd have to search all remaining backups in the set to see if the file had changed since then. Another disadvantage to this type of backup is the fact that you must have all backups in the set available in order to restore only one file.

If you're planning to use an incremental backup, you might consider starting a new backup set every Monday that would include the backups for Monday through Friday of that week. Of course, if your servers are heavily utilized on weekends, you can schedule Saturday and Sunday backups as well. You can also make the length of time between creating new backup sets as long or as short as your needs dictate.

Develop a backup strategy

Regular backups of local hard disks prevent data loss resulting from disk drive failures, disk controller errors, power outages, virus infection, and other possible problems. Backup operations that are based on careful planning and reliable equipment make file recovery easier and less time-consuming. There are several backup strategies, though the most common strategy is known as the Grandfather-Father-Son (GFS) strategy, which is described below. Your backup strategy usually uses some combination of normal, incremental, or differential backups.

Developing a backup strategy involves not only determining when to perform backups, but also testing the data with random and scheduled verification to make sure that tape devices and media are functioning properly. Also, make sure that, throughout the organization, the persons or departments responsible for handling backup and restore operations are well informed as to what exactly they should back up. You don't want to be caught in the awkward situation where someone asks you to restore a file that you didn't even know you were supposed to back up.

The Grandfather-Father-Son backup strategy

There are several generally accepted backup strategies, as illustrated in Exhibit 8-10. However, many of them are based on the popular *Grandfather-Father-Son* (*GFS*) backup strategy (otherwise known as the Child-Parent-Grandparent method). This backup strategy uses three sets of tapes for daily, weekly, and monthly backup sets, and you implement it as follows:

1 *Back up the "Son."* Label four tapes as "Monday" through "Thursday." These Son tapes are used for daily incremental backups during the week. For subsequent weeks, reuse these same tapes.

2 *Back up the "Father."* Label five tapes as "Week 1" through "Week 5." These Father tapes are used for weekly normal backups on Friday, the day you don't perform a Son backup. Once you make the tape, store it locally. Reuse the tapes when each tape's respective week arrives. Depending on your backup policy, periodically duplicate a Father tape for off-site storage. You can use another drive to perform a simultaneous backup, or some backup software might offer a tape copy feature.

3 *Back up the "Grandfather."* Grandfather tapes are used for a normal backup performed on the last business day of the month. No standard labeling scheme is stated, but consider labeling three tapes as "Month 1" through "Month 3." The tapes are valid for three months and are reused every quarter.

At a minimum, the GFS strategy requires 12 tapes if you add them all together, assuming that no one backup exceeds the capacity of a single cartridge.

Of course, you can modify this scheme as it suits your backup policy, but the GFS strategy is a logical, reliable place to start. For example, if you want to keep a year's data archived at all times, instead of only a quarter's, then for the Grandfather tapes you would label 12 tapes "Month 1" through "Month 12" and reuse the tapes every year. An illustration of the GFS rotation scheme appears in Exhibit 8-11.

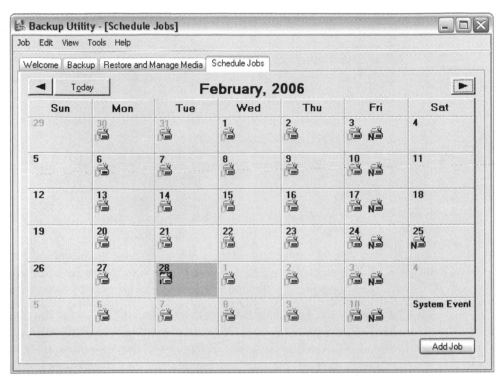

Exhibit 8-10: Windows 2003 software allows you to set a detailed backup schedule

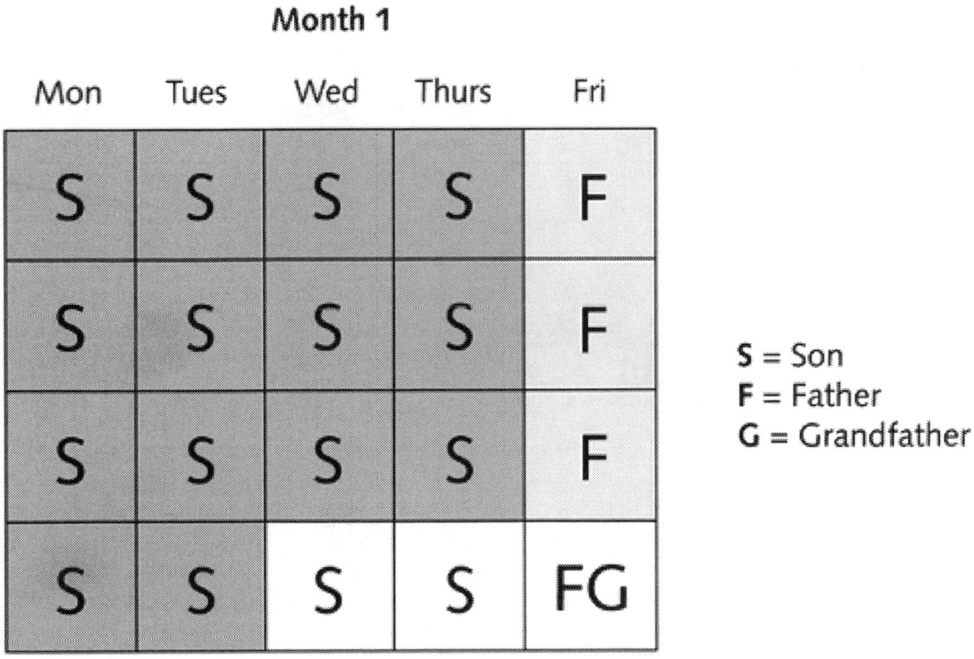

Month 1

Mon	Tues	Wed	Thurs	Fri
S	S	S	S	F
S	S	S	S	F
S	S	S	S	F
S	S	S	S	FG

S = Son
F = Father
G = Grandfather

Exhibit 8-11: The GFS tape rotation strategy

The six-cartridge backup

If you want to use fewer tapes, consider the *six-cartridge backup* strategy. This might be a better choice for smaller businesses or sites that don't generate large quantities of data. The disadvantage of the six-cartridge strategy is that you have a shorter archive history, only two weeks, whereas the GFS strategy has a quarter.

To perform a six-cartridge backup:

1 Label six cartridges "Friday 1," "Friday 2," "Monday," "Tuesday," "Wednesday," and "Thursday."

2 Perform the first normal backup onto the "Friday 1" tape. Store the tape off-site.

3 On Monday, perform an incremental backup onto the "Monday" tape. Store the tape on site.

4 Repeat the incremental backup onto tapes "Tuesday," "Wednesday," and "Thursday" on the corresponding days.

5 Perform the second normal backup onto the "Friday 2" tape. This completes the backup cycle. Store the cartridge off site. On each successive Friday, alternate between the "Friday 1" tape and the "Friday 2" tape.

Note that the Friday tapes are always stored off site, as illustrated in Exhibit 8-12. This can cause a problem when it's necessary to restore data, because you have to retrieve the tape physically, and this might not suit the time frame necessary to restore the data. As with the GFS method, you can modify the six-cartridge method to suit your needs.

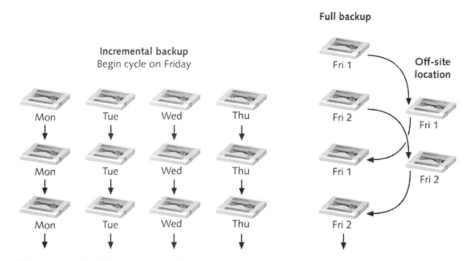

Exhibit 8-12: The six-cartridge backup strategy stores Friday tapes off-site

The Tower of Hanoi

Finally, there's the *Tower of Hanoi backup* method, borrowing from a mathematical logic game of the same name. Use five sets of media for this rotation, labeling them "A" through "E" and proceed as follows:

1 On day one, back up to "A." Reuse the "A" tape every other day.

2 On day two, back up to "B." Reuse the "B" tape every four days.

3 On day four, back up to "C." Reuse the "C" tape every eight days.

4 On day eight, back up to "D." Reuse the "D" tape every 16 days.

5 On day 16, back up to "E." Reuse the "E" tape every 32 days.

As a memory aid to the Tower of Hanoi rotation, just notice that each tape is reused in a pattern similar to binary notation. Look at the "reuse" schedule at the end of every step above. Notice that you reuse tapes every 2, 4, 8, 16, and 32 days.

An advantage of the Tower of Hanoi rotation is that you always have a daily history of data extending back 32 days. This is a flexible backup strategy requiring only five tapes (assuming each backup requires only one tape). If you want longterm archiving, you can remove a tape and store it off-site. Label the tape with the date and replace it with another. For example, if you want to archive the "E" tape, place a date on it, send it to storage, and label a new cartridge "E" that continues the rotation. Also, you can extend the history, if you like. By adding an "F" backup every 64 days, you now have a 64-day history. Keep adding letters until you reach the history you want.

The rotation scheme is best understood by viewing Exhibit 8-13.

1	2	3	4	5	6	7	8	9	10	11	12	13	14	15	16
A		A		A		A		A		A		A		A	
	B				B				B				B		
			C								C				
							D								
															E

Exhibit 8-13: Tower of Hanoi media rotation schedule

Document the process

Keeping accurate backup records is essential for locating backed-up data quickly, particularly if you have accumulated a large number of backup cartridges. Thorough records include cartridge labels, catalogs, and online log files and log books.

- *Cartridge label.* Cartridge labels for write-once cartridges should contain the backup date, the type of backup (normal, incremental, or differential), and a list of contents. If you're restoring from differential or incremental backups, you need to be able to locate the last normal backup and either the last differential backup or all incremental backups that have been created since the last normal backup. Label reusable media, such as tapes or removable disks, sequentially, and keep a log book in which you note the content of cartridges, the backup date, the type of backup, and the date the medium was placed in service. If you have to replace a defective cartridge, label it with the next unused sequential ID, and record it in the log book.

- *Catalogs.* Most backup software includes a mechanism for cataloging backup files. Backup software typically stores backup catalogs on the cartridge and temporarily loads them into memory. Catalogs are created for each backup set or for each collection of backed-up files from one drive.

- *Log files.* Log files include the names of all backed-up and restored files and directories. A log file is useful when you're restoring data, because you can print or read this file from any text editor. Keeping printed logs in a notebook makes it easier to locate specific files. For example, if the tape that contains the catalog of the backup set is corrupted, you can use the printed logs to locate a file.

Do it!

B-1: Discussing backup software and strategies

Questions and answers

1 What's the minimum number of tapes required in a GFS tape backup strategy?

2 Which backup strategy requires fewer tapes than the GFS method?

3 What's an advantage of the Tower of Hanoi rotation strategy?

Topic C: Server redundancy and other disaster precautions

This topic covers the following CompTIA Server+ exam objectives:

#	Objective
1.13	Know the attributes, purpose, function, and advantages of clustering, scalability, high availability, and fault tolerance.
3.6	Install service tools • Service tools include: • SNMP • System monitoring agents • Event logs • Supporting knowledge includes: • Identity, purpose, and function of service tools • How to set up SNMP • How system monitoring software and MIB's are implemented on hardware • Purpose of event logs
4.2	Add processors • Activities include: • Ensure proper ventilation
5.4	Perform physical housekeeping • Activities include: • Periodic checks for dust buildup
8.1	Read and follow the disaster recover plan • Supporting knowledge includes: • The need for redundancy (e.g. hard drives, power supplies, fans, NIC's, processors, UPS) • Ability to read and comprehend a disaster recovery plan

Clustering

File services, print services, and client-server applications rely not only on the availability of the computers running the services, but also on the availability of network services. In an environment where there's only one computer providing a particular service (file, print, or application), an outage involving that server eliminates the availability of the provided service.

To provide both load balancing and redundancy for these services, a group, or cluster, of computers can cooperate in providing these services. This cooperation is managed by clustering software that provides a service to clients in a client-server environment. For example, a public file share, a Web server, and a database application can all be managed as resources.

A cluster improves the availability of client-server applications by increasing the availability of server resources. Using a cluster, you can set up applications on two or more servers (nodes) in a cluster. Each node connects to a shared storage media. Clusters present a single, virtual image of the cluster to clients, as illustrated in Exhibit 8-14. If one node fails, the applications on the failed node are available on the other node. Throughout this process, client communications with applications usually continue with little or no interruption. In most cases, the interruption in service is detected in about five seconds, and services can be available again in as few as 30 seconds, depending on how long it takes to restart the application.

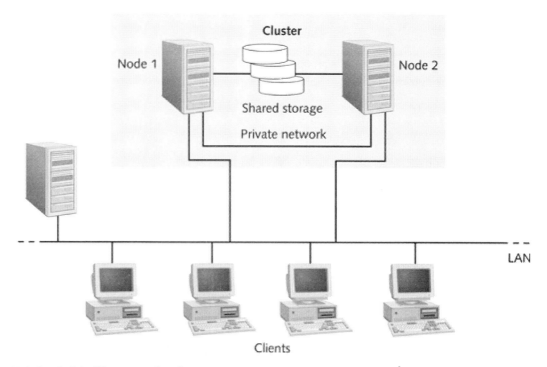

Exhibit 8-14: Cluster technology connects two or more servers to common shared storage

Clustering provides high availability and fault tolerance by keeping a backup of the primary system available. Static load balancing remains idle and unused until a failure occurs, which makes this an expensive solution. An active cluster is a clustering method in which all nodes perform normal, active functions and then perform additional functions for a failed cluster member.

For example, redundant systems might have one node in the cluster servicing Web clients while the other node provides access to a database. If either node fails, the resource (the Web server or the database server) fails over to the other node. The node that's still functioning responds to both Web and SQL requests from clients, as shown in Exhibit 8-15. In a passive cluster, a server with identical services as its failover partner would remain in an idle node state until such a time as the primary node fails.

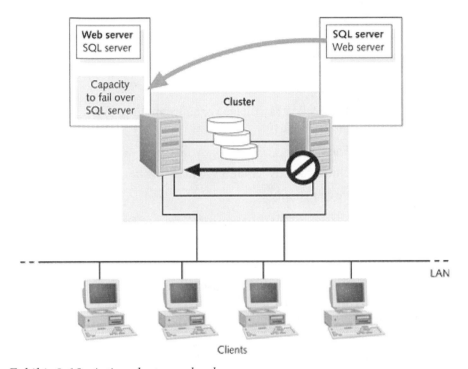

Exhibit 8-15: Active cluster redundancy

CPU, I/O, storage, and application resources can be added incrementally to expand capacity efficiently, making the solution highly scalable. This creates reliable access to system resources and data, as well as investment protection of both hardware and software resources. Clusters are relatively affordable, because they can be built with commodity hardware (high-volume components that are relatively inexpensive).

By clustering existing hardware with new computers, you protect your investment in both hardware and software: Instead of replacing an existing computer with a new one of twice the capacity, you can simply add another computer of equal capacity. For example, if performance degrades because of an increase in the number of clients using an application on a server, you can add a second server to a cluster, which improves performance and also increases availability.

Clients typically access network applications and resources through network names and IP addresses. When these network applications and resources are hosted within a Microsoft Cluster Server (MSCS), clients can continue to find and access the resources, even though they may move between nodes. MSCS enables this by failing over both the IP address and network name for a given resource.

Failover

Failover is the process of having cluster resources migrate from an unavailable node to an available node. A related process, *failback*, occurs when service transfers back to the node that's been offline after it's back online. The cluster automatically initiates failover when it detects a failure on one of the cluster nodes. Because each cluster node monitors both its own processes and the other node's, the need for failover is detected without delay.

Spare parts

For hardware failure recovery, having a number of spare parts available saves the time needed to order failed items from the original vendor. Also, as equipment ages, the availability of the parts needed to continue operation may diminish as well. All parts to be considered available as replacements for a given computer system must be compatible with both the operating system in use and other components within the system. The best strategy for mission-critical systems is to have a set of matching parts available. Some vendors, such as Intel, sell spare parts kits comprised of the most critical system components, including:

- 12 V VRM (a voltage regulator module that helps ensure clean power to the motherboard)
- Fans
- Hot-swap bay assembly with SCSI backplane
- Power supply
- CD-ROM drive
- Floppy drive
- Cables

Using the spare parts kit, you use parts as necessary and immediately call the vendor to replace the parts you use. That way, the spare parts kit is always ready for service. Be sure also to have additional spare parts, which might not be included in a spare parts kit, such as:

- Network card
- Memory modules
- Processor
- Hard disk
- Hard disk host adapter (EIDE or SCSI)
- Motherboard
- Video card
- Sound card (optional)
- Other miscellaneous I/O boards

Spare drives

The redundancy of a RAID system wouldn't be very useful if you couldn't easily replace a failed drive. RAID controllers and associated software usually indicate when a drive fails. You can then at least shut down the system and replace the drive. This is referred to as a cold spare. It's more likely, though, that the system allows hot swapping or hot spares.

Hot swapping allows you to pull the old drive and put in a new one without shutting down the system. The new drive isrebuilt automatically. You can also use a *hot spare* that's connected to the hard disk host adapter along with the other hard disks but is dormant until another device in the drive array fails. At that time, the system fails over to the hot spare automatically, rebuilding with the data that was on the failed drive. For example, if one member of a mirrored (RAID-1) array fails, the hot spare can automatically come online and the remaining member begin to duplicate to it. You can then replace the failed drive at your convenience. The main difference between a hot-swappable disk and a hot spare is that a hot spare is on the bus at the time of the failure, whereas a hot-swap drive is manually replaced.

A hot spare is called local when it's dedicated to one RAID logical drive. It's also possible to have a global spare, which is available to several RAID systems.

SNMP settings

Previously you learned the basics of SNMP. SNMP is a critical element for disaster avoidance, detection, and recovery. The following is a short list of common SNMP items for which you want to configure your SNMP management system to assist in disaster prevention and recovery:

- Network protocol identification and statistics
- Dynamic identification of devices attached to the network (discovery)
- Hardware and software configuration data
- Device performance and usage statistics
- Device error and event messages
- Program and application usage statistics

The items in the list can help to detect impending problems and verify that a proposed solution worked effectively. For example, if you suspect network traffic to be excessive on an Ethernet network, you could configure the SNMP agent to issue a trap when it detects over 30% network utilization on a given segment. After replacing a hub with a switch to increase throughput and reduce collisions, the same SNMP agent can confirm, by the absence of a trap, that the solution worked.

In general, agents don't originate messages; they only respond to messages. The exception is an SNMP trap triggered by a specific event, such as a system reboot or illegal access. Traps and trap messages provide a rudimentary form of security by notifying the management system any time such an event occurs. Typically, you configure the management system to issue an e-mail, fax, network message, or pager alert. For pager alerts, some systems require an external modem, but this requirement can be circumvented by using e-mail instead to send text messages to a cell phone or e-mail-capable pager.

If your cabinet and SNMP management software support it, you can add a layer of physical security to the server cabinet by configuring SNMP to issue a trap any time the cabinet door opens. If you're the only one who's supposed to access the cabinet and your pager receives an SNMP message while you're away at lunch, then you know somebody is illegitimately accessing the cabinet.

Server management and maintenance

Server management and disaster recovery are really two balancing components in the same overall server health management scheme. You use server management software and faithful physical management of the server to prevent disaster. Then, you use disaster recovery techniques to fix the inevitable problems that occur.

Server management software

There's a broad selection of server management software. We have mentioned third-party management products, such as IBM Tivoli or Computer Associates' Unicenter TNG. In this area, third-party products can still play a role, but servers also usually include less comprehensive software that provides basic system monitoring functions. These utilities often integrate with the system BIOS or CMOS settings, and display or issue an alert when a problem appears. For example, Exhibit 8-16 shows a very simple server monitoring utility that monitors temperature, fan speed, voltages, and more.

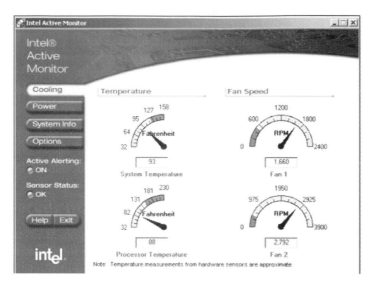

Exhibit 8-16: A monitoring utility displays basic server health issues

Server motherboards and management software usually offer such features as the following:

- *Failure detection.* Detects temperature and voltage changes, fan speed change or failure, disk drive problems or failure, power supply failure, processor status, and ECC memory errors.
- *Software monitoring.* Detects hung applications. For serious problems, you can use management software to perform a graceful shutdown or reboot.
- *Event logging.* Events are stored in NVRAM (nonvolatile RAM), so that, if power is lost, the records remain.
- *Emergency Management Port* (Intel boards). A feature that allows you to turn on, off, or reset the server and view the event log, all remotely. These features require an external modem and are very useful for remotely monitoring servers over a wide geographic area from a single location.
- *Security monitoring.* A jumper setting enables chassis intrusion detection. Some systems automatically blank the video when the chassis or cabinet is open, and a password is required to resume normal video.

Most server boards include a server management utility, but if yours doesn't, download a freeware monitoring utility such as the Motherboard Monitor from nearly any popular download site or from www.tweakfiles.com/diagnostic/motherboardmonitor.html.

Larger organizations need more than a local server management utility, so they opt for enterprise management software, such as HP's Openview or CA's Unicenter TNG. A significant advantage of this type of software is that you can manage the entire network from a single seat, regardless of the physical location of any one server. For example, in Exhibit 8-17, CA's Unicenter TNG is shown as being used to access the California network and, in Exhibit 8-18, the North American network. The figures are shown using a map feature of Unicenter in 2D, but you can also use 3D graphics. In the map view, you can click on any of your networks to access information and administer them.

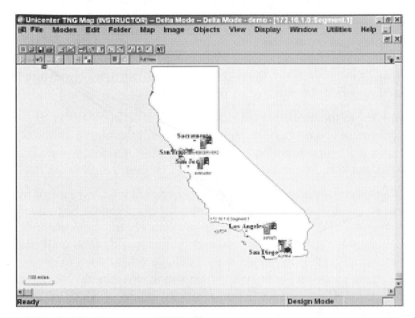

Exhibit 8-17: Unicenter TNG allows you to access your server visually

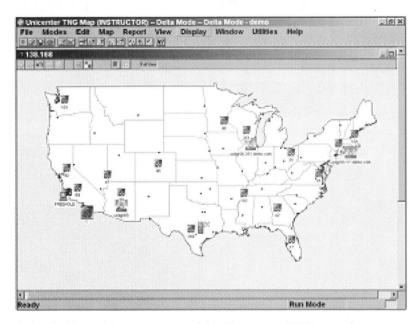

Exhibit 8-18: A demonstration of the Unicenter TNG map feature

Physical care and maintenance

Recall that two primary factors contribute to hardware device and computer peripheral failure: dirt and heat. Regular cleaning of computer equipment and adequate ventilation are necessary in order to maximize the lifetime of the equipment.

Hard disk drives, for example, are prone to failure in high-heat environments. Their mechanical nature causes a great deal of friction, as the platters can spin in excess of 15,000 revolutions per minute (rpm). Stack several disks inside of a single computer without proper ventilation, and the combined heat of several drives can damage the electrical components, leading to drive failure. If a drive fails and data is lost prior to a timely backup, an expensive data recovery service bureau needs to be employed to open the disks and attempt to extract the data from the failed device.

Consider checking into a server chassis that includes airflow guides. These guides are paddles near the cooling fans that allow you to direct the airflow as desired. This is very handy when the drives or other hot components are located some distance from the actual fans or aren't in the path of the normal airflow. For example, Supermicro offers airflow guides on some of its popular models.

Related to the heat and dust that accumulate during the normal use and function of your equipment is the age of the equipment and/or the time that this equipment has been in service. Regular monitoring of your system is necessary to note changes in I/O and other performance measures unrelated to changes in network access or activity.

If a device is performing slowly or experiencing an increase of random or unexplained errors, it may be in an early stage of failure and should be replaced as soon as possible. Some devices, such as a power supply, can't be easily monitored without server management software, but can lead to system-wide failures if performance begins to deteriorate. A power supply whose voltage is beginning to drop significantly or fluctuate can affect many components in the system, both in terms of quality and length of service. If you suspect a power supply failure, replace it immediately to avoid further damage to other system components.

Probably the most common maintenance issue for servers is planned downtime to blow out dust. The frequency of this task varies greatly depending on the environmental conditions at the site. Until you can determine the rate at which dust accumulates in the case, check accumulation weekly. Once you determine an optimum frequency for this planned downtime, be sure to schedule it regularly. When dusting, in order to avoid contaminating the environment, remember to remove the server from the server room if you're blowing out dust. Remove dust from every place you can, though the chassis fans and power supply fans accumulate dust most quickly.

Do it!

C-1: Discussing disaster precautions

Questions and answers

1 Which SNMP component should be configured in order to report errors, security breaches, or other event notification?

2 Why should spare network components be kept on site?

3 Server motherboards and management software usually offer which features?

Topic D: Developing a disaster recovery plan

This topic covers the following CompTIA Server+ exam objectives:

#	Objective
8.1	Read and follow the disaster recover plan • Activities include: • Find, read and implement the recover plan • Participate in testing of disaster recover • Supporting knowledge includes: • Ability to read and comprehend a disaster recovery plan • Concept of hot, cold, and warm sites

The disaster recovery plan

Explanation

A *disaster recovery plan* (*DRP*) for a large enterprise can amount to hundreds of pages with thousands of contingencies. These complicated details and scenarios, if left unplanned, can go unaccomplished, leading to an unacceptable extension of system outage. When putting together a DRP, there are many items that need to be considered and included. Practical implementations vary from one network to another, but the most important matter is to develop a disaster recovery plan in the first place.

The DRP is critical because, in a disaster, the tendency is to assemble hastily a short list of recovery steps that come to mind. This can actually extend the time it takes to recover from disaster, because it's difficult to account for every recovery procedure. A DRP specifies what actions need to be taken, and in what order, after the destructive event. Each scenario, from a single desktop computer failure to a complete outage of an entire site, should have a plan of action for those responsible. Depending on the severity of the event, these actions can include:

- Evacuation of facility and notification of emergency services
- Notification sequence for team leaders and backups
- Establishing a temporary business recovery command center
- Preliminary and detailed damage assessment
- Recall of vital records from off-site storage

In the event of a site-wide or catastrophic failure, longer-term issues must be addressed:

- Handling legal, financial, and insurance issues
- Dealing with the news media to mitigate misinformation
- Locating interim facilities to restart your business
- Recovery of PCs, LANs, and midrange systems
- Establishing voice and data communication
- Addressing human resource and accounts payable/receivable issues
- Replacement of equipment, furniture, and supplies
- Notification to clients, customers, suppliers, and stockholders

A disaster recovery plan is a possibility only when there's actually a team to develop it. Assemble members from each major branch or function of your organization, because disasters affect all aspects of the organization, not just the IT department. The disaster recovery team needs to work well together in order to minimize downtime and loss of productivity. Preparing a disaster recovery plan can take months and, depending on the size of the organization, perhaps over a year. For an example of comprehensive disaster recovery services, see BMS Catastrophes (www.bmscat.com). For help in planning a disaster recovery solution, see Davis Logic (www.davislogic.com).

Using alternate sites

In larger computing environments, it isn't practical to have enough computers in store and configured to replace most of the equipment all at once. Larger companies, universities, and institutions can't afford to carry more than 1% or 2% of the total hardware collection in recovery-based inventory. Also, in the event of facility-, site-, or campus-wide failure, there may be more than computers that need to be replaced: Facilities may also have to be recovered as in the case of a flood, tornado, or other natural disaster.

In preparation for large-scale recovery, consider alternate sites. They can range from simple data collection and warehousing services designed to return data as needed to continue business operations, to full-scale facility duplication (*hot sites*) designed to replicate all of the hardware, software, and data infrastructure necessary to assume all business functions in the event of a primary facility failure. These hot sites are very expensive to maintain, as they have nearly a complete replica of all computers in the central facility, but if a large-scale outage will cost the company its existence, the price is worth it.

Hot sites

Usually, a hot site is a shared facility with a number of subscribers from various geographic locations, each of which shares in the cost of maintaining the fully operational center. Each subscriber usually occupies the hot site for up to six weeks after a disaster. These facilities are also available for subscribers to exercise their recovery plan in test mode.

Hot site recovery is appropriate for a computer operation that has more than a 24-hour outage tolerance. Data centers requiring faster service restoration must invest in redundant (spare) equipment that's immediately available to satisfy this need. Conversely, facilities that can afford to wait several weeks before restoring service need not engage a hot site, for they have time to order and install new equipment.

Cold sites

Many service bureaus augment their hot site services with a *cold site* feature. This is a facility designed to receive computer equipment. All power, water, air conditioning, raised floor, and other items requiring a long lead-time to acquire, install, and make ready to house a computer center are in place.

Should a company be unable to return to its home computing center within a tolerable time frame, it would make arrangements to occupy this cold site. Computers, peripheral equipment, and related services would be ordered (purchased, leased, or rented) and made ready to assume the company's processing workload. Cold sites are used until the home site is repaired or rebuilt.

Site management

Business processes can be quite complex as remote sites, either hot or cold, are implemented. Bad planning in these areas leads to confusion and delay. Several important steps are necessary to determine the activities and timeframes surrounding service and equipment movement and delegation between the central (or original) site, hot sites, cold sites, and their return to the repaired or newly constructed site.

- Determine the extent of the damage and if additional equipment, services, or supplies are needed.

- Take care to cover telecommunications issues adequately. Most medium-sized and large organizations usually have a number of telecommunications services, such as leased lines and fiber, connecting campuses and other facilities. This means that, in the event of a disaster, such connections to other facilities may have to be abandoned, re-routed, or installed to the hot and/or cold sites in order to establish connectivity to other operational facilities. Detailed records of current operations must be carefully reviewed to be certain that your disaster recovery plan covers every conceivable technical aspect of recovering all critical services and data in the least amount of time.

- Obtain approval for expenditure of funds to bring in any needed equipment and supplies. One corporation set up an agreement with its bank so that, in the event of a catastrophic disaster, the bank would supply a mobile branch staffed with at least two tellers who would dispense the finances and keep all necessary records.

- Notify local vendor marketing and/or service representatives, if there's a need for immediate delivery of components to bring the computer systems to an operational level, even in a degraded mode.

If an alternate site is necessary, the following additional major tasks must be undertaken:

- Obtain governmental permissions and assistance, as necessary. For example, you are likely to need building permits to construct even a temporary site.

- Coordinate moving of equipment and support personnel into the alternate site. Be sure to hire the services of a dependable security firm to protect company assets, because looting is to be expected.

- Bring the tape backups from off-site storage to the alternate site.

- As soon as the hardware is up to specifications to run the operating system, load software and run necessary tests. One of the best solutions is to record recent images of server hard drives for a fast restore.

- Prepare backup materials and return these to the off-site storage area.

- Coordinate client activities to ensure that the most critical jobs are being supported as needed.

- Be sensitive to the employees involved in the relocation. For example, in a natural disaster, employees might be suffering from the death of friends or loved ones, or they might be without a home.

- As production begins, ensure that periodic backup procedures are being followed and materials are being placed in off-site storage periodically.

- Keep administration and clients informed of the status, progress, and problems.

Do it!   **D-1:   Discussing a disaster recovery plan**

Questions and answers
1 What's a hot site?
2 What's a cold site?
3 For recovery from a primary facility failure with less than 24-hour downtime tolerance, what alternate site strategy is most appropriate?

Unit summary: Disaster planning

Topic A

In this topic, you learned that factors to consider when you purchase a backup unit include the amount of data you need to back up, whether your backup software supports the unit, and the amount of money you want to spend. You learned that, for a large-scale enterprise, you should probably investigate an automated backup technology, such as tape libraries that use autoloaders to change tapes in a largely unattended fashion. You also learned that **automated tape libraries** have an **extensive online retention period (OLRP)**. There are a number of tape media standards. The most common for smaller tape devices is probably the **Quarter Inch Cartridge (QIC)**, which, as the name implies, is a quarter inch wide. For server use, you probably won't see QIC and **QIC Wide**, which is actually .315 inches (8 mm) wide, in common use anymore.

Topic B

In this topic, you learned that, on the whole, lower-cost tape drives and some disk-based devices intended for use with stand-alone PCs come bundled with backup software that provides only basic functionality. More sophisticated backup software is considerably more expensive. You also learned that a **normal backup** copies all selected files and clears their archive bit. An **incremental backup** backs up only those files that have been created or changed since the last normal or incremental backup, which can reduce the amount of time that's required to complete the backup process. It marks files as having been backed up. A **differential backup** copies files that have been created or changed since the last normal or incremental backup, which can reduce the amount of time that's required to complete the backup process. It doesn't mark files as having been backed up. A **copy backup** copies all selected files, but it doesn't mark each file as having been backed up. Copying is useful to back up files between normal and incremental backups because it doesn't affect other backup operations.

Topic C

In this topic, you learned that, to provide both load balancing and redundancy, a group of computers, or **cluster**, can cooperate in providing services. This cooperation is managed by clustering software that provides a service to clients in a client-server environment. If one **node** fails, the applications on the failed node are available on the other node. Throughout this process, client communications with applications usually continue with little or no interruption. You learned that, for hardware failure recovery, having a number of spare parts available saves the time needed to order failed items from the original vendor. Some vendors, such as Intel, sell spare parts kits comprised of the most critical system components. You also learned that **System monitoring software** can detect problems, such as failing hard drives, fans, and power supplies, as well as high temperatures.

Topic D

In this topic, you learned that it's essential to assemble a disaster recovery team and develop a disaster recovery plan. Practical implementations vary from one organization to another. You learned that, in preparation for large-scale recovery, you should consider alternate sites. These can range from simple data collection and warehousing services designed to return data as needed to continue business operations, to full-scale facility duplication (**hot site**) designed to replicate all of the hardware, software, and data infrastructure necessary to assume all business functions in the event of a primary facility failure. Hot sites are very expensive to maintain, as they have nearly a complete replica of all computers in the central facility.

Independent practice activity

In this activity, you'll learn more about disaster recovery.

1 In your Web browser, access www.davislogic.com. Davis Logic specializes in contingency planning and disaster recovery.

2 On the left side of the Davis Logic Web page, click the **Disaster Recovery** link. Notice several publications that would be excellent research guides in planning for disaster recovery.

3 On the Disaster Recovery page, scroll down the page and look for a bulleted list of possible disaster events. In this text, we've specified only a few types of disasters, such as natural ones, that could make your site unavailable. Write down some other types of events that could constitute a disaster.

4 Close the Web browser.

Review questions

1 What is the minimum number of tapes required in a GFS tape backup strategy?

A 12

B 24

C 48

D 60

2 You wish to back up all of the files on a hard disk in your computer. You have just replaced your old, single media tape device with a new, 12-tape automated tape library system. When you attempt to initiate the backup, the process fails. What should you do?

A Install the driver for the new device

B Restore the catalog from the old device, then re-try the backup

C Make sure that you use only new, blank tapes for the backup

D Reboot the computer

3 Your company's Internet servers are becoming overloaded due to an increase in commerce traffic to your web site. You decide to implement a clustering solution. What kind of clustering model should you implement in order to provide the desired load balancing?

A active

B passive

C disruptive

D peanut

4 Which of the following are necessary for disaster recovery?

A hot site

B hot swap implementation

C data backup

D fire drills

5 Which backup media type will provide the greatest storage capacity?

A DAT

B DLT

C Travan

D Ultrium

6 You want to have a separate location prepared to transfer all data management services immediately upon the failure of your network operations center. What type of site do you set up?

A alternate site

B backup storage site

C hot site

D cold site

7 Why should one or more backups be stored offsite?

A for security reasons

B backup data is not usually needed quickly

C so it is available to a remote site

D so that primary site disasters will not affect the data

8 Which of the following are not part of a disaster recovery plan?

A handling legal, financial and insurance issues

B Performing a tape backup immediately after disaster strikes

C locating interim facilities to restart your business

D recovery of PCs, LANs, and midrange systems

9 Which backup strategy provides the fastest backup time?

A Grandfather, Father, Son

B six cartridge

C Tower of Hanoi

D incremental backup

10 Which of the following utilizes a form of memory inside the tape? (Choose all that apply.)

A AIT

B DAT

C Ultrium

D Accelis

11 Which of the following backs up data and clears the archive bit?

A normal backup

B differential backup

C copy backup

D daily backup

12 Which of the following Travan tape formats offers the highest compressed capacity?

A Travan-8

B Travan NS-8

C TR-4

D Travan-5

13 Which backup strategy provides the least expensive media allocation?

A Grandfather, Father, Son

B Tower of Hanoi

C normal daily backup

D RAID-1

14 Which SNMP component should be configured in order to report errors, security breaches, or other event notification?

A SNMP trap

B SNMP Management Information Base

C SNMP community name

D SNMP host name

15 Why should spare network components be kept on site?

A to configure new computers on the network quickly

B to provide for efficient replacement of equipment as part of a maintenance cycle

C to allow for efficient replacement of failed components of similar types

D to allow for efficient replacement of failed components of dissimilar types

16 For large-scale recovery of failed components, what site strategy is most appropriate?

A hot site

B cold site

C no alternate site; keep required spare components at primary site

D no alternate site; implement an active clustering solution

17 A _____ site is a facility that has no equipment of its own, but has all the necessary facilities and environmental controls to accept server equipment?

A hot site

B cold site

C data center

D service bureau

18 For recovery from a primary facility failure with less than 24 hour downtime tolerance, what alternate site strategy is most appropriate?

A hot site

B cold site

C no alternate site; implement an active clustering solution

D no alternate site; implement a passive clustering solution

19 You want administrators to be notified of system failures as soon as possible, regardless of the time of day during which the failure occurs. You should implement a(n):

A SNMP management system

B tape backup strategy

C Management Information Base

D remote notification system

20 You have purchased hard disks for replacement of existing units if and when the existing units fail. You wish to be able to replace these hard disks without losing any system availability. Which elements are required to achieve this?

A hot swap device capability

B active clustering

C passive clustering

D hot site

E cold site

Unit 9

Performance monitoring and optimization

Unit time: 90 minutes

Complete this unit, and you'll know how to:

A Use performance monitoring tools effectively.

B Establish a baseline.

C Recognize acceptable and unacceptable performance thresholds, and provide solutions to performance bottlenecks.

Topic A: Monitoring the server

This topic covers the following CompTIA Server+ exam objective:

#	Objective
5.3	Adjust SNMP thresholds

Performance monitoring

Explanation

Performance monitoring, which is observing, measuring, and recording the performance of critical server and network resources, is essential for troubleshooting and maintaining a network. There are several reasons to monitor servers:

- To become familiar with your server's normal performance so you know when there's a problem.
- To notice impending problems and prevent them before they occur.
- To pinpoint existing problems and identify solutions.
- To aid in resource and capacity planning.

Performance monitoring is the best tool for systematic troubleshooting, capacity planning, and checking on the health of servers. It can mean the difference between being unprepared when a problem comes up and anticipating a problem and correcting it before users even notice.

The following table shows some typical server areas that can be monitored:

Monitor this...	To determine this...
CPU	CPU utilization and performance
RAM	Memory shortage or damaged memory
Hard disk	Disk performance, capacity, and errors
Paging	Page file size and performance
Caching	Cache allocation and performance
Process	Hung or stopped service or process using high CPU resources
Users	Number of users logged on and types of resources they're accessing

The operating systems discussed in this text use various tools to monitor the performance of server components listed in the previous table, but they're used in similar ways:

- To establish performance baselines.
- To measure current performance (and perhaps compare it to a baseline).
- To keep logs of performance over time.

There are many, many possible performance measures and results, and performance monitoring can, at first glance, be a little overwhelming. The key is to focus on the most significant resources. With performance monitoring, less is more. Focusing your attention on the most critical resources helps to achieve the most effective results.

Using monitoring tools

The performance monitoring concepts presented in the previous section are consistent across all platforms. The specific tools and functions vary according to operating system. We'll discuss tools for:

- Linux
- NetWare
- Windows NT 4.0
- Windows 2000

The main focus of performance monitoring should be the accurate gathering and interpretation of performance data regardless of which operating system or tool you use.

Among all the NOSs, there are literally hundreds of various measures of performance. Although it isn't practical to define each performance measure, you should be aware of the main tools and resource categories for each operating system. After a brief tour of the primary performance monitoring tools in several operating systems, you'll learn about establishing a baseline and how to use monitoring results for troubleshooting and planning. This unit also helps you to identify major performance bottlenecks and proposes solutions for each area.

Linux

UNIX tools are used to monitor performance on Linux systems. These tools are command-line utilities that provide statistics on CPU usage, memory, disk I/O, and network connections. Although there are multiple UNIX/Linux utilities available for specific monitoring purposes, some of the most commonly used are shown in the following table.

Command	Function
vmstat	Provides information on memory usage, CPU, and interrupts
ps	Lists all processes currently running on the system
df	Lists disk space used and available
top	Shows top several processes running and amount of resources they consume

Exhibit 9-1 shows the output from the *vmstat*, *ps*, and *df* commands.

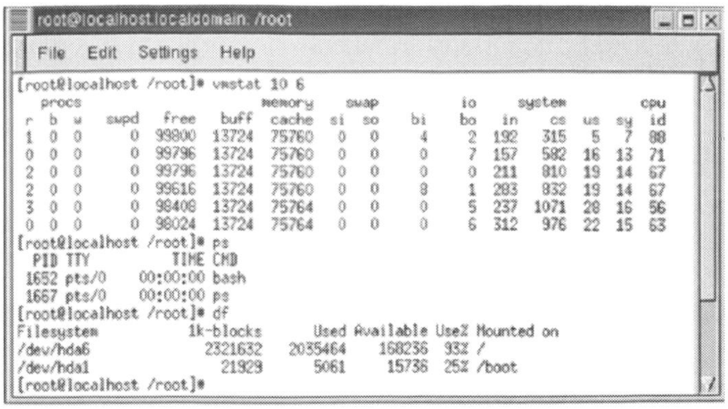

Exhibit 9-1: Output from UNIX utilities vmstat, ps, and df

The *vmstat* tool provides real-time performance statistics for several resources. For example, when system performance slows, you can use *vmstat* to provide a quick snapshot of CPU load average to determine what process is causing a bottleneck. The syntax for the utility looks like this:

> vmstat *seconds #OfReports*

If you wanted to take a snapshot every 10 seconds and create a total of six reports, you'd type *vmstat 10 6*, as illustrated in Exhibit 9-1. If you don't specify the number of reports, the utility runs continuously until you issue the Ctrl+C command.

In addition to displaying the top consuming resources, the *top* command also provides other information, such as the number of users logged on, the amount of memory consumed, and how much is swapped out to the swap file. Exhibit 9-2 shows sample output of the *top* command.

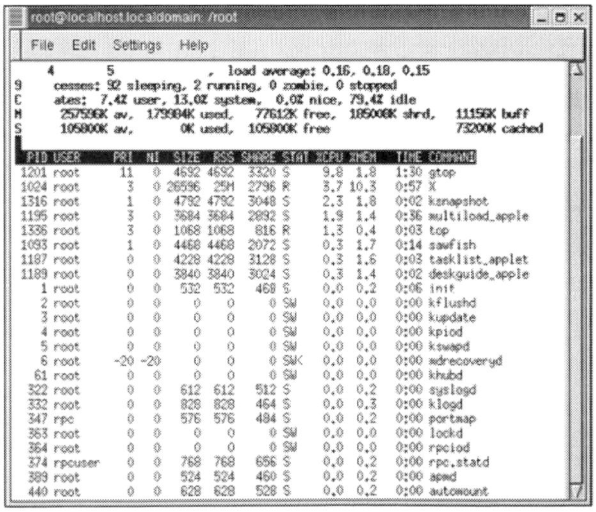

Exhibit 9-2: Sample output from the UNIX top command

The top command automatically refreshes. This can be advantageous when you're troubleshooting, but keep in mind that the refresh itself consumes resources. Remember this additional load when using the top command in heavily loaded systems.

If you also use graphical UNIX/Linux utilities, several other performance monitoring tools might be available to you, including the GNOME System Monitor, as illustrated in Exhibit 9-3, and the Stripchart Plotter, as illustrated in Exhibit 9-4, which provides a quick graphical snapshot of processor, swap file, network, and PPP activity.

Third-party tools that provide a graphical interface for monitoring are also useful. For example, Computer Associates' Unicenter TNG, an enterprise management software package, provides a graphical interface to monitor performance on Linux as well as on most flavors of UNIX.

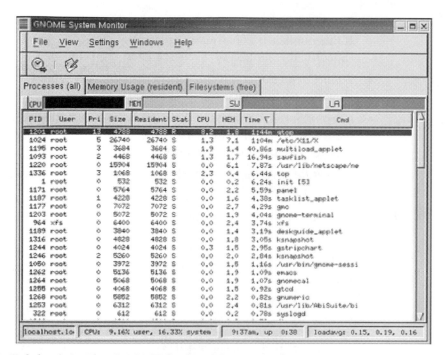

Exhibit 9-3: The GNOME System Monitor tool

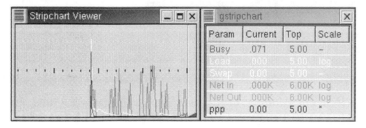

Exhibit 9-4: The Stripchart Plotter

NetWare

Novell NetWare uses a service known as Traffic Manager to monitor network traffic. Traffic Manager runs on Windows NT computers and uses Windows NT's Performance Monitoring tool to display its data.

The Monitor utility is included with NetWare to track server performance, as illustrated in Exhibit 9-5. Many Novell system administrators leave this screen on instead of a conventional screen saver. When Monitor is running, four performance indicators are shown:

- *Utilization*. This shows the CPU utilization rate for servicing network requests. If this number is consistently greater than 50–65%, your CPU is a bottleneck. (Specific thresholds are discussed later in this unit.)

- *Total Cache Buffers*. If this number is quite low, your system will suffer from slow file performance.

- *Current Service Processes*. This indicates outstanding read requests. If a read request is buffered, it means that resources weren't available. This may indicate that you need to upgrade your disk controller.

- *Packet Receive Buffers*. This is an indicator that shows packets that are being buffered from workstations.

For a GUI, use the Java-based ConsoleOne.

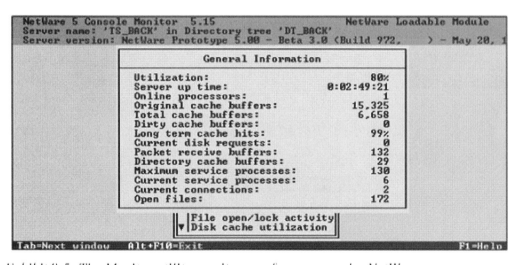

Exhibit 9-5: The Monitor utility monitors performance under NetWare

Administrators running Web or FTP services on NetWare servers probably rely on the Novell Internet Caching System (ICS) utility to track and optimize performance using the ICS caching facility, but it can also be useful for monitoring general server performance and network activity, as illustrated in Exhibit 9-6.

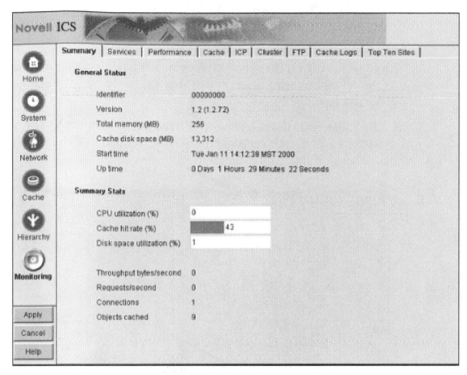

Exhibit 9-6: The Novell ICS utility

Windows NT 4.0

Performance monitoring on the Windows NT 4.0 operating system uses the Performance Monitor GUI tool. This tool uses objects, instances, and counters to measure performance on local servers or remote systems. Open Performance Monitor on a Windows NT system by clicking Start, pointing to Programs, pointing to Administrative Tools, and then clicking the Performance Monitor icon.

For best results, monitor an NT server from an NT workstation. Running Performance Monitor locally on the server creates an artificial load that can skew performance data. (Remotely monitoring a server can also add to the network load, although the impact is generally minimal.)

Chart View is the default view for Performance Monitor and provides real-time dynamic snapshots of server activity, as illustrated in Exhibit 9-7. Snapshots are taken in one-second intervals by default.

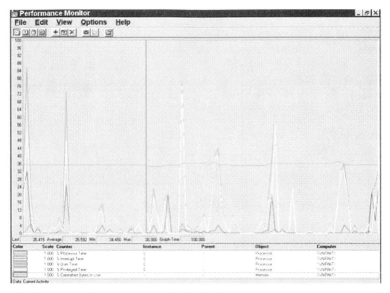

Exhibit 9-7: Chart View is the default for Windows NT 4.0 Performance Monitor

Performance is measured by choosing objects to monitor. In Performance Monitor, *objects* are resources such as Processor, Memory, PhysicalDisk, and Network Segment. After selecting an object to monitor, you choose specific *counters*, which are measures pertaining to Performance Monitor objects. For example, when monitoring the Processor object, you must specify exactly what it is about the processor you want to monitor by selecting a counter.

Some examples of Processor counters are:

- *% Processor Time*. A primary indicator of overall processor activity.
- *Interrupts/Se*. The average number of hardware interrupts the processor receives and services per second. During an interrupt, normal processes owned by applications, services, and so forth are unable to perform actions, so you want to be sure to watch this counter.
- *% User Time*. The percentage of processor time spent in user mode, which includes applications, environment subsystems, and integral subsystems. Despite the use of the word "user," this counter isn't always tied to user activities per se.
- *% Privileged Time*. The percentage of processor time spent in privileged mode, which is designed for hardware driver activity and operating system components. A high percentage might indicate a failing hardware device or driver that sends out excessive interrupts.

If there's more than one processor on the system, the Processor object also has multiple *instances* to distinguish one processor from the other. Instances also apply to other resources, such as multiple hard disks or multiple NICs. Using instances provides the capability to monitor processors or other components collectively or individually.

You can add objects and counters to the chart that are relevant to the tasks performed by the server. (Information concerning how to determine these objects is presented later in this unit.)

You can also save settings for objects and counters so that you can return to monitor the same objects and counters at a later date. The simplest way is to save a Performance Monitor file. Once your chart is set, press the F12 key. Enter a name for the file in the Save As dialog box.

Windows NT 4.0 also uses performance logs to measure historical performance data and to set alerts to call attention to specific threshold breaches. Performance logs are discussed more specifically in the Windows 2000 section.

Windows 2000/2003

Performance monitoring in Windows 2000/2003 uses the Microsoft Management Console (MMC) graphical interface. The monitoring tool uses objects, instances, and counters in a manner similar to Windows NT 4.0. The steps to open and use the Windows 2000 Performance console, like all management tools in Windows 2000, have changed from NT 4.0. The Performance console can be opened from Administrative Tools or added as a snap-in to an MMC containing other management tools.

A very handy feature of both Windows NT 4.0 and Windows 2000/2003 is the Explain button, as illustrated in Exhibit 9-8, that appears when you want to add a counter. By clicking it, an explanation appears for the otherwise cryptic counters in the list.

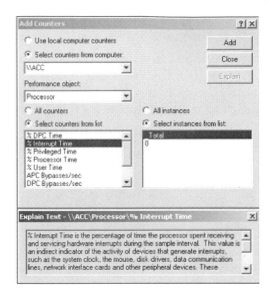

Exhibit 9-8: The Explain button describes each counter

The Performance console contains two snap-ins: System Monitor and Performance Logs and Alerts. System Monitor provides real-time snapshots of system resources on local or remote servers, as illustrated in Exhibit 9-9. The Performance Logs and Alerts snap-in offers two functions:

- Performance logs gather historical performance data over a period of time.
- Performance alerts send messages when designated thresholds are exceeded based on dynamic data.

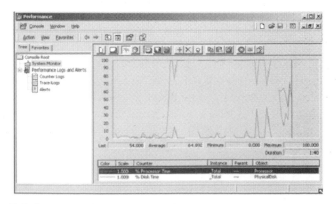

Exhibit 9-9: The Windows 2000 System Monitor gathering real-time performance data

System monitor

The System Monitor relies on objects and counters to display data in the chart. Click the plus sign (+) button in the toolbar above the chart to add objects and counters. From the Add Counters dialog box, you can choose to monitor the local server or a remote server. Exhibit 9-10 shows the Performance object, PhysicalDisk, selected from the dropdown list. The counter, % Disk Time, has also been chosen. By reading the information in the Instances list, we can see that the server named "infiniti" has two physical disks. The disks are labeled 0 and 1. The Instances box provides the capability to monitor the disks individually or collectively. Selecting "_Total" monitors both/all physical disks.

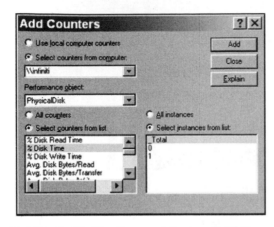

Exhibit 9-10: The System Monitor Add Counters dialog box

Performance logs and alerts

Performance logs monitor resources over a specific period of time. This is termed *historical performance monitoring*. The time can be hours, days, or weeks depending on the situation. The log records the data. When logging is complete, the data can display in a static format in the System Monitor screen.

To begin recording performance logs, you must create a log file:

1 Click the plus sign (+) button to the left of Performance Logs and Alerts.
2 Right-click Counter Logs. Select New Log Settings.
3 Give an intuitive name to the new log. Click OK.

Objects and counters must be added to the log for historical data, just as you add objects and counters to System Monitor for real-time data. (The objects and counters are the same in Performance Logs and Alerts as in System Monitor, except that they can be configured to record over a specific period of time and can issue alerts upon reaching a specified threshold.)

After choosing the objects and counters and returning to the Counter Log dialog box, there are multiple options for the time and frequency to gather data. Notice that the counter samples data every 15 seconds by default, because it's expected that performance logs record over a longer duration. You can adjust the data-sampling interval as you like, but if you make it too short, the log files can get quite large and unmanageable. Exhibit 9-11 shows the General tab of the Counter Log dialog box.

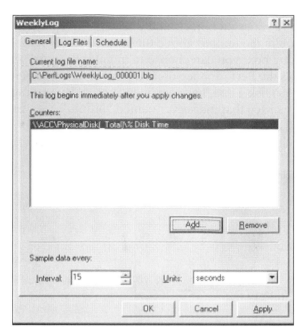

Exhibit 9-11: The General tab of the Counter Log dialog box

Besides adding counters from the General tab of the interface, you can also select the Log Files tab, as shown in Exhibit 9-12, to specify characteristics of the log file itself, such as maximum size, location, and naming preferences. The Schedule tab shows the total timeframe for the log to record data, as compared to the data-sampling interval shown on the General tab, which determines the frequency of system snapshots.

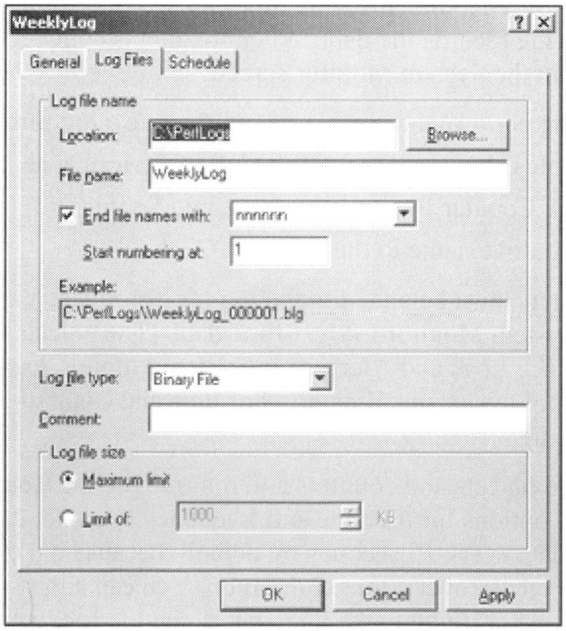

Exhibit 9-12: The options for the Log Files tab

From the Log Files tab, specify the following items:

- A file location, preferably not on the same disk or system you're monitoring, so as not to skew the results.

- An intuitive file name, so that you and others easily identify the file.

- "End file names with," to allow log files to be tagged with sequential numbers or dates.

- The default log file type, binary. Log files can also be saved in formats, such as .CSV, to enable simple import to databases or spreadsheets.

- Log file size, which, by default, allows growth potential limited only by the space on the hard disk. This can be limited to a specific size with this option.

Once all parameters are determined, you can start the log manually or schedule it to run automatically in the future. Initiate a manual start from the Performance console as follows:

1   Click the plus sign (+) button on Performance Logs and Alerts.
2   Click Counter Logs. This displays all eligible logs.
3   Right-click the log and select Start.
4   To stop the log manually, right-click the log and select Stop.

The options to schedule the log are illustrated in Exhibit 9-13. Start the log according to time and date. The log is stopped after a specific period of time has elapsed or at an exact time and date. There are also two options to indicate when the log completes. First, you can specify that, when a log file reaches a scheduled termination, another log file begins. This arrangement is useful for breaking the log files into smaller, more manageable chunks of data. Second, you could run an executable or batch file. For example, you might want to run a .bat file that includes the net send command to alert the administrator that the log is complete.

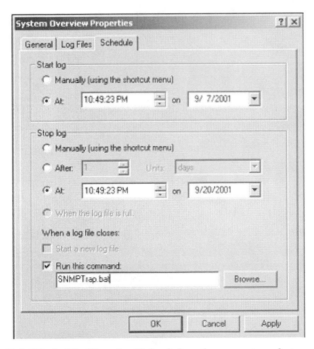

Exhibit 9-13: Use the Schedule tab to start and stop the log

Do it!

A-1: Discussing performance monitoring

Questions and answers

1 Which UNIX tool shows resources currently running that consume the most memory?

2 The Windows Performance Monitor relies on which two elements to measure performance?

3 The counter Interrupts/sec is associated with which object in Windows Performance Monitor?

4 Windows 2000/2003 real-time performance is observed with what?

Topic B: Establishing a baseline

This topic covers the following CompTIA Server exam objectives:

#	Objective

3.7	Perform server baseline
	• Supporting knowledge includes:
	  • Conditions under which different baselines might be useful
	  • When baselines should be updated

4.2	Add processors
	• Activities include:
	  • Perform upgrade checklist, including:
	    • Review and baseline

5.2	Create baseline and compare performance • Activities include • Regular comparisons to the original baseline
7.3	Identify bottlenecks • Activities include: • Run performance tool and compare against baseline

Baseline

One of the most important aspects of monitoring performance is establishing a baseline. A *baseline* is established by recording performance data when a server is healthy, or running normally. When problems occur, such as the slow logons in the opening scenario, use performance monitoring tools to observe dynamic real-time values. Compare the real-time output with historic performance data to determine the bottleneck in the system. This methodical approach to problem solving consistently yield faster results than a shotgun approach of random fixes based on experience and luck.

What is a bottleneck?

A *bottleneck* refers to the delay in transmission of data through the circuits of a computer's system. When you monitor performance to detect a bottleneck, you're looking for the resource (processor, memory, etc.) that's causing the delay in data transmission.

Most of us experience bottlenecks every day outside of information technology. Think of a freeway with four lanes heading in the same direction. If traffic is moving at 65 mph on average and a driver moves into the fast (far left) lane and proceeds at 50 mph, this creates a bottleneck. The analogy of a four-lane freeway also relates to servers because there are four basic resources to monitor to create a baseline:

- Processor
- Memory
- Disk subsystem
- Network segment

It's important to note that these are the basic resources, not a comprehensive, detailed picture of a server. We discuss each of these resources in more detail later in this unit.

When to create a baseline

The best time to create a baseline is while the server is experiencing maximum activity. Referencing the logon scenario again, you create a baseline for the logon server in this network. Record historical performance data during the period of time when most users are logging on to the system, such as 30–60 minutes after people arrive at work in the morning.

If you were creating a baseline for a database server, the timing might be completely different. Perhaps your company runs the majority of reports on a database server after business hours, between 7 P.M. and 9 P.M. This would be the best time to create the baseline for that server. You can begin to see why using scheduled performance monitoring, as opposed to using manually started monitoring, can be advantageous. In many instances, the optimal monitoring time isn't within normal business hours.

What if you aren't familiar enough with a server to know the optimal monitoring time? In such instances, use historical performance monitoring to discover the busiest periods of activity. Then create the baseline for that interval.

What to monitor in a baseline

Now that you've determined when to monitor performance, the next decision is what resources to monitor. As previously stated, the basics of Processor, Memory, PhysicalDisk, and Network Segment are a good place to start. There are exceptions, however, and there's often the need for greater detail.

Returning again to the logon scenario, monitoring the basic resources can provide important information for troubleshooting the slow logon problem. But, based on the specified problem, we can add more objects and create more relevant data. The following table illustrates possible objects and counters for creating a baseline in the logon scenario for Windows NT or Windows 2000.

Object	Counter
Processor	% Privileged Time
Processor	% User Time
Memory	% Committed Bytes in Use
Server	Logon Total
Server	Logons/sec
Network Segment	% Network Utilization

Note that, in addition to the basic four resources, we've chosen to monitor the Server object, with counters for logon statistics. These additional resources, when included in the baseline, provide specific data about the number of users who normally log on during the recorded time. Even more useful is the number of logons per second. This statistic gives an objective number to use for gauging logon speed. The nature of fast or slow is very subjective. Note also that the PhysicalDisk object is excluded from this baseline. Disk activity isn't a major factor in the logon process.

Putting the tools to work

Let's continue with the logon scenario to walk through how baseline data and monitoring tools can be used to solve a performance problem. The first table that follows shows the baseline measurements for the logon server, and the second table shows the comparative real-time data for the same objects during the Monday morning slowdown.

BASELINE DATA FOR THE LOGON SERVER

Object	Counter	Averages (over 30 minutes)
Processor	% Privileged Time	9%
Processor	% User Time	14%
Memory	% Committed Bytes in Use	37%
Server	Logon Total	510 (total over 30 minutes)
Server	Logons/sec	5
Network Segment	% Network Utilization	36%

REAL-TIME DATA FOR THE LOGON SERVER

Object	Counter	Real-time statistics
Processor	% Privileged Time	15%
Processor	% User Time	14%
Memory	% Committed Bytes in Use	39%
Server	Logon Total	1 (one-second snapshot)
Server	Logons/sec	1
Network Segment	% Network Utilization	76%

The first step in interpreting this data is to look for significant changes. In this case, you note the following:

- Processor: % Privileged Time increased by 6%.
- Processor: % User Time is unchanged.
- Memory: % Committed Bytes in Use increased by 2%.
- Server: Logons/sec decreased to 1.
- Network Segment: % Network Utilization increased by 40%.

The most significant changes occurred in the number of logons and network utilization. From this data, you can safely say that logons definitely are slow, and the bottleneck is the flow of data on the network interface. Solving the problem requires "drilling down" deeper into the specifics of network utilization. The value of the baseline is that you have eliminated processor time and memory as possible bottlenecks.

Capacity planning

The baseline measurements for a server can also be used for capacity planning. This is the practice of monitoring resources for the purpose of projecting the effect of increasing or decreasing workload on a server. By measuring the performance of a server under current conditions, we can project how it will perform under another set of conditions. In the current business environment of mergers and acquisitions, capacity planning makes for a smoother IT transition.

Using our logon scenario again, the current network has 750 users. Of these, 510 logged on during the performance monitoring that created the previous baseline table. You learn in a meeting that your company has acquired another company of equal size. Your IT staff has the task of merging IT departments and is responsible for user logons and security. You need to accommodate twice the current number of users on the network. That means 1500 users logging on. Can your server handle the load? Creating baselines for capacity planning helps answer these questions, not only for logon servers but also for many network resources.

Do it!

B-1:   Discussing a baseline

Questions and answer

1 What's a bottleneck?

2 To get the most effective comparisons, when is the best time to create a baseline?

3 What's capacity planning?

Topic C: Acceptable levels of performance

This topic covers the following CompTIA Server+ exam objectives:

#	Objective
1.2	Know the characteristics of adapter fault tolerance. • Adapter load balancing • Adapter teaming
1.13	Know the attributes, purpose, function, and advantages of clustering, scalability, high availability, and fault tolerance.

3.7	Perform server baseline
	
	• Supporting knowledge includes:
	  • Purpose and types of baseline
	    • Processor utilization
	    • Page file
	    • Disk utilization
	    • Memory utilization
	    • Network utilization

7.3	Identify bottlenecks
	
	• Bottlenecks include:
	  • Processor
	  • Bus transfer
	  • I/O
	  • Disk I/O
	  • Network I/O
	  • Memory
	• Supporting knowledge includes:
	  • How to run performance tools and compare against baseline
	    • Processor utilization
	    • Page file
	    • Disk utilization
	    • Memory utilization
	    • Network utilization

Processor

Explanation

Processor time is measured as a percentage of time that the processor is active, executing threads submitted by *processes* (running programs) on the system. (A *thread* is a main component of an application and is the means by which the application accesses memory and processor time). One hundred percent represents constant activity.

Acceptable processor performance

A processor running constantly at 100% is overworked, and server performance will deteriorate rapidly. Acceptable levels of processor activity extend up to 60–65% on a consistent basis. Levels exceeding 65% during performance monitoring usually indicate that the processor is the bottleneck in the system. However, the specific processor utilization percentage that's acceptable within an organization can vary. For example, perhaps you consider 65% processor utilization to be acceptable for the intranet Web server that company employees use. However, for the Internet Web transaction server, 65% is way too high, because online purchases take too long, and impatient buyers might cancel transactions. It's not unusual for the processor to peak or spike higher than 65% for a brief period of time. When new processes are started or when services are starting after rebooting a server, processor levels spiking to 100% are totally acceptable.

A bottleneck is indicated when known applications, processes, or services push processor levels beyond 65% for an extended period of time, and the processor doesn't return to lower levels until the applications, processes, or services are terminated.

Processor solutions

The following sections present various approaches to improving processor performance.

Implement SMP

If the processor is the bottleneck, additional CPUs can be added to a server to improve performance and handle increased loads. All major NOSs under discussion in this text support symmetric multiprocessing (SMP). Many 32-bit applications can benefit from SMP, if the code allows *multithreading*, which is the ability to run two or more program threads at once. For example, if a program runs two threads on an SMP system with two processors, each processor can handle a thread simultaneously. With a single processor, the program can still run multiple threads but the processor can execute only a single thread at one time.

Add servers

Sometimes the best solution to a processor bottleneck is simply to add another server, especially when a server is performing multiple tasks that may conflict with each other. For example, a company may be using a single database server to perform sales transactions and provide reports based on those transactions. Transactions and queries for reports may require multiple reads from tables simultaneously. While adding another processor (SMP) may improve performance, a better solution would be to add another server dedicated to running queries from which to create reports.

Remove compression

Compression is storing data in a format that requires less space than usual. Simply storing data doesn't place a greater load on the processor. However, when data is written to the compressed partition or folder, the processor must work harder to calculate the compression algorithms. Removing compression from partitions or folders where data is written frequently can free the processor to perform more critical tasks. The type of data that you choose to compress, if any, is also a factor. Some file types don't compress well, and processor utilization is wasted on these files. For example, multimedia files, such as movie and JPEG files, don't compress well.

Remove unnecessary encryption

Encryption uses any of several methods to protect sensitive data from prying eyes. However useful, encryption is processor-intensive and places a greater load on the processor. Just as with compression, the processor performs calculations to encrypt and decrypt data. The operative word in this solution is "unnecessary." Security is important and, when encryption is warranted, the better solution is upgrading or adding additional processors.

Although administrators are usually adept at understanding encryption, you should be careful about users implementing encryption. There are several encryption schemes and utilities available. You don't want users to place encrypted data on network resources where server processors must perform the encryption. In addition, some encryption schemes can make data permanently inaccessible.

Implement clustering

Clustering is a solution to performance issues that benefit from load balancing. Clustering is connecting two or more computers together in such a way that they behave like a single computer. As a solution to slow processor performance, clustering is essentially adding another computer to aggregate performance in addition to providing fault tolerance.

Remove software RAID (especially RAID-5)

RAID provides fault tolerance and in some cases can actually improve performance. Software RAID-5, however, can significantly diminish processor performance. As data is written to the hard disk, the processor must calculate the algorithms for the parity bit that creates fault tolerance. This requires considerable processor time and, consequently, other processes may suffer. If the RAID-5 array is primarily for reading data, this isn't an issue, because parity calculations aren't performed during reads. Hardware RAID-5 doesn't burden the server CPU, because the parity calculation occurs on a separate processor designed for RAID functionality.

Move processor-intensive applications or services

Moving applications or services that overwork the processor is called *load balancing*. It includes installing an application or service on a second server and deleting the application or service from the server that's overworked. For example, if one server is functioning as both the DHCP and WINS server, install WINS on another server and delete WINS from the server with DHCP.

You can also keep the application or service on the original server and then install it on a second server to balance the load between the two servers. This is a common practice in Web servers. Instead of overloading a single Web server, administrators place the same Web content on two or more other Web servers, and the Web servers take turns in servicing client requests.

Verify proper operation of applications and drivers

When not running normally, applications or bad drivers can cause excessive processor utilization. To detect problems with applications, monitor the individual process of the application. It's also useful to monitor the number of threads utilized by the application by using the following object/counter combination:

- Object: Process
- Counter: Thread Count

As an example, the Windows 2000 Performance Monitor, as illustrated in Exhibit 9-14, is monitoring the Diskeeper defragmentation utility running over four threads (numbered 0–4) and utilizing over 60% processor time. In this case, it's acceptable, because Diskeeper was deliberately set to run at a high priority, and there were no other pressing tasks to run at the time.

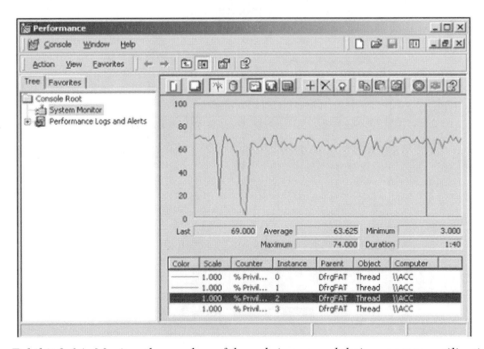

Exhibit 9-14: Monitor the number of threads in use and their processor utilization

A significant change in the number of threads used by an application, compared to a baseline, indicates problems in the application code. Some applications may run multiple instances, which can also increase the load on the processor.

Corrupted device drivers can also demand excessive processor time. An effective measurement for this problem is to monitor the following object/counter combinations:

- Object: Processor
- Counters: % Interrupt Time or Interrupts/sec

Compare the results to a baseline. Significant increases in the number of interrupts indicate problems with hardware devices and/or the drivers. A failing NIC (and several other types of hardware) often issues constant interrupts, because it isn't able to determine that the processor has responded to the interrupt requests.

Don't be too concerned if Interrupts/sec is over 100 when idle; the system clock accounts for this by sending regular interrupts every 10 milliseconds.

Set process priority

In Windows NT and Windows 2000, you can manually set a process or application to run at a specific priority to ensure that it doesn't dominate processor utilization at the expense of other applications. You can also adjust the process priority to force the processor to favor the process or application over others. Some applications allow you to adjust settings within the application, or you can use Task Manager to configure the application priority:

1 Press Ctrl+Shift+Esc to access Task Manager.

2 On the Process tab, select the application's process.

3 Right-click the process, click Set Priority, and choose a priority from Low to Realtime, as illustrated in Exhibit 9-15.

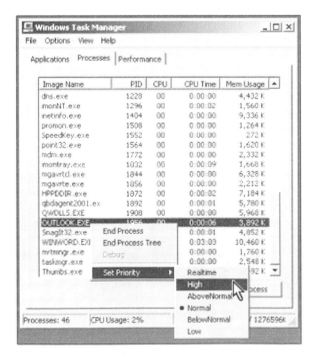

Exhibit 9-15: Changing the priority level of a process

Memory

The following sections present various approaches to improving memory performance. Memory is indirectly one of the most critical performance factors. A low memory condition causes higher disk utilization due to disk swapping. Low memory also affects stability. Some operating system information, such as passwords or other security-sensitive data, can never be swapped to hard disk. However, if you're out of memory, there's no place else for it to go, and the server might fail. It's critical to determine what acceptable memory performance is and how to remedy low memory conditions.

Acceptable memory performance

Defining acceptable memory performance is extremely subjective. What's tolerable to one organization may be completely unacceptable to another. Most of the time, memory performance, that is, speed, isn't an issue, because it performs in nanoseconds. However, not having enough memory clearly is a performance issue, because the NOS must then turn to virtual memory paging on the hard disk, the most common bottleneck component in the system.

The most important counters for memory are:

- Object: Memory
- Counter: % Committed Bytes in Use
- Counter: Page Faults/sec
- Counter: Available Bytes
- Counter: Pages/sec
- Counter: Pool Non-Paged Bytes

Committed Bytes in Use represents a percentage of the total system memory (physical memory plus virtual memory) currently used by processes running on the computer. The first general rule is that this percentage should remain relatively constant. Only slight variations are acceptable. When processes are stopped or started or the number of connected users changes, variation is normal. However, a steady increase of committed bytes, in the absence of additional processes or user load, frequently indicates a *memory leak*. A memory leak occurs when an application opens a thread but doesn't close it when the application is finished with it. At first, a memory leak starts more paging, which in itself deteriorates performance. Later, as both memory and available swap-file space become scarcer, the memory leak can eventually cause a system crash.

Available Bytes is the amount of physical memory available to processes running on the computer. It reflects the last observed value rather than an average.

Pages/sec is a good indicator of excessive paging in a virtual memory system. Paging is a technique to help ensure that the data needed is available as quickly as possible. Recall that the page file is designated space on the hard disk used as memory. Each time a page is needed that isn't currently in memory, a page fault occurs. When this value exceeds 20 per second on a consistent basis, performance deteriorates. Excessive page faults are normally due to insufficient memory or memory leaks.

Pool Non-Paged Bytes is the number of bytes in the nonpaged pool, an area of system memory for objects that can't be written to disk but must remain in physical memory as long as they're allocated. The Registry, for example, can't be paged to disk.

Memory solutions

All solutions to memory problems fall under one general category: add more memory. However, it's important to remember that all resources work hand in hand; no resource is independent. Increasing or decreasing one resource always has some impact on others. In the case of excessive paging, adding more memory reduces the need for paging and helps to reduce the hard disk bottleneck.

Add memory

Adding memory can never harm anything except the budget. There are many instances in which adding memory is the best and easiest solution. The best method to determine when additional memory is justified is through performance monitoring. Without this analysis, simply adding more memory can mask a more serious underlying problem.

Upgrade the motherboard to accept more memory

All motherboards have a limit on the amount and type of memory that can be installed. When this limit is reached, one solution is to upgrade to a motherboard that accommodates more and/or faster memory. Frequently, this is an expensive solution and in some instances not cost-effective, based on advances in technology. For example, a motherboard that has an older Pentium processor may be limited to 512 MB of RAM. Even if an upgraded motherboard accommodated 2 GB of RAM, significant performance improvements may not be achieved until the processor is also upgraded. Generally, upgrading the motherboard really means replacing the server. The original server becomes a collection of spare parts or is used in a less demanding role.

Increase or optimize swap file size

Swap file space goes by various names but is essentially space designated on a hard disk to act as memory. If all physical memory is used and there isn't enough swap space, the system reports out-of-memory errors. One solution is to increase the swap file space, but you should realize that this doesn't really improve performance, since the system is still making slower disk accesses instead of rapid memory accesses. Increasing swap file space merely prevents more out-of-memory errors.

Depending on the current space dedicated to the swap file, increasing its size may be only a temporary solution. If the swap space or paging file is increased to meet memory needs, performance monitoring also reveals a corresponding increase in the number of page faults.

Windows-based servers build a page file equal to the amount of RAM by default during installation. NT 4.0 Workstation and Windows 2000 Professional default to 1.5 times physical memory, because it's assumed that there's less physical memory in client workstations. The swap space or paging file functions best at a size of 300–500 MB. A previous general rule was 1.5 to 2 times the size of physical RAM, but with physical memory reaching into gigabytes on servers, this number is no longer reasonable. Too much space allotted to a swap file leads to fragmentation (discussed later in the unit).

You can improve overall system performance regarding swapping to the hard disk by placing the swap file in an optimum location. By default, most NOSs place the swap file on the same hard disk as the operating system itself, often referred to as the system disk. Because the system disk is often quite active running normal operating system services, the swap file must compete for disk access. If available, it's better to place the swap file on a separate physical disk that's less active; another partition on the same disk provides no benefit. Better yet, you can split the swap file between multiple disks (for example, in RAID-0 striping), so that multiple disks can service swap-file activity at once.

If you're trying to determine which of two disks would be best to store the swap file, and all other factors are equal, consider the number of heads the hard disks have. The drive with more heads will perform better.

If the swap file has the ability to grow, as is the case for Windows operating systems, it's better to set a fixed size for the swap file that's large enough to service present and future needs. This helps to prevent fragmentation as the swap file adjusts in size.

As a security precaution, you might consider clearing the swap file when the system reboots. If sensitive information is paged to the swap file, and someone is able to gain physical access to it, they might be able to retrieve information from it. This possibility is extremely remote for a number of reasons. However, some highly secure organizations require it. Note that clearing the swap file causes slower shutdown and startup times while the system clears and re-creates the swap file.

Use faster memory

As discussed previously, there are various kinds of RAM, some faster than others. SDRAM has almost entirely replaced EDO DRAM and is about twice as fast. SDRAM is capable of synchronizing with the CPU bus and reaching clock speeds of 133 MHz. RDRAM and DDR SDRAM appear to be the next generation of high-performance memory, each capable of more than 1 GBps of data throughput. Choosing faster memory usually requires a faster motherboard, unless, for example, you have 100 MHz SDRAM installed on a 133 MHz bus. In that case, upgrading to 133 MHz SDRAM takes advantage of the faster bus speed.

Distribute memory-intensive applications or services

As discussed with respect to processors, the best solution to memory problems can be load balancing, because you utilize the hardware resources of another server to alleviate the server load. Thorough performance monitoring and analysis tells you whether this is the best approach. When monitoring applications and services, pay close attention to which ones are processor-intensive and which are memory-intensive. A server providing basic file/print services is memory-intensive and probably doesn't place significant demand on the processor. In contrast, a database server providing report functions and servicing multiple queries is very processor-intensive. Familiarity with the relative needs of applications and services in your network will assist you in making the most efficient distribution of resources.

Check for memory leaks

Memory leaks were discussed earlier in this unit in relation to the % Committed Bytes in Use counter. This is perhaps the best indicator of a memory leak. Committed bytes should remain relatively constant. If they continue to increase gradually over time, yet no additional processes are introduced to the server, this is a strong indicator of a memory leak.

The best longterm solution to a memory leak is to contact the vendor, so that it can make alterations to the code to stop the leak. Usually, the fix is an update that you can download. The short-term solution is to terminate the application, reboot the server, and restart the application. This forces the application to free memory no longer being used.

Hard disk

As always, the hard disk seems to be the slowest performing of all the server components. Even with SCSI-3, Fibre Channel, and rotation speeds upward of 15,000 rpm, hard disks can't begin to compete with the speed of the processor and memory. However, you can still arrive at an acceptable level of performance given the physical limitations of hard disks.

Acceptable hard disk performance

Exact thresholds for determining an acceptable speed for the transfer of data from hard disks or any storage devices are even more subjective than memory or processor performance. The key is to obtain baseline numbers on current performance regardless of whether it's perceived to be slow or fast. To determine whether the hard disk is able to keep up reasonably with I/O requests, use the following object and counters:

- Object: PhysicalDisk
- Counter: % Disk Time
- Counter: Current Disk Queue Length
- Counter: Avg. Disk Bytes/Transfer

The % Disk Time counter represents the amount of time that the disk services read or write requests. You generally want to see less than 50% for this counter. Current Disk Queue Length represents the number of outstanding I/O requests waiting for the hard disk to become available. If the hard disk is overly taxed, then there will be several outstanding requests. You generally want to see no more than two requests queued. This counter is an instantaneous view. If you want to check an average over time, PhysicalDisk counters such as Avg. Disk Bytes/Transfer are also available.

Hard disk solutions

If the time comes when hard disk performance is deemed to be unacceptable, you can implement solutions such as the ones offered below.

Add or replace hard disks

Hardware or software RAID arrays can significantly increase disk performance and provide fault tolerance. Hardware RAID is superior to software RAID, but it's also more expensive. While arguments abound concerning whether software RAID provides true fault tolerance, this isn't the forum for that discussion: We're concerned with performance.

Both hardware and software RAID arrays increase performance by striping data across multiple disks. Because multiple drive heads are working simultaneously to write or read data, transfer speeds are faster than non-RAID disks. For example, let's say you have a software RAID-5 array consisting of three hard disks, and performance is unacceptably slow. By adding another disk, you aggregate total performance across four hard disks instead of three, assuming you're using SCSI, not IDE. The only potential problem might be processor utilization for the parity calculation, in which case you might also need to add a processor, upgrade the existing one, or switch to hardware RAID. (Software RAID-5 increases performance on disk reads. Performance suffers on disk writes, however, due to processor-intensive parity calculations.)

Defragment disks

Fragmentation on hard disks occurs through the normal processes of creating, moving, copying, and deleting files. The result, over time, is that single files are spread out in pieces across the disk. If the condition persists, disk transfer rates deteriorate, because the drive head must search around and across multiple sectors to read a single file. Comparing real-time and baseline disk activity can provide evidence of fragmentation.

On a Windows NT/2000 server, use the following object and counter to find evidence of fragmentation:

- Object: PhysicalDisk
- Counter: Disk Read Time

Defragmentation relocates fragmented files back into a contiguous layout. Running a defragmentation utility such as Executive Software's Diskeeper, as illustrated in Exhibit 9-16, on a regular schedule yields an appreciable increase in performance. Obviously, defragmentation is highly disk intensive, so you should run it only when disk utilization is at its lowest. You can set defragmentation to start on a schedule, or configure defragmentation to start automatically when the hard disk reaches a certain point of fragmentation. You want to use Diskeeper's capability to defragment other servers and workstations remotely.

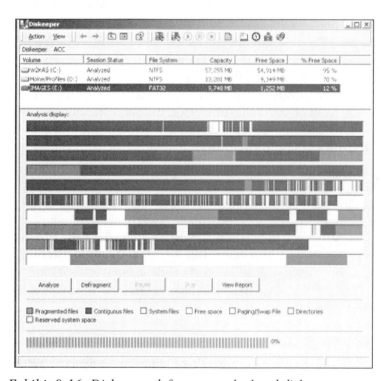

Exhibit 9-16: Diskeeper defragments the hard disk

Add faster or additional controllers

Adding controllers can solve performance problems. The process is very similar to adding another lane to a highway. More controllers accommodate more disks. More disks can balance the workload from multiple users. More controllers and/or disks also increase options for deploying RAID arrays.

The most dramatic and fundamental improvement to the disk subsystem is to upgrade from IDE disks to SCSI disks. Traditionally, SCSI controllers or interfaces have supported faster data transfer rates than IDE. The gap has narrowed with the introduction of EIDE, ATA-5, and the upcoming ATA-6. (Recall that SCSI-3 supports data transfer rates up to 320 MBps, while ATA-5 and ATA-6 support data transfer rates up to 100 MBps.)

Distribute files

Distributing files works to solve disk performance problems in a way similar to load balancing. Frequently accessed files are distributed over multiple servers instead of residing on a single server. All network operating systems have some form of distributed files. In the Microsoft environment, it's called the Distributed File System (Dfs). Distributing files has the following advantages:

- There's a single access point for users. In Microsoft Dfs, for example, user computers map to a single file share point and still access files on multiple servers. The share point is the Dfs server, which redirects the requests to the appropriate servers. The process is transparent to users, and security is maintained no differently from that of files accessed normally.

- Distributed files can be a cost-effective performance alternative to adding more servers or upgrading processor, memory, and/or disk resources.

Archive files to longterm backup media

As hard disks exceed 75–80% of capacity, performance starts to deteriorate. When large portions of data on a disk must be maintained but not frequently accessed, archiving files to longterm storage can both reduce the risk of running out of disk space and improve performance. Offline storage is available from many hardware and software vendors, but the main idea is that, when a given file hasn't been accessed for a specific period of time, the file is automatically moved to offline storage, such as an optical drive or tape. Users can still access the data, but it arrives more slowly as it's retrieved from the offline storage media. Windows 2000 Server integrates this capability into the operating system.

Check for disk errors

S.M.A.R.T. is an acronym for Self-Monitoring Analysis and Reporting Technology. It's an open standard for developing disk drives and software systems that automatically monitor the health of the drive and report potential problems. Potentially, this feature enables proactive solutions to disk errors before actual disk failure. To use S.M.A.R.T., you load software that's able to query and accept messages from the S.M.A.R.T. hard disk. The software is often provided by the disk manufacturer and included with the hard disk or host adapter. Exhibit 9-17 illustrates a hard disk monitoring utility included with Promise Technologies' FastTrak 100 IDE host adapter.

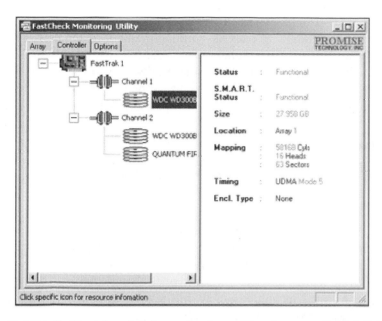

Exhibit 9-17: A hard disk monitoring utility that uses S.M.A.R.T. reporting

Network

Network performance on a server is contingent on the actual network interface card(s) installed and the components connecting the server to the network, such as cabling switches and/or hubs. Performance Monitor can measure only the traffic on the NICs local to the server.

Acceptable network performance

Network utilization is one of the most important network statistics. Most monitoring and reporting tools provide network utilization values as their primary reporting variable. Percentages of up to about 30% network utilization are acceptable. Collision networks (Ethernet) that exceed 30 50% utilization need to be monitored closely to prevent a larger increase of traffic that may cause network delays or low throughput. Server network utilization measures traffic on a specific NIC, and segment utilization measures all traffic on a given segment. Network and server traffic are monitored and analyzed separately, but the acceptable values are the same. Overall network utilization and server network utilization usually affect each other.

To measure the server's ability to send/receive data and handle network requests, monitor the following objects and counters:

- Object: Network Segment
- Counter: % Network Utilization
- Object: Network Interface
- Counter: Output Queue Length

The % Network Utilization counter represents a percentage of network bandwidth in use on the network segment. Each NIC is an instance of the segment. Output Queue Length measures the number of packets waiting to put out on the network. Values of 1 or 2 are acceptable, but anything higher means your NIC can't keep up with requests. Multihoming (discussed in the next section) can be a workable solution in this instance. (The Network Monitor Agent service must be installed on Windows NT 4.0/2000/2003 for the Network Segment object to be available in Performance Monitor.)

Network solutions

If you find that network utilization is too high, consider the following solutions.

Adapter teaming

For network operating systems, adapter-teaming techniques can be used to offer additional bandwidth and improved performance. *Adapter teaming* is the process of installing two or more network adapters in a server and then logically grouping them so that they appear to the operating system as a single network interface. There are several types of teaming techniques, including Adaptive Fault Tolerance (AFT), Adaptive Load Balancing (ALB), and link aggregation.

Adaptive Fault Tolerance (AFT)

Adaptive Fault Tolerance (AFT) can provide an easy and effective method for increasing the availability of network server connections. By simply installing two or more server network adapters and configuring AFT, you have an emergency backup connection between the server and the network. If there's any problem with a cable, NIC, switch port, or hub port on the primary adapter, the secondary adapter can kick in within seconds to provide transparent recovery for applications and users. AFT can be configured with just two server adapters. Certain vendors and manufacturers provide automatic AFT support when multiple server adapters are configured.

A critical point of vulnerability on your network is corporate or departmental servers, where a failure or bottleneck can be disastrous to productivity. AFT technology usually supports up to four adapter teams with two to four adapters on each team. Depending on the vendor, AFT solutions can be made up of various adapter types and speeds as long as there's at least one primary server adapter in the team. The primary server adapter generally passes its MAC and Layer 3 address to the failover adapter(s). This type of AFT requires the NIC vendor to provide a driver model that can take advantage of this technology.

Adaptive Load Balancing (ALB)

Adaptive Load Balancing (ALB) is a technique of guaranteeing a consistent level of high server throughput and transparent backup links by implementing multiple NICs and balancing the data transmission load across them. ALB is also known as asymmetric port aggregation. With Intel components, for example, you can use as many as four server adapters, connect them to a switch, and configure them to work as a team for an aggregate throughput of up to 400 Mbps with Fast Ethernet adapters or 8 Gbps with Gigabit Ethernet adapters. All of the adapters in a team must be connected to a switch, as illustrated in Exhibit 9-18, and the team is assigned a single network address. (ALB is designed to work with a switch, whereas AFT works with either a hub or a switch.) With ALB, all of the traffic moving from the network server is automatically balanced among up to four links. This balance can assure fast throughput with no need to restructure or reconfigure the network.

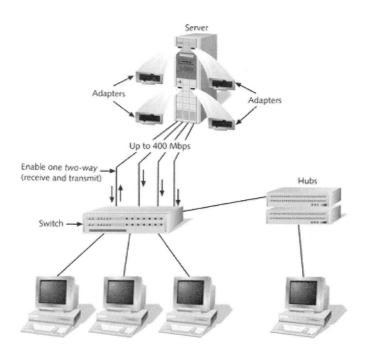

Exhibit 9-18: Adaptive Load Balancing

ALB offers a simpler and better way to move more data faster through the server than AFT does, by enabling each adapter essentially to add another 100 Mbps link, or channel. ALB also delivers the same fault-tolerance benefits as AFT technology, because if one link fails, the others continue to provide network connectivity. Therefore, with ALB technology, it's no longer necessary to segment the network if the server link becomes a bottleneck. Instead, you can eliminate the bottleneck quickly and easily by installing two adapters in your server and configuring ALB with the driver software. This requires no client configuration, and clients don't have to be routed to communicate with each other. In addition, traffic is balanced along all of the server adapters. As with AFT, an intelligent, adaptive agent is included with the software driver. This driver dynamically manages the server adapter team and evenly distributes the load among them by constantly analyzing the traffic flow from the server. One channel within an ALB team carries traffic to and from the server, while the others carry traffic from the server only. This load balancing of server traffic assures that all users enjoy the same network response from the server. By taking advantage of ALB, a four-link configuration can yield an aggregate throughput of approximately 400 Mbps.

An intelligent adaptive agent in the driver also continuously analyzes the traffic flow from the server and distributes the packets based on destination addresses. Load balancing can occur only on routed protocols (IP and NCP IPX). Multicast/broadcast and nonrouted protocols, such as NetBEUI and Microsoft IPX, are transmitted only over the primary adapter.

For AFT and ALB technologies, you can usually choose a primary and secondary role for selected adapters. The primary adapter carries the majority of the traffic. With AFT, it's the only adapter used until that link fails. With ALB and nonroutable protocols, it's the only adapter used. It's also the only adapter used for broadcast and multicast traffic.

Improve network equipment

Over the past decade, the lower cost and availability of networking equipment has created enormous growth in IT for small and medium-sized companies. One of the key pieces of equipment is the hub. Recall that the hub enables multiple nodes to be linked together on a single bus and communicate data to a common destination. Switches can replace hubs to improve network throughput and performance.

A hub with 16 ports accommodates 16 nodes. Using the analogy of highway traffic, think of each of those ports as a lane of traffic. The exit to the bus from the hub is a single lane. Consequently, a hub forces multiple lanes of traffic (in this example, 16) to a single lane. This results in multiple collisions while contesting for the single lane.

A switch with 16 ports also accommodates 16 nodes. However, a switch maintains each lane of traffic to the exit point on the bus. There are no collisions, as the lanes are merged. In Ethernet topology, reduced collisions dramatically improve throughput.

Some networks combine switch and hub technology. Hubs, rather than individual nodes, are connected to ports on a switch. While there's no absolute right or wrong to network design, without careful analysis of traffic patterns, arbitrarily connecting hubs to switches can erode the additional throughput provided by the switch.

Upgrade NICs

Ethernet technology as originally developed was capable of transferring data at speeds up to 10 Mbps. Accordingly, the components (NICs, hubs, bridges, routers) developed for networks provided the same throughput speed. In the mid-1990s, Fast Ethernet (100 Mbps) became more affordable and more prevalent in networks.

Upgrading a network card from 10 Mbps to 100 Mbps can boost server throughput and performance. Also consider utilizing full-duplex NICs instead of half-duplex NICs, if you're using hubs instead of switches. Recall that full-duplex uses an additional pair of wires and removes collision detection to double potential throughput. As with any other network equipment upgrade, it's effective only if the network bandwidth isn't oversubscribed.

Place the server on the other side of a network bottleneck

Simple server placement can sometimes eliminate network bottlenecks. You should perform network traffic analysis to identify a bottleneck, but some solutions are simple and logical.

For example, 12 engineers are working on a project and need to share data. Each engineer has a workstation that connects to the network through a hub to the backbone. The engineers have access to a dedicated server named ENGSRV1. This server is located and maintained in a server room, one among many in racks of servers. The engineers complain about slow response time when they save and access data on the server. System administrators analyze server performance and determine that the server is handling requests at an acceptable rate. So the problem doesn't appear to be in the hardware performance on ENGSRV1. The likely conclusion is a network bottleneck between the engineers and the server.

A possible solution to this bottleneck is to swap the hub where the engineers are connected for a 16-port switch. You can connect the server to the same switch with the engineer workstations and bypass the network bottleneck. This is a very simplified solution, but it introduces the logic to apply when monitoring and analyzing network performance.

Do it!   ## C-1: Discussing basic resources and performance

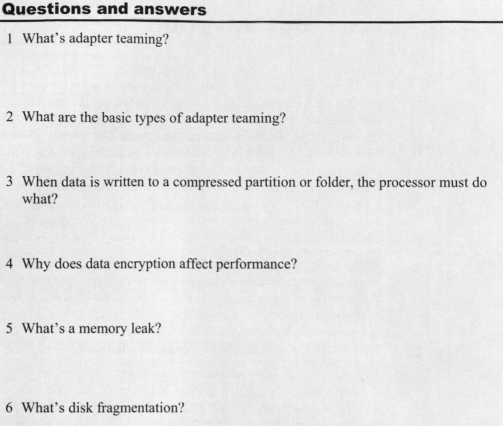

Questions and answers

1 What's adapter teaming?

2 What are the basic types of adapter teaming?

3 When data is written to a compressed partition or folder, the processor must do what?

4 Why does data encryption affect performance?

5 What's a memory leak?

6 What's disk fragmentation?

7 The server named Infinity is approaching 80% disk capacity. There's no budget to increase disk space at this time. Four other servers are available and can reasonably increase file capacity 10–15%. What's a possible solution?

Unit summary: Performance monitoring and optimization

Topic A

In this topic, you learned that performance monitoring concepts are consistent across all platforms, but the specific tools and functions vary according to operating system. UNIX/Linux text-based tools such as **vmstat**, **ps**, **df**, and **top** are used to monitor performance on Linux systems. NetWare uses the **Traffic Manager** tool to monitor network traffic. Traffic Manager works with a Windows NT computer within the Performance Monitor tool. Performance monitoring on the Windows NT operating system uses a GUI tool named **Performance Monitor**, and the default view is Chart View. Performance monitoring in Windows 2000 uses the **Microsoft Management Console** (**MMC**) graphical interface to the System Monitor, but the objects, counters, and instances are nearly identical to those in the Windows NT 4.0 Performance Monitor tool.

Topic B

In this topic, you learned that a **baseline** is established by recording performance data when a server is healthy or running normally. The best time to create a baseline is while the server is experiencing maximum activity. You learned that, when you monitor performance to detect a **bottleneck**, you're looking for the resource (processor, memory, etc.) that's causing the delay in the transmission of data. Baseline information for a server can also be used for **capacity planning**.

Topic C

In this topic, you learned that, within a server, there are limited resources that can affect the performance of a given system. You learned that each of these resources works hand in hand and is capable of influencing the behavior of one another. Finally, you learned that Processor, Memory, PhysicalDisk, and Network Segment are the basic resources to track in performance monitoring.

Independent practice activity

In this activity, you'll use Windows Performance Monitor.

1 Choose Start, Programs, Administrative Tools, Performance. The Performance tool opens. You can drag the window edges to make it larger.

2 Click the Add button (the one with the plus sign). The Add Counters dialog box opens.

3 Verify that Processor is selected in the Performance object list and that % Processor Time is in the counters list. Click the Explain button and read about the selected counter. Click Add to add the counter.

4 From the counters list, select, read about, and add Interrupts/sec.

5 From the Performance object list, scroll up and select Memory. Verify that Pages/sec is selected in the counters list and click Add. Click Close to exit the Add Counters dialog box.

6 Click the Properties button (the pointing finger icon). Examine the various tabs to see how you can adjust the look of the output and data sources.

7 Click the Data tab. Select each counter in turn and, in the width list, choose the third in the list. Click OK. Try opening and closing an application or two, such as pinball, paint, and your Web browser. Examine the Performance graph. It should look something like the illustration in Exhibit 9-19.

8 Open the properties sheet again and experiment with various counters, graph types, colors, and fonts.

9 If you have time, expand Performance Logs and Alerts and experiment with creating running logs and alerts for counter values. Close Performance Monitor when you're done.

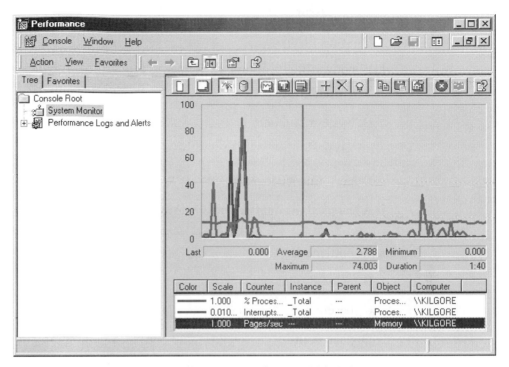

Exhibit 9-19: Performance Monitor in Windows 2000/2003

Review questions

1 The _____ UNIX tool shows resources currently running that consume the most memory.

   A vmstat

   B logging facility

   C top

   D Committed Bytes

2 The Windows NT Performance Monitor relies on which two elements to measure performance?

   A objects

   B cache

   C services

   D counters

3 The counter Interrupts/sec is associated with which object in NT Performance Monitor?

A Memory

B PhysicalDisk

C Processor

D LogicalDdisk

4 Windows 2000 real-time performance is observed with the:

A vmstat utility

B System Monitor

C MMC

D performance logs

5 A test used to compare performance of hardware/software on servers is called a _____

A bottleneck

B network segment

C baseline

D page fault

6 One or more system components that hinder the performance of the rest of the system is known as a:

A bottleneck

B baseline

C multihoming

D port aggregation

7 To get the most effective comparisons, the best time to create a baseline is during:

A the hours between 12:00-6:00 AM

B times of minimal activity

C immediately after rebooting

D periods of maximum activity

8 Predicting server performance using a current baseline and future conditions is called:

A network planning

B capacity planning

C server planning

D performance planning

9 When data is written to a compressed partition or folder, the processor must:

   A remove compression before writing to disk

   B hold the data permanently in memory

   C use multiple controllers

   D work harder to compress the data before it is written

10 Data encryption impacts performance because:

   A more memory is required to hold the private key

   B more hard disk space is required to store the encryption bits

   C additional protocols are necessary to transmit encrypted data over the network

   D the processor must perform calculations to encrypt and decrypt the data

11 PC133 SDRAM is capable of synchronizing with the _____ and reaching clock speeds of _____

   A warp core/20 GoogleHertz

   B page file/133 MHz

   C CPU bus/133 MHz

   D serial port/600 MHz

12 A _____ is a bug in an application or program that prevents it from freeing up memory that it no longer needs.

   A memory leak

   B page fault

   C SCSI

   D cluster

13 Software RAID 5 improves performance for _____operations.

   A write

   B delete

   C read

   D copy

14 When files exist in noncontiguous pieces on a hard disk, the condition is known as _____.

   A disk performance

   B defrag

   C disk fragmentation

   D IDE fault tolerance

15 SCSI-3 supports data transfer rates up to _____ .

A 320 MBps

B 40mbps

C 133MHz

D 600MHz

16 The server named Infinity is approaching 80% disk capacity. There is no budget to increase disk space at this time. Four other servers are available and can reasonably increase file capacity by 10-15%. What is a possible solution?

A add more memory

B upgrade to SCSI

C implement a distributed file system

D rename the server Finite

17 After monitoring a heavily used file server for 2 hours, the network analysis shows the Output Queue Length averaged a value of 5 and never fell below 3. What is a possible solution?

A add more memory

B upgrade processor

C upgrade the motherboard

D multihoming

18 Five illustrators work in a remote office across the city from the main office. They each use Windows 2000 Professional workstations. Currently each illustrator needs to access storyboards on a server in the main office. Only one person accesses the storyboard files from the main office. The illustrators consistently complain about slow access to the server. After monitoring the server you find it is performing within acceptable parameters. What is a possible solution?

A SCSI controller for the server

B Upgrade to faster memory

C Move the server to the remote location

D Print all files and hire a courier

19 _____ can replace _____ to improve network throughput and performance.

A IDE/SCSI

B hubs/routers

C switches/controllers

D switches/hubs

Unit 10

Troubleshooting and problem determination

Unit time: 120 minutes

Complete this unit, and you'll know how to:

A Utilize sound troubleshooting logic to determine and solve problems, document problems and solutions, and check for common causes of server failure.

B Utilize network, connectivity, NOS, and hardware diagnostic tools.

C Troubleshoot from a remote location.

D Recognize and solve boot, virus, and hardware problems.

E Locate help from vendors and peers.

Topic A: Troubleshooting

This topic covers the following CompTIA Server+ exam objectives:

#	Objective

3.6	Install service tools
	• Service tools include:
	  • Event logs
	• Supporting knowledge includes:
	  • Purpose of event logs

3.8	Document the configuration
	• Supporting knowledge includes:
	  • Document contents:
	    • What components are in the box
	    • Where components are located in the box
	    • What updates have been applied
	    • Warranty information
	    • Server configuration information (e.g. BIOS information, RAID levels used, what drives were put into what arrays, server network information)
	    • Install date

4.2	Add processors
	• Activities include:
	  • Perform upgrade checklist, including:
	    • Document upgrade

4.3	Add hard drives
	• Activities include:
	  • Perform upgrade checklist, including:
	    • Document upgrade
	• Supporting knowledge includes:
	  • Importance and use of maintenance logs and service logs (documentation)

4.4	Increase memory
	• Activities include:
	  • Perform upgrade checklist including:
	    • Document upgrade
	• Supporting knowledge includes:
	  • Importance and use of maintenance logs and service logs (documentation)

#	Objective

4.5 Upgrade BIOS/firmware

- Activities include:
  - Perform upgrade checklist including:
    - Document upgrade
  - Supporting knowledge includes:
    - Importance and use of maintenance logs and service logs (documentation)

4.6 Upgrade adapters (e.g. NIC's, SCSI cards, RAID, etc)

- Activities include:
  - Perform upgrade checklist including:
    - Document upgrade
  - Supporting knowledge includes:
    - Importance and use of Maintenance logs and service logs (documentation)

4.7 Upgrade peripheral devices, internal and external. Verify appropriate system resources (e.g. expansion slots, IRQ, DMA, etc.)

- Activities include:
  - Perform upgrade checklist including:
    - Document upgrade
  - Supporting knowledge includes
    - Importance and use of Maintenance logs and service logs (documentation)

4.8 Upgrade system monitoring agents

- Activities include:
  - Perform upgrade checklist including:
    - Document upgrade
  - Supporting knowledge includes
    - Importance and use of Maintenance logs and service logs (documentation)

4.9 Upgrade service tools (e.g. diagnostic tools, EISA configuration, diagnostic partition, SSU, etc.)

- Activities include:
  - Perform upgrade checklist including:
    - Document upgrade
  - Supporting knowledge includes
    - Importance and use of Maintenance logs and service logs (documentation)

4.10 Upgrade UPS

- Activities include:
  - Perform upgrade checklist including:
    - Document upgrade
  - Supporting knowledge includes
    - Importance and use of Maintenance logs and service logs (documentation)

#	Objective
5.1	Perform regular backup

* Supporting knowledge includes:

  * Importance and use of maintenance logs and service logs (documentation)

#	Objective
5.2	Create baseline and compare performance

* Supporting knowledge includes:

  * Importance and use of maintenance logs and service logs (documentation)

#	Objective
7.1	Perform problem determination

* Activities include:

  * Problem isolation

    * Determine whether the problem is hardware or software related

    * Use questioning techniques to determine what, how, when

    * Identify contact(s) responsible for problem resolution

    * Use senses to observe problem (e.g. smell of smoke, observation of unhooked cable, etc.)

    * Bringing it down to base

    * Removing one component at a time

#	Objective
7.2	Use diagnostic hardware and software tools and utilities

* Activities include:

  * Interpret error logs, operating system errors, health logs, and critical events

* Supporting knowledge includes:

  * Know common diagnostic tools

    * PING

    * IPCONFIG

  * Importance and use on maintenance logs and service logs (documentation)

Investigating problems

Explanation

Investigation is usually the most significant step in troubleshooting, and it can also be the most frustrating. However, all problems give you at least a starting point. For example, if the server won't turn on, at least initially you'd suspect a power problem. Unless the cause of the problem is immediately apparent, the investigation process involves several possible stages, and your primary resource (besides the obvious symptoms of the server problem) is the log records. Investigation includes at least checking and keeping accurate log records, checking server messages, and asking analytical questions.

Documentation

Documentation, a record of what hardware and software you have and what changes you make to them, is a critical part of server administration. Otherwise, you're likely to repeat the same configuration errors unnecessarily or troubleshoot using the same failed methods as before. Good documentation starts with keeping good log records prior to the occurrence of a problem. When configuring server equipment and software, record exactly what you do and the success or failure of each step. Then, the log records have useful meaning when it comes time to troubleshoot.

The server also has records of its own, in the system logs and RAID logs, for example. There's a limit to how large these logs can get. Many RAID cards, for example, have a limited amount of memory to store the data. Be sure that you print out existing logs before clearing them to make room for new events. Server logs are stored on the hard disk but can become quite large. You can usually print these out too, or archive them to tape backup or offline media, so they don't occupy too much space.

With proper documentation, you're ready to use log records to troubleshoot the server quickly and efficiently.

Check log records

We've discussed creating logs of any changes to the server or network electronically or on paper. Try using electronic logs; that way you can access the log from anywhere on the network. The method you choose isn't as important as the fact that you have a history of events that can affect the functionality of the server. Unfortunately, many administrators don't keep logs, because they're confident in their ability to remember their actions. However, this doesn't account for times when the administrator is unavailable, or in medium-sized or large networks where there are multiple administrators who might also need to know the history of a server. Documentation accounts for hardware assets and provides a progressive history that might reveal a series of actions that leads to a problem.

You should document the server hardware, software, and baseline performance from the first day you start running it. In addition, document every action performed on the server that could affect its functionality, including such events as:

- *Adding new peripherals.* Though external peripherals, especially a keyboard, mouse, and printer, might seem inconsequential, they can have a significant effect. For example, if a PS/2 mouse becomes unusable and an administrator replaces it temporarily with an old serial port mouse, a different set of resources is used, and an IRQ assigned to the serial port is now utilized, possibly conflicting with another device that previously accessed those resources. Also, these types of peripherals might include software that enables special features, such as a printer's double-sided printing capability. Any time you add software, you add hundreds or thousands of lines of code that could potentially interfere with other NOS functions. Peripherals, such as new devices added to a SCSI chain, become even more significant because of proper termination issues and ID assignments.

- *Installing software.* Although software packages interact with other packages and the NOS much better now than in the past, software bugs and interactions are always potentially problematic. That's another reason why it's so important to test and pilot software deployments.

- *Installing updates or upgrades.* One of the primary purposes of an update is to improve software and hardware compatibility. Nevertheless, some updates could cause more problems than they solve due to unforeseen incompatibilities. (In defense of programmers, it's nearly impossible for them to account for every possible software interaction that could present itself on a server.) Remember that documentation of upgrades might also be important for proper license tracking.

- *Installing hardware and drivers.* In a Plug and Play NOS, such as Windows 2000, allocating resources to various devices is much more flexible than in the past. Nevertheless, hardware devices sometimes still conflict with one another. For example, the COM1 serial port typically uses IRQ 4, and many UPS systems connect to COM1. If you add a device that requires IRQ 4 and a power outage occurs, the UPS system might not be able to communicate with the UPS software through COM1. An equally common problem arises from hardware device drivers, which can cause any number of undesirable interactions, such as incompatibility with the NOS, applications, or other devices. Note that, while new drivers sometimes cause problems, updated drivers can also resolve problems.

- *Baseline.* Carefully document baseline statistics both when you first bring the server online and every time you add or upgrade software or hardware.

- *Interacting directly with other servers.* Many types of servers directly interact with other servers. A problem with one server can affect the functionality of any of the other servers. For example, some servers synchronize some type of information with other servers: mail, database, DNS, and WINS to name a few. If an authoritative DNS server were to have a connectivity problem, then you know that none of the other DNS servers to which it replicates will receive DNS updates until the connectivity problem is resolved. This means that a problem with a single server can have widespread effects on other servers.

- *Stating server purpose.* Without documenting server purpose, various administrators can accidentally change a server's purpose beyond its original capabilities. Documenting a server's purpose can help to ensure that, over time, the server isn't repurposed beyond its capabilities, unless a compelling and deliberate reason dictates otherwise. For example, you might want a mail server with more resources than it really needs to be used exclusively for mail so that it's as responsive as possible to mail functionality and, more importantly, future growth. If another administrator comes along and sees your shiny mail server with plenty of power to spare, he or she might be tempted to use it to run another service or application also. As the company grows with more new employees using e-mail, you might be shocked to find that your more-than-capable mail server can't keep up because of its additional roles. Specially marking the server as dedicated to mail purposes might help to avoid this type of situation.

- *Identifying people performing work on the server.* If you run into a problem with the server, and the documentation doesn't seem to help, the person who last performed the work might have additional insight into the cause of the problem. Similarly, it's important to identify persons to contact should a problem occur. For example, let's say you're the administrator installing a new application on the server. Everything seems to work just fine, but you should document your name as the administrator who performed the installation. Better yet, enter the contact information of the vendor representative and/or technical support person.

- *Stating the purpose of the work on the server.* This allows other administrators to understand better the overall context of the server and the reasons for work that's performed on it.

- *Stating when the work started and finished.* This can help to develop a plan in performing similar tasks on other servers in the network and can help pinpoint problems that might be attributed to the actions performed on the server.

- *Labeling cables.* Although it isn't documentation in a log record, it's still prudent to label cables on both ends for easy identification. If you realize that the network cable to Server1 has a break in it, it's easy to find on the server end, but without labels on the other end, you might have to make random guesses as to which exact cable in the patch panel belongs to the server connection. Labeling isn't always possible or practical, particularly in very large installations. Trying to locate the correct unmarked cable requires a Fox and Hound tool (discussed later in this unit).

Check for server messages

Fortunately, all major NOSs include at least rudimentary, though often cryptic, server messages to indicate the successful start or stop of services, various functions, server or software errors, system conditions, and more. The Windows Event Viewer, as illustrated in Exhibit 10-1, records events by default system, security, and application events. If the server is performing other roles, such as acting as a DNS server, those events have their own category.

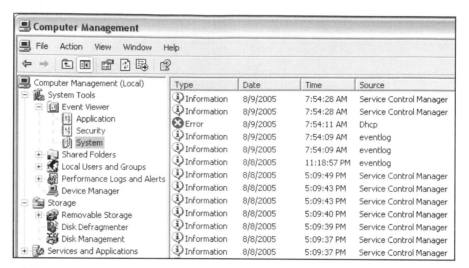

Exhibit 10-1: Windows 2000/2003 Event Viewer provides clues for troubleshooting

If you double-click the event, the Event Properties window opens, as illustrated in Exhibit 10-2, providing a more detailed description of the problem and often a hint as to how to solve it. Windows 2003 event properties also provide a hyperlink that opens the Help and Support Center and looks up the error of the Internet to more information.

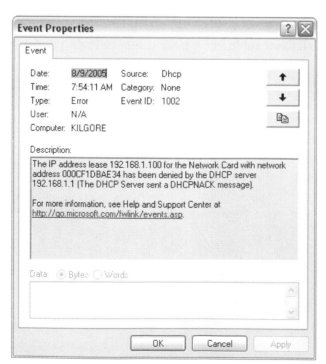

Exhibit 10-2: Event properties provide more information and sometimes a solution

Often, event logs and error messages are cryptic and difficult to interpret. When stumped about what a message means, you can attempt to interpret its meaning by:

- *Referring to events that precede it.* Previous messages might indicate other services or functions that affect the message you're studying.

- *Accessing the vendor's Web site.* The NOS and some applications report error events in the NOS error messaging facility. Many error events are numbered. So, if you visit the vendor's support Web pages and perform a search for the event number, you might find a white paper or some other solution.

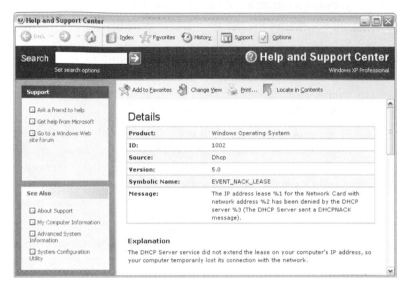

Exhibit 10-3: Windows 2003 event properties provide a link that opens the Help Center

Although all error messages should be investigated, some may be innocuous, and as long as they do not affect performance, reliability, or availability, you can ignore them. In these cases, the help center article will state, "This error message is only informational. You can safely ignore it."

Exactly what happens?

The important thing here is to track the root of the problem. Perhaps the problem initially presents itself through a few user calls saying that they're having trouble with e-mail. Now, you have to ask a series of questions that narrows down the scope of the problem. Otherwise, you're likely to chase problems that don't exist. In determining exactly what happens in the e-mail example, you might ask such things as:

- Are users having trouble sending, receiving, or both? If the user can only send, then SMTP over port 25 is probably working OK. If they can't receive, then perhaps another administrator accidentally blocked POP port 110 over the router, or the server's mail application has wrongly configured ports.

- What are the settings in the user's mail program? Though unlikely that each caller has identically configured the wrong mail settings, perhaps a deployment application that automatically configures the settings is incorrectly configuring each client. Or perhaps a new administrator spelled the name of the mail server incorrectly in the user's POP3 settings.

- Is the problem really with the server? Problems with users' e-mail are a common occurrence and often keep you pretty busy. However, user complaints about e-mail aren't always server-related. That's why you should ask specific questions about exactly what's happening. Most user issues revolve around incorrectly configured client e-mail settings or network connectivity to their computer.

Don't neglect user input into emerging server problems. Though users aren't typically server-savvy, their descriptions can help you to narrow down potential server problems, either as they occur or prior to an emerging problem. For example, if a user states that Internet access is too slow, don't dismiss the complaint because you have a high-speed T-1 Internet connection. Perhaps there's a problem with the Internet proxy software, hardware, or both. If the proxy software usually caches Internet content to a particular hard disk that's currently failing, that would explain the slowdown in Internet performance.

How does it happen?

Much of the time, a problem occurs as a result of a sequence of events. When troubleshooting user clients, technicians ask the user what the user did to alter the system. (The answer is almost always, "Nothing, I didn't change a thing.") With a server, there's usually nobody to ask if the event occurs during operations. That's when the log record comes in handy, so you can see if a previous change contributed to the problem. Also, look at logs generated by the application or NOS. They're often cryptic, but you might be able to distill enough useful information to determine a basic cause.

When does it happen?

Narrowing down the problem to a specific time or sequence of events helps you to determine what might be causing the problem. There are often scheduled events on the network that might contribute to the problem, or perhaps it's the result of peak traffic. Continuing the example of users with e-mail problems, you might also ask such questions as:

- Does the problem happen when the users dial up to the network? If so, perhaps the problem is actually related to a RAS server and not e-mail.

- Does it happen during a certain time of the day? Older backup programs can't back up open mail storage unless it's first closed, which makes it unavailable to users.

- Does the problem predictably repeat itself, or is it intermittent? Problems that repeat predictably are much easier to troubleshoot, because you can run performance monitoring applications or view logs to pinpoint when the problem occurs. You might also notice that predictable problems occur at the same time as another event. Intermittent problems are often baffling and difficult to diagnose, because the problem might happen when you aren't prepared to analyze its cause.

Check the obvious

It happens to every administrator eventually: You spend hours diagnosing the possible cause of a failed server using a full battery of tests, diagnostic software, and technical support calls. Finally, you discover the only reason the server won't function correctly is because of an obvious problem that would have taken only a few seconds to remedy.

Physical connections

It's easy to assume that, because a troubleshooting problem is severe, the solution must be equally severe. There's no logical reason for this, but it's just the way people sometimes react to problems in life and in technology. However, you can often save yourself hours (even days) of troubleshooting time if you check the obvious network cabling and physical connections first when troubleshooting hardware or connectivity problems.

Network cabling

As the network grows, it becomes even more important to remember the importance of a network diagram, which is only as useful as it is accurate. For example, a growing network starts with five segments, three of which have connected nodes and two of which connect only the hubs, and four hubs. Adding another hub and segment to the network results in breaking the 5-4-3 rule, and you're likely to have very poor connectivity with a high collision rate. A network diagram helps you to keep track of network growth and avoid overextending its limitations.

With coax and twisted-pair cable, you might also run into a *bend radius* limitation, which impairs signal transmission when the cable is bent at too tight an angle. Typically, the cable shouldn't bend more than four times its diameter to avoid signal loss. You're most likely to see exceeded bend radius where there's too much slack cable and it's all bunched up, or where the path of the cable run takes odd twists and turns.

Also remember not to exceed the maximum cable length for each respective cable type.

Connections

All kinds of connectors can come loose unless they include some kind of retention, such as thumbscrews, latches, or locks. RJ-45 connectors are particularly problematic due to a clip that easily snaps off or becomes overextended and weakened. Don't forget to add a boot to the ends of patch cables to protect the clip. Also check component connections. USB connectors are usually tight enough to stay by themselves, but moving other cables and equipment around the connector might accidentally wiggle a USB cord as well, causing it to loosen. The same applies to FireWire connections and serial, parallel, and video connectors, though, with the latter items, you can use thumbscrews to attach the cables securely.

The width of SCSI and IDE ribbon cables often impedes good airflow inside the case. You can try to flatten the cables as best you can, but inevitably you'll still have airflow problems. SCSI and IDE cables from Web sites, such as www.coolerguys.com, are round instead of ribbon. Replacing ribbon cable with round cable can significantly improve airflow. Also, it's easier to daisy-chain round cable. Sometimes you have to twist ribbon cable, because the number 1 pin is on the right on one device and on the left on the next device. This configuration makes the distance between connectors in ribbon cable shorter and sometimes strains the connectors.

Use your senses

Your senses can often alert you to problems in a proactive way to avoid trouble instead of as a reaction to disaster. Therefore, it's important not to ignore sight, sound, smell, and touch when troubleshooting.

People tend to depend on sight as the primary sense, and you may be able to observe when something's wrong. With sight, just remember not to take anything for granted and to stay alert. Assuming all server hardware is correctly installed and configured, you'd particularly want to observe any changes. For example, after sliding a server to the front of the rack, do any of the cables in the back come loose? Even with cable arms, cables sometimes loosen. Consider it a good practice to press in each connection when you reinsert the server.

Listen for unusual noises too, which usually come from the hard disk or a fan. When the hard disk starts to make unusual noises, failure is imminent and you should utilize redundancy measures such as RAID-1 or tape backup and immediately replace the drive. The noise is the result of mechanical failure, and it normally isn't worthwhile to attempt to open the case and repair the drive. IDE drives are very cheap to replace, and expensive SCSI disks normally have a warranty program promising overnight delivery of replacements.

When you hear noise in the power supply or case cooling fans, it's usually a result of failing bearings, which, under normal conditions, provide an extremely smooth, low-friction action). Failure to replace the fan could cause the system to overheat. Replace case cooling fans from your stock of spare parts. With the power supply, replace the entire power supply, as its design isn't intended for serviceability. Failure to replace a PSU can result in an overheated power supply, causing it to fail. Though the risk is slight, a fire hazard is also present.

Fans accumulate dust more quickly than any other single component of the system. Unusual noises might be the result of excessive dust impeding normal operation. See if blowing out the dust eliminates the sound.

Properly designed server rooms have very clean air and are probably one of the healthiest places for people to work. There's probably never cigarette smoke in the room, and even food and drink are usually against company policy. If you smell anything unusual in the server room, the most likely smell is probably the plastic-like smell of overheated components or the unmistakable smell of electrical smoke. The human sense of smell is likely to be able to detect these odors prior to a smoke alarm, so go into bloodhound mode and try to locate the source. Then, immediately power down the problem equipment. You may be able to catch an electrical fire in the early stages and prevent a halon dump and the resulting mess.

Finally, the sense of touch helps you to detect problems, such as an unusual amount of heat for potentially overheating components, such as the power supply.

Do it!

A-1: Discussing troubleshooting

Questions and answers

1 Why should an administrator keep server logs?

2 Why might it be important to record servers' interaction with one another?

3 Why should you document the person performing the work?

4 What should you do when you see a server message that's difficult to interpret?

Topic B: Diagnostic tools

This topic covers the following CompTIA Server+ exam objective:

#	Objective

7.2	Use diagnostic hardware and software tools and utilities
	• Activities include:
	    • Select the appropriate tool
	    • Use the selected tool effectively
	• Supporting knowledge includes:
	    • Know common diagnostic tools
	        • TRACEROUTE

Network cable diagnostic devices

When the network stops, so does your business. The common misconception is that most network issues are difficult to diagnose properly. The truth is that, with proper training, finding a network problem is usually a matter of using proper diagnostic equipment discussed here and the troubleshooting methods discussed in the first section of this unit.

Recall that a multimeter combines the functions of a voltmeter, which measures the potential difference, or voltage, between two points, and an ohmmeter, which measures resistance, as well as a few additional functions.

One common application of a multimeter is to diagnose and troubleshoot network errors on a typical thinnet or 10Base2 network. Recall that this cabling requires 50-ohm resistors placed on either end of the bus to reflect the signals properly down the wire. Should a resistor, a T-connector, or an individual segment fail, the entire cable segment fails as well. By using a multimeter, you can effectively troubleshoot by tracking each segment's resistance.

Also, you can use a *time domain reflectometer* (*TDR*), a tool that not only detects cable breaks but also provides the approximate distance to the break by measuring the time it takes for a signal to return. A TDR doesn't tell you exactly what the problem is, but it does tell you where the problem is located on the physical cable.

There's a formula to calculate the distance to the problem section of a cable. A signal is sent down the cable, and the TDR measures the time it takes for the signal to return, converting time to distance, which is then divided by the speed of light and multiplied by the proper velocity of propagation (VOP). (VOP is a measure of the speed of light multiplied by mitigating factors that affect this speed, such as the physical cable media. Twisted-pair cable has a VOP of about .65.) Finally, the result is divided by two. The resulting number is the distance to the problem location on the cable.

In addition to checking for cable breaks, also check cable lengths. If you exceed cable lengths only slightly, connectivity problems might appear periodically but not necessarily on a consistent basis. Similarly, inconsistency in network signaling could occur if you're within maximum cable lengths, but other factors, such as radio signals or EMI, compromise signal integrity.

Another device in your network diagnosis arsenal is a *Fox and Hound*, or *tone generator and locator*, used to identify cable. Imagine pulling several hundred cables through walls, raised floors, and conduit from the patch panel. Identifying each individual cable ahead of time would be fruitless, as the labeling might not survive the trip. By sending a tone, or a signal, down a cable segment, the Fox and Hound can easily identify each cable, and then you can appropriately label the cable. A Fox and Hound is actually a pair of network tools, a tone generator that applies a tone signal to a wire pair or single conductor (the "fox") and an inductive amplifier locator probe (the "hound") on the other end. At a crossconnection point, such as a patch panel, or even at the remote end, you can use the amplifier probe to identify the conductor within a bundle to which the tone has been applied.

The Fox and Hound can also be utilized to troubleshoot physical problems with the cables. For example, some tone generators also allow you to test resistance levels and provide audible tones to indicate the line condition.

Connectivity issues

To test for network connectivity on TCP/IP-based networks, the first tool most seasoned administrators turn to is the Ping utility, which verifies Network layer connectivity. (The Network layer is the third layer of the OSI network model. If you aren't familiar with this model, refer to the *Network+ Guide to Networks* by Tamara Dean, from Course Technology, ISBN 0-7600-1145-1). Recall that the Ping utility verifies remote host accessibility by sending small packets of data to which an accessible host responds. This functionality takes place by sending an echo request to a remote host, such as another computer or router. If the destination host doesn't respond, the interface displays some form of an error message, such as "destination host unreachable."

To determine if a host is properly configured on a TCP/IP network, execute the following sequence of steps:

1 Ping the IP address or host name of a network device that lies outside of your local router's interface, commonly referred to as your "default gateway." If the destination host replies, the system is properly configured. If the destination host is unreachable, it's time to locate the issue: Is it a local configuration issue, or is it on an intermediate system?

2 Ping the IP address of the local router's interface to your subnet (default gateway). If this IP address replies, the issue lies outside of the local subnet. Perhaps the destination host is offline, or there's a network issue somewhere in between. If the default gateway is unreachable, determine if the problem lies with the router or in the local system.

3 Ping a local host on the local subnet. If this host replies, the problem most likely resides with the router. Perhaps the router's interface into the LAN is down due to an administrative error, temporary maintenance, an error condition, or because the router itself is in the process of rebooting. Also check the IP address of the default gateway in the system's configuration, as it may be wrong. If the local host doesn't reply, you probably have an issue with the local system.

4 Ping the local host's IP address. A reply indicates you may have misconfigured your subnet mask. If you don't get a reply, ping the loopback address of 127.0.0.1. If you get a reply, you probably mistyped your IP address when configuring TCP/IP properties. If you don't get a reply, it's time to check the TCP/IP stack, which is often remedied with a simple reinstallation of the protocol. Finally, remember to check physical connectors and drivers:

- Is the network cable connected to your NIC?
- Is the network cable plugged into the hub or switch?
- Are the proper drivers loaded and running?

You can also use several command switches to extend the functionality of the Ping command, as shown in the following table.

Switch	Purpose	Use this switch when...
-t	Ping the specified host until interrupted	The standard four packets don't return data for an acceptable length of time. For example, you could run it continuously to identify when a router starts "flapping," which is becoming intermittently available/unavailable. (Linux Pings indefinitely by default.)
-a	Resolve addresses to host names	You want to verify the presence of DNS reverse lookup records.
-n count	*count* represents the number of echo requests to send	You want more Ping packets than in a typical Ping but do not want to Ping indefinitely.
-l size	*size* represents the size of the buffer	You want to test how network equipment handles packets of various sizes.

The Ping command isn't case-sensitive in most operating systems, but remember that UNIX/Linux is case sensitive, so you need to type "ping" in all lowercase to use the utility. Also, Ping isn't a separately loaded program; it's an integral part of the TCP/IP protocol stack. In other words, if you have TCP/IP loaded and functioning correctly, you also have Ping. There's no such thing as a "ping service" or "ping daemon." If you can otherwise access the server (logging in, for example) but can't successfully ping the server, this indicates that there's probably a problem with the TCP/IP stack on the server, and you need to reload TCP/IP by rebooting. If the TCP/IP stack is corrupt, you need to reinstall it.

Another commonly used network diagnostic utility is TRACERT (or TRACEROUTE). Depending upon the operating system or hardware platform, this utility traces the route your packets take to reach the destination host on a TCP/IP network. You may use this utility to determine if there's a network issue between your host and the destination host. The resulting output shows the path of the packet from one hop to another. This may diagnose a slow router, a dead router, or a misconfigured access list.

To speed up TRACERT, you can use the "-d" switch to stop resolving IP addresses to their associated host names. You may also wish to set a maximum trace length by minimizing the maximum number of hops to the target host by using the "-h *maximum_hops*" switch.

Operating system utilities

Performance monitoring is a big part of troubleshooting the server. For example, recall that a very high frequency of unaccounted-for interrupts usually indicates that a hardware device has failed. Performance monitoring tools detect such events. However, there are also utilities that you can use specifically for troubleshooting, many of which are listed in the sections that follow.

Novell NetWare utilities

The following table lists NetWare utilities that you can use to monitor system health and performance.

Utility	Purpose
VREPAIR	Repairs a volume.
CONLOG	Captures console messages to a text file for later viewing.
NWCONFIG	Modifies the server configuration, performs management operations, and installs additional products.
WAN Traffic Manager	Manages how and when WAN traffic is sent.
TPCON	Monitors TCP/IP activity.
NCMCON	Controls and monitors hot-plug PCI devices.
DSREPAIR	Repairs NDS database problems.

Besides these utilities, you can continue to use NetWare Administrator (NWADMIN or NWADMN32) or ConsoleOne to perform general administration.

Linux utilities

The following table shows graphical (KDE or GNOME) Linux utilities that you can use to monitor system health and performance.

Utility	Purpose
Tripwire	Detects changed files and directories.
KDE Control Center	Provides detailed system information about the system's applications, devices, and GUI interface.
Sysctlconfig	Configures specific settings for networking, file systems, virtual memory, and the kernel.
KDE Task Manager	Similar to Windows NT/2000 Task Manager, you can view each running process and adjust its priority level ("re-nice") or kill it.
tksysv and SysV Init Editor	A system process editor that allows you to add and delete services as well as adjust priority (see Exhibit 10-4)

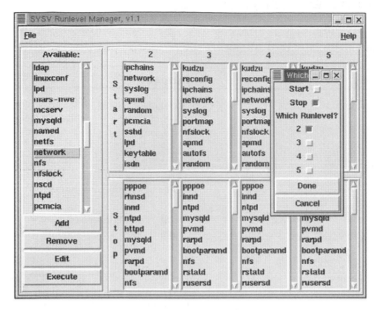

Exhibit 10-4: The Linux tksysv utility allows you to manipulate various processes

Windows NT 4.0 utilities

The following table shows Windows NT 4.0 utilities that you can use to monitor system health and performance.

Utility	Purpose
Disk Administrator	Manages disks and partitions; creates software RAID configurations.
Task Manager	Shows running applications and processes and allows you to adjust their priority or terminate. Displays realtime processor and memory utilization statistics.
System Properties	Adjusts how applications use memory, copies/deletes user profiles, configures virtual memory, and manages the boot menu.
Windows NT 4.0 Resource Kit	A collection of dozens of various utilities designed to make administration, troubleshooting, and performance monitoring more effective.
Windows NT Diagnostics	Accesses data regarding the system bus, BIOS, CPU(s), display adapter, memory usage, paging file usage, running services, system resources, and more.
Dr. Watson	Debugger for win32 applications. Might not make much sense to you unless you're a developer. Software vendors might ask for a copy of a Dr. Watson output to analyze their programs.
Network Monitor	A basic network sniffer useful for packet analysis.
The /SOS switch	Add this switch to the end of the Boot.ini file to view each driver as it loads, similar to the OS/2 Alt + F2 boot method.
Performance Monitor	Monitor the values of many system counters, such as percent processor and memory usage, interrupts/second and pages/second. Allows you to log values and set alerts to go off if specified counters go above or below a given value.

Windows 2000/2003 utilities

The following table shows Windows 2000/2003 utilities that you can use to monitor system health and performance.

Utility	Purpose
Computer Management	Broad management capability that includes event viewer, system information, device management, hard disk management, various services, and other functions.
Task Manager	Shows running applications and processes and allows you to adjust their priority or terminate. Displays real-time processor and memory utilization statistics.
Windows 2000 Resource Kit, Windows Server 2003 Resource Kit Tools	A collection of dozens of various utilities designed to make administration, troubleshooting, and performance monitoring more effective.
Dr. Watson	Debugger for win32 applications. Might not make much sense to you unless you're a developer. Software vendors might ask for a copy of a Dr. Watson output to analyze their programs.
Network Monitor	A basic network sniffer useful for packet analysis.
The /SOS switch	Add this switch to the end of the Boot.ini file to view each driver as it loads, similar to the OS/2 Alt + F2 boot method.
Active Directory Domains and Trusts	Establishes trust relationships between domains.
Active Directory Sites and Services	Manages Active Directory replication between sites.
Active Directory Users and Computers	Creates and manages Active Directory user, group, and computer accounts.
System Information	Comprehensive information about system hardware, components, and software.
Performance Monitor	Monitors the values of many system counters, such as percent processor and memory usage, interrupts/second and pages/second. Allows you to log values and set alerts to go off if specified counters go above or below a given value.

System and hardware diagnostic utilities

Because much of troubleshooting is actually a matter of ensuring proper configuration in the first place or correcting misconfigurations, using the right administration tool is important.

Besides the administrative utilities included in the NOS, performance monitoring utilities are also critical, because troubleshooting often involves improving the performance of a server. Sometimes a diagnostic utility is included with an installation package for a device, as seen in the screenshot for the Intel NIC illustrated in Exhibit 10-5.

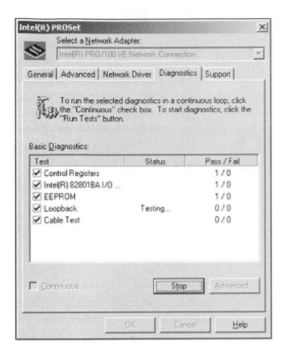

Exhibit 10-5: Running diagnostics on an Intel NIC

Most server vendors include utilities that perform low-level diagnosis of the server hardware. You can usually place these utilities in a directory and run them from there or copy the utility to a floppy disk. Floppies are useful for systems that can't boot properly or for file systems, such as Windows NT NTFS, that don't allow direct disk access from a conventional MS-DOS boot disk.

Third-party manufacturers also make utilities that diagnose hardware. There are several such products, many of which are designed for individual workstation use. One such useful product on servers is American Megatrends' AMIDiag, which performs extensive diagnostics for workstations or servers. Most utilities of this type can run only from MS-DOS, but AMIDiag offers a convenient and intuitive Windows interface as well. The latest version includes loopback plugs for serial and parallel port testing and reports detailed information about components, including the motherboard, chipset, memory, and processor. For server components you suspect might be faulty, you can run extensive diagnostics, as shown in Exhibit 10-6.

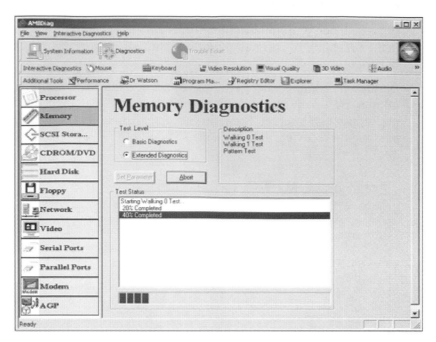

Exhibit 10-6: AMIDiag performing extensive tests on system memory

In some situations, you might also consider creating a small FAT partition on the hard disk that can be used for several purposes, especially when you need to perform administration on a system without loading the NOS. Typically, loading the NOS causes a problem, because the file systems of most NOSs are inaccessible from MS-DOS. You might store common MS-DOS utilities in the partition that are useful for disk management, moving or editing plain text files, and so forth. For example, start with:

- ATTRIB. Without ATTRIB to reset attributes on some files, you might not be able to view or change certain files.

- FDISK. For repairing the master boot record using the /MBR switch or adding additional partitions. In the worst case, you use FDISK to delete partitions.

- FORMAT. To format partitions after using FDISK.

- CHKDSK or SCANDISK. To check the health of partitions. CHKDSK has been around since early versions of DOS, but it has been updated with NTFS options. Run CHKDSK /? to see available options.

- MSCDEX. To load CD-ROM capability, also include the CD-ROM drivers.

The partition can also be useful for storing diagnostic software. For example, if the system won't boot, you can't access NOS diagnostics, and the CD-ROM is inaccessible as well. This means that third-party diagnostics are also unavailable. By storing an MS-DOS diagnostic utility in advance on a separate partition of the hard disk, you save yourself the headache of trying to work around the inaccessible NOS file system.

Do it!

B-1: Discussing diagnostic tools

Questions and answers

1 If you suspect a problem with the NIC, how can you diagnose it?

2 Besides checking for proper voltages, how else can you use a multimeter?

3 Which tool checks for breaks in the network cable?

Topic C: Working remotely

This topic covers the following CompTIA Server+ exam objectives:

#	Objective
3.9	Implement the server management plan (OS-dependent and OS-independent components)
	• Plans typically include:
	• Remote management hardware
7.2	Use diagnostic hardware and software tools and utilities
	• Activities include:
	• Use documentation from previous technician successfully
	• Supporting knowledge includes:
	• Know common diagnostic tools
	• Basic hard disk tools

Wake-on LAN

Explanation

Although most servers run 24/7, organizations that run mostly during business hours might choose to conserve power by putting servers and workstations into a low-power state during off hours, with only certain servers, such as Web or RAS, running constantly. If the administrator wants to perform administration or troubleshoot during off hours, he or she must typically wait until server utilization is low, which translates into a long day in the server room for the administrator. However, with various remote features such as wake-on LAN, you can administer servers from nearly anywhere, such as the comfort of your own home.

Wake-on LAN (*WOL*) is a technology that allows the administrator to wake a computer remotely from its low-power state. WOL allows administrators to "wake up" the server and perform tasks during times of reduced activity. You can use WOL on both Token Ring and Ethernet networks.

WOL works when a *magic packet*, or *wake-up packet*, consisting of 16 copies of the MAC address is sent to the host system from a server system that has a remote network management application installed. When the WOL NIC receives the magic packet, the server turns on. To enable WOL, you must have the following:

- A WOL network interface card. This card is always awake, listening for the magic packet. In order to do this, the adapter card draws continuous, low power from the motherboard.
- A WOL motherboard BIOS.
- WOL remote management software.

WOL functionality has several advantages, even for client workstations. For example, every workstation in your organization can be started up just before your employees arrive, saving the time and revenue lost while they boot and avoiding unnecessary energy costs associated with employees leaving systems on all night.

Remote administration tools

There are many utilities and tools available that allow you to administer the systems in your network remotely, whether they're across the room or in another state. On the traditional side of things, most NOS's can be set up as telnet servers, allowing you to log in at a command line and administer and troubleshoot from there. This method was available long before graphical user interfaces. One of the most widely used graphic utilities is Symantec's pcAnywhere (www.symantec.com), which allows you to connect to your server remotely to copy files, run remote applications, or perform any other actions that you'd normally do if seated locally at the server.

Another free method of remotely administering servers is Windows NT 4.0 or Windows 2000 Terminal Services. In Windows 2000, use Add/Remove Programs to add Terminal Services. A wizard asks you to specify the mode in which you want the server to run:

- *Application server mode* allows users to run the Windows 2000 desktop and applications from any Windows workstation, even Windows 3.x. The benefit is that you can use older hardware incapable of running Windows 2000 or more demanding applications on its own. Using an older version of Windows, clients can derive all the benefits of a Windows 2000 desktop. Application server mode requires the purchase of proper client licenses.

- *Remote administration mode*, as shown in Exhibit 10-7, allows up to two administrators to connect as if local to the server at no additional licensing expense. Of course, this is the mode we're interested in for purposes of remotely administering a server.

Either mode allows an administrator to "shadow" an ongoing session. You can see what applications the connected terminal services user is using and, if you like, operate his or her keyboard and mouse. For user sessions, this can be an excellent support tool. As a server administration tool, Terminal Services allows you to perform complete administration over a LAN, the Internet, or a dial-up connection. For example, if you're out of town and your pager receives an alert that a service has unexpectedly shut down, you could dial up from your hotel room, establish a terminal session, and restart the service. If the situation is drastic, you could even remotely reboot the server.

Another way that administrators can connect to and troubleshoot remote desktops and servers with a simple right-click is through the Computer Management console, as follows:

1 From the Windows 2003 desktop, choose Start, then right-click the My Computer and choose Manage. The Computer Management console appears and, by default, connects to the local computer.

2 Right-click the Computer Management node at the top of the left pane and select Connect to another computer.

3 Select Another computer and click Browse.

4 Click Advanced.

5 Click Find Now to search for other computers.

6 Select the computer of your choice from the interface, as shown in Exhibit 10-8, and click OK.

7 The Computer Management console now displays management nodes for the remote computer and functions for the most part as if you were locally seated at the server. Some features are disabled. For example, you can view Device Manager hardware settings, but you can't change them unless seated locally or running over a Terminal Services session.

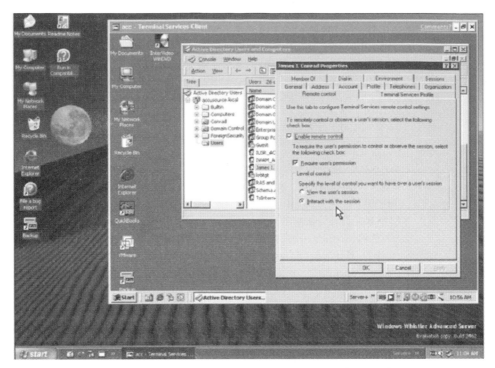

Exhibit 10-7: Remotely connecting to a Windows 2000 Advanced Server computer from Windows 2003 Server

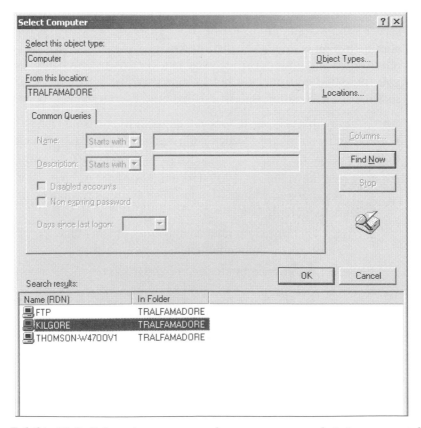

Exhibit 10-8: Select the computer that you want to administer remotely

The preceding steps apply to Windows 2000/2003, but most NOSs offer a similar remote management facility. For example, Windows NT 4.0 has a similar capability, and NetWare has ConsoleOne and Remote Management Facility for general administration and ZENworks for remote control capability. You can also use the RConsole or RConsoleJ. With OS/2, use the SystemView utility, also known as NetFinity.

In addition to software products, there are hardware solutions that provide a great deal of remote administration flexibility. These are usually PCI or ISA cards that occupy an available slot in the server and are connected via a network cable, internal or external modem, or both. One of the better products is MegaRAC (Remote Access Companion) from American Megatrends. Because of an onboard battery and WOL support, you can administer the server remotely, even in the event of a power failure. Some other remote administration tools require the server to be up and running, but this is of little use if you need to change BIOS settings or observe startup error messages, text sequences, and so forth remotely. With MegaRAC, you can still perform all of these actions from a remote station. Some of the features of MegaRAC are as follows:

- Captures the screen when the server crashes so that you can see error messages or what might have caused the problem. This is especially handy for error messages that might appear briefly before an unplanned reboot such as some instances of a BSOD. In addition, MegaRAC logs the probable cause of the crash.

- Monitors system health including temperatures, fan RPMs, voltages, and alerts for chassis intrusion.

- Allows you to view the graphics display of a remote server to see current activity.

- Allows you to reboot a server and watch the boot process, including POST.

- Provides a special boot to a separate partition that loads diagnostic utilities. You can also insert a floppy in your local computer and use it to boot the remote server! This is very handy for booting an unbootable server or running utilities or diagnostics that would otherwise require you to visit that server.

- Provides dead server management. When the server fails, MegaRAC can issue an alert to the supervisor and put itself in a special server mode to receive commands from the supervisor, such as performing a reboot or running special diagnostics. This is probably the single most powerful benefit of the product.

Using administrative tools that require the network and server to be up and running is sometimes referred to as *in-band management*, while using tools that can be used even when there is network or server failure is called *out-of-band management*.

Booting an unbootable server

At some point, the inevitable happens: the server refuses to boot. Numerous recovery options are available in each NOS, but here we primarily address basic boot functionality to provide you with a starting point for troubleshooting.

Typically, the first option is to uninstall any new hardware devices, device drivers, or software. Windows NT/2000/2003 allows you to boot to the last known good state, which bypasses changes made by devices/drivers/software in the last session. If the system still refuses to boot, try using a boot disk. Most operating systems come with one or more bootable floppies or CDs to use during setup. It's always wise to guard these diskettes closely and make backup copies. Instructions for returning to a basic bootable operating system for each respective NOS appear below.

To create boot floppies for a Red Hat Linux system from MS-DOS or Windows:

1 Change directories to the CD disk drive where the installation files are located.

2 Change to the dosutils directory.

3 Execute the *rawrite* command, which then prompts you for the file name of a disk image. Consult your Linux documentation for a suitable boot image. In Red Hat Linux, for example, use the \images\boot.img file on the Red Hat CD-ROM.

4 Specify the destination letter for the floppy disk (usually "A"). The contents of the image file copies to the floppy.

To create boot floppies for a Red Hat Linux system from Linux:

1 Mount the CD with the installation files.

2 Change directory to the desired image.

3 Execute the following command: *# dd if=boot.img of=/dev/fd0 bs=1440k.*

To create the boot floppies for a Windows NT-based system:

1 Have three labeled floppy disks ready.

2 Enter *rdisk* from the command prompt, and follow the onscreen directions that automatically appear, swapping disks as prompted.

3 Please note that the disks are inserted in reverse order, that is, disk 3 is inserted first, and disk 1 last.

The floppies that the RDISK utility creates aren't directly bootable but contain information that allows you to run setup in repair mode to restore critical boot and system information.

To create the boot floppies for a Windows 2000 system:

1 Have four floppy disks ready.

2 On any Windows or MS-DOS computer, insert the Windows 2000 CD into the CD-ROM drive.

3 Execute the *makeboot a:* command from the *bootdisk* directory of the CD, and follow the screen prompts to switch disks.

Booting to Windows NT or 2000 with the boot floppy disks doesn't provide full access to the operating system. It allows you only to use other recovery tools to repair the Registry or add/remove files. Prior to a server boot failure, however, you can create a special (unsupported) boot floppy to access the NOS desktop as follows:

1   Format a floppy disk from within the running Windows NT/2000 NOS. This is important, as it creates a boot sector that wouldn't appear if formatted under MS-DOS or Windows 9.x.

2   Copy the following files to the floppy:

- BOOT.INI
- NTLDR
- NTDETECT.COM
- [NTBOOTDD.SYS] (if a SCSI adapter is present)
- [BOOTSECT.DOS] (if the computer dual-boots)

3   Now, provided there are no other NOS problems, the system should boot as usual to the desktop. (Boot disks for many operating systems may be found at www.bootdisk.com.)

Recall that NetWare actually uses a conventional DOS partition to boot. If the boot files are corrupt, you can boot with any bootable MS-DOS floppy and manually create or edit Autoexec.bat and Config.sys files, which service the basic MS-DOS boot. Server boot files include Autoexec.ncf, Startup.ncf, and Config.ncf. As a reference for the correct commands to include, you can copy known good files from another properly functioning NetWare server.

NetWare requires at least 10–20% free disk space on the SYS volume to boot reliably. If you suspect disk space is an issue, run "NDIR /VOL," which shows total volume space that's in use and is free. If space is an issue, run "PURGE /ALL" for each volume, which permanently deletes previously erased files, which is similar to emptying the Recycle Bin on Windows operating systems. If you still haven't opened enough space, you may want to run FILER or NWAdmin to remove files manually.

More drastic measures

Finally, if server problems are so severe that you can't recover within a reasonable length of time, you might have to:

- Reinstall over an existing operating system. This is probably a better method than formatting the hard disk and starting over, because reinstallation usually replaces files that might have become corrupt, and applications usually remain intact. Use this method in situations where you're certain that there are missing or corrupt NOS files but can't identify each one and manually replace it within a reasonable length of time. This method is a bit more of a gamble if you're less certain that NOS files are missing or corrupt.

- Use cloning software. You can use imaging software to store the entire contents of a partition into a single file that you can later reapply to the same or another computer. Create an image of a known good NOS installation, so that if problems occur at a later time, you can reapply the known good NOS image and effectively roll back time. This restores the server in minutes, and you don't have to install applications or spend time configuring services and NOS settings.

- Format the hard disk and reinstall the NOS and all applications and then configure all services. While this isn't too disruptive for a workstation and might take between one and four hours, on a highly utilized server, this could take at least a day and be highly disruptive. If this is the method you use, server logs are again crucial: You wouldn't want to duplicate a series of events that led to the server corruption in the first place. Also, by looking at the recorded purpose of the server, you avoid running services and applications that are unnecessary.

Do it!

C-1: Discussing remote and on-site rebooting

Questions and answers

1 What can be sent to a WOL host to wake it up?

2 What's the difference between in-band and out-of-band management?

3 What does booting to Windows NT or 2000 with the boot floppy disks allow an administrator to do?

Topic D: Troubleshooting viruses and FRUs

This topic covers the following CompTIA Server+ exam objectives:

#	Objective
3.1	Check/upgrade BIOS/firmware levels (system board, RAID controller, hard drive, etc.)
7.2	Use diagnostic hardware and software tools and utilities

- Activities include:
  - Replace defective hardware components as appropriate
  - Identify defective FRU's and replace with correct part
  - Locate and effectively use hot tips (e.g. fixes, OS updates, E-support, web pages, CD's)
  - Gather resources to get problem solved
    - Identify situations requiring call for assistance
    - Acquire appropriate documentation

Viruses

Explanation

Viruses are programs that are sometimes harmless pranks but more often are self-propagating programs that perform damaging and wide-ranging actions on server and client computers. The most effective way of troubleshooting viruses is to use a preventive, constantly running virus-detection utility that recognizes the presence of a virus and cleans infected files if possible. Unfortunately, if a virus gets loose on a system, there's little that virus utilities can do to undo the damage. A few virus symptoms include:

- Unbootable or intermittently bootable systems. Many viruses, especially early viruses, attack the boot sector.
- Display problems. Some make screens unreadable, although they may or may not damage actual data.
- File destruction. Obviously this is the most comprehensive damage, though some viruses might also slightly alter data and, therefore, are more difficult to notice.
- Unexplained poor performance, for example, slow program load times or disk access times.
- Unexpected low-memory situations.
- Strange noises and/or graphics.
- Unexplained reduction in available disk space.
- Random drive letter reassignment.
- Odd error messages.
- A growing number of bad hard disk sectors.
- Mail servers handling an extremely high number of e-mails. Some particularly destructive viruses send copies of themselves to all persons in the client mail program's address book.

If a system becomes infected by a virus, you might be tempted to delete and recreate all partitions. If you then boot from a floppy and reinstall the OS from a CD, you might unwittingly reintroduce the virus if the floppy is also infected. Be sure to scan the boot floppy for infection prior to using it.

All major virus detection/protection software should work fine for you. The key is to make sure that the virus definition files that identify signs of a virus are up to date. All these antivirus programs are excellent:

- McAfee VirusScan (www.mcafee.com)
- Norton Antivirus (www.symantec.com)
- Innoculan (www.ca.com)

For more about viruses and their effects, refer to Jean Andrews' book, *Enhanced A+ Guide to Managing and Maintaining Your PC* (Course Technology, 2000).

Troubleshooting specific FRUs

Recall that an FRU is a Field Replaceable Unit. Depending on the context, an FRU can refer to the server as a whole or to the components themselves; for example, the power supply is a common FRU.

This section addresses some of the most common symptoms of FRU failure.

Power supply

Unless the system utilizes N+1 power supply redundancy, loss of a power supply means total loss of server function. Signs of a failing power supply include:

- Intermittent memory problems. Because clean, consistent power to the memory ensures its integrity, power problems can cause memory loss or corruption. If you regularly see errors that report a problem in the same memory address, the problem is more likely the actual memory.
- Systems that lock, hang, or reboot. Systems with overtaxed or failing power supplies sometimes exhibit these problems, especially when they get busy.
- Damaged or intermittently failing motherboards. Power irregularities are bad for all electrical components; the motherboard is no exception.
- Unusually hot case and power supply. Minutes and seconds without adequate cooling can damage the power supply, and failing fans are often the cause.

Use backprobing techniques to verify proper power supply voltages.

Memory

Memory problems can often be difficult to diagnose. Operating systems and applications are so complex that, when a crash occurs, it might be difficult to say for certain whether it was due to a software bug or memory problems. However, the following might help you to diagnose memory problems:

- *Varying part numbers*. Some cheaper memory is really made from manufacturer spare parts. In fact, some memory modules are actually a collection of chips from different manufacturers. In such a case, the markings on the chips are all different. However, recall that it's normal for one chip to have different markings if it's the parity chip. Memory timing is so tight that little if any variation can be tolerated. For server use, don't use modules with varying part numbers.

- *No POST*. There may be no POST if memory isn't properly seated, the memory is of poor quality, it uses mixed parts (as described above), or incompatible modules are installed (ECC and non-ECC in the same server, for example).

- *Memory errors in the same location each time*. Most servers include a reporting facility within the CMOS that shows the memory error. If not, and you have the opportunity otherwise to record the memory location, make a note of it. Later, if a memory error appears again in the same location, you know it's because of the memory module, not because of the NOS or applications. However, some device drivers might require the same location in memory, and a bad driver might be disguised as bad memory.

- *Memory-testing utilities*. AMIDiag is a good one, though there are several utilities that can do this for you. The utility might run from within the NOS, but try running it from a bare boot floppy with no memory management in effect (such as Himem.sys or loadhigh statements).

- *Physical symptoms*. Bad memory chips often run comparatively hotter than the others. Also inspect the system board slot contacts. If a contact is bent or misaligned, you might have to replace the motherboard.

- *Suspect modules*. When replacing suspect modules, replace them one at a time and test them each time to confirm which modules are bad.

- *Handle with care*. Exercise special care in handling memory modules, which are particularly susceptible to ESD problems.

Hard disks

Some hard disk problems are obvious, especially when they make that grinding noise that sounds like there's gravel in the drive. If the master boot record is damaged or corrupt (often due to virus infection), the system may not boot. Try booting from a floppy to verify that the system is bootable and to rule out other possible problems. Other hard disk problems include data loss or corruption and unusually high or growing numbers of bad sectors as reported by disk analysis utilities.

Use the FDISK /MBR switch to reconstruct the master boot record for Windows, MS-DOS, or any other NOS that starts from a DOS-compatible boot partition. Similarly, Windows 2000 allows you to boot to a special recovery console, which allows you direct disk access with the right password. Then, you can use additional boot utilities such as FIXMBR and FIXBOOT.

If you experience hard disk problems, consider the following solutions:

- Perform a thorough analysis of the hard disk. All major NOSs have such a utility included, such as Windows CHKDSK command. Also consider third-party utilities, but remember that the more thorough the utility, the longer it takes (perhaps hours) to analyze the hard disk. Most NOSs also have hot-fix capability to save data automatically away from detected bad sectors onto healthy disk space.

- Verify proper cabling. For IDE, make sure that the marked Pin1 on the cable is adjacent to the power connector. Also make sure that the power connector is inserted all the way. SCSI connections are a study of their own. Verify proper termination, signaling (HVD, LVD, or SE), and device ID settings.

- Check the POST. ATAPI drives display their presence during POST, and SCSI adapters, such as Adaptec's, show the specific drives in the setup BIOS of the adapter.

SCSI and RAID troubleshooting

Troubleshooting SCSI is a study of its own. This section addresses these issues specifically. Recall from earlier in this unit that troubleshooting is mostly configuring devices properly in the first place, and it could never be more true of any device than it is of SCSI drives. Adding to the obvious importance of properly configuring SCSI as an administrator, note that SCSI is heavily emphasized on the CompTIA Server+ exam.

The following subjects resolve the most common SCSI issues.

Termination

If someone tells you that the new SCSI drive isn't working, you can almost assume that it's a termination problem. Even experienced administrators occasionally forget to terminate the SCSI chain properly. Consider the following SCSI termination issues:

- Remember that both ends of a SCSI chain need to be terminated.

- If the drive doesn't support self-termination, then you must add a terminator to the end of the chain. (The cable might already have a built-in terminator.)

- Most newer drives, such as Ultra160 drives, don't self-terminate. Some older 50-pin drives offer self-termination.

- If there's no room for a terminator, use a pass-through terminator that both connects the drive to the chain and provides termination. Even better, use a cable that has a terminator already crimped to the end.

- Passive termination is generally considered the worst type of termination, because its resistance (132 ohms) varies too greatly from the standard cable resistance of 105 to 108 ohms. Make sure you use active termination instead of passive termination. Even better, use forced perfect termination whenever possible.

- Recall that, when adding 50-pin devices to a 68-pin bus, you must specially terminate for the additional pins that the 50-pin device doesn't use. Although there are 18 additional pins, nine are only for grounding and don't require special treatment. The remaining nine, known as the "high nine," are hot and require you to terminate properly.

Cabling

- Recall that 8-bit ("narrow") SCSI always uses 50-pin cables and connectors, and 16-bit ("wide") SCSI always uses 68-pin cables and connectors. Therefore, if you're combining various generations of SCSI technology on the same bus, make sure the cabling remains compatible. For example, Ultra2 SCSI devices, which are usually "wide" devices, use a 68-pin connector and so does Ultra3. In this case, you could mix the technologies.

- If the Ultra2 SCSI device is the more rare "narrow" version requiring a 50-pin connector, then you can't use it on an Ultra3 68-pin bus without an adapter.

- You can use special adapters to place 50-pin devices on a 68-pin cable.

- Likewise, you can use special adapters to place 68-pin devices on a 50-pin cable.

- This is important: If you mix 50-pin narrow devices with 68-pin wide devices, the net effect is that the 68-pin devices are effectively reduced to 50-pin narrow performance. There are all kinds of converters, custom cables, and so forth that allow you to mix and match devices and buses physically in countless ways, but conversion usually comes at the cost of performance.

- If you have 50-pin and 68-pin devices on a 68-pin bus, place the 68-pin devices nearest the host adapter. Then add and terminate the 50-pin devices.

Device ID

Recall that each device has a method to set the device ID, usually through jumpers, as is often the case with hard disks or with a dial.

- Especially on older SCSI, set the booting hard disk to ID 0, or else it might not be recognized as the boot drive.

- If you also have IDE drives in the system but want to boot from SCSI, then configure the system BIOS to boot from the SCSI host adapter as the first bootable device. Some systems may require you to connect the IDE drive to the secondary IDE interface instead of the primary IDE interface.

- Each SCSI device must have a unique ID number. Recall that, in order from highest to lowest, the priority order is 0, 7, 6, 5, 4, 3, 2, 1, and then if the bus is also wide, 15, 14, 13, 12, 11, 10, 9, 8.

- The SCSI host adapter is usually set at 7. It's best to leave it at this setting.

RAID

Keep the following RAID tips in mind:

- A RAID log records the state of the RAID array. This log can be in the host adapter BIOS, the system log of the NOS, or separate software.

- With RAID-5, you must keep the drives in the same order in which they were originally configured. For example, if a remote office sends you a preconfigured RAID-5 external array case but takes out the drives and ships them separately, you must place the drives back into the original locations on the SCSI chain. If the drives are placed in a different order, the RAID controller returns a message that the array configuration has changed and that you should reconfigure it.

- Don't move drives configured with one RAID adapter to another RAID adapter. RAID host adapters actually write data to track zero or the last track on the drive, and this information is often largely proprietary. Moving the drives could cause the RAID array not to recognize the drives or, worse, to destroy data.

- As a rule, any time you touch equipment that contains data, back it up first. For example, if you're asked to add an additional drive to the RAID array, back it up first! No exceptions.

- The host adapter BIOS automatically implements the hot spare when a RAID drive fails. The interim time between when the original drive fails and the hot spare is fully implemented is known as "degraded mode." For example, if a RAID-5 member fails, it takes time for the array to integrate the hot spare while it reconstructs data from the parity stripe of the other array members.

- If you want fast performance without redundancy, use RAID-0.

- If you want fast read performance and low overhead in terms of usable storage space in the array, use RAID-5. RAID-5 lags behind other RAID methods for write performance because of the parity calculation.

- If you want fast read and write performance at the expense of high disk overhead, use RAID-1.

Adapter cards

Although it may seem obvious (if the device stops working, it's defective), there are still questions and solutions you should look into for NIC problems.

- Move the card to another computer. If the problem repeats itself in a known good system, then you have isolated the card as problematic.
- Closely associated with the physical hardware is the device driver. Upgrade the driver to verify that the driver isn't corrupt and that it's the most compatible. Usually, the most recent version includes bug fixes for problems of which the vendor is aware.
- Move the device to a different slot. Some devices perform better when in a different slot, and high-performance devices work nominally better when closer to the processor.
- Check to see if the device is fully seated into the slot.

Processor

The processor might fail, but this is somewhat rare and is usually brought on by overheating. Usually when a processor fails, the system won't even POST. Motherboard failure is also rare but not unheard of, and it's usually brought on by power problems or overheating. If you suspect a motherboard problem, use an extensive diagnostic utility to analyze the board.

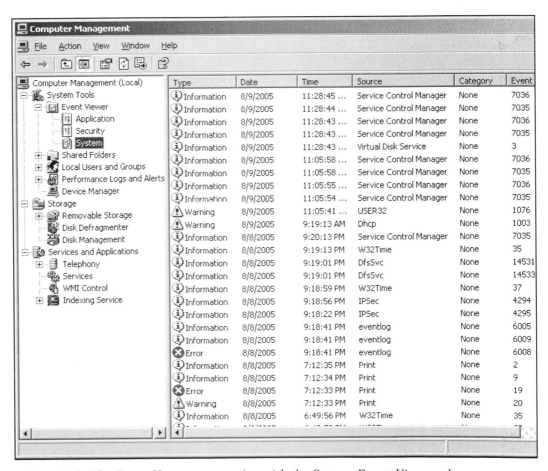

Exhibit 10-9: The Event Viewer categories with the System Event Viewer chosen

Do it!

D-1:   Viewing the Windows Server 2003 Event Log

Here's how

1 Log on as Administrator.

2 Right-click **My Computer** and choose **Manage**. The Computer Management console opens.

3 In the left pane, expand the **Event Viewer** underneath System Tools. You should see three or more log categories, depending on the roles of the server. The viewer should look something like the one shown in Exhibit 10-9.

4 Select a log category in the left pane. Then, double-click any event in the right pane. Look for errors rather than just information. Use the up and down arrows in the Event Properties dialog box to move up and down the list of messages.

5 Most servers probably have a warning or error of some kind. Click the more information hyperlink and answer the following questions: Does the event seem to be critical to the operation or performance of the server? How? Is there a resolution or additional information for the problem displayed in the Event Properties dialog box? If so, what's the resolution or information?

6 Close the Event Properties dialog box, and then close the Computer Management console.

Topic E: Troubleshooting tips and getting help

This topic covers the following CompTIA Server+ exam objectives:

#	Objective
7.1	Perform problem determination
	• Activities include:
	• Problem isolation
	• Determine whether the problem is hardware or software related
	• Use questioning techniques to determine what, how, when
	• Bringing it down to base
	• Removing one component at a time

Some general tips

Explanation

- *It usually takes longer than you think.* When you know what's causing a problem, it's easy quickly to review the steps that it takes to resolve it in your head. However, it's easy sometimes to leave out steps that you don't realize until you're in the thick of a repair. Also, in resolving one problem, other parts of the system are often affected.

- *Start with the simplest solution.* Save time and headaches by starting with the simple causes and solutions. Also, more complex troubleshooting steps tend to affect the rest of the system more significantly. For example, it's much less disruptive to uninstall the most recent application or hardware device than to reinstall the operating system.

- *Move hardware to see if the problem follows.* If you suspect a specific hardware device is problematic, move it from the original system to a known good system and see if the problem repeats itself. If so, you have confirmed the hardware problem. If not, you know that the problem is something else. It might also be possible that the hardware device interacts poorly with other hardware or software in the original system.

- *Always check for updates.* Periodically, installing a new software package on a server causes the system to lock on reboot. Be sure to check for software updates when installing new server software.

- *Troubleshoot one issue at a time, and apply one solution at a time.* The tendency is to attempt too many solutions at once. If you think a problem has three possible solutions, don't perform all three at once. Execute each solution individually to see if it's the proper solution. That way, you can enter the exact solution in the server log.

- *Fix or change one thing at a time.* Similar to the above issue, it isn't wise to try the "kill two birds with one stone" method of troubleshooting and maintenance. For example, if you install a new hardware device and driver, add new software, and apply an operating system patch all for the same session, how will you know which one caused a problem if the system doesn't function properly afterwards?

- *Progressively document troubleshooting steps.* Some administrators like to keep a legal pad or notebook nearby and write down the history of steps they take to troubleshoot an item. This record is unofficial, and once a successful solution appears, they enter it into the actual server log. Of course, any of the steps that change the system permanently must also be entered in the server log. The purpose of the history is that, if the troubleshooting session gets lengthy and tiresome, it's easy to forget whether or not a particular solution was already attempted. In addition, it's easier to backtrack a specific sequence of steps if they make the problem worse or add new problems. Some also make a note each time the system successfully reboots. If the server doesn't reboot successfully, then the administrator can look at the series of steps that led up to that point.

Getting help

Administrators have a tendency to be somewhat independent and determined to solve server ills single-handedly. If the administrator is solving a problem on a workstation or even a home PC, that approach might be OK. But when the network is at the mercy of a failed server, you can't take too long to resolve the issue. One of the best ways to resolve these problems quickly is to get outside help. You also want to get help if determining the cause of the problem and its solution requires more knowledge than you currently have. It isn't good timing to learn a new technology in the midst of a server disaster. Therefore, you should consult a source with more information. Somebody has probably already solved the problem you're dealing with. There's no need for you to reinvent the wheel on your own. Help is available from a number of sources, such as:

- *Web support.* This is usually the first place to go, because most vendors that really want to support the customer keep searchable white papers and other technical support documents. Using Web support also avoids those annoying automated phone menus and repeating messages about your value as a customer. The Web is also the main source for product updates, a grateful change from the days when administrators had to order and pay for updates to be mailed on a floppy disk.

- *FAQs.* A listing of frequently asked questions (FAQs) can appear on the application, NOS, or hardware installation disk. While you might not read the entire thing, it might be worthwhile at least to scan it to see if any of the issues it raises apply to your situation. A FAQ list might also appear on the vendor Web site.

- *Phone help.* Contact telephone technical support from the vendor of the product with which you're experiencing a problem. Although it seems that phone technical support persons can sometimes be much less knowledgeable overall than you are, they probably have enough specific knowledge about their product at least to offer some suggestions.

- *Newsgroups.* There are two main types of newsgroups. The first is vendor-moderated, which keeps the comments civil and apropos. The second is public and unmoderated, which might be less reverent about the vendor but might also be more truthful. In both cases, you use the newsgroup reader to track a problem to see what the vendor suggests, as well as what other administrators might be able to contribute. These can be excellent sources of peer help. Chances are that somebody else has experienced a troubleshooting problem similar to yours and can offer a solution. The disadvantage of newsgroups is that they often aren't instant solutions. You might post a message today and have to wait several days for an answer, if one returns at all. Similar to the newsgroup is the chat room in which others contribute their knowledge to solving your troubleshooting problem.

- *E-mail.* Many vendors offer e-mail support. Typically, you go to the support section of the vendor's Web site, and if your problem isn't solved there, a link might appear for you to contact technical support via e-mail. Sometimes you receive a response the same day, and sometimes never.

- *Newsletters.* Various e-mail newsletters are excellent sources of late-breaking product news and optimization and troubleshooting tips. Newsletters are distributed on a periodic basis. For example, Red Hat has several newsletter mailing lists available at www.redhat.com/mailing-lists, and an excellent Windows 2000 newsletter can be found at www.trainability.com.

Do it!

E-1: Getting peer help online

Here's how

1 Open your Web browser. You'll research some problems using newsgroups.

2 Go to www.google.com and click on **Groups**. Remember, public newsgroups are informal and unmediated, so there's no guarantee you'll find accurate information, or any, for that matter.

3 In the text box, enter words for a computer hardware or software problem you've had, or just make up a problem. The more specific words you use, the better. Vendor names or exact words and numbers from an error window, for instance, are more likely to produce useful information.

4 Click **Google Search**

5 Read through questions and answers that others have posted.

6 Refine or modify your search, or try some new ones.

7 Answer the following questions and discuss with the class:

What question/problem did you research?

Did you find good idea or leads?

How did you refine or modify your search to get better results?

8 Close the browser.

Unit summary: Troubleshooting and problem determination

Topic A   In this topic you learned that, by properly configuring server hardware and software, you largely avoid server problems. However, sometimes there's no way to predict what a combination of hardware and software interactions will produce, and problems arise. That's when troubleshooting begins. Whether you keep paper or electronic logs, it's crucial that you keep accurate log records so that others can learn the history of the server, avoid past problems, and retain the server's original purpose, unless a compelling and deliberate reason dictates otherwise. The log also records server interaction with other servers, changes relating to applications, updates, and drivers, and the persons performing work on the server. Server problems often occur as a result of obvious, easily overlooked problems, such as physical connections (network cable, network connections), as well as signs that your senses of sight, smell, sound, or touch can detect.

Topic B   In this topic you found that each respective server NOS has accompanying network tools, and third-party vendors also offer a rich assortment from which to choose. Important network diagnostic devices include a multimeter, Fox and Hound (tone generator and locator), and time domain reflectometer (TDR). Besides the hardware tools, you still have the ever-handy TCP/IP utilities, such as Ping and TRACERT. With Ping, you generally ping a device outside the local router's interface, ping the IP address of the local router on your subnet, ping another local host on your local subnet, ping the local IP address, and finally, ping the loopback address (127.x.x.x).

Topic C   In this topic you discovered that remote administration allows you to administer servers regardless of physical location. Several technologies allow this functionality, including **Wake-on LAN** network cards, third-party remote administration software, and remote administration hardware.

Topic D   In this topic you learned that viruses are a common cause of server failure and that you should use antivirus software to detect and clean infected files. There are many symptoms of virus infection, including rapid and comprehensive file deletion. You should also be sure to troubleshoot and replace any malfunctioning FRU, such as power supplies, memory, hard disks, and adapter cards.

Topic E   In this topic, you discovered that you should obtain help from other sources when it's taking too long to resolve the problem or you need more information about a technology. Helpful sources include Web support, FAQs, phone help, newsgroups, e-mail, chat, and newsletters.

Independent practice activity

In this activity, you'ill check a disk with command-line and graphical tools.

1 Choose Start, Run. In the Open text box, enter cmd, if necessary, and click OK. The command window opens. Drag the bottom of the window down so you can see more text at a time.

2 Enter chkdsk /? and then press Return. The question mark switch causes the command to display available switches. Read the descriptions.

3 Enter chkdsk and press Return. This checks the current partition by default. Examine the results.

4 If there are other partitions, check those by adding a drive letter to the command, for instance, chkdsk d:. The command doesn't work on a CD drive.

5 Close the command window.

6 On the desktop, double-click My Computer. Right-click the C: drive and choose Properties. Click the Tools tab and then click the Check Now button. Click Start to scan the disk. Unlike the command-line chkdsk, this doesn't give you any information unless there are problems.

7 Click OK to close the dialog box and click OK again to close the Properties window.

Review questions

1 Which of the following is not a valid reason to keep a server log record?

A To identify and contact persons who have previously worked on the server.

B To keep a history of actions performed on the server.

C To increase the administrator's already heavy workload.

D To track software, updates, hardware, and drivers installed on the server.

2 Why might it be important to record servers interact with one another?

A To see which other servers might be affected if this server stops functioning correctly.

B To redirect all network traffic to the other servers.

C So that you can move the RAID array to the most appropriate alternate.

D To find an alternate for failover purposes.

3 Why should you document the person performing the work?

A To properly assess blame for failed server administration.

B To consult that person for more information about the work they performed on the server.

C To verify that employees are being productive.

D To make sure that only that person works on the server in the future.

4 When you see a server message that is difficult to interpret, you should (choose two):

  A Ignore the message and tackle only the easier messages.

  B Refer to preceding events.

  C Access the vendor web site.

  D Clear the error log to get rid of the message.

5 Error messages are:

  A Always critical, interpret every message

  B Seldom critical, only interpret if the server fails

  C Usually critical, some are innocuous as long as they do not affect performance or server availability

  D Worthy of attention only if other people notice server problems

6 When analyzing server problems, you should ask which of the following? (Select all that apply.)

  A Exactly what happened?

  B Who does it affect?

  C How does it happen?

  D When does it happen?

7 Troubleshooting solutions are often as simple as:

  A Reprogramming the operating system

  B An unplugged or loose cable

  C A failed motherboard

  D The human genome

8 One of the first things you should check when troubleshooting failed hardware is:

  A The logs of the last few administrators who also worked on the server

  B The BIOS version of the system.

  C The warranty

  D The physical connection

9 Bend radius is:

  A A reference to the degree to which a cable can be bent before losing signal integrity

  B A yoga position

  C A reference to the number of token ring hosts permitted in any given ring

  D Accidentally overwriting a recent driver version with an older one

10 What is likely to happen if you break the 5-4-3 rule?

   A Host name resolution problems

   B Excessive collisions and poor connectivity

   C Counting to infinity router loops

   D SCSI ID conflicts

11 An unusual noise in the power supply:

   A Could indicate imminent power supply failure

   B Can be ignored until you smell smoke

   C Indicate a fan problem only, you can continue using the power supply

   D Is not a problem provided the power supply is not also hot to the touch

12 If you suspect a problem with the NIC, how can you diagnose it?

   A Use a packet sniffer to analyze each packet to see if the problem is consistent across all communications.

   B Copy a large file to a network share, and see if a CRC check indicates that the file is corrupt.

   C Use the NIC vendor's diagnosis utility

   D From a command prompt, type Ping 127.0.0.1

13 Besides checking for proper voltages, how else can you use a multimeter?

   A To check network cable amperages

   B To check the RPM speed of a cooling fan

   C To check the resistance on thinnet cable

   D To detect the location of a break in the cable

14 Which tool checks for breaks in the network cable?

   A TDR

   B PDQ

   C DMZ

   D PDC

15 Which of the following are valid loopback IP addresses? (Choose two)

   A 127.0.1.1

   B 172.168.0.1

   C 127.98.67.256

   D 127.254.254.254

16 What can be sent to a WOL host to wake it up?

A A shock packet

B A magic packet

C A sleep packet

D Any Ping packet

17 What do you use to create boot floppies for an OS/2 system?

A The MAKEBOOT utility

B The FORMAT A: /SYS command

C The INITIAL utility

D The Create Utility Diskette utility

18 The system periodically hangs without explanation. What might be a cause of this?

A Failing power supply

B Failing hard disk

C Improper SCSI termination

D Insufficient memory

19 One of the troubleshooting principles discussed is:

A Troubleshoot as many problems at once as possible to save time

B Troubleshoot only one issue at a time

C Apply as many solutions at once as possible

D When you have finished troubleshooting, try to remember everything you did and write it down.

Appendix A

Certification exam objectives map

This appendix covers these additional topics:

A CompTIA Server+ 2005 exam objectives with references to corresponding coverage in this course manual.

Topic A: Comprehensive exam objectives

Explanation

The following table lists all CompTIA Server+ 2005 exam objectives and indicates where each objective is covered in conceptual explanations, activities, or both.

Domain 1.0: General Server Hardware Knowledge

1.1 Know the characteristics, purpose, function, limitations, and performance of the following system bus architectures.

Topic	Conceptual information	Supporting activities
PCI Bus Mastering	Unit 1, Topic B	A-1
PCI Hot swap	Unit 1, Topic A	
PCI-Express	Unit 1, Topic A	A-1
PCI-X	Unit 1, Topic A	
Hierarchical PCI Bus	Unit 1, Topic A	A-1
Peer PCI Bus	Unit 1, Topic A	
I2O – Intelligent Input-Output	Unit 1, Topic A	
Hot Plug PCI	Unit 1, Topic A	
PCI Expansion Slots	Unit 1, Topic A	A-1
PCI Interrupts	Unit 1, Topic A	
EISA	Unit 1, Topic A	

1.2 Know the characteristics of adapter fault tolerance.

Topic	Conceptual information	Supporting activities
adapter load balancing	Unit 9, Topic C	C-1
adapter teaming	Unit 9, Topic C	C-1

1.3 Know the basic purpose and function of the following types of servers.

Topic	Conceptual information	Supporting activities
Server types include:		
Server as a Gateway	Unit 7, Topic C	
Server as a Router	Unit 7, Topic C	C-1
Server as a Bridge	Unit 7, Topic C	
Firewall Server	Unit 7, Topic C	
Proxy Server	Unit 7, Topic C	
Database Server	Unit 7, Topic C	
Client/Server	Unit 7, Topic A	
Application Server	Unit 7, Topic C	
Mail Server	Unit 7, Topic B	
FTP Server	Unit 7, Topic B	
SNA Server	Unit 7, Topic B	
RAS Server	Unit 7, Topic B	B-2
File and Print Server	Unit 7, Topic C	C-1
Fax Server	Unit 7, Topic B	B-3
DNS Server	Unit 7, Topic A	A-2
WINS Server	Unit 7, Topic A	
DHCP Server	Unit 7, Topic A	A-1, A-2
Web Server	Unit 7, Topic B	B-3
Hardware types, including module types, basic spec, limitations and requirements (especially power and cooling):		
Blade servers	Unit 4, Topic B	
Tower servers	Unit 4, Topic B	
Rack-mount servers	Unit 4, Topic B	B-1, B-2

1.4 Know the function of the following application server models.

Topic	Conceptual information	Supporting activities
Dedicated Application	Unit 7, Topic C	C-1
Distributed Application	Unit 7, Topic C	
Peer to peer application	Unit 7, Topic C	

1.5 Know the characteristics of the following types of memory and server memory requirements.

Topic	Conceptual information	Supporting activities
Memory types:		
EDO	Unit 1, Topic C	
SDRAM	Unit 1, Topic C	
DDR	Unit 1, Topic C	
DDR-2	Unit 1, Topic C	
RAMBUS	Unit 1, Topic C	
Memory Interleaving	Unit 1, Topic C	
ECC vs. Non ECC vs. Extended ECC	Unit 1, Topic C	
Unbuffered vs. buffered vs. registered	Unit 1, Topic C	
Hardware compatibility list	Unit 1, Topic B	B-2
Memory caching	Unit 1, Topic B	B-1

1.6 Know the differences between different SCSI solutions, their advantages, and their specifications.

Topic	Conceptual information	Supporting activities
SCSI-1, 2, & 3	Unit 2, Topic C	C-1
SCSI bus width (narrow and wide)	Unit 2, Topic D	
SCSI bus speed (Fast and Ultra, Ultra Wide, Ultra 2, Ultra 160, Ultra 320, iSCSI, SAS)	Unit 2, Topic C	C-1
SCSI connectors, cables, termination (passive, active, multi-mode)	Unit 2, Topic D	
SCSI ID's and LUN's	Unit 2, Topic D	D-1
Single-ended devices	Unit 2, Topic D	
Low voltage differential (LVD)	Unit 2, Topic D	D-1
High voltage differential (HVD)	Unit 2, Topic D	D-1
BUS lengths	Unit 2, Topic D	
Multi-tasking	Unit 2, Topic D	
Multi-threading	Unit 2, Topic D	
Disconnect and reconnect	Unit 2, Topic D	

1.7 Know the differences between different ATA (IDE) solutions, their advantages, limitations, and specifications

Topic	Conceptual information	Supporting activities
ATA 33	Unit 2, Topic B	
ATA 66	Unit 2, Topic B	
ATA 100	Unit 2, Topic B	B-1
ATA 133	Unit 2, Topic B	B-1
SATA (Serial ATA)	Unit 2, Topic B	B-1
SATA II (SATA II v1.2)	Unit 2, Topic B	B-1
Ultra DMA	Unit 2, Topic B	
Cabling and connectors	Unit 2, Topic B	
Master/slave/cable select (CSEL)	Unit 2, Topic B	
Jumper settings	Unit 2, Topic B	

1.8 Know the features and benefits of fibre channel hardware

Topic	Conceptual information	Supporting activities
Storage arrays	Unit 2, Topic E	E-1
Disk drives	Unit 2, Topic E	
Adapters	Unit 2, Topic E	
Cables, connectors, GBIC's, SFP GBIC's	Unit 2, Topic E	
Single- and Multi-mode	Unit 2, Topic E	
1 Gbit, 2 Gbit, 10 Gbit	Unit 2, Topic E	
Bus lengths	Unit 2, Topic E	E-1
Point-to-point vs. switched vs. LOOP	Unit 2, Topic E	

1.9 Know the features and benefits of iSCSI and FCIP

Topic	Conceptual information	Supporting activities
Storage arrays	Unit 2, Topic E	E-1
Adapters	Unit 2, Topic E	
Cables, connectors	Unit 2, Topic E	
1 Gbit, 2 Gbit, 10 Gbit	Unit 2, Topic E	
Bus lengths	Unit 2, Topic E	E-1

1.10 Know the features and capabilities of the following RAID levels, when they apply, and how each relates to fault tolerance and high availability (non-proprietary).

Topic	Conceptual information	Supporting activities
RAID 0	Unit 2, Topic F	
RAID 1	Unit 2, Topic F	
RAID 3	Unit 2, Topic F	
RAID 5	Unit 2, Topic F	
RAID 5+1	Unit 2, Topic F	
RAID 0+1	Unit 2, Topic F	
RAID 0+5	Unit 2, Topic F	
RAID 1+0	Unit 2, Topic F	
RAID 5+0	Unit 2, Topic F	
RADIOS	Unit 2, Topic F	
Zero Channel RAID	Unit 2, Topic F	
Differences between hardware RAID and software RAID and the advantages of one over the other.	Unit 2, Topic F	F-1

1.11 Know the characteristics of hot swap drives and hot plug boards.

Topic	Conceptual information
All	Unit 1, Topic A

1.12 Know the features, advantages, and disadvantages of multiprocessing

Topic	Conceptual information
All	Unit 1, Topic B

1.13 Know the attributes, purpose, function, and advantages of clustering, scalability, high availability, and fault tolerance.

Topic	Conceptual information	Supporting activities
All	Unit 2, Topic F	
	Unit 8, Topic C	C-1
	Unit 9, Topic C	C-1

1.14 Understand the processor subsystem of a server

Topic	Conceptual information	Supporting activities
Multiprocessing systems		
What they are	Unit 1, Topic B	
How they differ from dual-processor systems	Unit 1, Topic B	
64-bit server environments		
What they are	Unit 1, Topic B	B-1
Why and when they are important	Unit 1, Topic B	B-1
What are the different architectures	Unit 1, Topic B	B-1

1.15 Know the basic specifications of and differences between SAN and NAS

Topic	Conceptual information
Block and file	Unit 2, Topic E

Domain 2.0: Planning Installation

2.1 Conduct pre-installation planning activities

Topic	Conceptual information	Supporting activities
Activities include:		
Plan the installation	Unit 4, Topic A Unit 4, Topic B	A-1 B-1
Verify the installation plan	Unit 4, Topic A Unit 4, Topic B	
Verify hardware compatibility with the operating system	Unit 4, Topic A	
Verify power sources, space, UPS and network availability	Unit 4, Topic A	A-1, A-2
Verify network protocols, naming conventions, domain names	Unit 6, Topic A Unit 7, Topic A	A-2, A-3 A-2
Verify that all correct components and cables have been delivered	Unit 4, Topic A	
Supporting knowledge includes:		
How to get drivers and BIOS updates	Unit 5, Topic C	C-1
Cables and connectors required	Unit 4, Topic A	
UPS sizes and types	Unit 4, Topic A	A-2
Server power requirements	Unit 4, Topic A	A-1, A-2
Power issues (stability, spikes, etc.)	Unit 4, Topic B	
BTU's for the UPS and associated equipment	Unit 4, Topic A	A-1, A-2
Server storage issues (rack requirements, rack sizes)	Unit 4, Topic B	B-1, B-2
Uses of common server types (desk server, rack mount server, blade server) and the pros and cons of each	Unit 4, Topic B	

2.2 Install hardware using best practices

Topic		Conceptual information	Supporting activities
Hardware includes:	Boards	Unit 1, Topic A	
	Drives	Unit 2, Topic B Unit 2, Topic C	B-1 C-1, D-1
	Processors and power modules	Unit 1, Topic B Unit 5, Topic B Unit 5, Topic C	B-1 B-1
	Memory	Unit 1, Topic C Unit 5, Topic B	C-1 B-2
	Internal cable	Unit 5, Topic B	
	Internal fans	Unit 5, Topic B	
Installation activities include:			
Mount the rack installation (if appropriate)		Unit 4, Topic B	B-1
Cut and crimp the network cabling		Unit 4, Topic C	C-1
Install UPS (depending on environment)		Unit 4, Topic A	A-2
Verify the SCSI ID configuration and termination		Unit 2, Topic D	D-1
Install external devices (e.g. keyboards, monitors, subsystems, modem rack, etc.)		Unit 6, Topic A	B-2
Verify power-on via power-on sequence		Unit 1, Topic D	
Supporting knowledge includes:			
Physical infrastructure requirements (e.g. proper layout of equipment in the rack, adequate airflow, etc.)		Unit 4, Topic B	B-1
SCSI cabling, termination, and hot plug configuration		Unit 2, Topic C Unit 2, Topic D	D-1
Basic understanding of network cabling and connector types		Unit 4, Topic C	C-1
Cable management		Unit 4, Topic B	
KVM management		Unit 4, Topic B	B-2
Rack Mount security		Unit 4, Topic B	
Characteristics of common network interface protocols			
- Ethernet		Unit 6, Topic A	A-2
- Fast Ethernet		Unit 6, Topic A	A-2
- Gigabit Ethernet		Unit 6, Topic A	

2.3 Develop the server management plan (in-band and out-of-band management).

Topic	Conceptual information	Supporting activities
All	Unit 10, Topic C	C-1

Domain 3.0: Configuration

3.1 Check/upgrade BIOS/firmware levels (system board, RAID controller, hard drive, etc.)

Topic	Conceptual information	Supporting activities
All	Unit 5, Topic C Unit 10, Topic D	C-1

3.2 Configure RAID

Topic	Conceptual information
Activities include:	
Use manufacturer's tool to configure the array	Unit 2, Topic F
Testing (simulate failure)	Unit 2, Topic F
Supporting knowledge includes:	Unit 2, Topic F
Familiarity with OCE	Unit 2, Topic F
Characteristics of fail over and spare drive types (i.e. cold, hot, warm, dedicated, and global)	Unit 8, Topic C
Characteristics, purpose, and function of RAID cache including when to turn off write caching	Unit 2, Topic F
How to calculate storage capacity	Unit 2, Topic F
Functionality of RAID controller battery	Unit 2, Topic F

3.3 Install NOS

Topic	Conceptual information	Supporting activities
All	Unit 6, All Topics	B-1, C-1, D-1, E-1

3.4 Configure external peripherals

Topic	Conceptual information	Supporting activities
Peripherals include:		
UPS	Unit 4, Topic A	A-2
Backup device	Unit 8, Topic A	A-1
Data storage subsystems	Unit 2, Topic E Unit 8, Topic A	A-1
Supporting knowledge includes:		
Proper layout of equipment	Unit 4, Topic A	
Requirements of the server installation environment (UPS, network, availability, space, power)	Unit 4, Topic A	A-1, A-2
SCSI cabling and termination	Unit 2, Topic D	D-1
Fibre channel cabling	Unit 2, Topic E	E-1
Know available cable types for peripheral devices		
- Firewire	Unit 1, Topic A	
- USB	Unit 1, Topic A	
- Serial ATA (SATA)	Unit 1, Topic A	

3.5 Install NOS and driver updates to design specifications

Topic	Conceptual information	Supporting activities
Activities include:		
Obtain update	Unit 6, Topic E	
Ensure that there is a backup and recovery plan	Unit 6, Topic E	
Make sure that the old drivers are available for reinstallation	Unit 6, Topic E	
Lab testing	Unit 6, Topic E	
Installation	Unit 6, Topic E	
Testing	Unit 6, Topic E	
Supporting knowledge includes:		
Know how to obtain OS updates	Unit 6, Topic E	
Why updates might be needed	Unit 6, Topic E	E-3
How updates can be used	Unit 6, Topic E	E-3
How to decide whether an update is necessary	Unit 6, Topic E	E-3

3.6 Install service tools

Topic	Conceptual information	Supporting activities
Service tools include:		
SNMP	Unit 7, Topic C Unit 8, Topic C	C-1
Backup software	Unit 8, Topic B	B-1
System monitoring agents	Unit 8, Topic C	C-1
Event logs	Unit 8, Topic C Unit 10, Topic A	A-1
Supporting knowledge includes:		
Identity, purpose, and function of service tools	Unit 7, Topic C Unit 8, Topic C	C-1 C-1
How to set up SNMP	Unit 8, Topic C	
How system monitoring software and MIB's are implemented on hardware	Unit 7, Topic C Unit 8, Topic C	
Purpose of event logs	Unit 8, Topic B Unit 10, Topic A	

3.7 Perform server baseline

Topic	Conceptual information	Supporting activities
Supporting knowledge includes:		
Purpose and types of baseline		
- Processor utilization	Unit 9, Topic C	C-1
- Page file	Unit 9, Topic C	
- Disk utilization	Unit 9, Topic C	C-1
- Memory utilization	Unit 9, Topic C	C-1
- Network utilization	Unit 9, Topic C	
Conditions under which different baselines might be useful	Unit 9, Topic B	
When baselines should be updated	Unit 9, Topic B	

3.8 Document the configuration

Topic	Subtopic	Conceptual information	Supporting activities
Supporting knowledge includes:			
Document contents:			
	What components are in the box	Unit 10, Topic A	
	Where components are located in the box	Unit 10, Topic A	A-1
	What updates have been applied	Unit 10, Topic A	
	Warranty information	Unit 10, Topic A	
	Baseline	Unit 9, Topic B	B-1
	Server configuration information (e.g. BIOS information, RAID levels used, what drives were put into what arrays, server network information)	Unit 9, Topic C	
	Install date	Unit 9, Topic C	

3.9 Implement the server management plan (OS-dependent and OS-independent components)

Topic	Conceptual information	Supporting activities
Plans typically include:		
Server management software installation	Unit 6, Topic E	
Availability	Unit 6, Topic E	
Server change management requirements	Unit 6, Topic E	
Security plan	Unit 7, Topic B	
Remote management hardware	Unit 10, Topic C	
Supporting knowledge includes:		
Purpose and function of server management tools	Unit 6, Topic E Unit 10, Topic C	C-1

Domain 4: Upgrading

4.1 Perform backup

Topic	Conceptual information
Activities include:	
Update the ERD/recover disk (if applicable)	Unit 8, Topic B
Verify backup	Unit 8, Topic B
Supporting knowledge includes:	
When full backups might be necessary	Unit 8, Topic B
How to select the appropriate type of backup	
- Differential	Unit 8, Topic B
- Appended	Unit 8, Topic B
- Copy	Unit 8, Topic B
- Full	Unit 8, Topic B

4.2 Add processors

Topic	Conceptual information	Supporting activities
Activities include:		
On single processor upgrade, verify compatibility	Unit 5, Topic B	
Verify N+1 stepping	Unit 5, Topic B	
Verify speed and cache matching	Unit 5, Topic B	
Perform BIOS upgrade	Unit 5, Topic B Unit 5, Topic C	
Perform OS upgrade to support multiprocessors	Unit 5, Topic B	B-1
Ensure proper ventilation	Unit 5, Topic B Unit 8, Topic C	B-1
Perform upgrade checklist, including:		
Locate/obtain latest drivers, OS updates, software, etc.	Unit 6, Topic E	E-3
Review FAQ's, instruction, facts and issues	Unit 5, Topic A Unit 6, Topic E	
Test and pilot	Unit 5, Topic A Unit 6, Topic E	A-1
Schedule downtime	Unit 5, Topic A	

Objective 4.2 continues on next page...

4.2, continued

Topic	Conceptual information	Supporting activities
Activities include:		
Implement ESD best practices	Unit 5, Topic B	B-1
Confirm that upgrade has been recognized	Unit 1, Topic D Unit 5, Topic A	D-1
Review and baseline	Unit 5, Topic A Unit 9, Topic B	B-1
Document upgrade	Unit 10, Topic A	A-1
Supporting knowledge includes:		
What it means to verify stepping	Unit 5, Topic B	

4.3 Add hard drives

Topic	Conceptual information	Supporting activities
Activities include:		
Verify that the drives are the appropriate type	Unit 2, Topic A	A-1
Confirm SCSI termination and cabling	Unit 2, Topic D	D-1
For ATA/IDE drives, confirm cabling, master/slave and potential cross-brand compatibility	Unit 5, Topic B	
Verify connections on serial ATA drives	Unit 2, Topic B	
Upgrade mass storage	Unit 4, Topic B	
Make sure RAID controller can support additions	Unit 2, Topic F	
Add drives to array	Unit 2, Topic F	
Replace existing drives	Unit 2, Topic F	
Integrate into storage solution and make it available to the operating system	Unit 2, Topic F	

4.3, continued

Topic	Conceptual information	Supporting activities
Perform upgrade checklist, including:		
Locate/obtain latest drivers, OS updates, software, etc.	Unit 6, Topic E	E-3
Review FAQ's, instruction, facts and issues	Unit 5, Topic A Unit 6, Topic E	
Test and pilot	Unit 5, Topic A Unit 6, Topic E	A-1
Schedule downtime	Unit 5, Topic A	
Implement ESD best practices	Unit 5, Topic B	B-1
Confirm that the upgrade has been recognized	Unit 1, Topic D Unit 5, Topic A	D-1
Review and baseline	Unit 5, Topic A Unit 9, Topic B	B-1
Document upgrade	Unit 10, Topic A	A-1
Supporting knowledge includes:		
Available types of hard drive array additions and when they are appropriate	Unit 2, Topic F	
Expansions	Unit 4, Topic B	
Extensions	Unit 4, Topic B	
What "hot swappable" means	Unit 2, Topic F	
Difference between a RAID partition and an OS partition	Unit 2, Topic A Unit 2, Topic F	
Importance and use of maintenance logs and service logs (documentation)	Unit 10, Topic A	A-1

4.4 Increase memory

Topic	Conceptual information	Supporting activities
Activities include:		
Verify hardware and OS support for capacity increase	Unit 1, Topic C Unit 5, Topic A	C-1 A-1
Verify memory is on hardware/vendor comptibility list	Unit 1, Topic C Unit 5, Topic B	C-1
Verify memory compatibility		
Speed	Unit 5, Topic B	B-2
Brand	Unit 5, Topic B	B-2
Capacity	Unit 5, Topic B	B-2
EDO	Unit 5, Topic C	
DDR	Unit 5, Topic C	
RAMBUS	Unit 5, Topic C	
ECC/non-ECC	Unit 5, Topic C	
SDRAM/RDRAM	Unit 5, Topic C	
Perform upgrade checklist including:		
Locate/obtain latest drivers, OS updates, software, etc.	Unit 6, Topic E	E-3
Review FAQ's, instruction, facts and issues	Unit 5, Topic A Unit 6, Topic E	
Test and pilot	Unit 5, Topic A Unit 6, Topic E	A-1
Schedule downtime	Unit 5, Topic A	
Implement ESD best practices	Unit 5, Topic B	B-1
Confirm that the upgrade has been recognized	Unit 1, Topic D Unit 5, Topic A	D-1
Review and baseline	Unit 5, Topic A Unit 9, Topic B	B-1
Document upgrade	Unit 10, Topic A	A-1
Verify that server and OS recognize the added memory	Unit 1, Topic D Unit 5, Topic C	D-1
Perform server optimization to make use of the additional RAM (BIOS and OS level)	Unit 5, Topic C	

4.4, continued

Topic	Conceptual information	Supporting activities
Supporting knowledge includes:		
Number of pins on each type of memory	Unit 1, Topic C	
How servers deal with memory pairings	Unit 1, Topic C	
Importance and use of maintenance logs and service logs (documentation)	Unit 10, Topic A	A-1

4.5 Upgrade BIOS/firmware

Topic	Conceptual information	Supporting activities
Activities include:		
Perform upgrade checklist including:		
Locate/obtain latest drivers, OS updates, software, etc.	Unit 6, Topic E	E-3
Review FAQ's, instruction, facts and issues	Unit 5, Topic A Unit 6, Topic E	
Test and pilot	Unit 5, Topic A Unit 6, Topic E	A-1
Schedule downtime	Unit 5, Topic A	
Implement ESD best practices	Unit 5, Topic B	B-1
Confirm that the upgrade has been recognized	Unit 1, Topic D Unit 5, Topic A	D-1
Review and baseline	Unit 5, Topic A Unit 9, Topic B	B-1
Document upgrade	Unit 10, Topic A	A-1
Supporting knowledge includes:	Unit 5, Topic C	
When the BIOS/firmware upgrades should be performed	Unit 5, Topic C	
How to obtain the latest firmware	Unit 5, Topic C	
Be aware the most hardware companies include self-installing installation applications for their components	Unit 5, Topic C	

Objective 4.5 continues on following page…

4.5, continued

Topic	Conceptual information	Supporting activities
Supporting knowledge includes:	Unit 5, Topic C	
Implications of a failed firmware upgrade		
Multi-BIOS systems	Unit 5, Topic C	
Firmware recover options available	Unit 5, Topic C	
Backup flashing (when applicable)	Unit 5, Topic C	
Failed flash implies inoperable device	Unit 5, Topic C	
Issues surrounding multi-BIOS systems (how to properly upgrade, etc.)	Unit 5, Topic C	
Need to follow manufacturers flash instructions	Unit 5, Topic C	C-1
Importance and use of maintenance logs and service logs (documentation)	Unit 10, Topic A	A-1

4.6 Upgrade adapters (e.g. NIC's, SCSI cards, RAID, etc)

Topic	Conceptual information	Supporting activities
Activities include:		
Perform backup	Unit 8, Topic A	
Perform upgrade checklist including:		
Locate/obtain latest drivers, OS updates, software, etc.	Unit 6, Topic E	E-3
Review FAQ's, instruction, facts and issues	Unit 5, Topic A Unit 6, Topic E	
Test and pilot	Unit 5, Topic A Unit 6, Topic E	A-1
Schedule downtime	Unit 5, Topic A	
Implement ESD best practices	Unit 5, Topic B	B-1
Confirm that the upgrade has been recognized	Unit 1, Topic D Unit 5, Topic A	D-1
Review and baseline	Unit 5, Topic A Unit 9, Topic B	B-1
Document upgrade	Unit 10, Topic A	A-1

4.6, continued

Topic	Conceptual information	Supporting activities
Supporting knowledge includes		
Available bus types		
PCI-X	Unit 1, Topic A	
PCI-Express	Unit 1, Topic A	A-1
Hot swap PCI	Unit 1, Topic A	
PCI (bus architecture, bus speed)	Unit 1, Topic A	A-1
EISA	Unit 1, Topic A	
Implementation of hot swappable PCI in servers	Unit 1, Topic A	
Implications on the array of changing RAID controller types	Unit 2, Topic F	
Characteristics of SCSI		
Levels	Unit 2, Topic C	C-1
Cabling	Unit 2, Topic D	
Termination	Unit 2, Topic D	D-1
Signaling	Unit 2, Topic D	D-1
Importance and use of Maintenance logs and service logs (documentation)	Unit 10, Topic A	A-1

4.7 Upgrade peripheral devices, internal and external. Verify appropriate system resources (e.g. expansion slots, IRQ, DMA, etc.)

Topic	Conceptual information	Supporting activities
Peripheral devices include:		
Disk drives	Unit 2, Topic A	A-1, A-2
Backup devices	Unit 8, Topic A	A-1
Optical devices	Unit 8, Topic A	
KVM devices	Unit 4, Topic B	B-2
Resources include:		
Expansion slots	Unit 1, Topic A	
IRQ	Unit 5, Topic A	A-1
DMA	Unit 5, Topic A	
SCSI ID's	Unit 2, Topic D	D-1
Expansion cards	Unit 1, Topic A	
Activities include:		
Perform upgrade checklist including:		
Locate/obtain latest drivers, OS updates, software, etc.	Unit 6, Topic E	E-3
Review FAQ's, instruction, facts and issues	Unit 5, Topic A Unit 6, Topic E	
Test and pilot	Unit 5, Topic A Unit 6, Topic E	A-1
Schedule downtime	Unit 5, Topic A	
Implement ESD best practices	Unit 5, Topic B	B-1
Confirm that the upgrade has been recognized	Unit 1, Topic D Unit 5, Topic A	D-1
Review and baseline	Unit 5, Topic A Unit 9, Topic B	B-1
Document upgrade	Unit 10, Topic A	A-1

4.7, continued

Topic	Conceptual information	Supporting activities
Supporting knowledge includes:		
Potential effects on performance of adding devices	Unit 9, Topic C	
Importance and use of Maintenance logs and service logs (documentation)	Unit 10, Topic A	A-1
Validation via hardware compatibility list, tips, documentation, and FAQ's	Unit 1, Topic B Unit 4, Topic A Unit 6, Topic D, E	B-1

4.8 Upgrade system monitoring agents

Topic	Conceptual information	Supporting activities
Activities include:		
Perform upgrade checklist including:		
Locate/obtain latest drivers, OS updates, software, etc.	Unit 6, Topic E	E-3
Review FAQ's, instruction, facts and issues	Unit 5, Topic A Unit 6, Topic E	
Test and pilot	Unit 5, Topic A Unit 6, Topic E	A-1
Schedule downtime	Unit 5, Topic A	
Implement ESD best practices	Unit 5, Topic B	B-1
Confirm that the upgrade has been recognized	Unit 1, Topic D Unit 5, Topic A	D-1
Review and baseline	Unit 5, Topic A Unit 9, Topic B	B-1
Document upgrade	Unit 10, Topic A	A-1
Supporting knowledge includes		
Purpose and function of the following management protocols:		
- SNMP	Unit 7, Topic C	C-1
- DMI	Unit 7, Topic C	
- IPMI 1.5 and 2.0	Unit 7, Topic C	
Function and monitoring agents	Unit 7, Topic C	
Dependencies between SNMP and MIB's	Unit 7, Topic C	
Importance/use of maintenance logs and service logs (documentation)	Unit 10, Topic A	A-1

4.9 Upgrade service tools (e.g. diagnostic tools, EISA configuration, diagnostic partition, SSU, etc.)

Topic	Conceptual information	Supporting activities
Service tools include:		
RAID utility	Unit 2, Topic F	
SCSI utility	Unit 2, Topic C	
System configuration utility	Unit 5, Topic B	
External storage utility	Unit 2, Topic A Unit 2, Topic A	
Activities include:		
Perform upgrade checklist including:		
Locate/obtain latest drivers, OS updates, software, etc.	Unit 6, Topic E	E-3
Review FAQ's, instruction, facts and issues	Unit 5, Topic A Unit 6, Topic E	
Test and pilot	Unit 5, Topic A Unit 6, Topic E	A-1
Schedule downtime	Unit 5, Topic A	
Implement ESD best practices	Unit 5, Topic B	B-1
Confirm that the upgrade has been recognized	Unit 1, Topic D Unit 5, Topic A	D-1
Review and baseline	Unit 5, Topic A Unit 9, Topic B	B-1
Document upgrade	Unit 10, Topic A	
Supporting knowledge includes:		
Most utilities are vendor specific	Unit 2, Topic A	
Importance and use of maintenance logs and service logs (documentation)	Unit 10, Topic A	A-1

4.10 Upgrade UPS

Topic	Conceptual information	Supporting activities
Activities include:		
Firmware updates	Unit 5, Topic C	
Battery replacement	Unit 5, Topic C	
Battery disposal	Unit 5, Topic C	
Determine physical requirements	Unit 5, Topic C	
Determine load requirements	Unit 5, Topic C	
Verify whether UPS supports hot swap replacement	Unit 5, Topic C	C-1
Perform upgrade checklist including:		
Locate/obtain latest drivers, OS updates, software, etc.	Unit 6, Topic E	E-3
Review FAQ's, instruction, facts and issues	Unit 5, Topic A Unit 6, Topic E	
Test and pilot	Unit 5, Topic A Unit 6, Topic E	A-1
Schedule downtime	Unit 5, Topic A	
Implement ESD best practices	Unit 5, Topic B	B-1
Confirm that the upgrade has been recognized	Unit 1, Topic D Unit 5, Topic A	D-1
Review and baseline	Unit 5, Topic A Unit 9, Topic B	B-1
Document upgrade	Unit 10, Topic A	A-1
Supporting knowledge includes:		
Some UPS's support shot swap battery replacement	Unit 4, Topic A	A-2
Some UPS's support smart cabling	Unit 5, Topic C	
What can be upgraded		
UPS MIB's	Unit 5, Topic C	
Management card	Unit 5, Topic C	
Management software	Unit 5, Topic C	
Importance and use of maintenance logs and service logs (documentation)	Unit 10, Topic A	A-1

Domain 5.0: Proactive Maintenance

5.1 Perform regular backup

Topic	Conceptual information	Supporting activities
Activities include:		
Update the ERD/recovery disk (if applicable)	Unit 8, Topic B	
Verify backup	Unit 8, Topic B	
Supporting knowledge includes:	Unit 8, Topic B	
When full backups might be necessary	Unit 5, Topic A Unit 8, Topic B	A-1
How to select the appropriate type of backup		
Differential	Unit 8, Topic B	B-1
Appended	Unit 8, Topic B	
Copy	Unit 8, Topic B	
Full	Unit 8, Topic B	
Importance and use of maintenance logs and service logs (documentation)	Unit 10, Topic A	

5.2 Create baseline and compare performance

Topic	Conceptual information	Supporting activities
Activities include:		
Regular comparisons to the original baseline	Unit 5, Topic A Unit 9, Topic B	B-1
Supporting knowledge includes:		
Importance and use of maintenance logs and service logs (documentation)	Unit 10, Topic A	A-1

5.3 Adjust SNMP thresholds

Topic	Conceptual information
All	Unit 9, Topic A

5.4 Perform physical housekeeping

Topic	Conceptual information
Activities include:	
Periodic checks for dust buildup	Unit 8, Topic C
Cable management	Unit 4, Topic B

5.5 Monitor, maintain and follow the server management and service plan

Topic	Conceptual information
Activities include:	
Follow the changes management protocol	Unit 7, Topic C

Domain 6.0: Environment

6.1 Recognize and report of physical security issues

Topic	Conceptual information
Activities include:	
Limit access to the server room and backup tapes	Unit 3, Topic B
Ensure physical locks exist on doors	Unit 3, Topic B
Establish anti-theft devices for hardware (lock server racks)	Unit 3, Topic B
Supporting knowledge includes:	
Fundamentals of server security (importance of physically securing a server)	Unit 3, Topic B

6.2 Recognize and report on server room environment issues

Topic	Conceptual information	Supporting activities
Issues include:		
Temperature	Unit 3, Topic A	A-2
Humidity	Unit 3, Topic A	A-2
ESD	Unit 3, Topic A Unit 5, Topic B	B-1
Power surges	Unit 3, Topic A	A-3
Back-up generator	Unit 3, Topic A	A-3
Fire suppression	Unit 3, Topic B	B-1
Flood consideration	Unit 3, Topic B	

Domain 7.0: Troubleshooting and Problem Determination

7.1 Perform problem determination

Topic	Conceptual information	Supporting activities
Activities include:		
Problem isolation		
Determine whether the problem is hardware or software related	Unit 10, Topic A Unit 10, Topic D	D-1
Use questioning techniques to determine what, how, when	Unit 10, Topic A Unit 10, Topic D	A-1 D-1
Identify contact(s) responsible for problem resolution	Unit 10, Topic A	A-1
Use senses to observe problem (e.g. smell of smoke, observation of unhooked cable, etc.)	Unit 10, Topic A	
Bringing it down to base	Unit 10, Topic A	
Removing one component at a time	Unit 10, Topic A	

7.2 Use diagnostic hardware and software tools and utilities

Topic	Conceptual information	Supporting activities
Activities include:		
Perform shutdown across the following OS's: Microsoft Windows NT/2000/2003, Novell Netware, UNIX, Linux	Unit 6, All Topics	
Select the appropriate tool	Unit 10, Topic B	B-1
Use the selected tool effectively	Unit 10, Topic B	B-1
Replace defective hardware components as appropriate	Unit 10, Topic D	
Identify defective FRU's and replace with correct part	Unit 10, Topic D	
Interpret error logs, operating system errors, health logs, and critical events	Unit 10, Topic A Unit 10, Topic D	A-1 D-1
Use documentation from previous technician successfully	Unit 10, Topic A Unit 10, Topic C	A-1
Locate and effectively use hot tips (e.g. fixes, OS updates, E-support, web pages, CD's)	Unit 10, Topic D	
Gather resources to get problem solved		
Identify situations requiring call for assistance	Unit 10, Topic D	
Acquire appropriate documentation	Unit 10, Topic D	
Supporting knowledge includes:		
Know common diagnostic tools	Unit 10, Topic B	B-1
PING	Unit 10, Topic A	
IPCONFIG	Unit 10, Topic A	
TRACEROUTE	Unit 10, Topic B	
FDISK	Unit 2, Topic A	
Basic hard disk tools	Unit 2, Topic A Unit 10, Topic B	A-1
TELNET	Unit 10, Topic C	
NOS shutdown procedures		
Novell Netware	Unit 6, Topic B	
Microsoft Windows NT/2000/2003	Unit 6, Topic D Unit 6, Topic E	E-2
UNIX/Linux	Unit 6, Topic C	
Importance and use on maintenance logs and service logs (docs)	Unit 10, Topic A	A-1

7.3 Identify bottlenecks

Topic	Conceptual information	Supporting activities
Bottlenecks include:		
Processor	Unit 9, Topic C	
Bus transfer	Unit 9, Topic C	
I/O	Unit 9, Topic C	C-1
Disk I/O	Unit 9, Topic C	C-1
Network I/O	Unit 9, Topic C	
Memory	Unit 9, Topic C	C-1
Activities include:		
Run performance tool and compare against baseline	Unit 9, Topic B	B-1
Supporting knowledge includes:		
How to run performance tools and compare against baseline		
Processor utilization	Unit 9, Topic C	
Page file	Unit 9, Topic C	
Disk utilization	Unit 9, Topic C	C-1
Memory utilization	Unit 9, Topic C	C-1
Network utilization	Unit 9, Topic C	

Domain 8.0: Disaster Recovery

8.1 Read and follow the disaster recover plan

Topic	Conceptual information	Supporting activities
Activities include:		
Find, read and implement the recover plan	Unit 8, Topic D	
Confirm and use off site storage for backup	Unit 8, Topic B Unit 8, Topic D	D-1
Participate in testing of disaster recover	Unit 8, Topic D	
Supporting knowledge includes:		
The need for redundancy (e.g. hard drives, power supplies, fans, NIC's, processors, UPS)	Unit 8, Topic C	C-1
Ability to read and comprehend a disaster recovery plan	Unit 8, Topic D	D-1
Types of backup hardware and media		
DAT	Unit 8, Topic A	A-1
SDAT	Unit 8, Topic A	
DLT	Unit 8, Topic A	
Super DLT	Unit 8, Topic A	
Optical backup device	Unit 8, Topic A	A-1
AIT	Unit 8, Topic A	
LTO	Unit 8, Topic A	
Disk to disk	Unit 8, Topic A	
Libraries vs. stand-alones	Unit 8, Topic A	
Identify types of backup and restoration schemes		
Grandfather schemes	Unit 8, Topic B	B-1
Differential and incremental backups	Unit 8, Topic B	
Concept of hot, cold, and warm sites	Unit 8, Topic D	D-1

Course summary

This summary contains information to help you bring the course to a successful conclusion. Using this information, you'll be able to:

A Use the summary text to reinforce what you've learned in class.

B Determine the next courses in this series, if any, as well as any other resources that might help you continue to learn about server and network administration.

Topic A: Course summary

Use the following summary text to reinforce what you've learned in class.

Unit summaries

Unit 1

In this unit, you identified various **motherboard buses** and described how **clock frequency** affects performance. You also learned to identify common server processors and various types of memory, to configure the **BIOS**, what happens during **POST**, and to identify common server configuration items.

Unit 2

In this unit, you identified basic physical hard disk components, compared **physical** and **logical drives**, and identified major file systems. Next, you identified characteristics of **IDE** and **SCSI** interfaces, and learned about configuring IDE and SCSI cabling and connectors. Finally, you examined **Fibre Channel** technology, storage area networking, and various types of **RAID** configuration.

Unit 3

In this unit, you learned about optimum **server placement** and diagramming server plans. Then, you learned about planning the server environment, **physical site readiness**, and implementing sound physical server security practices.

Unit 4

In this unit, you identified features of server power supply and found how to implement an **uninterruptible power supply (UPS)** correctly. You also discovered that an administrator must plan the placement of equipment in a **server rack** and properly configure a keyboard, video, mouse (**KVM**) console to control multiple servers.

Unit 5

In this unit, you learned how to prepare for a server upgrade, verify availability of system resources, and adequately **test** and **pilot** the server upgrade. You also focused on upgrading the processor, memory, the BIOS, power supply, UPS, and adapters. Finally, you learned about **thinnet**, **shielded twisted-pair**, **unshielded twisted-pair**, and **fiber optic cable** characteristics, as well as **network adapter teaming** techniques.

Unit 6

In this unit, you learned to discuss general **network operating system (NOS)** characteristics and versions, list NOS hardware requirements, and perform NOS installations and upgrades. You also identified the major NOS characteristics and versions, listed hardware requirements, and examined proper **installation** and **shutdown** procedures for each NOS.

Unit 7

In this unit, you identified major network operating system services, discussed other **NOS services** such as **DNS**, **DHCP**, e-mail, Web, FTP, and fax, and discovered the various ways that servers run network applications. You also found out how to specify the functions of the server as a network device such as a **router** or a **firewall**.

Unit 8

In this unit, you examined the primary types of hardware used to back up critical data, and discussed the primary types of software used to back up that data. You also identified the need for high server availability/redundancy and key areas for **SNMP monitoring**. Finally, you discovered key server management and disaster recovery strategies for preserving system uptime.

Unit 9

In this unit, you learned to use **performance monitoring** tools effectively, to establish a **baseline** for acceptable server performance, to recognize acceptable and unacceptable performance thresholds, and to provide solutions to performance **bottlenecks**.

Unit 10

In this unit, you learned to utilize sound **troubleshooting** logic to determine and solve problems. You also discussed network, connectivity, NOS, and hardware diagnostic tools, examined troubleshooting from a **remote location**, and learned to recognize and solve boot, virus, and hardware problems.

Topic B: Continued learning after class

It's impossible to learn any subject effectively in only three days. To get the most out of this class, you should begin working with servers and networks to perform real tasks as soon as possible. Course Technology also offers resources for continued learning.

Next courses in this series

This is the only course in this series.

Other resources

For more information, visit www.course.com.

Glossary

"A" cable

8-bit, 50-conductor SCSI cable.

Accelerated Graphics Port (AGP)

A high-speed graphics port that relieves the system bus and CPU of video-processing traffic.

accelerated hub architecture

Connects buses to the system bus independently through a dedicated hub interface to the PCI bus, yielding throughput of up to 266 MBps.

access time

The time it takes for the hard disk drive head to arrive at the location of the data. Access time depends upon the spin rate of the hard disk.

active termination

A requirement for faster, single-ended SCSI, active termination adds voltage regulators to provide a more reliable and consistent termination. Another type of active termination is active negation termination, which uses a more complex circuit to stabilize the voltage supply level, further eliminating electrical noise from the signal.

actual power (true power)

The power in watts delivered from the utility company.

Adaptive Fault Tolerance (AFT)

Installing two or more server network adapters to provide an emergency backup connection between the server and the network. If there is any problem with a cable, NIC, switch port, or hub port on the primary adapter, the secondary adapter can kick in within seconds to provide transparent recovery for applications and users.

Adaptive Load Balancing (ALB)

A technique of guaranteeing a consistent level of high server throughput and transparent backup links by implementing multiple NICs and balancing the data transmission load across them. ALB is also known as "asymmetric port aggregation."

Advanced Transfer Cache (ATC)

L2 cache located on the processor die and running at full processor speed.

AFS

Refers to Carnegie-Mellon's Andrew File System, a UNIX file system.

apparent power

The power delivered to a device after passing through the power supply.

ARP (Address Resolution Protocol)

Displays the resolution between the IP address and physical (MAC) address on the NIC by building a table as IP addresses resolve to MAC addresses. You can also modify the ARP cache and table entries.

ATA (AT attachment)

Drive technology that attaches to the 16-bit AT bus.

ATA-1

An ATA standard that supports master, slave, or cable-select determination using jumpers and connecting to a 40-pin cable. The transfer rate is 3.3–8.3 MBps.

ATA-2

An ATA standard supporting large drive support up to 137 GB. Also known as Fast-ATA-2 and Enhanced IDE (EIDE).

ATA-3

An ATA standard that supports S.M.A.R.T. and transfer rates up to 16.6 MBps.

ATA-4

An ATA standard that introduced the optional 80-conductor/40-pin cable and transfer rates up to 33 MBps. Also known as Ultra-DMA and Ultra-ATA. In reference to the transfer rate, you might also see UDMA/33 or Ultra-ATA/33.

ATA-5

An ATA standard requiring the 80-conductor cable, also adding support for the IEEE-1394 (FireWire) specification and a 66 MBps transfer rate. Later implementations achieve 100 MBps and are also known as Ultra-DMA/100.

ATA-6

The upcoming official 100 MBps ATA standard.

ATAPI (ATA Packet Interface)

A specification that allows other devices besides hard disks to plug into the ATA interface.

authentication

Verification of a person's identity based on their credentials (usually a username and password).

authorization
Verification that an authenticated user is permitted to access a network resource.

back-end application
Applications that run on the server on behalf of the client.

back side bus
The data path used to access L2 cache.

backprobing
Inserting the probe alongside the live connection.

bandwidth
The transmission capacity of the network. For example, most Ethernet networks can transmit 10 Mbps or 100 Mbps.

baseline
Performance data that reflects an acceptable level of system performance.

BIOS (basic input/output system)
A series of input and output configuration settings for peripherals, adapters, and on-board components.

blind connector mating
Refers to the fact that you can't see the SCSI hot-plug connection take place inside the chassis.

buffer (read cache)
On a hard disk, memory that stores part of the data read from the hard disk. Later, the CPU can request the same data and it will be retrieved from the buffer, which is many times faster than mechanically retrieving it from the hard disk.

buffered memory
Re-drives (amplifies) signals entering the memory module.

bus
Set of wires or printed circuits that provides the data path to and from the processor, memory, hard disk, adapters, and peripherals.

bus mastering
A technology that allows devices to bypass the processor and directly access memory, resulting in an overall increase in processor performance. Bus mastering devices can also communicate among themselves without processor intervention. Bus mastering is actually a form of direct memory access (DMA).

bus queue entries
A Pentium Xeon technology that holds outstanding bus and memory operations.

bus width
The number of individual data wires that transmit data. The more wires the component such as the motherboard has, the more data it can transmit in a given period of time.

cable management arm (CMA)
Rack equipment that allows orderly arrangement of cables, and expands and contracts so that you can move equipment on the rack without accidentally unplugging it.

cable select
The IDE drive's position on the cable indicates whether it is a master or slave.

cache
Memory that assists performance by storing frequently used data for fast access. Processors and hard disks use cache, and cache is separate from main system memory (RAM).

cache memory
A small amount of memory that stores recently or frequently used program code or data.

centralized management
The ability to administer a given system from a single location instead of disparate locations.

chassis
The metal frame to which the motherboard is attached and which forms the case structure.

chipset
Circuitry that provides motherboard features and organizes the various buses.

client
A network workstation that requests and receives service from the server.

client-server
A network that begins with a LAN and one or more servers. The client-server network can also encompass a more complicated network configuration such as multiple, geographically distant LANs connected to one another across a relatively great distance known as a wide area network (WAN).

clock speed
The number of instructions the processor can execute in a single instruction, measured in megahertz (MHz)—which is one million cycles per second. Instructions sent to the processor require a certain number of cycles, so the more cycles the processor can handle per second, the faster it operates, or "thinks."

clustering

Redundant servers hosting the same application for the purpose of fault tolerance. If one of the servers fails, the remaining server(s) continues to serve the application to the network.

CMOS

Complimentary metal oxide semiconductor that includes a small amount of memory, the purpose of which is to store the BIOS settings.

command queuing

A method that allows the host adapter to send as many as 256 commands to the drive. The drive stores and sorts the commands for optimum efficiency and performance internally before responding to the host adapter.

compiler

Translates high-level programming language into the lowest language the computer can understand, machine language.

console

An inclusive term for the keyboard, video, mouse (KVM), and all attached servers.

cyclical redundancy check (CRC)

A calculation used by the sending device based on the data in the packet. The data arrives at the destination target and another calculation is performed using the same "formula." If the calculation in the packet matches the calculation performed by the destination device, the data is complete and considered error free.

datacenter

A term with two meanings, depending upon the context. It can refer to a consolidation of the majority of computer systems and data into a main location, or it can refer to one or more very powerful servers optimized as database servers—sometimes configured with as many as 32 processors.

data bus

The number of bits the processor can execute in a single instruction. Bandwidth is typically 32 bits. Some new processors offer 64-bit bandwidth.

DDR SDRAM (double data rate SDRAM)

Transfers data twice per clock cycle, similar to RDRAM, but at a lower cost because DDR SDRAM is an open standard charging no royalties.

density

A term used with equipment racks that describes consolidation of space because you can stack several servers and other network equipment into the rack in the same floor space.

digital multimeter (DMM)

A device that measures AC voltage, DC voltage, continuity, or electrical resistance.

Direct Memory Address (DMA)

A resource that ISA devices use to directly access memory without first having to access the processor, both increasing device performance and reducing processor load. There are eight DMA channels, numbered 0–7.

discrete L2 cache

L2 cache located inside the processor housing but not on the processor die.

disk mirroring

See RAID-1.

disk striping

See RAID-0.

Distributed File System (Dfs)

A Windows NT/2000 service that deploys what appears to be a single directory structure over multiple physical file servers.

domain validation

The determined SCSI transfer rate is tested, and if errors occur, the rate is incrementally reduced and again tested until no errors occur.

double transition (DT) clocking

Transmitting data on both the rising and falling edges of the clock cycle. On a 16-bit, 40 MHz bus, this yields a transfer rate of 160 MBps.

drive logic

The circuitry included in the floppy or hard drive that interfaces with the disk controller.

duplexing

Two host adapters with one drive on each adapter.

extended partition

A partition that provides the ability to store logical drives.

dynamic RAM (DRAM)

Main memory referred to as dynamic because the information requires continuous electrical refresh, or else the data can become corrupt or lost.

EEPROM (electrically erasable programmable read-only memory)

A chip that stores the BIOS programming. EEPROM has been mostly superceded by a similar memory known as flash BIOS.

EIA (Electronic Industries Alliance) unit (U)

A rack unit of measure equaling 1.75 vertical inches (4.45 cm).

electrostatic discharge (ESD)
Static electricity that can damage, destroy, or shorten the life of the server's electrical components.

enterprise
A geographically dispersed network under the jurisdiction of one organization. It often includes several different types of networks and computer systems from different vendors.

error correcting code (ECC)
Circuitry on the memory chip that uses check bits to verify the integrity of memory and corrects single bit errors.

Extended ISA (EISA)
An evolution of ISA, the EISA bus provides backward compatibility with older ISA devices and provides maximum bus bandwidth of about 33 MBps.

failover
An alternate system that takes over for a failed system.

Fast SCSI
SCSI operating at 10 MHz instead of 5 MHz.

FAT/FAT32
A Microsoft-based file system. FAT is capable of 2 GB partitions and FAT32 is capable of 2 TB partitions. Neither file system offers local security features.

fault tolerance
Continued service despite failure of a server or component.

FDISK
An MS-DOS utility used to create hard disk partitions.

Fibre Channel (FC)
A storage area network (SAN) SCSI technology that can use gigabit Ethernet networks, but is primarily intended for fiber optic cable as the name implies.

Fibre Channel Arbitrated Loop (FC-AL)
A connection of up to 126 devices on a shared bandwidth fiber hub.

field replaceable unit (FRU)
A system with replaceable CPU, CMOS, CMOS battery, RAM, and RAM cache.

File Allocation Table (FAT)
A Microsoft-based file system compatible with nearly any operating system.

file server
A server that provides a central location to store files for network clients.

File Transfer Protocol (FTP)
A TCP/IP protocol that manages file transfers. Usually used to download files over the Internet.

Filesystem Hierarchy Standard (FHS)
A UNIX directory structure to which Linux complies.

fill buffers
The interface between the CPU and main memory.

firewall
A hardware or software solution that protects internal LAN users from the public Internet.

FireWire
An extremely fast bus allowing up to 63 connected devices and up to 3200 Mbps throughput in the latest version.

flash BIOS
BIOS memory that can be reprogrammed without having to remove the chip. Instead, you download and run a program that updates the BIOS.

forced perfect termination (FPT)
An advanced form of SCSI termination in which termination is forced to a more exact voltage by means of diode clamps added to the terminator circuitry. FPT is very clean, and it's the best termination available for an SE bus.

front-end application
An application running on the client that retrieves information processed by a back-end application.

front side bus
A 64-bit data pathway that the processor uses to communicate with L1 cache, main memory, and the graphics card through the North Bridge chipset.

Graphics Memory Controller Hub (GMCH)
Replaces the North Bridge in newer chipsets, providing higher data throughput.

gray code
A binary code that identifies physical locations on the drive. Gray code is written to the drive by the drive manufacturer.

hierarchical bus
Various portions of the bus running at different speeds, with the slower buses hierarchically structured beneath the faster buses.

high byte
The dangling bits resulting from terminating only 8 bits on a 16-bit bus (also known as high 9). Use special terminators that will terminate both the 8 and 16 bits.

High Performance File System (HPFS)
The native file system of IBM OS/2.

high voltage differential (HVD) signaling

SCSI signaling circuitry that uses a comparatively high voltage to extend the length of the SCSI chain to as much as 82 feet (25 meters).

host

A network device (usually a computer) in a TCP/IP network.

host adapter

The more accurate term for what is usually referred to as an IDE or SCSI hard disk controller. The host adapter is the physical interface between the hard disk and the computer bus.

hot-plug (or hot-swap)

Add or remove a device without first powering down the computer.

hub

A network device that connects network cables together in a central, star configuration. Passive hubs simply make the connections, and active hubs (multiport repeaters) regenerate the signal to increase the distance it can travel.

HVD termination

High voltage termination for HVD signaling.

Industry Standard Architecture (ISA)

A bus interface that connects ISA devices to the ISA bus, which is 16 bits wide and accommodates both 16-bit devices and older 8-bit devices. The ISA bus only operates at 8.33 MHz and is capable of transfer speeds up to 8 MBps.

Integrated Drive Electronics (IDE)

Refers to any hard disk with an integrated controller. Closely associated with the ATA standard.

Intelligent Input/Output (I2O)

An I/O design initiative that allows improved I/O performance via an I2O processor using the I2O driver model.

interface

The hardware connecting the drive to the computer motherboard.

interleaving

A process that allows memory access between two or more memory banks and/or boards to occur alternately, minimizing wait states.

interrupt request (IRQ)

An electrical signal that obtains the CPU's attention in order to handle an event immediately, although the processor might queue the request behind other requests.

I/O Controller Hub (ICH)

Replaces the South Bridge in newer chipsets, allowing higher data throughput.

IPCONFIG

A Microsoft utility that displays a wide variety of IP configuration data for a Windows 98/ME/NT/2000 system, including the IP address, subnet mask, and default gateway and other information.

IPX/SPX (Internetwork Packet Exchange/Sequence Packet Exchange)

The default Novell protocol implementation for all versions of NetWare until 5.x, which can also use TCP/IP.

ISA bus

A 16-bit data pathway for slower expansion adapter cards and the floppy disk, mouse, keyboard, serial and parallel ports, and the BIOS via a Super I/O chip, which mitigates the need for a separate expansion card for each of the aforementioned items.

Journaled File System (JFS)

An OS/2 file system that contains its own backup and recovery capability. Using an indexing system and log to corroborate file changes, JFS can interoperate with the operating system to repair corrupt files.

keyboard, video, mouse (KVM)

A console that enables you to control multiple servers from a single keyboard, video monitor, and mouse.

L1 cache

A small amount of memory (usually 32–64 KB) that provides extremely fast access to its data because of its proximity to the processor and because it runs at the same speed as the processor itself—not at the speed of the motherboard.

L2 cache

Provides the same basic benefits as L1 cache, but it is larger, ranging from 256 KB to 2 MB.

line conditioner

A device that filters out power inconsistencies, temporarily bridges power in the event of a brief brownout, suppresses high voltage spikes, and provides overall buffering between building power and the system.

Linux

A version of UNIX that operates on PCs as well as Alpha RISC and PowerPC platforms.

load balancing

Distributing a network role between two or more servers.

local area network (LAN)

A collection of computers in close proximity to one another on a single network.

logical drive

A section on the hard disk that appears to the operating system as if it were a separate hard disk, and that has its own drive letter.

logical unit number (LUN)

A subunit of the SCSI device, used to identify items within the device.

low voltage differential (LVD) signaling

Similar to HVD except for use of lower voltage and shorter cable lengths (39 feet, or 12 meters).

LVD termination

Low voltage termination for LVD signaling.

mainframe

The most powerful level of computer classification, mainframes are extremely large and powerful computers. Also known as "big iron."

mean time between failure (MTBF)

The anticipated lifetime of a computer or one of its components.

memory address

Some devices reserve a dedicated region in system memory that is unavailable for use by any other device, application, or the operating system. This can help device stability by ensuring that nothing else trespasses the memory, which causes system errors.

mezzanine bus

An add-on bus used to increase the number of processors in a single system.

midrange computer (or minicomputer)

A broad computer classification that lies somewhere between desktop workstation and mainframe computer.

N+1

A term that describes the expandability of a given server component or components, or space provided for expandable components. "N" is a variable that refers to the quantity of a given component installed in a system, and "+1" refers to a spare component.

NetBEUI (NetBIOS Enhanced User Interface)

A small, fast protocol optimized for small networks.

NETSTAT

A command-line networking utility that shows TCP/IP protocol statistics using any of several options. One of the most useful options is –r, which shows the routing table. This is useful in verifying the efficiency of the routing tables.

NetWare File System

Novell's file system that offers large volume support, efficient cluster size, and local security.

network

A collection of two or more computers connected with transmission media such as network cable or wireless means, such as radio or infrared signals. Usually includes other devices such as printers.

network applications

Server-based programs that run in memory and on the processor on behalf of other servers or clients.

network attached storage (NAS)

One or more storage devices attached to a network, most commonly Ethernet. Simple to configure, you plug in the power, connect it to the network, and turn it on.

network device

Any device connected to the network for purposes of communicating with other network devices. (A network device is also known as a host in most networks.)

Network File System (NFS)

A UNIX file system that makes files accessible over a network.

network interface card (NIC)

The workstation's adapter card that connects to the network and through which network communication takes place.

network operating system (NOS)

Provides file and printer sharing, centralized file storage, security, and various services. Primary examples of a NOS include Microsoft Windows NT or 2000, Linux, IBM OS/2, or Novell NetWare.

network resource

An object users can access from across the network, such as printers, files, and folders.

network utilization

The percentage of bandwidth in use in a given period of time.

non-maskable interrupt (NMI)

An interrupt that takes priority over standard interrupt requests. An NMI is useful to stop the system or issue a message in the event of critical events or failures such as failing memory.

North Bridge

A chipset element that divides the processor bus from the PCI bus and manages data traffic to and from the South Bridge, and components on the FSB and PCI bus.

Novell Directory Services (NDS)
A hierarchical database of network resources that allows users from anywhere in the enterprise to access resources throughout the organization, as opposed to logging on to a single server and accessing only resources available from that server.

Novell Storage Service (NSS)
Operates alongside the traditional NetWare file system to support large files, improve performance, and provide flexible storage management.

NT File System (NTFS)
A Microsoft-based file system designed for Windows NT/2000, offering large volumes and local security.

null cable modem
A special cable that uses special crossed wires to simulate a modem presence, allowing data to travel between two hosts without an actual modem or network connection.

overclocking
Increasing the speed of the motherboard clock and/or the CPU to accelerate the clock speed, which can yield a performance increase. Not recommended on servers because of the higher risk associated with higher temperatures and a reduction in overall stability.

oversubscribe
A network connection with network utilization that exceeds an acceptable baseline for the available network bandwidth. The network utilization has a direct relationship to network bandwidth: the higher the network bandwidth, the lower the network utilization.

"P" cable
16-bit, 68-conductor SCSI cable.

packetization
A data transfer method that reduces the overall communication overhead. Previously, data was transferred over the SCSI bus using a series of phases to set up and transfer data. Packetization streamlines this process by combining the process into a packet, reducing overhead.

parallel bus
A SCSI reference meaning that multiple wires on the cable can transmit data at the same time.

parity
In SCSI, an encoding scheme that represents data appearing on other drives.

passive termination
The simplest type of SCSI termination, but also the least reliable. Passive terminators use resistors to terminate the SCSI chain, similar to the way terminators are used on coaxial Ethernet networks. Passive terminators usually work best on short, SE SCSI-1 buses. It is unlikely you will find many passive terminators in servers.

pass-through termination
If the last position on the SCSI chain is in use by a device that does not terminate itself, you can place a terminator over the connection, which allows signal transfer to and from the device while also providing the necessary termination.

PCI interrupts
Assignment of a designation to PCI devices that represent an actual ISA IRQ. The main benefit with PCI interrupts is that if no more IRQ addresses are available, PCI can use PCI steering to assign two or more PCI devices the same ISA IRQ.

PCI steering
Using PCI interrupts to assign two or more PCI devices the same ISA IRQ.

PCI-X (PCI-eXtended)
A 64-bit addendum to PCI 2.2 utilizing 64 bits and up to 133 MHz.

peer PCI bus
A bus architecture that increases available PCI bandwidth and expands the number of PCI expansion cards from the usual limit of four with a minimal impact on overall system bus bandwidth. This architecture usually involves dual peer PCI buses and two North Bridges, which connect to a primary PCI bus and a secondary PCI bus.

peer-to-peer network
A collection of networked computers with no logon server to verify the identity of users. Each network device has an equal (peer) level of authority.

Peripheral Components Interface (PCI) bus
A 32-bit data pathway for high-speed I/O for expansion adapter cards, USB, and IDE ports. The CMOS and system clock also connect to the PCI bus. The PCI bus connects to both the North Bridge and the South Bridge.

permissions
The configured level of access applied to a resource. For example, if a user can read a file but not change the file, then they have read-only permission.

Physical Address Extension (PAE)
Intel technology that allows the processor to utilize 36 bits to address up to 64 GB of memory.

Pin Grid Array (PGA)

An arrangement of pins on the underside of a processor. The pins fit inside a corresponding PGA socket.

plenum

The space between the dropped ceiling tiles and the actual ceiling, or the space between the raised floor surface and the concrete.

positive pressure

The internal environment of a server case or cabinet that utilizes one or more filtered fans to supply main internal airflow throughout the server. Internal server fans only draw upon this filtered air.

POST (power-on self-test)

Verifies functionality of motherboard hardware.

power distribution unit (PDU)

A device similar in function to a household power strip that connects multiple devices to a power supply, but it is capable of much higher power capacity.

power factor

The difference between actual power and apparent power.

power supply unit (PSU)

The internal power supply powering a server or servers.

Quick Arbitration and Selection (QAS)

Reduces overhead by reducing the number of times that arbitration must occur and by allowing a device waiting for bus access to do so more quickly.

rack

A cabinet that houses stacked network equipment, storage, and servers. A rack can store multiple items in the same floor space.

RAID-0

Also known as disk striping, a level of RAID that lays down data across two or more physical drives, benefiting from the combined performance of all drives in the array.

RAID-1

Also known as disk mirroring, a level of RAID in which the controller writes the exact same data to two disks at the same time (redundancy).

RAID-0+1

A level of RAID that offers the performance of RAID-0 and the redundancy of RAID-1. In this implementation, two channels and at least four drives are required. Data is striped across two or more disks in the first channel (RAID-0), and the data is mirrored to disks in the second channel (RAID-1).

RAID-5

A level of RAID that offers the performance benefits of RAID-0 striping but also adds redundancy by use of parity with less overhead.

RAID cache

A high-speed memory cache that fills with data sequentially beyond the actual requested data in anticipation that the next data will soon be requested. If the data is indeed required, the RAID cache serves data more quickly than if data must be retrieved directly from disk.

RDRAM (Rambus DRAM)

Memory manufactured under license to Rambus. RDRAM is very fast, transferring data on both leading and trailing clock cycles.

redundancy

The ability to continue providing service when something fails. For example, if a hard disk fails, a redundant hard disk can continue to store and serve files.

Redundant Array of Inexpensive (Independent) Disks (RAID)

Utilization of multiple disks to improve performance, provide redundancy, or both.

registered memory

Memory that re-drives (amplifies) signals entering the memory module. Registered memory also enacts a deliberate pause of one clock cycle in the module to ensure that all communication from the chipset arrives properly. Registered memory is useful on heavily loaded server memory, and was designed for SIMMs containing 32 or more chips.

remote user

A user connected to the LAN from a geographically distant location, usually over a modem or virtual private network (VPN).

run time

The number of minutes that batteries can power the system.

SATA

Serial ATA. The current generation of hard disk interface, it uses a 7-pin serial connection instead of the 40-pin parallel cable found on the ATA interface.

SAS

Serial Attached SCSI. A new SCSI interface that, like SATA, uses a serial connection instead of a parallel one.

SCSI-1

The original SCSI implementation.

SCSI-2

A version of SCSI that introduced Fast and Wide data transmission.

SCSI-3

A compilation of several different documents, SCSI-3 can be mostly equivalent to SCSI-2 in its features unless several of the various SCSI-3 features are applied. At present, SCSI-3 can be as fast as 320 MBps under Ultra320.

SCSI-3 Parallel Interface (SPI)

See SPI.

SCSI ID

Unique numbering for each SCSI device to ensure proper SCSI operation.

SCSI Interlock Protocol (SIP)

The SCSI-3 parallel command set.

server

A computer with more processing power, RAM, and hard disk capacity than typical workstations. A server has a server NOS such as Microsoft Windows NT or Novell NetWare, and provides file and printer sharing, centralized file storage, security, and various services.

services

A function of the NOS that provides server features to the network.

servo mechanism

Detects precise cylinder locations on the platter using gray code.

signaling

Transmission of data using electrical impulses or variations. These electrical transmissions represent data that the sender originates and the receiver translates based upon a mutually agreed-upon method.

Single Edge Contact Cartridge (SECC)

A slot format processor that stands upright inside a motherboard slot, similar to adapter or memory slots.

Single Edge Contact Cartridge2 (SECC2)

A longer form of the SECC slot that accommodates Pentium Xeon processors.

single sign-on

A single logon that allows transparent access to multiple servers. For example, a single sign-on might allow you to log on to a NetWare server and pass the logon credentials to an NT 4.0 server as well.

single-ended (SE) signaling

The original signaling method used on the SCSI-1 bus, uses a common signaling method in which a positive voltage represents a one and a zero voltage (ground) represents a zero, resulting in binary communication.

SMARTDRV.EXE

An MS-DOS-based caching utility that significantly speeds up file reads and writes.

South Bridge

A chipset element that divides the PCI bus from the ISA bus.

SPI

SCSI-3 parallel interface, defining SCSI-3 standards in SPI-1 through SPI-3 releases. The original SPI release has been renamed SPI-1 for clarity when comparing against other successive SPI versions. SPI-1 is also known as Ultra SCSI or Wide Ultra SCSI.

SPI-2

Also known as Ultra2 SCSI and Wide Ultra2 SCSI, a SCSI-3 standard that introduced SCA-2 connectors LVD signaling, and Fast-40 40 MBps transfer rate on a narrow (8-bit) channel or 80 MBps on a wide (16-bit) channel.

SPI-3

Still in draft stage at the time of this writing, a SCSI-3 standard that introduces CRCs for data integrity, domain validation, DT clocking, packetization, and QAS. Also known as Ultra3 SCSI.

SPI-4

The latest SCSI-3 specification, still in draft form at the time of this writing. Most hard disk and host adapter manufacturers have products using the standard's 320 MBps data rate. This data rate is accomplished by doubling the bus speed from 40 MHz to 80 MHz and using DT clocking. Manufacturers are calling this standard Ultra320.

Staggered Pin Grid Array (SPGA)

Same as a PGA processor or socket format, except in a staggered arrangement to squeeze more pins in the same space (as opposed to straight rows).

standby power supply (SPS)

A device or technique that detects an interruption in line power and switches to a large transformer that stores a small amount of power required to bridge the time it takes to switch to battery power.

storage area network (SAN)

Generally refers to Fibre Channel and any other type of network-based storage solution that is not server-based.

subnet

A division in the network useful for limiting network traffic to a particular location; also known as a segment in many contexts.

subnet mask

A series of network identification numbers which, when compared against the IP address, identifies the specific network to which the host belongs.

superscalar

A processor architecture that allows a processor to execute more than one instruction in a single clock cycle.

switch

Similar to a router in that it segments a network, and similar to a hub in that it connects network cables together in a central, star configuration. Switches forward traffic at very high speeds.

switched fabric

A somewhat inexact reference to the connection to the FC storage. The connection can use any number of connection routes, depending on which one is deemed best at that particular moment.

symmetric multiprocessing (SMP)

The simultaneous use of multiple processors on the same server.

synchronize

The process of making data in one location consistent with data in another location. Synchronization is necessary to ensure that user accounts, for example, are consistent from one logon server to another. Synchronization also applies to items such as data files.

synchronous dynamic RAM (SDRAM)

Memory that operates at system clock speed.

TCP/IP (Transmission Control Protocol/Internet Protocol)

A suite of protocols in common use on most networks and the Internet.

terminator

A connector placed at the end of a SCSI chain that absorbs the transmission signal to avoid signal bounce, making it appear to the devices as if the cable was of infinite length. Terminators also regulate the electrical load, and are therefore critical in establishing a reliable communications medium. Proper termination requires a terminator at both ends of the SCSI cable.

thermistor

A power supply thermostat that increases or decreases fan speed based on heat generated by the power supply.

thicknet

Based on the 10Base5 standard, which transmits data at 10 Mbps over a maximum distance of 500 meters (1640.4 feet). Thicknet is about 1 cm thick and has been used for backbone media because of its durability and maximum length.

thinnet

Based on the 10Base2 standard (10 Mbps/Baseband transmission), networking cable that utilizes RG-58 A/U or RG-58 C/U 50 ohm coaxial cable with maximum segment lengths of 185 meters (606.9 feet).

thin client

A computer that receives its operating system environment, including applications and data, from the server.

thin-film

A magnetic medium applied to disks in a near perfect, continuous vacuum.

throughput

A measure of the quantity of data sent or received in a second.

tower

An upright, free-standing computer case.

TRACERT

A command-line trace routing utility that works like Ping but shows the actual router hops taken to reach the remote host.

transistor

An electronic device that opens or closes, or turns on or off to provide a logic gate or switch. Transistors provide the "thinking" capability of the processor.

Ultra160, Ultra160+

A collection of SCSI-3 standards that ensure compliance with a minimum level of SCSI-3 standards, offering speeds of 160 MBps.

UNIX

An open server operating system that allows vendors to specially modify it to their servers. UNIX usually operates on more expensive RISC-based processors.

UNIX File System (UFS)

The UNIX file system, which supports large volumes and local security.

uptime

The continued operation of the overall server or specific components.

virtual private network (VPN)

A highly secured network connection over an otherwise unsecured network such as the Internet.

voice coil

A construction used by the hard disk actuator mechanism to move from one location to the next.

volume

In NetWare, a collection of files, directories, subdirectories, and even partitions.

wide area network (WAN)

Multiple, geographically distant LANs connected to one another across a relatively great distance.

Wide SCSI

Utilizing 16-bit transfer instead of 8-bit (which is "narrow" SCSI).

workstation

Desktop computer with only enough hardware to service the needs of a single user at a time. Synonymous in most contexts with PC, desktop computer, or client.

zero insertion force (ZIF)

A socket format that allows gravity alone to seat the processor. The processor is then locked into place with a locking lever.

Index

COMPUTERIZED ACCOUNTING WITH
QUICKBOOKS® 2021

Kathleen Villani, CPA
Queensborough Community College

James B. Rosa, CPA
Queensborough Community College

PARADIGM
EDUCATION SOLUTIONS

A DIVISION OF KENDALL HUNT
Minneapolis • Dubuque

Care has been taken to verify the accuracy of information presented in this book. However, the authors, editors, and publisher cannot accept responsibility for web, email, newsgroup, or chat room subject matter or content, or for consequences from the application of the information in this book, and make no warranty, expressed or implied, with respect to its content.

Trademarks: Intuit and QuickBooks are trademarks and service marks of Intuit Inc., registered in the United States and other countries. Microsoft is a trademark or registered trademark of Microsoft Corporation in the United States and/or other countries. Some of the product names and company names included in this book have been used for identification purposes only and may be trademarks or registered trade names of their respective manufacturers and sellers. The authors, editors, and publisher disclaim any affiliation, association, or connection with, or sponsorship or endorsement by, such owners.

Paradigm Education Solutions is independent from Intuit and Microsoft Corporation and not affiliated with Intuit or Microsoft in any manner.

Cover Photo Credit: ©Tarchyshnik Andrei/Shutterstock.com

We have made every effort to trace the ownership of all copyrighted material and to secure permission from copyright holders. In the event of any question arising as to the use of any material, we will be pleased to make the necessary corrections in future printings.

ISBN 978-1-7924-5249-9

© 2022 by Paradigm Education Solutions, a Division of Kendall Hunt
7900 Xerxes Avenue S STE 310
Minneapolis, MN 55431-1118
Email: CustomerService@ParadigmEducation.com
Website: ParadigmEducation.com

Published in the United States of America

Brief Contents

Contents

Preface

Computerized Accounting with QuickBooks® 2021 is designed to introduce both accounting and non-accounting students to QuickBooks, a popular general ledger software package for small- and medium-sized businesses. Students will learn to use the software to maintain a general ledger; track vendor, customer, and inventory activities; process payroll for company employees; prepare bank reconciliations; track time for employees and jobs; and complete other key accounting procedures.

In addition to learning how to use QuickBooks, students review the related accounting concepts as applied in the software. A background in accounting is not necessary, but to get the most out of this course, students should be familiar with basic accounting principles and practices. Students should also be familiar with file management and navigation in a Windows environment. The chapter problems, chapter exercises, and case problems must be performed using QuickBooks Desktop Premier: Accountant Edition 2021 installed on a PC. Students using QuickBooks Online or QuickBooks for Mac will not be able to use this course. See Chapter 1, pages 4–5, for instructions on how to download and install the free student trial copy of the software.

Course Objectives

A course using *Computerized Accounting with QuickBooks® 2021* will accomplish two main objectives. The first goal is to become proficient in using QuickBooks for common daily business transactions. Throughout the course, you will work hands-on in QuickBooks using sample company files. Step-by-step instructions and colorful screen captures guide you through the process of entering data and navigating the software interface.

The second objective is to understand the accounting performed by QuickBooks behind the scenes. You will review accounting concepts and T-account illustrations to gain an understanding of the differences between manual accounting and accounting with QuickBooks. In the workplace, the better you understand the flow of the activity as it is recorded in the system, the more accurate and efficient you will be in operating the software.

After completing this course, you should be able to do the following:
- Understand the differences and similarities between a manual accounting system and QuickBooks
- Identify and execute the four levels of operation within QuickBooks: New Company Setup, Lists/Centers, Activities, and Reports
- Set up and maintain the Vendor, Customer, and Employee Centers and the Chart of Accounts, Items, and Payroll Item Lists
- Enter daily activities as appropriate in the Enter Bills, Pay Bills, Write Checks, Create Invoices, Receive Payments, Enter Sales Receipts, Make Deposits, Pay Sales Tax, Adjust Quantity/Value on Hand, Create Purchase Orders, Pay Employees, and Pay Liabilities windows

- Set up and customize a new company file using the Detailed Start and Express Start methods, with and without the QuickBooks Desktop Setup window
- Set up and process payroll
- Transfer funds between accounts, record and pay credit card charges, and prepare a bank reconciliation
- Record revenues and expenses by job, with and without the Time-Tracking feature
- View and print management reports, accounting reports, and financial statements
- Customize the QuickBooks desktop, Lists, Activities windows, and Reports

Instructional Design

Computerized Accounting with QuickBooks® 2021 gets you working hands-on in QuickBooks from the first day of class. Using a free QuickBooks account and data files for our sample company, Kristin Raina Interior Designs, you will follow the steps in each chapter to complete typical daily, monthly, and yearly accounting tasks. End-of-chapter case problems allow you to apply your QuickBooks skills to build financial records for two additional companies, Lynn's Music Studio and Olivia's Web Solutions.

The online course includes video tutorials and automatically graded exercises, quizzes, and exams. As you work through the exercises and problems, you can upload your solutions to the Cirrus course platform for immediate feedback. See page xv for further description of the online course.

Course Content and Organization

Lessons in the course are organized to follow the four levels of operation in QuickBooks: New Company Setup, Lists/Centers, Activities, and Reports. As each level of operation is presented in the chapters, it is denoted with the appropriate margin icon shown at the left.

You can learn the New Company Setup more effectively if you understand the basic operations of the QuickBooks software. Therefore, Chapters 1–5 present how to use QuickBooks following a normal business flow. After the basic software operations are mastered in Chapters 1–5, the New Company Setup level of operation is explained in Chapters 6 and 7. Chapters 8 and 9 discuss the setup and processing of payroll transactions. Throughout these chapters, you will view and print many management and accounting reports and financial statements.

Upon successful completion of Chapters 1–9, you should have a thorough understanding of the four levels of operation in QuickBooks. Chapters 10–12 discuss banking, jobs accounting, time tracking, and customization features. The topics presented in each chapter build on content covered in previous chapters.

Student Courseware

The following visual guide shows features of the courseware that support mastery of skills and concepts.

Chapter Features

Chapter openers present an overview of the skills you can learn by completing the chapter. ——————

Objectives outline chapter learning goals. ——————

Step-by-step procedures with screen captures guide you to the desired outcome for each accounting procedure. Screen captures illustrate what the screen should look like at key points. ——————

Tables provide a description of the different links, buttons, and options in the various windows. Tables are also used to organize large amounts of data for entry in the software. ——————

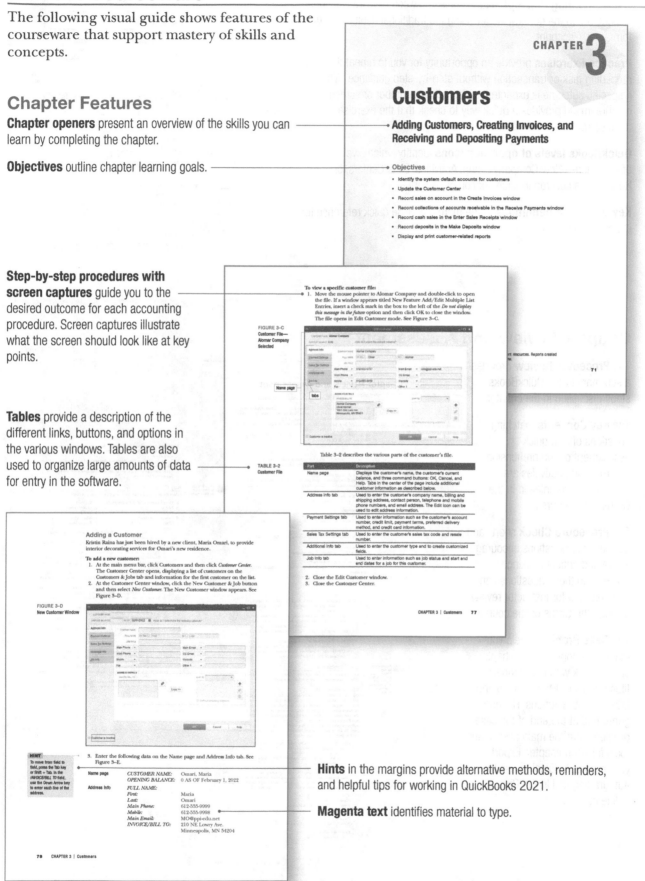

Hints in the margins provide alternative methods, reminders, and helpful tips for working in QuickBooks 2021.

Magenta text identifies material to type.

The **Accounting Concept** feature shows how common transactions are entered in the general ledger using the traditional debit and credit format, or T-account.

Practice Exercises provide an opportunity for you to repeat the preceding task or transaction without step-by-step guidance. When a specific outcome is expected, a *QuickCheck* number or screen capture image provides a quick way to check that the exercise was done correctly.

QuickBooks levels of operation icons identify which level of operation—New Company Setup, Activities, Lists/Centers, or Reports—is covered in each section of content.

Key terms and definitions in the margin provide quick reference for chapter vocabulary.

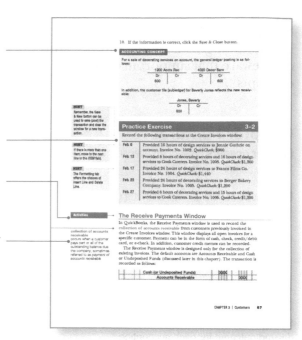

Chapter Review and Assessment

The **Procedure Review** provides a summary of the QuickBooks steps discussed in the chapter.

The **Key Concepts** matching questions offer a quick assessment of comprehension. The matching activities are available for completion in the Cirrus online course.

The **Procedure Check** short- and long-answer questions encourage active and critical thinking. Answers to these questions can be submitted for instructor review through the Cirrus online course.

The **Case Problems** help you master the topics of the chapter as you work with the company files for Lynn's Music Studio and Olivia's Web Solutions. Reports generated at the end of the case problems are the main assessment tools for each chapter. Export your reports to Excel to use the autograding tool in the Cirrus online course.

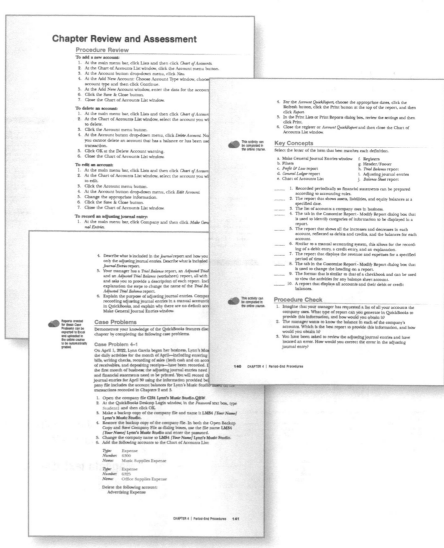

Cirrus for QuickBooks

Cirrus for QuickBooks is Paradigm's web-based training and assessment program and learning management system (LMS) for *Computerized Accounting with QuickBooks® 2021*. Cirrus offers rich content, a sophisticated grade book, and robust scheduling and analytics tools. The platform offers access to all course content and resources, including student files and instructor resources. Key features of the course are described below.

Watch and Learn video tutorials presented by QuickBooks ProAdvisor Hector Garcia, CPA, introduce tools and concepts featured in each chapter, allowing students to watch and learn before attempting the chapter exercises on their own. While providing step-by-step demonstrations, Hector explains the functionality and capabilities of the software, giving background about accounting concepts and practices as well as helpful tips and shortcuts. After viewing the Watch and Learn tutorial and reading chapter content, students complete an automatically graded quiz to assess their comprehension.

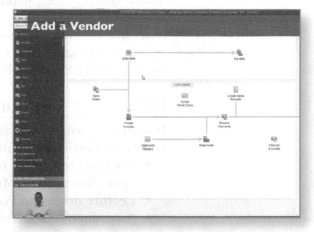

Chapter-based, multiple-choice quizzes and exams are preprogrammed in the Cirrus course with automatic feedback and grade book entry. Additional assessment activities for each chapter include the Key Concepts matching quiz and short-essay Procedure Check, both available for completion in the online course.

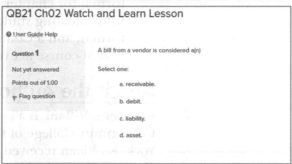

The end-of-chapter case problems have been programmed in the **Automatic Feedback and Scoring Tool**. After completing a case problem, export your reports to Microsoft® Excel® and upload each report to the corresponding activity in Cirrus. Cirrus for QuickBooks will compare your report against a model answer, generate a score that is added to the grade book, and make your report available to the instructor.

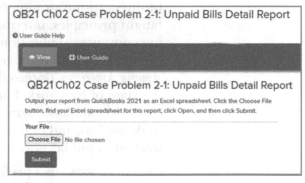

Chapter Problem Upload activities provide a way for you to upload the reports created for each Chapter Problem instead of printing them out. The uploaded files are then available for the instructor to review and grade, if desired.

A full **eBook and individual chapter files** are provided within the course, enabling content to be viewed electronically from any device.

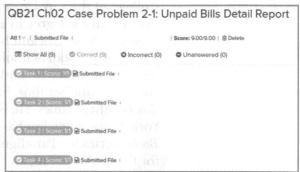

QuickBooks 2021 Trial Software and Data Files

Before you begin the course, you will need to install QuickBooks Desktop Premier: Accountant Edition 2021. Students taking this course through an accredited academic institution are eligible for a free five-month trial license of the software, provided by Intuit. (See pages 4–5 for instructions on how to register, download, and install your copy.) Sample company files to be used in chapter and end-of-chapter activities can be downloaded through the online course. (See Chapter 1, page 6, for detailed instructions.)

Note: Instructors should register with Intuit Education prior to class start to receive software and ensure their institution is eligible for free student licenses. Visit https://QB21.ParadigmEducation.com/InstructorRegistration.

Instructor Resources

Instructor resources are available through a link in the Cirrus online course and include the following:
- Planning resources, including instructions for downloading the QuickBooks 2021 software and sample course syllabi
- Lecture notes and PowerPoint presentations
- Assessment resources, including model answers in PDF and QBW file format for chapter work and end-of-chapter activities, answer keys for evaluating student work, chapter-based exam banks in RTF file format, and a Comprehensive Problem for use as a supplementary end-of-course activity.

About the Authors

Kathleen Villani is a professor of accounting at Queensborough Community College of the City University of New York in Queens, New York. Kathleen received her bachelor's degree in accounting from Queens College of the City University of New York and her master's degree in business administration from Hofstra University. Since 1984, Kathleen has taught principles, intermediate, and cost accounting, along with accounting computer applications, microcomputer applications, and business organization and management. Kathleen has been included in *Who's Who Among America's Teachers* three times. She is a certified public accountant in the state of New York. Kathleen has coauthored the *Computerized Accounting with QuickBooks®* series for Paradigm Education Solutions, including desktop, Pro, and online editions, since the year 2000. Kathleen previously worked in public, government, and private accounting.

James B. Rosa is a professor of accounting at Queensborough Community College of the City University of New York in Queens, New York. Jim received his bachelor's degree in accounting from Queens College of the City University of New York and his master's degree in business administration from the Peter J. Tobin School of Business, St. John's University. Since 1987, Jim has taught principles and intermediate accounting, tax law, and accounting computer applications. Jim has been included in *Who's Who Among America's Teachers* three times. He is a certified public accountant in the state of New York. Since 2000, Jim has coauthored the *Computerized Accounting with Quick-Books®* series for Paradigm Education Solutions, producing training materials for the desktop, Pro, and online editions of the software.

## CHAPTER 1

Introducing QuickBooks 2021

Installing and Opening QuickBooks, Opening a Company File, Creating and Restoring a Backup Copy, and Changing the Company Name

Objectives

- Describe the differences and similarities between manual and computerized accounting

- Identify the four levels of operation within QuickBooks

- Install your QuickBooks 2021 trial software

- Open QuickBooks

- Open a company file

- Make a backup copy of a company file

- Restore a backup copy of a company file

- Change the company name in a company file

The online course includes additional training and assessment resources.

Chapter Introduction

accounting the process of recording, summarizing, and presenting a company's financial information in the form of financial statements

Accounting for the financial activity of any company involves repetitive recording of day-to-day business activities. Recording common business activities such as paying bills, purchasing merchandise, selling merchandise, and processing payroll involves repeating the same steps again and again. Many of these activities can occur several times in the course of one day, requiring much repetitive recording.

When mainframe computers were introduced, certain processes such as payroll became simple to perform. Companies were created to process payrolls for local businesses using mainframe computers. Eventually, mainframe computers were used to process other accounting activities, such as maintaining the general ledger and journals. As personal computers became more common, computerized accounting software enabled routine business activities—including paying bills, buying and selling merchandise, and paying employees—to be processed without the need for a mainframe computer.

With a computerized accounting software package, as business activities are recorded, all necessary reports—from the journals to the general ledger to the payroll reports and the **financial statements**—are instantly prepared. This makes them available on a more timely basis. Also, if an error is noticed, it can be easily corrected and a revised report can be prepared immediately.

financial statements summaries of the financial information of a company, the most common of which are the income statement and the balance sheet

Originally, only people trained in accounting commonly used accounting software. As more people began to use personal computers, business owners and non-accountants started to record business activities on their own using accounting software.

QuickBooks® 2021 is an example of an accounting software package used to record all types of business and accounting activities and prepare a variety of reports, including financial statements. However, unlike many accounting software products, it is designed with the non-accountant in mind. Many of the data entry windows are described in everyday, non-accounting terms. Behind the scenes, QuickBooks uses traditional accounting procedures to record, summarize, and report financial information. Therefore, a basic understanding of accounting terms and procedures allows you to operate the software more efficiently. Throughout the text, to clarify the accounting principles behind the QuickBooks features, accounting terms are defined in the margins, and accounting concepts are presented after each QuickBooks activity.

transaction a monetary business event or activity

general journal the document in which transactions are initially recorded chronologically; at the end of the month, transactions in the general journal are posted (rewritten) to the general ledger

general ledger the document in which transactions are summarized by account

Accounting with QuickBooks versus Manual and Other Computerized Accounting Systems

In accounting, every **transaction** that involves money must be recorded. In a manual accounting system, all transactions are recorded chronologically in a **general journal**. At the end of the month, these transactions are posted (rewritten) in a book called the *general ledger*. The **general ledger** summarizes the information by descriptive names, called *accounts*. Examples of accounts are Cash, Accounts Receivable, and Inventory (assets); Accounts Payable and Notes Payable (liabilities); Capital and Drawings, and Stock and Retained Earnings (equity); Fees Earned and Sales (revenue); and Rent, Insurance, Salaries, and Depreciation (expenses). After routine transactions and any necessary adjustments are recorded in the journal and posted to the general ledger, a **trial balance** is prepared to confirm that the general ledger is in balance, and then the financial statements are prepared.

To facilitate the recording of so many transactions in a manual accounting system, several journals are used. Similar transactions are recorded in each journal. Typically, a purchases journal is used to record purchases of merchandise on account; a sales journal is used to record sales of merchandise on account; a cash receipts journal is used to record collections of sales on account, cash sales, and any other cash receipt activity; and a cash payments journal is used to record payment of purchases on account, cash purchases, and any other cash payment activity. These journals are often referred to as **special journals**. Any transaction that is not appropriately recorded in a special journal is recorded in the general journal. Month-end adjusting journal entries and fiscal year-end closing entries are recorded in the general journal.

Many computerized accounting software packages follow the procedures used in a manual accounting system. Transactions are recorded in special journals and the general journal as appropriate, and transactions from the journals are then posted to the general ledger. Users of other accounting software packages need to analyze the transaction, determine the correct journal in which to record the transaction, enter the data, view the journal entry for correctness, and then post the journal entry to the general ledger.

QuickBooks, on the other hand, is designed for the non-accountant as well as the accountant. QuickBooks does not do its recording in special journals; instead, it identifies transactions by business function: vendors, customers, employees, and banking. The language used in recording transactions is common business language: enter bills, pay bills, create invoices, receive payments, and so on. The user enters the transaction based on the nature of the activity, and then, behind the scenes, the software updates the appropriate accounting reports—the journal, general ledger, and trial balance—and financial statements, based on the activity entered into the system.

Four Levels of Operation

Although much of the accounting is conducted behind the scenes in Quick-Books, an understanding of the accounting concepts used by the software will help you determine how to record financial information correctly. The operations conducted by QuickBooks can be classified into four levels: New Company Setup, Lists/Centers, Activities, and Reports. See Figure 1–A.

FIGURE 1–A
Four Levels of Operation in QuickBooks

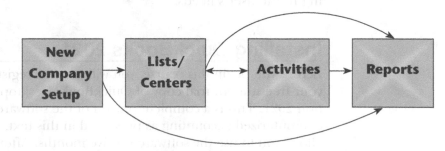

New Company Setup →

The first level of operation is creating and setting up a new company file with the background information for the new company. This involves recording the company name, address, identification numbers, fiscal periods, type of business, accounts, and balances.

Lists/Centers →

The second level of operation is recording background information in Lists and Centers. These Lists and Centers include Chart of Accounts, Item, Fixed Asset Item, Price Level, Billing Rate Level, Sales Tax Code, Payroll Item, Customer, Vendor, Employee, and so on. Information is initially recorded in Lists and Centers as part of New Company Setup, but it can be revised by adding, deleting, or editing information.

The Lists/Centers in QuickBooks function similarly to a database. Certain information is stored in these Lists/Centers, and as business activities involving any item in the Lists/Centers are processed, the information can simply be recalled and plugged into the windows rather than requiring you to retype the data.

In QuickBooks 2021, the difference between Lists and Centers lies in how the List information is accessed. For the Customer, Vendor, and Employee Lists, the information is accessed through their respective Centers. For the Chart of Accounts, Item, Fixed Asset Item, Price Level, Billing Rate Level, Sales Tax Code, and Payroll Item Lists, the Lists are accessed by clicking Lists on the main menu bar.

Activities →

The third level of operation is recording daily business activities in QuickBooks. This is where most of the routine accounting work is processed. Activities are identified using common language such as enter bills, write checks, create invoices, and receive payments. In addition, the information in Lists/Centers is frequently used to eliminate repetitive entering of data while recording daily activities.

Reports →

At certain times, it is necessary to display and print a variety of reports and financial statements based on information entered into QuickBooks. The fourth level of operation is using QuickBooks to display and print an assortment of Reports—for example, management reports related to each activity, such as vendor, customer, inventory, and payroll reports; accounting reports, such as the journal, general ledger, and trial balance; and financial statements, including the income statement and balance sheet.

Information that appears on the Reports is gathered during other operations within QuickBooks. As data is entered in the New Company Setup, Lists/Centers, and Activities levels of operation, the information is simultaneously recorded in the Reports level. QuickBooks provides for simple as well as more elaborate reporting. All the Reports can be customized according to the user's needs.

Installing QuickBooks 2021

Before you begin this course, you will need to register, download, and install your free student trial copy of QuickBooks Desktop Premier: Accountant Edition 2021. This is a complete version of the software that will be used to learn computerized accounting as presented in this text. The student trial license allows you to use the software for five months. After the five-month trial period, Intuit allows you to download a second trial license within 12 months of your initial activation.

First, you will register with Intuit online by answering a few questions about yourself and indicating the product you need. Once you are registered and verified with Intuit, you will receive a link to download your student trial copy of QuickBooks Accountant 2021 and the information you will need to activate the software.

HINT

The installation process takes a while to complete.

To install the student trial of QuickBooks 2021 on your computer:

1. Open an internet browser and type the following link into the address bar: https://QB21.ParadigmEducation.com/QuickBooksDownloadPage. The link takes you to a page on the Intuit website where you can register to get a student copy of QuickBooks.
2. Enter your information in the required fields.
3. At the QuickBooks Desktop Version drop-down list, select *2021*.
4. Click the Verify and Continue button and follow the instructions on the screen to complete the verification process. You will receive a link to download the software as well as license and product codes to activate the software.

Note: You may be asked to provide documentation of your student status. Be prepared with a document such as a transcript, class schedule, or tuition receipt showing your full name, college/university name, and a date within the last three months.

HINT

Step 5 may vary depending on the internet browser you use.

5. At the message asking whether you want to run or save the setup file, click Run.
6. At the User Account Control message, click Yes to allow QuickBooks to make changes to your computer. The Intuit Download Manager window appears. It will take a while for the files to download.
7. When the download is complete, confirm that the Intuit Download Manager window has closed.
8. Confirm that the InstallShield Wizard window is displayed on the screen. Follow the instructions on the screen.
9. When prompted, enter the license number and product code that you received from Intuit.
10. Continue to follow the instructions on the screen until you receive the message "Installation Complete." Click the Open QuickBooks button and then move to step 12. (You may need to close the window and restart your computer before opening QuickBooks.)
11. If you are prompted to activate QuickBooks, do so immediately by clicking the Begin Activation button. You should receive a message saying "Received Confirmation - Your activation is now complete." Click Start Using QuickBooks Now.
12. If you receive a message explaining how QuickBooks uses your internet connection, click OK. If the QuickBooks Desktop Setup window appears, close the window.
13. If you are prompted to register in order to activate the software, do this immediately.

Note: If you do not register and activate your trial of QuickBooks within 30 days, your trial will expire and you will no longer be able to use the software.

14. Close QuickBooks. If the Exiting QuickBooks message appears, click Yes.

Accessing the Company Files Needed for This Text

QuickBooks must be installed on your computer for you to use this book. In addition, you will need access to sample company files that you will use to work through chapter exercises and end-of-chapter case problems. These files can be downloaded through a link in your student ebook or Cirrus online course. Your instructor may also make the files available in some other directory on the hard drive, a network, or cloud storage location. There are company files for all chapters except Chapters 6 and 7, where you will learn to create a new company file.

By default, QuickBooks stores company files in the following path:

C:\Users\Public\Public Documents\Intuit\QuickBooks\Company Files.

The instructions in this textbook assume that you will store company files in the subfolder Company Files. However, you are not required to use this path. Your instructor may designate a different location for the company files, or you can save them in a location most convenient for you.

Opening QuickBooks

To open QuickBooks:

1. After you have installed the program, look for a shortcut to Quick-Books on your desktop. If there is none, type "QuickBooks" in the search bar at the bottom of the screen or click the Start button and look for a tile or icon for the QuickBooks Premier - Accountant Edition 2021. (You may need to scroll through the list of applications to find it.) See Figure 1–B.

FIGURE 1–B
Ways to Open
Quickbooks

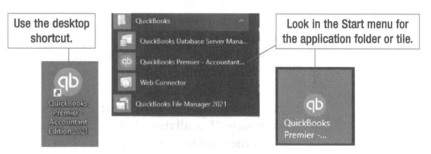

2. QuickBooks opens. If you receive a message explaining how Quick-Books uses your internet connection, click OK. If the QuickBooks Desktop Setup window appears, close the window.

   The QuickBooks main window is displayed. In addition, the No Company Open window appears. See Figure 1–C.

Note: If a company file was previously used on this computer, that company file may be opened automatically. In this case, click File and then click Close Company. If the QuickBooks Desktop Login window appears, click Cancel. You should see a window like the one shown in Figure 1–C.

The first time QuickBooks is opened, no company files are listed in the No Company Open window. Thereafter, company files previously opened are listed; you can use this window to select a company name and then click the Open button. If companies are listed, notice under the box listing the

HINT

You are not required to use this path. You can download the company files to a folder of your choice on your hard drive or network. A hard drive location is recommended.

HINT

To open QuickBooks, click on the shortcut or tile as shown in Figure 1–B, or open the Start menu and then choose the application QuickBooks Premier - Accountant Edition 2021.

FIGURE 1–C
QuickBooks Main
Window—No Company
Open Window

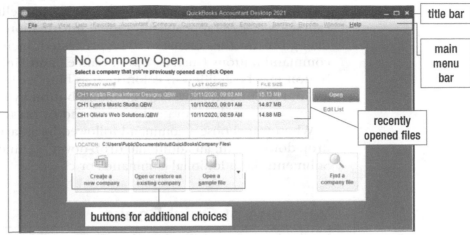

company files that the location path is indicated. This path will be useful later as you begin to open several different company files. You also have three additional choices: Create a new company, Open or restore an existing company, and Open a sample file.

In Chapters 1–5 and 8–12, you will open an existing company file from those provided in the *Student Data Files* that you have installed on the hard drive of your computer. In Chapters 6 and 7, you will learn how to create a new company file.

Using Drop-Down Menus and Dialog Boxes

Whether or not a company file is open, notice the QuickBooks main window shown in Figure 1–C. Along the top is the QuickBooks title bar, which includes a company name when a company file is open. Below the title bar is the main menu bar, which includes the menu choices of File, Edit, View, Lists, Favorites, Accountant, Company, Customers, Vendors, Employees, Banking, Reports, Window, and Help. When no company file is open, only the menus File and Help are active and can be chosen. You can choose a menu by clicking the menu name or by pressing the Alt key and the underlined letter from the menu name on the keyboard. Whenever you choose a menu, a drop-down menu appears that lists additional choices or commands. Choices on the menus vary depending on the data entered into the company file and depending on which of the open windows is active.

At the main menu bar, click File. The File drop-down menu appears, displaying commands or choices. See Figure 1–D.

FIGURE 1–D
File Menu in
QuickBooks

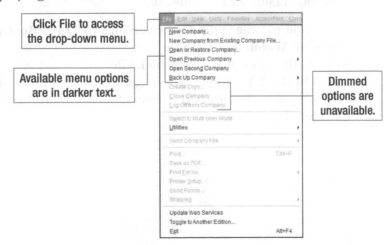

When you choose a command followed by an ellipsis (…), a window called a *dialog box* appears. Additional information must be entered in the dialog box for the command to be processed. Included in dialog boxes are command buttons (such as Open, Cancel, and Help). The active command button may be a different color, such as blue, or have a slightly darker line around it. You can activate a command button by clicking it. If the button is active, you can also activate the command by pressing the Enter key.

When you choose a command followed by an arrow (▸) from the File drop-down menu, an additional drop-down menu called a *submenu* appears. Submenus list additional commands or choices.

Versions of QuickBooks

Intuit, the maker of QuickBooks, offers several versions of the QuickBooks desktop software: Pro, Premier, and Enterprise Solutions. In addition, the QuickBooks Premier version is available in several editions: Accountant Edition, General Business Edition, Contractor Edition, and so on. The fundamentals of each version and edition of the QuickBooks software are the same. QuickBooks Pro is the basic version of the software with Premier and Enterprise Solutions offering additional features. Usually, small business owners will use QuickBooks Pro. Larger businesses, businesses that have large inventories, and specific industries may use the QuickBooks Enterprise Solutions or QuickBooks Premier versions of the software. The QuickBooks Premier Accountant Edition is often used by accountants who have clients that use various editions of QuickBooks. QuickBooks Premier Accountant Edition is a popular choice for accountants with multiple clients, as it allows the accountant to toggle (switch) to different editions of QuickBooks Premier depending on which edition the client uses.

QuickBooks also offers an online version of the software for a monthly fee. There are four versions available: QuickBooks Online Simple Start, QuickBooks Online Essentials, QuickBooks Online Plus, and QuickBooks Online Advanced. Although the functionality of the online version is similar to the QuickBooks desktop version, the graphic interface of the menus, data entry windows, and reports differs significantly.

This book was written using the QuickBooks Premier Accountant Edition, which is the version provided with this textbook. When schools license the Education packs of the software to install in computer labs, Intuit provides the schools with the QuickBooks Premier Accountant Edition version of the software.

To toggle to other editions or versions of QuickBooks in the QuickBooks Premier Accountant Edition:
1. At the main menu bar, click File.
2. On the File menu, click *Toggle to Another Edition.* The Select QuickBooks Desktop Industry-Specific Edition dialog box appears. See Figure 1–E.

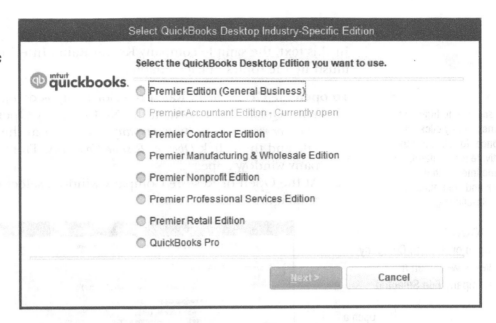

3. In the Select QuickBooks Desktop Industry-Specific Edition dialog box, click the desired edition of QuickBooks.
4. Click Next. The next window confirms the edition of QuickBooks that you selected.

   If you click Toggle, QuickBooks Premier - Accountant Edition closes and then reopens in the edition of QuickBooks that you have selected. Since the text is prepared using QuickBooks Premier - Accountant Edition, do not change to another version of the software.
5. Click Cancel.

There are several ways to determine which version or edition of Quick-Books you are using. The QuickBooks edition is listed in the title bar. In Figure 1–C on page 7, note that the title bar displays QuickBooks Accountant Desktop 2021. If you toggle to a different edition of QuickBooks, the title bar changes to reflect which edition you are using.

You can also determine the edition that is currently open in the Select QuickBooks Desktop Industry-Specific Edition dialog box. See Figure 1–E, which notes that the Premier Accountant Edition is currently open.

The Help menu also displays the version or edition of QuickBooks you are using.

HINT

Look at the title bar to see which edition of the software you are using.

To determine the version or edition of QuickBooks using the Help menu:
1. At the main menu bar, click Help.
2. At the drop-down menu, notice the last command.

   The last command on the drop-down Help menu displays the edition of QuickBooks that is open.
3. Click Help to remove the Help drop-down menu.

Opening a Company File

In this text, the sample company Kristin Raina Interior Designs is used to illustrate the topics in each chapter.

HINT

To *select* is to highlight something by clicking it once. To *choose* is to activate a command, sometimes with one click and sometimes by double-clicking.

To open the CH1 Kristin Raina Interior Designs company file:
1. With QuickBooks open, at the No Company Open window, click the *Open or restore an existing company* button, or at the main menu bar, click File and then click *Open or Restore Company.* The Open or Restore Company window appears.
2. At the Open or Restore Company window, select *Open a company file.* See Figure 1–F.

FIGURE 1–F
Open or Restore Company Window—Open a Company File Selected

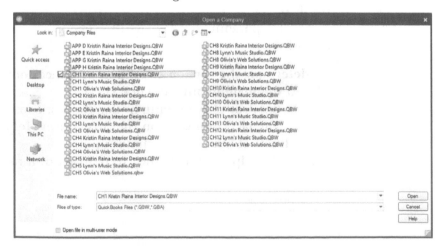

3. Click Next.

    The Open a Company dialog box appears. Most likely, the subfolder Company Files appears in the *Look in* text box. QuickBooks automatically assigns the extension .QBW to each company file. (If you cannot see the extensions, enable the display of file extensions using File Explorer.)
4. In the Open a Company dialog box, in the *Look in* text box, choose the Company Files subfolder or the subfolder where you stored the company files.
5. Select the company file named **CH1 Kristin Raina Interior Designs.QBW**.

    When you select a company file name, the name also appears in the *File name* text box. See Figure 1–G.

HINT

Refer to the instructions provided in Cirrus or your ebook to download the company files.

FIGURE 1–G
Open a Company Dialog Box—CH1 Kristin Raina Interior Designs Company File Selected

HINT

Occasionally when opening a company file, you may receive a warning that QuickBooks encountered a problem. Click OK at the warning and then open the company file again.

HINT

The password for all company files for this textbook is Student1. If you are prompted for the Security question, the Challenge Question is *First college roommate's name*, and the Challenge Answer is *Friend*.

6. Click Open.
7. At the QuickBooks Desktop Login window, in the *Password* text box, type Student1 and then click OK. Student1 is the password on all company files used in this textbook.

Pop-up messages may appear in QuickBooks at various times, such as when a company file is opened or another action is completed. In general, simply close the messages. On some occasions, you may be provided a choice not to show the message again. Also, in some situations, the QuickBooks default can be changed so the messages no longer appear. Throughout this book, suggestions are made to close the message, choose not to show the message again, or change the default.

For now, when opening a company file, if the Set Up an External Accountant User window appears, insert a check mark in the box to the left of *Don't show this again* and then click No to close the window. If the Accountant Center window appears, remove the check mark in the box to the left of *Show Accountant Center when opening a company file* and then click the X (close button) to close the window. If the Close Accountant Center window appears, click OK to close it. If the New Feature Tour window appears, click the X to close the window.

Once a company file is open, the QuickBooks main window changes. See Figure 1–H.

FIGURE 1–H
QuickBooks Main Window—Company File Open

title bar with company name

Left Icon bar

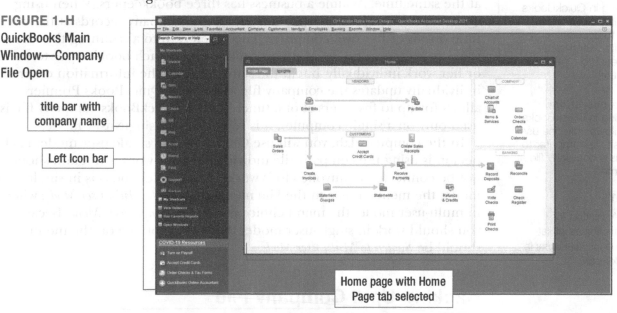

Home page with Home Page tab selected

The company file name, CH1 Kristin Raina Interior Designs, is now displayed in the title bar. Along the left side of the window is the Left Icon bar. The remainder of the window displays the Home page. The Left Icon bar and the Home page can also be used to access information in QuickBooks as alternatives to using the main menu bar. In this text, only the main menu bar is used. If a WHAT'S NEW pop-up message appears on the edge of the Home page, click the X to close it. If a Help message appears, it will fade away in a few seconds.

In this textbook, the Left Icon bar and the Home page will be closed to allow more screen space for the windows.

HINT

Chapter 12 illustrates customizing and using the Home page and Icon bars.

In a computer lab, the
Left Icon bar or Home
page may not appear
because another user
has changed the default
settings. To view the
Left Icon bar, at the main
menu bar, click View and
then click *Left Icon Bar*.
To view the Home page,
at the main menu bar,
click Company and then
click *Home Page*.

HINT

To close the Left Icon bar:
1. At the main menu bar, click View.
2. At the View menu, click *Hide Icon Bar*.

To close the Home page:
1. Click the X on the Home page.

You can change the default if you do not want the Home page window to open each time QuickBooks is opened.

To change the default to close the Home page window:
1. At the main menu bar, click Edit.
2. At the Edit menu, click *Preferences*.
3. In the left panel, click the Desktop View icon.
4. Choose the My Preferences tab.
5. Remove the check mark to the left of *Show Home page when opening a company file.*
6. Click OK.

Multi-User and Single-User Mode

multi-user mode
a setting in QuickBooks
that allows up to five
users to access a com-
pany file at the same
time, each on their own
computer

single-user mode
a setting in QuickBooks
that allows only one user
on a single computer to
access a company file at
one time

HINT

See Appendix I for
information about set-
ting up multiple users in
QuickBooks.

QuickBooks is designed so that several people can use one company file at the same time. Assume a business has three bookkeepers. When using QuickBooks, each bookkeeper can access the company records at the same time on his or her own computer. This is referred to as running the soft-ware in **multi-user mode**. Multi-user mode allows each bookkeeper to do his or her work individually, but at the same time, all the information entered individually updates the company file as a whole. QuickBooks Premier allows for up to five users at one time. When a QuickBooks company file is used only on a single computer, it is referred to as **single-user mode**.

In the computer lab, you will use QuickBooks in single-user mode. Each person is using the company file individually; your work is not and should not be connected to anyone else's work. When QuickBooks is in single-user mode, the menu choice in the File menu is *Switch to Multi-user Mode;* when in multi-user mode, the menu choice is *Switch to Single-user Mode.* Because you should work in single-user mode, the choice you see on the menu should be *Switch to Multi-user Mode.*

Backing Up a Company File

In business, it is advisable to make backup copies of records on a regular basis and store the backup copies in a safe place, such as an offsite or cloud storage location. In the event of damage to a company's computers and/or files, the backup copies can be used to restore the lost or damaged data.

Why Backing Up a File Is Important

In this text, you will use the Back Up command for two purposes. First, Back Up will be used to make a copy of the original company file. As pre-viously mentioned, company files are provided for the sample company Kristin Raina Interior Designs to illustrate topics in each chapter. Two other companies, Lynn's Music Studio and Olivia's Web Solutions, will be used in the case problems at the end of each chapter. To use the company files for practice, you will first open the company file and then make a copy of the company file using the Back Up command. The backup copy of the company file must then be restored for you to use it as a practice exercise. By making a backup copy and then restoring it, you preserve the original company file intact for others to use.

Second, as in business, you will use the Back Up command to make backup copies of your exercise company files on a removable storage device or a network directory. In the event your exercise company file is deleted from the hard drive that you are working on, you will have a backup copy. This copy will also be helpful in case you use a different computer each time in the computer lab.

Naming Backup Files

Two types of names are used in QuickBooks to identify a company file: the file name and the company name. When your backup copy is made and restored, it is recommended that you include your name or your initials as part of the company *file name* to distinguish your individual copy of the file from those of other students. In the restored copy (your exercise copy), the *company name* will also be changed to include your name or your initials to further identify the exercise copy of the company file as your copy.

In each chapter, the original company file name is preceded with the prefix CH1, CH2, and so on to represent the chapter number. For example, the company files needed for Chapter 1 are the following:

CH1 Kristin Raina Interior Designs.QBW
CH1 Lynn's Music Studio.QBW
CH1 Olivia's Web Solutions.QBW

When you create backup copies for your own use, you will rename the files by adding your name or initials and changing the prefixes. The prefix EX1, EX2, and so on will be used for all the chapter exercise files. (Use EX for exercise, along with the number of the chapter.) For the files used in the end-of-chapter case problems, you will use LMS and OWS along with the chapter number as your prefix. For example, here is how you will rename your backup files for Chapter 1:

EX1 [Your Name] Kristin Raina Interior Designs.QBB
LMS1 [Your Name] Lynn's Music Studio.QBB
OWS1 [Your Name] Olivia's Web Solutions.QBB

QuickBooks automatically assigns the extension .QBB to a backup copy and condenses the file. Condensed backup copies cannot be used for work; they are strictly for use as stored copies.

Backup copies can be made to the Company Files subfolder, to a subfolder of your choice, to a removable storage device, or to a cloud storage location as directed by your instructor. It is recommended that you create your own subfolder on the hard drive of the computer using File (or Windows) Explorer and that you use your subfolder to store your backup copy of the company file. The following instructions assume you have created your own subfolder.

To make a backup copy of the CH1 Kristin Raina Interior Designs company file:

1. At the main menu bar, click File and then click *Back Up Company.*
2. At the Back Up Company submenu, click *Create Local Backup.* The Create Backup window appears with the *Do you want to save your backup copy online or locally?* page displayed.

   The Create Backup window is a dialog box that presents you with a series of pages that ask for or inform you of additional information. Click Next to move from page to page. You will follow a similar step-by-step process at various times when working with QuickBooks.
3. At the *Do you want to save your backup copy online or locally?* page, confirm that *Local backup* is selected. See Figure 1–I.

FIGURE 1–I
Create Backup Window—Do You Want to Save Your Backup Copy Online or Locally?

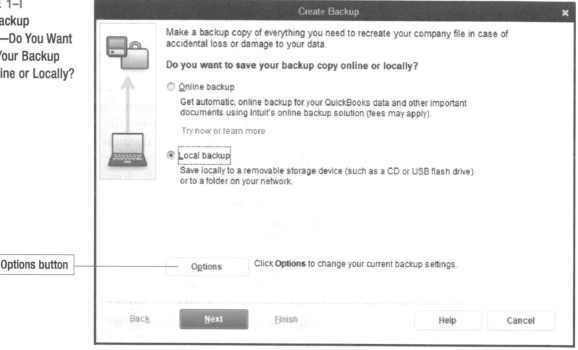

Options button

Create Backup

Make a backup copy of everything you need to recreate your company file in case of accidental loss or damage to your data.

Do you want to save your backup copy online or locally?

○ Online backup

Get automatic, online backup for your QuickBooks data and other important documents using Intuit's online backup solution (fees may apply).

Try now or learn more

◉ Local backup

Save locally to a removable storage device (such as a CD or USB flash drive) or to a folder on your network.

Options   Click **Options** to change your current backup settings.

Back   Next   Finish   Help   Cancel

4. Click Next. The Backup Options window appears. See Figure 1–J.

FIGURE 1–J
Backup Options
Window

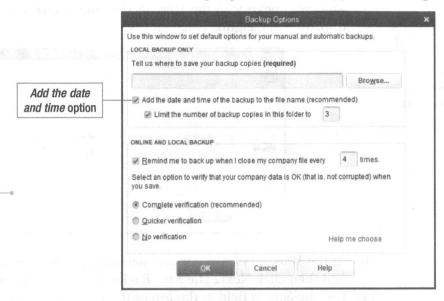

Add the date and time option

HINT
Use the Options button in the Create Backup window (see Figure 1–I) to open the Backup Options window when it does not open automatically. The Backup Options window is used for settings regarding backup.

Note: The first time you make a backup copy of a company file, the Backup Options window appears. For subsequent backup copies of the same file, this window will not appear; you will not need to do Steps 5–9 of this procedure.

5. At the Backup Options window, click the Browse button. The Browse for Folder window appears. See Figure 1–K.

FIGURE 1–K
Browse for Folder
Window

6. At the Browse for Folder window, choose your subfolder, a network directory designated by your instructor, or a removable storage device.
7. Click OK. You are returned to the Backup Options window, and the *Tell us where to save your backup copies (required)* field is completed.
   By default, the date and time are listed in the file name of the backup copy of a company file. When you make many backup copies of a company file, you will have several backup files, each with an individual date and time in the backup file name. You can remove this option by removing the check mark in the box to the left of *Add the date and time of the backup to the file name (recommended)*. See Figure 1–J. You then have only one backup copy of the file, which is replaced each time you update the backup copy. Additional settings can also be changed in this window.
8. Click OK.

9. At the QuickBooks message, click *Use this Location*. The Create Backup window appears with the *When do you want to save your backup copy?* page displayed. See Figure 1–L.

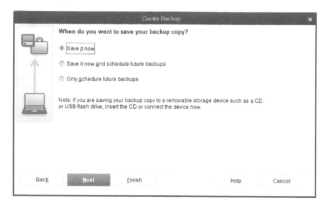

10. At the *When do you want to save your backup copy?* page, select *Save it now* and then click Next. The Save Backup Copy dialog box appears.
11. Use the *Save in* field at the top of the window to navigate to the folder, directory, or storage device where you want to save the backup file, if the correct location is not already selected.
12. In the *File name* text box, change the file name to EX1 *[Your Name] Kristin Raina Interior Designs*. You can leave the word *[Backup]* in the filename. See Figure 1–M.

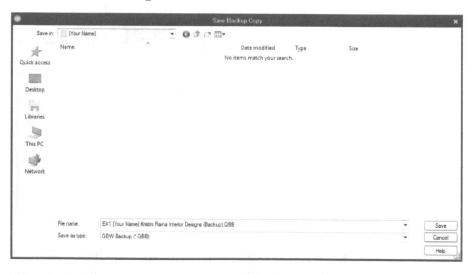

13. Click Save.

   If you use a file name that already exists, the message Confirm Save As appears and asks if you want to replace the existing file. If you want to replace or update the existing file, click Yes. If you do not want to replace the existing file, click No and then use a different file name in the Save Backup Copy dialog box.

   If the QuickBooks message appears, click *Use this Location*.
14. A QuickBooks Desktop Information message appears, informing you that the backup has been saved. Click OK.

You have now made a backup copy of the company file, but the original file is still open. To begin working, you must restore the backup copy that you just created.

HINT

When there is a Save or OK command button in a window, the button must be clicked to save the changes. If you exit from the window by clicking the X, all changes will be lost.

Restoring a Company File

You use the Restore command to open a backup copy of a company file. Recall that backup copies are automatically assigned the extension .QBB and that they are condensed copies of a company file. QuickBooks gives the restored copy a .QBW extension, which denotes it as a working copy of the company file. If you are using removable storage devices to store your backup copies of company files, it is recommended that you use the hard drive for the exercises and use the removable storage devices only for backup. Using removable storage devices for the exercises may be slow, and all your work for one company file may not fit onto one removable storage device.

Restoring a backup file is a two-step process. In the first step (Open Backup Copy), you determine which backup copy you wish to open; in the second step (Save Company File As), you indicate where you wish to restore the backup copy and what the file name should be. In business, the backup company file would be restored to the original company file name. In this book, however, the intent is to retain the original company file intact for others to use, so the backup company file will *not* be restored to the original company file name but rather to your exercise company file name, which includes your name or initials.

To restore the backup copy of the company file:

1. At the main menu bar, click File and then click *Open or Restore Company*. The Open or Restore Company window appears with the *What type of file do you want to open or restore?* page displayed.

    This is the same window that appeared earlier in the chapter when you first opened the CH1 Kristin Raina Interior Designs company file, as seen in Figure 1–F on page 10. This window is now also used to restore a backup copy of a company file. Whenever you use this window, be clear about whether you are opening a company file or restoring a backup copy of a company file so you make the correct choice.

2. At the page *What type of file do you want to open or restore?*, select *Restore a backup copy*. See Figure 1–N.

HINT

It is recommended that you restore your company file to a hard drive location. Working with a file on a removeable storage device may be slower, and if the file is located on a network drive, it could be damaged if a network error occurs.

FIGURE 1–N
Open or Restore Company Window—Restore a Backup Copy Selected

Restore a backup copy

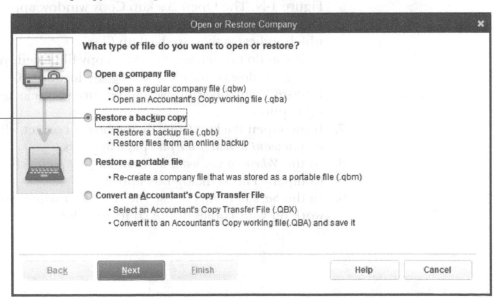

3. Click Next. The page *Is the backup copy stored locally or online?* appears.
4. At the page *Is the backup copy stored locally or online?*, choose *Local backup* and then click Next. The Open Backup Copy dialog box appears.
5. In the *Look in* field, choose the location where you saved your backup copy.
6. Select the company file **EX1** *[Your Name]* **Kristin Raina Interior Designs (Backup).QBB**. See Figure 1–O.

FIGURE 1–O
Open Backup Copy
Dialog Box—EX1
[Your Name] Kristin
Raina Interior Designs
(Backup).QBB
Selected

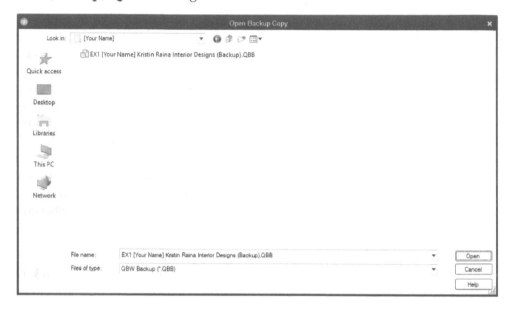

HINT

See Appendix A for a comparison of the windows used to open a company file and restore (open) a backup copy of a company file.

Look back at Figures 1-F and 1-G on page 10 and compare them with Figure 1-N and Figure 1-O. When you open a company file at the Open or Restore Company window, as in Figure 1-F, you choose the option *Open a company file*. The Open a Company dialog box appears, as shown in Figure 1-G. All the files in this dialog box have the extension.QBW.

In contrast, when you want to open a backup copy of a company file, you must restore the file. At the Open or Restore Company window, you choose the option *Restore a backup copy*, as shown in Figure 1-N. The Open Backup Copy window appears, as shown in Figure 1-O. All the files in this dialog box have the extension .QBB, which indicates they are backup files.

If you do not see your backup copy file listed, you may be in the wrong window or have the wrong file location. Go back to the Open or Restore Company window, and be sure you selected the *Restore a backup copy* option.

7. If the Open Backup Copy dialog box is correct, click Open. The *Where do you want to restore the file?* page appears.
8. At the *Where do you want to restore the file?* page, click Next. The Save Company File as dialog box appears.
9. In the *Save in* field, choose the subfolder where you will open and work on your copies of the company files.

10. In the *File name* text box, type EX1 *[Your Name]* Kristin Raina Interior Designs. The prefix EX followed by the chapter number and your name or initials will be used for the restored copies as well as the backup copies. See Figure 1–P.

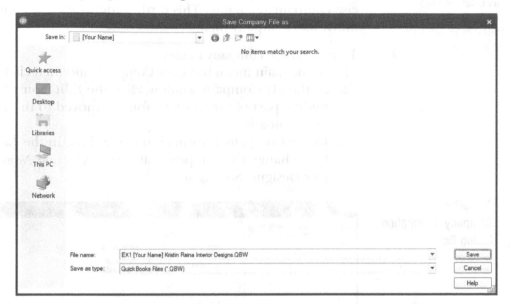

When a backup copy of a company file is restored, it becomes a working copy of the company file, and QuickBooks assigns it a .QBW extension.

11. If the information is correct, click Save.

If you use a file name that already exists, a Confirm Save As message appears to indicate that this company file exists and to ask if you want to replace it. If this is what you want to do, click Yes. You must type yes in the box in the Delete Entire File message and then click OK. If the name shown in the Confirm Save As message is not the correct file name, click No and then enter the correct file name in the Save Company File as dialog box.

12. At the QuickBooks Desktop Login window, in the *Password* text box, type Student1 and then click OK. If the Home page window appears, click the X to close it. If the Left Icon bar appears, click View at the main menu bar and then click *Hide Icon Bar* to remove it.

HINT

If you receive a QuickBooks Update Service message, click Install Later. See the following section on QuickBooks Updates for more information.

After your backup copy is successfully restored, your exercise copy of the company file appears in the QuickBooks window, but the title bar indicates the original company file name. Before you begin working, you should change the company name in the My Company window to match your exercise company file name. This further identifies this company file as your individual company file.

To change the company name:

1. At the main menu bar, click Company and then click *My Company.*
2. At the My Company window, click the Edit icon 🖉 in the upper middle part of the window. You are moved to the Company Information dialog box.
3. In the Company Information dialog box, in the *Company Name* text box, change the company name to EX1 *[Your Name]* Kristin Raina Interior Designs. See Figure 1–Q.

FIGURE 1–Q
Company Information Dialog Box

4. If the information is correct, click OK.
   You are returned to the My Company window with the company name updated. See Figure 1–R.

FIGURE 1–R
My Company Window—Updated

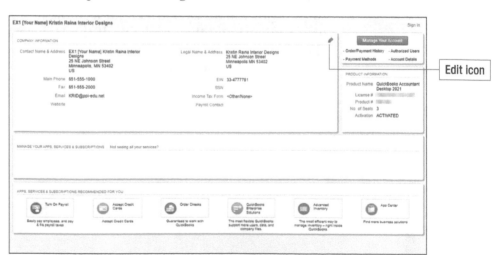

HINT

The *file name* appears in the Open a Company, Backup, and Restore dialog boxes and File or Windows Explorer. The *company name* appears in the title bar of QuickBooks and the reports. It is recommended that you use the same name in both locations to more easily keep track of your files.

5. Close the My Company window.

The company name is changed in the title bar. This company name now appears in the heading of the reports. The name in the title bar comes from the Company Information dialog box. The name of the company file in the Open a Company dialog box is based on the file name typed in the Backup and Restore dialog boxes. Be careful to type the same name in both places. Doing so will help you to more easily keep track of your files.

In business, backing up is used to maintain a copy of company financial records, and backup copies should be made on a regular basis. You would need to restore the backup copy only in the event your computer or files were damaged or you upgraded your computer system. An accountant may use backup and restore procedures when reviewing clients' accounting records.

Because you may work in a computer lab, where many students may work on the same company files, the backup and restore procedures are used to make your own personal copy of the company file so that you may practice the work in each chapter in your own file. You will also use the backup procedures to make a copy to your personal removable device in case your personal copy in a computer lab is deleted.

As you open company files and then do the backup and restore, you may become unsure as to which company file is open or in what location you are working. You can check the company file and the location path by viewing the Open Previous Company submenu.

To view which company file is open:

1. At the main menu bar, click File and then click *Open Previous Company*. The Open Previous Company submenu appears. The file listed at the top of the submenu list is the current file that is open. See Figure 1–S.

FIGURE 1–S Open Previous Company Submenu

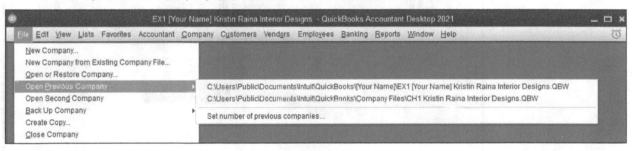

HINT

If you are unsure about the location of the company file in which you are working, click File and then click *Open Previous Company*. The file listed at the top of the submenu list is the current file that is open.

2. Click any open space on the computer screen to remove the File menu and Open Previous Company submenu.

QuickBooks Updates

QuickBooks occasionally provides updates to the current version of the software that you are using. Product updates, sometimes referred to as *maintenance releases* by QuickBooks, are delivered via the internet. Your computer can be set up so that the product updates are automatically downloaded (which is the default), or you can disable the automatic updates. If the updates are not set to install automatically, you will receive messages alerting you when updates are available. You can also check for QuickBooks updates using the Help menu.

To update QuickBooks using the Help menu:

1. At the main menu bar, click Help.
2. At the drop-down menu, click *Update QuickBooks Desktop*. The Update QuickBooks Desktop window appears.
3. At the Update QuickBooks Desktop window, click the Update Now button on the Overview tab, or click the Update Now tab. See Figure 1–T.

FIGURE 1–T
Update QuickBooks
Desktop Window

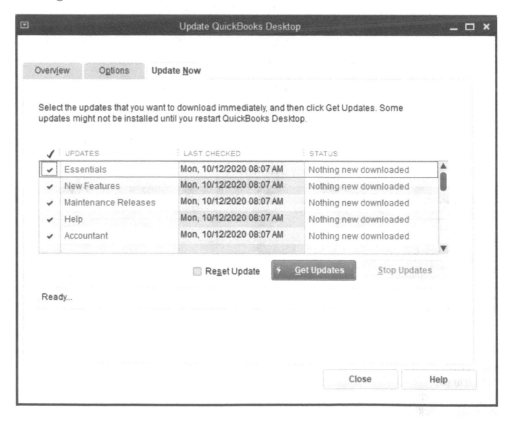

4. On the Update Now tab, click the Get Updates button. If any updates are available, they will be downloaded. Follow the instructions to download the updates.
5. Close the Update QuickBooks Desktop window.

Product updates are noted by release numbers, such as R2 and R3. To determine the most recent update downloaded onto your computer, press the F2 function key on the keyboard or press Ctrl + 1 to display the Product Information window which contains the product edition and latest release number. See Figure 1–U.

FIGURE 1–U
Product Information
Window

product edition
and release
number

Product Information   ✕

Product   QuickBooks Accountant Desktop 2021 Release R1P
License number   ▓▓▓▓▓▓▓▓   ACTIVATED
Product number   ▓▓▓▓▓▓   R1_13
User Licenses   3
Installed   10/04/2020

SERVICES INFORMATION
AuthID   ▓▓▓▓▓
Company Realm ID null
Online Billing Token
Shopping Source Token

USAGE INFORMATION
Date First Used   10/11/2013   Number of Uses 321
Audit Trail   Enabled since 12/31/2006 00:08:58

INTEGRATED APPLICATION INFORMATION
# of apps   0
Last accessed

FILE INFORMATION
Location   C:\Users\Public\Documents\Intuit\QuickBooks\[Your
           Name]\EX1 [Your Name] Kristin Raina Interior Designs.QBW

CONDENSE INFORMATION
Last run   None
Last as of date   None
Last payroll deleted   None
Last inventory deleted   None

		Versions Used on File
File Size	15260 K	V8.0D R2 06/10/2000
Page Size	4096	V10.0D R1 12/16/2001
Total Transactions	2	V12.0D Bw1 09/27/2002
Total Targets	5	V12.0D Bw3 11/13/2002
Total Links	0	V12.0D R1 12/20/2002
Dictionary Entries	0	V12.0D R2 03/19/2003
DB File Fragments	1	V15.0D R1 01/06/2005
Schema version	133.0	
Server Port	0	

List Information
Total Accounts: 24
Total Names: 0
  Customers: 0
  Vendors: 0
  Employees: 0

Server IP   ▓▓▓▓▓
Server Name   QB_data_engine_31
# of Users Logged In   1
Current Cache Size   513
Max Cache Size   1024

Free Memory   3164956 K

LOCAL SERVER INFORMATION
Hosting: Off   Server IP   DB Engine version   ▓▓▓▓
Initial Cache   512   Server Port   0
Cache   1024 Server Name

[OK]   [Review last Verify / Rebuild]

6. Close the Product Information window.

Exiting QuickBooks

Most work is automatically saved in QuickBooks when the correct command button is chosen. At the end of a session, it is recommended that you use the Back Up command to save your work onto a removable storage device or a network directory designated by your instructor. For the security of your work, you should also close your company file before exiting Quick-Books. However, it is not necessary to make a backup copy of the exercise file for this session.

At the end of each session, you should close the company file and then close QuickBooks.

To close the company file and exit QuickBooks:
1. At the main menu bar, click File and then click *Close Company*.
2. To exit QuickBooks, click the X on the QuickBooks title bar, or click File and then click *Exit*.

Chapter Review and Assessment

Procedure Review

To open a company file:
1. Open QuickBooks.
2. At the No Company Open window, click the *Open or restore an existing company* button, or at the main menu bar, click File and then click *Open or Restore Company.*
3. At the Open or Restore Company window, select *Open a company file* and then click Next.
4. In the Open a Company dialog box in the *Look in* text box, choose *Company Files* or the subfolder containing the company files for this course.
5. Select the company file **CH# Company Name.QBW**.
6. Click Open.
7. At the QuickBooks Desktop Login window, in the *Password* text box, type Student1 and then click OK.
8. If the Set Up an External Accountant User window appears, insert a check mark in the box to the left of *Don't show this again* and then click No to close the window. If the Accountant Center window appears, remove the check mark in the box to the left of *Show Accountant Center when opening a company file* and then click the X to close the window. If the New Feature Tour window appears, click the X (close button) to close the window. If the Help message appears, it will fade away in a few seconds. If the Home page window appears, click the X to close it. If the Left Icon bar appears, click View at the main menu bar and then click *Hide Icon Bar* to remove it.

To make a backup copy of a company file:
1. At the main menu bar, click File and then click *Back Up Company.*
2. At the Back Up Company submenu, click *Create Local Backup.*
3. At the Create Backup window with the page *Do you want to save your backup copy online or locally?* displayed, confirm that *Local backup* is selected and then click Next.

Note: The first time you make a backup copy of a company file, the Backup Options window appears. For subsequent backup copies of the same file, this window will not appear; you will not need to do Steps 4–7 of this procedure.

4. At the Backup Options window, click the Browse button.
5. At the Browse for Folder window, choose your subfolder, a network directory designated by your instructor, or a removable storage device and then click OK.
6. At the Backup Options window, if you do not want multiple backup copies of the company file, remove the check mark to the left of *Add the date and time of the backup to the file name* and then click OK.
7. At the QuickBooks message, click *Use this Location.*
8. At the Create Backup window with the page *When do you want to save your backup copy?* displayed, select *Save it now* and then click Next.
9. In the Save Backup Copy dialog box, use the *Save in* field at the top of the window to navigate to the folder, directory, or storage device where you want to save the backup file, if the correct location is not already selected.

10. In the *File name* text box, type EX# *[Your Name]* Company Name.
11. Click Save. If the QuickBooks message appears, click *Use this Location*.
12. A QuickBooks Desktop Information message appears, informing you that the backup has been saved. Click OK.

To restore the backup copy of the company file:
1. At the main menu bar, click File and then click *Open or Restore Company*.
2. At the Open or Restore Company window, with the page *What type of file do you want to open or restore?* displayed, select *Restore a backup copy* and then click Next.
3. At the page *Is the backup copy stored locally or online?*, choose *Local backup* and then click Next.
4. In the Open Backup Copy dialog box, in the *Look in* field, choose the location where you saved your backup copy.
5. Select the company file **EX# *[Your Name]* Company Name.QBB**.
6. Click Open.
7. At the page *Where do you want to restore the file?*, click Next.
8. In the Save Company File as dialog box, in the *Save in* field, choose the subfolder in which you will open and work on your copies of the company files.
9. In the *File name* text box, type EX# *[Your Name]* Company Name.
10. Click Save.
11. At the QuickBooks Desktop Login window, in the *Password* text box, type Student1 and then click OK. If the Home page window appears, click the X to close it. If the Left Icon bar appears, click View at the main menu bar and then click *Hide Icon Bar* to remove it.

To change the company name:
1. At the main menu bar, click Company and then click *My Company*.
2. At the My Company window, click the Edit icon. You are moved to the Company Information dialog box.
3. In the Company Information dialog box, in the *Company Name* text box, type EX# *[Your Name]* Company Name.
4. Click OK. You are returned to the My Company window with the company name updated.
5. Close the My Company window. The company name is updated in the title bar of QuickBooks.

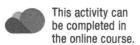 This activity can be completed in the online course.

Key Concepts

Select the letter of the item that best matches each definition.

a. Company name
b. Ellipsis
c. Activities
d. QuickBooks
e. File name

f. Reports
g. New Company Setup
h. Main menu bar
i. Back Up Company
j. Lists/Centers

_____ 1. A software package used to record business and accounting activities, designed with the non-accountant in mind.

_____ 2. The level of operation that creates a new company file.

_____ 3. The level of operation that records background information.

_____ 4. The level of operation where most routine work is processed.

_____ 5. The level of operation where information can be displayed and printed.

_____ 6. Follows a command on a menu and means additional information must be entered in a second window called a *dialog box*.

_____ 7. The name that appears in the title bar of QuickBooks. The source is the My Company window.

_____ 8. The part of the QuickBooks window where the File, Edit, View, Lists, Favorites, Accountant, Company, Customers, Vendors, Employees, Banking, Reports, Window, and Help menus are displayed.

_____ 9. The name indicated in the Backup and Restore dialog boxes.

_____ 10. The command used to make a copy of the original company file.

This activity can be completed in the online course.

Procedure Check

1. Describe QuickBooks. What kind of software is it? Who uses it, and how is it useful?
2. List the steps for opening a company file called Madeline's Shoe Club, stored in the Company Files subfolder on the hard drive.
3. Imagine that you have been instructed to work on a company file named **CH1 Edward's Electronics**. List the steps you need to take to make a backup copy called **EX1** *[Your Name]* **Edward's Electronics** and to restore the backup copy. Assume the company file is stored in the Company Files subfolder and backed up and restored in the *[Your Name]* subfolder. If you backed up the file to a removable storage device, how would the steps be different, and how would they be the same?
4. Imagine that you have been working on a company file previously backed up and restored as **EX1** *[Your Name]* **Travel Food Supplies** but are unable to finish the work today. Explain what you will need to do to open the company file and complete the work when you return the following day, assuming no additional backup copy was made.
5. Explain the difference between the file name and the company name.
6. Discuss the advantages of using a computerized accounting software package instead of using non-computerized accounting methods. Discuss the specific advantages of using QuickBooks.

Case Problems

Demonstrate your knowledge of the QuickBooks features discussed in this chapter by completing the following case problems.

Case Problem 1–1

Lynn Garcia, a music instructor, opened a new business called Lynn's Music Studio. A company file has been created for her in QuickBooks, with the date of April 1, 2022 as the opening date of her business.

1. Open the company file **CH1 Lynn's Music Studio.QBW**.

2. At the QuickBooks Desktop Login window, in the *Password* text box, type **Student1** and then click OK.
3. Make a backup copy of the company file and name it **LMS1** *[Your Name]* **Lynn's Music Studio**.
4. Restore the backup copy of the company file. In both the Open Backup Copy and Save Company File as dialog boxes, use the file name **LMS1** *[Your Name]* **Lynn's Music Studio** and enter **Student1** as the password.
5. Change the company name to **LMS1** *[Your Name]* **Lynn's Music Studio**.
6. Close the company file.
7. Exit QuickBooks.

Case Problem 1–2

Olivia Chen, an internet consultant and web designer, opened a business called Olivia's Web Solutions. A company file has been created for her using QuickBooks, reflecting the opening date of her business on June 1, 2022.

1. Open the company file **CH1 Olivia's Web Solutions.QBW**.
2. At the QuickBooks Desktop Login window, in the *Password* text box, type **Student1** and then click OK.
3. Make a backup copy of the company file and name it **OWS1** *[Your Name]* **Olivia's Web Solutions**.
4. Restore the backup copy of the company file. In both the Open Backup Copy and Save Company File as dialog boxes, use the file name **OWS1** *[Your Name]* **Olivia's Web Solutions** and enter **Student1** as the password.
5. Change the company name to **OWS1** *[Your Name]* **Olivia's Web Solutions**.
6. Close the company file.
7. Exit QuickBooks.

## CHAPTER 2

Vendors

Adding Vendors and Creating and Paying Bills

Objectives

- Identify the system default accounts for vendors

- Update the Vendor Center by adding and editing vendor information

- Record purchases on account in the Enter Bills window

- Process credit memos in the Enter Bills window

- Record payments of accounts payable in the Pay Bills window

- Record cash purchases in the Write Checks window

- Display and print vendor-related reports

 The online course includes additional training and assessment resources. Reports created for the Chapter Problem can be uploaded for instructor review.

Chapter Introduction

QuickBooks allows you to track all vendor transactions. A **vendor** is someone from whom a company buys goods or services, either on account or for cash. You should establish a file for each vendor before entering transactions for that vendor. The collection of all vendor files comprises the vendor list, which is contained in the Vendor Center (Lists/Centers).

Once a vendor file is established, transactions (Activities) such as receiving a bill from a vendor, paying that bill, and paying for a cash purchase can be entered in the Enter Bills, Pay Bills, and Write Checks windows, respectively. As transactions are recorded in the activities windows, QuickBooks simultaneously updates the vendor's file in the Vendor Center, as well as any related reports (Reports), with information about the transaction for a particular vendor.

In this chapter, you will record and pay bills received by our sample company, Kristin Raina Interior Designs, for non-inventory purchases of goods and services, such as operating expenses and assets acquisitions. In addition, you will record cash purchases when bills have not been previously received or entered.

QuickBooks versus Manual Accounting: Vendor Transactions

In a manual accounting system, all purchases of goods on account are recorded in a multicolumn **purchases journal**. At month end, the totals are posted to the affected asset, expense, and liability (Accounts Payable) accounts. As each purchase transaction is recorded, the appropriate vendor's account in the accounts payable subsidiary ledger is updated for the new liability on a daily basis. Payments for open accounts payable balances and payments for cash purchases of goods or services are recorded in a multicolumn **cash payments journal**. As in the purchases journal, monthly totals are posted to the general ledger accounts, while payment information is recorded daily in the vendor's subsidiary ledger record.

In QuickBooks, the Vendor Center serves as the accounts payable subsidiary ledger for the company. The Vendor Center contains a file for each company and individual from whom the company buys goods and services. Relevant information—such as name, address, contact person, and credit limit—should be entered at the time the vendor's file is created in the Vendor Center.

When the company receives a bill for goods or services, you record the bill in the Enter Bills window. The Enter Bills window is equivalent to the multicolumn purchases journal. QuickBooks automatically updates the **Chart of Accounts List** and general ledger; at the same time, it updates the vendor's file in the Vendor Center for the new liability. When the bill is to be paid, you enter the transaction in the Pay Bills window. This is equivalent to recording a payment of open accounts payable in a cash payments journal. QuickBooks updates the Chart of Accounts List, general ledger, and the vendor's file to reflect payment of the liability.

For a cash payment for a bill not previously entered, use the Write Checks window. This is equivalent to recording payment for cash purchases of goods or services in a cash payments journal. Again, the Chart of Accounts List, the general ledger, and the vendor's file are updated simultaneously.

---

vendor someone from whom a company buys goods or services, either on account or for cash

purchases journal a journal used to record all purchases of goods on account; can be in a single-column or multi-column format

cash payments journal a multicolumn journal used to record all cash payment activities, including payments of accounts payable

HINT

See Appendix B for a comparison of manual accounting versus QuickBooks.

Chart of Accounts List the list of accounts a company uses as it conducts its business

System Default Accounts

To process transactions expeditiously and organize data for reporting, Quick-Books establishes specific general ledger accounts as default accounts in each activity window. When you enter transactions, QuickBooks automatically increases or decreases certain account balances depending on the nature of the transaction. For example, when you enter a vendor invoice in the Enter Bills window, QuickBooks automatically increases (credits) the Accounts Payable account, because the Enter Bills window is used to record purchases on account. When you write a check in the Pay Bills window, QuickBooks automatically decreases (debits) the Accounts Payable account. Therefore, you do not have to enter the account numbers or names for these default accounts, because they have been pre-established by QuickBooks.

Throughout the text, the default accounts for each type of transaction, such as vendor, customer, inventory, and payroll, will be identified.

Chapter Problem

In this chapter, you will enter and track vendor transactions for Kristin Raina Interior Designs, a sole proprietorship that provides interior decorating and design services to both residential and commercial clients. The owner of the business, Kristin Raina, began operations on January 1, 2022 by investing $50,000 in the business. During January, Kristin Raina devoted most of her time to organizing the business, securing office space, and buying assets. Beginning February 1, 2022, she wishes to begin tracking vendor transactions. Information for several vendors has been entered in the Vendor Center. This information, along with February 1, 2022, beginning balances, is contained in the company file **CH2 Kristin Raina Interior Designs**.

To open the company file:
1. Open QuickBooks.
2. At the No Company Open window, click the *Open or restore an existing company* button, or click File and then click *Open or Restore Company*.
3. At the Open or Restore Company window, choose *Open a company file* and then click Next.
4. In the Open a Company dialog box, in the *Look in* field, choose the Company Files subfolder or the subfolder containing the company files.
5. Select the company file **CH2 Kristin Raina Interior Designs.QBW** and then click Open.
6. At the QuickBooks Desktop Login window, in the *Password* text box, type Student1 and then click OK.
7. Close all pop-up windows and messages.

HINT

Refer to page 11 in Chapter 1 for steps to close all unnecessary windows and messages.

To make a backup copy of the company file:
1. At the main menu bar, click File and then click *Back Up Company*.
2. At the Back Up Company submenu, click *Create Local Backup*.
3. At the Create Backup window—*Do you want to save your backup copy online or locally?* page, confirm that *Local backup* is selected and then click Next.
4. At the Backup Options window, click the Browse button.
5. At the Browse for Folder window, choose your subfolder, a network directory designated by your instructor, or a removable storage device and then click OK.

HINT

The first time you make a backup copy of a company file, the Backup Options window appears. For subsequent backup copies of the same file, this window will not appear; you will not need to complete Steps 4–7 of this procedure.

HINT

QuickBooks automatically assigns the extension .QBB to a backup copy.

6. At the Backup Options window, you can remove the check mark to the left of *Add the date and time of the backup to the file name* if you do not want multiple backup copies and then click OK.

7. At the QuickBooks message, click *Use this Location*.

8. At the Create Backup window—*When do you want to save your backup copy?* page, choose *Save it now* and then click Next.

9. In the Save Backup Copy dialog box, in the *Save in* field, choose your subfolder, a network directory designated by your instructor, or a removable storage device, if the location you want is not already selected.

10. In the *File name* text box, type EX2 *[Your Name]* Kristin Raina Interior Designs.

11. Click Save. If the QuickBooks message appears, click *Use this Location*.

12. At the QuickBooks Information message, click OK.

To restore the backup copy of the company file:

1. At the main menu bar, click File and then click *Open or Restore Company*.

2. At the Open or Restore Company window—*What type of file do you want to open or restore?* page, choose *Restore a backup copy* and then click Next.

3. At the *Is the backup copy stored locally or online?* page, choose *Local backup* and then click Next.

4. In the Open Backup Copy dialog box, in the *Look in* field, choose the location where you saved your backup copy.

5. Select the company file **EX2 *[Your Name]* Kristin Raina Interior Designs.QBB** and then click Open.

6. At the *Where do you want to restore the file?* page, click Next.

7. In the Save Company File as dialog box, in the *Save in* field, choose the subfolder in which you will open and work on your copies of the company file.

8. In the *File name* text box, type EX2 *[Your Name]* Kristin Raina Interior Designs and then click Save.

9. At the QuickBooks Desktop Login window, in the *Password* text box, type Student1 and then click OK

10. Close all pop-up windows and messages.

HINT

QuickBooks automatically assigns the extension .QBW to a restored copy.

The backup copy has been restored, but the company name still reads CH2 Kristin Raina Interior Designs.

To change the company name:

1. At the main menu bar, click Company and then click *My Company*.

2. At the My Company window, click the Edit icon.

3. In the Company Information dialog box, change the company name to **EX2 *[Your Name]* Kristin Raina Interior Designs** and then click OK.

4. Close the My Company window.

The Vendor Center

The Vendor Center contains a file for each vendor with which the company does business. For example, the utility company that supplies electricity, the company that provides advertising, and the company from which equipment for the business is purchased are all vendors. The Vendor Center contains important information on each vendor, such as company name, address, contact person, type of vendor, terms, credit limit, tax identification number, and current balance owed. All the vendors with which the company does business should be included in the Vendor Center.

You should enter the information for each vendor in the Vendor Center before recording transactions. However, if you inadvertently omit a vendor, you can add that vendor during the Activities level of operation with minimal disruption.

You need to periodically revise the Vendor Center to add new vendors, delete vendors no longer used in the business, and make modifications as background information on vendors changes. Making these adjustments to the vendor files in the Vendor Center is referred to as *updating* the Vendor Center, and doing so is part of the second level of operation in QuickBooks.

Kristin Raina has entered information for existing and anticipated vendors in the Vendor Center of her company file.

To review the Vendor Center:

1. At the main menu bar, click Vendors and then click *Vendor Center*. If a window appears titled New Feature - Attach Documents to QuickBooks, click OK or the X to close the window. The Vendor Center appears with the vendor file for Galeway Computers displayed. See Figure 2–A.

FIGURE 2–A Vendor Center—Galeway Computers Vendor File Displayed

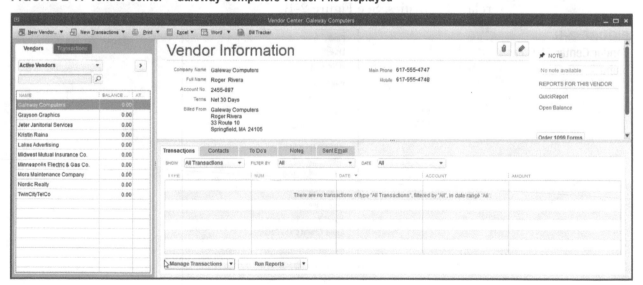

Table 2–1 describes the various parts of the Vendor Center.

TABLE 2–1
Vendor Center

Part	Description
Vendors tab	Lists all vendors with current balances owed. You can display all vendors, active vendors, or vendors with balances.
Transactions tab	Lists all transactions for a selected vendor. The Transactions tab in the Vendor Information section contains the same information.
New Vendor button	Used to add a new vendor or multiple vendors.
New Transactions button	Used to enter a bill or pay a bill.
Vendor Information section	Displays background and transaction information for the vendor selected on the Vendor tab.
Attach icon	Used to attach documents from your computer or scanner.
Edit icon	Used to edit background information for the vendor selected on the Vendors tab.
Reports for This Vendor section	Lists the reports available in the Vendor Center.
Contacts tab	Used to add a contact name for this vendor by clicking the Manage Contacts drop-down arrow and choosing *Add New*. You can designate the contact as primary, secondary, or additional.
To Do's tab	Used to view the To Do List for this vendor.
Notes tab	Used to include narrative information specific to a vendor.

In addition, after selecting a vendor, you can right-click the vendor name on the Vendors tab to display a shortcut menu to accomplish most vendor-related activities. See Figure 2–B.

FIGURE 2–B
Vendor Center Shortcut Menu

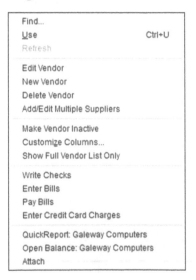

To view a specific vendor file:

1. Move the mouse pointer to *Jeter Janitorial Service* and then double-click to open the file. If a window appears titled New Feature Add/Edit Multiple List Entries, insert a check mark in the box to the left of the *Do not display this message in the future* option and then click OK to close the window. The file opens in Edit Vendor mode. See Figure 2–C.

FIGURE 2–C
Vendor File—Jeter Janitorial Services

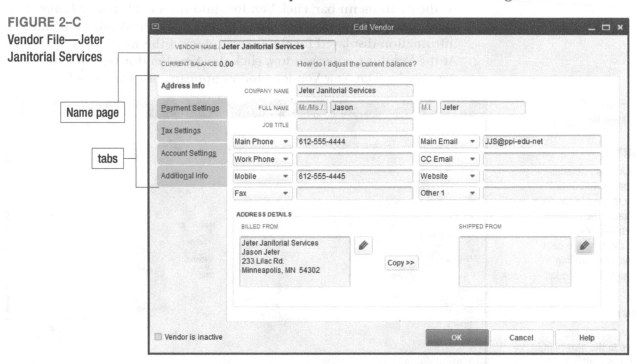

Table 2–2 describes the various parts of the vendor's file.

TABLE 2–2
Vendor File

Part	Description
Name page	Displays the vendor's name, the vendor's current balance, and three command buttons: OK, Cancel, and Help.
Address Info tab	Enter the vendor's company name, address, contact person, telephone and mobile numbers, and email address. The Edit icon can be used to edit address information.
Payment Settings tab	Enter information such as the vendor's account number, credit limit, payment terms, and name to be printed on checks.
Tax Settings tab	Enter the vendor's tax identification number and indicate if the vendor is to receive IRS Form 1099.
Account Settings tab	Identify up to three default general ledger posting accounts for each vendor. Once a vendor is selected in an activity window, the first account listed is identified as the general ledger posting account for that transaction. The use of this tab is optional.
Additional Info tab	Enter the vendor type and create customized fields.

2. Close the Edit Vendor window.
3. Close the Vendor Center.

Adding a Vendor

Kristin Raina has just hired a new accountant who will provide accounting services each month for the business. She wishes to add this vendor to the Vendor Center by creating a vendor file.

To add a new vendor:

1. At the main menu bar, click Vendors and then click *Vendor Center*. The Vendor Center opens with a list of vendors on the Vendor tab and information displayed for the first vendor on the list.

2. At the Vendor Center window, click the New Vendor button and select *New Vendor*. The New Vendor window appears. See Figure 2–D.

FIGURE 2–D
New Vendor Window

HINT

QuickBooks defaults to the current date. Be sure to change the date to match the problem. When entering a date, you can type the date instead of scrolling through the calendar.

HINT

Press the Tab key to move to the next field, or press Shift + Tab to move back a field. In the *BILLED FROM* field, at the end of each line in the address, use the Enter key or the Down Arrow key to move to the next line.

3. Enter the following data on the Name page and the Address Info tab. (The Edit button can be used to enter the address, but this is not necessary.)

Name page	*VENDOR NAME:*	*[Your Name]* Accounting Service
	OPENING BALANCE:	0 AS OF February 1, 2022
Address Info	*COMPANY NAME:*	*[Your Name]* Accounting Service
	FULL NAME:	
	First:	*[Your First Name]*
	Last:	*[Your Last Name]*
	Main Phone:	651-555-2222
	Mobile:	651-555-2223
	Main Email:	*[Your Initials]*@ppi-edu.net
	BILLED FROM:	One Main Plaza
		St. Paul, MN 53602

Your New Vendor window should look similar to Figure 2–E.

FIGURE 2–E
New Vendor Window—
Name Page and Address
Info Tab Completed

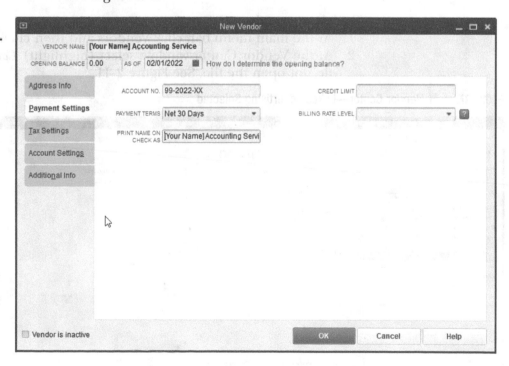

HINT
You can click the Edit icon ✐ to access the address information window.

4. Click the Payment Settings tab and enter the following information.

Payment Settings	ACCOUNT NO.:	99-2022-XX
	PAYMENT TERMS:	Net 30 Days
	PRINT NAME ON CHECK AS:	*[Your Name]* Accounting Service

See Figure 2–F.

FIGURE 2–F
New Vendor Window—
Payments Settings Tab
Completed

5. Click the Account Settings tab and enter the following information, as shown in Figure 2–G.

Account Settings   Select account to pre-fill transactions:
6020 Accounting Expense

FIGURE 2–G
New Vendor Window—
Account Settings Tab
Completed

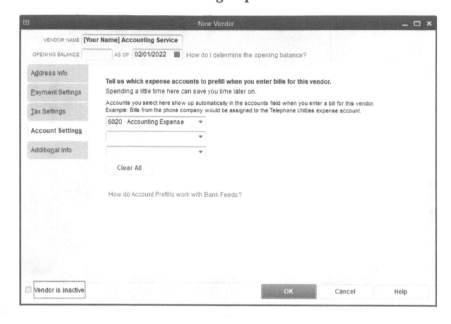

6. If the information is correct, click OK.
7. Close the Vendor Center.

Deleting a Vendor

Kristin Raina wishes to delete Lakes Advertising from the Vendor Center because the company has ceased to operate.

To delete a vendor:
1. At the main menu bar, click Vendors and then click *Vendor Center*.
2. At the Vendor Center window, select (highlight) *Lakes Advertising*, but do not open the file. See Figure 2–H.

FIGURE 2–H Vendor Center—Lakes Advertising Selected

3. At the main menu bar, click Edit and then click *Delete Vendor.*
4. At the Delete Vendor warning, click OK to delete the vendor file.
5. Close the Vendor Center.

QuickBooks cannot delete a vendor that has a balance or that has been part of a transaction for the fiscal period. If a vendor will no longer be used but there has been activity in the file for the period, you can insert a check mark in the *Vendor is inactive* box. The vendor's name is no longer displayed in the reports, but the vendor information is retained in QuickBooks and can be accessed as needed.

Editing a Vendor

HINT

An alternative method to access the Edit Vendor window is to select the Vendor in the Vendor Center and then click the Edit icon.

Kristin Raina needs to edit the file for Minneapolis Electric & Gas Co. because the billing address has changed.

To edit a vendor file:
1. At the main menu bar, click Vendors and then click *Vendor Center.*
2. At the Vendor Center window, double-click *Minneapolis Electric & Gas Co.* The vendor file opens in Edit Vendor mode. See Figure 2–I.

FIGURE 2–I
Edit Vendor Window

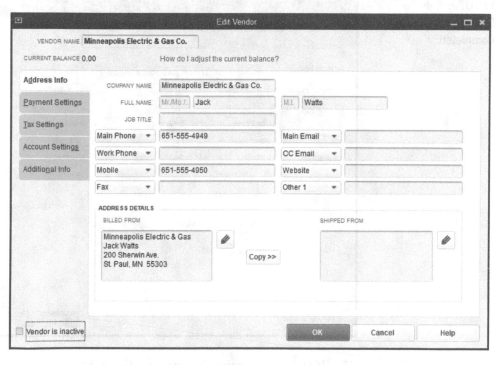

3. Since this is an edit of an address, click the Edit icon [pencil icon]. The Edit Address Information window appears. See Figure 2–J.

FIGURE 2–J
Edit Address Information
Window

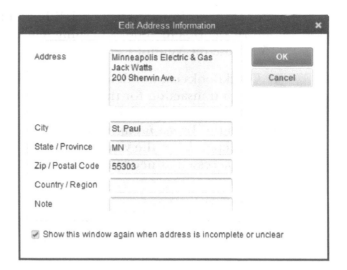

4. At the *Address* field, delete the current street address; in its place, type 150 Douglas Ave. and then click OK. See Figure 2–K.

FIGURE 2–K
Edit Vendor Window—
Completed

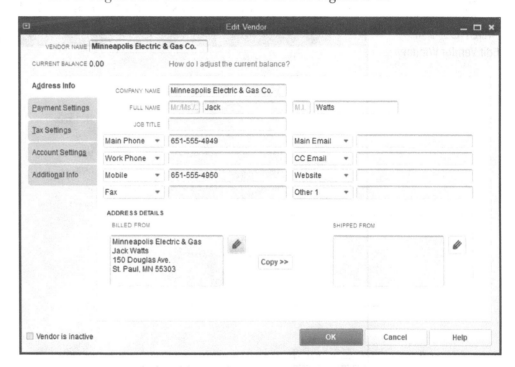

5. If the information is correct, click OK.
6. Close the Vendor Center.

Practice Exercise   2–1

Add the following vendor:

Name page	*VENDOR NAME:*	Williams Office Supply Company
	OPENING BALANCE:	0 AS OF February 1, 2022
Address Info	*COMPANY NAME:*	Williams Office Supply Company
	FULL NAME:	
	First:	Bernard
	Last:	Williams
	Main Phone:	612-555-2240
	Mobile:	612-555-2241
	Main Email:	Wilsup@ppi-edu.net
	BILLED FROM:	15 Grand Ave. S.
		Minneapolis, MN 55404
Payment Settings	*ACCOUNT NO.:*	55-8988
	PAYMENT TERMS:	Net 30 Days
	PRINT NAME ON	
	CHECK AS:	Williams Office Supply Company

Delete the following vendor:

Mora Maintenance Company

Edit the following vendor:

New phone/mobile for Grayson Graphics:

Main Phone:	612-555-0002
Mobile:	612-555-0003

QuickCheck: The updated Vendor Center appears in Figure 2–L.

FIGURE 2–L Updated Vendor Center

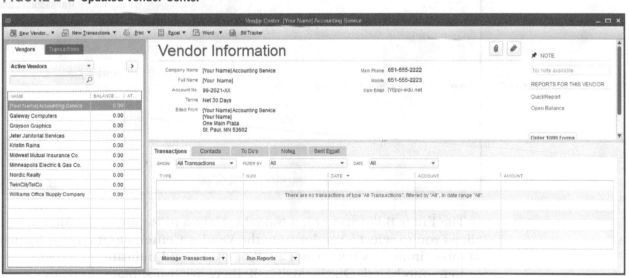

purchase on account
when a company
receives a bill for goods
or services from a vendor
but plans to pay it at a
later date

The Enter Bills Window

In QuickBooks, the Enter Bills window is used to record a **purchase on account**. This window allows you to identify the vendor sending the bill, the invoice date, due date, terms of payment, and nature of purchase (expense, asset, or item). QuickBooks uses the default Accounts Payable account from the Chart of Accounts to post all open bill liabilities. Certain recurring bills can be set up to be recorded automatically as they become due. In addition, you can use this window to record credit memos.

QuickBooks records a transaction that is a purchase on account as follows:

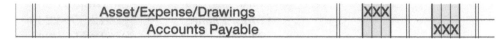

At the same time, QuickBooks updates the vendor's file in the Vendor Center to reflect the new liability.

Recall from Chapter 1 that the third level of operation in QuickBooks is Activities. In this case, the Activity is the recording of purchases on account in the Enter Bills window. Accounts Payable is the default general ledger posting account. All transactions entered in this window will result in a credit to the Accounts Payable account. The *ACCOUNT* field in this window is used to indicate the asset, expense, or drawings account to be debited.

The Enter Bills window appears in Figure 2–M.

FIGURE 2–M
Enter Bills Window—
Expenses Tab

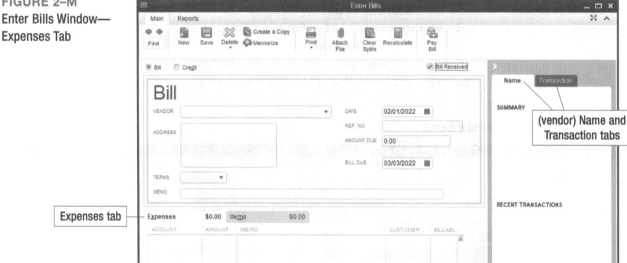

The Enter Bills window has two tabs: Main and Reports. The Main tab allows you to select a vendor from the Vendor Center, enter a bill reference number, indicate whether it is a bill or credit, and indicate the expense or item purchased. On the Main tab, there are two subtabs: Expenses and Items. The Expenses tab should be the active tab.

The Reports tab allows you to access various transactions reports. Most icons and data fields are self-explanatory, but take special note of the parts of the Main tab described in Table 2–3.

TABLE 2–3
Enter Bills Window,
Main Tab

Part	Description
Find button, Previous/Next arrows	Used to move from the current transaction to the previous ◄ or next ► transaction. The current transaction is saved before moving to the previous or next window. Also used to find previously recorded bills by vendor, date range, reference number, or amount.
New button	Used to open a blank transactions window and save a current transaction.
Delete button	Used to delete or void a transaction.
Clear Splits button	Used to erase entries on the Expenses and Items tabs.
Recalculate button	Used to add up multiple entries on the Expenses and Items tabs to fill the *AMOUNT DUE* field.
Pay Bill button	Used to open the Pay Bills window.
Bill Received check box	Indicates that the bill has been received for this expense or item. If unchecked, the expense or item was received, but the bill will follow at a later date.
Expenses/Items tabs	For non-item purchases, such as expenses and non-inventory assets, click the Expenses tab. For the purchase of an item, such as inventory, click the Items tab. The Items tab is covered in Chapter 5.
Save & Close button	Used to save (post) the transaction and close the window.
Save & New button	Used to save (post) the transaction and clear the window for a new transaction.
Clear button	Used to clear the entire screen if errors are made.
Vendor Name/Transaction tabs	Displays a summary of information about the vendor, recent transactions, and notes. Click the > arrow to hide the information, and click the < arrow to display it.
Edit icon 🖉	Allows you to edit vendor information while remaining in the Enter Bills window. The icon appears when a vendor is selected.
SUMMARY section	Lists the phone number, email address, and open balance for the selected vendor.
RECENT TRANSACTIONS section	Displays recent transactions for the selected vendor. Also allows you to access a Quick Report for this vendor.
NOTES section	Clicking the Edit icon 🖉 allows you to post notes concerning the selected vendor.

Entering a Bill

On February 2, 2022, Kristin Raina received a bill for utilities services from Minneapolis Electric & Gas Co. in the amount of $350, Ref. No. 125-55. The bill is due March 4, 2022, terms **Net 30 Days**.

Net 30 Days full payment of an invoice requested within 30 days of the invoice date

To enter a bill:

1. At the main menu bar, click Vendors and then click *Enter Bills*.
2. Click the *Bill* option and the *Bill Received* check box, if necessary.
3. At the *VENDOR* field, click the down arrow to display the VENDOR drop-down list and then click *Minneapolis Electric & Gas Co.*
4. At the *DATE* field, choose *02/02/2022*. (Click the Calendar icon, click through the months to find February 2022, and then click *2*.)
5. At the *REF. NO.* field, type 125-55.
6. At the *AMOUNT DUE* field, type 350.
7. At the *BILL DUE* field, choose *03/04/2022, if necessary.*
8. At the *TERMS* field, click *Net 30 Days*, if necessary.
9. Click the Expenses tab, if necessary, and then in the *ACCOUNT* field, click the first line to display the drop-down list arrow. At the account drop-down list, click *6500 Utilities Expense.* See Figure 2–N.

FIGURE 2–N
Enter Bills Window Completed

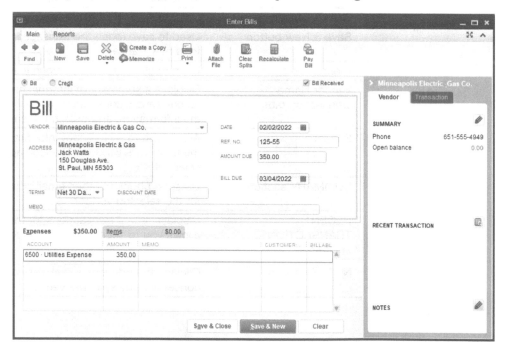

HINT

Click the > arrow on the Vendor Name/Transaction tabs to hide the tabs. Click the < arrow to display the tabs.

10. If the information is correct, click the Save & Close button.

Recall that the Save & Close button saves the information and closes the window. Clicking the Next arrow saves the information and then clears the fields for the next transaction. Clicking the Previous arrow displays the window for the previous transaction. Since this is the first transaction, the Previous arrow cannot yet be used.

For a purchase of an expense on account, the general ledger posting is as follows:

In addition, the vendor file (subledger) for Minneapolis Electric & Gas Co. reflects the new liability:

6500 Utilities Exp		2010 Accts Payable		Minn Electric & Gas	
Dr	Cr	Dr	Cr	Dr	Cr
350			350		350

Updating the Vendor Center While in an Activities Window

On February 2, 2022, Kristin Raina received a bill for prepaid advertising services from Cuza and Carl Associates in the amount of $600, Invoice No. X-145. The bill is due March 4, 2022, terms Net 30 Days. Cuza and Carl Associates is a new vendor.

To update the Vendor Center from the Enter Bills window:

1. At the main menu bar, click Vendors and then click *Enter Bills*.
2. At the VENDOR drop-down list, click < *Add New* >. The New Vendor window appears. This is the same window that appears after choosing the New Vendor button in the Vendor Center window.
3. Enter the following information for the new vendor.

Name page	*VENDOR NAME:*	Cuza and Carl Associates
	OPENING BALANCE:	0 AS OF February 2, 2022
Address Info	*COMPANY NAME:*	Cuza and Carl Associates
	FULL NAME:	
	First Name:	Carrie
	Last Name:	Cuza
	Main Phone:	651-555-8855
	Mobile:	651-555-8856
	Main Email:	CC@ppi-edu.net
	BILLED FROM:	23 W. University Ave.
		St. Paul, MN 53603
Payment Settings	*ACCOUNT NO.:*	KR569
	TERMS:	Net 30 Days
	PRINT NAME	
	ON CHECK AS:	Cuza and Carl Associates

HINT
You can display transactions previously entered by clicking the Previous arrow ◄ above the Find button; any errors can then be corrected. Clicking the Next arrow ► returns you to the current transaction or brings you to a clear window.

4. Click OK to save the information and exit the New Vendor window. The new vendor is now listed in the *VENDOR* field.
5. Complete the remaining fields of the Enter Bills window.
6. On the Expenses tab, click the account *1410 Prepaid Advertising* and key 600 in the *AMOUNT* field, if necessary.

    You use the Expenses tab to indicate which account should be debited. The account can be an asset, expense, or drawings account. Remember when using this window that by default, Accounts Payable is the account credited. See Figure 2–O.

FIGURE 2–O
Enter Bills Window—
Completed

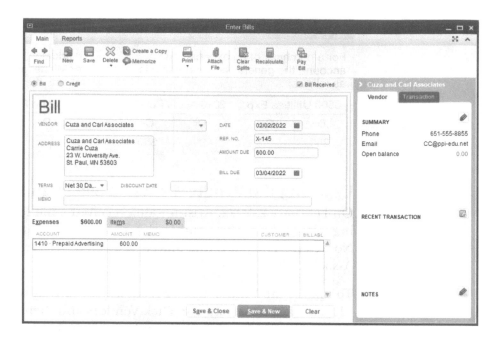

7. If the information is correct, click the Save & New button.

Correcting Errors

There are several ways to correct an error in a recorded transaction. One way is to open the window that contains the transaction and use the Previous arrow [ ] above the Find button to view it. You can then make the necessary correction and save the transaction by choosing the Save button at the top of the window. As an alternative to correcting an error in a transaction, you can delete the transaction by clicking the Delete button (in this example) or by selecting Edit at the main menu bar, clicking *Delete Bill,* and reentering the transaction correctly.

Assume that on February 2, 2022, Kristin Raina inadvertently records a Prepaid Advertising amount for $300, realizes the correct amount is $600, and further realizes the invoice had already been recorded. The bill is from Cuza and Carl Associates, Invoice No. X-145, due March 4, 2022, terms Net 30 Days.

To record an erroneous transaction, make corrections, and delete the transaction:

1. At the main menu bar, click Vendors and then click *Enter Bills* if the Enter Bills window is not already open.
2. At the VENDOR drop-down list, click *Cuza and Carl Associates.*
3. Enter information at the *DATE, REF. NO., BILL DUE, TERMS,* and *ACCOUNT* fields.
4. At the *AMOUNT DUE* field, type 300.
5. Click the Save & New button.
6. You will receive a warning that the Reference No. has already been used. This means that you are incorrectly recording an invoice for the second time. For now, ignore the warning and click Keep Number. The transaction is recorded.
7. Click the Previous arrow [ ].

   Upon reviewing the transaction, you realize the correct amount should have been $600.

8. At the *AMOUNT DUE* field, change the amount to 600. The *AMOUNT* field, on the Expenses tab, will automatically update. Click the Save & New button.
9. A message appears that says *You have changed the transaction. Do you want to record your changes?* Click Yes.

   If a window appears that asks *Want to reclassify several transactions at once?*, click OK to close the window. The corrected transaction is then saved with the new amount. But you now realize that this transaction is a duplicate transaction, and you wish to delete the transaction completely.
10. Click the Previous arrow to view the transaction.
11. Click the X on the Delete button.
12. You will receive another warning message that asks *Are you sure you want to delete this transaction?* Click OK. The duplicate transaction is deleted.

Practice Exercise 2–2

Record the following transactions in the Enter Bills window:

Feb. 3	Received bill from Nordic Realty for February rent, Invoice No. F-22, $800. Due date February 13, 2022 (charge to Rent Expense Account No. 6400).
Feb. 6	Received bill from Williams Office Supply Company for purchase of office supplies, Invoice No. K-222, $475. Due date March 8, 2022 (charge to Office Supplies Account No. 1305).
Feb. 9	Received bill from Midwest Mutual Insurance Co. for one-year insurance policy, Invoice No. 01-22, $2,400. Due date March 11, 2022 (charge to Prepaid Insurance Account No. 1420).
Feb. 13	Received bill from Galeway Computers for new computer, Invoice No. 556588, $3,600. Due date March 15, 2022 (charge to Computers, Cost Account No. 1825).
Feb. 23	Received bill from *[Your Name]* Accounting Service for accounting service, Invoice No. Feb22, $300. Due date March 25, 2022. (Note that Account 6020—Accounting Expense automatically filled the general ledger posting account line on the Expenses tab because the Account Settings tab was completed for this vendor.)

HINT

Click Save and New button after each transaction

Processing a Credit Memo

QuickBooks allows you to process a **credit memo** from a vendor using the Enter Bills window. The resulting credit reduces the balance owed to that vendor.

On February 24, 2022, Kristin Raina returned $75 of damaged office supplies to Williams Office Supply Company for credit, using credit memo CM-245.

credit memo
a reduction of Accounts Payable as a result of a return or an allowance by a vendor

To record a vendor credit:

1. At the main menu bar, click Vendors and then click *Enter Bills* if the Enter Bills window is not already open.
2. At the VENDOR drop-down list, click *Williams Office Supply Company.* Note on the Vendor tab the open balance and the bill for the purchase of supplies dated 02/06/22.
3. Click the *Credit* option. When this option is chosen, the default entry is a debit to Accounts Payable.
4. Enter the appropriate information at the *DATE, REF. NO.*, and *CREDIT AMOUNT* fields.
5. At the *MEMO* field, type Return damaged office supplies.
6. On the Expenses tab, in the *ACCOUNT* field, click *1305 Office Supplies.* See Figure 2–P. Click the Save & Close button.

FIGURE 2–P
Credit Memo—
Completed

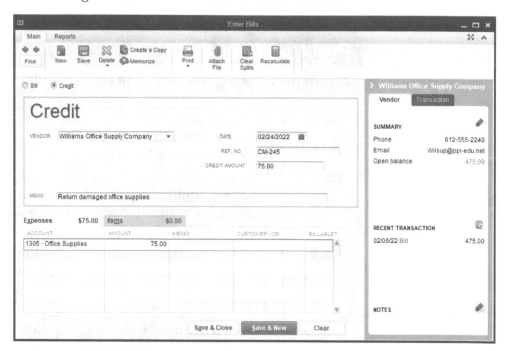

ACCOUNTING CONCEPT

For a return of office supplies for credit, the general ledger posting is as follows:

2010 Accts Payable		1305 Office Supplies	
Dr	Cr	Dr	Cr
75			75

In addition, the vendor file for Williams Office Supply Company reflects the reduced liability amount:

Williams Office Supply Co.		
Dr		Cr
CM 75	Bill	475
	Bal	400

payment on account
payment of an outstanding account payable

The Pay Bills Window

In QuickBooks, the Pay Bills window is used to record a **payment on account**. These are the bills previously recorded in the Enter Bills window. This window displays all open bills as of a selected date. Bills can be paid in full, or a partial payment can be made. Payment can be in the form of check, credit card, or online payment. In addition, several bills can be paid at one time.

The Pay Bills window is designed only for payments of existing bills. The default accounts are Accounts Payable and Cash. The transaction is recorded as follows:

Accounts Payable		XXX		
Cash				XXX

At the same time, the vendor's file in the Vendor Center is updated to reflect the payment. The QuickBooks Pay Bills window appears in Figure 2–Q.

FIGURE 2–Q Pay Bills Window

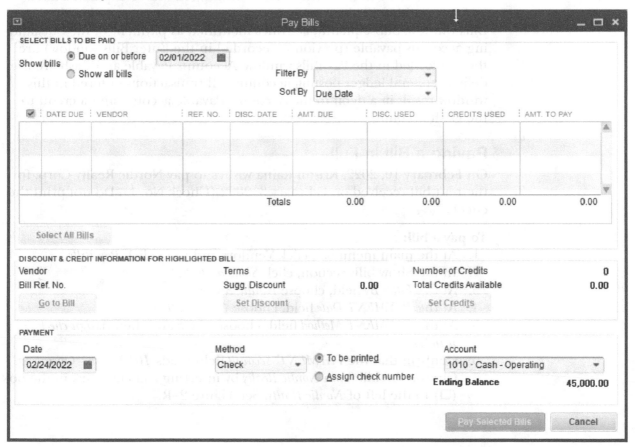

This window allows you to select a bill or bills to be paid, pay all or part of each bill, and designate checks to be printed by the computer. Table 2–4 describes the various parts of the Pay Bills window.

TABLE 2–4
Pay Bills Window

Part	Description
Show bills section	Allows you to display all bills or bills due by a certain date.
Filter By field	Allows you to display bills for all vendors or a selected vendor from the drop-down list.
Sort By field	Allows you to list bills by due date, discount date, vendor, or amount due.
Go to Bill button	Allows you to view the selected bill in the Enter Bills window.
Set Discount/Set Credits buttons	Used to activate any discount or credit for a bill selected for payment.
PAYMENT Date field	Indicates the date of payment that will appear on the payment check and on all reports.
PAYMENT Account field	Lists accounts from which this payment can be made.

If you make an error in this window and have clicked the Pay Selected Bills button, you cannot correct the error in this window. However, you can correct the error in the Write Checks window, as will be explained later.

Activities identified as purchases on account were recorded in the Enter Bills window. Subsequently, activities identified as payment of the outstanding accounts payable (previously recorded in the Enter Bills window) are then recorded in the Pay Bills window. Accounts Payable and Cash are the default general ledger posting accounts. All transactions entered in this window result in a debit to the Accounts Payable account and a credit to the Cash account.

Paying a Bill in Full

On February 10, 2022, Kristin Raina wishes to pay Nordic Realty Corp. for the rent bill received on February 3, 2022 (Check No. 1). Do not print the check.

To pay a bill:
1. At the main menu bar, click Vendors and then click *Pay Bills*.
2. In the Show bills section, click *Show all bills*.
3. At the *Filter By* field, choose *Nordic Realty*.
4. At the *PAYMENT Date* field, choose *02/10/2022*.
5. At the *PAYMENT Method* field, choose *Check* and then *Assign check number*.
6. Confirm that the *PAYMENT Account* field reads *1010 Cash - Operating*.
7. Choose the bill from *Nordic Realty* by inserting a check mark in the box (❑) to the left of *Nordic Realty*. See Figure 2–R.

FIGURE 2–R
Pay Bills Window—
Vendor Bill Selected

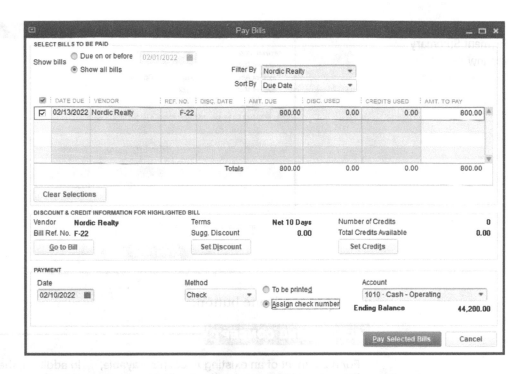

8. Click the Pay Selected Bills button. The Assign Check Numbers window appears.
9. Click the *Let me assign the check numbers below* option.
10. In the *CHECK* field, type 1. See Figure 2–S.

FIGURE 2–S
Assign Check Numbers
Window

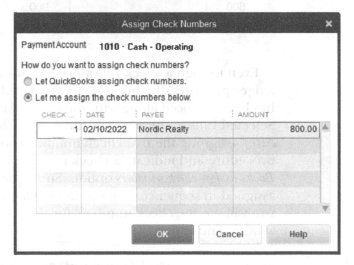

11. Click OK.
12. The Payment Summary window appears. See Figure 2–T.

HINT

If the information is incorrect, it cannot be corrected here. It can be corrected later in the Write Checks window.

FIGURE 2–T
Payment Summary
Window

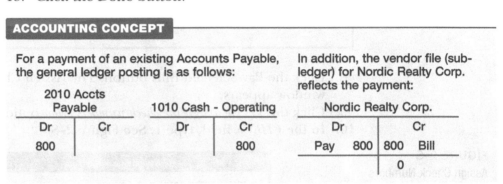

13. Click the Done button.

ACCOUNTING CONCEPT

For a payment of an existing Accounts Payable, the general ledger posting is as follows:

In addition, the vendor file (sub-ledger) for Nordic Realty Corp. reflects the payment:

2010 Accts Payable		1010 Cash - Operating		Nordic Realty Corp.	
Dr	Cr	Dr	Cr	Dr	Cr
800			800	Pay 800	800 Bill
					0

Even though a check is not printed, for accounts payable and general ledger purposes, the bill is now considered paid. The vendor balance owed has been reduced along with the cash balance. Each time you click Pay Selected Bills in this window, the Assign Check Numbers window appears. After assigning the first check number, you can either use the foregoing procedure and indicate a check number, or you can click the *Let Quick-Books assign check numbers* option. Subsequent check numbers will then be assigned in sequence. You will not see a check number in this window, but you will see the check numbers for these transactions in the Write Checks window and reports.

Making a Partial Payment of a Bill

QuickBooks allows a partial payment to be made toward an outstanding bill. On February 23, 2022, Kristin Raina wishes to make a partial payment of $200 toward the Cuza and Carl Associates outstanding bill of $600 (Check No. 2).

To make a partial payment:
1. At the main menu bar, click Vendors and then click *Pay Bills*.
2. In the Show bills section, click *Show all bills* to display all the bills.
3. At the *Filter By* field, choose *Cuza and Carl Associates*.
4. At the *PAYMENT Date* field, set the payment date for *02/23/2022*.

5. At the *PAYMENT Method* field, choose *Check,* if necessary; the *Assign check no.* option should be selected. Accept *1010 Cash - Operating* in the *PAYMENT Account* field.

6. In the *AMT. TO PAY* field, on the line for the Cuza and Carl Associates bill, type 200.

   When you move to another field, the bill is automatically checked off for payment. See Figure 2–U.

FIGURE 2–U
Pay Bills Window—
Partial Payment

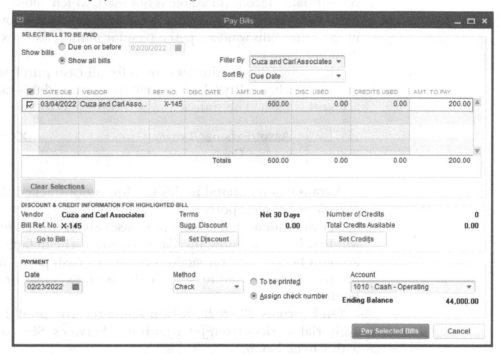

7. Click the Pay Selected Bills button.
8. At the Assign Check Numbers window, click the *Let QuickBooks assign check numbers* option.
9. Click OK.
10. At the Payment Summary window, notice the check number is 2.
11. Click Done.

Practice Exercise   2–3

Record the following transactions at the Pay Bills window:

Feb. 27	Paid *[Your Name]* Accounting Service bill in full (Check No. 3).
Feb. 27	Made a partial payment of $1,000 toward Galeway Computers bill of $3,600 (Check No. 4).

HINT

Use the Scroll Down arrow if you do not see the invoice in the Pay Bills window.

The Write Checks Window

cash purchase
payment of any bill or
item other than accounts
payable

In QuickBooks, the Write Checks window is used to record a **cash purchase** that has not been previously entered into the system. The Write Checks window is useful for companies that usually pay on account but occasionally receive bills and remit payments immediately and for companies that do not purchase goods or services on account and therefore do not need to track vendor data. Accounts Payable is not used, which allows for a cash purchase to be recorded in one step. The data fields in this window are similar to those in the Enter Bills window: payee (vendor name), date, expense, asset, and item purchased.

The Write Checks window is used for all cash purchases, whether the payment is by check, PayPal, electronic transfer, or debit card. The default account is Cash. The transaction is recorded as follows:

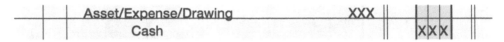

A transaction entered in this window is not tracked through the *Accounts Payable* or *Vendor* reports.

Activities identified as cash purchases are recorded in the Write Checks window. In this window, the Cash account is the default credit posting account because all transactions result in a cash payment. The account field in this window is used to indicate the asset, expense, or drawings account to be debited.

On February 28, 2022, Kristin Raina receives a bill for $125 for monthly janitorial services from Jeter Janitorial Services. She pays it with Check No. 5.

To write a check:
1. At the main menu bar, click Banking and then click *Write Checks.*
2. At the *BANK ACCOUNT* field, confirm that *1010 Cash - Operating* displays. Click to remove the check mark in the *Print Later* box, and in the check number field, type 5, if necessary.
3. At the *DATE* field, choose *02/28/2022.*
4. At the PAY TO THE ORDER OF drop-down list, click *Jeter Janitorial Services.*
5. At the *$* field, type 125.
6. On the Expenses tab, in the *ACCOUNT* field, click *6300 Janitorial Expenses* at the drop-down list. See Figure 2–V.

FIGURE 2-V
Write Checks Window—
Completed

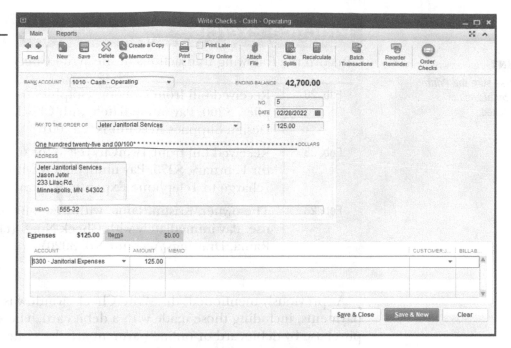

HINT

Errors can be corrected
in the Write Checks win-
dow, or you can click the
Delete button and choose
Delete Check.

7. If the information is correct, click the Save & New button. Even though a check is not printed, the bill is now considered paid.

ACCOUNTING CONCEPT

For a cash payment of an expense, the general ledger posting is as follows:

6300 Janitorial Expenses		1010 Cash - Operating	
Dr	Cr	Dr	Cr
125			125

The vendor file is unaffected because payment was made immediately.

If you click the Previous arrow at this time, you will see the payments recorded in this window as well as the payments recorded in the Pay Bills window. Activities recorded in the Pay Bills window are actually checks written that subsequently appear in the Write Checks window, in addition to the checks written in the Write Checks window. The payments are recorded in check number sequence. Since checks are not being printed, the program automatically assigns the next check number. Any errors recorded in the Pay Bills window cannot be corrected in the Pay Bills window, but they can be corrected in the Write Checks window.

To see an example of this, click the Previous arrow several times. Each time, notice that the payments include those entered in both the Write Checks and Pay Bills windows. As you scroll through the windows, notice the window is different for payments made in the Write Checks and Pay Bills windows. Notice also that the check numbers are in sequence.

Practice Exercise 2–4

Record the following transactions in the Write Checks window:

Feb. 28	Received bill from Grayson Graphics for design supplies, $200. Pay immediately with Check No. 6 (charge to Design Supplies Account No. 1300).
Feb. 28	Received bill from TwinCityTelCo for telephone service for February, $275. Pay immediately with Check No. 7 (charge to Telephone Expense Account No. 6450).
Feb. 28	The owner, Kristin Raina, withdrew $400 for personal use. Pay immediately with Check No. 8 (charge to Kristin Raina, Drawings Account No. 3020).

As previously mentioned, the Write Checks window is used for all cash payments, including those made with a debit card. The steps to enter a purchase by debit card or online payment are the same as the steps for payment by check, except instead of entering a check number in the *NO.* field, another identifier (such as DC-1 or DC-2) is used. All other steps are the same.

Vendor Reports and Accounting Reports

Reports, the fourth level of operation in QuickBooks, reflect the information and activities recorded in the various Lists/Centers and Activities windows. QuickBooks can display and print a variety of internal management reports as well as typical accounting and financial reports, many of which should be printed monthly.

Viewing and Printing Vendor Reports

The Accounts Payable and vendor-related reports help a company manage its liability payments, ensure timely and correct remittances, control cash flow, and retain an accurate record of all vendor-related transactions. Among these reports are the *Unpaid Bills Detail* report, the *Vendor Balance Detail* report, and the *Vendor Contact List* report.

Unpaid Bills Detail Report

The *Unpaid Bills Detail* report lists all unpaid bills for each vendor at a specific date. The report lists each open bill (with date and invoice number) for a vendor, along with any credit memos applied. The report may be customized to show all vendors or only those with outstanding bills.

To view and print the *Unpaid Bills Detail* report:
1. At the main menu bar, click Reports and then click *Vendors & Payables*.
2. At the Vendors & Payables submenu, click *Unpaid Bills Detail*.
3. At the *Date* calendar, choose *02/28/2022*. The *Unpaid Bills Detail* report appears. See Figure 2–W.

FIGURE 2–W
Unpaid Bills Detail Report

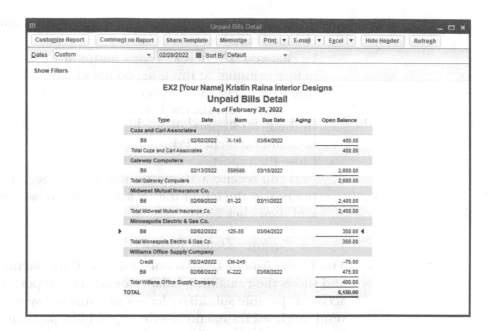

Along the top of the *Unpaid Bills Detail* report window are several buttons (e.g., Customize Report, Comment on Report, Share Template, Memorize, Print). Notice the vertical dotted bar before each column heading in the report text. If you wish to change the width of a column, you can click and drag the crossed arrows that appear in either direction.

4. To print the report, click the Print button at the top of the report and then click *Report*.

   If you receive a message about Printing Features, insert a check mark in the box to the left of the *Do not display this message in the future* option and then click OK. The Print Reports dialog box appears. See Figure 2–X.

FIGURE 2–X
Print Reports Dialog Box

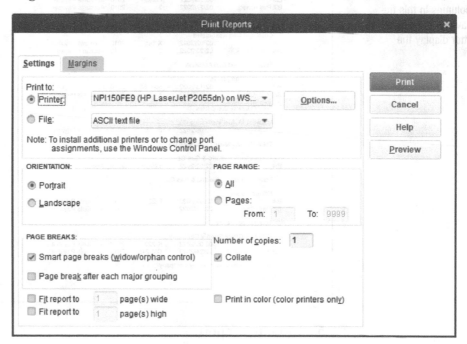

In the Print Reports dialog box, the settings and margins can be changed based on your printer. The orientation of the report can also be changed. There is a Preview button if you wish to preview the report before printing. At this time, do not change any settings other than the orientation. For most reports, the portrait orientation is fine, but for some wider reports, the landscape orientation may be more useful.

5. In the Print Reports dialog box, choose *Portrait* in the Orientation section and then click Print.
6. Close the report.

If you receive a Memorize Report message, insert a check mark in the box to the left of the *Do not display this message in the future* option and then click No.

Vendor Balance Detail Report

The *Vendor Balance Detail* report displays all transactions for each vendor and shows the remaining balance owed. This report is similar to an accounts payable subsidiary ledger in a manual system. The report shows all vendor-related transactions—that is, all bills, payments, and credit memos for each vendor—in chronological order.

To view and print the *Vendor Balance Detail* report:
1. At the main menu bar, click Reports and then click *Vendors & Payables*.
2. At the Vendors & Payables submenu, click *Vendor Balance Detail*.
3. Click the Print button at the top of the report and then click *Report*.
4. In the Print Reports dialog box, choose *Portrait* orientation and then click Print. Your printout should look like Figure 2–Y.

FIGURE 2–Y
Vendor Balance Detail Report

HINT
The columns in this figure have been widened to better display the data.

EX2 [Your Name] Kristin Raina Interior Designs					
Vendor Balance Detail					
All Transactions					
Type	Date	Num	Account	Amount	Balance
[Your Name] Accounting Service					
Bill	02/23/2022	Feb22	2010 · Accounts Payable	300.00	300.00
Bill Pmt -Check	02/27/2022	3	2010 · Accounts Payable	-300.00	0.00
Total [Your Name] Accounting Service				0.00	0.00
Cuza and Carl Associates					
Bill	02/02/2022	X-145	2010 · Accounts Payable	600.00	600.00
Bill Pmt -Check	02/23/2022	2	2010 · Accounts Payable	-200.00	400.00
Total Cuza and Carl Associates				400.00	400.00
Galeway Computers					
Bill	02/13/2022	556588	2010 · Accounts Payable	3,600.00	3,600.00
Bill Pmt -Check	02/27/2022	4	2010 · Accounts Payable	-1,000.00	2,600.00
Total Galeway Computers				2,600.00	2,600.00
Midwest Mutual Insurance Co.					
Bill	02/09/2022	01-22	2010 · Accounts Payable	2,400.00	2,400.00
Total Midwest Mutual Insurance Co.				2,400.00	2,400.00
Minneapolis Electric & Gas Co.					
Bill	02/02/2022	125-55	2010 · Accounts Payable	350.00	350.00
Total Minneapolis Electric & Gas Co.				350.00	350.00
Nordic Realty					
Bill	02/03/2022	F-22	2010 · Accounts Payable	800.00	800.00
Bill Pmt -Check	02/10/2022	1	2010 · Accounts Payable	-800.00	0.00
Total Nordic Realty				0.00	0.00
Williams Office Supply Company					
Bill	02/06/2022	K-222	2010 · Accounts Payable	475.00	475.00
Credit	02/24/2022	CM-245	2010 · Accounts Payable	-75.00	400.00
Total Williams Office Supply Company				400.00	400.00
TOTAL				6,150.00	6,150.00

5. Close the report.

Vendor Contact List Report

HINT
The *Vendor Contact List* report may also be accessed from the Vendors & Payables submenu.

The *Vendor Contact List* report displays information for all vendors that has been entered in each vendor's file. This report displays the name of each vendor, along with the vendor's account number, address, contact person, and telephone and mobile numbers. It also shows the present balance owed.

To view the *Vendor Contact List* report:

1. At the main menu bar, click Reports and then click *List.*
2. At the List submenu, click *Vendor Contact List.* The *Vendor Contact List* report appears. See Figure 2–Z.

FIGURE 2–Z Vendor Contact List

EX2 [Your Name] Kristin Raina Interior Designs
Vendor Contact List
February 28, 2022

Vendor	Account No.	Bill from	Primary Contact	Main Phone	Balance Total
[Your Name] Accounting S...	99-2022-XX	[Your Name] Accounting Service [Your Name]...		651-555-2222	0.00
Cuza and Carl Associates	KR569	Cuza and Carl Associates Carrie Cuza 23 W....		651-555-8855	400.00
Galeway Computers	2455-897	Galeway Computers Roger Rivera 33 Route 1...	Roger Rivera	617-555-4747	2,600.00
Grayson Graphics	33-2221	Grayson Graphics Gregg Grayson 56 Amity W...	Gregg Grayson	612-555-0002	0.00
Jeter Janitorial Services	555-32	Jeter Janitorial Services Jason Jeter 233 Lilac...	Jason Jeter	612-555-4444	0.00
Kristin Raina					0.00
Midwest Mutual Insurance...	54778784	Midwest Mutual Insurance Co. Mike Mills 3566...	Mike Mills	805-555-4545	2,400.00
Minneapolis Electric & Gas...	2001-23657	Minneapolis Electric & Gas Jack Watts 150 Do...	Jack Watts	651-555-4949	350.00
Nordic Realty	55-1212	Nordic Realty Carrie Marx 23 N. 12th Street Mi...	Melanie Marx	612-555-3232	0.00
TwinCityTelCo	666-6667	TwinCityTelCo Terry Ameche 3223 River Dr. S...	Terry Ameche	651-555-6667	0.00
Williams Office Supply Co...	55-8988	Williams Office Supply Company Bernard Wil...		612-555-2240	400.00

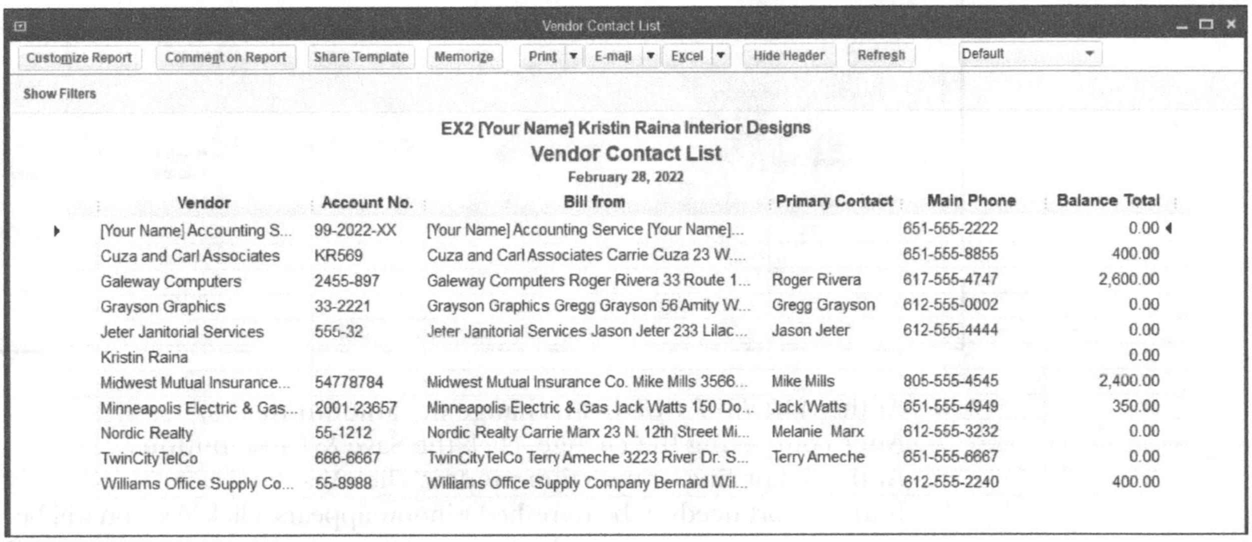

The format of your reports may vary slightly from the figures in the textbook. The reports in the figures are customized to display certain information. Chapter 12 will discuss customizing reports.

3. Close the report.

Drilling Down to a Transaction Window

HINT
You can view a vendor file by choosing the vendor name from the *Vendor Contact List* or by "drilling down" to the vendor file from within a vendor report.

While viewing reports, it is frequently helpful to see the originating transaction or document that gave rise to the report figures. Most of the reports provide a drill-down feature. When reviewing a report, QuickBooks, like many computerized accounting programs, allows you to "drill down" from a report to the original window where data has been entered. If the transaction is incorrect, you can edit or remove the transaction at that time. Any changes to the transactions are automatically reflected in subsequent reports.

When Kristin Raina reviewed the *Unpaid Bills Detail* report, she discovered that the bill from Minneapolis Electric & Gas Co. was entered incorrectly as $350, while the correct amount was $450.

To drill down from a report and correct an error:

1. At the main menu bar, click Reports and then click *Vendors & Payables.*
2. At the Vendors & Payables submenu, click *Unpaid Bills Detail.*
3. Set the date for *02/28/2022.*

4. Place the mouse pointer over the Minneapolis Electric & Gas Co. bill. Notice that the pointer turns into a magnifying glass with a Z in the center. This is called the *zoom glass.*

5. With the zoom glass positioned over the Minneapolis Electric & Gas Co. bill, double-click the bill. The original bill entry appears. See Figure 2–AA.

FIGURE 2–AA
Minneapolis Electric &
Gas Co. Bill Transaction

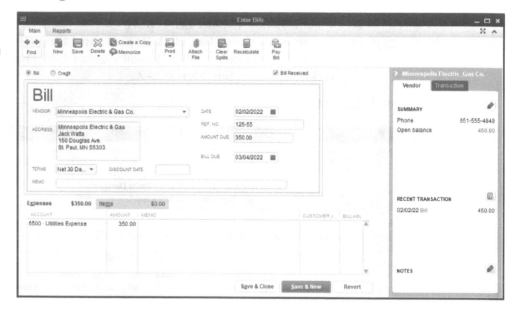

6. At the *AMOUNT DUE* field, change the amount to 450.
7. After completing the change, click the Save & Close button.
8. At the Recording Transaction window, click Yes.
9. If the Report needs to be refreshed window appears, click Yes. You will be returned to the report with the corrected figure in place. See Figure 2–BB.

FIGURE 2–BB
Corrected Unpaid
Bills Report

EX2 [Your Name] Kristin Raina Interior Designs
Unpaid Bills Detail
As of February 28, 2022

	Type	Date	Num	Due Date	Aging	Open Balance
Cuza and Carl Associates						
	Bill	02/02/2022	X-145	03/04/20...		400.00
Total Cuza and Carl Associates						400.00
Galeway Computers						
	Bill	02/13/2022	556588	03/15/20...		2,600.00
Total Galeway Computers						2,600.00
Midwest Mutual Insurance Co.						
	Bill	02/09/2022	01-22	03/11/20...		2,400.00
Total Midwest Mutual Insurance Co.						2,400.00
Minneapolis Electric & Gas Co.						
▶	Bill	02/02/2022	125-55	03/04/20...		450.00 ◀
Total Minneapolis Electric & Gas Co.						450.00
Williams Office Supply Company						
	Credit	02/24/2022	CM-245			-75.00
	Bill	02/06/2022	K-222	03/08/20...		475.00
Total Williams Office Supply Company						400.00
TOTAL						**6,250.00**

10. To print the corrected report, click the Print button at the top of the report.
11. In the Print Reports dialog box, choose *Landscape* orientation and then click Print.
12. Close the report.

Viewing and Printing Accounting Reports

As activities are entered in the windows, behind-the-scenes accounting activity is recorded in general journal format and posted to the general ledger, and then it flows into the financial statements. QuickBooks can display and print these standard accounting reports, such as the *Journal* report. The *Journal* report displays, in general journal format, all transactions recorded during a specified period of time.

To view and print the *Journal* report:
1. At the Reports menu, click *Accountant & Taxes*.
2. At the Accountant & Taxes submenu, click *Journal*.
3. At the *From* and *To* fields, choose *02/01/2022* and *02/28/2022*. The *Journal* report is displayed.
4. To print the report, click the Print button at the top of the report and then click *Report*.
5. In the Print Reports dialog box, choose *Landscape* orientation and then click Print. See Figure 2–CC.

FIGURE 2–CC
Journal Report

EX2 [Your Name] Kristin Raina Interior Designs
Journal
February 2022

Trans #	Type	Date	Num	Name	Memo	Account	Debit	Credit
3	Bill	02/02/2022	125...	Minneapolis Electri...		2010 · Accounts Payable		450.00
				Minneapolis Electri...		6500 · Utilities Expense	450.00	
							450.00	450.00
4	Bill	02/02/2022	X-1...	Cuza and Carl Ass...		2010 · Accounts Payable		600.00
				Cuza and Carl Ass...		1410 · Prepaid Advertising	600.00	
							600.00	600.00
6	Bill	02/03/2022	F-22	Nordic Realty		2010 · Accounts Payable		800.00
				Nordic Realty		6400 · Rent Expense	800.00	
							800.00	800.00
7	Bill	02/06/2022	K-2...	Williams Office Su...		2010 · Accounts Payable		475.00
				Williams Office Su...		1305 · Office Supplies	475.00	
							475.00	475.00
8	Bill	02/09/2022	01-22	Midwest Mutual Ins...		2010 · Accounts Payable		2,400.00
				Midwest Mutual Ins...		1420 · Prepaid Insurance	2,400.00	
							2,400.00	2,400.00
9	Bill	02/13/2022	556...	Galeway Computers		2010 · Accounts Payable		3,600.00
				Galeway Computers		1825 · Computers, Cost	3,600.00	
							3,600.00	3,600.00
10	Bill	02/23/2022	Feb...	[Your Name] Acco...		2010 · Accounts Payable		300.00
				[Your Name] Acco...		6020 · Accounting Expense	300.00	
							300.00	300.00
11	Credit	02/24/2022	CM...	Williams Office Su...		2010 · Accounts Payable	75.00	
				Williams Office Su...		1305 · Office Supplies		75.00
							75.00	75.00

Page 1

...continues

6. Close the report.

FIGURE 2–CC
Journal Report...
continued

EX2 [Your Name] Kristin Raina Interior Designs
Journal
February 2022

Trans #	Type	Date	Num	Name	Memo	Account	Debit	Credit
12	Bill Pmt -Check	02/10/2022	1	Nordic Realty	55-1212	1010 · Cash - Operating		800.00
				Nordic Realty	55-1212	2010 · Accounts Payable	800.00	
							800.00	800.00
13	Bill Pmt -Check	02/23/2022	2	Cuza and Carl Ass...	KR569	1010 · Cash - Operating		200.00
				Cuza and Carl Ass...	KR569	2010 · Accounts Payable	200.00	
							200.00	200.00
14	Bill Pmt -Check	02/27/2022	3	[Your Name] Acco...	99-2022-...	1010 · Cash - Operating		300.00
				[Your Name] Acco...	99-2022-...	2010 · Accounts Payable	300.00	
							300.00	300.00
15	Bill Pmt -Check	02/27/2022	4	Galeway Computers	2455-897	1010 · Cash - Operating		1,000.00
				Galeway Computers	2455-897	2010 · Accounts Payable	1,000.00	
							1,000.00	1,000.00
16	Check	02/28/2022	5	Jeter Janitorial Ser...	555-32	1010 · Cash - Operating		125.00
				Jeter Janitorial Ser...	555-32	6300 · Janitorial Expenses	125.00	
							125.00	125.00
17	Check	02/28/2022	6	Grayson Graphics	33-2221	1010 · Cash - Operating		200.00
				Grayson Graphics	33-2221	1300 · Design Supplies	200.00	
							200.00	200.00
18	Check	02/28/2022	7	TwinCityTelCo	666-6667	1010 · Cash - Operating		275.00
				TwinCityTelCo	666-6667	6450 · Telephone Expense	275.00	
							275.00	275.00
19	Check	02/28/2022	8	Kristin Raina		1010 · Cash - Operating		400.00
				Kristin Raina		3020 · Kristin Raina, Drawings	400.00	
							400.00	400.00
TOTAL							12,000.00	12,000.00

Page 2

HINT
See Appendix C for a
summary of journal
report types.

QuickBooks automatically assigns transaction numbers (Trans #). You cannot change them. Notice in Figure 2–CC that there is no transaction number 5 because this transaction was deleted earlier in the chapter. The software deletes the transaction but moves to the next transaction number for the next transaction. When comparing your work to the solutions, do not be concerned if you have different transaction numbers as long as you have the correct journal entries.

The *Type* column in Figure 2–CC indicates the window where the activity was recorded. In this column, the *Bill* entries represent transactions entered in the Enter Bills window. Notice that each *Bill* transaction has a credit to Accounts Payable because this is the default for that account. The *Credit* entry represents the credit memo entered in the Enter Bills window. Recall that when the credit memo option is chosen, the default account becomes a debit to Accounts Payable. The *Bill Pmt–Check* entries represent transactions entered in the Pay Bills window. Each of these transactions is a debit to Accounts Payable and a credit to Cash; these two accounts are the defaults for this window. The *Check* entries are from the Write Checks window. Each has a credit to Cash because that is the default account for this window.

Exiting QuickBooks

After completing this session, you should make a backup copy of your exercise company file on a removable storage device or network directory using the backup procedures explained in Chapter 1. When you back up to a removable storage device, be sure to change the *Save in* field to the location where you keep your backup files and then carefully type in the correct file name.

Close the company file and then exit QuickBooks.

Chapter Review and Assessment

Procedure Review

To add a vendor:
1. At the main menu bar, click Vendors and then click *Vendor Center.*
2. At the Vendor Center window, click the New Vendor button and then select *New Vendor.*
3. Enter the background data for the vendor.
4. Click OK.
5. Close the Vendor Center window.

To delete a vendor:
1. At the main menu bar, click Vendors and then click *Vendor Center.*
2. At the Vendor Center window, select the vendor you wish to delete.
3. At the main menu bar, click Edit and then click *Delete Vendor.*
4. Click OK at the warning.
5. Close the Vendor Center window.
   You cannot delete a vendor that has a balance or that was used in a transaction during the period. Instead, you can mark the vendor as inactive by checking the *Vendor is inactive* check box.

To edit a vendor:
1. At the main menu bar, click Vendors and then click *Vendor Center.*
2. At the Vendor Center window, select the vendor you wish to edit and then double-click the vendor name.
3. Change the appropriate information.
4. Click OK.
5. Close the Vendor Center window.

To enter a bill:
1. At the main menu bar, click Vendors and then click *Enter Bills.*
2. Click the *Bill* option.
3. At the VENDOR drop-down list, click the vendor name.
4. Enter the bill date in the *DATE* field.
5. Enter the invoice number in the *REF. NO.* field.
6. Enter the amount in the *AMOUNT DUE* field.
7. Enter the due date in the *BILL DUE* field.
8. Select the terms in the *TERMS* field.
9. Select the account to be debited on the Expenses tab.
10. Click Save & Close.

To update the Vendor Center while in an Activity window:
1. At the main menu bar, click Vendors and then click *Enter Bills.*
2. At the VENDOR drop-down list, click < *Add New* >.
3. Follow the procedures to add a vendor.
4. Click OK.

To correct an error in an Activity window:
1. Open the Activity window containing the error.
2. Use the Previous arrow to locate the transaction.
3. Make the necessary corrections.
4. Click the Save & Close button.

To process a credit memo:
1. At the main menu bar, click Vendors and then click *Enter Bills*.
2. Click the *Credit* option.
3. Follow the procedures for entering a bill.

To pay a bill:
1. At the main menu bar, click Vendors and then click *Pay Bills*.
2. Click *Show all bills*.
3. At the *Filter By* field, choose the appropriate vendor whose bill you wish to pay.
4. Enter the payment date in the *PAYMENT Date* field.
5. At the *PAYMENT Method* field, choose *Check* and the *Assign check no.* option.
6. At the *PAYMENT Account* field, choose the appropriate cash account.
7. Choose the bill to be paid by inserting a check mark in the box (❑) to the left of the bill. Accept the full amount or enter a partial amount.
8. Click the Pay Selected Bills button. The Assign Check Numbers dialog box appears.
9. Click the *Let me assign the check numbers below* option.
10. Enter the check number.
11. Click OK.
12. At the Payment Summary window, click Done.

To record a cash purchase:
1. At the main menu bar, click Banking and then click *Write Checks*.
2. At the *BANK ACCOUNT* field, choose the appropriate account.
3. Enter the payment date in the *DATE* field. Enter the check or identifying number in the *NO.* field.
4. Choose the payee from the PAY TO THE ORDER OF drop-down list.
5. At the *$* field, enter the amount of the payment.
6. On the Expenses tab, choose the account to be debited.
7. Click Save & Close.

To view and print vendor reports from the Reports menu:
1. At the main menu bar, click Reports and then click *Vendors & Payables*.
2. At the Vendors & Payables or List submenu, choose a report.
3. Indicate the appropriate dates for the report and then click the Refresh button at the top of the report.
4. Click the Print button at the top of the report and then click *Reports*.
5. In the Print Reports dialog box, review the settings and then click Print.
6. Close the report.

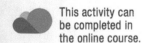

This activity can be completed in the online course.

Key Concepts

Select the letter of the item that best matches each definition.

a. *Journal* report
b. Write Checks window
c. System default account
d. Vendor Center
e. *Unpaid Bills* report

f. Credit memo
g. Pay Bills window
h. Vendor
i. Enter Bills window
j. *Vendor Contact List* report

_____ 1. Someone from whom the business buys goods or services.

_____ 2. Contains a file for all vendors with whom the company does business.

_____ 3. A report that lists all unpaid vendor bills at a specific date.

_____ 4. Processed through the Enter Bills window to reflect a reduction of the vendor's liability due to a credit for return or allowance.

_____ 5. Activity window used to record vendor bills to be paid at a later date.

_____ 6. Activities displayed in general journal format for a specified period of time.

_____ 7. Report that lists all vendors from which the company buys goods and services.

_____ 8. A pre-identified general ledger account that increases or decreases automatically, depending on the type of transaction entered.

_____ 9. Activity window used to record a cash purchase of goods or services from a vendor.

_____ 10. Activity window used to pay bills previously entered in the Enter Bills window.

This activity can be completed in the online course.

Procedure Check

1. Your company has changed its telephone carrier. Describe the steps to add the new vendor to the system.
2. Upper management requests a list of all businesses from which the company buys goods or services. How would you use QuickBooks to quickly produce this information?
3. You receive a batch of bills that must be paid immediately. You do not need to maintain an Accounts Payable record of these payments. How would you use QuickBooks to expeditiously enter these payments into the system and write the appropriate payment checks?
4. A vendor calls your company to complain that a bill sent 45 days ago remains unpaid. How would you use QuickBooks to verify this complaint?
5. You wish to view all the bills received from a vendor and all payments made to that vendor. How would you use QuickBooks to obtain the required information?
6. Compare and contrast a manual accounting system with a computerized accounting system for processing vendor transactions. How does the accounts payable subsidiary ledger compare with the Vendor Center?

Reports created for these Case Problems can be exported to Excel and uploaded in the online course to be automatically graded.

Case Problems

Demonstrate your knowledge of the QuickBooks features discussed in this chapter by completing the following case problems.

Case Problem 2–1

On April 1, 2022, Lynn Garcia started her business, Lynn's Music Studio, as a music instructor. She began by depositing $10,000 cash in a bank account in the business name. She also contributed a piano and some guitars. The musical instruments have an outstanding note balance of $2,000, which will now be assumed by the business. The cash, musical instruments, note payable, and capital have all been recorded in the opening balances of the books. Lynn anticipates setting up her studio in the beginning of the month and expects to provide piano and guitar lessons later in the month. Record the transactions listed below for the month of April.

1. Open the company file **CH2 Lynn's Music Studio.QBW**.
2. At the QuickBooks Desktop Login window, in the *Password* text box, type Student1 and then click OK.
3. Make a backup copy of the company file and name it **LMS2** *[Your Name]* **Lynn's Music Studio**.
4. Restore the backup copy of the company file. In both the Open Backup Copy and Save Company File as dialog boxes, use the file name **LMS2** *[Your Name]* **Lynn's Music Studio** and enter the password.
5. Change the company name to **LMS2** *[Your Name]* **Lynn's Music Studio**.
6. Add the following vendors to the Vendor Center:

VENDOR NAME:	Pioneer Phone
OPENING BALANCE:	0 AS OF April 1, 2022
COMPANY NAME:	Pioneer Phone
First Name:	Customer
Last Name:	Service
Main Phone:	570-555-6000
Mobile:	570-555-6500
Main Email:	pioph@ppi-edu.net
BILLED FROM:	1000 Route 6
	Carbondale, PA 18407
PAYMENT TERMS:	Net 15 Days

VENDOR NAME:	Steamtown Electric
OPENING BALANCE:	0 AS OF April 1, 2022
COMPANY NAME:	Steamtown Electric
First Name:	Customer
Last Name:	Service
Main Phone:	570-555-2500
Mobile:	570-555-3000
Main Email:	steam@ppi-edu.net
BILLED FROM:	150 Vine Lane
	Scranton, PA 18501
PAYMENT TERMS:	Net 15 Days

Delete the following vendor:
  Universal Electric

Edit the following vendor:
  Mutual Insurance Company main telephone number:
  570-555-5600

7. Using the appropriate window, record the following transactions for April 2022:

Apr. 2   Received bill for rent for the month of April from Viewhill Realty, $600, paid immediately, Check No. 1. Do not print check.

Apr. 2   Received a bill for a one-year insurance policy on account from Mutual Insurance Company, Invoice No. 4010102, $1,200, Net 30 Days.

Apr. 5   Purchased furniture on account from Mills Family Furniture, Invoice No. 1257, $2,500, Net 30 Days.

Apr. 6   Purchased a computer system on account from Computer Town, Invoice No. X234, $3,000, Net 30 Days.

Apr. 9   Purchased music supplies on account from Strings, Sheets, & Such, Invoice No. 1290, $500, Net 15 Days.

Apr. 9   Received bill for tuning of piano and guitars from Tune Tones, $100, paid immediately, Check No. 2. Tune Tones is a new vendor:

VENDOR NAME:	Tune Tones
OPENING BALANCE:	0 AS OF April 1, 2022
COMPANY NAME:	Tune Tones
First Name:	Tony
Last Name:	Tune
Main Phone:	570-555-1111
Mobile:	570-555-2222
Main Email:	TUNE@ppi-edu.net
BILLED FROM:	500 Monroe Ave.
	Dunmare, PA 18512
PAYMENT TERMS:	Net 30 Days

Apr. 9   Purchased office supplies on account from Paper Clips and More, Invoice No. 01-1599, $400, Net 30 Days.

Apr. 12   Received the telephone bill from Pioneer Phone, Invoice No. pp401, $50, Net 15 Days.

Apr. 13   Received utilities bill from Steamtown Electric, Invoice No. SE401, $70, Net 15 Days.

Apr. 20   Paid in full Strings, Sheets, & Such, Invoice No. 1290 (Check No. 3). Do not print check.

Apr. 23   Received a credit memo from Paper Clips, and More, Invoice No. CM250, $50, for office supplies returned.

Apr. 26   Paid in full Pioneer Phone, Invoice No. pp401 (Check No. 4).

Apr. 27   Paid in full Steamtown Electric, Invoice No. SE401 (Check No. 5).

Apr. 30   Made a partial payment of $1,000 to Mills Family Furniture (Check No. 6).

Apr. 30   Made a partial payment of $1,000 to Computer Town (Check No. 7).

Apr. 30   The owner, Lynn Garcia, withdrew $1,000 for personal use (Check No. 8).

8. Display and print the following reports for April 1, 2022, to April 30, 2022:
   a. *Unpaid Bills Detail*
   b. *Vendor Balance Detail*
   c. *Vendor Contact List*
   d. *Journal*

Case Problem 2–2

On June 1, 2022, Olivia Chen started her business, Olivia's Web Solutions, as an internet consultant and web page designer. She began by depositing $25,000 cash in a bank account in the business name. She also contributed a computer system. The computer has an outstanding note balance of $2,500 that will be assumed by the business. The cash, computer, note payable, and capital have all been recorded in the opening balances of the books. Olivia anticipates setting up her office in the beginning of the month and expects to provide web design and internet consulting services later in the month. You will record the transactions listed below for the month of June.

1. Open the company file **CH2 Olivia's Web Solutions.QBW**.
2. At the QuickBooks Desktop Login window, in the *Password* text box, type Student1 and then click OK.
3. Make a backup copy of the company file and name it **OWS2** *[Your Name]* **Olivia's Web Solutions**.
4. Restore the backup copy of the company file. In both the Open Backup Copy and Save Company File as dialog boxes, use the file name **OWS2** *[Your Name]* **Olivia's Web Solutions** and enter the password.
5. Change the company name to **OWS2** *[Your Name]* **Olivia's Web Solutions**.
6. Add the following vendors to the Vendor Center:

VENDOR NAME:	Comet Computer Supplies
OPENING BALANCE:	0 AS OF June 1, 2022
COMPANY NAME:	Comet Computer Supplies
First Name:	Customer
Last Name:	Service
Main Phone:	631-555-4444
Mobile:	631-555-4455
Main Email:	CometCs@ppi-edu.net
BILLED FROM:	657 Motor Parkway
	Center Island, NY 11488
PAYMENT TERMS:	Net 15 Days

VENDOR NAME:	Chrbet Advertising
OPENING BALANCE:	0 AS OF June 1, 2022
COMPANY NAME:	Chrbet Advertising
First Name:	Chris
Last Name:	Chrbet
Main Phone:	212-555-8777
Mobile:	212-555-8778
Main Email:	Cadv@ppi-edu.net

BILLED FROM:	201 East 10th Street New York, NY 10012
PAYMENT TERMS:	Net 30 Days

Delete the following vendor:
Johnson Ad Agency

Edit the address for Martin Computer Repairs:
366 North Franklin Street
Garden City, NY 11568

7. Using the appropriate window, record the following transactions for
June 2022:

Jun. 1	Received bill for rent for the month of June from ARC Management, $800, paid immediately. Check No. 1. Do not print check.
Jun. 4	Received a one-year insurance policy on account from Eastern Mutual Insurance, Invoice No. 87775, $1,800, Net 30 Days.
Jun. 4	Purchased software on account from Netsoft Development Co., Invoice No. 38745, $3,600, Net 30 Days.
Jun. 7	Purchased office furniture on account from Lewis Furniture Co., Invoice No. O9887, $3,200, Net 30 Days.
Jun. 8	Purchased six months of advertising services on account from Chrbet Advertising, Invoice No. O-989, $1,200, Net 30 Days.
Jun. 11	Purchased computer supplies on account from Comet Computer Supplies, Invoice No. 56355, $600, Net 15 Days.
Jun. 14	Received bill for online internet services from Systems Service, $150, paid immediately (Check No. 2). Systems Service is a new vendor:

VENDOR NAME:	Systems Service
OPENING BALANCE:	0 AS OF June 1, 2022
COMPANY NAME:	Systems Service
First Name:	Jeremy
Last Name:	Jones
Main Phone:	516-555-2525
Mobile:	516-555-2526
Main Email:	Sysser@ppi-edu.net
BILLED FROM:	36 Sunrise Lane Hempstead, NY 11004
PAYMENT TERMS:	Net 30 Days

Jun. 15	Purchased office supplies on account from Office Plus, Invoice No. 3665, $450, Net 30 Days.
Jun. 18	Received telephone bill from Eastel, Invoice No. 6-2568, $350, Net 30 Days.
Jun. 21	Received utilities bill from LI Power Company, Invoice No. OWS-23556, $125, Net 15 Days.
Jun. 21	Returned office supplies to Office Plus for $75 credit, CM789.

	Jun. 21	Paid in full Eastern Mutual Insurance, Invoice No. 87775 (Check No. 3). Do not print check.
	Jun. 25	Paid in full Comet Computer Supplies, Invoice No. 56355 (Check No. 4).
	Jun. 28	Paid in full LI Power Company, Invoice No. OWS-23556 (Check No. 5).
	Jun. 30	Made a partial payment of $2,000 to Netsoft Development Co. (Check No. 6).
	Jun. 30	Made partial payment of $1,500 to Lewis Furniture Co. (Check No. 7).
	Jun. 30	The owner, Olivia Chen, withdrew $500 for personal use (Check No. 8).

8. Display and print the following reports for June 1, 2022, to June 30, 2022:
   a. *Unpaid Bills Detail*
   b. *Vendor Balance Detail*
   c. *Vendor Contact List*
   d. *Journal*

Customers

Adding Customers, Creating Invoices, and Receiving and Depositing Payments

Objectives

- Identify the system default accounts for customers
- Update the Customer Center
- Record sales on account in the Create Invoices window
- Record collections of accounts receivable in the Receive Payments window
- Record cash sales in the Enter Sales Receipts window
- Record deposits in the Make Deposits window
- Display and print customer-related reports

 The online course includes additional training and assessment resources. Reports created for the Chapter Problem can be uploaded for instructor review.

Chapter Introduction

customer a person or business to which the company sells goods or services, either on account or for cash

QuickBooks allows you to track all customer transactions. A **customer** is a person or business to which the company sells goods or services, either on account or for cash. A file for a particular customer should be established before entering transactions for that customer. The collection of all the customer files comprises the customer list, which is contained in the Customer Center (Lists/Centers).

Once a customer file is established, transactions (Activities) such as creating an invoice for a customer, receiving payment from that customer, and making a cash sale can be entered in the Create Invoices, Receive Payments, Enter Sales Receipts, and Make Deposits windows. As transactions are recorded in these activities windows, QuickBooks simultaneously updates the customer's file in the Customer Center to include information about the transactions for that customer. At the same time, QuickBooks updates any related reports (Reports).

In this chapter, our sample company, Kristin Raina Interior Designs, will create invoices for design and decorating services, receive payments for invoices, make cash sales, and deposit funds.

QuickBooks versus Manual Accounting: Customer Transactions

sales journal a journal used to record all sales of goods or services on account; can be in single-column or multicolumn format

cash receipts journal a multicolumn journal used to record all cash receipt activities, including collections of accounts receivable

In a manual accounting system, all sales of goods or services on account are recorded in a multicolumn **sales journal**. At the conclusion of the month, the totals are posted to the accounts receivable and revenue accounts affected by the transactions. As each sales transaction is recorded, the appropriate customer's account in the accounts receivable subsidiary ledger is updated for the new receivable on a daily basis. Collections of open accounts receivable balances and cash sales of goods/services are recorded in a multicolumn **cash receipts journal**. As was done with the sales journal, monthly totals are posted to the general ledger accounts, while payment information is recorded daily in the customer's subsidiary ledger record.

In QuickBooks, the Customer Center serves as the accounts receivable subsidiary ledger for the company. The Customer Center contains a file for all companies and individuals to whom the company sells goods and services. Relevant information—such as name, address, contact person, and credit limit—is entered when the customer's file is created in the Customer Center.

When the company creates an invoice for goods or services, the invoice is created in the Create Invoices window. The Create Invoices window is equivalent to the multicolumn sales journal. This transaction updates the Chart of Accounts List and general ledger while simultaneously updating the customer's file in the Customer Center for the new receivable. When the customer pays the invoice, the company enters this transaction in the Receive Payments window. The Receive Payments window is equivalent to the part of the cash receipts journal that records the collection of open accounts receivable. QuickBooks automatically updates the Chart of Accounts List and general ledger while at the same time updating the customer's file in the Customer Center for the payment of the receivable.

To record a check received for an invoice not previously entered, the Enter Sales Receipts window is used. This window is equivalent to the remainder of the cash receipts journal, which records all cash receipts other than collection of accounts receivable. Again, the Chart of Accounts List and general ledger and the customer's file in the Customer Center are updated simultaneously.

System Default Accounts

As we saw in Chapter 2, to process transactions expeditiously and organize data for reporting, QuickBooks establishes specific general ledger accounts as default accounts in each window. When you enter a transaction, QuickBooks automatically increases or decreases certain account balances, depending on the nature of the transaction.

For example, for a vendor, when you enter a transaction in the Enter Bills window, QuickBooks automatically increases (credits) the Accounts Payable account; when you pay the bills in the Pay Bills window, Quick-Books automatically decreases (debits) the Accounts Payable account. Similarly, for a customer, when you enter a transaction in the Create Invoices window, QuickBooks automatically increases (debits) the Accounts Receivable account because the Create Invoices window is used to record sales on account. When you record a collection of accounts receivable in the Receive Payments window, QuickBooks automatically decreases (credits) the Accounts Receivable account. Therefore, you do not have to enter the account numbers or names for these default accounts because they have been pre-established by QuickBooks.

Chapter Problem

In this chapter, you will enter and track customer transactions for Kristin Raina Interior Designs. Kristin Raina provides interior design and decorating services both on account and for cash. Customers and clients remit payment for invoices; these funds are periodically deposited in the company checking account. Information for several customers has been entered in the Customer Center. This information, along with February 1, 2022, beginning balances and vendor activity from Chapter 2, is contained in the company file **CH3 Kristin Raina Interior Designs**.

To open the company file:
1. Open QuickBooks.
2. At the No Company Open window, click the Open or restore an existing company button, or click File and then click *Open or Restore Company*.
3. At the Open or Restore Company window, choose *Open a company file* and then click Next.
4. In the Open a Company dialog box, in the *Look in* text box, choose the Company Files subfolder or the subfolder containing the company files.
5. Select the company file **CH3 Kristin Raina Interior Designs.QBW** and then click Open.
6. At the QuickBooks Desktop Login window, in the *Password* text box, type Student1 and then click OK.
7. Close all pop-up windows and messages.

To make a backup copy of the company file:

1. At the main menu bar, click File and then click *Back Up Company*.
2. At the Back Up Company submenu, click *Create Local Backup*.
3. At the Create Backup window, at the *Do you want to save your backup copy online or locally?* page, confirm that *Local backup* is selected and then click Next.
4. At the Backup Options window, click the Browse button.
5. At the Browse for Folder window, choose your subfolder, a network directory designated by your instructor, or a removable storage device and then click OK.
6. At the Backup Options window, you can remove the check mark to the left of *Add the date and time of the backup to the file name* if you do not want multiple backups and then click OK.
7. At the QuickBooks message, click *Use this Location*.
8. At the Create Backup window, at the *When do you want to save your backup copy?* page, choose *Save it now* and then click Next.
9. In the Save Backup Copy dialog box, in the *Save in* field, choose your subfolder, a network directory designated by your instructor, or a removable storage device, if the correct location is not already selected.
10. In the *File name* text box, type EX3 *[Your Name]* Kristin Raina Interior Designs and then click Save.
11. At the QuickBooks Information message, click OK.

To restore the backup copy of the company file:

1. At the main menu bar, click File and then click *Open or Restore Company*.
2. At the Open or Restore Company window, at the *What type of file do you want to open or restore?* page, choose *Restore a backup copy* and then click Next.
3. At the *Is the backup copy stored locally or online?* page, choose *Local backup* and then click Next.
4. In the Open Backup Copy dialog box, in the *Look in* field, choose the location where you saved your backup copy.
5. Select the company file **EX3 *[Your Name]* Kristin Raina Interior Designs.QBB** and then click Open.
6. At the *Where do you want to restore the file?* page, click Next.
7. In the Save Company File as dialog box, in the *Save in* field, choose the subfolder in which you will open and work on your copy of the company file.
8. In the *File name* text box, type EX3 *[Your Name]* Kristin Raina Interior Designs and then click Save.
9. At the QuickBooks Desktop Login window, in the *Password* text box, type Student1 and then click OK.
10. Close all pop-up windows and messages.

The backup copy has been restored, but the company name still reads CH3 Kristin Raina Interior Designs.

To change the company name:
1. At the main menu bar, click Company and then click *My Company*.
2. At the My Company window, click the Edit icon.
3. In the Company Information dialog box, change the company name to **EX3** *[Your Name]* **Kristin Raina Interior Designs** and then click OK.
4. Close the My Company window.

Lists/Centers

The Customer Center

The Customer Center contains a file for each customer to whom the company sells goods or services. Each file contains important information, such as company name, address, contact person, type of customer, terms, credit limit, preferred payment method, and current balance owed. You should include all customers with which the company does business in the Customer Center.

Recall from Chapter 1 that the second level of operation in QuickBooks is recording background information in Lists/Centers. The Customer Center is revised periodically when new customers are added, customers not used in the business are deleted, and modifications are made to customer information. Making these adjustments to the customer files is referred to as *updating* the Customer Center.

As previously stated, the Customer Center contains a file for each customer with whom the company does business. You should try to enter the information for each customer in the Customer Center before recording transactions. However, if you inadvertently omit a customer, you can add that customer during the Activities level of operation with minimal disruption.

Kristin Raina has entered information for existing and anticipated customers in the Customer Center.

To view the Customer Center:
1. At the main menu bar, click Customers and then click *Customer Center*. If a window appears titled New Feature - Attach Documents to QuickBooks, click OK or click the X to close it.

   The Customer Center appears with the customer file for Alomar Company displayed. See Figure 3–A.

FIGURE 3–A Customer Center—Alomar Company File Displayed

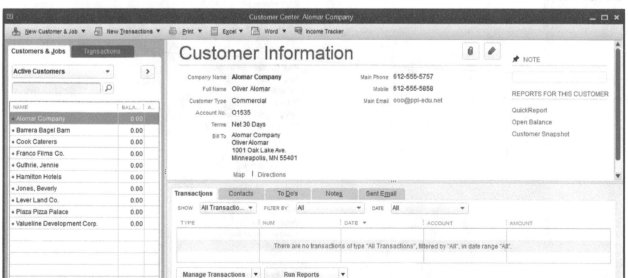

Table 3–1 describes the various parts of the Customer Center.

TABLE 3–1
Customer Center

Part	Description
Customers & Jobs tab	Lists all customers and jobs with current balances due. You can display all customers, active customers, or only customers with balances.
Transactions tab	Lists all transactions for a selected customer. The Transactions tab in the Customer Information section contains the same information.
New Customer & Job button	Used to add a new customer or job.
New Transactions button	Used to create invoices and to enter sales receipts, payments, and credit memos.
Customer Information section	Displays background and transaction information for the customer selected on the Customers & Jobs tab.
Attach icon	Used to attach documents via the QuickBooks Document Management feature.
Contacts tab	Used to add a contact name for this customer by clicking the Manage Contacts drop-down arrow and choosing *Add New*. You can designate the contact as primary, secondary, or additional.
Edit icon	Used to edit background information for the customer selected on the Customers & Jobs tab.
To Do's tab	Used to view the To Do List for this customer.
Notes tab	Used to include narrative information specific to a customer.
REPORTS FOR THIS CUSTOMER section	Lists the reports available in the Customer Center.

In addition to the foregoing, once a customer is selected, you can right-click the customer name on the Customers & Jobs tab to display a shortcut menu, as shown in Figure 3–B. Use this menu to perform most customer-related activities.

FIGURE 3–B
Customer Center
Shortcut Menu

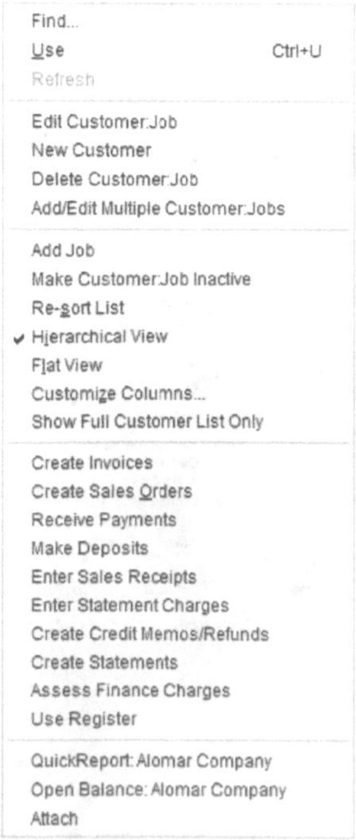

To view a specific customer file:

1. Move the mouse pointer to Alomar Company and double-click to open the file. If a window appears titled New Feature Add/Edit Multiple List Entries, insert a check mark in the box to the left of the *Do not display this message in the future* option and then click OK to close the window. The file opens in Edit Customer mode. See Figure 3–C.

FIGURE 3–C
Customer File—
Alomar Company
Selected

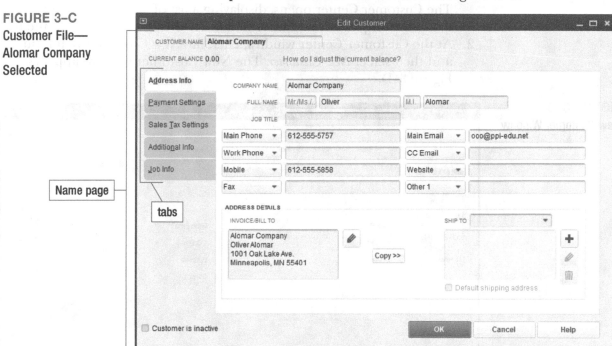

Table 3–2 describes the various parts of the customer's file.

TABLE 3–2
Customer File

Part	Description
Name page	Displays the customer's name, the customer's current balance, and three command buttons: OK, Cancel, and Help. Tabs in the center of the page include additional customer information as described below.
Address Info tab	Used to enter the customer's company name, billing and shipping address, contact person, telephone and mobile phone numbers, and email address. The Edit icon can be used to edit address information.
Payment Settings tab	Used to enter information such as the customer's account number, credit limit, payment terms, preferred delivery method, and credit card information.
Sales Tax Settings tab	Used to enter the customer's sales tax code and resale number.
Additional Info tab	Used to enter the customer type and to create customized fields.
Job Info tab	Used to enter information such as job status and start and end dates for a job for this customer.

2. Close the Edit Customer window.
3. Close the Customer Center.

Adding a Customer

Kristin Raina has just been hired by a new client, Maria Omari, to provide interior decorating services for Omari's new residence.

To add a new customer:

1. At the main menu bar, click Customers and then click *Customer Center*. The Customer Center opens, displaying a list of customers on the Customers & Jobs tab and information for the first customer on the list.
2. At the Customer Center window, click the New Customer & Job button and then select *New Customer*. The New Customer window appears. See Figure 3–D.

FIGURE 3–D
New Customer Window

3. Enter the following data on the Name page and Address Info tab. See Figure 3–E.

Name page	CUSTOMER NAME:	Omari, Maria
	OPENING BALANCE:	0 AS OF February 1, 2022
Address Info	FULL NAME:	
	First:	Maria
	Last:	Omari
	Main Phone:	612-555-9999
	Mobile:	612-555-9998
	Main Email:	MO@ppi-edu.net
	INVOICE/BILL TO:	210 NE Lowry Ave.
		Minneapolis, MN 54204

HINT

To move from field to field, press the Tab key or Shift + Tab. In the *INVOICE/BILL TO* field, use the Down Arrow key to enter each line of the address.

4. Click the Payment Settings tab and enter the following information.
   See Figure 3–F.

Payment Settings	*ACCOUNT NO:*	01545
	CREDIT LIMIT:	10,000
	PAYMENT TERMS:	Net 30 Days
	PREFERRED DELIVERY METHOD:	None
	PREFERRED PAYMENT METHOD:	Check

FIGURE 3–F
New Customer
Window—Payment
Settings Tab Completed

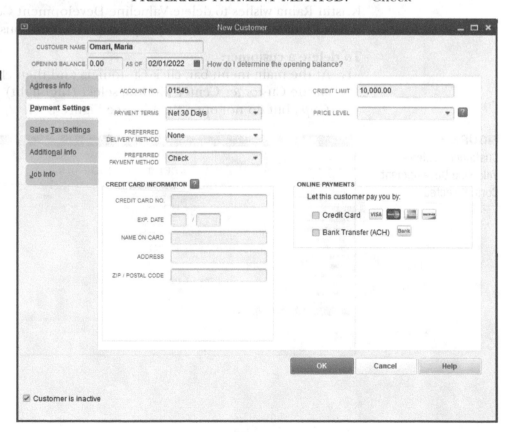

5. Click the Additional Info tab and enter the following information. See Figure 3–G.

Additional Info   *CUSTOMER TYPE:*   Residential

FIGURE 3–G
New Customer
Window—Additional
Info Tab Completed

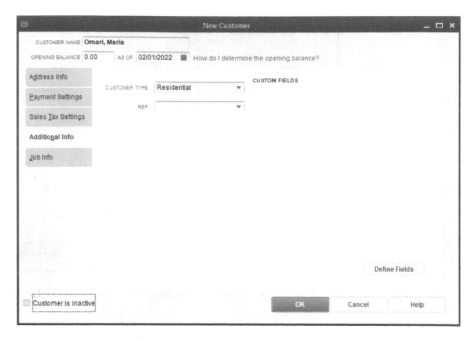

6. If the information is correct, click OK.
7. Close the Customer Center.

Deleting a Customer

Kristin Raina wishes to delete Valueline Development Corp. from the Customer Center because the company has gone out of business.

To delete a customer:

1. At the main menu bar, click Customers and then click *Customer Center.*
2. At the Customer Center window, select (highlight) *Valueline Development Corp.,* but do not open the file. See Figure 3–H.

FIGURE 3–H
Customer Center—
Valueline Development
Corp. Selected

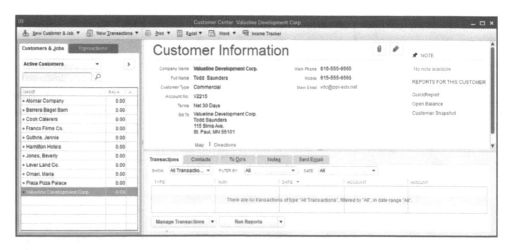

3. At the main menu bar, click Edit and then click *Delete Customer:Job.*
4. Click OK at the Delete Customer:Job warning. The customer file is now deleted.
5. Close the Customer Center window.

   A customer with a balance or a customer who has been part of a transaction for the current accounting period cannot be deleted but can be marked inactive. The customer's name is no longer displayed in the reports, but the information is retained in QuickBooks and can be accessed if needed.

Editing a Customer

Kristin Raina needs to edit the file for Plaza Pizza Palace because the contact person has changed.

To edit a customer file:
1. Open the Customer Center and double-click *Plaza Pizza Palace.* The customer file opens in Edit Customer mode.
2. At the *FULL NAME* field, delete the current first name and then type Mikey. See Figure 3–I.

HINT

Another way to access the Edit Customer window is to select the customer in the Customer Center and then click the Edit icon.

FIGURE 3–I
Edit Customer Window—
Plaza Pizza Palace

HINT

Changing the *FULL NAME* field will not change the name in the Address Details section.

3. If the information is correct, click OK.

CHAPTER 3 | Customers   **81**

Add the following customer:

Name page	*CUSTOMER NAME:*	Berger Bakery Company
	OPENING BALANCE:	0 AS OF February 1, 2022
Address Info	*COMPANY NAME:*	Berger Bakery Company
	First Name:	Barry
	Last Name:	Berger
	Main Phone:	612-555-2240
	Mobile:	612-555-2241
	Main Email:	BBC@ppi-edu.net
	INVOICE/BILL TO:	18 N Grand Ave.
		Minneapolis, MN 55403
Payment Settings	*ACCOUNT NO:*	R1825
	CREDIT LIMIT:	10,000
	PAYMENT TERMS:	Net 30 Days
	PREFERRED DELIVERY METHOD:	None
	PREFERRED PAYMENT METHOD:	Check
Additional Info	*CUSTOMER TYPE:*	Commercial

Delete the following customer:
   Lever Land Company

Edit the following customer:
   New phone/mobile for Barrera Bagel Barn:
      Main Phone: 612-555-1233
      Mobile: 612-555-1234

QuickCheck: The updated Customer Center appears in Figure 3–J.

FIGURE 3–J Updated Customer Center

The Create Invoices Window

Recall from Chapter 1 that the third level of operation in QuickBooks is Activities. In QuickBooks, Activities identified as **sales on account** are recorded in the Create Invoices window. Accounts Receivable is the default general ledger posting account. All transactions entered in this window result in a debit to the Accounts Receivable account. The account to be credited, usually a revenue account, is determined based on the item chosen.

QuickBooks records a sales-on-account transaction as follows:

Accounts Receivable		XXX		
Revenue				XXX

At the same time, QuickBooks updates the customer's file in the Customer Center to reflect the new receivable. The QuickBooks Create Invoices window appears in Figure 3–K.

FIGURE 3–K
Create Invoices
Window

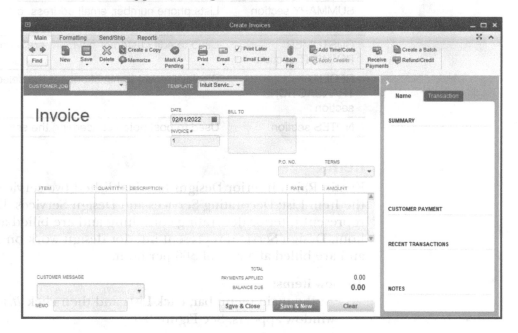

The Create Invoices window has four tabs: Main, Formatting, Send/Ship, and Reports. The Main tab allows you to select a customer from the Customer Center, enter an invoice number and terms of payment, and identify items sold or services provided. The Formatting tab allows you to customize the design and presentation of invoices. Customizing invoices will be covered in Chapter 12. The Send/Ship tab allows you to select a carrier for a shipment. The Reports tab accesses various transaction reports. Most icons and data fields are self-explanatory, but take special note of the various parts on the Main tab, as described in Table 3–3.

The Find button; Previous and Next arrows; and New, Save, Delete, Save & Close, Save & New, and Clear buttons all have the same functions in this window as in the Enter Bills window.

TABLE 3–3
Create Invoices
Window, Main Tab

Part	Description
TEMPLATE field	QuickBooks allows for eight types of invoice formats. Choose the one that best describes the items sold. For this chapter, the Intuit Service Invoice will be used. In addition, you can customize and download additional formats.
ITEM field	When you click in the ITEM field, a drop-down arrow appears, which allows you to access the Item List. Choose the item of service or inventory sold from the drop-down list. Once an item is selected, the description and rate are filled in automatically based on data entered in the Item List window.
Print button	Used to print this invoice immediately rather than using the Print Forms submenu of the File menu.
Customer Name/ Transaction tabs	Displays a summary of information about the customer, recent transactions, and notes. Click the > arrow to hide this information; click the < arrow to display it.
Edit icon	Used to edit customer information while remaining in the Create Invoices window.
SUMMARY section	Lists phone number, email address, credit limit, and open balance for the selected customer.
CUSTOMER PAYMENT section	Used to edit customer payment preferences.
RECENT TRANSACTIONS section	Displays recent transactions for the selected customer.
NOTES section	Used to post notes concerning the selected customer.

Items

Kristin Raina Interior Designs has established two service revenue items in the Item List: Decorating Services and Design Services. Decorating Services represent interior decorating consulting and are billed at a rate of $50 per hour. Design Services represent interior design work on specific projects and are billed at a rate of $60 per hour.

To view items:

1. At the main menu bar, click Lists and then click *Item List.* The Item List window appears. See Figure 3–L.

FIGURE 3–L
Item List Window

2. To view the data for the Decorating Services item, double-click the item. The Edit Item window appears. See Figure 3–M.

FIGURE 3–M
Edit Item Window—
Decorating Services

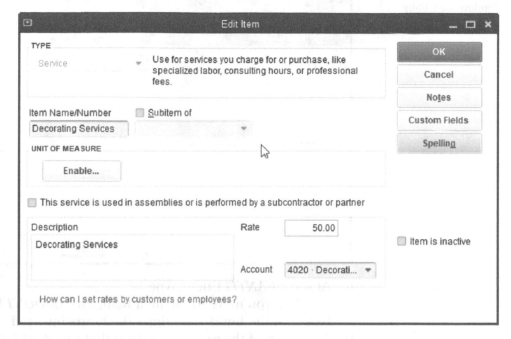

Decorating Services is indicated as a service item (rather than inventory or payroll). The window also contains a description, rate per unit (hour), and default general ledger posting account. QuickBooks uses this data when you create an invoice for a customer for this service.

3. Close the Edit Item and Item List windows.

Creating an Invoice

On February 1, 2022, Kristin Raina provided 12 hours of decorating services on account to Beverly Jones.

HINT

In the event a new customer needs to be added while you are in the Create Invoices window, click *< Add New >* from the CUSTOMER:JOB drop-down list.

To create an invoice:
1. At the main menu bar, click Customers and then click *Create Invoices*.
2. At the CUSTOMER:JOB drop-down list, click *Jones, Beverly*.
3. At the TEMPLATE drop-down list, accept the default choice, *Intuit Service Invoice*.
4. At the *DATE* field, choose *02/01/2022*.
5. At the *INVOICE* # field, type 1001.
6. At the TERMS drop-down list, accept the default choice, *Net 30 Days*.
7. At the *ITEM* field, click the first line to display the drop-down Item List and then click *Decorating Services*. The data from the Decorating Services file in the Item List complete the *DESCRIPTION* and *RATE* fields. See Figure 3–N.

FIGURE 3–N
Create Invoices
Window—Partially
Completed

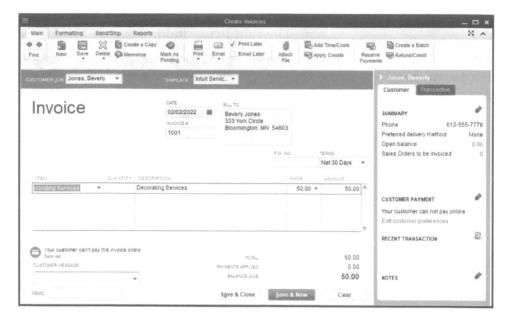

8. At the *QUANTITY* field, type 12.

   When you move to the next field, the *AMOUNT* box is completed based on the hourly rate times the hours invoiced.

9. At the top of the window, confirm that the *Print Later* and *Email Later* boxes do not contain check marks. In the lower left part of the window, the *Your customer can't pay this invoice online* command should remain off. See Figure 3–O.

FIGURE 3–O
Create Invoices
Window—Completed

HINT

You can display transactions previously entered by clicking the Previous arrow. You can correct errors in a transaction, or you can remove a transaction by clicking the Delete button and then either deleting or voiding the invoice.

As stated earlier, the default account to debit in the Create Invoices window is Accounts Receivable. An account to be credited is not indicated in this window. The item for Decorating Services in the Item List indicated the revenue account that should be credited when entering this item in an activity window. Once you choose the Decorating Services item in the Create Invoices window, QuickBooks knows from the Item List to credit the revenue account Decorating Services for this transaction.

10. If the information is correct, click the Save & Close button.

For a sale of decorating services on account, the general ledger posting is as follows:

1200 Accts Rec		4020 Decor Serv	
Dr	Cr	Dr	Cr
600			600

In addition, the customer file (subledger) for Beverly Jones reflects the new receivable:

Jones, Beverly	
Dr	Cr
600	

Practice Exercise 3–2

Record the following transactions at the Create Invoices window:

Feb. 6	Provided 16 hours of design services to Jennie Guthrie on account. Invoice No. 1002. *QuickCheck:* $960
Feb. 13	Provided 8 hours of decorating services and 16 hours of design services to Cook Caterers. Invoice No. 1003. *QuickCheck:* $1,360
Feb. 17	Provided 24 hours of design services to Franco Films Co. Invoice No. 1004. *QuickCheck:* $1,440
Feb. 23	Provided 24 hours of decorating services to Berger Bakery Company. Invoice No. 1005. *QuickCheck:* $1,200
Feb. 27	Provided 6 hours of decorating services and 15 hours of design services to Cook Caterers. Invoice No. 1006. *QuickCheck:* $1,200

The Receive Payments Window

In QuickBooks, the Receive Payments window is used to record the **collection of accounts receivable** from customers previously invoiced in the Create Invoices window. This window displays all open invoices for a specific customer. Payment can be in the form of cash, check, credit/debit card, or e-check. In addition, customer credit memos can be recorded.

The Receive Payments window is designed only for the collection of existing invoices. The default accounts are Accounts Receivable and Cash or Undeposited Funds (discussed later in this chapter). The transaction is recorded as follows:

			Cash (or Undeposited Funds)		XXX		
			Accounts Receivable			XXX	

At the same time, the customer's file in the Customer Center is updated to reflect the payment. The QuickBooks Receive Payments window appears in Figure 3–P.

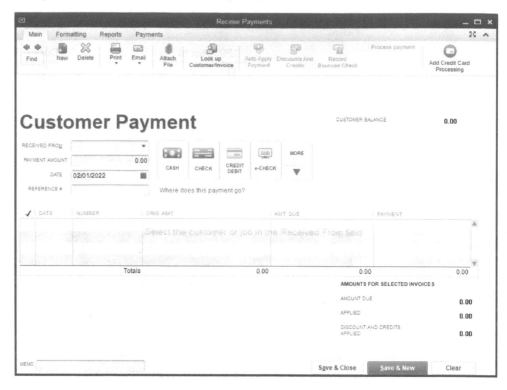

Once a customer is identified, a list of open invoices is displayed. Table 3–4 describes the various parts of the Receive Payments window.

Part	Description
CUSTOMER BALANCE field	Indicates the balance owed by the selected customer for all open invoices.
PAYMENT AMOUNT field	Used to enter the current payment. When an amount is entered, it is applied to the oldest invoice, and a check mark appears to the left of the invoice line. If you wish to have the payment applied to an alternate invoice, you need to select that invoice by inserting a check mark to the left of it.
CASH, CHECK, CREDIT/DEBIT, e-CHECK, MORE buttons	Used to indicate the customer's method of payment.
Look up Customer/Invoice button	Used to search for all open invoices. The search can be by invoice number, customer name, amount, date, and so on.
Auto Apply/Un-Apply Payment button	Auto Apply Payment is the default button. If no invoice has been selected, Auto Apply automatically applies a payment to the oldest invoice. When a payment is applied, the button switches to Un-Apply Payment, which allows you to select the invoice to be paid.
Discounts and Credits button	Used to apply discounts for early payments and unused credits.

Activities identified as sales on account were recorded in the Create Invoices window. Subsequently, Activities identified as collection of an outstanding account receivable (previously recorded in the Create Invoices window) are now recorded in the Receive Payments window. Cash or Undeposited Funds and Accounts Receivable are the default general ledger posting accounts. All transactions entered in this window result in a debit to the Cash or Undeposited Funds account and a credit to the Accounts Receivable account.

Receiving a Payment in Full

On February 13, 2022, Kristin Raina receives a $600 payment from Beverly Jones for Invoice No. 1001, her Check No. 6544.

To record a receipt of payment:
1. At the main menu bar, click Customers and then click *Receive Payments*.
2. At the RECEIVED FROM drop-down list, click *Jones, Beverly*. All the open invoices for Beverly Jones are displayed. See Figure 3–Q.

FIGURE 3–Q
Receive Payments Window—Beverly Jones

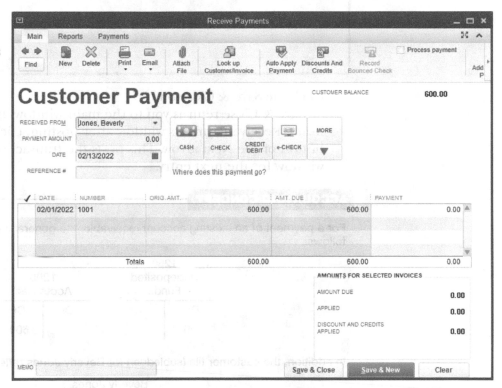

3. At the *PAYMENT AMOUNT* field, type 600.
    Once the amount is entered and you move to the next field, a check mark appears next to open Invoice No. 1001, indicating the $600 payment will be applied to that invoice automatically (since this is the only open invoice).
4. At the *DATE* field, choose *02/13/2022*.
5. Click the CHECK button.
6. At the *CHECK #* field, type 6544. See Figure 3–R.

FIGURE 3-R
Receive Payments
Window—Completed

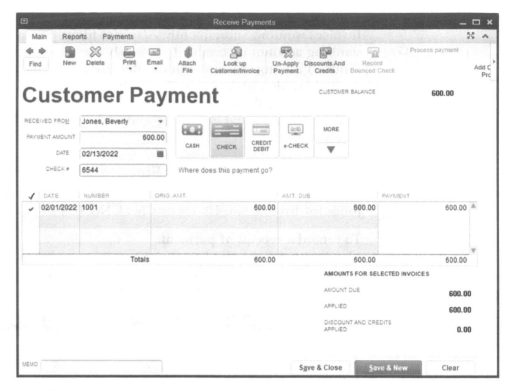

7. Click the Save & Close button.

   Save & Close returns you to the main window. If you wish to remain in the Receive Payments window after posting, click the Save & New button or the Next arrow. This posts the transaction and clears the window for the next entry.

ACCOUNTING CONCEPT

For a payment of an existing account receivable, the general ledger posting is as follows:

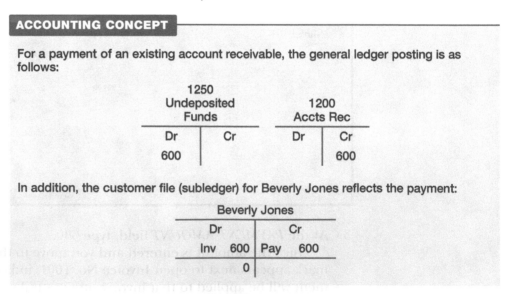

Entering a Partial Payment of an Invoice

The Receive Payments window allows you to record partial payments of open invoices. On February 20, 2022, Franco Films remits $500 toward its open Invoice No. 1004 in the amount of $1,440, its Check No. 1255. No discount is allowed.

To record a partial payment of an invoice:

1. At the main menu bar, click Customers and then click *Receive Payments*.
2. At the RECEIVED FROM drop-down list, click *Franco Films Co.* The open invoice is displayed along with the unpaid amount of $1,440 in the *CUSTOMER BALANCE* field.
3. At the *PAYMENT AMOUNT* field, type 500.

    When you move to the next field, the amount appears in the *PAYMENT* field. The *UNDERPAYMENT* box appears, indicating that $940 remains underpaid and asking if you want to leave it as an underpayment or write off the balance. Choose the *LEAVE THIS AS AN UNDERPAYMENT* option.
4. At the *DATE* field, choose *02/20/2022*.
5. Click the CHECK button.
6. At the *CHECK #* field, type 1255. See Figure 3–S.

FIGURE 3–S
Receive Payments Window—Partial Payment

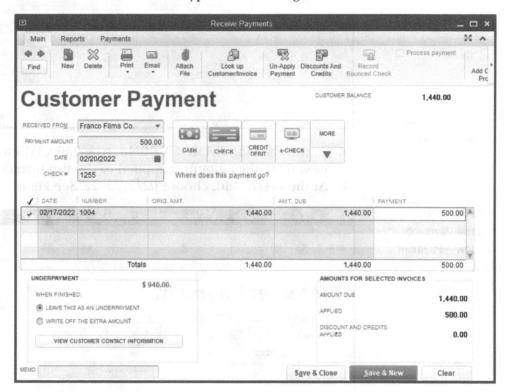

7. Click the Save & Close button.

Receiving Payment for More Than One Invoice

QuickBooks allows you to record the payment of several invoices at the same time. On February 27, 2022, Cook Caterers remits $2,560 in full payment of Invoice Nos. 1003 and 1006, its Check No. 655.

To record payment of more than one invoice:

1. At the main menu bar, click Customers and then click *Receive Payments*.
2. At the RECEIVED FROM drop-down list, click *Cook Caterers*. All the open invoices are displayed. See Figure 3–T.

FIGURE 3–T
Receive Payments
Window—Invoices
Displayed

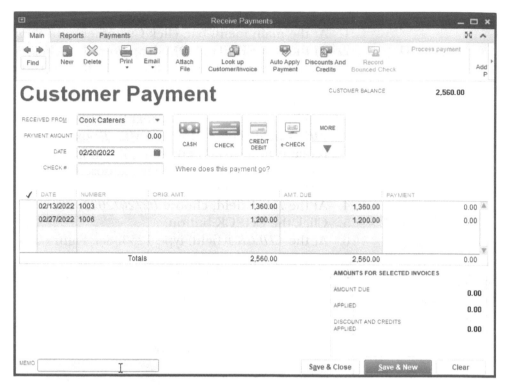

3. At the *PAYMENT AMOUNT* field, type 2560. When you move to the next field, the amount is applied to the two invoices.
4. At the *DATE* field, choose *02/27/2022*. See Figure 3–U.

FIGURE 3–U
Receive Payments
Window—Payment
Applied

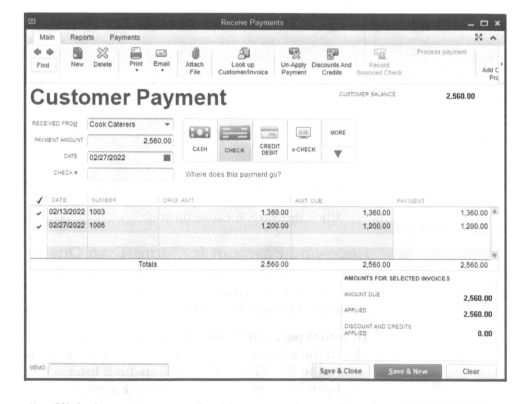

5. Click the payment method button and complete the *CHECK #* field. See Figure 3–V.

FIGURE 3-V
Receive Payments
Window—Completed

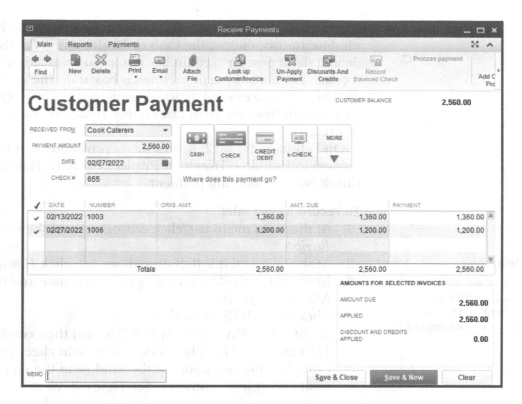

6. If the information is correct, click the Save & New button.

Practice Exercise   3–3

Record the following transactions at the Receive Payments window:

| Feb. 28 | Received $960 from Jennie Guthrie in full payment of Invoice No. 1002, her Check No. 674. |
| Feb. 28 | Received $600 from Berger Bakery Company in partial payment of Invoice No. 1005. Leave as underpayment, its Check No. 12458. |

The Enter Sales Receipts Window

In QuickBooks, you use the Enter Sales Receipts window to record sales for which the payments are received immediately. Since you do not use Accounts Receivable, this window allows you to record a **cash sale** in one step. The data fields in this window are similar to those in the Create Invoices window: customer, date, item sold, service provided, and so on.

The Enter Sales Receipts window is used for all cash sales of goods and services. As with the Receive Payments window, the default account is Cash or Undeposited Funds. The transaction is recorded as follows:

cash sale a sale for which payment is received immediately

| | Cash (or Undeposited Funds) | XXX | |
| | Revenue | | XXX |

A transaction entered in this window is not tracked through the *Accounts Receivable* or *Customer* reports.

Activities identified as cash sales are recorded in the Enter Sales Receipts window. In this window, the Cash or Undeposited Funds account is the default debit posting account because each transaction results in a cash receipt. The account to be credited is based on the item selected. As in the Create Invoices window, when an item is selected, QuickBooks uses the information from the Item List window to determine which account should be credited.

On February 24, 2022, Kristin Raina provided eight hours of design services to Hamilton Hotels on Invoice No. 1007. Hamilton Hotels issued Check No. 25546 in full payment.

To record a cash sale:

1. At the main menu bar, click Customers and then click *Enter Sales Receipts.*
2. At the CUSTOMER:JOB drop-down list, click *Hamilton Hotels.*
3. In the *DATE* field, enter the appropriate date and then in the *SALE NO.* field, type 1007.
4. Click the CHECK button.
5. At the *CHECK NO.* field, type 25546 and then confirm that the *Print Later* and *Email Later* boxes do not contain check marks.
6. Complete the remainder of the window in the same manner as you would complete an invoice. See Figure 3–W.

HINT

After entering the quantity, you must move to another field for the amount to be computed.

FIGURE 3–W
Enter Sales Receipts
Window—Completed

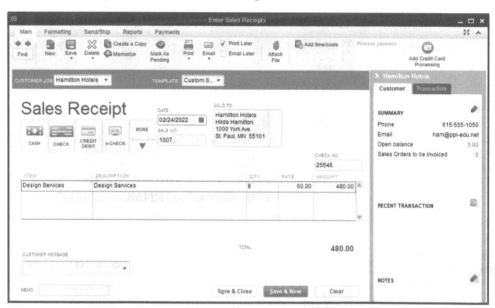

7. If the information is correct, click the Save & Close button.
   The customer file is unaffected because the payment was received at the point of sale.

ACCOUNTING CONCEPT

For a cash sale, the general ledger posting is as follows:

1250 Undeposited Funds		4010 Design Serv	
Dr	Cr	Dr	Cr
480			480

The Make Deposits Window

Most accounting textbooks assume that when cash is received, it is immediately posted to the Cash account. However, many businesses post to the Cash account only when funds are actually deposited in the checking account. This may occur several days after the funds are received. For these businesses, the receipt of funds is posted to a current asset account, titled Undeposited Funds, until a deposit is made. At that point, a second transaction is recorded to show the undeposited funds transferred to the Cash - Operating account. Debits to the Cash - Operating account should coincide with deposits recorded on the bank statement. This allows the company to more easily track deposits during the month-end bank reconciliation process.

When the Undeposited Funds account is used, cash receipts are recorded as follows:

| | Undeposited Funds | XXX | |
| | Accounts Receivable/Revenue | | XXX |

This entry results from activities entered in the Receive Payments and Enter Sales Receipts windows.

When funds previously received and recorded in the Receive Payments or Sales Receipts windows are subsequently deposited in the bank, the Make Deposits window is used. The default accounts are Cash and Undeposited Funds. The transaction is recorded as follows:

| | Cash | XXX | |
| | Undeposited Funds | | XXX |

Activities identified as deposits of funds are recorded in the Make Deposits window. In this window, Cash and Undeposited Funds are the default general ledger posting accounts. Each transaction entered in this window results in a debit to the Cash account and a credit to the Undeposited Funds account.

In the Receive Payments and Enter Sales Receipts windows, the default posting account for the receipt of cash is the Undeposited Funds account, rather than the Cash - Operating account. If you wish to allow for alternate debit posting accounts, you can change this default in the Payments Preferences of the Edit menu.

In this chapter, Kristin Raina will deposit all the receipts at one time at month-end. In a real-world setting, deposits are made more frequently depending on collection volume. Using this window allows you either to deposit each receipt individually or deposit several receipts or to deposit all the receipts at one time. On February 28, 2022, Kristin Raina deposits all the collections for the month.

To deposit all receipts collected and previously recorded as Undeposited Funds:

1. At the main menu bar, click Banking and then click *Make Deposits*. The Payments to Deposit window is displayed, showing all undeposited receipts.
2. At the Sort payments by drop-down list, click *Date*. See Figure 3–X.

HINT
In this text, the Undeposited Funds account will remain the default debit posting account.

FIGURE 3–X
Payments to Deposit
Window

3. Because all the receipts will be deposited, click the Select All button. All the receipts are checked for deposit. See Figure 3–Y.

FIGURE 3–Y
Payments to Deposit
Window—All Receipts
Selected

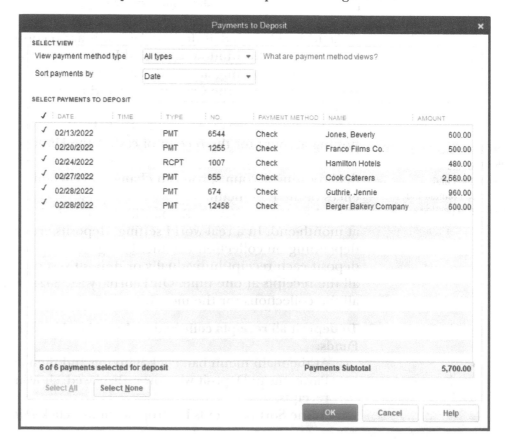

4. If the information is correct, click OK. You are forwarded to the Make Deposits window.
5. At the Deposit To drop-down list, click *1010 Cash - Operating*.
6. At the *Date* field, choose *02/28/2022*. See Figure 3–Z.

FIGURE 3–Z
Make Deposits
Window—Completed

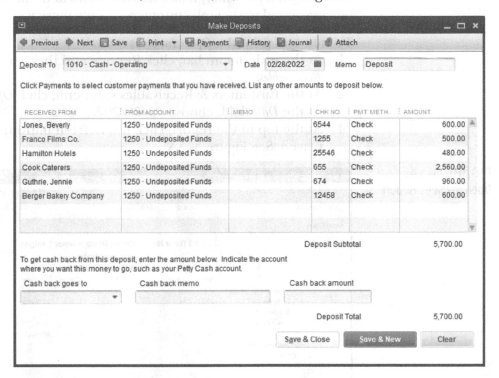

7. If the information is correct, click the Save & Close button.

HINT

If you make an error on the deposit, use the Previous arrow to display the deposit, click Edit, and then click *Delete Deposit*.

ACCOUNTING CONCEPT

The deposit of receipts as a separate transaction is recorded as follows:

1010 Cash - Operating		1250 Undeposited Funds	
Dr	Cr	Dr	Cr
5,700		5,700	5,700
			0

Reports

Customer Reports and Accounting Reports

Recall from Chapter 1 that Reports, the fourth level of operation, display the information and activities recorded in the various Lists/Centers and Activities windows. QuickBooks can display and print a variety of internal management reports as well as typical accounting and financial reports, many of which should be printed monthly.

Viewing and Printing Customer Reports

The Accounts Receivable and customer-related reports help the company to manage its collections, control cash flow, and retain an accurate record of all customer-related transactions. Among these reports are the *Open Invoices* report, the *Customer Balance Detail* report, and the *Customer Contact List* report.

Open Invoices Report

The *Open Invoices* report lists all unpaid invoices for each customer at a specific date. The report lists each open invoice, with the date and invoice number, for a customer; it also lists the terms and due date. The report may be customized to show all customers or only those with outstanding bills.

To view and print the *Open Invoices* report:

1. At the main menu bar, click Reports and then click *Customers & Receivables*.
2. At the Customers & Receivables submenu, click *Open Invoices*.
3. At the *Date* field, choose *02/28/2022*.
4. At the top of the report, click the Refresh button. The report is displayed. See Figure 3–AA.

FIGURE 3–AA
Open Invoices Report

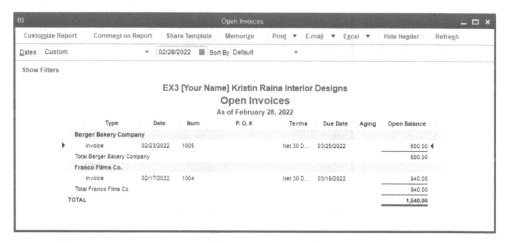

5. To print the report, click the Print button at the top of the report.
6. In the Print Reports dialog box, choose *Landscape* orientation and then click Print.
7. Close the report.

Customer Balance Detail Report

The *Customer Balance Detail* report displays all transactions for each customer with the remaining balance owed. This report is similar to an accounts receivable subsidiary ledger in a manual accounting system.

To view and print the *Customer Balance Detail* report:

1. At the main menu bar, click Reports and then click *Customers & Receivables*.
2. At the Customers & Receivables submenu, click *Customer Balance Detail*. The report shows all invoices, payments, and credit memos for each customer in chronological order.
3. To print the report, click the Print button at the top of the report and then click *Report*.
4. In the Print Reports dialog box, choose *Landscape* orientation and then click Print. Your printout should look like Figure 3–BB.

> **HINT**
> To change the width of a column, click and drag the vertical dotted bars between the column headings.

> **HINT**
> The format of your reports may vary slightly from the figures in the textbook. The reports in the figures are customized to display specific information. Chapter 12 will discuss customizing reports.

FIGURE 3–BB Customer Balance Detail Report

EX3 [Your Name] Kristin Raina Interior Designs
Customer Balance Detail
All Transactions

Type	Date	Num	Account	Amount	Balance
Berger Bakery Company					
Invoice	02/23/2022	1005	1200 · Accounts Receivable	1,200.00	1,200.00
Payment	02/28/2022	12458	1200 · Accounts Receivable	-600.00	600.00
Total Berger Bakery Company				600.00	600.00
Cook Caterers					
Invoice	02/13/2022	1003	1200 · Accounts Receivable	1,360.00	1,360.00
Invoice	02/27/2022	1006	1200 · Accounts Receivable	1,200.00	2,560.00
Payment	02/27/2022	655	1200 · Accounts Receivable	-2,560.00	0.00
Total Cook Caterers				0.00	0.00
Franco Films Co.					
Invoice	02/17/2022	1004	1200 · Accounts Receivable	1,440.00	1,440.00
Payment	02/20/2022	1255	1200 · Accounts Receivable	-500.00	940.00
Total Franco Films Co.				940.00	940.00
Guthrie, Jennie					
Invoice	02/06/2022	1002	1200 · Accounts Receivable	960.00	960.00
Payment	02/28/2022	674	1200 · Accounts Receivable	-960.00	0.00
Total Guthrie, Jennie				0.00	0.00
Jones, Beverly					
Invoice	02/01/2022	1001	1200 · Accounts Receivable	600.00	600.00
Payment	02/13/2022	6544	1200 · Accounts Receivable	-600.00	0.00
Total Jones, Beverly				0.00	0.00
TOTAL				1,540.00	1,540.00

5. Close the report.

Customer Contact List Report

The *Customer Contact List* report displays the information that has been entered in each customer's file in the Customer Center. This report displays the customer name, billing address, contact person, main phone and fax numbers, and present balance due.

HINT

The *Customer Contact List* report may also be accessed from the Customers & Receivables submenu.

To view the *Customer Contact List* report:

1. At the main menu bar, click Reports and then click *List*.
2. At the List submenu, click *Customer Contact List*. The Customer Contact List appears. See Figure 3–CC.

FIGURE 3–CC Customer Contact List Report

Customer Contact List					
Customize Report	Comment on Report	Share Template	Memorize	Print ▼ E-mail ▼ Excel ▼ Hide Header Refresh	Default ▼

Show Filters

EX3 [Your Name] Kristin Raina Interior Designs
Customer Contact List
February, 28, 2022

Customer	Bill to	Primary Contact	Main Phone	Fax	Balance Total
Alomar Company	Alomar Company Oliver Alomar 1001 Oak Lake Ave. Minneapolis, MN 55401	Oliver Alomar	612-555-5757		0.00
Barrera Bagel Barn	Barrera Bagel Barn Belinda Barrera 148 46th Ave. N Plymouth, MN 53406	Belinda Barrera	612-555-1233		0.00
Berger Bakery Company	Berger Bakery Company Barry Berger 18 N Grand Ave. Minneapolis, MN 55403		612-555-2240		600.00
Cook Caterers	Cook Caterers Stephen Cook 275 Oak Lake Ave. Minneapolis, MN 55401	Stephen Cook	612-555-7896		0.00
Franco Films Co.	Franco Films Co. Fred Franco 100 Pleasant Ave. S Minneapolis, MN 55409	Fred Franco	612-555-4566		940.00
Guthrie, Jennie	Jennie Guthrie 165 Terrace Ct. St. Paul, MN 55101	Jennie Guthrie	615-555-1515		0.00
Hamilton Hotels	Hamilton Hotels Hilda Hamilton 1000 York Ave. St. Paul, MN 55101	Hilda Hamilton	615-555-1050		0.00
Jones, Beverly	Beverly Jones 333 York Circle Bloomington, MN 54603	Beverly Jones	612-555-7778		0.00
Omari, Maria	Maria Omari 210 NE Lowry Ave. Minneapolis, MN 54204		612-555-9999		0.00
Plaza Pizza Palace	Plaza Pizza Palace Tony Plaza 360 Border Ave. N Minneapolis, MN 55401	Tony Plaza	612-555-9000		0.00

3. Close the report.

Viewing and Printing Accounting Reports

HINT

You can "drill down" from the reports to the activity window if you need to make any corrections.

As activities are entered in the windows, behind-the-scenes accounting activity is recorded in general journal format, posted to the general ledger, and flowed into the financial statements. You can display and print standard accounting reports showing these activities, such as the *Journal* report. The *Journal* report displays, in general journal format, all transactions recorded during a specified period of time.

To view and print the *Journal* report:

1. At the main menu bar, click Reports and then click *Accountant & Taxes.*
2. At the Accountant & Taxes submenu, click *Journal.*
3. At the *From* and *To* fields, choose *02/01/2022* to *02/28/2022.*
4. At the top of the report, click the Refresh button. The *Journal* report is displayed.
5. To print the report, click the Print button at the top of the report and then click *Report.*
6. In the Print Reports dialog box, choose *Landscape* orientation and then click Print. The last part of your printout should look like Figure 3–DD.
7. Close the report.

HINT

QuickBooks assigns transaction numbers that cannot be changed. Do not be surprised if your transaction numbers differ from those shown in the textbook, because you deleted transactions. The important thing is to make sure that the journal entries are correct.

HINT

If the name field displays *Multiple*, you can click the Expand button at the top of the report to display more detail.

Notice on your printout that all the activity for February is displayed in the order that it was entered. The earlier transactions are the vendor activities recorded in Chapter 2. The later transactions are the customer activities recorded in this chapter. Scroll down to the transactions for this chapter, and look in the *Type* column. This indicates the window where the activity was recorded. The *Invoice* type is from the Create Invoices window. Each of these transactions has a debit to Accounts Receivable, because this is the default for that window. The *Payment* type is from the Receive Payments window. Each of these transactions is a debit to Undeposited Funds and a credit to Accounts Receivable, which are the default accounts for this window. The *Sales Receipt* type is from the Enter Sales Receipts window. Each of these transactions has a debit to Undeposited Funds, because that is the default account for this window. The *Deposit* type is from the Make Deposits window. Each of these transactions by default is a debit to Cash and a credit to Undeposited Funds.

Exiting QuickBooks

Upon completing this session, make a backup copy of your practice exercise company file to a removable storage device using the Back Up command. Be sure to change the *Save in* field to the removable storage device and then carefully type the correct file name. Close the company file and then exit QuickBooks.

FIGURE 3–DD Journal Report—Partial

EX3 [Your Name] Kristin Raina Interior Designs
Journal
February 2022

Tran...	Type	Date	Num	Name	Account	Debit	Credit
3	Bill	02/02/2022	125-55	Minneapolis Electric &...	2010 · Accounts Payable		450.00
				Minneapolis Electric &...	6500 · Utilities Expense	450.00	
						450.00	450.00
4	Bill	02/02/2022	X-145	Cuza and Carl Associ...	2010 · Accounts Payable		600.00
				Cuza and Carl Associ...	1410 · Prepaid Advertising	600.00	
						600.00	600.00
6	Bill	02/03/2022	F-22	Nordic Realty	2010 · Accounts Payable		800.00
				Nordic Realty	6400 · Rent Expense	800.00	
						800.00	800.00
7	Bill	02/06/2022	K-222	Williams Office Suppl...	2010 · Accounts Payable		475.00
				Williams Office Suppl...	1305 · Office Supplies	475.00	
						475.00	475.00
8	Bill	02/09/2022	01-22	Midwest Mutual Insur...	2010 · Accounts Payable		2,400.00
				Midwest Mutual Insur...	1420 · Prepaid Insurance	2,400.00	
						2,400.00	2,400.00
9	Bill	02/13/2022	556588	Galeway Computers	2010 · Accounts Payable		3,600.00
				Galeway Computers	1825 · Computers, Cost	3,600.00	
						3,600.00	3,600.00
10	Bill	02/23/2022	Feb22	[Your Name] Accounti...	2010 · Accounts Payable		300.00
				[Your Name] Accounti...	6020 · Accounting Expen...	300.00	
						300.00	300.00
11	Credit	02/24/2022	CM-2...	Williams Office Suppl...	2010 · Accounts Payable	75.00	
				Williams Office Suppl...	1305 · Office Supplies		75.00
						75.00	75.00
12	Bill Pmt -Ch...	02/10/2022	1	Nordic Realty	1010 · Cash - Operating		800.00
				Nordic Realty	2010 · Accounts Payable	800.00	
						800.00	800.00
13	Bill Pmt -Ch...	02/23/2022	2	Cuza and Carl Associ...	1010 · Cash - Operating		200.00
				Cuza and Carl Associ...	2010 · Accounts Payable	200.00	
						200.00	200.00
14	Bill Pmt -Ch...	02/27/2022	3	[Your Name] Accounti...	1010 · Cash - Operating		300.00
				[Your Name] Accounti...	2010 · Accounts Payable	300.00	
						300.00	300.00
15	Bill Pmt -Ch...	02/27/2022	4	Galeway Computers	1010 · Cash - Operating		1,000.00
				Galeway Computers	2010 · Accounts Payable	1,000.00	
						1,000.00	1,000.00
16	Check	02/28/2022	5	Jeter Janitorial Services	1010 · Cash - Operating		125.00
				Jeter Janitorial Services	6300 · Janitorial Expenses	125.00	
						125.00	125.00
17	Check	02/28/2022	6	Grayson Graphics	1010 · Cash - Operating		200.00
				Grayson Graphics	1300 · Design Supplies	200.00	
						200.00	200.00
18	Check	02/28/2022	7	TwinCityTelCo	1010 · Cash - Operating		275.00
				TwinCityTelCo	6450 · Telephone Expense	275.00	
						275.00	275.00
19	Check	02/28/2022	8	Kristin Raina	1010 · Cash - Operating		400.00
				Kristin Raina	3020 · Kristin Raina, Dra...	400.00	
						400.00	400.00
20	Invoice	02/01/2022	1001	Jones, Beverly	1200 · Accounts Receiva...	600.00	
				Jones, Beverly	4020 · Decorating Services		600.00
						600.00	600.00
21	Invoice	02/06/2022	1002	Guthrie, Jennie	1200 · Accounts Receiva...	960.00	
				Guthrie, Jennie	4010 · Design Services		960.00
						960.00	960.00
22	Invoice	02/13/2022	1003	Cook Caterers	1200 · Accounts Receiva...	1,360.00	
				Cook Caterers	4020 · Decorating Services		400.00
				Cook Caterers	4010 · Design Services		960.00
						1,360.00	1,360.00
23	Invoice	02/17/2022	1004	Franco Films Co.	1200 · Accounts Receiva...	1,440.00	
				Franco Films Co.	4010 · Design Services		1,440.00
						1,440.00	1,440.00
24	Invoice	02/23/2022	1005	Berger Bakery Compa...	1200 · Accounts Receiva...	1,200.00	
				Berger Bakery Compa...	4020 · Decorating Services		1,200.00
						1,200.00	1,200.00
25	Invoice	02/27/2022	1006	Cook Caterers	1200 · Accounts Receiva...	1,200.00	
				Cook Caterers	4020 · Decorating Services		300.00
				Cook Caterers	4010 · Design Services		900.00
						1,200.00	1,200.00
26	Payment	02/13/2022	6544	Jones, Beverly	1250 · Undeposited Funds	600.00	
				Jones, Beverly	1200 · Accounts Receiva...		600.00
						600.00	600.00
27	Payment	02/20/2022	1255	Franco Films Co.	1250 · Undeposited Funds	500.00	
				Franco Films Co.	1200 · Accounts Receiva...		500.00
						500.00	500.00
28	Payment	02/27/2022	655	Cook Caterers	1250 · Undeposited Funds	2,560.00	
				Cook Caterers	1200 · Accounts Receiva...		2,560.00
						2,560.00	2,560.00
29	Payment	02/28/2022	674	Guthrie, Jennie	1250 · Undeposited Funds	960.00	
				Guthrie, Jennie	1200 · Accounts Receiva...		960.00
						960.00	960.00
30	Payment	02/28/2022	12458	Berger Bakery Compa...	1250 · Undeposited Funds	600.00	
				Berger Bakery Compa...	1200 · Accounts Receiva...		600.00
						600.00	600.00
31	Sales Receipt	02/24/2022	1007	Hamilton Hotels	1250 · Undeposited Funds	480.00	
				Hamilton Hotels	4010 · Design Services		480.00
						480.00	480.00
32	Deposit	02/28/2022			1010 · Cash - Operating	5,700.00	
				-MULTIPLE-	1250 · Undeposited Funds		5,700.00
						5,700.00	5,700.00
TOTAL						30,160.00	30,160.00

Chapter Review and Assessment

Procedure Review

To add a customer:
1. At the main menu bar, click Customers and then click *Customer Center*.
2. At the Customer Center window, click the New Customer & Job button and then select *New Customer*.
3. Enter the background data for the customer.
4. Click OK.
5. Close the Customer Center window.

To delete a customer:
1. At the main menu bar, click Customers and then click *Customer Center*.
2. At the Customer Center window, select the customer you wish to delete.
3. At the main menu bar, click Edit and then click *Delete Customer:Job*.
4. Click OK at the warning.
5. Close the Customer Center window.
    You cannot delete a customer who has a balance or who was used in a transaction during the current accounting period. Instead, you can mark the customer as inactive by checking the *Customer inactive* check box.

To edit a customer:
1. At the main menu bar, click Customers and then click *Customer Center*.
2. At the Customer Center window, double-click to select the customer you wish to edit.
3. Change the appropriate information.
4. Click OK.
5. Close the Customer Center window.

To create an invoice:
1. At the main menu bar, click Customers and then click *Create Invoices*.
2. At the CUSTOMER:JOB drop-down list, click the customer name.
3. At the TEMPLATE drop-down list, accept *Intuit Service Invoice*.
4. At the *DATE* field, enter the invoice date.
5. At the *INVOICE* # field, enter the invoice number.
6. At the TERMS drop-down list, select the terms.
7. At the *ITEM* field, click the first line to display the drop-down Item List and then click the appropriate item(s).
8. At the *QUANTITY* field, enter the quantity.
9. At the top of the window, confirm that the *Print Later* and *Email Later* boxes do not contain check marks. In the lower left part of the window, the *Your customer can't pay this invoice online* command should remain off.
10. Click the Save & Close button.

To receive a payment:
1. At the main menu bar, click Customers and then click *Receive Payments*.
2. At the RECEIVED FROM drop-down list, click the customer name.
3. At the *PAYMENT AMOUNT* field, enter the amount.
4. At the *DATE* field, enter the payment date.

5. Click the CHECK button.
6. At the *CHECK* # field, enter the check number.
7. Click the Save & Close button.

To enter a cash sale:
1. At the main menu bar, click Customers and then click *Enter Sales Receipts.*
2. At the CUSTOMER:JOB drop-down list, click the customer name.
3. Click the CHECK button and then enter the check number.
4. Complete the remainder of the window in the same manner as an invoice.
5. Click the Save & Close button.

To make a deposit:
1. At the main menu bar, click Banking and then click *Make Deposits.*
2. At the Payments to Deposit window, click Select All to deposit all the receipts.
3. Click OK.
4. At the Make Deposits window, at the Deposit To drop-down list, accept or choose the *1010 Cash - Operating* account.
5. Enter the deposit date in the *Date* field.
6. Click the Save & Close button.

To view and print customer reports from the Reports menu:
1. At the main menu bar, click Reports and then click *Customers & Receivables.*
2. At the Customers & Receivables submenu, choose a report.
3. Choose the appropriate dates for the report and then click the Refresh button at the top of the report.
4. Click the Print button at the top of the report and then click *Report.*
5. In the Print Reports dialog box, review the settings and then click Print.
6. Close the report.

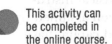
This activity can be completed in the online course.

Key Concepts

Select the letter of the item that best matches each definition.

a. Customer Center
b. Receive Payments window
c. Cash sales
d. Create Invoices window
e. *Open Invoices* report

f. Customer
g. Undeposited Funds
h. Enter Sales Receipts window
i. Make Deposits window
j. *Customer Balance Detail* report

_____ 1. Contains a file for each customer with whom the company does business.
_____ 2. A report that displays all the transactions for a customer.
_____ 3. Window used to record a deposit of funds collected.
_____ 4. A person or business to which the company provides services or sells a product.
_____ 5. Window used to record the payment of invoices.

_____ 6. Sales for which payment is received immediately.
_____ 7. Window used to record sales on account.
_____ 8. Collections not yet deposited in the bank.
_____ 9. A report that lists all the unpaid invoices for each customer.
_____ 10. Window used to record sales for cash.

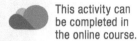
This activity can be completed in the online course.

Procedure Check

1. Your company has obtained a new major client. Describe the steps to add the new client to the system.
2. Your company has the type of business that makes cash sales to many customers and rarely tracks accounts receivable. How would you use QuickBooks to record your sales?
3. Your business wishes to track all the deposits made to the bank to facilitate the month-end bank reconciliation process. How would you record the collection of funds to accomplish this?
4. You wish to determine the oldest unpaid invoices. How would you use QuickBooks to obtain that information?
5. You wish to view all the invoices and collection activity for a customer. How would you use QuickBooks to obtain the required information?
6. Compare and contrast a manual accounting system with a computerized accounting system for processing customer transactions. Include an explanation of how the accounts receivable subsidiary ledger compares with the Customer Center.

Reports created for these Case Problems can be exported to Excel and uploaded in the online course to be automatically graded.

Case Problems

Demonstrate your knowledge of the QuickBooks features discussed in this chapter by completing the following case problems.

Case Problem 3–1

On April 1, 2022, Lynn Garcia started her business, Lynn's Music Studio. Lynn began by depositing $10,000 cash in a bank account in the business name. She also contributed a piano and some guitars. The musical instruments have an outstanding note balance of $2,000 that has been assumed by the business. The cash, musical instruments, note payable, and capital have all been recorded in the opening balances of the books. During the first part of the month, Lynn set up her studio. She has now begun providing piano and guitar lessons. Piano lessons are billed at $35 per hour, and guitar lessons are billed at $30 per hour. You will record the transactions listed below for the month of April. The company file for this chapter includes the beginning information for Lynn's Music Studio along with the transaction balances from Chapter 2.

1. Open the company file **CH3 Lynn's Music Studio.QBW**.
2. At the QuickBooks Desktop Login window, in the *Password* text box, type Student1 and then click OK.
3. Make a backup copy of the company file and name it **LMS3** *[Your Name]* **Lynn's Music Studio**.

4. Restore the backup copy of the company file. In both the Open Backup Copy and Save Company File as dialog boxes, use the file name **LMS3 *[Your Name]* Lynn's Music Studio** and enter the password.

5. Change the company name to **LMS3 *[Your Name]* Lynn's Music Studio**.

6. Add the following customer to the Customer Center:

CUSTOMER NAME:	Musical Youth Group
OPENING BALANCE:	0 AS OF April 1, 2022
COMPANY NAME:	Musical Youth Group
First Name:	Dana
Last Name:	Thompson
Main Phone:	570-555-6642
Mobile:	570-555-6700
Main Email:	myg@ppi-edu.net
INVOICE/BILL TO:	550 Marion Lane
	Scranton, PA 18504
CREDIT LIMIT:	20,000
PAYMENT TERMS:	Net 30 Days
TYPE:	Group

   Delete the following customer:
   Rivera Family

7. Using the appropriate window, record the following transactions for April 2022:

   Apr. 9   Provided 15 hours guitar lessons and 10 hours piano lessons on account to Jefferson High School, Invoice No. 2001, Net 10 Days. Be sure the Intuit Service Invoice is the active template.

   Apr. 12   Provided 3 hours piano lessons to the Schroeder Family, Invoice No. 2002. Received payment immediately, Check No. 478.

   Apr. 13   Provided 12 hours piano lessons to Highland School, Invoice No. 2003, Net 30 Days.

   Apr. 16   Provided 8 hours guitar lessons and 5 hours piano lessons to Twin Lakes Elementary School, Invoice No. 2004, Net 30 Days.

   Apr. 16   Provided 6 hours guitar lessons to the Patterson Family, Invoice No. 2005. Received payment immediately, Check No. 208.

   Apr. 20   Provided 5 hours guitar lessons and 7 hours piano lessons to Mulligan Residence, Invoice No. 2006, Net 30 Days.

   Apr. 20   Received payment in full from Jefferson High School for Invoice No. 2001, Check No. 28759.

Apr. 23 Provided 5 hours piano lessons to Douglaston Senior
Center, Invoice No. 2007, Net 30 Days. Douglaston Senior
Center is a new client:

CUSTOMER NAME:	Douglaston Senior Center
OPENING BALANCE:	0 AS OF April 1, 2022
COMPANY NAME:	Douglaston Senior Center
First Name:	Herbie
Last Name:	Richardson
Main Phone:	570-555-7748
Mobile:	570-555-8800
Main Email:	DSC@ppi-edu.net
INVOICE/BILL TO:	574 S Beech Street
	Scranton, PA 18506
CREDIT LIMIT:	25,000
PAYMENT TERMS:	Net 30 Days
TYPE:	Group

Apr. 23 Provided 10 hours guitar lessons and 10 hours piano lessons
to the Musical Youth Group, Invoice No. 2008. Received
payment immediately, Check No. 578.

Apr. 26 Provided 15 hours guitar lessons and 10 hours piano lessons
on account to Jefferson High School, Invoice No. 2009, Net
10 Days.

Apr. 26 Received payment in full from Highland School for Invoice
No. 2003, Check No. 75281.

Apr. 27 Provided 2 hours guitar lessons for the Patel Family, Invoice
No. 2010. Received payment immediately, Check No. 629.

Apr. 30 Provided 8 hours guitar lessons and 5 hours piano lessons
to Twin Lakes Elementary School, Invoice No. 2011, Net 30
Days.

Apr. 30 Received partial payment of $145 from Mulligan Residence
for Invoice No. 2006, Check No. 715.

Apr. 30 Deposited all receipts for the month.

8. Display and print the following reports for April 1, 2022, to April 30, 2022:
   a. *Open Invoices*
   b. *Customer Balance Detail*
   c. *Customer Contact List*
   d. *Journal*

Case Problem 3–2

On June 1, 2022, Olivia Chen began her business, Olivia's Web Solutions.
Olivia began by depositing $25,000 cash in a bank account in the business
name. She also contributed a computer. The computer has an outstanding
note balance of $2,500 that has been assumed by the business. The cash,
computer, note payable, and capital have all been recorded in the opening
balances of the books. During the first part of the month, Olivia set up her
office. She has now begun providing web design and internet consulting
services to individuals and small businesses. The Web Page Design Services

are billed at $125 per hour, and the Internet Consulting Services are billed at $100 per hour. You will record the transactions listed below for the month of June. The company file includes the beginning information for Olivia's Web Solutions along with the transaction balances from Chapter 2.

1. Open the company file **CH3 Olivia's Web Solutions.QBW**.
2. At the QuickBooks Desktop Login window, in the *Password* text box, type Student1 and then click OK.
3. Make a backup copy of the company file and name it **OWS3** *[Your Name]* **Olivia's Web Solutions**.
4. Restore the backup copy of the company file. In both the Open Backup Copy and Save Company File as dialog boxes, use the file name **OWS3** *[Your Name]* **Olivia's Web Solutions** and enter the password.
5. Change the company name to **OWS3** *[Your Name]* **Olivia's Web Solutions**.
6. Add the following customer to the Customer Center:

CUSTOMER NAME:	Thrifty Stores
OPENING BALANCE:	0 AS OF June 1, 2022
COMPANY NAME:	Thrifty Stores
First Name:	William
Last Name:	Way
Main Phone:	718-555-2445
Mobile:	718-555-2446
Main Email:	Thrifty@ppi-edu.net
INVOICE/BILL TO:	23 Boston Ave.
	Bronx, NY 11693
CREDIT LIMIT:	25,000
PAYMENT TERMS:	Net 30 Days
TYPE:	Commercial

Delete the following customer:
Printers Group

7. Using the appropriate window, record the following transactions for June 2022:

Jun. 11   Provided 8 hours Internet Consulting Services and 10 hours Web Page Design Services on account to Long Island Water Works, Invoice No. 1001, Net 30 Days. Be sure the Intuit Service Invoice is the active template.

Jun. 14   Provided 8 hours Web Page Design Services on account to Sehorn & Smith, Invoice No. 1002, Net 30 Days.

Jun. 15   Provided 8 hours Web Page Design Services on account to the Schneider Family, Invoice No. 1003, Net 15 Days.

Jun. 17   Provided 4 hours Internet Consulting Services and 8 hours Web Page Design Services on account to Miguel's Restaurant, Invoice No. 1004, Net 30 Days.

Jun. 18   Provided 4 hours Internet Consulting Services to the Singh Family, Invoice No. 1005. Received payment immediately, Check No. 687.

Jun. 21	Provided 8 hours Web Page Design Services on account to Breathe Easy, Invoice No. 1006, Net 30 Days.
Jun. 25	Received payment in full from Long Island Water Works for Invoice No. 1001, Check No. 124554.
Jun. 25	Provided 12 hours Web Page Design Services on account to Thrifty Stores, Invoice No. 1007, Net 30 Days.
Jun. 28	Provided 8 hours Internet Consulting Services on account to Artie's Auto Repair, Invoice 1008, Net 30 Days. Artie's Auto Repair is a new client:

CUSTOMER NAME:	Artie's Auto Repair
OPENING BALANCE:	0 AS OF June 1, 2022
COMPANY NAME:	Artie's Auto Repair
First Name:	Leon
Last Name:	Artie
Main Phone:	516-555-1221
Mobile:	516-555-1231
Main Email:	ArtieAuto@ppi-edu.net
INVOICE/BILL TO:	32 West 11th Street
	New Hyde Park, NY 11523
CREDIT LIMIT:	25,000
PAYMENT TERMS:	Net 30 Days
TYPE:	Commercial

Jun. 28	Received payment in full from Sehorn & Smith for Invoice No. 1002, Check No. 3656.
Jun. 29	Provided 12 hours of Internet Consulting Services on account to South Shore School District, Invoice No. 1009, Net 30 Days.
Jun. 29	Received payment in full from Miguel's Restaurant for Invoice No. 1004, Check No. 3269.
Jun. 30	Provided 8 hours of Internet Consulting Services on account to Sehorn & Smith, Invoice No. 1010, Net 30 Days.
Jun. 30	Received partial payment of $250 from Breathe Easy for Invoice No. 1006, Check No. 1455.
Jun. 30	Deposited all receipts for the month.

8. Display and print the following reports for June 1, 2022, to June 30, 2022:
   a. *Open Invoices*
   b. *Customer Balance Detail*
   c. *Customer Contact List*
   d. *Journal*

## CHAPTER 4

Period-End Procedures

Making General Journal Entries

Objectives

- Update the Chart of Accounts List
- Record adjustments in the Make General Journal Entries window
- View the effect of period-end adjustments on the trial balance
- Display and print period-end accounting reports
- Change the reports display using the Customize Report button
- Display and print accounting reports and financial statements

 The online course includes additional training and assessment resources. Reports created for the Chapter Problem can be uploaded for instructor review.

Chapter Introduction

QuickBooks allows you to record journal entries in general journal format. As shown in Chapters 2 and 3, QuickBooks records daily activities in windows such as Enter Bills, Pay Bills, Write Checks, Create Invoices, Receive Payments, and so on. However, behind the scenes, QuickBooks also records the activities in general journal format using debits and credits. The accounts used to record the activities come from the Chart of Accounts (Lists/Centers).

At times, some account balances (Activities) will need to be adjusted based on information that does not appear in the daily activities so that the financial statements can be properly prepared in accordance with **generally accepted accounting principles (GAAP)**. These adjustments to the accounts are **adjusting journal entries**, and they are recorded in the Make General Journal Entries window. As you record the daily activities and adjusting journal entries, QuickBooks simultaneously updates the accounting records and financial statements (Reports).

In this chapter, our sample company, Kristin Raina Interior Designs, will make the necessary adjusting journal entries for February—the end of the first month of operations.

QuickBooks versus Manual Accounting: General Journal Entries

In a manual accounting system, the general journal is the document in which transactions are initially recorded chronologically. For each transaction, the dollar value of at least one account must be recorded as a **debit** amount, and the dollar value of at least one account must be recorded as a **credit** amount. The total dollar value of debits must equal the total dollar value of credits. A company has the option of recording all transactions exclusively in the general journal or, alternatively, for frequent similar transactions, in special journals. In either case, at month-end, the transactions from all journals are posted to the general ledger.

Periodically, certain adjustments that are not daily business activities must be made to the accounts to update the balances. These adjustments, called *adjusting journal entries*, are always recorded in the general journal. They are then posted to the general ledger to update the balances in the accounts. The adjusted balances are used to prepare the financial statements. These adjusting journal entries must always be made on the date the financial statements are prepared, but they can be recorded more often. Most large companies typically prepare the adjusting journal entries monthly.

QuickBooks does not follow the format of the special journals for daily transactions. Instead, each activity is recorded in a different window depending on the nature of the activity. Behind the scenes, QuickBooks records the activity in general journal format, as seen in the *Journal* report. However, for adjusting journal entries, QuickBooks uses the Make General Journal Entries window in a manner similar to that of a manual accounting system. As you save the information entered in each window, including the Make General Journal Entries window, the general ledger balances, the Chart of Accounts List balances, the trial balance, and the financial statements are updated simultaneously. Because balances are easily updated in a computerized accounting system, even small companies can record adjusting journal entries monthly.

Chapter Problem

In this chapter, you will record the adjusting journal entries for the end of the first month of business, February 28, 2022, for Kristin Raina Interior Designs. The February 1, 2022, beginning balances, along with all the vendor and customer activities for the month of February, as illustrated in Chapters 2 and 3, are contained in the company file **CH4 Kristin Raina Interior Designs**.

Before you begin, open the company file **CH4 Kristin Raina Interior Designs.QBW**. Enter the password, *Student1*. Make a backup copy of the file, name it **EX4 *[Your Name]* Kristin Raina Interior Designs**, and then restore the file. Enter the password, *Student1*. Finally, change the company name in the file to **EX4 *[Your Name]* Kristin Raina Interior Designs**.

Lists/Centers

The Chart of Accounts List

Recall from Chapter 1 that the second level of operation in QuickBooks is recording background information in Lists/Centers. Lists and Centers need to be revised periodically when new accounts need to be added, accounts not used in the business need to be deleted, or modifications need to be made to an account. When you make these revisions to the accounts, you are updating the Chart of Accounts List.

The **Chart of Accounts List** is the list of accounts a company uses as it conducts its business. In a manual accounting system, all the individual accounts are placed together in a book called the **general ledger**. Each account in the general ledger shows all the increases and decreases in the account, reflected as debits and credits, and the balance in each account. In computerized accounting systems, a general ledger is also maintained showing the increases and decreases in each account, reflected as debits and credits, and the balance for each account. In addition, the Chart of Accounts List displays the balance next to each account name. Because of this, the Chart of Accounts List has become synonymous with the general ledger in computerized systems, although it indicates the balances for only the assets, liabilities, and equity accounts and does not display all the detail activities.

In QuickBooks, the Chart of Accounts List consists of the account numbers, names, types, and balances. The account numbers are optional but are used in this text. The name you assign an account is the name that appears in the windows and reports. The balance is determined by the original amount entered (if any) when the account is first created and then subsequently updated by Activities entered in the windows.

The software uses account types to determine where to place each account name and balance on the financial statements and to establish the system default accounts. The account types consist of:

> **Chart of Accounts List** the list of accounts a company uses as it conducts its business
>
> **general ledger** the document in which transactions are summarized by account

Assets:	Liabilities:	Income and Expenses:	Equity:
Bank	Accounts Payable	Income	Equity
Accounts Receivable	Credit Card	Cost of Goods Sold	
Other Current Asset	Other Current Liability	Expense	
Fixed Asset	Long-Term Liability	Other Income	
Other Asset		Other Expenses	

As shown in Chapters 2 and 3, QuickBooks identifies certain accounts as system default accounts and uses them to identify the transactions recorded in the windows. For example, the Accounts Payable account type is used to identify the Accounts Payable liability account when transactions are recorded in the Enter Bills window. The Accounts Receivable account type is used to identify the Accounts Receivable asset account when transactions are recorded in the Create Invoices window. When QuickBooks looks for an account, it looks for the account type, not the account name.

Kristin Raina previously entered information to establish the Chart of Accounts List, which was then used for the February activities recorded in Chapters 2 and 3.

To review the Chart of Accounts List:
1. At the main menu bar, click Reports and then click *List.*
2. At the List submenu, click *Account Listing.* The *Account Listing* report is displayed. See Figure 4–A.

FIGURE 4–A Account Listing Report

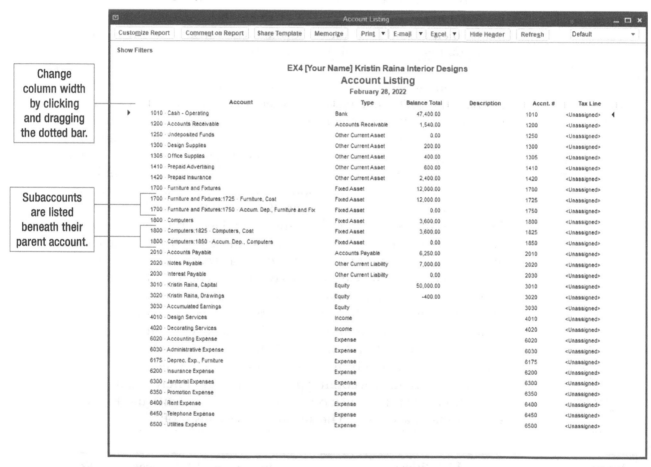

In QuickBooks, the account balances that flow into the financial statements are based on the account types. If you want to subtotal two or more accounts on the financial statements, you can identify an account as a subaccount. A subaccount shows a subtotal amount on the financial statements in addition to the regular account balances. A parent account is an account that has a subaccount.

In Kristin Raina's Chart of Accounts List, the fixed asset cost and accumulated depreciation accounts were marked as subaccounts of the related asset account. This was done to see the accumulated depreciation account as a deduction from the cost of an asset on the financial statements and to display the net amount.

In the *Account Listing* report, when parent and subaccounts are used, the parent account is listed first, with subaccounts beneath it. Each subaccount listing includes the name of the parent account followed by a colon and the subaccount name. Review the *Account Listing* report in Figure 4–A on page 112. Look at the 1700 Furniture and Fixtures account. The accounts below it are as follows: 1700 Furniture and Fixtures: 1725 - Furniture, Cost 1700 Furniture and Fixtures: 1750 - Accum. Dep., Furniture and Fix. This means accounts 1725 and 1750 are subaccounts of 1700. Account 1700 is a parent account because it has subaccounts. Notice the same setup with accounts 1800, 1825, and 1850 in the *Account Listing* report.

To view a specific account:

1. With the *Account Listing* report open, place the zoom glass over the Cash - Operating account.
2. Choose *Cash - Operating* by double-clicking it. The Edit Account window for Cash - Operating is displayed. See Figure 4–B.

FIGURE 4–B
Edit Account Window

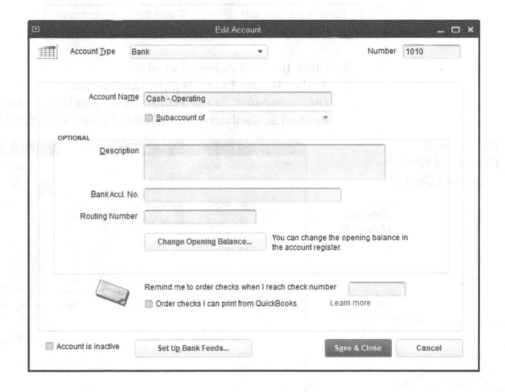

Table 4–1 describes the account information contained in the Edit Account window (Figure 4–B on the previous page).

TABLE 4–1
Edit Account Window

Field	Description
Account Type	Use the drop-down list to display and choose the account type. QuickBooks uses the account type for system default accounts in windows and for placement on financial statements.
Number	An account number is optional. Account numbers will be used in this text and have been established in the company files.
Account Name	Enter an account name of your choice. The software uses the account type, not the account name, for necessary identification (default accounts and placement on financial statements). The name typed in this field appears in the windows and on reports.
Subaccount of	An account can be identified as a subaccount of another account. To activate this field, click to insert a check mark in the box. Once this box is activated, use the drop-down list to determine in which account this will become a subaccount.
Description	This field is optional. A description entered here appears on certain reports.
Bank Acct. No. and Routing Number	These fields are optional. They are listed as references for the user.

3. Close the Edit Account window.
4. At the *Account Listing* report, double-click *1800 Computers: 1850 - Accum. Dep., Computers.* At the Edit Account window, notice how this account is marked as a subaccount of 1800 - Computers. See Figure 4–C.

FIGURE 4–C
Edit Account Window— Subaccount Checked

5. Close the Edit Account window.
6. Close the *Account Listing* report.

Adding an Account

In preparation for recording month-end adjusting journal entries, Kristin Raina has determined that she needs to add an Advertising Expense account to the Chart of Accounts List.

To add a new account:

1. At the main menu bar, click Lists and then click *Chart of Accounts.* The Chart of Accounts List window appears. See Figure 4–D.

FIGURE 4–D
Chart of Accounts List Window

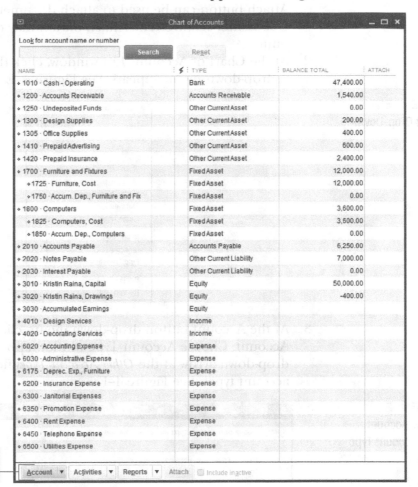

NAME		TYPE	BALANCE TOTAL	ATTACH
1010 · Cash - Operating		Bank	47,400.00	
1200 · Accounts Receivable		Accounts Receivable	1,540.00	
1250 · Undeposited Funds		Other Current Asset	0.00	
1300 · Design Supplies		Other Current Asset	200.00	
1305 · Office Supplies		Other Current Asset	400.00	
1410 · Prepaid Advertising		Other Current Asset	600.00	
1420 · Prepaid Insurance		Other Current Asset	2,400.00	
1700 · Furniture and Fixtures		Fixed Asset	12,000.00	
1725 · Furniture, Cost		Fixed Asset	12,000.00	
1750 · Accum. Dep., Furniture and Fix		Fixed Asset	0.00	
1800 · Computers		Fixed Asset	3,600.00	
1825 · Computers, Cost		Fixed Asset	3,600.00	
1850 · Accum. Dep., Computers		Fixed Asset	0.00	
2010 · Accounts Payable		Accounts Payable	6,250.00	
2020 · Notes Payable		Other Current Liability	7,000.00	
2030 · Interest Payable		Other Current Liability	0.00	
3010 · Kristin Raina, Capital		Equity	50,000.00	
3020 · Kristin Raina, Drawings		Equity	-400.00	
3030 · Accumulated Earnings		Equity		
4010 · Design Services		Income		
4020 · Decorating Services		Income		
6020 · Accounting Expense		Expense		
6030 · Administrative Expense		Expense		
6175 · Deprec. Exp., Furniture		Expense		
6200 · Insurance Expense		Expense		
6300 · Janitorial Expenses		Expense		
6350 · Promotion Expense		Expense		
6400 · Rent Expense		Expense		
6450 · Telephone Expense		Expense		
6500 · Utilities Expense		Expense		

List window drop-down menu buttons

Account ▾ Activities ▾ Reports ▾ Attach ☐ Include inactive

Notice that most of the account names are left-aligned. In the Chart of Accounts List window, when parent and subaccounts are used, by default the parent account name is left-aligned, and the subaccount names are indented under the parent account name. For example, account 1700 is the parent account, and subaccounts 1725 and 1750 are indented under account 1700.

The presentation of parent accounts and subaccounts in the Chart of Accounts List window is different from the presentation of parent and subaccounts on the *Account Listing* report. Recall that in the *Account Listing* report in Figure 4–A on page 112, for each subaccount listed, both the parent account and subaccount are listed on one line, with the parent account name left-aligned and the subaccount name listed to the right of the parent account name.

The Chart of Accounts List is displayed in a List window. Each List window has drop-down menu buttons at the bottom of the window.

The first menu button in all List windows represents the name of the list—in this case, Account. In almost all List windows, there is also a Reports button. The remaining buttons vary according to the List window displayed. In the Chart of Accounts List window, the first menu button is Account, the second menu button is Activities, the third menu button is Reports, and the fourth menu button is Attach. The Activities and Reports buttons are shortcuts you can use instead of using the main menu bar drop-down menus to access commands. The Attach button can be used to attach documents using the QuickBooks Doc Center feature. The Attach button may or may not be an active button.

2. At the Chart of Accounts List window, click the Account menu button. A drop-down menu appears. See Figure 4–E.

FIGURE 4–E
Account Drop-Down
Menu

3. At the Account button drop-down menu, click *New*. The Add New Account: Choose Account Type window appears. You can click the drop-down arrow at the *Other Account Types* field to display additional account types. See Figure 4–F.

FIGURE 4–F
Add New Account:
Choose Account Type
Window

4. Click *Expense* and then click Continue. The Add New Account window appears with the Account Type drop-down list completed with *Expense*. See Figure 4–G.

If you chose an incorrect account type, you can simply change it here. Click the Account Type arrow and a drop-down list displays all the account types. See Figure 4–H.

5. Enter the following data as the account number and name.

Number: 6050
Account Name: Advertising Expense

See Figure 4–I.

FIGURE 4–I
Add New Account
Window—Completed

6. If the information is correct, click the Save & Close button. Notice the account was added to the Chart of Accounts List.
7. Close the Chart of Accounts List window.

Deleting an Account

Kristin Raina has decided the Promotion Expense account is not necessary and should be deleted.

To delete an account:
1. At the main menu bar, click Lists and then click *Chart of Accounts*.
2. At the Chart of Accounts List window, select (highlight) *6350 Promotion Expense*. See Figure 4–J.

FIGURE 4–J
Chart of Accounts List
Window—Promotion
Expense Selected

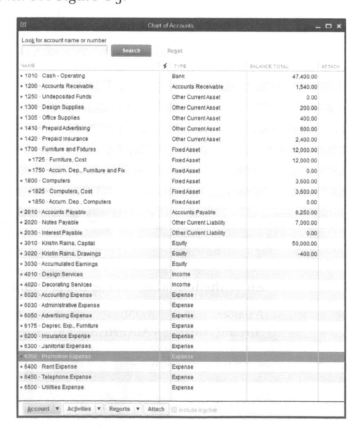

HINT

If you delete the wrong account, immediately click Edit on the main menu bar and then click *Undo Delete Account*; if you do not do this immediately, you will not be able to undo the deletion.

3. Click the Account menu button.
4. At the Account button drop-down menu, click *Delete Account*.
5. When the Delete Account warning appears, click OK. The account is deleted.
6. Close the Chart of Accounts List window.

An account with a balance or an account that has been used in a transaction cannot be deleted. It can instead be marked inactive and will no longer appear in reports.

Editing an Account

Kristin Raina has decided to change the account name Furniture and Fixtures to simply Furniture.

HINT

To edit an account, you must click the Account menu button and then click *Edit Account*. Do *not* double-click the account name in the Chart of Accounts List window.

To edit an account:
1. Open the Chart of Accounts List and select the *1700 Furniture and Fixtures* account.
2. At the Chart of Accounts List window, click the Account menu button.
3. At the Account button drop-down menu, click *Edit Account*. The Edit Account window appears.
4. At the *Account Name* field, delete the text *and Fixtures*. See Figure 4–K.

FIGURE 4–K
Edit Account Window—
Completed

5. If the information is correct, click the Save & Close button.
6. Close the Chart of Accounts List window.

Add the following accounts:

Type: Expense
Number: 6325
Name: Office Supplies Expense

Type: Other Expense
Number: 7000
Name: Interest Expense

Delete the following account:
     6030 Administrative Expense

Edit the following account:
     Change the name of account 1750 to *Accum. Dep., Furniture.*

QuickCheck: The updated Chart of Accounts List window appears in
Figure 4–L.

FIGURE 4–L
Updated Chart of
Accounts List Window

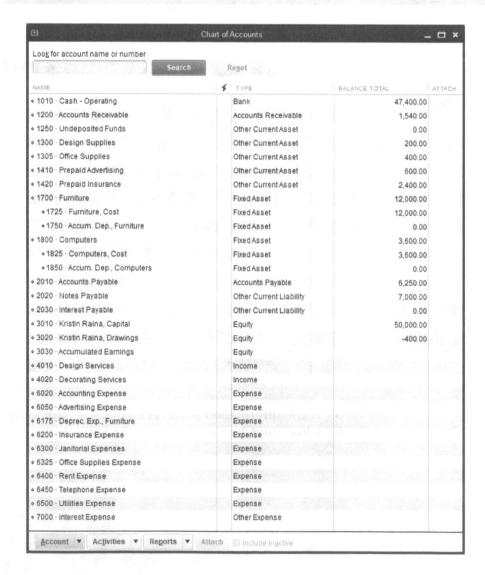

NAME	TYPE	BALANCE TOTAL	ATTACH
1010 · Cash - Operating	Bank	47,400.00	
1200 · Accounts Receivable	Accounts Receivable	1,540.00	
1250 · Undeposited Funds	Other Current Asset	0.00	
1300 · Design Supplies	Other Current Asset	200.00	
1305 · Office Supplies	Other Current Asset	400.00	
1410 · Prepaid Advertising	Other Current Asset	600.00	
1420 · Prepaid Insurance	Other Current Asset	2,400.00	
1700 · Furniture	Fixed Asset	12,000.00	
1725 · Furniture, Cost	Fixed Asset	12,000.00	
1750 · Accum. Dep., Furniture	Fixed Asset	0.00	
1800 · Computers	Fixed Asset	3,600.00	
1825 · Computers, Cost	Fixed Asset	3,600.00	
1850 · Accum. Dep., Computers	Fixed Asset	0.00	
2010 · Accounts Payable	Accounts Payable	6,250.00	
2020 · Notes Payable	Other Current Liability	7,000.00	
2030 · Interest Payable	Other Current Liability	0.00	
3010 · Kristin Raina, Capital	Equity	50,000.00	
3020 · Kristin Raina, Drawings	Equity	-400.00	
3030 · Accumulated Earnings	Equity		
4010 · Design Services	Income		
4020 · Decorating Services	Income		
6020 · Accounting Expense	Expense		
6050 · Advertising Expense	Expense		
6175 · Deprec. Exp., Furniture	Expense		
6200 · Insurance Expense	Expense		
6300 · Janitorial Expenses	Expense		
6325 · Office Supplies Expense	Expense		
6400 · Rent Expense	Expense		
6450 · Telephone Expense	Expense		
6500 · Utilities Expense	Expense		
7000 · Interest Expense	Other Expense		

The Trial Balance

In a manual accounting system, errors can occur when journal entries are recorded and posted to the general ledger or when doing arithmetic computations. The **trial balance** is used to verify that the total debits equal the total credits, which means the general ledger is in balance. In a computerized system, on the other hand, there is less chance of the accounts being out of balance because the postings to the general ledger and arithmetic computations occur automatically.

trial balance a report containing all the general ledger account names, their debit or credit balances, and the total debits and credits

But a trial balance is still useful. It allows you to view the accounts and their debit or credit balances without having to look at all the details in the general ledger. It is often useful to review the trial balance before recording the adjusting journal entries.

To view and print the trial balance:
1. At the main menu bar, click Reports and then click *Accountant & Taxes*.
2. At the Accountant & Taxes submenu, click *Trial Balance*.
3. At the *From* and *To* fields, choose *01/01/2022* and *02/28/2022* and then click the Refresh button at the top of the report. The trial balance is displayed. See Figure 4–M.

FIGURE 4–M
Trial Balance Report

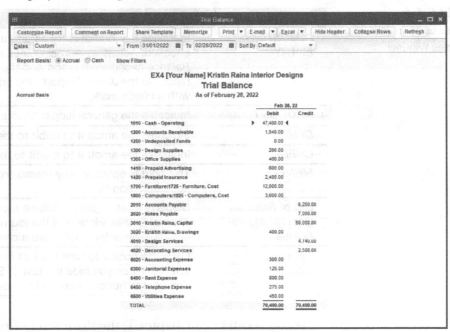

HINT

Print the trial balance at this time. Once you record adjusting journal entries, you will no longer be able to view and print a preadjusted trial balance.

4. Print the report.
5. Close the report.

The Make General Journal Entries Window

To adjust account balances based on accounting rules, you usually need to enter adjusting journal entries before preparing financial statements. In QuickBooks, adjusting journal entries are recorded in the Make General Journal Entries window. This window is set up similarly to that for a manual accounting system. It lists the account and amount of the debit entry, the account and amount of the credit entry, and an explanation.

The QuickBooks Make General Journal Entries window is shown in Figure 4–N.

FIGURE 4–N
Make General Journal
Entries Window

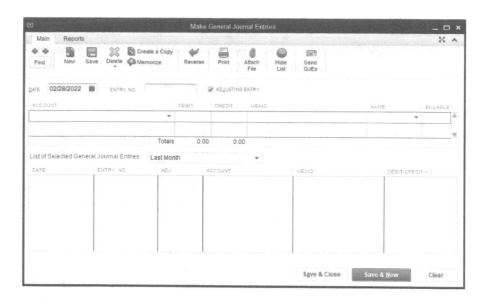

Table 4–2 describes the various parts of the Make General Journal Entries window.

TABLE 4–2
Make General Journal
Entries Window

Part	Description
ADJUSTING ENTRY	Identifies the journal entry as an adjusting journal entry when checked. Adjusting journal entries appear on the *Adjusted Trial Balance* (worksheet) report and the *Adjusting Journal Entries* report. In the *Journal* report, any adjusting entry will be noted with a check mark.
ACCOUNT	Indicates the general ledger account to be adjusted.
DEBIT	Indicates the amount to debit to the account.
CREDIT	Indicates the amount to credit to the account.
MEMO	This field is optional. Any memo entry recorded here will appear in reports.
List of Selected General Journal Entries	Displays a list of journal entries recorded in the Make General Journal Entries window. If the journal entry was checked off as an adjusting entry, it will have a check mark in this list.
Hide List button	Click this button to hide the List of Selected General Journal Entries. When you hide the List of Selected General Journal Entries, the button changes to Show List.

As you recall from Chapter 1, the third level of operation in QuickBooks is Activities. Activities identified as adjustments to account balances are entered in the Make General Journal Entries window. There are no default accounts in this window because each adjusting journal entry is different. The account to debit and the account to credit must be indicated. Adjusting journal entries are usually dated the last day of the month.

The first adjusting journal entry Kristin Raina makes on February 28, 2022, is to record (debit) Advertising Expense and reduce (credit) the Prepaid Advertising account for one month of service. The prepaid advertising was originally purchased on February 1 for $600 and represents a six-month prepayment. One month of Advertising Expense is $100 ($600/6 months).

HINT

Look at the Trial Balance in Figure 4–M on page 121. Notice the Prepaid Advertising account with a balance of $600.

To record an adjusting journal entry:

1. At the main menu bar, click Company and then click *Make General Journal Entries.*

   The Assigning Numbers to Journal Entries message may appear. As you know, QuickBooks automatically assigns a transaction number (Trans #) to each transaction recorded in each window. You cannot change the transaction number. If a transaction is deleted, that transaction number is also deleted; the next transaction is assigned the next transaction number in sequence. QuickBooks allows the user to assign a journal entry number to each transaction. In this book, journal entry numbers are used for the adjusting journal entries. Once you start a sequence of numbers in the Make General Journal Entries window, QuickBooks automatically assigns the next adjusting journal entry number in sequence; however, you can edit or delete the automatically assigned journal entry number. If you receive the message box, insert a check mark in the box to the left of *Do not display this message in the future* and then click OK.

   The Make General Journal Entries window appears.

2. At the *DATE* field, choose *02/28/2022.*

3. At the *ENTRY NO.* field, type AJE1.

4. Insert a check mark in the box to the left of *ADJUSTING ENTRY,* if necessary.

5. In the first line of the *ACCOUNT* field, click the drop-down arrow, scroll down, and then click *6050 Advertising Expense.*

6. At the *DEBIT* field, type 100.

7. Move to the second line in the *ACCOUNT* field, click the drop-down arrow, and then click *1410 Prepaid Advertising.*

8. At the *CREDIT* field, type 100, if necessary.

9. At the *MEMO* field, type To record one month of advertising expense. The *MEMO* field is optional; you do not have to enter an explanation. See Figure 4–O.

HINT

In QuickBooks Premier Accountant Edition, the *Make General Journal Entries* choice is also available on the Accountant menu.

HINT

Use the scroll arrow in the drop-down list to find the account.

FIGURE 4–O
Make General Journal Entries Window— Completed

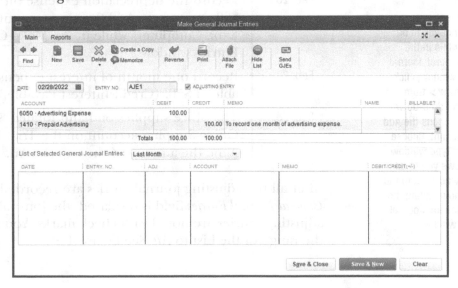

As in the other windows, the Find button and Previous and Next arrows can be used to view previous and subsequent journal entries. Choosing one of the arrows saves the entry. The Save & New button can be used when entering more than one journal entry.

For this adjusting journal entry, the general ledger posting is as follows:

6050 Advertising Exp		1410 Prepaid Advertising	
Dr	Cr	Dr	Cr
100		Bill 600	100 Adj
		Bal 500	

10. If the entry is correct, click the Save & Close button.

In each journal entry, the total dollar value of debits must equal the total dollar value of credits. At the Make General Journal Entries window, if you attempt to save an entry that is not in balance, a warning window appears that gives you the opportunity to correct the journal entry. If the journal entry is not corrected, you will not be able to save it.

Practice Exercise 4–2

Record the following adjusting journal entries in the Make General Journal Entries window. Record each adjusting journal entry separately, and continue with the *ENTRY NO.* sequence of AJE2, AJE3, and so on:

Feb. 28	Record one month of insurance expense. The insurance was purchased for $2,400 in February and recorded as Prepaid Insurance. It is a one-year policy effective February 1. *QuickCheck:* $200
Feb. 28	Record the depreciation expense on the Furniture of $100 per month.
Feb. 28	Record the depreciation expense on the Computer of $60 per month. Add the new account 6185 Deprec. Exp., Computers while in the Make General Journal Entries window.
Feb. 28	Record one month of interest expense on the note payable of $50. (Credit Interest Payable.)
Feb. 28	The office supplies on hand totaled $225. Refer to the Office Supplies account on the Trial Balance to determine the amount of the adjustment. *QuickCheck:* $175

After all the adjusting journal entries are recorded, if the *List of Selected General Journal Entries* field is displayed, the journal entries identified as adjusting entries are noted with check marks. You may need to change the range of the List to *All*. See Figure 4–P.

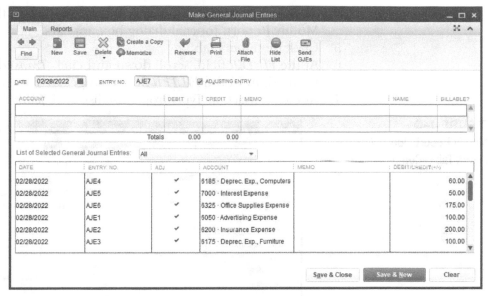

Reports

Period-End Accounting Reports and Financial Statements

Reports, the fourth level of operation in QuickBooks, reflect the activities and adjustments recorded in the windows as well as the information compiled in the Lists/Centers. When you complete the adjusting journal entries, you should display and print the period-end accounting reports and financial statements.

Viewing and Printing Accounting Reports

The period-end accounting reports consist of the *Journal*, the *General Ledger*, and the *Adjusted Trial Balance* reports. These reports should be printed at the end of each month.

Journal Report

In the previous chapters, the *Journal* report was printed for the entire month. However, it is not necessary to reprint all the journal entries when you wish to view only the adjusting journal entries. All reports can be customized to modify the appearance of the report or the fields of information to be displayed. In this case, we will customize the report using the Filter feature, which displays only the adjusting journal entries in the *Journal* report.

To view and print only the adjusting journal entries in the *Journal* report:
1. At the main menu bar, click Reports and then click *Accountant & Taxes*.
2. At the Accountant & Taxes submenu, click *Journal*.

Note: Do not choose the Adjusting Journal Entries *report at this time.*

3. At the *From* and *To* fields, choose *02/01/2022* and *02/28/2022* and then click the Refresh button at the top of the report. The *Journal* report is displayed.

   All transactions for February, from all windows, are displayed. Scroll to the bottom of the entries. Notice the account type General Journal on the last six journal entries. These are the adjusting journal entries entered in the Make General Journal Entries window.

4. Click the Customize Report button at the top of the report. The Modify Report: Journal dialog box appears.
5. Click the Filters tab.
6. At the *FILTER* field, scroll down and click *TransactionType*. The box to the right of the *FILTER* field changes to *Transaction Type*.
7. At the Transaction Type drop-down list, click *Journal*. See Figure 4–Q.

FIGURE 4–Q
Modify Report: Journal—
Filters Tab—Completed

8. Click OK. Only the journal entries recorded in the Make General Journal Entries window are displayed.
9. Above the heading of the report, click Show Filters. The Filters bar indicates that in this report, a *Custom* date is used and only *Journal* transaction type entries are displayed. See Figure 4–R.

FIGURE 4–R
Journal Report—Filtered
for Adjusting Journal
Entries

Show Filters/
Hide Filters

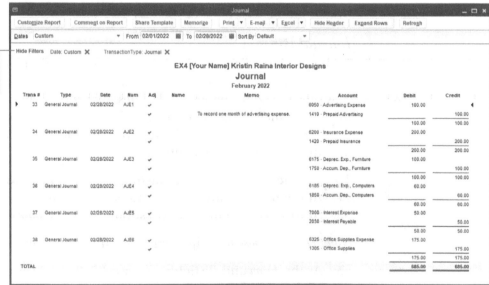

10. To remove the Filters bar, click Hide Filters.
11. Print the report.
12. Close the report.

Because it is usually the accountant who views the adjusting journal entries, instead of displaying the *Journal* report and filtering the adjusting journal entries, QuickBooks Premier Accountant Edition provides an *Adjusting Journal Entries* report.

To view and print the *Adjusting Journal Entries* report in QuickBooks Premier Accountant Edition:

1. At the main menu bar, click Reports and then click *Accountant & Taxes.*
2. At the Accountant & Taxes submenu, click *Adjusting Journal Entries.*
3. At the *From* and *To* fields, choose *02/01/2022* and *02/28/2022* and then click the Refresh button at the top of the report. The *Adjusting Journal Entries* report is displayed.

   This report displays the adjusting journal entries recorded in the Make General Journal Entries window that were checked off as an Adjusting Entry. The adjusting journal entries are the same entries displayed in the *Journal* report in Figure 4–R on page 126. Notice, however, that in this report, the title of the report is *Adjusting Journal Entries,* and the columns labeled *Trans #, Type,* and *Adj* are not displayed.
4. Print the report.
5. Close the report.

General Ledger Report

All transactions recorded in any of the windows are posted to the general ledger. The *General Ledger* report displays all the activity in each account as a debit or a credit and then lists the balance after each activity.

To view and print the *General Ledger* report:

1. At the main menu bar, click Reports and then click *Accountant & Taxes.*
2. At the Accountant & Taxes submenu, click *General Ledger.*
3. At the *From* and *To* fields, choose *01/01/2022* and *02/28/2022* and then click the Refresh button at the top of the report. The general ledger is displayed. See Figure 4–S.

Type	Date	Num	Adj	Name	Memo	Split	Debit	Credit	Balance
1010 · Cash - Operating									0.00
General Journal	01/01/2022					3010 · Kristin Raina, Capital	50,000.00		50,000.00
General Journal	01/31/2022					1725 · Furniture, Cost		5,000.00	45,000.00
Bill Pmt -Check	02/10/2022	1		Nordic Realty	55-1212	2010 · Accounts Payable		800.00	44,200.00
Bill Pmt -Check	02/23/2022	2		Cuza and Carl Associates	KR589	2010 · Accounts Payable		200.00	44,000.00
Bill Pmt -Check	02/27/2022	3		[Your Name] Accounting Service	99-2022-XX	2010 · Accounts Payable		300.00	43,700.00
Bill Pmt -Check	02/27/2022	4		Galeway Computers	2455-897	2010 · Accounts Payable		1,000.00	42,700.00
Check	02/28/2022	5		Jeter Janitorial Services	555-32	6300 · Janitorial Expenses		125.00	42,575.00
Check	02/28/2022	6		Grayson Graphics	33-2221	1300 · Design Supplies		200.00	42,375.00
Check	02/28/2022	7		TwinCityTelCo	666-6667	6450 · Telephone Expense		275.00	42,100.00
Check	02/28/2022	8		Kristin Raina		3020 · Kristin Raina, Drawings		400.00	41,700.00
Deposit	02/28/2022				Deposit	-SPLIT-	5,700.00		47,400.00
Total 1010 · Cash - Operating							55,700.00	8,300.00	47,400.00
1200 · Accounts Receivable									0.00
Invoice	02/01/2022	1001		Jones, Beverly		4020 · Decorating Services	600.00		600.00
Invoice	02/06/2022	1002		Guthrie, Jennie		4010 · Design Services	960.00		1,560.00
Invoice	02/13/2022	1003		Cook Caterers		-SPLIT-	1,360.00		2,920.00
Payment	02/13/2022	6544		Jones, Beverly		1250 · Undeposited Funds		600.00	2,320.00
Invoice	02/17/2022	1004		Franco Films Co.		4010 · Design Services	1,440.00		3,760.00
Payment	02/20/2022	1255		Franco Films Co.		1250 · Undeposited Funds		500.00	3,260.00
Invoice	02/23/2022	1005		Berger Bakery Company		4020 · Decorating Services	1,200.00		4,460.00
Invoice	02/27/2022	1006		Cook Caterers		-SPLIT-	1,200.00		5,660.00
Payment	02/27/2022	655		Cook Caterers		1250 · Undeposited Funds		2,560.00	3,100.00
Payment	02/28/2022	674		Guthrie, Jennie		1250 · Undeposited Funds		960.00	2,140.00
Payment	02/28/2022	12450		Berger Bakery Company		1250 · Undeposited Funds		600.00	1,540.00
Total 1200 · Accounts Receivable							6,760.00	5,220.00	1,540.00
1250 · Undeposited Funds									0.00

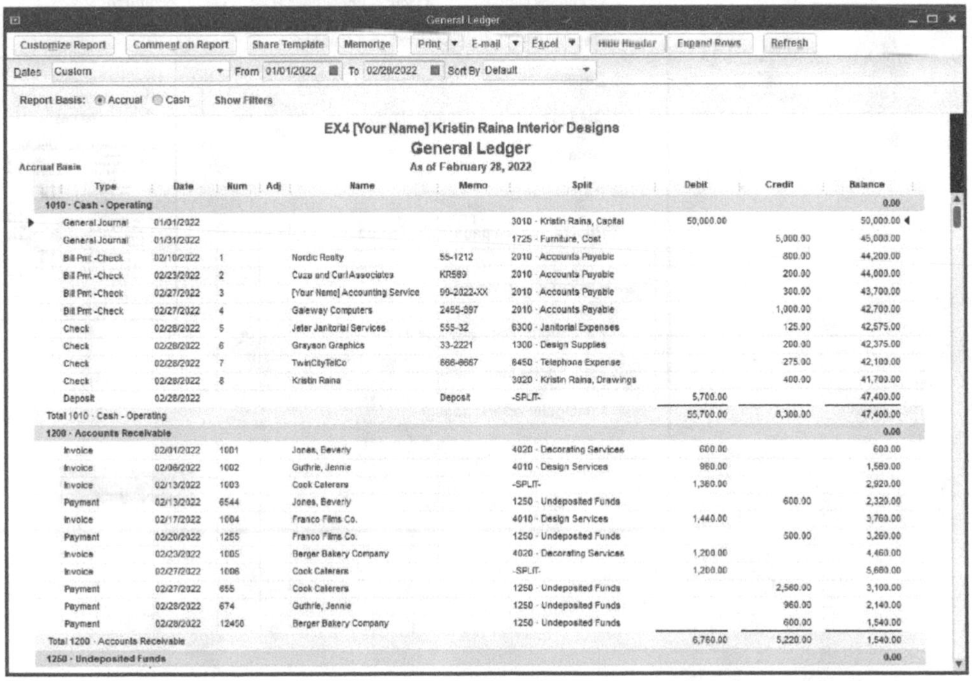

FIGURE 4–S
General Ledger Report—Partial

4. Print the report.
5. Close the report.

Adjusted Trial Balance Report

HINT

Once you record the adjusting journal entries, you can no longer create a pre-adjusted trial balance.

The trial balance of February 28, 2022 (Figure 4–M, page 121), was reviewed before the adjusting journal entries were prepared. Typically, the trial balance is printed again after the adjusting journal entries have been recorded. The second trial balance is referred to as the *Adjusted Trial Balance* report. To distinguish between the two printed trial balances, you will modify the report by changing the name in the heading of the second trial balance to *Adjusted Trial Balance*.

To view and print the *Adjusted Trial Balance* report:

1. At the main menu bar, click Reports and then click *Accountant & Taxes*.
2. At the Accountant & Taxes submenu, click *Trial Balance*.

Note: Do not choose the Adjusted Trial Balance *report at this time.*

3. At the *From* and *To* fields, choose *01/01/2022* and *02/28/2022* and then click the Refresh button at the top of the report. The trial balance is displayed. Notice that the heading includes the default heading *Trial Balance*. You will use the Customize Report button to change the heading to *Adjusted Trial Balance*.
4. At the top of the report, click the Customize Report button. The Modify Report: Trial Balance dialog box appears.
5. Click the Header/Footer tab.
6. At the *Report Title* field, type the word Adjusted before the text *Trial Balance*. See Figure 4–T.

FIGURE 4–T
Modify Report: Trial Balance—Header/Footer Tab Completed

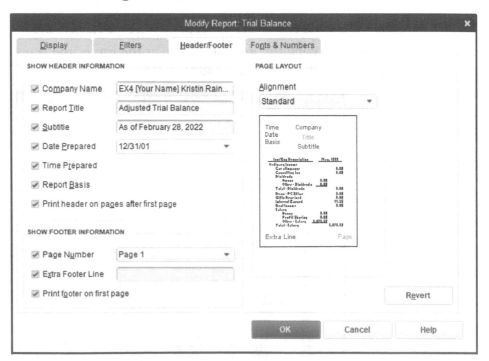

7. If the information is correct, click OK. The *Trial Balance* heading is now displayed as *Adjusted Trial Balance.* See Figure 4–U.

FIGURE 4–U
Trial Balance Report—
Renamed Adjusted
Trial Balance

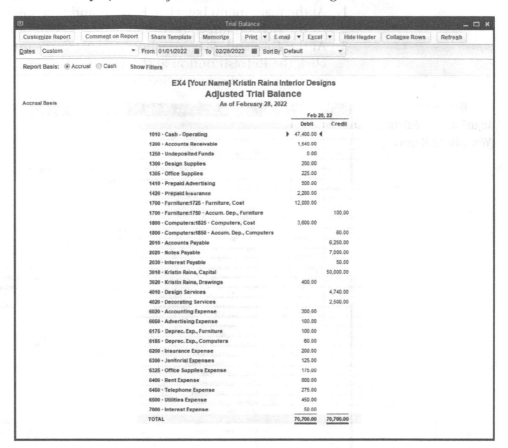

8. Print the report.
9. Close the report.

Compare the effect of the adjusting journal entries on the account balances by comparing the trial balance (Figure 4–M, page 121) to the adjusted trial balance (Figure 4–U).

Note: The trial balance showed $70,490, while the adjusted trial balance now shows $70,700.

Once again, the text is using the Accountant edition of the QuickBooks software. So instead of displaying the *Trial Balance* report and modifying the report to display the name *Adjusted Trial Balance,* QuickBooks Premier Accountant Edition provides an *Adjusted Trial Balance* (worksheet) report. Not only does this report have the name *Adjusted Trial Balance,* but it also displays the original trial balance, the adjusting journal entries, and the adjusted trial balance. It is similar to a worksheet an accountant might prepare.

To view, make a correction, and print the *Adjusted Trial Balance* **(worksheet) report in QuickBooks Premier Accountant Edition:**

1. At the main menu bar, click Reports and then click *Accountant & Taxes.*
2. At the Accountant & Taxes submenu, click *Adjusted Trial Balance.*
3. At the *From* and *To* fields, choose *01/01/2022* and *02/28/2022* and then click the Refresh button at the top of the report. The *Adjusted Trial Balance* report is displayed. See Figure 4–V.

FIGURE 4–V
Adjusted Trial Balance
(Worksheet) Report

	Unadjusted Balance		Adjustments		Adjusted Balance	
	Debit	Credit	Debit	Credit	Debit	Credit
1010 · Cash - Operating	47,400.00				47,400.00	
1200 · Accounts Receivable	1,540.00				1,540.00	
1250 · Undeposited Funds	0.00				0.00	
1300 · Design Supplies	200.00				200.00	
1305 · Office Supplies	400.00			175.00	225.00	
1410 · Prepaid Advertising	600.00			100.00	500.00	
1420 · Prepaid Insurance	2,400.00			200.00	2,200.00	
1700 · Furniture:1725 · Furniture, Cost	12,000.00				12,000.00	
1700 · Furniture:1750 · Accum. Dep., Furniture				100.00		100.00
1800 · Computers:1825 · Computers, Cost	3,600.00				3,600.00	
1800 · Computers:1850 · Accum. Dep. Computers				60.00		60.00
2010 · Accounts Payable		6,250.00				6,250.00
2020 · Notes Payable		7,000.00				7,000.00
2030 · Interest Payable				50.00		50.00
3010 · Kristin Raina, Capital		50,000.00				50,000.00
3020 · Kristin Raina, Drawings	400.00				400.00	
4010 · Design Services		4,740.00				4,740.00
4020 · Decorating Services		2,500.00				2,500.00
6020 · Accounting Expense	300.00				300.00	
6050 · Advertising Expense			100.00		100.00	
6175 · Deprec. Exp., Furniture			100.00		100.00	
6185 · Deprec. Exp., Computers			60.00		60.00	
6200 · Insurance Expense			200.00		200.00	
6300 · Janitorial Expenses	125.00				125.00	
6325 · Office Supplies Expense			175.00		175.00	
6400 · Rent Expense	800.00				800.00	
6450 · Telephone Expense	275.00				275.00	
6500 · Utilities Expense	450.00				450.00	
7000 · Interest Expense			50.00		50.00	
TOTAL	70,490.00	70,490.00	685.00	685.00	70,700.00	70,700.00

Look at the first two columns labeled *Unadjusted Balance.* This is the original trial balance of February 28, 2022. Compare this balance to the one in Figure 4–M on page 121. Next, look at the third and fourth columns, which are labeled *Adjustments.* These are the adjusting journal entries displayed in the *Journal* report in Figure 4–R on page 126. Finally, look at the fifth and sixth columns of this report. This is the adjusted trial balance that was displayed in Figure 4–U on page 129.

Recall that in most reports in QuickBooks, you can "drill down" to the original window where an activity was recorded and make any necessary changes. This can also be done in this report. Assume that you realize the Office Supplies on hand is $250, not $225 as noted in the practice exercise on page 124. The last adjusting journal entry originally recorded as $175 needs to be changed to $150 ($400 Office Supplies – $250 supplies on hand = $150 Supplies Expense).

4. In the *Adjustments - Debit* column, on the line that displays *6325 Office Supplies Expense*, double-click *175.00*. This drills down to the *Transactions by Account* report.

5. In the *Transactions by Account* report, on the line that displays *AJE6*, double-click *175.00*. This drills down to the Make General Journal Entries window, where the adjusting journal entry for Supplies Expense was originally recorded.

6. Change the amount to 150.00 in both the *DEBIT* column and the *CREDIT* column. See Figure 4–W.

FIGURE 4–W
Make General Journal
Entries Window—
Correction Completed

The List of Selected General Journal Entries still displays *175* for *AJE6*. This list will be updated after the change to the adjusting journal entry is saved.

7. If the information is correct, click the Save & New button. At the Recording Transaction message, click Yes. The correction is saved and the fields are cleared for a new transaction. Notice in the List of Selected Entries in the Make General Journal Entries window AJE6 is updated to $150.

8. Close the Make General Journal Entries window. You are returned to the *Transactions by Account* report with the adjusting journal entry updated for the correction.

9. Close the *Transactions by Account* report.

10. You are returned to the *Adjusted Trial Balance* (worksheet) report. Click the Refresh button. The report is updated. See Figure 4–X.

FIGURE 4–X
Adjusted Trial Balance
(Worksheet) Report—
Correction Completed

HINT

Compare the *Adjusted Trial Balance* (worksheet) report to Figure 4–R on page 126, Figure 4–U on page 129, and Figure 4–V on page 130. Notice the TOTALs in the *Adjustments* columns have changed due to the change in AJE6. Notice the TOTALs in the *Adjusted Balance* columns are the same, but the balances in the Office Supplies account and the Office Supplies Expense account have changed.

EX4 [Your Name] Kristin Raina Interior Designs
Adjusted Trial Balance
January through February 2022

	Unadjusted Balance Debit	Unadjusted Balance Credit	Adjustments Debit	Adjustments Credit	Adjusted Balance Debit	Adjusted Balance Credit
1010 · Cash - Operating	47,400.00				47,400.00	
1200 · Accounts Receivable	1,540.00				1,540.00	
1250 · Undeposited Funds	0.00				0.00	
1300 · Design Supplies	200.00				200.00	
1305 · Office Supplies	400.00			150.00	250.00	
1410 · Prepaid Advertising	600.00			100.00	500.00	
1420 · Prepaid Insurance	2,400.00			200.00	2,200.00	
1700 · Furniture:1725 · Furniture, Cost	12,000.00				12,000.00	
1700 · Furniture:1750 · Accum. Dep., Furniture				100.00		100.00
1800 · Computers:1825 · Computers, Cost	3,600.00				3,600.00	
1800 · Computers:1850 · Accum. Dep., Computers				60.00		60.00
2010 · Accounts Payable		6,250.00				6,250.00
2020 · Notes Payable		7,000.00				7,000.00
2030 · Interest Payable				50.00		50.00
3010 · Kristin Raina, Capital		50,000.00				50,000.00
3020 · Kristin Raina, Drawings	400.00				400.00	
4010 · Design Services		4,740.00				4,740.00
4020 · Decorating Services		2,500.00				2,500.00
6020 · Accounting Expense	300.00				300.00	
6050 · Advertising Expense			100.00		100.00	
6175 · Deprec. Exp., Furniture			100.00		100.00	
6185 · Deprec. Exp., Computers			60.00		60.00	
6200 · Insurance Expense			200.00		200.00	
6300 · Janitorial Expenses	125.00				125.00	
6325 · Office Supplies Expense			▶ 150.00 ◀		150.00	
6400 · Rent Expense	800.00				800.00	
6450 · Telephone Expense	275.00				275.00	
6500 · Utilities Expense	450.00				450.00	
7000 · Interest Expense			50.00		50.00	
TOTAL	70,490.00	70,490.00	660.00	660.00	70,700.00	70,700.00

11. Print the report.
12. Close the report.

Viewing and Printing Financial Statements

The financial statements include the income statement and the balance sheet. A company must prepare financial statements at least once a year, but they can be prepared more frequently, such as quarterly or even monthly.

Profit & Loss Standard Report (Income Statement)

The income statement is known as the *Profit & Loss* report in QuickBooks. The *Profit & Loss* report displays revenue and expenses for a specified period of time. The *Profit & Loss* report can be displayed in a standard or comparative format. In addition, a detailed *Profit & Loss* report can be produced that lists all the transactions affecting a particular item on the report.

To view and print a year-to-date *Profit & Loss Standard* **report:**
1. At the main menu bar, click Reports and then click *Company & Financial.*
2. At the Company & Financial submenu, click *Profit & Loss Standard.*
3. At the *From* and *To* fields, choose *01/01/2022* and *02/28/2022* and then click the Refresh button at the top of the report. The report for the period is displayed. See Figure 4–Y.

FIGURE 4–Y
Profit & Loss Standard
Report

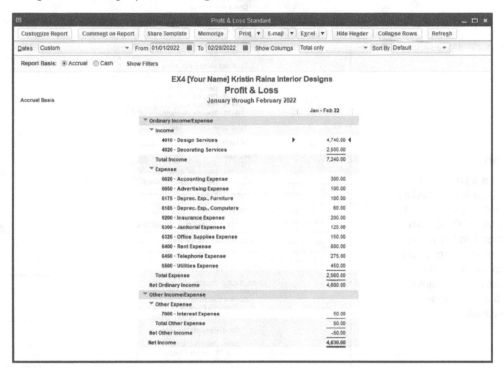

4. Print the report.
5. Close the report.

Balance Sheet Standard Report

In QuickBooks, the *Balance Sheet* report, which shows the assets, liabilities, and equity balances as of a certain date, may be displayed in a standard, summary, or comparative format. In addition, a detailed report, showing all the transactions affecting balance sheet accounts, can be produced.

To display and print a *Balance Sheet Standard* **report:**
1. At the main menu bar, click Reports and then click *Company & Financial.*
2. At the Company & Financial submenu, click *Balance Sheet Standard.*
3. At the *As of* field, choose *02/28/2022* and then click the Refresh button at the top of the report. The balance sheet in standard format is displayed.

4. Print the report. See Figure 4–Z.

FIGURE 4–Z
Balance Sheet
Standard Report

EX4 [Your Name] Kristin Raina Interior Designs
Balance Sheet
As of February 28, 2022

Accrual Basis

	Feb 28, 22
ASSETS	
Current Assets	
Checking/Savings	
1010 · Cash - Operating	47,400.00
Total Checking/Savings	47,400.00
Accounts Receivable	
1200 · Accounts Receivable	1,540.00
Total Accounts Receivable	1,540.00
Other Current Assets	
1300 · Design Supplies	200.00
1305 · Office Supplies	250.00
1410 · Prepaid Advertising	500.00
1420 · Prepaid Insurance	2,200.00
Total Other Current Assets	3,150.00
Total Current Assets	52,090.00
Fixed Assets	
1700 · Furniture	
1725 · Furniture, Cost	12,000.00
1750 · Accum. Dep., Furniture	-100.00
Total 1700 · Furniture	11,900.00
1800 · Computers	
1825 · Computers, Cost	3,600.00
1850 · Accum. Dep., Computers	-60.00
Total 1800 · Computers	3,540.00
Total Fixed Assets	15,440.00
TOTAL ASSETS	67,530.00
LIABILITIES & EQUITY	
Liabilities	
Current Liabilities	
Accounts Payable	
2010 · Accounts Payable	6,250.00
Total Accounts Payable	6,250.00
Other Current Liabilities	
2020 · Notes Payable	7,000.00
2030 · Interest Payable	50.00
Total Other Current Liabilities	7,050.00
Total Current Liabilities	13,300.00
Total Liabilities	13,300.00
Equity	
3010 · Kristin Raina, Capital	50,000.00
3020 · Kristin Raina, Drawings	-400.00
Net Income	4,630.00
Total Equity	54,230.00
TOTAL LIABILITIES & EQUITY	67,530.00

HINT

This is a printout of the *Balance Sheet Standard* report. The Fixed Assets section of the *Balance Sheet Standard* report on the computer screen lists the balances of all Fixed Assets—parent and subaccounts—in a single column.

Look at the Fixed Assets section on the printout of the *Balance Sheet Standard* report. Recall that in the Chart of Accounts List, parent and subaccounts were used for the fixed assets. When parent and subaccounts flow into the financial statements, the parent account name becomes a heading and a total for the related subaccounts. Under the parent account name heading, the subaccount names are indented on the financial statements. The account balances for the subaccounts are displayed and subtotaled and then shown as the total for the parent account. For example, the parent account 1700 Furniture is a heading; the subaccounts 1725 Furniture, Cost and 1750 Accum. Dep., Furniture are indented and displayed under the parent account; and then the parent account 1700 Furniture is again displayed, this time as the total for the subaccounts. On the printout of the report, the balances of the subaccounts (12,000 and –100) are displayed to the left of the dollar-value column, and the subtotal of these subaccounts (11,900) is displayed in the dollar-value column and labeled as the total for the parent account.

5. Close the report.

Registers

Because QuickBooks is designed for the non-accountant, it includes an alternative method for reviewing daily activity by using registers. Registers are available for any balance sheet account—that is, any asset, liability, or equity account. Registers are not available for income and expense accounts.

The register format is similar to that of a personal checkbook, but the information displayed in a register is similar to the information displayed in the general ledger.

To view a register:

1. At the main menu bar, click Lists and then click *Chart of Accounts.*
2. At the Chart of Accounts List window, double-click the *1010 Cash - Operating* account. The 1010 Cash - Operating register appears. See Figure 4–AA.

FIGURE 4–AA
1010 Cash - Operating Register

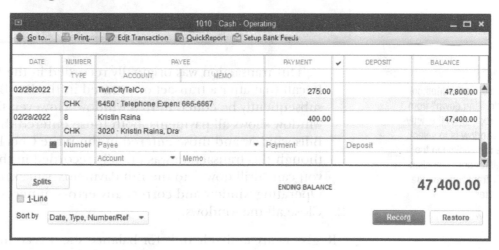

Transactions that were entered in any of the other windows that affected the 1010 Cash - Operating account are also displayed in the register. Scroll through the transactions and compare them with those in the 1010 Cash - Operating account in the general ledger (see Figure 4–S on page 127).
You can use the register to correct any activity already recorded by "drilling down" to the source of the activity.

To "drill down" using the register:

1. At the 1010 Cash - Operating register, double-click the *February 23, Cuza and Carl Associates* transaction. The Bill Payments(Check) window appears. See Figure 4–BB.

FIGURE 4–BB
Bill Payments(Check)
Window

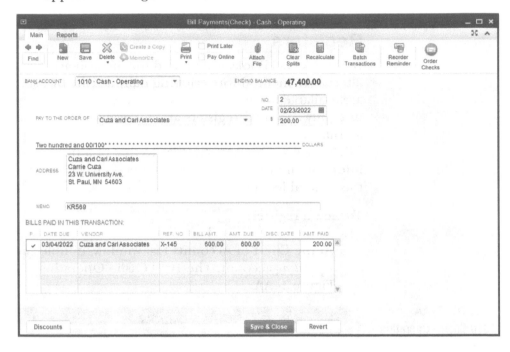

HINT

An alternative method of "drilling down" from the register to the activity window is to select the transaction in the register and then click Edit Transaction in the register.

This transaction was originally recorded in the Pay Bills window. Recall that after a transaction is saved in the Pay Bills window, it cannot subsequently be edited in that window. However, the Write Checks window shows all payments, both those entered through the Pay Bills window and those entered in the Write Checks window. So even though this transaction was initially recorded in the Pay Bills window, you can "drill down" to the Bill Payments(Check) - Cash - Operating window and correct any errors, if necessary.

2. Close all the windows.

Registers are available only for balance sheet accounts. For income statement accounts—that is, income and expenses—registers are not available, but an *Account QuickReport* is available that displays all the activity to the account—again, similar to the general ledger information.

To view an income *Account QuickReport*:

1. At the main menu bar, click Lists and then click *Chart of Accounts*.
2. At the Chart of Accounts window, double-click *4020 Decorating Services*.
3. At the *From* and *To* fields, choose *02/01/2022* and *02/28/2022* and then click the Refresh button at the top of the report. The *Account QuickReport* is displayed, listing all the activity to this account during the time period chosen. See Figure 4–CC.

FIGURE 4–CC Account QuickReport

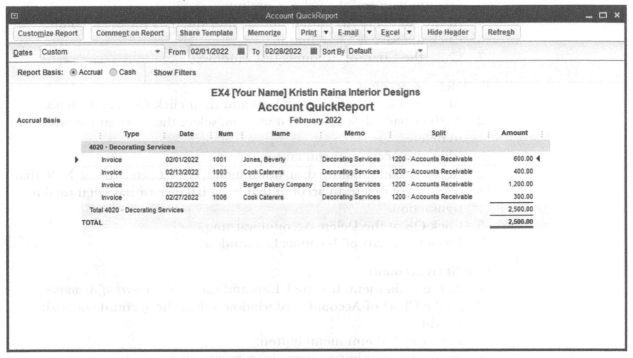

From this report, as with others, you can "drill down" to the window where the original activity was recorded.

4. Close the report.
5. Close the Chart of Accounts List window.

Exiting QuickBooks

Upon completing this session, make a backup copy of your practice exercise company file to a removable storage device using the Back Up command. Be sure to change the *Save in* field to the removable storage device and then carefully type the correct file name. Close the company file and then exit QuickBooks.

Chapter Review and Assessment

Procedure Review

To add a new account:
1. At the main menu bar, click Lists and then click *Chart of Accounts*.
2. At the Chart of Accounts List window, click the Account menu button.
3. At the Account button drop-down menu, click *New*.
4. At the Add New Account: Choose Account Type window, choose the account type and then click Continue.
5. At the Add New Account window, enter the data for the account.
6. Click the Save & Close button.
7. Close the Chart of Accounts List window.

To delete an account:
1. At the main menu bar, click Lists and then click *Chart of Accounts*.
2. At the Chart of Accounts List window, select the account you wish to delete.
3. Click the Account menu button.
4. At the Account button drop-down menu, click *Delete Account*. Note that you cannot delete an account that has a balance or has been used in a transaction.
5. Click OK at the Delete Account warning.
6. Close the Chart of Accounts List window.

To edit an account:
1. At the main menu bar, click Lists and then click *Chart of Accounts*.
2. At the Chart of Accounts List window, select the account you wish to edit.
3. Click the Account menu button.
4. At the Account button drop-down menu, click *Edit Account*.
5. Change the appropriate information.
6. Click the Save & Close button.
7. Close the Chart of Accounts List window.

To record an adjusting journal entry:
1. At the main menu bar, click Company and then click *Make General Journal Entries*.
2. At the *DATE* field, enter the date.
3. At the *ENTRY NO.* field, type in the original journal entry number, if necessary; thereafter, QuickBooks assigns the entry numbers in sequence.
4. Insert a check mark in the box to the left of *ADJUSTING ENTRY*.
5. In the first line of the *ACCOUNT* field, click once to access the drop-down list of accounts and then choose the account to debit.
6. Enter the amount to debit at the *DEBIT* field.
7. On the second line in the *ACCOUNT* field, from the drop-down list of accounts, choose the account to credit.
8. At the *CREDIT* field, enter the amount to credit.
9. At the *MEMO* field, type in a brief explanation (optional).
10. Click the Save & Close button.

To view and print accounting reports from the Reports menu:

1. At the main menu bar, click Reports and then click *Accountant & Taxes*.
2. At the Accountant & Taxes submenu, choose a report.
3. Choose the appropriate dates for the report and then click the Refresh button at the top of the report.
4. Print the report.
5. Close the report.

To view and print financial statements from the Reports menu:

1. At the main menu bar, click Reports and then click *Company & Financial*.
2. At the Company & Financial submenu, choose a financial statement.
3. Choose the appropriate dates for the statement and then click the Refresh button at the top of the report.
4. Print the report.
5. Close the report.

To filter the information displayed in a report or financial statement:

1. Open a report or financial statement, enter the correct dates, and then click the Refresh button.
2. At the top of the report, click the Customize Report button.
3. In the Modify Report dialog box, click the Filters tab.
4. At the *FILTER* field, select the category of information you wish to filter—for example, transaction type. The field to the right changes to the filter chosen.
5. Choose the specific information you wish to filter; for example, in transaction type, you might choose *Journal*.
6. Click OK. The report now displays the information chosen on the Filters tab.
7. Above the heading of the report, click *Show Filters*. The filters selected for this report are displayed.
8. To remove the Filters bar, click *Hide Filters*.
9. Close the report.

To change the heading in a report or financial statement:

1. Open a report or financial statement, enter the correct dates, and then click the Refresh button.
2. At the top of the report, click the Customize Report button.
3. In the Modify Report dialog box, click the Header/Footer tab.
4. At the *Report Title* field, change the name of the report to the desired title.
5. Click OK. The report now displays the new title of the report.
6. Close the report.

To view and print a register or *Account QuickReport* from the Lists menu:

1. At the main menu bar, click Lists and then click *Chart of Accounts*.
2. Double-click the account for which you want the register or *Account QuickReport*. (Registers are used for assets, liabilities, and equity accounts; *Account QuickReports* are used for revenues and expenses accounts.)
3. For the registers, click the Print icon, enter the dates in the Print Register dialog box, and then click OK.

4. For the *Account QuickReport*, choose the appropriate dates, click the Refresh button, click the Print button at the top of the report, and then click *Report.*
5. In the Print Lists or Print Reports dialog box, review the settings and then click Print.
6. Close the register or *Account QuickReport* and then close the Chart of Accounts List window.

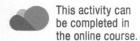

This activity can be completed in the online course.

Key Concepts

Select the letter of the item that best matches each definition.

a. Make General Journal Entries window
b. Filters
c. *Profit & Loss* report
d. *General Ledger* report
e. Chart of Accounts List

f. Registers
g. Header/Footer
h. *Trial Balance* report
i. Adjusting journal entries
j. *Balance Sheet* report

_____ 1. Recorded periodically so financial statements can be prepared according to accounting rules.
_____ 2. The report that shows assets, liabilities, and equity balances at a specified date.
_____ 3. The list of accounts a company uses in business.
_____ 4. The tab in the Customize Report - Modify Report dialog box that is used to identify categories of information to be displayed in a report.
_____ 5. The report that shows all the increases and decreases in each account, reflected as debits and credits, and the balances for each account.
_____ 6. Similar to a manual accounting system, this allows for the recording of a debit entry, a credit entry, and an explanation.
_____ 7. The report that displays the revenue and expenses for a specified period of time.
_____ 8. The tab in the Customize Report - Modify Report dialog box that is used to change the heading on a report.
_____ 9. The format that is similar to that of a checkbook and can be used to view the activities for any balance sheet account.
_____ 10. A report that displays all accounts and their debit or credit balances.

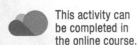

This activity can be completed in the online course.

Procedure Check

1. Imagine that your manager has requested a list of all your accounts the company uses. What type of report can you generate in QuickBooks to provide this information, and how would you obtain it?
2. The manager wants to know the balance in each of the company's accounts. Which is the best report to provide this information, and how would you obtain it?
3. You have been asked to review the adjusting journal entries and have located an error. How would you correct the error in the adjusting journal entry?

4. Describe what is included in the *Journal* report and how you would display only the adjusting journal entries. Describe what is included in the *Adjusting Journal Entries* report.

5. Your manager has a *Trial Balance* report, an *Adjusted Trial Balance* report, and an *Adjusted Trial Balance* (worksheet) report, all with the same date, and asks you to provide a description of each report. Include in your explanation the steps to change the name of the *Trial Balance* report to *Adjusted Trial Balance* report.

6. Explain the purpose of adjusting journal entries. Compare and contrast recording adjusting journal entries in a manual accounting system and in QuickBooks, and explain why there are no default accounts in the Make General Journal Entries window.

Case Problems

Reports created for these Case Problems can be exported to Excel and uploaded in the online course to be automatically graded.

Demonstrate your knowledge of the QuickBooks features discussed in this chapter by completing the following case problems.

Case Problem 4–1

On April 1, 2022, Lynn Garcia began her business, Lynn's Music Studio. All the daily activities for the month of April—including entering and paying bills, writing checks, recording of sales (both cash and on account), collection of receivables, and depositing receipts—have been recorded. It is the end of the first month of business; the adjusting journal entries need to be recorded, and financial statements need to be printed. You will record the adjusting journal entries for April 30 using the information provided below. The company file includes the account balances for Lynn's Music Studio based on the transactions recorded in Chapters 2 and 3.

1. Open the company file **CH4 Lynn's Music Studio.QBW**.
2. At the QuickBooks Desktop Login window, in the *Password* text box, type Student1 and then click OK.
3. Make a backup copy of the company file and name it **LMS4 *[Your Name]* Lynn's Music Studio**.
4. Restore the backup copy of the company file. In both the Open Backup Copy and Save Company File as dialog boxes, use the file name **LMS4 *[Your Name]* Lynn's Music Studio** and enter the password.
5. Change the company name to **LMS4 *[Your Name]* Lynn's Music Studio**.
6. Add the following accounts to the Chart of Accounts List:

   Type: Expense
   Number: 6300
   Name: Music Supplies Expense

   Type: Expense
   Number: 6325
   Name: Office Supplies Expense

   Delete the following account:
   Advertising Expense

7. Display and print the *Trial Balance* report before preparing the adjusting journal entries (April 1, 2022–April 30, 2022).
8. Use the information that follows to prepare adjusting journal entries. Record each adjusting journal entry separately, and use April 30, 2022, for the date.
   a. The prepaid insurance represents a one-year policy. Record insurance expense for one month. Refer to the trial balance to determine the amount in the Prepaid Insurance account. For Entry No., use AJE1.
   b. Monthly depreciation on the assets: $60 for the Music Instruments, $40 for the Furniture, and $35 for the Computers. Record each depreciation expense as a separate adjusting journal entry.
   c. The music supplies on hand total $430. Compare this amount with the amount in the Music Supplies account to determine how many of the music supplies have been used, then record the music supplies expense.
   d. The office supplies on hand total $300. Compare this amount with the amount in the Office Supplies account to determine how many of the supplies have been used and then record the office supplies expense.
   e. The interest on the note payable for one month is $51. Record the interest expense. Add to the Chart of Accounts List the Interest Payable account Other Current Liability, number 2030.
9. Display and print the following reports for April 30, 2022:
   a. *Adjusted Trial Balance* (worksheet): Change Interest Expense to $15 (April 1, 2022–April 30, 2022)
   b. *Journal:* Only the adjusting journal entries (April 30, 2022–April 30, 2022)
   c. *Trial Balance:* Change name in header of the report to *Adjusted Trial Balance* (April 1, 2022–April 30, 2022)
   d. *Profit & Loss Standard* (April 1, 2022–April 30, 2022)
   e. *Balance Sheet Standard* (April 30, 2022)

Case Problem 4–2

On June 1, 2022, Olivia Chen began her business, Olivia's Web Solutions. All daily activities for the month of June—including entering and paying bills, writing checks, recording of sales (both cash and on account), collection of receivables, and depositing receipts—have been recorded. It is the end of the first month of business; the adjusting journal entries need to be recorded, and financial statements need to be printed. You will record the adjusting journal entries for June 30 using the information provided below. The company file includes the account balances for Olivia's Web Solutions based on the transactions recorded in Chapters 2 and 3.

1. Open the company file **CH4 Olivia's Web Solutions.QBW**.
2. At the QuickBooks Desktop Login window, in the *Password* text box, type Student1 and then click OK.
3. Make a backup copy of the company file and name it **OWS4** *[Your Name]* **Olivia's Web Solutions**.

4. Restore the backup copy of the company file. In both the Open Backup Copy and Save Company File as dialog boxes, use the file name **OWS4** *[Your Name]* **Olivia's Web Solutions** and enter the password.

5. Change the company name to **OWS4** *[Your Name]* **Olivia's Web Solutions**.

6. Add the following accounts to the Chart of Accounts List:

   Type: Expense
   Number: 6300
   Name: Computer Supplies Expense

   Type: Expense
   Number: 6325
   Name: Office Supplies Expense

   Delete the following account:
   Repair Expense

7. Display and print the *Trial Balance* report before preparing the adjusting journal entries (June 1, 2022–June 30, 2022).

8. Use the information below to prepare adjusting journal entries. Record each adjusting journal entry separately, and use June 30, 2022, for the date.

   a. The prepaid insurance represents a one-year policy. Record insurance expense for one month. Refer to the trial balance to determine the amount in the Prepaid Insurance account. For Entry No., use AJE1.

   b. The prepaid advertising represents a six-month contract. Record the advertising expense for one month.

   c. Monthly depreciation on the assets: $75 for the Computer, $50 for the Furniture, and $100 for the Software. Record each depreciation expense as a separate adjusting journal entry.

   d. The computer supplies on hand total $350. Compare this amount with the amount in the Computer Supplies account to determine how much of the computer supplies has been used and then record the computer supplies expense.

   e. The office supplies on hand total $325. Compare this amount with the amount in the Office Supplies account to determine how many of the office supplies have been used and then record the office supplies expense.

   f. The interest on the note payable for one month is $52. Record the interest expense. Add to the Chart of Accounts List the Interest Payable account Other Current Liability, number 2030.

9. Display and print the following reports for June 30, 2022:

   a. *Adjusted Trial Balance* (worksheet): Change Interest Expense to $25 (June 1, 2022–June 30, 2022)

   b. *Journal:* Only the adjusting journal entries: (June 30, 2022–June 30, 2022)

   c. *Trial Balance:* Change name in header of the report to *Adjusted Trial Balance* (June 1, 2022–June 30, 2022)

   d. *Profit & Loss Standard* (June 1, 2022–June 30, 2022)

   e. *Balance Sheet Standard* (June 30, 2022)

## CHAPTER 5

Inventory

Receiving and Selling Items, Processing Sales Discounts, Adjusting Quantity/Value on Hand, and Paying Sales Tax

Objectives

- Identify the two main types of inventory accounting systems: periodic and perpetual
- Update the Item List to add, delete, or edit items
- Record purchases of inventory items in the Enter Bills and Write Checks windows
- Identify transactions requiring sales tax
- Process sales discounts
- Record adjustments to Inventory items in the Adjust Quantity/Value on Hand window
- Record payment of sales tax in the Pay Sales Tax window
- Display and print inventory-related reports
- Display and print accounting reports and financial statements

The online course includes additional training and assessment resources. Reports created for the Chapter Problem can be uploaded for instructor review.

Chapter Introduction

QuickBooks allows you to track inventory transactions. **Inventory** is ready-made merchandise that is sold to customers for a profit. Before you can enter inventory transactions, you must establish a file for each inventory item. Inventory item files are included in the Item List (Lists/Centers).

Once you establish an inventory item file, transactions for the item (Activities) can be entered in the Enter Bills, Write Checks, Create Invoices, Enter Sales Receipts, and Adjust Quantity/Value on Hand activity windows in much the same manner as was done in prior chapters. Every time the company receives merchandise for resale, sells merchandise, or adjusts the inventory because of loss or damage, QuickBooks records that information in the Item List. This allows you to accurately determine inventory quantity, value, and profit on sales. In addition, QuickBooks automatically changes balance sheet and income statement accounts based on the inventory information in the Item List (Reports).

In this chapter, our sample company, Kristin Raina Interior Designs, begins purchasing and selling decorative accessories to clients in addition to providing design and decorating services. This means that Kristin Raina must now be concerned with keeping an inventory.

QuickBooks versus Manual Accounting: Inventory Transactions

As discussed in previous chapters, in a manual accounting system, purchases on account are recorded in a purchases journal while sales on account are recorded in a sales journal. This is true whether the purchase or sale is for services or for merchandise. Cash transactions are recorded in the cash receipts or cash payments journals, again for both inventory and non-inventory items.

In QuickBooks, the Item List serves as an inventory subsidiary ledger for the company. The list includes all the items the company sells, both inventory and service items. Relevant information for each inventory item, such as name/number, type, description, cost, sales price, and related general ledger accounts, is entered at the time the item file is created and is updated as necessary.

When the company purchases an inventory item from a vendor on account, the transaction is recorded in the Enter Bills activity window in much the same manner as non-inventory purchases have been recorded. When the inventory items are sold on account, the invoice is recorded in the Create Invoices activity window in a manner similar to that for other revenues. When you enter these transactions, QuickBooks updates the Chart of Accounts List (general ledger) and at the same time updates each vendor and customer file. In addition, it updates the Item List to reflect the purchase and sale of the inventory items. Cash purchases of inventory items are recorded in the Write Checks activity window, while cash sales of inventory are recorded in the Enter Sales Receipts activity window. Changes in inventory that are not the result of a sale or purchase are recorded in the Adjust Quantity/Value on Hand window. In each instance when inventory items are purchased, sold, or adjusted, the Item List is updated to reflect the new inventory quantity and value.

Accounting for Inventory Transactions

periodic inventory system a system in which inventory is valued periodically based on a physical count of the merchandise; usually done once a year

perpetual inventory system a system in which inventory is valued after every purchase or sale of inventory items

There are two types of inventory systems: periodic and perpetual. Under the **periodic inventory system**, separate records are *not* maintained for inventory items, and no attempts are made to adjust the inventory account for purchases and sales. Instead, inventory is counted periodically to determine inventory quantity, value, cost of goods sold, and gross profit. In the past, the periodic system was often used by businesses that sold high-volume, low-cost goods, for which keeping individual inventory records was not practical.

Under the **perpetual inventory system**, accounting records are maintained that continuously show the current inventory quantity and value. When inventory is purchased, the inventory (asset) account is increased. When inventory is sold, the inventory account is reduced. In addition, the cost of goods sold is simultaneously computed to arrive at gross profit. Before the availability of low-cost computer hardware and software, only businesses with low-volume, high-cost goods used the perpetual system. Now, with computers pervasive in business, most companies are able to use a perpetual inventory system.

QuickBooks, like almost all general ledger accounting software programs, uses the perpetual system for two reasons. It not only allows the user to know the current inventory quantity and value at any given moment, but it also calculates the cost of goods sold and gross profit after each sale without the need for a periodic physical inventory count.

Chapter Problem

In this chapter, you will track inventory transactions for Kristin Raina Interior Designs, which will begin selling decorative inventory items in addition to providing decorating and design services. Information for inventory items has been entered in the Item List. This information, along with the March 1, 2022, beginning balances, is contained in the company file **CH5 Kristin Raina Interior Designs**.

Before you begin, open the company file **CH5 Kristin Raina Interior Designs.QBW**. Enter the password, *Student1*. Make a backup copy of the file, name it **EX5** *[Your Name]* **Kristin Raina Interior Designs**, and then restore the file. Enter the password, *Student1*. Finally, change the company name in the file to **EX5** *[Your Name]* **Kristin Raina Interior Designs**.

Lists/Centers

The Item List

Recall from Chapter 1 that the second level of operation in QuickBooks is to record background information in Lists/Centers. The Item List contains a file for each type of service or inventory item sold by the company. If the item sold is an inventory product, QuickBooks calls this an *inventory part* as opposed to a *service item*. You should enter the information for each inventory item in the Item List before recording transactions. This will make the Activities function run more smoothly. However, if you inadvertently omit an item, you can add that item during the Activities level of operation with minimal disruption.

The Item List contains important information on each product, such as type of item; number; descriptions; cost; general ledger posting accounts for inventory asset, cost of goods sold, and sales; preferred vendor; and sales tax status. All products or services sold by the company should be included in the Item List. Periodically, these files need to be updated as products are added or discontinued or as background information changes.

Kristin Raina has entered information for various inventory items in the Item List.

To review the Item List:
1. At the main menu bar, click Lists and then click *Item List*. The Item List appears. See Figure 5–A.

FIGURE 5–A Item List

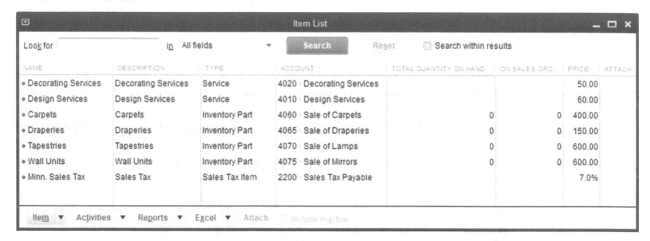

To view a specific inventory item file:
1. Double-click the *Carpets* item name. The inventory item file opens in Edit Item mode. See Figure 5–B.

FIGURE 5–B
Edit Item Window

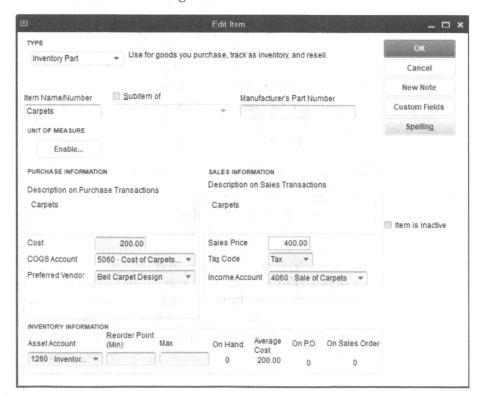

Table 5–1 describes the various fields of the Edit Item window.

TABLE 5–1
Edit Item Window

Field	Description
TYPE	If this is an inventory item, select *Inventory Part*. Other selections include *Service* for service revenue items, *Non-inventory Part* for products sold that are not maintained in inventory, *Inventory Assembly, Other Charge*, and so on.
Item Name/Number	Used to assign an identifying name or number to each item.
Subitem of	Used if an item is a component of another item, such as in a construction or manufacturing company.
Description on Purchase Transactions/Description on Sales Transactions	Used to enter a description of the item for the purchase or sales activity windows.
Cost	Used to enter the typical unit cost for the item. This amount will appear in the purchase activity windows (Enter Bills and Write Checks) as the default cost amount. Can override this entry as needed.
COGS Account	Lists the default general ledger posting account for cost of goods sold when the item is sold. Can override this account as needed.
Sales Price	This is the default selling price per unit that appears in the sales activity windows (Create Invoices and Enter Sales Receipts). Can override this entry as needed.
Tax Code	Used to indicate if the item is taxable or nontaxable for sales tax purposes.
Income Account	This is the default general ledger posting account for revenue when the item is sold. Can override this account as needed.
Asset Account	This is the default general ledger posting account for the inventory balance sheet account when an item is purchased. Can override this entry as needed.

2. Close the Edit Item window.
3. Close the Item List window.

The Item List is revised periodically when new inventory items are added, unused items are deleted, or modifications are made to inventory items. Making these adjustments to the inventory item files is referred to as *updating the Item List.*

Adding an Item

The company has decided to sell a line of modern lamps to its clients and needs to add this inventory item to the Item List.

To add an item:

1. With Decorating Services highlighted, at the main menu bar, click Lists and then click *Item List.*
2. At the Item List window, click the Item menu button. The Item drop-down menu appears. See Figure 5–C.

FIGURE 5–C
Item Drop-Down Menu

3. At the Item button drop-down menu, click *New.* The New Item window appears. See Figure 5–D.

FIGURE 5–D
New Item Window

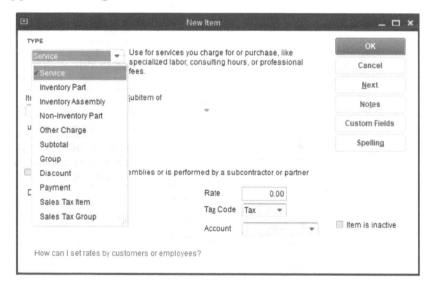

4. At the TYPE drop-down list, click *Inventory Part.*
5. Complete the remainder of the window with the following information:

Item Name/Number:	Lamps
Description on	
Purchase/Sales Transactions:	Lamps
Cost:	100
COGS Account:	5070 Cost of Lamps Sold
Preferred Vendor:	Lumiare Lighting Company
Sales Price:	200
Tax Code:	Tax – Taxable Sales
Income Account:	4070 Sale of Lamps
Asset Account:	1270 Inventory of Lamps
Date:	March 1, 2022

Your screen should look like Figure 5–E.

FIGURE 5–E
New Item Window—
Completed

6. If the information is correct, click OK.
7. Close the Item List window.

Deleting an Item

Kristin Raina wishes to delete Tapestries from the Item List because the company has decided not to sell this product.

To delete an item:
1. At the main menu bar, click Lists and then click *Item List*.
2. At the Item List window, select *Tapestries* but do not open the file. See Figure 5–F.

FIGURE 5–F
Item List—Tapestries
Selected

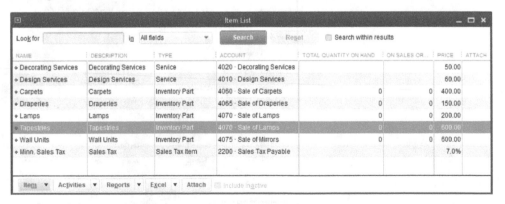

HINT

If you delete the wrong item, immediately click Edit and then *Undo Delete Item*. If you do not do this immediately, you will not be able to undo the deletion, and you will have to enter the record again.

3. Click the Item menu button. At the Item button drop-down menu, click *Delete Item*.
4. A warning screen appears. Click OK. The item file is deleted.
5. Close the Item List window.

You cannot delete an item with a balance or an item that has been part of a transaction for the period.

Editing an Item

Kristin Raina needs to edit the file for Draperies because the unit cost has increased to $125 and the sales price to $250.

To edit an item file:
1. At the main menu bar, click Lists and then click *Item List*.
2. Double-click the *Draperies* item file. The file opens in Edit Item mode. See Figure 5–G.

FIGURE 5–G
Edit Item Window—
Draperies

3. At the *Cost* and *Sales Price* fields, delete the current information and then enter the new amounts shown in Figure 5–H.

FIGURE 5–H
Edit Item Window—
Draperies—Updated

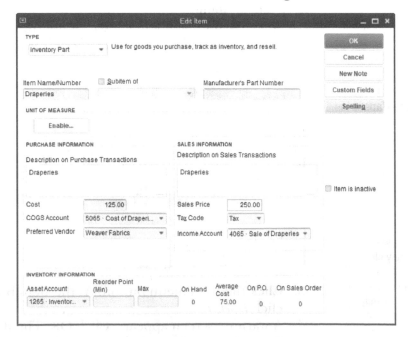

4. If the information is correct, click OK.
5. Close the Item List window.

Add the following item:

Type:	Inventory Part
Item Name/Number:	Mirrors
Description on Purchase/Sales Transactions:	Decorative Mirrors
Cost:	150
COGS Account:	5075 Cost of Mirrors Sold
Preferred Vendor:	Ace Glass Works
Sales Price:	300
Tax Code:	Tax – Taxable Sales
Income Account:	4075 Sale of Mirrors
Asset Account:	1275 Inventory of Mirrors
Date:	March 1, 2022

Delete the following item:

    Wall Units

QuickCheck: The updated Item List appears in Figure 5–I.

FIGURE 5–I Updated Item List

NAME	DESCRIPTION	TYPE	ACCOUNT	TOTAL QUANTITY ON HAND	ON SALES OR...	PRICE	ATTACH
◇ Decorating Services	Decorating Services	Service	4020 · Decorating Services			50.00	
◇ Design Services	Design Services	Service	4010 · Design Services			60.00	
◇ Carpets	Carpets	Inventory Part	4060 · Sale of Carpets	0	0	400.00	
◇ Draperies	Draperies	Inventory Part	4065 · Sale of Draperies	0	0	250.00	
◇ Lamps	Lamps	Inventory Part	4070 · Sale of Lamps	0	0	200.00	
◇ Mirrors	Decorative Mirrors	Inventory Part	4075 · Sale of Mirrors	0	0	300.00	
◇ Minn. Sales Tax	Sales Tax	Sales Tax Item	2200 · Sales Tax Payable			7.0%	

Inventory Center

Many of the procedures reviewed in this chapter, such as adding and editing an inventory item and recording a sale of inventory, can be accomplished through the Inventory Center. The Inventory Center can be found by clicking the Vendors menu, clicking *Inventory Activities*, and then clicking *Inventory Center.* See Figure 5–J.

The Inventory Center window is similar to the Vendor Center and Customer Center windows. The Inventory Center window contains a file for each inventory item. Each file contains important information, such as inventory item name, description, cost, sales price, and quantity on hand. The Inventory Center duplicates the information contained in the Item List. However, the Inventory Center maintains only files for Inventory Part items as seen on the Item List. The Inventory Center does not display non-inventory part items from the Item List.

FIGURE 5-J Inventory Center

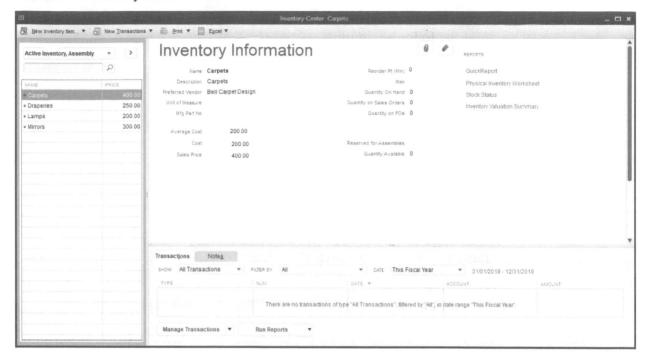

Purchasing Inventory

Recall from Chapter 1 that the third level of operation in QuickBooks is Activities, in which you record the daily business activities. Activities identified as purchases of inventory items on account are recorded in the Enter Bills window. Activities identified as purchases of inventory items for cash are recorded in the Write Checks window.

Recording Inventory Purchases Using the Enter Bills Window

HINT

If you click *Enter Bills* instead of *Receive Items and Enter Bill*, simply click the Items tab in the Enter Bills window.

In Chapter 2, you used the Enter Bills activity window when goods and services were purchased on account from a vendor. There are two subtabs on the Main tab of the Enter Bills window: Expenses and Items. When you chose *Enter Bills* from the Vendors drop-down menu, you used the Expenses tab to record your non-inventory purchases. When a company wishes to use the inventory feature, the Vendors drop-down menu offers an additional choice of *Receive Items and Enter Bill.* When you click *Receive Items and Enter Bill,* the Enter Bills window opens, but you use the Items tab to record an inventory purchase. In the Enter Bills window, the Items tab is similar to the Expenses tab but provides for additional fields that relate to inventory. In addition, you will find buttons that can be used when purchase orders are used in the purchase of inventory.

In some instances, items are received before the vendor forwards a bill. If this occurs, a different procedure is employed to record the transactions. However, for this chapter, it is assumed that a bill from the vendor accompanies the receipt of the inventory item and that you will record the transaction in the Enter Bills window—Items tab by clicking Vendors on the main menu bar and then *Receive Items and Enter Bill.* See Figure 5–K.

FIGURE 5–K
Enter Bills Window—
Items Tab

Table 5–2 describes the various fields on the Items tab in the Enter Bills window.

TABLE 5–2
Enter Bills Window—
Items Tab

Field	Description
ITEM	Click the inventory item purchased from the drop-down list. Once an item is chosen, the *DESCRIPTION* and *COST* fields are automatically filled based on information in the item file.
QTY	Enter the quantity purchased. QuickBooks multiplies the quantity purchased by the unit cost to arrive at the *AMOUNT* and *AMOUNT DUE* figures. In the *QTY* field, an icon ⬛ appears. Clicking the icon allows you to view the current availability information for this item, such as quantity available and quantity on purchase order. You can enter the quantity amount in the field while this icon is displayed. This icon appears any time an inventory part item is selected.

Notice that a field for the general ledger accounts is not displayed. Recall that when you entered items in the Item List, the general ledger accounts for the purchase (inventory asset account) and sale (income account and COGS account) of inventory items were indicated. QuickBooks uses the information in the Item List and the information entered in the Enter Bills window to adjust the correct accounts automatically.

The Enter Bills window—Items tab is designed for purchases of inventory items on account. The default accounts are the Inventory asset account and the Accounts Payable account. QuickBooks uses the information on the Item List to correctly record the amount and account for the inventory asset. The transaction is recorded as follows:

	Inventory	XXX	
	Accounts Payable		XXX

Recording a Purchase and Receipt of an Inventory Item on Account

On March 1, 2022, Kristin Raina purchases and receives 10 mirrors from Ace Glass Works at a cost of $150 each. The purchase is billed on Invoice No. K-588. The bill is due March 31, 2022, terms Net 30 Days.

To record a purchase and receipt of inventory items on account:

1. At the main menu bar, click Vendors and then click *Receive Items and Enter Bill.*
2. At the VENDOR drop-down list, click *Ace Glass Works.*
3. Complete the *DATE, REF. NO., BILL DUE,* and *TERMS* fields in the same way you would for a non-inventory purchase. Make sure the Items tab is the active tab. See Figure 5–L.

FIGURE 5–L
Enter Bills Window—
Partially Completed

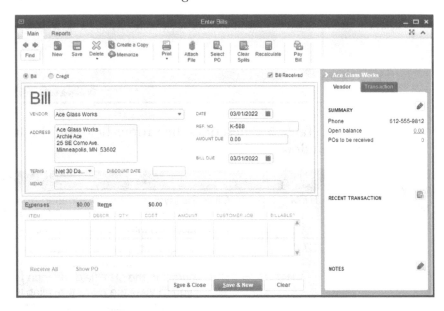

4. At the ITEM drop-down list, click *Mirrors.* The *DESCRIPTION* and *COST* fields fill automatically.
5. At the *QTY* field, type 10 and then move to the next field. The *AMOUNT* and *AMOUNT DUE* fields are completed automatically. See Figure 5–M.

FIGURE 5–M
Enter Bills Window—
Completed

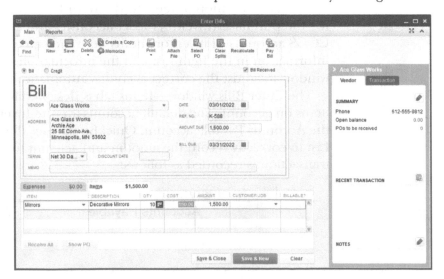

HINT

Remember, you can enter the quantity while the inventory icon is displayed.

For a purchase of inventory on account, the general ledger posting is as follows:

1275 Mirrors Inventory		2010 Accts Payable	
Dr	Cr	Dr	Cr
1,500			1,500

In addition, the vendor file (subledger) for Ace Glass Works reflects the new liability.

Ace Glass Works	
Dr	Cr
	1,500

6. If all the data is correct, click the Save & Close button.

In addition to the general ledger and vendor file changes, this transaction updates the item file for Mirrors to reflect a quantity of 10 on hand with an inventory value of $1,500.

Recording Inventory Purchases Using the Write Checks Window

Like the Enter Bills window, the Write Checks window has an Expenses tab and an Items tab. For the purchase of inventory items for cash, you switch to the Items tab after opening the Write Checks window. The fields in which to enter information for inventory items in the Write Checks window—Items tab are similar to those in the Enter Bills window—Items tab.

The Write Checks window—Items tab is designed for purchases of inventory items for cash. The default accounts are the Inventory asset account and the Cash account. QuickBooks uses the information on the Item List to correctly record the amount and account for the inventory asset. The transaction is recorded as follows:

	Inventory		XXX	
	Cash			XXX

Recording a Purchase and Receipt of an Inventory Item for Cash

On March 2, 2022, Kristin Raina purchases and receives 16 lamps from Lumiare Lighting Company at a cost of $100 each. The purchase is billed on Invoice No. 6844 and paid with Check No. 9.

To record a purchase and receipt of inventory items for cash:
1. At the main menu bar, click Banking and then click *Write Checks*.
2. At the Write Checks window, confirm that the *Print Later* and *Pay Online* boxes are not checked; at the *BANK ACCOUNT* field, confirm that *1010 Cash - Operating* is displayed; and at the *NO.* field, confirm that *9* is displayed.
3. At the *DATE* field, choose *03/02/2022.*
4. At the PAY TO THE ORDER OF drop-down list, click *Lumiare Lighting Company.*

5. Click the Items tab.
6. At the ITEM drop-down list, click *Lamps*.
7. At the *QTY* field, type 16 and then move to the next field. QuickBooks completes the *AMOUNT* field. See Figure 5–N.

FIGURE 5–N
Write Checks Window—
Completed

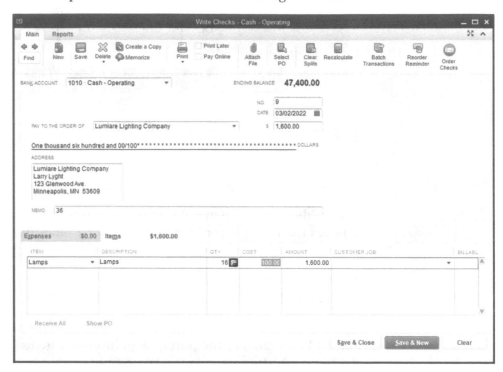

8. Click the Save & Close button.

ACCOUNTING CONCEPT

For a cash payment for the purchase of inventory, the general ledger posting is as follows:

1270 Lamps Inventory		1010 Cash - Operating	
Dr	Cr	Dr	Cr
1,600			1,600

In addition, the item file for Lamps is updated to reflect the new purchase.

Practice Exercise   5–2

Record the following transactions at the Enter Bills or Write Checks window:

Mar. 6	Purchased and received 10 carpets from Bell Carpet Design at a cost of $200 each, its Invoice No. 12-5585. The bill is due April 5, 2021. *QuickCheck:* $2,000
Mar. 13	Purchased and received 12 sets of draperies from Weaver Fabrics at a cost of $125 each. Pay immediately with Check No. 10. *QuickCheck:* $1,500

HINT

Many companies use purchase order forms to order inventory items from their suppliers. After completing Chapter 5, refer to Appendix D to see how QuickBooks uses purchase orders as part of the inventory purchase cycle.

Sales Tax

When a company sells a product to a customer, it is usually required to collect sales tax on the sale. The sales tax amount charged is added to the invoice price of the product. For example, a customer purchases an item with a retail price of $1,000, and the applicable sales tax rate is 6%. The retailer adds $60 to the invoice and collects $1,060 from the customer. At a later date, the retailer remits the tax collected from this and other customers to the appropriate state sales tax collection agency. Rules for applying and collecting sales tax are complex and beyond the scope of this text. For examples and cases in this text, assume every customer pays sales tax. QuickBooks, like most general ledger software programs, is equipped to track taxable sales transactions and to facilitate the collection and payment of taxes due.

In this chapter, Kristin Raina Interior Designs will sell decorative accessories to its customers. All sales of these products are subject to a sales tax charge of 7%, which is added to the invoice total. The tax will be payable to the Minnesota Department of Revenue at the end of each month. Sales tax will not be collected on services (decorating and design) in this text, because services generally are not subject to sales tax. Note, however, that in some localities, services also are subject to sales tax.

As you know from Chapter 3, a sale on account is recorded in the Create Invoices window, and a sale for cash is recorded in the Enter Sales Receipts window. The default account in the Create Invoices window is a debit to Accounts Receivable, and the default account in the Enter Sales Receipts window is a debit to Cash or Undeposited Funds. When sales tax is charged on the sale of an item, a default Sales Tax Payable account is credited in both the Create Invoices and Enter Sales Receipts windows. The sale of taxable products either for cash or on account results in the following general ledger posting:

Accounts Receivable/Cash (or Undeposited Funds)	XXX			
Sales			XXX	
Sales Tax Payable			XXX	

Sale of Inventory

Activities identified as sales of inventory items on account are recorded in the Create Invoices window. Activities identified as sales of inventory items for cash are recorded in the Enter Sales Receipts window. Activities recorded in these windows are similar to those in Chapter 3, but additional fields in the window are used that relate to inventory.

Inventory Sales on Account in the Create Invoices Window

When you record the sale of inventory items in the Create Invoices window, you use a template to access the additional fields needed for inventory items. In Chapter 3, for the sale of services, you used the Intuit Service Invoice Template. For the sale of inventory items on account, you will use the Intuit Product Invoice Template.

The Create Invoices window—Intuit Product Invoice is designed for the sale of inventory items on account. The default accounts are Accounts Receivable, Cost of Goods Sold, Inventory, Sales Tax Payable, and Sales.

QuickBooks uses the inventory Item List to determine the correct amount and account for the Cost of Goods Sold, Inventory, and Sales accounts. If an item is marked as taxable, QuickBooks uses the Item List to determine the correct amount of sales tax to be recorded in the Sales Tax Payable account. The transaction is recorded as follows:

Accounts Receivable	XXX		
Cost of Goods Sold	XXX		
Inventory			XXX
Sales Tax Payable			XXX
Sales			XXX

Recording a Sale of an Inventory Item on Account

On March 15, 2022, Kristin Raina sells the following items to Jennie Guthrie on account, Invoice No. 1008, Terms 2/10, Net 30 Days:

2 lamps	$ 400.00
3 carpets	1,200.00
1 mirror	300.00
Total sale of merchandise	$ 1,900.00
sales tax (0.07 × $1,900)	133.00
decorating services (8 hours)	400.00
Total sale on account	$ 2,433.00

To record a sale of inventory on account:

1. At the main menu bar, click Customers and then click *Create Invoices*.
2. At the CUSTOMER:JOB drop-down list, click *Guthrie, Jennie*.
3. At the TEMPLATE drop-down list, click *Intuit Product Invoice*. Additional fields for inventory item information appear.
4. Enter the information listed above for the *DATE* and *INVOICE #* fields.
5. At the TERMS drop-down list, click *2/10, Net 30 Days*, if necessary.
6. At the *QUANTITY* field, type 2.
7. Click the *ITEM CODE* field. At the ITEM CODE drop-down list, click *Lamps*. QuickBooks automatically fills the *DESCRIPTION, PRICE EACH, AMOUNT,* and *TAX* fields. See Figure 5–O.

FIGURE 5–O
Create Invoices Window—Partially Completed

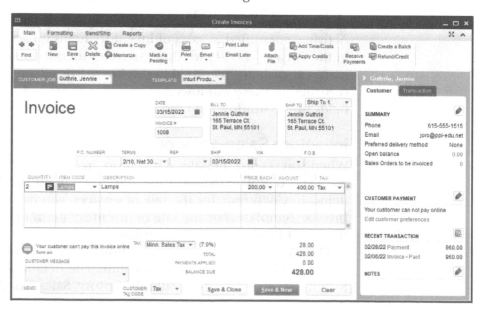

Note that the word *Tax* should appear in the *TAX* field for the taxable items, and *Non* should appear for the nontaxable service item. If the correct coding for the tax does not appear, use the drop-down list in the field to indicate the correct tax code.

8. Move to the second line of the *QUANTITY* field and type 3.

HINT

You may need to press the Tab key to move to additional lines in the Create Invoices window, or you can enlarge the Create Invoices window.

9. At the ITEM CODE drop-down list, click *Carpets*. QuickBooks fills the *DESCRIPTION, PRICE EACH, AMOUNT,* and *TAX* fields.

10. Move to the third line of the *QUANTITY* field and type 1.

11. At the ITEM CODE drop-down list, click *Mirrors*. QuickBooks fills the remaining fields.

12. Move to the fourth line of the *QUANTITY* field and type 8.

HINT

If you miss an item, click *Insert Line* from the Edit menu; if you wish to erase a line, click *Delete Line* from the Edit menu.

13. At the ITEM CODE drop-down list, click *Decorating Services*. QuickBooks fills the rcmaining fields. Note that the *TAX* field indicates *Non* because Decorating Services are not subject to sales tax.

14. Click the arrow at the TAX drop-down list and then click *Minn. Sales Tax*, if necessary. Confirm that the *Print Later* and *Email Later* boxes do not contain check marks. The *Your customer can't pay this invoice online* command should remain off. At the CUSTOMER TAX CODE drop-down list, confirm that *Tax* is selected. See Figure 5–P.

FIGURE 5–P
Create Invoices Window—Completed

15. If the information is correct, click the Save & Close button.

For a sale of inventory products on account, the general ledger posting is as follows:

1200 Accts Receivable			4060-4075 Sale of Inventory			
Dr	Cr		Dr	Cr	2 lamps @ 200 =	400
2,433				1,900	3 carpets @ 400 =	1,200
					1 mirror @ 300 =	300
						1,900

2200 Sales Tax Payable			4010-4020 Service Revenue	
Dr	Cr		Dr	Cr
	133			400

The cost of the inventory sold and resulting decline in the inventory is recorded as follows:

5060-5075 Cost of Goods Sold			1260-1275 Inventory			
Dr	Cr		Dr	Cr	2 lamps @ 100 =	200
950				950	3 carpets @ 200 =	600
					1 mirror @ 150 =	150
						950

Inventory Sales for Cash in the Enter Sales Receipts Window

The Enter Sales Receipts window is designed for cash received for both the sale of services and the sale of inventory items for cash. Once an inventory item is chosen, QuickBooks uses the information from the Item List to correctly record the Cost of Goods Sold, Inventory, and Sales accounts. If an item is marked as taxable, QuickBooks uses the Item List to determine the correct amount of sales tax to be recorded in the Sales Tax Payable account. The transaction is recorded as follows:

		Cash (or Undeposited Funds)	XXX		
		Cost of Goods Sold	XXX		
		Inventory			XXX
		Sales Tax Payable			XXX
		Sales			XXX

Recording a Sale of an Inventory Item for Cash

On March 22, 2022, Kristin Raina sells the following items to Beverly Jones, Invoice No. 1009, receiving payment immediately, her Check No. 5477.

1 carpet	$ 400.00
2 draperies	500.00
Total sale of merchandise	$ 900.00
sales tax (0.07 × $900)	63.00
decorating services (4 hrs)	200.00
Total sale for cash	$ 1,163.00

To record a sale of inventory for cash:

1. At the main menu bar, click Customers and then click *Enter Sales Receipts.*
2. At the CUSTOMER:JOB drop-down list, click *Jones, Beverly.*
3. Choose the appropriate date and then type 1009 in the *SALE NO.* field.
4. Click the CHECK button and then type 5477 in the *CHECK NO.* field. Confirm that the *Print Later* and *Email Later* boxes do not contain check marks and that *Tax* is selected in the CUSTOMER TAX CODE drop-down list.
5. Complete the remainder of the Enter Sales Receipts window for each item in the same manner as you would in the Create Invoices window. See Figure 5–Q.

FIGURE 5–Q Enter Sales Receipts Window—Completed

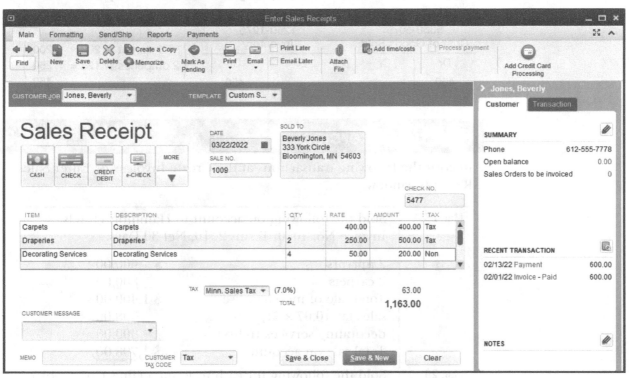

6. If all the information is correct, click the Save & Close button.

Companies that have cash sales of numerous low-cost items use the Sales Receipts window to enter these sales in batches on a periodic basis, such as weekly or semimonthly.

For a sale of inventory products for cash, the general ledger posting is as follows:

1250 Undeposited Funds			4060-4075 Sale of Inventory		
Dr	Cr		Dr	Cr	1 carpet @ 400 = 400
1,163				900	2 draperies @ 250 = 500
					900

2200 Sales Tax Payable			4010-4020 Service Revenue	
Dr	Cr		Dr	Cr
	63			200

The cost of the inventory sold and resulting decline in the inventory is recorded as follows:

5060-5075 Cost of Goods Sold			1260-1275 Inventory		
Dr	Cr		Dr	Cr	1 carpet @ 200 = 200
450				450	2 draperies @ 125 = 250
					450

Practice Exercise 5–3

Record the following transactions at the Create Invoices or Enter Sales Receipts window:

Mar. 27	Sold the following on account to Hamilton Hotels, Invoice No. 1010, Terms 2/10, Net 30 Days:	
	2 mirrors	$ 600.00
	2 carpets	800.00
	Total sale of merchandise	$ 1,400.00
	sales tax (0.07 × $1,400)	98.00
	decorating services (6 hrs)	300.00
	Total sale on account	$ 1,798.00
Mar. 29	Sold the following for cash to Franco Films Co., Invoice No. 1011, its Check No. 1361:	
	4 lamps	$ 800.00
	2 draperies	500.00
	Total sale of merchandise	$ 1,300.00
	sales tax (0.07 × $1,300)	91.00
	design services (4 hrs)	240.00
	Total sale for cash	$ 1,631.00

Sales Discounts

sales discount
a reduction in the selling price that is offered if the invoice payment is made shortly after the invoice date

Sales discounts are offered to customers to encourage early payment of outstanding invoices. Generally, companies provide for a 1% or 2% reduction of the invoice amount if the payment is made within 10 days of the invoice date. The terms, written as *2/10, Net 30*, would indicate a 2% discount within 10 days with the entire amount due in 30 days.

On March 23, 2022, Kristin Raina receives full payment from Jennie Guthrie for Invoice No. 1008, her Check No. 2453, less the appropriate discount.

To record a receipt of payment within the discount period:

1. At the main menu bar, click Customers and then click *Receive Payments*.
2. At the RECEIVED FROM drop-down list, click *Guthrie, Jennie*. The open invoice in the full amount for Jennie Guthrie appears.
3. At the *DATE* field, choose *03/23/2022*. Select the payment method and then enter the check number. See Figure 5–R.

FIGURE 5–R
Receive Payments Window—Jennie Guthrie—Partially Completed

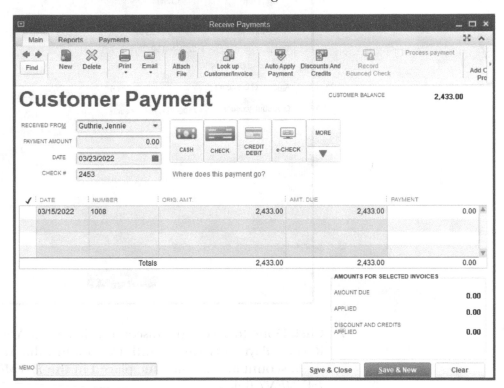

4. Select the invoice by clicking in the ✓ field next to the open invoice. The Automatically Calculate Payments window warning appears, inquiring if the *Automatically calculate payments* option should be selected in the Company Preferences for Payments. Insert a check mark in the box to the left of *Do not display this message in the future* and then click Yes. If you choose No in error, go to Edit, click *Preferences*, and then choose Payments. On the Company Preferences tab, insert a check mark next to the *Automatically calculate payments* option.

5. Click the Discounts and Credits button. The Discount and Credits window appears.

   This window displays information concerning the selected invoice, including the date the discount is available. The window computes the default discount amount based on information contained in the customer file.

6. At the Discount Account drop-down list, click *4100 Sales Discounts.* See Figure 5–S.

FIGURE 5–S
Discount and Credits Window

7. Click Done to accept the discount calculation. You are returned to the Receive Payments window with the amount due recalculated based on the discount and the net due placed in the *PAYMENT AMOUNT* and *PAYMENT* fields.

8. At the ✓ field, insert a check mark next to the selected invoice again, if necessary. See Figure 5–T.

FIGURE 5-T
Receive Payments
Window—Completed

HINT

See Appendix E for the steps to record a customer credit for returned inventory and to write off uncollectable receivables.

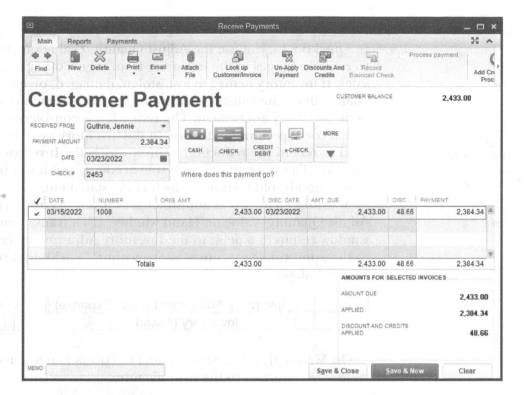

HINT

If you make an error on the payment, you can correct changes and resave, or you can click Edit and then *Delete Payment* and start over.

9. If the information is correct, click the Save & Close button.

ACCOUNTING CONCEPT

For a collection of an accounts receivable with a sales discount, the general ledger posting is as follows:

1010 Cash - Operating		1200 Accts Receivable		4100 Sales Discounts	
Dr	Cr	Dr	Cr	Dr	Cr
2,384.34		Bill 2,433	Coll 2,433	48.66	
		Bal 0			

In addition, the customer file (subledger) for Jennie Guthrie reflects the new collection.

Practice Exercise   **5–4**

Record the following transaction at the Receive Payments window:

Mar. 30	Received full payment from Hamilton Hotels for Invoice No. 1010, paid with Check No. 6555, less applicable discount. *QuickCheck:* $1,762.04

The Adjust Quantity/Value on Hand Window

inventory adjustment
an amount recorded in an expense or loss account to reflect the reduction of inventory value and/or quantity due to loss, theft, damage, or spoilage

In QuickBooks, you use the Adjust Quantity/Value on Hand activity window to record changes in the inventory from events other than purchases or sales. If inventory items are lost, stolen, damaged, or spoiled, the resulting change in the inventory quantity and/or value is recorded in this window as an **inventory adjustment**. The reduction is considered a loss or expense with a corresponding reduction in the inventory asset account. The account used to record the reduction to inventory is the Inventory Adjustment account. This is a cost of goods sold account, and it will be included in the cost of goods sold section of the income statement.

Activities identified as adjustments to inventory are recorded in the Adjust Quantity/Value on Hand window. Each transaction entered in this window results in a debit to the Inventory Adjustment account and a credit to the appropriate inventory asset account. QuickBooks records the transaction as follows:

	Inventory Adjustment (Loss/Expense)	XXX	
	Inventory (Asset)		XXX

On March 31, 2022, Kristin Raina discovers that a mirror is damaged and cannot be returned to the manufacturer.

To record an inventory adjustment:
1. At the main menu bar, click Vendors and then click *Inventory Activities.*
2. At the Inventory Activities submenu, click *Adjust Quantity/Value on Hand.*
3. At the Adjustment Type drop-down list, choose *Quantity and Total Value.*
4. At the *Adjustment Date* field, choose *03/31/2022.*
5. At the *Reference No.* field, type Inv. Adj. 1.
6. At the Adjustment Account drop-down list, click *5900 Inventory Adjustment.* If the Income or Expense expected window appears, insert a check mark next to *Do not display this message in the future* and then click OK.
7. At the ITEM drop-down list, click *Mirrors.* The description and current quantity are displayed. See Figure 5–U.

HINT

After selecting the Adjustment Account, if the reference number changes, go back and correct it.

FIGURE 5–U
Adjust Quantity/Value on Hand Window

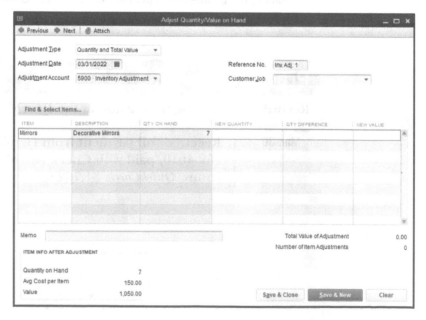

8. At the *NEW QUANTITY* field, type 6. When you move to the next field, QuickBooks fills the *QTY DIFFERENCE* and *NEW VALUE* fields and enters the Total Value of Adjustment amount. See Figure 5–V.

FIGURE 5–V
Adjust Quantity/Value on Hand Window— Completed for Quantity

9. If the information is correct, click the Save & Close button.

HINT
If you make an error in this window, click Edit and then *Delete Inventory Adjustment* and redo the transaction.

If the inventory adjustment was a result of a change in value only, without a change in quantity, you would choose *Total Values* at the Adjustment Type drop-down list. This allows you to adjust the value without changing the quantity.

ACCOUNTING CONCEPT

For an adjustment to inventory, the general ledger posting is as follows:

5900 Invent Adj		1275 Inv of Mirrors	
Dr	Cr	Dr	Cr
150		Prev Bal 1,050	Adj 150
		Bal 900	

In addition, the item file (subledger) for Mirrors reflects the new balance.

The Pay Sales Tax Window

In QuickBooks, the Pay Sales Tax window is used to record the remittance of sales tax charged to customers to the proper tax agency. QuickBooks uses the default accounts Sales Tax Payable and Cash.

The Pay Sales Tax window is designed for Activities identified as payment of sales tax charged to customers. The default accounts are Sales Tax Payable and Cash. QuickBooks records the transaction as follows:

		Sales Tax Payable	XXX	
		Cash		XXX

At the conclusion of each month, Kristin Raina remits the sales tax collected from customers to the appropriate state agency.

To pay the sales tax collected:
1. At the main menu bar, click Vendors and then click *Sales Tax*.
2. At the Sales Tax submenu, click *Pay Sales Tax*. The Pay Sales Tax window appears. See Figure 5–W.

FIGURE 5–W
Pay Sales Tax Window

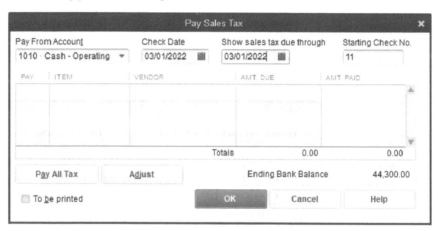

3. At the *Check Date* field, choose *03/31/2022*. In the *Pay From Account* field, confirm that the *1010 Cash - Operating* account is selected. Confirm that the *To be printed* box does not contain a check mark.
4. Confirm that the *Starting Check No.* is *11*.
5. At the *Show sales tax due through* field, choose *03/31/2022*.
6. Click the Pay All Tax button to select the liability. The sales tax liabilities to date is displayed.
7. At the *PAY* field, insert a check mark, if necessary. See Figure 5–X.

FIGURE 5–X
Pay Sales Tax Window—
Liabilities Displayed

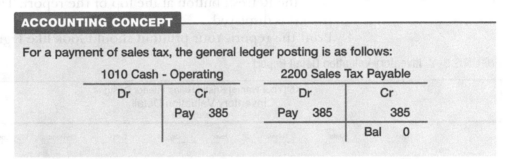

8. If the information is correct, click OK. The liability is now paid.

ACCOUNTING CONCEPT

For a payment of sales tax, the general ledger posting is as follows:

1010 Cash - Operating		2200 Sales Tax Payable	
Dr	Cr	Dr	Cr
	Pay 385	Pay 385	385
			Bal 0

Activities

Make Deposits

Recall from Chapter 3 that Kristin Raina Interior Designs deposits all funds collected from customers at the end of the month. Before the reports for the month are reviewed, the deposits should be recorded.

Practice Exercise   5–5

Record the following transaction at the Make Deposits window:

Mar. 31	Deposit all undeposited funds to the Cash - Operating account. *QuickCheck:* $6,940.38

Reports

Inventory Reports, Accounting Reports, and Financial Statements

Recall from Chapter 1 that Reports, the fourth level of operation, reflect the activities recorded in the various Lists/Centers and Activities windows. Inventory activities entered in the various windows flow into the reports, many of which should be displayed and printed at the end of the month.

Viewing and Printing Inventory Reports from the Reports Menu

Inventory reports, such as the *Inventory Valuation Detail* report, *Inventory Stock Status by Item* report, and *Purchases by Item Detail* report, help the company track and manage its inventory.

Inventory Valuation Detail Report

The *Inventory Valuation Detail* report displays the transactions affecting each inventory item along with the quantity and value on hand for each.

To view and print the *Inventory Valuation Detail* report:

1. At the main menu bar, click Reports and then click *Inventory*.
2. At the Inventory submenu, click *Inventory Valuation Detail*.
3. At the *From* and *To* fields, choose *03/01/2022* and *03/31/2022* and then click the Refresh button at the top of the report. The report for the period is displayed.
4. Print the report. Your printout should look like Figure 5–Y.

FIGURE 5–Y Inventory Valuation Detail Report

Type	Date	Name	Num	Qty	Cost	On Hand	Avg Cost	Asset Value
EX5 [Your Name] Kristin Raina Interior Designs								
Inventory Valuation Detail								
March 2022								
Inventory								
Carpets (Carpets)								
Bill	03/06/2022	Bell Carpet Design	12-5585	10	2,000.00	10	200.00	2,000.00
Invoice	03/15/2022	Guthrie, Jennie	1008	-3		7	200.00	1,400.00
Sales Receipt	03/22/2022	Jones, Beverly	1009	-1		6	200.00	1,200.00
Invoice	03/27/2022	Hamilton Hotels	1010	-2		4	200.00	800.00
Total Carpets (Carpets)						4.00		800.00
Draperies (Draperies)								
Check	03/13/2022	Weaver Fabrics	10	12	1,500.00	12	125.00	1,500.00
Sales Receipt	03/22/2022	Jones, Beverly	1009	-2		10	125.00	1,250.00
Sales Receipt	03/29/2022	Franco Films Co.	1011	-2		8	125.00	1,000.00
Total Draperies (Draperies)						8.00		1,000.00
Lamps (Lamps)								
Check	03/02/2022	Lumiare Lighting ...	9	16	1,600.00	16	100.00	1,600.00
Invoice	03/15/2022	Guthrie, Jennie	1008	-2		14	100.00	1,400.00
Sales Receipt	03/29/2022	Franco Films Co.	1011	-4		10	100.00	1,000.00
Total Lamps (Lamps)						10.00		1,000.00
Mirrors (Decorative Mirrors)								
Bill	03/01/2022	Ace Glass Works	K-588	10	1,500.00	10	150.00	1,500.00
Invoice	03/15/2022	Guthrie, Jennie	1008	-1		9	150.00	1,350.00
Invoice	03/27/2022	Hamilton Hotels	1010	-2		7	150.00	1,050.00
Inventory Adjust	03/31/2022		1	-1		6	150.00	900.00
Total Mirrors (Decorative Mirrors)						6.00		900.00
Total Inventory						28.00		3,700.00
TOTAL						28.00		3,700.00

5. Close the report.

Inventory Stock Status by Item Report

The *Inventory Stock Status by Item* report displays the on-hand status of each inventory item. The report indicates whether an item should be ordered based upon on-hand quantity and the reorder amount.

To view and print the *Inventory Stock Status by Item* report:

1. At the main menu bar, click Reports and then click *Inventory*.
2. At the Inventory submenu, click *Inventory Stock Status by Item*.
3. At the *From* and *To* fields, choose *03/01/2022* and *03/31/2022* and then click the Refresh button at the top of the report. The report for the period is displayed. See Figure 5–Z.

FIGURE 5–Z
Inventory Stock Status
by Item Report

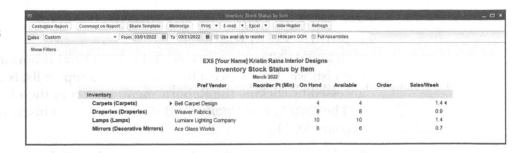

4. Print the report.
5. Close the report.

Purchases by Item Detail Report

The *Purchases by Item Detail* report displays all purchase information for each inventory item. The report shows the vendor name, cost per unit, quantity purchased, and total cost.

To view and print the *Purchases by Item Detail* report:
1. At the main menu bar, click Reports and then click *Purchases*.
2. At the Purchases submenu, click *Purchases by Item Detail.*
3. At the *From* and *To* fields, choose *03/01/2022* and *03/31/2022* and then click the Refresh button at the top of the report. The report for the period is displayed.
4. Print the report. Your printout should look like Figure 5–AA.

FIGURE 5–AA Purchases by Item Detail Report

EX5 [Your Name] Kristin Raina Interior Designs
Purchases by Item Detail
March 2022

Accrual Basis

Type	Date	Num	Memo	Source Name	Qty	Cost Price	Amount	Balance
Inventory								
Carpets (Carpets)								
Bill	03/06/2022	12-5585	Carpets	Bell Carpet Design	10	200.00	2,000.00	2,000.00
Total Carpets (Carpets)					10		2,000.00	2,000.00
Draperies (Draperies)								
Check	03/13/2022	10	Draperies	Weaver Fabrics	12	125.00	1,500.00	1,500.00
Total Draperies (Draperies)					12		1,500.00	1,500.00
Lamps (Lamps)								
Check	03/02/2022	9	Lamps	Lumiare Lighting Company	16	100.00	1,600.00	1,600.00
Total Lamps (Lamps)					16		1,600.00	1,600.00
Mirrors (Decorative Mirrors)								
Bill	03/01/2022	K-588	Decorative Mirrors	Ace Glass Works	10	150.00	1,500.00	1,500.00
Total Mirrors (Decorative Mirrors)					10		1,500.00	1,500.00
Total Inventory					48		6,600.00	6,600.00
TOTAL					48		6,600.00	6,600.00

This report, like several of those reviewed in prior chapters, allows you to "drill down" to view the source transaction. Kristin Raina wishes to see the detail of the purchase of carpets on March 6, 2022.

To "drill down" to the purchase transaction of carpets:
1. Hover the mouse pointer over the carpet purchase transaction until the zoom glass appears.
2. Double-click the transaction. The Enter Bills window for this transaction is displayed.
3. Close the Enter Bills window and the report.

Viewing and Printing Inventory Reports from the Lists Menu

QuickBooks allows you to view and print several inventory reports from the Lists windows. Once a list is accessed, a report list is available that is accessed by clicking the Reports menu button in the List window.

The *Sales by Item Detail* report shows sales of all inventory items both on account and for cash.

To view and print an Item List report such as *Sales by Item Detail*:

1. At the main menu bar, click Lists and then click *Item List*.
2. At the Item List window, click the Reports menu button.
3. At the Reports menu, click *Reports on All Items*.
4. At the Reports on all Items submenu, click *Sales Reports*.
5. At the Sales Reports submenu, click *By Item Detail*.
6. At the *From* and *To* fields, choose *03/01/2022* and *03/31/2022* and then click the Refresh button at the top of the report. The report for the period is displayed.
7. Print the report. Your printout should look like Figure 5–BB.

FIGURE 5–BB Sales by Item Detail Report

EX5 [Your Name] Kristin Raina Interior Designs
Sales by Item Detail
March 2022

Accrual Basis

Type	Date	Num	Memo	Name	Qty	Sales Price	Amount	Balance
Inventory								
Carpets (Carpets)								
Invoice	03/15/2022	1008	Carpets	Guthrie, Jennie	3	400.00	1,200.00	1,200.00
Sales Receipt	03/22/2022	1009	Carpets	Jones, Beverly	1	400.00	400.00	1,600.00
Invoice	03/27/2022	1010	Carpets	Hamilton Hotels	2	400.00	800.00	2,400.00
Total Carpets (Carpets)					6		2,400.00	2,400.00
Draperies (Draperies)								
Sales Receipt	03/22/2022	1009	Draperies	Jones, Beverly	2	250.00	500.00	500.00
Sales Receipt	03/29/2022	1011	Draperies	Franco Films Co.	2	250.00	500.00	1,000.00
Total Draperies (Draperies)					4		1,000.00	1,000.00
Lamps (Lamps)								
Invoice	03/15/2022	1008	Lamps	Guthrie, Jennie	2	200.00	400.00	400.00
Sales Receipt	03/29/2022	1011	Lamps	Franco Films Co.	4	200.00	800.00	1,200.00
Total Lamps (Lamps)					6		1,200.00	1,200.00
Mirrors (Decorative Mirrors)								
Invoice	03/15/2022	1008	Decorative Mirrors	Guthrie, Jennie	1	300.00	300.00	300.00
Invoice	03/27/2022	1010	Decorative Mirrors	Hamilton Hotels	2	300.00	600.00	900.00
Total Mirrors (Decorative Mirrors)					3		900.00	900.00
Total Inventory					19		5,500.00	5,500.00
Service								
Decorating Services (Decorating Services)								
Invoice	03/15/2022	1008	Decorating Services	Guthrie, Jennie	8	50.00	400.00	400.00
Sales Receipt	03/22/2022	1009	Decorating Services	Jones, Beverly	4	50.00	200.00	600.00
Invoice	03/27/2022	1010	Decorating Services	Hamilton Hotels	6	50.00	300.00	900.00
Total Decorating Services (Decorating Services)					18		900.00	900.00
Design Services (Design Services)								
Sales Receipt	03/29/2022	1011	Design Services	Franco Films Co.	4	60.00	240.00	240.00
Total Design Services (Design Services)					4		240.00	240.00
Total Service					22		1,140.00	1,140.00
TOTAL					41		6,640.00	6,640.00

8. Close the report and the Item List.

In addition to the *Sales* reports, *Purchase, Inventory, Item,* and *Price* reports can be viewed from the Reports menu of the Item List.

1. From the Inventory Reports menu, view and print the *Inventory Stock Status by Vendor* report for March.
2. From the Item List window, view and print the *Item Profitability* report (from the Reports on All Items—Project submenu).

Viewing and Printing Accounting Reports and Financial Statements

At the end of each month, the *Journal, Profit & Loss Standard* (or *Income Statement*), and *Balance Sheet Standard* reports should be viewed and printed. Your printouts should look like Figures 5–CC, 5–DD, and 5–EE, respectively.

FIGURE 5–CC Journal Report—Partial March 1, 2022–March 31, 2022

EX5 [Your Name] Kristin Raina Interior Designs
Journal
March 2022

Trans #	Type	Date	Num	Name	Memo	Account	Debit	Credit
39	Bill	03/01/2022	K-588	Ace Glass Works		2010 · Accounts Payable		1,500.00
				Ace Glass Works	Decorative Mirrors	1275 · Inventory of Mirrors	1,500.00	
							1,500.00	1,500.00
40	Check	03/02/2022	9	Lumiare Lighting Company	36	1010 · Cash - Operating		1,600.00
				Lumiare Lighting Company	Lamps	1270 · Inventory of Lamps	1,600.00	
							1,600.00	1,600.00
41	Bill	03/06/2022	12-5585	Bell Carpet Design		2010 · Accounts Payable		2,000.00
				Bell Carpet Design	Carpets	1260 · Inventory of Carpets	2,000.00	
							2,000.00	2,000.00
42	Check	03/13/2022	10	Weaver Fabrics	9878	1010 · Cash - Operating		1,500.00
				Weaver Fabrics	Draperies	1265 · Inventory of Draperies	1,500.00	
							1,500.00	1,500.00
43	Invoice	03/15/2022	1008	Guthrie, Jennie		1200 · Accounts Receivable	2,433.00	
				Guthrie, Jennie	Lamps	4070 · Sale of Lamps		400.00
				Guthrie, Jennie	Lamps	1270 · Inventory of Lamps		200.00
				Guthrie, Jennie	Lamps	5070 · Cost of Lamps Sold	200.00	
				Guthrie, Jennie	Carpets	4060 · Sale of Carpets		1,200.00
				Guthrie, Jennie	Carpets	1260 · Inventory of Carpets		600.00
				Guthrie, Jennie	Carpets	5060 · Cost of Carpets Sold	600.00	
				Guthrie, Jennie	Decorative Mirrors	4075 · Sale of Mirrors		300.00
				Guthrie, Jennie	Decorative Mirrors	1275 · Inventory of Mirrors		150.00
				Guthrie, Jennie	Decorative Mirrors	5075 · Cost of Mirrors Sold	150.00	
				Guthrie, Jennie	Decorating Services	4020 · Decorating Services		400.00
				Minn. Dept. of Revenue	Sales Tax	2200 · Sales Tax Payable		133.00
							3,383.00	3,383.00
44	Sales Receipt	03/22/2022	1009	Jones, Beverly		1250 · Undeposited Funds	1,163.00	
				Jones, Beverly	Carpets	4060 · Sale of Carpets		400.00
				Jones, Beverly	Carpets	1260 · Inventory of Carpets		200.00
				Jones, Beverly	Carpets	5060 · Cost of Carpets Sold	200.00	
				Jones, Beverly	Draperies	4065 · Sale of Draperies		500.00
				Jones, Beverly	Draperies	1265 · Inventory of Draperies		250.00
				Jones, Beverly	Draperies	5065 · Cost of Draperies Sold	250.00	
				Jones, Beverly	Decorating Services	4020 · Decorating Services		200.00
				Minn. Dept. of Revenue	Sales Tax	2200 · Sales Tax Payable		63.00
							1,613.00	1,613.00

...continues

FIGURE 5–CC Journal Report...*continued*

EX5 [Your Name] Kristin Raina Interior Designs
Journal
March 2022

Trans #	Type	Date	Num	Name	Memo	Account	Debit	Credit
45	Invoice	03/27/2022	1010	Hamilton Hotels		1200 · Accounts Receivable	1,798.00	
				Hamilton Hotels	Decorative Mirrors	4075 · Sale of Mirrors		600.00
				Hamilton Hotels	Decorative Mirrors	1275 · Inventory of Mirrors		300.00
				Hamilton Hotels	Decorative Mirrors	5075 · Cost of Mirrors Sold	300.00	
				Hamilton Hotels	Carpets	4060 · Sale of Carpets		800.00
				Hamilton Hotels	Carpets	1260 · Inventory of Carpets		400.00
				Hamilton Hotels	Carpets	5060 · Cost of Carpets Sold	400.00	
				Hamilton Hotels	Decorating Services	4020 · Decorating Services		300.00
				Minn. Dept. of Revenue	Sales Tax	2200 · Sales Tax Payable		98.00
							2,498.00	2,498.00
46	Sales Receipt	03/29/2022	1011	Franco Films Co.		1250 · Undeposited Funds	1,631.00	
				Franco Films Co.	Lamps	4070 · Sale of Lamps		800.00
				Franco Films Co.	Lamps	1270 · Inventory of Lamps		400.00
				Franco Films Co.	Lamps	5070 · Cost of Lamps Sold	400.00	
				Franco Films Co.	Draperies	4065 · Sale of Draperies		500.00
				Franco Films Co.	Draperies	1265 · Inventory of Draperies		250.00
				Franco Films Co.	Draperies	5065 · Cost of Draperies Sold	250.00	
				Franco Films Co.	Design Services	4010 · Design Services		240.00
				Minn. Dept. of Revenue	Sales Tax	2200 · Sales Tax Payable		91.00
							2,281.00	2,281.00
47	Payment	03/23/2022	2453	Guthrie, Jennie		1250 · Undeposited Funds	2,384.34	
				Guthrie, Jennie		1200 · Accounts Receivable		2,433.00
				Guthrie, Jennie		4100 · Sales Discounts	48.66	
							2,433.00	2,433.00
48	Payment	03/30/2022	6555	Hamilton Hotels		1250 · Undeposited Funds	1,762.04	
				Hamilton Hotels		1200 · Accounts Receivable		1,798.00
				Hamilton Hotels		4100 · Sales Discounts	35.96	
							1,798.00	1,798.00
49	Inventory Adjust	03/31/2022	1			5900 · Inventory Adjustment	150.00	
					Mirrors Inventory Adju...	1275 · Inventory of Mirrors		150.00
							150.00	150.00
50	Sales Tax Pay...	03/31/2022	11	Minn. Dept. of Revenue		1010 · Cash - Operating		385.00
				Minn. Dept. of Revenue		2200 · Sales Tax Payable	385.00	
							385.00	385.00
51	Deposit	03/31/2022			Deposit	1010 · Cash - Operating	6,940.38	
				-MULTIPLE-	Deposit	1250 · Undeposited Funds		6,940.38
							6,940.38	6,940.38
TOTAL							28,081.38	28,081.38

EX5 [Your Name] Kristin Raina Interior Designs
Profit & Loss
Accrual Basis   January through March 2022

	Jan - Mar 22
Ordinary Income/Expense	
Income	
4010 · Design Services	4,980.00
4020 · Decorating Services	3,400.00
4060 · Sale of Carpets	2,400.00
4065 · Sale of Draperies	1,000.00
4070 · Sale of Lamps	1,200.00
4075 · Sale of Mirrors	900.00
4100 · Sales Discounts	-84.62
Total Income	13,795.38
Cost of Goods Sold	
5060 · Cost of Carpets Sold	1,200.00
5065 · Cost of Draperies Sold	500.00
5070 · Cost of Lamps Sold	600.00
5075 · Cost of Mirrors Sold	450.00
5900 · Inventory Adjustment	150.00
Total COGS	2,900.00
Gross Profit	10,895.38
Expense	
6020 · Accounting Expense	300.00
6050 · Advertising Expense	100.00
6175 · Deprec. Exp., Furniture	100.00
6185 · Deprec. Exp., Computers	60.00
6200 · Insurance Expense	200.00
6300 · Janitorial Expenses	125.00
6325 · Office Supplies Expense	150.00
6400 · Rent Expense	800.00
6450 · Telephone Expense	275.00
6500 · Utilities Expense	450.00
Total Expense	2,560.00
Net Ordinary Income	8,335.38
Other Income/Expense	
Other Expense	
7000 · Interest Expense	50.00
Total Other Expense	50.00
Net Other Income	-50.00
Net Income	8,285.38

FIGURE 5–EE Balance Sheet Standard Report March 31, 2022

EX5 [Your Name] Kristin Raina Interior Designs
Balance Sheet

Accrual Basis   As of March 31, 2022

	Mar 31, 22
ASSETS	
Current Assets	
Checking/Savings	
1010 · Cash - Operating	50,855.38
Total Checking/Savings	50,855.38
Accounts Receivable	
1200 · Accounts Receivable	1,540.00
Total Accounts Receivable	1,540.00
Other Current Assets	
1260 · Inventory of Carpets	800.00
1265 · Inventory of Draperies	1,000.00
1270 · Inventory of Lamps	1,000.00
1275 · Inventory of Mirrors	900.00
1300 · Design Supplies	200.00
1305 · Office Supplies	250.00
1410 · Prepaid Advertising	500.00
1420 · Prepaid Insurance	2,200.00
Total Other Current Assets	6,850.00
Total Current Assets	59,245.38
Fixed Assets	
1700 · Furniture	
1725 · Furniture, Cost	12,000.00
1750 · Accum. Dep., Furniture	-100.00
Total 1700 · Furniture	11,900.00
1800 · Computers	
1825 · Computers, Cost	3,600.00
1850 · Accum. Dep., Computers	-60.00
Total 1800 · Computers	3,540.00
Total Fixed Assets	15,440.00
TOTAL ASSETS	74,685.38
LIABILITIES & EQUITY	
Liabilities	
Current Liabilities	
Accounts Payable	
2010 · Accounts Payable	9,750.00
Total Accounts Payable	9,750.00
Other Current Liabilities	
2020 · Notes Payable	7,000.00
2030 · Interest Payable	50.00
Total Other Current Liabilities	7,050.00
Total Current Liabilities	16,800.00
Total Liabilities	16,800.00
Equity	
3010 · Kristin Raina, Capital	50,000.00
3020 · Kristin Raina, Drawings	-400.00
Net Income	8,285.38
Total Equity	57,885.38
TOTAL LIABILITIES & EQUITY	74,685.38

Exiting QuickBooks

Upon completing this session, make a backup copy of your practice exercise company file to a removable storage device using the Back Up command. Be sure to change the *Save in* field to the removable storage device and then carefully type the correct file name. Close the company file and then exit QuickBooks.

Chapter Review and Assessment

Procedure Review

To add an item:
1. At the main menu bar, click Lists and then click *Item List*.
2. At the Item List window, click the Item menu button.
3. At the Item button drop-down menu, click *New*.
4. Enter the background data for the item.
5. Click OK.
6. Close the Item List window.

To delete an item:
1. At the main menu bar, click Lists and then click *Item List*.
2. At the Item List window, select the item you wish to delete.
3. Click the Item menu button.
4. At the Item button drop-down menu, click *Delete Item*.
5. Click OK at the warning.
6. Close the Item List window.
    You cannot delete an item that has a balance or is used in a transaction.

To edit an item:
1. At the main menu bar, click Lists and then click *Item List*.
2. At the Item List window, select the item you wish to edit.
3. Click the Item menu button.
4. At the Item button drop-down menu, click *Edit Item*.
5. Change the appropriate information.
6. Click OK.
7. Close the Item List window.

To record a purchase and receipt of an inventory item on account:
1. At the main menu bar, click Vendors and then click *Receive Items and Enter Bill*.
2. At the VENDOR drop-down list, click the vendor name.
3. Enter data into the *DATE, REF. NO., BILL DUE,* and *TERMS* fields in the usual manner.
4. Click the item from the ITEM drop-down list.
5. Enter the quantity; the *AMOUNT* and *AMOUNT DUE* fields fill automatically.
6. Click the Save & Close button.

To record a purchase and receipt of an inventory item for cash:
1. At the main menu bar, click Banking and then click *Write Checks*.
2. At the Write Checks window, click the appropriate bank account.
3. Enter the check date in the *DATE* field.
4. Click the vendor from the PAY TO THE ORDER OF drop-down list.
5. Click the Items tab.
6. Click the item from the ITEM drop-down list.
7. Enter the quantity. The *AMOUNT* field fills automatically.
8. Click the Save & Close button.

To record a sale of inventory on account:
1. At the main menu bar, click Customers and then click *Create Invoices*.
2. At the CUSTOMER:JOB drop-down list, click the customer name.
3. At the TEMPLATE drop-down list, click *Intuit Product Invoice*.
4. Enter data into the *DATE, INVOICE* #, and *TERMS* fields in the usual manner.
5. Enter the quantity.
6. Click the item from the ITEM drop-down list; the *DESCRIPTION, PRICE EACH*, and *AMOUNT* fields fill automatically.
7. At the TAX drop-down list, click the applicable sales tax. Make sure that *Tax* from the CUSTOMER TAX CODE drop-down list is selected.
8. Click the Save & Close button.

To enter a cash sale of inventory:
1. At the main menu bar, click Customers and then click *Enter Sales Receipt.*
2. At the CUSTOMER:JOB drop-down list, click the customer name.
3. Enter the date, invoice number, payment method, and check number.
4. Complete the remainder of the window in the same manner as a sale on account.
5. Click the Save & Close button.

To record a receipt of payment within the discount period:
1. At the main menu bar, click Customers and then click *Receive Payments.*
2. At the RECEIVED FROM drop-down list, click the customer name.
3. Enter the payment date in the *DATE* field. Enter the payment method and check number.
4. Select the invoice by clicking in the ✓ field next to the open invoice.
5. Click Yes at the warning and then click the Discounts and Credits button.
6. At the Discount Account drop-down list, click the *Sales Discounts* account.
7. Click Done to accept the discount calculation.
8. At the ✓ field, insert a check mark next to the selected invoice again, if necessary.
9. Click the Save & Close button.

To record an inventory adjustment:
1. At the main menu bar, click Vendors and then click *Inventory Activities.*
2. At the Inventory Activities menu, click *Adjust Quantity/Value on Hand.*
3. At the Adjustment Type drop-down list, choose *Quantity and Total Value.*
4. Enter data into the *DATE* and *REFERENCE NO.* fields.
5. At the Adjustment Account drop-down list, click *Inventory Adjustment.*
6. Select the item from the drop-down list.
7. Enter the new quantity in the *NEW QUANTITY* field.
8. Click the Save & Close button.

To pay sales tax:
1. At the main menu bar, click Vendors and then click *Sales Tax*.
2. At the Sales Tax submenu, click *Pay Sales Tax*.
3. Enter the payment date.
4. Click the *Cash* account.
5. Enter the correct date in the *Show sales tax due through* field.
6. Click the Pay All Tax button.
7. Insert a check mark in the *PAY* field.
8. Click OK.

To view and print inventory reports from the Reports menu:
1. At the main menu bar, click Reports and then click *Inventory*.
2. At the Inventory submenu, choose a report.
3. Indicate the appropriate dates for the report.
4. Click the Print button at the top of the report and then click *Report*.
5. Print the report.
6. Close the report.

To view and print inventory reports from the Lists menu:
1. At the main menu bar, click Lists and then click *Item List*.
2. Click the Reports menu button.
3. Click *Reports on All Items*.
4. From the submenu, click a category.
5. From the second submenu, click a report.
6. Indicate the appropriate dates for the report.
7. Click the Print button at the top of the report.
8. Print the report.
9. Close the report.

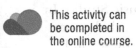
This activity can be completed in the online course.

Key Concepts

Select the letter of the item that best matches each definition.

a. Enter Bills window—Items tab
b. Adjust Quantity/Value on Hand activity window
c. Item List
d. Sales discount
e. *Purchases by Item Detail* report
f. Sales tax
g. Pay Sales Tax window
h. *Inventory Valuation Detail* report
i. *Sales by Item Detail* report
j. *Inventory Stock Status by Item* report

_____ 1. Report that displays all transactions affecting each inventory item.
_____ 2. Reduction of the invoice amount due when the customer pays by a specific date.
_____ 3. Window used to record purchases and receipt of inventory items.
_____ 4. Window used to adjust the quantity or value of inventory as a result of damage or loss.
_____ 5. Contains a file of all inventory items.
_____ 6. Window used to remit sales tax collected from customers to the appropriate state tax agency.

_____ 7. Report that displays each purchase transaction for inventory items.

_____ 8. Report that displays the on-hand status of each inventory item.

_____ 9. Report from the Item List that shows sales information for each inventory item.

_____ 10. Tax collected by a retailer from a customer on the sales of goods.

This activity can be completed in the online course.

Procedure Check

1. Your company will be selling a new product. Describe the steps that must be taken to add the new item to the system.
2. Explain the difference between using *Enter Bills* or *Receive Items and Enter Bills* from the Vendors drop-down menu.
3. Your company wishes to determine which inventory items generate the most revenue. How could you use QuickBooks to develop this information?
4. At year-end, you wish to confirm the quantity on hand for each inventory item. How would you use QuickBooks reports to determine the quantity and value of the ending inventory?
5. Your company wishes to view the profitability of each inventory item. How could you use QuickBooks to develop this information?
6. Discuss the advantages of using a computerized accounting system to maintain a perpetual inventory system.

Reports created for these Case Problems can be exported to Excel and uploaded in the online course to be automatically graded.

Case Problems

Demonstrate your knowledge of the QuickBooks features discussed in this chapter by completing the following case problems.

Case Problem 5–1

On April 1, 2022, Lynn Garcia began her business, Lynn's Music Studio. In the first month of business, Lynn set up the music studio, provided guitar and piano lessons, and recorded month-end activity. In May, the second month of business, Lynn will purchase and sell inventory items of guitars, keyboards, music stands, and sheet music. For customers that purchase merchandise inventory, the terms of payment are 2/10, Net 30 Days. For illustration purposes, assume a 7% sales tax is charged on the sales of all inventory items. The company file includes the information for Lynn's Music Studio as of May 1, 2022.

1. Open the company file **CH5 Lynn's Music Studio.QBW**.
2. At the QuickBooks Desktop Login window, in the *Password* text box, type Student1 and then click OK.
3. Make a backup copy of the company file and name it **LMS5** *[Your Name]* **Lynn's Music Studio** and enter the password.
4. Restore the backup copy of the company file. In both the Open Backup Copy and Save Company File as dialog boxes, use the file name **LMS5** *[Your Name]* **Lynn's Music Studio**.
5. Change the company name to **LMS5** *[Your Name]* **Lynn's Music Studio**.

6. Add the following inventory items to the Item List:

Type:	Inventory Part
Item Name/Number:	Keyboards
Description on	
* Purchase/Sales Transactions:*	Keyboards
Cost:	75
COGS Account:	5065 Cost of Keyboards Sold
Preferred Vendor:	Katie's Keyboards
Sales Price:	150
Tax Code:	Tax – Taxable Sales
Income Account:	4065 Sale of Keyboards
Asset Account:	1265 Inventory of Keyboards

Type:	Inventory Part
Item Name/Number:	Sheet Music
Description on	
* Purchase/Sales Transactions:*	Sheet Music
Cost:	3
COGS Account:	5075 Cost of Sheet Music Sold
Preferred Vendor:	Strings, Sheets & Such
Sales Price:	6
Tax Code:	Tax – Taxable Sales
Income Account:	4075 Sale of Sheet Music
Asset Account:	1275 Inventory of Sheet Music

Delete the following inventory item:
    Harmonicas

7. Using the appropriate window, record each of the following transactions for May:

May 3   Purchased 30 guitars on account from Music Instruments, Inc., at $50 each, its Invoice No. GU75998.

May 3   Purchased 30 keyboards on account from Katie's Keyboards at $75 each, its Invoice No. 10089-30.

May 3   Purchased 30 music stands from Melody Music Equipment at $20 each, paid immediately, Check No. 9. Do not print check.

May 3   Purchased 300 sheets of music of various themes from Strings, Sheets & Such at $3 each, paid immediately, Check No. 10. Do not print check.

May 4   Sold 15 guitars for $100 each, 15 keyboards for $150 each, and 15 music stands for $40 each to Jefferson High School, Invoice No. 2012, terms 2/10, Net 30 Days. In addition, provided 15 hours of guitar lessons and 10 hours of piano lessons.

May 4   Sold 10 keyboards for $150 each to Highland School, Invoice No. 2013, terms 2/10, Net 30 Days. In addition, provided 12 hours of piano lessons.

> **HINT**
> Remember to use the Intuit Product Invoice template in the Create Invoices window.

May 7	Received full payment from Jefferson High School for Invoice 2009, Check No. 30531. (No discount.)
May 10	Record the weekly cash sales of sheet music, 75 sheets at $6 each, Sale No. 2014. Leave the *CUSTOMER:JOB* field blank.
May 11	Sold 3 guitars for $100 each, 3 keyboards for $150 each, and 3 music stands for $40 each to Mulligan Residence, Invoice No. 2015, terms 2/10, Net 30 Days. In addition, provided 5 hours of guitar lessons and 7 hours of piano lessons.
May 11	Received full payment net of discount from Jefferson High School for Invoice No. 2012, Check No. 30711.
May 14	Received full payment net of discount from Highland School, Check No. 76115.
May 17	Purchased 20 keyboards on account from Katie's Keyboard Company at $75 each, its Invoice No. 10758-20.
May 17	Purchased 10 music stands from Melody Music Equipment at $20 each, paid immediately, Check No. 11. Do not print check.
May 17	Record the weekly cash sales of sheet music, 100 sheets at $6 each, Sale No. 2016.
May 21	Sold 5 guitars for $100 each, 5 keyboards for $150 each, and 5 music stands for $40 each to Twin Lakes Elementary, Invoice No. 2017, terms 2/10, Net 30 Days. In addition, provided 8 hours of guitar lessons and 5 hours of piano lessons.
May 24	Received a payment of $830 from Twin Lakes Elementary for Invoice Nos. 2004 and 2011, Check No. 7266.
May 24	Record the weekly cash sales of sheet music, 115 sheets at $6 each, Sale No. 2018.
May 24	Purchased 300 sheets of music of various themes from Strings, Sheets, & Such at $3 each, paid immediately, Check No. 12. Do not print check.
May 25	Received full payment net of discount from Twin Lakes Elementary for Invoice No. 2017, Check No. 7384.
May 25	Paid in full Music Instruments, Inc. (Check No. 13). Do not print check.
May 25	Paid in full Katie's Keyboard Company, Invoice No. 10089-30 (Check No. 14). Do not print check.
May 31	Record the weekly cash sales of sheet music, 145 sheets at $6 each, Invoice No. 2019.
May 31	Upon reviewing the inventory, Lynn discovers that one guitar is damaged, through no fault of the manufacturer, and cannot be sold. Adjust the inventory on hand to remove the one guitar from the inventory. Inv. Adj. 1.
May 31	Remit all sales tax collected to the PA Dept. of Revenue, Check No. 15.
May 31	Deposit all undeposited funds to the Cash - Operating account.

8. Display and print the following reports for May 1, 2022, to May 31, 2022:
   a. *Inventory Valuation Detail*
   b. *Inventory Stock Status by Item*
   c. *Purchases by Item Detail*
   d. *Sales by Item Detail*
   e. *Journal*
   f. *Profit & Loss Standard* (April 1, 2022–May 31, 2022)
   g. *Balance Sheet Standard*

Case Problem 5–2

On June 1, 2022, Olivia Chen began her business, Olivia's Web Solutions. In the first month of business, Olivia set up the office, provided web page design and internet consulting services, and recorded month-end activity. In July, the second month of business, Olivia will purchase and sell inventory items of computer hardware and software. For customers that purchase merchandise inventory, the terms of payment are 2/10, Net 30 Days. For illustration purposes, assume an 8% sales tax is charged on the sales of all inventory items. The company file includes the information for Olivia's Web Solutions as of July 1, 2022.

1. Open the company file **CH5 Olivia's Web Solutions.QBW**.
2. At the QuickBooks Desktop Login window, in the *Password* text box, type Student1 and then click OK.
3. Make a backup copy of the company file and name it **OWS5 *[Your Name]* Olivia's Web Solutions**.
4. Restore the backup copy of the company file. In both the Open Backup Copy and Save Company File as dialog boxes, use the file name **OWS5 *[Your Name]* Olivia's Web Solutions** and enter the password.
5. Change the company name to **OWS5 *[Your Name]* Olivia's Web Solutions**.
6. Add the following inventory items to the Item List:

Type:	Inventory Part
Item Name/Number:	Scanners
Description on	
Purchase/Sales Transactions:	Scanners
Cost:	300
COGS Account:	5065 Cost of Scanners Sold
Preferred Vendor:	Scanntronix
Sales Price:	600
Tax Code:	Tax – Taxable Sales
Income Account:	4065 Sale of Scanners
Asset Account:	1265 Inventory of Scanners
Type:	Inventory Part
Item Name/Number:	Desktop Publishing Software
Description on	
Purchase/Sales Transactions:	Desktop Publishing Software
Cost:	100

COGS Account:	5075 Cost of Desktop Pub. Software
Preferred Vendor:	Textpro Software, Inc.
Sales Price:	200
Tax Code:	Tax – Taxable Sales
Income Account:	4075 Sale of Desktop Pub. Soft.
Asset Account:	1275 Inventory of Desktop Pub. Soft.

Delete the following inventory item:
   Printers

7. Using the appropriate window, record each of the following transactions for July:

Jul. 2	Purchased 10 computers on account from Computec Computers at $1,000 each, its Invoice No. 068788.
Jul. 2	Purchased 20 scanners on account from Scanntronix at $300 each, its Invoice No. 10089-30.
Jul. 2	Purchased 10 desktop publishing software packages from Textpro Software, Inc. at $100 each, paid immediately, Check No. 9. Do not print check.
Jul. 2	Purchased 20 HTML software packages from InterSoft Development Co. at $75 each, paid immediately, Check No. 10. Do not print check.
Jul. 5	Sold 3 computers for $2,000 each, 2 scanners for $600 each, and 1 desktop publishing software package for $200 on account to Long Island Water Works, Invoice No. 1011, terms 2/10, Net 30 Days. In addition, provided 10 hours of internet consulting services.
Jul. 6	Sold 2 computers on account to Miguel's Restaurant for $2,000 each, Invoice No. 1012, terms 2/10, Net 30 Days. In addition, provided 8 hours of web page design services.
Jul. 9	Sold 1 scanner for $600 and 1 desktop publishing software package for $200 to the Singh family, Invoice No. 1013. Received payment immediately, their Check No. 901.
Jul. 12	Sold 1 computer for $2,000, 2 scanners for $600 each, and 1 HTML software package for $150 on account to Breathe Easy, Invoice No. 1014, Net 30 Days. In addition, provided 12 hours of internet consulting services.
Jul. 13	Received full payment net of discount from Long Island Water Works for Invoice No. 1011, Check No. 125671.
Jul. 16	Purchased 5 computers on account from Computec Computers at $1,000 each, its Invoice No. 072445.
Jul. 16	Purchased 5 desktop publishing software packages from Textpro Software, Inc. at $100 each, paid immediately, Check No. 11. Do not print check.

Jul. 19   Sold 1 computer for $2,000 and 1 desktop publishing software package for $200 to the Schneider Family, Invoice No. 1015. Received payment immediately, their Check No. 899.

Jul. 20   Sold 3 computers for $2,000 each, 3 scanners for $600 each, and 2 desktop publishing software packages for $200 each to South Shore School District, Invoice No. 1016, terms 2/10, Net 30 Days. In addition, provided 16 hours of web page design services.

Jul. 26   Received full payment, no discount, from Miguel's Restaurant for Invoice No. 1012, Check No. 4110.

Jul. 27   Received full payment, no discount, from Breathe Easy for Invoice Nos. 1006 (remaining balance) and 1014, Check No. 1874.

Jul. 30   Purchased 5 computers on account from Computec Computers at $1,000 each, its Invoice No. 073111.

Jul. 30   Paid in full Computec Computers Invoice No. 068788 (Check No. 12). Do not print check.

Jul. 30   Paid in full Scanntronix, Invoice No. 10089-30 (Check No. 13). Do not print check.

Jul. 30   Upon reviewing the inventory, Olivia discovers one HTML software package was damaged, through no fault of the manufacturer, and cannot be sold. Adjust the inventory on hand to remove the one HTML software package from the inventory. Inv. Adj. 1.

Jul. 31   Remit all sales tax collected to New York State, Check No. 14.

Jul. 31   Deposit all undeposited funds to the Cash - Operating account.

8. Display and print the following reports for July 1, 2022, to July 31, 2022:
   a. *Inventory Valuation Detail*
   b. *Inventory Stock Status by Item*
   c. *Purchases by Item Detail*
   d. *Sales by Item Detail*
   e. *Journal*
   f. *Profit & Loss Standard* (June 1, 2022–July 31, 2022)
   g. *Balance Sheet Standard*

## CHAPTER 6

New Company Setup— Detailed Start

Using EasyStep Interview and QuickBooks Desktop Setup

Objectives

- Create a new company file and establish preferences using the QuickBooks Detailed Start method and EasyStep Interview window

- Set up the Customer Center, Vendor Center, and Item List using the QuickBooks Desktop Setup window

- Review information recorded in the EasyStep Interview and QuickBooks Desktop Setup windows

- Customize the Chart of Accounts List, system default accounts, and Terms List

- Update the Chart of Accounts and Item Lists

- Update the Customer and Vendor Centers

- Adjust the new company file to follow the accrual basis of accounting

- Display and print accounting reports and financial statements

 The online course includes additional training and assessment resources. Reports created for the Chapter Problem can be uploaded for instructor review.

Chapter Introduction

In this chapter, you will learn how to create a new company file in QuickBooks. As you know, the four levels of operation for QuickBooks are New Company Setup, Lists/Centers, Activities, and Reports. In Chapters 2 through 5, you learned about and used the Lists/Centers, Activities, and Reports levels for both a service company and a merchandise company. In those chapters, you opened an existing company file, updated Lists/Centers, recorded Activities in the various windows, and viewed and printed Reports. You will now learn the first level of operation for QuickBooks: New Company Setup.

QuickBooks provides two methods of New Company Setup: Detailed Start and Express Start. Chapter 6 presents the Detailed Start method, and Chapter 7 presents the Express Start method.

QuickBooks provides two windows to assist with New Company Setup. One window is the QuickBooks Desktop Setup window which is where you select the method of New Company Setup.

When you choose the Detailed Start method at the QuickBooks Desktop Setup window, you are moved to the EasyStep Interview window, which is designed to assist you in creating and setting up a new company file. The EasyStep Interview window asks for basic information about your company and then asks a series of questions to help you customize QuickBooks for your company.

After completing the EasyStep Interview, you return to the QuickBooks Desktop Setup window, which then further assists you in setting up your new company file. The QuickBooks Desktop Setup window can be used to enter information on customers, vendors, services, and inventory part items. You do not have to use the QuickBooks Desktop Setup window to enter this information. However, the QuickBooks Desktop Setup window will be used in this chapter. Using the EasyStep Interview and QuickBooks Desktop Setup windows is only part of the process of setting up a company file. You then take the information set up in the EasyStep Interview and QuickBooks Desktop Setup windows and customize and update the information according to your company preferences. Finally, the new company file is prepared for the accrual basis of accounting.

In this chapter, you will create and set up a new company file for our sample company, Kristin Raina Interior Designs. It is assumed that Kristin Raina Interior Designs has been recording accounting activities using a manual accounting system and now will convert the company accounting records to QuickBooks.

QuickBooks versus Manual Accounting: New Company Setup

In a manual accounting system, a company's records are set up by creating the Chart of Accounts and the general ledger. The Chart of Accounts is the list of accounts (assets, liabilities, equity, revenues, and expenses) the company intends to use. The general ledger is the book of all accounts with the beginning balance for each account. If desired, subsidiary ledgers are also created and beginning balances recorded. The subsidiary ledgers typically include accounts receivable and accounts payable. If the perpetual inventory system is used, an inventory subsidiary ledger is also created.

In QuickBooks, a company's records are set up by creating a new company file and establishing the Chart of Accounts List. As the opening balances are entered, QuickBooks simultaneously sets up the general ledger. The Customer Center and Vendor Center are set up; these centers are equivalent to the accounts receivable and accounts payable subsidiary ledgers. The Item List, which is equivalent to an inventory subsidiary ledger, is set up. However, in QuickBooks, the Item List includes service revenue items and sales tax items in addition to inventory items.

In this chapter, you will first use the EasyStep Interview window to create a new company file, establish some preferences, and begin the Item List and Chart of Accounts List. After creating the company file, you leave the EasyStep Interview and then use the QuickBooks Desktop Setup window to enter information on customers, vendors, and inventory part items. This sets up the Customer Center and Vendor Center and adds to the Item List that was started in the EasyStep Interview. You will next customize and update the company file. Finally, you need to make three journal entries to complete the New Company Setup. One journal entry records the opening balance in the accounts that were not included in the EasyStep Interview or QuickBooks Desktop Setup windows; the other two journal entries reverse accounts QuickBooks sets up during New Company Setup that are not used in the accrual basis of accounting.

Chapter Problem

In this chapter, there is no prepared company file to open from the company files. Instead, you will create and set up the company file for Kristin Raina Interior Designs.

Assume that Kristin Raina began operating her interior design business in January 2022 and has maintained accounting records with a manual accounting system for January through March. Effective April 1, 2022, Kristin Raina will convert the company's accounting records to QuickBooks using the Detailed Start method.

As you set up the new company file, you will enter company information (name, address, tax identification numbers); general ledger account names and account numbers; customer information (name, address, telephone numbers, and so on) and outstanding balances; vendor information (name, address, telephone numbers, and so on) and outstanding balances; service items and billing amounts; inventory part items (name, cost, selling price, and quantity on hand); and sales tax information.

To begin New Company Setup:
1. Open QuickBooks.
2. At the No Company Open window, click *Create a new company* or click File and then click *New Company*. The QuickBooks Desktop Setup window appears with the *Let's set up your business!* page displayed. This is the page where you select the method of New Company Setup. See Figure 6–A.

Detailed
Start button

Detailed Start and EasyStep Interview Window

In New Company Setup, the first level of operation in QuickBooks, you will enter the information needed to create and set up a company file for Kristin Raina Interior Designs using the Detailed Start method, which uses the EasyStep Interview window.

The EasyStep Interview window is designed to guide you through the steps needed to create and set up a new company file. (EasyStep Interview is not the only way to create a company file in QuickBooks; an alternative method is covered in Chapter 7.)

With EasyStep Interview, you proceed through a series of pages by clicking the Next button. On each page, you enter basic company information and answer questions that QuickBooks uses to create the new company file. As you answer the questions, QuickBooks establishes some preferences for your company. Company preferences enable or disable features available in QuickBooks. When a feature is enabled, you will see that choice listed on the drop-down menu and on the Home page. If a feature is disabled, you will not see that choice on the drop-down menu or Home page.

The company information can later be edited by clicking Company and then *My Company*. The preferences can be edited by clicking Edit and then *Preferences*.

At any time, you can click the Leave button to leave the EasyStep Interview window. However, you are advised not to leave before saving the company file. If you leave the window before saving the company file, all the information will be lost.

If you leave the EasyStep Interview after saving the company file, QuickBooks goes to the No Company Open window. The next time you open the company file, you return to the EasyStep Interview window at the same page you left.

HINT

See Appendix F for a summary of using the Detailed Start method for New Company Setup.

To create a new company file using the Detailed Start method and the EasyStep Interview window:

1. At the QuickBooks Desktop Setup window, at the *Let's set up your business!* page, click the Detailed Start button. The EasyStep Interview window appears with the *Enter your company information* page displayed.

2. At the *Enter your company information* page, at the *Company name* field, type the company name CH6 *[Your Name]* Kristin Raina Interior Designs.

    When you tab to the *Legal name* field, the same name is automatically filled in. The legal name is the name that will be used on tax forms. If the company name and legal name are not the same, you can make any necessary changes. For our sample company, the company name and legal name are the same.

<table>
<tr><td>HINT</td></tr>
</table>

HINT

If you type the letter **M** in the *State* field, the first state that begins with *M (MA)* is displayed. To choose *MN,* keep pressing the M key. You will scroll through all the states beginning with M. An alternative is to click the drop-down arrow to display the list of states.

3. At the *Enter your company information* page, type the following information:

Tax ID:	33-4777781
Street address:	25 NE Johnson Street
City:	Minneapolis
State:	MN
Zip:	53402
Country:	U.S.
Phone:	651-555-1000
Fax:	651-555-2000
E-mail address:	KRID@ppi-edu.net

See Figure 6–B.

FIGURE 6–B
EasyStep Interview Window—Enter Your Company Information Page

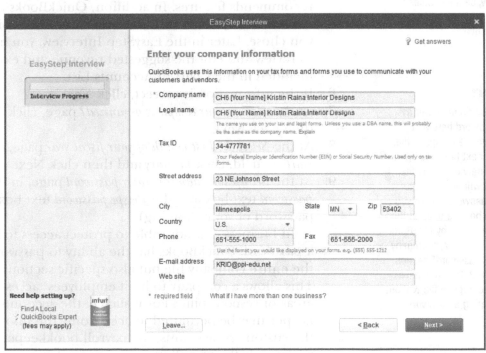

HINT

If you want to activate the Next button using the keyboard, press Alt + N.

4. If the information is correct, click Next. You are moved to the *Select your industry* page.

5. At the *Select your industry* page, scroll down the INDUSTRY list and click *General Product-based Business*. See Figure 6–C.

FIGURE 6–C
EasyStep Interview
Window—*Select Your
Industry* Page

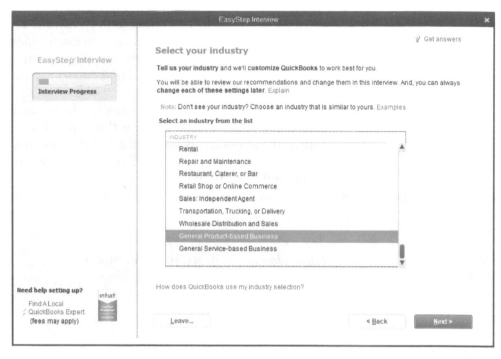

HINT

When you are in the EasyStep Interview window, all the choices at the main menu bar are inactive.

QuickBooks provides a list of sample industries to assist in creating your new company file. Based on the industry you select, QuickBooks asks a series of questions, and based on the responses, activates or recommends features. In addition, QuickBooks creates the Chart of Accounts List, which includes some accounts typical for the industry you chose. Later in the EasyStep Interview, you have the opportunity to review and edit the suggested revenue and expense accounts to be included in the Chart of Accounts List.

6. If the information is correct, click Next.
7. At the *How is your company organized?* page, click *Sole Proprietorship* and then click Next.
8. At the *Select the first month of your fiscal year* page, at the *My fiscal year starts in* field, click *January* and then click Next.
9. At the *Set up your administrator password* page, in the *Administrator password* text box and the *Retype password* text box, type Student1 (or a password of your choosing).

HINT

If you do not enter a password here and leave the company file, the next time you open the new company file, you will need to enter a password before you will be able to open the new company file. Refer to Chapter 7, "Company File Password" section, page 272, if you leave the company file without creating a password.

In business, it is advisable to protect access to financial records with a password. QuickBooks has the ability to password protect not only the entire company file but also specific sections of the company file. This allows a company to limit employees' access to their respective areas of responsibility. For instance, the accounts receivable bookkeeper may be permitted to access only the information pertaining to the customers' accounts, the payroll bookkeeper may be permitted to access only the payroll information, and so on.

10. Click Next.

HINT

See Appendix J for information on how to set up users.

HINT

In the *File name* text box, use the arrow keys to scroll through the entire name.

11. At the *Create your company file* page, click Next. The Filename for New Company dialog box appears.

12. Choose your subfolder in the *Save in* text box, and accept the file name **CH6 *[Your Name]* Kristin Raina Interior Designs.QBW**.

13. If the information is correct, click Save. The new company file has been created and saved.

    At this point, the company file has been saved. It is now safe to use the Leave button at any time from this point on. If you do leave the EasyStep Interview at this point, QuickBooks closes the company file. The next time you open QuickBooks and the company file, you are returned to the EasyStep Interview window and the last page you opened.

14. At the *Customizing QuickBooks for your business* page, read the page and then click Next.

15. At the *What do you sell?* page, click *Both services and products* and then click Next.

16. At the *Do you charge sales tax?* page, click *Yes* and then click Next.

17. At the *Do you want to create estimates in QuickBooks?* page, click *No* and then click Next.

18. At the *Tracking customer orders in QuickBooks* page, click *No* and then click Next.

19. At the *Using statements in QuickBooks* page, click *No* and then click Next.

20. At the *Using invoices in QuickBooks* page, click *Yes* and then click Next.

21. At the *Using progress invoicing* page, click *No* and then click Next.

22. At the *Managing bills you owe* page, click *Yes* and then click Next.

23. At the *Tracking inventory in QuickBooks* page, click *Yes* and then click Next.

24. At the *Tracking time in QuickBooks* page, click *No* and then click Next.

25. At the *Do you have employees?* page, click *No* and then click Next.

26. At the *Using accounts in QuickBooks* page, read the page and then click Next.

27. At the *Select a date to start tracking your finances* page, click *Use today's date or the first day of the quarter or month* and then choose *04/01/2022*.

    This identifies the date the company began to use QuickBooks. For our sample company, Kristin Raina Interior Designs, the fiscal start date is January 1, 2022. The QuickBooks start date is April 1, 2022. You will enter the balances as of April 1, which represent January 1 to March 31 activities, in the new company file as part of the New Company Setup. See Figure 6–D.

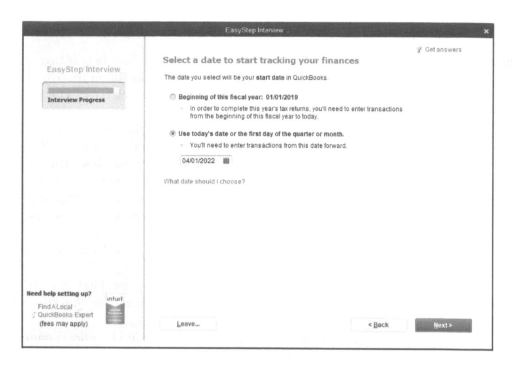

28. If the information is correct, click Next.

The *Review income and expense accounts* page appears. See Figure 6–E.

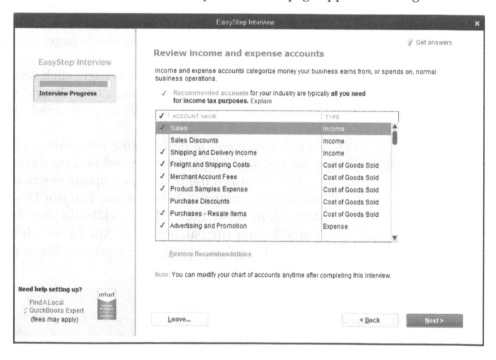

This page lists common Chart of Accounts income and expense accounts names. Each account with a check mark to the left of the account name is an account that QuickBooks recommends for your company based on the industry type you selected earlier in the EasyStep Interview window. You can remove the check mark for any account your company does not use, and you can insert a check mark for any account your company does use. At any time, you can click the

Restore Recommendations button to replace the original check marks inserted by QuickBooks.

Any account checked is created in the Chart of Accounts List by QuickBooks. After you finish the EasyStep Interview window, you can add, delete, and modify any account on the Chart of Accounts List using the procedures presented in Chapter 4.

29. Remove the check mark from each of the following accounts by clicking the check mark, since Kristin Raina Interior Designs does not use these accounts:

> Shipping and Delivery Income
> Freight and Shipping Costs
> Merchant Account Fees
> Product Samples Expense
> Purchases - Resale Items
> Automobile Expense
> Bank Service Charges
> Computer and Internet Expenses
> Dues and Subscriptions
> Meals and Entertainment
> Postage and Delivery
> Professional Fees
> Repairs and Maintenance
> Travel Expense

30. Insert a check mark to the left of each of the following accounts, as these are accounts Kristin Raina Interior Designs uses:

> Sales Discounts
> Janitorial Expense

31. Click Next. The EasyStep Interview is complete. The *Congratulations!* page appears.

32. Click Go to Setup.

After completing the EasyStep Interview window, you are returned to the QuickBooks Desktop Setup window with the *Get all the details into QuickBooks Desktop* page displayed. See Figure 6–F.

FIGURE 6–F
QuickBooks Desktop Setup Window—*Get All the Details into QuickBooks Desktop* Page

HINT
The Add button may change to Add More.

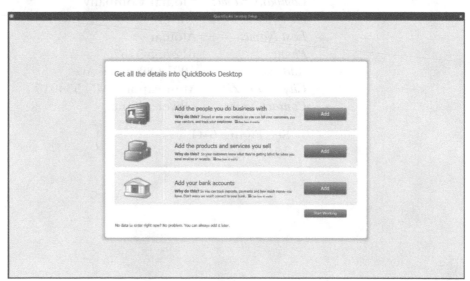

QuickBooks Desktop Setup Window

You can use the QuickBooks Desktop Setup window—*Get all the details into QuickBooks Desktop* page to enter your customers (Customer Center), vendors (Vendor Center), service items and inventory items (Item List), and banking (Cash - Operating) information, or you can go directly into QuickBooks (Start Working).

For Kristin Raina Interior Designs, you will use the QuickBooks Desktop Setup window to continue setting up the new company file and to create the Customer Center, create the Vendor Center, and add to the Item List that begins in EasyStep Interview.

If you wish to leave the QuickBooks Desktop Setup window, click the X. You will enter QuickBooks in the new company file. To return to the QuickBooks Desktop Setup window, click Company at the main menu bar and then click *Bulk Enter Business Details*.

HINT

See Appendix F for a summary of using the QuickBooks Desktop Setup window to enter data in New Company Setup.

HINT

If you leave the QuickBooks Desktop Setup window and the New Feature Tour window appears, click the X to close it. You can remove the Left Icon bar by clicking View and then clicking *Hide Icon Bar*. You can close the Home page by clicking the X.

Setting Up the Customer Center

The Customer Center records the information for all the customers with whom the company does business. Kristin Raina has 10 customers. Two of the customers have outstanding balances. When you record the outstanding balance, QuickBooks creates the accounts receivable for that customer.

To add customers to the Customer Center using the QuickBooks Desktop Setup window:

1. At the QuickBooks Desktop Setup window, at the *Get all the details into QuickBooks Desktop* page, in the *Add the people you do business with* section, click the Add button.
2. At the next *Add the people you do business with* page, click the *Paste from Excel or enter manually* button and then click Continue.
3. At the next *Add the people you do business with* page, in the *Customer* column, click *Select all* and all the circles are filled in the *Customer* column.
4. At the *Name* field in the first row, type Alomar Company. Press the Tab key to move to the next field.
5. Enter the following information in the appropriate columns:

Company Name:	Alomar Company
First Name:	Oliver
Last Name:	Alomar
Phone:	612-555-5757
Address:	1001 Oak Lake Ave.
City, State, Zip:	Minneapolis, MN 55401
Contact Name:	Oliver Alomar

   See Figure 6–G.

Select all

6. Add the remaining customers using the information in Table 6–1.

TABLE 6–1
Customers

Customer/ Company Name	Name/Contact	Phone	Address/ City, State, Zip
Barrera Bagel Barn	Belinda Barrera	612-555-1233	148 46th Ave. N Plymouth, MN 53406
Berger Bakery Company	Barry Berger	612-555-2240	18 N. Grand Ave. Minneapolis, MN 55403
Cook Caterers	Stephen Cook	612-555-7896	275 Oak Lake Ave. Minneapolis, MN 55401
Franco Films Co.	Fred Franco	612-555-4566	100 Pleasant Ave. S. Minneapolis, MN 55409
Guthrie, Jennie	Jennie Guthrie	651-555-1515	165 Terrace Ct. St. Paul, MN 55101
Hamilton Hotels	Hilda Hamilton	651-555-1050	1000 York Ave. St. Paul, MN 55101
Jones, Beverly	Beverly Jones	612-555-7778	333 York Circle Bloomington, MN 54603
Omari, Maria	Maria Omari	612-555-9999	210 NE Lowry Ave. Minneapolis, MN 54204
Plaza Pizza Palace	Mikey Plaza	612-555-9000	360 Border Ave. N Minneapolis, MN 46877

HINT

If you have information in an Excel spreadsheet, you can copy an entire column and paste it into the *Add the people you do business with* page. If you have difficulty pasting, press CTRL + V to paste.

After entering the information in Table 6–1, your screen should look like Figure 6–H.

7. If the information is correct, click Continue. At the next *Add the people you do business with* page, it should indicate that 10 contacts are ready to be added. If that is incorrect, you will have an opportunity to make corrections later. See Figure 6–I.

*Enter opening
balances* link

8. Click the *Enter opening balances* link. At the *Enter opening balances for your customers and vendors* page, enter the balances for the following customers and change all the dates to 04/01/2022:

Berger Bakery Company $600
Franco Films Co.   940

     See Figure 6–J.

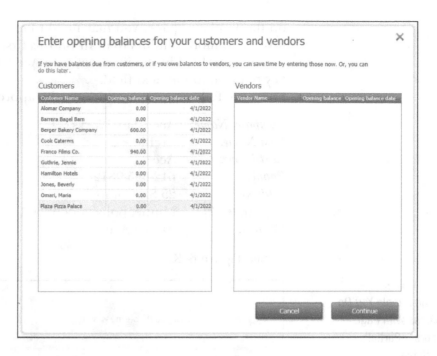

9. If the information is correct, click Continue. You are returned to the
    Add the people you do business with page.
10. Click Continue. If you don't click Continue here, none of the customers and opening balances will be saved.
11. You are returned to the QuickBooks Desktop Setup window—*Get all the details into QuickBooks* page.

ACCOUNTING CONCEPT

1200 Accounts Receivable		49900 Uncategorized Income	
Dr	Cr	Dr	Cr
600			600
940			940
Bal 1,540			Bal 1,540

Setting Up the Vendor Center

The Vendor Center records the information for all the vendors with whom the company does business. Kristin Raina has 17 vendors. Seven of the vendors have outstanding balances. When you record the outstanding balance, QuickBooks creates the accounts payable for that vendor.

To add vendors to the Vendor Center using the QuickBooks Desktop Setup window:

1. At the QuickBooks Desktop Setup window, at the *Get all the details into QuickBooks Desktop* page, in the Add the people you do business with section, click the Add More button.
2. At the *Add the people you do business with* page, click the Paste from Excel or enter manually button and then click Continue.
3. At the next *Add the people you do business with* page, in the *Vendor* column, click *Select all,* and all the circles are filled in the *Vendor* column

on the displayed page. You may need to check the *Vendor* column again if you add more vendors than fit on this first page.

4. At the *Name* field in the first row, type Ace Glass Works. Press the Tab key to move to the next field.

5. Enter the following information in the appropriate columns:

Company Name:	Ace Glass Works
First Name:	Archie
Last Name:	Ace
Phone:	612-555-9812
Address:	25 SE Como Ave.
City, State, Zip:	Minneapolis, MN 53602
Contact:	Archie Ace

See Figure 6–K.

FIGURE 6–K
Add the People You Do Business With Page—Vendors—Partially Completed

6. Add the remaining vendors using the information in Table 6–2.

TABLE 6–2
Vendors

Vendor/ Company Name	Name/Contact	Phone	Address/ City, State, Zip
Bell Carpet Design	Bill Bell	651-555-8823	55 North Main Ave. St. Paul, MN 54603
Cuza and Carl Associates	Carrie Cuza	651-555-8855	23 W. University Ave. St. Paul, MN 54603
Darren Tapestry	Donna Darren	612-555-2221	10 W. Larpenteur Ave. Minneapolis, MN 52604
Galeway Computers	Roger Rivera	617-555-4747	33 Route 10 Springfield, MA 24105
Grayson Graphics	Gregg Grayson	612-555-0002	56 Amity Way Bloomington, MN 53608
Jeter Janitorial Services	Jason Jeter	612-555-4444	233 Lilac Rd. Minneapolis, MN 54302
Kristin Raina	Kristin Raina		
Lumiare Lighting Company	Larry Lyght	612-555-4790	123 Glenwood Ave. Minneapolis, MN 53609

...continues

TABLE 6–2
Vendors...*continued*

Vendor/ Company Name	Name/Contact	Phone	Address/ City, State, Zip
Midwest Mutual Insurance Co.	Mike Mills	805-555-4545	3566 Broadway Chicago, IL 58303
Minn. Dept. of Revenue			
Minneapolis Electric & Gas Co.	Jack Watts	651-555-4949	150 Douglas Ave. St. Paul, MN 55303
Nordic Realty	Melanie Marx	612-555-3232	23 N. 12th St. Minneapolis, MN 53604
TwinCityTelCo	Terry Ameche	651-555-6667	3223 River Dr. St. Paul, MN 53908
Weaver Fabrics	Jon Weaver	612-555-8777	355 W. 70th St. Minneapolis, MN 53604
Williams Office Supply Company	Bernard Williams	612-555-2240	15 Grand Ave. S Minneapolis, MN 55404
[Your Name] Accounting Service	[Your Name]	612-555-2222	One Main Plaza St. Paul, MN 53602

Note: In the event that you do not have a person's name but instead have a department as a contact, you can still enter the information on the Address Info tab in the FULL NAME *field. For example, if the contact is* Customer Service, *you can enter* Customer *in the* First Name *field and* Service *in the* Last Name *field.*

After entering the information in Table 6–2, your screen should look like Figure 6–L.

FIGURE 6–L
Add the People You Do Business With Page— Vendors—Completed

Confirm that this number is *17.* Scroll down the list of vendors and make sure the *Vendor* option is selected in each line.

7. Scroll down the list of vendors and make sure the *Vendor* option is selected in each line.
8. If the information is correct, click Continue. At the next *Add the people you do business with* page, it should indicate that 17 contacts are ready to be added. If that is incorrect, you will have an opportunity to make corrections later.

HINT

Exercise care in clicking the *Enter opening balances* link. If you do not click the *Enter opening balances* link here, you will subsequently have to reenter the vendors with balances.

9. Click the *Enter opening balances* link. At the *Enter opening balances for customers and vendors* page, enter the balances for the following vendors and change all of the dates to 04/01/2022:

Ace Glass Works	$1,500
Bell Carpet Design	2,000
Cuza and Carl Associates	400
Galeway Computers	2,600
Midwest Mutual Insurance Co.	2,400
Minneapolis Electric & Gas Co.	450
Williams Office Supply Company	400

See Figure 6–M.

FIGURE 6–M
Enter Opening Balances for Your Customers and Vendors Page— Vendors—Completed

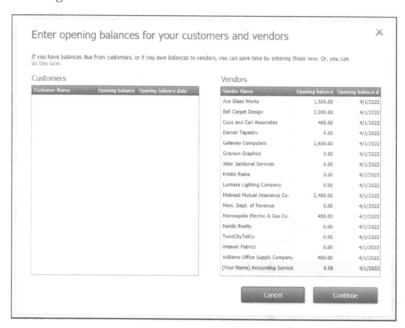

10. If the information is correct, click Continue. You are returned to the *Add the people you do business with* page.
11. Click Continue. If you don't click Continue here, none of the vendors and opening balances will be saved.
12. You are returned to the QuickBooks Desktop Setup window—*Get all the details into QuickBooks Desktop* page.

ACCOUNTING CONCEPT

69800 Uncategorized Expenses		2010 Accounts Payable	
Dr	Cr	Dr	Cr
1,500			1,500
2,000			2,000
400			400
2,600			2,600
2,400			2,400
450			450
400			400
Bal 9,750			Bal 9,750

Adding to the Item List

The Item List stores information about the service items, the inventory part items, and the sales tax. As transactions are recorded in the Activities windows, QuickBooks uses information in the Item List to record the transaction in the correct accounts. Kristin Raina has two service items and four inventory part items. When you record the quantity on hand for an inventory part, QuickBooks creates the inventory asset for that inventory part.

To add service items to the Item List using the QuickBooks Desktop Setup window:

1. At the QuickBooks Desktop Setup window, at the *Get all the details into QuickBooks Desktop* page, in the Add the products and services you sell section, click the Add button.
2. At the *Add the products and services you sell* page, click the *Service* option and then click Continue.
3. At the *Name* field in the first row, type Design Services.
4. At the *Description* field, type Design Services.
5. At the *Price* field, type 60.
6. Enter the following information for the next service item:

Name:	Decorating Services
Description:	Decorating Services
Price:	50

See Figure 6–N.

FIGURE 6–N
Add the Products and Services You Sell Page—Services Items—Completed

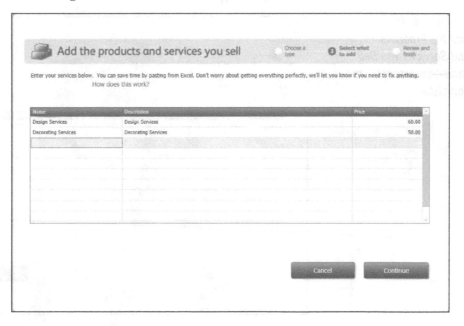

7. If the information is correct, click Continue. You are returned to the *Add the products and services you sell* page, which should indicate 2 Items are ready to be added. If that is incorrect, you will have an opportunity to make corrections later.
8. Click Continue. If you don't click Continue here, none of the service items will be saved. You are returned to the QuickBooks Desktop Setup window—*Get all the details into QuickBooks Desktop* page.

To add inventory part items to the Item List using the QuickBooks Desktop Setup window:

1. At the QuickBooks Desktop Setup window, at the *Get all the details into QuickBooks Desktop* page, in the *Add the products and services you sell* section, click the Add More button.
2. At the *Add the products and services you sell* page, click the *Inventory part* option and then click Continue.
3. At the *Name* field in the first row, type Carpets.
4. At the *Description* field, type Carpets.
5. At the *Price* field, type 400.
6. At the *Cost* field, type 200.
7. At the *On Hand* field, type 4. When you move to the next field, the amount in the *Total Value* field is computed automatically based on cost multiplied by quantity.
8. At the *As of date* field, choose *04/01/2022*.
9. Add the remaining inventory part items using the information in Table 6–3.

TABLE 6–3
Inventory Part Items

Name and Description	Price	Cost	On Hand	Total Value
Draperies	$250	$125	8	$1,000
Lamps	200	100	10	1,000
Mirrors	300	150	6	900

After entering the information in Table 6–3, your screen should look like Figure 6–O.

FIGURE 6–O
Add the Products and Services You Sell Page—Inventory Parts—Completed

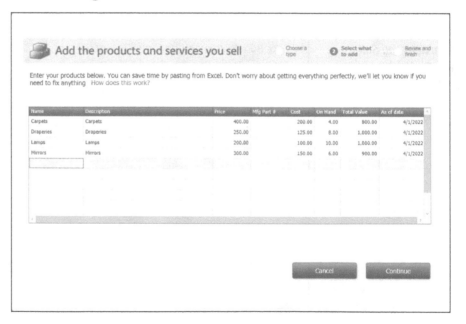

10. If the information is correct, click Continue. You are returned to the *Add the products and services you sell* page, which should indicate 4 Items are ready to be added. If that is incorrect, you will have an opportunity to make corrections later.
11. Click Continue. If you don't click Continue here, none of the inventory part items and opening balances will be saved. You are returned to the QuickBooks Desktop Setup window—*Get all the details into Quick-Books Desktop* page.

ACCOUNTING CONCEPT

Inventory Asset		Opening Balance Equity	
Dr	Cr	Dr	Cr
800			800
1,000			1,000
1,000			1,000
900			900

HINT

Recall that you can change the default so the Home page does not appear when opening a company file. Click Edit at the main menu bar and then click *Preferences*. In the left panel, click the Desktop View icon. Choose the My Preferences tab. Remove the check mark to the left of *Show Home page when opening a company file* and then click OK.

12. Exit the QuickBooks Desktop Setup window by clicking the X. You enter QuickBooks in the new company file. If the New Feature Tour window appears, click the X to close it. The QuickBooks Home page and the Left Icon bar appear. Close the Home page by clicking the X, and remove the Left Icon bar by clicking View and then clicking *Hide Icon Bar*.

Reviewing EasyStep Interview and QuickBooks Desktop Setup Information

The EasyStep Interview created the Chart of Accounts List and the Item List. It also established preferences that enabled certain features in QuickBooks. The activated preferences provide for choices to be listed on the drop-down menus and the Home page, and they allow for accessing activity windows. The QuickBooks Desktop Setup created the Customer Center and Vendor Center and added the service items and inventory part items to the Item List.

Chart of Accounts List

Reviewing the Chart of Accounts List allows you to see the accounts set up as part of the EasyStep Interview and QuickBooks Desktop Setup.

To view the Chart of Accounts List:
1. At the main menu bar, click Lists and then click *Chart of Accounts*. The Chart of Accounts List appears. See Figure 6–P.

FIGURE 6–P
Chart of Accounts List
Window

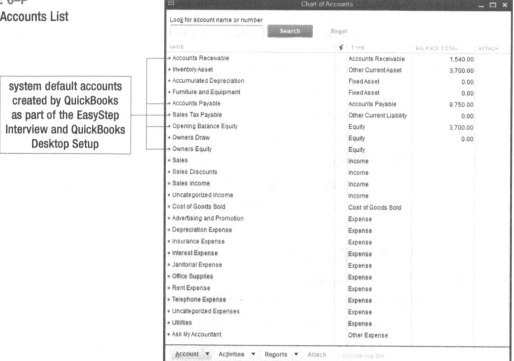

system default accounts created by QuickBooks as part of the EasyStep Interview and QuickBooks Desktop Setup

You can correct any errors by adding, deleting, or editing an account, as illustrated in Chapter 4.

Upon reviewing the Chart of Accounts List, observe that Kristin Raina Interior Designs uses many more accounts that are not included in the Chart of Accounts List created by the EasyStep Interview and QuickBooks Desktop Setup or uses different account names. Notice also that an account number was not assigned to each account.

2. Close the Chart of Accounts List.

Item List

Reviewing the Item List allows you to see the items set up as part of the EasyStep Interview and QuickBooks Desktop Setup.

To view the Item List:

1. At the main menu bar, click Lists and then click *Item List.* The Item List appears. See Figure 6–Q.

FIGURE 6–Q
Item List Window

At the QuickBooks Desktop Setup window, at the *Add new products and services* page, when you added service items and inventory part items, these items were added to the Item List.

2. Double-click the *Decorating Services* service item. The Edit Item window appears. See Figure 6–R.

FIGURE 6–R
Edit Item Window—
Service Item

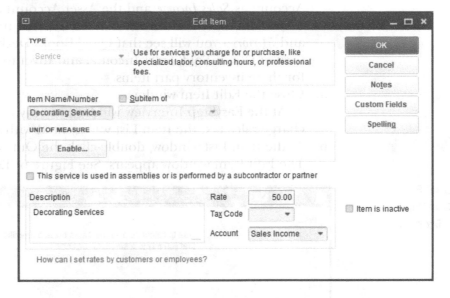

When this service item was created, QuickBooks Desktop Setup recorded *Sales Income* in the *Account* field. If you double-click *Design Services* at the Item List window, you will see that QuickBooks Desktop Setup also uses Sales Income as the account for Design Services.

3. Close the Edit Item window.
4. At the Item List window, double-click the *Carpets* inventory part item. The Edit Item window appears. See Figure 6–S.

FIGURE 6–S
Edit Item Window—
Inventory Part Item

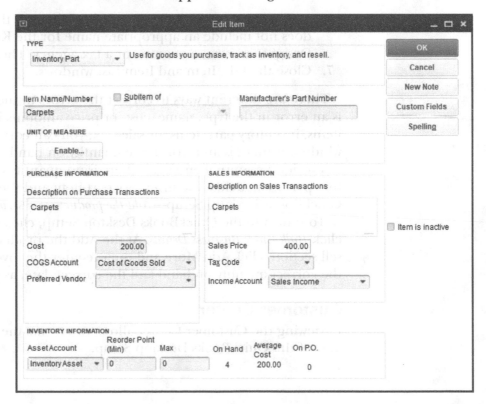

When this inventory part item was created, QuickBooks Desktop Setup recorded the COGS Account as *Cost of Goods Sold*, the Income Account as *Sales Income*, and the Asset Account as *Inventory Asset*. If you double-click each of the other inventory part items—*Draperies, Lamps,* and *Mirrors*—you will see that QuickBooks Desktop Setup also used Cost of Goods Sold, Sales Income, and Inventory Asset as the accounts for these inventory part items.

5. Close the Edit Item window.

At the EasyStep Interview window, when you indicated *Yes*, you do charge sales tax, the Item List was created with this sales tax item.

6. At the Item List window, double-click the Out of State Sales Tax item. The Edit Item window appears. See Figure 6–T.

FIGURE 6–T
Edit Item Window—
Sales Tax Item

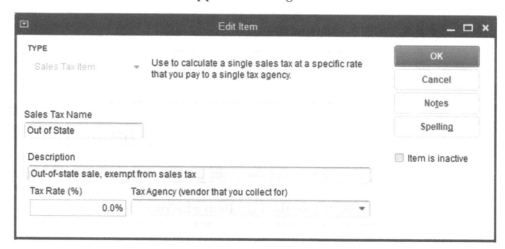

The EasyStep Interview created this item in the Item List, but it does not include an appropriate name for the Kristin Raina Interior Designs tax item, a tax rate, or a tax agency. These will be added later.

7. Close the Edit Item and Item List windows.

There are different ways to correct the errors in the Item List. If there is an error in the type, name, cost, or price amounts in any of the service items, inventory part items, or sales tax, you can correct it in the Edit Item window. If there is an error in the quantity on hand, you can correct it when viewing journal entries. If there is no quantity on hand for an inventory part item, delete the inventory part item and then go back to the QuickBooks Desktop Setup—*Add the products and services you sell* page.

To return to the QuickBooks Desktop Setup, click Company and then click *Bulk Enter Business Details*. At the Add the products and services you sell section, click Add More and then reenter the inventory part item with the correct quantity on hand and the correct date, as previously illustrated.

Customer Center

Reviewing the Customer Center allows you to see the customers set up as part of the QuickBooks Desktop Setup.

To review the Customer Center:

1. At the main menu bar, click Customers and then click *Customer Center*. The Customer Center appears. See Figure 6–U.

FIGURE 6–U
Customer Center Window

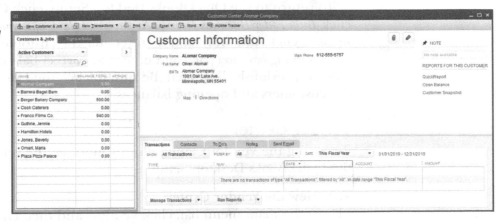

2. Double-click *Berger Bakery Company*. The Edit Customer window appears. See Figure 6–V.

FIGURE 6–V
Edit Customer Window

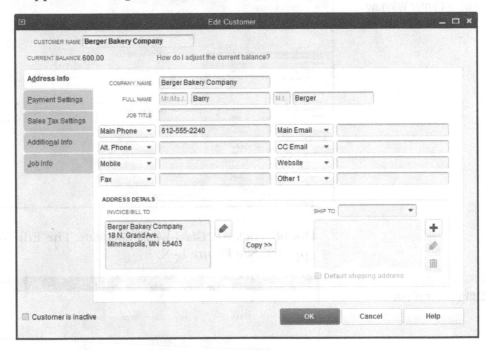

QuickBooks created this customer based on the information entered in QuickBooks Desktop Setup—*Add the people you do business with* pages. If you entered an opening balance, the balance is displayed in the *CURRENT BALANCE* field. If you did not enter an opening balance, the *CURRENT BALANCE* field indicates a zero. You can correct all the information in the Edit Customer window except the current balance.

3. Close the Edit Customer window and the Customer Center window.

There are different ways to correct the errors in the Customer Center. If there is an error in the name, address, or phone number for any of the customers, you can correct it in the Edit Customer window. If there is an error in the current balance, you can correct it when viewing journal entries. If there is no current balance for a customer with an outstanding balance, delete the customer and then go back to the QuickBooks Desktop Setup—*Add the people you do business with* pages.

To return to the QuickBooks Desktop Setup, click Company and then click *Bulk Enter Business Details.* At the *Add the people you do business with* section, click Add More and then reenter the customer. Continue to the *Enter opening balances* page and enter the correct balance and the correct date, as previously illustrated. Be sure to click the Continue button to save the customers and opening balances.

Vendor Center

Reviewing the Vendor Center allows you to see the vendors set up as part of the QuickBooks Desktop Setup.

To review the Vendor Center:

1. At the main menu bar, click Vendors and then click *Vendor Center.* The Vendor Center appears. See Figure 6–W.

FIGURE 6–W
Vendor Center Window

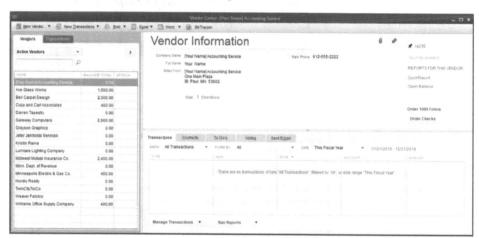

2. Double-click *Ace Glass Works Company.* The Edit Vendor window appears. See Figure 6–X.

FIGURE 6–X
Edit Vendor Window

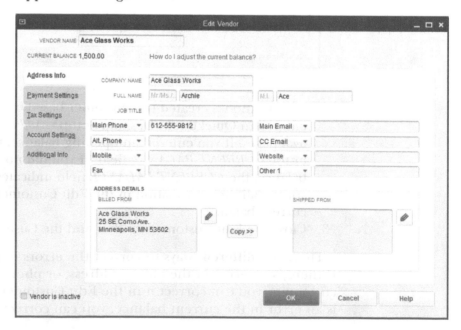

QuickBooks created this vendor based on the information entered in QuickBooks Desktop Setup—*Add the people you do business with* pages. If you entered an opening balance, the balance is displayed in the *CURRENT BALANCE* field. If you did not enter an opening balance, the *CURRENT BALANCE* field indicates a zero. You can correct all the information in the Edit Vendor window except the current balance.

3. Close the Edit Vendor window and the Vendor Center window.

There are different ways to correct an error in the Vendor Center. If there is an error in the company name, address, or phone number for any of the vendors, you can correct it in the Edit Vendor window. If there is an error in the current balance, you can correct it when viewing journal entries. If there is no current balance for a vendor with an outstanding balance, delete the vendor and then go back to the QuickBooks Desktop Setup—*Add the people you do business with* pages.

To return to the QuickBooks Desktop Setup, click Company and then click *Bulk Enter Business Details.* At the *Add the people you do business with* section, click Add More and then reenter the vendor. Continue to the *Enter opening balances* page and enter the correct balance and the correct date, as previously illustrated. Be sure to click the Continue button to save the vendors and opening balances.

Journal Report

Reviewing the *Journal* report allows you to see the journal entries created as part of the QuickBooks Desktop Setup.

To view and print the *Journal* report:
1. At the main menu bar, click Reports and then click *Accountant & Taxes.*
2. At the Accountant & Taxes submenu, click *Journal.* If the Collapsing and Expanding Transactions message appears, read the message, insert a check mark in the box to the left of *Do not display this message in the future,* and then click OK.
3. At the *From* and *To* fields, choose *04/01/2022* and *04/01/2022* and then click the Refresh button at the top of the report.
4. Print the report. Your printout should look like Figure 6–Y.

FIGURE 6–Y
Journal Report

CH6 [Your Name] Kristin Raina Interior Designs
Journal
April 1, 2022

Trans #	Type	Date	Num	Adj	Name	Memo	Account	Debit	Credit
1	Invoice	04/01/2022			Berger Bakery Company	Opening balance	Accounts Receivable	600.00	
					Berger Bakery Company	Opening balance	Uncategorized Income		600.00
								600.00	600.00
2	Invoice	04/01/2022			Franco Films Co.	Opening balance	Accounts Receivable	940.00	
					Franco Films Co.	Opening balance	Uncategorized Income		940.00
								940.00	940.00
3	Bill	04/01/2022			Ace Glass Works	Opening balance	Accounts Payable		1,500.00
					Ace Glass Works	Opening balance	Uncategorized Expenses	1,500.00	
								1,500.00	1,500.00
4	Bill	04/01/2022			Bell Carpet Design	Opening balance	Accounts Payable		2,000.00
					Bell Carpet Design	Opening balance	Uncategorized Expenses	2,000.00	
								2,000.00	2,000.00
5	Bill	04/01/2022			Cuza and Carl Associates	Opening balance	Accounts Payable		400.00
					Cuza and Carl Associates	Opening balance	Uncategorized Expenses	400.00	
								400.00	400.00
6	Bill	04/01/2022			Galeway Computers	Opening balance	Accounts Payable		2,600.00
					Galeway Computers	Opening balance	Uncategorized Expenses	2,600.00	
								2,600.00	2,600.00
7	Bill	04/01/2022			Midwest Mutual Insurance Co.	Opening balance	Accounts Payable		2,400.00
					Midwest Mutual Insurance Co.	Opening balance	Uncategorized Expenses	2,400.00	
								2,400.00	2,400.00
8	Bill	04/01/2022			Minneapolis Electric & Gas Co.	Opening balance	Accounts Payable		450.00
					Minneapolis Electric & Gas Co.	Opening balance	Uncategorized Expenses	450.00	
								450.00	450.00
9	Bill	04/01/2022			Williams Office Supply Company	Opening balance	Accounts Payable		400.00
					Williams Office Supply Company	Opening balance	Uncategorized Expenses	400.00	
								400.00	400.00
10	Inventory Adjust	04/01/2022			Carpets Opening balance	Opening Balance Equity			800.00
					Carpets Opening balance	Inventory Asset		800.00	
								800.00	800.00
11	Inventory Adjust	04/01/2022			Draperies Opening balance	Opening Balance Equity			1,000.00
					Draperies Opening balance	Inventory Asset		1,000.00	
								1,000.00	1,000.00
12	Inventory Adjust	04/01/2022			Lamps Opening balance	Opening Balance Equity			1,000.00
					Lamps Opening balance	Inventory Asset		1,000.00	
								1,000.00	1,000.00
13	Inventory Adjust	04/01/2022			Mirrors Opening balance	Opening Balance Equity			900.00
					Mirrors Opening balance	Inventory Asset		900.00	
								900.00	900.00
TOTAL								14,990.00	14,990.00

As you added customers, vendors, and inventory part items at the appropriate pages in QuickBooks Desktop Setup, behind the scenes, QuickBooks recorded the information in general journal format and updated the appropriate balances.

In the *Journal* report, QuickBooks recorded 13 journal entries based on information recorded in the QuickBooks Desktop Setup. The journal entries can be categorized as follows:

- The two journal entries labeled as *Invoice* were created when customers with balances were recorded at the *Add the people you do business with* pages. QuickBooks debits the Accounts Receivable with the customers' outstanding balances and credits an account called *Uncategorized Income*.
- The seven journal entries labeled as *Bill* were created when vendors with outstanding balances were recorded at the *Add the people you do business with* pages. QuickBooks credits the Accounts Payable with the vendors' outstanding balances and debits an account called *Uncategorized Expenses*.
- The four journal entries labeled as *Inventory Adjust* were created when the inventory part items with balances were recorded at the *Add the products and services you sell* page. QuickBooks credits the Opening Balance Equity account and debits the Inventory Asset account with the total value for each inventory part item.

5. Close the *Journal* report. If you receive the Memorize Report message, insert a check mark to the left of *Do not display this message in the future* and then click No.

If you determine there is an error in the *Journal* report, you can "drill down" to the original source, as shown in prior chapters. The original source you "drill down" to is based on the transaction type. The transaction type is the same as shown in prior chapters.

For a transaction type of Invoice, if you double-click that transaction, you are drilled down to the Create Invoices window. You can make corrections to a customer's opening balance or date in this window.

For a transaction type of Bill, if you double-click that transaction, you are drilled down to the Enter Bills window. You can make corrections to a vendor's opening balance or date in this window.

For a transaction type of Inventory Adjust, if you double-click that transaction, you are drilled down to the Adjust Quantity/Value on Hand window. You can make corrections to an inventory part quantity on hand or date in this window. The value of the inventory part item is automatically computed by QuickBooks as the quantity on hand multiplied by the cost for the inventory part. If you change the quantity on hand in the Adjust Quantity/Value on Hand window but the value does not change to the correct amount, go to the Item List, edit the inventory part item, and make sure the cost is the correct amount.

Trial Balance

Reviewing the Trial Balance allows you to see the balances in the accounts you created as part of the QuickBooks Desktop Setup.

To view the Trial Balance:
1. At the main menu bar, click Reports and then click *Accountant & Taxes*.
2. At the Accountant & Taxes submenu, click *Trial Balance*.
3. At the *From* and *To* fields, choose *04/01/2022* and *04/01/2022* and then click the Refresh button at the top of the report. See Figure 6–Z.

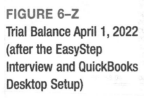

FIGURE 6–Z
Trial Balance April 1, 2022 (after the EasyStep Interview and QuickBooks Desktop Setup)

Note the following on the Trial Balance:
• The amount in the Accounts Receivable account equals the amount in the Uncategorized Income account.

- The amount in the Inventory Asset account equals the amount in the Opening Balance Equity account.
- The amount in the Accounts Payable account equals the amount in the Uncategorized Expenses account.

4. Close the report.

Figure 6–AA shows the Trial Balance from **EX5** *[Your Name]* **Kristin Raina Interior Designs**. It reflects the activities of January 1 to March 31, 2022, which were recorded in Chapters 2 through 5. Compare the Trial Balance of April 1, 2022 (Figure 6–Z, page 215) with the Trial Balance of March 31, 2022 (Figure 6–AA).

FIGURE 6–AA
Trial Balance
March 31, 2022
(from Chapter 5)

EX5 [Your Name] Kristin Raina Interior Designs
Trial Balance
As of March 31, 2022

Accrual Basis

	Mar 31, 22	
	Debit	Credit
1010 · Cash - Operating	50,855.38	
1200 · Accounts Receivable	1,540.00	
1250 · Undeposited Funds	0.00	
1260 · Inventory of Carpets	800.00	
1265 · Inventory of Draperies	1,000.00	
1270 · Inventory of Lamps	1,000.00	
1275 · Inventory of Mirrors	900.00	
1300 · Design Supplies	200.00	
1305 · Office Supplies	250.00	
1410 · Prepaid Advertising	500.00	
1420 · Prepaid Insurance	2,200.00	
1700 · Furniture:1725 · Furniture, Cost	12,000.00	
1700 · Furniture:1750 · Accum. Dep., Furniture		100.00
1800 · Computers:1825 · Computers, Cost	3,600.00	
1800 · Computers:1850 · Accum. Dep., Computers		60.00
2010 · Accounts Payable		9,750.00
2020 · Notes Payable		7,000.00
2030 · Interest Payable		50.00
2200 · Sales Tax Payable	0.00	
3010 · Kristin Raina, Capital		50,000.00
3020 · Kristin Raina, Drawings	400.00	
4010 · Design Services		4,980.00
4020 · Decorating Services		3,400.00
4060 · Sale of Carpets		2,400.00
4065 · Sale of Draperies		1,000.00
4070 · Sale of Lamps		1,200.00
4075 · Sale of Mirrors		900.00
4100 · Sales Discounts	84.62	
5060 · Cost of Carpets Sold	1,200.00	
5065 · Cost of Draperies Sold	500.00	
5070 · Cost of Lamps Sold	600.00	
5075 · Cost of Mirrors Sold	450.00	
5900 · Inventory Adjustment	150.00	
6020 · Accounting Expense	300.00	
6050 · Advertising Expense	100.00	
6175 · Deprec. Exp., Furniture	100.00	
6185 · Deprec. Exp., Computers	60.00	
6200 · Insurance Expense	200.00	
6300 · Janitorial Expenses	125.00	
6325 · Office Supplies Expense	150.00	
6400 · Rent Expense	800.00	
6450 · Telephone Expense	275.00	
6500 · Utilities Expense	450.00	
7000 · Interest Expense	50.00	
TOTAL	**80,840.00**	**80,840.00**

Although the EasyStep Interview and QuickBooks Desktop Setup guide you in creating a new company file, they do not enter all the information for a company. Upon completion of the next parts of New Company Setup—customizing and updating the new company file and preparing for the accrual basis of accounting—the trial balance of April 1 in this chapter will be the same as the trial balance of March 31 from Chapter 5.

Profit & Loss Standard (Income Statement) Report

Reviewing the *Profit & Loss Standard* report allows you to see the balances created as part of the QuickBooks Desktop Setup that flow into the *Profit & Loss Standard* report.

To view the *Profit & Loss Standard* report:

1. At the main menu bar, click Reports and then click *Company & Financial.*
2. At the Company & Financial submenu, click *Profit & Loss Standard.*
3. At the *From* and *To* fields, choose *01/01/2022* and *04/01/2022* and then click the Refresh button at the top of the report. See Figure 6–BB.

FIGURE 6–BB
Profit & Loss Standard Report

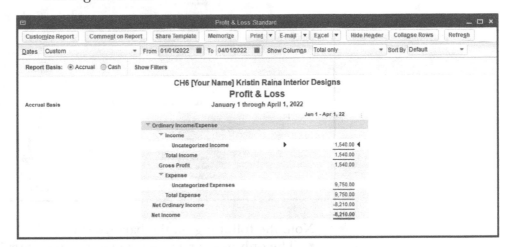

The *Profit & Loss Standard* report indicates only Uncategorized Income and Uncategorized Expenses. These amounts are off-setting amounts of the Accounts Receivable and Accounts Payable accounts, respectively. This is not a proper representation of the income and expenses of this company.

4. Close the report.

Balance Sheet Standard Report

Reviewing the *Balance Sheet Standard* report allows you to see the balances created as part of the QuickBooks Desktop Setup that flow into the *Balance Sheet Standard* report.

To display the *Balance Sheet Standard* report:

1. At the main menu bar, click Reports and then click *Company & Financial.*
2. At the Company & Financial submenu, click *Balance Sheet Standard.*
3. At the *As of* field, choose *04/01/2022* and then click the Refresh button at the top of the report. See Figure 6–CC.

FIGURE 6–CC
Balance Sheet Standard
Report

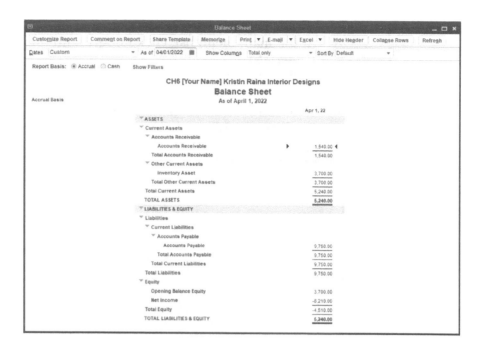

Note the following on the balance sheet:
- The only assets recorded so far are Accounts Receivable and Inventory Asset.
- The only liability recorded so far is Accounts Payable.
- The balance in the Opening Balance Equity account is the amount in Inventory Asset.
- The net income is incorrect as seen in the Income Statement (*Profit & Loss* report) because of incomplete information.

4. Close the report.

New Company Setup

Customizing the New Company File

When you use the EasyStep Interview and QuickBooks Desktop Setup windows, only part of the New Company Setup is completed. The EasyStep Interview window is used to create the new company file; enable or disable some preferences; record a sales tax item, which begins the Item List; and begin the setup of the Chart of Accounts List. When you enter information in the QuickBooks Desktop Setup window, you create the Customer Center, create the Vendor Center, and update the Item List to include service items and inventory part items. At the same time, the information entered in the QuickBooks Desktop Setup window records opening balances for Accounts Receivable, Accounts Payable, and Inventory Asset.

The next part of the process is to continue with the information set up in the EasyStep Interview and QuickBooks Desktop Setup windows to customize the new company file according to your company's preferences, update the Lists/Centers as needed, and prepare the company file for the accrual basis of accounting by recording three journal entries.

Customizing the Chart of Accounts List

You will customize the Chart of Accounts for Kristin Raina by enabling the account numbers feature and then editing the account numbers and names assigned by QuickBooks.

Adding Account Numbers

By default, QuickBooks does not use account numbers. This can be seen in the Chart of Accounts List and in the individual accounts.

To view an account in Edit mode:
1. At the main menu bar, click Lists and then click *Chart of Accounts*.
2. At the Chart of Accounts window, select the *Accounts Receivable* account.
3. Click the Account menu button.
4. At the Account button drop-down menu, click *Edit Account*. Notice that there is no field in which to place an account number.
5. Close the Edit account and Chart of Accounts List windows.

To add account numbers to the Chart of Accounts List, you must activate the account numbers feature in the Preferences window.

To activate the account numbers feature:
1. At the main menu bar, click Edit and then click *Preferences*. The Preferences window appears.

    In the left panel of the window are 23 icons, which represent the different categories of features. For each category, there is a My Preferences tab and a Company Preferences tab. The Company Preferences tab is used for most customizations when setting up a new company file. The My Preferences tab records the preferences for each user on their own personal computer. When using the EasyStep Interview window, most preferences are established based on the responses to the questions in the EasyStep Interview.
2. In the left panel of the Preferences window, click the Accounting icon.
3. Click the Company Preferences tab.
4. In the ACCOUNTS section, insert a check mark in the box to the left of *Use account numbers* to turn on the account numbers feature. See Figure 6–DD.

FIGURE 6–DD
Preferences Window—
Accounting—Company
Preferences Tab

Use account numbers option

warning options

5. If the information is correct, click OK. The account *Number* field now appears in the New Account and Edit Account windows in the Chart of Accounts List.

Editing Account Numbers and Names

When you activate the account numbers feature, QuickBooks assigns account numbers to most accounts. You can change or delete these numbers.

To edit the account numbers and names:

1. At the main menu bar, click Lists and then click *Chart of Accounts.*
2. At the Chart of Accounts window, select the *Furniture and Equipment* account.
3. Click the Account menu button.
4. At the Account button drop-down menu, click *Edit Account.* Notice that a *Number* field has been added.
5. At the *Number* field, type 1700, and at the *Account Name* field, delete the text *and Equipment.* See Figure 6–EE.

FIGURE 6–EE
Edit Account Window—
Furniture—Number
Added and Account
Name Edited

6. If the information is correct, click the Save & Close button.
7. Edit each of the accounts created by QuickBooks, changing the account number and name as listed on the next page. If an edited name is not listed, keep the name assigned by QuickBooks.

HINT

To edit an account in the Chart of Accounts List window, select the account, click the Account button, and then click the Edit button. Do not double-click the account.

QuickBooks		Edited	
Number	Account Name	Number	Account Name
17000	Accumulated Depreciation	1750	Accum. Dep., Furniture [Subaccount of 1700 Furniture]
30800	Owners Draw	3020	Kristin Raina, Drawings
	Sales Income	4060	Sale of Carpets
48300	Sales Discounts	4100	
60000	Advertising and Promotion	6050	Advertising Expense
62400	Depreciation Expense	6175	Deprec. Exp., Furniture
63300	Insurance Expense	6200	
63400	Interest Expense	7000	[Account Type: Other Expense]
63500	Janitorial Expense	6300	
64900	Office Supplies	6325	Office Supplies Expense
67100	Rent Expense	6400	
68100	Telephone Expense	6450	
68600	Utilities	6500	Utilities Expense
80000	Ask My Accountant	6020	Accounting Expense [Account Type: Expense]

HINT

As an alternative to selecting an account and then clicking the Account button, you can right-click an account and then choose *Edit Account* from the shortcut menu.

8. Close the Chart of Accounts List.

Deleting an Account

As part of the EasyStep Interview and QuickBooks Desktop Setup, QuickBooks created two sales accounts: Sales Income and 47900 Sales. The Sales Income account was not assigned an account number by QuickBooks but was the revenue account QuickBooks used in the Item List whenever an income account was needed. This account now has the number *4060*, and the name has been changed to *Sale of Carpets*. Kristin Raina does not need the 47900 Sales account and will delete it.

To delete an account:

1. At the main menu bar, click Lists and then click *Chart of Accounts.*
2. At the Chart of Accounts window, select the *47900 Sales* account.
3. Click the Account menu button.
4. At the Account button drop-down menu, click *Delete Account.*
5. At the Delete Account warning, click OK. The account is now deleted from the Chart of Accounts.

The customized Chart of Accounts List appears in Figure 6–FF.

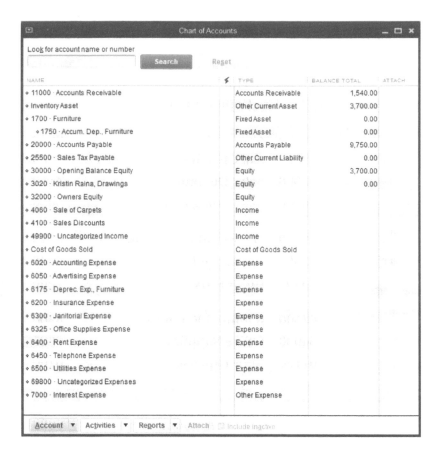

6. Close the Chart of Accounts List window.

Customizing System Default Accounts

As you saw in prior chapters, QuickBooks establishes default accounts and uses those accounts when recording transactions in the Activities windows. QuickBooks looks for these accounts in the Chart of Accounts List; if it cannot find an account, it creates one. Some system default accounts you have learned so far are Accounts Receivable, Undeposited Funds, Accounts Payable, Sales Tax Payable, Inventory Asset, and Cost of Goods Sold. Other system default accounts include the equity accounts (capital and accumulated earnings).

When you created the company file using the EasyStep Interview and QuickBooks Desktop Setup, QuickBooks created some of the system default accounts (Accounts Receivable, Accounts Payable, Sales Tax Payable, and the equity accounts) as part of the Chart of Accounts, as shown in Figure 6–P on page 208. You will customize the system default accounts that were created as part of the EasyStep Interview (Sales Tax Payable and the equity accounts) and QuickBooks Desktop Setup (Accounts Receivable and Accounts Payable) by editing the account names and numbers to follow the company's pattern for naming and numbering accounts on the Chart of Accounts List. You will then learn how to force QuickBooks to create additional system default accounts that were not created as part of the EasyStep Interview or QuickBooks Desktop Setup (Undeposited Funds, Inventory Asset, and Cost of Goods Sold). After QuickBooks creates the additional system default accounts, you will then customize these account names and numbers.

Customizing System Default Accounts
Created in a New Company File

When you created the company file and indicated the company was a sole proprietorship, QuickBooks automatically created three equity accounts: Opening Balance Equity, Owners Draw, and Owners Equity. When you activated the sales tax feature in the EasyStep Interview window, QuickBooks created a Sales Tax Payable account. When you added each customer in QuickBooks Desktop Setup, QuickBooks created the Accounts Receivable account. When you added each vendor in QuickBooks Desktop Setup, QuickBooks created the Accounts Payable account. When you added each inventory part in QuickBooks Desktop Setup, QuickBooks created the Inventory Asset and Cost of Goods Sold accounts. The numbers and names for all these accounts can be edited. The Opening Balance Equity account will be renamed as *Kristin Raina, Capital*, and the Owners Draw account was already renamed *Kristin Raina, Drawings*. QuickBooks uses the Opening Balance Equity account as an offsetting account when certain opening balances are entered in the accounts. The Owners Equity account is created to capture net income at the end of the fiscal year. In Chapter 12, you will see how QuickBooks uses the Owner's Equity account in a company file. This account will be renamed *Accumulated Earnings*.

As you will soon see, QuickBooks recognizes the Accounts Receivable; Accounts Payable; Sales Tax Payable; Kristin Raina, Capital (Opening Balance Equity); and Accumulated Earnings (Owners Equity) accounts as system default accounts, but QuickBooks does not recognize the Inventory Asset and Cost of Goods Sold accounts as system default accounts. QuickBooks usually identifies a system default account by graying, or dimming, the account type. As you edit each account, notice that the account type is dimmed.

To edit system default account numbers and account names:

1. At the main menu bar, click Lists and then click *Chart of Accounts*.
2. At the Chart of Accounts window, select *30000 Opening Balance Equity*.
3. Click the Account menu button.
4. At the Account button drop-down menu, click *Edit Account*. In the Edit Account window, notice that the Account Type drop-down list is dimmed.
5. At the *Number* field, delete *30000* and then type 3010.
6. At the *Account Name* field, delete the text *Opening Balance Equity* and then type Kristin Raina, Capital. See Figure 6–GG.

FIGURE 6–GG
Edit Account Window—
System Default Account

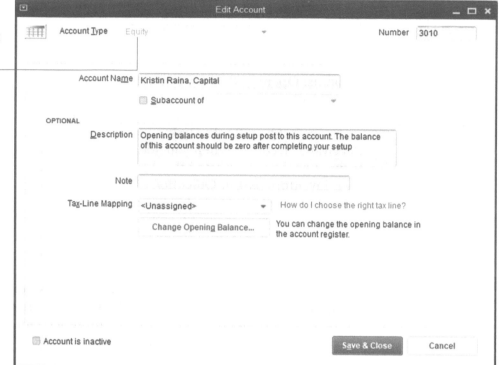

The Account Type drop-down list is dimmed because this is a system default account.

7. If the information is correct, click the Save & Close button.
8. Edit the other system default accounts created by the EasyStep Interview and QuickBooks Desktop Setup as follows:

QuickBooks		Edited	
Number	Account Name	Number	Account Name
11000	Accounts Receivable	1200	
20000	Accounts Payable	2010	
25500	Sales Tax Payable	2200	
32000	Owners Equity	3030	Accumulated Earnings

Notice that for the Accounts Receivable account, *Accounts Receivable* is both the account name and the account type. Similarly, notice that for the Accounts Payable account, *Accounts Payable* is both the account name and the account type. When QuickBooks looks for a system default account, it looks for the account type, not the account name.

9. Close the Chart of Accounts List window.

Customizing System Default Accounts
Created for Use in Activities Windows

Recall that in the Create Invoices window, the system default account is a debit to Accounts Receivable; in the Enter Bills window, the system default is a credit to Accounts Payable. When you chose an inventory item in any of the activity windows, QuickBooks knew—from the Item List—which inventory asset account, cost of goods sold account, and sale of inventory account was the system default account to use for properly recording the transaction. You also know that you can create accounts in the Chart of Accounts List. However, sometimes QuickBooks does not find an account already created; you must let QuickBooks create the account for the software to identify it as a system default account.

To illustrate how QuickBooks creates its own system default accounts, you will first add an account to the Chart of Accounts List and then open some activity windows and the Item List. You will see that QuickBooks cannot locate the account you created and some accounts created in QuickBooks Desktop Setup and that it creates its own accounts.

To add a new account:
1. Click Lists and then click *Chart of Accounts.*
2. At the Chart of Accounts window, click the Account menu button and then click *New.* The Add New Account: Choose Account Type window appears.
3. Click *Other Account Types.* The drop-down list appears. See Figure 6–HH.

FIGURE 6–HH
Add New Account:
Choose Account Type
Window

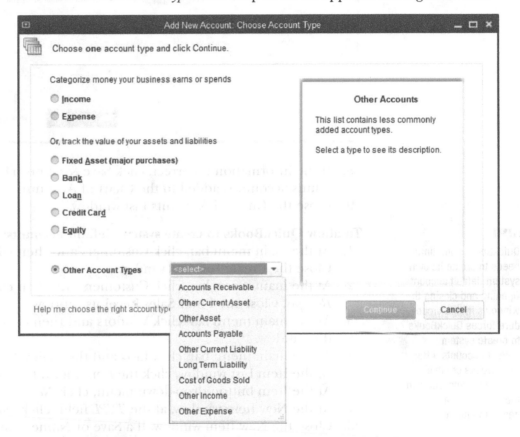

4. At the Other Account Types drop-down list, click *Other Current Asset.*
5. Click Continue. The Add New Account window appears.
6. At the *Number* field, type 1250.
7. At the *Account Name* field, type Undeposited Funds. See Figure 6–II.

FIGURE 6–II
Add New Account
Window—Completed

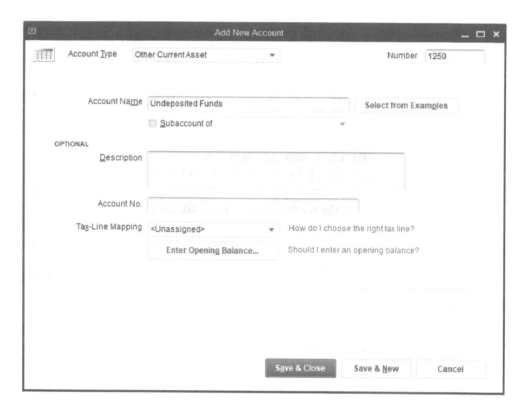

8. If the information is correct, click Save & Close. The Undeposited Funds account is added to the Chart of Accounts List.
9. Close the Chart of Accounts List window.

To allow QuickBooks to create system default accounts:
1. At the main menu bar, click Customers and then click *Create Invoices*. Close the Create Invoices window.
2. At the main menu bar, click Customers and then click *Enter Sales Receipts*. Close the Enter Sales Receipts window.
3. At the main menu bar, click Vendors and then click *Enter Bills*. Close the window.
4. At the main menu bar, click Lists and then click *Item List*.
5. At the Item List window, click the Item menu button.
6. At the Item button drop-down menu, click *New*.
7. At the New Item window, at the *TYPE* field, click *Inventory Part*.
8. Close the New Item window. If a Save or Name cannot be blank message appears, click No. Close the Item List.

As you opened each window, QuickBooks looked for certain system default accounts; when they could not be identified, QuickBooks created new system default accounts. Review the Chart of Accounts List and observe that QuickBooks created the following accounts, as shown in Figure 6–JJ: 12000 *Undeposited Funds, 12100 *Inventory Asset, and 50000 *Cost of Goods Sold.

HINT
QuickBooks sometimes needs to create its own system default accounts. Opening and closing the windows in this procedure forces QuickBooks to create system default accounts. After QuickBooks creates these accounts, you can then edit each account name and number.

HINT
When QuickBooks creates an account with an account name already in use, it precedes the new account name with an asterisk (*).

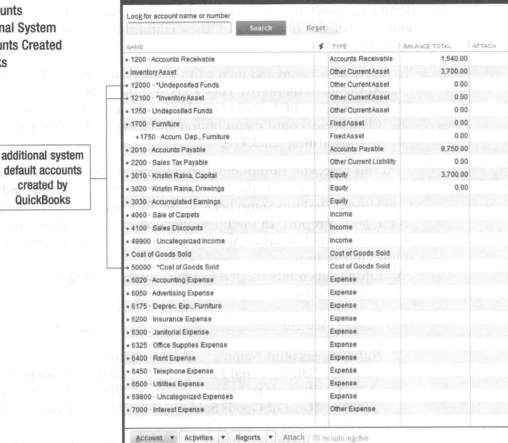

NAME	⚡	TYPE	BALANCE TOTAL	ATTACH
◦ 1200 · Accounts Receivable		Accounts Receivable	1,540.00	
◦ Inventory Asset		Other Current Asset	3,700.00	
◦ 12000 · *Undeposited Funds		Other Current Asset	0.00	
◦ 12100 · *Inventory Asset		Other Current Asset	0.00	
◦ 1250 · Undeposited Funds		Other Current Asset	0.00	
◦ 1700 · Furniture		Fixed Asset	0.00	
◦ 1750 · Accum. Dep., Furniture		Fixed Asset	0.00	
◦ 2010 · Accounts Payable		Accounts Payable	9,750.00	
◦ 2200 · Sales Tax Payable		Other Current Liability	0.00	
◦ 3010 · Kristin Raina, Capital		Equity	3,700.00	
◦ 3020 · Kristin Raina, Drawings		Equity	0.00	
◦ 3030 · Accumulated Earnings		Equity		
◦ 4060 · Sale of Carpets		Income		
◦ 4100 · Sales Discounts		Income		
◦ 49900 · Uncategorized Income		Income		
◦ Cost of Goods Sold		Cost of Goods Sold		
◦ 50000 · *Cost of Goods Sold		Cost of Goods Sold		
◦ 6020 · Accounting Expense		Expense		
◦ 6050 · Advertising Expense		Expense		
◦ 6175 · Deprec. Exp., Furniture		Expense		
◦ 6200 · Insurance Expense		Expense		
◦ 6300 · Janitorial Expense		Expense		
◦ 6325 · Office Supplies Expense		Expense		
◦ 6400 · Rent Expense		Expense		
◦ 6450 · Telephone Expense		Expense		
◦ 6500 · Utilities Expense		Expense		
◦ 69800 · Uncategorized Expenses		Expense		
◦ 7000 · Interest Expense		Other Expense		

additional system default accounts created by QuickBooks

When you opened the Create Invoices window, QuickBooks looked for the Accounts Receivable account and was able to locate it because of the accounts receivable account type in that account. Similarly, when you opened the Enter Bills window, QuickBooks looked for the Accounts Payable account and was able to locate it because of the accounts payable account type.

But when you opened the Enter Sales Receipts window, QuickBooks looked for an Undeposited Funds account; even though you created this account, QuickBooks could not locate it and created the new account 12000 *Undeposited Funds. Likewise, when you chose the new inventory part type in the Item List, QuickBooks looked for an inventory asset account and cost of goods sold account. Even though an Inventory Asset account and Cost of Goods Sold account were created when you entered inventory part items in the QuickBooks Desktop Setup window, QuickBooks did not identify these accounts as system default accounts and therefore did not locate them; thus, it created a new account 12100 *Inventory Asset account and a new account 50000 *Cost of Goods Sold. In situations like these, you must allow QuickBooks to create its own accounts; then you can edit them to your liking. In all cases, the system default accounts created by QuickBooks will have dimmed account types; you cannot change the account types, but you can change the account numbers and account names.

Before you can edit the accounts that QuickBooks created, delete the 1250 Undeposited Funds account that you created. This account name and number can then be used when editing the accounts created by QuickBooks.

To delete an account and then edit the accounts created by QuickBooks:
1. At the main menu bar, click Lists and then click *Chart of Accounts*.
2. At the Chart of Accounts window, select *1250 Undeposited Funds*.
3. Click the Account menu button and then click *Delete Account*.
4. At the warning, click OK.

At this time, you cannot delete the Inventory Asset account and Cost of Goods Sold account (the accounts without numbers) created in QuickBooks Desktop Setup because they are used in the Item List and in the *Journal* report. In the upcoming section on updating the Item List with the updated Chart of Accounts, you will be able to delete these two duplicated accounts.
5. Edit the accounts created by QuickBooks, noting that the account types are dimmed:

QuickBooks		Edited	
Number	Account Name	Number	Account Name
12000	*Undeposited Funds	1250	Undeposited Funds
12100	*Inventory Asset	1260	Inventory of Carpets
50000	*Cost of Goods Sold	5060	Cost of Carpets Sold

After QuickBooks creates an Inventory account and a Cost of Goods Sold account, you can create as many additional inventory and cost of goods sold accounts as desired. You will do this in the upcoming section "Updating the Chart of Accounts List."
6. Close the Chart of Accounts List window.

Customizing Payment Terms

In QuickBooks, a list with payment terms is accessed in customer files, vendor files, and activities windows when needed. As shown in prior chapters, payment terms such as Net 30 Days and 2/10, Net 30 Days can be identified in both the customer and vendor files if they relate to a particular customer or vendor.

When you create a new company file, QuickBooks automatically creates a list of payment terms. As with all other Lists in QuickBooks, you can add, delete, or edit the Terms List to customize it for your company.

To add a payment term:
1. At the main menu bar, click Lists and then click *Customer & Vendor Profile Lists*.
2. At the Customer & Vendor Profile Lists submenu, click *Terms List*. The Terms List window appears with the terms of payment that were created by QuickBooks. See Figure 6–KK.

FIGURE 6–KK
Terms List Created by
QuickBooks

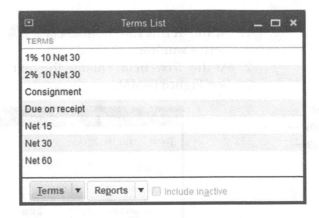

3. At the Terms List window, click the Terms menu button.
4. At the Terms menu, click *New.* The New Terms window appears.
5. At the *Terms* field, type Net 10 Days.
6. At the *Net due in days* field, type 10. See Figure 6–LL.

FIGURE 6–LL
New Terms Window—
Net 10 Days—Completed

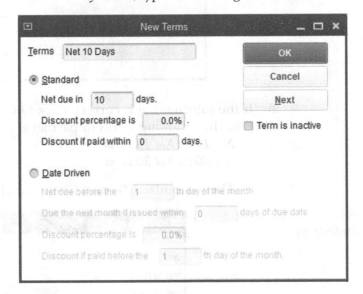

7. If the information is correct, click OK.

To delete a payment term:
1. At the Terms List, select *1% 10 Net 30*, but do not open it.
2. Click the Terms menu button. At the Terms menu, click *Delete Terms.*
3. A Delete Terms warning screen appears. Click OK. The payment term is deleted.
4. Delete the following terms of payment:
   Consignment
   Due on receipt
   Net 60

To edit a payment term:

1. At the Terms List, double-click *2% 10 Net 30* terms to open the Edit Terms window.
2. At the *Terms* field, change the text to 2/10, Net 30 Days. See Figure 6–MM.

FIGURE 6–MM
Edit Terms Window—
2/10, Net 30 Days—
Completed

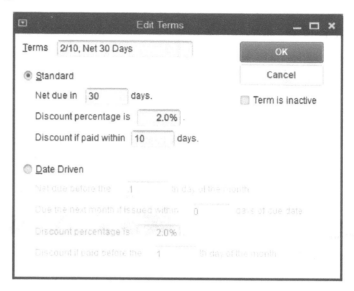

3. If the information is correct, click OK.
4. Edit the following terms of payment:
   Net 15 to *Net 15 Days*
   Net 30 to *Net 30 Days*

The customized Terms List appears in Figure 6–NN.

FIGURE 6–NN
Terms List—Customized

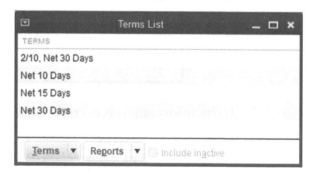

5. Close the Terms List window.

Lists/Centers

Updating Lists/Centers

In the EasyStep Interview and QuickBooks Desktop Setup windows, QuickBooks created the Chart of Accounts List, which has now been customized for Kristin Raina Interior Designs. But our sample company uses many more accounts that must be added to the Chart of Accounts List. Also, as part of the EasyStep Interview and QuickBooks Desktop Setup, the Item List was created, but it requires some modifications.

The QuickBooks Desktop Setup created the Customer Center and the Vendor Center, which may also require some modifications. Thus, the next part of customizing the company file is to update the Chart of Accounts and Item Lists as well as the Customer and Vendor Centers.

Updating the Chart of Accounts List

As just noted, QuickBooks has already created some accounts in the new company file. However, many additional accounts must be added to the Chart of Accounts List for Kristin Raina Interior Designs. Most of these accounts have opening balances, which will be entered later by a general journal entry.

Using the information in Table 6–4, enter all remaining accounts. The updated Chart of Accounts List appears in Figure 6–OO.

TABLE 6–4
Chart of Accounts List

Account Type	Number	Account Name
Bank	1010	Cash - Operating
Other Current Asset	1265	Inventory of Draperies
Other Current Asset	1270	Inventory of Lamps
Other Current Asset	1275	Inventory of Mirrors
Other Current Asset	1300	Design Supplies
Other Current Asset	1305	Office Supplies
Other Current Asset	1410	Prepaid Advertising
Other Current Asset	1420	Prepaid Insurance
Fixed Asset	1725	Furniture, Cost [Subaccount of 1700]
Fixed Asset	1800	Computers
Fixed Asset	1825	Computers, Cost [Subaccount of 1800]
Fixed Asset	1850	Accum. Dep., Computers [Subaccount of 1800]
Other Current Liability	2020	Notes Payable
Other Current Liability	2030	Interest Payable
Income	4010	Design Services
Income	4020	Decorating Services
Income	4065	Sale of Draperies
Income	4070	Sale of Lamps
Income	4075	Sale of Mirrors
Cost of Goods Sold	5065	Cost of Draperies Sold
Cost of Goods Sold	5070	Cost of Lamps Sold
Cost of Goods Sold	5075	Cost of Mirrors Sold
Cost of Goods Sold	5900	Inventory Adjustment
Expense	6185	Deprec. Exp., Computers

HINT
In the *Account Type* field, instead of looking for the type in the drop-down list, press the first letter of the type.

HINT
If a message appears stating that the account number is being used, click Cancel. You have recorded an account incorrectly; review the Chart of Accounts List to locate your error and then edit the account to correct it.

FIGURE 6–OO
Chart of Accounts List—
Updated

HINT

If you incorrectly labeled an account as a parent account or subaccount, you can edit the account or move the entry. To move the entry, click the diamond to the left of the account number. If you drag the diamond to the left, a subaccount becomes a parent account. If you drag the diamond to the right, a parent account becomes a subaccount. You can also click and drag up or down to reorganize the list.

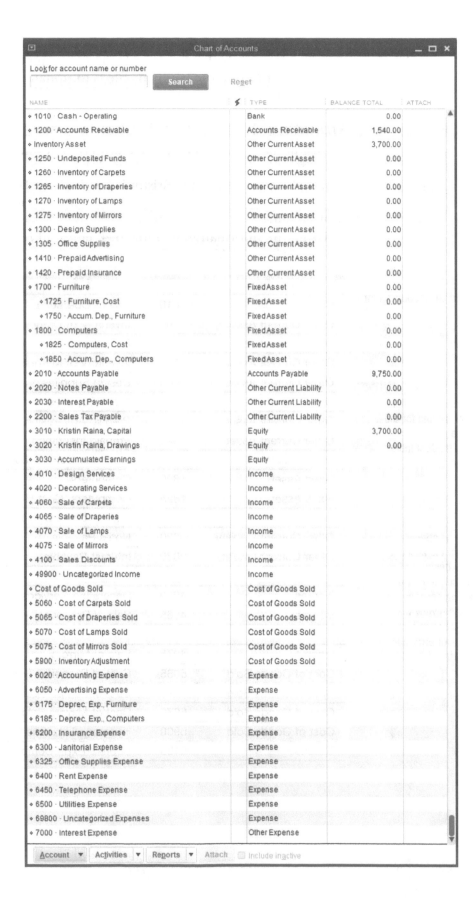

NAME	⚡	TYPE	BALANCE TOTAL	ATTACH
◇ 1010 · Cash - Operating		Bank	0.00	
◇ 1200 · Accounts Receivable		Accounts Receivable	1,540.00	
◇ Inventory Asset		Other Current Asset	3,700.00	
◇ 1250 · Undeposited Funds		Other Current Asset	0.00	
◇ 1260 · Inventory of Carpets		Other Current Asset	0.00	
◇ 1265 · Inventory of Draperies		Other Current Asset	0.00	
◇ 1270 · Inventory of Lamps		Other Current Asset	0.00	
◇ 1275 · Inventory of Mirrors		Other Current Asset	0.00	
◇ 1300 · Design Supplies		Other Current Asset	0.00	
◇ 1305 · Office Supplies		Other Current Asset	0.00	
◇ 1410 · Prepaid Advertising		Other Current Asset	0.00	
◇ 1420 · Prepaid Insurance		Other Current Asset	0.00	
◇ 1700 · Furniture		Fixed Asset	0.00	
◇ 1725 · Furniture, Cost		Fixed Asset	0.00	
◇ 1750 · Accum. Dep., Furniture		Fixed Asset	0.00	
◇ 1800 · Computers		Fixed Asset	0.00	
◇ 1825 · Computers, Cost		Fixed Asset	0.00	
◇ 1850 · Accum. Dep., Computers		Fixed Asset	0.00	
◇ 2010 · Accounts Payable		Accounts Payable	9,750.00	
◇ 2020 · Notes Payable		Other Current Liability	0.00	
◇ 2030 · Interest Payable		Other Current Liability	0.00	
◇ 2200 · Sales Tax Payable		Other Current Liability	0.00	
◇ 3010 · Kristin Raina, Capital		Equity	3,700.00	
◇ 3020 · Kristin Raina, Drawings		Equity	0.00	
◇ 3030 · Accumulated Earnings		Equity		
◇ 4010 · Design Services		Income		
◇ 4020 · Decorating Services		Income		
◇ 4060 · Sale of Carpets		Income		
◇ 4065 · Sale of Draperies		Income		
◇ 4070 · Sale of Lamps		Income		
◇ 4075 · Sale of Mirrors		Income		
◇ 4100 · Sales Discounts		Income		
◇ 49900 · Uncategorized Income		Income		
◇ Cost of Goods Sold		Cost of Goods Sold		
◇ 5060 · Cost of Carpets Sold		Cost of Goods Sold		
◇ 5065 · Cost of Draperies Sold		Cost of Goods Sold		
◇ 5070 · Cost of Lamps Sold		Cost of Goods Sold		
◇ 5075 · Cost of Mirrors Sold		Cost of Goods Sold		
◇ 5900 · Inventory Adjustment		Cost of Goods Sold		
◇ 6020 · Accounting Expense		Expense		
◇ 6050 · Advertising Expense		Expense		
◇ 6175 · Deprec. Exp., Furniture		Expense		
◇ 6185 · Deprec. Exp., Computers		Expense		
◇ 6200 · Insurance Expense		Expense		
◇ 6300 · Janitorial Expense		Expense		
◇ 6325 · Office Supplies Expense		Expense		
◇ 6400 · Rent Expense		Expense		
◇ 6450 · Telephone Expense		Expense		
◇ 6500 · Utilities Expense		Expense		
◇ 69800 · Uncategorized Expenses		Expense		
◇ 7000 · Interest Expense		Other Expense		

Updating the Item List

In QuickBooks, the Item List stores information about the service items, the inventory part items, and the sales tax. As each transaction is recorded in an Activity window, QuickBooks uses information in the Item List to record the transaction in the correct accounts.

Open and review the Item List. In the EasyStep Interview, when you responded *Yes* to the question of whether sales tax is used, QuickBooks created a sales tax item. In the QuickBooks Desktop Setup, service and inventory part items were added on the *Add products and services you sell* pages. As this information was entered in the EasyStep Interview and QuickBooks Desktop Setup windows, QuickBooks recorded the information in the Item List. Earlier in the chapter, you reviewed the Item List (Figure 6–Q, page 208) and saw that for the service items and inventory part items (Figure 6–R and Figure 6–S, page 209), QuickBooks used the same Sales Income account as the income account for each item. In addition, for each inventory part item (Figure 6–S), QuickBooks used the same Cost of Goods Sold account and Inventory Asset account. When customizing the system default accounts, some of the account names and numbers were changed. *Sales Income* was changed to *4060 Sale of Carpets, 12100 Inventory Asset* was changed to *1260 Inventory of Carpets,* and *50000 Cost of Goods Sold* was changed to *5060 Cost of Carpets Sold.* In addition, when updating the Chart of Accounts List, you added additional inventory accounts, income accounts, and cost of goods sold accounts. When you changed the account names and numbers of the system default accounts, these changes flowed into the Item List. You will now edit the service items and inventory part items to reflect the accounts used by Kristin Raina Interior Designs.

When you entered each service item and inventory part item in the QuickBooks Desktop Setup window, you were not allowed to indicate if the item was taxable or nontaxable. When you edit each service and inventory part item for the correct accounts, you will also indicate if the item is taxable or nontaxable. In addition, the sales tax item (see Figure 6–T on page 210) does not have the necessary information for Kristin Raina Interior Designs sales tax and must be edited.

To edit a service item:

1. At the main menu bar, click Lists and then click *Item List.*
2. At the Item List window, double-click the *Decorating Services* service item. The Edit Item window appears.
3. At the *Tax Code* field, click *Non* (for *Non-Taxable Sales*).
4. At the *Account* field, click *4020 Decorating Services.* See Figure 6–PP.

FIGURE 6–PP
Edit Item Window—
Service—Completed

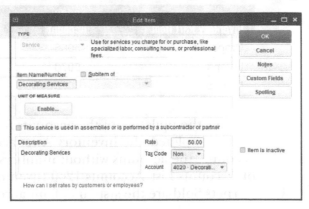

5. If the information is correct, click OK. At the Account Change message, click Yes.
6. Double-click the *Design Services* service item.
7. At the *Tax Code* field, click *Non* (for *Non-Taxable Sales*), and at the *Account* field, click *4010 Design Services.*
8. Click OK, and then at the Account Change message, click Yes.

To edit an inventory part item:
1. At the Item List window, double-click the *Carpets* inventory part item. The Edit Item window appears.
2. At the *COGS Account* field, click *5060 Cost of Carpets Sold.*
3. At the *Tax Code* field, click *Tax* (for *Taxable Sales*).
4. At the *Income Account* field, click *4060 Sale of Carpets*, if necessary.
5. At the *Asset Account* field, click *1260 Inventory of Carpets.* See Figure 6–QQ.

FIGURE 6–QQ
Edit Item Window—
Inventory Part—
Completed

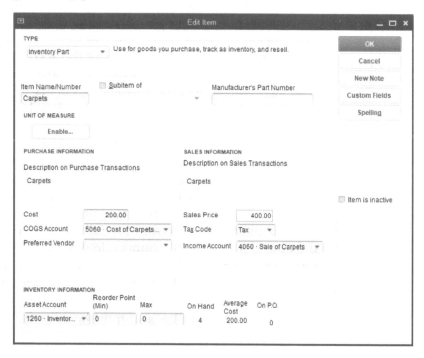

HINT

If a warning appears about the minimum quantity, click OK at the warning and then delete the zero in the *Reorder Point (min)* field.

6. If the information is correct, click OK. If the Account Change message appears, click Yes.
7. Using the information in Table 6–5, update the remainder of the inventory part items. All inventory part items are taxable.

TABLE 6–5
Update Inventory
Part Items

Inventory Part Item	COGS Account	Income Account	Asset Account
Draperies	5065	4065	1265
Lamps	5070	4070	1270
Mirrors	5075	4075	1275

After the updating of the accounts for the inventory part items has been completed, the Inventory Asset account and Cost of Goods Sold account (the accounts without numbers) can be deleted from the Chart of Accounts List. Accounts 1260 Inventory of Carpets and 5060 Cost of Carpets Sold are the system default accounts created by QuickBooks, as indicated by the dimmed account types. Inventory accounts and cost of goods sold accounts can be added or deleted, since QuickBooks will always find the two system default accounts.

To edit the sales tax item:

1. Double-click the *Sales Tax* item. The Edit Item window appears.
2. At the *Sales Tax Name* field, delete the text *Out of State* and type Minn. Sales Tax.
3. At the *Description* field, delete the description and type Sales Tax.
4. At the *Tax Rate (%)* field, type 7.
5. At the Tax Agency drop-down list, click *Minn. Dept. of Revenue.* The Edit Item window is complete. See Figure 6–RR.

FIGURE 6–RR
Edit Item Window—Sales Tax Item—Completed

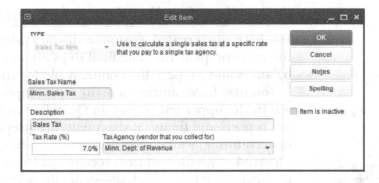

6. If the information is correct, click OK.
   The updated Item List appears in Figure 6–SS. Compare it with the list shown in Figure 6–Q on page 208.

FIGURE 6–SS Item List—Updated

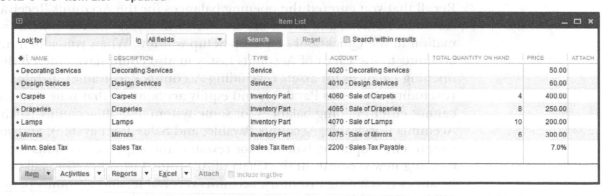

7. Close the Item List window.

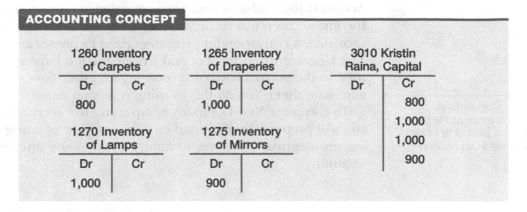

ACCOUNTING CONCEPT

1260 Inventory of Carpets		1265 Inventory of Draperies		3010 Kristin Raina, Capital	
Dr	Cr	Dr	Cr	Dr	Cr
800		1,000			800
					1,000
1270 Inventory of Lamps		**1275 Inventory of Mirrors**			1,000
Dr	Cr	Dr	Cr		900
1,000		900			

Updating the Customer Center and Vendor Center

The Customer Center and Vendor Center were created when information was entered in the QuickBooks Desktop Setup window—*Add the people you do business with* pages. You reviewed them when the QuickBooks Desktop Setup was complete. (See Figures 6–U and 6–W on pages 211 and 212, respectively.) At this time, if you want to include additional information in the Customer Center or Vendor Center that was not included in the Quick-Books Desktop Setup—such as terms of payment, email addresses, and account numbers—you can edit each customer or vendor to add the additional information.

Adjusting for the Accrual Basis of Accounting

accrual basis of accounting
an accounting method that requires the recording of revenue when it is earned and the recording of expenses when they are incurred, regardless of cash receipts and cash payments

You have now created, customized, and updated the Lists and Centers in the new company file. The final steps are to enter the remaining opening balances and prepare the company file for the accrual basis of accounting.

You may have noticed in many of the reports that the label *accrual basis* was in the upper left corner. In QuickBooks, by default, the accounting reports and financial statements are prepared using the accrual basis of accounting, which records revenue when earned and expenses when incurred, regardless of cash receipts and cash payments. The accrual basis of accounting follows GAAP—generally accepted accounting principles—and is the basis used in this text.

Completing New Company Setup Using the Accrual Basis of Accounting

Recall that you entered the opening balances for the Accounts Receivable, Accounts Payable, and Inventory accounts when you entered the information in the QuickBooks Desktop Setup window. When you added new accounts to the Chart of Accounts List, you also could have entered the opening balances for assets (excluding Accounts Receivable), liabilities (excluding Accounts Payable), and equity accounts at that time. But you cannot enter opening balances for some system default accounts (such as Accounts Receivable, Accounts Payable, and Sales Tax Payable), and you cannot enter opening balances for revenue and expense accounts when creating new accounts in the Chart of Accounts List. Therefore, all opening balances (excluding inventory, accounts receivable, and accounts payable) will be entered in one journal entry.

As you saw in the *Journal* report (Figure 6–Y on page 214), every time an Accounts Receivable account was recorded, a corresponding Uncategorized Income account was recorded; every time an Accounts Payable account was recorded, a corresponding Uncategorized Expenses account was recorded. The Uncategorized Income and Uncategorized Expenses accounts are not used in the accrual basis of accounting and therefore must be reversed to eliminate them. You do this by using reversing entries.

reversing entries
entries recorded in the general journal to offset a balance in an account

To complete New Company Setup using the accrual basis of accounting, you will prepare three journal entries: entering opening balances, reversing uncategorized income account, and reversing uncategorized expenses account.

Entering Opening Balances

You will enter all opening balances for Kristin Raina Interior Designs—excluding inventory, accounts receivable, and accounts payable—as one large compound journal entry.

HINT

Enlarge the Make General Journal Entries window and click the Hide List button before recording this journal entry so that you can see more of the entries.

To enter opening balances in the Make General Journal Entries window:

1. At the main menu bar, click Company and then click *Make General Journal Entries*. At the Assigning Numbers to Journal Entries message, insert a check mark in the box to the left of *Do not display this message in the future* and then click OK. The Make General Journal Entries window appears.
2. At the *DATE* field, choose *04/01/2022*.
3. At the *ENTRY NO.* field, accept the default *1*.
4. Remove the check mark next to *ADJUSTING ENTRY* and then click the Hide List button to allow more space to record this large journal entry.
5. Enter the following accounts and amounts as debits:

HINT

You can type in the account number for each account or use the drop-down list.

HINT

It may be easier to type the account number and then use the Tab key to move to the debit or credit column. After typing in the amount, use the Tab key to move to the next row. It is not necessary to delete the balancing amount in the credit (or debit) column; just type in the correct amount in the debit or credit column. When appropriate, type over the balancing amount.

Number	Account Name	Balance
1010	Cash - Operating	$50,855.38
1300	Design Supplies	200.00
1305	Office Supplies	250.00
1410	Prepaid Advertising	500.00
1420	Prepaid Insurance	2,200.00
1725	Furniture, Cost	12,000.00
1825	Computers, Cost	3,600.00
3020	Kristin Raina, Drawings	400.00
4100	Sales Discounts	84.62
5060	Cost of Carpets Sold	1,200.00
5065	Cost of Draperies Sold	500.00
5070	Cost of Lamps Sold	600.00
5075	Cost of Mirrors Sold	450.00
5900	Inventory Adjustment	150.00
6020	Accounting Expense	300.00
6050	Advertising Expense	100.00
6175	Deprec. Exp., Furniture	100.00
6185	Deprec. Exp., Computers	60.00
6200	Insurance Expense	200.00
6300	Janitorial Expense	125.00
6325	Office Supplies Expense	150.00
6400	Rent Expense	800.00
6450	Telephone Expense	275.00
6500	Utilities Expense	450.00
7000	Interest Expense	50.00

QuickCheck: $75,600.00

6. Enter the following accounts and amounts as credits:

Number	Account Name	Balance
1750	Accum. Dep., Furniture	$ 100.00
1850	Accum. Dep., Computers	60.00
2020	Notes Payable	7,000.00

...continues

...continued

Number	Account Name	Balance
2030	Interest Payable	50.00
4010	Design Services	4,980.00
4020	Decorating Services	3,400.00
4060	Sale of Carpets	2,400.00
4065	Sale of Draperies	1,000.00
4070	Sale of Lamps	1,200.00
4075	Sale of Mirrors	900.00

QuickCheck: $54,510.00

7. Record the credit balance of $54,510.00 as a credit to account 3010 Kristin Raina, Capital. See Figure 6–TT.

FIGURE 6–TT
Make General Journal Entries Window— Opening Balances

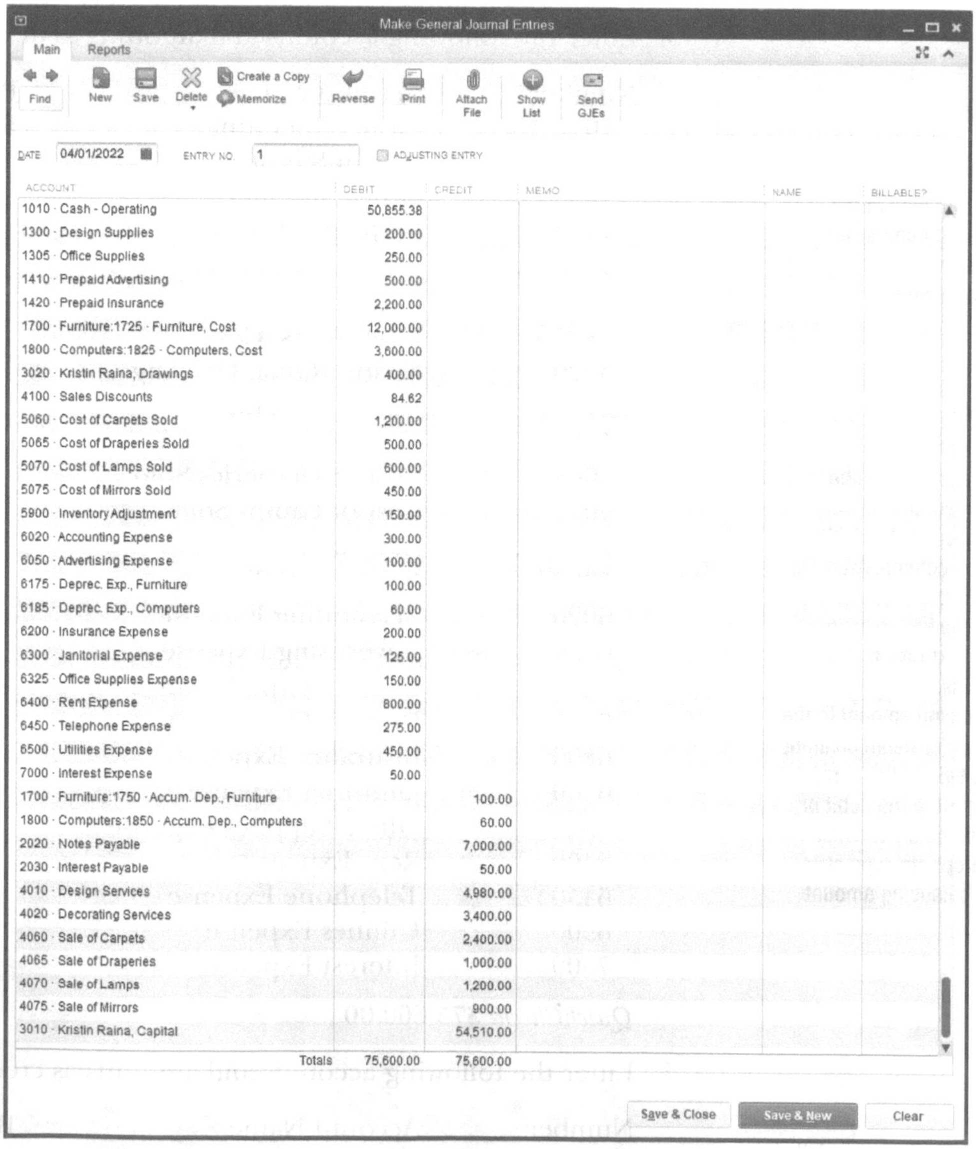

HINT

If the Future Transactions message appears, click Yes. To change this preference, click Edit at the main menu bar and then click *Preferences*. In the left panel of the Preferences window, click the Accounting icon. Choose the Company Preferences tab. Remove the check marks in the warning options and then click OK.

8. If the information is correct, click the Save & New button. If a message appears about Tracking fixed assets, insert a check mark in the box to the left of *Do not display this message in the future* and then click OK.

The effects of recording the opening balances are as follows:

1010-1825 Assets			
Dr		**Cr**	
Cash - Operating	50,855.38		
Design Supplies	200.00		
Office Supplies	250.00		
Prepaid Advertising	500.00		
Prepaid Insurance	2,200.00		
Furniture	12,000.00		
Computers	3,600.00		
	69,605.38		

1750-1850 Accum Dep	
Dr	**Cr**
	100.00
	60.00
	160.00

2020-2030 Payables		
Dr	**Cr**	
	7,000.00	Notes
	50.00	Interest
	7,050.00	

3010 Kristin Raina, Capital	
Dr	**Cr**
	54,510.00

3020 Kristin Raina, Drawings	
Dr	**Cr**
400.00	

4010-4020 Service Revenue		
Dr	**Cr**	
	Design	4,980.00
	Decor	3,400.00
		8,380.00

4060-4075 Sale of Inventory		
Dr	**Cr**	
	Carpets	2,400.00
	Draperies	1,000.00
	Lamps	1,200.00
	Mirrors	900.00
		5,500.00

4100 Sales Discounts	
Dr	**Cr**
84.62	

5060-5075,5900 Cost of Goods Sold		
Dr		**Cr**
Carpets	1,200.00	
Draperies	500.00	
Lamps	600.00	
Mirrors	450.00	
Invent Adj	150.00	
	2,900.00	

6020-6500 Expenses		
Dr		**Cr**
Accounting	300.00	
Advertising	100.00	
Dep Exp, Furniture	100.00	
Dep Exp, Computers	60.00	
Insurance	200.00	
Janitorial	125.00	
Office Supplies	150.00	
Rent	800.00	
Telephone	275.00	
Utilities	450.00	
	2,560.00	

7000 Interest Exp	
Dr	**Cr**
50.00	

Reversing the Uncategorized Income Account

Recall that in the *Journal* report in Figure 6–Y on page 214, two journal entries are recorded that debit Accounts Receivable and credit Uncategorized Income for two customers as follows:

Berger Bakery Company	$ 600
Franco Films Co.	940
	$1,540

The debit entries to the Accounts Receivable account are correct and will stay in that account. The credits to the Uncategorized Income account will be reversed by debiting Uncategorized Income for the total of $1,540 and crediting the account 3010 Kristin Raina, Capital (formerly the Opening Balance Equity account) for $1,540.

HINT

As part of customizing the Chart of Accounts, the account Opening Balance Equity, created by QuickBooks, was renamed *3010 Kristin Raina, Capital.*

To reverse the Uncategorized Income account:

1. At the Make General Journal Entries window, choose the date *04/01/2022,* and at the *ENTRY NO.* field, accept *2.*
2. Remove the check mark next to *ADJUSTING ENTRY,* if necessary.
3. Debit account 49900 Uncategorized Income for 1,540 and credit account 3010 Kristin Raina, Capital, for 1,540. See Figure 6–UU.

FIGURE 6–UU
Make General Journal
Entries Window—
Reverse Uncategorized
Income

4. If the information is correct, click the Save & New button.

ACCOUNTING CONCEPT

49900 Uncategorized Income		3010 Kristin Raina, Capital	
Dr	Cr	Dr	Cr
Rev 1,540	1,540		1,540
	0		

Reversing the Uncategorized Expenses Account

In the *Journal* report shown in Figure 6–Y on page 214, there are seven journal entries that credit Accounts Payable and debit Uncategorized Expenses for seven vendor balances as follows:

Ace Glass Works	$1,500
Bell Carpet Design	2,000
Cuza and Carl Associates	400
Galeway Computers	2,600
Midwest Mutual Insurance Co.	2,400
Minneapolis Electric & Gas Co.	450
Williams Office Supply Company	400
	$9,750

The credit entries to the Accounts Payable account are correct and will stay in that account. The debits to the Uncategorized Expenses, however, have to be reversed by crediting Uncategorized Expenses for the total of $9,750 and debiting the 3010 Kristin Raina, Capital, account for $9,750.

To reverse the Uncategorized Expenses account:
1. At the Make General Journal Entries window, choose the date *04/01/2022*, and at the *ENTRY NO.* field, accept *3*.
2. Remove the check mark next to *ADJUSTING ENTRY*, if necessary.
3. Debit account 3010 Kristin Raina, Capital, for 9,750 and credit account 69800 Uncategorized Expenses for 9,750. See Figure 6–VV.

FIGURE 6–VV
Make General Journal Entries Window— Reverse Uncategorized Expenses

4. If the information is correct, click the Save & Close button.

ACCOUNTING CONCEPT

69800 Uncategorized Expenses		3010 Kristin Raina, Capital	
Dr	Cr	Dr	Cr
9,750	Rev 9,750	9,750	
0			

Accounting Reports and Financial Statements

Upon completing the New Company Setup, you should display and print the accounting reports and financial statements.

Accounting Reports

The accounting reports you need to print and review consist of the *Journal* and the *Trial Balance*.

Journal Report

You displayed and printed the *Journal* report after the EasyStep Interview and QuickBooks Desktop Setup windows were completed (Figure 6–Y on page 214). After recording the opening balances and reversing the Uncategorized Income and Uncategorized Expenses accounts, you added three more journal entries to the *Journal* report. View and print all the journal entries for April 1, 2022. The total debits and credits is $101,880. Figure 6–WW displays only the additional three journal entries.

HINT
To display only the last three journal entries in the *Journal* report, click the Customize Report button and then click the Filters tab. In the *FILTER* field, click *Transaction Type*. In the *Transaction Type* field, click *Journal* and then click OK.

FIGURE 6–WW Journal Report - Filtered - Additional Journal Entries

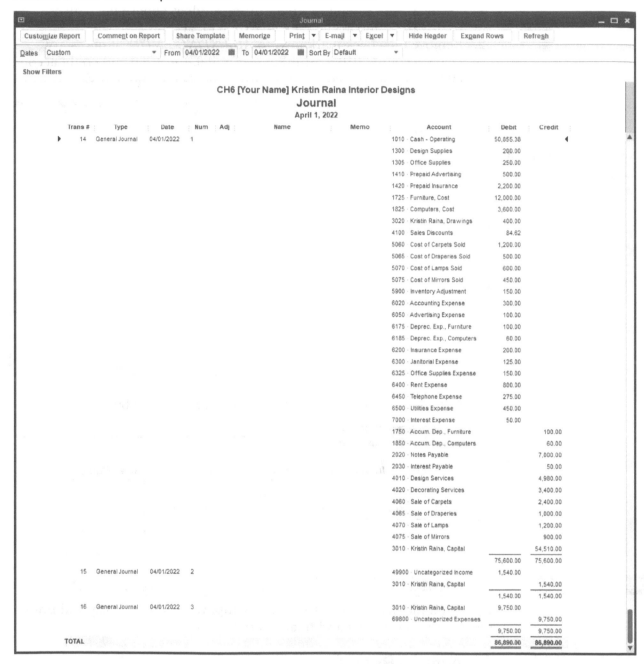

Trial Balance **Report**

Next, view and print the *Trial Balance* report for April 1, 2022.
See Figure 6–XX.

FIGURE 6–XX Trial Balance Report

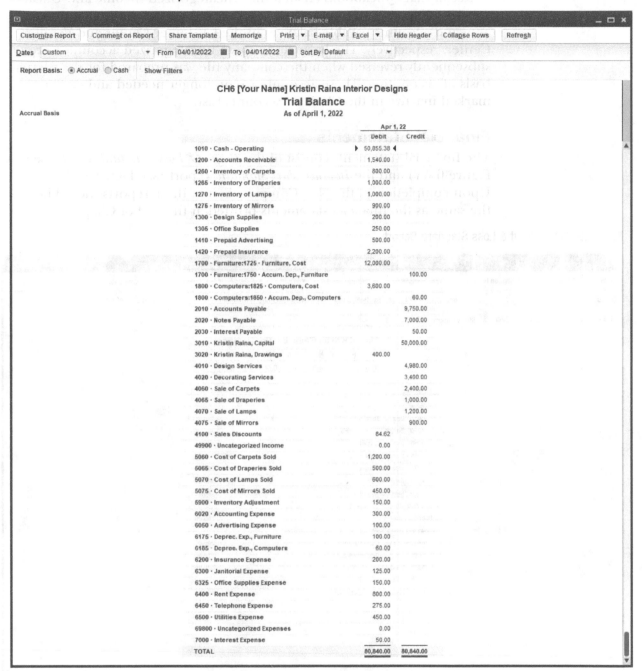

Trial Balance

| Customize Report | Comment on Report | Share Template | Memorize | Print ▼ | E-mail ▼ | Excel ▼ | Hide Header | Collapse Rows | Refresh |

Dates Custom ▼ From 04/01/2022 📅 To 04/01/2022 📅 Sort By Default ▼

Report Basis: ● Accrual ○ Cash   Show Filters

CH6 [Your Name] Kristin Raina Interior Designs
Trial Balance
As of April 1, 2022

Accrual Basis

	Apr 1, 22	
	Debit	Credit
1010 · Cash - Operating	▶ 50,855.38 ◀	
1200 · Accounts Receivable	1,540.00	
1260 · Inventory of Carpets	800.00	
1265 · Inventory of Draperies	1,000.00	
1270 · Inventory of Lamps	1,000.00	
1275 · Inventory of Mirrors	900.00	
1300 · Design Supplies	200.00	
1305 · Office Supplies	250.00	
1410 · Prepaid Advertising	500.00	
1420 · Prepaid Insurance	2,200.00	
1700 · Furniture:1725 · Furniture, Cost	12,000.00	
1700 · Furniture:1750 · Accum. Dep., Furniture		100.00
1800 · Computers:1825 · Computers, Cost	3,600.00	
1800 · Computers:1850 · Accum. Dep., Computers		60.00
2010 · Accounts Payable		9,750.00
2020 · Notes Payable		7,000.00
2030 · Interest Payable		50.00
3010 · Kristin Raina, Capital		50,000.00
3020 · Kristin Raina, Drawings	400.00	
4010 · Design Services		4,980.00
4020 · Decorating Services		3,400.00
4060 · Sale of Carpets		2,400.00
4065 · Sale of Draperies		1,000.00
4070 · Sale of Lamps		1,200.00
4075 · Sale of Mirrors		900.00
4100 · Sales Discounts	84.62	
49900 · Uncategorized Income	0.00	
5060 · Cost of Carpets Sold	1,200.00	
5065 · Cost of Draperies Sold	500.00	
5070 · Cost of Lamps Sold	600.00	
5075 · Cost of Mirrors Sold	450.00	
5900 · Inventory Adjustment	150.00	
6020 · Accounting Expense	300.00	
6050 · Advertising Expense	100.00	
6175 · Deprec. Exp., Furniture	100.00	
6185 · Deprec. Exp., Computers	60.00	
6200 · Insurance Expense	200.00	
6300 · Janitorial Expense	125.00	
6325 · Office Supplies Expense	150.00	
6400 · Rent Expense	800.00	
6450 · Telephone Expense	275.00	
6500 · Utilities Expense	450.00	
69800 · Uncategorized Expenses	0.00	
7000 · Interest Expense	50.00	
TOTAL	**80,840.00**	**80,840.00**

The accounts and balances on this trial balance should match the trial balance of March 31, 2022 (Figure 6–AA on page 216), after transactions were recorded in Chapters 2 through 5.

Recall that QuickBooks created the Uncategorized Income and Uncategorized Expenses accounts when you entered outstanding accounts receivable and accounts payable balances in the Customer Center and Vendor Center, respectively. The balances in these uncategorized accounts were subsequently reversed when the company file was prepared for the accrual basis of accounting. These accounts are no longer needed and can be marked inactive in the Chart of Accounts List.

Financial Statements

The financial statements consist of the *Profit & Loss Standard* report (see Figure 6–YY) and the *Balance Sheet Standard* report (see Figure 6–ZZ). Upon completion of the New Company Setup, these reports should be the same as the financial statements printed at the end of Chapter 5.

FIGURE 6–YY Profit & Loss Standard Report

FIGURE 6–ZZ
Balance Sheet
Standard Report

Backing Up the New Company File and Exiting QuickBooks

You should make a backup copy of the new company file in the event there is damage to the file or the computer or you work on a different computer at some point. Using the procedures learned in previous chapters, make a backup copy of the new company file to your subfolder and/or a removable storage device and name it **EX6** *[Your Name]* **Kristin Raina Interior Designs**. Restore the backup copy and change the company name to **EX6** *[Your Name]* **Kristin Raina Interior Designs**.

Upon completing the New Company Setup level of operation, customizing and updating the Lists/Centers, recording the appropriate journal entries, viewing and printing Reports, and making a backup copy of the new company file, your accounting records are now ready for recording daily activities. Activities should be recorded in the new company file using the procedures illustrated in prior chapters.

Close the company file and then exit QuickBooks.

Chapter Review and Assessment

Procedure Review

To begin the New Company Setup and create a new company file using the Detailed Start method and the EasyStep Interview window:
1. Open QuickBooks.
2. At the No Company Open window, click *Create a new company*, or click File and then click *New Company*. The QuickBooks Desktop Setup window appears with the *Let's set up your business!* page displayed. This is the page where you select the method of New Company Setup.
3. At the QuickBooks Desktop Setup window, at the *Let's set up your business!* page, click the Detailed Start button. The EasyStep Interview window appears.
4. At the EasyStep Interview window, read and complete each page. Click Next after completing each page.
5. At the *Congratulations!* window, click Go to Setup. Continue the New Company Setup using the QuickBooks Desktop Setup window, or exit the QuickBooks Desktop Setup window and go directly into the new company file.

To leave the EasyStep Interview window:
1. Click the Leave button.
2. Click OK at the EasyStep Interview message.
   You should not leave the EasyStep Interview window until the new company file has been saved.

To reenter the EasyStep Interview window:
1. At the No Company Open window, click *Open or Restore an existing company* or click File and then click *Open Company*.
2. Open the new company file.
3. Enter the password at the QuickBooks Desktop Login window.
4. Click OK at the QuickBooks Desktop Information message.
   When you open the company file, you are returned to the page you used last.

To enter the QuickBooks Desktop Setup window:
1. At the main menu bar, click Company and then click *Bulk Enter Business Details*.

To add customers to the Customer Center using the QuickBooks Desktop Setup window:
1. At the QuickBooks Desktop Setup window, at the *Get all the details into QuickBooks Desktop* page, in the *Add the people you do business with* section, click the Add button.
2. At the next *Add the people you do business with* page, click the Paste from Excel or enter manually button and then click Continue.
3. At the next *Add the people you do business with* page, in the *Customer* column, click *Select all* to fill in all the circles in the *Customer* column.
4. Enter the information for the customers in the appropriate columns.
5. After entering all the customer information, click Continue.
6. At the next *Add the people you do business with* page, click the *Enter opening balances* link.

7. At the *Enter opening balances for customers and vendors* page, enter the balances for the customers and enter the correct date.
8. Click Continue. You are returned to the *Add the people you do business with* page.
9. Click Continue. If you do not click Continue, the customers and opening balances will not be saved. You are returned to the QuickBooks Desktop Setup window—*Get all the details into QuickBooks Desktop* page.
10. Click Add More to enter additional customers, vendors, or items, or close the QuickBooks Desktop Setup window.

To add vendors to the Vendor Center using the QuickBooks Desktop Setup window:
1. At the QuickBooks Desktop Setup window, at the *Get all the details into QuickBooks Desktop* page, in the Add the people you do business with section, click the Add or Add More button.
2. At the next *Add the people you do business with* page, click the Paste from Excel or enter manually button and then click Continue.
3. At the next *Add the people you do business with* page, in the *Vendor* column, click *Select all* to fill in all the circles in the *Vendor* column.
4. Enter the information for the vendors in the appropriate columns.
5. After entering all the vendor information, click Continue.
6. At the next *Add the people you do business with* page, click the *Enter opening balances* link.
7. At the *Enter opening balances for customers and vendors* page, enter the balances for the vendors and enter the correct date.
8. Click Continue. You are returned to the *Add the people you do business with* page.
9. Click Continue. If you do not click Continue, the vendors and opening balances will not be saved. You are returned to the QuickBooks Desktop Setup window—*Get all the details into QuickBooks Desktop* page.
10. Click Add More to enter additional vendors, customers, or items, or close the QuickBooks Desktop Setup window.

To add service items to the Item List using the QuickBooks Desktop Setup window:
1. At the QuickBooks Desktop Setup window, at the *Get all the details into QuickBooks Desktop* page, in the *Add the products and services you sell* section, click the Add or Add More button.
2. At the *Add the products and services you sell* page, click the *Service* option and then click Continue.
3. Enter the information for the service items in the appropriate columns.
4. After entering all the service items information, click Continue. You are returned to the *Add the products and services you sell* page.
5. Click Continue. If you do not click Continue, the service items will not be saved. You are returned to the QuickBooks Desktop Setup window— *Get all the details into QuickBooks Desktop* page.
6. Click Add More to enter additional items, customers, or vendors, or close the QuickBooks Desktop Setup window.

To add inventory part items to the Item List using QuickBooks Desktop Setup:

1. At the QuickBooks Desktop Setup window, at the *Get all the details into QuickBooks Desktop* page, in the Add the products and services you sell section, click the Add or Add More button.
2. At the *Add the products and services you sell* page, click the *Inventory part* option and then click Continue.
3. Enter the information for the inventory part items in the appropriate columns and choose the correct date.
4. After entering all the inventory part items information, click Continue. You are returned to the *Add the products and services you sell* page.
5. Click Continue. If you do not click Continue, the inventory part items and opening balances will not be saved. You are returned to the QuickBooks Desktop Setup window—*Get all the details into QuickBooks Desktop* page.
6. Click Add More to enter additional items, customers, or vendors, or close the QuickBooks Desktop Setup window.

To correct an error in the *Journal* report:

1. In the *Journal* report, double-click the transaction with the error. The Invoice type will bring you to the Create Invoices window. The Bill type will bring you to the Enter Bills window. The Inventory Adjust type will bring you to the Adjust Quantity/Value on Hand window.
2. Make the correction in the appropriate window and then click Save & Close.
3. At the warning, click Yes.

To activate the account numbers feature:

1. At the main menu bar, click Edit and then click *Preferences*.
2. In the left panel of the Preferences window, click the Accounting icon.
3. Click the Company Preferences tab.
4. In the ACCOUNTS section, insert a check mark in the box to the left of *Use account numbers* to turn on the account numbers feature.
5. Click OK.

To customize the accounts on the Chart of Accounts List created in the EasyStep Interview and QuickBooks Desktop Setup windows and change account numbers and names:

1. At the main menu bar, click Lists and then click *Chart of Accounts*.
2. Select the account to edit.
3. Click the Account menu button.
4. At the Account button drop-down menu, click *Edit Account*.
5. Make any necessary changes to the account and then click Save & Close.

To allow QuickBooks to create system default accounts:

1. Open and close Activities windows, such as the Create Invoices, Enter Sales Receipts, and Enter Bills windows. Also open the Item List and the New Item window and then select *Inventory Part*.

    This process creates the system default accounts Undeposited Funds, Inventory Asset, and Cost of Goods Sold. After QuickBooks creates these accounts, you can edit each account number and name. If you created an accounts receivable–type account and an accounts payable–type account, QuickBooks will accept the accounts. If you did not previously create them, when you open and close the Create Invoices and Enter Bills windows, QuickBooks will create the accounts receivable and accounts payable accounts, respectively.

2. Follow the steps to customize the Chart of Accounts List and to customize the numbers and names of the system default accounts created by QuickBooks.

To customize the payment terms created in the EasyStep window:

1. At the main menu bar, click Lists and then click *Customer & Vendor Profile Lists*.
2. At the Customer & Vendor Profile Lists submenu, click *Terms List*.
3. At the Terms List window, click the Terms menu button.
4. At the Terms button drop-down menu, click *New*.
5. At the New Terms window, type the appropriate information for any terms QuickBooks did not create that you wish to create.
6. Click Next or OK.
7. At the Terms List window, select the terms created by QuickBooks that you wish to delete.
8. Click the Terms menu button and then click *Delete Terms*. Click OK at the warning.
9. At the Terms List window, select the terms created by QuickBooks that you wish to edit.
10. Click the Terms menu button and then click *Edit Terms*.
11. Change the appropriate information and then click OK.

To update the Chart of Accounts List:

1. At the main menu bar, click Lists and then click *Chart of Accounts*.
2. Click the Account menu button.
3. At the Account button drop-down menu, click *New*.
4. At the Add New Account: Choose Account Type window, choose the type and then click Continue.
5. At the Add New Account window, type in the information and then click Save & New or Save & Close.

To edit the Item List for service items created in the QuickBooks Desktop Setup window:

1. At the main menu bar, click Lists and then click *Item List*.
2. At the Item List window, double-click the service item. The Edit Item window appears.
3. At the *Tax Code* field, click *Non (Non-Taxable Sales)*.
4. At the *Account* field, click the correct account.
5. If the information is correct, click OK.
6. At the Account Change message, click Yes.

To edit an inventory part item created in the QuickBooks Desktop Setup window:

1. At the main menu bar, click Lists and then click *Item List*.
2. At the Item List window, double-click the inventory part item. The Edit Item window appears.
3. At the *COGS Account* field, click the correct account.
4. At the *Tax Code* field, click *Tax (Taxable Sales)*.
5. At the *Income Account* field, click the correct account.
6. At the *Asset Account* field, click the correct account.
7. If the information is correct, click OK.
8. At the Account Change message, click Yes.

To edit the Item List for sales tax created in EasyStep Interview:

1. At the main menu bar, click Lists and then click *Item List*.
2. At the Item List window, double-click the sales tax item to display the Edit window for that item.
3. Review the sales tax information and make any necessary changes.
4. Click OK.

To enter opening balances in the Make General Journal Entries window:

1. At the main menu bar, click Company and then click *Make General Journal Entries*.
2. Choose the date and make or accept the entry in the *ENTRY NO.* field.
3. Remove the check mark next to *ADJUSTING ENTRY*.
4. Enter the accounts and amounts to be debited.
5. Enter the accounts and amounts to be credited.
6. Record the balancing amount as a credit (or debit) to the capital account.
7. Click the Save & Close button.

To reverse the Uncategorized Income account:

1. At the main menu bar, click Company and then click *Make General Journal Entries*.
2. Choose the date and check the entry in the *ENTRY NO.* field.
3. Remove the check mark next to *ADJUSTING ENTRY*.
4. Debit the Uncategorized Income account for the full amount in that account and credit the Capital account for the same amount.
5. Click the Save & Close button.

To reverse the Uncategorized Expenses account:

1. At the main menu bar, click Company and then click *Make General Journal Entries*.
2. Choose the date and check the entry in the *ENTRY NO.* field.
3. Remove the check mark next to *ADJUSTING ENTRY*.
4. Debit the Capital account for the full amount in the Uncategorized Expenses account and credit the Uncategorized Expenses account for the same amount.
5. Click the Save & Close button.

To view and print accounting reports from the Reports menu:

1. At the main menu bar, click Reports and then click *Accountant & Taxes*.
2. At the Accountant & Taxes submenu, choose a report.

3. Indicate the start and end dates for the report.
4. Print the report.
5. Close the report.

To view and print financial statements from the Reports menu:
1. At the main menu bar, click Reports and then click *Company & Financial.*
2. At the Company & Financial submenu, choose a financial report.
3. Indicate the start and end dates for the report.
4. Print the report.
5. Close the report.

Key Concepts

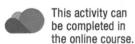
This activity can be completed in the online course.

Select the letter of the item that best matches each definition.

a. System default accounts
b. EasyStep Interview
c. Account numbers
d. Uncategorized Expenses
e. Customizing the Chart of Accounts List
f. Inventory Asset and Cost of Goods Sold

g. Lists - Customer & Vendor Profile Lists - Terms
h. Uncategorized Income
i. Edit - Preferences
j. Dimmed account type

_____ 1. The way QuickBooks identifies system default accounts.
_____ 2. A feature in a company file to identify accounts; must be activated in the Preferences window.
_____ 3. Menu choice used to customize payment terms.
_____ 4. Window where a new company file is created when using the Detailed Start method of New Company Setup.
_____ 5. Account created by QuickBooks as an offsetting amount for Accounts Receivable.
_____ 6. Accounts created by QuickBooks to be used in the Activities windows and journal entries.
_____ 7. Menu choice used to make account numbers active.
_____ 8. Adding and editing account numbers and names.
_____ 9. Accounts created by QuickBooks as an offsetting amount of Accounts Payable.
_____ 10. System default accounts QuickBooks looks for when an inventory part item is set up.

Procedure Check

This activity can be completed in the online course.

1. What is New Company Setup? What is one method of New Company Setup?
2. You have switched your company accounting records to QuickBooks using the EasyStep Interview window and QuickBooks Desktop Setup window. What would you do to customize the Chart of Accounts List created by QuickBooks?
3. How and why would you adjust the Uncategorized Income and Uncategorized Expenses accounts?

4. You are reviewing the new company file you created in QuickBooks using EasyStep Interview and QuickBooks Desktop Setup, and you notice that there are no balances in the revenue and expense accounts. Why is this, and how would you correct it?

5. You have created an Inventory account and a Cost of Goods Sold account, but every time you add a new inventory part item to the Item List, QuickBooks creates an Inventory Asset account and Cost of Goods Sold account. Why does this happen, and how can you correct it?

6. Your manager is just learning QuickBooks. She has asked you to explain EasyStep Interview and QuickBooks Desktop Setup. Provide the manager with a written explanation of the EasyStep Interview and QuickBooks Desktop Setup windows. Be sure to explain what is included in the EasyStep Interview window and QuickBooks Desktop Setup window, and describe the additional procedures necessary to complete the New Company Setup after completing the EasyStep Interview and QuickBooks Desktop Setup windows.

Case Problems

Reports created for these Case Problems can be exported to Excel and uploaded in the online course to be automatically graded.

Demonstrate your knowledge of the QuickBooks features discussed in this chapter by completing the following case problems.

Case Problem 6–1

On April 1, 2022, Lynn Garcia began her business, Lynn's Music Studio. In the first month of business, Lynn set up the music studio, provided guitar and piano lessons, and recorded month-end activity. In May, the second month of business, Lynn started purchasing and selling inventory items of guitars, keyboards, music stands, and sheet music. In April and May, Lynn recorded the financial activities using a manual accounting system. On June 1, 2022, Lynn decides to switch her accounting method to QuickBooks. Lynn has organized the information about the company but has hired you to convert the accounting records to QuickBooks.

1. Use the following information to create the company file and record the information for the company using the Detailed Start method and the EasyStep Interview window. Where no specific information is given, accept the EasyStep Interview window default setting.

Company Name:	CH6 *[Your Name]* Lynn's Music Studio
Tax ID:	45-6123789
Address:	228 Pearl Street
	Scranton, PA 18501
Country:	U.S.
Phone:	570-555-0400
Fax:	570-555-0500
E-mail:	LYNN@ppi-edu.net
Industry:	General Product-based Business
Company:	Sole Proprietorship
Fiscal Year Start:	January
Password:	Student1
Save As:	CH6 *[Your Name]* Lynn's Music Studio

Sell:	Both services and products
Sales Tax:	Yes
Estimates:	No
Tracking Customer Orders:	No
Statements:	No
Invoices:	Yes
Progress Invoicing:	No
Bills You Owe:	Yes
Tracking Inventory:	Yes
Tracking Time:	No
Employees:	No
Start Tracking:	06/01/2022

Remove the check mark from each of the following accounts:
    Shipping and Delivery Income
    Freight and Shipping Costs
    Merchant Account Fees
    Product Samples Expense
    Purchases - Resale Items
    Advertising and Promotion
    Automobile Expense
    Bank Service Charges
    Computer and Internet Expenses
    Dues and Subscriptions
    Meals and Entertainment
    Postage and Delivery
    Professional Fees
    Repairs and Maintenance
    Travel Expense
    Ask My Accountant

Insert a check mark to the left of the following account:
    Sales Discounts

2. Use the information in Table LMS—Customers to create and update the Customer Center using the QuickBooks Desktop Setup window. Be sure to use the date *June 1, 2022*.

TABLE LMS Customers

Customer/Company Name	Name/Contact	Phone	Address/ City, State, Zip	Balance
Douglaston Senior Center	Herbie Richardson	570-555-7749	574 S Beech Street Scranton, PA 18506	$175.00
Highland School	Asst. Principal Office	570-555-6963	115 Forrest Street Waymart, PA 18472	
Jefferson High School	Music Department	570-555-9600	500 Apple Street Dunmore, PA 18512	

...continues

Customer/Company Name	Name/Contact	Phone	Address/ City, State, Zip	Balance
Mulligan Residence	Adam Smith	570-555-3325	299 Hickory Lane Scranton, PA 18504	$1,575.90
Musical Youth Group	Dana Thompson	570-555-6642	550 Marion Lane Scranton, PA 18504	
Patel Family	Ari Patel	570-555-1132	574 Kenwood Drive Dickson City, PA 18519	
Patterson Family	Jonathan Patterson	570-555-6321	650 Memory Lane Dickson City, PA 18519	
Schroeder Family	Betty Schroeder	570-555-1897	98 Belmont Rd. Carbondale, PA 18407	
Twin Lakes Elementary	Miss Brooks	570-555-4474	515 Hobson Street Honesdale, PA 18431	

3. Use the information in Table LMS—Vendors to create and update the Vendor Center using the QuickBooks Desktop Setup window. Be sure to use the date *June 1, 2022.*

TABLE LMS Vendors

Vendor/Company Name	Name/Contact	Phone	Address/ City, State, Zip	Balance
Computer Town	Customer Service	570-555-1500	1000 Carbondale Highway Scranton, PA 18502	$2,000.00
Katie's Keyboards	Katie Shea	570-555-7777	158 Clay Road Scranton, PA 18505	1,500.00
Lynn Garcia				
Melody Music Equipment	Melody Arhmand	570-555-1120	780 Roselyn Ave. Scranton, PA 18505	
Mills Family Furniture	Edna Mills	570-555-7144	150 Amelia Street Scranton, PA 18503	1,500.00
Music Instruments, Inc.	Matilda Molloy	570-555-9630	25 Monroe Ave. Scranton, PA 18505	
Mutual Insurance Company	Bob Maxwell	570-555-5600	1 Main Street Honesdale, PA 18431	1,200.00
PA Dept. of Revenue				
Paper, Clips, and More	Justin Daves	570-555-8558	157 Waymart Lane Waymart, PA 18472	350.00
Pioneer Phone	Customer Service	570-555-6000	1000 Route 6 Carbondale, PA 18407	
Steamtown Electric	Customer Service	570-555-2500	150 Vine Lane Scranton, PA 18501	
Strings, Sheets & Such	Manuela Perez	570-555-3636	250 Lincoln St. Scranton, PA 18505	
Tune Tones	Tony Tune	570-555-1111	500 Monroe Ave. Dunmore, PA 18512	
Viewhill Realty	Matt Snyder	570-555-1000	100 Commerce Blvd. Scranton, PA 18501	

4. Use the information in Table LMS—Items to update the Item List using the QuickBooks Desktop Setup window. Be sure to use the date *June 1, 2022*.

TABLE LMS
Items

Item Name and Description	Price	Cost	On Hand	Total Value
Service Items:				
Guitar Lessons	$ 30			
Piano Lessons	35			
Inventory Part Items:				
Guitars	100	$50	6	$ 300
Keyboards	150	75	17	1,275
Music Stands	40	20	17	340
Sheet Music	6	3	165	495

5. Activate the account numbers feature. Use the following information to customize the Chart of Accounts List:

	QuickBooks		Edited
Number	Account Name	Number	Account Name
15000	Furniture and Equipment	1700	Music Instruments
17000	Accumulated Depreciation	1750	Accum. Dep., Music Instruments [Subaccount of 1700 Music Instruments]
30800	Owners Draw	3020	Lynn Garcia, Drawings
	Sales Income	4060	Sale of Guitars
48300	Sales Discounts	4100	
62400	Depreciation Expense	6075	Deprec. Exp., Music Instruments
63300	Insurance Expense	6200	
63400	Interest Expense	7000	[Account Type: Other Expense]
64900	Office Supplies	6325	Office Supplies Expense
67100	Rent Expense	6400	
68100	Telephone Expense	6450	
68600	Utilities	6500	Utilities Expense

6. Delete the following account:
   47900 Sales

7. Open and close the following windows to allow QuickBooks to create default accounts:
   Create Invoices
   Enter Sales Receipts
   Enter Bills
   Item List: New Item: Inventory Part

8. Customize the system default accounts:

QuickBooks		Edited	
Number	Account Name	Number	Account Name
11000	Accounts Receivable	1200	
12000	Undeposited Funds	1250	
12100	*Inventory Asset	1260	Inventory of Guitars
20000	Accounts Payable	2010	
25500	Sales Tax Payable	2200	
30000	Opening Balance Equity	3010	Lynn Garcia, Capital
32000	Owners Equity	3030	Accumulated Earnings
50000	*Cost of Goods Sold	5060	Cost of Guitars Sold

9. Customize the payment Terms List to list only the following:
   2/10, Net 30 Days
   Net 10 Days
   Net 15 Days
   Net 30 Days

10. Use the information in Table LMS—New Accounts to update the Chart of Accounts List.

TABLE LMS
New Accounts

Account Type	Number	Account Name
Bank	1010	Cash - Operating
Other Current Asset	1265	Inventory of Keyboards
Other Current Asset	1270	Inventory of Music Stands
Other Current Asset	1275	Inventory of Sheet Music
Other Current Asset	1300	Music Supplies
Other Current Asset	1305	Office Supplies
Other Current Asset	1410	Prepaid Advertising
Other Current Asset	1420	Prepaid Insurance
Fixed Asset	1725	Music Instruments, Cost [Subaccount of 1700]
Fixed Asset	1800	Furniture
Fixed Asset	1825	Furniture, Cost [Subaccount of 1800]
Fixed Asset	1850	Accum. Dep., Furniture [Subaccount of 1800]
Fixed Asset	1900	Computers
Fixed Asset	1925	Computers, Cost [Subaccount of 1900]
Fixed Asset	1950	Accum. Dep., Computers [Subaccount of 1900]
Other Current Liability	2020	Notes Payable
Other Current Liability	2030	Interest Payable
Income	4010	Piano Lessons
Income	4020	Guitar Lessons
Income	4065	Sale of Keyboards
Income	4070	Sale of Music Stands
Income	4075	Sale of Sheet Music

...continues

Account Type	Number	Account Name
Cost of Goods Sold	5065	Cost of Keyboards Sold
Cost of Goods Sold	5070	Cost of Music Stands Sold
Cost of Goods Sold	5075	Cost of Sheet Music Sold
Cost of Goods Sold	5900	Inventory Adjustment
Expense	6085	Deprec. Exp., Furniture
Expense	6095	Deprec. Exp., Computers
Expense	6150	Instrument Tuning Expense
Expense	6300	Music Supplies Expense

11. Use the information in Table LMS—Update Item List to update the Item List for items created as part of the QuickBooks Desktop Setup.

TABLE LMS
Update Item List

Item Name and Description	COGS Account	Income Account	Asset Account
Service Items (nontaxable):			
Guitar Lessons		4020	
Piano Lessons		4010	
Inventory Part Items (taxable):			
Guitars	5060	4060	1260
Keyboards	5065	4065	1265
Music Stands	5070	4070	1270
Sheet Music	5075	4075	1275

After updating the Item List, you can delete the Inventory Asset account and Cost of Goods Sold account (the accounts with no numbers).

12. Edit the Item List for the sales tax item created in the EasyStep Interview:

Sales Tax Name: PA Sales Tax
Description: Sales Tax
Tax Rate: 7%
Tax Agency: PA Dept. of Revenue

13. Make three journal entries on June 1, 2022 (accept the default Entry Nos.):
    a. Enter the opening balances listed below. Enter the following accounts and amounts as debits:

Number	Account Name	Balance
1010	Cash - Operating	$14,615.18
1300	Music Supplies	430.00
1305	Office Supplies	300.00
1420	Prepaid Insurance	1,100.00
1725	Music Instruments, Cost	4,000.00
1825	Furniture, Cost	2,500.00
1925	Computers, Cost	3,000.00

...continues

...continued

Number	Account Name	Balance
3020	Lynn Garcia, Drawings	1,000.00
4100	Sales Discounts	188.92
5060	Cost of Guitars Sold	1,150.00
5065	Cost of Keyboards Sold	2,475.00
5070	Cost of Music Stands Sold	460.00
5075	Cost of Sheet Music Sold	1,305.00
5900	Inventory Adjustment	50.00
6075	Deprec. Exp., Music Instruments	60.00
6085	Deprec. Exp., Furniture	40.00
6095	Deprec. Exp., Computers	35.00
6150	Instrument Tuning Expense	100.00
6200	Insurance Expense	100.00
6300	Music Supplies Expense	70.00
6325	Office Supplies Expense	50.00
6400	Rent Expense	600.00
6450	Telephone Expense	50.00
6500	Utilities Expense	70.00
7000	Interest Expense	15.00

Enter the following accounts and amounts as credits:

Number	Account Name	Balance
1750	Accum. Dep., Music Instruments	$ 60.00
1850	Accum. Dep., Furniture	40.00
1950	Accum. Dep., Computers	35.00
2020	Notes Payable	2,000.00
2030	Interest Payable	15.00
4010	Piano Lessons	3,535.00
4020	Guitar Lessons	2,910.00
4060	Sale of Guitars	2,300.00
4065	Sale of Keyboards	4,950.00
4070	Sale of Music Stands	920.00
4075	Sale of Sheet Music	2,610.00

    b. Make a journal entry to reverse the Uncategorized Income account.

    c. Make a journal entry to reverse the Uncategorized Expenses account.

14. Display and print the following reports for June 1, 2022:

    a. *Journal*

    b. *Trial Balance*

    c. *Profit & Loss Standard* (04/01/2022–06/01/2022)

    d. *Balance Sheet Standard*

    e. *Item Listing*

    f. *Customer Contact List*

    g. *Vendor Contact List*

15. Make a backup copy of the new company file. Use the name **LMS6** *[Your Name]* **Lynn's Music Studio**. Restore the backup copy and change the company name to **LMS6** *[Your Name]* **Lynn's Music Studio**.

Case Problem 6–2

On June 1, 2022, Olivia Chen began her business, Olivia's Web Solutions. In the first month of business, Olivia set up the office, provided web page design and internet consulting services, and recorded month-end activity. In July, the second month of business, Olivia began to purchase and sell inventory items of computer hardware and software. In June and July, Olivia recorded the financial activities using a manual accounting system. On August 1, 2022, Olivia decides to switch her accounting method to QuickBooks. Olivia has organized the information about the company but has hired you to convert the accounting records to QuickBooks.

1. Use the information below to create the company file and record the information for the company using the Detailed Start method and the EasyStep Interview window. Where no specific information is given, accept the EasyStep Interview window default setting.

Company Name:	CH6 *[Your Name]* Olivia's Web Solutions
Tax ID:	55-5656566
Address:	547 Miller Place
	Westport, NY 11858
Country:	U.S.
Phone:	516-555-5000
Fax:	516-555-6000
E-mail:	LIV@ppi-edu.net
Industry:	General Product-based Business
Company:	Sole Proprietorship
Fiscal Year Start:	January
Password:	Student1
Save As:	CH6 *[Your Name]* Olivia's Web Solutions
Sell:	Both services and products
Sales Tax:	Yes
Estimates:	No
Tracking Customer	
Orders:	No
Statements:	No
Invoices:	Yes
Progress Invoicing:	No
Bills You Owe:	Yes
Tracking Inventory:	Yes
Tracking Time:	No
Employees:	No
Start Tracking:	08/01/2022

Remove the check mark from each of the following accounts:
    Shipping and Delivery Income
    Freight and Shipping Costs
    Merchant Account Fees
    Product Samples Expense
    Purchases - Resale Items
    Automobile Expense
    Bank Service Charges   *...continues*

...continued

Computer and Internet Expenses
Dues and Subscriptions
Meals and Entertainment
Postage and Delivery
Professional Fees
Repairs and Maintenance
Travel Expense
Ask My Accountant

Insert a check mark to the left of the following account:
Sales Discounts

2. Use the information in Table OWS—Customers to create and update the Customer Center using the QuickBooks Desktop Setup window. Be sure to use the date *August 1, 2022.*

TABLE OWS Customers

Customer/ Company Name	Name/Contact	Phone	Address/ City, State, Zip	Balance
Artie's Auto Repair	Leon Artie	516-555-1221	32 W. 11th Street New Hyde Park, NY 11523	$ 800.00
Breathe Easy A/C Contractors	Allen Scott	516-555-6868	556 Atlantic Ave. Freeport, NY 11634	
Long Island Water Works	Customer Service	516-555-4747	87-54 Bayview Ave. Glen Cove, NY 11536	
Miguel's Restaurant	Miguel Perez	516-555-3236	30 Willis Ave. Roslyn, NY 11541	
Schneider Family	Johnny Schneider	516-555-8989	363 Farmers Rd. Syosset, NY 11547	1,000.00
Sehorn & Smith Attorneys	Jerry Sehorn	212-555-3339	510 Fifth Ave. New York, NY 10022	800.00
Singh Family	David Singh	718-555-3233	363 Marathon Parkway Little Neck, NY 11566	
South Shore School District	Joseph Porter	516-555-4545	3666 Ocean Ave. South Beach, NY 11365	12,056.00
Thrifty Stores	William Way	718-555-2445	23 Boston Ave. Bronx, NY 11693	1,500.00

3. Use the information in Table OWS—Vendors to create and update the Vendor Center using the QuickBooks Desktop Setup window. Be sure to use the date *August 1, 2022.*

TABLE OWS Vendors

Vendor/Company Name	Name/Contact	Phone	Address/ City, State, Zip	Balance
ARC Management	Alvin R. Clinton	516-555-6363	668 Lakeville Ave. Garden City, NY 11678	
Chrbet Advertising	Chris Chrbet	212-555-8777	201 E. 10th Street New York, NY 10012	$1,200.00

...continues

Vendor/Company Name	Name/Contact	Phone	Address/ City, State, Zip	Balance
Comet Computer Supplies	Customer Service	631-555-4444	657 Motor Parkway Center Island, NY 11488	
Computec Computers	Customer Service	702-555-6564	3631 Gate Blvd. Greenboro, NC 27407	$10,000.00
Eastel	Customer Service	212-555-6565	655 Fifth Ave. New York, NY 10012	350.00
Eastern Mutual Insurance	Customer Service	212-555-6363	55 Broadway, Room 55 New York, NY 10001	
InterSoft Development Co.	Customer Service	361-555-3634	556 Route 347 Hauppauge, NY 11654	
Lewis Furniture Co.	Manny Lewis	631-555-6161	1225 Route 110 Farmingdale, NY 11898	1,700.00
LI Power Company	Customer Service	516-555-8888	5444 Northern Ave. Plainview, NY 11544	
Martin Computer Repairs	Ken Martin	516-555-7777	366 N. Franklin St. Garden City, NY 11568	
Netsoft Development Co.	Customer Service	974-555-7873	684 Mountain View Rd Portland, OR 68774	1,600.00
NYS Tax Dept.				
Office Plus	Customer Service	516-555-3214	45 Jericho Tpke. Jericho, NY 11654	375.00
Olivia Chen				
Scanntronix	Customer Service	617-555-8778	2554 Bedford Rd. Boston, MA 02164	
Systems Service	Jeremy Jones	516-555-2525	36 Sunrise Lane Hempstead, NY 11004	
Textpro Software, Inc.	Customer Service	615-555-4545	877 Route 5 Ft. Lauderdale, FL 70089	

4. Use the information in Table OWS—Items to update the Item List using the QuickBooks Desktop Setup window. Be sure to use the date *August 1, 2022*.

TABLE OWS
Items

Item Name and Description	Price	Cost	On Hand	Total Value
Service Items:				
Internet Consulting Services	$100			
Web Page Design Services	125			
Inventory Part Items:				
Computers	2,000	$1,000	10	$10,000
Scanners	600	300	12	3,600
HTML Software	150	75	18	1,350
Desktop Pub. Software	200	100	10	1,000

5. Activate the account numbers feature. Use the following information to customize the Chart of Accounts List:

	QuickBooks		Edited
Number	**Account Name**	**Number**	**Account Name**
15000	Furniture and Equipment	1700	Computers
17000	Accumulated Depreciation	1750	Accum. Dep., Computers Subaccount of 1700]
30800	Owners Draw	3020	Olivia Chen, Drawings
	Sales Income	4060	Sale of Computers
48300	Sales Discounts	4100	
60000	Advertising and Promotion	6050	Advertising Expense
62400	Depreciation Expense	6075	Deprec. Exp., Computers
63300	Insurance Expense	6100	
63400	Interest Expense	7000	[Account Type: Other Expense]
64900	Office Supplies	6325	Office Supplies Expense
67100	Rent Expense	6400	
68100	Telephone Expense	6450	
68600	Utilities	6500	Utilities Expense

6. Delete the following account:
   47900 Sales

7. Open and close the following windows to allow QuickBooks to create default accounts:
   Create Invoices
   Enter Sales Receipts
   Enter Bills
   Item List: New Item: Inventory Part

8. Customize the system default accounts:

	QuickBooks		Edited
Number	**Account Name**	**Number**	**Account Name**
11000	Accounts Receivable	1200	
12000	Undeposited Funds	1250	
12100	*Inventory Asset	1260	Inventory of Computers
20000	Accounts Payable	2010	
25500	Sales Tax Payable	2200	
30000	Opening Balance Equity	3010	Olivia Chen, Capital
32000	Owners Equity	3030	Accumulated Earnings
50000	*Cost of Goods Sold	5060	Cost of Computers Sold

9. Customize the payment Terms List to list only the following:
   2/10, Net 30 Days
   Net 10 Days
   Net 15 Days
   Net 30 Days

10. Use the information in Table OWS—New Accounts to update the Chart of Accounts List.

TABLE OWS
New Accounts

Account Type	Number	Account Name
Bank	1010	Cash - Operating
Other Current Asset	1265	Inventory of Scanners
Other Current Asset	1270	Inventory of HTML Software
Other Current Asset	1275	Inventory of Desktop Pub. Soft.
Other Current Asset	1300	Computer Supplies
Other Current Asset	1305	Office Supplies
Other Current Asset	1410	Prepaid Advertising
Other Current Asset	1420	Prepaid Insurance
Fixed Asset	1725	Computers, Cost [Subaccount of 1700]
Fixed Asset	1800	Furniture
Fixed Asset	1825	Furniture, Cost [Subaccount of 1800]
Fixed Asset	1850	Accum. Dep., Furniture [Subaccount of 1800]
Fixed Asset	1900	Software
Fixed Asset	1925	Software, Cost [Subaccount of 1900]
Fixed Asset	1950	Accum. Dep., Software [Subaccount of 1900]
Other Current Liability	2020	Notes Payable
Other Current Liability	2030	Interest Payable
Income	4010	Web Page Design Fees
Income	4020	Internet Consulting Fees
Income	4065	Sale of Scanners
Income	4070	Sale of HTML Software
Income	4075	Sale of Desktop Pub. Software
Cost of Goods Sold	5065	Cost of Scanners Sold
Cost of Goods Sold	5070	Cost of HTML Software Sold
Cost of Goods Sold	5075	Cost of Desktop Pub. Soft. Sold
Cost of Goods Sold	5900	Inventory Adjustment
Expense	6085	Deprec. Exp., Furniture
Expense	6095	Deprec. Exp., Software
Expense	6300	Computer Supplies Expense
Expense	6350	Online Service Expense

11. Use the information in Table OWS—Update Item List to update the Item List for items created as part of QuickBooks Desktop Setup.

TABLE OWS
Update Item List

Item Name and Description	COGS Account	Income Account	Asset Account
Service Items (nontaxable):			
Internet Consulting Services		4020	
Web Page Design Services		4010	
Inventory Part Items (taxable):			
Computers	5060	4060	1260
Scanners	5065	4065	1265
HTML Software	5070	4070	1270
Desktop Pub. Software	5075	4075	1275

After updating the Item List, you can delete the Inventory Asset account and Cost of Goods Sold account (the accounts with no numbers).

12. Edit the Item List for the sales tax item created in the EasyStep Interview:

Sales Tax Name: NY Sales Tax
Description: Sales Tax
Tax Rate: 8%
Tax Agency: NYS Tax Dept.

13. Make three journal entries on August 1, 2022 (accept the default Entry Nos.):
   a. Enter the opening balances listed below. Enter the following accounts and amounts as debits:

Number	Account Name	Balance
1010	Cash - Operating	$24,489.16
1300	Computer Supplies	350.00
1305	Office Supplies	325.00
1410	Prepaid Advertising	1,000.00
1420	Prepaid Insurance	1,650.00
1725	Computers, Cost	5,000.00
1825	Furniture, Cost	3,200.00
1925	Software, Cost	3,600.00
3020	Olivia Chen, Drawings	500.00
4100	Sales Discounts	179.84
5060	Cost of Computers Sold	10,000.00
5065	Cost of Scanners Sold	2,400.00
5070	Cost of HTML Software Sold	75.00
5075	Cost of Desktop Pub. Soft. Sold	500.00
5900	Inventory Adjustment	75.00
6050	Advertising Expense	200.00
6075	Deprec. Exp., Computers	75.00
6085	Deprec. Exp., Furniture	50.00
6095	Deprec. Exp., Software	100.00
6100	Insurance Expense	150.00

...continues

...continued

Number	Account Name	Balance
6300	Computer Supplies Expense	250.00
6325	Office Supplies Expense	50.00
6350	Online Service Expense	150.00
6400	Rent Expense	800.00
6450	Telephone Expense	350.00
6500	Utilities Expense	125.00
7000	Interest Expense	25.00

Enter the following accounts and amounts as credits:

Number	Account Name	Balance
1750	Accum. Dep., Computers	$ 75.00
1850	Accum. Dep., Furniture	50.00
1950	Accum. Dep., Software	100.00
2020	Notes Payable	2,500.00
2030	Interest Payable	25.00
4010	Web Page Design Fees	9,750.00
4020	Internet Consulting Fees	6,600.00
4060	Sale of Computers	20,000.00
4065	Sale of Scanners	4,800.00
4070	Sale of HTML Software	150.00
4075	Sale of Desktop Pub. Software	1,000.00

   b. Make a journal entry to reverse the Uncategorized Income account.

   c. Make a journal entry to reverse the Uncategorized Expenses account.

14. Display and print the following reports for August 1, 2022:

   a. *Journal*

   b. *Trial Balance*

   c. *Profit & Loss Standard* (06/01/2022–08/01/2022)

   d. *Balance Sheet Standard*

   e. *Item Listing*

   f. *Customer Contact List*

   g. *Vendor Contact List*

15. Make a backup copy of the new company file. Use the name **OWS6 *[Your Name]* Olivia's Web Solutions**. Restore the backup copy and change the company name to **OWS6 *[Your Name]* Olivia's Web Solutions**.

New Company Setup— Express Start

Setting Up Company Preferences and Lists and Centers

Objectives

- Create a new company file using the QuickBooks Express Start Method

- Set up a company file password

- Establish preferences

- Update the Chart of Accounts List

- Customize the system default accounts and Terms List

- Update the Item List

- Update the Customer and Vendor Centers

- Adjust the new company file to follow the accrual basis of accounting

- Display and print accounting reports and financial statements

 The online course includes additional training and assessment resources. Reports created for the Chapter Problem can be uploaded for instructor review.

Chapter Introduction

In this chapter, you will learn an alternative method for creating a new company file in QuickBooks. As you know, the four levels of operation for QuickBooks are New Company Setup, Lists/Centers, Activities, and Reports. In Chapters 2 through 5, the Lists, Activities, and Reports levels were presented for both a service company and a merchandise company. In those chapters, you opened an existing company file, updated the Lists/Centers, recorded Activities in the various windows, and viewed and printed Reports. You will now learn another method for New Company Setup.

QuickBooks provides two methods of New Company Setup: Detailed Start and Express Start. In Chapter 6, the New Company Setup level of operation was presented using the Detailed Start method, which moves you to the EasyStep Interview window. In addition, you used the QuickBooks Desktop Setup window to continue with the New Company Setup.

In Chapter 7, you will learn how to conduct New Company Setup using the Express Start method. With this method you are not moved to the EasyStep Interview window, but rather enter some basic information to create your company file, set up a password, and then directly enable the features you desire. In addition, in this Chapter, you will not use the QuickBooks Desktop Setup window to enter the detailed information for the company but instead you will use many of the procedures you learned earlier for updating the List/Centers to directly enter information in the new company file. Finally, the new company file will be prepared for the accrual basis of accounting.

In this chapter, you will again create and set up a new company file for our sample company, Kristin Raina Interior Designs. It is assumed that Kristin Raina Interior Designs has been recording accounting activities using a manual accounting system and will convert the company's accounting records to QuickBooks.

QuickBooks versus Manual Accounting: New Company Setup

As explained in Chapter 6, in a manual accounting system, a company's records are set up by creating the Chart of Accounts and a general ledger. The Chart of Accounts is the list of accounts (assets, liabilities, equity, revenues, and expenses) the company intends to use. The general ledger is the book of all accounts, with the beginning balance for each account. If desired, subsidiary ledgers can also be created and beginning balances recorded. The subsidiary ledgers typically include accounts receivable and accounts payable. If the perpetual inventory system is used, an inventory subsidiary ledger is also created.

In QuickBooks, a company's records are set up by creating a new company file and establishing the Chart of Accounts List. As the opening balances are entered, QuickBooks simultaneously sets up the general ledger. The Customer Center and Vendor Center are set up; these centers are equivalent to the accounts receivable and accounts payable subsidiary ledgers. The Item List, which is equivalent to an inventory subsidiary ledger, is set up. However, in QuickBooks, the Item List includes service revenue items and sales tax items in addition to inventory items.

When you set up a new company file using the Express Start method—which does not use the Easy Step Interview window—you first set up a company file password, and then you identify certain company preferences. After that, you customize parts of the company file. You can use the QuickBooks Desktop Setup window to enter the information for customers, vendors, and items as illustrated in Chapter 6, but doing so is not required. If you choose not to use the QuickBooks Desktop Setup window to enter information, you will then use the Lists/Centers windows to continue with the setup of the new company file.

Entering information in the Lists/Centers is similar to creating a Chart of Accounts, general ledger, and subsidiary ledgers in a manual accounting system. Finally, you need to make three journal entries to complete the New Company Setup. One journal entry records the opening balances in the accounts that were not included when you set up the Lists/Centers; the other two journal entries reverse accounts set up by QuickBooks during the New Company Setup that are not used in the accrual basis of accounting.

Chapter Problem

In this chapter, there is no prepared company file to open from the company files. Instead, you will create and set up the company file for Kristin Raina Interior Designs.

Assume that Kristin Raina began her interior design business in January 2022 and has maintained accounting records with a manual accounting system for January through March. Effective April 1, 2022, Kristin Raina will convert the company's accounting records to QuickBooks using the Express Start method.

When setting up the new company file, you will enter company information (name, address, tax identification numbers) and create a password. Once the file is created and saved, you'll establish preferences and enter the rest of the information, including general ledger account names and account numbers; customer information (name, address, telephone numbers, and so on) and outstanding balances; vendor information (name, address, telephone numbers, and so on) and outstanding balances; service items and billing amounts; inventory part items (name, cost, selling price, and quantity on hand); and sales tax information.

To begin the New Company Setup:
1. Open QuickBooks.
2. At the No Company Open window, click Create a new company or click File and then click *New Company*. The QuickBooks Desktop Setup window appears with the *Let's set up your business!* page displayed. This is the page where you select the method of New Company Setup. See Figure 7–A.

FIGURE 7–A
QuickBooks Desktop
Setup Window—*Let's Set
Up Your Business!* Page

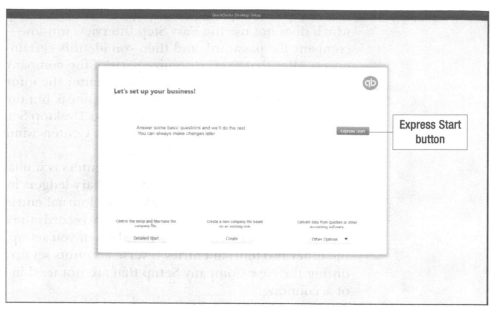

Let's set up your business!

Answer some basic questions and we'll do the rest
You can always make changes later

Express Start

**Express Start
button**

Control the setup and fine-tune the company file.

Create a new company file based on an existing one.

Convert data from Quicken or other accounting software.

Detailed Start

Create

Other Options ▼

New Company Setup

HINT

See Appendix F for a summary of this method for New Company Setup.

Express Start

In the New Company Setup, the first level of operation in QuickBooks, you will enter the information needed to create and setup a company file for Kristin Raina Interior Designs using the Express Start method. With this method of New Company Setup, you will enter some basic information about the company, identify the type of industry for your company, and save the company file.

To create a new company file using the Express Start method without the EasyStep Interview:

1. At the QuickBooks Desktop Setup window, at the *Let's set up your business!*, click the Express Start button. The *Glad you're here* page appears.
2. At the *Glad you're here* page, at the *Business Name* field, type CH7 *[Your Name]* Kristin Raina Interior Designs.
3. At the *Industry* field, click *Help me choose.* The Select Your Industry page appears.
4. At the Select Your Industry page, at the *Industry* field, scroll to the bottom and select *Other/None.* See Figure 7–B.

FIGURE 7–B
Select Your Industry Page

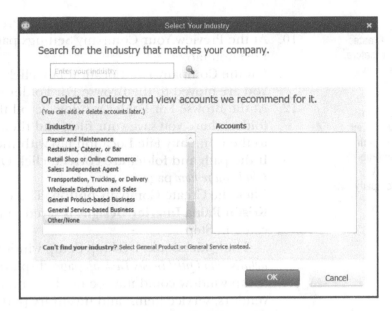

5. If the information is correct, click OK. You are returned to the *Glad you're here* page.
6. At the *Business Type* field, choose *Sole Proprietorship* from the drop-down menu.
7. At the *Employer Identification Number (EIN)* field, type 33-4777781.
8. Enter the following business contact information:

Phone:	651-555-1000
Business Address:	25 NE Johnson Street
City:	Minneapolis
ZIP:	53402
State:	MN
Country:	U.S.

When you are finished, your screen should look like Figure 7–C.

FIGURE 7–C
Glad You're Here Page—
Completed

HINT

If you click the Create Company button before clicking the Preview Your Settings button, QuickBooks will save your file in the most recent folder you used or in the default path C:\Users\Public\(Public) Documents\Intuit\ QuickBooks\Company Files.

9. If the information is correct, click the Preview Your Settings button.
10. At the Preview Your Company Settings page, click the Company File Location tab.
11. On the Company File Location tab, click the Change Location button. You are moved to the Browse For Folder window.
12. At the Browse For Folder window, scroll through the list, choose the folder where you save your files, and then click OK. You are returned to the Company File Location tab with the path and folder displayed.
13. If the path and folder are correct, click OK. You are returned to the *Glad you're here* page.
14. Click the Create Company button. The company file **CH7** *[Your Name]* **Kristin Raina Interior Designs** is saved in the path and folder you indicated in Step 12.

    The QuickBooks Desktop Setup window appears with the *Get all the details into QuickBooks Desktop* page displayed. The QuickBooks Desktop Setup window could now be used to enter information for customers, vendors, service items, and inventory part items, as was illustrated in Chapter 6. However, in this chapter, you will not use the QuickBooks Desktop Setup window. Instead, you will enter information directly into Lists and Centers.
15. Close the QuickBooks Desktop Setup window. If the New Feature Tour window appears, click the X to close it. The Home page and Left Icon bar appear. Close the Home page. To remove the Left Icon bar, click View and then click *Hide Icon Bar*.

You will now continue setting up the company file. To do this, you will take the following steps: set up a company file password; establish Preferences; update the Chart of Accounts List; customize the system default accounts and the Terms List; and update the Item List, Customer Center, and Vendor Center with beginning balances. Finally, you will adjust for the accrual basis of accounting by entering opening balances in accounts by journal entry and recording two journal entries to offset two accounts created by QuickBooks that are not used in the accrual basis of accounting.

New Company Setup → ## Company File Password

In business, it is advisable to protect access to financial records with a password. QuickBooks has the ability to password protect not only the entire company file but also specific sections of the company file. This allows a company to limit employees' access to their respective areas of responsibility. For instance, the accounts receivable bookkeeper may be permitted to access only the information pertaining to customers' accounts; the payroll bookkeeper may be permitted to access only the payroll information; and so on.

Originally, it was optional for the user to password protect a company file. But in recent versions of QuickBooks, password protection has become mandatory. There are a few instances when a password can be optional (such as when a business identification number has not been entered), but in most situations, a password is now required to open a company file.

HINT

In both Chapter 6 and Chapter 7, if you close a new company file without setting up a password, you will be required to create a password the next time you open the company file.

When you create a new company file using the EasyStep Interview window as you did in Chapter 6, you are prompted to set up a password. In this chapter, you are not using the EasyStep Interview and will not be prompted. However, if you close a new company file without setting up a password, you will be required to create one the next time you open the company file. Therefore, it is always a good practice to set up a password before leaving a new company file.

To create a company file password:

1. At the main menu bar, click Company and then click *Setup Users and Passwords.*
2. At the Setup Users and Passwords submenu, click *Change Your Password.* The Change Your Password window appears. See Figure 7–D.

FIGURE 7–D
Change Your Password Window

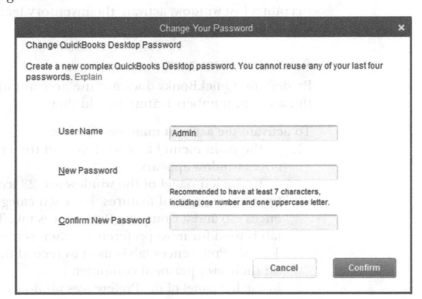

HINT

If you use your own password, challenge question, and answer, be sure to keep a record of them in a safe place, or you will be unable to open the new company file. In this textbook, for all company files, the password is *Student1.*

3. In the *New Password* and *Confirm New Password* text boxes, type Student1 or a password of your choosing.
4. If the information is correct, click Confirm. At the QuickBooks Desktop Information message, click OK. Close the Home page if it appears. The password is now created for the new company file, and you will need to enter the password each time you open the company file.

If you closed the company file before creating a password, the next time you open the company file, a window labeled Sensitive Data Protection Setup appears where you must enter a password. While the title of the window is different than the Change Your Password window, the fields of information in both windows are the same for entering the password.

Establishing Preferences

When you use the EasyStep Interview window in the Detailed Start method of New Company Setup, as seen in Chapter 6, QuickBooks asks questions and, based on your responses, establishes preferences for your company. When you choose the Express Start method, you do not use EasyStep Interview window. Therefore, you must establish the preferences for the new company file yourself. Company preferences enable or disable features available in QuickBooks. When a feature is enabled, it allows for choices to be listed on the drop-down menus and the Home page. If a feature is disabled, some choices will not be listed on the drop-down menus and the Home page.

You set these preferences in the Preferences window. You will use the Preferences window to activate the account *Number* field in the Chart of Accounts List window, activate the inventory feature, activate sales tax, and disable the payroll feature.

Account Numbers

By default, QuickBooks does not use account numbers. You must activate the account numbers feature to add them.

To activate the account numbers feature:

1. At the main menu bar, click Edit and then click *Preferences*. The Preferences window appears.

   In the left panel of the window are 23 icons that represent the different categories of features. For each category, there is a My Preferences tab and a Company Preferences tab. The Company Preferences tab is used for most preferences when setting up a new company file. The My Preferences tab is used to record the preferences for each user on their own personal computer.

2. In the left panel of the Preferences window, click the Accounting icon.

3. Click the Company Preferences tab.

4. In the Accounts section, insert a check mark in the box to the left of *Use account numbers* to turn on the account numbers feature. See Figure 7–E.

FIGURE 7–E
Preferences Window—
Accounting—Company
Preferences Tab

Use account numbers option

DATE WARNINGS options

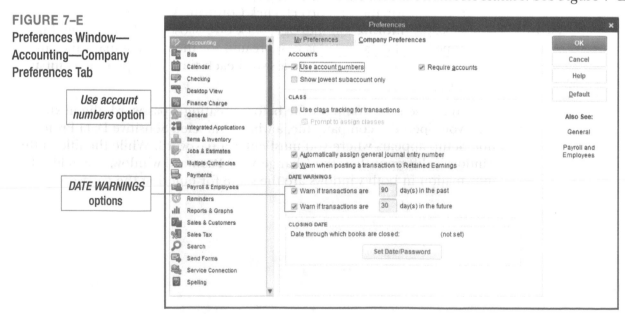

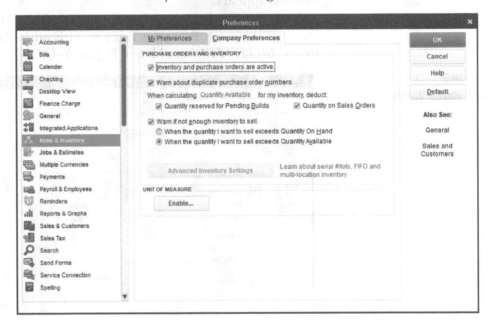

HINT

If you receive warnings about dates, remove the check marks from the DATE WARNINGS section.

5. If the information is correct, click OK. The account *Number* field now appears in the New Account and Edit Account windows in the Chart of Accounts List.

Inventory

QuickBooks provides you with the ability to maintain inventory records, but the inventory feature must be activated.

To activate the inventory feature:

1. At the main menu bar, click Edit and then click *Preferences*. The Preferences window appears.
2. In the left panel of the Preferences window, click the Items & Inventory icon.
3. Click the Company Preferences tab.
4. In the PURCHASE ORDERS AND INVENTORY section, insert a check mark in the box to the left of *Inventory and purchase orders are active* to turn on the inventory feature. See Figure 7–F.

FIGURE 7–F
Preferences Window—
Items & Inventory—
Company Preferences
Tab

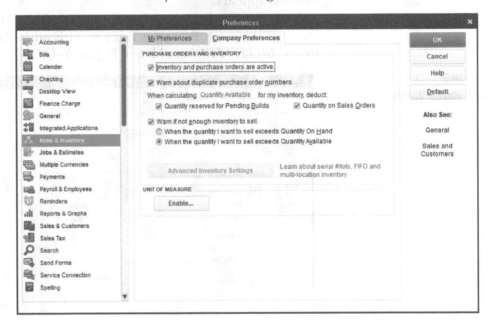

5. If the information is correct, click OK. The inventory feature is now activated, and fields of information relevant to inventory appear in the Activities windows.

Sales Tax

QuickBooks also provides you with the ability to charge and maintain sales tax information, but the sales tax feature must be activated.

To activate the sales tax feature:

1. At the main menu bar, click Edit and then click *Preferences*.
2. In the left panel of the Preferences window, click the Sales Tax icon.
3. Click the Company Preferences tab.
4. At the *Do you charge sales tax?* field, click *Yes*. The other fields of information that were dimmed are now activated.
   You must complete the *Your most common sales tax item* field.

HINT

You could also click
the Add sales tax item
button.

5. At the *Your most common sales tax item* field, click the drop-down arrow. Because this is a new company, there is no information regarding sales tax. You will add it in this window.

6. Click *< Add New >*.
   The New Item window appears. This allows you to add sales tax to the Item List.

7. Enter the following sales tax item information:

TYPE:	Sales Tax Item
Sales Tax Name:	Minn. Sales Tax
Description:	Sales Tax
Tax Rate (%):	7

8. At the *Tax Agency (vendor that you collect for)* field, click the drop-down arrow. Again, because this is a new company file, vendors have not yet been entered into the file.

9. At the Tax Agency drop-down list, click *< Add New >*. The New Vendor window appears.

10. At both the *VENDOR NAME* and *COMPANY NAME* fields, type Minn. Dept. of Revenue. Press the Tab key. This adds Minn. Dept. of Revenue to the *BILLED FROM* field. See Figure 7–G.

FIGURE 7–G
New Vendor Window

11. If the information is correct, click OK. The Minn. Dept. of Revenue has been added to the Vendor Center, and the New Item window is complete. See Figure 7–H.

FIGURE 7–H
New Item Window—Completed

12. If the information is correct, click OK. The Preferences window for sales tax is complete. See Figure 7–I.

FIGURE 7–I
Preferences Window—
Sales Tax—Completed

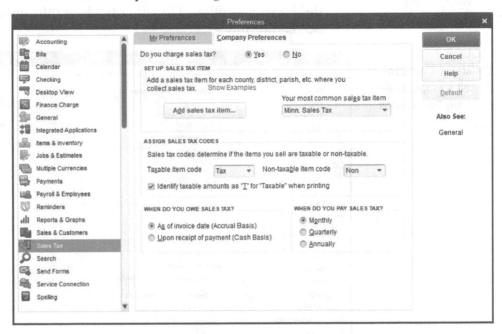

13. If the information is correct, click OK. The Updating Sales Tax dialog box appears. In this dialog box, QuickBooks is inquiring if all existing customers and all non-inventory and inventory parts should be made taxable. See Figure 7–J.

FIGURE 7–J
Updating Sales Tax
Dialog Box

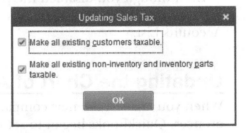

14. In the Updating Sales Tax dialog box, click OK. The sales tax item is established and added to the Item List.

Payroll

When you set up a new company file using the Express Start method, QuickBooks assumes you will be using the Payroll feature and activates it by default. When QuickBooks activates the payroll feature, it automatically creates a Payroll Liabilities account and Payroll Expenses account in the Chart of Accounts List. Our sample company, Kristin Raina Interior Designs, has not yet used the payroll feature and does not need it activated.

To disable the payroll feature:
1. At the main menu bar, click Edit and then click *Preferences*.
2. In the left panel of the Preferences window, click the Payroll & Employees icon.

<hr>

HINT

When you use the Detailed Start method of New Company Setup, you have the choice to enable or disable the payroll feature.

3. Click the Company Preferences tab.
4. In the QUICKBOOKS DESKTOP PAYROLL FEATURES section, click the *No payroll* option. The other fields of information are now dimmed. See Figure 7–K.

FIGURE 7–K
Preferences Window—
Payroll & Employees—
Company Preferences
Tab

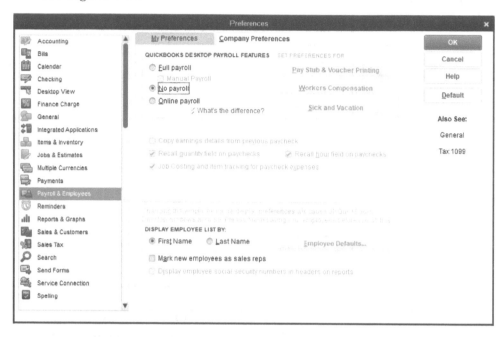

5. If the information is correct, click OK.

Even though you disabled the payroll feature, the Payroll Liabilities account and the Payroll Expenses account still appear on the Chart of Accounts List.

Lists/Centers

Updating the Chart of Accounts List

When you created the new company file and established some of the preferences, QuickBooks began to set up the Chart of Accounts List. Open the Chart of Accounts List and review it.

To open and review the Chart of Accounts List:
1. At the main menu bar, click Lists and then click *Chart of Accounts*. See Figure 7–L.

FIGURE 7–L
Chart of Accounts List
Window

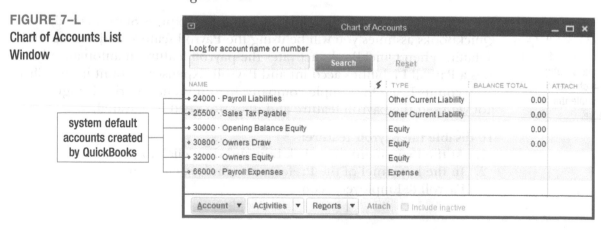

Many additional accounts must be added to the Chart of Accounts List for Kristin Raina Interior Designs. Most of these accounts have opening balances. These balances will be entered later by journal entry.

You add accounts to the Chart of Accounts List by using the Chart of Accounts List window, as illustrated in prior chapters.

To add a new account:

1. Open the Chart of Accounts List, if it is not already open.
2. At the Chart of Accounts window, click the Account menu button and then click *New*. The Add New Account: Choose Account Type window appears.
3. At the Choose Account Type window, click *Bank* and then click Continue. The Add New Account window appears.
4. At the Add New Account window, enter the following information:

   Number: 1010
   Account Name: Cash - Operating

   Your screen should look like Figure 7–M.

FIGURE 7–M
Add New Account Window

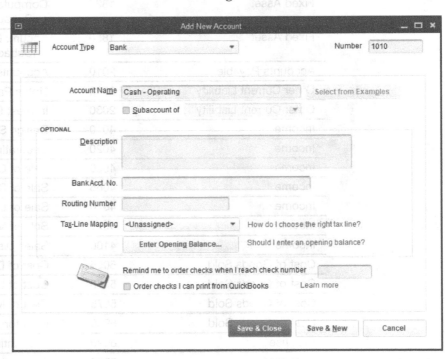

5. If the information is correct, click Save & New. The Add New Account window is displayed, with the fields cleared for the next account.
6. Using the information in Table 7–1, type in all the accounts.

TABLE 7–1
Chart of Accounts List

Account Type	Number	Account Name
Accounts Receivable	1200	Accounts Receivable
Other Current Asset	1250	Undeposited Funds
Other Current Asset	1265	Inventory of Draperies
Other Current Asset	1270	Inventory of Lamps
Other Current Asset	1275	Inventory of Mirrors
Other Current Asset	1300	Design Supplies
Other Current Asset	1305	Office Supplies
Other Current Asset	1410	Prepaid Advertising
Other Current Asset	1420	Prepaid Insurance
Fixed Asset	1700	Furniture
Fixed Asset	1725	Furniture, Cost [Subaccount of 1700]
Fixed Asset	1750	Accum. Dep., Furniture [Subaccount of 1700]
Fixed Asset	1800	Computers
Fixed Asset	1825	Computers, Cost [Subaccount of 1800]
Fixed Asset	1850	Accum. Dep., Computers [Subaccount of 1800]
Accounts Payable	2010	Accounts Payable
Other Current Liability	2020	Notes Payable
Other Current Liability	2030	Interest Payable
Income	4010	Design Services
Income	4020	Decorating Services
Income	4060	Sale of Carpets
Income	4065	Sale of Draperies
Income	4070	Sale of Lamps
Income	4075	Sale of Mirrors
Income	4100	Sales Discounts
Cost of Goods Sold	5065	Cost of Draperies Sold
Cost of Goods Sold	5070	Cost of Lamps Sold
Cost of Goods Sold	5075	Cost of Mirrors Sold
Cost of Goods Sold	5900	Inventory Adjustment
Expense	6020	Accounting Expense
Expense	6050	Advertising Expense
Expense	6175	Deprec. Exp., Furniture
Expense	6185	Deprec. Exp., Computers
Expense	6200	Insurance Expense
Expense	6300	Janitorial Expense
Expense	6325	Office Supplies Expense
Expense	6400	Rent Expense
Expense	6450	Telephone Expense
Expense	6500	Utilities Expense
Other Expense	7000	Interest Expense

HINT

In the *Account Type* field, instead of looking for the type in the drop-down list, type the first letter of the type name.

HINT

The Inventory of Carpets and Cost of Carpets Sold accounts will be added in the next section of this chapter.

The updated Chart of Accounts List appears in Figure 7–N.

FIGURE 7–N
Chart of Accounts List—
Updated

If you incorrectly labeled an account as a parent account or subaccount, you can edit the account or move the entry. To move the entry, click the diamond to the left of the account number. If you drag the diamond to the left, a subaccount becomes a parent account. If you drag the diamond to the right, a parent account becomes a subaccount. You can also click and drag up or down to reorganize the list.

HINT

If the account 90000 Estimates is displayed, click Edit and then click *Preferences*. At the Preferences window, click the Jobs & Estimates icon and then click the Company Preferences tab. At the *DO YOU CREATE ESTIMATES?* field, click No and then click OK. In the Chart of Accounts List, delete the account 90000 Estimates.

NAME		TYPE	BALANCE TOTAL	ATTACH
1010 · Cash - Operating		Bank	0.00	
1200 · Accounts Receivable		Accounts Receivable	0.00	
1250 · Undeposited Funds		Other Current Asset	0.00	
1265 · Inventory of Draperies		Other Current Asset	0.00	
1270 · Inventory of Lamps		Other Current Asset	0.00	
1275 · Inventory of Mirrors		Other Current Asset	0.00	
1300 · Design Supplies		Other Current Asset	0.00	
1305 · Office Supplies		Other Current Asset	0.00	
1410 · Prepaid Advertising		Other Current Asset	0.00	
1420 · Prepaid Insurance		Other Current Asset	0.00	
1700 · Furniture		Fixed Asset	0.00	
1725 · Furniture, Cost		Fixed Asset	0.00	
1750 · Accum. Dep., Furniture		Fixed Asset	0.00	
1800 · Computers		Fixed Asset	0.00	
1825 · Computers, Cost		Fixed Asset	0.00	
1850 · Accum. Dep., Computers		Fixed Asset	0.00	
2010 · Accounts Payable		Accounts Payable	0.00	
2020 · Notes Payable		Other Current Liability	0.00	
2030 · Interest Payable		Other Current Liability	0.00	
24000 · Payroll Liabilities		Other Current Liability	0.00	
25500 · Sales Tax Payable		Other Current Liability	0.00	
30000 · Opening Balance Equity		Equity	0.00	
30800 · Owners Draw		Equity	0.00	
32000 · Owners Equity		Equity		
4010 · Design Services		Income		
4020 · Decorating Services		Income		
4060 · Sale of Carpets		Income		
4065 · Sale of Draperies		Income		
4070 · Sale of Lamps		Income		
4075 · Sale of Mirrors		Income		
4100 · Sales Discounts		Income		
5065 · Cost of Draperies Sold		Cost of Goods Sold		
5070 · Cost of Lamps Sold		Cost of Goods Sold		
5075 · Cost of Mirrors Sold		Cost of Goods Sold		
5900 · Inventory Adjustment		Cost of Goods Sold		
6020 · Accounting Expense		Expense		
6050 · Advertising Expense		Expense		
6175 · Deprec. Exp., Furniture		Expense		
6185 · Deprec. Exp., Computers		Expense		
6200 · Insurance Expense		Expense		
6300 · Janitorial Expense		Expense		
6325 · Office Supplies Expense		Expense		
6400 · Rent Expense		Expense		
6450 · Telephone Expense		Expense		
6500 · Utilities Expense		Expense		
66000 · Payroll Expenses		Expense		
7000 · Interest Expense		Other Expense		

7. Close the Add New Account and Chart of Accounts windows.

New Company Setup

Customizing the New Company File

As previously stated, when setting up a new company file using the Express Start method of New Company Setup, you first set up the preferences for the company file. As you do this, accounts are set up on the Chart of Accounts List. Then the Chart of Accounts List is updated to add more of the accounts the company uses. The next step is to customize the new company file. This consists of customizing the system default accounts and payment terms created by QuickBooks.

Customizing System Default Accounts

As you learned in prior chapters, QuickBooks establishes default accounts and uses those accounts when recording transactions in the Activities windows. QuickBooks looks for these system default accounts in the Chart of Accounts List; if it cannot find an account, it will create one. Some of the system default accounts you have learned so far are Accounts Receivable, Undeposited Funds, Accounts Payable, Sales Tax Payable, Inventory Asset, and Cost of Goods Sold. Other system default accounts include the equity accounts (capital and accumulated earnings) and payroll accounts (payroll liabilities and payroll expenses).

When you created the company file and established some of the company preferences, QuickBooks created some of the system default accounts, as you saw in Figure 7–L on page 278.

You will now customize the system default accounts that were created by QuickBooks (sales tax payable and equity accounts) by editing the account names and numbers to follow the company's pattern for naming and numbering accounts on the Chart of Accounts List. The payroll accounts that QuickBooks creates cannot be deleted, but since they will not be used in our sample company file, they can be marked as inactive to hide them on the Chart of Accounts List. Then you will learn how to force QuickBooks to create additional system default accounts that were not created when you created the company file and established the preferences (undeposited funds, inventory asset, and cost of goods sold). After QuickBooks creates the additional system default accounts, you will then customize these account names and numbers.

Customizing System Default Accounts Created in a New Company File and Company Preferences

When you created the company file and indicated the company was a sole proprietorship, QuickBooks automatically created three equity accounts: Opening Balance Equity, Owners Draw, and Owners Equity. When you activated the sales tax feature in the Preferences window, QuickBooks created a Sales Tax Payable account. The numbers and names for each of these accounts can be edited. The Opening Balance Equity account will be renamed as *Kristin Raina, Capital,* and the Owners Draw account will be renamed *Kristin Raina, Drawings.* The Opening Balance Equity account is used by QuickBooks as an offsetting account when certain opening balances are entered in the accounts. The Owners Equity account is created to capture net income at the end of the fiscal year. In Chapter 12, you will see how QuickBooks uses the Owner's Equity account in a company file. This account will be renamed *Accumulated Earnings.*

As you will soon see, QuickBooks recognizes the Accounts Receivable; Accounts Payable; Sales Tax Payable; Kristin Raina, Capital (Opening Balance Equity); and Accumulated Earnings (Owners Equity) accounts as system default accounts, but QuickBooks does not recognize the Undeposited Funds, Inventory Asset, and Cost of Goods Sold accounts as system default accounts. QuickBooks usually identifies a system default account by graying, or dimming, the account type. As you edit each of these accounts, notice that the account type is dimmed.

To edit account numbers and account names:

1. At the main menu bar, click Lists and then click *Chart of Accounts*.
2. At the Chart of Accounts window, select *30000 Opening Balance Equity* but do not open the account.
3. Click the Account menu button.
4. At the Account button drop-down menu, click *Edit Account*.
5. At the *Number* field, delete *30000* and then type 3010.
6. At the *Account Name* field, delete the text *Opening Balance Equity* and then type Kristin Raina, Capital. See Figure 7–O.

FIGURE 7–O
Edit Account Window—
System Default Account

account type dimmed

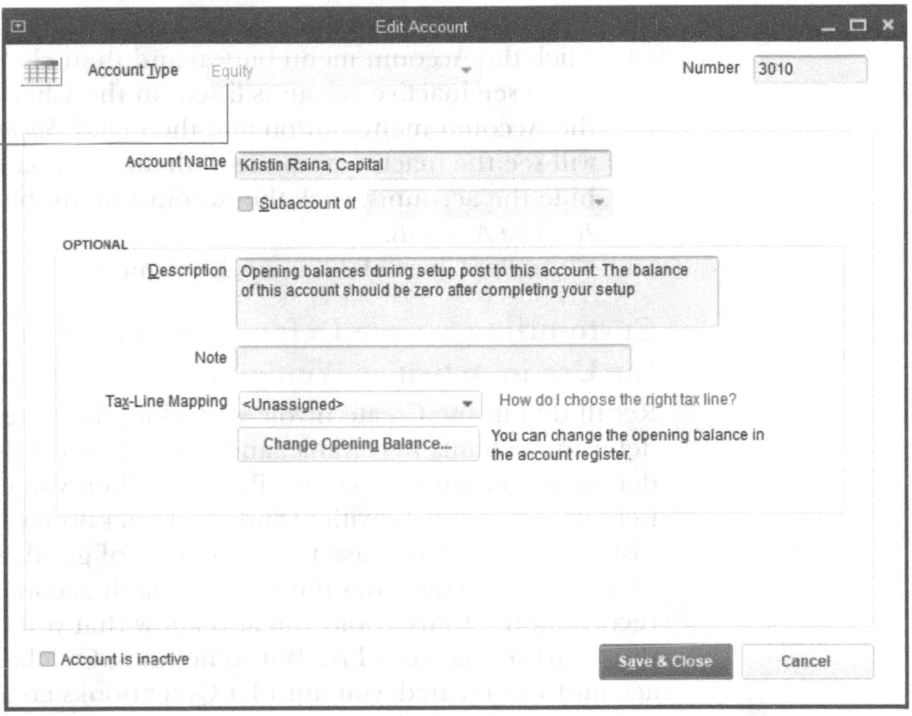

HINT

After the New Company Setup has been completed, the account 3010 Kristin Raina, Capital shows a balance of $50,000, which is the amount Kristin Raina originally invested in the company.

7. If the information is correct, click the Save & Close button.
8. Edit the two other equity accounts and the Sales Tax Payable account as follows:

QuickBooks		Edited	
Number	Account Name	Number	Account Name
30800	Owners Draw	3020	Kristin Raina, Drawings
32000	Owners Equity	3030	Accumulated Earnings
25500	Sales Tax Payable	2200	

HINT

Owners Draw is not a system default account but is customized here to match Kristin Raina's pattern for naming and numbering accounts.

Hiding Inactive System Default Accounts Created in a New Company File

When you create a new company file using the Express Start method, QuickBooks assumes by default that you will be using the payroll feature and automatically creates a Payroll Liabilities account and a Payroll Expenses account. Even though you subsequently turned off the payroll feature in the Preferences window, once you have created the payroll accounts in QuickBooks, you cannot delete them.

In addition, once you turned on the account numbers feature, QuickBooks assigned the account numbers *24000* to the Payroll Liabilities account and

66000 to the Payroll Expenses account. Because payroll has not yet been covered, you will not be using the payroll accounts at this time. You can make them inactive, and they will not display in the reports.

To mark an account as inactive:
1. At the Chart of Accounts List window, select the *24000 Payroll Liabilities* account but do not open it.
2. Click the Account menu button and then click *Make Account Inactive*. The Payroll Liabilities account is no longer displayed in the Chart of Accounts List.
3. Select the *66000 Payroll Expenses* account.
4. Click the Account menu button and then click *Make Account Inactive*.

    To see inactive accounts listed on the Chart of Accounts List, click the Account menu button and then click *Show Inactive Accounts*. You will see the inactive accounts with an ✖ next to the account names. To hide the accounts, click the Account menu button and then click *Hide Inactive Accounts*.
5. Close the Chart of Accounts List window.

Customizing System Default Accounts Created for Use in Activities Windows

Recall that in the Create Invoices window, the system default account is a debit to Accounts Receivable, and in the Enter Bills window, the system default is a credit to Accounts Payable. When you chose an inventory item in any of the Activities windows, QuickBooks knew—from the Item List—which inventory asset account, cost of goods sold account, and sale of inventory account was the system default account to use for properly recording the transaction. You also know that you can create accounts in the Chart of Accounts List. But sometimes, QuickBooks does not find the account you created; you must let QuickBooks create the account for the software to identify it as a system default account.

You have just updated the Chart of Accounts List to add accounts that will be used by Kristin Raina Interior Designs, including Accounts Receivable, Undeposited Funds, Inventory, Accounts Payable, and Cost of Goods Sold. To illustrate how QuickBooks creates its own system default accounts, you will open some Activities windows and the Item List. You will then see that QuickBooks cannot locate some of the accounts you created and will create its own accounts.

To allow QuickBooks to create system default accounts:
1. At the main menu bar, click Customers and then click *Create Invoices*. Close the Create Invoices window.
2. At the main menu bar, click Customers and then click *Enter Sales Receipts*. Close the Enter Sales Receipts window.
3. At the main menu bar, click Vendors and then click *Enter Bills*. Close the Enter Bills window.
4. At the main menu bar, click Lists and then click *Item List*.
5. At the Item List window, click the Item menu button.
6. At the Item button drop-down menu, click *New*.
7. At the New Item window, at the *TYPE* field, click *Inventory Part*.
8. Close the New Item window. If a Save message appears, click No. Close the Item List.

HINT

QuickBooks sometimes needs to create its own system default accounts. Opening and closing the windows in Steps 1–8 forces QuickBooks to create system default accounts. After QuickBooks creates these accounts, you can edit the account names and numbers.

HINT

At the New Item window, in the *TYPE* field, if *Inventory Part* does not appear, then the Inventory feature was not enabled. Go to the "Inventory" section on page 275 and follow the steps to enable the Inventory feature.

As you opened each of these windows, QuickBooks looked for certain accounts; when they could not be identified, QuickBooks created new system default accounts. Review the Chart of Accounts List and observe that QuickBooks created the following accounts:

12000	*Undeposited Funds
12100	Inventory Asset
50000	Cost of Goods Sold

See Figure 7–P.

FIGURE 7–P
Chart of Accounts
List—Additional System
Default Accounts Created
by QuickBooks

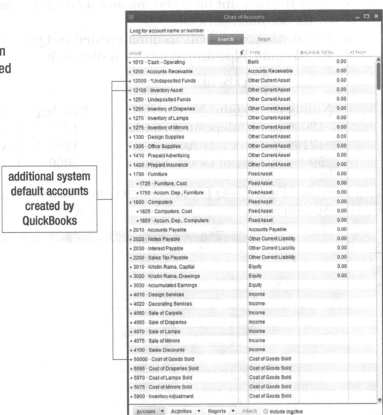

additional system default accounts created by QuickBooks

HINT

When QuickBooks creates an account with an account name already in use, it precedes the account name with an asterisk (*).

HINT

Notice for the Accounts Receivable account that *Accounts Receivable* is both the account name and the account type. Similarly, notice that for the Accounts Payable account that *Accounts Payable* is both the account name and the account type. When QuickBooks looks for a system default account, it is looking for the account type, not the account name.

HINT

If you did not already create the Accounts Receivable and Accounts Payable accounts, when you open the Create Invoices and Enter Bills windows, these two accounts are automatically created and the account types dimmed. You need to edit only the account numbers.

When you opened the Create Invoices window, QuickBooks looked for the Accounts Receivable account and was able to locate it because of the accounts receivable account type in that account. Similarly, when you opened the Enter Bills window, QuickBooks looked for the Accounts Payable account and was able to locate it because of the accounts payable account type.

But when you opened the Enter Sales Receipts window, QuickBooks looked for an Undeposited Funds account, and even though you created this account, QuickBooks could not locate it and created a new account 12000 *Undeposited Funds. Similarly, when you chose the *New Inventory Part* type in the New Item window in the Item List, QuickBooks looked for an inventory asset account and cost of goods sold account. Even though you had previously created three inventory accounts and three cost of goods sold accounts, again, QuickBooks did not identify these accounts as system default accounts and thus created a new account 12100 Inventory Asset and a new account 50000 Cost of Goods Sold. In situations like these, you must allow QuickBooks to create its own accounts and then edit them to your liking. In all cases, accounts created by QuickBooks will have dimmed account types;

you cannot change an account type, but you can change an account number and account name.

Before you can edit the accounts that QuickBooks created, delete the 1250 Undeposited Funds account you created. This account name and number can then be used when editing the accounts created by QuickBooks.

To delete an account and then edit the accounts created by QuickBooks:

1. At the main menu bar, click Lists and then click *Chart of Accounts.*
2. At the Chart of Accounts window, select *1250 Undeposited Funds.*
3. Click the Account menu button and then click *Delete Account.*
4. At the warning, click OK.
5. Edit the system default accounts created by QuickBooks, noting that the Account Type drop-down list is dimmed:

QuickBooks		Edited	
Number	Account Name	Number	Account Name
12000	*Undeposited Funds	1250	Undeposited Funds
12100	Inventory Asset	1260	Inventory of Carpets
50000	Cost of Goods Sold	5060	Cost of Carpets Sold

See Figure 7–Q for the updated and customized Chart of Accounts List.

FIGURE 7–Q
Chart of Accounts List—
Updated and Customized
System Default Accounts

6. Close the Chart of Accounts window.

Customizing Payment Terms

In QuickBooks, a list with payment terms can be accessed in customer files, vendor files, and activities windows when needed. As shown in prior chapters, payment terms such as Net 30 Days; 2/10, Net 30 Days; and so on can be identified in both the customer and vendor files if they relate to a particular customer or vendor.

When you create a new company file, QuickBooks automatically creates a list of payment terms. As with all the other Lists/Centers in QuickBooks, you can add, delete, or edit the Terms List to customize it for your company.

To add a payment term:
1. At the main menu bar, click Lists and then click *Customer & Vendor Profile Lists.*
2. At the Customer & Vendor Profile Lists submenu, click *Terms List.* The Terms List window appears with the terms of payment that were created by QuickBooks. See Figure 7–R.

FIGURE 7–R
Terms List Created by QuickBooks

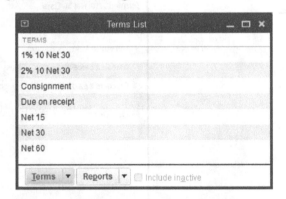

3. At the Terms List window, click the Terms menu button.
4. At the Terms button drop-down menu, click *New.* The New Terms window appears.
5. At the *Terms* field, type Net 10 Days.
6. At the *Net due in days* field, type 10. See Figure 7–S.

FIGURE 7–S
New Terms Window—Net 10 Days—Completed

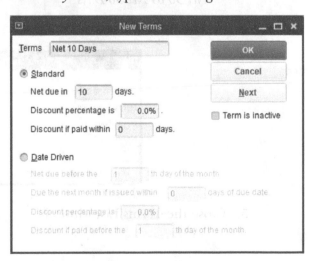

7. If the information is correct, click OK.

To delete a payment term:

1. At the Terms List, select *1% 10 Net 30* but do not open it.
2. Click the Terms menu button and then click *Delete Terms*.
3. A Delete Terms warning appears. Click OK. The payment term is deleted.
4. Delete the following terms of payment:
   Consignment
   Due on receipt
   Net 60

To edit a payment term:

1. At the Terms List, double-click *2% 10 Net 30* to open the Edit Terms window.
2. At the *Terms* field, change the text to 2/10, Net 30 Days. See Figure 7–T.

FIGURE 7–T
Edit Terms Window—
2/10, Net 30 Days—
Completed

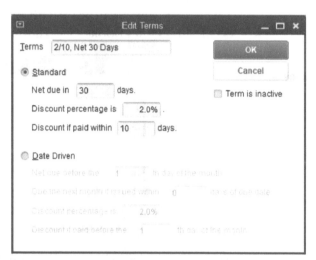

3. If the information is correct, click OK.
4. Edit the following terms of payment:
   Net 15 to *Net 15 Days*
   Net 30 to *Net 30 Days*

   The updated Terms List appears in Figure 7–U.

FIGURE 7–U
Terms List—Updated

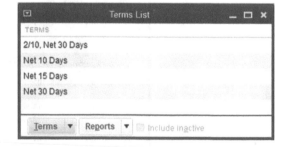

5. Close the Terms List window.

Updating Lists and Centers

At this point, the company file has been created, a company file password has been set up, preferences have been established, the Chart of Accounts List has been updated, and the system default accounts and payment terms have been customized. Since you did not use the QuickBooks Desktop Setup window to create the Customer and Vendor Centers or update the Item List, the next step is to update the Item List and the Customer and Vendor Centers using the procedures learned in prior chapters. In addition, when you update the Item List and Customer and Vendor Centers, you will enter the beginning balances.

Updating the Item List

In QuickBooks, the Item List stores information about the service items, inventory part items, and sales tax. As transactions are recorded in the Activities windows, QuickBooks uses the information in the Item List to record the transaction in the correct accounts.

Open and review the Item List. Notice that QuickBooks recorded the sales tax item when the sales tax feature was activated at the Preferences window. The Item List needs to be updated to include the service items and inventory part items that describe the services and inventory that Kristin Raina Interior Design provides or stocks to conduct business. These items are added to the Item List using the Item List window, as illustrated in Chapter 5. The only additional step is to add the quantity on hand for each inventory part item.

To add a service item:
1. At the main menu bar, click Lists and then click *Item List*.
2. At the Item List window, click the Item menu button.
3. At the Item button drop-down menu, click *New*. The New Item window appears.
4. At the *TYPE* field, click *Service*.
5. At the *Item Name/Number* and *Description* fields, type Design Services.
6. At the *Rate* field, type 60.
7. At the *Tax Code* field, click *Non* for *Non-Taxable Sales*.
8. At the *Account* field, click *4010 Design Services*. Your screen should look like Figure 7–V.

FIGURE 7–V
New Item Window—
Service

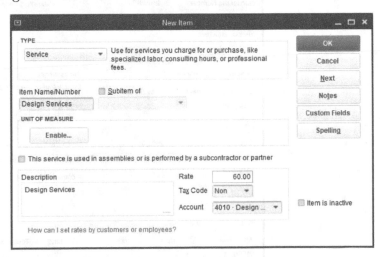

9. If the information is correct, click Next.

10. Enter the following information for the next service item:

  TYPE: Service
  Item Name/Number: Decorating Services
  Description: Decorating Services
  Rate: 50
  Tax Code: Non Non-Taxable Sales
  Account: 4020 Decorating Services

11. Click OK.

To add inventory part items:
1. Open the Item List, if necessary, and then click *New* at the Item button drop-down menu.
2. At the *TYPE* field, click *Inventory Part.*
3. Enter the following information for the carpets inventory:

  Item Name/Number: Carpets
  Description on Purchase
  and Sales Transactions: Carpets
  Cost: 200
  COGS Account: 5060 Cost of Carpets Sold
  Sales Price: 400
  Tax Code: Tax Taxable Sales
  Income Account: 4060 Sale of Carpets
  Asset Account: 1260 Inventory of Carpets
  On Hand: 4
  As of: 04/01/2022

HINT

In the account fields, you can type in the account number instead of using the drop-down list.

The amount *800.00* in the *Total Value* field is computed automatically based on the cost multiplied by the quantity on hand ($200 × 4). See Figure 7–W.

FIGURE 7–W
New Item Window—Inventory Part

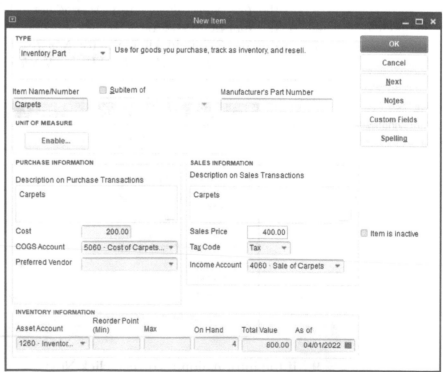

HINT

If the Future Transactions message appears, click Yes. To avoid this message, click Edit at the main menu bar and then click *Preferences*. In the left panel, click the Accounting icon and then click the Company Preferences tab. Remove the check marks from the date warning options and then click OK.

4. If the information is correct, click Next. If the Future Transactions message appears, click Yes. The New Item window is displayed with the fields cleared for the next item.
5. Using the information in Table 7–2, type in the remainder of the inventory part items. All the inventory part items are taxable. Be sure to have the date as of *04/01/2022* for each item. The updated Item List appears in Figure 7–Y.
6. After entering the information from Table 7–2 and comparing it to Figure 7–X, close the New Item and Item List windows.

TABLE 7–2 Inventory Part Items

Item Name, Description on Purchase and Sales Transactions	Cost	COGS Account	Sales Price	Income Account	Asset Account	On Hand	Total Value
Draperies	$125	5065	$250	4065	1265	8	$1,000
Lamps	100	5070	200	4070	1270	10	1,000
Mirrors	150	5075	300	4075	1275	6	900

FIGURE 7–X
Item List—Updated

HINT

If you inadvertently do not enter the quantity on hand, delete the inventory item and then reenter the inventory item along with the quantity on hand and the correct date.

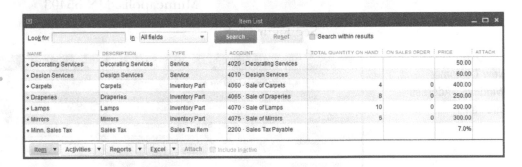

NAME	DESCRIPTION	TYPE	ACCOUNT	TOTAL QUANTITY ON HAND	ON SALES ORDER	PRICE	ATTACH
Decorating Services	Decorating Services	Service	4020 · Decorating Services			50.00	
Design Services	Design Services	Service	4010 · Design Services			60.00	
Carpets	Carpets	Inventory Part	4060 · Sale of Carpets	4	0	400.00	
Draperies	Draperies	Inventory Part	4065 · Sale of Draperies	8	0	250.00	
Lamps	Lamps	Inventory Part	4070 · Sale of Lamps	10	0	200.00	
Mirrors	Mirrors	Inventory Part	4075 · Sale of Mirrors	6	0	300.00	
Minn. Sales Tax	Sales Tax	Sales Tax Item	2200 · Sales Tax Payable			7.0%	

ACCOUNTING CONCEPT

1260 Inventory of Carpets		1265 Inventory of Draperies		1270 Inventory of Lamps	
Dr	Cr	Dr	Cr	Dr	Cr
800		1,000		1,000	

1275 Inventory of Mirrors		3010 Kristin Raina, Capital	
Dr	Cr	Dr	Cr
900			800
			1,000
			1,000
			900

Updating the Customer Center

The Customer Center records the information for all the customers with whom the company does business. You can update the Customer Center using the procedures learned in Chapter 3 to add a new customer. The only additional step you need to take is to enter outstanding balances for some of these customers when recording the new customer files.

Kristin Raina has 10 customers. Two of the customers have outstanding balances.

To add a customer with an outstanding balance:

1. At the main menu bar, click Customers and then click *Customer Center*.
2. At the Customer Center window, click the New Customer & Job button and then click *New Customer*. The New Customer window appears.
3. At the *CUSTOMER NAME* field, type Berger Bakery Company.
4. At the *OPENING BALANCE* field, type 600.
5. At the *AS OF* field, choose *04/01/2022*.
6. Enter the information listed below on the Address Info tab:

COMPANY NAME:	Berger Bakery Company
FULL NAME:	
First:	Barry
Last:	Berger
Main Phone:	612-555-2240
Mobile:	612-555-2241
INVOICE/BILL TO:	18 N. Grand Ave.
	Minneapolis, MN 55403

See Figure 7–Y.

FIGURE 7–Y
New Customer Window—Address Info Tab

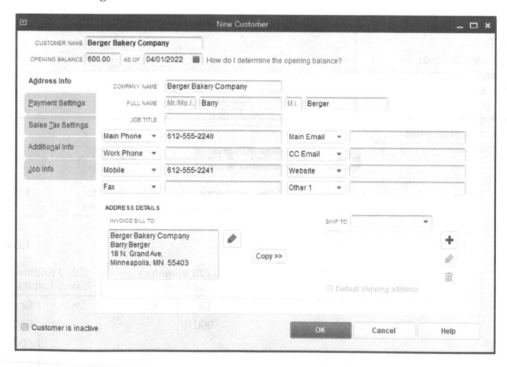

7. On the Payment Settings tab, at the *ACCOUNT NO.* field, type R1825.
8. At the PAYMENT TERMS drop-down list, click *Net 30 Days*.
9. Click OK. The new customer is added to the Customer Center.
10. Using the information in Table 7–3, enter the remaining customers. Be sure to have the date *as of 04/01/2022* for the customer with the opening balance.

TABLE 7–3 Customers

Customer/ Company Name	Opening Balance	Full Name	Main Phone/ Mobile	Invoice/Bill To	Account No.	Payment Terms
Alomar Company		Oliver Alomar	612-555-5757 612-555-5858	1001 Oak Lake Ave. Minneapolis, MN 55401	O1535	Net 30 Days
Barrera Bagel Barn		Belinda Barrera	612-555-1233 612-555-1234	148 46th Ave. N Plymouth, MN 53406	B0250	Net 30 Days
Cook Caterers		Stephen Cook	612-555-7896 612-555-7599	275 Oak Lake Ave. Minneapolis, MN 55401	C0360	Net 30 Days
Franco Films Co.	$940	Fred Franco	612-555-4566 612-555-4567	100 Pleasant Ave. S. Minneapolis, MN 55409	F0660	Net 30 Days
Guthrie, Jennie		Jennie Guthrie	651-555-1515	165 Terrace Ct. St. Paul, MN 55101	O1565	2/10, Net 30 Days
Hamilton Hotels		Hilda Hamilton	651-555-1050 651-555-1060	1000 York Ave. St. Paul, MN 55101	H0830	2/10, Net 30 Days
Jones, Beverly		Beverly Jones	612-555-7778	333 York Circle Bloomington, MN 54603	J1013	Net 30 Days
Omari, Maria		Maria Omari	612-555-9999 612-555-9998	210 NE Lowry Ave. Minneapolis, MN 54204	O1545	Net 30 Days
Plaza Pizza Palace		Mikey Plaza	612-555-9000 612-555-9800	360 Border Ave. N Minneapolis, MN 55401	P1650	Net 30 Days

The updated Customer Center appears in Figure 7–Z.

FIGURE 7–Z
Customer Center—
Updated

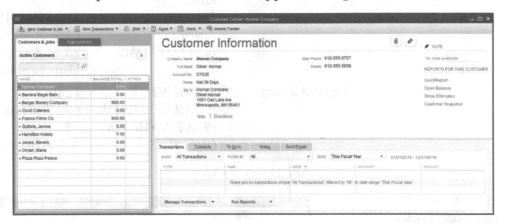

11. Close the Customer Center window.

ACCOUNTING CONCEPT

1200 Accounts Receivable		49900 Uncategorized Income	
Dr	Cr	Dr	Cr
600			600
940			940
Bal 1,540			Bal 1,540

Updating the Vendor Center

The Vendor Center records the information for all the vendors with whom the company does business. Open and review the Vendor Center. There is one vendor, Minn. Dept. of Revenue, that was added to the Vendor Center when you set up the sales tax item. All the other vendors need to be added to the Vendor Center.

The Vendor Center is updated using the procedures learned in Chapter 2 to add a new vendor. The only additional step you need to take is to enter outstanding balances for some of these vendors when recording the new vendor files.

Kristin Raina has 17 vendors. Seven of the vendors have outstanding balances.

To add a vendor with an outstanding balance:

1. At the main menu bar, click Vendors and then click *Vendor Center.*
2. At the Vendor Center window, click the New Vendor menu button and then click *New Vendor.* The New Vendor window appears.
3. At the *VENDOR NAME* field, type Ace Glass Works.
4. At the *OPENING BALANCE* field, type 1500.
5. At the *AS OF* field, choose *04/01/2022.*
6. Enter the following information:

Address Info	COMPANY NAME:	Ace Glass Works
	FULL NAME:	
	First:	Archie
	Last:	Ace
	Main Phone:	612-555-9812
	Mobile:	612-555-6813
	BILLED FROM:	25 SE Como Ave.
		Minneapolis, MN 53602
Payment Settings	*ACCOUNT NO.:*	1245
	PAYMENT TERMS:	Net 30 Days
	PRINT NAME ON	
	CHECK AS:	Ace Glass Works

See Figure 7–AA.

FIGURE 7–AA
New Vendor Window—
Payment Settings Tab

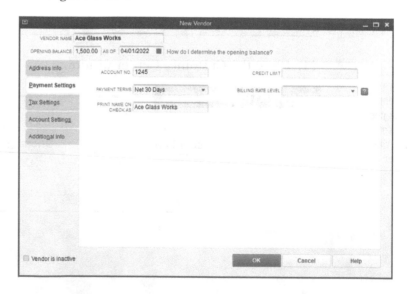

7. If the information is correct, click OK. The new vendor is added to the Vendor Center.
8. Using the information in Table 7–4, enter the remaining vendors. Be sure to have the date *as of 04/01/2022* for the vendors with opening balances.

TABLE 7–4 Vendors

Vendor/ Company Name	Opening Balance	Full Name	Main Phone/ Mobile	Billed From	Account No.	Payment Terms
Bell Carpet Design	$2,000	Bill Bell	651-555-8823 651-555-8824	55 North Main Ave. St. Paul, MN 54603	66-87874	Net 30 Days
Cuza and Carl Associates	400	Carrie Cuza	651-555-8855 651-555-8856	23 W. University Ave. St. Paul, MN 54603	KR569	Net 30 Days
Darren Tapestry		Donna Darren	612-555-2221 612-555-2222	10 W. Larpenteur Ave. Minneapolis, MN 52604	2365	Net 30 Days
Galeway Computers	2,600	Roger Rivera	617-555-4747 617-555-4748	33 Route 10 Springfield, MA 24105	2455-897	Net 30 Days
Grayson Graphics		Gregg Grayson	612-555-0002 612-555-0003	56 Amity Way Bloomington, MN 53608	33-2221	Net 30 Days
Jeter Janitorial Services		Jason Jeter	612-555-4444 612-555-4445	233 Lilac Rd. Minneapolis, MN 54302	555-32	Net 30 Days
Kristin Raina		Kristin Raina				
Lumiare Lighting Company		Larry Lyght	612-555-4790 612-555-4795	123 Glenwood Ave. Minneapolis, MN 53609	36	Net 30 Days
Midwest Mutual Insurance Co.	2,400	Mike Mills	805-555-4545 805-555-4546	3566 Broadway Chicago, IL 58303	54778784	Net 30 Days
Minneapolis Electric & Gas Co.	450	Jack Watts	651-555-4949 651-555-4950	150 Douglas Ave. St. Paul, MN 55303	2001-23657	Net 30 Days
Nordic Realty		Melanie Marx	612-555-3232 612-555-3233	23 N. 12th Street Minneapolis, MN 53604	55-1212	Net 10 Days
TwinCityTelCo		Terry Ameche	651-555-6667 651-555-6668	3223 River Dr. St. Paul, MN 53908	666-6667	Net 30 Days
Weaver Fabrics		Jon Weaver	612-555-8777 612-555-8778	355 W. 70th Street Minneapolis, MN 53604	9878	Net 30 Days
Williams Office Supply Company	400	Bernard Williams	612-555-2240 612-555-2241	15 Grand Ave. S Minneapolis, MN 55404	55-8988	Net 30 Days
[Your Name] Accounting Service		Your Name	612-555-2222 612-555-2223	One Main Plaza St. Paul, MN 53602	99-2022-XX	Net 30 Days

Note: In the event that you do not have a person's name but instead have a department as a contact, you can still enter the information on the Address Info tab at the FULL NAME field. For example, if the contact is Customer Service, you can enter Customer at the First Name field and Service at the Last Name field.

The updated Vendor Center appears in Figure 7–BB.

FIGURE 7–BB Vendor Center—Updated

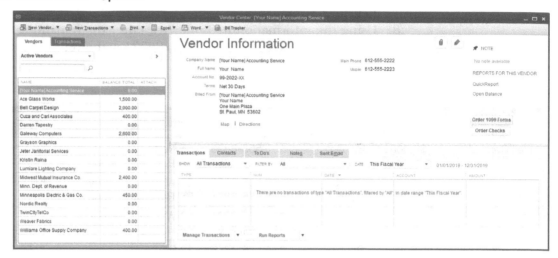

9. Close the New Vendor and Vendor Center windows.

ACCOUNTING CONCEPT

69800 Uncategorized Expenses		2010 Accounts Payable	
Dr	Cr	Dr	Cr
1,500			1,500
2,000			2,000
400			400
2,600			2,600
2,400			2,400
450			450
400			400
Bal 9,750			Bal 9,750

Interim Review of the New Company Setup

So far in setting up your new company file, you have created the company file, set up a company file password, established preferences, updated and customized the Chart of Accounts, and updated the Item List and Customer and Vendor Centers.

As you added the inventory items, customers, and vendors with balances to the Lists and Centers, behind the scenes QuickBooks recorded the information in general journal format and updated the appropriate account balances. Now, display the *Journal, Profit & Loss Standard,* and *Balance Sheet Standard* reports to see the activity taking place behind the scenes up to this point.

Journal Report

To view the *Journal* report:

1. At the main menu bar, click Reports and then click *Accountant & Taxes.*
2. At the Accountant & Taxes submenu, click *Journal.* At the Collapsing and Expanding Transactions message, read the message, insert a check mark in the box to the left of *Do not display this message in the future,* and then click OK.

3. At the *From* and *To* fields, choose *04/01/2022* and then click the Refresh button at the top of the report. See Figure 7–CC.

FIGURE 7–CC
Journal Report

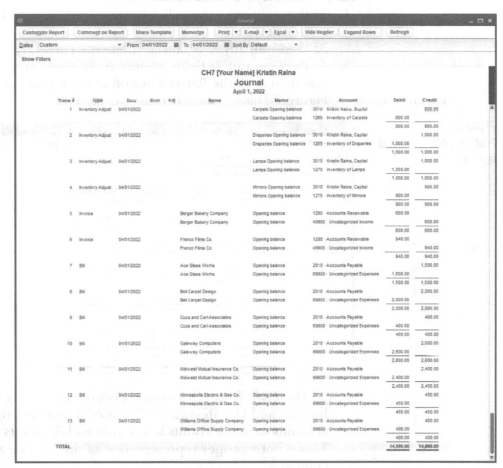

Review the journal entries. They can be categorized as follows:
- For items that are debit entries to the inventory accounts, the corresponding credit entry is to the Kristin Raina, Capital (Opening Balance Equity) account.
- For entries that are debits to Accounts Receivable, the corresponding credit is to Uncategorized Income.
- For entries that are credits to Accounts Payable, the corresponding debit is to Uncategorized Expenses.
4. Close the report. If you receive the Memorize Report message, insert a check mark in the box to the left of *Do not display this message in the future* and then click No.

Profit & Loss Standard (Income Statement) Report

To view the *Profit & Loss Standard* report:

1. At the main menu bar, click Reports and then click *Company & Financial.*
2. At the Company & Financial submenu, click *Profit & Loss Standard.*
3. At the *From* and *To* fields, choose *01/01/2022* and *04/01/2022* and then click the Refresh button at the top of the report. See Figure 7–DD.

FIGURE 7–DD
Profit & Loss Standard Report

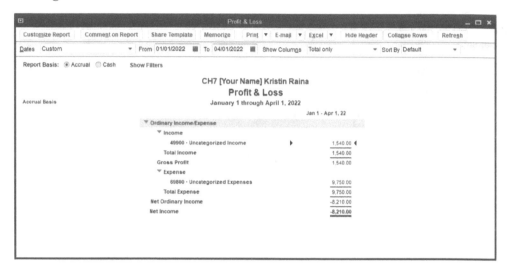

The *Profit & Loss Standard* report indicates only Uncategorized Income and Uncategorized Expenses. These amounts are offsetting amounts of the Accounts Receivable and Accounts Payable accounts. This is not a proper representation of the income and expenses of this company.

4. Close the report.

Balance Sheet Standard Report

To display the *Balance Sheet Standard* report:

1. At the main menu bar, click Reports and then click *Company & Financial.*
2. At the Company & Financial submenu, click *Balance Sheet Standard.*
3. At the *As of* field, choose *04/01/2022* and then click the Refresh button at the top of the report. See Figure 7–EE.

    A review of the balance sheet indicates the following:
    * The only assets recorded so far are Accounts Receivable and the Inventory accounts.
    * The only liabilities recorded so far are the Accounts Payable.
    * The balance in the Kristin Raina, Capital (Opening Balance Equity) account is the same as the sum of the total inventory.
    * The net income is incorrect as seen in the *Profit & Loss Standard* report.

4. Close the report.

FIGURE 7–EE
Balance Sheet Standard
Report

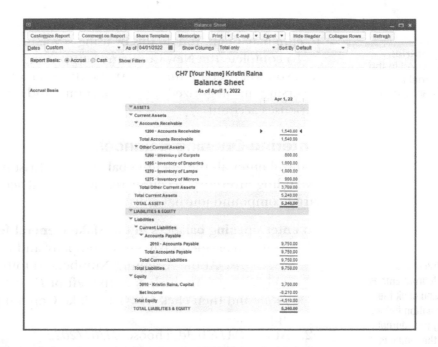

Adjusting for the Accrual Basis of Accounting

You have now created the new company file, set up a company file password, established preferences, and updated and customized the Lists and Centers. The final step is to enter the remaining opening balances and prepare the company file for the **accrual basis of accounting**.

accrual basis of accounting
an accounting method that requires the recording of revenue when it is earned and the recording of expenses when they are incurred, regardless of cash receipts and cash payments

You may have noticed the label *accrual basis* in the upper left corner of many reports. In QuickBooks, by default, the accounting reports and financial statements are prepared using the accrual basis of accounting, which records revenue when earned and expenses when incurred regardless of cash receipts and cash payments. The accrual basis of accounting follows GAAP—generally accepted accounting principles—and is the basis used in this text.

Completing the New Company Setup Using the Accrual Basis of Accounting

Recall that you entered the opening balances for the Inventory accounts, Accounts Receivable, and Accounts Payable accounts when you set up and updated the Lists/Centers. When you set up the Chart of Accounts List, you also could have entered the opening balances for assets (excluding Accounts Receivable and Inventory), liabilities (excluding Accounts Payable), and equity accounts at that time. But you cannot enter opening balances for some system default accounts (such as Accounts Receivable, Accounts Payable, and Sales Tax Payable), and you cannot enter opening balances for revenue and expense accounts when creating new accounts in the Chart of Accounts List. Therefore, all the opening balances (excluding inventory, accounts receivable, and accounts payable) will be entered in one journal entry.

As you saw in the *Journal* report (Figure 7–CC on page 297), every time an Accounts Receivable account was recorded, a corresponding Uncategorized Income account was recorded, and every time an Accounts Payable account was recorded, a corresponding Uncategorized Expenses account was recorded. The Uncategorized Income and Uncategorized Expenses accounts

reversing entries
entries recorded in the general journal to offset a balance in an account

are not used in the accrual basis of accounting and therefore must be reversed to eliminate them. You do this by using reversing entries.

To complete the New Company Setup using the accrual basis of accounting, you will prepare three journal entries: entering opening balances, reversing uncategorized income account, and reversing uncategorized expenses account.

Entering Opening Balances

You will enter all the opening balances for Kristin Raina Interior Designs—excluding inventory, accounts receivable, and accounts payable—as one large compound journal entry.

To enter opening balances in the Make General Journal Entries window:

1. At the main menu bar, click Company and then click *Make General Journal Entries*. At the Assigning Numbers to Journal Entries message, insert a check mark in the box to the left of *Do not display this message in the future* and then click OK. The Make General Journal Entries window appears.
2. At the *DATE* field, choose *04/01/2022*.
3. At the *ENTRY NO.* field, accept the default *1*.
4. Remove the check mark next to *ADJUSTING ENTRY* and click the Hide List button to allow more space to record this large journal entry.
5. Enter the following accounts and amounts as debits:

Number	Account Name	Balance
1010	Cash - Operating	$50,855.38
1300	Design Supplies	200.00
1305	Office Supplies	250.00
1410	Prepaid Advertising	500.00
1420	Prepaid Insurance	2,200.00
1725	Furniture, Cost	12,000.00
1825	Computers, Cost	3,600.00
3020	Kristin Raina, Drawings	400.00
4100	Sales Discounts	84.62
5060	Cost of Carpets Sold	1,200.00
5065	Cost of Draperies Sold	500.00
5070	Cost of Lamps Sold	600.00
5075	Cost of Mirrors Sold	450.00
5900	Inventory Adjustment	150.00
6020	Accounting Expense	300.00
6050	Advertising Expense	100.00
6175	Deprec. Exp., Furniture	100.00
6185	Deprec. Exp., Computers	60.00
6200	Insurance Expense	200.00
6300	Janitorial Expense	125.00
6325	Office Supplies Expense	150.00
6400	Rent Expense	800.00
6450	Telephone Expense	275.00
6500	Utilities Expense	450.00
7000	Interest Expense	50.00

QuickCheck: $75,600

HINT

Enlarge the Make General Journal Entries window and click the Hide List button before recording this journal entry so that you can see more of the entries.

HINT

You can type in the account number for each account or use the drop-down list.

HINT

It may be easier to type the account number and then use the Tab key to move to the debit or credit column, type in the amount, and then use the Tab key to move to the next row. It is not necessary to delete the balancing amount in the credit (or debit) column; just type in the correct amount in the debit or credit column. When appropriate, type over the balancing amount.

6. Enter the following accounts and amounts as credits:

Number	Account Name	Balance
1750	Accum. Dep., Furniture	$100.00
1850	Accum. Dep., Computers	60.00
2020	Notes Payable	7,000.00
2030	Interest Payable	50.00
4010	Design Services	4,980.00
4020	Decorating Services	3,400.00
4060	Sale of Carpets	2,400.00
4065	Sale of Draperies	1,000.00
4070	Sale of Lamps	1,200.00
4075	Sale of Mirrors	900.00

QuickCheck: $54,510

7. Record the credit balance of $54,510 as a credit to account 3010 Kristin Raina, Capital. See Figure 7–FF.

FIGURE 7–FF
Make General Journal Entries Window—Opening Balances

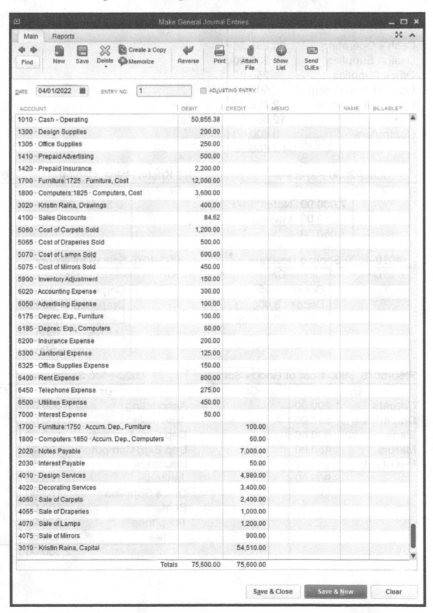

Chapter 7 | New Company Setup—Express Start

HINT

If the Future Transactions message appears, click Yes. To change this preference, click Edit at the main menu bar and then click *Preferences*. In the left panel of the Preferences window, click the Accounting icon. Choose the Company Preferences tab. Remove the check marks from the warning options and then click OK.

8. If the information is correct, click Save & New. If the Tracking fixed assets message appears, insert a check mark next to *Do not display this message in the future* and then click OK.

ACCOUNTING CONCEPT

The effects of recording the opening balances are as follows:

1010-1825 Assets	Dr	Cr
Cash - Operating	50,855.38	
Design Supplies	200.00	
Office Supplies	250.00	
Prepaid Advertising	500.00	
Prepaid Insurance	2,200.00	
Furniture	12,000.00	
Computers	3,600.00	
	69,605.38	

1750-1850 Accum Dep	Dr	Cr
		100.00
		60.00
		160.00

2020-2030 Payables	Dr	Cr	
		7,000.00	Notes
		50.00	Interest
		7,050.00	

3010 Kristin Raina, Capital	Dr	Cr
		54,510.00

3020 Kristin Raina, Drawings	Dr	Cr
	400.00	

4010-4020 Service Revenue	Dr	Cr	
		Design	4,980.00
		Decor	3,400.00
			8,380.00

4060-4075 Sale of Inventory	Dr	Cr	
		Carpets	2,400.00
		Draperies	1,000.00
		Lamps	1,200.00
		Mirrors	900.00
			5,500.00

4100 Sales Discounts	Dr	Cr
	84.62	

5060-5075, 5900 Cost of Goods Sold	Dr	Cr
Carpets	1,200.00	
Draperies	500.00	
Lamps	600.00	
Mirrors	450.00	
Invent Adj	150.00	
	2,900.00	

6020-6500 Expenses	Dr	Cr
Accounting	300.00	
Advertising	100.00	
Dep Exp. Furniture	100.00	
Dep Exp. Computers	60.00	
Insurance	200.00	
Janitorial	125.00	
Office Supplies	150.00	
Rent	800.00	
Telephone	275.00	
Utilities	450.00	
	2,560.00	

7000 Interest Exp	Dr	Cr
	50.00	

Reversing the Uncategorized Income Account

Recall that in the *Journal* report, shown in Figure 7–CC on page 297, two journal entries are recorded that debit Accounts Receivable and credit Uncategorized Income for two customers as follows:

Berger Bakery Company	$ 600
Franco Films Co.	940
	$1,540

The debit entries to the Accounts Receivable account are correct and will stay in that account. The credits to the Uncategorized Income account will be reversed by debiting Uncategorized Income for $1,540 and crediting the account 3010 Kristin Raina, Capital (formerly the Opening Balance Equity account) for $1,540.

HINT

As part of customizing the Chart of Accounts, the account Opening Balance Equity, created by QuickBooks, was changed to 3010 Kristin Raina, Capital.

To reverse the Uncategorized Income account:
1. At the Make General Journal Entries window, choose the date *04/01/2022*, and at the *ENTRY NO.* field, accept *2*.
2. Remove the check mark next to *ADJUSTING ENTRY*, if necessary.
3. Debit account 49900 Uncategorized Income for 1,540 and credit account 3010 Kristin Raina, Capital for 1,540. See Figure 7–GG.

FIGURE 7–GG
Make General Journal Entries Window—Reverse Uncategorized Income

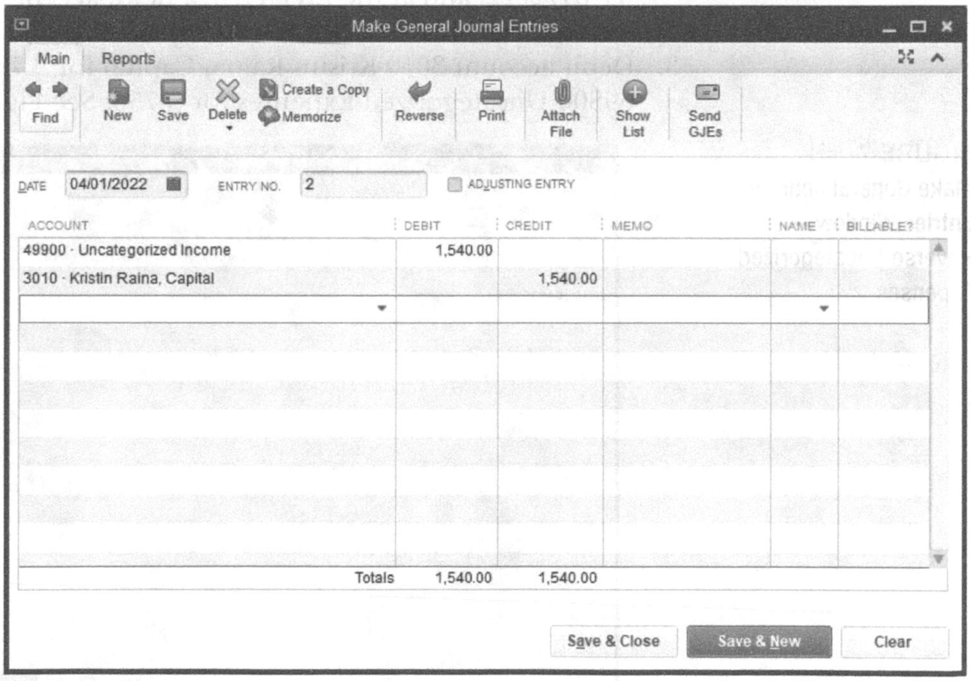

4. If the information is correct, click Save & New.

ACCOUNTING CONCEPT

49900 Uncategorized Income		3010 Kristin Raina, Capital	
Dr	Cr	Dr	Cr
Rev 1,540	1,540		1,540
	0		

Reversing the Uncategorized Expenses Account

In the *Journal* report shown in Figure 7–CC on page 297, there are seven journal entries that credit Accounts Payable and debit Uncategorized Expenses for seven vendors as follows:

Ace Glass Works	$1,500
Bell Carpet Design	2,000
Cuza and Carl Associates	400
Galeway Computers	2,600
Midwest Mutual Insurance Co.	2,400
Minneapolis Electric & Gas Co.	450
Williams Office Supply Company	400
	$9,750

The credit entries to the Accounts Payable account are correct and will stay in that account. The debits to the Uncategorized Expenses, however, have to be reversed by crediting Uncategorized Expenses for $9,750 and debiting the 3010 Kristin Raina, Capital account for $9,750.

To reverse the Uncategorized Expenses account:
1. At the Make General Journal Entries window, choose the date *04/01/2022*, and at the *ENTRY NO.* field, accept *3*.
2. Remove the check mark next to *ADJUSTING ENTRY*, if necessary.
3. Debit account 3010 Kristin Raina, Capital for *9,750* and credit account 69800 Uncategorized Expenses for *9,750*. See Figure 7–HH.

FIGURE 7–HH
Make General Journal Entries Window—Reverse Uncategorized Expenses

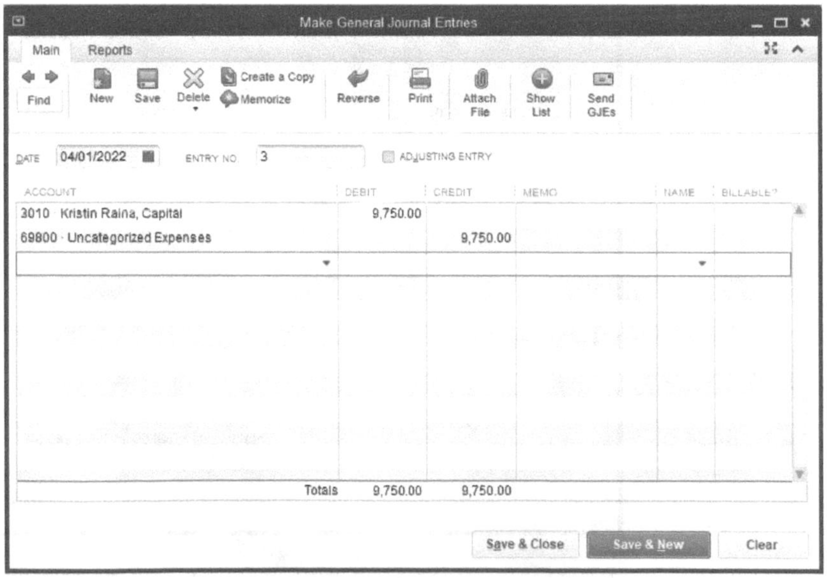

4. If the information is correct, click the Save & Close button.

ACCOUNTING CONCEPT

69800 Uncategorized Expenses		3010 Kristin Raina, Capital	
Dr	Cr	Dr	Cr
9,750	Rev 9,750	9,750	
0			

Accounting Reports and Financial Statements

Upon completing the New Company Setup, you should display and print the accounting reports and financial statements.

Accounting Reports

The accounting reports you need to print and review include the *Journal* and the *Trial Balance*.

Journal Report

You displayed and printed the *Journal* report after the initial company setup was completed (Figure 7–CC, page 297). After recording the opening balances and reversing the Uncategorized Income and Uncategorized Expenses accounts, you added three more journal entries to the *Journal* report. You can view and print all the journal entries for April 1, 2022. Figure 7–II displays only the additional three journal entries.

HINT

To display only the last three journal entries in the *Journal* report, click the Customize Report button and then click the Filters tab. At the *FILTER* field, click *Transaction Type*. At the *Transaction Type* field, click *Journal* and then click OK.

FIGURE 7–II
Journal Report—
Filtered—Additional
Journal Entries

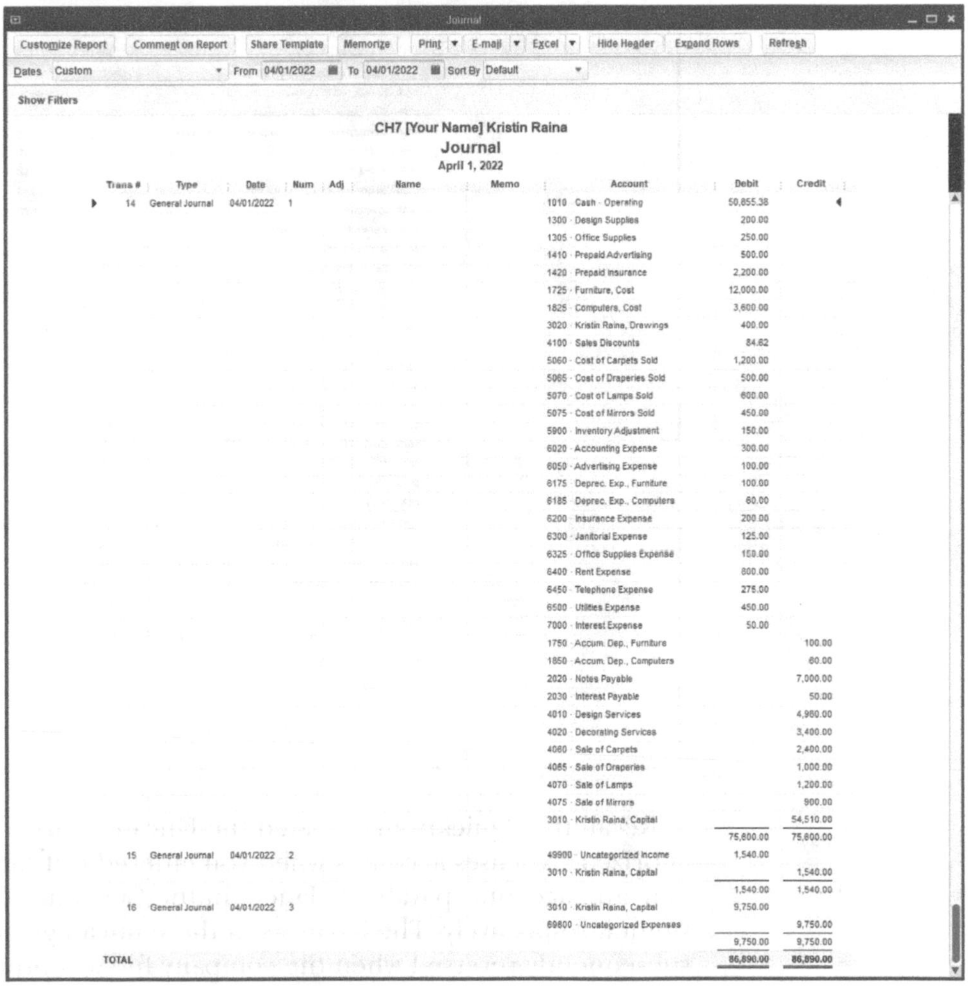

HINT

If you display all the journal entries, the total debits and total credits is $101,880.

Trial Balance Report

Review and print the *Trial Balance* report for April 1, 2022. (It should look like Figure 7–JJ.) The accounts and balances on this trial balance should match those on the trial balance of March 31, 2022, after transactions were recorded in Chapters 2 through 5.

FIGURE 7–JJ
Trial Balance Report

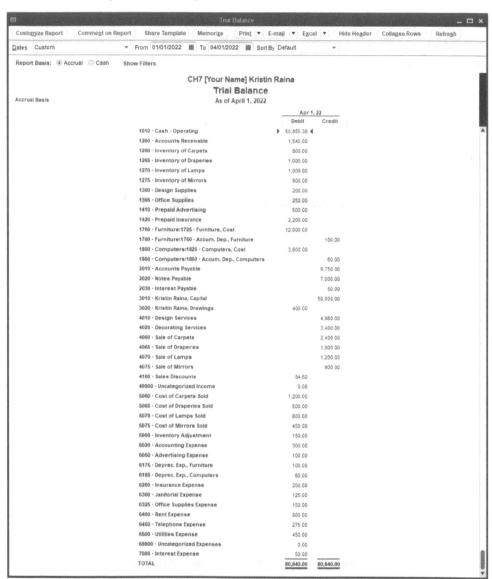

CH7 [Your Name] Kristin Raina
Trial Balance
Accrual Basis
As of April 1, 2022

	Apr 1, 22 Debit	Credit
1010 · Cash - Operating	50,855.38	
1200 · Accounts Receivable	1,540.00	
1260 · Inventory of Carpets	800.00	
1265 · Inventory of Draperies	1,000.00	
1270 · Inventory of Lamps	1,000.00	
1275 · Inventory of Mirrors	900.00	
1300 · Design Supplies	200.00	
1305 · Office Supplies	250.00	
1410 · Prepaid Advertising	500.00	
1420 · Prepaid Insurance	2,200.00	
1700 · Furniture:1725 · Furniture, Cost	12,000.00	
1700 · Furniture:1750 · Accum. Dep., Furniture		100.00
1800 · Computers:1825 · Computers, Cost	3,600.00	
1800 · Computers:1850 · Accum. Dep., Computers		60.00
2010 · Accounts Payable		9,750.00
2020 · Notes Payable		7,000.00
2030 · Interest Payable		50.00
3010 · Kristin Raina, Capital		50,000.00
3020 · Kristin Raina, Drawings	400.00	
4010 · Design Services		4,980.00
4020 · Decorating Services		3,400.00
4060 · Sale of Carpets		2,400.00
4065 · Sale of Draperies		1,000.00
4070 · Sale of Lamps		1,200.00
4075 · Sale of Mirrors		900.00
4100 · Sales Discounts	84.62	
49900 · Uncategorized Income	0.00	
5060 · Cost of Carpets Sold	1,200.00	
5065 · Cost of Draperies Sold	500.00	
5070 · Cost of Lamps Sold	600.00	
5075 · Cost of Mirrors Sold	450.00	
5900 · Inventory Adjustment	150.00	
6020 · Accounting Expense	300.00	
6050 · Advertising Expense	100.00	
6175 · Deprec. Exp., Furniture	100.00	
6185 · Deprec. Exp., Computers	60.00	
6200 · Insurance Expense	200.00	
6300 · Janitorial Expense	125.00	
6325 · Office Supplies Expense	150.00	
6400 · Rent Expense	800.00	
6450 · Telephone Expense	275.00	
6500 · Utilities Expense	450.00	
69800 · Uncategorized Expenses	0.00	
7000 · Interest Expense	50.00	
TOTAL	**80,840.00**	**80,840.00**

Recall that QuickBooks created the Uncategorized Income and Uncategorized Expenses accounts when you entered outstanding accounts receivable and accounts payable balances in the Customer Center and Vendor Center, respectively. The balances in these uncategorized accounts were subsequently reversed when the company file was prepared for the accrual basis of accounting. These accounts are no longer needed and can be marked inactive in the Chart of Accounts List.

Financial Statements

The financial statements consist of the *Profit & Loss Standard* report (see Figure 7–KK) and the *Balance Sheet Standard* report (see Figure 7–LL). Upon completion of the New Company Setup, these reports should be the same as the financial reports printed at the end of Chapter 5.

FIGURE 7–KK
Profit & Loss Standard Report

FIGURE 7–LL

Balance Sheet Standard Report

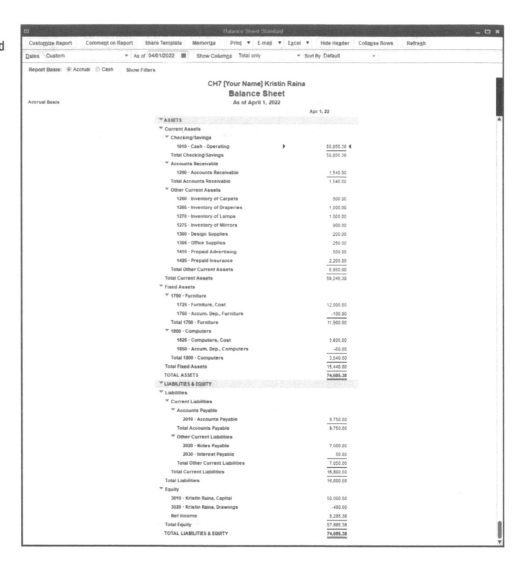

Hybrid Method of New Company Setup and QuickBooks Desktop Setup Window

You have learned two methods of New Company Setup: Detailed Start and Express Start without the EasyStep Interview. In addition, in Chapter 6, you learned how to use the QuickBooks Desktop Setup window to enter information for customers, vendors, and items. The QuickBooks Desktop Setup window also could have been used in Chapter 7. Instead, in Chapter 7, you learned to enter service items and inventory part items, customers, and vendors by going directly to the Item List, Customer Center, and Vendor Center to enter the appropriate information, bypassing the QuickBooks Desktop Setup window.

Whichever method you use to create the new company file, you can use any combination of entering company information for service items, inventory part items, customers, and vendors. That is, you can use the QuickBooks Desktop Setup window or the Lists/Centers in any combination. For instance, you could use the QuickBooks Desktop Setup window to enter the customers and vendors but use the Item List to enter the service and inventory part items, or you could use the QuickBooks Desktop Setup window to enter the inventory part items and use the Item List to enter the service items. QuickBooks will accept any variation of using the QuickBooks Desktop Setup window or Lists/Centers for entering the information for customers, vendors, service items, and inventory part items.

Backing Up the New Company File and Exiting QuickBooks

You should make a backup copy of the new company file in the event there is damage to the file or the computer or at some time you work on a different computer. Using the procedures learned in previous chapters, make a backup copy of the new company file to your subfolder and/or a removable storage device and name it **EX7** *[Your Name]* **Kristin Raina Interior Designs**. Restore the backup copy and change the company name to **EX7** *[Your Name]* **Kristin Raina Interior Designs**.

Upon completion of the New Company Setup level of operation, customizing and updating the Lists/Centers, viewing and printing Reports, and making a backup copy of the new company file, your accounting records are now ready for recording daily activities. Activities should be recorded in the new company file using the procedures illustrated in the prior chapters.

Close the company file and then exit QuickBooks.

Chapter Review and Assessment

Procedure Review

To begin the New Company Setup and create a new company file using Express Start:

1. Open QuickBooks.
2. At the No Company Open window, click the Create a new company button or click File and then click *New Company*. The QuickBooks Desktop Setup window appears with the *Let's set up your business!* page displayed. This is the page where you select the method of New Company Setup.
3. At the QuickBooks Desktop Setup window, at the *Let's set up your business!* page, click the Express Start button. The *Glad you're here* page appears.
4. At the *Glad you're here* page, at the *Business Name* field, type the company name.
5. At the *Industry* field, click *Help me choose*. The Select Your Industry page appears.
6. At the Select Your Industry page, at the *Industry* field, scroll to the bottom and select *Other/None*.
7. Click OK. You are returned to the *Glad you're here* page.
8. At the *Business Type* field, click the drop-down arrow and choose *Sole Proprietorship*.
9. At the *Employer Identification Number (EIN)* field, type in the tax identification number.
10. Enter your business contact information.
11. Click the Preview Your Settings button.
12. At the Preview Your Company Settings page, click the Company File Location tab.
13. On the Company File Location tab, click the Change Location button. You are moved to the Browse For Folder window.
14. At the Browse For Folder window, scroll through the list and choose the folder where you save your files and then click OK. You are returned to the Company File Location tab, with the path and folder displayed.
15. If the path and folder are correct, click OK. You are returned to the *Glad you're here* page.
16. Click the Create Company button. The company file is saved in the path and folder you indicated in Step 17. The QuickBooks Desktop Setup window appears.
17. Close the QuickBooks Desktop Setup window. If the New Feature Tour window appears, click the X to close it. The Home page and Left Icon bar appear. Close the Home page. To remove the Left Icon bar, click View and then click *Hide Icon Bar*.

To create a company file password:

1. At the main menu bar, click Company and then click *Setup Users and Passwords*.
2. At the Setup Users and Passwords submenu, click *Change Your Password*. The Change Your Password window appears.
3. At the *New Password* and *Confirm New Password* text boxes, type Student1 or a password of your choosing.

4. If the information is correct, click Confirm. At the QuickBooks Desktop message, click OK. Close the Home page if it appears. The password has now been created for the company file, and you will need to enter the password each time you open the company file.

To activate the account numbers feature:
1. At the main menu bar, click Edit and then click *Preferences.*
2. In the left panel of the Preferences window, click the Accounting icon.
3. Click the Company Preferences tab.
4. At the *ACCOUNTS* field, insert a check mark in the box to the left of *Use account numbers* to turn on the account numbers feature.
5. Click OK.

To activate the inventory feature:
1. At the main menu bar, click Edit and then click *Preferences.*
2. In the left panel of the Preferences window, click the Items & Inventory icon.
3. Click the Company Preferences tab.
4. In the PURCHASE ORDERS AND INVENTORY section, insert a check mark in the box to the left of *Inventory and purchase orders are active* to turn on the inventory feature.
5. Click OK.

To activate the sales tax feature:
1. At the main menu bar, click Edit and then click *Preferences.*
2. In the left panel of the Preferences window, click the Sales Tax icon.
3. Click the Company Preferences tab.
4. At the *Do You Charge Sales Tax?* field, click *Yes.*
5. At the *Your most common sales tax item* field, click the drop-down arrow.
6. Click < *Add New* >. The New Item window appears.
7. Type in the sales tax item information.
8. At the *Tax Agency (vendor that you collect for)* field, click the drop-down arrow.
9. At the Tax Agency drop-down list, click < *Add New* >. The New Vendor window appears.
10. Enter the appropriate vendor information and then click OK.
11. Click OK at the completed New Item window and then click OK at the Preferences window.
12. In the Updating Sales Tax dialog box, click OK.

To disable the payroll feature:
1. At the main menu bar, click Edit and then click *Preferences.*
2. In the left panel of the Preferences window, click the Payroll & Employees icon.
3. Click the Company Preferences tab.
4. In the QUICKBOOKS DESKTOP PAYROLL FEATURES section, click the *No payroll* option.
5. Click OK.

To update the Chart of Accounts List:
1. At the main menu bar, click Lists and then click *Chart of Accounts.*
2. Click the Account menu button.
3. At the Account button drop-down menu, click *New.*

4. At the Add New Account: Choose Account Type window, choose the type and then click Continue.
5. At the Add New Account window, type the information and then click Save & New or Save & Close.

To allow QuickBooks to create system default accounts:
1. Open and close some Activities windows, such as the Create Invoices, Enter Sales Receipts, and Enter Bills windows. Open the Item List and the New Item window and then select *Inventory Part*.

   This process creates the system default accounts Undeposited Funds, Inventory Asset, and Cost of Goods Sold. After QuickBooks creates these accounts, you can edit the account numbers and names. If you created an accounts receivable–type account and an accounts payable–type account, QuickBooks will accept the accounts. If you did not previously create them, when you open and close the Create Invoices and Enter Bills windows, QuickBooks will create the accounts receivable and accounts payable accounts, respectively.
2. Follow the steps to customize the system default accounts.

To customize the system default accounts:
1. At the main menu bar, click Lists and then click *Chart of Accounts*.
2. Select the account to edit.
3. Click the Account menu button.
4. At the Account button drop-down menu, click *Edit Account*.
5. Make any necessary changes to the account and then click Save & Close.

To mark an account inactive:
1. At the main menu bar, click Lists and then click *Chart of Accounts*.
2. Select the account to make inactive.
3. Click the Account menu button.
4. At the Account button drop-down menu, click *Make Account Inactive*.
5. To view the inactive accounts, click the Account menu button and then click S*how Inactive Accounts*. Inactive accounts are displayed with an X to the left of the account names.
6. Close the Chart of Accounts List window.

To customize payment terms:
1. At the main menu bar, click Lists and then click *Customer & Vendor Profile Lists*.
2. At the Customer & Vendor Profile Lists submenu, click *Terms List*.
3. At the Terms List window, click the Terms menu button.
4. At the Terms button drop-down menu, click *New*.
5. At the New Terms window, type the appropriate information for any terms QuickBooks did not create that you wish to create.
6. Click Next or OK.
7. At the Terms List window, select the terms created by QuickBooks that you wish to delete.
8. Click the Terms menu button, and then from the Terms button drop-down menu, click *Delete Terms*. Click OK at the warning.
9. At the Terms List window, select the terms created by QuickBooks that you wish to edit.

10. Click the Terms menu button, and then from the Terms button drop-down menu, click *Edit Terms*.
11. Change the appropriate information and then click OK.

To update the Item List:
1. At the main menu bar, click Lists and then click *Item List*.
2. At the Item List window, click the Item menu button.
3. At the Item button drop-down menu, click *New*.
4. At the New Item window, select an option in the *TYPE* field and then type the information.
5. Click Next or OK.

To update the Customer Center:
1. At the main menu bar, click Customers and then click *Customer Center*.
2. At the Customer Center window, click the New Customer & Job button and then click *New Customer*.
3. At the New Customer window, enter the background data for the customer, including the opening balance, if any, and the correct date.
4. Click Next or OK.

To update the Vendor Center:
1. At the main menu bar, click Vendors and then click *Vendor Center*.
2. At the Vendor Center window, click the New Vendor menu button and then click *New Vendor*.
3. At the New Vendor window, enter the background data for the vendor, including the opening balance, if any, and the correct date.
4. Click Next or OK.

To enter opening balances in the Make General Journal Entries window:
1. At the main menu bar, click Company and then click *Make General Journal Entries*.
2. Choose the date and make or accept an entry at the *ENTRY NO.* field.
3. Remove the check mark next to *ADJUSTING ENTRY*.
4. Enter the accounts and amounts to be debited.
5. Enter the accounts and amounts to be credited.
6. Record the balancing amount as a credit (or debit) to the capital account.
7. Click the Save & Close button.

To reverse the Uncategorized Income account:
1. At the main menu bar, click Company and then click *Make General Journal Entries*.
2. Choose the date and check the entry at the *ENTRY NO.* field.
3. Remove the check mark next to *ADJUSTING ENTRY*.
4. Debit the Uncategorized Income account for the full amount in that account and credit the Capital account for the same amount.
5. Click the Save & Close button.

To reverse the Uncategorized Expenses account:
1. At the main menu bar, click Company and then click *Make General Journal Entries*.
2. Choose the date and check the entry at the *ENTRY NO.* field.

3. Remove the check mark next to *ADJUSTING ENTRY*.
4. Debit the Capital account for the full amount in the Uncategorized Expenses account and credit the Uncategorized Expenses account for the same amount.
5. Click the Save & Close button.

To view and print accounting reports from the Reports menu:
1. At the main menu bar, click Reports and then click *Accountant & Taxes*.
2. At the Accountant & Taxes submenu, choose a report.
3. Indicate the start and end dates for the report.
4. Print the report.
5. Close the report.

To view and print financial statements from the Reports menu:
1. At the main menu bar, click Reports and then click *Company & Financial*.
2. At the Company & Financial submenu, choose a financial report.
3. Indicate the start and end dates for the report.
4. Print the report.
5. Close the report.

This activity can be completed in the online course.

Key Concepts

Select the letter of the item that best matches each definition.

a. Most common sales tax
b. Make account inactive
c. Uncategorized Income
d. Preferences - Accounting
e. Inventory Asset and Cost of Goods Sold

f. Preferences - Items & Inventory
g. Express Start
h. System default accounts
i. Uncategorized Expenses
j. Customer & Vendor Profile Lists

_____ 1. To set up your company file more quickly, click this button instead of choosing Detailed Start.
_____ 2. Accounts automatically created by QuickBooks when you choose an inventory item part in the New Item window.
_____ 3. An option you can choose so accounts not in use are not displayed in the reports.
_____ 4. The window used to activate account numbers.
_____ 5. Accounts automatically created by QuickBooks.
_____ 6. The account created by QuickBooks as an offsetting amount of Accounts Receivable.
_____ 7. The window used to activate the inventory feature.
_____ 8. The submenu used to open the Terms List window.
_____ 9. The field that must be completed to activate the sales tax feature.
_____ 10. The account created by QuickBooks as an offsetting amount of Accounts Payable.

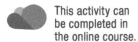

This activity can be completed in the online course.

Procedure Check

1. You are creating a new company file using the Express Start method. Should you set up a password? Which preferences should you establish before recording data?

2. When you first choose *Inventory Part* in the *TYPE* field in the New Item window of the Item List, which two accounts does QuickBooks look for on the Chart of Accounts List? Can you customize these accounts? If so, explain how.

3. What is the Opening Balance Equity account? Can you customize this account? If so, explain how.

4. Why would you mark an account inactive, and how would you do it? What would you do to display inactive accounts in the Chart of Accounts List?

5. If you set up a new company file using the Express Start method described in this chapter (without using the EasyStep Interview or QuickBooks Desktop Setup), which journal entries would you most likely record to complete the New Company Setup process?

6. Your manager is just learning QuickBooks. She has asked you if it is necessary to use the Detailed Start method for New Company Setup. Provide the manager with a written explanation of how she could set up the new company file without using the EasyStep Interview or QuickBooks Desktop Setup windows.

Case Problems

Reports created for these Case Problems can be exported to Excel and uploaded in the online course to be automatically graded.

Demonstrate your knowledge of the QuickBooks features discussed in this chapter by completing the following case problems.

Case Problem 7–1

On April 1, 2022, Lynn Garcia began her business, Lynn's Music Studio. In the first month of business, Lynn set up the music studio, provided guitar and piano lessons, and recorded month-end activity. In May, the second month of business, Lynn started purchasing and selling inventory items of guitars, keyboards, music stands, and sheet music. In April and May, Lynn recorded the financial activities using a manual accounting system. On June 1, 2022, Lynn decided to switch her accounting method to QuickBooks. Lynn has organized the information about the company but has hired you to convert the accounting records to QuickBooks.

1. Use the information below to create and set up the company file using the Express Start method. (Skip the QuickBooks Desktop Setup window after the new company file is created.)

Business Name:	CH7 *[Your Name]* Lynn's Music Studio
Industry:	Other/None
Business Type:	Sole Proprietorship
Employer Identification Number (EIN):	45-6123789
Phone:	570-555-0400

Business Address:	228 Pearl Street		
City:	Scranton		
ZIP:	18501		
State:	PA		
Country:	U.S.		

2. Set up the company file password.

New Password:	Student1
Confirm New Password:	Student1

3. Activate the account numbers, inventory, and sales tax features. For sales tax, use the following information:

TYPE:	Sales Tax Item
Sales Tax Name:	PA Sales Tax
Description:	Sales Tax
Tax Rate (%):	7
Tax Agency:	PA Dept. of Revenue

4. Disable the payroll.
5. Open and close the following windows to allow QuickBooks to create system default accounts:
   Create Invoices
   Enter Sales Receipts
   Enter Bills
   Item List: New Item: Inventory Part

6. Use the following information to customize the system default accounts:

QuickBooks		Edited	
Number	Account Name	Number	Account Name
11000	Accounts Receivable	1200	
12000	Undeposited Funds	1250	
12100	Inventory Asset	1260	Inventory of Guitars
20000	Accounts Payable	2010	
25500	Sales Tax Payable	2200	
30000	Opening Balance Equity	3010	Lynn Garcia, Capital
30800	Owners Draw	3020	Lynn Garcia, Drawings
32000	Owners Equity	3030	Accumulated Earnings
50000	Cost of Goods Sold	5060	Cost of Guitars Sold

7. Mark the Payroll Liabilities and Payroll Expenses accounts as inactive.
8. Customize the payment Terms List to list only the following:
   2/10, Net 30 Days
   Net 10 Days
   Net 15 Days
   Net 30 Days

9. Use the information in Table LMS—Accounts to update the Chart of Accounts List.

TABLE LMS
Accounts

Account Type	Number	Account Name
Bank	1010	Cash - Operating
Other Current Asset	1265	Inventory of Keyboards
Other Current Asset	1270	Inventory of Music Stands
Other Current Asset	1275	Inventory of Sheet Music
Other Current Asset	1300	Music Supplies
Other Current Asset	1305	Office Supplies
Other Current Asset	1410	Prepaid Advertising
Other Current Asset	1420	Prepaid Insurance
Fixed Asset	1700	Music Instruments
Fixed Asset	1725	Music Instruments, Cost [Subaccount of 1700]
Fixed Asset	1750	Accum. Dep., Music Instruments [Subaccount of 1700]
Fixed Asset	1800	Furniture
Fixed Asset	1825	Furniture, Cost [Subaccount of 1800]
Fixed Asset	1850	Accum. Dep., Furniture [Subaccount of 1800]
Fixed Asset	1900	Computers
Fixed Asset	1925	Computers, Cost [Subaccount of 1900]
Fixed Asset	1950	Accum. Dep., Computers [Subaccount of 1900]
Other Current Liability	2020	Notes Payable
Other Current Liability	2030	Interest Payable
Income	4010	Piano Lessons
Income	4020	Guitar Lessons
Income	4060	Sale of Guitars
Income	4065	Sale of Keyboards
Income	4070	Sale of Music Stands
Income	4075	Sale of Sheet Music
Income	4100	Sales Discounts
Cost of Goods Sold	5065	Cost of Keyboards Sold
Cost of Goods Sold	5070	Cost of Music Stands Sold
Cost of Goods Sold	5075	Cost of Sheet Music Sold
Cost of Goods Sold	5900	Inventory Adjustment
Expense	6075	Deprec. Exp., Music Instruments
Expense	6085	Deprec. Exp., Furniture
Expense	6095	Deprec. Exp., Computers
Expense	6150	Instrument Tuning Expense
Expense	6200	Insurance Expense
Expense	6300	Music Supplies Expense
Expense	6325	Office Supplies Expense
Expense	6400	Rent Expense
Expense	6450	Telephone Expense
Expense	6500	Utilities Expense
Other Expense	7000	Interest Expense

10. Use the information in Table LMS—Items to update the Item List. For the Inventory Part Items, be sure to use the date *June 1, 2022*.

TABLE LMS Items

Item Name and Description on Purchase and Sales Transactions	Cost	COGS Account	Rate/ Sales Price	Income Account	Asset Account	On Hand	Total Value
Service Items (nontaxable):							
Guitar Lessons			$ 30	4020			
Piano Lessons			35	4010			
Inventory Part Items (taxable):							
Guitars	$50	5060	100	4060	1260	6	$ 300
Keyboards	75	5065	150	4065	1265	17	1,275
Music Stands	20	5070	40	4070	1270	17	340
Sheet Music	3	5075	6	4075	1275	165	495

11. Use the information in Table LMS—Customers to update the Customer Center. Be sure to use the date *June 1, 2022*, for each customer with an opening balance.

TABLE LMS Customers

Customer/ Company Name	Opening Balance	Full Name	Main Phone/ Mobile	Invoice/Bill To	Payment Terms
Douglaston Senior Center	$175.00	Herbie Richardson	570-555-7748 570-555-8800	574 S Beech Street Scranton, PA 18506	Net 30 Days
Highland School		Asst. Principal Office	570-555-6963 570-555-6970	115 Forrest Street Waymart, PA 18472	2/10, Net 30 Days
Jefferson High School		Music Department	570-555-9600 570-555-9700	500 Apple Street Dunmore, PA 18512	2/10, Net 30 Days
Mulligan Residence	1575.90	Adam Smith	570-555-3325 570-555-3500	299 Hickory Lane Scranton, PA 18504	2/10, Net 30 Days
Musical Youth Group		Dana Thompson	570-555-6642 570-555-6700	550 Marion Lane Scranton, PA 18504	Net 30 Days
Patel Family		Ari Patel	570-555-1132	574 Kenwood Drive Dickson City, PA 18519	Net 30 Days
Patterson Family		Jonathan Patterson	570-555-6321	650 Memory Lane Dickson City, PA 18519	Net 30 Days
Schroeder Family		Betty Schroeder	570-555-1897	98 Belmont Rd. Carbondale, PA 18407	Net 30 Days
Twin Lakes Elementary		Miss Brooks	570-555-4474 570-555-4485	515 Hobson Street Honesdale, PA 18431	2/10, Net 30 Days

12. Use the information in Table LMS—Vendors to update the Vendor Center. Be sure to use the date *June 1, 2022*, for each vendor with an outstanding balance.

TABLE LMS Vendors

Vendor/ Company Name	Opening Balance	Full Name	Main Phone/ Mobile	Billed From	Payment Terms
Computer Town	$2,000.00	Customer Service	570-555-1500 570-555-1550	1000 Carbondale Highway Scranton, PA 18502	Net 30 Days
Katie's Keyboards	1,500.00	Katie Shea	570-555-7777 570-555-8888	158 Clay Road Scranton, PA 18505	Net 30 Days
Lynn Garcia					
Melody Music Equipment		Melody Arhmand	570-555-1120 570-555-1125	780 Roselyn Ave. Scranton, PA 18505	Net 30 Days
Mills Family Furniture	1,500.00	Edna Mills	570-555-7144 570-555-7200	150 Amelia Street Scranton, PA 18503	Net 30 Days
Music Instruments, Inc.		Matilda Molloy	570-555-9630 570-555-9635	25 Monroe Ave. Scranton, PA 18505	Net 30 Days
Mutual Insurance Company	1,200.00	Bob Maxwell	570-555-5600 570-555-5900	1 Main Street Honesdale, PA 18431	Net 30 Days
Paper, Clips, and More	350.00	Justin Daves	570-555-8558 570-555-5555	157 Waymart Lane Waymart, PA 18472	Net 30 Days
Pioneer Phone		Customer Service	570-555-6000 570-555-6500	1000 Route 6 Carbondale, PA 18407	Net 15 Days
Steamtown Electric		Customer Service	570-555-2500 570-555-3000	150 Vine Lane Scranton, PA 18501	Net 15 Days
Strings, Sheets & Such		Manuela Perez	570-555-3636 570-555-3700	250 Lincoln St. Scranton, PA 18505	Net 30 Days
Tune Tones		Tony Tune	570-555-1111 570-555-2222	500 Monroe Ave. Dunmore, PA 18512	Net 30 Days
Viewhill Realty		Matt Snyder	570-555-1000 570-555-1200	100 Commerce Blvd. Scranton, PA 18501	Net 15 Days

13. Make three journal entries on June 1, 2022 (accept the default Entry Nos.):
    a. Enter the opening balances listed below. Enter the following accounts and amounts as debits:

Number	Account Name	Balance
1010	Cash - Operating	$14,615.18
1300	Music Supplies	430.00
1305	Office Supplies	300.00
1420	Prepaid Insurance	1,100.00
1725	Music Instruments, Cost	4,000.00
1825	Furniture, Cost	2,500.00
1925	Computers, Cost	3,000.00
3020	Lynn Garcia, Drawings	1,000.00

...continues

...continued

Number	Account Name	Balance
4100	Sales Discounts	188.92
5060	Cost of Guitars Sold	1,150.00
5065	Cost of Keyboards Sold	2,475.00
5070	Cost of Music Stands Sold	460.00
5075	Cost of Sheet Music Sold	1,305.00
5900	Inventory Adjustment	50.00
6075	Deprec. Exp., Music Instruments	60.00
6085	Deprec. Exp., Furniture	40.00
6095	Deprec. Exp., Computers Expense	35.00
6150	Instrument Tuning	100.00
6200	Insurance Expense	100.00
6300	Music Supplies Expense	70.00
6325	Office Supplies Expense	50.00
6400	Rent Expense	600.00
6450	Telephone Expense	50.00
6500	Utilities Expense	70.00
7000	Interest Expense	15.00

Enter the following accounts and amounts as credits:

Number	Account Name	Balance
1750	Accum. Dep., Music Instruments	$ 60.00
1850	Accum. Dep., Furniture	40.00
1950	Accum. Dep., Computers	35.00
2020	Notes Payable	2,000.00
2030	Interest Payable	15.00
4010	Piano Lessons	3,535.00
4020	Guitar Lessons	2,910.00
4060	Sale of Guitars	2,300.00
4065	Sale of Keyboards	4,950.00
4070	Sale of Music Stands	920.00
4075	Sale of Sheet Music	2,610.00

   b. Make a journal entry to reverse the Uncategorized Income account.
   c. Make a journal entry to reverse the Uncategorized Expenses account.
14. Display and print the following reports for June 1, 2022:
   a. *Journal*
   b. *Trial Balance*
   c. *Profit & Loss Standard* (04/01/2022–06/01/2022)
   d. *Balance Sheet Standard*
   e. *Item Listing*
   f. *Customer Contact List*
   g. *Vendor Contact List*
15. Make a backup copy of the new company file and name it **LMS7** *[Your Name]* **Lynn's Music Studio**. Restore the backup copy and change the company name to **LMS7** *[Your Name]* **Lynn's Music Studio**.

Case Problem 7–2

On June 1, 2022, Olivia Chen began her business, Olivia's Web Solutions. In the first month of business, Olivia set up the office, provided web page design and internet consulting services, and recorded month-end activity. In July, the second month of business, Olivia began to purchase and sell inventory items of computer hardware and software. In June and July, Olivia recorded the financial activities using a manual accounting system. On August 1, 2022, Olivia decides to switch her accounting method to Quick-Books. Olivia has organized the information about the company but has hired you to convert the accounting records to QuickBooks.

1. Use the information below to create and set up the company file using the Express Start method. (Skip the Quickbooks Desktop Setup window after the new company file is created.)

Business Name:	CH7 *[Your Name]* Olivia's Web Solutions
Industry:	Other/None
Business Type:	Sole Proprietorship
Employer Identification Number (EIN):	55-5656566
Phone:	516-555-5000
Business Address:	547 Miller Place
City:	Westport
ZIP:	11858
State:	NY
Country:	U.S.

2. Set up the company file password.

New Password:	Student1
Confirm New Password:	Student1

3. Activate the account numbers, inventory, and sales tax features. For sales tax, use the following information:

TYPE:	Sales Tax Item
Tax Name:	NYS Sales Tax
Description:	Sales Tax
Tax Rate (%):	8
Tax Agency:	NYS Tax Dept.

4. Disable the payroll.
5. Open and close the following windows to allow QuickBooks to create system default accounts:
    Create Invoices
    Enter Sales Receipts
    Enter Bills
    Item List: New Item: Inventory Part

6. Use the following information to customize the system default accounts:

	QuickBooks		Edited
Number	Account Name	Number	Account Name
11000	Accounts Receivable	1200	
12000	Undeposited Funds	1250	
12100	Inventory Asset	1260	Inventory of Computers
20000	Accounts Payable	2010	
25500	Sales Tax Payable	2200	
30000	Opening Balance Equity	3010	Olivia Chen, Capital
30800	Owners Draw	3020	Olivia Chen, Drawings
32000	Owners Equity	3030	Accumulated Earnings
50000	Cost of Goods Sold	5060	Cost of Computers Sold

7. Mark the Payroll Liabilities and Payroll Expenses accounts as inactive.
8. Customize the payment Terms List to list only the following:
   2/10, Net 30 Days
   Net 10 Days
   Net 15 Days
   Net 30 Days

9. Use the information in Table OWS—Accounts to update the Chart of Accounts List.

TABLE OWS
Accounts

Account Type	Number	Account Name
Bank	1010	Cash - Operating
Other Current Asset	1265	Inventory of Scanners
Other Current Asset	1270	Inventory of HTML Software
Other Current Asset	1275	Inventory of Desktop Pub. Soft.
Other Current Asset	1300	Computer Supplies
Other Current Asset	1305	Office Supplies
Other Current Asset	1410	Prepaid Advertising
Other Current Asset	1420	Prepaid Insurance
Fixed Asset	1700	Computers
Fixed Asset	1725	Computers, Cost [Subaccount of 1700]
Fixed Asset	1750	Accum. Dep., Computers [Subaccount of 1700]
Fixed Asset	1800	Furniture
Fixed Asset	1825	Furniture, Cost [Subaccount of 1800]
Fixed Asset	1850	Accum. Dep., Furniture [Subaccount of 1800]
Fixed Asset	1900	Software
Fixed Asset	1925	Software, Cost [Subaccount of 1900]
Fixed Asset	1950	Accum. Dep., Software [Subaccount of 1900]
Other Current Liability	2020	Notes Payable
Other Current Liability	2030	Interest Payable

continues...

Account Type	Number	Account Name
Income	4010	Web Page Design Fees
Income	4020	Internet Consulting Fees
Income	4060	Sale of Computers
Income	4065	Sale of Scanners
Income	4070	Sale of HTML Software
Income	4075	Sale of Desktop Pub. Software
Income	4100	Sales Discounts
Cost of Goods Sold	5065	Cost of Scanners Sold
Cost of Goods Sold	5070	Cost of HTML Software Sold
Cost of Goods Sold	5075	Cost of Desktop Pub. Soft. Sold
Cost of Goods Sold	5900	Inventory Adjustment
Expense	6050	Advertising Expense
Expense	6075	Deprec. Exp., Computers
Expense	6085	Deprec. Exp., Furniture
Expense	6095	Deprec. Exp., Software
Expense	6100	Insurance Expense
Expense	6300	Computer Supplies Expense
Expense	6325	Office Supplies Expense
Expense	6350	Online Service Expense
Expense	6400	Rent Expense
Expense	6450	Telephone Expense
Expense	6500	Utilities Expense
Other Expense	7000	Interest Expense

10. Use the information in Table OWS—Items to update the Item List. For the Inventory Part Items, be sure to use the date *August 1, 2022.*

TABLE OWS Items

Item Name and Description on Purchase and Sales Transactions	Cost	COGS Account	Rate/ Sales Price	Income Account	Asset Account	On Hand	Total Value
Service Items (nontaxable):							
Internet Consulting Services			$ 100	4020			
Web Page Design Services			125	4010			
Inventory Part Items (taxable):							
Computers	$1,000	5060	2,000	4060	1260	10	$10,000
Scanners	300	5065	600	4065	1265	12	3,600
HTML Software	75	5070	150	4070	1270	18	1,350
Desktop Pub. Software	100	5075	200	4075	1275	10	1,000

11. Use the information in Table OWS—Customers to update the Customer Center. Be sure to use the date *August 1, 2022*, for each customer with an opening balance.

TABLE OWS Customers

Customer/ Company Name	Opening Balance	Full Name	Main Phone/ Mobile	Invoice/Bill To	Payment Terms
Artie's Auto Repair	$800.00	Leon Artie	516-555-1221 516-555-1231	32 W. 11th Street New Hyde Park, NY 11523	Net 30 Days
Breathe Easy A/C Contractors		Allen Scott	516-555-6868 516-555-6869	556 Atlantic Ave. Freeport, NY 11634	Net 30 Days
Long Island Water Works		Customer Service	516-555-4747 516-555-4748	87-54 Bayview Ave. Glen Cove, NY 11563	2/10, Net 30 Days
Miguel's Restaurant		Miguel Perez	516-555-3236 516-555-3237	30 Willis Ave. Roslyn, NY 11541	2/10, Net 30 Days
Schneider Family	1,000.00	Johnny Schneider	516-555-8989 516-555-8990	363 Farmers Rd. Syosset, NY 11547	Net 15 Days
Sehorn & Smith Attorneys	800.00	Jerry Sehorn	212-555-3339 212-555-3338	510 Fifth Ave. New York, NY 10022	Net 30 Days
Singh Family		David Singh	718-555-3233 718-555-3239	363 Marathon Parkway Little Neck, NY 11566	Net 15 Days
South Shore School District	12,056.00	Joseph Porter	516-555-4545 516-555-4546	3666 Ocean Ave. South Beach, NY 11365	2/10, Net 30 Days
Thrifty Stores	1,500.00	William Way	718-555-2445 718-555-2446	23 Boston Ave. Bronx, NY 11693	Net 30 Days

12. Use the information in Table OWS—Vendors to update the Vendor Center. Be sure to use the date of *August 1, 2022*, for each vendor with an opening balance.

TABLE OWS Vendors

Vendor/Company Name	Opening Balance	Full Name	Main Phone/ Mobile	Billed To	Payment Terms
ARC Management		Alvin R. Clinton	516-555-6363 516-555-6364	668 Lakeville Ave. Garden City, NY 11678	Net 30 Days
Chrbet Advertising	$1,200.00	Chris Chrbet	212-555-8777 212-555-8778	201 E. 10th Street New York, NY 10012	Net 30 Days
Comet Computer Supplies		Customer Service	631-555-4444 631-555-4455	657 Motor Parkway Center Island, NY 11488	Net 15 Days
Computec Computers	10,000.00	Customer Service	702-555-6564 702-555-6563	3631 Gate Blvd. Greensboro, NC 27407	Net 30 Days
Eastel	350.00	Customer Service	212-555-6565 212-555-6566	655 Fifth Ave. New York, NY 10012	Net 30 Days
Eastern Mutual Insurance		Customer Service	212-555-6363 212-555-6364	55 Broadway, Room 55 New York, NY 10001	Net 30 Days
InterSoft Development Co.		Customer Service	631-555-3634 631-555-3635	556 Route 347 Hauppauge, NY 11654	Net 30 Days

continues...

Vendor/Company Name	Opening Balance	Full Name	Main Phone/ Mobile	Billed To	Payment Terms
Lewis Furniture Co.	1,700.00	Manny Lewis	631-555-6161 631-555-6162	1225 Route 110 Farmingdale, NY 11898	Net 30 Days
LI Power Company		Customer Service	516-555-8888 516-555-8889	5444 Northern Ave. Plainview, NY 11544	Net 15 Days
Martin Computer Repairs		Ken Martin	516-555-7777 516-555-7778	366 N. Franklin St. Garden City, NY 11568	Net 30 Days
Netsoft Development Co.	1,600.00	Customer Service	974-555-7873 974-555-7874	684 Mountain View Rd. Portland, OR 68774	Net 30 Days
Office Plus	375.00	Customer Service	516-555-3214 516-555-3213	45 Jericho Tpke. Jericho, NY 11654	Net 30 Days
Olivia Chen					
Scanntronix		Customer Service	617-555-8778 617-555-8776	2554 Bedford Rd. Boston, MA 02164	Net 30 Days
Systems Service		Jeremy Jones	516-555-2525 516-555-2526	36 Sunrise Lane Hempstead, NY 11004	Net 30 Days
Textpro Software, Inc.		Customer Service	615-555-4545 615-555-4546	877 Route 5 Ft. Lauderdale, FL 70089	Net 30 Days

13. Make three journal entries on August 1, 2022 (accept the default Entry Nos.):

    a. Enter the opening balances listed below. Enter the following accounts and amounts as debits:

Number	Account Name	Balance
1010	Cash - Operating	$24,489.16
1300	Computer Supplies	350.00
1305	Office Supplies	325.00
1410	Prepaid Advertising	1,000.00
1420	Prepaid Insurance	1,650.00
1725	Computers, Cost	5,000.00
1825	Furniture, Cost	3,200.00
1925	Software, Cost	3,600.00
3020	Olivia Chen, Drawings	500.00
4100	Sales Discounts	179.84
5060	Cost of Computers Sold	10,000.00
5065	Cost of Scanners Sold	2,400.00
5070	Cost of HTML Software Sold	75.00
5075	Cost of Desktop Pub. Soft. Sold	500.00
5900	Inventory Adjustment	75.00
6050	Advertising Expense	200.00
6075	Deprec. Exp., Computers	75.00
6085	Deprec. Exp., Furniture	50.00
6095	Deprec. Exp., Software	100.00
6100	Insurance Expense	150.00
6300	Computer Supplies Expense	250.00

...continues

...continued

Number	Account Name	Balance
6325	Office Supplies Expense	50.00
6350	Online Service Expense	150.00
6400	Rent Expense	800.00
6450	Telephone Expense	350.00
6500	Utilities Expense	125.00
7000	Interest Expense	25.00

Enter the following accounts and amounts as credits:

Number	Account Name	Balance
1750	Accum. Dep., Computers	$ 75.00
1850	Accum. Dep., Furniture	50.00
1950	Accum. Dep., Software	100.00
2020	Notes Payable	2,500.00
2030	Interest Payable	25.00
4010	Web Page Design Fees	9,750.00
4020	Internet Consulting Fees	6,600.00
4060	Sale of Computers	20,000.00
4065	Sale of Scanners	4,800.00
4070	Sale of HTML Software	150.00
4075	Sale of Desktop Pub. Software	1,000.00

   b. Make a journal entry to reverse the Uncategorized Income account.
   c. Make a journal entry to reverse the Uncategorized Expenses account.
14. Display and print the following reports for August 1, 2022:
   a. *Journal*
   b. *Trial Balance*
   c. *Profit & Loss Standard* (06/01/2022–08/01/2022)
   d. *Balance Sheet Standard*
   e. *Item Listing*
   f. *Customer Contact List*
   g. *Vendor Contact List*
15. Make a backup copy of the new company file and name it **OWS7** *[Your Name]* **Olivia's Web Solutions**. Restore the backup copy and change the company name to **OWS7** *[Your Name]* **Olivia's Web Solutions**.

## CHAPTER 8

Payroll Setup

Customizing Payroll Setup

Objectives

- Review payroll terminology
- Activate the payroll feature and manual payroll option
- Customize payroll system default accounts
- Customize and update the Chart of Accounts List for payroll
- Customize the Payroll Item List for payroll items created by QuickBooks
- Update the Payroll Item List
- Display and print the *Payroll Item Listing* report

 The online course includes additional training and assessment resources. Reports created for the Chapter Problem can be uploaded for instructor review.

Chapter Introduction

QuickBooks allows you to process payroll and track payroll information for your company's employees. The company that hires the workers is called the **employer**. The person hired by a company who will receive salary or wages on a regular basis is called the **employee**. **Payroll** involves computing each employee's gross earnings, determining each employee's **withholdings** and **deductions**, and calculating each employee's net pay. It also involves preparing employees' paychecks or setting up direct deposits, properly recording payroll-related transactions (journal entries), submitting payroll withholdings and deductions to the appropriate tax agency or other entity, and preparing payroll compliance reports.

To process payroll in QuickBooks, it must first be set up. Payroll setup involves enabling the payroll feature, customizing and adding payroll accounts to the Chart of Accounts List, choosing a QuickBooks payroll service or activating the manual entries feature, customizing pre-established payroll items, and establishing payroll items such as compensation and payroll taxes or payroll deductions. These payroll items comprise the Payroll Item List.

In this chapter, our sample company, Kristin Raina Interior Designs, will set up the payroll in anticipation of hiring two employees beginning April 1, 2022. After the payroll setup is complete and the employees are hired, the payroll transactions for Kristin Raina Interior Designs will then be illustrated in Chapter 9.

QuickBooks versus Manual Accounting: Payroll

In a manual accounting system, the process of preparing a payroll is laborious and time consuming. For each employee, the company has to tally the hours worked in a pay period, compute the gross pay for the pay period, and then determine all the withholdings and deductions from that employee's pay. After completing these computations, the company has to prepare a paycheck or direct deposit, along with a pay stub showing all the earnings, withholdings, and deductions for the pay period, as well as all the year-to-date earnings, withholdings, and deductions. When computers are not used, payroll withholdings are calculated manually using preprinted withholding tables. The gross pay, withholdings, and deductions for all employees then have to be totaled to record the payroll in a payroll journal, which subsequently is posted to the general ledger accounts. In addition, year-to-date earnings and withholdings need to be accumulated and used in preparing government-required quarterly and year-end reports. In dealing with such a quantity and variety of computations, it is easy to make a mistake.

Payroll was one of the first accounting tasks to be available on computers. Payroll preparation firms were formed for this sole purpose. A company simply prepares a list of each employee's name and the hours that person worked during a pay period. This information is submitted to the payroll processing firm and—usually overnight—the payroll is prepared; the company receives its properly completed paychecks or list of direct deposits and a summary report the next morning. The paychecks are distributed to the employees or the direct deposits are processed, and the summary report is used to record the appropriate journal entries for the payroll. The payroll processing firm also accumulates the necessary information for preparing

---

employer the company or individual that hires workers

employee the person hired by a company who will receive salary or wages on a regular basis

payroll involves computing each employee's gross earnings, withholdings and deductions, and net pay; preparing employees' paychecks or setting up direct deposits; properly recording payroll-related transactions; submitting payroll withholdings and deductions to the appropriate agencies; and preparing payroll compliance reports

withholdings generally refer to the payroll taxes the employer is required to take out of the employee's paycheck and submit to the appropriate government agency

deductions generally refer to amounts taken out of the employee's paycheck for various fringe benefits, such as insurance, pension, and so on

government compliance reports. As personal computers and accounting software packages became available, companies were able to process their payroll in-house as part of their routine accounting tasks without needing to use an outside payroll preparation firm.

QuickBooks includes a payroll feature that, once activated, allows processing a payroll with employees' gross earnings, withholdings, deductions, and net pay both quickly and easily. Simultaneously, the payroll transactions are recorded in the journal. In addition, the paychecks can be immediately printed when the printer is set up to do so, or the direct deposit can be set up and immediately processed. QuickBooks also simultaneously prepares reports that summarize all quarterly and annual information needed for required filings and for required payments of employee withholdings to the appropriate agencies.

Part of what makes payroll processing easier in QuickBooks than in a manual system is the use of Lists/Centers, which you will recall function as a database. Typical gross earnings, withholdings, and deductions are detailed in the Payroll Item List. In addition, exact payroll taxes are maintained within the payroll feature and QuickBooks payroll services. When employees are to be paid, QuickBooks calls on the information in the Payroll Item List, along with information about the employee (discussed in Chapter 9), and quickly does all the computations and prepares all the related reports. But because QuickBooks computes the employee's pay by accessing information from the Payroll Item List, it is important that the Payroll Item List be accurate and complete. Any errors in the Payroll Item List will result in inaccurate computations in the payroll and the subsequent recording of incorrect entries in the general journal.

Using QuickBooks Payroll Services versus Calculating Payroll Manually

Like most computerized accounting packages, QuickBooks offers several desktop payroll services, available by subscription for a fee: QuickBooks Core Payroll, QuickBooks Premium Payroll, and QuickBooks Elite Payroll. A company would choose the service that best fits its needs, from the Core service, which allows the company to prepare and issue paychecks or next day direct deposits, to the Premium service, which also provides setup review and same day direct deposits. If a company prefers, it could use the Elite service, which does the payroll setup and then does the same as the Premium service but also provides additional support and protection. If a company chooses to use one of the QuickBooks payroll services, it subscribes to the service and pays a monthly fee, and then the taxes imposed on the employer and the employees' withholdings are automatically computed based on the information in the Payroll Item List, the employee's file (Chapter 9), and the QuickBooks payroll service. If a company has not subscribed to a QuickBooks payroll service, then the firm's payroll withholdings, deductions, and payroll taxes must be entered by typing the amounts into QuickBooks. This is referred to as calculating payroll manually.

Part of the payroll setup is to indicate either that a specific QuickBooks payroll service will be used or that the payroll will be processed manually. In business, it is commonly advisable to subscribe to a payroll service.

However, in the classroom environment, the payroll withholdings, deductions, and payroll taxes will be entered manually.

Payroll Definitions and Terms

Whether payroll is processed manually or with a software package, the laws, procedures, filing requirements, definitions, and terminology remain the same. The following is a brief review of the more common payroll definitions.

Employee Payroll Information

To properly determine an employee's gross pay, tax withholdings, deductions, and net pay and to meet federal and state record-keeping requirements, the employer needs specific information about the employee. This information includes but is not limited to the following:

- Name
- Address
- Social Security number
- Marital status
- Gross pay amount or hourly rate
- State tax withholding allowances
- Voluntary deductions (pension, 401(k), insurance, and so on)

The employer uses this information along with the applicable tax rates to compute the employee's paycheck and track the employee's pay information.

Gross Pay

gross pay total earnings for an employee for a specific pay period before withholdings and deductions

Gross pay, also known as *gross earnings*, is the total earnings for the employee for a specific pay period before any withholdings and deductions. Compensation can be in the form of a salary, hourly wages, tips, commissions, bonus, and overtime earned during a pay period. If the employee is paid based on an annual salary, the annual amount is divided over the number of pay periods in the year. Gross pay for an hourly worker is determined based on the number of hours worked during the pay period multiplied by the employee's hourly pay rate. The gross pay will be subject to payroll taxes for both the employer and the employee.

FICA Tax (Social Security) and Medicare Tax

The Federal Insurance Contribution Act (FICA) tax, also known as Social Security, is a tax imposed on both the employer and the employee at a rate of 6.2% of the first $137,700 (year 2020) of wages for each employee. Medicare tax is also imposed on both the employer and the employee at a rate of 1.45% each; there is no wage maximum for the Medicare tax. Beginning in 2013, an Additional Medicare Tax of 0.9% (0.009) was imposed, which has different thresholds for different taxpayers ($250,000/$200,000). The employer periodically remits both the employer and the employee portions of the tax to the federal government.

Federal Income Tax (FIT)

Employers are required to withhold from each employee's pay the appropriate amount of federal income tax (FIT). The Internal Revenue Service (IRS) publishes tables and instructions to assist employers in determining the proper withholding amount for each employee. The withholding amount is determined based on the employee's gross pay and marital status. The employer periodically forwards the tax withheld to the federal government along with the Social Security and Medicare taxes.

State Income Tax (SIT)

Many states impose an income tax and require employers to withhold the tax from employees' pay in a manner similar to that used for FIT. The withholding amount is determined based on the employee's gross pay, marital status, and exemption allowances claimed. The employer will remit this tax periodically to the appropriate state taxing authority. Some local governments (city, county) may also impose income taxes. Rules for withholding local taxes for local governments are similar to those used by federal and state governments.

Federal Unemployment Tax Act (FUTA)

The Federal Unemployment Tax Act (FUTA) imposes a tax on the employer only. The tax is used to fund unemployment insurance programs administered by the federal government. The effective rate of the tax is 0.6% of the first $7,000 of each employee's wages.

State Unemployment Insurance (SUI)

In addition to paying the FUTA tax, employers are required by all states to contribute to a state unemployment insurance (SUI) fund. Rates and regulations vary from state to state. However, most states impose the tax only on the employer. The rate can vary from 1% to 11% based on the employer's location and unemployment experience, and the taxable amount varies from state to state.

State Disability Insurance (SDI)

Most states require employers to purchase an insurance policy, sometimes called *state disability insurance* (SDI), that compensates employees if they are unable to work for an extended period due to illness or injury. Some states allow the employer to withhold a small amount from each employee's pay to defray the employer's insurance premium cost.

Company Deductions

Many employers sponsor various fringe benefit programs and deduct amounts from an employee's pay to fund or offset the costs of the benefits. Programs such as 401(k) plans, medical and dental insurance, pension and profit-sharing plans, long-term disability, life insurance, and so on may be partially funded by a deduction made by the company from an employee's paycheck.

Net Pay

net pay total gross earnings for an employee minus all employee withholdings and deductions

Net pay is the amount of the employee's gross pay less all employee withholdings and deductions. As anyone who has worked knows, net pay is only a fraction of the gross pay earned.

United States Treasury

The United States Treasury is the tax-collecting agency of the federal government. The United States Treasury is responsible for collecting the FICA tax, Medicare tax, FIT, and FUTA tax. Most states have a similar department for collecting SIT, SUI, and SDI.

Chapter Problem

In this chapter, Kristin Raina Interior Designs will set up the payroll in anticipation of hiring two employees during April 2022. The April 1 beginning balances for the company are contained in the company file **CH8 Kristin Raina Interior Designs**.

Before you begin, open the company file **CH8 Kristin Raina Interior Designs.QBW**. Enter the password, *Student1*. Make a backup copy of the file, name it **EX8** *[Your Name]* **Kristin Raina Interior Designs**, and then restore the file. Enter the password, *Student1*. Finally, change the company name in the file to **EX8** *[Your Name]* **Kristin Raina Interior Designs**.

New Company Setup

Payroll Setup—Activate the Payroll Feature and Manual Payroll Option

To set up payroll in QuickBooks, you must first activate the payroll feature. If you set up a new company file using the Detailed Start method—which means you are using the EasyStep Interview window (Chapter 6)—you have the choice of disabling the payroll feature as part of the New Company Setup. However, if you set up a new company file using the Express method (Chapter 7), QuickBooks automatically activates the payroll feature. In the company file for this chapter problem, the payroll feature was disabled in New Company Setup and needs to be activated at the Preferences window on the Edit menu.

In addition, as noted earlier, part of Payroll Setup is to indicate if the company will subscribe to a payroll service or process payroll manually. Choosing the manual payroll option is also made at the Preferences window where the payroll feature is enabled.

To activate the QuickBooks payroll feature and manual payroll option:
1. At the main menu bar, click Edit and then click *Preferences*.
2. In the left panel of the Preferences window, click the Payroll & Employees icon.
3. Click the Company Preferences tab. If the payroll processing feature is not activated, the *No payroll* option is selected.
4. Click the *Full payroll* option. This will enable the Payroll feature.
5. Click the *Manual Payroll* option to insert a check mark in the box.
6. At the *Get payday peace of mind* message, click Next.
7. At the Confirm Manual Payroll message, click Activate.
8. At the QuickBooks Desktop Information window informing you that Manual Payroll has been activated, click OK. See Figure 8–A.

FIGURE 8–A
Preferences Window—
Payroll & Employees—
Company Preferences

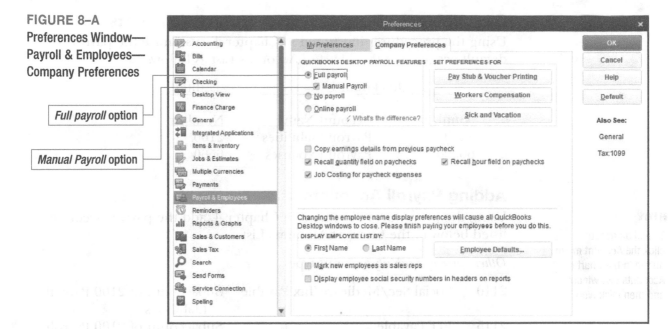

Full payroll option

Manual Payroll option

9. Click OK at the Preferences window to accept the defaults.

Once you have activated the payroll feature, QuickBooks automatically creates two default general ledger accounts in the Chart of Accounts list: Payroll Liabilities and Payroll Expenses. Once you activate the Manual Payroll option, QuickBooks creates the Payroll Item List. You will review and customize the Chart of Accounts and the Payroll Item list on the following pages.

Lists/Centers

Updating the Chart of Accounts List for Payroll

When the payroll feature is activated, QuickBooks establishes one default general ledger liability posting account for *all* payroll-related liabilities and one expense account for *all* payroll expenses. Open and review the Chart of Accounts List. The accounts created by QuickBooks are 24000 Payroll Liabilities and 66000 Payroll Expenses. When these accounts are created, each account type is dimmed in the Edit Account window to indicate that QuickBooks has created each account and that each account is a system default account. Recall that you must allow QuickBooks to create its own accounts in some situations, but then you can edit the account names and account numbers.

QuickBooks creates one payroll liability account and one payroll expense account to be used in the payroll processing transactions (Chapter 9). However, most companies usually create separate payroll liability accounts for FIT, SIT, Social Security, Medicare, and so on. Similarly, most companies usually create separate payroll expense accounts for Social Security, Medicare, FUTA, SUI, and so on. For our sample company, Kristin Raina Interior Designs, you will create separate payroll liability accounts that will be subaccounts of the system default Payroll Liabilities account created by QuickBooks. Similarly, you will create separate payroll expense accounts that will be subaccounts of the system default Payroll Expenses account created by QuickBooks. Before creating the additional payroll accounts, you will customize the system default accounts to change the account numbers to follow the company pattern for numbering accounts on the Chart of Accounts List.

HINT

Notice that on the Chart of Accounts List, there is a Cash - Payroll account. Many companies use a separate checking account for payroll transactions. Periodically, funds are transferred into this account from the Cash - Operating account. Transfer of funds between cash accounts is covered in Chapter 10.

Customize the Payroll System Default Accounts

Using the procedures illustrated in Chapter 4, customize the payroll system default accounts in the Chart of Accounts List as follows:

	QuickBooks	Edited
Number	Account Name	Number
24000	Payroll Liabilities	2100
66000	Payroll Expenses	6560

Adding Payroll Accounts

HINT

To add an account, click the Account menu button in the Chart of Accounts List window and then click *New*.

Using the procedures illustrated in Chapter 4, add the payroll accounts listed below to the Chart of Accounts List.

Other Current Liability account type:

2110	Social Sec/Medicare Tax Payable	Subaccount of 2100 Payroll Liabilities
2115	FIT Payable	Subaccount of 2100 Payroll Liabilities
2120	SIT Payable	Subaccount of 2100 Payroll Liabilities
2125	FUTA Payable	Subaccount of 2100 Payroll Liabilities
2130	SUI Payable	Subaccount of 2100 Payroll Liabilities

Expense account type:

HINT

Use *Edit* from the Account menu in the Chart of Accounts List window to correct any errors.

6565	Salaries and Wages Expense	Subaccount of 6560 Payroll Expenses
6610	Social Sec/Medicare Tax Expense	Subaccount of 6560 Payroll Expenses
6625	FUTA Expense	Subaccount of 6560 Payroll Expenses
6630	SUI Expense	Subaccount of 6560 Payroll Expenses

QuickCheck: The updated Chart of Accounts List appears in Figure 8–B.

FIGURE 8–B
Updated Chart of Accounts List

Chart of Accounts

Look for account name or number

[Search] [Reset]

NAME	TYPE	BALANCE TOTAL	ATTACH
1010 · Cash - Operating	Bank	43,355.38	
1020 · Cash - Payroll	Bank	7,500.00	
1200 · Accounts Receivable	Accounts Receivable	1,540.00	
1250 · Undeposited Funds	Other Current Asset	0.00	
1260 · Inventory of Carpets	Other Current Asset	800.00	
1265 · Inventory of Draperies	Other Current Asset	1,000.00	
1270 · Inventory of Lamps	Other Current Asset	1,000.00	
1275 · Inventory of Mirrors	Other Current Asset	900.00	
1300 · Design Supplies	Other Current Asset	200.00	
1305 · Office Supplies	Other Current Asset	250.00	
1410 · Prepaid Advertising	Other Current Asset	500.00	
1420 · Prepaid Insurance	Other Current Asset	2,200.00	
1700 · Furniture	Fixed Asset	11,900.00	
1725 · Furniture, Cost	Fixed Asset	12,000.00	
1750 · Accum. Dep., Furniture	Fixed Asset	-100.00	
1800 · Computers	Fixed Asset	3,540.00	
1825 · Computers, Cost	Fixed Asset	3,600.00	
1850 · Accum. Dep., Computers	Fixed Asset	-60.00	
2010 · Accounts Payable	Accounts Payable	9,750.00	
2020 · Notes Payable	Other Current Liability	7,000.00	
2030 · Interest Payable	Other Current Liability	50.00	
2100 · Payroll Liabilities	Other Current Liability	0.00	
2110 · Social Sec/Medicare Tax Payable	Other Current Liability	0.00	
2115 · FIT Payable	Other Current Liability	0.00	
2120 · SIT Payable	Other Current Liability	0.00	
2125 · FUTA Payable	Other Current Liability	0.00	
2130 · SUI Payable	Other Current Liability	0.00	
2200 · Sales Tax Payable	Other Current Liability	0.00	
3010 · Kristin Raina, Capital	Equity	50,000.00	
3020 · Kristin Raina, Drawings	Equity	-400.00	
3030 · Accumulated Earnings	Equity		
4010 · Design Services	Income		
4020 · Decorating Services	Income		
4060 · Sale of Carpets	Income		
4065 · Sale of Draperies	Income		
4070 · Sale of Lamps	Income		
4075 · Sale of Mirrors	Income		
4100 · Sales Discounts	Income		
5060 · Cost of Carpets Sold	Cost of Goods Sold		
5065 · Cost of Draperies Sold	Cost of Goods Sold		
5070 · Cost of Lamps Sold	Cost of Goods Sold		
5075 · Cost of Mirrors Sold	Cost of Goods Sold		
5900 · Inventory Adjustment	Cost of Goods Sold		
6020 · Accounting Expense	Expense		
6050 · Advertising Expense	Expense		
6175 · Deprec. Exp., Furniture	Expense		
6185 · Deprec. Exp., Computers	Expense		
6200 · Insurance Expense	Expense		
6300 · Janitorial Expenses	Expense		
6325 · Office Supplies Expense	Expense		
6400 · Rent Expense	Expense		
6450 · Telephone Expense	Expense		
6500 · Utilities Expense	Expense		
6560 · Payroll Expenses	Expense		
6565 · Salaries and Wages Expense	Expense		
6610 · Social Sec/Medicare Tax Expense	Expense		
6625 · FUTA Expense	Expense		
6630 · SUI Expense	Expense		
7000 · Interest Expense	Other Expense		

Payroll Liabilities—parent account and subaccounts

Payroll Expenses—parent account and subaccounts

[Account ▼] [Activities ▼] [Reports ▼] Attach ☐ Include inactive

The Payroll Item List

Once you have activated the payroll feature and the manual calculations feature, QuickBooks automatically sets up a Payroll Item List, which you may now access. The Payroll Item List contains a file for each type of payroll item that affects both the company and the employees. QuickBooks automatically creates several standard payroll items, including Social Security Company (FICA tax), Social Security Employee, Medicare Company (Medicare tax), Medicare Employee, federal withholding, and so on. Typically, you must modify the Payroll Item List based on your company's geographic location, company deductions, and pay policies.

As you know, the second level of operation in QuickBooks is to update the background information in the Lists/Centers. In earlier chapters, you added, deleted, or edited vendor files, customer files, accounts, and inventory item files to keep the Lists/Centers current for your company. Now you will customize and update the Payroll Item List to match the payroll information unique to your company.

HINT

The Payroll Item List was not a choice on the Lists menu in earlier chapters because the payroll and manual calculations features had not been activated.

To review the Payroll Item List created by QuickBooks:

1. At the main menu bar, click Lists and then click *Payroll Item List*. The Payroll Item List appears. See Figure 8–C.

FIGURE 8–C Payroll Item List

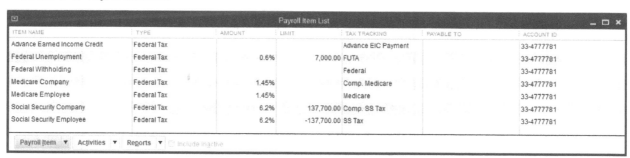

Notice that the payroll items initially created by QuickBooks are the ones generally applicable to all payroll situations, such as Social Security tax, Medicare tax, Federal Withholding tax, and Federal Unemployment tax.

The tax rates (amounts) and limits displayed on the Payroll Item List are those that were in effect when this book was prepared. As the government revises tax rates and limits, QuickBooks should update them in the Payroll Item List accordingly. The tax rates and limits in the Payroll Item List and subsequent windows illustrated in this chapter may be different from what appears on your computer screen. In general, accept the tax rates and limits on your computer screen.

To view a specific payroll item, such as Federal Withholding:

1. Double-click *Federal Withholding*. The Edit payroll item (Federal Withholding) window appears. See Figure 8–D.

FIGURE 8–D
Edit Payroll Item (Federal Withholding) Window— Name Used in Paychecks and Payroll Reports Page

HINT

An alternative method of displaying this window is to select (highlight) the payroll item, click the Payroll Item button, and then click *Edit Payroll Item*.

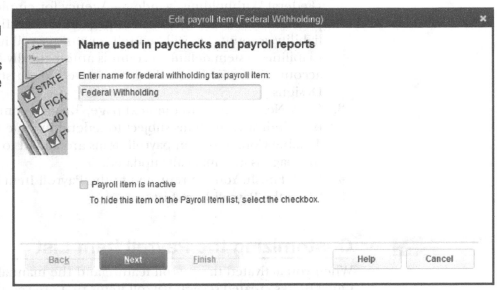

This window displays the name used in paychecks and payroll reports. The Edit payroll item window for each payroll item file displays several pages of information that are displayed each time you click Next.

2. Click Next and the Agency for employee-paid liability page appears. See Figure 8–E. On this page, you will select the government agency to which the employee's federal income tax payment should be forwarded as well as the general ledger account for the tax liability. (This information will be filled in later.)

FIGURE 8–E
Edit Payroll Item (Federal Withholding) Window— Agency for Employee- Paid Liability Page

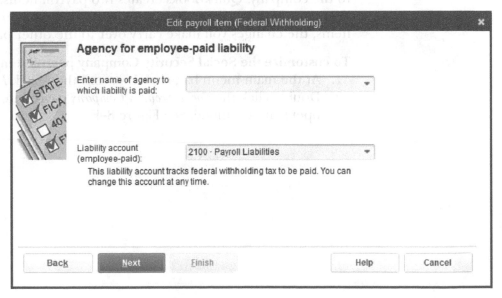

Remember that federal income tax withheld from the employee's paycheck is counted as a liability to the employer that must at some time be paid to the appropriate tax agency. The Edit payroll item (Federal Withholding) window—Agency for employee-paid liability page identifies that agency. This page also identifies the general ledger liability account that will be used for this payroll item. The 2100 Payroll Liabilities system default account is automatically listed as the liability account. This account will be customized for Kristin Raina Interior Designs.

3. Click Next to move to the next page, Taxable compensation. This page indicates all items subject to federal income tax withholdings. As Taxable Compensation payroll items are added to the Payroll Item List, this page is automatically updated.

4. Click Finish. You are returned to the Payroll Item List window.

5. Close the Payroll Item List.

Lists/Centers ## Customizing the Payroll Item List

When you activated the payroll feature and the manual calculations feature, QuickBooks created several payroll items that are required of all companies, as shown in Figure 8–C on page 336. You will customize these items for Kristin Raina Interior Designs to include identifying the government agency to which payment will be directed, the appropriate liability account, and the appropriate expense account for each pre-established payroll item.

Kristin Raina wishes to enter the vendor for Social Security Company tax payments. She also wants to change the general ledger posting accounts for the liability and the expense for this payroll item.

Recall that Social Security tax is withheld from the employee's paycheck and that the employer must also pay an equal amount, which is an expense to the company. QuickBooks creates two payroll items: Social Security Company and Social Security Employee. When you edit one of these payroll items, the changes you make carry over to the other payroll item.

To customize the Social Security Company payroll item:

1. At the main menu bar, click Lists and then click *Payroll Item List.*

2. Double-click the *Social Security Company* payroll item. The payroll item opens in Edit mode. See Figure 8–F.

FIGURE 8–F

Edit Payroll Item
(Social Security Taxes)
Window—Name Used in
Paychecks and Payroll
Reports Page

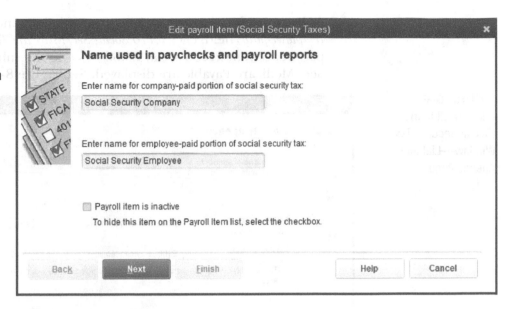

3. Accept the default names and then click Next. The Liability agency page appears.

This payroll item, Social Security Company, represents the Social Security tax that the employer must pay. This tax—both the employee's withholding and the employer's portion—is subsequently paid to the United States Treasury. Since the company will write a check to this government agency, QuickBooks considers it a vendor of the company; thus, it must be included in the Vendor Center. Once the agency is included in the Vendor Center, it can be selected from this drop-down list.

HINT

If the vendor is not on the Vendor List, click *< Add New >* to add the new vendor.

4. At the *Enter name of agency to which liability is paid* field, click *United States Treasury* at the drop-down list.

For each payroll item, you will need to indicate general ledger accounts. For some payroll items, you will select a liability account, for some you will select an expense account, and for some you will select both a liability account and an expense account. When selecting accounts, be careful to choose the correct liability account or expense account, and then be careful to choose the proper subaccount. Quick-Books eventually uses the general ledger accounts in the Payroll Item List to record the payroll journal entries. If an incorrect general ledger account is recorded in the Payroll Item List, the payroll journal entries will be incorrect.

The Liability agency page also asks for the liability account that will be used for both the amount to be paid by the employer and the amount withheld from the employees' paychecks. These can be different liability accounts, but Kristin Raina uses the same liability account for both the employer and the employee. Notice that you must enter two liability accounts on this page.

5. At both the *Liability account (company-paid)* field and the *Liability account (employee-paid)* field, click *2110 Social Sec/Medicare Tax Payable.* Both the parent account 2100 Payroll Liabilities and the subaccount 2110 Social Sec/Medicare Payable are displayed. See Figure 8–G.

FIGURE 8–G
Edit Payroll Item
(Social Security Taxes)
Window—Liability
Agency Page

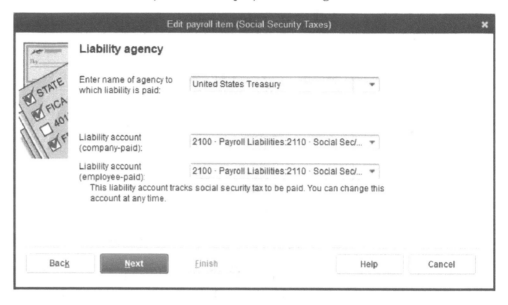

6. If the information is correct, click Next. The Expense account page appears.

Only the employer's portion of Social Security and Medicare is considered an expense for the company. The portion withheld from the employee's paycheck is not.

7. At the *Enter the account for tracking this expense* field, click *6610 Social Sec/Medicare Tax Expense.* Both the parent account 6560 Payroll Expenses and the subaccount 6610 Social Sec/Medicare Expense are displayed. See Figure 8–H.

FIGURE 8–H
Edit Payroll Item
(Social Security Taxes)
Window—Expense
Account Page

8. If the information is correct, click Next. The Company and employee tax rates page appears, displaying the current tax rates. Notice that

these tax rates are dimmed. The federal government establishes the tax rates for the current year, and they cannot be changed.

9. Click Next to accept. The Taxable compensation page appears.
10. Click Finish. You will be returned to the Payroll Item List with all changes saved.

As stated previously, QuickBooks creates both a Social Security Company payroll item and a Social Security Employee payroll item. Changes made to one payroll item carry over to the other payroll item. Review the Social Security Employee payroll item to observe that the changes were carried over.

To review the Social Security Employee payroll item:
1. Open the Payroll Item List, if necessary.
2. Double-click the *Social Security Employee* item.
3. Review all the pages and compare them with Figures 8–F to 8–H on pages 339 and 340.
4. Close the Edit payroll item (Social Security Taxes) and the Payroll Item List windows.

Practice Exercise	8–1

On the Payroll Item List, customize the Medicare Company and Medicare Employee payroll items.

Liability Agency:	United States Treasury
Liability Account:	2110 Social Sec/Medicare Tax Payable
(for both company-paid and employee-paid)	
Expense Account:	6610 Social Sec/Medicare Tax Expense

Kristin Raina wishes to enter the vendor for the Federal Unemployment tax payments. She also wants to change the general ledger posting accounts for the expense and liability for this payroll item.

To customize the Federal Unemployment payroll item:
1. At the main menu bar, click Lists and then click *Payroll Item List.*
2. Double-click the *Federal Unemployment* payroll item. The payroll item opens in Edit mode.
3. Accept the default name *Federal Unemployment* by clicking Next. The Agency for company-paid liability page appears.
4. At the *Enter name of agency to which the liability is paid* field, click *United States Treasury* at the drop-down list.
5. At the *Liability account* field, click *2125 FUTA Payable.* Both the parent account 2100 Payroll Liabilities and the subaccount 2125 FUTA Payable are displayed.
6. At the *Expense account* field, click *6625 FUTA Expense.* Both the parent account 6560 Payroll Expenses and the subaccount 6625 FUTA Expense are displayed. Notice that on this page, you are listing one liability account and one expense account. See Figure 8–I.

FIGURE 8–I
Edit Payroll Item
(Federal Unemployment)
Window—Agency for
Company-Paid Liability
Page

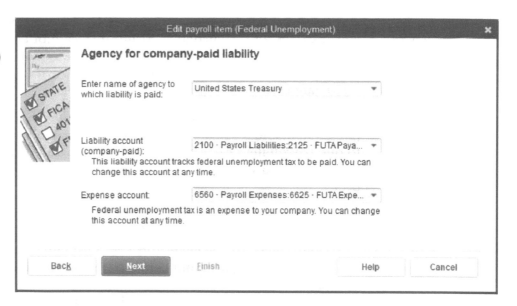

Notice that for this payroll item, the liability and expense accounts are recorded on the same page, whereas with the Social Security and Medicare items, two liability accounts were recorded on one page and the expense account was recorded on a second page.

7. If the information is correct, click Next.
8. At the Federal unemployment tax rate page, accept the default rate by clicking Next.
9. At the Taxable compensation page, click Finish.
10. Close the Payroll Item List.

Practice Exercise   8–2

On the Payroll Item List, customize the Federal Withholding payroll item.

Liability Agency:	United States Treasury
Liability Account:	2115 FIT Payable

Lists/Centers

Updating the Payroll Item List

In QuickBooks, there are two methods for adding a payroll item: EZ Setup and Custom Setup. The EZ Setup method guides you in setting up payroll items using the QuickBooks Payroll Setup window. The Custom Setup method allows you to directly enter information in the Payroll Item List. The Custom Setup method is used in this chapter.

In Custom Setup, the steps to set up the Payroll Items of salary and wages are slightly different from the steps to set up the Payroll Items of payroll withholdings and employer payroll taxes.

HINT

See Appendix G for the steps to set up payroll, including the Payroll Item List, using the alternative method of the QuickBooks Payroll Setup window.

Adding a Salary and Wage Payroll Item

Kristin Raina wishes to add Salary to the Payroll Item List.

To add Salary to the Payroll Item List:

1. At the main menu bar, click Lists and then click *Payroll Item List.*
2. At the Payroll Item List window, click the Payroll Item menu button.
3. At the Payroll Item button drop-down menu, click *New*. The Add new payroll item window with the Select setup method page appears.
4. At the Select setup method page, click the *Custom Setup* option. See Figure 8–J.

FIGURE 8–J

Add New Payroll Item Window—Select Setup Method Page

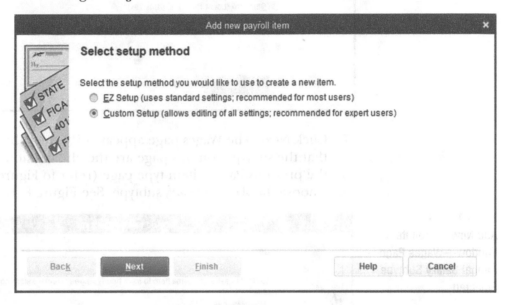

5. Click Next.

    Similar to what happens in editing a payroll item when you create a new payroll item, a new page of information displays each time you click Next.

    The second page in the Add new payroll item window—the Payroll item type page—lists the types of payroll items you can create. There are seven payroll item types: Wage, Addition, Deduction, Company Contribution, Federal Tax, State Tax, and Other Tax. For each type, several subtypes are listed in parentheses next to it. When adding a new payroll item, you will first select the payroll item type on this page; then, on the next page, you will select the subtype.

6. At the Payroll item type page, click *Wage (Hourly Wages, Annual Salary, Commission, Bonus)*. See Figure 8–K.

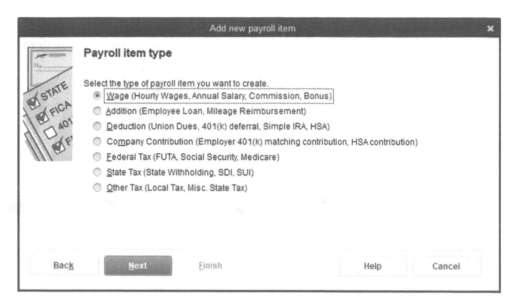

7. Click Next. The Wages page appears with the subtypes listed. Observe that the subtypes on this page are the choices noted in parentheses on the previous Payroll item type page (refer to Figure 8–K).
8. Choose the *Annual Salary* subtype. See Figure 8–L.

9. Click Next. The next page lets you indicate the form of pay: regular, sick, or vacation.
10. Choose the *Regular Pay* option. See Figure 8–M.

FIGURE 8–M

Add New Payroll Item
(Salary) Window—Wages
Page—Regular Pay
Selected

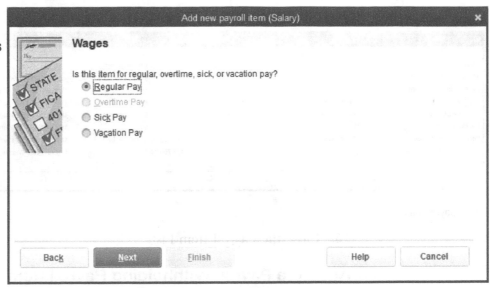

11. Click Next. The Name used in paychecks and payroll reports page
appears. This step is where you assign a name for the item on paychecks and reports.

12. At the *Enter name for salary item* field, type Salary and then click Next.
The Expense account page appears. This step is where you assign the
general ledger account for Salary expense.

13. At the *Enter the account for tracking this expense* field, click *6565 Salaries
and Wages Expense* at the drop-down list. Both the parent account 6560
Payroll Expenses and the subaccount 6565 Salaries and Wages are
displayed. See Figure 8–N.

FIGURE 8–N

Add New Payroll Item
(Salary:Salary) Window—
Expense Account Page

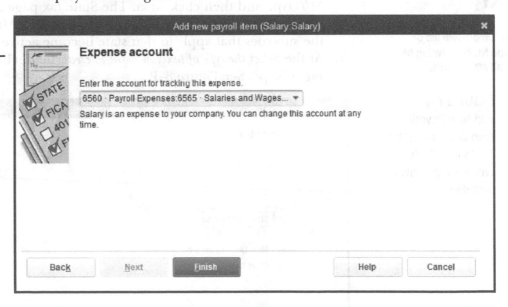

14. If the information is correct, click Finish. You are returned to the Payroll
Item List window with the new payroll item included. See Figure 8–O.

FIGURE 8–O Payroll Item List Window with New Payroll Item

ITEM NAME	TYPE	AMOUNT	LIMIT	TAX TRACKING	PAYABLE TO	ACCOUNT ID
Salary	Yearly Salary			Compensation		
Advance Earned Income Credit	Federal Tax			Advance EIC Payment	United States Treasury	33-4777781
Federal Unemployment	Federal Tax	0.6%	7,000.00	FUTA	United States Treasury	33-4777781
Federal Withholding	Federal Tax			Federal	United States Treasury	33-4777781
Medicare Company	Federal Tax	1.45%		Comp. Medicare	United States Treasury	33-4777781
Medicare Employee	Federal Tax	1.45%		Medicare	United States Treasury	33-4777781
Social Security Company	Federal Tax	6.2%	137,700.00	Comp. SS Tax	United States Treasury	33-4777781
Social Security Employee	Federal Tax	6.2%	-137,700.00	SS Tax	United States Treasury	33-4777781

Payroll Item ▼   Activities ▼   Reports ▼   Include inactive

new payroll item

15. Close the Payroll Item List.

Adding a Payroll Withholding Payroll Item

Kristin Raina wishes to add Minnesota state income tax to the Payroll Item List.

To add Minnesota state income tax to the Payroll Item List:

1. At the main menu bar, click Lists and then click *Payroll Item List.*
2. At the Payroll Item List window, click the Payroll Item menu button.
3. At the Payroll Item button drop-down menu, click *New.* The Add new payroll item window with the Select setup method page appears.
4. At the Select a setup method page, click the *Custom Setup* option and then click Next. The Payroll item type page appears.
5. At the Payroll item type page, click the *State Tax (State Withholding, SDI, SUI)* type and then click Next. The State tax page appears.
6. At the Enter the state drop-down list, click *MN.* After you select a state, the subtypes that apply to that state become active.
7. At the *Select the type of tax you want to create* field, click the *State Withholding* subtype. See Figure 8–P.

HINT

To choose the state, use the drop-down list or type **M**. Keep typing **M** until *MN* appears.

FIGURE 8–P
Add New Payroll
Item Window—State
Tax Page—State
Withholding Subtype
Selected

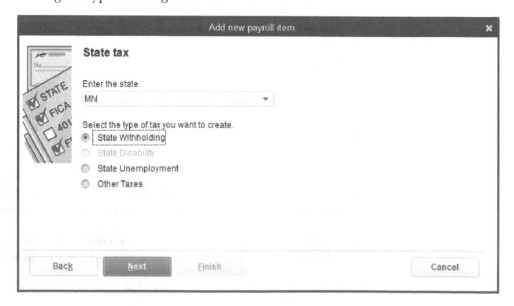

8. If the information is correct, click Next. The Name used in paychecks and payroll reports page appears; it assigns a name for the tax for paycheck and payroll reporting purposes.

9. Accept the default name assigned and click Next. The Agency for employee-paid liability page, which lets you record information for tax vendors and general ledger posting accounts, appears.

10. At the *Enter name of agency to which liability is paid* field, click *Minn. Dept. of Revenue* at the drop-down list.

    This payroll item, Minnesota State Withholding Tax, represents the state income tax withheld from the employee's paycheck that must subsequently be paid to the Minnesota Department of Revenue. Since the company will write a check to this government agency, QuickBooks identifies it as a vendor of the company; therefore, it must be included in the Vendor Center.

11. At the *Enter the number that identifies you to agency* field, type 33-4777781.

12. At the *Liability account (employee-paid)* field, click *2120 SIT Payable.* Both the parent account 2100 Payroll Liabilities and the subaccount 2120 SIT Payable are displayed. See Figure 8–Q.

FIGURE 8–Q

Add New Payroll Item (MN-State Withholding Tax) Window—Agency for Employee-Paid Liability Page

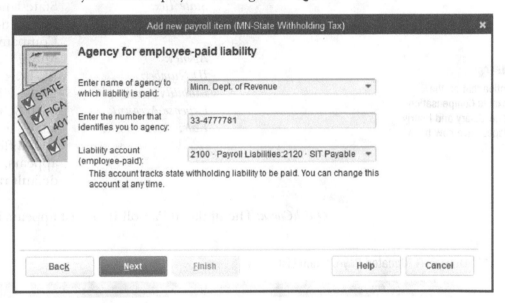

13. If the information is correct, click Next. The Taxable compensation page appears; it shows the types of income subject to the tax. At this time, the only payroll item for Kristin Raina Interior Designs subject to state income tax is Salary. This item should be checked.

14. Click Finish. At the Schedule Payments message, click OK. You are returned to the Payroll Item List window with the new tax included.

15. Close the Payroll Item List.

HINT

QuickBooks provides a Schedule Payments feature if you subscribe to one of the QuickBooks payroll services. The Schedule Payments feature allows you to keep track of your payroll tax and other payroll liabilities amounts, due dates, and payments.

On the Payroll Item List, add the following two new payroll items:

Hourly Wages	*Payroll Item Type:*	Wage (Hourly Wages, Annual Salary, Commission, Bonus)
	Payroll Item Subtype—	
	Wages:	Hourly Wages
	Wages:	Regular Pay
	Name:	Hourly Wages
	Expense Account:	6565 Salaries and Wages Expense
Minnesota State Unemployment (SUI)	*Payroll Item Type:*	State Tax (State Withholding, SDI, SUI)
	State:	MN
	Payroll Item Subtype—	
	State Tax:	State Unemployment
	Name:	MN - Unemployment Company
	Agency:	Minn. Dept. of Revenue
	ID Number:	ER-12343
	Liability Account:	2130 SUI Payable
	Expense Account:	6630 SUI Expense
	Rate:	1.96% each quarter (If a different rate appears, accept the default rate.)

> **HINT**
>
> Notice that on the Taxable Compensation page, Salary and Hourly Wages have now been added.

QuickCheck: The updated Payroll Item List appears in Figure 8–R.

FIGURE 8–R Updated Payroll Item List

ITEM NAME	TYPE	AMOUNT	LIMIT	TAX TRACKING	PAYABLE TO	ACCOUNT ID
Salary	Yearly Salary			Compensation		
Hourly Wages	Hourly Wage			Compensation		
Advance Earned Income Credit	Federal Tax			Advance EIC Payment	United States Treasury	33-4777781
Federal Unemployment	Federal Tax	0.6%	7,000.00	FUTA	United States Treasury	33-4777781
Federal Withholding	Federal Tax			Federal	United States Treasury	33-4777781
Medicare Company	Federal Tax	1.45%		Comp. Medicare	United States Treasury	33-4777781
Medicare Employee	Federal Tax	1.45%		Medicare	United States Treasury	33-4777781
Social Security Company	Federal Tax	6.2%	137,700.00	Comp. SS Tax	United States Treasury	33-4777781
Social Security Employee	Federal Tax	6.2%	-137,700.00	SS Tax	United States Treasury	33-4777781
MN - Withholding	State Withholding Tax			SWH	Minn. Dept. of Revenue	33-4777781
MN - Unemployment Company	State Unemployment Tax	1.96%	35,000.00	Comp. SUI	Minn. Dept. of Revenue	ER-12343

Payroll Item ▼   Activities ▼   Reports ▼   ☐ Include inactive

Payroll Reports

Reports, the fourth level of operation in QuickBooks, allows you to display and print a number of payroll reports, both for internal payroll management and for government and payroll tax compliance.

The payroll management reports provide the company with valuable information, most of which reflects payroll processing (Chapter 9). One of the reports reflects payroll setup—the *Payroll Item Listing* report—which lists the payroll item, type, rates, and limits for some of the mandatory taxes and the expense and liability accounts relating to the payroll item.

To view the *Payroll Item Listing* report:
1. At the main menu bar, click Reports and then click *Employees & Payroll.*
2. At the Employees & Payroll submenu, click *Payroll Item Listing.* The *Payroll Item Listing* report is displayed. See Figure 8–S.
3. Close the report.

FIGURE 8–S Payroll Item Listing Report

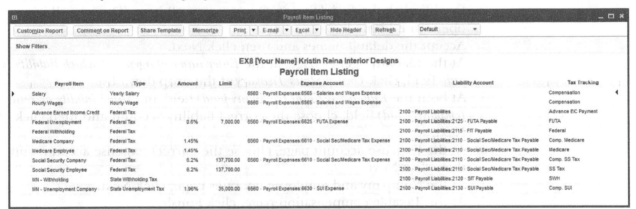

Exiting QuickBooks

Upon completing this session, make a backup copy of your practice exercise company file to a removable storage device using the Back Up command. Be sure to change the *Save in* field to the removable storage device and then carefully type the correct file name. Close the company file and then exit QuickBooks.

Chapter Review and Assessment

Procedure Review

To activate the QuickBooks payroll feature and activate the manual payroll option:
1. At the main menu bar, click Edit and then click *Preferences.*
2. In the left panel of the Preferences window, click the Payroll & Employees icon.
3. Click the Company Preferences tab.
4. Click the *Full payroll* option.
5. Click *Manual Payroll.*
6. At the *Get payday peace of mind* message, click Next.
7. At the Confirm Manual Payroll message, click Activate.
8. At the QuickBooks Desktop message, click OK.
9. At the Preferences window, accept the defaults and click OK.

To customize the Social Security Company payroll item:
1. At the main menu bar, click Lists and then click *Payroll Item List.*
2. Double-click the *Social Security Company* payroll item. The payroll item opens in Edit mode.
3. Accept the default names and then click Next.
4. At the Liability agency page, at the *Enter name of agency to which liability is paid* field, click *United States Treasury* at the drop-down list.
5. At both the *Liability account (company-paid)* field and the *Liability account (employee-paid)* field, choose the correct liability account and then click Next.
6. At the Expense account page, choose the correct expense account and then click Next.
7. At the Company and employee tax rates page, click Next.
8. At the Taxable compensation page, click Finish.
9. Close the Payroll Item List.

To add a salary or wages payroll item:
1. At the main menu bar, click Lists and then click *Payroll Item List.*
2. At the Payroll Item List window, click the Payroll Item menu button.
3. At the Payroll Item button drop-down menu, click *New.*
4. At the Select setup method page, click the *Custom Setup* option and then click Next.
5. At the Payroll item type page, click the *Wage (Hourly Wages, Annual Salary, Commission, Bonus)* type and then click Next.
6. At the Wages page, choose the *Annual Salary* or *Hourly Wages* subtype and then click Next.
7. Choose *Regular Pay* and then click Next.
8. At the Name used in paychecks and payroll reports page, at the *Enter name for salary item* field, type Salary or Hourly Wages and then click Next.
9. At the Expense account page, choose the expense account to track this item and then click Finish.
10. Close the Payroll Item List.

To add a state withholding or tax payroll item:
1. At the main menu bar, click Lists and then click *Payroll Item List*.
2. At the Payroll Item List window, click the Payroll Item menu button.
3. At the Payroll Item button drop-down menu, click *New*.
4. At the Select setup method page, click the *Custom Setup* option and then click Next.
5. At the Payroll item type page, choose the *State Tax (State Withholding, SDI, SUI)* type and then click Next.
6. At the State page, enter the state. After you select a state, the subtypes that apply to that state become active.
7. At the *Select the type of tax you want to create* field, click the appropriate withholding or tax subtype and then click Next.
8. At the Name used in paychecks and payroll reports page, at the *Enter name for state withholding tax* field, accept the default and then click Next.
9. At the Agency for employee-paid liability page, at the *Enter name of agency* field, click the tax agency at the drop-down list.
10. Type the tax ID number.
11. At the *Liability account* field, choose the liability account for the tax. If it is a tax payroll item, choose the expense account and then click Next.
12. If it is a tax payroll item, accept the default tax rates and then click Next.
13. The Taxable compensation page shows which types of income are subject to tax. Click Finish to accept.
14. Close the Payroll Item List.

To view and print the *Payroll Item Listing* report from the Reports menu:
1. At the main menu bar, click Reports and then click *Employees & Payroll*.
2. At the Employees & Payroll submenu, click *Payroll Item Listing*. The *Payroll Item Listing* report is displayed.
3. Print the report.
4. Close the report.

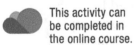
This activity can be completed in the online course.

Key Concepts

Select the letter of the item that best matches each definition.

a. Payroll
b. Social Security tax, Medicare tax, FUTA, and SUI
c. Manual Payroll
d. Payroll Item List
e. Social Security tax, Medicare tax, federal withholding, and state withholding
f. Payroll items
g. Payroll Liabilities and Payroll Expenses
h. Government agency
i. Social Security and Medicare
j. QuickBooks Payroll Services

_____ 1. Payroll taxes imposed on the employer.

_____ 2. A variety of services offered by QuickBooks; includes automatic processing of payroll and requires a monthly service fee.

_____ 3. Two default general ledger accounts created by QuickBooks when the payroll feature is activated.

_____ 4. Payroll taxes imposed on the employee and collected by the employer.

_____ 5. Contains a file for each type of payroll item that affects the payroll computation.

_____ 6. Included in the Vendor Center and selected when creating a new payroll item identifying the entity to which the payroll liability is paid.

_____ 7. An option that must be activated to access the Payroll Item List when a company does not subscribe to QuickBooks Payroll Services.

_____ 8. Payroll items that require identifying two liability accounts and one expense account in the Payroll Item List.

_____ 9. Compensation, payroll taxes, and payroll withholdings created by QuickBooks that you can customize or add to; each requires identifying the related liability accounts, expense accounts, and government agency.

_____ 10. Involves computing each employee's gross earnings, withholdings and deductions, and net pay; preparing paychecks or setting up direct deposits; recording payroll journal entries; and submitting payroll withholdings to the appropriate agency.

This activity can be completed in the online course.

Procedure Check

1. What is the Payroll Item List and how do you access it?

2. You have decided to use the payroll feature of QuickBooks. How do you activate the payroll feature and manual payroll option in an existing company file? Which default ledger accounts are set up by QuickBooks once the payroll feature is activated?

3. What items on the Payroll Item List are automatically created by QuickBooks, and how would you customize them for your company?

4. What types of payroll items does QuickBooks allow to be created, and which types and subtypes would a company be interested in adding to the Payroll Item List?

5. Which payroll items have two liability accounts and one expense account, and which payroll items have one liability account and one expense account? How many pages are used to enter the liability accounts and expense accounts?

6. Your company has been using the services of an outside payroll processing firm. You, as a junior accountant, know that QuickBooks has a payroll feature; you wish to recommend to your manager that your company process payroll within the company. Prepare a summary of the steps involved in setting up payroll in QuickBooks.

Reports created for these Case Problems can be exported to Excel and uploaded in the online course to be automatically graded.

Case Problems

Demonstrate your knowledge of the QuickBooks features discussed in this chapter by completing the following case problems.

Case Problem 8–1

In June, the third month of business for Lynn's Music Studio, Lynn Garcia has decided to hire two employees. To prepare for this, Lynn wishes to set up the payroll feature. The company file includes information for Lynn's Music Studio as of June 1, 2022.

1. Open the company file **CH8 Lynn's Music Studio.QBW**.
2. At the QuickBooks Desktop Login window, in the *Password* text box, type Student1 and then click OK.
3. Make a backup copy of the company file and name it **LMS8 *[Your Name]* Lynn's Music Studio**.
4. Restore the backup copy of the company file. In both the Open Backup Copy and Save Company File as dialog boxes, use the file name **LMS8 *[Your Name]* Lynn's Music Studio** and enter the password.
5. Change the company name to **LMS8 *[Your Name]* Lynn's Music Studio**.
6. Activate the payroll feature and manual payroll option for Lynn's Music Studio.
7. Customize the system default accounts:

	QuickBooks	Edited
Number	Account Name	Number
24000	Payroll Liabilities	2100
66000	Payroll Expenses	6560

8. Add the following accounts to the Chart of Accounts List:

2110	Social Sec/Medicare Tax Payable	Subaccount of 2100 Payroll Liabilities
2115	FIT Payable	Subaccount of 2100 Payroll Liabilities
2120	SIT Payable	Subaccount of 2100 Payroll Liabilities
2125	FUTA Payable	Subaccount of 2100 Payroll Liabilities
2130	SUI Payable	Subaccount of 2100 Payroll Liabilities
6565	Salaries and Wages Expense	Subaccount of 6560 Payroll Expenses
6611	Social Sec/Medicare Tax Expense	Subaccount of 6560 Payroll Expenses
6625	FUTA Expense	Subaccount of 6560 Payroll Expenses
6630	SUI Expense	Subaccount of 6560 Payroll Expenses

9. Customize each of the payroll items listed below. For each item, proceed as follows:
   - Accept the name listed.
   - Choose *United States Treasury* as the agency to which the liability will be paid.
   - Select the liability and expense accounts indicated below.
   - Accept all tax rates.
   - Accept all taxable compensation defaults.

Payroll Item	Liability Account	Expense Account
Federal Unemployment	2125 FUTA Payable	6625 FUTA Expense
Federal Withholding	2115 FIT Payable	
Medicare Company	2110 Social Sec/ Medicare Tax Payable	6611 Social Sec/ Medicare Tax Expense
Medicare Employee	2110 Social Sec/ Medicare Tax Payable	6611 Social Sec/ Medicare Tax Expense
Social Security Company	2110 Social Sec/ Medicare Tax Payable	6611 Social Sec/ Medicare Tax Expense
Social Security Employee	2110 Social Sec/ Medicare Tax Payable	6611 Social Sec/ Medicare Tax Expense

10. Add the following payroll items:

Salary

Payroll Item Type:	Wage (Hourly Wages, Annual Salary, Commission, Bonus)
Payroll Item Subtype—Wages:	Annual Salary
Wages:	Regular Pay
Name:	Salary
Expense Account:	6565 Salaries and Wages Expense

Wages

Payroll Item Type:	Wage (Hourly Wages, Annual Salary, Commission, Bonus)
Payroll Item Subtype—Wages:	Hourly Wages
Wages:	Regular Pay
Name:	Hourly Wages
Expense Account:	6565 Salaries and Wages Expense

State Tax Withholding

Payroll Item Type:	State Tax (State withholding, SDI, SUI)
State:	PA
Payroll Item Subtype—State Tax:	State Withholding
Name Used in Paychecks:	PA – Withholding
Agency for Liabilities:	PA Dept. of Revenue
Identifying Number:	45-6123789
Liability Account:	2120 SIT Payable
Taxable Compensation:	Accept defaults

SUI

Payroll Item Type:	State Tax (State withholding, SDI, SUI)
State:	PA
Payroll Item Subtype—State Tax:	State Unemployment
Names Used in Paychecks:	PA – Unemployment Company/ Employee
Agency for Liabilities:	PA Dept. of Revenue
Identifying Number:	ER-76558
Liability Accounts:	2130 SUI Payable
Expense Account:	6630 SUI Expense
Company Tax Rate:	3.689% each quarter (or accept the default)
Employee Tax Rate:	.06% each quarter
Taxable Compensation:	Accept defaults

11. Display and print the *Payroll Item Listing* report.

Case Problem 8–2

In August, the third month of business for Olivia's Web Solutions, Olivia Chen has decided to hire two employees. To prepare for this, Olivia wishes to set up the payroll feature. The company file includes information for Olivia's Web Solutions as of August 1, 2022.

1. Open the company file **CH8 Olivia's Web Solutions.QBW**.
2. At the QuickBooks Desktop Login window, in the *Password* text box, type Student1 and then click OK.
3. Make a backup copy of the company file and name it **OWS8 *[Your Name]* Olivia's Web Solutions**.
4. Restore the backup copy of the company file. In both the Open Backup Copy and Save Company File as dialog boxes, use the file name **OWS8 *[Your Name]* Olivia's Web Solutions** and enter the password.
5. Change the company name to **OWS8 *[Your Name]* Olivia's Web Solutions**.
6. Activate the payroll feature and manual payroll option for Olivia's Web Solutions.
7. Customize the system default accounts:

QuickBooks		Edited
Number	Account Name	Number
24000	Payroll Liabilities	2100
66000	Payroll Expenses	6560

8. Add the following accounts to the Chart of Accounts List:

2110	Social Sec/Medicare Tax Payable	Subaccount of 2100 Payroll Liabilities
2115	FIT Payable	Subaccount of 2100 Payroll Liabilities
2120	SIT Payable	Subaccount of 2100 Payroll Liabilities
2125	FUTA Payable	Subaccount of 2100 Payroll Liabilities
2130	SUI Payable	Subaccount of 2100 Payroll Liabilities
6565	Salaries and Wages Expense	Subaccount of 6560 Payroll Expenses
6611	Social Sec/Medicare Tax Expense	Subaccount of 6560 Payroll Expenses
6625	FUTA Expense	Subaccount of 6560 Payroll Expenses
6630	SUI Expense	Subaccount of 6560 Payroll Expenses

9. Customize each of the payroll items listed below. For each item, proceed as follows:
   - Accept the name listed.
   - Choose *United States Treasury* as the agency to which the liability will be paid.
   - Select the liability and expense accounts indicated below.
   - Accept all tax rates.
   - Accept all taxable compensation defaults.

Payroll Item	Liability Account	Expense Account
Federal Unemployment	2125 FUTA Payable	6625 FUTA Expense
Federal Withholding	2115 FIT Payable	
Medicare Company	2110 Social Sec/ Medicare Tax Payable	6611 Social Sec/ Medicare Tax Expense
Medicare Employee	2110 Social Sec/ Medicare Tax Payable	6611 Social Sec/ Medicare Tax Expense
Social Security Company	2110 Social Sec/ Medicare Tax Payable	6611 Social Sec/ Medicare Tax Expense
Social Security Employee	2110 Social Sec/ Medicare Tax Payable	6611 Social Sec/ Medicare Tax Expense

10. Add the following payroll items:

Salary

Payroll Item Type:	Wage (Hourly Wages, Annual Salary, Commission, Bonus)
Payroll Item Subtype—Wages:	Annual Salary
Wages:	Regular Pay
Name:	Salary
Expense Account:	6565 Salaries and Wages Expense

Wages

Payroll Item Type:	Wage (Hourly Wages, Annual Salary, Commission, Bonus)
Payroll Item Subtype—Wages:	Hourly Wages
Wages:	Regular Pay
Name:	Hourly Wages
Expense Account:	6565 Salaries and Wages Expense

State Tax Withholding

Payroll Item Type:	State Tax (State Withholding, SDI, SUI)
State:	NY
Payroll Item Subtype—State Tax:	State Withholding
Name Used on Paychecks:	NY – Withholding
Agency for Liabilities:	NYS Tax Department
Identifying Number:	55-5656566
Liability Account:	2120 SIT Payable
Taxable Compensation:	Accept defaults

SUI

Payroll Item Type:	State Tax (State Withholding, SDI, SUI)
State:	NY
Payroll Item Subtype—State Tax:	State Unemployment
Name Used on Paychecks:	NY – Unemployment Company
Agency for Liabilities:	NYS Tax Department
Identifying Number:	ER-4877
Liability Account:	2130 SUI Payable
Expense Account:	6630 SUI Expense
Company Tax Rate:	3.125% each quarter (or accept the default)
Taxable Compensation:	Accept defaults

11. Display and print the *Payroll Item Listing* report.

## CHAPTER 9

Payroll Processing

Paying Employees, Paying Payroll Liabilities, and Processing Payroll Forms

Objectives

- Review accounting for payroll transactions
- Update the Employee Center
- Record payroll in the Pay Employees windows
- Record payments of payroll taxes in the Pay Liabilities window
- Display and print payroll-related reports, accounting reports, and financial statements

 The online course includes additional training and assessment resources. Reports created for the Chapter Problem can be uploaded for instructor review.

Chapter Introduction

In Chapter 8, you learned to activate the payroll feature, customize and update the Chart of Accounts List to include the appropriate payroll accounts required for payroll processing, set up the payroll to accept manual entries, and customize and add various payroll items to the Payroll Item List. Once payroll has been activated and set up, QuickBooks allows you to process payroll and track payroll information for your company's employees. You can establish a file for each employee and then process payroll transactions. These employee files comprise the Employee Center.

Once you have established an employee file, you can enter transactions for payroll (Activities) in the Pay Employees and Pay Liabilities windows. Every time your company processes payroll for employees in the activities windows, QuickBooks simultaneously updates the information in the Employee Center. In addition, QuickBooks changes balance sheet and income statement accounts based on payroll transactions entered in the payroll activities windows.

In this chapter, our sample company, Kristin Raina Interior Designs, will hire and pay two employees beginning April 1, 2021. Kristin Raina will have to establish an employee file for each employee in the Employee List.

QuickBooks versus Manual Accounting: Payroll Transactions

payroll journal (register) a journal used to calculate payroll and record payroll entries for each employee

In a manual accounting system, employee pay transactions are usually recorded in a **payroll journal** or **register**. The employee's gross pay, tax withholdings, and other payroll deductions are calculated in the journal using the employee's background information (pay rate, marital status, state of residency, and so on) along with the applicable tax schedules. Payroll checks and tax remittance checks are usually recorded in a cash payments journal.

In QuickBooks, the Employee Center contains background information for each employee, such as name, address, Social Security number, pay rate, and applicable tax deductions. The Payroll Item List contains a file for all the payroll items, such as taxes and withholdings, that affect pay computations for the company (Chapter 8).

When the company processes payroll, the transactions are recorded in the Pay Employees windows. QuickBooks uses the information entered in the Employee Center, along with the items on the Payroll Item List applicable to the employee, to determine gross pay, payroll deductions, and net pay in the Pay Employees windows.

When payroll tax liabilities are paid, the Pay Liabilities window is used to record the transaction. These transactions update the Chart of Accounts List (general ledger) and at the same time update the employee's file.

In both manual and computerized systems, payroll reports are generated and forwarded periodically to the appropriate federal and state tax authorities. In QuickBooks, these payroll forms are prepared using the Process Payroll Forms window if you subscribe to a QuickBooks payroll service.

Accounting for Payroll Transactions

When a company generates a paycheck, the transaction affects a number of expense and liability accounts.

The employee's gross pay is an expense the company records at the payroll date. Additional expenses for the company include the various taxes imposed on the employer, including but not limited to Social Security tax (FICA), Medicare tax, Federal Unemployment Tax Act (FUTA) tax, and state unemployment insurance (SUI). All of these taxes are recorded in the appropriate expense accounts at the payroll date.

The employee, at a minimum, will have amounts for FICA, Medicare, federal income tax (FIT), and state income tax (SIT) (if applicable) deducted from their paycheck by the employer. These withheld taxes, along with the taxes imposed on the employer, are recorded as liabilities on the company books, because the company is responsible for remitting these taxes to the appropriate government tax-collecting agency at a later date.

The gross pay less the employee deductions results in a net payroll check to the employee. The following example illustrates the effect that issuing one paycheck has on the general ledger:

> Company A has one employee who earns an annual salary of $48,000. The company pays its employees semimonthly on the 15th and last day of the month. Therefore, there are 24 pay periods in the year. Consequently, that employee will earn $2,000 of salary income for each pay period. The employee is subject to FICA (6.2% of $2,000 = $124), Medicare tax (1.45% of $2,000 = $29), FIT ($300), and SIT ($100)—with a resulting net pay of $1,447. The employer is also subject to the matching FICA tax and Medicare tax along with FUTA (0.6% of $2,000 = $12) and SUI (3% of $2,000 = $60).

The journal entry to record the employee's earnings, deductions, and net pay is as follows:

Salaries Expense		2 0 0 0		
Social Sec/Medicare Tax Payable				1 5 3
($124 + $29)				
FIT Payable				3 0 0
SIT Payable				1 0 0
Cash – Payroll				1,4 4 7

Many companies use a separate checking account for payroll transactions. Periodically, funds are transferred into this account from the operating account. Having a separate checking account helps track payroll transactions.

In addition, the journal entry of the employer's payroll tax expenses is recorded on the paycheck date as follows:

Social Sec/Medicare Tax Expense		1 5 3		
FUTA Expense (.006 × $2,000)		1 2		
SUI Expense (.03 × $2,000)		6 0		
Social Sec/Medicare Tax Payable				1 5 3
FUTA Payable				1 2
SUI Payable				6 0

When the company remits the employer and employee taxes to the federal and local governments, it records several journal entries. Payment for the employer and employee Social Security tax and Medicare tax, the employee federal withholding, and the FUTA tax will be forwarded to the federal government. The journal entry is as follows:

		Social Sec/Medicare Tax Payable		3 0 6				
		($153 + $153)						
		FIT Payable		3 0 0				
		FUTA Payable		1 2				
		Cash – Payroll				6 1 8		

Payment for the state withholding tax and the SUI is usually made with one check payable to the state taxing authority responsible for these taxes. In some states, two checks have to be sent because two different tax agencies are responsible. The journal entry is as follows:

		SIT Payable		1 0 0				
		SUI Payable		6 0				
		Cash – Payroll				1 6 0		

As you can see, the journal entries for the foregoing transactions can be complex, as several general ledger accounts are affected. In addition, federal and state payroll and compliance laws are detailed and burdensome, with costly penalties for noncompliance. As a result, payroll accounting is a time-consuming process that can result in costly errors and omissions.

Before the availability of low-cost, off-the-shelf accounting software, most small companies either processed payroll manually or used outside computerized payroll services that charged per check. With the coming of QuickBooks and other general ledger software packages, small companies can now process payroll; determine gross pay, tax expenses, and tax liabilities; and prepare employee paychecks and payroll data in compliance with federal and state payroll regulations.

Chapter Problem

In this chapter, Kristin Raina Interior Designs will hire two employees and begin to process payroll during the month of April 2022. You will enter information for each employee in the Employee Center. The April 1 beginning balances for the company are contained in the company file **CH9 Kristin Raina Interior Designs**.

Before you begin, open the company file **CH9 Kristin Raina Interior Designs.QBW**. Make a backup copy of the file, name it **EX9** *[Your Name]* **Kristin Raina Interior Designs**, and restore the file. Enter the password, *Student1*. Finally, change the company name in the file to **EX9** *[Your Name]* **Kristin Raina Interior Designs**.

The Employee Center

The Employee Center contains a file for each employee of the company. Information such as name, address, Social Security number, hire date, pay rate, and applicable payroll taxes are indicated for each employee. Quick-Books uses the information contained in each employee's file, along with the information in the Payroll Item List, to calculate the employee's gross pay, deductions, and net paycheck.

HINT

See Appendix G for the steps to set up the payroll, including the Employee Center, using the alternative method of the QuickBooks Payroll Setup window.

Like all the other Lists and Centers, in QuickBooks, the Employee Center needs to be updated as new employees are hired, employees leave the company, or information about an employee changes and needs to be revised.

To view the Employee Center:

1. Click Employees and then click *Employee Center*. The Employee Center appears. See Figure 9–A.

FIGURE 9–A Employee Center

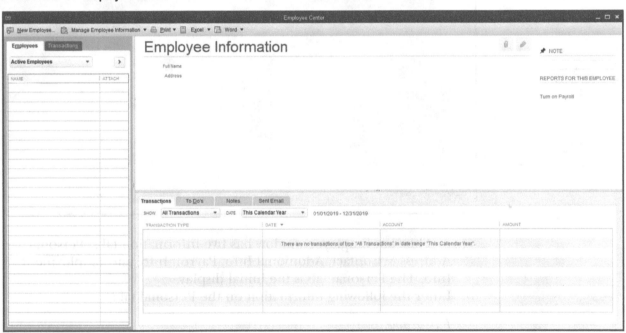

Table 9–1 describes the various parts of the Employee Center.

TABLE 9–1
Employee Center

Part	Description
Employees tab	Lists all current employees. You can display active employees, all employees, or only released employees.
Transactions tab	Lists all transactions for selected employees.
New Employee button	Used to add a new employee.
Employee Information section	Displays background and transaction information for the employee selected on the Employees tab.
Edit icon	Used to edit background information for the employee selected on the Employees tab.
Notes tab	Used to include narrative information specific to an employee.

Kristin Raina has hired two employees, Harry Renee and Richard Henderson, beginning April 1, 2022. Since our sample company did not previously have employees, the only update to the Employee Center at this time is to add the new employees.

To add an employee:

1. Open the Employee Center, if necessary.
2. At the Employee Center window, click the New Employee button. The New Employee window appears. See Figure 9–B.

FIGURE 9–B
New Employee Window

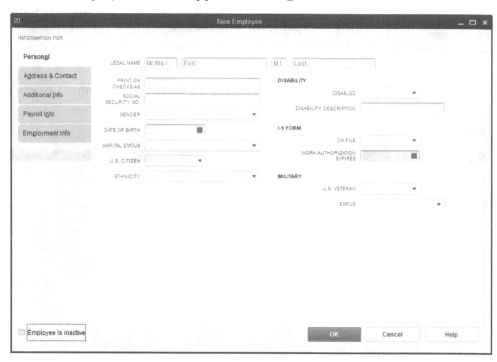

The New Employee window has five information tabs: Personal, Address & Contact, Additional Info, Payroll Info, and Employment Info. The Personal tab is the initial display.

3. Enter the following information on the Personal tab:

First Name:	Harry
Last Name:	Renee
PRINT ON CHECKS AS:	Harry Renee
SOCIAL SECURITY NO.:	112-55-9999
GENDER:	Male
DATE OF BIRTH:	02/17/88

See Figure 9–C.

FIGURE 9–C
New Employee
Window—Personal
Tab—Completed

4. Enter the following information on the Address & Contact tab:

ADDRESS:	323 S. Main Ave.
	St. Paul, MN 54120
MAIN PHONE:	651-555-3311
Mobile:	651-555-0001

See Figure 9–D.

FIGURE 9–D
New Employee
Window—Address
& Contact Tab—
Completed

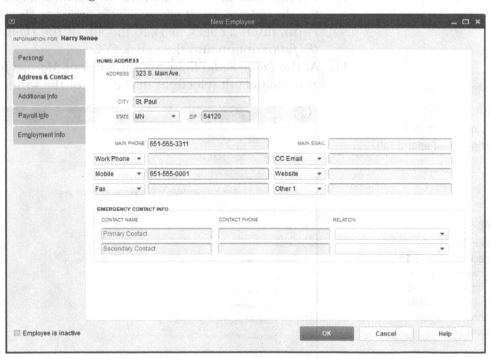

5. Click the Payroll Info tab.
6. At the *PAY FREQUENCY* field, click *Semimonthly* at the drop-down list.
7. In the EARNINGS section, at the *ITEM NAME* field, click *Salary* at the drop-down list.
8. At the *HOURLY/ANNUAL RATE* field, type 24000. See Figure 9–E.

FIGURE 9–E
New Employee Window—Payroll Info Tab—Partially Completed

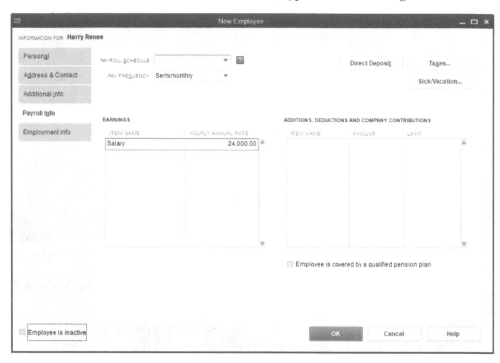

9. Click the Taxes button. The Taxes for Harry Renee window appears.
10. On the Federal tab, at the *Form W-4* field, select *2020 and Later* from the drop-down list. If you receive a message about Federal W-4 2020 Form, insert a check mark to the left of the *Do not display this message in the future* option and then click OK.
11. At the *Filing Status* field, accept *Single or Married filing separately* option and the default selections in the rest of the window. See Figure 9–F.

FIGURE 9–F
Taxes for Harry Renee Window—Federal Tab

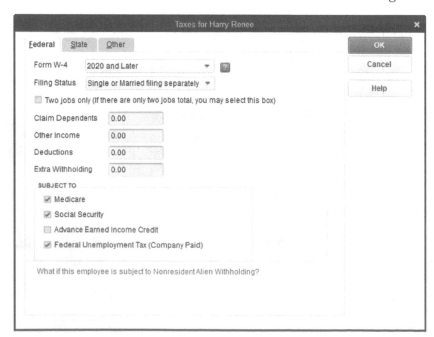

HINT

If you inadvertently uncheck a SUBJECT TO tax, a window appears warning of a possible setup error. To restore the check mark, click Reselect.

12. Click the State tab. In both the STATE WORKED and STATE SUB-JECT TO WITHHOLDING sections, click *MN* at the *State* field. When you move to the next field, additional fields appear. Confirm there is a check mark next to the *SUI (Company Paid)* option.
13. Accept *Single* at the *Filing Status* field; at the *Allowances* field, type 1. See Figure 9–G.

FIGURE 9–G
Taxes for Harry Renee Window—State Tab

14. If the information is correct, click OK. If the QuickBooks Information window appears, read the information and then click OK. Click the Delete button to remove the tax added by the QuickBooks program.
15. Click OK to close the window. At the QuickBooks for Windows message, click No. You are returned to the Payroll Info tab.
16. Click OK. The New Employee: Payroll Info (other) window appears.
17. Click Leave As Is. You are returned to the Employee Center.

Add the following employee:

Personal tab	*First Name:*	Richard
	Last Name:	Henderson
	PRINT ON CHECKS AS:	Richard Henderson
	SOCIAL SECURITY NO.:	333-44-5555
	GENDER:	Male
	DATE OF BIRTH:	08/1/95
Address & Contact tab	*ADDRESS:*	23 Ashland Rd.
		St. Paul, MN 54120
	MAIN PHONE:	651-555-6868
	Mobile:	651-555-2541
Payroll Info tab	*PAY FREQUENCY:*	Semimonthly
	EARNINGS-ITEM NAME:	Hourly Wages
	HOURLY/ANNUAL RATE:	20
Taxes	*Form W-4:*	2020 and Later
	Federal Filing Status:	Married filing jointly
	State Worked/Subject to Withholding:	MN
	SUI (Company Paid):	(Insert a check mark, if necessary.)
	State Filing Status:	Married
	State Allowances:	2

Delete the taxes added by QuickBooks on the Other tab and confirm No when prompted.

QuickCheck: The updated Employee Center appears in Figure 9–H.

FIGURE 9–H Updated Employee Center

The Pay Employees Windows

You use the Pay Employees windows to calculate gross pay, taxes, and net payroll for employees—a daily business activity that is part of the third order of operations in QuickBooks. As you would in a manual accounting system, when you process payroll through the Pay Employees windows, a number of general ledger accounts are affected by the transaction.

As illustrated earlier in the chapter, it is common in a manual accounting system to record payroll using two journal entries. One journal entry records the salaries/wages expense, the employees' withholdings as liabilities, and the net pay. The second journal entry usually records the employer's related tax expense and related liabilities.

In QuickBooks, the transaction is recorded as one compound journal entry instead of two separate journal entries. The transaction is recorded as follows:

Salaries Expense (Gross pay)	XXX		
Social Sec/Medicare Tax Expense	XXX		
FUTA Expense	XXX		
SUI Expense	XXX		
Social Sec/Medicare Tax Payable			XXX
Federal Withholding Tax Payable			XXX
State Withholding Tax Payable			XXX
FUTA Payable			XXX
SUI Payable			XXX
Cash – Payroll			XXX

At the same time the transaction is recorded, QuickBooks updates the Employee Center and payroll reports to reflect the pay earned to date and taxes withheld.

There are three Pay Employees windows: Enter Payroll Information, Preview Paycheck, and Review and Create Paychecks. The Enter Payroll Information window is used to select the employee(s) to be paid at the current pay date. See Figure 9–I.

FIGURE 9–I
Enter Payroll Information Window

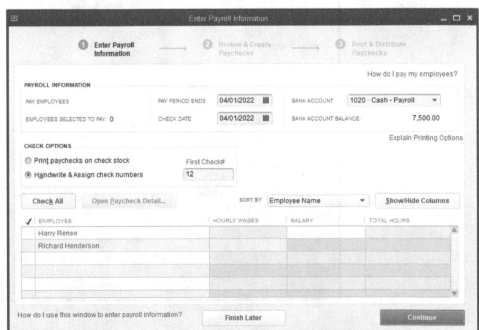

After selecting an employee, you move to the Preview Paycheck window. See Figure 9–J.

FIGURE 9–J
Preview Paycheck Window

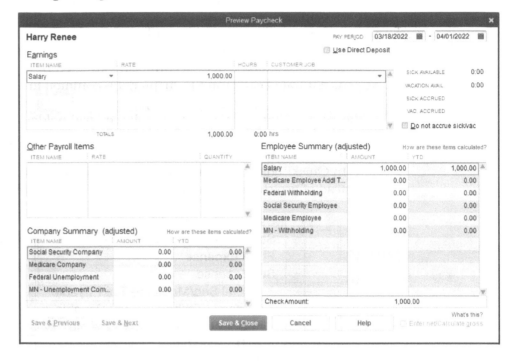

If the company has subscribed to a QuickBooks payroll service, tax figures and deductions will be calculated and displayed automatically in the taxes and deductions columns. If you do not subscribe to a payroll service, which is assumed in this text, you will need to type in the amount for the taxes in the Preview Paycheck window. Once all the payroll information has been entered, you will move to the Review and Create Paychecks window. See Figure 9–K.

FIGURE 9–K
Review and Create Paychecks Window

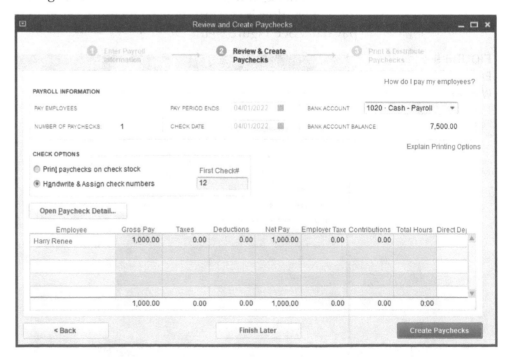

Paying an Employee

On April 15, 2022, Kristin Raina will pay the company's two employees. Harry Renee will be paid first. When Harry Renee was entered in the Employee Center, an annual salary of $24,000 was entered and the semi-monthly pay period was indicated. Semimonthly pay periods result in 24 paychecks per year. Based on this information, QuickBooks determines that Harry Renee is to be paid $1,000 ($24,000/24 pay periods) per pay period.

HINT

Remember that many companies set up a separate checking account dedicated to payroll transactions.

To pay an employee:

1. At the main menu bar, click Employees and then click *Pay Employees*. The Enter Payroll Information window appears.
2. At the *PAY PERIOD ENDS* and *CHECK DATE* fields, choose *04/15/2022*.
3. At the *BANK ACCOUNT* field, click *1020 Cash - Payroll*.
4. In the CHECK OPTIONS section, choose the *Handwrite & Assign check numbers* option and then type 1, if necessary, in the *First Check#* field.
5. Select *Harry Renee* by inserting a check mark next to the name. See Figure 9–L.

FIGURE 9–L
Enter Payroll Information Window—Completed

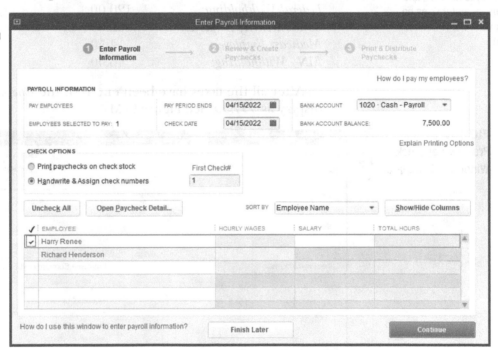

6. If the information is correct, click the Open Paycheck Detail button. The Preview Paycheck window appears.
7. Confirm that the *ITEM NAME* field in the EARNINGS section lists *Salary*, that the *RATE* field shows *1,000*, and that the *PAY PERIOD* fields display *04/01/2022* and *04/15/2022*.
8. Move to the Company Summary (adjusted) section.

   In the Company Summary (adjusted) section, you enter the employer's payroll-related tax expenses. When you type information in this section, use the mouse or press the Tab key, *not* the Enter key, to move to each field. If you press the Enter key, QuickBooks will assume the pay information is complete and close the window. Click the Open Paycheck Detail button to reenter the window, if necessary.

9. Type the employer's taxes in the Company Summary (adjusted) section using the following information:

Social Security Company:	62.00
Medicare Company:	14.50
Federal Unemployment:	6.00
MN - Unemployment Company:	40.00

HINT

The *YTD* fields display the total taxes imposed or collected from this employee for the entire year to date.

10. Move to the Employee Summary (adjusted) section.

In the Employee Summary (adjusted) section, you enter the amount of taxes withheld from the employee's paycheck. As in the Company Summary (adjusted) section, use the mouse or press the Tab key to move to each field; do *not* press the Enter key. You do not have to precede the amount with a minus sign; QuickBooks automatically enters the minus sign before each amount.

HINT

If the *Medicare Employee Addl Tax* line appears, enter **0**, as no tax will be due in this text.

11. Type the employee's taxes in the Employee Summary (adjusted) section using the following information:

Federal Withholding:	120.00
Social Security Employee:	62.00
Medicare Employee:	14.50
MN - Withholding:	46.00

After all the taxes have been entered, the *Check Amount* total should display as *757.50*. See Figure 9–M.

FIGURE 9–M
Preview Paycheck Window—Completed

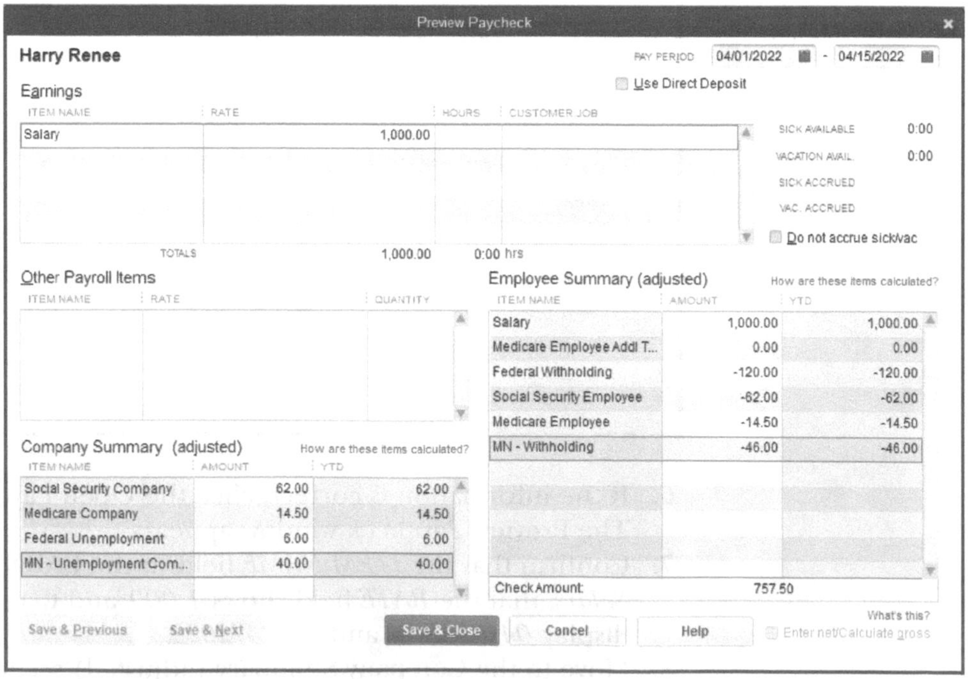

12. If the information is correct, click the Save & Close button. You are returned to the Enter Payroll Information window.
13. Click Continue. You move to the Review and Create Paychecks window, with the taxes columns completed. See Figure 9–N.

FIGURE 9–N
Review and Create
Paychecks Window—
Completed

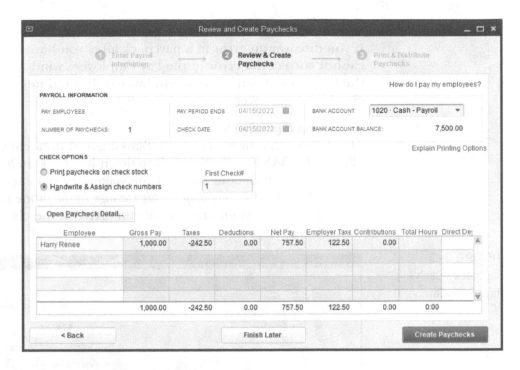

14. If the information is correct, click the Create Paychecks button.
15. At the Confirmation and Next Steps window, click Close.

ACCOUNTING CONCEPT

For the processing of a paycheck, the general ledger posting is as shown below.
(The taxes payable accounts consist of both the employee and employer taxes;
er represents the employer's share, and *ee* represents the employee's share.)

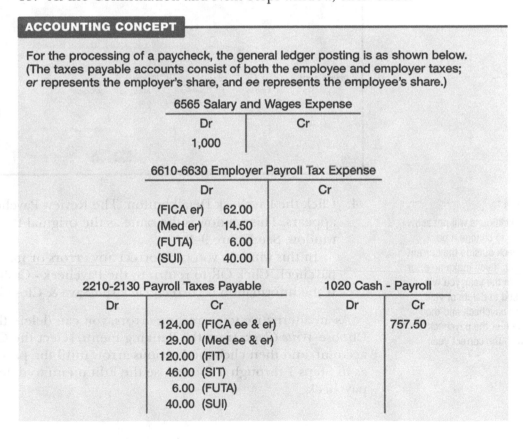

6565 Salary and Wages Expense	
Dr	Cr
1,000	

6610-6630 Employer Payroll Tax Expense	
Dr	Cr
(FICA er) 62.00	
(Med er) 14.50	
(FUTA) 6.00	
(SUI) 40.00	

2210-2130 Payroll Taxes Payable		1020 Cash - Payroll	
Dr	Cr	Dr	Cr
	124.00 (FICA ee & er)		757.50
	29.00 (Med ee & er)		
	120.00 (FIT)		
	46.00 (SIT)		
	6.00 (FUTA)		
	40.00 (SUI)		

Correcting an Error in a Paycheck

If you discover an error in a paycheck after you have created the check, you cannot correct the error in the Pay Employees window. You will have to use the Paycheck - Cash - Payroll window to edit or, if necessary, delete the paycheck and start over.

To correct a paycheck:

1. At the main menu bar, click Banking and then click *Write Checks*.
2. At the BANK ACCOUNT drop-down list, click *1020 Cash - Payroll*. At the Setting Default Accounts message, insert a check mark in the box to the left of *Do not display this message in the future* and then click OK.
3. Click the Previous arrow until you arrive at the check for Harry Renee. See Figure 9–O.

FIGURE 9–O
Paycheck - Cash - Payroll Window

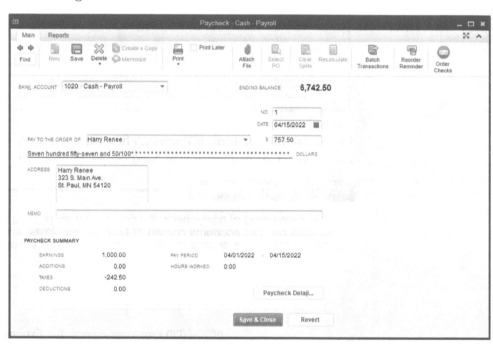

4. Click the Paycheck Detail button. The Review Paycheck window appears. This window is the same as the original Preview Paycheck window. See Figure 9–P.

    In this window, you can correct any errors or make changes to the paycheck. Click OK to return to the Paycheck - Cash - Payroll window.
5. If the information is correct, click the Save & Close button.

As an alternative to correcting errors, you can delete the entire paycheck. Choose *Write Checks* from the Banking menu, select the Cash - Payroll account, and then click the Previous arrow until the paycheck is displayed, as in Steps 1 through 3 above. Use the Edit menu to delete or void the paycheck.

> **HINT**
>
> QuickBooks will not allow you to change a paycheck outside the current year. If you make an error with the year, you will need to delete or void the paycheck and then reenter the paycheck with the correct year.

FIGURE 9–P
Review Paycheck
Window

Practice Exercise 9–2

Process the pay for Richard Henderson for the pay period ending April 15, 2022, in the Pay Employees windows using the information listed below.

Richard Henderson's pay information:

Item Name:	Hourly Wages
Rate:	20
Hours:	80

Richard is an hourly employee. You must type the actual number of hours he has worked at the *HOURS* field. QuickBooks then computes the gross pay by multiplying his hourly pay rate (previously entered in the Employee Center and displayed in this window) by the number of hours worked for this pay period.

Company Taxes	Social Security Company:	99.20
	Medicare Company:	23.20
	Federal Unemployment:	9.60
	MN - Unemployment Company:	64.00
Employee Taxes	Medicare Employee Addl Tax:	0
	Federal Withholding:	120.00
	Social Security Employee:	99.20
	Medicare Employee:	23.20
	MN - Withholding:	54.00

QuickCheck: The check amount should be $1,303.60.

Additional Payroll Journal Entries

For the pay date April 30, 2022, the pay information shown below is for Kristin Raina's two employees for the pay period April 16 to April 30, 2022. Record the payroll for April 30, 2022, in the Pay Employees window using the information listed for each employee.

Harry Renee's pay information:

Check Number:	3
Item Name:	Salary
Rate:	1,000
Company Taxes:	
Social Security Company:	62.00
Medicare Company:	14.50
Federal Unemployment:	6.00
MN - Unemployment Company:	40.00
Employee Taxes:	
Federal Withholding:	120.00
Social Security Employee:	62.00
Medicare Employee:	14.50
MN - Withholding:	46.00

QuickCheck: The check amount should be $757.50.

Richard Henderson's pay information:

Check Number:	4
Item Name:	Hourly Wages
Rate:	20
Hours:	88
Company Taxes:	
Social Security Company:	109.12
Medicare Company:	25.52
Federal Unemployment:	10.56
MN - Unemployment Company:	70.40
Employee Taxes:	
Federal Withholding:	132.00
Social Security Employee:	109.12
Medicare Employee:	25.52
MN - Withholding:	61.00

QuickCheck: The check amount should be $1,432.36.

Activities

The Pay Liabilities Window

Activities identified as paying employees were recorded in the Pay Employees window. Subsequently, Activities identified as paying payroll liabilities are then recorded in the Pay Liabilities window. As you process paychecks in the Pay Employees windows, QuickBooks tracks all the payroll liabilities as they accumulate from each paycheck. The Pay Liabilities window then displays all the payroll liabilities existing at a specified date and allows you to pay each liability to its appropriate tax-collecting agency.

The Pay Liabilities window is designed for the payment of federal and local payroll tax liabilities. The default accounts are the various payroll tax liability accounts that have been credited during payroll processing in the Pay Employees window. Once a liability has been selected for payment, the transaction is recorded as follows:

		Payroll Tax Payable		XXX				
		Cash – Payroll					XXX	

The QuickBooks Pay Liabilities window appears in Figure 9–Q.

FIGURE 9–Q
Pay Liabilities Window

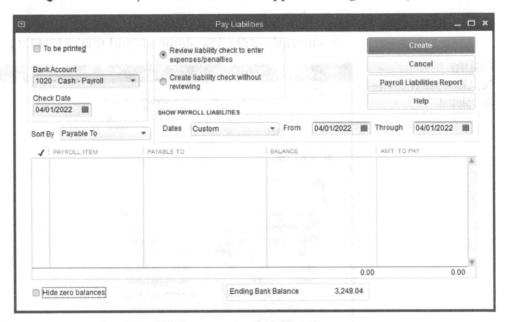

Once you enter the period of time, QuickBooks displays all the payroll tax liabilities accrued during that period that remain unpaid. With this information, you can pay all the liabilities payable to a given taxing authority with a single check.

On April 30, 2021, Kristin Raina wishes to remit the federal employer and employee payroll taxes owed to the United States Treasury for the April payroll. The company and employee FICA, the company and employee Medicare tax, the employee's FIT, and the employer's FUTA tax are to be remitted to the federal government.

To pay the federal payroll tax liabilities:
1. At the main menu bar, click Employees and then click *Payroll Taxes and Liabilities.*
2. At the Payroll Taxes and Liabilities submenu, click *Pay Payroll Liabilities.*
3. In the Select Date Range For Liabilities dialog box, choose *04/01/2022* and *04/30/2022* and then click OK. The Pay Liabilities window appears, showing all the payroll tax liabilities accumulated during the selected period. The company can pay the entire liability or only a portion as needed.

4. Confirm that the *To be printed* box is unchecked, that the *Review liability check to enter expenses/penalties* option is selected, and that the correct date range appears.
5. At the Bank Account drop-down list, click *1020 Cash - Payroll.*
6. At the *Check Date* field, choose *04/30/2022.*
7. Insert a check mark next to each of the following liabilities, all of which are payable to the United States Treasury:
   Federal Unemployment
   Federal Withholding
   Medicare Company
   Medicare Employee
   Social Security Company
   Social Security Employee

The *AMT. TO PAY* column should total $1,344.24. See Figure 9–R.

FIGURE 9–R
Pay Liabilities Window—Completed

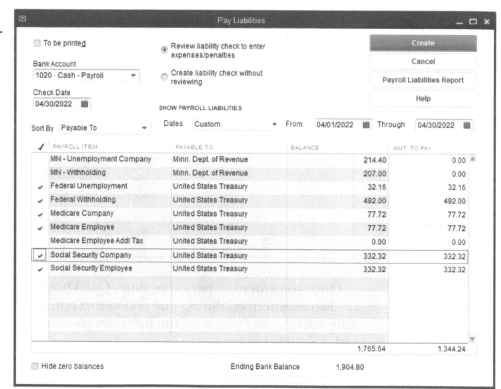

8. If all the information is correct, click the Create button. The Liability Check - Cash - Payroll window is displayed. See Figure 9–S.
9. If the information on the check is correct, click the Save & Close button.

As in the other Write Check windows in QuickBooks, even though a check is not printed, the liability is considered paid and a check is recorded in the system.

FIGURE 9–S
Liability Check - Cash -
Payroll Window

HINT

If you make an error
in the Pay Liabilities
window, you cannot cor-
rect it in that window
once you have saved
the information. You
must use the Liability
Check - Cash - Payroll
window *(Write Checks)*
in the Banking menu.
Click the Cash - Payroll
account and then click
the Previous arrow until
the check with the error
is displayed. Make any
corrections or delete the
entire check using the
Edit menu.

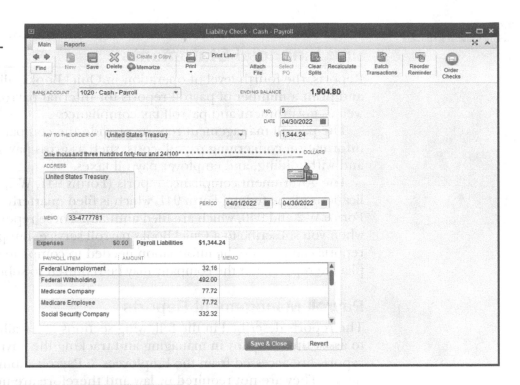

ACCOUNTING CONCEPT

For a payment of payroll liabilities, the general ledger posting is as follows:

2110 Social Security/Medicare Taxes Payable

Dr		Cr
Pmt 820.08		820.08
	Bal 0	

2115 FIT Payable

Dr		Cr
Pmt 492.00		492.00
	Bal 0	

2125 FUTA Payable

Dr		Cr
Pmt 32.16		32.16
	Bal 0	

1020 Cash in Bank - Payroll

Dr		Cr
		1,344.24

Practice Exercise   9–3

On April 30, 2022, pay the payroll tax liabilities for MN - Unemployment
Company and MN-Withholding.

QuickCheck: The amount due and to pay is $421.40.

Payroll Reports, Accounting Reports, and Financial Statements

Reports, the fourth level of operation in QuickBooks, allows you to display and print a number of payroll reports for internal payroll management as well as government and payroll tax compliance.

The payroll management reports provide the company with valuable information concerning payroll costs, such as gross pay, payroll liabilities and withholding, and employer payroll taxes.

The government compliance reports (Forms 941, W-2, and 940) are replications of the federal Form 941, which is filed quarterly, and the federal Forms W-2 and 940, which are filed annually. These reports are available only when you subscribe to a QuickBooks payroll service, but payroll management reports can provide the information needed to complete state and local compliance reports that the company may be required to submit.

Payroll Management Reports

The reports described in the following sections are available in QuickBooks to assist the company in managing and tracking the payroll process. These reports are accessed from the Employees & Payroll submenu of the Reports menu. They are not required by law and therefore are not forwarded to a government agency. However, the information contained in these reports is sometimes used to complete government-mandated payroll reports, especially at the state or local level.

Payroll Summary Report

The *Payroll Summary* report lists the earnings, deductions, and employer payroll taxes for each employee for a specified period of time.

HINT

You can also view payroll management reports from the Reports menu of the Payroll Item List or the Employee Center window.

To view and print the *Payroll Summary* report:

1. At the main menu bar, click Reports and then click *Employees & Payroll*.
2. At the Employees & Payroll submenu, click *Payroll Summary*.
3. At the *From* and *To* fields, choose *04/01/2022* and *04/30/2022* and then click Refresh. The report is displayed for the period.
4. Print the report. Your report should look like Figure 9–T.
5. Close the report.

FIGURE 9–T Payroll Summary Report

EX9 [Your Name] Kristin Raina Interior Designs
Payroll Summary
April 2022

	Harry Renee			Richard Henderson			TOTAL		
	Hours	Rate	Apr 22	Hours	Rate	Apr 22	Hours	Rate	Apr 22
Employee Wages, Taxes and Adjustments									
Gross Pay									
Salary			2,000.00			0.00			2,000.00
Hourly Wages			0.00	168	20.00	3,360.00	168.00		3,360.00
Total Gross Pay			2,000.00	168		3,360.00	168.00		5,360.00
Adjusted Gross Pay			2,000.00	168		3,360.00	168.00		5,360.00
Taxes Withheld									
Federal Withholding			-240.00			-252.00			-492.00
Medicare Employee			-29.00			-48.72			-77.72
Social Security Employee			-124.00			-208.32			-332.32
MN - Withholding			-92.00			-115.00			-207.00
Medicare Employee Addl Tax			0.00			0.00			0.00
Total Taxes Withheld			-485.00			-624.04			-1,109.04
Net Pay			1,515.00	168		2,735.96	168.00		4,250.96
Employer Taxes and Contributions									
Federal Unemployment			12.00			20.16			32.16
Medicare Company			29.00			48.72			77.72
Social Security Company			124.00			208.32			332.32
MN - Unemployment Company			80.00			134.40			214.40
Total Employer Taxes and Contributions			245.00			411.60			656.60

Payroll Liability Balances Report

The *Payroll Liability Balances* report lists all the payroll liabilities owed and unpaid for a specified period of time. If liabilities have been accrued and paid, a zero will appear for that liability.

To view and print the *Payroll Liability Balances* report:

1. At the main menu bar, click Reports and then click *Employees & Payroll.*
2. At the Employees & Payroll submenu, click *Payroll Liability Balances.*
3. At the *From* and *To* fields, choose *04/01/2022* and *04/30/2022* and then click Refresh. The report is displayed for the period. See Figure 9–U.
4. Print the report.
5. Close the report.

FIGURE 9–U Payroll Liability Balances Report

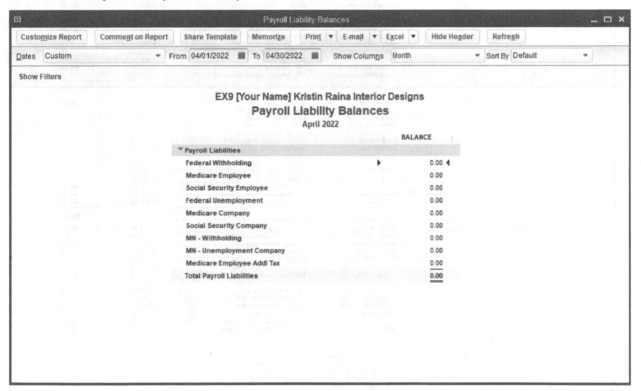

Payroll Transaction Detail Report

The *Payroll Transaction Detail* report provides detailed information for each payroll transaction (paychecks and payroll liability payments) recorded during the period. Information such as employee salary per paycheck, tax withholdings, net pay, employer-paid taxes, and taxes remitted are presented in this report.

To view and print the *Payroll Transaction Detail* report:

1. At the main menu bar, click Reports and then click *Employees & Payroll.*
2. At the Employees & Payroll submenu, click *Payroll Transaction Detail.*
3. At the *From* and *To* fields, choose *04/01/2022* and *04/30/2022* and then click Refresh. The report displays all the payroll transactions recorded during the specified period.
4. Print the report. See Figure 9–V.
5. Close the report.

FIGURE 9–V Payroll Transaction Detail Report

EX9 [Your Name] Kristin Raina Interior Designs
Payroll Transaction Detail
April 2022

Date	Num	Type	Source Name	Payroll Item	Wage Base	Amount
04/15/2022	1	Paycheck	Harry Renee	Salary	0.00	1,000.00
			Harry Renee	Medicare Employee Addl Tax	0.00	0.00
			Harry Renee	Federal Withholding	1,000.00	-120.00
			Harry Renee	Social Security Company	1,000.00	62.00
			Harry Renee	Social Security Company	1,000.00	-62.00
			Harry Renee	Social Security Employee	1,000.00	-62.00
			Harry Renee	Medicare Company	1,000.00	14.50
			Harry Renee	Medicare Company	1,000.00	-14.50
			Harry Renee	Medicare Employee	1,000.00	-14.50
			Harry Renee	Federal Unemployment	1,000.00	6.00
			Harry Renee	Federal Unemployment	1,000.00	-6.00
			Harry Renee	MN - Withholding	1,000.00	-46.00
			Harry Renee	MN - Unemployment Company	1,000.00	40.00
			Harry Renee	MN - Unemployment Company	1,000.00	-40.00
						757.50
04/15/2022	2	Paycheck	Richard Henderson	Hourly Wages	0.00	1,600.00
			Richard Henderson	Federal Withholding	1,600.00	-120.00
			Richard Henderson	Social Security Company	1,600.00	99.20
			Richard Henderson	Social Security Company	1,600.00	-99.20
			Richard Henderson	Social Security Employee	1,600.00	-99.20
			Richard Henderson	Medicare Company	1,600.00	23.20
			Richard Henderson	Medicare Company	1,600.00	-23.20
			Richard Henderson	Medicare Employee	1,600.00	-23.20
			Richard Henderson	Federal Unemployment	1,600.00	9.60
			Richard Henderson	Federal Unemployment	1,600.00	-9.60
			Richard Henderson	MN - Withholding	1,600.00	-54.00
			Richard Henderson	MN - Unemployment Company	1,600.00	64.00
			Richard Henderson	MN - Unemployment Company	1,600.00	-64.00
						1,303.60
04/30/2022	3	Paycheck	Harry Renee	Salary	0.00	1,000.00
			Harry Renee	Medicare Employee Addl Tax	0.00	0.00
			Harry Renee	Federal Withholding	1,000.00	-120.00
			Harry Renee	Social Security Company	1,000.00	62.00
			Harry Renee	Social Security Company	1,000.00	-62.00
			Harry Renee	Social Security Employee	1,000.00	-62.00
			Harry Renee	Medicare Company	1,000.00	14.50
			Harry Renee	Medicare Company	1,000.00	-14.50
			Harry Renee	Medicare Employee	1,000.00	-14.50
			Harry Renee	Federal Unemployment	1,000.00	6.00
			Harry Renee	Federal Unemployment	1,000.00	-6.00
			Harry Renee	MN - Withholding	1,000.00	-46.00
			Harry Renee	MN - Unemployment Company	1,000.00	40.00
			Harry Renee	MN - Unemployment Company	1,000.00	-40.00
						757.50
04/30/2022	4	Paycheck	Richard Henderson	Hourly Wages	0.00	1,760.00
			Richard Henderson	Medicare Employee Addl Tax	0.00	0.00
			Richard Henderson	Federal Withholding	1,760.00	-132.00
			Richard Henderson	Social Security Company	1,760.00	109.12
			Richard Henderson	Social Security Company	1,760.00	-109.12
			Richard Henderson	Social Security Employee	1,760.00	-109.12
			Richard Henderson	Medicare Company	1,760.00	25.52
			Richard Henderson	Medicare Company	1,760.00	-25.52
			Richard Henderson	Medicare Employee	1,760.00	-25.52
			Richard Henderson	Federal Unemployment	1,760.00	10.56
			Richard Henderson	Federal Unemployment	1,760.00	-10.56
			Richard Henderson	MN - Withholding	1,760.00	-61.00
			Richard Henderson	MN - Unemployment Company	1,760.00	70.40
			Richard Henderson	MN - Unemployment Company	1,760.00	-70.40
						1,432.36
04/30/2022	5	Liability Check	United States Treasury	Federal Unemployment		32.16
			United States Treasury	Federal Withholding		492.00
			United States Treasury	Medicare Company		77.72
			United States Treasury	Medicare Employee		77.72
			United States Treasury	Social Security Company		332.32
			United States Treasury	Social Security Employee		332.32
						1,344.24
04/30/2022	6	Liability Check	Minn. Dept. of Revenue	MN - Unemployment Company		214.40
			Minn. Dept. of Revenue	MN - Withholding		207.00
						421.40
TOTAL						**6,016.60**

Employee State Taxes Detail Report

As mentioned previously, federal and state compliance reports are available only when you subscribe to a QuickBooks payroll service. However, the *Employee State Taxes Detail* report provides most if not all the information most states will require a company to submit periodically. Information such as type of state tax, amount of income subject to tax, and amount of each tax will be displayed in this report.

To view and print the *Employee State Taxes Detail* report:

1. At the main menu bar, click Reports and then click *Employees & Payroll.*
2. At the Employees & Payroll submenu, click *Employee State Taxes Detail.*
3. Since most states require quarterly filings, at the *From* and *To* fields, choose *04/01/2022* and *06/30/2022* and then click Refresh. The report is displayed for the period. See Figure 9–W.

FIGURE 9–W Employee State Taxes Detail Report

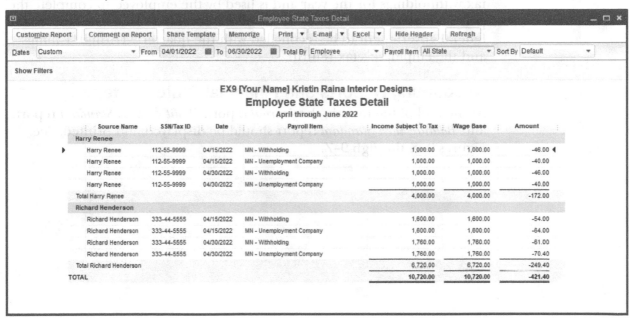

4. Print the report.
5. Close the report.

HINT

Remember that the "drill-down" feature is available if the zoom glass appears.

Government Compliance Reports for Payroll

The Employees menu contains the basic government compliance reports that all companies with payroll are required to file with the federal government (Internal Revenue Service). To display and print government payroll compliance reports, you need to subscribe to a QuickBooks payroll service.

If you have not subscribed to a QuickBooks payroll service, you can use worksheets provided by QuickBooks to prepare the tax forms manually. These worksheets can be accessed at the Tax Form Worksheets in Excel submenu of either the Employee menu or the Reports menu.

Form 941

Form 941—Employer's Quarterly Federal Tax Return is forwarded to the Internal Revenue Service quarterly. This form is used to report the total wages paid to all employees for the quarter, along with the federal tax withheld and the employer's and employees' Social Security and Medicare tax liabilities.

Form 940

Form 940—Employer's Annual Federal Unemployment (FUTA) Tax Return is filed annually with the Internal Revenue Service. This form is used to compute the FUTA tax liability for the company for the year and reconciles the amount to the tax payments made by the company toward the tax during the year.

Form W-2

Form W-2—Wage and Tax Statement is prepared annually and furnished to each employee. The W-2 is a record of the employee's total earnings and tax withholdings for the year and is used by the employee to complete their personal income tax return. A copy of this form is also forwarded to the federal government to be reconciled with the quarterly Form 941 filings and the employee's tax return.

Accounting Reports and Financial Statements

At the end of the month, the *Journal* report, *Profit & Loss Standard* report, and *Balance Sheet Standard* report should be displayed and printed. See Figures 9–X through 9–Z.

FIGURE 9–X Journal Report—April 1, 2022–April 30, 2022

EX9 [Your Name] Kristin Raina Interior Designs
Journal
April 2022

Trans #	Type	Date	Num	Name	Memo	Account	Debit	Credit
52	Transfer	04/01/2022			Funds Transfer	1010 · Cash - Operating		7,500.00
					Funds Transfer	1020 · Cash - Payroll	7,500.00	
							7,500.00	7,500.00
53	Paycheck	04/15/2022	1	Harry Renee		1020 · Cash - Payroll		757.50
				Harry Renee		6565 · Salaries and Wages Expense	1,000.00	
				Harry Renee		2100 · Payroll Liabilities	0.00	
				Harry Renee		2115 · FIT Payable		120.00
				Harry Renee		6610 · Social Sec/Medicare Tax Expense	76.50	
				Harry Renee		2110 · Social Sec/Medicare Tax Payable		153.00
				Harry Renee		6625 · FUTA Expense	6.00	
				Harry Renee		2125 · FUTA Payable		6.00
				Harry Renee		2120 · SIT Payable		46.00
				Harry Renee		6630 · SUI Expense	40.00	
				Harry Renee		2130 · SUI Payable		40.00
							1,122.50	1,122.50
54	Paycheck	04/15/2022	2	Richard Henderson		1020 · Cash - Payroll		1,303.60
				Richard Henderson		6565 · Salaries and Wages Expense	1,600.00	
				Richard Henderson		2115 · FIT Payable		120.00
				Richard Henderson		6610 · Social Sec/Medicare Tax Expense	122.40	
				Richard Henderson		2110 · Social Sec/Medicare Tax Payable		244.80
				Richard Henderson		6625 · FUTA Expense	9.60	
				Richard Henderson		2125 · FUTA Payable		9.60
				Richard Henderson		2120 · SIT Payable		54.00
				Richard Henderson		6630 · SUI Expense	64.00	
				Richard Henderson		2130 · SUI Payable		64.00
							1,796.00	1,796.00
55	Paycheck	04/30/2022	3	Harry Renee		1020 · Cash - Payroll		757.50
				Harry Renee		6565 · Salaries and Wages Expense	1,000.00	
				Harry Renee		2100 · Payroll Liabilities	0.00	
				Harry Renee		2115 · FIT Payable		120.00
				Harry Renee		6610 · Social Sec/Medicare Tax Expense	76.50	
				Harry Renee		2110 · Social Sec/Medicare Tax Payable		153.00
				Harry Renee		6625 · FUTA Expense	6.00	
				Harry Renee		2125 · FUTA Payable		6.00
				Harry Renee		2120 · SIT Payable		46.00
				Harry Renee		6630 · SUI Expense	40.00	
				Harry Renee		2130 · SUI Payable		40.00
							1,122.50	1,122.50
56	Paycheck	04/30/2022	4	Richard Henderson		1020 · Cash - Payroll		1,432.36
				Richard Henderson		6565 · Salaries and Wages Expense	1,760.00	
				Richard Henderson		2100 · Payroll Liabilities	0.00	
				Richard Henderson		2115 · FIT Payable		132.00
				Richard Henderson		6610 · Social Sec/Medicare Tax Expense	134.64	
				Richard Henderson		2110 · Social Sec/Medicare Tax Payable		269.28
				Richard Henderson		6625 · FUTA Expense	10.56	
				Richard Henderson		2125 · FUTA Payable		10.56
				Richard Henderson		2120 · SIT Payable		61.00
				Richard Henderson		6630 · SUI Expense	70.40	
				Richard Henderson		2130 · SUI Payable		70.40
							1,975.60	1,975.60
57	Liability Check	04/30/2022	5	United States Treas...	33-4777781	1020 · Cash - Payroll		1,344.24
				United States Treas...	33-4777701	2126 · FUTA Payable	32.16	
				United States Treas...	33-4777781	2115 · FIT Payable	492.00	
				United States Treas...	33-4777781	2110 · Social Sec/Medicare Tax Payable	820.08	
							1,344.24	1,344.24
58	Liability Check	04/30/2022	6	Minn. Dept. of Reve...	ER-12343, 33-...	1020 · Cash - Payroll		421.40
				Minn. Dept. of Reve...	ER-12343, 33-...	2130 · SUI Payable	214.40	
				Minn. Dept. of Reve...	ER-12343, 33-...	2120 · SIT Payable	207.00	
							421.40	421.40
TOTAL							15,282.24	15,282.24

EX9 [Your Name] Kristin Raina Interior Designs
Profit & Loss
Accrual Basis   January through April 2022

	Jan - Apr 22
Ordinary Income/Expense	
Income	
4010 · Design Services	4,980.00
4020 · Decorating Services	3,400.00
4060 · Sale of Carpets	2,400.00
4065 · Sale of Draperies	1,000.00
4070 · Sale of Lamps	1,200.00
4075 · Sale of Mirrors	900.00
4100 · Sales Discounts	-84.62
Total Income	13,795.38
Cost of Goods Sold	
5060 · Cost of Carpets Sold	1,200.00
5065 · Cost of Draperies Sold	500.00
5070 · Cost of Lamps Sold	600.00
5075 · Cost of Mirrors Sold	450.00
5900 · Inventory Adjustment	150.00
Total COGS	2,900.00
Gross Profit	10,895.38
Expense	
6020 · Accounting Expense	300.00
6050 · Advertising Expense	100.00
6175 · Deprec. Exp., Furniture	100.00
6185 · Deprec. Exp., Computers	60.00
6200 · Insurance Expense	200.00
6300 · Janitorial Expenses	125.00
6325 · Office Supplies Expense	150.00
6400 · Rent Expense	800.00
6450 · Telephone Expense	275.00
6500 · Utilities Expense	450.00
6560 · Payroll Expenses	
6565 · Salaries and Wages Expense	5,360.00
6610 · Social Sec/Medicare Tax Expense	410.04
6625 · FUTA Expense	32.16
6630 · SUI Expense	214.40
Total 6560 · Payroll Expenses	6,016.60
Total Expense	8,576.60
Net Ordinary Income	2,318.78
Other Income/Expense	
Other Expense	
7000 · Interest Expense	50.00
Total Other Expense	50.00
Net Other Income	-50.00
Net Income	2,268.78

FIGURE 9–Z Balance Sheet Standard Report April 30, 2022

EX9 [Your Name] Kristin Raina Interior Designs
Balance Sheet

Accrual Basis

As of April 30, 2022

	Apr 30, 22
ASSETS	
Current Assets	
Checking/Savings	
1010 · Cash - Operating	43,355.38
1020 · Cash - Payroll	1,483.40
Total Checking/Savings	44,838.78
Accounts Receivable	
1200 · Accounts Receivable	1,540.00
Total Accounts Receivable	1,540.00
Other Current Assets	
1260 · Inventory of Carpets	800.00
1265 · Inventory of Draperies	1,000.00
1270 · Inventory of Lamps	1,000.00
1275 · Inventory of Mirrors	900.00
1300 · Design Supplies	200.00
1305 · Office Supplies	250.00
1410 · Prepaid Advertising	500.00
1420 · Prepaid Insurance	2,200.00
Total Other Current Assets	6,850.00
Total Current Assets	53,228.78
Fixed Assets	
1700 · Furniture	
1725 · Furniture, Cost	12,000.00
1750 · Accum. Dep., Furniture	-100.00
Total 1700 · Furniture	11,900.00
1800 · Computers	
1825 · Computers, Cost	3,600.00
1850 · Accum. Dep., Computers	-60.00
Total 1800 · Computers	3,540.00
Total Fixed Assets	15,440.00
TOTAL ASSETS	68,668.78
LIABILITIES & EQUITY	
Liabilities	
Current Liabilities	
Accounts Payable	
2010 · Accounts Payable	9,750.00
Total Accounts Payable	9,750.00
Other Current Liabilities	
2020 · Notes Payable	7,000.00
2030 · Interest Payable	50.00
Total Other Current Liabilities	7,050.00
Total Current Liabilities	16,800.00
Total Liabilities	16,800.00
Equity	
3010 · Kristin Raina, Capital	50,000.00
3020 · Kristin Raina, Drawings	-400.00
Net Income	2,268.78
Total Equity	51,868.78
TOTAL LIABILITIES & EQUITY	68,668.78

Exiting QuickBooks

Upon completing this session, make a backup copy of your practice exercise company file to a removable storage device using the Back Up command. Be sure to change the *Save in* field to the removable storage device and then carefully type the correct file name. Close the company file and then exit QuickBooks.

Chapter Review and Assessment

Procedure Review

To add an employee:
1. At the main menu bar, click Employees and then click *Employee Center.*
2. At the Employee Center window, click the New Employee button.
3. Enter the information on the Personal tab.
4. Click the Address & Contact tab. Enter the information.
5. Click the Payroll Info tab.
6. On the Payroll Info tab, enter the information at the *ITEM NAME, HOURLY/ANNUAL RATE,* and *PAY FREQUENCY* fields.
7. Click the Taxes button. The Taxes window is displayed.
8. On the Federal tab, enter the information for federal withholding tax.
9. Click the State tab and enter the state withholding tax information.
10. Click OK. If the Information window appears, click OK to close it, and click the Delete button to remove the tax added by the program.
11. Click OK.
12. At the question box, click No.
13. Click OK.
14. Click Leave As Is.
15. Close the Employee Center.

To pay an employee:
1. At the main menu bar, click Employees and then click *Pay Employees.* Click *No* at the QuickBooks Payroll Services message if it appears. The Enter Payroll Information window appears.
2. Enter the correct dates at the *PAY PERIOD ENDS* and *CHECK DATE* fields.
3. At the *BANK ACCOUNT* field, click *1020 Cash - Payroll.*
4. In the CHECK OPTIONS section, choose the *Handwrite & Assign check numbers* option and then type the check number in the *First Check#* field.
5. Select the employee to be paid by inserting a check mark next to the name.
6. If the information is correct, click the Open Paycheck Detail button. The Preview Paycheck window appears.
7. Enter the needed information in the EARNINGS section.
8. In the Company Summary (adjusted) section, enter the company tax information.
9. In the Employee Summary (adjusted) section, enter the employee taxes.
10. If the information is correct, click the Save & Close button. You are returned to the Enter Payroll Information window.
11. Click Continue. The Review and Create Paychecks window appears with the taxes columns completed.
12. If the information is correct, click the Create Paychecks button.

To pay payroll liabilities:
1. At the main menu bar, click Employees and then click *Payroll Taxes and Liabilities.*
2. At the Payroll Taxes and Liabilities submenu, click *Pay Payroll Liabilities.*
3. In the Select Date Range For Liabilities dialog box, choose the date range and then click OK.

4. Confirm that the *To be printed* box is unchecked, the *Review liability check to enter expenses/penalties* option is selected, and the correct date range appears.
5. At the Bank Account drop-down list, click *1020 Cash - Payroll.*
6. Enter the payment date.
7. Insert a check mark next to each liability you wish to pay.
8. If the information is correct, click the Create button. The liability check is displayed.
9. If the information on the check is correct, click the Save & Close button.

To view and print reports from the Reports menu:
1. At the Reports menu, click *Employees & Payroll.*
2. At the Employees & Payroll submenu, click a report.
3. Indicate the appropriate dates.
4. Print the report.
5. Close the report.

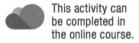 This activity can be completed in the online course.

Key Concepts

Select the letter of the item that best matches each definition.

a. Pay Employees windows
b. Payroll Info tab
c. Employee Center
d. Preview Paycheck window
e. New Employee button

f. *Payroll Summary* report
g. Form 941
h. *Employee State Taxes Detail* report
i. *Payroll Liability Balances* report
j. Pay Liabilities window

_____ 1. The tab in the New Employee window on which pay information is entered.

_____ 2. Quarterly payroll report forwarded to the Internal Revenue Service.

_____ 3. The series of three windows used to calculate gross pay, taxes, and net pay for an employee.

_____ 4. The button in the Employee Center used to access the New Employee window.

_____ 5. The Pay Employees window used to enter pay and tax information to calculate net pay.

_____ 6. Report that lists all the payroll liabilities unpaid as of a specified date.

_____ 7. Contains a file with each employee's payroll background information.

_____ 8. Report that displays information concerning state taxes imposed on the employer and employee.

_____ 9. Window used to pay payroll liabilities accumulated when pay is processed.

_____ 10. Report that displays the earnings, deductions, and employer payroll taxes for each employee.

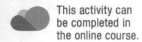
This activity can be completed in the online course.

Procedure Check

1. Your company plans to convert from a manual payroll process to a computerized payroll processing system. What information must be assembled before you can process the first payroll check?
2. Your company has hired a new employee. Describe the steps to add this employee to the Employee Center.
3. After setting up a new employee in the Employee Center, you want to prepare a paycheck for the employee. Describe the steps to pay an employee.
4. Your company's management wishes to have a report that shows the amount of each local payroll tax to which the company is subject. How would you use QuickBooks to gather this information?
5. Your company wishes to have a report that displays the earnings, deductions, and employer payroll taxes paid for each employee for a specific period of time. Describe how you would use QuickBooks to obtain this information.
6. Your company's newly hired college intern has just received her first paycheck. She is disappointed that her net check is only a fraction of what she thought she was earning. Prepare a brief memo describing the taxes that must be withheld from her check.

Reports created for these Case Problems can be exported to Excel and uploaded in the online course to be automatically graded.

Case Problems

Demonstrate your knowledge of the QuickBooks features discussed in this chapter by completing the following case problems.

Case Problem 9–1

In June, the third month of business for Lynn's Music Studio, Lynn Garcia decides to hire two employees. One employee will be the studio manager, who will be paid a salary. The other employee, an assistant instructor, will be paid on an hourly basis. The company file includes information for Lynn's Music Studio as of June 1, 2022.

1. Open the company file **CH9 Lynn's Music Studio.QBW**.
2. At the QuickBooks Desktop Login window, in the *Password* text box, type Student1 and then click OK.
3. Make a backup copy of the company file and name it **LMS9 *[Your Name]* Lynn's Music Studio**.
4. Restore the backup copy of the company file. In both the Open Backup Copy and Save Company File as dialog boxes, use the file name **LMS9 *[Your Name]* Lynn's Music Studio** and enter the password.

5. Change the company name to **LMS9** *[Your Name]* **Lynn's Music Studio**.
6. Add the following employees:

First Name:	Wei
Last Name:	Chan
PRINT ON CHECKS AS:	Wei Chan
SOCIAL SECURITY NO.:	159-89-2527
GENDER:	Female
DATE OF BIRTH:	3/23/80
ADDRESS:	417 Willow Street
	Scranton, PA 18505
MAIN PHONE:	570-555-3980
Mobile:	570-555-9898
PAY FREQUENCY:	Semimonthly
ITEM NAME:	Salary
HOURLY/ANNUAL RATE:	$28,800
Form W-4:	2020 and Later
Federal Filing Status:	Married filing jointly
State Worked/	
Subject to Withholding:	PA
SUI (Company Paid):	Yes
State Filing Status:	Withhold
State Allowances:	1
Not Subject to Other Taxes	

First Name:	Michelle
Last Name:	Auletta
PRINT ON CHECKS AS:	Michelle Auletta
SOCIAL SECURITY NO.:	291-08-7433
GENDER:	Female
DATE OF BIRTH:	8/9/85
ADDRESS:	23 Grand Ave.
	Scranton, PA 18505
MAIN PHONE:	570-555-4872
Mobile:	570-555-4949
PAY FREQUENCY:	Semimonthly
ITEM NAME:	Hourly Wages
HOURLY/ANNUAL RATE:	20
Form W-4:	2020 and Later
Federal Filing Status:	Single or Married filing separately
State Worked/	
Subject to Withholding:	PA
SUI (Company Paid):	Yes
State Filing Status:	Withhold
State Allowances:	1
Not Subject to Other Taxes	

7. Process pay for June 15, 2022, using the following information:

Check No.:	1
Check Date:	06/15/2022
Pay Period Ends:	06/15/2022
Employee:	Michelle Auletta
Item Name:	Hourly Wages
Rate:	20
Hours:	30
Company Taxes:	
Social Security Company:	37.20
Medicare Company:	8.70
Federal Unemployment:	3.60
PA - Unemployment Company:	24.00
Employee Taxes:	
Federal Withholding:	66.00
Social Security Employee:	37.20
Medicare Employee:	8.70
PA - Withholding:	18.00
PA - Unemployment Employee:	0

Check No.:	2
Check Date:	06/15/2022
Pay Period Ends:	06/15/2022
Employee:	Wei Chan
Item Name:	Salary
Rate:	1,200.00
Company Taxes:	
Social Security Company:	74.40
Medicare Company:	17.40
Federal Unemployment:	7.20
PA - Unemployment Company:	48.00
Employee Taxes:	
Federal Withholding:	132.00
Social Security Employee:	74.40
Medicare Employee:	17.40
PA - Withholding:	36.00
PA - Unemployment Employee:	0

8. Process pay for June 30, 2022, using the following information:

Check No.:	3
Check Date:	06/30/2022
Pay Period Ends:	06/30/2022
Employee:	Michelle Auletta
Item Name:	Hourly Wages
Rate:	20
Hours:	45

Company Taxes:

Social Security Company:	55.80
Medicare Company:	13.05
Federal Unemployment:	5.40
PA - Unemployment Company:	36.00

Employee Taxes:

Federal Withholding:	99.00
Social Security Employee:	55.80
Medicare Employee:	13.05
PA - Withholding:	27.00
PA - Unemployment Employee:	0

Check No.:	4
Check Date:	06/30/2022
Pay Period Ends:	06/30/2022
Employee:	Wei Chan
Item Name:	Salary
Rate:	1,200.00

Company Taxes:

Social Security Company:	74.40
Medicare Company:	17.40
Federal Unemployment:	7.20
PA - Unemployment Company:	48.00

Employee Taxes:

Federal Withholding:	132.00
Social Security Employee:	74.40
Medicare Employee:	17.40
PA - Withholding:	36.00
PA - Unemployment Employee:	0

9. On June 30, 2022, pay all payroll tax liabilities owed to the United States Treasury for the period June 1, 2022, to June 30, 2022, Check No. 5.

10. Display and print the following reports for June 1, 2022, to June 30, 2022:
   a. *Payroll Summary*
   b. *Payroll Transaction Detail*
   c. *Journal*
   d. *Employee State Taxes Detail*

Case Problem 9–2

In August, the third month of business for Olivia's Web Solutions, Olivia Chen decides to hire two employees. One employee will be a web page designer, who will be paid hourly. The other employee, an administrative assistant, will be paid on a salary. The company file includes information for Olivia's Web Solutions as of August 1, 2022.

1. Open the company file **CH9 Olivia's Web Solutions.QBW**.
2. At the QuickBooks Desktop Login window, in the *Password* text box, type Student1 and then click OK.
3. Make a backup copy of the company file and name it **OWS9 *[Your Name]* Olivia's Web Solutions**.
4. Restore the backup copy of the company file. In both the Open Backup Copy and Save Company File as dialog boxes, use the file name **OWS9 *[Your Name]* Olivia's Web Solutions** and enter the password.
5. Change the company name to **OWS9 *[Your Name]* Olivia's Web Solutions**.
6. Add the following employees:

First Name:	Fiona
Last Name:	Ferguson
PRINT ON CHECKS AS:	Fiona Ferguson
SOCIAL SECURITY NO.:	449-99-3333
GENDER:	Female
DATE OF BIRTH:	8/8/91
ADDRESS:	23 E. 14th Street
	Westport, NY 11858
MAIN PHONE:	631-555-1020
Mobile:	631-555-3814
PAY FREQUENCY:	Semimonthly
ITEM NAME:	Salary
HOURLY/ANNUAL RATE:	30,000
Form W-4:	2020 and Later
Federal Filing Status:	Single or Married filing separately
State Worked/	
Subject to Withholding:	NY
SUI (Company Paid):	Yes
SDI:	(Remove check mark.)
	(Click Continue at the potential setup error window.)
State Filing Status:	Single
State Allowances:	1
Not Subject to Other Taxes	(Click the Delete button six times to remove other taxes and then click No at the warning window.)

First Name:	Gary
Last Name:	Glenn
PRINT ON CHECKS AS:	Gary Glenn
SOCIAL SECURITY NO.:	101-55-3333
GENDER:	Male
DATE OF BIRTH:	12/23/95
ADDRESS:	1050 York Ave.
	Westport, NY 11858
MAIN PHONE:	631-555-5447
Mobile:	631-555-7111
PAY FREQUENCY:	Semimonthly
ITEM NAME:	Hourly Wages

HOURLY ANNUAL RATE:	25
Form W-4:	2020 and Later
Federal Filing Status:	Married filing jointly
State Worked/	
Subject to Withholding:	NY
SUI (Company Paid):	Yes
SDI:	(Remove check mark.)
State Filing Status:	Married
State Allowances:	2
Not Subject to Other Taxes	(Click the Delete button six times to remove other taxes and click No at the warning window.)

7. Process pay for August 15, 2022, using the following information:

Check No.:	1
Check Date:	08/15/2022
Pay Period Ends:	08/15/2022
Employee:	Fiona Ferguson
Item Name:	Salary
Rate:	1,250.00
Company Taxes:	
Social Security Company:	77.50
Medicare Company:	18.12
Federal Unemployment:	7.50
NY - Unemployment	
Company:	50.00
Employee Taxes:	
Federal Withholding:	190.00
Social Security Employee:	77.50
Medicare Employee:	18.12
NY - Withholding:	62.50

Check No.:	2
Check Date:	08/15/2022
Pay Period Ends:	08/15/2022
Employee:	Gary Glenn
Item Name:	Hourly Wages
Rate:	25
Hours:	80
Company Taxes:	
Social Security Company:	124.00
Medicare Company:	29.00
Federal Unemployment:	12.00
NY - Unemployment	
Company:	80.00
Employee Taxes:	
Federal Withholding:	360.00
Social Security Employee:	124.00
Medicare Employee:	29.00
NY - Withholding:	98.00

8. Process pay for August 31, 2022, using the following information:

Check No.:	3
Check Date:	08/31/2022
Pay Period Ends:	08/31/2022
Employee:	Fiona Ferguson
Item Name:	Salary
Rate:	1,250.00
Company Taxes:	
Social Security Company:	77.50
Medicare Company:	18.12
Federal Unemployment:	7.50
NY - Unemployment Company:	50.00
Employee Taxes:	
Federal Withholding:	190.00
Social Security Employee:	77.50
Medicare Employee:	18.12
NY - Withholding:	62.50

Check No.:	4
Check Date:	08/31/2022
Pay Period Ends:	08/31/2022
Employee:	Gary Glenn
Item Name:	Hourly Wages
Rate:	25
Hours:	88
Company Taxes:	
Social Security Company:	136.40
Medicare Company:	31.90
Federal Unemployment:	13.20
NY - Unemployment Company:	88.00
Employee Taxes:	
Federal Withholding:	400.00
Social Security Employee:	136.40
Medicare Employee:	31.90
NY - Withholding:	105.00

9. On August 31, 2022, pay all payroll tax liabilities owed to the United States Treasury for the period August 1, 2022, to August 31, 2022, Check No. 5.

10. Display and print the following reports for August 1, 2022, to August 31, 2022:
   a. *Payroll Summary*
   b. *Payroll Transaction Detail*
   c. *Journal*
   d. *Employee State Taxes Detail*

## CHAPTER 10

Banking

Transferring Funds, Reconciling Accounts, and Entering Credit Card Charges

Objectives

- Transfer funds between accounts using the Transfer Funds window

- Reconcile cash accounts using the Reconcile window

- Enter credit card charges using the Enter Credit Card Charges window

- Pay credit card charges using the Write Checks window

- Display and print banking-related reports, accounting reports, and financial statements

 The online course includes additional training and assessment resources. Reports created for the Chapter Problem can be uploaded for instructor review.

Chapter Introduction

An integral part of operating any business is effectively managing cash. This usually involves maintaining cash in one or more bank accounts. In addition, it involves transferring funds among the bank accounts, reconciling account balances, using credit cards for business purchases, and making credit card payments. QuickBooks allows you to transfer funds from one bank account to another, process the month-end bank reconciliation, and enter and pay credit card charges using the Banking menu at the main menu bar.

Many companies have more than one checking account. The regular checking account, commonly known as the *operating account*, is used to pay bills and collect and deposit receivables and other funds. Usually, a company maintains a separate checking account solely for payroll transactions. Periodically, funds from the operating checking account are transferred to the payroll checking account to pay employees and payroll taxes.

As a business grows in complexity, the need for special-purpose accounts grows correspondingly. For example, many companies have interest-bearing money market accounts that are designed to hold excess funds temporarily. These funds earn interest until they are needed for an operating activity, at which time they are transferred to a checking account.

transfer funds to move money from one account to another account

Companies can **transfer funds** as needed among the different accounts, often via online banking connections. With QuickBooks, you can use the Transfer Funds Between Accounts window to record and monitor the transfer of funds between accounts.

A company typically receives a statement from the bank at the end of the month detailing the activity the bank has recorded in the company's checking account, along with a month-end balance. Often, this balance does not agree with the company's records. Differences in the account balance usually occur because the bank has recorded transactions that the company does not know about. **Bank reconciliation** is a procedure used to determine the correct cash balance by accounting for these differences and ensuring that they are not a result of errors, either by the bank or the company, or from theft of funds. In addition, if the bank makes changes to the company's account, the company will have to record transactions in the general ledger accounts to reflect these changes. In QuickBooks, the Reconcile window is used to reconcile the balance per the bank statement to the balance per the accounting records.

bank reconciliation a procedure used to determine the correct cash balance in an account by comparing the activity recorded in the account with the activity recorded on the bank statement

Many companies use credit cards to pay bills. These **credit card charges** allow the company to track expenses of a specific nature, such as travel and entertainment expenses, and to defer payment of expenses as needed. In QuickBooks, the Enter Credit Card Charges window is used to record credit card expenditures.

credit card charges expenditures charged to a credit card to be paid at a later date

In this chapter, our sample company, Kristin Raina Interior Designs, will transfer funds between accounts, process bank reconciliations, and use a credit card to pay for expenses.

QuickBooks versus Manual Accounting: Banking

Banking activities in both manual and computerized accounting systems require a company to record transfers of funds among bank accounts, reconcile each bank account balance to the company's balances, and track charges and payments by credit card.

Transfer Funds

In a manual accounting system, when funds are transferred to or from one cash account to another, the transaction can be handled in several ways. Transfers from the company's operating account can be recorded in the cash payments journal or the general journal. If the cash payments journal is used for transfers out of the cash accounts, the cash receipts journal will be used for transfers into the cash accounts. Similarly, if the general journal is used to record transfers out of the cash accounts, it also will be used to record transfers into the cash accounts. A cash payments journal procedure is used when a check is drawn from a cash account to accomplish the transfer. If the transfer is accomplished via a bank credit and debit memo, electronic transfer, or phone transfer, the general journal procedure is used.

In QuickBooks, transfers among bank accounts that are not done by check are recorded in the Transfer Funds Between Accounts activity window. This window indicates the cash accounts involved in the transfer and the amount of the transfer.

Bank Reconciliation

The steps to completing a bank reconciliation in QuickBooks are similar to those in a manual accounting system. The company receives a statement from the bank detailing the activity in the account for the month. The statement shows the deposits (or other additions) to the account along with the checks that have cleared (were paid by) the bank. If the account has earned interest, the amount is added to the balance by the bank. If the bank has charged any fees, called *service charges*, they will be deducted from the account. Other items that may appear are checks returned for non-sufficient funds (NSF checks), credit memos (additions), and debit memos (subtractions).

The bank statement is compared with the company's accounting records, and any differences are identified. Generally, these differences, called **reconciling items**, fall into three categories: timing differences, such as **deposits in transit** and **outstanding checks**; omissions, such as the interest recorded by the bank not yet recorded by the company; and errors by either party. The first two are normal differences that are expected as part of the reconciliation process. If all timing differences and omissions are accounted for and there are no errors, the adjusted bank balances will agree with the adjusted balance for the company's books. The account is then said to be *reconciled*. However, if there is an error, a difference will remain until the source of the mistake is found.

In QuickBooks, the bank reconciliation procedure is carried out using the Reconcile windows. Once a cash account has been identified, the windows display all activity to the account, including deposits or other additions (debits) and checks or other reductions (credits). This information is compared with that in the bank statement to reconcile the account.

reconciling items
differences between the bank statement and the company's records that have to be reconciled so that the cash balance in the company's accounting records agrees with the balance in its bank statement

deposit in transit
a deposit recorded on the company's books, usually at the end of the month, yet deposited too late to be on the current month's bank statement

outstanding check
a check written and recorded by the company that has not yet been paid by the bank

Credit Card Charges

In a manual accounting system, a credit card charge is usually recorded when the bill is paid by the company or tracked as part of accounts payable. Doing so often results in expenses being recorded in periods after they are actually incurred. In QuickBooks, a credit card charge can be recorded immediately when it is incurred by using the Enter Credit Card Charges window. The program also tracks the resulting credit card liability, which will be paid at a later date and separate from accounts payable. Using this method ensures that each asset and/or expense is recorded in the proper time period and that the credit card liability is tracked.

Chapter Problem

In this chapter, Kristin Raina Interior Designs will transfer funds among the company's bank accounts, prepare a reconciliation of the cash accounts, and enter credit card transactions. The balances as of April 30, 2022, are contained in the company file **CH10 Kristin Raina Interior Designs**. Open that file, make a backup copy, name it **EX10** *[Your Name]* **Kristin Raina Interior Designs**, restore the backup copy, and then enter the password. Change the company name to **EX10** *[Your Name]* **Kristin Raina Interior Designs**.

Lists/Centers ────•

Updating the Chart of Accounts List

Kristin Raina has decided to open and fund a money market cash account, because the bank offers a higher rate of interest on money market funds than it offers on a Cash - Operating account. Typically, a company will have a separate general ledger account for each bank account to facilitate the bank reconciliation process. Kristin Raina needs to add another cash account as well as accounts that reflect the adjustments resulting from the bank reconciliation. Kristin also will begin using a credit card to pay for travel-related expenses, so accounts must be added for this additional expense and liability. You will need to update Kristin Raina's Chart of Accounts List to include the new accounts needed for the additional banking procedures.

Follow the procedures presented in Chapter 4 to add these accounts:

Type	Number	Account Name
Bank	1050	Cash - Money Market
Credit Card	2015	American Travel Card
Expense	6100	Bank Service Charges
Expense	6475	Travel Expense
Other Income	6900	Interest Income

The revised Account Listing appears in Figure 10–A.

FIGURE 10–A Updated Account Listing

EX10 [Your Name] Kristin Raina Interior Designs
Account Listing
April 30, 2022

Account	Type	Balance Total	Accnt. #	Tax Line
1010 · Cash - Operating	Bank	43,355.38	1010	<Unassigned>
1020 · Cash - Payroll	Bank	1,483.40	1020	<Unassigned>
1050 · Cash - Money Market	Bank	0.00	1050	<Unassigned>
1200 · Accounts Receivable	Accounts Receivable	1,540.00	1200	<Unassigned>
1250 · Undeposited Funds	Other Current Asset	0.00	1250	<Unassigned>
1260 · Inventory of Carpets	Other Current Asset	800.00	1260	<Unassigned>
1265 · Inventory of Draperies	Other Current Asset	1,000.00	1265	<Unassigned>
1270 · Inventory of Lamps	Other Current Asset	1,000.00	1270	<Unassigned>
1275 · Inventory of Mirrors	Other Current Asset	900.00	1275	<Unassigned>
1300 · Design Supplies	Other Current Asset	200.00	1300	<Unassigned>
1305 · Office Supplies	Other Current Asset	250.00	1305	<Unassigned>
1410 · Prepaid Advertising	Other Current Asset	500.00	1410	<Unassigned>
1420 · Prepaid Insurance	Other Current Asset	2,200.00	1420	<Unassigned>
1700 · Furniture	Fixed Asset	11,900.00	1700	<Unassigned>
1700 · Furniture:1725 · Furniture, Cost	Fixed Asset	12,000.00	1725	<Unassigned>
1700 · Furniture:1750 · Accum. Dep., Furniture	Fixed Asset	-100.00	1750	<Unassigned>
1800 · Computers	Fixed Asset	3,540.00	1800	<Unassigned>
1800 · Computers:1825 · Computers, Cost	Fixed Asset	3,600.00	1825	<Unassigned>
1800 · Computers:1850 · Accum. Dep., Computers	Fixed Asset	-60.00	1850	<Unassigned>
2010 · Accounts Payable	Accounts Payable	9,750.00	2010	<Unassigned>
2015 · American Travel Card	Credit Card	0.00	2015	<Unassigned>
2020 · Notes Payable	Other Current Liability	7,000.00	2020	<Unassigned>
2030 · Interest Payable	Other Current Liability	50.00	2030	<Unassigned>
2100 · Payroll Liabilities	Other Current Liability	0.00	2100	<Unassigned>
2100 · Payroll Liabilities:2110 · Social Sec/Medicare Tax Pa...	Other Current Liability	0.00	2110	<Unassigned>
2100 · Payroll Liabilities:2115 · FIT Payable	Other Current Liability	0.00	2115	<Unassigned>
2100 · Payroll Liabilities:2120 · SIT Payable	Other Current Liability	0.00	2120	<Unassigned>
2100 · Payroll Liabilities:2125 · FUTA Payable	Other Current Liability	0.00	2125	<Unassigned>
2100 · Payroll Liabilities:2130 · SUI Payable	Other Current Liability	0.00	2130	<Unassigned>
2200 · Sales Tax Payable	Other Current Liability	0.00	2200	<Unassigned>
3010 · Kristin Raina, Capital	Equity	50,000.00	3010	<Unassigned>
3020 · Kristin Raina, Drawings	Equity	-400.00	3020	<Unassigned>
3030 · Accumulated Earnings	Equity		3030	<Unassigned>
4010 · Design Services	Income		4010	<Unassigned>
4020 · Decorating Services	Income		4020	<Unassigned>
4060 · Sale of Carpets	Income		4060	<Unassigned>
4065 · Sale of Draperies	Income		4065	<Unassigned>
4070 · Sale of Lamps	Income		4070	<Unassigned>
4075 · Sale of Mirrors	Income		4075	<Unassigned>
4100 · Sales Discounts	Income		4100	<Unassigned>
5060 · Cost of Carpets Sold	Cost of Goods Sold		5060	<Unassigned>
5065 · Cost of Draperies Sold	Cost of Goods Sold		5065	<Unassigned>
5070 · Cost of Lamps Sold	Cost of Goods Sold		5070	<Unassigned>
5075 · Cost of Mirrors Sold	Cost of Goods Sold		5075	<Unassigned>
5900 · Inventory Adjustment	Cost of Goods Sold		5900	<Unassigned>
6020 · Accounting Expense	Expense		6020	<Unassigned>
6050 · Advertising Expense	Expense		6050	<Unassigned>
6100 · Bank Service Charges	Expense		6100	<Unassigned>
6175 · Deprec. Exp., Furniture	Expense		6175	<Unassigned>
6185 · Deprec. Exp., Computers	Expense		6185	<Unassigned>
6200 · Insurance Expense	Expense		6200	<Unassigned>
6300 · Janitorial Expenses	Expense		6300	<Unassigned>
6325 · Office Supplies Expense	Expense		6325	<Unassigned>
6400 · Rent Expense	Expense		6400	<Unassigned>
6450 · Telephone Expense	Expense		6450	<Unassigned>
6475 · Travel Expense	Expense		6475	<Unassigned>
6500 · Utilities Expense	Expense		6500	<Unassigned>
6560 · Payroll Expenses	Expense		6560	<Unassigned>
6560 · Payroll Expenses:6565 · Salaries and Wages Expense	Expense		6565	<Unassigned>
6560 · Payroll Expenses:6610 · Social Sec/Medicare Tax Ex...	Expense		6610	<Unassigned>
6560 · Payroll Expenses:6625 · FUTA Expense	Expense		6625	<Unassigned>
6560 · Payroll Expenses:6630 · SUI Expense	Expense		6630	<Unassigned>
6900 · Interest Income	Other Income		6900	<Unassigned>
7000 · Interest Expense	Other Expense		7000	<Unassigned>

The Transfer Funds Window

As you know, the third level of operations in QuickBooks is to record the daily transactions of the business. In QuickBooks, you use the Transfer Funds Between Accounts window (or Transfer Funds window, for short) to record the movement of funds among the cash accounts of the business. If you transfer funds by writing a check from one cash account to be deposited into another cash account, you can use the Write Checks window. However, when you transfer funds via bank memo, telephone, ATM, or online services, you use the Transfer Funds window to record the transaction. In this window, since there are no default accounts, you identify the source (transferor) cash account, the receiving account (transferee), and the amount to be transferred. The transaction is recorded as follows:

| | | Transferee Cash Account | | XXX | | |
| | | Transferor Cash Account | | | XXX | |

The Transfer Funds window appears in Figure 10–B.

FIGURE 10–B
Transfer Funds Between Accounts Window

In addition to displaying the source and receiving cash accounts, the Transfer Funds window also displays the current balance of the source account, thus preventing you from overdrawing it. The Previous and Next arrows, as well as the Save & Close, Save & New, and Clear buttons, all have the same functions in this window as in other Activity windows.

On April 30, 2022, Kristin Raina wants you to transfer $7,000 from the company's Cash - Operating account to its Cash - Payroll account so there are sufficient funds in that account to pay the payroll and payroll tax liabilities for May.

HINT

Remember, all payroll and payroll taxes are paid from the Cash - Payroll account.

To transfer funds:

1. At the main menu bar, click Banking and then click *Transfer Funds*.
2. At the *DATE* field, choose *04/30/2022*.
3. At the TRANSFER FUNDS FROM drop-down list, click *1010 Cash - Operating*. The balance in the account is displayed.
4. At the TRANSFER FUNDS TO drop-down list, click *1020 Cash - Payroll*.
5. At the *TRANSFER AMOUNT* field, type *7000*. See Figure 10–C.

FIGURE 10–C
Transfer Funds Between Accounts Window— Completed

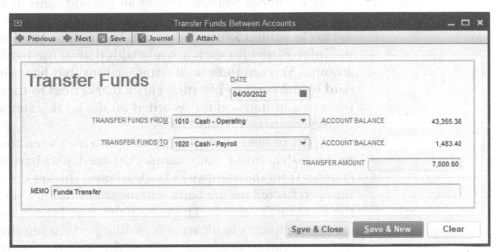

6. If the information is correct, click Save & New.

ACCOUNTING CONCEPT

For a transfer of funds between accounts, the general ledger posting is as follows:

1010 Cash - Operating				1020 Cash - Payroll			
	Dr		Cr		Dr		Cr
Bal	43,355.38	Trf	7,000	Bal	1,472.68		
				Trf	7,000.00		
Bal	36,355.38			Bal	8,472.68		

Practice Exercise 10–1

On April 30, 2022, transfer $10,000 from the Cash - Operating account to the Cash - Money Market account.

The Reconcile Windows

In QuickBooks, activities identified as bank reconciliations are processed in the Reconcile windows. The reconciliation procedure in QuickBooks accomplishes two purposes. First, it ensures that the company's cash records are correct and agree with the bank's records. Second, transactions that are missing from the company's records and discovered during the reconciling process can be recorded at this time.

The Reconcile windows display all the additions to a given account, such as deposits and transfers in, and all reductions to the account, such as checks written and transfers out. Using these windows, you can compare the information for each account with that in the bank statement for that account. You can indicate the transactions that have cleared or have been paid by the bank by inserting check marks next to these transactions, and you can add transactions recorded on the bank statement that are not yet on the company's books.

As part of the reconciling process, you may need to make adjustments to the cash account. For example, the bank may have deducted service charges from the company's bank account during the month. This deduction is reflected on the bank statement but has not yet been recorded in the company's records. The same holds true for any interest income earned on the company's bank account. While performing the bank reconciliation in the Reconcile windows, you have the opportunity to identify and record these transactions and adjust the company's accounts accordingly.

When you add service charges, the default accounts are the Bank Service Charges account and the Cash account. QuickBooks records the transaction as follows:

	Bank Service Charges (expense)	XXX		
	Cash			XXX

When you record interest income, the default accounts are the Cash account and the Interest Income account. QuickBooks records the transaction as follows:

	Cash	XXX		
	Interest Income			XXX

If the bank records an NSF check from a customer, QuickBooks does not automatically record the transaction. Instead, you must record the transaction in the Create Invoices window to reestablish the accounts receivable for this customer and deduct the cash that was never actually collected.

Recall that the system default account in the Create Invoices window is a debit to Accounts Receivable. When you select an item, usually a service or inventory part item, the appropriate revenue account is credited. If you are using QuickBooks to reconcile accounts, you create an item for NSFs in the Item List. When you establish an NSF item, you will identify the default account as Cash. When you record an NSF item in the Create Invoices window, Accounts Receivable is debited for the amount of the NSF still due the company; the corresponding credit, based on the NSF item, will be to Cash.

The QuickBooks Reconcile window has two parts. The first window, the Begin Reconciliation window, allows you to select a bank account to reconcile, add transactions such as service charges and interest income, and enter the bank statement balance. See Figure 10–D.

FIGURE 10–D
Begin Reconciliation Window

Table 10–1 describes the key parts of the Begin Reconciliation window.

TABLE 10–1
Begin Reconciliation Window

Part	Description
Account field	QuickBooks allows you to reconcile all the cash accounts set up by the company. Once you select an account at the drop-down list, all the activity for only that account is displayed.
Beginning Balance	Indicates the opening balance for the bank statement. If this is the first time you are reconciling the account, the figure will be zero. *You cannot edit this number*.
Ending Balance field	Used to enter the ending balance that appears on the bank statement.
Service Charge field	Used to enter the amount of the service charges on the bank statement. You also indicate the service charge general ledger posting account. When you click the Reconcile Now button at the Reconcile window, QuickBooks automatically posts the expense and reduces the Cash account.
Interest Earned field	Used to enter the amount of interest shown on the bank statement along with the appropriate income account for interest. When you click the Reconcile Now button at the Reconcile window, QuickBooks automatically posts the increase to both Cash and Interest Income.
Locate Discrepancies button	Used to locate changes to previously cleared transactions.
Undo Last Reconciliation button	Used to undo the previous reconciliation to correct errors or omissions.

Once the information has been entered in the first window, the second window, called the Reconcile window, will be used to indicate which transactions recorded on the company's books have cleared the bank. Once all the cleared and missing transactions have been accounted for, the *Difference* amount should be zero. See Figure 10–E.

FIGURE 10–E
Reconcile Window

Table 10–2 describes the key parts of the Reconcile window.

TABLE 10–2
Reconcile Window

Part	Description
Difference amount	If all items have been accounted for in the reconciliation, the difference will be zero. If a difference remains after the reconciliation process has been completed, it is probably due to an error by either the bank or the company. You must identify the error and correct it before completing the reconciliation.
Reconcile Now button	Click this button if the *Difference* amount is zero. The account is now reconciled, and a *Reconciliation* report can be printed.

On April 30, 2022, Kristin Raina receives the bank statement for the Cash - Operating account. After reviewing the bank statement, you determine the following:

1. The cash balance per the bank statement is $20,675.00.
2. The cash balance per the company's books is $26,355.38.
    You can review the Chart of Accounts List, the trial balance, or the general ledger for the Cash - Operating account to determine the balance on the company's books.
3. The bank charged the account $35 for bank service charges.
4. The bank credited the account $10 for interest income.

5. All deposits except the deposit of March 31, 2022, have cleared the bank.
6. All checks and payments except Check Nos. 10 and 11 have cleared the bank.
7. A check for $600 from Berger Bakery Company, which was included in the deposit of February 28, 2022, was returned for non-sufficient funds (NSF). The bank deducted the amount from the bank statement.

To reconcile the Cash - Operating account with the bank statement:

<table>
<tr><td>**HINT**</td></tr>
<tr><td>You cannot edit the *Beginning Balance* figure.</td></tr>
</table>

1. At the main menu bar, click Banking and then click *Reconcile*. The Begin Reconciliation window appears.
2. At the Account drop-down list, click *1010 Cash - Operating*.
3. At the *Statement Date* field, choose *04/30/2022*.
4. At the *Ending Balance* field, type 20,675.
5. At the *Service Charge* field, type 35.
6. At the *Service Charge Date* field, choose *04/30/2022*.
7. At the Service Charge Account drop-down list, click *6100 Bank Service Charges*.
8. At the *Interest Earned* field, type 10.
9. At the *Interest Earned Date* field, choose *04/30/2022*.
10. At the Interest Earned Account drop-down list, click *6900 Interest Income*. See Figure 10–F.

**FIGURE 10–F
Begin Reconciliation
Window—Completed**

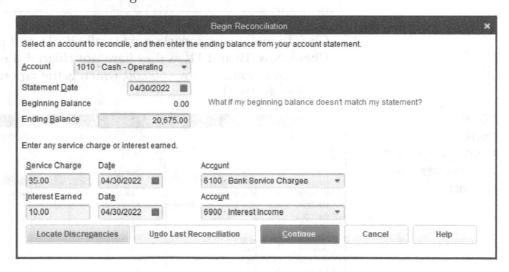

11. If the information is correct, click Continue. The Reconcile - Cash - Operating window appears. The activity for that account is displayed.
12. Click to insert check marks for all deposits and credits except the deposit of March 31, which has not yet cleared. See Figure 10–G.

FIGURE 10–G
Reconcile - Cash - Operating Window with Cleared Deposits

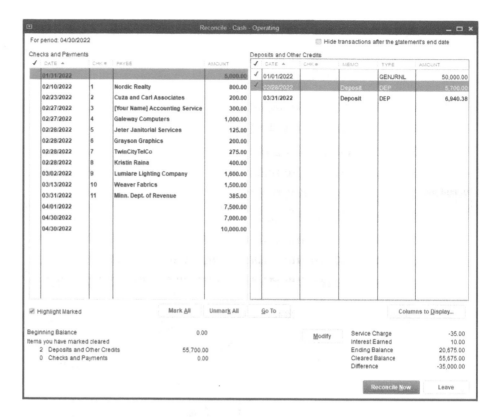

13. Click to insert check marks next to all checks and payments except Check Nos. 10 and 11, as they have not cleared the bank. The *Difference* amount is now *-600.00*, which is the amount of the NSF. See Figure 10–H.

FIGURE 10–H
Reconcile - Cash - Operating Window with Cleared Checks and Payments

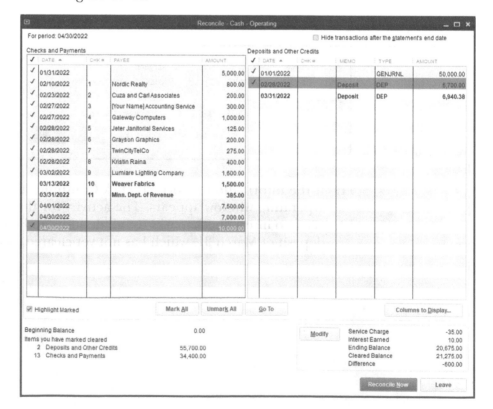

14. Click the *02/28/2022* deposit to select it and then click the Go To button. The Make Deposits window appears, listing the checks that were included in the deposit of February 28. Notice that the $600 check from Berger Bakery Company is included in the deposit. See Figure 10–I.

FIGURE 10–I
Make Deposits Window

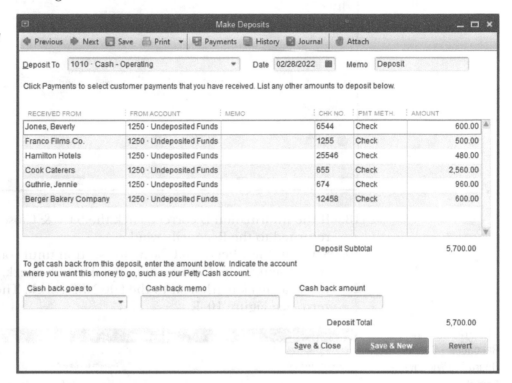

HINT

If you leave the Reconcile window at this point, the items checked off will be saved; however, all the other information—such as ending balance, service charge, and interest income—will be lost.

When this deposit was made on February 28, the bank recorded the total deposit and increased the bank balance by $5,700. When the Berger Bakery Company check was returned due to NSFs, the bank then deducted the $600 from the bank balance. To reconcile with the bank account, the $600 must be deducted from the Cash - Operating account.

15. Close the Make Deposits window. If the check mark was removed from the February 28 deposit, click the deposit to replace the check mark.

16. With the Reconcile window open, at the main menu bar, click Customers and then click *Create Invoices*.

17. At the Create Invoices window, enter the following information:

CUSTOMER:JOB:	Berger Bakery Company
Date:	04/30/2022
Invoice #:	NSF1
ITEM CODE:	NSF
AMOUNT:	600
TAX:	Non

See Figure 10–J.

FIGURE 10–J
Create Invoices Window

18. If the information is correct, click the Save & Close button. You are returned to the Reconcile window.
19. Scroll in the Checks and Payments section until you locate the $600 adjustment to the Cash account for the NSF check.
20. Insert a check mark next to the 600 NSF check. The difference is now zero. See Figure 10–K.

FIGURE 10–K
Reconcile - Cash -
Operating Window—
Completed

✓	DATE ▲	CHK #	PAYEE	AMOUNT
✓	01/31/2022			5,000.00
✓	02/10/2022	1	Nordic Realty	800.00
✓	02/23/2022	2	Cuza and Carl Associates	200.00
✓	02/27/2022	3	[Your Name] Accounting Service	300.00
✓	02/27/2022	4	Galeway Computers	1,000.00
✓	02/28/2022	5	Jeter Janitorial Services	125.00
✓	02/28/2022	6	Grayson Graphics	200.00
✓	02/28/2022	7	TwinCityTelCo	275.00
✓	02/28/2022	8	Kristin Raina	400.00
✓	03/02/2022	9	Lumiare Lighting Company	1,600.00
	03/13/2022	10	Weaver Fabrics	1,500.00
	03/31/2022	11	Minn. Dept. of Revenue	385.00
✓	04/01/2022			7,500.00
✓	04/30/2022			7,000.00
✓	04/30/2022			10,000.00
✓	04/30/2022		Berger Bakery Company	600.00

✓	DATE ▲	CHK #	MEMO	TYPE	AMOUNT
✓	01/01/2022			GENJRNL	50,000.00
✓	02/28/2022		Deposit	DEP	5,700.00
	03/31/2022		Deposit	DEP	6,940.38

For period: 04/30/2022

Checks and Payments

Deposits and Other Credits

☑ Hide transactions after the statement's end date

☑ Highlight Marked   Mark All   Unmark All   Go To   Columns to Display...

Beginning Balance	0.00		Service Charge	-35.00
Items you have marked cleared		Modify	Interest Earned	10.00
2 Deposits and Other Credits	55,700.00		Ending Balance	20,675.00
14 Checks and Payments	35,000.00		Cleared Balance	20,675.00
			Difference	0.00

Reconcile Now   Leave

21. If the information is correct, click Reconcile Now. If the Information message appears, click OK. The account is now reconciled, and the missing transactions for service charges and interest are now posted to the appropriate accounts.
22. In the Select Reconciliation Report dialog box, click *Detail* and then click Print.
23. In the Print Lists dialog box, choose the *Portrait* orientation and then click Print. The report should look like Figure 10–L.

FIGURE 10–L Reconciliation Detail Report—Cash - Operating Account

EX10 [Your Name] Kristin Raina Interior Designs
Reconciliation Detail
1010 · Cash - Operating, Period Ending 04/30/2022

Type	Date	Num	Name	Clr	Amount	Balance
Beginning Balance						0.00
Cleared Transactions						
Checks and Payments - 15 items						
General Journal	01/31/2022			X	-5,000.00	-5,000.00
Bill Pmt -Check	02/10/2022	1	Nordic Realty	X	-800.00	-5,800.00
Bill Pmt -Check	02/23/2022	2	Cuza and Carl Associates	X	-200.00	-6,000.00
Bill Pmt -Check	02/27/2022	4	Galeway Computers	X	-1,000.00	-7,000.00
Bill Pmt -Check	02/27/2022	3	[Your Name] Accounting Service	X	-300.00	-7,300.00
Check	02/28/2022	8	Kristin Raina	X	-400.00	-7,700.00
Check	02/28/2022	7	TwinCityTelCo	X	-275.00	-7,975.00
Check	02/28/2022	6	Grayson Graphics	X	-200.00	-8,175.00
Check	02/28/2022	5	Jeter Janitorial Services	X	-125.00	-8,300.00
Check	03/02/2022	9	Lumiare Lighting Company	X	-1,600.00	-9,900.00
Transfer	04/01/2022			X	-7,500.00	-17,400.00
Transfer	04/30/2022			X	-10,000.00	-27,400.00
Transfer	04/30/2022			X	-7,000.00	-34,400.00
Invoice	04/30/2022	NSF1	Berger Bakery Company	X	-600.00	-35,000.00
Check	04/30/2022			X	-35.00	-35,035.00
Total Checks and Payments					-35,035.00	-35,035.00
Deposits and Credits - 3 items						
General Journal	01/01/2022			X	50,000.00	50,000.00
Deposit	02/28/2022			X	5,700.00	55,700.00
Deposit	04/30/2022			X	10.00	55,710.00
Total Deposits and Credits					55,710.00	55,710.00
Total Cleared Transactions					20,675.00	20,675.00
Cleared Balance					20,675.00	20,675.00
Uncleared Transactions						
Checks and Payments - 2 items						
Check	03/13/2022	10	Weaver Fabrics		-1,500.00	-1,500.00
Sales Tax Payment	03/31/2022	11	Minn. Dept. of Revenue		-385.00	-1,885.00
Total Checks and Payments					-1,885.00	-1,885.00
Deposits and Credits - 1 item						
Deposit	03/31/2022				6,940.38	6,940.38
Total Deposits and Credits					6,940.38	6,940.38
Total Uncleared Transactions					5,055.38	5,055.38
Register Balance as of 04/30/2022					25,730.38	25,730.38
Ending Balance					25,730.38	25,730.38

Note: You should print the Reconciliation Detail *report immediately. It is only available in the Reports menu until you do the next reconciliation.*

For a bank reconciliation, the postings to the general ledger are as follows:

Cash - Operating			Accts Rec	
Dr	Cr		Dr	Cr
26,355.38	600 NSF		600	
Int Inc 10.00	35 SC			
Bal 25,730.38				

Bank Service Charges			Interest Income	
Dr	Cr		Dr	Cr
35.00				10.00

Adjusted Bank Statement Balance:

Ending Balance		$20,675.00
Deposit-in-Transit		6,940.38
Outstanding Checks:		
No. 10	1,500.00	
No. 11	385.00	(1,885.00)
		$25,730.38

In addition, the customer file for Berger Bakery Company reflects the increased asset amount:

Berger Bakery Company	
Dr	Cr
600	

Practice Exercise   10–2

On April 30, 2022, reconcile the company's Cash - Payroll account. The following information relates to this account:
1. The cash figure per the bank statement is $3,224.04 as of April 30, 2022.
2. The bank charged the account $25 for bank service charges.
3. No interest was earned on this account.
4. The deposit of $7,000 on April 30, 2022, did not clear the bank statement.
5. Check Nos. 5 and 6 did not clear the bank.

QuickCheck: See the bank *Reconciliation Detail* report in Figure 10–M.

FIGURE 10–M Reconciliation Detail Report—Cash - Payroll Account

EX10 [Your Name] Kristin Raina Interior Designs
Reconciliation Detail
1020 · Cash - Payroll, Period Ending 04/30/2022

Type	Date	Num	Name	Clr	Amount	Balance
Beginning Balance						0.00
Cleared Transactions						
Checks and Payments - 5 items						
Paycheck	04/15/2022	2	Richard Henderson	X	-1,303.60	-1,303.60
Paycheck	04/15/2022	1	Harry Renee	X	-757.50	-2,061.10
Paycheck	04/30/2022	4	Richard Henderson	X	-1,432.36	-3,493.46
Paycheck	04/30/2022	3	Harry Renee	X	-757.50	-4,250.96
Check	04/30/2022			X	-25.00	-4,275.96
Total Checks and Payments					-4,275.96	-4,275.96
Deposits and Credits - 1 item						
Transfer	04/01/2022			X	7,500.00	7,500.00
Total Deposits and Credits					7,500.00	7,500.00
Total Cleared Transactions					3,224.04	3,224.04
Cleared Balance					3,224.04	3,224.04
Uncleared Transactions						
Checks and Payments - 2 items						
Liability Check	04/30/2022	5	United States Treasury		-1,344.24	-1,344.24
Liability Check	04/30/2022	6	Minn. Dept. of Revenue		-421.40	-1,765.64
Total Checks and Payments					-1,765.64	-1,765.64
Deposits and Credits - 1 item						
Transfer	04/30/2022				7,000.00	7,000.00
Total Deposits and Credits					7,000.00	7,000.00
Total Uncleared Transactions					5,234.36	5,234.36
Register Balance as of 04/30/2022					8,458.40	8,458.40
Ending Balance					8,458.40	8,458.40

If there are errors in a previous bank reconciliation, QuickBooks allows you to undo that reconciliation and make corrections.

To undo the last reconciliation of the Cash - Operating account:
1. At the main menu bar, click Banking and then click *Reconcile.* The Begin Reconciliation window appears.
2. At the Account drop-down list, click *1010 Cash - Operating.*
3. Confirm that the *Statement Date* field displays *May 31, 2022.*
4. Confirm that the *Beginning Balance* field displays *$20,675.* See Figure 10–N.

FIGURE 10–N
Begin Reconciliation Window

5. If the information is correct, click the Locate Discrepancies button. The Locate Discrepancies window appears. See Figure 10–O.

FIGURE 10–O
Locate Discrepancies Window

6. Click the Undo Last Reconciliation button. At the Undo Previous Reconciliation message, click Cancel.

If you wished to undo the April reconciliation, you would click Continue. At this time, do not click Continue. If you undo the April reconciliation, the service charge, interest income, and NSF transactions entered as part of the original reconciliation would not be removed, although their cleared status would be changed to unclear. If you wish to reconcile the April bank statement again, do not reenter these items; instead, check them off as cleared in the Reconcile window.

7. Close the Locate Discrepancies window.

The Enter Credit Card Charges Window

Activities identified as credit card purchases of goods and services are recorded in the Enter Credit Card Charges window. When a credit card is used to purchase goods from a vendor, the asset purchased or expense incurred is recorded as if the goods were purchased with cash or on account. The purchase creates a liability in the form of a credit card balance that will be paid at a later date. The default account is the Credit Card Liability account. Since the liability is not posted to the Accounts Payable account, Accounts Payable is not used to track the credit card liability. The transaction is recorded as follows:

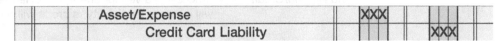

When the credit card bill is paid, the credit card liability is reduced by a cash payment. The default accounts are the Credit Card Liability account and the Cash account. The journal entry is as follows:

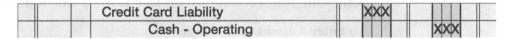

The QuickBooks Enter Credit Card Charges window appears in Figure 10–P.

FIGURE 10–P
Enter Credit Card Charges Window

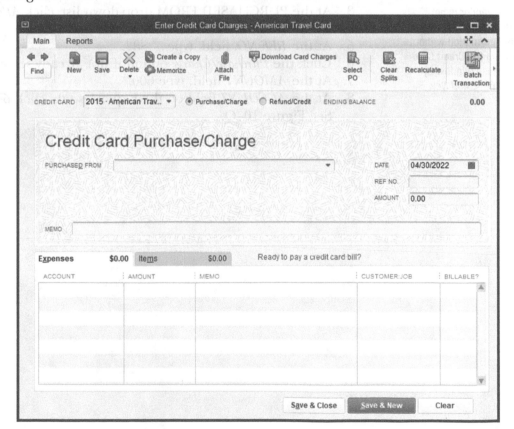

The procedures for entering information in this window are similar to those for the Enter Bills and Write Checks windows. Table 10–3 describes key parts of the Enter Credit Card Charges window.

TABLE 10–3
Enter Credit Card
Charges Window

Part	Description
CREDIT CARD	QuickBooks allows you to track the activity of more than one credit card. Choose the credit card for the current transaction at the drop-down list.
PURCHASED FROM	Used to choose the vendor that the item or expense was purchased from with the selected credit card.
Purchase/Charge and Refund/Credit	If this is a purchase, click *Purchase/Charge*. If you are processing a vendor credit, click *Refund/Credit*. A charge will increase the liability; a credit will reduce the liability.

Entering a Credit Card Charge

On May 1, 2022, Kristin Raina travels to a decorator's convention in Las Vegas, Nevada. She spends three days attending meetings and conferences. The travel expenses of $600 are paid to Atlantis Business Travel with the American Travel credit card on May 1, 2022. The Ref. No. is 47887.

To enter a credit card charge:

1. At the main menu bar, click Banking and then click *Enter Credit Card Charges*.
2. At the CREDIT CARD drop-down list, accept *2015 American Travel Card*.
3. At the PURCHASED FROM drop-down list, click *Atlantis Business Travel*.
4. At the *DATE* field, choose *05/01/2022*.
5. At the *REF NO.* field, type 47887.
6. Click the *Purchase/Charge* option if not already selected.
7. At the *AMOUNT* field, type 600.
8. At the *ACCOUNT* field on the Expenses tab, click *6475 Travel Expense*. See Figure 10–Q.

HINT

If the vendor is not listed, you can enter the information without leaving the Credit Card Purchase window by clicking *< Add New >*.

FIGURE 10–Q
Enter Credit Card
Charges Window—
Completed

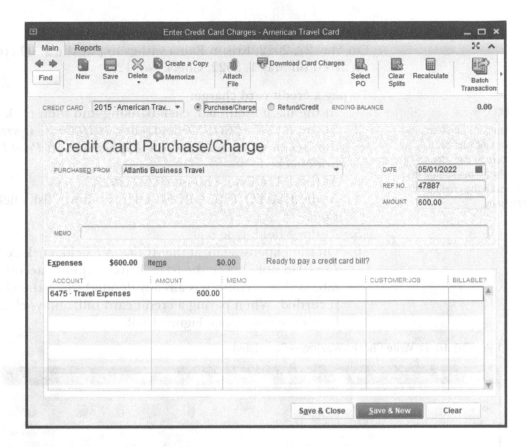

9. If the information is correct, click Save & New.

ACCOUNTING CONCEPT

For a credit card charge for a travel expense, the general journal posting is as follows:

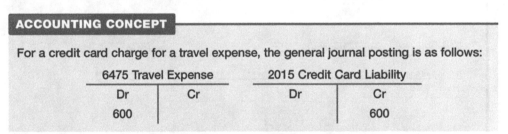

6475 Travel Expense		2015 Credit Card Liability	
Dr	Cr	Dr	Cr
600			600

Practice Exercise 10–3

On May 17, 2022, Kristin Raina travels to St. Louis, Missouri, to meet with a new client. The travel costs of $350 are paid to Atlantis Business Travel with the American Travel Card, Ref. No. 84441.

Paying a Credit Card Charge

On May 22, 2022, Kristin Raina wishes to pay the $600 credit card charge incurred on May 1, 2022, Check No. 12.

To pay a credit card charge:

1. At the main menu bar, click Banking and then click *Write Checks*.
2. At the *BANK ACCOUNT* field, click *1010 Cash - Operating*. Confirm that the *NO.* field reads *12* and the *Pay Online* and *Print Later* options are not checked.
3. At the *DATE* field, choose *05/22/2022*.
4. At the PAY TO THE ORDER OF drop-down list, click *American Travel Card*.
5. At the *$* field, type *600*.
6. On the Expenses tab, at the *ACCOUNT* field, click *2015 American Travel Card*. Do not choose the 6475 Travel Expense account on the Expenses tab, as that account was already debited when the charges were recorded. When paying a credit card bill, always choose the credit card liability account. See Figure 10–R.

> **HINT**
>
> Remember that since the vendor was paid via a credit card, the liability for the charge is now with the credit card company.

FIGURE 10–R Write Checks Window—Completed

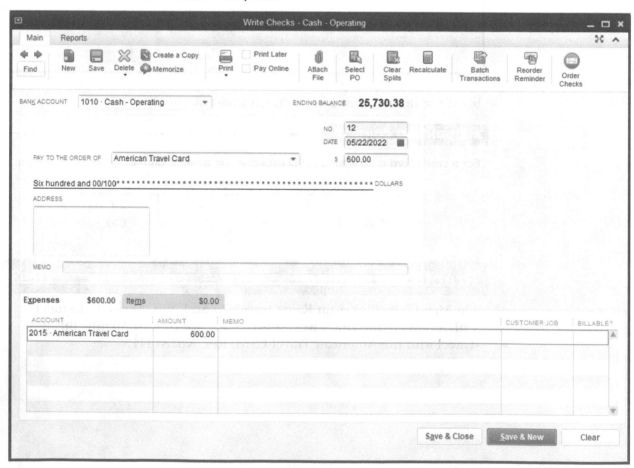

7. If the information is correct, click Save & New.

For a payment of a credit card charge, the general ledger posting is as follows:

2015 Credit Card Liability		1010 Cash - Operating	
Dr	Cr	Dr	Cr
Pmt 600	600		600
	Bal 0		

Practice Exercise 10–4

On May 31, 2022, pay the remaining credit card balance to American Travel, $350, Check No. 13.

Banking Reports, Accounting Reports, and Financial Statements

As you know, in QuickBooks, the fourth level of operation is to view and print reports. As described in prior chapters, the reports for an activity can be accessed from both the Reports menu and the Lists menu.

Banking Reports from the Reports Menu

The *Reconciliation Detail* report is printed as part of the reconciliation process. In addition to this report, the company uses the following reports:

Deposit Detail Report

The *Deposit Detail* report displays the components of each deposit to each cash account for a specified period of time. The report shows the payee's name, amount of payment, nature of payment, and date of payment and deposit. This report is helpful in tracing a collection from a customer to the actual bank deposit.

To view and print the *Deposit Detail* report:
1. At the main menu bar, click Reports and then click *Banking*.
2. At the Banking submenu, click *Deposit Detail*.
3. At the *From* and *To* fields, choose *02/01/2022* and *04/30/2022*.
4. Click Refresh. The report for the period is displayed. See Figure 10–S.
5. Close the report.

FIGURE 10–S Deposit Detail Report

EX10 [Your Name] Kristin Raina Interior Designs
Deposit Detail
February through April 2022

Type	Num	Date	Name	Account	Amount
Deposit		02/28/2022		1010 · Cash - Operating	5,700.00
Payment	6544	02/13/2022	Jones, Beverly	1250 · Undeposited Funds	-600.00
Payment	1255	02/20/2022	Franco Films Co.	1250 · Undeposited Funds	-500.00
Sales Receipt	1007	02/24/2022	Hamilton Hotels	1250 · Undeposited Funds	-480.00
Payment	655	02/27/2022	Cook Caterers	1250 · Undeposited Funds	-2,560.00
Payment	674	02/28/2022	Guthrie, Jennie	1250 · Undeposited Funds	-960.00
Payment	12458	02/28/2022	Berger Bakery Company	1250 · Undeposited Funds	-600.00
TOTAL					-5,700.00
Deposit		03/31/2022		1010 · Cash - Operating	6,940.38
Sales Receipt	1009	03/22/2022	Jones, Beverly	1250 · Undeposited Funds	-1,163.00
Payment	2453	03/23/2022	Guthrie, Jennie	1250 · Undeposited Funds	-2,384.34
Sales Receipt	1011	03/29/2022	Franco Films Co.	1250 · Undeposited Funds	-1,631.00
Payment	6555	03/30/2022	Hamilton Hotels	1250 · Undeposited Funds	-1,762.04
TOTAL					-6,940.38
Deposit		04/30/2022		1010 · Cash - Operating	10.00
				6900 · Interest Income	-10.00
TOTAL					-10.00

Missing Checks Report

The title of this report is somewhat misleading. The *Missing Checks* report actually displays detailed information for all checks written from a specified cash account. The report includes the check number, date written, payee, and purpose (type) of check. Since the report lists all checks, it is useful in finding missing and duplicate checks.

To view and print the *Missing Checks* report:
1. At the main menu bar, click Reports and then click *Banking*.
2. At the Banking submenu, click *Missing Checks*. The Missing Checks dialog box appears. See Figure 10–T.

FIGURE 10–T
Missing Checks
Dialog Box

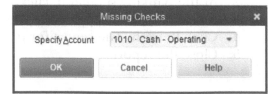

3. At the Specify Account drop-down list, click *1010 Cash - Operating* and then click OK. The report displays all checks written since the account was opened. See Figure 10–U.
4. Close the report.

FIGURE 10–U Missing Checks Report

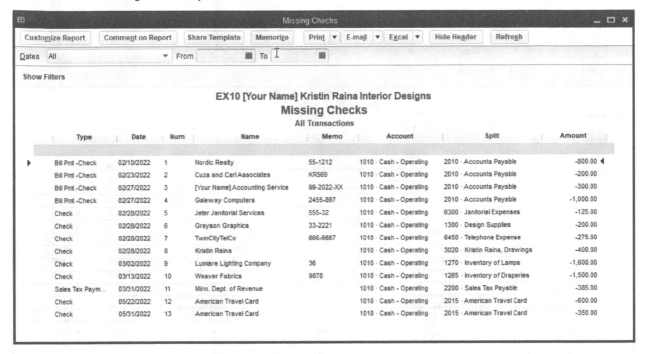

Banking Reports from the Lists Menu

HINT

An *Account QuickReport* can be displayed for any cash account and for any time period specified.

QuickBooks allows you to view and print banking reports from the Lists windows. Once you access a list, you can view a list of available reports by clicking the Reports button in the List window.

To view and print an *Account QuickReport* of the cash account:

1. At the main menu bar, click Lists and then click *Chart of Accounts*.
2. Select (highlight) *1010 Cash - Operating*, but do not open the account.
3. Click the Reports menu button.
4. At the Reports button drop-down menu, click *QuickReport: 1010 Cash - Operating*. The report is displayed. See Figure 10–V.

FIGURE 10–V Account QuickReport—1010 Cash - Operating

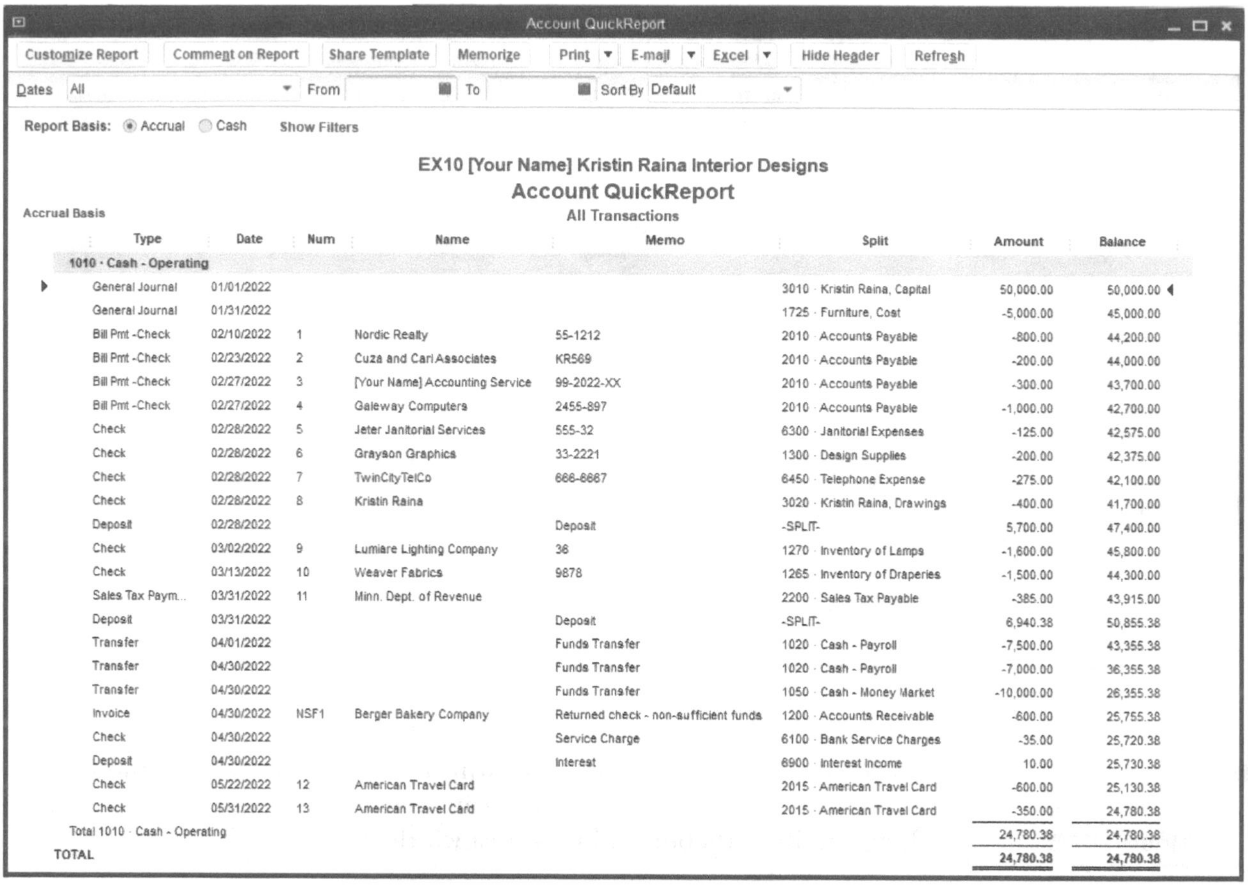

Account QuickReport

Customize Report | Comment on Report | Share Template | Memorize | Print | E-mail | Excel | Hide Header | Refresh

Dates All | From | To | Sort By Default

Report Basis: Accrual Cash Show Filters

EX10 [Your Name] Kristin Raina Interior Designs

Account QuickReport

Accrual Basis

All Transactions

Type	Date	Num	Name	Memo	Split	Amount	Balance
1010 · Cash - Operating							
General Journal	01/01/2022				3010 · Kristin Raina, Capital	50,000.00	50,000.00
General Journal	01/31/2022				1725 · Furniture, Cost	-5,000.00	45,000.00
Bill Pmt -Check	02/10/2022	1	Nordic Realty	55-1212	2010 · Accounts Payable	-800.00	44,200.00
Bill Pmt -Check	02/23/2022	2	Cuza and Carl Associates	KR569	2010 · Accounts Payable	-200.00	44,000.00
Bill Pmt -Check	02/27/2022	3	[Your Name] Accounting Service	99-2022-XX	2010 · Accounts Payable	-300.00	43,700.00
Bill Pmt -Check	02/27/2022	4	Galeway Computers	2455-897	2010 · Accounts Payable	-1,000.00	42,700.00
Check	02/28/2022	5	Jeter Janitorial Services	555-32	6300 · Janitorial Expenses	-125.00	42,575.00
Check	02/28/2022	6	Grayson Graphics	33-2221	1300 · Design Supplies	-200.00	42,375.00
Check	02/28/2022	7	TwinCityTelCo	666-6667	6450 · Telephone Expense	-275.00	42,100.00
Check	02/28/2022	8	Kristin Raina		3020 · Kristin Raina, Drawings	-400.00	41,700.00
Deposit	02/28/2022			Deposit	-SPLIT-	5,700.00	47,400.00
Check	03/02/2022	9	Lumiare Lighting Company	36	1270 · Inventory of Lamps	-1,600.00	45,800.00
Check	03/13/2022	10	Weaver Fabrics	9878	1265 · Inventory of Draperies	-1,500.00	44,300.00
Sales Tax Paym...	03/31/2022	11	Minn. Dept. of Revenue		2200 · Sales Tax Payable	-385.00	43,915.00
Deposit	03/31/2022			Deposit	-SPLIT-	6,940.38	50,855.38
Transfer	04/01/2022			Funds Transfer	1020 · Cash - Payroll	-7,500.00	43,355.38
Transfer	04/30/2022			Funds Transfer	1020 · Cash - Payroll	-7,000.00	36,355.38
Transfer	04/30/2022			Funds Transfer	1050 · Cash - Money Market	-10,000.00	26,355.38
Invoice	04/30/2022	NSF1	Berger Bakery Company	Returned check - non-sufficient funds	1200 · Accounts Receivable	-600.00	25,755.38
Check	04/30/2022			Service Charge	6100 · Bank Service Charges	-35.00	25,720.38
Deposit	04/30/2022			Interest	6900 · Interest Income	10.00	25,730.38
Check	05/22/2022	12	American Travel Card		2015 · American Travel Card	-600.00	25,130.38
Check	05/31/2022	13	American Travel Card		2015 · American Travel Card	-350.00	24,780.38
Total 1010 · Cash - Operating						24,780.38	24,780.38
TOTAL						24,780.38	24,780.38

This report displays all the activity affecting the account. The default setting is for all transactions for the fiscal year. However, you can set any period. If you scroll down the window, you will notice that the transactions for bank service charges and interest income have been included in the account activity.

5. Close the report.
6. Close the Chart of Accounts list.

Accounting Reports and Financial Statements

In addition to the banking reports, other reports related to the company's banking can be viewed and printed at the end of the month.

Transaction Detail by Account Report

An additional report that can be useful in the reconciliation process is the *Transaction Detail by Account* report. This report will display for the cash accounts all the checks written by the company. It will also indicate if each check has cleared the bank. This report is similar to the *General Ledger* report.

To view the *Transaction Detail by Account* report:

1. At the main menu bar, click Reports and then click *Accountant & Taxes*.
2. At the Accountant & Taxes submenu, click *Transaction Detail by Account*.
3. At the *From* and *To* fields, choose *01/01/2022* and *05/31/2022* and then click Refresh. The report for the period is displayed. See Figure 10–W for a partial listing.

FIGURE 10–W Transaction Detail by Account Report—Partial

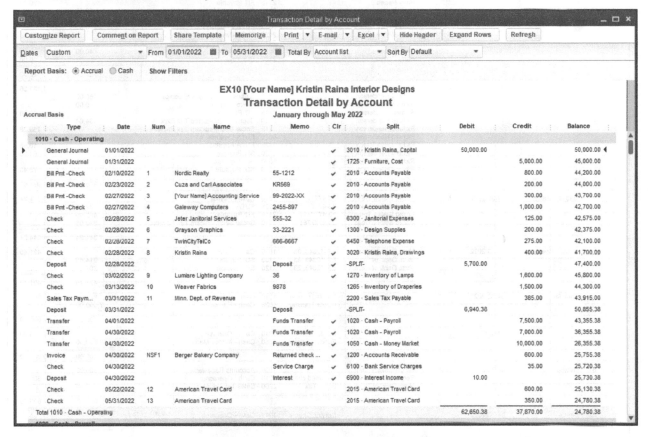

Notice that in the 1010 Cash - Operating account and the 1020 Cash - Payroll account, the cleared items have a check mark in the *Clr* column to indicate that they have cleared.

4. Close the report.

Journal Report and Financial Statements

At the end of each month, the *Journal* report, the *Profit & Loss Standard* report, and the *Balance Sheet Standard* report should be viewed and printed. These reports are displayed in Figures 10–X, 10–Y, and 10–Z.

FIGURE 10–X Journal Report April 30, 2022–May 31, 2022

EX10 [Your Name] Kristin Raina Interior Designs
Journal
April 30 through May 31, 2022

Trans #	Type	Date	Num	Name	Memo	Account	Debit	Credit
55	Paycheck	04/30/2022	3	Harry Renee		1020 · Cash - Payroll		757.50
				Harry Renee		6565 · Salaries and Wages Expense	1,000.00	
				Harry Renee		2100 · Payroll Liabilities	0.00	
				Harry Renee		2115 · FIT Payable		120.00
				Harry Renee		6610 · Social Sec/Medicare Tax Expense	76.50	
				Harry Renee		2110 · Social Sec/Medicare Tax Payable		153.00
				Harry Renee		6625 · FUTA Expense	6.00	
				Harry Renee		2125 · FUTA Payable		6.00
				Harry Renee		2120 · SIT Payable		46.00
				Harry Renee		6630 · SUI Expense	40.00	
				Harry Renee		2130 · SUI Payable		40.00
							1,122.50	1,122.50
56	Paycheck	04/30/2022	4	Richard Henderson		1020 · Cash - Payroll		1,432.36
				Richard Henderson		6565 · Salaries and Wages Expense	1,760.00	
				Richard Henderson		2100 · Payroll Liabilities	0.00	
				Richard Henderson		2115 · FIT Payable		132.00
				Richard Henderson		6610 · Social Sec/Medicare Tax Expense	134.64	
				Richard Henderson		2110 · Social Sec/Medicare Tax Payable		269.28
				Richard Henderson		6625 · FUTA Expense	10.56	
				Richard Henderson		2125 · FUTA Payable		10.56
				Richard Henderson		2120 · SIT Payable		61.00
				Richard Henderson		6630 · SUI Expense	70.40	
				Richard Henderson		2130 · SUI Payable		70.40
							1,975.60	1,975.60
57	Liability Check	04/30/2022	5	United States Treas...	33-4777781	1020 · Cash - Payroll		1,344.24
				United States Treas...	33-4777781	2125 · FUTA Payable	32.16	
				United States Treas...	33-4777781	2115 · FIT Payable	492.00	
				United States Treas...	33-4777781	2110 · Social Sec/Medicare Tax Payable	820.08	
							1,344.24	1,344.24
58	Liability Check	04/30/2022	6	Minn. Dept. of Reve...	ER-12343, 33...	1020 · Cash - Payroll		421.40
				Minn. Dept. of Reve...	ER-12343, 33...	2130 · SUI Payable	214.40	
				Minn. Dept. of Reve...	ER-12343, 33...	2120 · SIT Payable	207.00	
							421.40	421.40
59	Transfer	04/30/2022			Funds Transfer	1010 · Cash - Operating		7,000.00
					Funds Transfer	1020 · Cash - Payroll	7,000.00	
							7,000.00	7,000.00
60	Transfer	04/30/2022			Funds Transfer	1010 · Cash - Operating		10,000.00
					Funds Transfer	1050 · Cash - Money Market	10,000.00	
							10,000.00	10,000.00
61	Invoice	04/30/2022	NSF1	Berger Bakery Com...		1200 · Accounts Receivable	600.00	
				Berger Bakery Com...	Returned che...	1010 · Cash - Operating		600.00
				Minn. Dept. of Reve...	Sales Tax	2200 · Sales Tax Payable	0.00	
							600.00	600.00
62	Check	04/30/2022			Service Charge	1010 · Cash - Operating		35.00
					Service Charge	6100 · Bank Service Charges	35.00	
							35.00	35.00
63	Deposit	04/30/2022			Interest	1010 · Cash - Operating	10.00	
					Interest	6900 · Interest Income		10.00
							10.00	10.00
64	Check	04/30/2022			Service Charge	1020 · Cash - Payroll		25.00
					Service Charge	6100 · Bank Service Charges	25.00	
							25.00	25.00
65	Credit Card Charge	05/01/2022	47887	Atlantis Business Tr...		2015 · American Travel Card		600.00
				Atlantis Business Tr...		6475 · Travel Expenses	600.00	
							600.00	600.00
66	Credit Card Charge	05/17/2022	84441	Atlantis Business Tr...		2015 · American Travel Card		350.00
				Atlantis Business Tr...		6475 · Travel Expenses	350.00	
							350.00	350.00
67	Check	05/22/2022	12	American Travel Card		1010 · Cash - Operating		600.00
				American Travel Card		2015 · American Travel Card	600.00	
							600.00	600.00
68	Check	05/31/2022	13	American Travel Card		1010 · Cash - Operating		350.00
				American Travel Card		2015 · American Travel Card	350.00	
							350.00	350.00
TOTAL							24,433.74	24,433.74

FIGURE 10–Y Profit & Loss Standard Report January 1, 2022–May 31, 2022

EX10 [Your Name] Kristin Raina Interior Designs
Profit & Loss

Accrual Basis   January through May 2022

	Jan - May 22
Ordinary Income/Expense	
Income	
4010 · Design Services	4,980.00
4020 · Decorating Services	3,400.00
4060 · Sale of Carpets	2,400.00
4065 · Sale of Draperies	1,000.00
4070 · Sale of Lamps	1,200.00
4075 · Sale of Mirrors	900.00
4100 · Sales Discounts	-84.62
Total Income	**13,795.38**
Cost of Goods Sold	
5060 · Cost of Carpets Sold	1,200.00
5065 · Cost of Draperies Sold	500.00
5070 · Cost of Lamps Sold	600.00
5075 · Cost of Mirrors Sold	450.00
5900 · Inventory Adjustment	150.00
Total COGS	**2,900.00**
Gross Profit	**10,895.38**
Expense	
6020 · Accounting Expense	300.00
6050 · Advertising Expense	100.00
6100 · Bank Service Charges	60.00
6175 · Deprec. Exp., Furniture	100.00
6185 · Deprec. Exp., Computers	60.00
6200 · Insurance Expense	200.00
6300 · Janitorial Expenses	125.00
6325 · Office Supplies Expense	150.00
6400 · Rent Expense	800.00
6450 · Telephone Expense	275.00
6475 · Travel Expenses	950.00
6500 · Utilities Expense	450.00
6560 · Payroll Expenses	
6565 · Salaries and Wages Expense	5,360.00
6610 · Social Sec/Medicare Tax Expense	410.04
6625 · FUTA Expense	32.16
6630 · SUI Expense	214.40
Total 6560 · Payroll Expenses	**6,016.60**
Total Expense	**9,586.60**
Net Ordinary Income	**1,308.78**
Other Income/Expense	
Other Income	
6900 · Interest Income	10.00
Total Other Income	**10.00**
Other Expense	
7000 · Interest Expense	50.00
Total Other Expense	**50.00**
Net Other Income	**-40.00**
Net Income	**1,268.78**

FIGURE 10–Z Balance Sheet Standard Report May 31, 2022

EX10 [Your Name] Kristin Raina Interior Designs
Balance Sheet
Accrual Basis | As of May 31, 2022

	May 31, 22
ASSETS	
Current Assets	
Checking/Savings	
1010 · Cash - Operating	24,780.38
1020 · Cash - Payroll	8,458.40
1050 · Cash - Money Market	10,000.00
Total Checking/Savings	43,238.78
Accounts Receivable	
1200 · Accounts Receivable	2,140.00
Total Accounts Receivable	2,140.00
Other Current Assets	
1260 · Inventory of Carpets	800.00
1265 · Inventory of Draperies	1,000.00
1270 · Inventory of Lamps	1,000.00
1275 · Inventory of Mirrors	900.00
1300 · Design Supplies	200.00
1305 · Office Supplies	250.00
1410 · Prepaid Advertising	500.00
1420 · Prepaid Insurance	2,200.00
Total Other Current Assets	6,850.00
Total Current Assets	52,228.78
Fixed Assets	
1700 · Furniture	
1725 · Furniture, Cost	12,000.00
1750 · Accum. Dep., Furniture	-100.00
Total 1700 · Furniture	11,900.00
1800 · Computers	
1825 · Computers, Cost	3,600.00
1850 · Accum. Dep., Computers	-60.00
Total 1800 · Computers	3,540.00
Total Fixed Assets	15,440.00
TOTAL ASSETS	67,668.78
LIABILITIES & EQUITY	
Liabilities	
Current Liabilities	
Accounts Payable	
2010 · Accounts Payable	9,750.00
Total Accounts Payable	9,750.00
Other Current Liabilities	
2020 · Notes Payable	7,000.00
2030 · Interest Payable	50.00
Total Other Current Liabilities	7,050.00
Total Current Liabilities	16,800.00
Total Liabilities	16,800.00
Equity	
3010 · Kristin Raina, Capital	50,000.00
3020 · Kristin Raina, Drawings	-400.00
Net Income	1,268.78
Total Equity	50,868.78
TOTAL LIABILITIES & EQUITY	67,668.78

Exiting QuickBooks

Upon completing this session, make a backup copy of your practice exercise company file to a removable storage device using the Back Up command. Be sure to change the *Save in* field to the removable storage device and then carefully type the correct file name. Close the company file and then exit QuickBooks.

Chapter Review and Assessment

Procedure Review

To transfer funds between accounts:
1. At the main menu bar, click Banking and then click *Transfer Funds.*
2. At the *DATE* field, enter the transfer date.
3. At the TRANSFER FUNDS FROM drop-down list, click the cash account from which the funds are transferring.
4. At the TRANSFER FUNDS TO drop-down list, click the cash account to which the funds are transferring.
5. Enter the transfer amount at the *TRANSFER AMOUNT* field.
6. Click the Save & Close button.

To reconcile a cash account:
1. At the main menu bar, click Banking and then click *Reconcile.*
2. At the Begin Reconciliation window, at the Account drop-down list, click the account to reconcile.
3. Enter the date at the *Statement Date* field.
4. Enter the bank statement ending balance at the *Ending Balance* field.
5. Enter the bank service charges at the *Service Charge* field.
6. Enter the reconciliation date at the *Service Charge Date* field.
7. Click the expense account for the service charges at the Service Charge Account drop-down list.
8. Enter the interest income at the *Interest Earned* field.
9. Enter the reconciliation date at the *Interest Earned Date* field.
10. Click the revenue account for interest income at the Interest Earned Account drop-down list.
11. If the information is correct, click Continue. The Reconcile window appears. The activity for that account is displayed.
12. Insert a check mark next to each deposit that has cleared the bank.
13. Insert a check mark next to each of the checks and payments that have cleared the bank.
14. If there are any NSF checks, record them at the Create Invoices window while the Reconcile window is open.
15. At the Create Invoices window, click the Save & Close button and then return to the Reconcile window.
16. Insert a check mark next to any NSF amounts at the *Checks and Payments* field.
17. Confirm that the *Difference* amount reads zero.
18. If the information is complete and the difference is zero, click the Reconcile Now button.
19. In the Select Reconciliation Detail Report dialog box, click *Detail* and then click Print.
20. In the Print dialog box, click Print.

To enter a credit card charge:
1. At the main menu bar, click Banking and then click *Enter Credit Card Charges.*
2. At the CREDIT CARD drop-down list, click the appropriate credit card.
3. At the PURCHASED FROM drop-down list, click the vendor name.
4. Choose the charge date at the *DATE* field.

5. Enter the vendor reference number at the *REF NO.* field.
6. Click the *Purchase/Charge* option.
7. Enter the charge amount at the *AMOUNT* field.
8. At the *ACCOUNT* field on the Expenses tab, click the account to be debited.
9. Click Save & Close.

To pay a credit card charge:
1. At the main menu bar, click Banking and then click *Write Checks.*
2. At the *BANK ACCOUNT* field, click the appropriate cash account.
3. Choose the check date at the *DATE* field.
4. Click the credit card vendor at the PAY TO THE ORDER OF drop-down list.
5. At the *$* field, enter the amount of the check.
6. At the *ACCOUNT* field on the Expenses tab, click the appropriate credit card liability account.
7. Click Save & Close.

To view and print banking reports from the Reports menu:
1. At the main menu bar, click Reports and then click *Banking.*
2. At the Banking submenu, click a report.
3. Indicate the appropriate dates of the report.
4. Click Refresh.
5. Click the Print button at the top of the report.
6. Close the report.

To view and print banking reports from the Lists menu:
1. At the main menu bar, click Lists and then click *Chart of Accounts.*
2. Highlight the appropriate cash account.
3. Click the Reports menu button.
4. Click a report.
5. Indicate the appropriate dates for the report, if necessary.
6. Click the Print button at the top of the report.
7. Close the report.

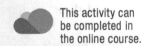
This activity can be completed in the online course.

Key Concepts

Select the letter of the item that best matches each definition.

a. Bank reconciliation
b. *Missing Checks* report
c. Reconcile windows
d. Reconciling items
e. *Deposit Detail* report

f. Transfer Funds Between Accounts window
g. Banking menu
h. Enter Credit Card Charges window
i. Cleared checks
j. *Account QuickReport*

_____ 1. The menu on the main menu bar that contains the *Write Checks, Reconcile,* and *Transfer Funds* choices.

_____ 2. The procedure to account for all differences between the company's cash account record and the bank statement.

_____ 3. Report from the Chart of Accounts List window that displays all the activity within an account.

_____ 4. Activity windows used to reconcile a cash account.
_____ 5. Activity window used to transfer funds among cash accounts.
_____ 6. Report that displays detailed information for each check written.
_____ 7. Activity window used to enter credit card charges.
_____ 8. Report from the Reports menu that displays details of each deposit for a specified period of time.
_____ 9. Items such as deposits in transit, outstanding checks, bank charges, and interest income that account for differences in cash between the company's books and the bank statement.
_____ 10. Checks written by the company that have cleared the bank.

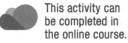

This activity can be completed in the online course.

Procedure Check

1. Your company has four cash accounts. How would you use QuickBooks to move funds from one account to another without having to write a check?
2. Your company wishes to verify the accuracy of the accounting records concerning its cash accounts. How would you use QuickBooks to accomplish this?
3. What is an NSF item, and how is it treated?
4. Your company has given all sales personnel a company credit card for travel and entertainment expenses. How would you use QuickBooks to record the sales force's expenses?
5. You wish to print a list of all the checks written for the year. How would you use QuickBooks to prepare this list?
6. Describe the steps to prepare a bank reconciliation that are common to both a manual accounting system and QuickBooks.

Case Problems

Reports created for these Case Problems can be exported to Excel and uploaded in the online course to be automatically graded.

Demonstrate your knowledge of the QuickBooks features discussed in this chapter by completing the following case problems.

Case Problem 10–1

On June 30, 2022, Lynn's Music Studio will open a new bank account and transfer funds among the various cash accounts. At the end of June, after receiving the bank statement for the company's Cash - Operating account, Lynn Garcia will prepare a bank reconciliation. In addition, during the month of July, Lynn Garcia will begin using a credit card for travel and seminar expenses. The company file includes the information for Lynn's Music Studio as of June 30, 2022.

1. Open the company file **CH10 Lynn's Music Studio.QBW**.
2. At the QuickBooks Desktop Login window, in the _Password_ text box, type **Student1** and then click OK.
3. Make a backup copy of the company file and name it **LMS10** _[Your Name]_ **Lynn's Music Studio**.
4. Restore the backup copy of the company file. In both the Open Backup Copy and Save Company File as dialog boxes, use the file name **LMS10** _[Your Name]_ **Lynn's Music Studio** and enter the password.

5. Change the company name to **LMS10** *[Your Name]* **Lynn's Music Studio**.
6. Add the following accounts:

Type	Number and Name
Bank	1050 Cash - Money Market
Credit Card	2015 Harmony Club Card
Expense	6060 Bank Service Charges
Expense	6475 Travel and Seminars
Other Income	6900 Interest Income

7. Using the Transfer Funds Between Accounts window, record the following transactions:

   Jun. 30   Transfer $3,000 from the Cash - Operating account to the Cash - Payroll account.

   Jun. 30   Transfer $4,000 from the Cash - Operating account to the Cash - Money Market account.

8. Using the Reconcile window, prepare a bank reconciliation for the Cash - Operating account as of June 30, 2022, based on the information listed below. Remember, since this is the first reconciliation, the opening balance is zero.
   a. The cash figure per the bank statement is $5,464.78 as of June 30.
   b. The cash balance per the company's books is $2,615.18.
   c. The bank charged the account $20 for bank service charges.
   d. The bank credited the account $10 for interest income.
   e. All the deposits cleared the bank.
   f. Check Nos. 14 and 15 did not clear the bank.
   g. A check from Mulligan Residence included in the April 30 deposit was returned NSF (nontaxable).
9. Print a *Reconciliation Detail* report. The statement closing date is June 30, 2022.
10. Using the Enter Credit Card Charges window, enter the following transaction:

    Jul. 16   Travel and seminar expenses of $400 to attend an instructor's convention in Philadelphia were paid to Express Business Travel with the Harmony Club credit card. Ref. No. 2718.

11. Using the Write Checks window, enter the following transaction:

    Jul. 27   Paid in full: $400 for the Harmony Club Card charge incurred on July 16; Check No. 16.

12. Display and print the following reports:
    a. *Deposit Detail* for April 1, 2022, to June 30, 2022
    b. *Missing Checks* for the Cash - Operating account
    c. *Journal* for June 30, 2022, to July 31, 2022

Case Problem 10–2

On August 31, 2022, Olivia's Web Solutions will open a new bank account and transfer funds among the various cash accounts. At the end of August, after receiving the bank statement for the company's Cash - Operating account, Olivia Chen will prepare a bank reconciliation. In addition, during the month of September, Olivia Chen will begin using a credit card for travel and entertainment expenses. The company file includes the information for Olivia's Web Solutions as of August 31, 2022.

1. Open the company file **CH10 Olivia's Web Solutions.QBW**.
2. At the QuickBooks Desktop Login window, in the *Password* text box, type Student1 and then click OK.
3. Make a backup copy of the company file and name it **OWS10 *[Your Name]* Olivia's Web Solutions**.
4. Restore the backup copy of the company file. In both the Open Backup Copy and the Save Company File as dialog boxes, use the file name **OWS10 *[Your Name]* Olivia's Web Solutions** and enter the password.
5. Change the company name to **OWS10 *[Your Name]* Olivia's Web Solutions**.
6. Add the following accounts:

Type	Number and Name
Bank	1050 Cash - Money Market
Credit Card	2015 Travelers Express Card
Expense	6060 Bank Service Charges
Expense	6475 Travel & Entertainment
Other Income	6900 Interest Income

7. Using the Transfer Funds Between Accounts window, record the following transactions:

    Aug. 31   Transfer $7,000 from the Cash - Operating account to the Cash - Payroll account.

    Aug. 31   Transfer $2,500 from the Cash - Operating account to the Cash - Money Market account.

8. Using the Reconcile window, prepare a bank reconciliation for the Cash - Operating account as of August 31, 2022, based on the information below. Remember, since this is the first reconciliation, the opening balance is zero.
    a. The cash figure per the bank statement was $13,487.16 as of August 31.
    b. The cash balance per the company's books was $6,989.16.
    c. The bank charged the account $30 for bank service charges.
    d. The bank credited the account $20 for interest income.
    e. All the deposits cleared the bank.
    f. Check Nos. 12 and 14 did not clear the bank.
    g. A check from Breathe Easy from the July 31 deposit was returned NSF (nontaxable).
9. Print a *Reconciliation Detail* report. The statement closing date is August 31, 2022.

10. Using the Enter Credit Card Charges window, enter the following transaction:

   Sep. 15   Travel and entertainment expenses of $750 to attend a sales convention in Florida were paid to Reliable Business Travel with the Travelers Express credit card. Ref. No. 6554.

11. Using the Write Checks window, enter the following transaction:

   Sep. 28   Paid $400 toward the Travelers Express credit card charge incurred on September 15; Check No. 15.

12. Display and print the following reports:
   a. *Deposit Detail* for June 1, 2022, to August 31, 2022
   b. *Missing Checks* for the Cash - Operating account
   c. *Journal* for August 31, 2022, to September 30, 2022

Jobs and Time Tracking

Recording Job Income and Job Payroll Expenses; Tracking Time for Employees and Jobs; and Creating Customer Statements

Objectives

- Add a job to the Customer Center
- Record and allocate payroll incurred for a specific job in the Pay Employees windows
- Record and allocate services rendered for a specific job in the Create Invoices windows
- Set up Time Tracking
- Track employee time for each job using the Weekly Timesheet window
- Pay employees using Time-Tracking data
- Create invoices using Time-Tracking data
- Create customer statements
- Display and print job and time-tracking reports, accounting reports, and financial statements

 The online course includes additional training and assessment resources. Reports created for the Chapter Problem can be uploaded for instructor review.

Chapter Introduction

QuickBooks allows you to allocate income and expenses for a specific job for a customer. A job is a project, assignment, or any identifiable segment of work for a customer. Identifying jobs allows the company to measure the profitability of individual customer projects and assignments. When you record revenue in windows such as the Create Invoices and Enter Sales Receipts windows, you can indicate the job for which the revenue was earned. When you record expenses such as payroll in the Pay Employees windows, you can also allocate employee pay and payroll tax expenses to a job.

Most service businesses track employee hours as part of the invoicing process. Customers are billed, usually at an hourly rate, for services provided by various company personnel. This is called *billable time* or *billable hours*. Time tracking mechanisms can vary from a simple manual system using handwritten timesheets to stand-alone time-and-billing software. The billable hours are used to allocate expenses to a job, determine the invoice to be billed for the job, and ultimately determine the profit (job revenue less job expenses) for the job.

To allocate the revenue and expenses to a specific job, you can either maintain the details manually or use the QuickBooks Time-Tracking feature. When activated, this feature allows you to record time spent by company personnel for customers and specific jobs by entering data in the Weekly Timesheet window. This data is then used to allocate payroll expenses to those jobs and to bill customers for work done.

QuickBooks versus Manual Accounting: Jobs and Time Tracking

In a manual accounting system, when revenue is recorded in a sales or cash receipts journal, an additional step must be taken to identify the job earning the revenue and to record that revenue in a jobs subsidiary ledger. Similarly, when job expenses are recorded in the purchases, cash payments, or payroll journals, they also must be posted to the jobs subsidiary ledger. These steps must be taken in addition to the customer and vendor subsidiary ledger posting.

In QuickBooks, the job file in the Customer Center serves as the jobs subsidiary ledger for the company. When it is desirable to track revenues and expenses for a particular job, that job is created as part of the customer's file in the Customer Center. Relevant information—such as job name, status, start date, and job description—is entered when the job file is created and updated as necessary.

When the company earns revenue from the job, the revenue is recorded in much the same manner as previously recorded in the Create Invoices window or the Enter Sales Receipts window. However, when the revenue is identified with a particular job in each window, it is automatically allocated to the job while the transaction is recorded. These transactions simultaneously update the general ledger for the revenue earned, the customer file for the account receivable (in the Create Invoices window), and the job file for the job revenue. If employees work on a specific job, the Pay Employees windows allow you to identify the time spent or salary expense related to the job.

In addition, QuickBooks has a Time-Tracking feature that is integrated into the existing accounting software. Time-Tracking is used to track the billable time allocated to the jobs. Billable time by job is recorded in the Weekly Timesheet window for each employee. This information is then carried to the Pay Employees window when payroll is processed; there, the payroll expense is allocated to the identified jobs. This information is also used in the Create Invoices and Enter Sales Receipts windows to bill customers by job based on the billable time.

Chapter Problem

In this chapter, our sample company, Kristin Raina Interior Designs, will track revenue and expenses for several jobs for a customer. As revenue is generated, you will identify the job earning the revenue and allocate the revenue to that job. You will also charge selected payroll to a specific job. Although not an employee, Kristin Raina also will track and allocate her time to specific jobs.

The Time-Tracking feature is an optional feature; you can track revenue and expenses with or without using it. For the first half of the month, you will allocate revenues and expenses to jobs without using the Time-Tracking feature. In the second half of the month, you will activate the Time-Tracking feature and then use it to allocate revenues and expenses to jobs. Additionally, at the end of the month, Kristin Raina will display and print a customer statement for the company that she is invoicing for the jobs.

Beginning balances for May 1, 2022, along with banking activity from Chapter 10, are contained in the company file **CH11 Kristin Raina Interior Designs**. Open that file, enter the password, make a backup copy, name it **EX11 *[Your Name]* Kristin Raina Interior Designs**, restore the backup copy, and then enter the password. Change the company name to **EX11 *[Your Name]* Kristin Raina Interior Designs**.

Lists/Centers ●────

The Customer Center

As you know, the Customer Center contains a file for each customer with which the company does business. If there are specific jobs for a customer or multiple jobs for that customer, you identify those jobs in the customer file. *A job must always be associated with a customer.* Once a job has been added, it will have its own file—separate but part of the customer's file. The job file carries over the customer information from the customer's file (name, address, telephone, and so on). In addition, the job file will contain important information such as the job name, description, start and expected completion dates, and status.

On May 1, 2022, Kristin Raina Interior Designs was awarded a contract to redesign the lobbies of three hotels owned by Hamilton Hotels. Kristin Raina wishes to track the revenue and payroll expenses for each of the three jobs by using the Job feature of QuickBooks.

To add a job:
1. At the main menu bar, click Customers and then click *Customer Center*.
2. At the Customer Center window, select (highlight) *Hamilton Hotels*, but do not open the file. See Figure 11–A.

HINT
To *select* is to highlight something by clicking once. To *choose* is to activate a command, usually by double-clicking.

FIGURE 11-A Hamilton Hotels File Selected

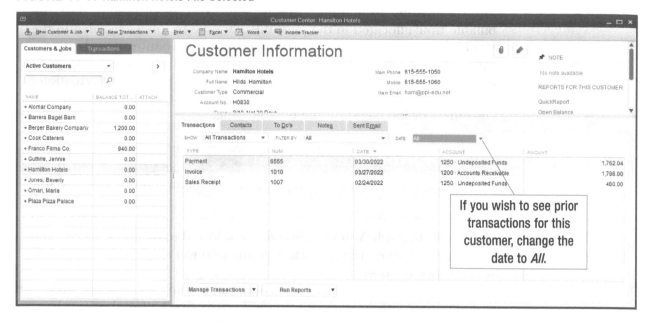

3. Click the New Customer & Job button.
4. At the New Customer & Job menu, click *Add Job*. The New Job window opens. Notice that the New Job window carries over information from the Hamilton Hotels file. See Figure 11-B.

FIGURE 11-B
New Job Window

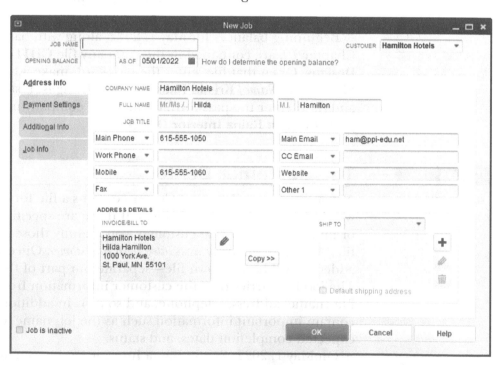

5. At the *JOB NAME* field, type Lakeside Hotel.

6. On the Job Info tab, enter the following data:

JOB DESCRIPTION:	Lakeside Hotel Lobby Redesign
JOB STATUS:	Awarded
START DATE:	05/01/2022
PROJECTED END DATE:	08/31/2022

See Figure 11–C.

FIGURE 11–C
New Job Window—Completed

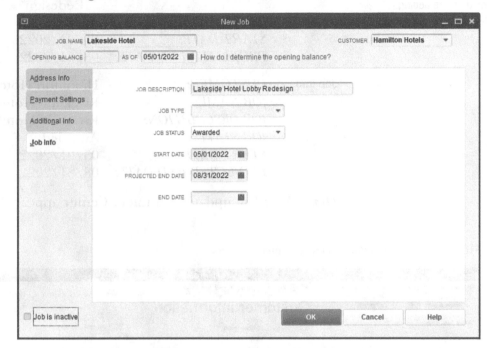

7. If the information is correct, click OK. You are returned to the Customer Center. Notice that the Lakeside Hotel job is listed below the Hamilton Hotels file as a subfile and the job data is displayed on the Job Information page. See Figure 11–D.

FIGURE 11–D Customer Center

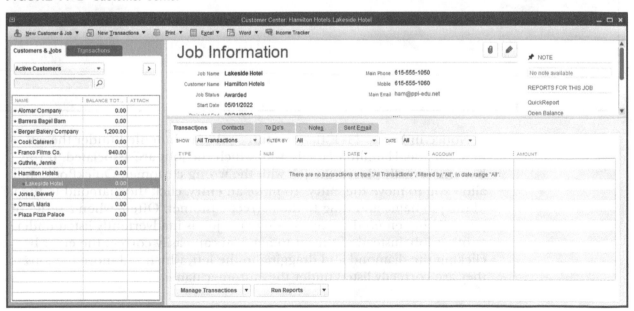

Add the following new jobs:

Job Info	*CUSTOMER:*	Hamilton Hotels
	JOB NAME:	Mountainside Hotel
	JOB DESCRIPTION:	Mountainside Hotel Lobby Redesign
	JOB STATUS:	Awarded
	START DATE:	05/01/2022
	PROJECTED END DATE:	08/31/2022
Job Info	*CUSTOMER:*	Hamilton Hotels
	JOB NAME:	Riverside Hotel
	JOB DESCRIPTION:	Riverside Hotel Lobby Redesign
	JOB STATUS:	Awarded
	START DATE:	05/01/2022
	PROJECTED END DATE:	08/31/2022

QuickCheck: The updated Customer Center appears in Figure 11–E.

FIGURE 11–E Updated Customer Center

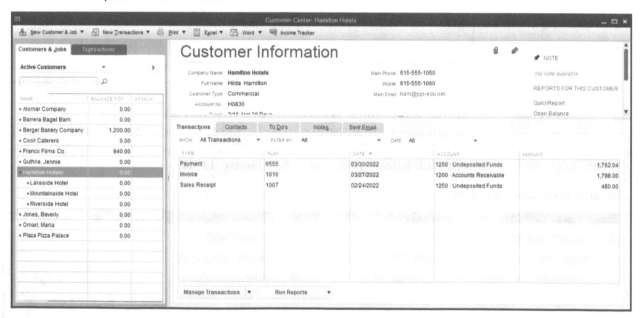

Notice in Figure 11–E that the three jobs are indented under the customer name, Hamilton Hotels, with which the jobs are associated. If you have incorrectly placed the job with the wrong customer, QuickBooks will allow you to move the entry. To move an entry, click the diamond to the left of the job name and drag to the correct customer. Often, when a series of jobs is being entered for one customer, a job is inadvertently listed under another job, instead of the customer. You can easily correct the error by clicking the diamond and dragging to the left, which will move the jobs so they are correctly listed under the customer name.

The Item List

Beginning this month, Kristin Raina will bill customers for design and decorating work done by both her and one of her employees. Recall that the rate for Design Services is $60 per hour and that the rate for Decorating Services is $50 per hour. These rates apply to work done by Kristin Raina, the owner. Work done by the employee, Richard Henderson, will be billed at $40 per hour for both Design and Decorating Services.

Since the company will now bill customers at different rates depending on who is doing the work, a separate item has to be set up for each rate. The Item List in the company file has been modified to reflect the foregoing changes. The Design Services item has been changed to Design Services - Owner. The Decorating Services item has been similarly changed. A new item, Decorating Services - Assistant, has been added that reflects the services performed and billed for Richard Henderson, with a rate of $40 per hour. See Figure 11-F.

FIGURE 11-F Item List

NAME	DESCRIPTION	TYPE	ACCOUNT	TOTAL QUANTITY ON HAND	ON SAL...	PRICE	ATTACH
Decorating Services - Assistant	Decorating Services - Assis...	Service	4020 · Decorating Services			40.00	
Decorating Services - Owner	Decorating Services - Owner	Service	4020 · Decorating Services			50.00	
Design Services - Owner	Design Services - Owner	Service	4010 · Design Services			60.00	
Carpets	Carpets	Inventory Part	4060 · Sale of Carpets	4	0	400.00	
Draperies	Draperies	Inventory Part	4065 · Sale of Draperies	8	0	250.00	
Lamps	Lamps	Inventory Part	4070 · Sale of Lamps	10	0	200.00	
Mirrors	Decorative Mirrors	Inventory Part	4075 · Sale of Mirrors	6	0	300.00	
NSF	Returned check - non-suffic...	Other Charge	1010 · Cash - Operating			0.00	
Minn. Sales Tax	Sales Tax	Sales Tax Item	2200 · Sales Tax Payable			7.0%	

Item ▾ Activities ▾ Reports ▾ Excel ▾ Attach ☐ Include inactive

Practice Exercise   11-2

Using the procedures you learned in Chapter 5, add the following item:

Type: Service
Item Name/Number: Design Services - Assistant
Description: Design Services - Assistant
Rate: 40
Tax Code: Non-taxable Sales
Account: 4010 Design Services

QuickCheck: The updated Item List appears in Figure 11-G.

FIGURE 11–G Item List—Updated

NAME	DESCRIPTION	TYPE	ACCOUNT	TOTAL QUANTITY ON HAND	ON SA	PRICE	ATTACH
◆ Decorating Services - Assistant	Decorating Services - Assistant	Service	4020 · Decorating Services			40.00	
◆ Decorating Services - Owner	Decorating Services - Owner	Service	4020 · Decorating Services			50.00	
◆ Design Services - Assistant	Design Services - Assistant	Service	4010 · Design Services			40.00	
◆ Design Services - Owner	Design Services - Owner	Service	4010 · Design Services			60.00	
◆ Carpets	Carpets	Inventory Part	4060 · Sale of Carpets	4	0	400.00	
◆ Draperies	Draperies	Inventory Part	4065 · Sale of Draperies	8	0	250.00	
◆ Lamps	Lamps	Inventory Part	4070 · Sale of Lamps	10	0	200.00	
◆ Mirrors	Decorative Mirrors	Inventory Part	4075 · Sale of Mirrors	6	0	300.00	
◆ NSF	Returned check - non-sufficient f...	Other Charge	1010 · Cash - Operating			0.00	
◆ Minn. Sales Tax	Sales Tax	Sales Tax Item	2200 · Sales Tax Payable			7.0%	

Activities

Allocating Payroll Expenses to a Job

As you recall from Chapter 9 on payroll, Kristin Raina has two employees, Harry Renee and Richard Henderson. Harry Renee is an administrative assistant whose time is not billable. Richard Henderson is a design assistant who, along with the owner Kristin Raina, provides design and decorating services to customers. Both Richard Henderson and Kristin Raina, will spend billable time working on the Hamilton Hotels projects.

Kristin Raina wishes to charge the payroll expense to each project to measure the profitability of the project. For the first payroll in May, Kristin Raina has used a manual system to keep track of the hours spent on each job by both Richard Henderson and by herself.

On May 15, 2022, Kristin Raina pays Richard Henderson, who spent all of his time during the pay period working on the Hamilton Hotels jobs. He worked 25 hours at Lakeside Hotel, 35 hours at Mountainside Hotel, and 28 hours at Riverside Hotel, for a total of 88 hours. In preparing the payroll for May 15, 2022, allocate the 88 hours he worked to the different jobs. This will allow you to keep track of the payroll costs by job.

To pay an employee and allocate hours to jobs:
1. At the main menu bar, click Employees and then click *Pay Employees.* The Enter Payroll Information window appears.
2. At the *PAY PERIOD ENDS* and *CHECK DATE* fields, choose *05/15/2022.*
3. At the *BANK ACCOUNT* field, click *1020 Cash - Payroll.*
4. Confirm that the *First Check#* box reads *7.*
5. Select *Richard Henderson* by inserting a check mark next to the name.
6. If the information is correct, click the Open Paycheck Detail button. You move to the Preview Paycheck window.
7. Confirm that the item name is *Hourly Wages,* the rate is *20,* and the pay period is *05/01/2022* to *05/15/2022.*
8. At the first line of the *HOURS* field, type *25.*
9. At the CUSTOMER:JOB drop-down list, click *Lakeside Hotel.* See Figure 11–H.

FIGURE 11–H
Preview Paycheck
Window

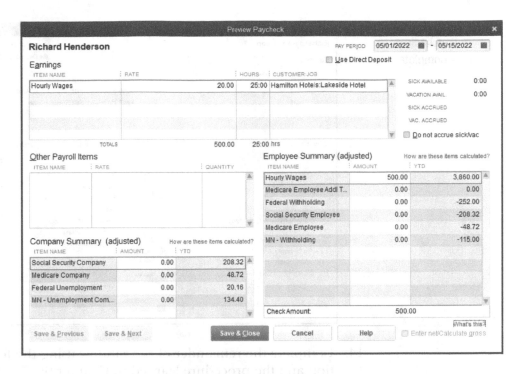

10. Move to the second line of the *ITEM NAME* field and then click *Hourly Wages* at the drop-down list.
11. At the *HOURS* field, type 35.
12. At the CUSTOMER:JOB drop-down list, click *Mountainside Hotel*. Notice that there are now two hourly wages totals. See Figure 11–I.

FIGURE 11–I
Preview Paycheck
Window

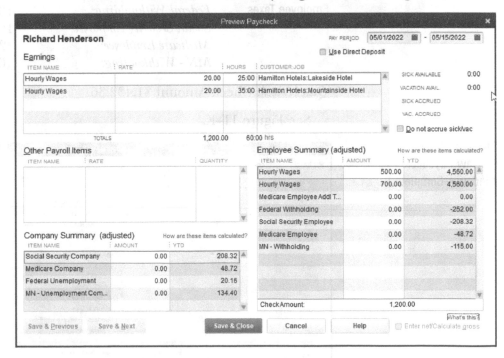

13. Move to the next line and complete the information for Riverside Hotel for 28 hours. Notice that there are three hourly wage amounts, totaling $1,760 (88 hours @ $20 per hour). See Figure 11–J.

FIGURE 11–J
Preview Paycheck Window—Completed

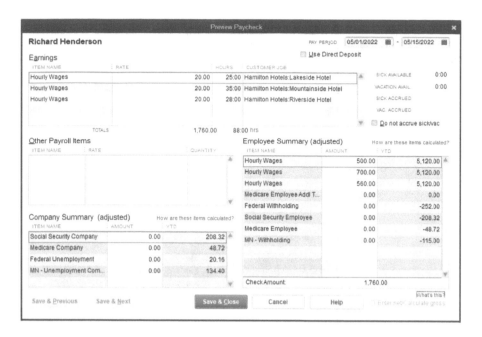

14. Complete the remainder of the window using the following information and the procedure learned in Chapter 9:

Company Taxes	*Social Security Company:*	109.12
	Medicare Company:	25.52
	Federal Unemployment:	10.56
	MN - Unemployment Company:	70.40
Employee Taxes	*Federal Withholding:*	132.00
	Social Security Employee:	109.12
	Medicare Employee:	25.52
	MN - Withholding:	61.00

QuickCheck: Check Amount $1,432.36.

See Figure 11–K.

FIGURE 11–K
Preview Paycheck Window—Completed

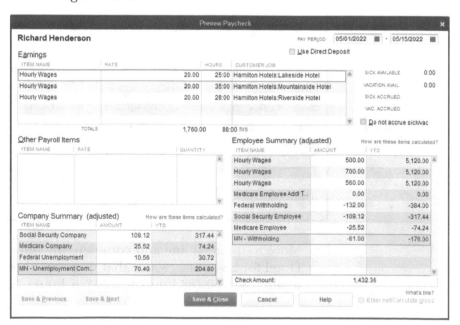

15. If the information is correct, click the Save & Close button. You are returned to the Enter Payroll Information window.
16. Click Continue. You move to the Review and Create Paychecks window, and the deductions and net pay columns are now completed.
17. If the information is correct, click the Create Paychecks button.
18. At the Confirmation and Next Steps window, click Close.

As a result of this transaction, payroll expense (including the employer payroll tax expense) is allocated to each job in proportion to the hours worked on it.

ACCOUNTING CONCEPT

For the processing of a paycheck, the general ledger posting is as shown below. (The taxes payable accounts consist of both the employee and employer taxes; *er* represents the employer's share, and *ee* represents the employee's share.)

6565 Salaries and Wages Expense			6610-6630 Employer Payroll Tax Expense		
Dr	Cr		Dr		Cr
(88 hrs @ $20) 1,760			(FICA er)	109.12	
			(Med er)	25.52	
			(FUTA)	10.56	
			(SUI)	70.40	
			Bal	215.60	

2210-2130 Payroll Taxes Payable			1020 Cash - Payroll	
Dr	Cr		Dr	Cr
	218.24 (FICA ee & er)			1,432.36
	51.04 (Med ee & er)			
	132.00 (FIT)			
	61.00 (SIT)			
	10.56 (FUTA)			
	70.40 (SUI)			
	Bal 543.24			

In addition, the job files keep track of the expenses as follows:

Lakeside			Mountainside		
Dr		Cr	Dr		Cr
(25 hrs @ $20)	500.00		(35 hrs @ $20)	700.00	
er taxes	61.25		er taxes	85.75	
Bal	561.25		Bal	785.75	

Riverside		
Dr		Cr
(28 hrs @ $20)	560.00	
er taxes	68.60	
Bal	628.60	

Employer taxes are allocated to the jobs as follows:

Lakeside:	25/88 × 215.60 =	$61.25
Mountainside:	35/88 × 215.60 =	85.75
Riverside:	28/88 × 215.60 =	68.60
		$215.60

Creating an Invoice for a Job

In Chapter 3, you learned how to create an invoice using the Create Invoices window. When invoices are prepared for specific jobs, the procedure will be similar but with one important difference. At the Customer:Job drop-down list, you will select the job rather than the customer.

On May 15, 2022, Kristin Raina is preparing an invoice for the Lakeside Hotel job. During the period from May 1, 2022, to May 15, 2022, Kristin Raina and Richard Henderson spent the following time on Design Services for each job:

Job	Kristin Raina Hours	Richard Henderson Hours
Lakeside Hotel	15	25
Mountainside Hotel	5	35
Riverside Hotel	20	28

The hours for Richard are the same hours you used to record the payroll, which allocates the payroll expenses to each job. QuickBooks now uses these hours to bill the customer for the job, which will record the revenue to each job.

Kristin Raina will invoice the client for the work done on the Lakeside Hotel project by her and her staff, Invoice No. 1011.

To create an invoice for a job:

1. At the main menu bar, click Customers and then click *Create Invoices*.
2. At the CUSTOMER:JOB drop-down list, click *Lakeside Hotel*. Although the Lakeside Hotel job is selected, the bill will be forwarded to Hamilton Hotels.
3. At the Billable Time/Costs window, choose the second option, *Exclude outstanding billable time and costs at this time?*, and then click OK.
4. At the TEMPLATE drop-down list, click *Intuit Service Invoice*.
5. At the *Date* field, choose the date *05/15/2022*, and at the *Invoice #* field, type 1011. Accept the terms shown.
6. At the ITEM drop-down list, click *Design Services - Owner*.
7. At the *QUANTITY* field, type 15.
8. Move to the second line of the *ITEM* field and then click *Design Services - Assistant* at the drop-down list.

HINT

Do not place a check mark next to the *Save this as a preference* option.

Recall that when you processed pay for the period, Richard Henderson, the design assistant, spent 25 hours on this project. Kristin Raina will invoice the customer for these hours at a rate of $40 per hour. *At present, this information is maintained manually.* Later in the chapter, we will use the QuickBooks Time-Tracking feature to incorporate this information into the company file.

9. At the *QUANTITY* field, type 25. See Figure 11–L.

FIGURE 11–L
Create Invoices
Window—Completed

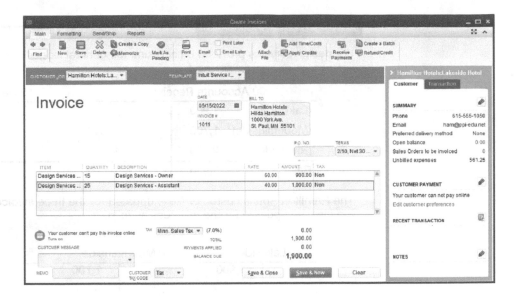

10. Confirm that the *Print Later* and *Email Later* boxes do not contain check marks and that the *Your customer can't pay this invoice online* command remains off.

11. If the information is correct, click Save & New.

Practice Exercise 11–3

May 15	Create Invoice No. 1012 for Mountainside Hotel for work done from May 1, 2022, to May 15, 2022, based on hours devoted to that job by Kristin Raina and Richard Henderson.
	QuickCheck: Total Invoice $1,700.
May 15	Create Invoice No. 1013 for Riverside Hotel for work done from May 1, 2022, to May 15, 2022, based on hours devoted to that job by Kristin Raina and Richard Henderson.
	QuickCheck: Total Invoice $2,320.

ACCOUNTING CONCEPT

For design services provided on account, the general ledger postings are as follows:

1200 Accounts Receivable				4010 Design Services	
(Lakeside)	1,900				1,900
(Mountainside)	1,700				1,700
(Riverside)	2,320				2,320
Bal	5,920			Bal	5,920

The Hamilton Hotels customer file is updated for the three invoices. In addition, the job files are updated for the revenues as follows:

Lakeside		Mountainside		Riverside	
	1,900		1,700		2,320

The Time-Tracking feature of QuickBooks allows you to track hours worked by both employees and owners. Tracking time means recording the hours worked by company personnel while identifying the customer or job for which the personnel spend their working hours. Many companies maintain manual timesheets or timecards to record employee time. The QuickBooks Time-Tracking feature automates that process and enables you to use the resulting data in a number of ways. You can use it to bill clients by job for work done by company personnel, allocate income and expenses to jobs, and process payroll by job.

You set up the Time-Tracking feature in the Preferences window. Once you have done that, the Weekly Timesheet window is available, and you can then input hourly and daily work activities for customers and/or jobs.

To set up the Time-Tracking feature:
1. At the main menu bar, click Edit and then click *Preferences.* The Preferences window appears.
2. In the left panel of the Preferences window, click the Time & Expenses icon. You may have to scroll down to find it.
3. Click the Company Preferences tab.
4. At the *Do you track time?* field, click the *Yes* option. Accept *Monday* at the *First Day of Work Week* field.
5. Insert a check mark in the box next to *Mark all time entries as billable,* if necessary. See Figure 11–M.

FIGURE 11–M
Preferences Window—
Time & Expenses—
Company Preferences
Tab

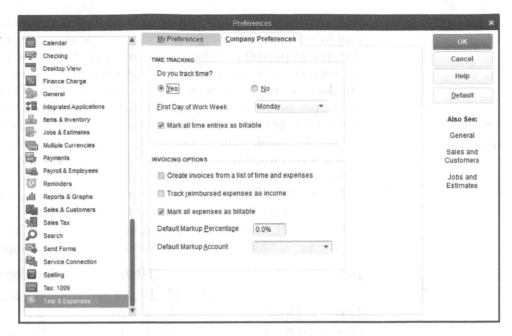

6. If the information is correct, click OK. Click OK at the Warning window, if necessary.

The Weekly Timesheet Window

In QuickBooks, you can use the Weekly Timesheet window to enter the daily work activities of employees and owners on a weekly basis. Each employee or owner indicates the number of hours worked for a customer or job. You enter the daily hours along with the customer or job name and the type of service that is performed in the Weekly Timesheet window. This information does not by itself generate a transaction or journal entry. Instead, when you wish to invoice a customer for the work and to prepare the payroll for employees, QuickBooks uses the information in the Weekly Timesheet to automatically complete fields at the Create Invoices, Enter Sales Receipts, and Pay Employee windows. The QuickBooks Weekly Timesheet window appears in Figure 11–N.

FIGURE 11–N
Weekly Timesheet
Window

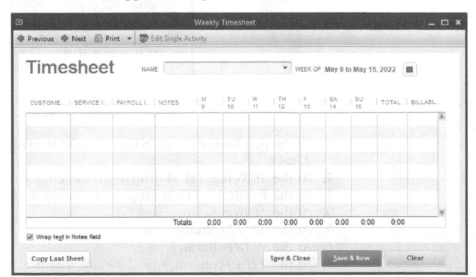

The Weekly Timesheet window allows you to select the name of the employee or owner doing the work, the type of service to be invoiced, the type of payroll item (salary or hourly pay), and the daily hours spent for each customer or job. Ideally, this information is entered daily by the employee or owner. However, in this chapter, you will enter the data for an entire pay period at one time. The *BILLABLE?* check box contains a check mark if the hours are billable to a customer. The hours for employees always default as billable. The hours for the owner always default as non-billable. When recording data for the owner, insert a check mark in the box to indicate that the hours are billable.

Kristin Raina has been tracking time manually. Beginning May 16, 2022, she wants to use the Time-Tracking feature and the Weekly Timesheet.

On May 31, 2022, Richard Henderson submitted the following time data for the period May 16, 2022, to May 31, 2022, for design services:

Job												Hours per Job for May by Date
	16	17	18	19	20	24	24	25	26	27	31	Totals
Lakeside Hotel	2	2	2	3			2	4	2	2	2	21
Mountainside Hotel	3	4	4	1		4	2	2	4	4		28
Riverside Hotel	3	2	2	4	8	4	4	2	2	2	6	39

To enter Time-Tracking data in the Weekly Timesheet:

1. At the main menu bar, click Employees and then click *Enter Time.*
2. At the Enter Time submenu, click *Use Weekly Timesheet.*
3. At the NAME drop-down list, click *Richard Henderson.* Click *Yes* at the Transfer Activities to Payroll message.
4. Click the Calendar icon next to the *WEEK OF* date range. The Set Date dialog box appears.
5. Choose *05/16/2022.* See Figure 11–O.

FIGURE 11–O
Set Date Dialog Box

6. At the first line of the CUSTOMER:JOB drop-down list, click *Lakeside Hotel.*
7. At the SERVICE ITEM drop-down list, click *Design Services - Assistant.*
8. At the PAYROLL ITEM drop-down list, click *Hourly Wages.*
9. At the *M 16* column, type 2.
10. At the *TU 17* column, type 2.
11. At the *W 18* column, type 2.
12. At the *TH 19* column, type 3. Notice that the *BILLABLE?* box correctly indicates billable. See Figure 11–P.

FIGURE 11–P Weekly Timesheet Window—Partially Completed

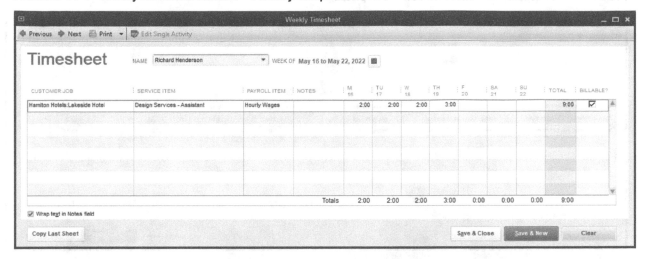

13. Move to the second line, and at the CUSTOMER:JOB drop-down list, click *Mountainside Hotel.*
14. At the SERVICE ITEM drop-down list, click *Design Services - Assistant.*
15. Accept the *Hourly Wages* default at the PAYROLL ITEM drop-down list.
16. Type the hours for the appropriate dates. See Figure 11–Q.

FIGURE 11–Q Weekly Timesheet Window—Partially Completed

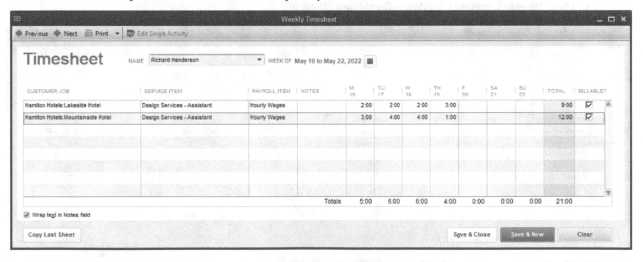

17. Move to the third line, and at the CUSTOMER:JOB drop-down list, click *Riverside Hotel.*
18. Complete the balance of the line by repeating steps similar to Steps 14 through 16. See Figure 11–R.

FIGURE 11–R Weekly Timesheet Window—Completed

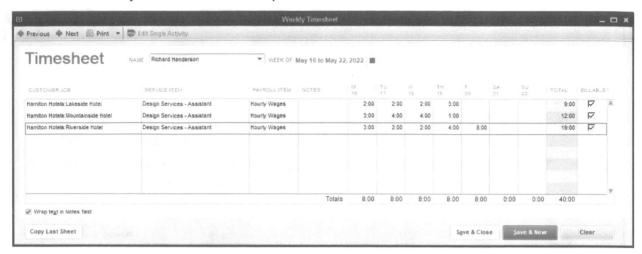

<table>
<tr><td style="vertical-align:top">HINT

It is not necessary to enter a zero where no work is indicated for a job.</td><td style="vertical-align:top">19. If the information is correct, click the Next arrow. You are moved to the next week for the same employee.

Note: If you click Save & New, you move to a new blank window.

20. Enter the information for May 23, 2022, through May 29, 2022, for all three jobs. See Figure 11–S.</td></tr>
</table>

FIGURE 11–S Weekly Timesheet Window—Completed (Week 2)

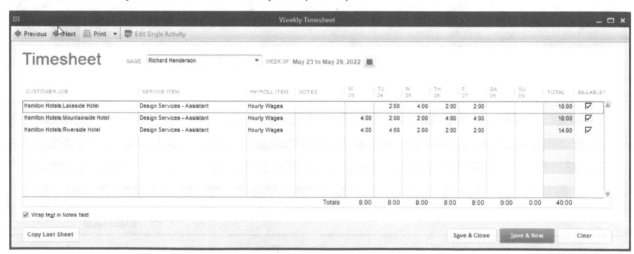

21. If the information is correct, click the Next arrow.

22. Enter the information for May 30, 2022 through June 5, 2022 for all three jobs. See Figure 11-T.

FIGURE 11–T Weekly Timesheet Window—Completed (Week 3)

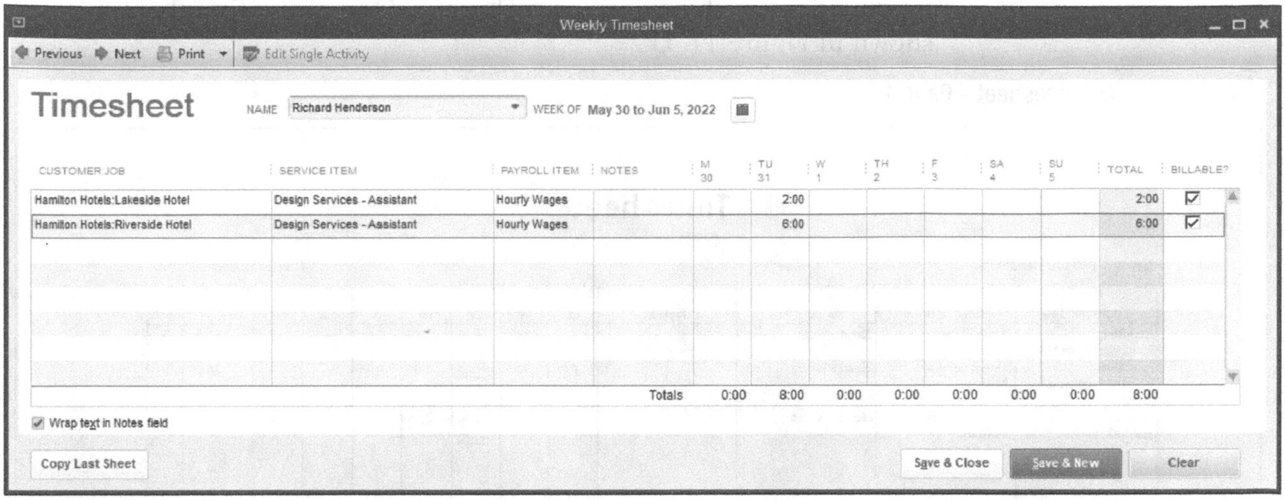

23. If the information is correct, click Save & Close.

The time records for Richard Henderson are now stored in the system for later use. When you bill Hamilton Hotels for the work done, Quick-Books will retrieve this information to assist in calculating billable time as part of creating an invoice for the work. In addition, this information will be part of the payroll processing and job allocation procedures. Since the time is billable, this information will be needed to create invoices for this customer.

Practice Exercise 11–4

May 31	On May 31, 2022, Kristin Raina submitted the following data for Design Services time spent on each project. Enter the information in the Weekly Timesheet window. Since the *Mark all time entries as billable* box is checked in the Time & Expenses icon at the Preferences window, the *BILLABLE?* box will automatically fill.

Job	\multicolumn{11}{c}{Hours per Job for May by Date}
	16	17	18	19	20	23	24	25	26	27	31	Totals
Lakeside Hotel	2	1	2				4				2	11
Mountainside Hotel		1			1	1	3	2	2			10
Riverside Hotel	1		2	1	1	2	1	3	4	1	3	19

To review the data entered in the Weekly Timesheet, you can print the timesheets:

1. If necessary, open the Weekly Timesheet window and then click the Print button. The Select Timesheets to Print dialog box appears.
2. At the *Dated* fields, choose *05/23/2022* through *05/29/2022* and then move to the next field. All the personnel for whom time data has been entered are listed and selected.
3. Click OK. The Print Timesheets dialog box appears.

4. At the Print Timesheets dialog box, click the Print button. A timesheet is printed for each person for each week. One of the timesheets is shown in Figure 11–U.

FIGURE 11–U Timesheet - Page 1

Timesheet

Printed on:

Name: Richard Henderson

May 23 to May 29, 2022

Customer:Job	Service Item	Payroll Item	Notes	M	Tu	W	Th	F	Sa	Su	Total	Bill*
Hamilton Hotels:Lakeside Hotel	Design Services - Assistant	Hourly Wages			2:00	4:00	2:00	2:00			10:00	B
Hamilton Hotels:Mountainside Hotel	Design Services - Assistant	Hourly Wages		4:00	2:00	2:00	4:00	4:00			16:00	B
Hamilton Hotels:Riverside Hotel	Design Services - Assistant	Hourly Wages		4:00	4:00	2:00	2:00	2:00			14:00	B
			Totals	8:00	8:00	8:00	8:00	8:00	0:00	0:00	40:00	

Signature _____

5. Close the Weekly Timesheet window.

Review the timesheets to make sure the hours are correct and the correct service item is listed for each employee. The data on these timesheets will flow through to the Pay Employees and Create Invoices windows. If there is an error, the payroll and invoices generated will be incorrect. Once you have recorded payroll and invoices, any subsequent changes you make to the timesheets will *not* flow through to correct them.

Activities

Paying an Employee and Allocating Payroll Expenses to a Job

On May 15, 2022, when Kristin Raina processed the pay for Richard Henderson, she manually entered the hours spent for each job at the Review Paycheck window. This was necessary because the QuickBooks Time-Tracking feature had not yet been set up. Now the Time-Tracking feature has been set up, and daily work activity has been entered at the Weekly Timesheet window. This information can now be used to assist in the payroll process and to allocate employee payroll costs to specific customer jobs.

On May 31, 2022, Kristin Raina will process the pay for Richard Henderson, who worked on all three jobs during the pay period.

To pay an employee and allocate payroll costs using Time-Tracking data:

1. At the main menu bar, click Employees and then click *Pay Employees*. The Enter Payroll Information window appears.
2. At the *PAY PERIOD ENDS* and *CHECK DATE* fields, choose *05/31/2022*. At the Pay Period Change message, click Yes to update the hours for the new pay period.
3. At the *BANK ACCOUNT* field, click *1020 Cash - Payroll* and confirm that the *First Check#* is *8*.
4. Select *Richard Henderson* by inserting a check mark next to the name.
5. If the information is correct, click the Open Paycheck Detail button. You move to the Preview Paycheck window. Notice that QuickBooks has automatically filled in the data for the hours worked on each job and for the amount paid. See Figure 11–V.

FIGURE 11–V
Preview Paycheck Window—Partially Completed

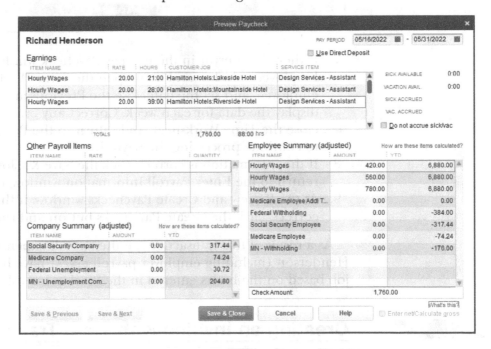

6. Complete the tax information with the following information and the procedures you learned in Chapter 9:

Company Taxes	*Social Security Company:*	109.12
	Medicare Company:	25.52
	Federal Unemployment:	10.56
	MN - Unemployment Company:	70.40
Employee Taxes	*Federal Withholding:*	132.00
	Social Security Employee:	109.12
	Medicare Employee:	25.52
	MN - Withholding:	61.00

QuickCheck: Check Amount $1,432.36.

See Figure 11–W.

FIGURE 11–W
Preview Paycheck
Window—Completed

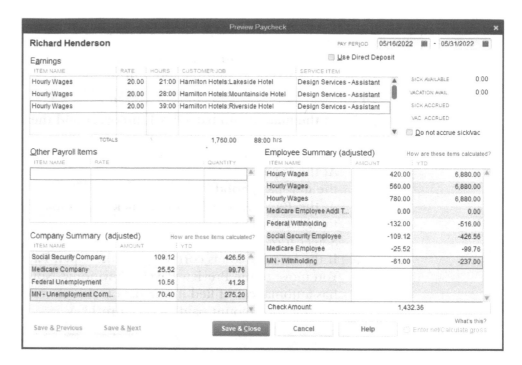

7. If there is an error in the Preview Paycheck window, close the Pay Employees window and then open the Time Worksheet, choose the employee, and set the date. Use the Previous and Next buttons to display the data for each week. Correct any errors, save the corrections, close the Time Worksheet, and return to the Pay Employees windows to continue processing the payroll.

8. If the information is correct, click the Save & Close button. When you return to the Enter Payroll Information window, click Continue.

9. At the Review and Create Paychecks window, if the information is correct, click the Create Paychecks button and then click Close.

As a result of this transaction, all the payroll expenses for Richard Henderson (including employer payroll taxes) have been allocated to each job based on the hours entered in the Weekly Timesheet window.

Activities

Creating an Invoice with Time Tracking

You have entered the daily work information for Kristin Raina and Richard Henderson at the Weekly Timesheet window. When you processed the payroll for Richard Henderson, QuickBooks used the information from the Weekly Timesheet window to total the hours spent on each job and to allocate the payroll expense accordingly. QuickBooks also uses the timesheet data to bill customers for services rendered and to allocate revenue earned to each job.

On May 31, 2022, Kristin Raina will bill Hamilton Hotels for work done by company personnel from May 16, 2022, to May 31, 2022, for each job at the rates established in the Item List for Design Services, Invoice Nos. 1014, 1015, and 1016.

To create an invoice using Time-Tracking data:

1. At the main menu bar, click Customers and then click *Create Invoices.*
2. At the *Date* field, choose *05/31/2022.*
3. Confirm that the invoice number is 1014 and that *Intuit Service Invoice* is selected at the Template drop-down list.
4. At the CUSTOMER:JOB drop-down list, click *Lakeside Hotel.* The Billable Time/Costs window appears. See Figure 11–X.

FIGURE 11–X
Billable Time/Costs
Window

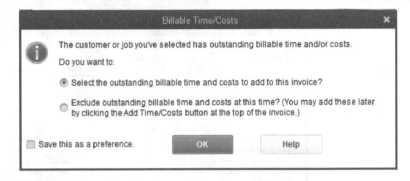

5. At the Billable Time/Costs window, accept the first option: *Select the outstanding billable time and costs to add to this invoice?*
6. Click OK. The Choose Billable Time and Costs window appears with the time information for Richard Henderson and Kristin Raina entered on the Time tab. See Figure 11–Y.

FIGURE 11–Y
Choose Billable Time and
Costs Window—Time Tab

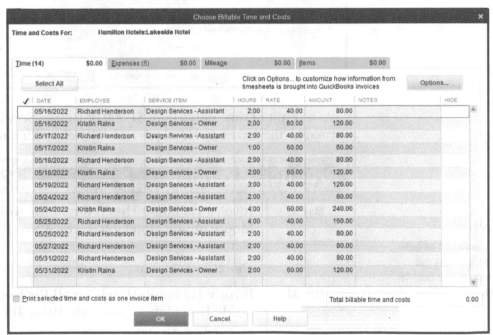

HINT
Scroll down to view all
the daily activity.

7. Click the Select All button. A check mark is inserted next to each item listed.

8. Click OK and then click OK at the Invoicing for Vendor Time window. You are returned to the Create Invoices window with all the billable hours entered at the appropriate rates and times. See Figure 11–Z.
9. If the information is correct, click Save & New.

FIGURE 11–Z
Create Invoices
Window—Completed

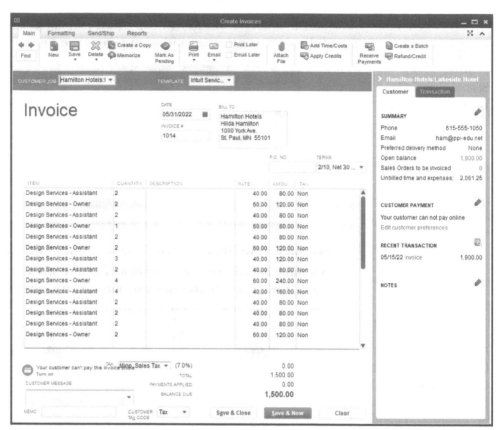

As a result of this transaction, $1,500 of Design Services revenue has been earned by the Lakeside Hotel job and will be credited to that job file.

Practice Exercise 11–5

May 31	Invoice Hamilton Hotels for all the work done on the Mountainside Hotel job. Invoice No. 1015. Terms 2/10, Net 30. *QuickCheck:* $1,720
May 31	Invoice Hamilton Hotels for all the work done on the Riverside Hotel job. Invoice No. 1016. Terms 2/10, Net 30. *QuickCheck:* $2,700

HINT
Use the Select All button on the Time tab to allocate all the time to a job.

Creating a Customer Statement

As part of the management of accounts receivable, it is often advisable to forward a statement of activity to a customer. The statement will list all the activity for that customer's account, such as sales on account or sales for cash, collections of receivables, and open balances, if any. This will act as a reminder to the customer if there is a balance due, especially if the balance is more than 30 days old. Often, the presentation of a statement will result in the payment of open invoices.

In QuickBooks, customer statements are prepared using the Create Statements window accessed from the Customers menu. Statements can be prepared for specific periods and for selected customers. Alternatively, statements can be prepared for all customers at one time, whether or not they have an open balance.

On May 31, 2022, Kristin Raina wishes to forward a statement to Hamilton Hotels, due to the increased activity with that customer during May.

To create a customer statement:

1. At the main menu bar, click Customers and then click *Create Statements*.
2. At the *Statement Date* field, choose *05/31/2022*.
3. At the *Statement Period From* and *To* fields, choose *02/01/2022* and *05/31/2022*.
4. In the SELECT CUSTOMERS section, click the *One Customer* option, and then at the drop-down list, click *Hamilton Hotels*. See Figure 11–AA.

**FIGURE 11–AA
Create Statements
Window—Hamilton
Hotels Selected**

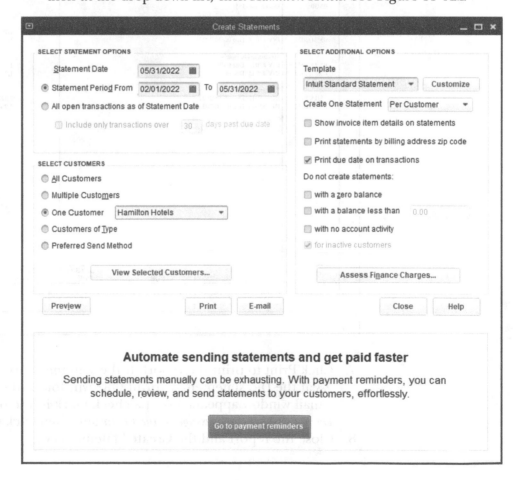

5. In the SELECT ADDITIONAL OPTIONS section, confirm that *Intuit Standard Statement* is selected at the Template drop-down list and the *Print due date on transactions* box is checked.

6. If the information is correct, click the Preview button. The statement displays all the activity for this customer along with an aging of open receivables. See Figure 11–BB.

Statement

EX11 [Student Name] Kristin Raina Interior Designs
25 NE Johnson Street
Minneapolis, MN 53402

Date
5/31/2022

To:

Hamilton Hotels
Hilda Hamilton
1000 York Ave.
St. Paul, MN 55101

	Amount Due	Amount Enc.
	$11,840.00	

Date	Transaction	Amount	Balance
01/31/2022	Balance forward		0.00
03/27/2022	INV #1010. Due 04/26/2022.	1,798.00	1,798.00
03/30/2022	PMT #6555.	-1,762.04	35.96
03/30/2022	Discount #6555.	-35.96	0.00
	Lakeside Hotel-		
05/15/2022	INV #1011. Due 06/14/2022.	1,900.00	1,900.00
05/31/2022	INV #1014. Due 06/30/2022.	1,500.00	3,400.00
	Mountainside Hotel-		
05/15/2022	INV #1012. Due 06/14/2022.	1,700.00	5,100.00
05/31/2022	INV #1015. Due 06/30/2022.	1,720.00	6,820.00
	Riverside Hotel-		
05/15/2022	INV #1013. Due 06/14/2022.	2,320.00	9,140.00
05/31/2022	INV #1016. Due 06/30/2022.	2,700.00	11,840.00

CURRENT	1-30 DAYS PAST DUE	31-60 DAYS PAST DUE	61-90 DAYS PAST DUE	OVER 90 DAYS PAST DUE	Amount Due
11,840.00	0.00	0.00	0.00	0.00	$11,840.00

7. Click Print to print the report. If the statement printed correctly, click *Yes* at the Did statement(s) print OK? window. If the Sending forms by e-mail window appears, insert a check mark in the box to the left of *Do not display this message in the future* and then click OK.

8. Close the report and the Create Statements window.

Job and Time-Tracking Reports, Accounting Reports, and Financial Statements

Both the Job and Time-Tracking features produce reports that companies find useful in measuring job profit and managing employee time. The job reports focus on profitability, while the Time-Tracking reports analyze time spent by each person or for each job.

Job and Time-Tracking Reports

Several reports can be accessed from the Reports menu that analyze information related to jobs. Two of these reports are the *Profit & Loss by Job* report and the *Time by Job Summary* report.

Profit & Loss by Job Report

The *Profit & Loss by Job* report provides information on the profitability of customer and job activity. The report shows the type of revenue earned and the expenses incurred for each job for a specified period of time.

To view and print the *Profit & Loss by Job* report:

1. At the main menu bar, click Reports and then click *Jobs, Time & Mileage*.
2. At the Jobs, Time & Mileage submenu, click *Profit & Loss by Job*.
3. At the *From* and *To* fields, choose *05/01/2022* and *05/31/2022* and then click Refresh. The report for the three jobs is displayed.
4. Print the report. See Figure 11–CC.

FIGURE 11–CC Profit & Loss by Job Report

EX11 [Your Name] Kristin Raina Interior Designs
Profit & Loss by Job
May 2022

Accrual Basis

	Lakeside Hotel (Hamilton Hotels)	Mountainside Hotel (Hamilton Hotels)	Riverside Hotel (Hamilton Hotels)	Total Hamilton Hotels	TOTAL
Ordinary Income/Expense					
Income					
4010 · Design Services	3,400.00	3,420.00	5,020.00	11,840.00	11,840.00
Total Income	3,400.00	3,420.00	5,020.00	11,840.00	11,840.00
Gross Profit	3,400.00	3,420.00	5,020.00	11,840.00	11,840.00
Expense					
6560 · Payroll Expenses					
6565 · Salaries and Wages Expense	920.00	1,260.00	1,340.00	3,520.00	3,520.00
6610 · Social Sec/Medicare Tax Expense	70.38	96.39	102.51	269.28	269.28
6625 · FUTA Expense	5.52	7.56	8.04	21.12	21.12
6630 · SUI Expense	36.80	50.40	53.60	140.80	140.80
Total 6560 · Payroll Expenses	1,032.70	1,414.35	1,504.15	3,951.20	3,951.20
Total Expense	1,032.70	1,414.35	1,504.15	3,951.20	3,951.20
Net Ordinary Income	2,367.30	2,005.65	3,515.85	7,888.80	7,888.80
Net Income	2,367.30	2,005.65	3,515.85	7,888.80	7,888.80

5. Close the report.

Time by Job Summary Report

The *Time by Job Summary* report lists hours spent by job for a specified period of time. The report lists the job and the time each employee devoted to each job.

To view and print the *Time by Job Summary* report:
1. At the main menu bar, click Reports and then click *Jobs, Time & Mileage*.
2. At the Jobs, Time & Mileage submenu, click *Time by Job Summary*.
3. At the *From* and *To* fields, choose *05/01/2022* and *05/31/2022* and then click Refresh. The report is displayed for the period. See Figure 11–DD.

FIGURE 11–DD Time by Job Summary Report

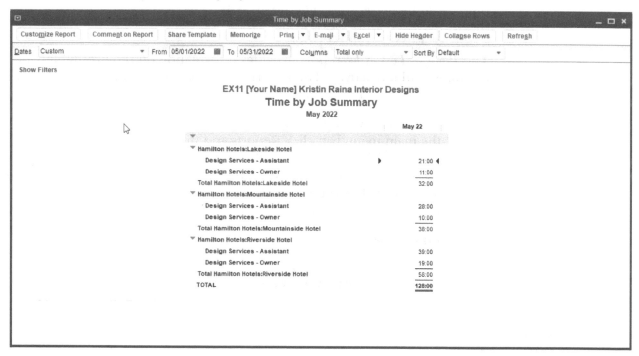

4. Print the report.
5. Close the report.

Accounting Reports and Financial Statements

At the end of the month, the *Journal* report, *Profit & Loss Standard* report, and *Balance Sheet Standard* report should be viewed and printed. The *Journal* report is displayed in Figure 11–EE, the *Profit & Loss Standard* report is displayed in Figure 11–FF, and the *Balance Sheet Standard* report is displayed in Figure 11–GG.

FIGURE 11-EE Journal Report May 1, 2022–May 31, 2022

EX11 [Your Name] Kristin Raina Interior Designs
Journal
May 2022

Trans #	Type	Date	Num	Name	Memo	Account	Debit	Credit
65	Credit Card ...	05/01/2022	47887	Atlantis Business Tr...		2015 · American Travel Card		600.00
				Atlantis Business Tr...		6475 · Travel Expenses	600.00	
							600.00	600.00
66	Credit Card ...	05/17/2022	84441	Atlantis Business Tr...		2015 · American Travel Card		350.00
				Atlantis Business Tr...		6475 · Travel Expenses	350.00	
							350.00	350.00
67	Check	05/22/2022	12	American Travel Card		1010 · Cash - Operating		600.00
				American Travel Card		2015 · American Travel Card	600.00	
							600.00	600.00
68	Check	05/31/2022	13	American Travel Card		1010 · Cash - Operating		350.00
				American Travel Card		2015 · American Travel Card	350.00	
							350.00	350.00
69	Paycheck	05/15/2022	7	Richard Henderson		1020 · Cash - Payroll		1,432.36
				-MULTIPLE-		6565 · Salaries and Wages Expense	1,760.00	
				Richard Henderson		2100 · Payroll Liabilities	0.00	
				Richard Henderson		2115 · FIT Payable		132.00
				-MULTIPLE-		6610 · Social Sec/Medicare Tax Expense	134.64	
				Richard Henderson		2110 · Social Sec/Medicare Tax Payable		269.28
				-MULTIPLE-		6625 · FUTA Expense	10.56	
				Richard Henderson		2125 · FUTA Payable		10.56
				Richard Henderson		2120 · SIT Payable		61.00
				-MULTIPLE-		6630 · SUI Expense	70.40	
				Richard Henderson		2130 · SUI Payable		70.40
							1,975.60	1,975.60
70	Invoice	05/15/2022	1011	Hamilton Hotels:Lak...		1200 · Accounts Receivable	1,900.00	
				Hamilton Hotels:Lak...	-MULTIPLE-	4010 · Design Services		1,900.00
				Minn. Dept. of Reve...	Sales Tax	2200 · Sales Tax Payable	0.00	
							1,900.00	1,900.00
71	Invoice	05/15/2022	1012	Hamilton Hotels:Mo...		1200 · Accounts Receivable	1,700.00	
				Hamilton Hotels:Mo...	-MULTIPLE-	4010 · Design Services		1,700.00
				Minn. Dept. of Reve...	Sales Tax	2200 · Sales Tax Payable	0.00	
							1,700.00	1,700.00
72	Invoice	05/15/2022	1013	Hamilton Hotels:Riv...		1200 · Accounts Receivable	2,320.00	
				Hamilton Hotels:Riv...	-MULTIPLE-	4010 · Design Services		2,320.00
				Minn. Dept. of Reve...	Sales Tax	2200 · Sales Tax Payable	0.00	
							2,320.00	2,320.00
73	Paycheck	05/31/2022		Richard Henderson		1020 · Cash - Payroll		1,432.36
				-MULTIPLE-		6565 · Salaries and Wages Expense	1,760.00	
				Richard Henderson		2100 · Payroll Liabilities	0.00	
				Richard Henderson		2115 · FIT Payable		132.00
				-MULTIPLE-		6610 · Social Sec/Medicare Tax Expense	134.64	
				Richard Henderson		2110 · Social Sec/Medicare Tax Payable		269.28
				-MULTIPLE-		6625 · FUTA Expense	10.56	
				Richard Henderson		2125 · FUTA Payable		10.56
				Richard Henderson		2120 · SIT Payable		61.00
				-MULTIPLE-		6630 · SUI Expense	70.40	
				Richard Henderson		2130 · SUI Payable		70.40
							1,975.60	1,975.60
74	Invoice	05/31/2022	1014	Hamilton Hotels:Lak...		1200 · Accounts Receivable	1,500.00	
				Hamilton Hotels:Lak...		4010 · Design Services		1,500.00
				Minn. Dept. of Reve...	Sales Tax	2200 · Sales Tax Payable	0.00	
							1,500.00	1,500.00
75	Invoice	05/31/2022	1015	Hamilton Hotels:Mo...		1200 · Accounts Receivable	1,720.00	
				Hamilton Hotels:Mo...		4010 · Design Services		1,720.00
				Minn. Dept. of Reve...	Sales Tax	2200 · Sales Tax Payable	0.00	
							1,720.00	1,720.00
76	Invoice	05/31/2022	1016	Hamilton Hotels:Riv...		1200 · Accounts Receivable	2,700.00	
				Hamilton Hotels:Riv...		4010 · Design Services		2,700.00
				Minn. Dept. of Reve...	Sales Tax	2200 · Sales Tax Payable	0.00	
							2,700.00	2,700.00
TOTAL							17,691.20	17,691.20

EX11 [Your Name] Kristin Raina Interior Designs
Profit & Loss
Accrual Basis

January through May 2022

	Jan - May 22
Ordinary Income/Expense	
Income	
4010 · Design Services	16,820.00
4020 · Decorating Services	3,400.00
4060 · Sale of Carpets	2,400.00
4065 · Sale of Draperies	1,000.00
4070 · Sale of Lamps	1,200.00
4075 · Sale of Mirrors	900.00
4100 · Sales Discounts	-84.62
Total Income	25,635.38
Cost of Goods Sold	
5060 · Cost of Carpets Sold	1,200.00
5065 · Cost of Draperies Sold	500.00
5070 · Cost of Lamps Sold	600.00
5075 · Cost of Mirrors Sold	450.00
5900 · Inventory Adjustment	150.00
Total COGS	2,900.00
Gross Profit	22,735.38
Expense	
6020 · Accounting Expense	300.00
6050 · Advertising Expense	100.00
6100 · Bank Service Charges	60.00
6175 · Deprec. Exp., Furniture	100.00
6185 · Deprec. Exp., Computers	60.00
6200 · Insurance Expense	200.00
6300 · Janitorial Expenses	125.00
6325 · Office Supplies Expense	150.00
6400 · Rent Expense	800.00
6450 · Telephone Expense	275.00
6475 · Travel Expenses	950.00
6500 · Utilities Expense	450.00
6560 · Payroll Expenses	
6565 · Salaries and Wages Expense	8,880.00
6610 · Social Sec/Medicare Tax Expense	679.32
6625 · FUTA Expense	53.28
6630 · SUI Expense	355.20
Total 6560 · Payroll Expenses	9,967.80
Total Expense	13,537.80
Net Ordinary Income	9,197.58
Other Income/Expense	
Other Income	
6900 · Interest Income	10.00
Total Other Income	10.00
Other Expense	
7000 · Interest Expense	50.00
Total Other Expense	50.00
Net Other Income	-40.00
Net Income	9,157.58

FIGURE 11-GG Balance Sheet Standard Report May 31, 2022

EX11 [Your Name] Kristin Raina Interior Designs
Balance Sheet
As of May 31, 2022

Accrual Basis

	May 31, 22
ASSETS	
Current Assets	
Checking/Savings	
1010 · Cash - Operating	24,780.38
1020 · Cash - Payroll	5,593.68
1050 · Cash - Money Market	10,000.00
Total Checking/Savings	40,374.06
Accounts Receivable	
1200 · Accounts Receivable	13,980.00
Total Accounts Receivable	13,980.00
Other Current Assets	
1260 · Inventory of Carpets	800.00
1265 · Inventory of Draperies	1,000.00
1270 · Inventory of Lamps	1,000.00
1275 · Inventory of Mirrors	900.00
1300 · Design Supplies	200.00
1305 · Office Supplies	250.00
1410 · Prepaid Advertising	500.00
1420 · Prepaid Insurance	2,200.00
Total Other Current Assets	6,850.00
Total Current Assets	61,204.06
Fixed Assets	
1700 · Furniture	
1725 · Furniture, Cost	12,000.00
1750 · Accum. Dep., Furniture	-100.00
Total 1700 · Furniture	11,900.00
1800 · Computers	
1825 · Computers, Cost	3,600.00
1850 · Accum. Dep., Computers	-60.00
Total 1800 · Computers	3,540.00
Total Fixed Assets	15,440.00
TOTAL ASSETS	76,644.06
LIABILITIES & EQUITY	
Liabilities	
Current Liabilities	
Accounts Payable	
2010 · Accounts Payable	9,750.00
Total Accounts Payable	9,750.00
Other Current Liabilities	
2020 · Notes Payable	7,000.00
2030 · Interest Payable	50.00
2100 · Payroll Liabilities	
2110 · Social Sec/Medicare Tax Payable	538.56
2115 · FIT Payable	264.00
2120 · SIT Payable	122.00
2125 · FUTA Payable	21.12
2130 · SUI Payable	140.80
Total 2100 · Payroll Liabilities	1,086.48
Total Other Current Liabilities	8,136.48
Total Current Liabilities	17,886.48
Total Liabilities	17,886.48
Equity	
3010 · Kristin Raina, Capital	50,000.00
3020 · Kristin Raina, Drawings	-400.00
Net Income	9,157.58
Total Equity	58,757.58
TOTAL LIABILITIES & EQUITY	76,644.06

Reconciliation of Data to Reports

As you have seen in this chapter, income and expenses can be allocated to jobs either by entering data directly into the Create Invoices window and Payroll window or by activating the Time-Tracking feature and using the Weekly Timesheet. When data is entered manually or into the Weekly Timesheet, QuickBooks operates behind the scenes to calculate the amounts per job that appear in the Create Invoice window, Payroll windows, Job files, and Job reports. To better understand some of the behind-the-scenes computations, see Figure 11–HH, which displays how the amounts are calculated by QuickBooks.

FIGURE 11–HH Reconciliation of Data to Reports

RECONCILIATION OF DATA TO REPORTS

		Lakeside Hotel		Mountainside Hotel		Riverside Hotel		Total
Design Services:								
May 15, 2022	Kristin Raina	(15 x $60) =	$900	(5 x $60) =	$300	(20 x $60) =	$1,200	$2,400
	Richard Henderson	(25 x $40) =	1,000	(35 x $40) =	1,400	(28 x $40) =	1,120	3,520
			$1,900		$1,700		$2,320	$5,920
May 31, 2022	Kristin Raina	(11 x $60) =	$660	(10 x $60) =	$600	(19 x $60) =	$1,140	$2,400
	Richard Henderson	(21 x $40) =	840	(28 x $40) =	1,120	(39 x $40) =	1,560	3,520
			$1,500		$1,720		$2,700	$5,920
	Total Income		*$3,400*		*$3,420*		*$5,020*	*$11,840*
Payroll Expenses:								
May 15, 2022	Salaries Expense	(25 x $20) =	500.00	(35 x $20) =	700.00	(28 x $20) =	560.00	$1,760.00
	PR Tax Expense		$61.25		85.75		68.60	215.60
			561.25		785.75		628.60	$1,975.60
May 31, 2022	Salaries Expense	(21 x $20) =	420.00	(28 x $20) =	560.00	(39 x $20) =	780.00	$1,760.00
	PR Tax Expense		51.45		68.60		95.55	215.60
			471.45		628.60		875.55	$1,975.60
	Total Expenses		*1,032.70*		*1,414.35*		*1,504.15*	*3,951.20*
	Net Income		*$2,367.30*		*$2,005.65*		*$3,515.85*	*$7,888.80*

Allocation of Payroll Tax Expense:

	Company Payroll Tax Expense:		Allocation of payroll tax expense based on hours to each job:			
May 15, 2022	Social Security Company	$109.12				
	Medicare Company	25.52	Lakeside Hotel	(25 ÷ 88) x	$215.60 =	$61.25
	Federal Unemployment	10.56	Mountainside Hotel	(35 ÷ 88) x	$215.60 =	85.75
	MN - Unemployment Company	70.40	Riverside Hotel	(28 ÷ 88) x	$215.60 =	68.60
		$215.60	Total			$215.60
May 31, 2022	Social Security Company	$109.12				
	Medicare Company	25.52	Lakeside Hotel	(21 ÷ 88) x	$215.60 =	$51.45
	Federal Unemployment	10.56	Mountainside Hotel	(28 ÷ 88) x	$215.60 =	$68.60
	MN - Unemployment Company	70.40	Riverside Hotel	(39 ÷ 88) x	$215.60 =	$95.55
		$215.60	Total			$215.60

Exiting QuickBooks

Upon completing this session, make a backup copy of your practice exercise company file to a removable storage device using the Back Up command. Be sure to change the *Save in* field to the removable storage device and then carefully type the correct file name. Close the company file and then exit QuickBooks.

Chapter Review and Assessment

Procedure Review

To add a job:

1. At the main menu bar, click Customers and then click *Customer Center.*
2. At the Customer Center window, select (highlight) the customer with which the job is associated, but do not open the file.
3. Click the New Customer & Job button.
4. At the New Customer & Job menu, click *Add Job.* The New Job window opens. The New Job window carries over information from the customer's file.
5. At the *JOB NAME* field, type the job name.
6. On the Job Info tab, type the appropriate data in the following fields:

   JOB DESCRIPTION
   JOB STATUS
   START DATE
   PROJECTED END DATE

7. If the information is correct, click OK.

To allocate payroll expenses to a job (without using the Time-Tracking feature):

1. At the main menu bar, click Employees and then click *Pay Employees.* Click *No* at the QuickBooks Payroll Services message, if necessary. The Enter Payroll Information window appears.
2. Enter the appropriate dates in the *PAY PERIOD ENDS* and *CHECK DATE* fields.
3. At the *BANK ACCOUNT* field, click the appropriate bank account.
4. Select the appropriate employee by inserting a check mark next to the name.
5. Click the Open Paycheck Detail button. You move to the Preview Paycheck window.
6. Confirm that the correct payroll item appears.
7. At the first line of the *HOURS* field, type the hours for the first job.
8. At the CUSTOMER:JOB drop-down list, click the job name.
9. Move to the second line of the *ITEM NAME* field and then click the payroll item at the drop-down list.
10. At the *HOURS* field, type the hours for the second job.
11. At the CUSTOMER:JOB drop-down list, click the second job name.
12. Repeat this procedure for all remaining jobs.
13. Complete the remainder of the window in the manner explained in Chapter 9 for company taxes and employee taxes.
14. If the information is correct, click the Save & Close button. You are returned to the Enter Payroll Information window.
15. Click Continue. The Review and Create Paychecks window appears, with the taxes columns completed.
16. If the information is correct, click the Create Paychecks button.
17. At the Confirmation and Next Steps window, click Close.

To create an invoice for a job (without using the Time-Tracking feature):
1. At the main menu bar, click Customers and then click *Create Invoices*.
2. At the CUSTOMER:JOB drop-down list, click the job name.
3. At the Billable Time/Costs window, choose *Exclude outstanding billable time and costs at this time?* and then click OK.
4. At the TEMPLATE drop-down list, click *Intuit Service Invoice*.
5. Enter the date and invoice number and accept the terms.
6. Click the appropriate items at the ITEM drop-down list.
7. Enter the quantity. Confirm that the *Print Later* and *Email Later* boxes do not contain check marks and the *Your customer can't pay this invoice online* command remains off.
8. Click the Save & Close button.

To set up the Time-Tracking feature:
1. At the main menu bar, click Edit and then click *Preferences*. The Preferences window appears.
2. In the left panel of the Preferences window, click the Time & Expenses icon.
3. Click the Company Preferences tab.
4. At the *Do you track time?* field, click the *Yes* option. Accept *Monday* as the first day of the work week.
5. Insert a check mark in the *Mark all time entries as billable* box.
6. If the information is correct, click OK.

To enter Time-Tracking data:
1. At the main menu bar, click Employees and then click *Enter Time*.
2. At the Enter Time submenu, click *Use Weekly Timesheet*.
3. At the NAME drop-down list, click the employee name and then click *Yes* at the Transfer Activities to Payroll message.
4. Click the Calendar icon. The Set Date dialog box appears.
5. Choose the start date.
6. Click the date on the calendar to return to the Weekly Timesheet window.
7. At the first line of the CUSTOMER:JOB drop-down list, click the job name.
8. At the SERVICE ITEM drop-down list, click the service item.
9. At the PAYROLL ITEM drop-down list, click the payroll item for this employee.
10. At the column for the first day of work, type the hours for that job.
11. Continue entering the hours for that job for the period of time displayed.
12. Confirm that the *BILLABLE?* box is checked.
13. Move to the second line, and at the CUSTOMER:JOB drop-down list, click the next job.
14. Repeat the process for all successive jobs for this time period.
15. If the information is correct, click the Next arrow.
16. Repeat the process for the employee for the next week.
17. If this is the final period of work, click the Save & Close button.

To pay an employee and allocate time using Time-Tracking data:

1. At the main menu bar, click Employees and then click *Pay Employees*. The Enter Payroll Information window appears.
2. Enter the appropriate dates in the *PAY PERIOD ENDS* and *CHECK DATE* fields. At the Pay Period Change message, click Yes to update the hours for the new pay period.
3. At the *BANK ACCOUNT* field, click the appropriate bank account.
4. Select the appropriate employee by inserting a check mark next to the name.
5. Click the Open Paycheck Detail button. You move to the Preview Paycheck window. Notice that the data for the hours worked on each job and for the pay amount have been filled automatically.
6. Complete the tax information in the usual manner.
7. If the information is correct, click the Save & Close button. You are returned to the Enter Payroll Information window.
8. Click Continue. The Review and Create Paychecks window appears with the taxes columns completed.
9. If the information is correct, click the Create Paychecks button.
10. At the Confirmation and Next Steps window, click Close.

To create an invoice using Time-Tracking data:

1. At the main menu bar, click Customers and then click *Create Invoices*.
2. Select the date, invoice number, and template.
3. At the CUSTOMER:JOB drop-down list, click the job name.
4. At the Billable Time/Costs window, choose the first option: *Select the outstanding billable time and costs to add to this invoice?*
5. Click OK. The Choose Billable Time and Costs window appears, and the hours billed by all the company employees for the job are displayed.
6. Click the Select All button. A check mark is inserted next to each item listed.
7. Click OK and then click OK at the message. You are returned to the Create Invoices window with all the billable hours entered at the appropriate rate and time.
8. Click the Save & Close button.

To create a customer statement:

1. At the main menu bar, click Customers and then click *Create Statements*.
2. At the *Statement Date* field, choose the statement date.
3. At the *Statement Period From* and *To* fields, enter the dates for the period of time covered by the statement.
4. In the SELECT CUSTOMERS section, click the option for the statement you wish to create.
5. Confirm that the *Intuit Standard Statement* is selected at the Template drop-down list and the *Print due date on transactions* box is checked.
6. If the information is correct, click the Preview button. The statement displays all the activity for this customer along with an aging of open receivables.
7. Click Print to print the report. If the statement printed OK, click *Yes* at the Did statement(s) print OK? window.
8. Close the report and the Create Statements window.

To view and print the *Profit & Loss by Job* report:
1. At the main menu bar, click Reports and then click *Jobs, Time & Mileage*.
2. At the Jobs, Time & Mileage submenu, click *Profit & Loss by Job*.
3. Enter the report dates.
4. Print the report and then close it.

To view and print the *Time by Job Summary* report:
1. At the main menu bar, click Reports and then click *Jobs, Time & Mileage*.
2. At the Jobs, Time & Mileage submenu, click *Time by Job Summary*.
3. Enter the dates of the report.
4. Print the report and then close it.

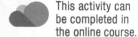
This activity can be completed in the online course.

Key Concepts

Select the letter of the item that best matches each definition.

a. Job
b. Time Tracking
c. Customer Center
d. Job revenue
e. Time tab

f. Weekly Timesheet window
g. Job profit
h. *Profit & Loss by Job* report
i. *Time by Job Summary* report
j. Billable time

_____ 1. Tab at the Choose Billable Time and Costs window that lists billable hours worked for a specific job.
_____ 2. The center that contains a file for each customer job.
_____ 3. Report that displays the revenues, expenses, and net profit for each job for a specified period of time.
_____ 4. The time worked by company personnel that can be billed to customers.
_____ 5. The process by which a company maintains records of time worked by employees for various customers or jobs.
_____ 6. Job revenue less job expenses.
_____ 7. The report that displays employee time spent on each job.
_____ 8. It can be a project, assignment, or any identifiable segment of work for a customer.
_____ 9. The window where time worked by company personnel is entered.
_____ 10. The income earned for a particular job.

This activity can be completed in the online course.

Procedure Check

1. Your company is a construction contractor and working on several projects for one customer. How would you use QuickBooks to determine which jobs are making money?
2. Describe the steps to add a job to the Customer Center.
3. Your company wishes to keep a record of the time worked by company personnel to bill customers for services provided. How would you use QuickBooks to track time information?

4. Upper management requests a report showing the profit or loss for each project on which the company is currently working. How would you use QuickBooks to obtain this information?
5. Explain to your company's new accounts receivable clerk how QuickBooks is used to inform customers of their account activity.
6. Explain why it is so important for a service business to keep accurate records of the time employees and others spend for each job or customer.

Case Problems

Reports created for these Case Problems can be exported to Excel and uploaded in the online course to be automatically graded.

Demonstrate your knowledge of the QuickBooks features discussed in this chapter by completing the following case problems.

Case Problem 11–1

In July, the fourth month of business for Lynn's Music Studio, one of Lynn Garcia's clients, Highland School, has asked her to organize, coordinate, and supervise an eight-week intensive music program. All the classes will be held at the school, but they will be offered to three levels of students: beginner, intermediate, and progressive. Highland School needs a separate invoice each month for each level of students, so Lynn has decided that it is necessary to track income and expenses for each level. To aid in this process, she has decided to activate the Time-Tracking feature of QuickBooks so that the time spent by her and one of her employees, Michelle Auletta, can be tracked and allocated to each level of student and then billed to the client, Highland School. Lynn has added two service items to the Item List for Michelle Auletta's billable time as an assistant. The company file includes information for Lynn's Music Studio as of July 1, 2022.

1. Open the company file **CH11 Lynn's Music Studio.QBW**.
2. At the QuickBooks Desktop Login window, in the *Password* text box, type Student1 and then click OK.
3. Make a backup copy of the company file and name it **LMS11 *[Your Name]* Lynn's Music Studio**.
4. Restore the backup copy of the company file. In both the Open Backup Copy and Save Company File as dialog boxes, use the file name **LMS11 *[Your Name]* Lynn's Music Studio** and enter the password.
5. Change the company name to **LMS11 *[Your Name]* Lynn's Music Studio**.
6. Set up the Time-Tracking feature for Lynn's Music Studio. Monday is the first day of the work week.
7. Add the following jobs to the Customer Center:

CUSTOMER:	Highland School
JOB NAME:	Beginner Level
JOB DESCRIPTION:	Beginner Level Summer Program
JOB STATUS:	Awarded
START DATE:	07/01/2022
PROJECTED END DATE:	08/31/2022

JOB NAME:	Intermediate Level
JOB DESCRIPTION:	Intermediate Level Summer Program
JOB STATUS:	Awarded
START DATE:	07/01/2022
PROJECTED END DATE:	08/31/2022

JOB NAME:	Progressive Level
JOB DESCRIPTION:	Progressive Level Summer Program
JOB STATUS:	Awarded
START DATE:	07/01/2022
PROJECTED END DATE:	08/31/2022

8. Enter the following hours worked for Highland School in the Weekly Timesheet window. (Remember to click *Yes* at the Transfer Activities to Payroll message.)

Michelle Auletta: Piano Lessons—Assistant

Job	Hours per Job for July by Date									
	5	6	7	8	11	12	13	14	15	Totals
Beginner Level	2	2	2	2	2	2	2	2	2	18
Intermediate Level						2		2		4
Progressive Level				2					2	4

Lynn Garcia: Piano Lessons—Owner

Job	Hours per Job for July by Date									
	5	6	7	8	11	12	13	14	15	Totals
Beginner Level		2	2				2			6
Intermediate Level	2	2	2	2	2	2	2	2	2	18
Progressive Level	2	2	2	2	2	2	2	2	2	18

9. Process pay and allocate time for July 15, 2022, for Michelle Auletta. (Click *Yes* at the Pay Period Change window.)

Check No.:	6
Item Name:	Hourly Wages
Rate:	20
Company Taxes:	
Social Security Company:	32.24
Medicare Company:	7.54
Federal Unemployment:	3.12
PA - Unemployment Company:	20.80
Employee Taxes:	
Federal Withholding:	57.00
Social Security Employee:	32.24
Medicare Employee:	7.54
PA - Withholding:	16.00
PA - Unemployment Employee:	0.00

10. Create the following invoices:

Jul. 15   Create invoice for Highland School Beginner Level piano lessons provided by Lynn Garcia and Michelle Auletta for the period July 1, 2022, to July 15, 2022. Invoice No. 2020. Terms 2/10, Net 30 Days.

Jul. 15   Create invoice for Highland School Intermediate Level piano lessons provided by Lynn Garcia and Michelle Auletta for the period July 1, 2022, to July 15, 2022. Invoice No 2021. Terms 2/10, Net 30 Days.

Jul. 15   Create invoice for Highland School Progressive Level piano lessons provided by Lynn Garcia and Michelle Auletta for the period July 1, 2022, to July 15, 2022. Invoice No. 2022. Terms 2/10, Net 30 Days.

11. Enter the following hours worked in the Weekly Timesheet window:

Michelle Auletta: Piano Lessons—Assistant

Job											Totals

Job — **Hours per Job for July by Date**

Job	18	19	20	21	22	25	26	27	28	29	Totals
Beginner Level	3	3	2	3	2	3	2	2	2	2	24
Intermediate Level	3		3			3		3			12
Progressive Level			2		2	2		3		3	2	14

Lynn Garcia: Piano Lessons—Owner

Job — **Hours per Job for July by Date**

Job	18	19	20	21	22	25	26	27	28	29	Totals
Beginner Level	2				2					2	6
Intermediate Level	2	2	2	2	2	2	2		2	2	18
Progressive Level	2	3	2	2	2	3	2	2	2	2	22

12. Process pay and allocate time for July 31, 2022, for Michelle Auletta:

Check No.:	7
Item Name:	Hourly Wages
Rate:	20
Company Taxes:	
Social Security Company:	62.00
Medicare Company:	14.50
Federal Unemployment:	6.00
PA - Unemployment Company:	40.00
Employee Taxes:	
Federal Withholding:	110.00
Social Security Employee:	62.00
Medicare Employee:	14.50
PA - Withholding:	30.00
PA - Unemployment Employee:	0.00

13. Create the following invoices:

Jul. 31   Create invoice for Highland School Beginner Level piano lessons provided by Lynn Garcia and Michelle Auletta for the period July 16, 2022, to July 31, 2022. Invoice No. 2023. Terms Net 30 Days.

Jul. 31   Create invoice for Highland School Intermediate Level piano lessons provided by Lynn Garcia and Michelle Auletta for the period July 16, 2022, to July 31 2022. Invoice No. 2024. Terms Net 30 Days.

Jul. 31   Create invoice for Highland School Progressive Level piano lessons provided by Lynn Garcia and Michelle Auletta for the period July 16, 2022, to July 31, 2022. Invoice No. 2025. Terms Net 30 Days.

14. Display and print a customer statement for Highland School for July 1, 2022, to July 31, 2022.

15. Display and print the following reports for July 1, 2022, to July 31, 2022:
    a. *Profit & Loss by Job*
    b. *Time by Job Summary*

Case Problem 11–2

In September, the fourth month of business for Olivia's Web Solutions, one of Olivia Chen's customers, Thrifty Stores, has decided to expand to three stores. Each store will need its own web page design services, as the stores carry different products. Olivia Chen has decided that it is necessary to track income and expenses for each store. In addition, she wishes to activate the Time-Tracking feature of QuickBooks so that the time spent by her and one of her employees, Gary Glenn, can be tracked and allocated to each job and then billed to the customer. She has added two service items to the Item List for Gary Glenn's billable time as an assistant. The company file includes information for Olivia's Web Solutions as of September 1, 2022.

1. Open the company file **CH11 Olivia's Web Solutions.QBW**.
2. At the QuickBooks Desktop Login window, in the *Password* text box, type Student1 and then click OK.
3. Make a backup copy of the company file and name it **OWS11 *[Your Name]* Olivia's Web Solutions**.
4. Restore the backup copy of the company file. In both the Open Backup Copy and the Save Company File as dialog boxes, use the file name **OWS11 *[Your Name]* Olivia's Web Solutions** and enter the password.
5. Change the company name to **OWS11 *[Your Name]* Olivia's Web Solutions**.
6. Set up the Time-Tracking feature for Olivia's Web Solutions. Monday is the first day of the work week.

7. Add the following jobs to the Customer Center:

CUSTOMER:	Thrifty Stores
JOB NAME:	Bronx Store
JOB DESCRIPTION:	Thrifty Bronx Store Web Page Design
JOB STATUS:	Awarded
START DATE:	09/01/2022
PROJECTED END DATE:	10/31/2022

JOB NAME:	Brooklyn Store
JOB DESCRIPTION:	Thrifty Brooklyn Store Web Page Design
JOB STATUS:	Awarded
START DATE:	09/01/2022
PROJECTED END DATE:	10/31/2022

JOB NAME:	Queens Store
JOB DESCRIPTION:	Thrifty Queens Store Web Page Design
JOB STATUS:	Awarded
START DATE:	09/01/2022
PROJECTED END DATE:	10/31/2022

8. Enter the following hours worked for Thrifty Stores in the Weekly Timesheet window. (Remember to click *Yes* at the Transfer Activities to Payroll message.)

Gary Glenn: Web Page Design—Assistant

HINT
You will need to start with the Weekly Timesheet for the week of August 30, 2022.

Job	Hours per Job for September by Date									
	1	2	6	7	8	9	12	13	14	15	Totals
Bronx Store	4	3	1		5	2	4		1	2	22
Brooklyn Store		1	4	4	3	2	1	6	4	6	31
Queens Store	4	4	3	4			4	3	2	3	27

Olivia Chen: Web Page Design—Owner

Job	Hours per Job for September by Date									
	1	2	6	7	8	9	12	13	14	15	Totals
Bronx Store		2		2	2	2	1	4	2		15
Brooklyn Store		1	2		3		1	2	2	4	15
Queens Store	2	1	1	2		1	2	2	3		14

9. Process pay and allocate time for September 15, 2022, for Gary Glenn. (Click *Yes* at the Pay Period Change window.)

Check No.:	6
Item Name:	Hourly Wages
Rate:	25
Company Taxes:	
Social Security Company:	124.00
Medicare Company:	29.00
Federal Unemployment:	12.00
NY - Unemployment Company:	80.00
Employee Taxes:	
Federal Withholding:	360.00
Social Security Employee:	124.00
Medicare Employee:	29.00
NY - Withholding:	98.00

10. Create the following invoices:

Sep. 15   Create invoice for Web Page Design Services for Thrifty Bronx Store for services provided by Olivia Chen and Gary Glenn for the period September 1, 2022, to September 15, 2022. Invoice No. 1017. Terms Net 30 Days.

Sep. 15   Create invoice for Web Page Design Services for Thrifty Brooklyn Store for services provided by Olivia Chen and Gary Glenn for the period September 1, 2022, to September 15, 2022. Invoice No. 1018. Terms Net 30 Days.

Sep. 15   Create invoice for Web Page Design Services for Thrifty Queens Store for services provided by Olivia Chen and Gary Glenn for the period September 1, 2022, to September 15, 2022. Invoice No. 1019. Terms Net 30 Days.

11. Enter the following hours worked in the Weekly Timesheet window. (Remember to click *Yes* at the Transfer Activities to Payroll message.)

Gary Glenn: Web Page Design—Assistant

Job	Hours per Job for September by Date										
	19	20	21	22	23	26	27	28	29	30	Totals
Bronx Store	4	3	6	4	2		1	2	3		25
Brooklyn Store	2	3	1	2	4	6	5	5	4	1	33
Queens Store	2	2	1	2	2	2	2	1	1	7	22

Olivia Chen: Web Page Design—Owner

Job	Hours per Job for September by Date										
	19	20	21	22	23	26	27	28	29	30	Totals
Bronx Store	1	2	5	2	3	4		2	2		21
Brooklyn Store	2	2	2	2	2		4		2		16
Queens Store	4	3		3	1	4	2	1	1		19

12. Process pay and allocate time for September 30, 2022, for Gary Glenn:

Check No.:	7
Item Name:	Hourly Wages
Rate:	25
Company Taxes:	
Social Security Company:	124.00
Medicare Company:	29.00
Federal Unemployment:	12.00
NY - Unemployment Company:	80.00
Employee Taxes:	
Federal Withholding:	360.00
Social Security Employee:	124.00
Medicare Employee:	29.00
NY - Withholding:	98.00

13. Create the following invoices:

Sep. 30   Create invoice for Web Page Design Services for Thrifty Bronx Store for services provided by Olivia Chen and Gary Glenn for the period September 16, 2022, to September 30, 2022. Invoice No. 1020. Terms Net 30 Days.

Sep. 30   Create invoice for Web Page Dcsign Services for Thrifty Brooklyn Store for services provided by Olivia Chen and Gary Glenn for the period September 16, 2022, to September 30, 2022. Invoice No. 1021. Terms Net 30 Days.

Sep. 30   Create invoice for Web Page Design Services for Thrifty Queens Store for services provided by Olivia Chen and Gary Glenn for the period September 16, 2022, to September 30, 2022. Invoice No. 1022. Terms Net 30 Days.

14. Display and print a customer statement for Thrifty Stores for September 1, 2022, to September 30, 2022.

15. Display and print the following reports for September 1, 2022, to September 30, 2022:
    a. *Profit & Loss by Job*
    b. *Time by Job Summary*

## CHAPTER 12

Customization of Your Company File

Customizing the Desktop, Invoices, Letters, Memorized Transactions, Graphs, and Fiscal Year

Objectives

- Customize the desktop to set viewing preferences for the Home page and Icon bars

- Customize Lists/Centers (including subaccounts), merge entries, and create custom fields

- Customize Activities (including an Activity window display and related invoice), prepare a QuickBooks Letter in Microsoft Word, and ask QuickBooks to memorize transactions

- Customize Reports (including the appearance of reports), instruct QuickBooks to memorize settings, export a report into Microsoft Excel, process multiple reports, change report default settings, and view and print a graph

- View fiscal year closing, set a closing date, and prepare for a new fiscal year

The online course includes additional training and assessment resources. Reports created for the Chapter Problem can be uploaded for instructor review.

Chapter Introduction

At this point, you should have a good understanding of how to use QuickBooks and be able to create and set up a new company file, update the Lists and Centers, record transactions in the Activities windows, and view and print a variety of management reports, accounting reports, and financial statements.

In this final chapter, you will learn how to customize features in QuickBooks to suit your needs. You will change viewing preferences for the QuickBooks desktop and Home page; customize Lists/Centers by changing subaccount default settings, merging entries, and creating custom fields; and customize Activities by personalizing the Create Invoices window and related printed invoices. You will then learn how to prepare a QuickBooks Letter in Microsoft Word and how to instruct QuickBooks to memorize transactions so they can be used again. Next, you will learn how to customize Reports and ask QuickBooks to memorize the settings, export a report to Microsoft Excel, process multiple reports, change report default settings, and view and print graphs. Finally, you will conclude the accounting cycle in QuickBooks by viewing the fiscal year closing, setting the closing date, and preparing for the new fiscal year.

Chapter Problem

Begin by opening the company file **CH12 Kristin Raina Interior Designs**. Enter the password, *Student1*. Make a backup copy and name it **EX12 *[Your Name]* Kristin Raina Interior Designs**. Restore the backup copy, enter the password *Student1*, and then change the company name to **EX12 *[Your Name]* Kristin Raina Interior Designs**.

Customize the Desktop

There are many different ways to access Lists/Centers, Activities windows, and Reports in QuickBooks. Throughout the text, only the main menu bar was used, but you can customize your QuickBooks desktop to use the Home page and the Icon bars as alternative ways to access these items.

Home Page

By default, when you create a new company file and each time you open a company file, the Home page is displayed. If the default was changed and the Home page is not automatically displayed, it can be accessed for the current work session, or the default can be changed so that the Home page displays each time the company file is opened. In addition, the Home page can be customized according to your choices.

Using the Home Page
To display the Home page if it is not displayed:
1. At the main menu bar, click Company.
2. Click *Home Page*. The Home Page appears.
   QuickBooks provides two tabs on the Home page: the Home Page tab and the Insights tab. The Home Page tab is shown in Figure 12–A.

The Insights tab provides information at a glance about the company's Profit & Loss, Income, and Expenses.

3. If necessary, click the Home Page tab. See Figure 12–A for the Home page—Home Page tab.

FIGURE12–A Home Page—Home Page Tab

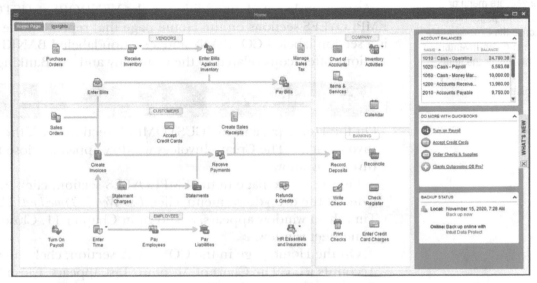

There are five sections of the Home page, and they are labeled with tabs: VENDORS, CUSTOMERS, EMPLOYEES, COMPANY, and BANKING. Recall that VENDORS, CUSTOMERS, and EMPLOYEES are the Centers presented in prior chapters. If you click any of these tabs, you are moved to the respective center.

The Home page also displays icons for certain tasks and the workflow related to each center. You can click the icon to move to the respective window. In some cases, a drop-down menu will appear with additional choices.

To access a window using the icons on the Home page:
1. On the Home page in the VENDORS section, click the Enter Bills icon. The Enter Bills window appears.

   In Chapter 2: Vendors, when a non-inventory item was purchased, the transaction was recorded in the Enter Bills window using the Expenses tab. The Enter Bills window was accessed by using the Vendors menu and choosing *Enter Bills.*
2. Close the Enter Bills window.
3. On the Home page, in the VENDORS section, click the Receive Inventory icon. A drop-down menu displays two choices: *Receive Inventory with Bill* and *Receive Inventory without Bill.* See Figure 12–B.

FIGURE 12–B
Receive Inventory
Drop-Down Menu

 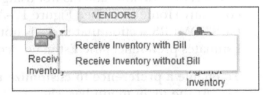

4. At the Receive Inventory drop-down menu, click *Receive Inventory with Bill.* The Enter Bills window appears.

HINT

Recall that there is only one Enter Bills window. To open it, choose *Enter Bills* or *Receive Items and Enter Bill* from the Vendors menu or the Home page. Then choose the Expenses tab to record non-inventory purchases or the Items tab to record inventory purchases.

In Chapter 5: Inventory, when inventory was purchased and received, the transaction was recorded in the Enter Bills window using the Items tab. The Enter Bills window was accessed by using the Vendors menu and choosing *Receive Items and Enter Bill*.

5. Close the Enter Bills window.

As previously noted, in addition to the VENDORS, CUSTOMERS, and EMPLOYEES sections on the Home page that represent the Centers, there is a section labeled COMPANY and a section labeled BANKING. These sections offer icons related to the Company and the Banking tasks.

Practice Exercise 12-1

On the Home page in the CUSTOMERS section, click the Create Invoices icon. The Create Invoices window appears. Close the Create Invoices window.

On the Home page in the EMPLOYEES section, click the Enter Time icon. At the drop-down menu, click *Use Weekly Timesheet*. The Weekly Timesheet window appears, as shown in Chapter 11. Close the Weekly Timesheet window.

On the Home page in the COMPANY section, click the Chart of Accounts icon. The Chart of Accounts List appears. Close the Chart of Accounts List.

On the Home page in the BANKING section, click the Reconcile icon. The Begin Reconciliation window appears, as shown in Chapter 10. Close the Begin Reconciliation window.

Customizing the Home Page

Icons are added to or removed from the Home page depending on the preferences for the company file. Recall in the New Company Setup chapters that when you create a new company file, the QuickBooks preferences, or features, are turned on (enabled) or turned off (disabled). In Chapter 6, the preferences were enabled or disabled as you answered questions in the EasyStep Interview window. In Chapter 7, you went directly to the Preferences window to enable or disable preferences. As a preference is enabled, choices appear on the drop-down menus on the main menu bar and also on the Home page. If a preference is enabled, you cannot remove the icon from the Home page.

In Chapter 12, most preferences for our sample company, Kristin Raina Interior Designs, have been enabled. If you look at the Home page for a company file in the earlier chapters, you will see fewer icons. For example, look at Figure 1–H on page 11.

Currently, Kristin Raina is not using the Estimates feature. Look at the company Home page (see Figure 12–A on page 479) and observe in the CUSTOMERS section that there is not an Estimates icon. Upon enabling the Estimates preference, the Estimates icon will appear on the Home page.

To enable a preference to customize the Home page:

1. At the main menu bar, click Edit and then click *Preferences*.
2. In the left panel of the Preferences window, click the Desktop View icon.
3. Click the Company Preferences tab. See Figure 12–C.

FIGURE 12–C
Preferences Window—
Desktop View—Company
Preferences Tab

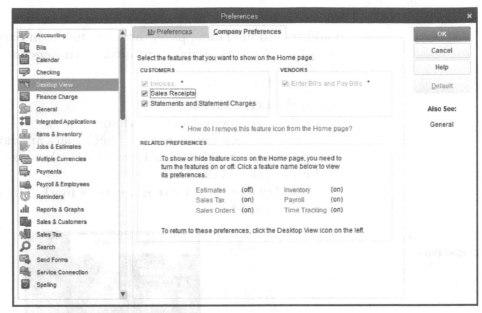

The RELATED PREFERENCES section of this page indicates if a feature is enabled (on) or disabled (off). If a preference is enabled, you cannot remove the icon from the Home page. To remove the icon from the Home page, you would have to disable (turn off) the preference. The Estimates preference is turned off. When it is enabled, the Estimates icon appears on the Home page.

4. In the RELATED PREFERENCES section, click *Estimates.* You are moved to the Jobs & Estimates page.

5. In the DO YOU CREATE ESTIMATES? section, click the *Yes* option and then click OK. At the warning, click OK.

6. Open the Home page from the Company menu. The Estimates feature is now enabled, and the Estimates icon appears on the Home page in the CUSTOMERS section.

Along the right side of the Home page are three areas of information: ACCOUNT BALANCES, DO MORE WITH QUICKBOOKS, and BACKUP STATUS. While you cannot remove these categories from the Home page, you can minimize the detail below each heading by clicking the up arrow ⋀. When you click this arrow, only the information title is displayed. To see the information below the title, click the down arrow ⋁.

Changing the Default for the Home Page

The Preferences window is used to change the default setting for displaying the Home page when opening a new company file.

To change the default setting for the Home page:

1. At the main menu bar, click Edit and then click *Preferences.* The Preferences window appears.

2. In the left panel of the Preferences window, click the Desktop View icon.

3. Click the My Preferences tab.

4. Depending on your preference, insert or remove a check mark in the box to the left of *Show Home page when opening a company file.*

5. Click OK to save the setting.

6. Close the Home page.

Icon Bars

In addition to the Home page, there are two Icon bars that can be used to access Lists/Centers, Activities windows, and Reports.

Left Icon Bar

To view the Left Icon bar:

1. At the main menu bar, click View.

    On the View menu, when a check mark appears to the left of *Left Icon Bar*, the Left Icon bar is enabled. If there is no check mark, the Left Icon bar is disabled.

2. Click *Left Icon Bar* if there is no check mark. The Left Icon bar displays. See Figure 12–D.

FIGURE 12–D
Left Icon Bar

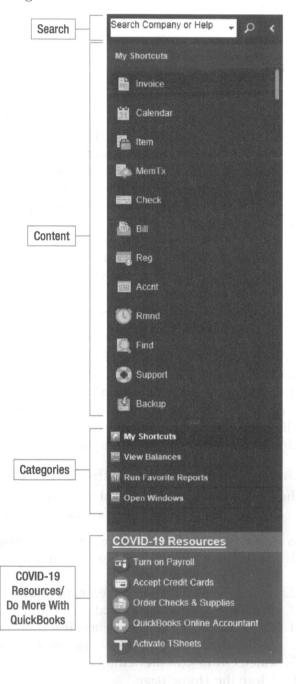

Search

Content

Categories

COVID-19
Resources/
Do More With
QuickBooks

There are four sections on the Left Icon bar: Search, Content, Categories, and COVID-19 Resources/Do More With QuickBooks. The information in the Content section changes depending on which category is selected. By default, the My Shortcuts category is selected. The Left Icon bar can be customized to add, delete, or edit the icons in the My Shortcuts Content section.

3. In the Content section, with the My Shortcuts content displayed, scroll up and down the list.

Notice that next to each icon in the Content section is part of the text name for the icon. Hover the mouse pointer over each icon listed in the Content section, and the entire text name for the icon is displayed. Notice the Accnt and Calendar icons. Also notice that the list of icons does not appear to be in any particular order.

To add an icon to the Left Icon bar:

1. At the main menu bar, click View and then click *Customize Icon Bar*. The Customize Icon Bar window appears. See Figure 12–E.

On the left in the ICON BAR CONTENT section is a list of the icons you just scrolled through on the Left Icon bar. Notice that at the bottom of the list is an option to reorder the icons. Buttons are also provided to Add, Edit, and Delete icons from the Left Icon bar.

2. At the Customize Icon Bar window, click the Add button. The Add Icon Bar Item window appears.

3. At the Add Icon Bar Item window, scroll through the list on the left until you see *Calculator*.

4. Click *Calculator*.

5. Click OK at the Add Icon Bar Item window and then click OK at the Customize Icon Bar window to save the change. The Calc icon is added to the Left Icon bar at the bottom of the list in the Content section.
6. On the Left Icon bar, scroll to the bottom of the My Shortcuts content to see the addition of the Calc icon.

You can also add icons to the Left Icon bar when a QuickBooks window is open. For many windows, when the window is open, you can click the View menu and there will be a choice to *Add Window to Icon Bar.*

To edit an icon on the Left Icon bar:
1. At the main menu bar, click View and then click *Customize Icon Bar.*
2. At the Customize Icon Bar window, in the ICON BAR CONTENT section, scroll through the list, click *Accnt* once to highlight it, and then click the Edit button.
3. At the Edit Icon Bar Item window, at the *Label* field, delete the text *Accnt* and then type Chart Accts.
4. Click OK at the Edit Icon Item Bar window and then click OK at the Customize Icon Bar window. In the Content section of the Left Icon bar, the Accnt icon text changes to Chart Accts.

To remove an icon from the Left Icon bar:
1. At the main menu bar, click View and then click *Customize Icon Bar.*
2. At the Customize Icon Bar window, in the ICON BAR CONTENT section, scroll through the list and then click *Reg* once to highlight it.
3. Click the Delete button. The Reg (Register) icon is removed from the Left Icon bar.
4. Delete the following items from the Left Icon bar:
   User Licenses
   Add Payroll
   Docs
   Client Review
5. Click OK to save the changes.

In the Categories section of the Left Icon bar, after My Shortcuts, other choices are View Balances, which allows you to view the balances in cash/bank accounts, accounts receivable, and liabilities accounts; Run Favorite Reports, which allows you to list customized reports that have been saved as favorites; and Open Windows, which provides a list of windows that may be open.

The last section, COVID-19 Resources/Do More With QuickBooks, provides additional features that QuickBooks offers online. The Account Balances and Do More With QuickBooks sections also appear on the Home page when the Left Icon bar is not displayed.

Top Icon Bar

To view the Top Icon bar:
1. At the main menu bar, click View.

    On the View menu, when a check mark appears to the left of *Top Icon Bar*, the top icon bar is enabled. If there is no check mark, then the Top Icon bar is disabled.
2. Click *Top Icon bar* if there is no check mark.

The Top Icon bar is displayed under the main menu bar when it is enabled. When the Top Icon bar is chosen, the Left Icon bar is no longer displayed. Under each icon is the text name for the icon on the Top Icon bar. See Figure 12–F.

FIGURE 12–F Top Icon Bar

The Top Icon bar can be customized to add, edit, and delete icons the same way the Left Icon bar was customized. Changes made to the icons on the Left Icon bar carry over to the Top Icon bar. In addition, the Top Icon bar can be customized to add spaces and vertical lines between the icons. This is done using the Add Separator button at the Customize Icon Bar window. The background color of the Top Icon bar can be changed using the Preferences window, Desktop View icon, and My Preferences tab.

To remove the Left Icon bar or Top Icon bar:
1. At the main menu bar, click View.
2. Click *Hide Icon Bar*.

Lists/Centers

Customize the View of Subaccounts and Parent Accounts

As you know, accounts in the Chart of Accounts List can be denoted as subaccounts. When an account is a subaccount, the account of which it is a subaccount is referred to as the *parent account*. Accounts are marked as subaccounts to show a subtotal or net amount of the parent account on the financial statements. This procedure was illustrated with fixed assets, where the accumulated depreciation account (subaccount) was deducted from the fixed asset cost account (subaccount) to show the net book value of the fixed asset account (parent) on the *Balance Sheet*.

When there is a parent account and related subaccounts in the Chart of Accounts list, *Account Listing* report, and some activity windows, by default QuickBooks displays the parent account followed by the subaccount on one line. Sometimes when you are reviewing the *Account Listing* report or choosing an account in an Activity window, the default listing of first the parent account and then the subaccount can be cumbersome. Therefore, you can change the default settings to simplify the presentation of the parent account and subaccounts.

Chart of Accounts List Window Presentation

Open the Chart of Accounts List window by clicking Lists and then clicking *Chart of Accounts*. Scroll down to the fixed asset section. Look at the cost and accumulated depreciation accounts. These subaccounts are indented under the parent accounts. This is referred to as the *hierarchical view*. See Figure 12–G.

FIGURE 12–G
Chart of Accounts Window—Hierarchical View

parent accounts and subaccounts for fixed assets

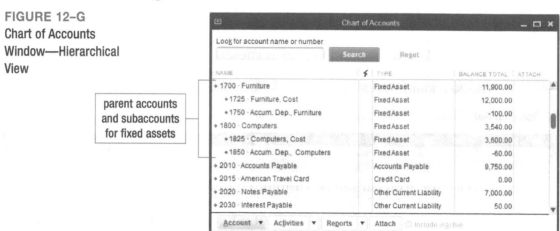

If you do not like the subaccounts indented, you can change the format to list all the accounts aligned at the left of the window. This is referred to as the *flat view*.

To change to the flat or hierarchical view:
1. At the Chart of Accounts List window, click the Account menu button. Notice that *Hierarchical View* is checked.
2. Click *Flat View*.
3. Scroll down the Chart of Accounts List window until the fixed assets are again displayed. The subaccounts are no longer indented; they are now left-aligned in the window. Notice that each line lists both the parent account and the subaccount. See Figure 12–H.

FIGURE 12–H
Chart of Accounts Window—Flat View

parent accounts and subaccounts for fixed assets

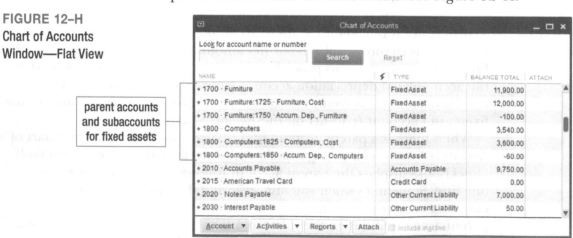

4. Click the Account menu button and then click *Hierarchical View*. If you receive the Hierarchical View message, insert a check mark in the box to the left of *Do not display this message in the future* and then click Yes. The presentation changes back to indent the subaccounts.
5. Close the window.

These changes to the view settings in the Chart of Accounts List window affect only this window.

Lists and Activities Windows Presentation

Open the *Account Listing* report by clicking Reports and then clicking *List*. See Figure 12–I.

FIGURE 12–I
Account Listing Report—Parent Accounts Listed to Left of Subaccounts

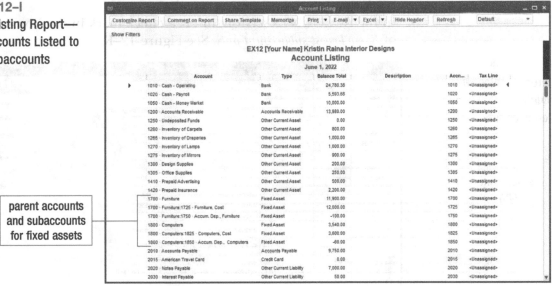

parent accounts and subaccounts for fixed assets

Review the subaccounts listed in the *Account Listing* report in Figure 12–I. Notice that the subaccounts 1725, 1750, 1825, and 1850—the cost and accumulated depreciation accounts—are listed next to their respective parent accounts, 1700 and 1800. Close the *Account Listing* report.

Open the Make General Journal Entries window by clicking Company and then clicking *Make General Journal Entries*. At the *ACCOUNT* field, on the first line, click the account *Furniture 1725, Cost,* and then tab to the next field. In the *ACCOUNT* field, the parent account is listed first. Because the field is small, you see the parent account and only a small part of the subaccount. See Figure 12–J.

FIGURE 12–J
Make General Journal Entries Window—Subaccount Selected—Parent Account Displayed

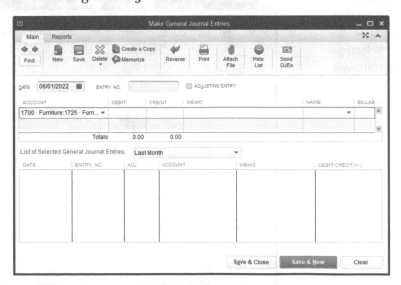

Close the Make General Journal Entries window.

In the Activities and Reports windows, the default setting is to display the subaccounts to the right of the parent account. This default setting can be changed in the Preferences window.

To change the default setting of subaccounts:
1. At the main menu bar, click Edit and then click *Preferences*.
2. In the left panel of the Preferences window, click the Accounting icon.
3. Click the Company Preferences tab.
4. In the ACCOUNTS section, insert a check mark in the box to the left of *Show lowest subaccount only*. See Figure 12–K.

FIGURE 12-K
Preferences Window—
Accounting—Company
Preferences Tab

Show lowest subaccount only

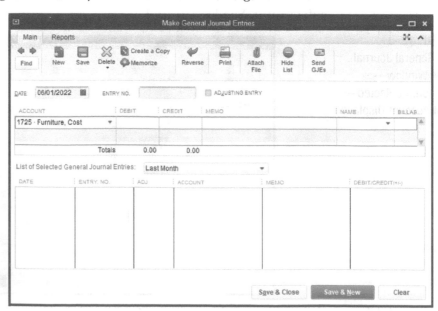

5. If the information is correct, click OK.

To see the effect of this default setting change, reopen the Make General Journal Entries window, and on the first line of the *ACCOUNT* field, click the account *1725 Furniture, Cost*. Notice that the parent account is no longer listed, only the subaccount. See Figure 12–L.

FIGURE 12-L
Make General Journal
Entries Window—
Subaccount Selected—
Subaccount Displayed

6. Close the Make General Journal Entries window.
7. View the *Account Listing* report. See Figure 12–M.

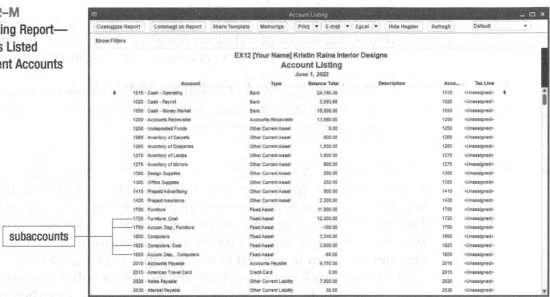

subaccounts

The subaccounts are listed on lines without the parent accounts.
Compare Figure 12–M to Figure 12–I on page 487.

8. Close the *Account Listing* report.

Lists/Centers

Merge Entries

You have previously learned to add, delete, and edit vendors, customers/
jobs, accounts, service items, and inventory part items in the appropriate Lists/Centers. You can also combine or merge vendors, customers,
accounts, service items, and inventory part items. To do so, you simply use a
name or number already in use, and QuickBooks will inquire if you wish to
merge the two items.

Kristin Raina currently has a 6450 Telephone Expense account and a
6500 Utilities Expense account. She decides to combine—that is, merge—
the two accounts into 6500 Utilities Expense.

Open the *Journal* report from 02/28/2022 to 02/28/2022. Scroll
through the journal entries until you see the TwinCityTelCo journal entry
(Trans #18), which records $275 to the account 6450 Telephone Expense.
Leave the *Journal* report open.

To merge two accounts:
1. Open the Chart of Accounts List by clicking Lists and then clicking
   Chart of Accounts. Scroll down the accounts and notice the accounts
   6450 Telephone Expense and 6500 Utilities Expense.
2. Select *6450 Telephone Expense*, but do not open it.
3. Click the Account menu button and then click *Edit Account*. The Edit
   Account window opens.
4. At the *Number* field, change the account number to 6500 and then
   click Save & Close. A Merge message informs you that the account is
   already in use and asks if you wish to merge the accounts.

5. At the Merge message, click Yes. Look at the Chart of Accounts List. Notice that there is no longer an account 6450 Telephone Expense.

6. Close the Chart of Accounts List.

Look at the *Journal* report for February 28, 2022. Notice that the transaction for TwinCityTelCo (Trans# 18) now has the transaction recorded as 6500 Utilities Expense instead of 6450 Telephone Expense.

7. Close the *Journal* report.

The same process can be used to combine vendors, customers/jobs, service items, and inventory part items. QuickBooks will update all the information based on the merge.

Lists/Centers → ## Create Custom Fields

In prior chapters, you displayed and printed reports, including filtering reports using fields of information already included in the report. QuickBooks allows you to create your own custom fields of information for later display in a report. Custom fields for customers, vendors, employees, and items can be created in the appropriate List or Center.

Most of Kristin Raina's customers are located in either Minneapolis or St. Paul. She would like to sort her customers by region so when she and her assistant visit the customers, they can each go to all the customers in one city at a time. To do this, Kristin Raina will create a custom field named *Region* and then edit each customer's account to identify the region for that customer. Finally, Kristin Raina will filter the Customer Center to list only the customers in a specified region.

To create a custom field:

1. Open the Customer Center by clicking Customers and then clicking *Customer Center.* Choose the first customer, Alomar Company, by double-clicking the customer name. The Edit Customer window appears. Notice that the city in the ADDRESS DETAILS section for this customer is Minneapolis.

2. Click the Additional Info tab.

3. On the Additional Info tab, in the CUSTOM FIELDS section, click the Define Fields button. The Set up Custom Fields for Names window appears.

4. On the first line in the *Label* column, type Region.

5. At the *Use for:* field, insert a check mark in the *Cust* (customer) column. See Figure 12–N.

FIGURE 12–N
Set Up Custom Fields for Names Window

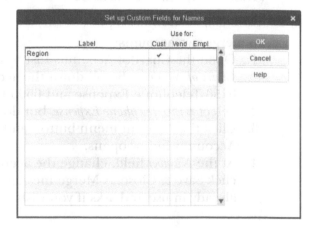

6. If the information is correct, click OK.
7. At the Information message, insert a check mark in the box to the left of *Do not display this message in the future* and then click OK. The *REGION* text box is now displayed in the CUSTOM FIELDS section on the Additional Info tab.
8. In the *REGION* text box, type Minneapolis. See Figure 12–O.

FIGURE 12–O
Edit Customer Window—
Additional Info Tab—
REGION Text Box Added
and Completed

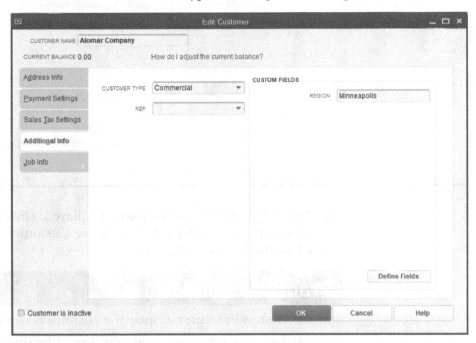

9. If the information is correct, click OK to save it.
10. Edit each customer and type in each customer's city in the *REGION* text box on the Additional Info tab.

Keep the Customer Center open for the next activity.

The Customer Center can now be customized to display only the customers in a specified region.

To display customers in the Customer Center in the Minneapolis region:
1. Open the Customer Center, if necessary.
2. On the Customer & Jobs tab, click the Search icon 🔍. The Custom Filter dialog box appears.
3. In the Customer Filter dialog box, click or type the following information:

Search: Active Customers
in: Custom fields
For: Minneapolis

4. Click Go. The Customer Center is updated to display only the six customers that have Minneapolis as their region on the Additional Info tab. See Figure 12–P.

HINT

The *REGION* text box can also be viewed in the *Customer Contact List* report. Open the report and click the Customize Report button. In the Modify Report dialog box, click the Filters tab. In the *FILTER* field, scroll through the list and choose *Region*. In the *REGION* text box, type **Minneapolis** and then click OK. The *Customer Contact List* report is updated to display only the six customers that have Minneapolis as their region.

FIGURE 12-P Customer Center Filtered for Minneapolis Region

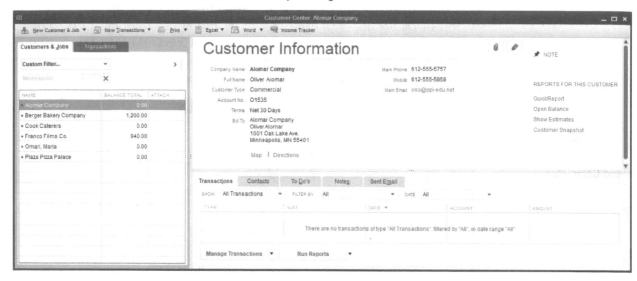

5. At the field where *Minneapolis* is displayed, click the X. The Customer Center returns to the list of all Active Customers.
6. Close the Customer Center.

Practice Exercise   12-2

In the Customer Center, display the customers in the St. Paul region.

QuickCheck: Five customers and jobs should be displayed in the Customer Center.

Similar procedures can be used to create custom fields for vendors, employees, and items. If you want to include the *REGION* field in the Vendor Center, open any vendor in the Edit Vendor window. On the Additional Info tab, click the Define Fields button. The Set up Custom Fields for Names window will appear with the *Region* label listed. Insert a check mark in the *Vend* (vendor) column and then click OK, which will activate the *REGION* text box on the Additional Info tab for each vendor.

Activities

Customize Activities Windows and Printed Documents

In all chapters, the Activities windows displayed were based on default settings. QuickBooks allows you to change the default settings of a window as well as those of a document that can be printed as a result of data entered in a window.

Recall in Chapter 11 that when you used the Time-Tracking feature, the data you entered in the Weekly Timesheet window was carried forward to the Create Invoices window. The Create Invoices window displayed by default did not show all the relevant information carried over to that window. By changing the default settings in the Create Invoices window, more of the important information can be displayed.

To view the default settings and preview an invoice:
1. At the main menu bar, click Customers and then click *Create Invoices*.
2. Click the Find Previous arrow to display Invoice No. 1016. Click the Formatting tab. See Figure 12–Q.

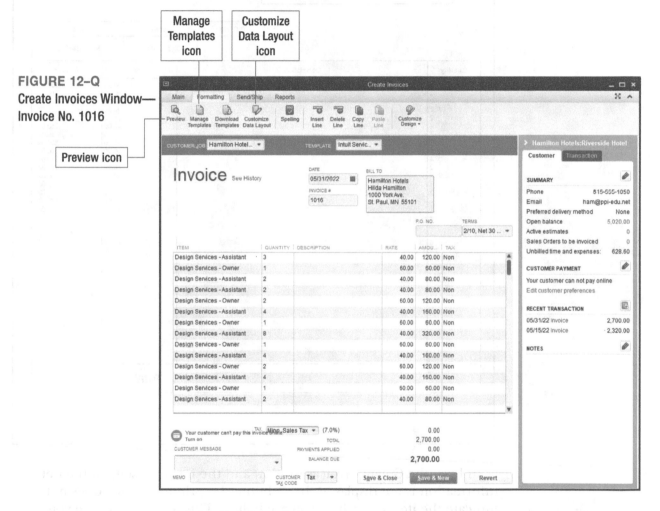

FIGURE 12–Q
Create Invoices Window—
Invoice No. 1016

In QuickBooks you can preview and print invoices that can be sent to customers.
3. On the Formatting tab, click the Preview icon. The invoice should look like Figure 12–R.

FIGURE 12–R
Invoice No. 1016

EX12 [Your Name] Kristin Raina Interior Designs	**Invoice**
25 NE Johnson Street	
Minneapolis, MN 53402	

Date	Invoice #
5/31/2022	1016

Bill To

Hamilton Hotels
Hilda Hamilton
1000 York Ave.
St. Paul, MN 55101

P.O. No.	Terms	Project
	2/10, Net 30 Days	Riverside Hotel

Quantity	Description	Rate	Amount
3		40.00	120.00
1		60.00	60.00
2		40.00	80.00
2		40.00	80.00
2		60.00	120.00
4		40.00	160.00
1		60.00	60.00
8		40.00	320.00
1		60.00	60.00
4		40.00	160.00
2		60.00	120.00
4		40.00	160.00
1		60.00	60.00
2		40.00	80.00
3		60.00	180.00
2		40.00	80.00
4		60.00	240.00
2		40.00	80.00
1		60.00	60.00
6		40.00	240.00
3		60.00	180.00
	Sales Tax	7.00%	0.00

Total	$2,700.00

In both the Create Invoices window and the invoice itself, all the detail information is not displayed. In addition, the printed invoice does not indicate the items for which you are billing. This is not an invoice you would want to send to a customer. You can customize both the Create Invoices window and the invoice so that all the detailed information is adequately displayed. QuickBooks provides several pre-established invoices. Two invoices previously used are the Intuit Service Invoice and Intuit Product Invoice. These invoices are based on templates. You can create your own invoice by customizing a template. To do this, you will first make a copy of the existing template and then customize the copy. This is done using the Manage Templates icon on the Formatting tab at the Create Invoices window.

4. Close the Print Preview window.

To customize the Create Invoices window and a printed invoice:

1. With the Create Invoices window open and Invoice No. 1016 displayed, on the Formatting tab, click the Manage Templates icon. You are moved to the Manage Templates window.

2. In the SELECT TEMPLATE section, select *Intuit Service Invoice* and then click the Copy button. A copy of the Intuit Service Invoice is made. It is labeled *Copy of: Intuit Service Invoice* in both the SELECT TEMPLATE section and the PREVIEW section—*Template Name* field. See Figure 12–S.

FIGURE 12–S
Manage Templates Window—Template Name—Copy of: Intuit Service Invoice

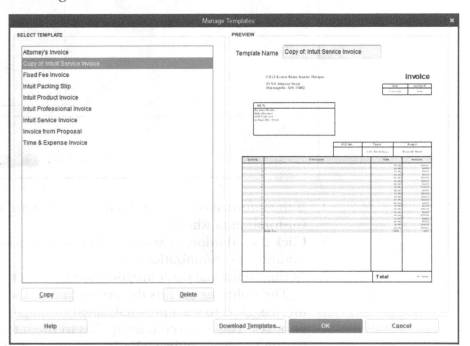

You will create your own invoice using the Copy of: Intuit Service Invoice as a guideline. But you will first assign a new name to the invoice.

3. In the PREVIEW section, at the *Template Name* field, delete the text *Copy of: Intuit Service Invoice*, type Job Invoice, and then press the Tab key. Notice that the invoice name is also changed in the SELECT TEMPLATE section. See Figure 12–T.

FIGURE 12–T
Manage Templates
Window—Template
Name—Job Invoice

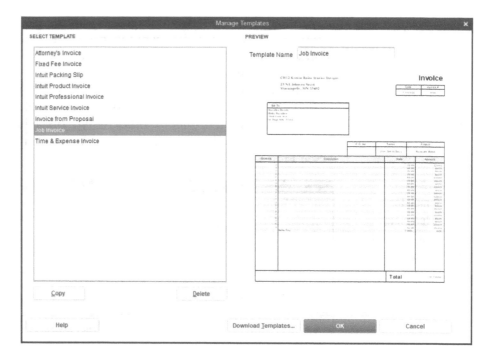

4. If the information is correct, click OK. You are moved to the Basic Customization window.
5. Click the Additional Customization button. You are moved to the Additional Customization window.
6. At the Additional Customization window, click the Columns tab.

    The Columns tab lists the pre-established settings for the service invoice. Next to each pre-established setting, you will see four columns of boxes. The *Screen* column applies to the settings that appear in the Create Invoices window. The *Print* column applies to the settings that appear on the printed invoice. Whether a specific setting will appear on the screen in the Create Invoices window, on the printed invoice, or both is indicated by which box or boxes contain check marks. The *Order* column applies to the order of display on both the screen and the printed invoice. The *Title* column is the title for the column to be displayed on both the screen and the printed invoice.

    Since nothing was listed in the *Description* field, we will remove this column from both the Create Invoice window and the printed invoice; this will allow more room for the columns in which data is displayed. In addition, we will indicate that the *Item* field should appear on the printed invoice.

7. At the *Description* field, in the *Screen* column, remove the check mark. At the Layout Designer message, insert a check mark to the left of *Do not display this message in the future* and then click OK.
8. At the *Description* field, in the *Print* column, remove the check mark.
9. Insert a check mark in the *Print* column box to the right of the *Item* field. At the Overlapping Fields message, click Continue.
10. At the *Service Date* field, insert a check mark in both the *Screen* and the *Print* columns. At the Overlapping Fields message, click Continue. QuickBooks automatically assigns an order number of *4*. See Figure 12–U.

FIGURE 12–U
Additional Customization
Window—Columns Tab

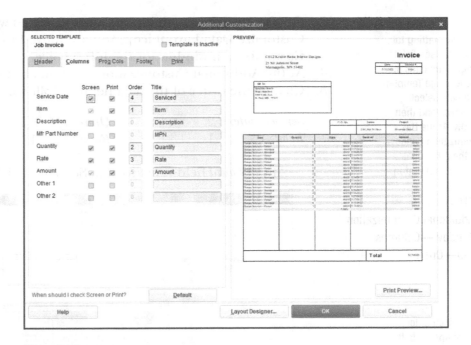

11. If the information is correct, click OK. You are returned to the Basic Customization window.
12. Click OK. You are returned to the Create Invoices window. The *TEMPLATE* field displays the new format created: *Job Invoice*. The *Description* column has been removed, and the *Serviced* column has been added. See Figure 12–V and compare it with Figure 12–Q on page 493.

FIGURE 12–V
Create Invoices
Window—Job Invoice—
Serviced Dates Added

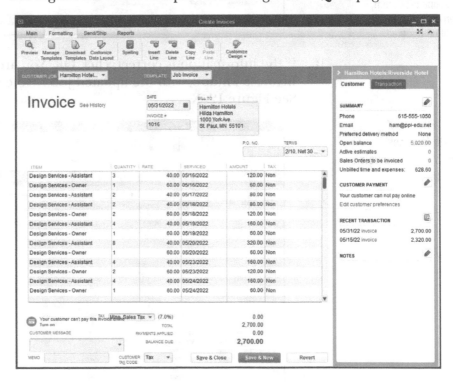

Upon reviewing the Create Invoices window, you realize that the order of data fields should be different. You will further customize the Job Invoice you just created.

HINT

On the Formatting tab, you could also click the Manage Templates icon. In the Manage Template dialog box, select *Job Invoice* and then click OK. At the Basic Customization window, click the Additional Customization button.

13. On the Formatting tab in the Create Invoices window, click the Customize Data Layout icon. You are moved to the Additional Customization window for the Job Invoice.
14. At the Additional Customization window, click the Columns tab.
15. Change the order of the data fields as follows:

Service Date:	2	*Quantity:*	3
Item:	1	*Rate:*	4

The *Amount* field remains at 5. See Figure 12–W.

FIGURE 12–W
Additional Customization Window—Columns Tab—Order

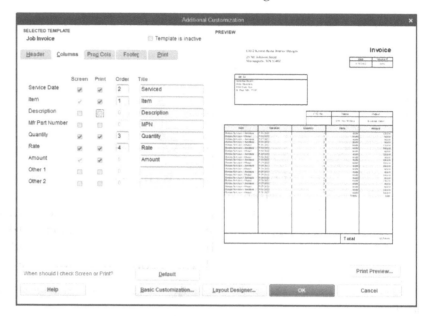

HINT

If the revised order does not appear in the PREVIEW section, at the Additional Customization window for the Job Invoice, click the Columns tab, recheck the *Description* field in the *Screen* and *Print* columns, uncheck them, and then click OK. The order will be updated.

16. If the information is correct, click OK. You are returned to the Create Invoices window, with the updated Job Invoice data displayed. See Figure 12–X.

FIGURE 12–X
Create Invoices Window—Job Invoice—Updated Order

17. If the information is correct, on the Formatting tab, click the Preview icon. If the Recording Transaction message appears, click Yes to save the Job Invoice format for this invoice.

18. The invoice is displayed using the custom-designed Job Invoice format. See Figure 12–Y and compare it with Figure 12–R on page 494.

compare it with Figure 12–R on page 494.

FIGURE 12–Y
Invoice No. 1016—
Job Invoice Format

EX12 [Your Name] Kristin Raina Interior Designs

25 NE Johnson Street
Minneapolis, MN 53402

Invoice

Date	Invoice #
5/31/2022	1016

Bill To

Hamilton Hotels
Hilda Hamilton
1000 York Ave.
St. Paul, MN 55101

P.O. No.	Terms	Project
	2/10, Net 30 Days	Riverside Hotel

Item	Serviced	Quantity	Rate	Amount
Design Services - Assistant	5/16/2022	3	40.00	120.00
Design Services - Owner	5/16/2022	1	60.00	60.00
Design Services - Assistant	5/17/2022	2	40.00	80.00
Design Services - Assistant	5/18/2022	2	40.00	80.00
Design Services - Owner	5/18/2022	2	60.00	120.00
Design Services - Assistant	5/19/2022	4	40.00	160.00
Design Services - Owner	5/19/2022	1	60.00	60.00
Design Services - Assistant	5/20/2022	8	40.00	320.00
Design Services - Owner	5/20/2022	1	60.00	60.00
Design Services - Assistant	5/23/2022	4	40.00	160.00
Design Services - Owner	5/23/2022	2	60.00	120.00
Design Services - Assistant	5/24/2022	4	40.00	160.00
Design Services - Owner	5/24/2022	1	60.00	60.00
Design Services - Assistant	5/25/2022	2	40.00	80.00
Design Services - Owner	5/25/2022	3	60.00	180.00
Design Services - Assistant	5/26/2022	2	40.00	80.00
Design Services - Owner	5/26/2022	4	60.00	240.00
Design Services - Assistant	5/27/2022	2	40.00	80.00
Design Services - Owner	5/27/2022	1	60.00	60.00
Design Services - Assistant	5/31/2022	6	40.00	240.00
Design Services - Owner	5/31/2022	3	60.00	180.00
			7.00%	0.00

Total	$2,700.00

HINT

If the revised order does not appear on the printed invoice, go back to the Additional Customization window for the Job Invoice, click the Columns tab, recheck the *Description* field in the *Screen* and *Print* columns, uncheck them, and then click OK.

19. Close the Preview and Create Invoices windows. If the Recording Transaction message appears, click Yes.

After creating this new format for an invoice, you could review the other invoices in the Create Invoices window that used Time-Tracking data and apply the new Job Invoice format to those invoices.

Practice Exercise   12–3

In the Create Invoices window, change Invoice #1015 and Invoice #1014 to the Job Invoice format by selecting *Job Invoice* at the *TEMPLATE* field. Save the changes.

FIGURE 12–Z
QuickBooks Bounced Check Letter Exported to Microsoft Word

QuickBooks Letters

QuickBooks provides preformatted letters that may be used in certain business circumstances. You can use these letters as they are or customize them based on your personal preferences. You must have Microsoft Word installed on your computer to use the QuickBooks Letters feature.

Kristin Raina wants to send a letter to Berger Bakery Company regarding the check that was returned as non-sufficient funds (NSF) with the April 30 bank statement. She will use QuickBooks Letters to do this.

To prepare a business letter using QuickBooks Letters:

1. At the main menu bar, click Company and then click *Prepare Letters with Envelopes.*
2. At the Prepare Letters with Envelopes submenu, click *Customer Letters.*If the Find Letter Templates message appears, click the Copy button. The Letters and Envelopes window appears.
3. At the Review and Edit Recipients page, click the Unmark All button to remove all the check marks from the customer names.
4. Click *Berger Bakery Company* to select that customer and then click Next.
5. At the Choose a Letter Template page, click *Bounced check* and then click Next.
6. At the Enter a Name and Title page, enter the following data:

   Name: [Your Name]
   Title: Assistant Accountant

7. Click Next. Microsoft Word opens, and the bounced check letter is displayed with your company name, the current date, and the customer name included. See Figure 12–Z.

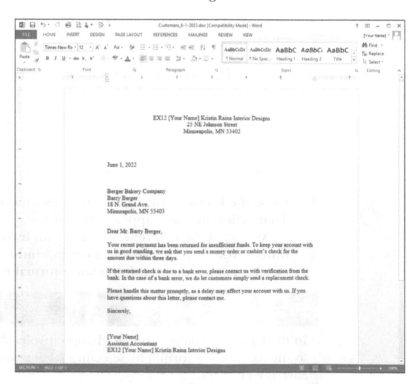

8. Close Microsoft Word. Do not save the letter.
9. Close the Letters and Envelopes window.

Memorized Transactions

Many routine business activities are repeated, often at daily, weekly, and monthly intervals. QuickBooks allows you to memorize repetitive transactions. Once a transaction has been memorized, you can recall the transaction at the appropriate time to record it, or you can have QuickBooks automatically record the transaction on certain dates.

An example of a transaction that could be memorized is the monthly rent Kristin Raina Interior Designs pays for its space. On June 1, 2022, Kristin Raina Interior Designs is ready to pay the monthly rent of $800 to Nordic Realty. Because this is a routine bill, Kristin Raina decides to have you set it up as a memorized transaction. To memorize a transaction, you first enter the data for the transaction as a regular transaction, and then before saving it, you set it up as a memorized transaction.

To set up and memorize a transaction:

1. At the main menu bar, click Banking and then click *Write Checks*.
2. Enter the following data for the rent expense, as you have previously learned:

Bank Account:	1010 - Cash - Operating
No.:	14
Date:	06/01/2022
Pay to the Order of:	Nordic Realty
Amount:	800
Memo:	(none)
Account:	6400 Rent Expense

See Figure 12–AA.

FIGURE 12–AA
Write Checks - Cash - Operating Window— Rent Expense

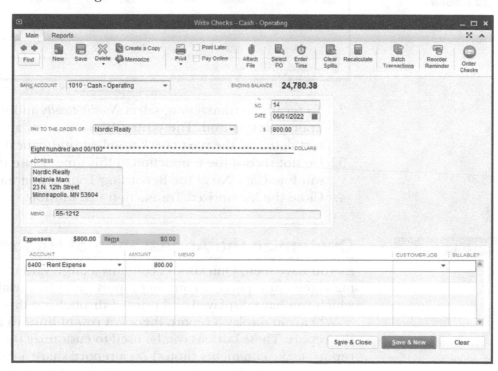

3. If the information is correct, click Edit at the main menu bar and then click *Memorize Check*. The Memorize Transaction dialog box appears.
4. At the *How Often* field, click *Monthly*.
5. At the *Next Date* field, choose *07/01/2022*. See Figure 12–BB.

FIGURE 12–BB
Memorize Transaction
Dialog Box

6. If the information is correct, click OK. The transaction is memorized.
7. At the Write Checks window, click the Save & Close button.

Assume that it is now July 1, 2022, and time to pay the rent for July. You can recall the memorized transaction.

To recall a memorized transaction:
1. At the main menu bar, click Lists and then click *Memorized Transaction List*. The Memorized Transaction List window appears. See Figure 12–CC.

FIGURE 12–CC
Memorized Transaction
List Window

2. To recall the transaction, select *Nordic Realty* and then click the Enter Transaction button. The Write Checks window appears, with the correct date and the next check number automatically entered.
3. Do not record the transaction at this time. Close the Write Checks window. Click No at the Recording Transaction message.
4. Close the Memorized Transaction List window.

Reports ➝ ## Customize the Appearance of Reports

As you have seen, QuickBooks contains a large variety of pre-established management reports, accounting reports, and financial statements, many of which you have displayed and printed throughout this text.

When you display a report, there is a row of buttons along the top of the report. These buttons can be used to customize the presentation of a report, make comments (notes) on a report, share a customized report template, memorize settings in a report, email a report, export a report into an Excel spreadsheet, hide the header of a report, and collapse or expand the numbers on a report. In prior chapters, you displayed and printed reports using the pre-established settings—except in Chapter 4, in which you modified the report using the Filters and Header/Footer tabs of the Customize Report button. In this chapter, you will use most of the remaining buttons along the top of the report.

Customize Report Button

The Customize Report button is used to adjust the appearance of the report. The Customize Report button moves you to the Modify Report dialog box, which has four tabs: Display, Filters, Header/Footer, and Fonts & Numbers. A report can be modified to add or delete fields of information displayed in a report (Display tab); to filter (select) which categories of information should be included in a report (Filters tab); to indicate which information should be displayed in the headers or footers (Header/Footer tab); and to indicate the fonts and formats of the numbers in the reports (Fonts & Numbers tab).

Modify Report—Display Tab

Open the *Account Listing* report by clicking Reports and then clicking *List*. See Figure 12–DD.

FIGURE 12–DD
Account Listing Report

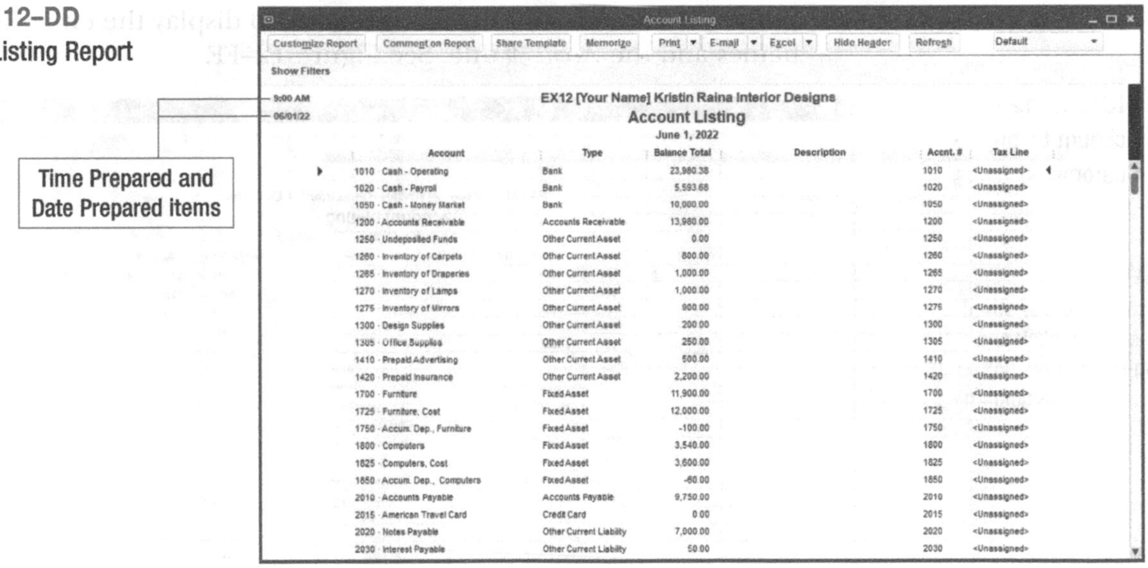

Time Prepared and Date Prepared items

To modify a report using the Display tab:

1. In the *Account Listing* report, click the Customize Report button at the top of the report. The Modify Report: Account Listing dialog box appears.

    In the Modify Report dialog box, the default tab is Display. The Display tab is used to indicate the fields of information that can be displayed in the columns in a report. Any column title that is checked is displayed.

    When adding new accounts to the Chart of Accounts List, you did not use the *Description* field; therefore, this field of information is blank. In the *Tax Line* field, all the accounts are marked unassigned. Since you do not need the information in these two fields, you can remove them from this report.

2. Remove the check marks from the field titles *Description* and *Tax Line*. See Figure 12–EE.

FIGURE 12–EE
Modify Report: Account
Listing—Display Tab

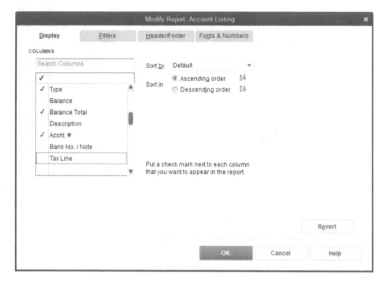

3. If the information is correct, click OK. The report is revised to exclude those two fields of information.
4. Widen the *Account* and *Accnt. #* columns to display the entire account names and the *Accnt. #* title. See Figure 12–FF.

FIGURE 12–FF
Account Listing—
Customized

HINT

To change the width of the column, click and drag the vertical dotted bar next to the column title.

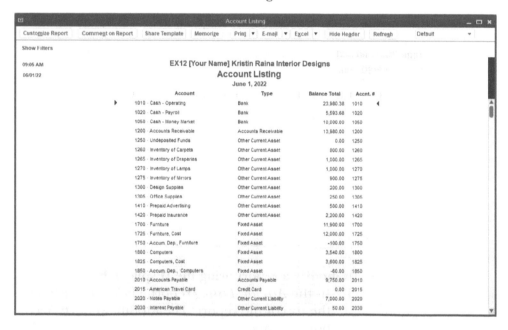

Modify Report—Header/Footer Tab

The Header/Footer tab is used to establish the presentation of the headers (including titles) and footers (including page numbers) to be displayed in a report. Two items in the heading of a report you can format are the Date Prepared and Time Prepared items. You may have noticed that when reports are displayed, by default, the date and time the report is prepared are always displayed in the upper left corner. The *Date Prepared* and *Time Prepared* fields are where you tell the software to display the current date and time on each report. This field is activated by default, which tells the software to display the current date and time as maintained by your computer.

If you print reports often, it is useful to have the date and time you print a report listed to avoid confusion among the many printouts. But there may be times you do not want the date or time displayed on a report. None of the printouts reproduced in this text included a current date or time because the *Date Prepared* and *Time Prepared* fields defaults were disabled.

To disable or change the format of the Date Prepared and Time Prepared items and change a title in a report:

1. In the *Account Listing* report, click the Customize Report button at the top of the report. The Modify Report: Account Listing dialog box appears.
2. In the Modify Report: Account Listing dialog box, click the Header/ Footer tab. The Header/Footer tab appears.
3. Click the Date Prepared drop-down list. You can use this drop-down list to change the format of the date.
4. To disable the Date Prepared item, remove the check mark from the box to the left of the *Date Prepared* field.
5. To disable the Time Prepared item, remove the check mark from the box to the left of the *Time Prepared* field.

    In the Header/Footer dialog box, you can also change or remove the company name, report title, subtitle, and footer information of the report.
6. At the *Subtitle* field, delete the date provided and then type June 30, 2022. See Figure 12–GG.

FIGURE 12–GG
Modify Report: Account Listing—Header/Footer Tab

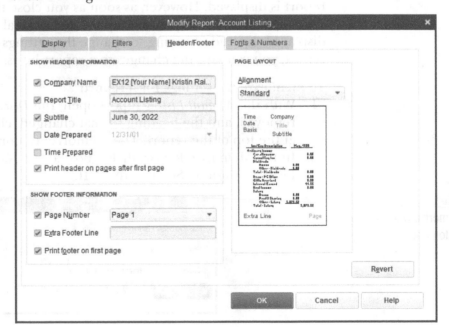

7. If the information is correct, click OK. You are returned to the *Account Listing* report. The Date Prepared and Time Prepared items have been removed, and the subtitle date has been changed. See Figure 12–HH.

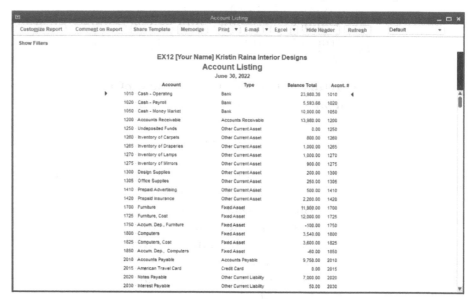

Keep the *Account Listing* report open for the next activity.

Memorize Button

The changes you just made to the report remain in place as long as the report is displayed. However, as soon as you close the report, those changes are lost. When you reopen the report, the original default settings are again displayed. Instead of having to change the settings each time you open the report, you can save the changes to a report by using the Memorize button.

To memorize the settings for a report:
1. With the *Account Listing* report open, the *Description* and *Tax Line* fields removed, and the heading format changed, click the Memorize button at the top of the report. The Memorize Report dialog box appears.
2. In the Memorize Report dialog box, at the *Name* field, type Account Listing - Custom. See Figure 12–II.

3. If the information is correct, click OK.
4. Close the *Account Listing* report.

Reopen the *Account Listing* report by clicking Reports and then *List.* Notice that all the original default settings are used to display the report. Close the *Account Listing* report. If you wish to see the memorized report, you must open it.

To open a memorized report:

1. At the main menu bar, click Reports and then click *Memorized Reports.*
2. At the Memorized Reports submenu, click *Memorized Report List.* The Memorized Report List appears. See Figure 12–JJ.

FIGURE 12–JJ
Memorized Report List

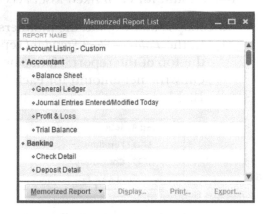

The first report on the list is the *Account Listing - Custom* memorized report. The other reports listed are the same reports that can be accessed from the Reports menu, but QuickBooks has organized them into groups for easy retrieval.

3. Double-click the report *Account Listing - Custom.*

The *Account Listing* report appears with all the changes intact. If you make any changes to a memorized report, they will be stored only while the report is displayed. If you wish to memorize the new changes, you must click Memorize again. You will then be given a choice to replace the memorized report with the new changes or to create an additional memorized report.

> **HINT**
> The memorized report can also be accessed at the Memorized Reports submenu.

4. Close the report and then close the Memorized Report List.

Collapse/Expand Button

Open the *Balance Sheet Standard* report for June 30, 2022, by clicking Reports and then clicking *Company & Financial.* Notice that the Date Prepared and Time Prepared items appear in the report window. Remove the Date Prepared and Time Prepared items using the Customize Report button (Header/Footer tab) at the top of the report. Notice how the fixed assets section appears on the screen. See Figure 12–KK.

FIGURE 12–KK
Balance Sheet Standard
Report—Fixed Assets
Section Expanded

Fixed Assets	
1700 · Furniture	
1725 · Furniture, Cost	12,000.00
1750 · Accum. Dep., Furniture	-100.00
Total 1700 · Furniture	11,900.00
1800 · Computers	
1825 · Computers, Cost	3,600.00
1850 · Accum. Dep., Computers	-60.00
Total 1800 · Computers	3,540.00
Total Fixed Assets	15,440.00

Recall that in the fixed assets section, the fixed asset account is the parent account, and the related cost and accumulated depreciation accounts are subaccounts of the fixed asset. On the *Balance Sheet Standard* report displayed on the screen, in the fixed asset section, the parent account is listed as a heading, the two subaccounts are listed under the parent account, and the parent account is listed again—this time with a subtotal of the two subaccounts. This format is referred to as *expanded*. As an alternative, you can collapse the accounts and numbers, so that only the net amount for each fixed asset account is displayed.

To collapse and expand the numbers in a report:

1. In the *Balance Sheet Standard* report, click the Collapse Rows button at the top of the report. Notice how the fixed assets are now displayed. Only the net amount for each fixed asset is displayed. See Figure 12–LL.

FIGURE 12–LL
Balance Sheet Standard Report—
Fixed Assets Collapsed Rows

Fixed Assets	
▷ 1700 · Furniture	11,900.00
▷ 1800 · Computers	3,540.00
Total Fixed Assets	15,440.00

Notice that the Collapse Rows button at the top of the report changed into the Expand Rows button.

2. To expand the numbers, click the Expand Rows button at the top of the report. The report returns to the original presentation.

Keep the *Balance Sheet Standard* report open for the next activity.

Excel Button

QuickBooks allows you to export a report to a Microsoft Excel worksheet, where you can incorporate the report into another Excel file you may have or create a new worksheet. You can then use Excel to further customize the report. Excel must be installed on your computer to export the report.

To export a report to a new Microsoft Excel worksheet:

1. With the *Balance Sheet Standard* report (expanded) for June 30, 2022, displayed, click the Excel button at the top of the report. A drop-down list appears that offers two choices: *Create New Worksheet* and *Update Existing Worksheet*.

2. Choose *Create New Worksheet*. The Send Report to Excel dialog box appears. See Figure 12–MM.

FIGURE 12–MM
Send Report to Excel
Dialog Box

HINT

If you previously made an incorrect choice at the drop-down list, you can change to the correct choice in this dialog box.

In this dialog box, you also have these choices: *Create new worksheet in new workbook* or *in existing workbook, Update an existing worksheet, Replace an existing worksheet,* and *Create a comma separated values (.csv) file.*

3. Click the Advanced button. The Advanced Excel Options dialog box appears. See Figure 12–NN.

FIGURE 12–NN
Advanced Excel Options
Dialog Box

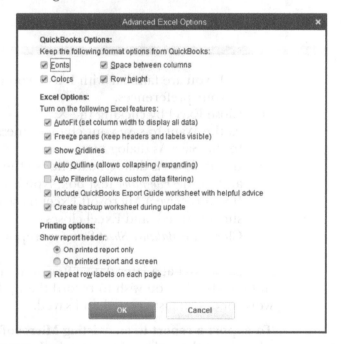

The Advanced Excel Options dialog box allows you to carry over formatting from QuickBooks to Excel and to turn on Excel options and printing options. You can make these choices in QuickBooks, or you can make them directly in the Excel worksheet after the report is exported into Excel.

4. In the Advanced Excel Options dialog box, click Cancel.
5. In the Send Report to Excel dialog box, with *Create new worksheet* and *in new workbook* selected, click Export. Excel opens and a worksheet is prepared, with the *Balance Sheet Standard* report exported into the worksheet. See Figure 12–OO.

FIGURE 12-OO Balance Sheet Standard Report Exported to Microsoft Excel

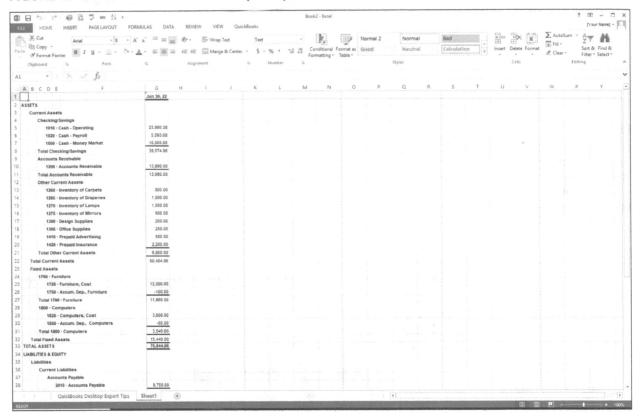

If you are familiar with Excel, you may revise the report according to your preferences.

6. Close Excel by clicking the X.
7. At the Want to save your changes message, click Save. You are moved to the Save As dialog box.
8. In the Save As dialog box, choose the folder where you save your files, and in the *File name* text box, type EX12 *(Your Name)* QB-BS. Click Save. If you receive a Microsoft Excel message, click Yes. The Excel worksheet is saved, and Excel closes.
9. Close the *Balance Sheet Standard* report.

Assume that at a later date, after more activities have been recorded in QuickBooks, you wish to record the updated information in the Excel worksheet you just created and saved.

To export a report to an existing Microsoft Excel worksheet:

1. Open the *Balance Sheet Standard* report and use the date *July 31, 2022.*
2. Click the Excel button.
3. At the drop-down list, click *Update Existing Worksheet.*
4. In the Send Report to Excel dialog box, click the Browse button. You are moved to the Open Microsoft Excel File dialog box.
5. Select the folder where you save your files, select the file **EX12** *(Your Name)* **QB-BS**, and then click Open. You are returned to the Send Report to Excel dialog box, with the path filled in the first box in the *Select workbook* field.

6. In the second box in the *Select workbook* field, click the drop-down list, choose *Sheet1*, and then click Export.

An Export Report Alert message appears, inquiring if you want the existing worksheet updated with new data. If you want to update the existing worksheet, click Yes. If you prefer to retain the existing worksheet intact, click No, which will end the process. Start over again using the previous steps to export a report to a new worksheet.

7. At the Export Report Alert message, click Yes. Excel opens the existing worksheet updated with the new data. The only change in this worksheet is that the date has been updated to *July 31, 2022*. Any previous changes in the formatting of the Excel worksheet will have been retained.
8. Close Excel. Do not save the changes.
9. Close the *Balance Sheet Standard* report.

Share Template Button

HINT

You can also access customized report templates from the Reports menu. Click Reports and then click *Contributed Reports*. From the Contributed Reports menu, select any report category. You are moved to the Report Center–Contributed tab.

In addition to the Reports menu, QuickBooks includes a Report Center. The Report Center provides the same choices of reports that appear on the Reports menu. The Report Center also allows you to memorize reports, save favorites, and view recent reports. An added feature to the Report Center is a forum where customized report templates can be shared among QuickBooks users. The customized report templates are provided by both Intuit and QuickBooks users. An internet connection is required to use the Report Center.

To access the Report Center, click Reports and then click *Report Center*. By default, the Intuit report templates are displayed on the Standard tab. The customized report templates are accessed on the Contributed tab in the Report Center. Click the Contributed tab. To access report templates prepared by other QuickBooks users, in the Report Center, on the Contributed tab, at the *SORT BY* field, choose *Community created* at the drop-down menu. You can select a customized report template by double-clicking on a report. When you customize any of these reports, the Share Template button in the report is activated, which then allows you to share your report with the community. Only the format of a report is shared, not the financial details. Close the Reports Center.

Process Multiple Reports

Reports

In each chapter, as various reports were displayed, each report was opened one at a time. QuickBooks also allows you to open several reports at the same time. For example, Kristin Raina wishes to display the *Trial Balance*, *Profit & Loss Standard*, and *Balance Sheet Standard* reports for the period January 1, 2022, through June 30, 2022.

To display multiple reports:
1. At the main menu bar, click Reports and then click *Process Multiple Reports*. The Process Multiple Reports window is displayed.
2. At the Select Memorized Reports From drop-down list, click *<All Reports>*. See Figure 12–PP.

FIGURE 12–PP
Process Multiple
Reports Window

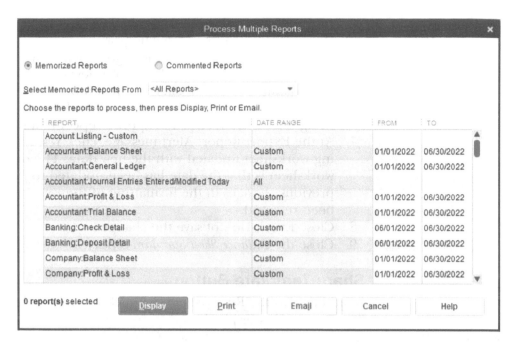

All the reports are listed. In the *From* and *To* fields, the current month or the current fiscal year-to-date is displayed. QuickBooks includes pre-established groups with which reports are classified. Custom groups can be created and reports can be memorized in a custom group. The name to the left of each report lists the pre-established group where QuickBooks locates the report. These classifications do not affect the display of the report.

3. Insert a check mark to the left of *Accountant: Balance Sheet*, *Accountant: Profit & Loss*, and *Accountant: Trial Balance*.

4. At the *From* and *To* fields for each report, choose *01/01/2022* and *06/30/2022* and then click Display. All three reports are displayed for the period of time indicated.

5. Close all the reports.

Reports

Set Default Settings in Reports

You saw that each time you display a report, you can modify the display by using the Customize Report (Display, Filters, Header/Footer tabs) and Collapse/Expand buttons. You also saw that these changes are only temporary. To save the changes, you can memorize the report. Or you can change the default settings for *all* reports using the Preferences window. For example, you can change the Date Prepared and Time Prepared items default settings.

To turn off or change the Date Prepared and Time Prepared items default settings:

1. At the main menu bar, click Edit and then click *Preferences*.
2. In the left panel of the Preferences window, click the Reports & Graphs icon.
3. Click the Company Preferences tab. See Figure 12–QQ.

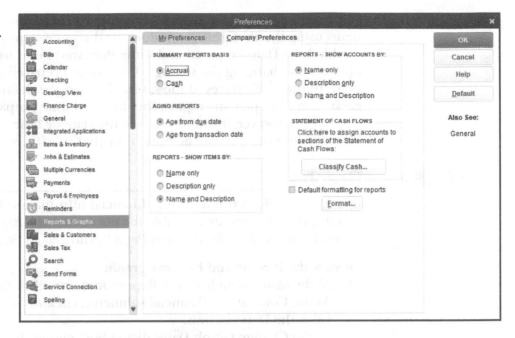

4. Click the Format button. The Report Format Preferences dialog box appears; it has two tabs: Header/Footer and Fonts & Numbers.
5. Click the Header/Footer tab, if necessary. You can change the default formats or disable any field of information for all the reports on this tab.
6. To disable the Date Prepared item, remove the check mark from the box to the left of the *Date Prepared* field.
7. To disable the Time Prepared item, remove the check mark from the box to the left of the *Time Prepared* field. See Figure 12–RR.

FIGURE 12–RR
Report Format
Preferences Dialog
Box—Header/Footer
Tab—Date Prepared and
Time Prepared Items
Disabled

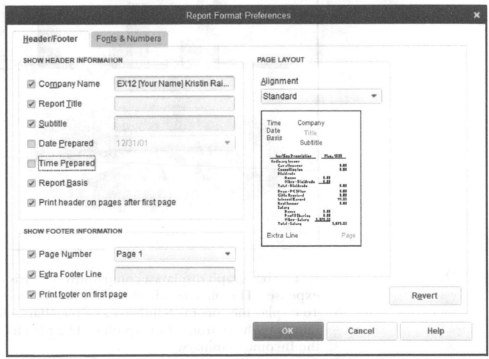

8. Click OK in the Report Format Preferences dialog box. You are returned to the Preferences window.
9. Click OK.

The steps you used to disable the Date Prepared and Time Prepared items using the Preferences window are the same steps you took when you disabled the Date Prepared and Time Prepared items while a report was opened. By changing the settings of the Date Prepared and Time Prepared items in the Preferences window, you changed the default settings. Now, each time you open any report, the date and time prepared are no longer displayed. However, if you wish to see the date or time prepared in an individual report, you can activate it for that specific report.

Reports

Graphs

QuickBooks allows you to display financial information in graph format. Graph presentations are available for the *Income and Expense, Net Worth, Accounts Receivable, Sales, Accounts Payable,* and *Budget vs. Actual* reports.

To view the Income and Expense graph:
1. At the main menu bar, click Reports and then click *Company & Financial.*
2. At the Company & Financial submenu, click *Income & Expense Graph.*
3. Click the Dates button.
4. In the Change Graph Dates dialog box, choose from *01/01/2022* to *05/31/2022* and then click OK. The Income and Expense graphs for that period of time appear. See Figure 12–SS.

FIGURE 12–SS
Income and Expense Graph Window

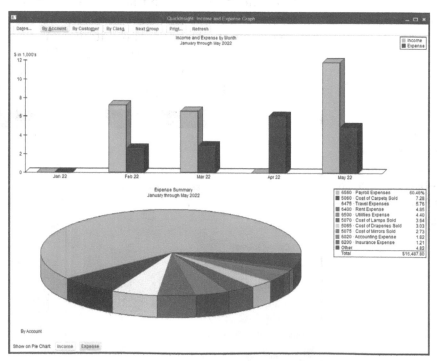

The bar graph displays a comparative analysis of income and expenses. The pie chart, by default, displays the Expense Summary.
5. To display the Income Summary as a pie chart, click the Income button at the bottom of the window. The pie chart changes to display the Income Summary.
6. Close the graph.

All graphs are displayed in the same manner. The graphs that are available can be accessed using the Reports menu at the main menu bar or the Reports button in the List windows.

Fiscal Year

Businesses must prepare their financial statements, including the *Profit & Loss* report and the *Balance Sheet* report, at least once per year. The year can be the calendar year or any other 12-month period. This 12-month financial reporting year for the company is called the fiscal year.

In QuickBooks, the start of the fiscal year is displayed in the Company Information—Report Information window.

To view the fiscal year for Kristin Raina Interior Designs:
1. At the main menu bar, click Company and then click *My Company*.
2. At the My Company window, click the Edit icon. The Company Information window appears.
3. At the Company Information window, on the left, click *Report Information*.
    The fiscal year for this company begins in January, which implies that the fiscal year for Kristin Raina is January 1 through December 31.
4. Close the Company Information and My Company windows.

Fiscal Year Closing

In a manual accounting system and in most other computerized accounting software packages, the books are closed on fiscal year-end. When the books are closed, each of the temporary accounts—usually revenues, expenses, and some equity accounts—is brought to a zero balance, and the net income for the year is transferred into a capital or retained earnings equity account for the next year. After the books are closed, preclosing balances in the temporary accounts are no longer accessible.

QuickBooks does not require you to close the books on fiscal year-end. However, QuickBooks automatically creates an Owner's Equity system default account, and at the start of a new fiscal year, automatically transfers the net income for the previous fiscal year into it. In addition, at the beginning of the new fiscal year, all the revenue and expense accounts will begin with zero balances so the net income for the new fiscal year can be accumulated.

When the new company file was created for Kristin Raina Interior Designs, the fiscal year was designated as beginning on January 1, which is displayed in the Company Information—Report Information window, as previously illustrated. Recall that in New Company Setup (Chapters 6 and 7), the Owner's Equity system default account created by QuickBooks was renamed *Accumulated Earnings*. When you move to the new fiscal year, January 1, 2023, QuickBooks transfers the net income for 2022 into the equity account called *Accumulated Earnings*. For example, look at the *Profit & Loss Standard* report for the period January 1, 2022, to June 30, 2022. There is a net income of $8,357.58. See Figure 12–TT.

FIGURE 12–TT
Profit & Loss
Standard Report—
January 1, 2022–
June 30, 2022—
Net Income Section

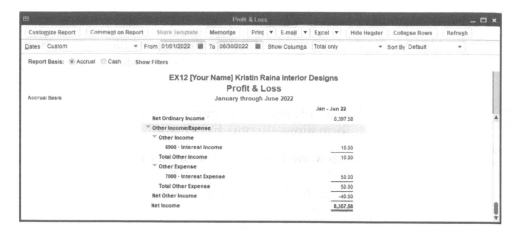

The net income is carried over to the *Balance Sheet Standard* report for June 30, 2022. See Figure 12–UU.

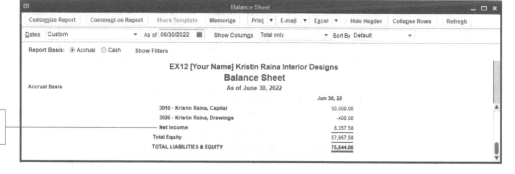

Assuming no other activity for the year 2022, look at the *Balance Sheet Standard* and *Profit & Loss Standard* reports for the first day of the new fiscal year, January 1, 2023. On the *Balance Sheet Standard* report, notice that there is no longer a line labeled *net income*, but the $8,357.58 has been transferred into the Accumulated Earnings account. See Figure 12–VV.

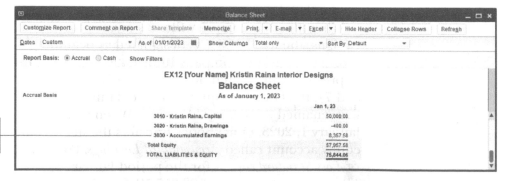

In addition, on the *Profit & Loss Standard* report, the revenue and expenses accounts all begin with zero balances for the start of the new fiscal year. Since there are no revenues or expenses on January 1, 2023, there is no income. See Figure 12–WW.

At this point, if you wanted to close the Drawings account, you would have to record an adjusting journal entry in the Make General Journal Entries window. Close all the windows.

FIGURE 12–WW
Profit & Loss
Standard Report—
January 1, 2023

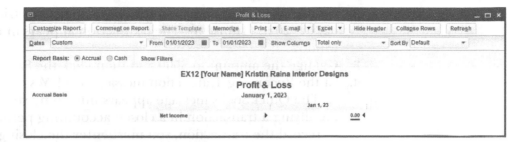

Set the Closing Date

HINT

You may want to make a backup copy of the company file and label it *preclosing* before following the steps to set the closing date or condense the company file.

Because QuickBooks does not actually close the books, you still have access to all the records for prior years. As a precaution, however, you can protect the data for a fiscal year by restricting access to the records so no changes can be made after fiscal year-end. This is accomplished when you set the closing date.

To set the closing date:

1. At the main menu bar, click Company and then click *Set Closing Date*. The Preferences window appears at the Accounting page—Company Preferences tab.
2. Click the Set Date/Password button. The Set Closing Date and Password dialog box appears.
3. Read the page, and then at the *Closing Date* field, choose *12/31/2022*.
4. In the *Closing Date Password* and *Confirm Password* text boxes, type Student1 or a password of your choosing. See Figure 12–XX.

FIGURE 12–XX
Set Closing Date and Password Dialog Box

HINT

As a matter of convenience, we are using the same password that has been used for all the company files for this textbook: *Student1*. You do not have to use the same password in the Set Closing Date and Password dialog box that was used for the company file.

5. If the information is correct, click OK.
6. At the Preferences window, click OK.

If you need to make a change to a transaction in the company file after you set the closing date, you will receive a warning that the company file is closed, and you will need to enter the password to save any changes.

To enter updated information in a company file that is closed:

1. Open the *Journal* report and enter the dates from *02/01/2022* to *2/28/2022*.

2. Double-click the transaction for Minneapolis Electric and Gas dated 02/02/2022 (Trans# 3). The transaction appears in the Enter Bills window.
3. Change the amount to $500 and then click the Save & Close button.
4. At the Recording Transaction message, click Yes.

    The QuickBooks message appears informing you that you are modifying a transaction in a closed accounting period. If you still wish to record the transaction, you must enter the closing date password (*Student1*).

5. Do not save the change. Click Cancel at the QuickBooks message and then close the Enter Bills window.
6. At the Recording Transaction message, click No.
7. Close the *Journal* report.

New Fiscal Year

In QuickBooks, the accounting records are not closed, so all the activities previously recorded will be retained in the company file. If you wish to continue with the company file in the new fiscal year but do not want to carry forward the prior fiscal year activities into the new fiscal year, QuickBooks provides the Condense Data utility. When you condense the data in a company file, the prior year activities are removed from the company file, but all the preferences previously established remain intact.

    As part of the process, QuickBooks makes a copy of the company file before condensing it. Note that this process is normally done in the year after the fiscal year-end. The company file for Kristin Raina Interior Designs is for 2022. If you attempt to do this process before January 1, 2023, it may not be completed.

To condense the company file to prepare for the new fiscal year:
1. At the main menu bar, click File and then click *Utilities*.
2. At the Utilities submenu, click *Condense Data*. The Condense your company file window appears with the *How do you want to condense your company file?* page displayed.
3. Accept the default *Remove the transactions you select from your company file* and click Next. The Condense Data dialog box appears with the *What transactions do you want to remove?* page displayed.
4. Choose the *Transactions before a specific date* option and choose *January 1, 2023*. See Figure 12–YY.

FIGURE 12–YY
Condense Data
Dialog Box

5. If the information is correct, click Next.
6. At the How Should Transactions Be Summarized? page, accept the default *Create one summary journal entry (recommended)* and then click Next.
7. At the How Should Inventory Be Condensed? page, accept the default *Summarize inventory transactions (recommended)* and then click Next.
8. At the Do You Want To Remove The Following Transactions? page, accept the defaults and then click Next.
9. At the Do You Want To Remove Unused List Entries? page, accept the defaults and then click Next.
10. At the Begin Condense page, click Begin Condense. It will take several minutes, and then you will see a QuickBooks Desktop Information message. Note that QuickBooks makes a copy of the company file. See Figure 12–ZZ.

FIGURE 12–ZZ
QuickBooks Desktop
Information Window—
Condense Complete

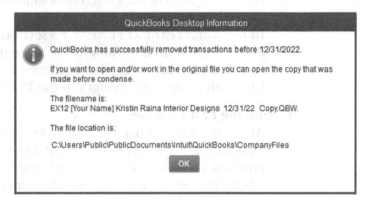

11. At the QuickBooks Desktop Information message, click OK.
12. In the condensed company file, if you view the *Balance Sheet Standard* report for January 1, 2023, you will notice that QuickBooks created an equity account 32000 Retained Earnings. Edit the account in the Chart of Accounts List and change it to 3030 Accumulated Earnings to match the company's pattern for numbering accounts.

The effect of condensing the file is similar to making the closing entries in a manual accounting system. A closing journal entry is recorded in the general journal. Balances in asset, liability, and equity accounts are carried forward into the new fiscal year in the general ledger. Balances in revenue and expense accounts are closed, and these accounts begin with zero balances in the general ledger in the new fiscal year. The company file is now ready for the activities for the new fiscal year.

Exiting QuickBooks

Upon completing this session, make a backup copy of your practice exercise company file to a removable storage device using the Back Up command and label it postclosing. Be sure to change the *Save in* field to the removable storage device and then carefully type the correct file name. Close the company file and then exit QuickBooks.

Chapter Review and Assessment

Procedure Review

To display the Home page, if it is not displayed:
1. At the main menu bar, click Company.
2. Click *Home Page* and then click the Home Page tab.

To access a window using the icons on the Home page:
1. On the Home page, click an icon. Either a window opens or a drop-down list appears.
2. If a drop-down list appears, select the appropriate option.

To enable a preference to customize the Home page:
1. At the main menu bar, click Edit and then click *Preferences.*
2. In the left panel of the Preferences window, click the Desktop View icon.
3. Click the Company Preferences tab.
4. In the RELATED PREFERENCES section, click the item marked *off,* and you are moved to the window to enable the preference. When you enable a preference, the icon or icons appear on the Home page.
5. Click OK to save the changes in the Preferences window.

To view the Left Icon bar:
1. At the main menu bar, click View. At the View drop-down menu, when a check mark appears to the left of *Left Icon Bar,* the Left Icon bar is enabled. If there is no check mark, the Left Icon bar is disabled.
2. Click *Left Icon Bar* if there is no check mark.

To view the Top Icon bar:
1. At the main menu bar, click View. On the View drop-down menu, when a check mark appears to the left of *Top Icon Bar,* the Top Icon bar is enabled. If there is no check mark, the Top Icon bar is disabled.
2. Click *Top Icon Bar* if there is no check mark. If the Left Icon bar was displayed, it would be removed when the Top Icon bar was displayed. (Only one Icon bar can be displayed.)

To add an icon to an Icon bar:
1. At the main menu bar, click View and then click *Customize Icon Bar.* The Customize Icon Bar window appears.
2. At the Customize Icon Bar window, click the Add button. The Add Icon Bar Item window appears.
3. At the Add Icon Bar Item window, scroll through the list on the left until you see the icon you wish to add.
4. Click the icon you wish to add.
5. Click OK at the Add Icon Bar Item window and then click OK at the Customize Icon Bar window to save the changes. The icon is now added to the Icon bar.

To edit an icon on an Icon bar:
1. At the main menu bar, click View and then click *Customize Icon Bar.* The Customize Icon Bar window appears.
2. At the Customize Icon Bar window, in the ICON BAR CONTENT section, scroll through the list and then click once on the icon you wish to edit to highlight it.

3. Click the Edit button.
4. At the Edit Icon Bar Item window, at the *Label* field, delete the name and then type the edited name.
5. Click OK at the Edit Icon Bar window and then click OK at the Customize Icon Bar window. The icon text is updated to the edited name on the Icon bar.

To remove an icon from an Icon bar:
1. At the main menu bar, click View and then click *Customize Icon Bar*. The Customize Icon Bar window appears.
2. At the Customize Icon Bar window, in the ICON BAR CONTENT section, scroll through the list and then click once on the icon you wish to delete to highlight it.
3. Click the Delete button.
4. Click OK to save the changes. The icon is removed from the Icon bar.

To change to flat or hierarchical view at the Chart of Accounts List window:
1. At the Chart of Accounts List window, click the Account menu button. By default, *Hierarchical View* is checked.
2. Click *Flat View*. The subaccounts are no longer indented; they are now left-aligned in the window.
3. Click the Account menu button and then click *Hierarchical View*. The presentation changes to indent the subaccounts.
4. Close the window.

To change the default setting of subaccounts:
1. At the main menu bar, click Edit and then click *Preferences*.
2. In the left panel of the Preferences window, click the Accounting icon.
3. Click the Company Preferences tab.
4. In the ACCOUNTS section, insert a check mark in the box to the left of *Show lowest subaccount only*.
5. Click OK. In the *Account Listing* report and the Activities window, only the subaccount will display (not the parent account followed by the subaccount).

To merge two accounts:
1. Open the Chart of Accounts List.
2. Select the account you wish to merge, but do not open it.
3. Click the Account menu button and then click *Edit Account*. The Edit Account window opens.
4. At the Edit Account window, change the name or number to the desired account to merge and then click the Save & Close button. A Merge message informs you that the account is already in use and asks if you wish to merge the accounts.
5. At the Merge message, click Yes. The two accounts are merged. All the information in QuickBooks is updated accordingly.
6. Close the Chart of Account List.

To create a custom field:
1. Open a center and then choose a customer or vendor by double-clicking the name. The Edit window appears.
2. Click the Additional Info tab.

3. On the Additional Info tab, in the CUSTOM FIELDS section, click the Define Fields button. The Set up Custom Fields for Names window appears.
4. On the first line in the *Label* column, type the name of the new field you wish to create.
5. At the *Use for:* field, insert a check mark in the appropriate column.
6. If the information is correct, click OK.
7. At the Information message, insert a check mark in the box to the left of *Do not display this message in the future* and then click OK. The new field text box is now displayed in the CUSTOM FIELDS section on the Additional Info tab.
8. In the new field text box, type the appropriate information.
9. If the information is correct, click OK to save it.
10. Edit each customer or vendor and type in the information in the new field text box on the Additional Info tab.
11. Close the Center.

To display customers or vendors in the Customer Center or Vendor Center for the custom field:
1. Open the Center.
2. Click the Search icon. The Custom Filter dialog box appears.
3. In the Custom Filter dialog box, click or type the appropriate information.
4. Click Go. The Center is updated to display only the customers or vendors that have been identified for the custom field on the Additional Info tab.
5. To remove the custom filter, click the X that replaced the Search icon.
6. Close the Center.

To customize the Create Invoices window and a printed invoice:
1. With the Create Invoices window open, on the Formatting tab, click the Manage Templates icon.
2. In the SELECT TEMPLATE section, make sure that *Intuit Service Invoice* is selected and then click the Copy button.
3. In the PREVIEW section, at the *Template Name* field, type Job Invoice.
4. Click OK.
5. At the Basic Customization window, click the Additional Customization button.
6. At the Additional Customization window, click the Columns tab.
7. Add or delete check marks for the different fields of information.
8. Change the order of the fields, if necessary.
9. Click OK at the Additional Customization and Basic Customization windows.
10. At the Create Invoices window, click the Save & Close button.

To prepare a business letter using QuickBooks Letters:
1. At the main menu bar, click Company and then click *Prepare Letters with Envelopes.*
2. At the Prepare Letters with Envelopes submenu, click *Customer Letters.* If the Find Letter Templates message appears, click the Copy button. The Letters and Envelopes window appears.

3. At the Review and Edit Recipients page, click the Unmark All button to remove all the check marks from the customer names.
4. Select the desired name and then click Next.
5. At the Choose a Letter Template page, select a letter and then click Next.
6. At the Enter a Name and Title page, enter the appropriate data.
7. If the information is correct, click Next. Microsoft Word opens, and the chosen letter is displayed with your company name and customer name included.
8. Save and print the letter and then close Microsoft Word.
9. Close the Letters and Envelopes window.

To set up and memorize a transaction:
1. Record a transaction as usual in an Activity window but do not click Save.
2. At the main menu bar, click Edit and then click *Memorize Check*.
3. At the *How Often* field, click *Monthly*.
4. At the *Next Date* field, choose the date to start the memorized transaction.
5. Click OK. The transaction is memorized.
6. At the Activity window, click the Save & Close button.

To recall a memorized transaction:
1. At the main menu bar, click Lists and then click *Memorized Transaction List*.
2. At the Memorized Transaction List window, select the transaction you wish to record and then click the Enter Transaction button.
3. The Activity window appears with the correct date and other information automatically entered. You may make changes, if necessary.
4. If you wish to record the transaction, click the Save & Close button.
5. Close the Memorized Transaction List window.

To modify a report using the Display tab:
1. Open the report and then click the Customize Report button at the top of the report.
2. In the Modify Report dialog box, the default tab is Display.
3. Insert or remove check marks from the column titles you wish to add or hide.
4. Click OK in the Modify Report dialog box.
5. Memorize the report if desired and then close the report.

To disable or change the format of the Date Prepared and Time Prepared items and change a subtitle in a report:
1. Open the report and then click the Customize Report button at the top of the report.
2. In the Modify Report dialog box, click the Header/Footer tab.
3. Remove the check marks from the boxes to the left of the *Date Prepared* and *Time Prepared* fields.
4. At the *Subtitle* field, delete the date provided and then type the new subtitle.
5. Click OK in the Modify Report dialog box.
6. Memorize the report if desired and then close the report.

To memorize the settings for a report:
1. Open the report and then make the desired changes.
2. Click the Memorize button at the top of the report.
3. In the Memorize Report dialog box, type the new report name in the *Name* field.
4. Click OK.
5. Close the report.

To open a memorized report:
1. At the main menu bar, click Reports and then click *Memorized Reports*.
2. At the Memorized Reports submenu, click *Memorized Report List*. The Memorized Reports List appears.
3. At the Memorized Reports List, double-click the desired report name. The memorized report appears.

To collapse and expand the numbers in a report:
1. Open the report and then click the Collapse Rows button at the top of the report. Any account that has subaccounts is collapsed into one net amount. The Collapse Rows button changes to the Expand Rows button.
2. To expand the numbers, click the Expand Rows button at the top of the report. The report returns to the original presentation, which lists the amounts for the subaccounts along with the net amount.
3. Close the report.

To export a report to a new Microsoft Excel worksheet:
1. Open the report and then click the Excel button at the top of the report. A drop-down list appears.
2. Choose *Create new worksheet*. The Send Report to Excel dialog box appears.
3. In the Send Report to Excel dialog box, click the Advanced button if you wish to review any Excel options and then click OK or Cancel.
4. In the Send Report to Excel dialog box, with *Create new worksheet* and *in new workbook* selected, click Export. Excel opens, and a worksheet is prepared using the report.
5. If you are familiar with Excel, you may revise the report according to your preferences.
6. Close Excel by clicking the X.
7. At the Do you want to save the changes message, click Save. You are moved to the Save As dialog box.
8. In the Save As dialog box, choose the folder where you save your files, and in the *File name* text box, type the file name and then click Save. The Excel worksheet is saved and Excel closes.

To export a report to an existing Microsoft Excel worksheet:
1. Open the report and enter the correct dates.
2. Click the Excel button. A drop-down list appears.
3. Click *Update Existing Worksheet*. The Send Report to Excel dialog box appears.
4. In the Send Report to Excel dialog box, with *Update Existing Worksheet* selected, click the Browse button. You are moved to the Open Microsoft Excel File dialog box.

5. Select the folder where you save your files, select the file, and then click Open. You are returned to the Send Report to Excel dialog box, with the path filled in the first box in the *Select workbook* field.
6. In the second box in the *Select workbook* field, choose *Sheet1* at the drop-down list and then click Export.
7. At the Export Report Alert message, click Yes. Excel opens the existing worksheet updated with the new data. Any previous changes in the formatting of the Excel worksheet will have been retained.
8. Close Excel and then close the report.

To display multiple reports:
1. At the main menu bar, click Reports and then click *Process Multiple Reports*. The Process Multiple Reports window is displayed.
2. At the Select Memorized Reports From drop-down list, click *<All Reports>*.
3. Insert a check mark to the left of each report you wish to view.
4. At the *From* and *To* fields for each report, choose the appropriate dates and then click Display. All the reports are displayed for the period of time indicated.
5. Close all the reports.

To disable or change the Date Prepared and Time Prepared items default settings:
1. At the main menu bar, click Edit and then click *Preferences*.
2. In the left panel of the Preferences window, click the Reports & Graphs icon.
3. Click the Company Preferences tab.
4. Click the Format button.
5. Click the Header/Footer tab. You can change the default formats or disable any field of information for all the reports on this tab.
6. To disable the Date Prepared item, remove the check mark from the box to the left of the *Date Prepared* field.
7. To disable the Time Prepared item, remove the check mark from the box to the left of the *Time Prepared* field.
8. Click OK in the Report Format Preferences dialog box. You are returned to the Preferences window.
9. Click OK.

To view a graph:
1. Use the Reports menu from the main menu bar or the Reports button in a List window to choose a graph.
2. Click the Dates button.
3. Choose the dates and then click OK. The graph for that period of time is displayed.
4. At the Income and Expense graph, to display the income as a pie chart, click the Income button. The pie chart changes to display the income analysis.
5. Close the graph.

To view the fiscal year:
1. At the main menu bar, click Company and then click *My Company*.
2. At the My Company window, click the Edit icon. The Company Information window appears.
3. At the Company Information window, on the left, click *Report Information*.
4. Close the Company Information and My Company windows.

To set the closing date:
1. At the main menu bar, click Company and then click *Set Closing Date*. The Preferences window appears at the Accounting page—Company Preferences tab.
2. Click the Set Date/Password button. The Set Closing Date and Password dialog box appears.
3. Read the page, and then at the *Closing Date* field, choose the closing date.
4. In the *Closing Date Password* and *Confirm Password* text boxes, type a password of your choosing.
5. If the information is correct, click OK.
6. At the Preferences window, click OK.

To enter updated information in a company file that is closed:
1. Open the *Journal* report and enter the appropriate dates.
2. Double-click the transaction. The transaction appears in the appropriate window.
3. Change the information and then click the Save & Close button.
4. At the Recording Transaction message, click Yes.
5. The QuickBooks message appears informing you that you are modifying a transaction in a closed accounting period. If you still wish to record the transaction, you must enter the closing date password.
6. Click OK or Cancel.
7. Close the Activity window and then click No at the Recording Transaction message.
8. Close the report.

To condense the company file to prepare for the new fiscal year:
1. At the main menu bar, click File and then click *Utilities*.
2. At the Utilities submenu, click *Condense Data*. The Condense your company file window appears with the *How do you want to condense your company file?* page displayed.
3. Accept the default *Remove the transactions you select from your company file* and then click Next. The Condense Data dialog box appears with the *What transactions do you want to remove?* page displayed.
4. Choose the *Transactions before a specific date* option, click the date of the new fiscal year, and then click Next.
5. At the How Should Transactions Be Summarized? page, accept the default *Create one summary journal entry (recommended)* and then click Next.
6. At the How Should Inventory Be Condensed? page, accept the default *Summarize inventory transactions (recommended)* and then click Next.
7. At the Do You Want To Remove The Following Transactions? page, accept the defaults and then click Next.
8. At the Do You Want To Remove Unused List Entries? page, accept the defaults and then click Next.

9. At the Begin Condense page, click Begin Condense. It will take several minutes, and then you will see a QuickBooks Information message. Note that QuickBooks made a copy of the company file.
10. At the QuickBooks Information message, click OK.
11. In the condensed company file, QuickBooks has created an equity account 32000 Retained Earnings. Edit the account in the Chart of Accounts List and change it to 3030 Accumulated Earnings to match the company's pattern for numbering accounts.

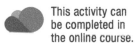

This activity can be completed in the online course.

Key Concepts

Select the letter of the item that best matches each definition.

a. Excel button
b. Additional Customization window—Columns tab
c. Header/Footer tab
d. Edit menu - Memorize Check
e. Accumulated Earnings
f. Display tab
g. Memorize button at the top of the report
h. Prepare Letters with Envelopes
i. Manage Templates icon
j. Collapse Rows/Expand Rows button

_____ 1. Used to choose fields of information and order of appearance in the Create Invoices window and on a printed invoice.
_____ 2. Command choice to use preformatted business letters available in QuickBooks.
_____ 3. Button used to save the changes made to the settings in a report.
_____ 4. Used to customize a pre-established invoice in QuickBooks.
_____ 5. Buttons used in a report to display all the parent accounts and their respective subaccounts or to display only the net value of the parent accounts and subaccounts.
_____ 6. Command used to save a routine transaction so you can recall it for later use.
_____ 7. Tab used to add or delete the fields of information displayed in each column in a report.
_____ 8. Account created and used by QuickBooks at the start of the new fiscal year to automatically transfer the net income of the previous year into it.
_____ 9. Button used to export a report into a spreadsheet.
_____ 10. Tab used to establish or edit the headers and footers to be displayed in a report.

This activity can be completed in the online course.

Procedure Check

1. In the Activities windows, when you choose an account with a subaccount, the parent account is displayed first in the account field, followed by the subaccount. How can you modify this display of account names?
2. You would like to prepare a list of all of your customers that live in the New York City area. How would you do this?
3. On the first of each month, you write a check for $100 for the liability insurance premium. How can you use QuickBooks to simplify this monthly process?

4. You change the columns of information displayed in the Customer Contact List every time you display it. What steps could you take to eliminate this repetitive formatting each time you view the List?
5. You wish to display a graph representing the sales for the first quarter of the year. How can you use QuickBooks to accomplish this?
6. Your manager is new to QuickBooks and has just used the Time-Tracking feature. However, when the data was transferred into the Create Invoices window, your manager found it difficult to read the information in the window. Explain how to change the settings in the Create Invoices window to display the information in a more useful way.

 Reports created for these Case Problems can be exported to Excel and uploaded in the online course.

Case Problems

Demonstrate your knowledge of the QuickBooks features discussed in this chapter by completing the following case problems.

Case Problem 12–1

Lynn's Music Studio recorded the income earned on the Highland School jobs for the month of July 2022 in the Create Invoices window, but Lynn Garcia has not yet sent the invoices to the school. It is now August 1, 2022, and she is ready to send the invoices for the first half of July but wishes to present the detail in a more desirable format. You have been requested to prepare a Job Invoice format and print Invoice Nos. 2020, 2021, and 2022.

1. Open the company file **CH12 Lynn's Music Studio.QBW**.
2. At the QuickBooks Desktop Login window, in the *Password* text box, type Student1 and then click OK.
3. Make a backup copy of the company file and name it **LMS12 *[Your Name]* Lynn's Music Studio**.
4. Restore the backup copy of the company file. In both the Open Backup Copy and Save Company File as dialog boxes, use the file name **LMS12 *[Your Name]* Lynn's Music Studio** and enter the password.
5. Change the company name to **LMS12 *[Your Name]* Lynn's Music Studio**.
6. Open the Create Invoices window and then display Invoice No. 2020.
7. Create a Job Invoice based on the Intuit Service Invoice, using the following information:
   a. Save the new invoice as *Job Invoice*.
   b. Delete the *Description* column.
   c. Add the *Item* column (Print).
   d. Add the *Service Date* column.
   e. Put the invoice columns in the following order:

Item:	1
Service Date:	2
Quantity:	3
Rate:	4

   The *Amount* field remains at 5.

8. Print Invoice No. 2020 and then save the invoice.
9. Open Invoice No. 2021, change it to the Job Invoice format, print the invoice, and then save the change.
10. Open Invoice No. 2022, change it to the Job Invoice format, print the invoice, and then save the change.

Case Problem 12–2

Olivia's Web Solutions recorded the income earned on the Thrifty Stores jobs for the month of September 2022 in the Create Invoices window, but Olivia Chen has not yet sent the invoices to the store. It is now October 1, 2022, and she is ready to send the invoices for the first half of September but wishes to present the detail in a more desirable format. You have been requested to prepare a Job Invoice format and print Invoice Nos. 1017, 1018, and 1019.

1. Open the company file **CH12 Olivia's Web Solutions.QBW**.
2. At the QuickBooks Desktop Login window, in the *Password* text box, type Student1 and then click OK.
3. Make a backup copy of the company file and name it **OWS12 *[Your Name]* Olivia's Web Solutions**.
4. Restore the backup copy of the company file. In both the Open Backup Copy and Save Company File as dialog boxes, use the file name **OWS12 *[Your Name]* Olivia's Web Solutions** and enter the password.
5. Change the company name to **OWS12 *[Your Name]* Olivia's Web Solutions**.
6. Open the Create Invoices window and display Invoice No. 1017.
7. Create a Job Invoice based on the Intuit Service Invoice, using the following information:
   a. Save the new invoice as *Job Invoice*.
   b. Delete the *Description* column.
   c. Add the *Item* column (Print).
   d. Add the *Service Date* column.
   e. Put the invoice columns in the following order:

Item:	1
Service Date:	2
Quantity:	3
Rate:	4

   The *Amount* field remains at 5

8. Print Invoice No. 1017 and then save the invoice.
9. Open Invoice No. 1018, change it to the Job Invoice format, print the invoice, and then save the change.
10. Open Invoice No. 1019, change it to the Job Invoice format, print the invoice, and then save the change.

Appendices

APPENDIX A
Open or Restore a Company File

At the Open or Restore Company window, it is important to understand the difference between the *Open a company file* option and the *Restore a backup copy* option. The following summarizes and compares opening a company file with restoring (opening a backup copy of) a company file. Compare Figure 1–F with Figure 1–N, and compare Figure 1–G with Figure 1–O below and on the next page. (These figures are the same illustrations that appear in Chapter 1.)

To *open* a company file, at the Open or Restore Company window, choose the *Open a company file* option. See Figure 1–F.

FIGURE 1–F

Open or Restore Company Window—Open a Company File Selected

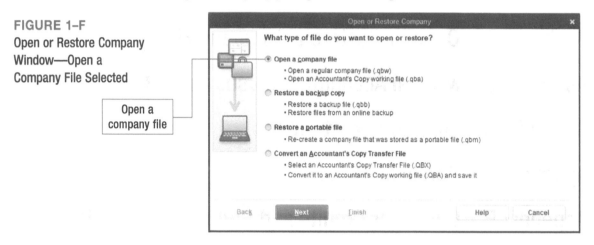

This window is followed by the Open a Company dialog box. See Figure 1–G.

FIGURE 1–G

Open a Company Dialog Box—CH1 Kristin Raina Interior Designs Company File Selected

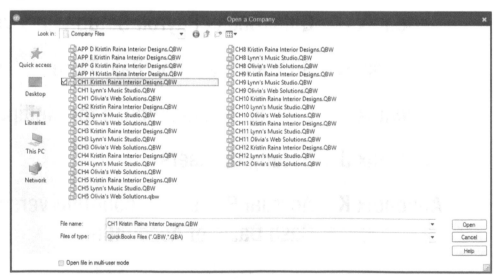

Notice that all the company files have the extension .QBW.

In contrast, when you want to open a backup copy of a file, you must restore the file. To *restore* a company file, at the Open or Restore Company window, choose the *Restore a backup copy* option. See Figure 1–N.

FIGURE 1–N
Open or Restore
Company Window—
Restore a Backup Copy
Selected

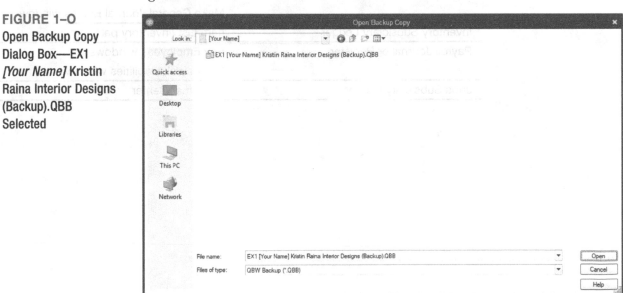

Restore a backup copy

This window is followed by the Open Backup Copy dialog box. See Figure 1–O.

FIGURE 1–O
Open Backup Copy
Dialog Box—EX1
[Your Name] Kristin
Raina Interior Designs
(Backup).QBB
Selected

Notice that any company files listed here will have the extension .QBB. If you do not see your backup copy file listed, you may be in the wrong dialog box. Go back to the Open or Restore Company window and be sure you selected the *Restore a backup copy* option.

APPENDIX B
Manual Accounting versus QuickBooks

A manual accounting system uses journals and ledgers. QuickBooks uses Lists/Centers, Activity windows, and Reports. Table B–1 summarizes and compares the journals and ledgers used in a manual accounting system with the Lists/Centers, Activity windows, and Reports used in QuickBooks, as explained in the chapters.

TABLE B–1
Manual Accounting versus QuickBooks

Manual Accounting System	QuickBooks
Accounts Payable Subsidiary Ledger	Vendor Center
Purchases Journal	Enter Bills window
	Enter Credit Card Charges window
Cash Payments Journal	Pay Bills window
	Write Checks window
	Pay Sales Tax window
Accounts Receivable Subsidiary Ledger	Customer Center
Sales Journal	Create Invoices window
Cash Receipts Journal	Receive Payments window
	Enter Sales Receipts window
General Ledger	*General Ledger* report
General Journal	*Journal* report
	Make General Journal Entries window
Inventory Subsidiary Ledger	Item List (inventory part items)
Payroll Journal or Register	Pay Employees windows
	Pay Payroll Liabilities window
Jobs Subsidiary Ledger	Customer Center

Journal Report Types

In a *Journal* report, the *Type* column indicates the window in which the activity was recorded. The System Default Account indicates the account that QuickBooks automatically uses to record activity. Table C–1 summarizes the Activity window and system default accounts for each journal entry type.

TABLE C–1 Journal Report Types

Type	Activity Window	System Default Account	
		Debit	Credit
Bill	Enter Bills		Accounts Payable
Credit	Enter Bills	Accounts Payable	
Bill Pmt — Check	Pay Bills	Accounts Payable	Cash — Operating
Check	Write Checks		Cash — Operating
Invoice	Create Invoices	Accounts Receivable	
Payment	Receive Payments	Undeposited Funds	Accounts Receivable
Sales Receipt	Enter Sales Receipts	Undeposited Funds	
Deposit	Make Deposits	Cash	Undeposited Funds
General Journal	Make General Journal Entries		
Inventory Adjust	Adjust Quantity/Value on Hand		
Sales Tax Payment	Pay Sales Tax	Sales Tax Payable	Cash
Paycheck	Pay Employees	Salaries and Wages Expense Payroll Tax Expenses	Payroll Liabilities Cash — Payroll
Liability Check	Pay Payroll Liabilities	Payroll Liabilities	Cash — Payroll
Transfer	Transfer Funds Between Accounts		
Credit Card Charge	Enter Credit Card Charges		Credit Card Liability
Credit Memo	Create Credit Memos/Refunds		Accounts Receivable
Discount	Receive Payments		Accounts Receivable

Purchase Orders

Businesses commonly use a purchase order document as part of the inventory process. The purchase order (PO) initiates an order from a supplier of goods and services and at the same time gives the purchasing company a record of goods on order but not yet received. In QuickBooks, the information contained in the PO documents (items ordered, quantity, cost, vendor name, and so on) serves as the basis for completing the Receive Items and Enter Bill or Write Checks windows when goods are received.

Appendix Problem

Before you begin, open the company file **APP D Kristin Raina Interior Designs.QBW**. Enter the password, *Student1*. Make a backup copy of the file, name it **EXD** *[Your Name]* **Kristin Raina Interior Designs**, and then restore the file and enter the password. Finally, change the company name to **EXD** *[Your Name]* **KR Interior Designs**.

Note: The company name is changed to KR Interior Designs *to fit the name in the PO ship to field.*

Activities

Creating a Purchase Order for Inventory Items

On April 1, 2022, Kristin Raina orders 10 carpets from Bell Carpet Design, as the *Stock Status by Item* report indicates that there are only 4 carpets in inventory. The Purchase Order No. is 1.

To create a purchase order:
1. At the main menu, click Vendors and then click *Create Purchase Orders*.
2. At the VENDOR drop-down list, click *Bell Carpet Design*.
3. At the *Date* field, choose *04/01/2022*.
4. At the *P.O. NO.* field, type 1, if necessary.
5. Complete the balance of the window in the same manner as you would the Receive Items and Enter Bill window. Note that the *Ship to* field contains the shipping address for Kristin Raina. See Figure D–1.

FIGURE D–1

Create Purchase Orders Window—Completed

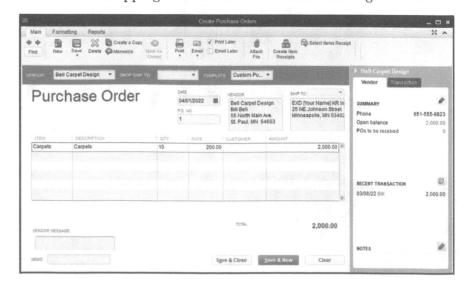

6. If the information is correct, click Save & Close.

The creation of a purchase order is not a transaction that changes general ledger posting accounts. No balances are affected. Kristin Raina can track open purchase orders through the *Open Purchase Orders* report contained in the Purchases submenu of the Reports menu. See Figure D–2.

FIGURE D–2 Open Purchase Orders Report

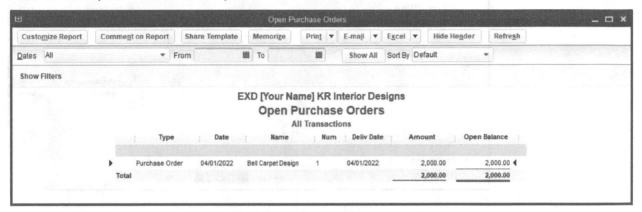

Recording Receipt of Inventory on Purchase Order

On April 5, 2022, Kristin Raina receives the carpets ordered on April 1 from Bell Carpet Design, its Invoice 12-5791. The bill is due May 5, 2022.

HINT

You can also access the Open Purchase Orders window by clicking the Select PO button at the Receive Items and Enter Bill window.

To record a purchase and receipt of inventory on order:

1. At the main menu bar, click Vendors and then click *Receive Items and Enter Bill.*
2. At the VENDOR drop-down list, click *Bell Carpet Design.* A window appears alerting you that open purchase orders exist for this vendor and asking *Do you want to receive against one or more of these orders?*
3. At the message, click Yes. The Open Purchase Orders window appears.
4. Choose the open purchase order by clicking in the ✓ column. See Figure D–3.

FIGURE D–3
Open Purchase Orders
Window—Open Purchase
Order Selected

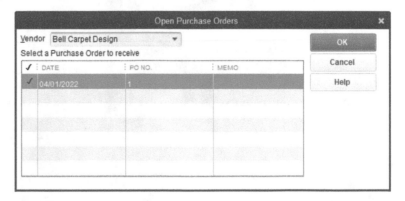

5. Click OK. The information from the Purchase Order window fills the appropriate fields in the Enter Bills window. See Figure D–4.

6. Complete the *DATE, REF. NO., BILL DUE,* and *TERMS* fields in the same way as illustrated in Chapter 5.
7. If the information is correct, click Save & Close.

   The same procedure can be employed if the purchase is recorded in the Write Checks window.

Customer Credits and Bad Debt Write-Offs

In Chapters 3 and 5, you learned to record sales of services and inventory on account in the Create Invoices window. This transaction created an accounts receivable from the customer, which you tracked through the *Customer Center* and *Customer & Receivables* reports. Collection of receivables was recorded in the Receive Payments window.

In Appendix E, you will record a credit memo for a customer return of inventory in the Create Credit Memos/Refunds window. The credit memo will reduce the balance owed by the customer and reduce sales revenue, while restoring the returned item to inventory.

In addition, in this appendix you will record the write-off of an accounts receivable that is determined to be uncollectible using the Receive Payments window. The write-off will result in the elimination of an accounts receivable and the recognition of a bad debt expense.

Appendix Problem

Before you begin, open the company file **APP E Kristin Raina Interior Designs.QBW**. Enter the password, *Student1*. Make a backup copy of the file, name it **EXE *[Your Name]* Kristin Raina Interior Designs**, and then restore the file and enter the password. Finally, change the company name to **EXE *[Your Name]* Kristin Raina Interior Designs**.

Activities

Record a Sale of Inventory on Account

1. Record the following transaction at the Create Invoices window. Refer back to the procedure in the section "Recording a Sale of an Inventory Item on Account" in Chapter 5 on pages 160–161.

Mar. 31, 2022	Sold the following on account to Maria Omari. Invoice No. 1020, Terms Net 30 Days.	
	4 lamps	$ 800.00
	2 carpets	800.00
	Total sale of merchandise	$ 1,600.00
	sales tax (.07 × $1,600)	112.00
	decorating services (6 hrs)	300.00
	Total sale on account	$ 2,012.00

See Figure E–1.

FIGURE E–1
Create Invoices Window—Maria Omari

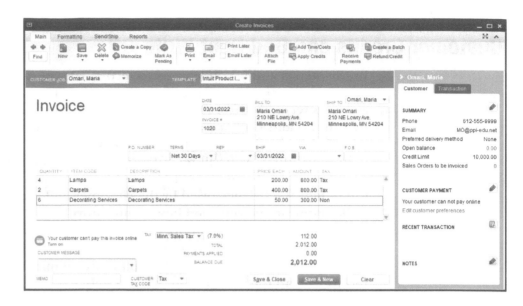

2. If the information is correct, click Save & Close.

Activities

Record a Customer Credit in the Create Credit Memos/Refund Window

The Create Credit Memos/Refund window is used to record a credit to a customer's account as a result of transactions such as returned inventory items from prior sales and allowances against prior invoicing. The credit can be in the form of a cash refund or credit available for use against future sales, or it can be applied to a specific open invoice. If a cash refund is made, a check can be created as part of the credit memo process. If the credit is applied to an open invoice, accounts receivable for that customer will be reduced.

The journal entry is as follows:

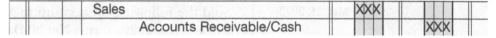

	Sales	XXX	
	Accounts Receivable/Cash		XXX

If the credit is a result of a returned inventory item, an additional journal entry will be made to return the item into the inventory account:

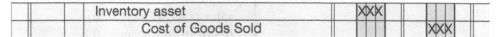

	Inventory asset	XXX	
	Cost of Goods Sold		XXX

On April 15, 2022, Maria Omari returns a lamp purchased on March 31, 2022, and a credit memo will be issued, No. 001. Because Invoice No. 1020 is still open, the credit memo will be applied against the unpaid balance.

To record a credit memo:
1. At the main menu bar, click Customers and then click *Create Credit Memos/Refunds.*

2. At the CUSTOMER:JOB drop-down list, click *Omari, Maria.* The invoice of March 31 is listed in the RECENT TRANSACTION section on the right, and the open balance of $2,012.00 appears in the SUMMARY section. See Figure E–2.

FIGURE E–2
**Create Credit Memos/
Refunds Window—Maria
Omari**

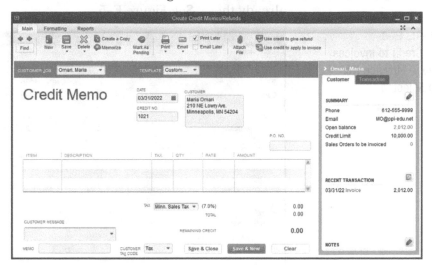

3. Enter the information provided on page 540 at the *DATE* and *CREDIT NO.* fields.
4. At the ITEM drop-down list, click *Lamps.*
5. At the *QTY* field, type 1. The word *Tax* should appear in the *CUSTOMER TAX CODE* field, and the *Print Later* and *Email Later* boxes should not be checked. See Figure E–3.

FIGURE E–3
**Create Credit Memos/
Refunds Window**

6. If the information is correct, click Save & Close. The Available Credit window appears and asks you how this credit should be used. See Figure E–4.

FIGURE E–4
Available Credit Window

7. Click the *Apply to an invoice* option and then click OK. The Apply Credit to Invoices window appears and lists the open invoices for this customer.

8. Insert a check mark on the line of Invoice No. 1020 if one is not already there. See Figure E–5.

FIGURE E–5
Apply Credit to Invoices
Window—Invoice No.
1020 Selected

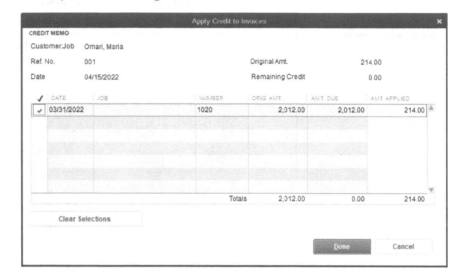

9. If the information is correct, click the Done button.
10. Open the Customer Center.
11. Select (highlight) *Maria Omari*.
12. At the DATE drop-down list, click *All*. A review of Maria Omari's customer file in the Customer Center shows the $214 credit, reducing her balance to $1,798. See Figure E–6.

FIGURE E–6 Customer Center—Maria Omari File

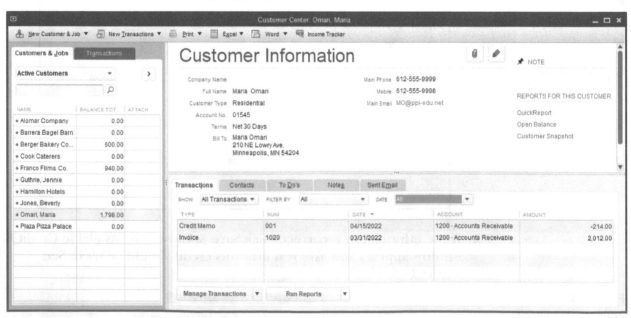

13. Close the Customer Center.

Inventory Valuation Detail Report

The cost of one lamp has been added back into inventory. View the *Inventory Valuation Detail* report for the period March 1, 2022, to April 30, 2022. Refer back to the procedure on page 172 in Chapter 5, if necessary. See Figure E–7.

FIGURE E–7
Inventory Valuation Detail Report

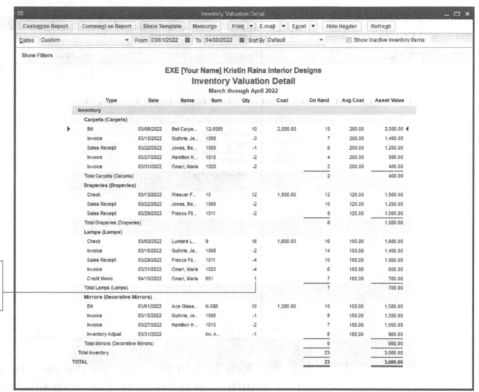

lamps inventory adjustment due to return

Recording the Write-Off of an Accounts Receivable (Bad Debt)

Often, companies that make sales on account must write off a receivable that will not be collected. Companies make every attempt to limit their losses by doing credit checks on customers, reviewing collection policies, and tracking the aging of receivables. However, despite a company's best efforts, a receivable may prove uncollectible. In QuickBooks, the write-off of an uncollectible account, called a *bad debt*, is accomplished using the Receive Payments window.

On April 30, 2022, Kristin Raina determines that the remaining balance owed by Franco Films Co. has become uncollectible, and she writes off the receivable and records a bad debt expense.

HINT

If the *PMT. METHOD* indicates *CHECK*, the *Reference* field will be called *CHECK #*. Changing the *PMT. METHOD* to *CASH* will change the title back to *Reference #*.

To record a bad debt:
1. At the main menu bar, click Customers and then click *Receive Payments*.
2. At the RECEIVED FROM drop-down list, click *Franco Films Co.* The open invoice for the customer is displayed.
3. At the *DATE* field, choose *04/30/2022*.
4. Leave the *AMOUNT* field at *0*.
5. At the *REFERENCE* # field, type Bad Debt 1.

6. Select the invoice by clicking in the ✓ column next to the open invoice.
7. Click the Discount and Credits button. This displays the Discount and Credits window.
8. At the *Amount of Discount* field, type 940.
9. At the Discount Account drop-down list, click *6075 Bad Debt Expense*. See Figure E–8.

FIGURE E–8
Discounts and Credits Window—Completed

10. Click the Done button to accept the discount (write-off) calculation. You are returned to the Receive Payments window, with the write-off amount in the *DISCOUNT* field. See Figure E–9.

FIGURE E–9
Receive Payments Window—Completed

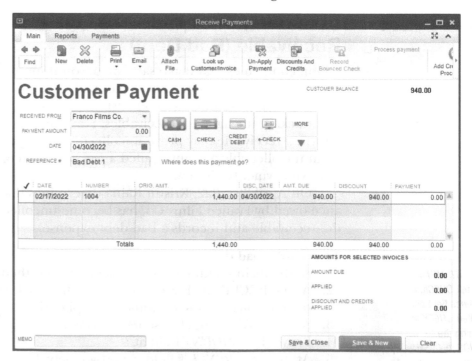

11. If the information is correct, click Save & Close.

Customer Balance Detail Report
and Profit & Loss Standard Report

1. View the *Customer Balance Detail* report. Refer back to the procedure on page 98, if necessary. See Figure E–10. Note that the balance for Franco Films Co. is now 0.

FIGURE E–10
Customer Balance Detail Report

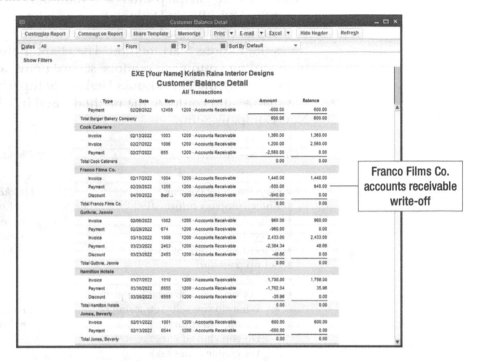

Franco Films Co. accounts receivable write-off

2. View a *Profit & Loss Standard* report for the period January 1, 2022, to April 30, 2022. Note the Bad Debt Expense for $940. See Figure E–11.

FIGURE E–11
Profit & Loss Standard Report January 1, 2022–April 30, 2022

Franco Films Co. write-off

APPENDIX F
New Company Setup Methods

New Company Setup → Users have two options for New Company Setup in QuickBooks: Detailed Start and Express Start. Chapter 6 illustrates the Detailed Start method, which uses the EasyStep Interview window. In addition, Chapter 6 illustrates using the QuickBooks Desktop Setup window to enter information for customers, vendors, service items, and inventory part items. Chapter 7 illustrates the Express Start method. The chapter also demonstrates the process of recording customers, vendors, service items, and inventory part items without using the QuickBooks Desktop Setup window. The following charts summarize and compare the methods used in Chapter 6 and Chapter 7 for New Company Setup.

Chapter 6—Detailed Start
↓

EasyStep Interview Window
- Enter company information
- Select industry
- Select business type
- Select first month of fiscal year
- Set up password
- Create company file
- Answer questions to establish preferences
  - ➤ What do you sell? (choosing products enables inventory)
  - ➤ Do you charge sales tax? (choosing Yes enables sales tax)
  - ➤ Do you have employees? (choosing No disables payroll)
- Provide start date for using QuickBooks
- Review income and expense accounts
  - ➤ Creates accounts in the Chart of Accounts List

↓

QuickBooks Desktop Setup Window*
- Enter customer information and opening balances
- Enter vendor information and opening balances
- Enter service items
- Enter inventory part items and opening balances

↓

Customize Chart of Accounts List
- Add account numbers
- Edit account numbers and names of accounts created by QuickBooks as part of the EasyStep Interview and QuickBooks Desktop Setup window

Chapter 7—Express Start
↓

QuickBooks Desktop Setup Window
- Enter company name
- Select industry
- Select business type
- Enter company information
- Create company file

↓

Create Company File Password
- Enter password

↓

Establish Preferences
- Add account numbers
- Enable inventory
- Enable sales tax
- Disable payroll

↓

Update Chart of Accounts List

continues...

...continued

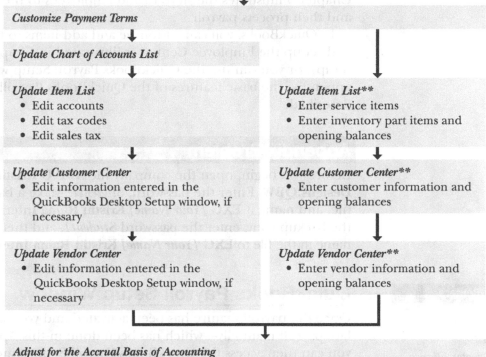

Customize System Default Accounts
- Edit account numbers and names of system default accounts created by QuickBooks
- Open and close windows to force QuickBooks to create additional system default accounts
- Edit additional system default accounts created by QuickBooks

Customize Payment Terms

Update Chart of Accounts List

Update Item List
- Edit accounts
- Edit tax codes
- Edit sales tax

Update Item List**
- Enter service items
- Enter inventory part items and opening balances

Update Customer Center
- Edit information entered in the QuickBooks Desktop Setup window, if necessary

Update Customer Center**
- Enter customer information and opening balances

Update Vendor Center
- Edit information entered in the QuickBooks Desktop Setup window, if necessary

Update Vendor Center**
- Enter vendor information and opening balances

Adjust for the Accrual Basis of Accounting
- Enter opening balances
- Reverse uncategorized income
- Reverse uncategorized expenses

* The QuickBooks Desktop Setup window can be used with either the Detailed Start method or the Express Start method of New Company Setup to enter information for customers, vendors, service items, and inventory part items, or it does not have to be used at all.

** All the information and balances can be entered directly into the Item List, Customer Center, and Vendor Center if you choose not to do so using the QuickBooks Desktop Setup window.

APPENDIX G
QuickBooks Payroll Setup Window

Chapter 8 illustrates the steps to activate the payroll feature and manual payroll option in QuickBooks, update the Chart of Accounts List for payroll, and customize and add payroll items to the Payroll Item List. Chapter 9 illustrates the steps to add employees to the Employee Center and then process payroll.

In QuickBooks, you can customize and add items to the Payroll Item List and set up the Employee Center, as illustrated in Chapters 8 and 9 (custom setup), or you can use the QuickBooks Payroll Setup window. In this appendix, the basic features of the QuickBooks Payroll Setup window are described.

Appendix Problem

Before you begin, open the company file **APP G Kristin Raina Interior Designs.QBW**. Enter the password, *Student1*. Make a backup copy of the file, and name it **EXG** *[Your Name]* **Kristin Raina Interior Designs**. Restore the backup copy, enter the password *Student1*, and then change the company name in the file to **EXG** *[Your Name]* **Kristin Raina Interior Designs**.

Lists/Centers

QuickBooks Payroll Setup Window

Once the payroll feature has been activated and you have chosen to calculate payroll manually—which has been done in this Appendix Problem—you can then access the QuickBooks Payroll Setup window. As part of this activation process, the Payroll Item List was created, as seen in, the section "The Payroll Item List" in Chapter 8 on pages 336–338. View the Payroll Item List in **EXG** *[Your Name]* **Kristin Raina Interior Designs**. The Payroll Item List includes typical federal tax items that generally apply to most payroll situations, such as Social Security, Medicare, federal withholding, and federal unemployment. As you enter information in the QuickBooks Payroll Setup window, additional items will be added to the Payroll Item List. In addition, in the Payroll Setup window, employees are added to the Employee Center.

To update the Payroll Item List and the Employee Center using the QuickBooks Payroll Setup window:

1. At the main menu bar, click Employees and then click *Payroll Setup*. The QuickBooks Payroll Setup window appears. See Figure G–1.

> **HINT**
>
> See Chapter 8 (pages 332–338) for the procedures on how to activate the payroll feature and set up processing payroll manually.

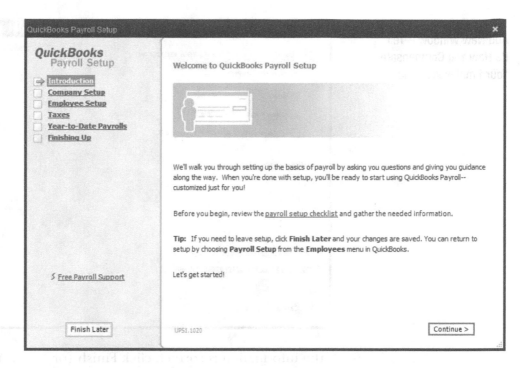

2. Read the page.

    At the QuickBooks Payroll Setup window, you move through pages; enter information when appropriate; and click Continue, Next, or Finish. As you proceed, you complete the six steps listed in the left panel of the QuickBooks Payroll Setup window. Notice the *payroll setup checklist* link. You can click this link to review a checklist provided by QuickBooks. (An internet connection is needed.)

3. Click Continue. You are moved to the *Set up your company compensation and benefits* page.

4. Read the page and then click Continue. You are moved to the Add New window—*Tell us how you compensate your employees* page. At this window, you add employee compensation items, which are added to the Payroll Item List.

5. At the *Tell us how you compensate your employees* page, choose *Salary* and *Hourly wage and overtime,* if necessary. Remove any other check marks. See Figure G–2.

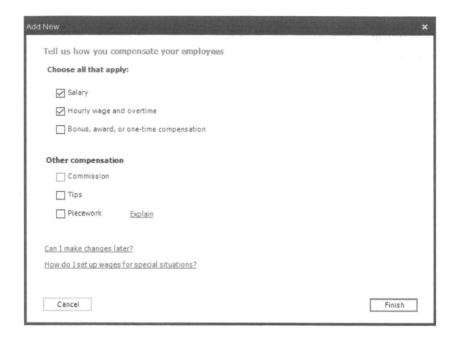

6. If the information is correct, click Finish (or Next). You are moved to the *Review your Compensation list* page.
7. Choose the Hourly compensation item by double-clicking *Hourly*. You are moved to the Edit: Hourly window.
8. At the Edit: Hourly window, at the *Show on paychecks as* field, type Hourly Wages.
9. In the Expense account section, at the Account name drop-down list, choose *Payroll Expenses: Salaries and Wages Expense*. See Figure G–3.

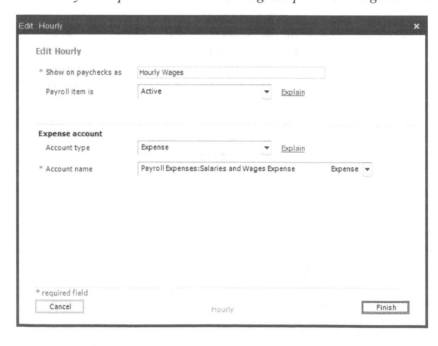

10. If the information is correct, click Finish. You are returned to the *Review your Compensation list* page.

11. Double-click the Salary item at the *Review your Compensation list* page to open the Edit Salary page, choose the Account name *Payroll Expenses: Salaries and Wages Expense,* and then click Finish. You are returned to the *Review your Compensation list* page.

   Our sample company, Kristin Raina Interior Designs, uses only the Salary and Hourly Wages compensation items. QuickBooks created the Double-time hourly and Overtime (×1.5) hourly items, which Kristin Raina will not use. You will delete these two items.

12. Click *Double-time hourly* once to select the item and then click the Delete button. At the Delete Payroll Item message, click Yes. The Double-time hourly item is deleted.

13. Delete the Overtime (×1.5) hourly item.

14. After you edit or delete each compensation item, click Continue. You are moved to the *Set up employee benefits* page.

15. Read the page and then click Continue. You are moved to the Add New window—S*et up insurance benefits* page.

16. Accept the default *My company does not provide insurance benefits* and then click Finish. You are moved to the *Review your Insurance Benefits list* page.

17. Click Continue. You are moved to the Add New window—*Tell us about your company retirement benefits* page.

18. Accept the default *My company does not provide retirement benefits* and then click Finish. You are moved to the *Review your Retirement Benefits list* page.

19. Click Continue. You are moved to the Add New window—*Set up paid time off* page.

20. At the *Set up paid time off* page, choose *Paid sick time off* and *Paid vacation time off.* See Figure G–4.

FIGURE G–4
Add New Window—Set Up Paid Time Off Page

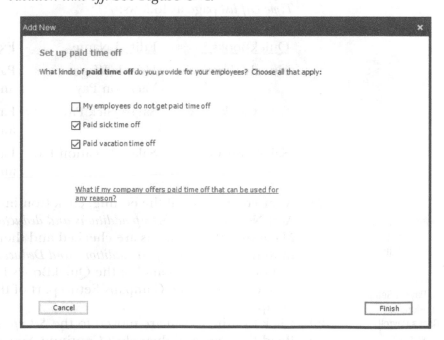

21. If the information is correct, click Finish. You are moved to the *Review your Paid Time Off list* page.

22. Choose the Hourly Sick paid time off item by double-clicking *Hourly Sick.* You are moved to the Edit: Sick Taken window.
23. At the *Show on paychecks as* field, type Hourly Wages Sick Pay.
24. At the Account name drop-down list, choose *Payroll Expenses:Salaries and Wages Expense.* See Figure G–5.

FIGURE G–5
Edit: Sick Taken Window

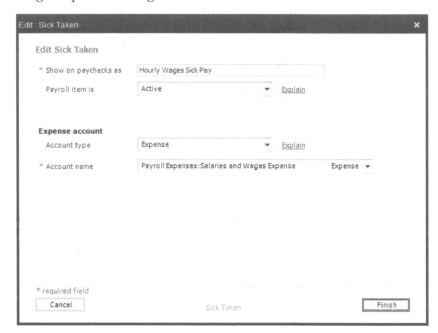

25. If the information is correct, click Finish. You are returned to the *Review your Paid Time Off list* page.
26. Repeat the steps to edit the remaining items at the *Review your Paid Time Off list* page as follows:

QuickBooks	Edited Name	Expense Account
Hourly Vacation	Hourly Wages Vacation Pay	Payroll Expenses: Salaries and Wages Expense
Salary Sick	Salary Sick Pay	Payroll Expenses: Salaries and Wages Expense
Salary Vacation	Salary Vacation Pay	Payroll Expenses: Salaries and Wages Expense

HINT

In the QuickBooks Payroll Setup window, at any time, you can click the Finish Later button, which will close the QuickBooks Payroll Setup window. To return to the QuickBooks Payroll Setup window, click Employees and then click *Payroll Setup.* You will be returned to the page where you left off.

27. After completing all the editing, click Continue. You are moved to the Add New window—*Set up additions and deductions* page.
28. Make sure that no items are checked and then click Finish. You are moved to the *Review your Additions and Deductions list* page.

    Look in the left panel of the QuickBooks Payroll Setup window. You have completed the Company Setup part of the QuickBooks Payroll Setup.
29. Click Continue. You are moved to the *Set up your employees* page.
30. Read the page and then click Continue. You are moved to the New Employee window. The information you enter here will be entered in the Employee Center.

31. Type in the following information:

First name:	Harry
Last name:	Renee
Print on check as:	Harry Renee
Employee status:	Active
Home Address:	323 S. Main Ave.
City:	St. Paul
State:	MN
Zip Code:	54120

See Figure G–6.

FIGURE G–6
Employee Harry Renee
Window—Enter
Employee's Name and
Address Page

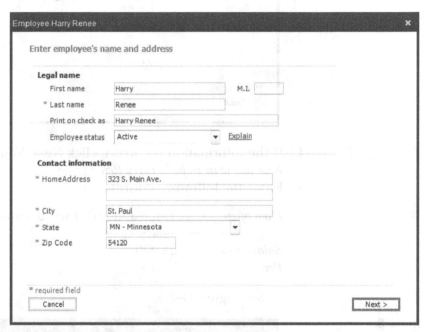

32. If the information is correct, click Next. You are moved to the Employee Harry Renee window—*Enter Harry Renee's hiring information* page.

33. Enter the following information:

Employee type:	Regular
Social Security #:	112-55-9999
Hire date:	4/1/2022
Birth date:	2/17/1988
Gender:	Male

See Figure G–7.

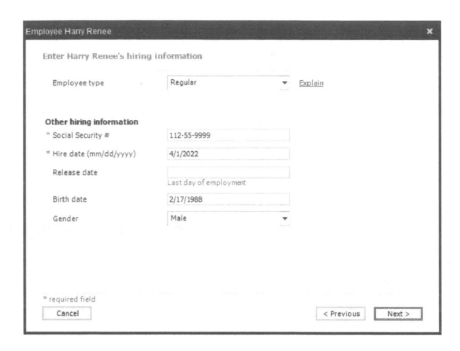

34. If the information is correct, click Next. You are moved to the *Tell us how you plan to pay Harry Renee* page.

35. Enter the following information:

How often?:	Twice a month (Semimonthly)
	Salary
Salary amount:	24,000
Per:	Year

See Figure G–8.

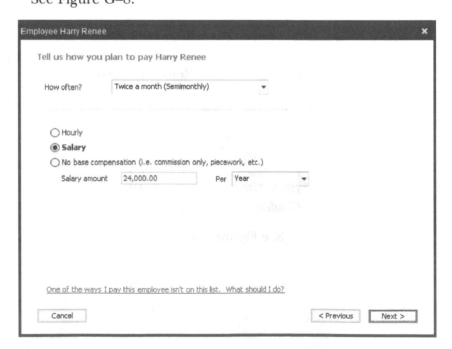

36. If the information is correct, click Next. You are moved to the *How is sick time off calculated for Harry Renee?* page.

37. Enter the following information, using the drop-down lists when necessary:

Calculation

Harry Renee earns:	48 hours at beginning of year
Unused sick hours:	must be used or lost by end of year
Sick time accrual year starts:	January 1
Harry Renee earns:	no time off until
Earn sick time hours starting:	4/1/2022

Current balances

Hours available as of (current date):	48
Hours used as of (current date):	0

See Figure G–9.

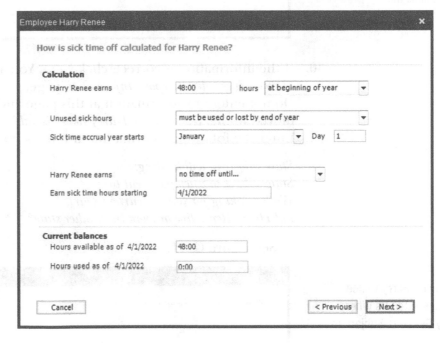

38. If the information is correct, click Next. You are moved to the *How is vacation time off calculated for Harry Renee?* page.

39. Enter the following information, using the drop-down lists when necessary:

Calculation

Harry Renee earns:	96 hours at beginning of year
Unused vacation hours:	must be used or lost by end of year
Vacation accrual year starts:	January 1
Harry Renee earns:	no time off until
Earn vacation hours starting:	4/1/2022

Current balances

Hours available as of (current date):	96
Hours used as of (current date):	0

See Figure G–10.

FIGURE G–10
Employee Harry Renee
Window—How Is
Vacation Time Off
Calculated for Harry
Renee? Page

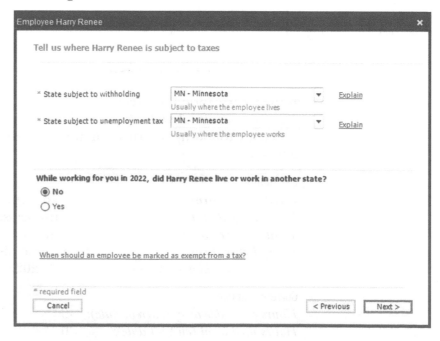

HINT

The date of the current
balances will be the
date on your computer.
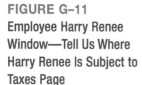

40. If the information is correct, click Next. You are moved to the *Set Up Harry Renee's direct deposit information* page.

41. Do not enter any information at this page and click Next. You are moved to the *Tell us where Harry Renee is subject to taxes* page.

42. Enter the following information, if it does not already appear:

State subject to withholding: MN - Minnesota
State subject to unemployment tax: MN - Minnesota
While working for you in (current year),
did Harry Renee live or work in another state?   No

See Figure G–11.

HINT

The year displayed will
be the year on your
computer.

43. If the information is correct, click Next. You are moved to the *Enter federal tax information for Harry Renee* page.

44. Enter the following information:

Filing Status: Single
Allowances: 1

See Figure G–12.

FIGURE G–12
Employee Harry Renee Window—Enter Federal Tax Information for Harry Renee Page

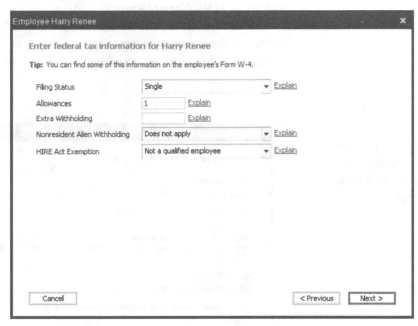

45. If the information is correct, click Next. You are moved to the *Enter additional federal tax information for Harry Renee* page.
46. Enter the following information, if necessary:

Subject to Medicare and
Medicare Employee Addl Tax: ✓
Subject to Social Security: ✓
Subject to Federal Unemployment: ✓

47. Accept all other defaults. See Figure G–13.

FIGURE G–13
Employee Harry Renee Window—Enter Additional Federal Tax Information for Harry Renee Page

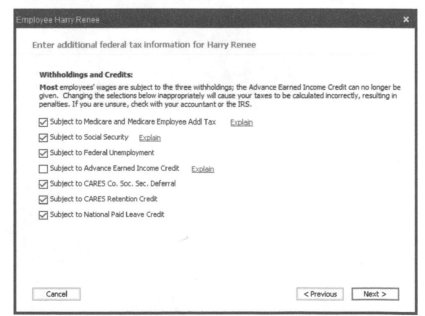

48. If the information is correct, click Next. You are moved to the *Enter state tax information for Harry Renee* page.

49. Enter the following information:

Filing Status:	Single
Allowances:	1
Subject to MN - Unemployment:	✓
Subject to MN - Workforce Enhancement Fee:	✓
Is this employee subject to any special local taxes not shown above?	No

See Figure G–14.

FIGURE G–14
Employee Harry Renee
Window—Enter State
Tax Information for Harry
Renee Page

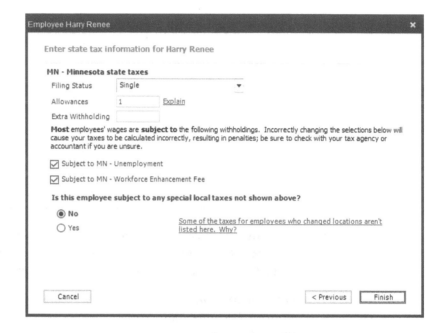

50. If the information is correct, click Finish. You are moved to the *Review your Employee list* page.

51. Click Add New. The New Employee window appears. Using Practice Exercise 9–1 on page 368, along with the information in Steps 52 and 53 below, enter the information for Richard Henderson, who was hired April 1, 2022.

52. At the Employee Richard Henderson window—*How is sick time off calculated for Richard Henderson?* page, enter the following information:

   Calculation

Richard Henderson earns:	48 hours at beginning of year
Unused sick hours:	must be used or lost by end of year
Sick time accrual year starts:	January 1
Richard Henderson earns:	no time off until
Earn sick time hours starting:	4/1/2022

   Current balances

Hours available as of (current date):	48
Hours used as of (current date):	0

53. At the Employee Richard Henderson window—*How is vacation time off calculated for Richard Henderson?* page, enter the following information:

   Calculation

Richard Henderson earns:	96 hours at beginning of year
Unused vacation hours:	must be used or lost by end of year
Vacation accrual year starts:	January 1
Richard Henderson earns:	no time off until
Earn vacation hours starting:	4/1/2022

   Current balances

Hours available as of (current date):	96
Hours used as of (current date):	0

   Do not enter any information on the *Set Up Richard Henderson's direct deposit information* page. Complete the tax information from the Practice Exercise on page 368.

54. After entering the information for Richard Henderson, click Finish. You are moved to the *Review your Employee list* page that lists both Harry Renee and Richard Henderson.

   Look at the list in the left panel of the QuickBooks Payroll Setup window. You have completed the Employee Setup part of the QuickBooks Payroll Setup.

55. Click Continue. You are moved to the *Set up your payroll taxes* page.

56. Read the page and then click Continue. You are moved to the *Here are the federal taxes we set up for you* page.

   The federal taxes that QuickBooks set up on the Payroll Item List are the ones common to most companies. While you have the choice here to edit these payroll items, you are not able to edit all the information at this time. Therefore, the federal taxes will not be edited here but later in this Appendix.

57. Click Continue. You are moved to the *Review your state taxes* page, and the Set up state payroll taxes window—*MN - Minnesota UI Fund payment* page appears. If the *MN - Minnesota UI Fund payment* page does not appear, double-click *MN-Unemployment* and then click Next.

58. At the *MN-Unemployment Company Rate* field, type 1.96.

59. Click Finish. You are returned to the *Review your state taxes* page.

60. Click Continue. You are moved to the Schedule Payments—*Set up payment schedule for Federal 940* page.

QuickBooks provides a Schedule Payments feature if you subscribe to one of the QuickBooks payroll services. The Schedule Payments feature allows you to keep track of your payroll tax and other payroll liabilities amounts, due dates, and payments.

61. At the Schedule Payments window—*Set up payment schedule for Federal 940* page, enter the following information, if necessary:

Payee:	United States Treasury
Payment (deposit) frequency:	Quarterly

See Figure G–15.

FIGURE G–15
Schedule Payments Window—Set Up Payment Schedule for Federal 940 Page

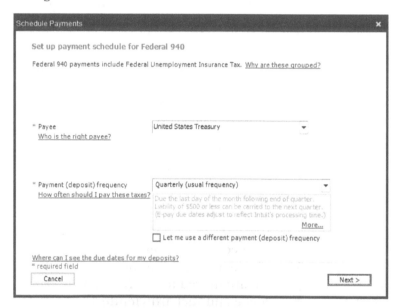

62. If the information is correct, click Next. You are moved to the Schedule Payments window—*Set up payment schedule for Federal 941/944/943* page.

63. Enter the following information:

Payee:	United States Treasury
Payment (deposit) frequency:	After Each Payroll (Semiweekly)

64. Click Next. You are moved to the Schedule Payments window—*Set up payment schedule for MN Withholding* page.

65. Enter the following information:

Payee:	Minn. Dept. of Revenue
MN Dept of Revenue Tax ID No.:	4777781
Payment (deposit) frequency:	After Each Payroll (Semiweekly)

See Figure G–16.

See Figure G–16.

FIGURE G–16
Schedule Payments
Window—Set Up
Payment Schedule for
MN Withholding Page

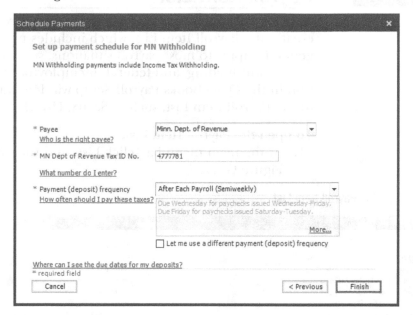

66. Click Next. You are moved to the Schedule Payments window—*Set up payment schedule for MN UI and Workforce Enhancement Fee* page.
67. Enter the following information:

    Payee: Minnesota UI Fund
    MN Dept of Emp and Economic
    Dev UI Tax Acct No: 04777781-0123
    Payment (deposit) frequency: Quarterly

68. If the information is correct, click Finish. You are moved to the *Review your Scheduled Tax Payments list* page.
    Look at the list in the left panel of the QuickBooks Payroll Setup window. You have completed the Taxes part of the QuickBooks Payroll Setup.
69. Click Continue. You are moved to the *Year-to-date payrolls* page. If you are setting up payroll in QuickBooks and have paid employees for the current year, you will have to enter the year-to-date payroll information for each employee.
70. Read the page and then click Continue. You are moved to the *Determine if you need to set up year-to-date payroll* page.
71. At the question *Has your company issued paychecks this year?*, click No and then click Continue. You are moved to the *You have finished payroll setup!* page.
    Look at the list in the left panel of the QuickBooks Payroll Setup window. You have completed the Year-to-Date Payrolls part of the QuickBooks Payroll Setup.
72. Click *Go to Payroll Center.*
    If you subscribe to a QuickBooks Payroll Service, you are moved to a Payroll Center window. If you compute payroll manually, you are moved to the Employee Center window. The Employee Center should be the same as was updated in Chapter 9. See Figure 9–H on page 368.
73. Close the Employee Center.

Payroll Item List

As previously noted, when you activate the payroll feature, QuickBooks creates the Payroll Item List, which includes typical federal tax items that generally apply to most payroll situations, such as Social Security, Medicare, federal withholding, and federal unemployment. As you entered information in the QuickBooks Payroll Setup window, additional items were added to the Payroll Item List, such as Salary, Hourly Wage, and State Taxes.

To open the Payroll Item List:
1. At the main menu bar, click Lists and then click *Payroll Item List*. See Figure G–17.

FIGURE G–17 Payroll Item List

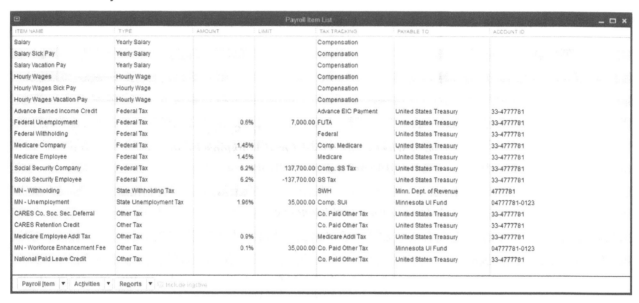

ITEM NAME	TYPE	AMOUNT	LIMIT	TAX TRACKING	PAYABLE TO	ACCOUNT ID
Salary	Yearly Salary			Compensation		
Salary Sick Pay	Yearly Salary			Compensation		
Salary Vacation Pay	Yearly Salary			Compensation		
Hourly Wages	Hourly Wage			Compensation		
Hourly Wages Sick Pay	Hourly Wage			Compensation		
Hourly Wages Vacation Pay	Hourly Wage			Compensation		
Advance Earned Income Credit	Federal Tax			Advance EIC Payment	United States Treasury	33-4777781
Federal Unemployment	Federal Tax	0.6%	7,000.00	FUTA	United States Treasury	33-4777781
Federal Withholding	Federal Tax			Federal	United States Treasury	33-4777781
Medicare Company	Federal Tax	1.45%		Comp. Medicare	United States Treasury	33-4777781
Medicare Employee	Federal Tax	1.45%		Medicare	United States Treasury	33-4777781
Social Security Company	Federal Tax	6.2%	137,700.00	Comp. SS Tax	United States Treasury	33-4777781
Social Security Employee	Federal Tax	6.2%	-137,700.00	SS Tax	United States Treasury	33-4777781
MN - Withholding	State Withholding Tax			SWH	Minn. Dept. of Revenue	4777781
MN - Unemployment	State Unemployment Tax	1.96%	35,000.00	Comp. SUI	Minnesota UI Fund	04777781-0123
CARES Co. Soc. Sec. Deferral	Other Tax			Co. Paid Other Tax	United States Treasury	33-4777781
CARES Retention Credit	Other Tax			Co. Paid Other Tax	United States Treasury	33-4777781
Medicare Employee Addl Tax	Other Tax	0.9%		Medicare Addl Tax	United States Treasury	33-4777781
MN - Workforce Enhancement Fee	Other Tax	0.1%	35,000.00	Co. Paid Other Tax	Minnesota UI Fund	04777781-0123
National Paid Leave Credit	Other Tax			Co. Paid Other Tax	United States Treasury	33-4777781

Payroll Item ▼   Activities ▼   Reports ▼   Include inactive

In the QuickBooks Payroll Setup window, you were generally but not always able to edit item names and account names. If there are item names and account names that you were not able to edit in the QuickBooks Payroll Setup window, you can do so in the Payroll Item List.

Follow the steps in the section "Customizing the Payroll Item List" in Chapter 8 on pages 338–342, including Practice Exercises 8–1 and 8–2, to customize the federal tax items of Social Security (Company and Employee), Medicare (Company and Employee), Federal Unemployment, and Federal Withholding.

After customizing the federal tax items, use the same procedures to customize the state tax items that were created in the QuickBooks Payroll Setup window:

State Tax Item	Liability Account	Expense Account
MN - Withholding	2120 SIT Payable	
MN - Unemployment	2130 SUI Payable	6630 SUI Expense

2. Close the Payroll Item List.

Payroll Item Listing Report

The *Payroll Item Listing* report lists the payroll item, type, rate, and limit for some of the mandatory taxes, as well as the expense and liability accounts relating to the payroll item.

To view the *Payroll Item Listing* report:

1. At the main menu bar, click Reports and then click *Employees & Payroll.*
2. At the Employees & Payroll submenu, click *Payroll Item Listing.* See Figure G–18.

FIGURE G–18 Payroll Item Listing Report

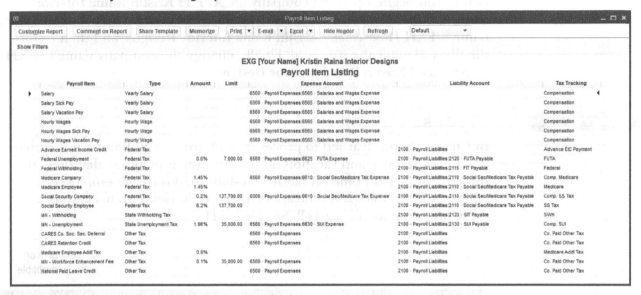

Payroll Item	Type	Amount	Limit	Expense Account	Liability Account	Tax Tracking
Salary	Yearly Salary			6560 · Payroll Expenses:6565 · Salaries and Wages Expense		Compensation
Salary Sick Pay	Yearly Salary			6560 · Payroll Expenses:6565 · Salaries and Wages Expense		Compensation
Salary Vacation Pay	Yearly Salary			6560 · Payroll Expenses:6565 · Salaries and Wages Expense		Compensation
Hourly Wages	Hourly Wage			6560 · Payroll Expenses:6565 · Salaries and Wages Expense		Compensation
Hourly Wages Sick Pay	Hourly Wage			6560 · Payroll Expenses:6565 · Salaries and Wages Expense		Compensation
Hourly Wages Vacation Pay	Hourly Wage			6560 · Payroll Expenses:6565 · Salaries and Wages Expense		Compensation
Advance Earned Income Credit	Federal Tax				2100 · Payroll Liabilities	Advance EIC Payment
Federal Unemployment	Federal Tax	0.6%	7,000.00	6560 · Payroll Expenses:6625 · FUTA Expense	2100 · Payroll Liabilities:2125 · FUTA Payable	FUTA
Federal Withholding	Federal Tax				2100 · Payroll Liabilities:2115 · FIT Payable	Federal
Medicare Company	Federal Tax	1.45%		6560 · Payroll Expenses:6610 · Social Sec/Medicare Tax Expense	2100 · Payroll Liabilities:2110 · Social Sec/Medicare Tax Payable	Comp. Medicare
Medicare Employee	Federal Tax	1.45%			2100 · Payroll Liabilities:2110 · Social Sec/Medicare Tax Payable	Medicare
Social Security Company	Federal Tax	6.2%	137,700.00	6560 · Payroll Expenses:6610 · Social Sec/Medicare Tax Expense	2100 · Payroll Liabilities:2110 · Social Sec/Medicare Tax Payable	Comp. SS Tax
Social Security Employee	Federal Tax	6.2%	137,700.00		2100 · Payroll Liabilities:2110 · Social Sec/Medicare Tax Payable	SS Tax
MN - Withholding	State Withholding Tax				2100 · Payroll Liabilities:2120 · SIT Payable	SWH
MN - Unemployment	State Unemployment Tax	1.96%	35,000.00	6560 · Payroll Expenses:6630 · SUI Expense	2100 · Payroll Liabilities:2130 · SUI Payable	Comp. SUI
CARES Co. Soc. Sec. Deferral	Other Tax			6560 · Payroll Expenses	2100 · Payroll Liabilities	Co. Paid Other Tax
CARES Retention Credit	Other Tax			6560 · Payroll Expenses	2100 · Payroll Liabilities	Co. Paid Other Tax
Medicare Employee Addl Tax	Other Tax	0.9%			2100 · Payroll Liabilities	Medicare Addl Tax
MN - Workforce Enhancement Fee	Other Tax	0.1%	35,000.00	6560 · Payroll Expenses	2100 · Payroll Liabilities	Co. Paid Other Tax
National Paid Leave Credit	Other Tax			6560 · Payroll Expenses	2100 · Payroll Liabilities	Co. Paid Other Tax

3. Close the report.

APPENDIX H
Sick and Vacation Paid Time

In Appendix G, you learned to set up paid time off for Kristin Raina's employees. In this appendix, you will process payroll when one employee uses sick or vacation time. You will also process payroll reports that track paid time used and paid time available.

Appendix Problem

Before you begin, open the company file **APP H Kristin Raina Interior Designs.QBW**. Enter the password, *Student1*. Make a backup copy of the file, name it **EXH** *[Your Name]* **Kristin Raina Interior Designs**, and then restore the file and enter the password. Finally, change the company name to **EXH** *[Your Name]* **Kristin Raina Interior Designs**.

Activities

Process Payroll

In Chapter 9, you learned to process payroll for Kristin Raina's two employees. Employee sick and vacation hours were not available at that time. In this appendix, paid time off has been established for each employee. The amount of available paid time appears in the Preview Paycheck window every time you process payroll. See Figure H–1.

FIGURE H–1
Preview Paycheck Window—Paid Time Off Hours Displayed

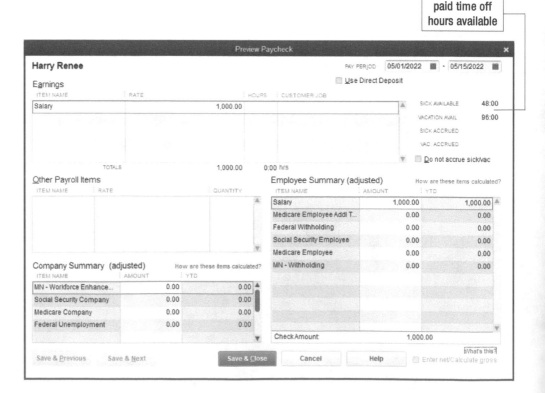

paid time off hours available

Using Banked Vacation Time Off Hours

Harry Renee plans to take a one-week vacation during the pay period ending May 15, 2022. Because he has 96 hours of paid vacation time available, he will use 40 of those hours and be paid during his time off.

To record the use of paid vacation time off:

1. At the main menu bar, click Employees and then click *Pay Employees*. The Enter Payroll Information window appears.
2. At the *PAY PERIOD ENDS* and *CHECK DATE* fields, choose *05/15/2022*.
3. At the *BANK ACCOUNT* field, click *1020 Cash - Payroll*.
4. At the *CHECK OPTIONS* field, choose the *Handwrite & Assign check numbers* option and then type 5 at the *First Check#* field.
5. Select *Harry Renee* by inserting a check mark next to the name.
6. If the information is correct, click the Open Paycheck Detail button. The Preview Paycheck window appears.
7. At the *ITEM NAME* field, confirm that the *Salary* item automatically fills for Harry Renee and that the *VACATION AVAIL.* hours are 96.
8. Move to the next line and choose *Salary Vacation Pay* at the *ITEM NAME* field. Notice that the $1,000 salary is now split between regular salary and vacation pay. See Figure H–2.

FIGURE H–2
Preview Paycheck Window—Salary Vacation Pay Entered

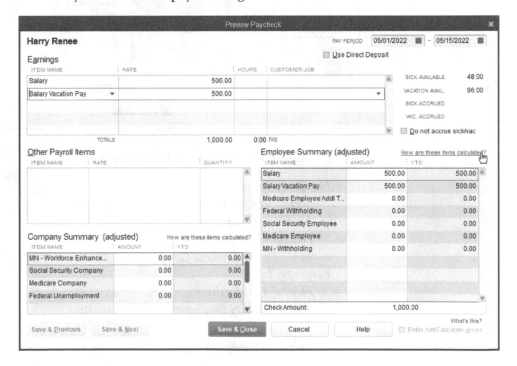

9. On both the *Salary* and *Salary Vacation Pay* lines at the *HOURS* field, type 40.

When you move to the next field, the *VACATION AVAIL.* hours will be reduced from 96 to 56, as 40 hours of paid vacation time have now been used. In addition, the $1,000 salary for the period is now divided between the Salary item and the Salary Vacation Pay item in the Employee Summary (adjusted) section. See Figure H–3.

FIGURE H–3
Preview Paycheck Window—Vacation Hours Used

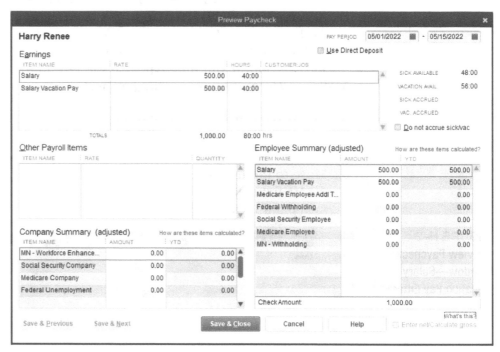

10. Complete Harry Renee's pay information:

Company Taxes:
   Social Security Company: 62.00
   Medicare Company: 14.50
   Federal Unemployment: 6.00
   MN - Unemployment Company: 40.00
Employee Taxes:
   Federal Withholding: 120.00
   Social Security Employee: 62.00
   Medicare Employee: 14.50
   MN - Withholding: 46.00

QuickCheck: The check amount should be $757.50.

11. Complete the process for Harry Renee's pay.

Activities

Using Banked Sick Time Off Hours

During the pay period ending May 15, 2022, Richard Henderson used two days (16 hours) of paid sick time. His pay will be processed for that pay period with 16 of the 80 hours allocated to Hourly Wages Sick Pay and only 64 hours allocated to Hourly Wages.

To record the use of paid sick time off:

1. At the main menu bar, click Employees and then click *Pay Employees*. The Enter Payroll Information window appears.
2. At the *PAY PERIOD ENDS* and *CHECK DATE* fields, choose *05/15/2022*. The Bank Account should be *1020 Cash - Payroll,* and the Check# should be *6.*
3. Select *Richard Henderson* and then click the Open Paycheck Detail button. Note that *SICK AVAILABLE* hours are 48.
4. At the *HOURS* field, on the *Hourly Wages* line, type 64.
5. Move to the next line and choose *Hourly Wages Sick Pay* at the *ITEM NAME* field.
6. At the *HOURS* field, type 16.

Note that the *SICK AVAILABLE* hours are now 32, reduced from 48. In addition, in the Employee Summary (adjusted) section, the gross pay is now split between Hourly Wages of $1,280 (64 hours at $20 per hour) and Hourly Wages Sick Pay of $320 (16 hours at $20 per hour). See Figure H–4.

FIGURE H–4
Preview Paycheck Window—Sick Hours Used

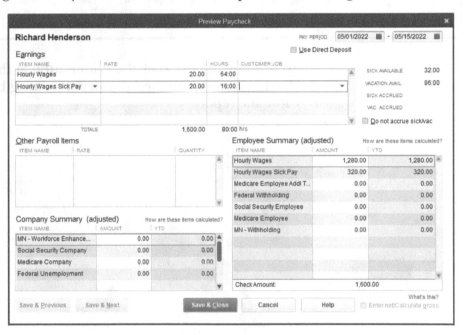

7. Complete Richard Henderson's pay information:

   Company Taxes:

Social Security Company:	99.20
Medicare Company:	23.20
Federal Unemployment:	9.60
MN - Unemployment Company:	64.00

   Employee Taxes:

Federal Withholding:	120.00
Social Security Employee:	99.20
Medicare Employee:	23.20
MN - Withholding:	54.00

   QuickCheck: The check amount should be $1,303.60.

8. Complete the process for Richard Henderson's pay.

Tracking Paid Time Off

The *Paid Time Off List* is a report that allows you to track the sick and vacation time used and the time available for each employee.

To view and print the *Paid Time Off List*:

1. At the main menu bar, click Reports and then click *Employees & Payroll*.
2. At the Employees & Payroll submenu, click *Paid Time Off List*. The report is displayed with the updated information. See Figure H–5.

FIGURE H–5 Paid Time Off List

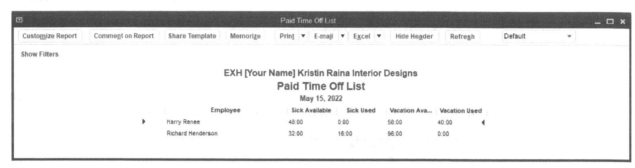

3. To print the report, click the Print button at the top of the report, check the settings in the Print Reports dialog box, and then click Print.
4. Close the report.

APPENDIX I
Setting Up QuickBooks for Multiple Users

There are many examples of businesses in which multiple employees need access to company files to record information. QuickBooks Pro and QuickBooks Premier allow up to three or five people, respectively, to access the company files, each from their own computer. This is referred to as *multi-user mode*. Computers for all the users must be networked within the company. One computer is designated as the host computer. To prepare for using the company file by multiple users, QuickBooks must be installed on each computer, multi-user access must be set up, and the company files must be prepared for multi-user access.

Install QuickBooks

To use QuickBooks in multi-user mode, QuickBooks must be installed separately on each computer. Additional license fees are required for each computer. A company usually purchases the multi-user QuickBooks software, which includes the license fees for the additional users. If a company purchased single-user QuickBooks software, additional licenses can be purchased from QuickBooks.

Install QuickBooks on each computer, as described in Chapter 1. For the computer designated as the host computer, select *Multi-User Host Installation* when prompted. For all the other computers, select a standard installation.

Set Up Multi-User Access

There are several ways to set up multi-user access for a company file. One way, as stated above, is to choose *Multi-User Host Installation* when installing QuickBooks. If QuickBooks was previously installed, you can set up the host computer for multi-user access.

Complete the steps below with QuickBooks open but with no company file open.

To set up the host computer for multi-user access:
1. At the main menu bar, click File and then click *Utilities.*
2. At the Utilities drop-down menu, click *Host Multi-User Access.* The Host multi-user access window appears.
3. Read the Start hosting multi-user access message and then click Yes.
4. If the Company file must be closed message appears, click Yes.
5. If the Administrator Permissions Needed message appears, click Continue.
6. If a User Account Control message appears, click Yes.
7. You are moved to the Set up multiple users information window. Read the message and then click OK.

The host computer is now set up in multi-user mode. The company files need to be scanned for multi-user access.

HINT

To view the number of user licenses, press the F2 function key or Ctrl + 1.

HINT

If the choice is *Stop Hosting Multi-User Access*, then you are already in multi-user mode. Move to the next section, "Scan Company Files for Multi-User Access."

Scan Company Files for Multi-User Access

QuickBooks provides a database server manager to scan the computer files and prepare them for multiple users.

To scan the company files:

1. In Windows 10, click the Windows Start button, and then in the apps menu, scroll down and click *QuickBooks File Manager 2021*.

   In Windows 8, click the Search charm. In the *Search* text box, type QuickBooks Database Server Manager. The QuickBooks Database app tile should appear. Click the QuickBooks Database app tile.

2. At the QuickBooks File Manager 2021 window, click the Launch QuickBooks File Manager button.

3. If the Create Password Vault Login dialog box appears, type or select the following:

Username:	Admin
Password:	Student1
Confirm Password:	Student1
Challenge Question:	First college roomate's name
Answer:	Friend
Alternate Question:	Favorite restaurant in college
Answer:	Local Place

   See Figure I–1.

FIGURE I–1
Create Password Vault Login Window— Completed

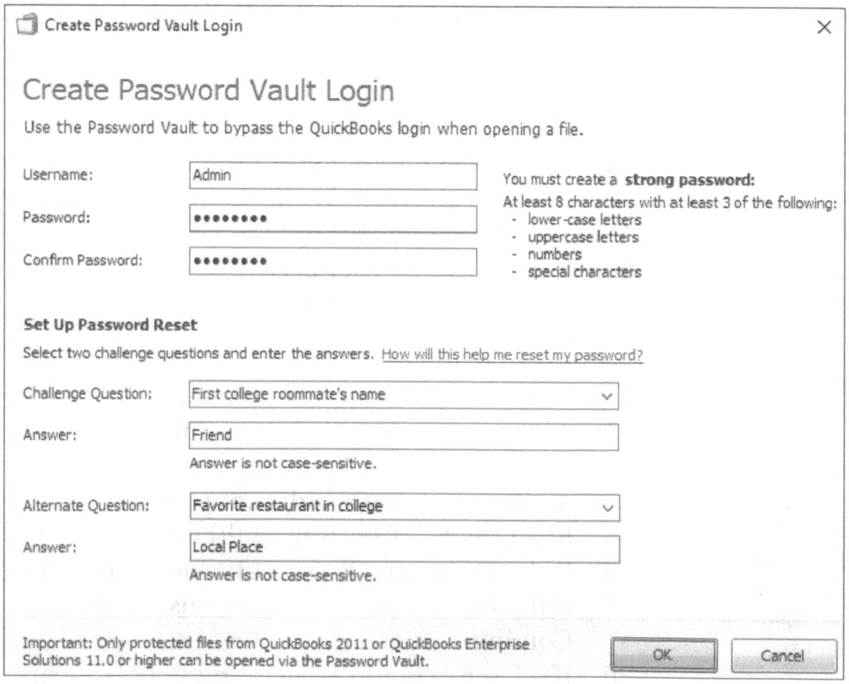

4. If the information is correct, click OK.
5. If the User Account Control message appears, click Yes.
6. If the 3-ways to Add Clients & Shortcuts to their Files message appears, click Add/Update Clients Wizard.
7. At the *Building your client list and adding shortcuts to their files... 1 - How should we name your clients?* page, click Next.

8. At the *Building your client list and adding shortcuts to their files...*
   2 - From QuickBooks File Names page, click the Browse button.
9. At the Browse for Folder window, select the folder where your
   QuickBooks files are located and then click OK. You are returned
   to the *Building your client list and adding shortcuts to their files...2 - From
   QuickBooks File Names* page with the path for your QuickBooks files
   listed.
10. Click Finish. The Updating Client List window appears. It will take
    a few minutes for the list to populate. The files now appear in the
    Clients section of the QuickBooks File Manager 2021 window. The
    company files are now ready to be used in multi-user mode.
11. Click the X to close the QuickBooks File Manager 2021 window.

You then set up the users that are allowed access to the company files.
See Appendix J for setting up users.

Accessing the Company File in Multi-User Mode

After the host computer has been set up to allow multi-users and the
company files have been set up to be accessed in multi-user mode, when
opening a company file, you must indicate that you will use the company
file in multi-user mode. You do this at the Open a Company window. In the
lower left corner of the Open a Company window, insert a check mark in
the box to the left of *Open file in multi-user mode*.

At the QuickBooks Desktop Login, enter the password. You may
be prompted to enter a user name or to Create New Users. If you are
prompted, click No. When the file opens, you will have access to the
company file as a multi-user.

If you did not open the company file in multi-user mode, you can switch
to multi-user mode when the company file is open. Click File and then click
Switch to Multi-user Mode. If the choice is *Switch to Single-user Mode*, then you
are already in multi-user mode.

APPENDIX J
Setting Up Users

As you have seen throughout this book, a company file password is set up to protect the company file. In addition, a company can further protect the company file by allowing limited access to the company file by users. The original person who creates the company file is the Administrator (Admin) of the file. The Administrator is the person who determines and sets up users so they may access the company file. When the Administrator creates a user, the Administrator can then restrict access to parts of the company file or restrict access to former company information.

To set up users in a company file:

1. At the main menu bar, click Company and then click *Set Up Users and Passwords*.
2. At the Set Up Users and Passwords submenu, click *Set Up Users*.
3. At the QuickBooks Desktop Login, type in the password Student1 and then click OK.
4. In the User List dialog box, click *Add User*. The Set Up user password and access dialog box appears.
5. In the Set Up user password and access dialog box, at the *User Name* field, type User1.
6. At the *Password* and *Confirm Password* fields, type User1PW. See Figure J–1.

HINT

You can use any Company File or Exercise File to set up users in a company file. You many want to use a File from one of the later chapters, and you may want to make a copy of the Company File or Exercise File.

FIGURE J–1

Set Up User Password and Access Dialog Box—User Name and Password Page Completed

7. If the information is correct, click Next.
8. At the *Access for user: User1* page, choose the *Selected areas of QuickBooks* option and then click Next.
9. At the Sales and Accounts Receivable page, choose the *Full Access* option and then click Next.
10. At the next several pages—Purchases and Accounts Payable, Checking and Credit Cards, Inventory, Time Tracking (if displayed), and Payroll and Employees (if displayed)—choose the *No Access* option and click Next.
11. At the Sensitive Accounting Activities page, choose the *Selective Access* option, choose the *Create transactions and create reports* option, and then click Next.

HINT

Depending on which features are enabled in a company file, some of these pages may not appear.

12. At the Sensitive Financial Reporting page, choose the *No Access* option and then click Next.
13. At the Changing or Deleting Transactions page, choose *Yes* at the first option, choose *No* at the second option, and then click Next. You are moved to the *Access for user: User1* page, which summarizes the user's access rights. See Figure J–2.

FIGURE J–2
Set Up User Password and Access Dialog Box— Access for User Page

14. If the information is correct, click Finish. If you receive a warning, click OK.
15. Close the User List dialog box.
16. Close the company file.

Open the same company file as User1:
1. Open the company file. The QuickBooks Desktop Login dialog box appears.
2. In the QuickBooks Login dialog box, at the *User Name* field, type User1; at the *Password* field, type User1PW; and then click OK.
3. If the Sensitive Data Protection Setup dialog box appears, type the following:

User Name:	User1
Current Password:	User1PW
New Password:	U1PassW
Confirm New Password:	U1PassW

4. Click Confirm.
5. At the QuickBooks Desktop Information message, click OK.

    Recall that for User1, permission was granted only for Sales and Accounts Receivable. Open the Create Invoices window and the Enter Sales Receipts window. These windows can be opened by User1. Now try opening other windows, such as Enter Bills, Pay Employees, *Journal* report, *Profit & Loss Standard* report, and so on. A message warns that you need permission to open these parts of the company file.
6. Click OK at the warnings for each window and then close the company file.
7. Close QuickBooks.

Accrual Basis of Accounting versus Cash Basis of Accounting

accrual basis of accounting
an accounting method that requires the recording of revenue when it is earned and the recording of expenses when they are incurred regardless of cash receipts or cash payments

cash basis of accounting
an accounting method that records revenue when cash is received for services provided or for a product sold and records expenses only when payments have been made

You may have noticed in many of the reports that there is an *accrual basis* label in the upper left corner of the report. In QuickBooks, by default, the accounting reports (such as the trial balance) and financial statements (such as the Profit & Loss and Balance Sheet) are prepared using the **accrual basis of accounting**, which records revenue when earned and expenses when incurred regardless of cash receipts and cash payments. The accrual basis of accounting follows generally accepted accounting principles and is the basis used in this text.

An alternative accounting method is called the **cash basis of accounting**, which records revenue only when the cash has been received for services provided or for a product sold and records expenses only when cash payments have been made. QuickBooks allows you to switch individual reports from the accrual basis to the cash basis of accounting. When you convert the financial statements to the cash basis of accounting, the accounts that are typically affected are Accounts Receivable, Accounts Payable, revenues, and expenses.

To view a report using the cash basis of accounting:
1. Open the company file, **EX5** *[Your Name]* **Kristin Raina Interior Designs**.
2. Open the *Profit & Loss Standard* report for the period 01/01/2022 through 03/31/2022.
   The report should match Figure 5–DD on page 177. Notice that the Net Income is *$8,285.38.*
3. In the *Profit & Loss Standard* report, click the Customize Report button.
4. In the Modify Report: Profit & Loss window, click the Display tab, if necessary.
5. On the Display tab, in the REPORT BASIS section, click the *Cash* option. See Figure K–1.

FIGURE K–1
Modify Report: Profit & Loss Window—Display Tab—Cash Report Basis Selected

6. Click OK. The *Profit & Loss Standard* report is converted to the cash basis of accounting. See Figure K–2.

In Figure K–2, the Net Income is *$7,195.38*. Compare this to Figure 5–DD on page 177, which displays a Net Income of *$8,285.38*. There is a difference in the Net Income values of $1,090.

The difference consists of the Total Income of $1,540, ($13,795.38 – $12,255.38), which is the amount of the Accounts Receivable balance (this balance represents non-cash income), and the Utilities Expense of $450, which is part of Accounts Payable because this expense has not yet been paid. The difference of the Total Income and Expenses is the difference in the Net Income ($1,540 – $450 = $1,090).

Now open the *Balance Sheet Standard* report for March 31, 2022. The report should match Figure 5–EE on page 178. Convert the *Balance Sheet Standard* report to the cash basis of accounting following Steps 3–6. See Figure K–3.

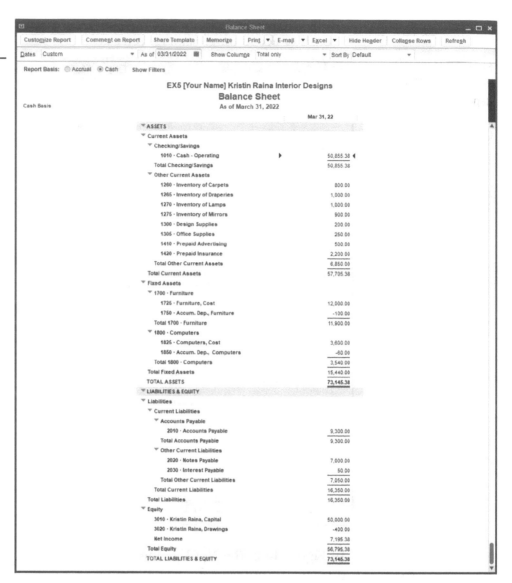

In Figure K–3 the balance is *$73,145.38*. Compare to Figure 5–EE on page 178, which displays a balance of *$74,685.38*. The difference is *$1,540*.

In the Asset section of the *Balance Sheet Standard* report, the difference consists of the difference in Accounts Receivable of $1,540. This balance is not included on the cash basis *Balance Sheet Standard* report because this balance relates to non-cash income.

In the Liabilities and Owner's Equity section of the *Balance Sheet Standard* report, the difference consists of the difference in Accounts Payable of $450, which is the not-yet-paid Utilities Expense (this expense is removed from Accounts Payable on the cash basis *Balance Sheet Standard* report) and the difference in the Net Income of *$1,090*, which is the cash basis Net Income reflected in Figure K–2 ($450 + $1,090 = $1,540).

When QuickBooks converts the *Profit & Loss* and *Balance Sheet* reports to the cash basis, it adjusts only the items that affect revenue and expenses and the related Accounts Receivable and Accounts Payable accounts.

The reports in Figures K–2 and K–3 were adjusted to the cash basis. When you close the report, the conversion to the cash basis of accounting is not retained. If you wish to preserve these settings, you will need to instruct QuickBooks to memorize the report as explained in Chapter 12.

Alternatively, if you wish for the reports to always display the cash basis of accounting, you can change the default settings for the reports in the Preferences window. To change the report defaults, click Edit and then click *Preferences*. Choose the Reports & Graphs icon and the Company Preferences tab. The *SUMMARY REPORTS BASIS* field can be used to change to the cash basis of accounting.

Index

I

Icon bars
  Left
    adding icon to, 483–484
    editing icon on, 484
    removing icon from, 484
    viewing, 482–483
  removing, 485
  Top, viewing, 485
icons
  accessing window using, from Home page, 479–480
  enable/disable preference to add/remove icons from Home page, 480–481
  Left and Top Icon bars, 482–485
inactive accounts
  hiding, system default accounts, 283–284
  making customer inactive, 80–81
  making vendor inactive, 39
Income Account field, 149
Income and Expense graph, 514
Income and Expenses account type, 111
Income Statement report
  reviewing after new company setup, 216–217, 298, 307
  viewing and printing, 132–133, 177, 307
installation of QuickBooks Desktop trial, 4–5
insurance
  state disability insurance (SDI), 331
  state unemployment insurance (SUI), 331, 361–362
interest earned
  field in Begin Reconciliation window, 405
  reconciling process, 399, 404
inventory, 146. *See also* inventory transactions
inventory adjustment
  defined, 168
  recording, 168–169
Inventory Adjustment account, 168
inventory asset account
  automatic adjustment to Accounts Payable account, 155
  automatic adjustment to Cash account, 157
  as system default account, 222, 282
Inventory Center
  accessing, 153
  overview of function, 153
Inventory Center window, 153–154
inventory feature, activating, 275
inventory item file
  editing, 152
  viewing specific, 148–149
inventory part items
  adding, 290–291
  creating purchase order for, 536–537
  editing, 234–235
  merging, 489–490
  using QuickBooks Desktop Setup window to add to Item List, 206–207
inventory reports
  Inventory Stock Status by Item report, 172–173
  Inventory Valuation Detail report, 172, 543
  Purchases by Item Detail report, 173
  Sales by Item Detail report, 174
Inventory Stock Status by Item report, 172–173
inventory subsidiary ledger, 190–191
  QuickBooks counterpart, 534
inventory transactions
  accounting for
    periodic inventory system, 147
    perpetual inventory system, 147
  activate inventory feature, 275
  inventory adjustments, 168–169
  inventory reports, 171–174
  Item List
    adding item, 149–151
    deleting item, 151
    editing, 152
    product information included, 147–148
    updating, 289–291
    viewing specific inventory file, 148–149
  make deposits, 171
  overview of, 146
  purchasing inventory, 154–158
    Enter Bills window to record on account, 156–157
    Write Checks window to record cash purchases, 157–158
  QuickBooks versus manual accounting, 146
  recording purchase and receipt of, on purchase order, 537–538
  record sale of inventory on account, 539–540
  sale of inventory, 159–167
    Create Invoices window to record on account, 159–161
    Enter Sales Receipt window to record for cash, 162–163
  sales tax, 159
    paying sales tax collected, 170–171
Inventory Valuation Detail report, 172, 543
invoice. *See also* Create Invoices window
  creating invoice, 85–87
    for job, 444–445
    with time-tracking data, 454–456
  customizing printed, 495–499
  Open Invoices report, 98
  previewing, 493–494
  receiving payment for
    in full, 89–90
    for more than one, 91–93
    partial payment, 90–91
Item List
  correcting errors in, 210
  editing, 85, 210, 233–235
  elements and features of, 147–148
  information contained, 153
  inventory part item
    adding, 149–151, 290–291
    adding with QuickBooks Desktop Setup window, 206–207
    create custom fields for, 490–492
    deleting item, 151
    editing, 152, 234–235
    information included about, 147–148
    reviewing list, 148
    sale of inventory and, 160
    updating, 149
    viewing specific inventory file, 148–149
  as inventory subsidiary ledger, 146
  manual accounting counterpart, 534
  overview of function, 146, 233
  reviewing, 208–210
  sales tax item
    activating sales tax feature, 275–277
    editing, 235
  service item
    adding, 289–290
    adding with QuickBooks Desktop Setup window, 205
    changing rates for, 439

create custom fields for, 490–492
    editing, 233–234
    updating after New Company Setup-Detailed Start,
        233–235
    viewing items, 84–85
Item List window, 83, 208
Items tab, 43
    of Enter Bills window
        elements of, 154–155
        to record inventory purchases, 154–155
    Write Checks window
        to record inventory items for cash, 157–158

J

job(s)
    associated with customer, 435
    automatic allocation of revenue to particular, 434
    creating invoice for, 444–445
    Customer Center, adding job to, 435–438
    defined, 434
    entering time in Weekly Timesheet window for, 448–451
    Item List for different services and rates, 439
    overview of, 434
    pay employee and allocate hours to job, 440–443
    pay employee and allocate payroll expense to, 453–454
    in Pay Employees window, 434
    Profit & Loss by Job report, 459
    QuickBooks versus manual accounting, 434–435
    Time by Job Summary report, 460
Job Info tab, 77, 437
jobs subsidiary ledger, 534
journal. See general journal; special journals
journal entry. See adjusting journal entries
Journal report
    banking transactions, 424
    customer, 100–101
    inventory, 175–176
    job and time tracking, 461
    list of types, 535
    manual accounting counterpart, 534
    merge entries, 489–490
    number of entries, 214–215
    payroll processing, 385
    as period-end accounting report, 125–127
    printing, 61–62, 213
    reviewing after new company setup, 213–215,
        241–242, 296–297, 305
    viewing, 61–62, 100–101
    viewing and printing only adjusting journal entries,
        125–127

L

Left Icon bar, 482–484
letters, preparing using QuickBooks Letters, 500
Liabilities account type, 111–112
Liability agency, Social Security tax setting, 339–340
Liability Check - Cash - Payroll window, 379
List of Selected General Journal Entries field, 122
Lists and Centers
    create custom fields, 490–492
    level of operation described, 3–4
    viewing banking reports from, 421–422
List windows
    menu buttons for Chart of Accounts List, 115–116
    view and print reports from, 174

Locate Discrepancies button, 405, 414
Locate Discrepancies window, 414
Look up Customer/Invoice button, 88

M

main menu bar, 7–8
Make Deposits window
    automatic adjustment to Cash or Undeposited
        account, 95
    deposit all receipts collected and previously recorded
        in Undeposited Funds account, 95–97
    making deposit and inventory transactions, 171
    viewing while reconciling bank account, 408–409
Make General Journal Entries window
    assigning numbers to journal entries, 123
    elements and features of, 122
    entering opening balances in, 237–239, 300–302
    manual accounting counterpart, 534
    overview of function, 121–122
    recording adjusting journal entry, 123–124
    view prior journal entry, 123
    warning message for entry not in balance, 124
Manage Templates icon, 495
Manage Templates window, 495–496
manual accounting systems
    compared to QuickBooks
        banking transactions, 398–400
        bank reconciliation, 399
        credit card charges, 400
        customer transactions, 72–73
        fiscal year closing, 515–517
        funds transfer, 399
        general journal entries, 110
        general ledger, 110, 111
        inventory transactions, 146
        jobs and time tracking, 434–435
        journals and recording transactions overview,
            2–3, 534
        New Company Setup, 190–191, 268–269
        payroll, 328–329
        payroll transactions, 360
        vendor transactions, 30
Medicare tax
    accounting for payroll transactions, 361–362
    defined, 330
    paying, 378
MEMO field, 122
Memorize button, 506–507
memorized report, 506–507
Memorized Transaction dialog box, 502
Memorized Transaction List, 502
memorized transactions, 501–502
Missing Checks report, 420–421
Modify Report dialog box
    Display tab, 503–504
    Header/Footer tab, 504–506
multi-user mode
    defined, 12
    scan company files for, 570–571
    setting up access for, 569
My Company window, 20

N

Name page, 35, 37, 77
Net 30 Days, 44
net pay, 331